THE ESSENTIAL
FRENCH
DICTIONARY

THE ESSENTIAL
FRENCH
DICTIONARY

CHANCELLOR
PRESS

First published in Great Britain in 1976 by
Hamlyn, a division of Octopus Publishing Group
under the title *French Dictionary*

Published in 1988 by Chancellor Press
an imprint of Bounty Books a division of
Octopus Publishing Group Ltd

Compiled by Laurence Urdang Associates Limited Aylesbury, Bucks

ISBN 0 7537 0645 8

Printed in England by Mackays of Chatham

Foreword

This dictionary aims to give concise and accurate definitions of 24,000 of the most important words in use in the English and French languages today.

A pronunciation system based on the International Phonetic Alphabet is used (see *Key to symbols used in pronunciation*). Pronunciation is given for all headwords in both sections of the dictionary, and also for selected subentries in the French-English section.

Modern technical, commercial, and informal usage is given particular attention, in preference to outmoded terms or other expressions not in common contemporary use. Definitions are numbered in order to distinguish senses, and abbreviations are used to indicate use in specific technical, scientific, or commercial fields (see *Abbreviations used in the Dictionary*). An additional feature is the inclusion of idiomatic expressions and phrases, so necessary for the understanding and use of the foreign language.

This dictionary, with its emphasis on modernity, together with its compact form and clear typeface, should prove indispensable in the home, at school, in the office, and abroad.

Abbreviations used in the Dictionary

adj	adjective	*indef art*	indefinite article	*poss*	possessive
adv	adverb	*inf*	informal	*pref*	prefix
anat	anatomy	*infin*	infinitive	*prep*	preposition
arch	architecture	*interj*	interjection	*pron*	pronoun
aux	auxiliary	*invar*	invariable	*rel*	religion
aviat	aviation	*lit*	literature	*s*	singular
bot	botany	*m*	masculine	*sci*	science
cap	capital	*math*	mathematics	*sl*	slang
comm	commerce	*med*	medical	*suff*	suffix
conj	conjunction	*mil*	military	*tab*	taboo
cul	culinary	*min*	minerals	*Tdmk*	trademark
def art	definite article	*mod*	modal	*tech*	technical
derog	derogatory	*mot*	motoring	*Th*	theatre
dom	domestic	*mus*	music	*US*	United States
educ	education	*n*	noun	*v*	verb
fam	familiar	*naut*	nautical	*vi*	intransitive verb
fml	formal	*neg*	negative	*v imp*	impersonal verb
game	cards, chess, etc.	*pers*	person	*vr*	reflexive verb
gram	grammar	*phot*	photography	*vt*	transitive verb
geog	geography	*pol*	politics	*zool*	zoology

Key to symbols used in pronunçiation

English
Vowels

iː	meet	u	put	ai	fly		
i	bit	uː	shoot	au	how		
e	get	ʌ	cut	ɔi	boy		
æ	hat	ə	ago	iə	here		
ɑː	heart	əː	sir	ɛə	air		
ɔ	hot	ei	late	uə	poor		
ɔː	ought	ou	go				

Consonants

θ	thin
ð	then
ŋ	sing
j	yes
ʃ	ship
ʒ	measure
tʃ	chin
dʒ	gin

' indicates that the following syllable is stressed, as in ago (ə'gou).

ˌ placed under an n or l indicates that the n or l is pronounced as a syllable, as in button ('bʌtn̩) and flannel ('flænl̩).

French
Vowels

iː	il	uː	ou	ã	blanc	
eː	été	y	tu	ɥ	lui	
ɛ	elle	œ	sœur	iːj	fille	
a	patte	ə	le	ɛj	soleil	
ɑ	âge	ɛ̃	vin	aj	travail	
ɔ	mort	œ̃	un	œj	feuille	
o	rôle	ɔ̃	bon			

Consonants

j	hier
ʃ	chat
ʒ	je
ɲ	agneau

' indicates that the following syllable is stressed, as in été (e:'te:).

Notes on the use of the Dictionary

Irregular plural forms of French nouns and adjectives are shown in the headword list of the French-English section and in the text of the English-French section: for example, *journal, -aux; jeu, jeux; ail, aulx*. A plural is considered to be irregular if it is not formed by adding *-s* to the singular. Exceptions are nouns and adjectives ending in *-x*, such as *vieux*, which do not vary in the plural.

The abbreviation *invar* means that a noun or adjective does not vary in the plural.

Irregular feminine forms are shown in the same way: for example, *lion, lionne; sec, sèche; relatif, -ive*. A feminine is considered to be irregular if it is not formed by adding *-e* to the masculine. Exceptions are nouns and adjectives ending in *-e*, such as *brave*, which do not vary in the feminine.

Variant masculine forms of adjectives used before an initial vowel sound are shown in the French-English section: for example, *vieux, vieil, vieille* (as in *un vieil homme*); *beau, bel, belle, beaux, belles* (as in *un bel arbre*).

Irregular verbs are marked with an asterisk in the headword lists of both sections of the dictionary. The principal parts of these verbs are shown in the verb tables. For compounds, see the base form in the table; for example, for *comprendre*, see *prendre*. Verbs ending in *-e + consonant + er*, such as *appeler* and *mener*, which either double the consonant or take a grave accent before mute endings, are not considered to be irregular.

Adverbs derived from adjectives are not shown in either section of the dictionary unless a separate translation is required, or unless the formation is not regular. French adverbs are considered regular if they add the suffix *-ment* to the feminine singular of the adjective; English adverbs are considered regular if they add *-ly* to the adjective.

When the same word may be both an adjective and a noun, the gender of the noun is given only when it is fixed. Thus, **coopératif, -ive** ... *adj,nf* ... (cooperative) indicates that the word may be an adjective or a feminine noun (*la coopérative*); **métis, -isse** ... *adj,n* ... (half-breed) indicates that the word may be an adjective and a masculine or feminine noun (*le métis, la métisse*).

A swung dash (~) before a change of part of speech indicates that the part of speech refers to the headword, not the preceding subentry in heavy type.

Infinitive	Past Tense	Past Participle	Infinitive	Past Tense	Past Participle
abide	abode *or* abided	abode *or* abided	draw	drew	drawn
arise	arose	arisen	dream	dreamed *or* dreamt	dreamed *or* dreamt
awake	awoke *or* awaked	awoke *or* awaked	drink	drank	drunk
			drive	drove	driven
be	was	been	dwell	dwelt	dwelt
bear[1]	bore	borne *or* born	eat	ate	eaten
beat	beat	beaten	fall	fell	fallen
become	became	become	feed	fed	fed
begin	began	begun	feel	felt	felt
bend	bent	bent	fight	fought	fought
bet	bet	bet	find	found	found
beware[2]			flee	fled	fled
bid	bid	bidden *or* bid	fling	flung	flung
bind	bound	bound	fly	flew	flown
bite	bit	bitten *or* bit	forbid	forbade *or* forbad	forbidden *or* forbid
bleed	bled	bled	forget	forgot	forgotten *or* forgot
blow	blew	blown			
break	broke	broken	forgive	forgave	forgiven
breed	bred	bred	forsake	forsook	forsaken
bring	brought	brought	freeze	froze	frozen
build	built	built	get	got	got
burn	burnt *or* burned	burnt *or* burned	give	gave	given
burst	burst	burst	go	went	gone
buy	bought	bought	grind	ground	ground
can	could		grow	grew	grown
cast	cast	cast	hang[3]	hung *or* hanged	hung *or* hanged
catch	caught	caught	have	had	had
choose	chose	chosen	hear	heard	heard
cling	clung	clung	hide	hid	hidden *or* hid
come	came	come	hit	hit	hit
cost	cost	cost	hold	held	held
creep	crept	crept	hurt	hurt	hurt
crow	crowed *or* crew	crowed	keep	kept	kept
cut	cut	cut	kneel	knelt	knelt
deal	dealt	dealt	knit	knitted *or* knit	knitted *or* knit
dig	dug *or* digged	dug *or* digged	know	knew	known
do	did	done			

English irregular verbs

Infinitive	Past Tense	Past Participle	Infinitive	Past Tense	Past Participle
lay	laid	laid	shear	sheared	sheared or shorn
lead	led	led			
lean	leant or leaned	leant or leaned	shed	shed	shed
leap	leapt or leaped	leapt or leaped	shine	shone	shone
learn	learnt or learned	learnt or learned	shoe	shod	shod
leave	left	left	shoot	shot	shot
lend	lent	lent	show	showed	shown
let	let	let	shrink	shrank or shrunk	shrunk or shrunken
lie	lay	lain			
light	lit or lighted	lit or lighted	shut	shut	shut
lose	lost	lost	sing	sang	sung
make	made	made	sink	sank	sunk
may	might		sit	sat	sat
mean	meant	meant	sleep	slept	slept
meet	met	met	slide	slid	slid
mow	mowed	mown	sling	slung	slung
must			slink	slunk	slunk
ought			slit	slit	slit
panic	panicked	panicked	smell	smelt or smelled	smelt or smelled
pay	paid	paid			
picnic	picnicked	picnicked	sow	sowed	sown or sowed
put	put	put	speak	spoke	spoken
quit	quitted or quit	quitted or quit	speed	sped or speeded	sped or speeded
read	read	read			
rid	rid or ridded	rid or ridded	spell	spelt or spelled	spelt or spelled
ride	rode	ridden	spend	spent	spent
ring	rang	rung	spill	spilt or spilled	spilt or spilled
rise	rose	risen	spin	spun	spun
run	ran	run	spit	spat or spit	spat or spit
saw	sawed	sawn or sawed	split	split	split
say	said	said	spread	spread	spread
see	saw	seen	spring	sprang	sprung
seek	sought	sought	stand	stood	stood
sell	sold	sold	steal	stole	stolen
send	sent	sent	stick	stuck	stuck
set	set	set	sting	stung	stung
sew	sewed	sewn or sewed	stink	stank or stunk	stunk
shake	shook	shaken	stride	strode	stridden
shall	should		strike	struck	struck

Infinitive	Past Tense	Past Participle	Infinitive	Past Tense	Past Participle
string	strung	strung	wake	woke	woken
strive	strove	striven	wear	wore	worn
swear	swore	sworn	weave	wove	woven or wove
sweep	swept	swept	weep	wept	wept
swell	swelled	swollen or swelled	will	would	
			win	won	won
swim	swam	swum	wind	wound	wound
swing	swung	swung	wring	wrung	wrung
take	took	taken	write	wrote	written
teach	taught	taught			
tear	tore	torn			
tell	told	told			
think	thought	thought			
throw	threw	thrown			
thrust	thrust	thrust			
traffic	trafficked	trafficked			
tread	trod	trodden or trod			

[1] when *bear* means *give birth to,* the past participle is always *born.*

[2] used only in the infinitive or as an imperative.

[3] the preferred form of the past tense and past participle when referring to death by hanging is *hanged.*

French irregular verbs

Infinitive	Present Indicative	Present Participle	Imperfect	Past Participle	Future
absoudre	absous	absolvant	absolvais	absous	absoudrai
acquérir	acquiers	acquérant	acquérais	acquis	acquerrai
aller	vais	allant	allais	allé	irai
apercevoir[1]	aperçois	apercevant	apercevais	aperçu	apercevrai
assaillir	assaille	assaillant	assaillais	assailli	assaillirai
asseoir	assieds *or* assois	asseyant	asseyais *or* assoyais	assis	assiérai *or* assoirai
atteindre[2]	atteins	atteignant	atteignais	atteint	atteindrai
avoir	ai	ayant	avais	eu	aurai
battre	bats	battant	battais	battu	battrai
boire	bois	buvant	buvais	bu	boirai
bouillir	bous	bouillant	bouillais	bouilli	bouillirai
circoncire	circoncis	circoncisant	circoncisais	circoncis	circoncirai
clore	clos	closant		clos	clorai
conclure	conclus	concluant	concluais	conclu	conclurai
conduire[3]	conduis	conduisant	conduisais	conduit	conduirai
confire	confis	confisant	confisais	confit	confirai
conquérir	conquiers	conquérant	conquérais	conquis	conquerrai
contraindre	contrains	contraignant	contraignais	contraint	contraindrai
coudre	couds	cousant	cousais	cousu	coudrai
courir	cours	courant	courais	couru	courrai
couvrir	couvre	couvrant	couvrais	couvert	couvrirai
craindre	crains	craignant	craignais	craint	craindrai
croire	crois	croyant	croyais	cru	croirai
croître	crois	croissant	croissais	crû	croîtrai
cueillir	cueille	cueillant	cueillais	cueilli	cueillerai
cuire	cuis	cuisant	cuisais	cuit	cuirai
devoir	dois	devant	devais	dû	devrai
dire	dis	disant	disais	dit	dirai
dissoudre	dissous	dissolvant	dissolvais	dissous	dissoudrai
dormir	dors	dormant	dormais	dormi	dormirai
échoir	il échoit *or* échet	échéant		échu	il échoira *or* écherra
écrire[4]	écris	écrivant	écrivais	écrit	écrirai
envoyer	envoie	envoyant	envoyais	envoyé	enverrai
être	suis	étant	étais	été	serai
exclure	exclus	excluant	excluais	exclu	exclurai
faillir		faillant		failli	faillirai
faire	fais	faisant	faisais	fait	ferai
falloir	il faut		il fallait	fallu	il faudra
férir				féru	
frire	fris			frit	frirai

Infinitive	Present Indicative	Present Participle	Imperfect	Past Participle	Future
fuir	fuis	fuyant	fuyais	fui	fuirai
gésir	gis	gisant	gisais		
haïr	haïs	haïssant	haïssais	haï	haïrai
importer	il importe	important		importé	
inclure	inclus	incluant	incluais	inclus	inclurai
joindre	joins	joignant	joignais	joint	joindrai
lire	lis	lisant	lisais	lu	lirai
luire	luis	luisant	luisais	lui	luirai
maudire	maudis	maudissant	maudissais	maudit	maudirai
mentir	mens	mentant	mentais	menti	mentirai
messeoir	il messied	messéant	il messeyait		il messiéra
mettre	mets	mettant	mettais	mis	mettrai
moudre	mouds	moulant	moulais	moulu	moudrai
mourir	meurs	mourant	mourais	mort	mourrai
mouvoir	meus	mouvant	mouvais	mû	mouvrai
naître	nais	naissant	naissais	né	naîtrai
nuire	nuis	nuisant	nuisais	nui	nuirai
offrir	offre	offrant	offrais	offert	offrirai
ouïr		oyant		ouï	ouïrai
ouvrir	ouvre	ouvrant	ouvrais	ouvert	ouvrirai
paître	pais	paissant	paissais		paîtrai
paraître[5]	parais	paraissant	paraissais	paru	paraîtrai
partir	pars	partant	partais	parti	partirai
plaindre	plains	plaignant	plaignais	plaint	plaindrai
plaire	plais	plaisant	plaisais	plu	plairai
pleuvoir	il pleut	pleuvant	il pleuvait	plu	il pleuvra
pourvoir	pourvois	pourvoyant	pourvoyais	pourvu	pourvoirai
pouvoir	peux or puis	pouvant	pouvais	pu	pourrai
prendre	prends	prenant	prenais	pris	prendrai
repaître	repais	repaissant	repaissais	repu	repaîtrai
se repentir	me repens	se repentant	me repentais	repenti	me repentirai
requérir	requiers	requérant	requérais	requis	requerrai
résoudre	résous	résolvant	résolvais	résolu	résoudrai
rire	ris	riant	riais	ri	rirai
saillir	il saillit or saille	saillissant or saillant	il saillissait or saillait	sailli	il saillira or saillera
savoir	sais	sachant	savais	su	saurai
sentir	sens	sentant	sentais	senti	sentirai
seoir	il sied	séant ou seyant	il seyait	sis	il siéra
servir	sers	servant	servais	servi	servirai
sortir	sors	sortant	sortais	sorti	sortirai

French irregular verbs

Infinitive	Present Indicative	Present Participle	Imperfect	Past Participle	Future
souffrir	souffre	souffrant	souffrais	souffert	souffrirai
suffire	suffis	suffisant	suffisais	suffi	suffirai
suivre	suis	suivant	suivais	suivi	suivrai
surseoir	sursois	sursoyant	sursoyais	sursis	surseoirai
taire	tais	taisant	taisais	tu	tairai
tenir	tiens	tenant	tenais	tenu	tiendrai
traire	trais	trayant	trayais	trait	trairai
tressaillir	tressaille	tressaillant	tressaillais	tressailli	tressaillirai
vaincre	vaincs	vainquant	vainquais	vaincu	vaincrai
valoir	vaux	valant	valais	valu	vaudrai
venir	viens	venant	venais	venu	viendrai
vêtir	vêts	vêtant	vêtais	vêtu	vêtirai
vivre	vis	vivant	vivais	vécu	vivrai
voir	vois	voyant	voyais	vu	verrai
vouloir	veux	voulant	voulais	voulu	voudrai

[1] All other verbs ending in -cevoir are conjugated like apercevoir.
[2] All other verbs ending in -eindre are conjugated like atteindre.
[3] All other verbs ending in -uire are conjugated like conduire.
[4] All other verbs ending in -crire are conjugated like écrire.
[5] All other verbs ending in -aître are conjugated like paraître.

A

a (a) v see **avoir**.
à (a) prep **1** to. **2** at. **3** in. **4** by. **5** from. **6** for. **7** according to.
abaisser (abɛ'se:) vt **1** lower, let down. **2** reduce. **s'abaisser** vr **1** humble oneself. **2** decrease. **abaissement** nm **1** humiliation, degradation. **2** lowering.
abandon (abã'dɔ̃) nm **1** desertion. **2** surrender. **3** neglect. **à l'abandon** uncared for.
abandonner (abãdɔ'ne:) vt **1** abandon, desert. **2** give up, surrender. **3** let go. **s'abandonner à** vr **1** give way to. **2** indulge in.
abasourdir (abasu:r'di:r) vt **1** astound, dumbfound. **2** bewilder.
abats (a'ba) nm pl offal.
abattoir (aba'twar) nm abattoir, slaughterhouse.
abattre° (a'batr) vt **1** knock or pull down. **2** slaughter. **3** lay. **4** shoot down. **s'abattre** vr **1** fall, collapse. **2** abate. **3** become depressed. **abat-jour** nm invar lampshade. **abattu** adj depressed, disheartened.
abbaye (abɛ'ji:) nf abbey, monastery.
abbé (a'be:) nm **1** abbot. **2** priest. **abbesse** (a'bɛs) nf abbess.
abcès (ap'sɛ) nm abscess.
abdiquer (abdi:'ke:) vt **1** abdicate. **2** renounce.
abdomen (abdɔ'mɛn) nm abdomen.
abeille (a'bɛj) nf bee.
abhorrer (abɔ're:) vt abhor, loathe.
abimer (abi:'me:) vt **1** spoil, damage. **2** injure. **s'abimer** vr **1** be engulfed. **2** get damaged. **abîme** nm abyss.
abnégation (abnɛga'sjɔ̃) nf self-sacrifice.
aboi (a'bwa) nm bark. **aux abois** in a desperate situation. **aboiement** nm **1** barking. **2** bark.
abolir (abɔ'li:r) vt abolish. **abolition** nf **1** abolition. **2** repeal.
abominable (abɔmi:'nabl) adj abominable.
abonder (abɔ̃'de:) vi abound, be plentiful. **abondamment** adv abundantly. **abondance**

nf **1** abundance. **2** wealth. **abondant** adj abundant, plentiful.
s'abonner (sabɔ'ne:) vr subscribe. **abonnement** nm **1** subscription. **2** season ticket.
abord (a'bɔr) nm access, approach. **d'abord** adv at first.
aborder (abɔr'de:) vi land. vt **1** approach, accost. **2** collide with. **3** deal with. **abordable** adj **1** approachable. **2** accessible. **3** reasonable.
aborigène (abɔri:'ʒɛn) adj **1** Aboriginal. **2** native. nm,f Aborigine.
abortif, -ive (abɔr'ti:f, -'ti:v) adj abortive.
aboutir (abu:'ti:r) vi **1** end. **2** lead, result. **3** succeed.
aboyer (abwa'je:) vi bark.
abrasif, -ive (abra'zi:f, -'zi:v) adj,nm abrasive.
abréger (abre:'ʒe:) vt **1** abbreviate. **2** abridge, cut down. **abrégé** nm precis, summary.
abreuver (abrœ've:) vt **1** water (animals). **2** soak. **s'abreuver** vr quench one's thirst.
abréviation (abre:vja'sjɔ̃) nf abbreviation.
abri (a'bri:) nm shelter. **à l'abri 1** sheltered, under cover. **2** safe.
abriter (abri:'te:) vt shelter, protect. **s'abriter** vr take cover or shelter.
abricot (abri:'ko) nm apricot. **abricotier** nm apricot tree.
abrutissant (abryti:'sã) adj **1** stunning. **2** extremely tedious.
absence (ap'sãs) nf absence. **absent** adj absent, missing.
abside (ap'si:d) nf apse.
absinthe (ap'sɛ̃t) nf absinthe.
absolu (apsɔ'ly) adj absolute, complete, utter. **absolument** adv absolutely.
absolvant (apsɔl'vã) v see **absoudre**.
absorber (apsɔr'be:) vt **1** absorb. **2** engross, occupy.
absoudre° (ap'su:dr) vt absolve, forgive.
absous (ap'su:) v see **absoudre**.
s'abstenir (sapstə'ni:r) vr **s'abstenir de** abstain or refrain from. **abstention** nf abstention. **abstinence** nf abstinence.

abstrait (ap'strɛ) *adj* abstract.
absurde (ap'syrd) *adj* absurd, ridiculous.
abus (a'by) *nm* 1 abuse, misuse. 2 error.
Abyssinie (abɪːsiːˈniː) *nf* Abyssinia. **abyssinien, -ienne** (abɪːsiːˈnjɛ̃, -ˈnjɛn) *adj,n* Abyssinian.
académie (akadeˈmiː) *nf* 1 academy. 2 college, school. **académique** *adj* academic.
acajou (akaˈʒu) *nm* mahogany.
accabler (akɑˈble) *vt* 1 overwhelm. 2 overload. **accablé** *adj* 1 overwhelmed, overcome. 2 tired out.
accaparer (akapaˈre) *vt* 1 monopolize, take possession of. 2 hoard.
accéder (akseˈde) *vi* **accéder à** 1 agree to, comply with. 2 have access to.
accélérer (akseleˈre) *vt* accelerate, quicken. **accélérateur** (akseleraˈtœr) *nm* accelerator.
accent (ak'sɑ̃) *nm* 1 accent. 2 stress. 3 pronunciation. 4 expression.
accentuer (aksɑ̃ˈtɥe) *vt* stress, accentuate, emphasize.
accepter (aksɛpˈte) *vt* accept. *vi* agree. **acceptable** *adj* 1 acceptable, reasonable. 2 welcome.
accès (ak'sɛ) *nm* 1 access. 2 fit, attack.
accessoire (aksɛˈswar) *adj,nm* accessory.
accident (aksiˈdɑ̃) *nm* accident, mishap. **accidenté** *adj* 1 uneven. 2 eventful. **accidentel, -elle** *adj* accidental.
acclamer (aklaˈme) *vt* acclaim, applaud, cheer. **acclamation** *nf* 1 acclamation. 2 *pl* cheers.
acclimater (akliːmaˈte) *vt* acclimatize. **s'acclimater** *vr* get acclimatized.
accommoder (akɔmɔˈde) *vt* 1 suit. 2 cook. 3 adapt. **s'accommoder à** *vr* 1 adapt oneself to. 2 come to an agreement with. **s'accommoder de** *vr* put up with. **accommodant** *adj* easygoing.
accompagner (akɔ̃paˈɲe) *vt* accompany. **accompagnement** *nm* 1 accompaniment. 2 *pl* trimmings.
accomplir (akɔ̃ˈpliːr) *vt* 1 complete. 2 accomplish, achieve. 3 fulfil. **accompli** *adj* 1 accomplished, perfect. 2 finished.
accord (aˈkɔr) *nm* 1 agreement. 2 *mus* chord. **d'accord!** agreed! **être d'accord** agree.
accorder (akɔrˈde) *vt* grant. **s'accorder** *vr* 1 agree. 2 correspond, tally.
accordéon (akɔrdeˈɔ̃) *nm* accordion.
accoucher (akuˈʃe) *vi* give birth.
accoutumer (akutyˈme) *vt* accustom. **s'accoutumer à** *vr* get used to.

accrocher (akrɔˈʃe) *vt* 1 hook, catch. 2 hang up. 3 collide with. **s'accrocher** *vr* cling or hang on. **accrocheur, -euse** (akrɔˈʃœr, -ˈʃœz) *adj* 1 tenacious. 2 eye-catching.
accroître (aˈkrwatr) *vt* 1 increase. 2 add to.
s'accroupir (sakruˈpiːr) *vr* crouch, squat.
accueil (aˈkœj) *nm* 1 reception. 2 welcome.
accueillir (akœˈjiːr) *vt* 1 receive. 2 welcome. 3 greet.
accumuler (akymyˈle) *vt* 1 accumulate, amass. 2 hoard.
accuser (akyˈze) *vt* 1 accuse. 2 accentuate. 3 indicate. **accuser réception de** acknowledge receipt of. **accusation** *nf* accusation, charge. **accusé** *adj* prominent. *nm* accused (person).
acerbe (aˈsɛrb) *adj* 1 harsh. 2 bitter.
s'acharner (saʃarˈne) *vr* persist. **s'acharner à** keep at. **acharné** *adj* 1 eager, keen. 2 desperate. **acharnement** (aʃarnəˈmɑ̃) *nm* 1 eagerness. 2 relentlessness.
achat (aˈʃa) *nm* purchase. **faire des achats** go shopping.
acheminer (aʃəmiˈne) *vt* dispatch, forward. **s'acheminer** *vr* make one's way.
acheter (aʃˈte) *vt* buy.
achever (aʃˈve) *vt* complete, finish. **achevé** *adj* accomplished. **achèvement** (aʃɛvˈmɑ̃) *nm* completion.
acide (aˈsiːd) *adj* 1 acid. 2 sour, sharp. *nm* acid.
acier (aˈsje) *nm* steel.
acné (akˈne) *nf* acne.
acompte (aˈkɔ̃t) *nm* instalment.
acoustique (akuˈstiːk) *adj* acoustic. *nf* acoustics.
acquérir (akeˈriːr) *vt* 1 acquire. 2 secure, get.
acquiers (akiˈɛr) *v* see **acquérir.**
acquiescer (akjɛˈse) *vt* acquiesce, agree.
acquis (aˈkɪ) *v* see **acquérir.**
acquit (aˈkɪ) *nm comm* receipt.
acquitter (akiˈte) *vt* 1 acquit. 2 pay off. 3 receipt. **s'acquitter de** *vr* fulfil, carry out.
âcre (ɑkr) *adj* 1 bitter, sharp. 2 pungent.
acrilique (akriˈliːk) *adj* acrylic.
acrimonie (akriːmɔˈniː) *nf* acrimony, bitterness.
acrobate (akrɔˈbat) *nm,f* acrobat. **acrobatique** *adj* acrobatic.
acte[1] (akt) *nm* 1 act, action, deed. 2 record. **acte de décès/mariage/naissance** death/marriage/birth certificate.
acte[2] (akt) *nm* Th act.
acteur, -trice (ak'tœr, -'triːs) *nm,f* actor, actress.

actif, -ive (ak'ti:f, -'ti:v) adj 1 active, busy. 2 brisk. nm comm credit.

action (ak'sjɔ̃) nf 1 action, act. 2 effect. 3 comm share.

activer (akti:'ve:) vt 1 stir up, activate. 2 quicken. **activiste** nm activist. **activité** nf activity, industry.

actuaire (ak'tɥɛr) nm actuary.

actualité (aktɥali:'te:) nf 1 reality. 2 topical event or question. 3 pl news, current events.

actuel, -elle (ak'tɥɛl) adj 1 current, present, topical. 2 real. **à l'heure actuelle** at the present time.

acuponcture (akypɔ̃k'tyr) nf acupuncture.

adapter (adap'te:) vt 1 adjust, fit. 2 adapt.

addenda (adɛ̃'da) nm invar addendum.

addition (adi:'sjɔ̃) nf 1 addition. 2 bill.

additionner (adi:sjɔ̃'ne:) vt add up.

adénoïde (ade:nɔ'i:d) adj adenoidal. **végétations adénoïdes** nf pl adenoids.

adhérer (ade:'re:) vi adhere, stick. **adhérer à** join (a party). **adhérent** adj adherent, sticky.

adhésion (ade:'zjɔ̃) nf 1 adhesion. 2 membership. **adhésif, -ive** (ade:'zi:f, -'zi:v) adj adhesive.

adieu, -eux (a'djœ) interj goodbye! farewell! nm farewell. **faire ses adieux à** say goodbye to, take one's leave of.

adjacent (adʒa'sɑ̃) adj adjacent.

adjectif, -ive (adʒɛk'ti:f, -'ti:v) nm adjective. adj adjectival.

adjoint (a'dʒwɛ̃) nm assistant, deputy.

adjudication (adʒydi:ka'sjɔ̃) nf adjudication, award. **mettre en adjudication** put up for auction.

adjuger (adʒy'ʒe:) vt 1 award. 2 allocate. **une fois! deux fois! trois fois! adjugé!** going! going! gone!

admettre (ad'mɛtr) vt 1 admit. 2 allow. 3 suppose. 4 acknowledge.

administrer (admi:ni:'stre:) vt administer, manage. **administrateur** nm administrator, manager. **administratif, -ive** (admi:ni:stra'ti:f, -'ti:v) adj administrative. **administration** nf 1 administration, management. 2 civil service.

admirer (admi:'re:) vt 1 admire. 2 wonder at. **admirable** adj admirable, wonderful. **admiration** nf admiration.

admission (admi:'sjɔ̃) nf admission. **admissible** (admi:'si:bl) adj 1 allowable. 2 eligible.

adolescence (adɔlɛs'sɑ̃s) nf adolescence. **ado-**lescent adj teenage, adolescent. nm teenager, adolescent.

s'adonner (sadɔ'ne:) vr **s'adonner à** 1 devote oneself to, go in for. 2 become addicted to.

adopter (adɔp'te:) vt 1 adopt. 2 take up. 3 pol pass, carry. **adopté** nm adopted child.

adorer (adɔ're:) vt 1 adore. 2 worship.

adoucir (adu:'si:r) vt 1 soften. 2 alleviate. 3 pacify, calm.

adrénaline (adrɛna'li:n) nf adrenaline.

adresser (adrɛ'se:) vt address, direct. **s'adresser à** vr 1 apply to. 2 speak to. **adresse** nf 1 address. 2 skill.

adriatique (adri:a'ti:k) adj Adriatic. **(Mer) Adriatique** nf Adriatic (Sea).

adroit (a'drwa) adj 1 skilful, dexterous, adroit. 2 shrewd.

adulation (adyla'sjɔ̃) nf adulation, flattery.

adulte (a'dylt) adj,n adult.

adultère (adyl'tɛr) nm adultery.

adultérer (adylte:'re:) vt adulterate.

advenir (advə'ni:r) v imp 1 occur to. 2 happen to.

adverbe (ad'vɛrb) nm adverb. **adverbial, -aux** (advɛr'bjal, -'bjo) adj adverbial.

adverse (ad'vɛrs) adj 1 adverse. 2 opposite. **adversaire** nm 1 opponent. 2 enemy.

aérer (ae:'re:) vt ventilate, air. **aérien, -ienne** (ae:'rjɛ̃, -'rjɛn) adj aerial, air.

aérodynamique (ae:rɔdi:na'mi:k) adj aerodynamic. nf aerodynamics.

aéroglisseur (ae:rɔgli:'sœr) nm hovercraft.

aéronautique (ae:rɔno'ti:k) adj aeronautical. nf aeronautics.

aéroport (ae:rɔ'pɔr) nm airport.

aéroporté (ae:rɔpɔr'te:) adj airborne.

aérosol (e:rɔ'sɔl) nm aerosol.

affable (a'fabl) adj affable.

affaiblir (afɛ'bli:r) vt 1 weaken. 2 impair. 3 reduce. **s'affaiblir** vr become weak, flag.

affaire (a'fɛr) nf 1 business. 2 matter. 3 trouble. 4 pl belongings, things. **avoir affaire à** have to do with. **faire l'affaire de** suit. **affairé** adj busy.

s'affaisser (safɛ'se:) vr 1 subside. 2 collapse.

affamer (afa'me:) vt starve. **affamé** adj hungry, ravenous.

affecter[1] (afɛk'te:) vt 1 feign, affect. 2 be partial to. 3 assume.

affecter[2] (afɛk'te:) vt allocate.

affecter[3] (afɛk'te:) vt move, touch, affect.

affecter[4] (afɛk'te:) vt concern.

affection (afɛk'sjɔ̃) nf 1 affection, liking. 2

3

ailment. **affectueux, -euse** (afɛk'tɥœ, -'tɥœz) *adj* loving, affectionate.

affiche (a'fiːʃ) *nf* 1 placard. 2 poster, bill.

affilier (afi'lje:) *vt* affiliate. **s'affilier à** *vr* affiliate oneself to, join.

affinité (afiːniːˈte:) *nf* 1 affinity. 2 resemblance.

affirmer (afiːrˈme:) *vt* 1 affirm. 2 assert. **affirmatif, -ive** (afiːrmaˈtiːf, -ˈtiːv) *adj* 1 affirmative. 2 positive. **affirmation** *nf* affirmation, assurance.

affliction (afliːkˈsjɔ̃) *nf* affliction, grief.

affliger (afliˈʒe:) *vt* 1 afflict. 2 distress. **s'affliger** *vr* grieve.

affluence (aflyˈɑ̃s) *nf* 1 abundance, plenty. 2 crowd.

affoler (afɔˈle:) *vt* 1 distract. 2 drive crazy. **s'affoler** *vr* 1 panic. 2 be infatuated. **affolé** *adj* crazy, frantic.

affranchir (afrɑ̃ˈʃiːr) *vt* 1 (set) free. 2 stamp.

affréter (afreˈte:) *vt* charter (a ship).

affreux, -euse (a'frœ, -ˈfrœz) *adj* 1 horrible, dreadful. 2 atrocious.

affront (a'frɔ̃) *nm* affront, insult.

Afghanistan (afganiːˈstɑ̃) *nm* Afghanistan. **afghan** *adj,n* Afghan.

afin (a'fɛ̃) **afin de** *prep* to, in order to. **afin que** *conj* so that, in order that.

Afrique (a'friːk) *nf* Africa. **Afrique du Sud** South Africa. **africain** *adj,n* African.

agacer (agaˈse:) *vt* 1 annoy. 2 jar, set on edge. **agaçant** *adj* annoying.

âge (ɑʒ) *nm* 1 age. 2 period. **d'un certain âge** middle-aged. **quel âge avez-vous?** how old are you? **âgé** *adj* aged, elderly.

agence (a'ʒɑ̃s) *nf* agency. **agence de voyages** travel agency. **agent** *nm* agent. **agent de change** stockbroker. **agent de police** policeman. **agent immobilier** estate agent.

s'agenouiller (saʒnuˈje:) *vr* kneel down.

agglomération (aglɔmɛraˈsjɔ̃) *nf* 1 built-up area. 2 mass.

aggraver (agraˈve:) *vt* 1 aggravate. 2 worsen. 3 increase.

agile (a'ʒiːl) *adj* 1 agile, nimble. 2 quick.

agir (a'ʒiːr) *vi* 1 act, do. 2 behave. 3 influence. **s'agir de** *v imp* concern, be a question of. **de quoi s'agit-il?** what's it all about?

agiter (aʒiːˈte:) *vt* 1 wave, shake. 2 agitate. 3 discuss. **s'agiter** *vr* fidget.

agneau, -aux (a'ɲo) *nm* lamb.

agnostique (agnɔˈstiːk) *adj,n* agnostic.

agonie (agɔˈniː) *nf* death agony. **à l'agonie** dying.

agrafe (a'graf) *nf* 1 hook, clasp. 2 clamp. 3 staple.

agraire (a'grɛr) *adj* agrarian.

agrandir (agrɑ̃ˈdiːr) *vt* 1 enlarge. 2 increase, magnify.

agréer (agreˈe:) *vt* 1 accept. 2 approve. 3 please. **agréable** *adj* 1 agreeable, pleasant. 2 comfortable. **agrément** *nm* 1 pleasure. 2 consent, approval. 3 amenities.

agression (agrɛˈsjɔ̃) *nf* agression. **agressif, -ive** (agrɛˈsiːf, -ˈsiːv) *adj* aggressive.

agricole (agriːˈkɔl) *adj* agricultural.

agriculture (agriːkylˈtyr) *nf* agriculture. **agriculteur** *nm* farmer.

agrumes (a'grym) *nm pl* citrus fruits.

aguets (a'gɛ) *nm pl* **aux aguets** watchful.

ahurir (ay'riːr) *vt* 1 astound, flabbergast. 2 bewilder.

ai (ɛ) *v* see **avoir.**

aider (ɛ'de:) *vt* help, assist, aid. **aide** *nf* 1 help, aid. 2 assistant. 3 relief. **à l'aide!** help! **venir en aide à** come to the help of

aïeul (a'jœl) *nm* 1 *pl* **aïeuls** grandfather. 2 *pl* **aïeux** forefather.

aigle (ɛgl) *nm* 1 eagle. 2 genius. 3 lectern.

aiglefin (ɛgləˈfɛ̃) *nm* haddock.

aigrir (ɛ'griːr) *vt* 1 sour. 2 embitter. *vi* turn sour. **aigre** *adj* 1 sour, tart. 2 shrill. **aigreur** *nf* 1 sourness. 2 bitterness.

aigu, -uë (e:'gy) *adj* 1 sharp, pointed. 2 acute. 3 shrill.

aiguille (e:'gɥiːj) *nf* 1 needle. 2 hand (of a clock). **aiguille à tricoter** knitting needle.

aiguillon (e:gɥiˈjɔ̃) *nm* 1 incentive. 2 sting.

aiguiser (e:gɥiːˈze:) *vt* 1 sharpen, point. 2 stimulate.

ail (aj) *nm, pl* **aulx** garlic.

aile (ɛl) *nf* 1 wing (of bird, building, car, or aircraft). 2 aisle. **ailé** *adj* winged. **aileron** (ɛl'rɔ̃) *nm* fin.

ailleurs (a'jœr) *adv* elsewhere. **d'ailleurs** besides.

aimant (ɛ'mɑ̃) *nm* magnet.

aimer (ɛ'me:) *vt* 1 like, care for. 2 love. **aimer mieux** prefer. **aimable** *adj* amiable, kind.

aine (ɛn) *nf* groin.

aîné (ɛ'ne:) *adj* 1 elder. 2 eldest. 3 senior.

ainsi (ɛ̃'siː) *adv* thus, in this way. **et ainsi de suite** and so on. **pour ainsi dire** so to speak. ~*conj* so. **ainsi que** 1 just as. 2 as well as.

air[1] (ɛr) *nm* 1 air, atmosphere. 2 wind.

air[2] (ɛr) *nm* 1 look, appearance. 2 way. **avoir l'air** look, seem.

4

air³ (εr) *nm* tune, melody.
airain (ε'rἔ) *nm* brass.
aire (εr) *nf* area.
aise (εz) *nf* ease, comfort. **être à l'aise 1** be comfortable. **2** be well off. ~*adj* glad, pleased. **aisé** *adj* easy.
aisselle (ε'sεl) *nf* armpit.
ajonc (a'ʒɔ̃) *nm* gorse.
ajourner (aʒu:r'ne:) *vt* **1** adjourn. **2** postpone.
ajouter (aʒu:'te:) *vt* **1** add. **2** add up.
ajuster (aʒy'ste:) *vt* **1** adjust, fit. **2** put in order.
alarme (a'larm) *nf* **1** alarm. **2** fear.
Albanie (alba'ni:) *nf* Albania. **albanais** *adj,n* Albanian.
albatros (alba'trɔs) *nm* albatross.
album (al'bɔm) *nm* album.
alcali (alka'li:) *nm* alkali.
alchimie (alʃi:'mi:) *nf* alchemy.
alcool (al'kɔl) *nm* **1** alcohol. **2** spirits. **alcoolique** *adj,n* alcoholic.
aléatoire (ale:a'twar) *adj* **1** contingent. **2** risky.
alentour (alã'tu:r) *adv* around, about. **alentours** *nm pl* **1** neighbourhood. **2** surroundings.
alerte (a'lεrt) *adj* alert, agile. *nf* alarm, warning. **fin d'alerte** *nf* all clear.
algèbre (al'ʒεbr) *nf* algebra.
Algérie (alʒe:'ri:) *nf* Algeria. **algérien, -ienne** (alʒe:'rjἔ, -'rjεn) *adj,n* Algerian.
algue (alg) *nf* seaweed.
alibi (ali:'bi:) *nm* alibi.
aliéner (alje:'ne:) *vt* alienate. **aliénable** *adj* transferable. **aliéné** *adj* mad, mentally ill.
aligner (ali:'ɲe:) *vt* align, put in a row.
aliment (ali:'mã) *nm* food. **alimentaire** *adj* alimentary. **alimentation** *nf* **1** nourishment, feeding. **2** foodstuffs.
alinéa (ali:ne:'a) *nm* paragraph.
aliter (ali:'te:) *vt* confine to bed.
allée (a'le:) *nf* garden path.
alléger (ale:'ʒe:) *vt* **1** relieve, alleviate. **2** lighten.
allégorie (alle:gɔ'ri:) *nf* allegory.
allègre (al'lεgr) *adj* **1** lively. **2** cheerful, light-hearted. **3** brisk.
alléguer (ale:'ge:) *vt* **1** allege. **2** plead, urge.
alléluia (ale:ly'ja) *nm* hallelujah.
Allemagne (al'maɲ) *nf* Germany. **allemand** (al'mã) *adj,n* German. *nm* German (language).
aller¹ (a'le:) *vi (aux* être) **1** go. **2** suit, fit. **aller chercher** fetch. **ça va!** OK! **comment allez-vous?** how are you? **vas-y! allez-y!** go on! **y aller de** stake, be at stake. **s'en aller** *vr* go away, depart. ~*nm* **1** single ticket. **2**

outward journey. **au pis aller** if the worst comes to the worst.
allergie (alεr'ʒi:) *nf* allergy. **allergique** *adj* allergic.
allier (a'lje:) *vt* **1** unite. **2** mix, blend. **alliage** *nm* alloy. **alliance** *nf* **1** alliance. **2** marriage. **3** wedding ring. **allié** *adj* **1** allied. **2** related by marriage. *nm* ally.
alligator (ali:ga'tɔr) *nm* alligator.
allitération (alli:te:ra'sjɔ̃) *nf* alliteration.
allô (a'lo) *interj* (on the telephone) hello!
allocation (allɔka'sjɔ̃) *nf* **1** allocation. **2** allowance.
allocution (allɔky'sjɔ̃) *nf* address, short speech.
allonger (alɔ̃'ʒe:) *vt* **1** lengthen. **2** thin (a sauce). **3** stretch out. **allonger une gifle à** slap.
allouer (a'lwe:) *vt* **1** grant. **2** allocate.
allumer (aly'me:) *vt* **1** light. **2** excite. **s'allumer** *vr* catch fire. **allumé** *adj* alight. **allume-feu** *nm invar* firelighter. **allumette** *nf* match.
allure (a'lyr) *nf* **1** pace, speed. **2** gait. **3** behaviour. **4** look. **à toute allure** at top speed.
allusion (ally'zjɔ̃) *nf* allusion. **faire allusion à** refer to.
almanach (alma'na) *nm* almanac.
aloi (a'lwa) *nm* quality. **de bon aloi** genuine.
alors (a'lɔr) *adv* **1** then, at that time. **2** so, in that case. **alors même que** even when. **alors que** when.
alouette (a'lwεt) *nf* lark.
alourdir (alu:r'di:r) *vt* **1** make heavy. **2** make stupid.
aloyau, -aux (alwa'jo) *nm* sirloin.
Alpes (alp) *nf pl* Alps. **alpestre** *adj* alpine. **alpin** *adj* alpine. **alpiniste** *nm* mountaineer.
alphabet (alfa'bε) *nm* alphabet. **alphabétique** (alfabe:'ti:k) *adj* alphabetical.
altercation (altεrka'sjɔ̃) *nf* dispute, squabble.
altérer (alte:'re:) *vt* **1** alter. **2** adulterate, corrupt. **3** make thirsty.
alterner (altεr'ne:) *vi* alternate, take turns. *vt* alternate. **alternatif, -ive** (altεrna'ti:f, -'ti:v) alternative, alternate. *nf* alternative.
Altesse (al'tεs) *nf* Highness.
altier, -ière (al'tje:, -'tjεr) *adj* haughty, arrogant.
altitude (alti:'tyd) *nf* altitude.
alto (al'to) *nm* **1** alto. **2** viola.
aluminium (alymi:'njɔm) *nm* aluminium.
amadouer (ama'dwe:) *vt* coax.
amaigrir (amε'gri:r) *vt* make thin, emaciate.

amalgamer (amalga'me:) *vt* amalgamate, blend.
amande (a'mãd) *nf* almond.
amant (a'mã) *nm* lover.
amarrer (ama're:) *vt* 1 moor. 2 tie up.
amas (a'ma) *nm* pile, heap, mass. **amasser** (ama'se:) *vt* 1 pile up. 2 amass.
amateur, -trice (ama'tœr, -'tri:s) *nm,f* 1 enthusiast. 2 patron. 3 amateur.
ambassade (ãba'sad) *nf* embassy. **ambassadeur** *nm* ambassador.
ambiance (ã'bjãs) *nf* 1 surroundings. 2 atmosphere.
ambidextre (ãbi'dɛkstr) *adj* ambidextrous.
ambigu, -uë (ãbi:'gy) *adj* ambiguous. **ambiguïté** *nf* ambiguity.
ambition (ãbi:'sjɔ̃) *nf* ambition. **ambitieux, -euse** (ãbi:'sjœ, -'sjœz) *adj* ambitious.
ambivalent (ãbi:va'lã) *adj* ambivalent.
ambre (ãbr) *nm* amber.
ambulance (ãby'lãs) *nf* ambulance.
ambulant (ãby'lã) *adj* 1 wandering. 2 travelling.
âme (am) *nf* 1 soul. 2 spirit. 3 mind. 4 feeling. 5 person. 6 core. 7 bore (of a gun).
améliorer (ame:ljɔ're:) *vt* improve. **amélioration** *nf* improvement.
aménager (amɛna'ʒe:) *vt* arrange, lay out. **aménagement** *nm* 1 fittings. 2 development.
amender (amã'de:) *vt* 1 improve. 2 amend. **amende** *nf* fine.
amener (am'ne:) *vt* 1 bring. 2 lead. 3 induce.
amer, -ère (a'mɛr) *adj* bitter. **amertume** *nf* bitterness.
Amérique (ame:'ri:k) *nf* America. **Amérique du Nord/Sud** North/South America. **américain** *adj,n* American.
améthyste (ame:'ti:st) *nf* amethyst.
ameublement (amœblə'mã) *nm* 1 furnishing. 2 furniture.
ami (a'mi:) *nm* 1 friend. 2 boyfriend. *adj* friendly. **amiable** *adj* amicable, friendly. **amical, -aux** (ami:'kal, -'ko) *adj* friendly. **amitié** *nf* 1 friendship. 2 kindness, favour.
amiante (a'mjãt) *nm* asbestos.
amibe (a'mi:b) *nf* amoeba.
amidon (ami:'dɔ̃) *nm* starch.
amiral, -aux (ami:'ral, -'ro) *nm* admiral. **amirauté** *nf* admiralty.
ammoniaque (amɔ'njak) *nf* ammonia.
amnistie (amni:'sti:) *nf* amnesty.
amoindrir (amwɛ̃'dri:r) *vt* reduce, diminish.
amollir (amɔ'li:r) *vt* 1 soften. 2 weaken.
amonceler (amɔ̃'sle:) *vt* heap up. **s'amonceler**

vr gather. **amoncellement** *nm* 1 heap. 2 accumulation.
amont (a'mɔ̃) **en amont** *adv* upstream. **en amont de** above.
amoral, -aux (amɔ'ral, -'ro) *adj* amoral.
amorcer (amɔr'se:) *vt* 1 bait. 2 begin. **amorce** *nf* 1 bait. 2 beginning.
amorphe (a'mɔrf) *adj* amorphous.
amortir (amɔr'ti:r) *vt* 1 deaden, soften. 2 pay off. **amortissement** *nm* 1 deadening. 2 redemption. **amortisseur** *nm* shock absorber.
amour (a'mu:r) *nm* love, affection. **amoureux, -euse** (amu'rœ, -'rœ:z) *adj* loving. **être amoureux de** be in love with. **amour-propre** *nm* 1 self-respect. 2 vanity.
ampère (ã'pɛr) *nm* ampere.
amphétamine (ãfe:ta'mi:n) *nf* amphetamine.
amphibie (ãfi:'bi:) *adj* amphibious. *nm* amphibian.
ample (ãpl) *adj* 1 ample. 2 full. 3 spacious. **ampleur** *nf* fullness.
amplifier (ãpli:'fje:) *vt* 1 amplify. 2 magnify. **amplificateur** (ãpli:fi:ka'tœr) *nm* amplifier.
ampoule (ã'pu:l) *nf* 1 bulb. 2 blister.
amputer (ãpy'te:) *vt* 1 amputate. 2 cut, reduce.
amuser (amy'ze:) *vt* amuse, entertain. **s'amuser** *vr* enjoy oneself. **amusement** *nm* 1 pastime. 2 recreation.
amygdale (ami:'dal) *nf* tonsil. **amygdalite** *nf* tonsillitis.
an (ã) *nm* year. **avoir six ans** be six years old. **tous les ans** every year.
anachronisme (anakrɔ'ni:sm) *nm* anachronism.
anal, -aux (a'nal, -'no) *adj* anal.
analogie (analɔ'ʒi:) *nf* analogy.
analphabète (analfa'bɛt) *adj* illiterate.
analyser (anali:'ze:) *vt* analyse. **analyse** *nf* analysis.
ananas (ana'na) *nm* pineapple.
anarchie (anar'ʃi:) *nf* anarchy. **anarchiste** *adj,n* anarchist.
anatomie (anatɔ'mi:) *nf* anatomy.
ancêtre (ã'sɛtr) *nm,f* 1 ancestor. 2 forefather.
anchois (ã'ʃwa) *nm* anchovy.
ancien, -ienne (ã'sjɛ̃, -'sjɛn) *adj* 1 ancient. 2 old, past. 3 former. 4 senior. **ancienneté** *nf* 1 antiquity. 2 seniority.
ancre (ãkr) *nf* anchor.
Andorre (ã'dɔr) *nm* Andorra. **andorran** *adj,n* Andorran.
âne (an) *nm* 1 donkey, ass. 2 fool.
anéantir (ane:ã'ti:r) *vt* annihilate, destroy.

s'anéantir vr 1 come to nothing. 2 humble oneself. **anéanti** adj 1 exhausted. 2 prostrate.

anecdote (anɛk'dɔt) nf anecdote.

anémie (ane:'mi:) nf anaemia. **anémique** adj anaemic.

anémone (ane:'mɔn) nf anemone.

anesthésier (anɛste:'zje:) vt anaesthetize. **anesthésique** adj,nm anaesthetic.

anfractueux, -euse (ãfrak'tɥœ, -'tɥœz) adj 1 winding. 2 irregular, rugged.

ange (ãʒ) nm angel.

angélique[1] (ãʒe:'li:k) adj angelic.

angélique[2] (ãʒe:'li:k) nf angelica.

angine (ã'ʒi:n) nf sore throat, tonsillitis.

angle (ãgl) nm 1 angle. 2 corner. 3 point of view. **angle droit** right angle.

Angleterre (ãglə'tɛr) nf England. **anglais** (ã'glɛ) adj English. nm 1 Englishman. 2 English (language).

anglican (ãgli:'kã) adj,n Anglican.

angoisse (ã'gwas) nf 1 anguish. 2 distress. **angoissant** (ãgwa'sã) adj 1 distressing. 2 alarming.

anguille (ã'gɪːj) nf eel.

anguleux, -euse (ãgy'lœ, -'lœz) adj 1 angular. 2 bony.

anhydride (ani:'dri:d) nm **anhydride carbonique** carbon dioxide.

animal, -aux[1] (ani:'mal, -'mo) nm animal.

animal, -aux[2] (ani:'mal, -'mo) adj 1 animal. 2 brutal. 3 sensual.

animer (ani:'me:) vt 1 animate. 2 prompt. 3 brighten. **s'animer** vr 1 come to life. 2 become excited. **animé** adj 1 lively. 2 bright.

animosité (ani:mɔzi:'te:) nf spite.

anis (a'ni:) nm aniseed.

annales (an'nal) nf pl annals.

anneau, -aux (a'no) nm 1 ring. 2 link. 3 ringlet.

année (a'ne:) nf year. **bonne année!** Happy New Year!

annexer (anɛk'se:) vt 1 annex. 2 attack. **annexe** nf annexe.

annihiler (ani:i:'le:) vt annihilate, destroy.

anniversaire (ani:vɛr'sɛr) adj anniversary. nm 1 birthday. 2 anniversary.

annoncer (anõ'se:) vt 1 announce. 2 advertise. 3 indicate. **s'annoncer bien** vr look promising. **annonce** nf 1 announcement. 2 advertisement. **petites annonces** nf pl classified advertisements.

annoter (anɔ'te:) vt annotate.

annuaire (a'nɥɛr) nm 1 almanac. 2 annual. 3 telephone directory.

annuel, -elle (a'nɥɛl) adj annual.

annuler (any'le:) vt annul, cancel.

anode (a'nɔd) nf anode.

anomalie (anɔma'li:) nf anomaly.

anonyme (anɔ'ni:m) adj anonymous. nm anonymity.

anormal, -aux (anɔr'mal, -'mo) adj 1 abnormal. 2 irregular.

anse (ãs) nf 1 handle. 2 cove.

antagonisme (ãtagɔ'ni:sm) nm antagonism. **antagoniste** adj antagonistic. nm opponent.

antarctique (ãtar'ti:k) adj antarctic. nm cap Antarctic.

antenne (ã'tɛn) nf 1 aerial. 2 antenna. 3 horn.

antérieur (ãte:'rjœr) adj 1 former, previous, prior. 2 fore.

anthologie (ãtɔlɔ'ʒi:) nf anthology.

anthropologie (ãtrɔpɔlɔ'ʒi:) nf anthropology.

anti-aérien, -ienne (ãti:ae:'rjɛ̃, -'rjɛn) adj anti-aircraft.

antialcoolique (ãti:alkɔ'li:k) adj teetotal. nm,f teetotaller.

antibiotique (ãti:bjɔ'ti:k) adj, nm antibiotic.

anticiper (ãti:si:'pe:) vt,vi anticipate. **anticipation** nf anticipation.

anticonceptionnel, -elle (ãti:kõsɛpsjɔ'nɛl) adj contraceptive.

anticorps (ãti:'kɔr) nm antibody.

anticyclone (ãti:si:'klon) nm anticyclone.

antidater (ãti:da'te:) vt backdate.

antidote (ãti:'dɔt) nm antidote.

anti-gel (ãti:'ʒɛl) nm invar antifreeze.

Antilles (ã'ti:j) nf pl West Indies. **antillais** adj,n West Indian.

antilope (ãti:'lɔp) nf antelope.

antique (ã'ti:k) adj 1 ancient. 2 antique. nf antique. **antiquaire** nm antique dealer. **antiquité** nf 1 antiquity. 2 pl antiques.

antisémitique (ãti:se:mi:'ti:k) adj anti-Semitic.

antiseptique (ãti:sɛp'ti:k) adj,nm antiseptic.

antisocial, -aux (ãti:sɔ'sjal, -'sjo) adj antisocial.

antithèse (ãti:'tɛz) nf antithesis.

antonyme (ãtɔ'ni:m) nm antonym.

antre (ãtr) nm 1 cave. 2 den.

anus (a'nys) nm anus.

anxiété (ãksje:'te:) nf anxiety, worry. **anxieux, -euse** (ãk'sjœ, -'sjœz) adj anxious, concerned.

août (u:) nm August.

apaiser (apɛ'ze:) vt 1 calm, appease. 2 alleviate. 3 quench. **s'apaiser** vr 1 calm down. 2 abate.

apathie (apa'ti:) nf apathy. **apathique** adj apathetic.

apercevoir* (apɛrsə'vwar) vt 1 perceive. 2 catch

7

sight of. **s'apercevoir** vr 1 notice. 2 realize. **aperçu** nm 1 glimpse. 2 outline.

apéritif (ape:ri'ti:f) nm aperitive.

aphis (a'fi:s) nm greenfly.

aplanir (apla'ni:r) vt 1 smooth, plane. 2 level.

aplatir (apla'ti:r) vt flatten. **s'aplatir** vr 1 go flat. 2 grovel.

aplomb (a'plɔ̃) nm 1 equilibrium. 2 uprightness. 3 self-assurance. **d'aplomb** upright, vertical.

apogée (apɔ'ʒe:) nm apex, climax.

apologie (apɔlɔ'ʒi:) nf 1 defence. 2 justification.

apostrophe (apɔ'strɔf) nf apostrophe.

apôtre (a'potr) nm apostle.

apparaître* (apa'rɛtr) vi (aux être) appear, become visible.

apparat (apa'ra) nm pomp, show. **d'apparat** formal.

appareil (apa'rɛj) nm 1 display. 2 apparatus. 3 machine, appliance. 4 inf phone. **appareil photo** camera.

apparence (apa'rãs) nf appearance, look. **en apparence** apparently. **apparent** adj 1 visible. 2 obvious. 3 apparent.

apparenter (aparã'te:) vt connect (by marriage).

appartement (apartə'mã) nm flat.

appartenir* (apartə'ni:r) vi **appartenir à** belong to. v imp concern.

appas (a'pa) nm pl charm, attraction.

appât (a'pɑ) nm bait.

appel (a'pɛl) nm 1 appeal. 2 call. **appel d'incendie** fire alarm.

appeler (ap'le:) vt 1 call. 2 summon. 3 appeal. 4 ring, telephone. **faire appeler** send for. **s'appeler** vr be called.

appendice (apɛ̃'di:s) nm appendix. **appendicite** nf appendicitis.

appentis (apã'ti:) nm 1 penthouse. 2 shed, outhouse.

appétit (ape:'ti:) nm 1 appetite. 2 desire. **bon appétit!** enjoy your meal!

applaudir (aplo'di:r) vt 1 applaud. 2 commend. 3 praise. **applaudissement** nm applause.

appliquer (apli'ke:) vt 1 apply. 2 enforce. **application** nf 1 application. 2 diligence. **applicable** adj 1 applicable. 2 appropriate. **appliqué** adj 1 applied. 2 studious.

appointements (apwɛ̃t'mã) nm pl salary.

apporter (apɔr'te:) vt 1 bring. 2 provide.

apposer (apo'ze:) vt affix.

apprécier (apre:'sje:) vt 1 appreciate. 2 appraise, value. **appréciable** adj appreciable. **appréciation** nf 1 estimate. 2 appreciation.

appréhender (apre:ã'de:) vt 1 seize. 2 apprehend, fear. **apprehensif, -ive** (apre:-ãsi:f, -'si:v) adj apprehensive, timid.

apprendre* (a'prãdr) vt 1 learn. 2 teach. 3 inform.

apprenti (aprã'ti:) nm apprentice.

apprivoiser (apri:vwa'ze:) vt 1 tame. 2 domesticate. **s'apprivoiser** vr grow tame.

approbation (aprɔba'sjɔ̃) nf consent, approval.

approcher (aprɔ'ʃe:) vt approach, bring near. vi approach, draw near. **s'approcher de** vr approach, come near to. **approche** nf approach.

approfondir (aprɔfɔ̃'di:r) vt 1 make deeper. 2 examine thoroughly. **approfondi** adj 1 deep. 2 thorough.

approprier (aprɔpri:'e:) vt 1 appropriate. 2 fit. **s'approprier à** vr adapt oneself to.

approuver (apru:'ve:) vt 1 approve. 2 agree to.

approximatif, -ive (aprɔksi:ma'ti:f, -'ti:v) adj approximate, rough.

appui (a'pɥi:) nm prop, support.

appuyer (apɥi:'je:) vt 1 support. 2 rest. 3 hold. **appuyer sur** 1 lean or press on. 2 emphasize. **s'appuyer sur** vr 1 lean on. 2 rely on.

âpre (ɑpr) adj 1 rough, harsh. 2 sharp. 3 keen. 4 greedy.

après (a'prɛ) prep after. **d'après** according to. ~adv afterwards, later. **après que** after, when. **et après?** what then? **après-demain** adv the day after tomorrow. **après-midi** nm invar afternoon.

à-propos (aprɔ'po) nm aptness.

apte (apt) adj 1 suited. 2 capable. **aptitude** nf 1 aptitude. 2 capacity.

aquarelle (akwa'rɛl) nf watercolour.

aquarium (akwa'rjɔm) nm aquarium.

aquatique (akwa'ti:k) adj aquatic.

aqueux, -euse (a'kœ, -'kœz) adj watery.

Arabie (ara'bi:) nf Arabia. **Arabie Séoudite** Saudi Arabia. **arabe** adj 1 Arab. 2 Arabic. nm 1 Arab. 2 Arabic (language).

arable (a'rabl) adj arable.

arachide (ara'ʃi:d) nf peanut.

araignée (arɛ'ɲe:) nf spider.

arbitre[1] (ar'bi:tr) nm umpire, referee.

arbitre[2] (ar'bi:tr) nm **libre arbitre** free will.

arbitrer (arbi:'tre:) vt 1 arbitrate. 2 umpire. **arbitraire** (arbi:'trɛr) adj arbitrary.

arbre (arbr) nm 1 tree. 2 shaft, axle. **arbre de Noël** Christmas tree. **arbre vert** evergreen.

arbuste (ar'byst) nm 1 bush. 2 shrub.

arc (ark) *nm* **1** bow. **2** arc. **3** arch. **arc-en-ciel** *nm, pl* **arcs-en-ciel** rainbow.

arcade (ar'kad) *nf* **1** archway. **2** arcade.

archaïque (arka'i:k) *adj* archaic.

arche¹ (arʃ) *nf* ark.

arche² (arʃ) *nf* **1** arch. **2** hoop.

archéologie (arke:ɔlɔ'ʒi:) *nf* archaeology. **archéologique** *adj* archaeological. **archéologue** *nm,f* archaeologist.

archet (ar'ʃɛ) *nm* mus bow.

archevêque (arʃə'vɛk) *nm* archbishop.

archi- (arʃi:) *pref* **1** arch. **2** utterly. **archibondé** (arʃi:bɔ̃'de:) *adj* crammed full. **archifou** (arʃi:'fu:) *adj* stark mad. **archiplein** (arʃi:'plɛ̃) *adj* packed.

archiduc (arʃi:'dyk) *nm* archduke.

archipel (arʃi:'pɛl) *nm* archipelago.

architecte (arʃi:'tɛkt) *nm,f* architect. **architecture** *nf* architecture.

archives (ar'ʃi:v) *nf pl* **1** archives. **2** public records.

arctique (ark'ti:k) *adj* arctic. *nm cap* Arctic.

ardent (ar'dã) *adj* **1** burning. **2** ardent, keen. **ardemment** (arda'mã) *adv* ardently, eagerly.

ardeur (ar'dœr) *nf* **1** heat. **2** ardour, eagerness.

ardoise (ar'dwaz) *nf* slate.

ardu (ar'dy) *adj* **1** steep. **2** difficult, arduous.

are (ar) *nm* unit of measure, equal to 100 square metres.

arène (a'rɛn) *nf* arena, ring.

arête (a'rɛt) *nf* **1** fish bone. **2** edge. **3** ridge.

argent (ar'ʒã) *nm* **1** silver. **2** money. **argent comptant** cash. **argent liquide** ready money. **argenté** *adj* silvered. **argenterie** *nf* plate.

Argentine (arʒã'ti:n) *nf* Argentina. **argentin** *adj* Argentine, Argentinian. *nm* Argentinian.

argile (ar'ʒi:l) *nf* clay.

argot (ar'go) *nm* slang.

argument (argy'mã) *nm* **1** argument. **2** synopsis.

aride (a'ri:d) *adj* **1** arid, dry. **2** barren.

aristocratie (ari:stɔkra'si:) *nf* aristocracy. **aristocrate** *nm,f* aristocrat. **aristocratique** *adj* aristocratic.

arithmétique (ari:tme:'ti:k) *nf* arithmetic.

armer (ar'me:) *vt* **1** arm. **2** strengthen. **3** equip. **4** load (a gun). **arme** *nf* **1** arm, weapon. **2** *pl* coat of arms. **armée** *nf* army. **armée de l'air** air force. **armure** *nf* armour.

armoire (ar'mwar) *nf* **1** wardrobe. **2** cupboard.

arome (a'rom) *nm* aroma.

arpenter (arpã'te:) *vt* **1** measure. **2** pace up and down.

arquer (ar'ke:) *vt* arch, bend. *vi* become bent, sag. **arqué** *adj* bent, curved.

arracher (ara'ʃe:) *vt* **1** tear away. **2** snatch, seize. **d'arrache-pied** *adv* steadily.

arranger (arã'ʒe:) *vt* **1** arrange. **2** settle. **3** accommodate. **s'arranger** *vr* **1** manage. **2** come to an agreement. **arrangement** *nm* **1** arrangement. **2** agreement.

arrérages (arɛ'raʒ) *nm pl* arrears.

arrestation (arɛsta'sjɔ̃) *nf* arrest.

arrêt (a'rɛ) *nm* **1** stop. **2** decree.

arrêter (arɛ'te:) *vt* **1** stop. **2** restrain. **3** arrest. **4** fix. *vi* stop. **s'arrêter** *vr* stop, halt. **s'arrêter sur** dwell on. **arrêté** *adj* fixed. *nm* **1** decision. **2** decree.

arrhes (ar) *nf pl* deposit (of money).

arrière (a'rjɛr) *nm* invar **1** back, back part of. **2** sport back. **en arrière 1** behind. **2** arrears. **3** backwards. ~*adj* invar back, rear. **arriéré** *adj* **1** backward. **2** old-fashioned. **arrière-garde** *nf, pl* **arrière-gardes** rearguard. **arrière-plan** *nm, pl* **arrière-plans** background.

arriver (ari:'ve:) *vi* (aux être) **1** arrive. **2** come. **3** succeed. **4** happen. **arrivée** *nf* arrival. **arriviste** *nm,f* social climber.

arrogance (arɔ'gãs) *nf* arrogance. **arrogant** *adj* arrogant, haughty.

arrondissement (arɔ̃di:s'mã) *nm* **1** district of a town. **2** division of a French department.

arroser (aro'ze:) *vt* **1** water. **2** sprinkle. **arrosoir** *nm* watering-can.

arsenic (arsə'ni:k) *nm* arsenic.

art (ar) *nm* **1** art. **2** skill.

artère (ar'tɛr) *nf* **1** artery. **2** thoroughfare. **tension artérielle** *nf* blood pressure.

arthrite (ar'tri:t) *nf* arthritis.

artichaut (arti:'ʃo) *nm* globe artichoke.

article (ar'ti:kl) *nm* **1** article. **2** item, commodity. **article-réclame** *nm, pl* **articles-réclame** special offer. **articles de Paris** fancy goods.

articuler (arti:ky'le:) *vt* articulate. **articulation** *nf* **1** *anat* joint. **2** link. **3** articulation. **articulation du doigt** knuckle. **articulé** *adj* articulate, distinct.

artifice (arti:'fi:s) *nm* **1** guile. **2** deceit.

artificiel, -elle (arti:fi:'sjɛl) *adj* **1** artificial. **2** imitation.

artillerie (arti:j'ri:) *nf* artillery.

artisan (arti:'zã) *nm* craftsman.

artiste (ar'ti:st) *nm,f* **1** artist. **2** performer. **3** actor. **artistique** *adj* artistic.

as¹ (ɑs) *nm* **1** ace. **2** expert, first-rate performer.

as² (a) *v* see **avoir.**

asbeste (az'bɛst) nm asbestos.

ascendance (asɑ̃'dɑ̃s) nf 1 ascent. 2 ancestry.

ascendant adj upward.

ascenseur (asɑ̃'sœr) nm lift.

Asie (a'zi:) nf Asia. **asiatique** adj Asiatic, Asian. nm Asian.

asile (a'zi:l) nm 1 refuge. 2 asylum. **sans asile** homeless.

aspect (a'spɛ) nm 1 sight. 2 appearance. 3 point of view. 4 aspect.

asperge (a'spɛrʒ) nf asparagus.

asphalte (as'falt) nm asphalt.

aspirer (aspi:'re:) vt 1 aspire. 2 inhale. **aspirant** nm candidate. **aspirateur** nm vacuum cleaner.

aspirine (aspi:'ri:n) nf aspirin.

assaillir (asa'ji:r) vt attack.

assainir (asɛ'ni:r) vt 1 make healthier. 2 cleanse.

assaisonner (asɛzɔ'ne:) vt season.

assassin (asa'sɛ̃) nm murderer, assassin. **assassinat** nm assassination, murder.

assassiner (asasi:'ne:) vt assassinate, murder.

assaut (a'so) nm attack, assault.

assembler (asɑ̃'ble:) vt 1 assemble. 2 gather, collect. 3 put together. **assemblage** nm assembling. **assemblée** nf assembly. **Assemblée Nationale** Lower Chamber of French Parliament.

assentiment (asɑ̃ti:'mɑ̃) nm assent.

asseoir (a'swar) vt 1 seat, set. 2 establish. **s'asseoir** vr sit down.

assez (a'se:) adv 1 enough, sufficient. 2 fairly, rather. **j'en ai assez!** I'm fed up with it!

asseyant (asɛ'jɑ̃) v see **asseoir.**

assidu (asi:'dy) adj 1 industrious, diligent. 2 regular. **assidûment** adv 1 diligently. 2 constantly.

assieds (a'sjɛ) v see **asseoir.**

assiéger (asje:'ʒe:) vt 1 besiege. 2 surround.

assiette (a'sjɛt) nf 1 plate. 2 seat, position. 3 situation. 4 base. **assiette creuse** soup plate. **assiette plate** dinner plate.

assigner (asi:'ɲe:) vt 1 assign. 2 appoint. 3 summon. **assignation** nf 1 assignment. 2 summons.

assimiler (asi:mi:'le:) vt assimilate, digest.

assis (a'si:) v see **asseoir.** adj seated. **assises** nf pl assizes.

assister (asi:'ste:) vt help, assist. **assister à** attend, be present. **assistance** nf 1 audience. 2 congregation. 3 assistance. **assistant** nm 1 onlooker. 2 assistant.

associer (asɔ'sje:) vt associate, connect. **s'as-**

socier à vr 1 join in. 2 go into partnership with. **association** nf 1 association. 2 society, company. 3 partnership. **associé** nm 1 partner. 2 associate member.

assommer (asɔ'me:) vt 1 knock senseless, overpower. 2 inf bore. **assommant** adj 1 overwhelming. 2 boring.

assortir (asɔr'ti:r) vt 1 assort. 2 match. 3 stock. **assorti** adj 1 assorted. 2 matched. **assortiment** nm 1 assortment. 2 set.

assoupir (asu:'pi:r) vt 1 make sleepy. 2 allay. **s'assoupir** vr doze off.

assourdir (asu:r'di:r) vt 1 make deaf. 2 deaden. 3 muffle.

assujettir (asyʒe:'ti:r) vt 1 subdue. 2 subject. 3 fasten.

assurer (asy're:) vt 1 assure. 2 make secure. 3 affirm. 4 insure. **assurance** nf 1 assurance. 2 insurance. **assuré** adj 1 sure. 2 safe. 3 certain. 4 confident. 5 insured.

astérisque (aste:'ri:sk) nm asterisk.

asthme (asm) nm asthma.

astre (astr) nm star.

astreindre* (a'strɛ̃dr) vt 1 force. 2 subject. **s'astreindre à** vr keep to.

astrologie (astrɔlɔ'ʒi:) nf astrology. **astrologique** adj astrological.

astronomie (astrɔnɔ'mi:) nf astronomy. **astronomique** adj astronomical.

astronaute (astrɔ'not) nm astronaut.

astucieux, -euse (asty'sjœ, -'sjœz) adj 1 astute. 2 artful.

atelier (atə'lje:) nm 1 workshop. 2 studio.

athée (a'te:) nm atheist. **athéisme** nm atheism.

Athènes (a'tɛn) nf Athens.

athlète (at'lɛt) nm athlete. **athlétique** adj athletic. **athlétisme** nm athletics.

atlantique (atlɑ̃'ti:k) adj Atlantic. **(Océan) Atlantique** nm Atlantic (Ocean).

atlas (at'las) nm atlas.

atmosphère (atmɔ'sfɛr) nf atmosphere. **atmosphérique** adj atmospheric.

atome (a'tom) nm atom. **atomique** (atɔ'mi:k) adj atomic.

atout (a'tu:) nm trump.

âtre (ɑtr) nm hearth.

atroce (a'trɔs) adj 1 atrocious. 2 terrible. **atrocité** nf atrocity.

s'attabler (sata'ble) vr sit down to table.

attacher (ata'ʃe:) vt 1 attach. 2 fasten. **s'attacher** vr 1 cling. 2 apply oneself. **attache** nf 1 fastening. 2 tie. 3 leash. **attaché** adj attached. nm pol attaché.

attaquer (ata'ke:) vt 1 attack. 2 assault. 3 begin. **s'attaquer à** vr 1 attack, tackle. 2 grapple with. **attaque** nf 1 attack. 2 bout, fit. 3 stroke.

attarder (atar'de:) vt keep late. **s'attarder** vr linger, delay.

atteignant (atɛ'ɲã) v see **atteindre**.

atteindre* (a'tɛ̃dr) vt 1 reach. 2 touch, hit. 3 attain.

atteint (a'tɛ̃) v see **atteindre**. **atteinte** (a'tɛ̃t) nf 1 reach. 2 blow, hit, attack. **hors d'atteinte** out of reach.

attenant (at'nã) adj adjacent, next.

attendre (a'tãdr) vt 1 wait for. 2 expect. **en attendant** in the meantime. **faire attendre** keep waiting. **s'attendre** vr expect. **attendu** adj expected. prep considering. **attendu que** seeing that.

attendrir (atã'dri:r) vt 1 make tender, soften. 2 move. **s'attendrir** vr 1 become tender. 2 be moved. **attendrissement** nm 1 emotion. 2 pity.

attentat (atã'ta) nm 1 criminal attempt. 2 outrage.

attente (a'tãt) nf 1 waiting. 2 expectation.

attention (atã'sjɔ̃) nf 1 attention. 2 care. **faire attention à** pay attention to. ~interj look out! **attentif, -ive** (atã'ti:f, -'ti:v) adj 1 attentive. 2 careful.

atténuer (ate'nɥe:) vt 1 weaken, lessen. 2 make allowance for.

atterrer (atɛ're:) vt overwhelm.

atterrir (atɛ'ri:r) vi land. **atterrissage** nm landing.

attester (atɛ'ste:) vt testify.

attirail (ati'raj) nm 1 apparatus, outfit. 2 show. 3 inf stuff, rubbish.

attirer (ati:'re:) vt 1 attract. 2 bring on. 3 lure. **attirant** adj 1 attractive. 2 engaging.

attitré (ati:'tre:) adj 1 appointed. 2 regular.

attitude (ati:'tyd) nf 1 attitude. 2 posture.

attraction (atrak'sjɔ̃) nf attraction. **attractif, -ive** (atrak'ti:f, -'ti:v) adj attractive.

attrait (a'trɛ) nm 1 attraction. 2 charm.

attraper (atra'pe:) vt 1 catch. 2 trap. 3 trick. 4 seize. **attrape** nm 1 trap. 2 trick. **attrape-nigaud** nm, pl **attrape-nigauds** practical joke.

attrayant (atrɛ'jã) adj attractive.

attribuer (atri'bɥe:) vt 1 assign. 2 attribute. **s'attribuer** vr 1 assume. 2 claim. **attribut** (atri'by) nm attribute.

au, aux (o) contraction of **à le, à les**.

aubaine (o'bɛn) nf windfall, piece of good luck.

aube[1] (ob) nf dawn.

aube[2] (ob) nf paddle.

aubépine (obe'pi:n) nf hawthorn.

auberge (o'bɛrʒ) nf inn. **auberge de la jeunesse** youth hostel.

aubergine (obɛr'ʒi:n) nf aubergine, eggplant.

aucun (o'kœ̃) pron,adj any. **ne...aucun** 1 none, no. 2 no-one. **aucunement** adv in no way, not at all.

audace (o'das) nf 1 audacity. 2 impudence. **audacieux, -euse** (oda'sjœ, -'sjœz) adj 1 audacious, bold. 2 impudent.

au-delà (o'dla) adv beyond. nm next world. **au-delà de** beyond, on the other side of.

au-dessous (od'su:) adv below, underneath. **au-dessous de** below, under.

au-dessus (od'sy) adv above, over. **au-dessus de** above, over, beyond.

au-devant (od'vã) adv **aller au-devant** go to meet.

audible (o'di:bl) adj audible.

audience (o'djãs) nf 1 audience, hearing. 2 session.

auditeur (odi'tœr) nm listener.

audition (odi:'sjɔ̃) nf 1 audition. 2 hearing.

auditoire (odi:'twar) nm 1 auditorium. 2 audience.

auge (oʒ) nf trough.

augmenter (ɔgmã'te:) vt,vi 1 increase. 2 raise. **augmentation** nf 1 increase. 2 rise.

aujourd'hui (oʒu:r'dɥi) adv 1 today. 2 nowadays. **d'aujourd'hui en huit** today week.

aumône (o'mon) nf alms. **aumônier** nm chaplain.

auparavant (opara'vã) adv 1 before, first. 2 previously.

auprès (o'prɛ) adv close by, near. **auprès de** 1 close to, near. 2 beside. 3 in comparison with.

auquel, auxquels (o'kɛl) contraction of **à lequel, à lesquels**.

aurai (ɔ'rɛ) v see **avoir**.

aurais (ɔ'rɛ) v see **avoir**.

auréole (ɔre:'ɔl) nf 1 halo. 2 glory.

aurore (ɔ'rɔr) nf dawn, daybreak.

aussi (o'si:) adv 1 as, so. 2 also, too. conj therefore, consequently. **aussi bien que** as well as. **aussitôt** (osi:'to) adv immediately, at once. **aussitôt que** as soon as.

austère (ɔ'stɛr) adj 1 austere, severe. 2 stern.

Australie (ɔstra'li:) nf Australia. **australien, -ienne** (ɔstra'ljɛ̃, -'ljɛn) adj,n Australian.

autant (o'tã) adv 1 as much. 2 as many. **autant**

11

que 1 as much as. 2 as far as. **d'autant plus/moins** the more/less. **d'autant que** more especially as.

autel (o'tɛl) nm altar.

auteur (o'tœr) nm 1 author. 2 inventor, maker.

authentique (otã'tɪːk) adj authentic, genuine.

autistique (otɪ'stɪːk) adj also **autiste**. autistic.

auto (ɔ'to) nf car. **auto-école** nf, pl **auto-écoles** driving school. **faire de l'auto-stop** hitchhike.

autobiographie (otɔbjɔgra'fiː) nf autobiography. **autobiographique** adj autobiographical.

autobus (otɔ'bys) nm bus. **autobus à impériale** double-decker bus.

autographe (otɔ'graf) nm autograph.

automatique (otɔma'tɪːk) adj automatic.

automatisation (ɔtɔmatɪza'sjɔ̃) nf automation.

automne (o'tɔn) nm autumn.

automobile (otɔmɔ'bɪːl) nf motor car. **automobiliste** nm motorist.

autonome (otɔ'nɔm) adj autonomous.

autopsie (otɔp'siː) nf post-mortem.

autoriser (otɔri'zeː) vt authorize.

autorité (otɔri'teː) nf authority. **autoritaire** adj domineering.

autoroute (otɔ'ruːt) nf motorway.

autour (o'tuːr) adv round, about. **autour de** around, about.

autre (otr) adj 1 other. 2 different. pron other. **autre chose** something else. **autre part** elsewhere. **d'autre part** on the other hand. **d'un moment à l'autre** from one moment to the next. **l'un et l'autre** both. **quelqu'un d'autre** someone else. **tout autre** quite different. **autrement** (otra'mã) adv otherwise.

autrefois (otra'fwa) adv formerly, in the past.

Autriche (o'triːʃ) nf Austria. **autrichien, -ienne** (otri'ʃjɛ̃, -ʃjɛn) adj,n Austrian.

autruche (o'tryʃ) nf ostrich.

autrui (o'trɥiː) pron invar others, other people.

aux (o) see **au**.

auxiliaire (ɔksi'ljɛr) adj auxiliary. nm 1 auxiliary. 2 assistant.

avais (a'vɛ) v see **avoir**.

aval (a'val) nm lower part. **en aval** downstream.

avalanche (ava'lãʃ) nf avalanche.

avaler (ava'leː) vt swallow.

avancer (avã'seː) vt advance, put forward. vi advance. **s'avancer** vr 1 move forward. 2 progress. **avance** nf 1 advance. 2 loan. **à l'avance** or **d'avance** beforehand. **être en**

avance 1 be early. 2 be fast. **avancement** nm 1 promotion. 2 progress.

avant[1] (a'vã) prep before. adv 1 before. 2 far, deep. **en avant** forward, in front.

avant[2] (a'vã) nm 1 naut bow. 2 sport forward. adj invar fore. In the following compounds **avant** is invar; the noun or adjective takes the plural. **avant-bras** nm forearm. **avant-centre** nm sport centre-forward. **avant-cour** nf forecourt. **avant-coureur** nm forerunner. **avant-dernier, -ière** adj last but one. **avant-goût** nm foretaste. **avant-hier** adv day before yesterday. **avant-main** nm sport forehand. **avant-propos** nm preface.

avantage (avã'taʒ) nm advantage. **avantageux, -euse** (avãta'ʒœ, -'ʒœz) adj advantageous.

avare (a'var) adj miserly. nm,f miser.

avarie (ava'riː) nf damage.

avec (a'vɛk) prep with. adv with it.

avènement (avɛn'mã) nm 1 coming. 2 accession.

avenir (av'niːr) nm future. **à l'avenir** in future, henceforth.

Avent (a'vã) nm Advent.

aventure (avã'tyr) nf 1 adventure. 2 chance. **à l'aventure** at random. **dire la bonne aventure** tell fortunes. **aventureux, -euse** (avãty'rœ, -'rœz) adj 1 adventurous. 2 risky.

avenue (av'ny) nf avenue.

averse (a'vɛrs) nf downpour.

aversion (avɛr'zjɔ̃) nf aversion, dislike.

avertir (avɛr'tiːr) vt 1 warn. 2 notify. **avertissement** nm 1 warning. 2 notice.

aveu, aveux (a'vœ) nm confession.

aveugler (avœ'gleː) vt 1 blind. 2 dazzle. **s'aveugler sur** vr shut one's eyes to. **aveugle** (a'vœgl) adj blind. nm,f blind person.

avez (a'vɛ) v see **avoir**.

aviateur (avja'tœr) nm airman. **aviation** nf aviation.

avide (a'viːd) adj 1 greedy, avid. 2 grasping.

avilir (avi'liːr) vt 1 degrade. 2 depreciate. **s'avilir** vr disgrace oneself.

avion (a'vjɔ̃) nm 1 aircraft. 2 plane. **par avion** by airmail.

aviron (avi'rɔ̃) nm 1 oar. 2 rowing. **faire de l'aviron** row.

avis ('aviː) nm 1 opinion. 2 advice. 3 notice. **changer d'avis** change one's mind.

aviser (avi'zeː) vt 1 perceive, catch a glimpse of. 2 comm advise, inform. **aviser à** see about. **s'aviser de** vr take it into one's head to. **avisé** adj **1** prudent. **2** shrewd.

avocat[1] (avɔ'ka) nm barrister.

avocat[2] (avɔ'ka) nm avocado.

avoine (a'vwan) nf oats.

avoir[*][1] (a'vwar) vt **1** have, possess. **2** get. v aux have. **en avoir à** or **contre** bear a grudge against. **il y a 1** there is, are. **2** ago. **il n'y a pas de quoi** don't mention it. **qu'est ce-qu'il y a?** what's the matter?

avoir[2] (a'vwar) nm **1** possession. **2** property.

avoisiner (avwazı:'ne:) vt be near, border on.

avons (a'vɔ̃) v see **avoir.**

avorter (avɔr'te:) vi **1** miscarry. **2** fail. **avortement** nm abortion.

avouer (a'vwe:) vt **1** admit. **2** acknowledge. **avoué** nm solicitor.

avril (a'vri:l) nm April.

axe (aks) nm **1** axis. **2** axle.

ayant (ɛ'jã) v see **avoir.**

ayez (a'je:) v see **avoir.**

ayons (ɛ'jɔ̃) v see **avoir.**

azalée (aza'le:) nf azalea.

azote (a'zɔt) nm nitrogen.

B

babiller (babı:'je:) vi **1** chatter, prattle. **2** babble. **babillage** nm chatter, prattle. **babillard** adj talkative.

bâbord (ba'bɔr) nm naut port (side).

babouin (ba'bwɛ̃) nm baboon.

bac (bak) nm **1** ferry. **2** ferryboat.

baccalauréat (bakalɔre:'a) nm school leaving examination.

bâche (baʃ) nf **1** canvas cover. **2** tank, cistern.

bachelier, -ière (baʃə'lje:, -'ljɛr) nm,f one who has passed the school leaving examination.

bâcler (ba'kle:) vt **1** bar, bolt. **2** do in a slapdash way.

bactérie (bakte:'rı:) nf bacteria.

badigeonner (badi:ʒɔ'ne:) vt **1** whitewash. **2** paint.

badiner (badi:'ne:) vi trifle, joke. **badinage** nm **1** jest. **2** play. **badine** nf cane.

bafouiller (bafu:'je:) vi,vt **1** stammer. **2** splutter.

bagage (ba'gaʒ) nm **1** baggage. **2** pl luggage. **bagages à main** nm pl hand luggage. **bagages non accompagnés** nm pl luggage in advance.

bagarre (ba'gar) nf brawl, scuffle.

bagatelle (baga'tɛl) nf trifle.

bagne (baɲ) nm prison.

bagnole (ba'ɲɔl) nf inf old car.

bague (bag) nf (jewellery) ring.

baguette (ba'gɛt) nf **1** rod, stick. **2** wand. **3** long thin loaf of French bread.

bahut (ba'y) nm **1** cupboard. **2** sl school.

bai (bɛ) adj bay.

baie[1] (bɛ) nf geog bay.

baie[2] (bɛ) nf arch bay. **fenêtre en baie** nf bay window.

baie[3] (bɛ) nf berry.

baigner (bɛ'ɲe:) vt **1** bathe. **2** wash. vi soak, steep. **se baigner** vr **1** have a bath. **2** bathe. **baigneur, -euse** (bɛ'ɲœr, -'ɲœz) nm,f bather. **baignoire.** nf bath.

bail (baj) nm, pl **baux** lease.

bâiller (ba'je:) vi **1** yawn. **2** be ajar. **bâillemer.** nm yawn.

bâillon (ba'jɔ̃) nm gag.

bâillonner (bajɔ'ne:) vt gag.

bain (bɛ̃) nm **1** bath. **2** bathe. **prendre un bain** have a bath.

baïonnette (bajɔ'nɛt) nf bayonet.

baiser (bɛ'ze:) vt kiss. nm kiss.

baisser (bɛ'se:) vt **1** lower. **2** bend. vi go down, decline. **se baisse r** vr bend down. **baisse** nf **1** fall. **2** decline. **3** ebb.

bal (bal) nm ball, dance. **bal travesti** fancy-dress ball.

balader (bala'de:) vi saunter. **se balader** vr stroll. **se balader en auto** go for a drive.

balafrer (bala'fre:) vt gash. **balafre** nf **1** gash. **2** scar. **balafré** adj scarred.

balai (ba'lɛ) nm broom, brush.

balancer (balã'se:) vt **1** balance. **2** swing, rock. vi **1** swing. **2** hesitate. **se balancer** vr sway, swing. **balance** nf **1** balance. **2** pair of scales. **3** cap Libra. **4** hesitation. **être en balance** be in suspense. **balancier** nm **1** pendulum. **2** beam. **balançoire.** nf **1** swing. **2** seesaw.

balayer (balɛ'je:) vt sweep.

balbutier (balby'sje:) vi,vt stammer, mumble.

balcon (bal'kɔ̃) nm **1** balcony. **2** Th dress circle.

baldaquin (balda'kɛ̃) nm canopy.

baleine (ba'lɛn) nf whale.

balise (ba'li:z) nf **balise flottante** buoy.

balistique (bali:'stı:k) adj ballistic.

baliverne (bali:'vɛrn) nf **1** idle story. **2** nonsense.

ballade (ba'lad) nf ballad.

balle (bal) nf **1** ball. **2** bullet. **3** bale. **à l'épreuve des balles** bullet-proof. **balle de golf** golfball.

ballet

ballet (ba'lɛ) *nm* ballet.
ballon (ba'l5) *nm* 1 balloon. 2 football.
ballotter (balɔ'te:) *vt* toss about, shake. *vi* 1 rattle. 2 toss.
balnéaire (balne:'ɛr) *adj* bathing. **station balnéaire** *nf* seaside resort.
Baltique (bal'tiːk) *adj* Baltic. (**Mer**) **Baltique** *nf* Baltic (Sea).
balustrade (baly'strad) *nf* handrail.
balustre (ba'lystr) *nm* banister.
ʾambou (bã'bu:) *nm* bamboo.
an (bã) *nm* 1 ban. 2 proclamation. 3 *pl* banns. 4 banishment.
ɔanal, -aux (ba'nal, -'no) *adj* 1 common, banal. 2 commonplace, trite.
banane (ba'nan) *nm* banana. **bananier** *nm* banana tree.
banc (bã) *nm* 1 bench. 2 pew. 3 bed. 4 bank. **banc des prévenus** *law* dock. **bancal** *adj* 1 bandy-legged. 2 wobbly.
bandage (bã'daʒ) *nm* 1 bandage. 2 tyre.
bande[1] (bãd) *nf* band, strip. **bande magnétique** recording tape. **bande sonore** soundtrack.
bande[2] (bãd) *nf* party, gang, group.
bander (bã'de:) *vt* 1 bandage, bind. 2 tighten. **bander les yeux à** blindfold. **bandé** *adj* 1 bandaged. 2 taut.
bandit (bã'di:) *nm* 1 bandit. 2 ruffian.
banlieue (bã'ljœ) *nf* 1 suburb. 2 outskirts.
banne (ban) *nf* 1 hamper. 2 awning.
bannière (ba'njɛr) *nf* banner.
bannir (ba'niːr) *vt* 1 banish, exile. **banni** *adj* banished, outlawed. *nm* exile, outlaw.
banque (bãk) *nf* 1 bank. 2 banking. **banquier, -ière** (bã'kje:, -'kjɛr) *adj* banking. *nm* banker.
banqueroute (bãk'ru:t) *nf* bankruptcy. **faire banqueroute** go bankrupt.
banquet (bã'kɛ) *nm* banquet, feast.
banquette (bã'kɛt) *nf* 1 seat. 2 bench.
baptême (ba'tɛm) *nm* baptism, christening.
baptiser (bati:'ze:) *vt* baptize, christen.
bar (bar) *nm* 1 public bar. 2 pub.
baragouiner (baragwi:'ne:) *vi,vt* gabble.
baraque (ba'rak) *nf* 1 hut, shanty. 2 stall, booth.
baratte (ba'rat) *nf* churn.
barbare (bar'bar) *adj* 1 barbaric. 2 barbarous, cruel. *nm,f* barbarian. **barbarie** *nf* barbarity.
barbe (barb) *nf* 1 beard. 2 whiskers (of an animal). **quelle barbe!** what a nuisance! **se faire la barbe** shave. **barbu** *adj* bearded.
barbecue (barbə'kju:) *nm* barbecue.

barbier (bar'bje:) *nm* barber.
barbiturate (barbity'rat) *nm* barbiturate.
barboter (barbɔ'te:) *vi* 1 paddle. 2 bubble. 3 *inf* get confused. *vt sl* steal.
barbouiller (barbu:'je:) *vt* 1 smear. 2 blot. 3 scribble.
barème (ba'rɛm) *nm* scale, schedule.
bariolé (barjɔ'le:) *adj* gaudy.
baromètre (barɔ'mɛtr) *nm* barometer.
baron (ba'r5) *nm* baron.
baronnet (barɔ'nɛ) *nm* baronet.
baroque (ba'rɔk) *adj* odd, quaint.
barque (bark) *nf* boat.
barrage (ba'raʒ) *nm* 1 obstruction. 2 dam.
barrer (ba're:) *vt* 1 fasten with bars. 2 bar, obstruct. 3 *naut* steer. 4 cross. 5 cross out. **barre** *nf* 1 bar, rod. 2 tiller, helm. 3 stroke. **barreau, -aux** 1 small wooden or metal bar. 2 prison bar. 3 *law* bar. **barrière** *nf* 1 barrier. 2 tollgate.
barricade (bari:'kad) *nf* barricade.
baryton (bari:'t5) *adj,nm* baritone.
bas, basse (ba, bas) *adj* 1 low. 2 deep. 3 mean, base. **bas** *adv* 1 low. 2 quietly. *nm* 1 bottom, lower part. 2 stocking. **à bas** down. **en bas** 1 below. 2 downstairs. **en bas de** at the foot of. **mettre bas** lay down. **basse** *nf* mus bass. **basse-cour** *nf* farmyard.
basculer (basky'le:) *vi,vt* 1 rock. 2 tip. **bascule** *nf* seesaw.
base-ball (bas'bal) *nm* baseball.
baser (ba'ze:) *vt* 1 base. 2 ground. **se baser** *vr* 1 be founded. 2 rely. **base** *nf* 1 base. 2 basis.
basilic (bazi:'li:k) *nm* basil.
basket-ball (baskɛt'bal) *nm also* **basket** basketball.
bassin (ba'sɛ̃) *nm* 1 basin. 2 dock. 3 ornamental pond. 4 *anat* pelvis.
basson (ba's5) *nm* bassoon.
bastille (ba'stiːj) *nf* small fortress.
bataclan (bata'klã) *nm inf* belongings.
bataille (ba'taj) *nf* battle. **bataillon** *nm* battalion.
bâtard (ba'tar) *adj,n* bastard.
bateau, -aux (ba'to) *nm* boat. **bateau à vapeur** steamship. **bateau à voiles** sailing boat. **bateau de sauvetage** lifeboat.
bâtir[1] (ba'tiːr) *vt* build, construct. **bâti** *nm* frame. **bien bâti** well-built. **bâtiment** *nm* 1 building, construction. 2 building trade. 3 ship. **bâtisse** *nf* ramshackle building.
bâtir[2] (ba'tiːr) *vt* (sewing) tack.

14

bâton (baˈtɔ̃) *nm* stick. **à bâtons rompus** by fits and starts.

batterie (baˈtriː) *nf* **1** fight. **2** *mil* battery. **3** set. **4** drums.

battre* (batr) *vt* **1** beat, thrash. **2** shuffle. *vi* beat. **se battre** *vr* fight. **battant** *adj* **1** beating. **2** pelting. **à dix heures battant** on the stroke of ten. **tout battant neuf** brand-new. ~*nm* **1** leaf (of a table). **2** clapper (of a bell). **battement** *nm* **1** banging. **2** throbbing. **3** interval. **battement de paupières** blink.

battu (baˈty) *v* see **battre**.

bavard (baˈvar) *adj* talkative.

bavarder (bavarˈde:) *vi* **1** chatter. **2** gossip. **bavardage** *nm* chatter.

baver (baˈve:) *vi* dribble. **bave** *nf* dribble. **bavette** *nf* bib.

béant (be:ˈɑ̃) *adj* open, gaping.

béat (be:ˈa) *adj* complacent, smug.

beau, bel, belle, beaux, belles (bo, bɛl, bɛl, bo, bɛl) *adj* **1** beautiful, handsome, good-looking. **2** fine. **au beau milieu** right in the middle. **bel et bien** well and truly. **beauté** *nf* beauty.

beaucoup (boˈkuː) *adv* **1** much. **2** many. **3** a great deal, a lot. **de beaucoup** by far.

beau-fils *nm*, *pl* **beaux-fils 1** son-in-law. **2** stepson.

beau-frère *nm*, *pl* **beaux-frères** brother-in-law.

beau-père *nm*, *pl* **beaux-pères 1** father-in-law. **2** stepfather.

beaux-arts *nm pl* fine arts.

bébé (be:ˈbe:) *nm* baby.

bec (bɛk) *nm* **1** beak. **2** spout. **3** mouthpiece. **bec de plume** pen nib. **prise de bec** *nf* argument, row.

bécane (be:ˈkan) *nf inf* bicycle.

bécasse (be:ˈkas) *nf* woodcock. **bécassine** *nf* snipe.

bêcher (bɛˈʃe:) *vt* dig. **bêche** *nf* spade.

becqueter (bɛkˈte:) *vt* **1** peck at. **2** *inf* kiss.

bedaine (bəˈdɛn) *nf* paunch.

bée (be:) *adj* **bouche bée** open-mouthed.

beffroi (beˈfrwa) *nm* belfry.

bégayer (be:gɛˈje:) *vi* stutter, stammer.

bégueule (be:ˈgœl) *nf* prude.

béguin (be:ˈgɛ̃) *nm* hood. **avoir un béguin pour** have a fancy for.

beige (bɛʒ) *adj* **1** beige. **2** natural coloured. *nf* beige.

beignet (bɛˈɲɛ) *nm* **1** fritter. **2** doughnut.

bel (bɛl) *adj* see **beau**.

bêler (bɛˈle:) *vi* bleat.

belette (bəˈlɛt) *nf* weasel.

Belgique (bɛlˈʒiːk) *nf* Belgium. **belge** *adj,n* Belgian.

bélier (be:ˈlje:) *nm* **1** ram. **2** *cap* Aries.

belle (bɛl) *adj* see **beau**.

belle-fille *nf*, *pl* **belles-filles 1** daugher-in-law. **2** stepdaughter.

belle-mère *nf*, *pl* **belles-mères 1** mother-in-law. **2** stepmother.

belle-sœur *nf*, *pl* **belles-sœurs** sister-in-law.

bémol (be:ˈmɔl) *nm mus* flat.

bénédicité (be:ne:di:si:ˈte:) *nm* grace (before meals). **bénédiction** *nf* blessing.

bénéficier (be:ne:fi:ˈsje:) *vi* **1** benefit. **2** make a profit. **bénéfice** *nm* **1** profit. **2** benefit.

bénévole (be:ne:ˈvɔl) *adj* **1** benevolent, kind. **2** voluntary.

benin, -igne (be:ˈnɛ̃, -ˈniːɲ) *adj* **1** kindly. **2** mild, gentle.

bénir (be:ˈniːr) *vt* **1** bless. **2** consecrate. **bénit** *adj* consecrated, holy.

béquille (be:ˈkiːj) *nf* crutch.

bercer (bɛrˈse:) *vt* **1** rock. **2** lull. **se bercer** *vr* delude oneself. **berceau, -aux** *nm* cradle. **berceuse** *nf* lullaby.

berger, -ère (bɛrˈʒe:, -ˈʒɛr) *n* shepherd, shepherdess.

besogne (bəˈzɔɲ) *nf* **1** work. **2** task. **besogneux, -euse** (bəzɔˈɲœ, -ˈɲœz) *adj* needy, poor.

besoin (bəˈzwɛ̃) *nm* **1** want, need. **2** necessity. **au besoin** if necessary. **avoir besoin de** need.

bétail (be:ˈtaj) *nm*, *pl* **bestiaux** (bɛˈstjo) **1** cattle. **2** livestock.

bête (bɛt) *nf* **1** beast, animal. **2** fool. *adj* stupid. **bête à bon Dieu** ladybird. **bête noire** pet aversion. **bêtise** (be:ˈtiːz) *nf* **1** stupidity. **2** stupid remark. **3** trifle. **4** blunder. **5** *pl* nonsense.

béton (be:ˈtɔ̃) *nm* concrete.

betterave (be:ˈtrav) *nf* beet. **betterave rouge** beetroot. **betterave sucré** sugarbeet.

beugler (bœˈgle:) *vi* **1** low. **2** bellow. *vt* bellow.

beurre (bœr) *nm* butter.

bévue (be:ˈvy) *nf* blunder.

biais (bjɛ) *adj* **1** sloping. **2** askew. **3** oblique. *nm* **1** slant. **2** bias. **3** expedient. **de biais** sideways. **en biais.** on the slant.

bibelot (biːˈblo) *nm* knick-knack.

biberon (biːˈbrɔ̃) *nm* feeding bottle.

Bible (biːbl) *nf* Bible. **biblique** *adj* biblical.

bibliographie (bɪːbliːɔgraˈfiː) *nf* bibliography. **bibliographique** *adj* bibliographical.

bibliothécaire (bɪːbliːɔteːˈkɛr) *nm,f* librarian.

bibliothèque (bɪːbliːɔˈtɛk) *nf* **1** library. **2** bookcase.

biceps (bɪːˈsɛps) *adj,nm* biceps.

biche (bɪːʃ) *nf* **1** *zool* hind. **2** *inf* darling.

bicyclette (bɪːsiːˈklɛt) *nf* bicycle.

bidon (bɪːˈdɔ̃) *nm* can, drum.

bien (bjɛ̃) *adv* **1** well. **2** properly. **3** good. **4** very. **5** many. **6** quite. **eh bien!** well then! **bien que** although. ~*nm* **1** good. **2** property. **3** *pl* belongings.

bien-aimé *adj* or *n, pl* **bien-aimés** darling.

bien-être *nm* well-being.

bienfaisant (bjɛ̃fɛˈzã) *adj* charitable, kind.

bienheureux, -euse (bjɛ̃nœˈrœ, -ˈrœz) *adj* **1** happy. **2** fortunate.

biennal, -aux (bɪːɛˈnal, -ˈno) *adj* biennial.

bienséance (bjɛ̃seˈãs) *nf* propriety. **bienséant** *adj* proper, seemly.

bientôt (bjɛ̃ˈto) *adv* soon, before long. **à bientôt!** so long!

bienveillance (bjɛ̃vɛˈjãs) *nf* goodwill. **bienveillant** *adj* kind, benevolent.

bienvenu (bjɛ̃vəˈny) *adj* welcome. **bienvenue** *nf* welcome.

bière[1] (bjɛr) *nf* beer. **bière à la pression** draught beer. **bière blonde 1** pale ale. **2** lager.

bière[2] (bjɛr) *nf* coffin.

biffer (bɪːˈfe) *vt* delete.

bifteck (bɪːfˈtɛk) *nm* steak.

bifurcation (bɪːfyrkaˈsjɔ̃) *nf* fork (in a road).

bigamie (bɪːgaˈmiː) *nf* bigamy.

bigorneau, -aux (bɪːgɔrˈno) *nm* winkle.

bigot (bɪːˈgo) *adj* **1** devout. **2** bigoted.

bijou, -oux (bɪːˈʒu) *nm* **1** jewel. **2** *inf* darling. **bijouterie** *nf* **1** jewellery. **2** jeweller's shop. **bijoutier** *nm* jeweller.

bikini (bɪːkiːˈniː) *nm* bikini.

bilan (bɪːˈlæ) *nm comm* balance sheet.

bile (bɪːl) *nf* **1** bile. **2** anger. **se faire de la bile** fret.

bilingue (biˈlɛ̃g) *adj* bilingual.

billard (bɪːˈjar) *nm* billiards.

bille (bɪːj) *nf* **1** marble. **2** billiard ball.

billet (biˈjɛ) *nm* **1** note. **2** ticket. **billet d'aller et retour** return ticket. **billet de banque** banknote. **billet de faveur** free ticket. **billet simple** single ticket.

billot (bɪːˈjo) *nm* block (of wood).

binaire (biːˈnɛr) *adj* binary.

biner (bɪːˈne) *vt* hoe. **binette** *nf* hoe.

biographie (bɪːɔgraˈfiː) *nf* biography. **biographique** *adj* biographical.

biologie (bɪːɔlɔˈʒiː) *nf* biology. **biologique** *adj* biological.

bis (bɪːs) *adv* **1** twice. **2** repeat. *interj* encore!

bisannuel, -elle (bɪːzaˈnɥɛl) *adj* biennial.

biscornu (bɪːskɔrˈny) *adj* **1** irregular. **2** *inf* odd, queer.

biscotte (bɪːˈskɔt) *nf* French toast, rusk.

biscuit (bɪːˈskɥiː) *nm* biscuit.

bise[1] (bɪːz) *nf* north wind.

bise[2] (bɪːz) *nf inf* kiss:

bisque (bɪːsk) *nf* shellfish soup.

bissextile (bɪːsɛkˈstiːl) **année bissextile** *nf* leap year.

bistro (bɪːˈstro) *nm also* **bistrot 1** French cafe. **2** pub.

bizarre (bɪːˈzar) *adj* **1** peculiar. **2** strange.

blafard (blaˈfar) *adj* **1** dim. **2** pale.

blaguer (blaˈge) *vi* **1** tell lies. **2** tease. **blague** *nf* **1** hoax. **2** joke. **sans blaque?** really?

blaireau, -aux (blɛˈro) *nm* **1** badger. **2** shaving brush.

blâmer (blɑˈme) *vt* blame. **blâme** *nm* blame.

blanc, blanche (blã, blãʃ) *adj* **1** white. **2** clean. **3** pale. **4** blank. *nm* white. *nf mus* minim. **blancheur** *nf* whiteness.

blanchir (blãˈʃiːr) *vt* **1** whiten. **2** bleach. **3** wash. **4** whitewash. *vi* turn white. **blanchissage** *nm* washing. **blanchisserie** *nf* laundry.

blanquette (blãˈkɛt) *nf* veal stew.

blaser (blaˈze) *vt* **1** blunt. **2** surfeit. **se blaser** *vr* become indifferent.

blason (blaˈzɔ̃) *nm* **1** coat of arms. **2** heraldry.

blasphémer (blasfeˈme) *vi,vt* blaspheme.

blatte (blat) *nf* cockroach.

blé (ble) *nm* **1** corn. **2** wheat.

blêmir (bleˈmiːr) *vi* turn pale. **blême** (blɛm) *adj* very pale.

blesser (blɛˈse) *vt* **1** wound. **2** injure. **3** hurt. **blessé** *adj* wounded. *nm* casualty. **blessure** *nf* **1** wound. **2** injury.

blet, blette (blɛ, blɛt) *adj* (of fruit) soft, over-ripe.

bleu (blœ) *adj* blue. *nm* **1** blue. **2** bruise. **3** novice. **bleu clair/foncé** light/dark blue. **bleuet** *nm also* **bluet** cornflower.

blindé (blɛ̃ˈde) *adj* armour-plated.

bloc (blɔk) *nm* **1** block. **2** lump. **3** *pol* coalition. **à bloc** thoroughly. **en bloc** in one piece.

blocus (blɔˈkys) *nm* blockade.

blond (blɔ̃) *adj* **1** fair, blond. **2** light.

16

blondir (blɔ̃'di:r) vi turn yellow. vt bleach.
bloquer (blɔ'ke:) vt 1 block up. 2 obstruct. 3 jam.
se blottir (blɔ'ti:r) vr 1 squat, crouch. 2 nestle.
blouse (blu:z) nf 1 blouse. 2 overall.
bluff (blœf, blyf) nm bluff.
bobine (bɔ'bi:n) nf 1 reel, spool. 2 coil.
bocage (bɔ'kaʒ) nm grove.
bock (bɔk) nm glass of beer.
bœuf (bœf) nm 1 bullock. 2 beef.
bohème (bɔ'ɛm) adj unconventional, bohemian. nf group of artists.
boire (bwar) vt 1 drink. 2 absorb. **boire à petits coups** sip.
bois (bwa) nm 1 wood, woodland. 2 timber, wood. 3 pl antlers. 4 woodwind instruments. **bois contre-plaqué** plywood. **de** or **en bois** wooden. **boiserie** (bwaz'ri:) nf woodwork.
boisson (bwa'sɔ̃) nf drink, beverage.
boîte (bwat) nf 1 box. 2 tin. 3 inf nightclub, discotheque. **boîte aux lettres** letter-box. **boîte d'allumettes** matchbox. **boîte de vitesses** gearbox.
boiter (bwa'te:) vi 1 limp. 2 be lame. **boiteux, -euse** (bwa'tœ, -'tœz) adj lame. nm,f cripple.
bol (bɔl) nm bowl, basin.
bombarder (bɔ̃bar'de:) vt 1 bombard. 2 bomb. **bombardier** nm aviat bomber.
bombe (bɔ̃b) nf bomb. **bombe atomique** atom bomb.
bomber (bɔ̃'be:) vt 1 stick out. 2 arch. vi bulge. **bombé** adj bulging.
bon, bonne (bɔ̃, bɔn) adj 1 good. 2 kind. 3 right. 4 nice. nm 1 good. 2 voucher. 3 comm bond. **à quoi bon?** what's the use? **pour de bon** for good. ~interj right!
bonasse (bɔ'nas) adj 1 simple. 2 silly.
bonbon (bɔ̃'bɔ̃) nm sweet.
bond (bɔ̃) nm 1 leap, jump. 2 bounce.
bondé (bɔ̃'de:) adj packed, crowded.
bondir (bɔ̃'di:r) vi 1 jump, leap. 2 bounce.
bonheur (bɔ'nœr) nm 1 happiness. 2 good fortune. **au petit bonheur** in a haphazard way. **par bonheur** fortunately.
bonhomie (bɔnɔ'mi:) nf good nature.
bonhomme (bɔ'nɔm) nm 1 good-humoured man. 2 old man.
boni (bɔ'ni:) nm 1 surplus. 2 profit.
bonjour (bɔ̃'ʒu:r) interj, nm good morning, good afternoon.
bonne (bɔn) nf housemaid.
bonne-maman nf, pl **bonnes-mamans** granny.
bonnet (bɔ'nɛ) nm 1 cap. 2 bonnet. **c'est bonnet blanc et blanc bonnet** it's six of one and half a dozen of the other. **gros bonnet** inf bigwig. **bonneterie** nf hosiery. **bonnetier** nm hosier.
bon-papa nm, pl **bons-papas** grandad.
bonsoir (bɔ̃'swar) interj, nm good evening.
bonté (bɔ̃'te:) nf 1 kindness. 2 goodness.
bord (bɔr) nm 1 edge. 2 rim. 3 hem. 4 bank. 5 side. **à bord** on board, aboard. **au bord de la mer** at the seaside. **bordure** nf 1 border. 2 edging. 3 kerb.
bordeaux (bɔr'do) nm 1 Bordeaux wine. 2 cap Bordeaux. **bordeaux rouge** nm claret.
bordel (bɔr'dɛl) nm brothel.
border (bɔr'de:) vt 1 line. 2 edge, skirt.
bordereau, -aux (bɔrdə'ro) nm 1 memorandum. 2 account, statement.
borgne (bɔrɲ) adj 1 blind in one eye. 2 (of a cafe, hotel, etc.) disreputable.
borner (bɔr'ne:) vt 1 mark out the boundary. 2 limit. **borne** nf boundary, limit. **borne milliaire** milestone. **borné** adj 1 limited. 2 narrow-minded.
bosquet (bɔ'skɛ) nm grove.
bosse (bɔs) nf 1 bump. 2 hump. **avoir la bosse de** have a gift for.
bosseler (bɔ'sle:) vt 1 emboss. 2 dent. **bosselure** nf dent.
bossu (bɔ'sy) adj hunchbacked. nm hunchback.
bot (bo) **pied bot** nm 1 club foot. 2 club-footed person.
botanique (bɔta'ni:k) nf botany. adj botanical.
botte[1] (bɔt) nf bunch.
botte[2] (bɔt) nf high boot. **bottier** nm shoemaker.
botte[3] (bɔt) nf (fencing) thrust.
botteler (bɔt'le:) vt put in bunches.
botter (bɔ'te:) vt 1 put boots on. 2 kick.
Bottin (bɔ'tɛ̃) nm Tdmk French street and trade directory.
bouc (bu:k) nm billy-goat. **bouc émissaire** scapegoat.
boucaner (bu:ka'ne:) vt cul cure.
bouche (bu:ʃ) nf 1 mouth. 2 opening. **bouchée** nf mouthful.
boucher[1] (bu:'ʃe:) vt 1 stop or fill up. 2 cork.
boucher[2] (bu:'ʃe:) nm butcher. **boucherie** nf butcher's shop.
bouchon (bu:'ʃɔ̃) nm 1 cork, stopper. 2 wisp (of straw).
boucler (bu:'kle:) vt 1 buckle, fasten. 2 curl. vi be curly. **boucle** nf 1 buckle 2 loop. 3 ring. 4

17

curl. **boucle d'oreille** earring. **bouclier** nm shield.

bouddhisme (bu:ˈdi:sm) nm Buddhism. **bouddhiste** adj,n Buddhist.

bouder (bu:ˈde:) vi sulk. **boudeur, -euse** (bu:ˈdœr, -ˈdœz) adj sulky.

boudin (bu:ˈdɛ̃) nm black pudding.

boue (bu:) nf 1 mud. 2 filth, dirt. **boueur** nm 1 dustman. 2 roadsweeper. **boueux, -euse** (bu:ˈœ, -ˈœz) adj muddy.

bouée (bu:ˈe:) nf buoy. **bouée de sauvetage** lifebuoy.

bouffer (bu:ˈfe:) vi,vt 1 puff out. 2 eat greedily. **bouffant** adj 1 puffed. 2 baggy. **bouffée** nf 1 puff. 2 gust. 3 whiff.

bouffir (bu:ˈfi:r) vi,vt swell. **bouffissure** nf swelling.

bouffon, -onne (bu:ˈfɔ̃, -ˈfɔn) adj comical. nm,f clown, fool.

bouger (bu:ˈʒe:) vi move, stir. vt move.

bougie (bu:ˈʒi:) nf candle. **bougeoir** nm candlestick.

bouillabaisse (bu:jaˈbɛs) nf Provençal fish stew.

bouillir* (bu:ˈji:r) vi boil. **bouillant** adj 1 boiling. 2 hot-tempered. **bouilloire** nf kettle.

bouillon nm 1 bubble. 2 soup. 3 stock.

bouillonner (bu:jɔˈne:) vi 1 bubble. 2 seethe.

bouillotte (bu:ˈjɔt) nf hot-water bottle.

boulangerie (bu:lɑ̃ʒˈri:) nf 1 bakery. 2 baking. **boulanger** nm baker.

boule (bu:l) nf 1 ball. 2 bulb. 3 sl face. **partie de boules** nf game of bowls.

bouleau, -aux (bu:ˈlo) nm birch tree.

bouledogue (bu:lˈdɔg) nm bulldog.

boulevard (bu:lˈvar) nm avenue.

bouleverser (bu:lvɛrˈse:) vt 1 overturn. 2 upset. 3 astound. **bouleversement** nm 1 overturning. 2 confusion, upheaval.

boulon (bu:ˈlɔ̃) nm bolt.

boulot[1], **-otte** (bu:ˈlo, -ˈlot) adj chubby, plump. nm inf food.

boulot[2] (bu:ˈlo) nm inf job, work.

boulotter (bu:lɔˈte:) vi jog along. vt inf eat.

bouquet (bu:ˈkɛ) nm 1 bunch. 2 clump. 3 aroma.

bouquin (bu:ˈkɛ̃) nm 1 old book. 2 inf book. **bouquiniste** nm second-hand bookseller.

bourbe (bu:rb) nf mud.

bourdon (bu:rˈdɔ̃) nm 1 mus drone. 2 bumble bee.

bourdonner (bu:rdɔˈne:) vi 1 buzz. 2 hum. **bourdonnement** nm buzz.

bourg (bu:r) nm 1 market town. 2 borough.

bourgeois (bu:rˈʒwa) adj 1 middle-class. 2 plain. 3 common. nm citizen. **bourgeoisie** nf middle class.

bourgeon (bu:rˈʒɔ̃) nm bud.

bourgeonner (bu:rʒɔˈne:) vi come into bud.

Bourgogne (bu:rˈgɔɲ) nf Burgundy. **(vin de) Bourgogne** nm Burgundy wine.

bourrade (bu:ˈrad) nf blow, thump.

bourrage (bu:ˈraʒ) nm padding, stuffing.

bourrasque (bu:ˈrask) nf gust of wind.

bourreau, -aux (bu:ˈro) nm 1 executioner. 2 torturer.

bourrelet (bu:rˈlɛ) nm 1 pad. 2 fold, swelling.

bourrer (bu:ˈre:) vt 1 stuff. 2 cram.

bourriche (bu:ˈriːʃ) nf hamper.

bourru (bu:ˈry) adj 1 surly. 2 gruff.

bourse (bu:rs) nf 1 purse. 2 scholarship. 3 cap Stock Exchange.

boursoufler (bu:rsu:ˈfle:) vt 1 swell. 2 blister. **boursouflure** nf swelling.

bousculer (bu:skyˈle:) vt 1 jostle. 2 upset, knock over. **bousculade** nf scuffle.

bousiller (bu:ziˈje:) vt 1 hurry through. 2 inf smash.

boussole (bu:ˈsɔl) nf compass.

bout (bu:) nm 1 end. 2 tip. 3 bit. **à bout de forces** exhausted. **à bout portant** pointblank. **au bout de** 1 at the end of. 2 after. **au bout du compte** after all. **de bout en bout** through and through. **venir à bout** 1 manage. 2 overcome. **boutade** nf 1 whim. 2 outburst. 3 flash of wit.

bouteille (bu:ˈtɛj) nf bottle. **bouteille Thermos** Tdmk Thermos flask.

boutique (bu:ˈtiːk) nf shop. **boutiquier, -ière** (bu:tiˈkjeː, -ˈkjɛr) n shopkeeper.

bouton (bu:ˈtɔ̃) nm 1 button. 2 bud. 3 handle. 4 spot, pimple. **bouton à pression** press-stud. **bouton de col** stud. **bouton d'or** buttercup. **boutons de manchettes** cufflinks. **boutonnière** nf buttonhole.

boutonner (bu:tɔˈne:) vt button.

bouvier (bu:ˈvje:) nm cowhand.

boxer (bɔkˈse:) vi,vt sport box. **boxe** nf boxing.

boyau, -aux (bwaˈjo) nm 1 bowel, guts. 2 passage, trench.

boycotter (bɔjkɔˈte:) vt boycott.

bracelet (braˈslɛ) nm 1 bracelet, bangle. 2 (watch) strap.

braconner (brakɔˈne:) vi,vt poach. **braconnier** nm poacher.

braguette (braˈgɛt) nf fly (of trousers).

braille (brɑj) *nm* braille.
brailler (brɑ'je:) *vi* bawl, shout.
braire (brɛr) *vi* bray.
braise (brɛz) *nf* embers.
braiser (brɛ'ze:) *vt* braise.
brancard (brɑ̃'kar) *nm* 1 stretcher. 2 shaft.
brancher (brɑ̃'ʃe:) *vi* perch. *vt tech* connect, plug in. **branche** *nf* 1 branch. 2 division.
brandir (brɑ̃'di:r) *vt* flourish, wave.
branler (brɑ̃'le:) *vi,vt* 1 shake. 2 move. **branle** *nm* motion.
braquer (brɑ'ke:) *vt* aim, point.
bras (brɑ) *nm* 1 arm. 2 handle. 3 *pl* labour. **bras dessus bras dessous** arm in arm.
brasier (brɑ'zje:) *nm* fire, blaze.
brasse (bras) *nf* 1 *naut* fathom. 2 stroke. 3 breaststroke.
brassée (brɑ'se:) *nf* armful.
brasser (brɑ'se:) *vt* 1 brew, mash. 2 stir. *nf* 1 brewery. 2 restaurant, café.
braver (brɑ've:) *vt* brave, face. **brave** *adj* 1 brave. 2 honest. 3 good. **bravoure** *nf* bravery, courage.
brebis (brə'bi:) *nf* 1 ewe. 2 sheep.
brèche (brɛʃ) *nf* 1 breach. 2 gap.
bredouiller (brədu:'je:) *vt,vi* mumble, stammer.
bref, brève (brɛf, brɛv) *adj* brief, short. **bref** *adv* briefly. **en bref** in short.
breloque (brə'lɔk) *nf* charm, trinket.
Bretagne (brə'taɲ) *nf* Brittany. **breton, -onne** (brə'tɔ̃, -'tɔn) *adj,n* Breton.
bretelle (brə'tɛl) *nf* 1 strap. 2 *pl* braces.
breuvage (brœ'vaʒ) *nm* drink, beverage.
brevet (brə'vɛ) *nm* 1 patent. 2 certificate.
breveter (brəv'te:) *vt* 1 grant a patent to. 2 patent.
bribes (bri:b) *nf pl* scraps, fragments.
bricoler (bri:kɔ'le:) *vi* do odd jobs, tinker about. *vt* arrange.
brider (bri:'de:) *vt* 1 bridle. 2 check. 3 fasten. **bride** *nf* 1 bridle. 2 rein. 3 strap. **à bride abattue** at full speed.
bridge (bri:dʒ) *nm* game bridge.
brièvement (brjɛv'mɑ̃) *adv* briefly.
brigade (bri:'gad) *nf* 1 brigade. 2 gang.
brigand (bri:'gɑ̃) *nm* 1 robber. 2 rascal.
brigue (bri:g) *nf* intrigue.
briller (bri:'je:) *vi* shine, sparkle. **brillamment** *adv* brilliantly. **brillant** *adj* 1 brilliant. 2 shining. *nm* 1 brilliance. 2 shine.
brin (brɛ̃) *nm* 1 blade. 2 sprig. 3 strand. **brindille** *nf* 1 twig. 2 sprig.
brioche (bri:'ɔʃ) *nf cul* bun.

brique (bri:k) *nf* brick. **briquet** *nm* cigarette lighter.
brise (bri:z) *nf* breeze.
briser (bri:'ze:) *vt* break, smash.
britannique (bri:ta'ni:k) *adj* British.
broc (brɔ) *nm* jug.
brocanter (brɔkɑ̃'te:) *vi* deal in second-hand goods. *vi* 1 barter. 2 sell. **brocanteur** *nm* second-hand dealer.
broche (brɔʃ) *nf* 1 *cul* spit. 2 peg. 3 brooch.
broché (brɔ'ʃe:) *adj* stitched. **livre broché** *nm* hardback book.
brochet (brɔ'ʃɛ) *nm zool* pike.
brochette (brɔ'ʃɛt) *nf* 1 skewer. 2 kebab.
brochure (brɔ'ʃyr) *nf* brochure, leaflet.
brocoli (brɔkɔ'li:) *nm* broccoli.
broder (brɔ'de:) *vt* 1 embroider. 2 embellish. **broderie** *nf* 1 embroidery. 2 embellishment.
broncher (brɔ̃'ʃe:) *vi* 1 stumble. 2 shy. 3 falter.
bronchite (brɔ̃'ʃi:t) *nf* bronchitis.
bronzer (brɔ̃'ze:) *vt* 1 bronze. 2 tan. **bronze** *nm* bronze.
brosser (brɔ'se:) *vt* brush. **brosse** *nf* brush. **brosse à cheveux/dents/habits** hairbrush/toothbrush/clothes brush. **brosse dure** *nf* scrubbing brush.
brouette (bru:'ɛt) *nf* wheelbarrow.
brouhaha (bru:a'a) *nm* uproar, din.
brouillard (bru:'jar) *nm* fog, mist.
brouiller (bru:'je:) *vt* 1 mix up. 2 confuse. **se brouiller** *vr* 1 get confused. 2 quarrel, fall out. **brouille** *nf* quarrel.
brouillon (bru:'jɔ̃) *nm* rough copy.
broussaille (bru:'saj) *nf* undergrowth.
brouter (bru:'te:) *vt* graze.
broyer (brwa'je:) *vt* 1 pound. 2 pulverize.
bru (bry) *nf* daughter-in-law.
bruiner (brɥi:'ne:) *v imp* drizzle.
bruire (brɥi:r) *vi* rustle.
bruit (brɥi:) *nm* 1 noise, din. 2 rumour. 3 fuss.
brûler (bry'le:) *vi* 1 be on fire, burn. 2 be eager. *vt* 1 burn. 2 scorch. **brûlure** *nf* 1 burn. 2 scald.
brume (brym) *nf* mist, fog. **brumeux, -euse** (bry'mœ, -'mœz) *adj* foggy.
brun (brœ̃) *adj* 1 brown. 2 dark. *nm* brown. **brune** *nf* dusk.
brunir (bry'ni:r) *vi* become dark. *vt* brown, darken, tan.
brusque (brysk) *adj* 1 abrupt, brusque. 2 sudden. 3 sharp.
brut (bryt) *adj* 1 raw. 2 rough. 3 *comm* gross. **brute** *nf* brute, beast.

19

brutal

brutal, -aux (bry'tal, -'to) *adj* 1 brutal. 2 coarse. 3 rough. 4 blunt. **brutalité** *nf* brutality.
brutaliser (brytali:'ze:) *vt* 1 ill-treat. 2 bully.
Bruxelles (bry'sɛl) *nf* Brussels.
bruyant (bry'jã) *adj* noisy.
bruyère (bry'jɛr) *nf* 1 heather. 2 heath.
bu (by) *v* see **boire.**
bucarde (by'kard) *nf* cockle.
buccin (byk'sɛ̃) *nm* whelk.
bûche (byʃ) *nf* 1 log. 2 idiot.
bûcher¹ (by'ʃe:) *nm* 1 woodshed. 2 stake. **bûcheron** *nm* lumberjack.
bûcher² (by'ʃe:) *vi,vt inf* work hard, swot.
budget (by'dʒɛ) *nm* budget.
buée (bɥe:) *nf* steam, vapour.
buffet (by'fɛ) *nm* 1 sideboard. 2 refreshment room. **buffet de cuisine** 'dresser.
buffle (byfl) *nm* buffalo.
buisson (bɥi:'sɔ̃) *nm* 1 bush. 2 thicket. **faire l'école buissonnière** play truant.
bulbe (bylb) *nf bot* bulb.
Bulgarie (bylga'ri:) *nf* Bulgaria. **bulgare** *adj,n* Bulgarian.
bulle (byl) *nf* bubble.
bulletin (byl'tɛ̃) *nm* 1 bulletin. 2 report. 3 ticket. **bulletin de vote** voting paper. **bulletin météorologique** weather forecast.
bungalow (bɛ̃ga'lo) *nm* bungalow.
bureau, -aux (by'ro) *nm* 1 desk. 2 office. 3 board, committee. **bureau de poste** post office.
bureaucratie (byrokra'si:) *nf* 1 bureaucracy. 2 *inf* red tape. **bureaucrate** (byro'krat) *nm* bureaucrat.
buriner (byri:'ne:) *vt* engrave.
burlesque (byr'lɛsk) *adj* comical, ludicrous.
buste (byst) *nm* bust.
but (byt) *nm* 1 aim. 2 purpose. 3 target. 4 goal.
buter (by'te:) *vi* 1 knock. 2 strike. 3 stumble. **se buter** *vr* 1 prop oneself up. 2 be set on.
butin (by'tɛ̃) *nm* plunder, loot.
butoir (by'twar) *nm* buffer.
butte (byt) *nf* mound. **être en butte à** be exposed to.
buvant (by'vã) *v* see **boire.**
buvard (by'var) *adj* **papier buvard** *nm* blotting paper.
buvette (by'vɛt) *nf* refreshment bar.
buveur (by'vœr) *nm* drinker.
byzantin (bi:zã'tɛ̃) *adj* Byzantine.

C

c' *pron* see **ce**¹.
ça (sa) *pron inf* contraction of **cela.**
çà (sa) *adv* here. **çà et là** here and there.
cabale (ka'bal) *nf* intrigue, plot.
cabane (ka'ban) *nf* hut.
cabaret (kaba'rɛ) *nm* 1 public house. 2 restaurant. 3 cabaret.
cabillaud (kabi:'jo) *nm* fresh cod.
cabine (ka'bi:n) *nf* 1 cabin. 2 callbox. 3 cab (of a lorry). **cabine d'essayage** cubicle, fitting room. **cabinet** *nm* 1 closet. 2 office. 3 collection. 4 *pol* cabinet. 5 lavatory. **cabinet de toilette** dressing-room. **cabinet de travail** study.
câbler (ka'ble:) *vt* 1 cable. 2 wire up. **câble** *nm* cable, rope. **câblogramme** *nm* cable.
cabosser (kabɔ'se:) *vt* 1 bump. 2 dent.
se cabrer (ka'bre:) *vr* 1 rear. 2 revolt against.
cabriole (kabri:'ɔl) *nf* 1 leap. 2 somersault.
cacahouette (kaka'wɛt) *nf also* **cacahuète** peanut.
cacao (kaka'o) *nm* cocoa.
cachemire (kaʃ'mi:r) *nm* cashmere.
cacher (ka'ʃe:) *vt* hide, conceal. **se cacher de** *vr* hide from. **cache-cache** *nm* hide-and-seek. **cache-nez** *nm invar* scarf.
cachet (ka'ʃɛ) *nm* 1 seal. 2 stamp. 3 mark. 4 style.
cacheter (kaʃ'te:) *vt* seal.
cachette (ka'ʃɛt) *nf* hiding place. **en cachette** on the quiet.
cachot (ka'ʃo) *nm* dungeon.
cactus (kak'tys) *nm* cactus.
cadavre (ka'davr) *nm* 1 corpse. 2 carcass.
cadeau, -aux (ka'do) *nm* present, gift.
cadenas (kad'na) *nm* padlock.
cadence (ka'dãs) *nf* 1 cadence. 2 rhythm. **cadencé** *adj* rhythmical.
cadet, -ette (ka'dɛ, -'dɛt) *adj* 1 younger. 2 junior. *nm* cadet.
cadran (ka'drã) *nm* dial. **cadran solaire** sundial.
cadrer (ka'dre:) *vi* agree, tally. **cadre** *nm* 1 frame. 2 framework. 3 executive. 4 limits. 5 plan.
caduc, -uque (ka'dyk) *adj* 1 decayed. 2 infirm.
cafard (ka'far) *adj* hypocritical. *nm* 1 cockroach. 2 *inf* sneak, telltale. **avoir le cafard** be fed up.

café (ka'fe:) nm 1 coffee. 2 cafe. café crème or au lait white coffee. café nature or noir black coffee.

caféine (kafe:'i:n) nf caffeine.

cafetier, -ière (kaf'tje:, -'tjɛr) nm,f owner of a cafe. nf coffee pot.

cage (kaʒ) nf 1 cage. 2 casing. cage à poules coop.

cagnotte (ka'ɲɔt) nf game kitty.

cagoule (ka'gu:l) nf hood.

cahier (ka'je:) nm exercise book.

cahin-caha (kaĕka'a) adv so-so.

cahot (ka'o) nm 1 jolt. 2 bump.

cahoter (kaɔ'te:) vi,vt 1 jolt. 2 bump.

caille (kɑj) nf quail.

cailler (kɑ'je:) vt 1 clot. 2 curdle. 3 congeal. caillot nm clot.

caillou, -oux (kɑ'ju:) nm pebble, stone.

caisse (kɛs) nf 1 case. 2 box. 3 tub. 4 till, cash desk. 5 mus drum. caisse d'épargne savings bank. caissier, -ière (kɛ'sje:, -'sjɛr) nm,f cashier.

cajoler (kaʒɔ'le:) vt coax.

calamité (kalamɪ:'te:) nf disaster.

calcaire (kal'kɛr) adj chalky. nm limestone.

calcium (kal'sjɔm) nm calcium.

calcul (kal'kyl) nm 1 calculation. 2 arithmetic.

calculer (kalky'le:) vt 1 calculate. 2 reckon. calculé adj 1 premeditated. 2 deliberate.

cale (kal) nf 1 naut hold. 2 chock, wedge.

caleçon (kal'sɔ̃) nm men's pants. caleçon de bain bathing trunks.

calembour (kalɑ̃'bu:r) nm pun.

calendrier (kalɑ̃dri:'je:) nm 1 calendar. 2 diary.

calepin (kal'pɛ̃) nm notebook.

caler (ka'le:) vt 1 wedge. 2 stall. 3 adjust. vi stall.

calfeutrer (kalfœ'tre:) vt block up.

calibre (ka'li:br) nm 1 calibre. 2 bore (of a gun). 3 size.

califourchon (kali:fu:r'ʃɔ̃) à califourchon adv astride.

câlin (kɑ'lɛ̃) adj 1 caressing. 2 winning.

câliner (kɑli:'ne:) vt caress, fondle.

calleux, -euse (ka'lœ, -'lœz) adj horny, callous.

calmar (kal'mar) nm squid.

calmer (kal'me:) vt 1 calm. 2 quiet. 3 soothe. se calmer vr calm down. calmant nm sedative. calme adj 1 calm. 2 still. nm 1 calm. 2 peace.

calomnier (kalɔm'nje:) vt slander. calomnie nf libel, slander.

calorie (kalɔ'ri:) nf calorie.

calorifère (kalɔri:'fɛr) nm 1 central heating apparatus. 2 stove.

calorifuger (kalɔri:fy'ʒe:) vt insulate.

calquer (kal'ke:) vt trace.

calvitie (kalvi:'si:) nf baldness.

camarade (kama'rad) nm,f comrade, mate, friend.

Cambodge (kɑ̃'bɔdʒ) nm Cambodia. cambodgien, -ienne (kɑ̃bɔ'dʒjɛ̃, -'dʒjɛn) adj,n Cambodian.

cambrer (kɑ̃'bre:) vt 1 bend. 2 arch. se cambrer vr brace oneself.

cambrioler (kɑ̃bri:ɔ'le:) vt burgle. cambriolage nm burglary. cambrioleur, -euse (kɑ̃bri:ɔ-'lœr, -'lœz) nm,f burglar.

caméléon (kame:le:'ɔ̃) nm chameleon.

camelote (kam'lɔt) nf rubbish, junk.

camembert (kamɑ̃'bɛr) nm a French cheese.

caméra (kame:'ra) nf cinecamera.

camion (ka'mjɔ̃) nm lorry. camionnette nf van.

camoufler (kamu:'fle:) vt disguise, camouflage. camouflage nm camouflage.

camp (kɑ̃) nm 1 camp. 2 side.

campagne (kɑ̃'paɲ) nf 1 country, countryside. 2 campaign. en rase campagne in the heart of the country. campagnard adj 1 rustic. 2 country.

camper (kɑ̃'pe:) vt camp. camping nm 1 camping. 2 camping ground.

campus (kɑ̃'pys) nm campus.

Canada (kana'da) nm Canada. canadien, -ienne (kana'djɛ̃, -'djɛn) adj,n Canadian.

canaille (ka'naj) nf inf 1 rabble. 2 scoundrel. adj vulgar, coarse.

canal, -aux (ka'nal, -'no) nm 1 canal. 2 channel. 3 pipe.

canapé (kana'pe:) nm couch, sofa.

canard (ka'nar) nm 1 duck. 2 drake. 3 false report.

canari (kana'ri:) nm canary.

Canaries (kana'ri:) îles Canaries nf pl Canary Islands.

cancan (kɑ̃'kɑ̃) nm 1 gossip. 2 pl scandal.

cancer (kɑ̃'sɛr) nm 1 cancer. 2 cap Cancer.

cancre (kɑ̃kr) nm 1 crab. 2 dunce.

candeur (kɑ̃'dœr) nf 1 frankness. 2 artlessness.

candidat (kɑ̃di:'da) nm 1 candidate. 2 applicant.

candide (kɑ̃'di:d) adj 1 frank. 2 open.

cane (kan) nf duck. caneton nm duckling.

canevas (kan'va) nm 1 canvas. 2 outline.

caniche (ka'ni:ʃ) nm,f poodle.

canif (ka'ni:f) nm penknife.

canin (ka'nɛ̃) adj canine.
caniveau, -aux (kanɪ:'vo) nm gutter.
canne (kan) nf 1 cane. 2 walking stick. canne
à pêche fishing rod. canne à sucre sugar
cane.
canneler (kan'le:) vt 1 groove. 2 flute. cannelure nf groove, channel.
cannelle (ka'nɛl) nf cinnamon.
canon¹ (ka'nɔ̃) nm mil 1 cannon. 2 barrel.
canon² (ka'nɔ̃) nm canon.
cañon (ka'ɲɔ̃) nm canyon.
canoniser (kanɔnɪ:'ze:) vt canonize.
canot (ka'no) nm 1 canoe. 2 boat. canot de
sauvetage lifeboat. canot glisseur speedboat. canotage nm boating. faire du canotage row. canotier nm 1 oarsman. 2 straw
hat.
cantatrice (kāta'trɪ:s) nf singer.
cantine (kā'tɪ:n) nf canteen.
canton (kā'tɔ̃) nm district, canton. cantonade
nf Th wings.
cantonnier (kātɔ'nje:) nm road mender.
caoutchouc (kau'tʃu:) nm 1 rubber. 2 mackintosh.
cap (kap) nm geog cape.
capable (ka'pabl) adj able, fit, capable.
capacité (kapasɪ:'te:) nf 1 capacity. 2 ability.
cape (kap) nf cape, cloak.
capitaine (kapɪ:'tɛn) nm captain.
capital, -aux (kapɪ:'tal, -'to) adj 1 capital. 2
principal. nm comm capital. nf capital (city).
capitalisme nm capitalism.
capitaliser (kapɪ:talɪ:'ze:) vt 1 capitalize. 2 save.
capiteux, -euse (kapɪ:'tœ, -'tœz) adj 1 (of
wine) strong. 2 sensuous.
capitonner (kapi:tɔ'ne:) vt pad. capitonnage
nm upholstery.
caporal, -aux (kapɔ'ral, -'ro) nm corporal.
capot (ka'po) nm 1 cover. 2 bonnet.
capote (ka'pɔt) nf 1 overcoat. 2 mot hood.
câpre (kɑpr) nf caper.
caprice (ka'prɪ:s) nm whim. capricieux, -euse
(kapri:'sjœ, -'sjœz) adj 1 capricious. 2 temperamental. 3 wayward.
Capricorne (kaprɪ:'kɔrn) nm Capricorn.
capsule (kap'syl) nf capsule.
capter (kap'te:) vt 1 obtain by fraud. 2 win
over. 3 tune in. captieux, -euse (kap'sjœ,
-'sjœz) adj 1 cunning. 2 insidious.
captif, -ive (kap'tɪ:f, -'tɪ:v) adj,n captive. captivité nf captivity.
captiver (kaptɪ:'ve:) vt captivate, charm.
capuchon (kapy'ʃɔ̃) nm 1 hood. 2 cap.

capucine (kapy'sɪ:n) nf nasturtium.
caquet (ka'kɛ) nm cackle.
caqueter (kak'te:) vi 1 cackle. 2 inf chatter.
car¹ (kar) conj because, for, as.
car² (kar) nm bus.
carabine (kara'bɪ:n) nf rifle.
caractère (karak'tɛr) nm 1 character. 2 nature.
3 type. 4 letter. d'un caractère facile good-
humoured. caractéristique adj 1 characteristic. 2 typical. nm characteristic.
carafe (ka'raf) nf decanter.
caramel (kara'mɛl) nm caramel. caramel au
beurre butterscotch.
carapace (kara'pas) nf shell.
carat (ka'ra) nm carat.
caravane (kara'van) nf caravan.
carbone (kar'bɔn) nm carbon.
carboniser (karbɔnɪ:'ze:) vt 1 char. 2 carbonize.
carburant (karby'rā) nm motor fuel.
carburateur (karbyra'tœr) nm carburettor.
carcasse (kar'kas) nf 1 carcass. 2 framework.
cardiaque (kar'djak) adj cardiac.
cardinal, -aux (kardɪ:'nal, -'no) adj cardinal. nm
rel cardinal.
carême (ka'rɛm) nm Lent.
carène (ka'rɛn) nf naut hull.
caresser (karɛ'se:) vt 1 caress. 2 cherish.
caresse nf caress.
cargaison (kargɛ'zɔ̃) nf 1 cargo. 2 freight.
caricaturer (karɪ:katy're:) vt caricature. caricature nf caricature.
carier (ka'rje:) vt rot. carie nf decay.
carillon (karɪ:'jɔ̃) nm 1 chime. 2 peal of bells.
carillonner (karɪ:jɔ'ne:) vi 1 chime. 2 peal.
carillonneur nm bellringer.
carnage (kar'naʒ) nm slaughter.
carnassier, -ière (karna'sje:, -'sjɛr) adj carnivorous.
carnaval (karna'val) nm carnival.
carnet (kar'nɛ) nm notebook. carnet de chèques chequebook.
carnivore (karnɪ:'vɔr) adj carnivorous.
carotte (ka'rɔt) nf 1 carrot. 2 inf trick.
carpette (kar'pɛt) nf rug.
carquois (kar'kwa) nm sport quiver.
carreau, -aux (ka'ro) nm 1 small square. 2 tile.
3 pane. 4 game diamonds.
carrefour (kar'fu:r) nm 1 crossroads. 2 square.
carreler (karle:) vt 1 pave. 2 tile. 3 draw
squares. carrelage nm tiling. carrelé adj
checked.
carrelet (karlɛ) nm plaice.
carrer (kɑ're:) vt square. se carrer vr swagger.

carré adj 1 square. 2 plain. nm 1 square. 2 landing. **carrément** adv 1 squarely. 2 bluntly, straightforwardly.

carrière[1] (ka'rjɛr) nf quarry.

carrière[2] (ka'rjɛr) nf career.

carrosse (ka'rɔs) nm coach. **carrosserie** nf mot body.

carrousel (karu:'zɛl) nm 1 tournament. 2 merrygo-round.

carrure (ka'ryr) nf 1 breadth (across shoulders). 2 stature.

cartable (kar'tạbl) nm satchel.

carte (kart) nf 1 map. 2 card. 3 playing card. 4 list. 5 menu. **carte à jouer** playing card. **carte d'abonnement** season ticket. **carte de crédit** credit card. **carte d'identité** identity card. **carte postale** postcard. **donner carte blanche à** give a free hand to.

cartilage (karti'laʒ) nm 1 cartilage. 2 gristle.

carton (kar'tɔ̃) nm 1 cardboard. 2 cardboard box. 3 cartoon. **carton-pâte** nm invar papiermâché.

cartouche (kar'tu:ʃ) nf 1 cartridge. 2 carton. 3 refill.

carvi (kar'vi:) nm caraway.

cas (ka) nm 1 case. 2 matter. 3 circumstance. **cas urgent** emergency. **faire cas de** value. **le cas échéant** should the occasion arise.

cascade (ka'skad) nf 1 cascade. 2 waterfall.

caser (ka'ze:) vt 1 put away. 2 inf find a place for. **se caser** vr settle down. **case** nf 1 hut. 2 compartment.

caserne (ka'zɛrn) nf barracks.

casino (kazi:'no) nm casino.

casque (kask) nm helmet. **casque protecteur** crash-helmet. **casque téléphonique** headphones. **casquette** nf cap.

casse (kas) nf breakage, damage.

casser (ka'se:) vt 1 break. 2 cashier. 3 quash. **se casser la tête** rack one's brains. **cassant** adj 1 brittle. 2 crisp. 3 abrupt. **cassé** adj 1 broken. 2 worn out. **casse-cou** nm invar 1 reckless fellow. 2 danger spot. **casse-croûte** nm invar snack. **casse-noisette** nm invar nutcrackers. **cassure** nf 1 break. 2 fracture.

casserole (ka'srɔl) nf 1 saucepan. 2 stew.

cassette (ka'sɛt) nf 1 case. 2 moneybox.

cassis (ka'si:s) nm 1 blackcurrant. 2 blackcurrant bush.

cassonade (kasɔ'nad) nf brown sugar.

castagnettes (kasta'ɲɛt) nf pl castanets.

caste (kast) nf caste.

castor (ka'stɔr) nm beaver.

casuel, -elle (ka'zɥɛl) adj 1 accidental. 2 casual.

cataloguer, (katalɔ'ge:) vt catalogue, list. **catalogue** nm 1 catalogue. 2 list.

catamaran (katama'rɑ̃) nm catamaran.

Cataphote (kata'fɔt) nm Tdmk mot cat's eye.

cataplasme (kata'plasm) nm poultice.

cataracte (kata'rakt) nf cataract.

catarrhe (ka'tar) nm catarrh.

catastrophe (kata'strɔf) nf catastrophe, disaster.

catéchisme (kate'ʃism) nm catechism.

catégoriser (kategɔri:'ze:) vt categorize. **catégorie** nf category. **catégorique** adj 1 categorical. 2 explicit.

cathédrale (kate'dral) nf cathedral.

cathode (ka'tɔd) nf cathode.

catholique (katɔ'li:k) adj 1 catholic. 2 orthodox. adj,n Roman Catholic.

cauchemar (kɔ'ʃmar) nm nightmare.

causer[1] (ko'ze:) vt cause, bring about. **cause** nf 1 cause. 2 law brief, suit. **à cause de** on account of. **et pour cause** for a very good reason.

causer[2] (ko'ze:) vi chat, talk. **causerie** nf chat.

caustique (ko'sti:k) adj 1 caustic. 2 cutting. nm sci caustic.

cauteleux, -euse (kot'lœ, -'lœz) adj cunning, sly.

caution (ko'sjɔ̃) nf 1 security. 2 guarantee.

cautionnement (kosjɔn'mɑ̃) nm 1 comm guarantee. 2 deposit. **cautionnement judiciaire** bail.

cavalerie (kaval'ri:) nf cavalry. **cavalier, -ière** (kava'lje:, -'ljɛr) adj offhand. nm 1 horseman. 2 partner. 3 game knight.

cave[1] (kav) adj hollow.

cave[2] (kav) nf cellar. **caveau, -aux** (ka'vo) nm 1 small cellar. 2 vault. **caverne** nf 1 cave. 2 den.

caviar (ka'vjar) nm caviar.

cavité (kavi:'te:) nf cavity, hollow.

cayenne (ka'jɛn) nf cayenne.

ce[1] (sə) pron he, she, it. **ce que** what, which. **pour ce qui est de** as regards. **sur ce** thereupon.

ce[2], **cet, cette** (sə, sɛt, sɛt) adj this, that. **ce dernier** the latter. **ceci** pron this.

cécité (se:si:'te:) nf blindness.

céder (se:'de:) vt 1 give up, surrender. 2 make over. vi yield. **le céder à** be inferior to.

cédille (se:'di:j) nf cedilla.

cèdre (sɛdr) nm cedar.

ceindre* (sɛ̃dr) vt 1 encircle. 2 put on.

ceinture (sɛ̃'tyr) *nf* 1 belt. 2 girdle. 3 sash. 4 waist. **ceinture de sécurité** safety belt.

cela (sə'la, sla) *pron also inf* **ça** 1 that. 2 it. 3 so. **c'est ça** that's right. **comme ci comme ça** so-so. **où ça?** where?

célèbre (se:'lɛbr) *adj* famous. **célébrité** *nf* celebrity.

célébrer (se:le:'bre:) *vt* 1 celebrate. 2 observe.

celer (sə'le:) *vt* conceal.

céleri (se:l'ri:) *nm* celery.

céleste (se:'lɛst) *adj* celestial, heavenly.

célibataire (se:li:ba'tɛr) *adj* celibate, single. *nm* bachelor.

celle (sɛl) *pron* see **celui.**

Cellophane (sɛlɔ'fan) *nf Tdmk* Cellophane.

cellule (sɛ'lyl) *nf* cell.

celte (sɛlt) *nm,f* Celt.

celui, celle (sə'lɥi:, sɛl) *pron* 1 he, she. 2 the one. **celui-ci, celle-ci** 1 this one. 2 the latter. **celui-là, celle-là** 1 that one. 2 the former.

cendre (sãdr) *nf* 1 ash. 2 cinder. **cendrier** *nm* ashtray.

cène (sɛn) *nf* Last Supper.

censé (sã'se:) *adj* supposed.

censeur (sã'sœr) *nm* 1 critic. 2 censor.

censurer (sãsy're:) *vt* 1 censure. 2 censor. **censure** *nf* censure, blame.

cent (sã) *adj* one hundred. *nm* 1 hundred. 2 cent. **faire les cent pas** walk up and down. **centaine** *nf* about a hundred. **centième** *adj* hundredth.

centenaire (sãt'nɛr) *nm* centenary.

centigrade (sãti:'grad) *adj* centigrade.

centime (sã'ti:m) *nm* centime.

centimètre (sãti:'mɛtr) *nm* 1 centimetre. 2 *inf* tape measure.

central, -aux (sã'tral, -'tro) *adj* 1 central, middle. 2 principal.

centraliser (sãtrali:'ze:) *vt* centralize.

centre (sãtr) *nm* centre, middle.

cep (sɛp) **cep de vigne** *nm* vine plant.

cependant (səpã'dã) *adv* meanwhile. *conj* however, still, yet.

céramique (se:ra'mi:k) *adj* ceramic. *nf* ceramics.

cerceau, -aux (sɛr'so) *nm* hoop.

cercle (sɛrkl) *nm* 1 circle. 2 club.

cercueil (sɛr'kœj) *nm* coffin.

céréale (se:re:'al) *adj* cereal. **céréales** *nf pl* cereals, corn.

cérébral, -aux (se:re:'bral, -'bro) *adj* of the brain.

cérémonie (se:re:mɔ'ni:) *nf* ceremony. **sans**

24

cérémonie informally. **cérémonieux, -euse** (se:re:mo'njœ, -'njœz) ceremonious, formal.

cerf (sɛr) *nm* stag. **cerf-volant** *nm, pl* **cerfs-volants** kite.

cerise (sə'ri:z) *nf* cherry. **cerisier** *nm* cherry tree.

cerner (sɛr'ne:) *vt* encircle, surround. **avoir les yeux cernés** have bags under one's eyes.

certain (sɛr'tɛ̃) *adj* 1 certain, sure. 2 fixed. *pron pl* some, certain.

certes (sɛrt) *adv* indeed, most certainly.

certifier (sɛrti:'fje:) *vt* 1 certify. 2 witness. **certificat** *nm* certificate.

certitude (sɛrti:'tyd) *nf* certainty.

cerveau, -aux (sɛr'vo) *nm* 1 brain. 2 mind. 3 intellect.

cervelle (sɛr'vɛl) *nf anat* brain. **avoir une cervelle de lièvre** have a brain like a sieve.

Cervin (sɛr'vɛ̃) **Mont Cervin** *nm* Matterhorn.

ces (se:, sɛ) *adj pl* these, those.

cesser (sɛ'se:) *vi,vt* cease, stop. **faire cesser** put a stop to. **cesse** *nf* cease, respite.

cet (sɛt) *adj* see **ce**[2].

cette (sɛt) *adj* see **ce**[2].

ceux (sœ) *pron pl* those. **ceux-ci** 1 these. 2 the latter. **ceux-là** 1 those. 2 the former.

Ceylan (se:'lã) *nm* Ceylon.

chacal (ʃa'kal) *nm* jackal.

chacun (ʃa'kœ̃) *pron* 1 each. 2 everybody, everyone.

chagrin[1] (ʃa'grɛ̃) *adj* 1 sad, downcast. 2 peevish.

chagrin[2] (ʃa'grɛ̃) *nm* 1 grief, sorrow. 2 worry.

chagriner (ʃagri:'ne:) *vt* 1 grieve. 2 vex.

chahut (ʃa'y) *nm* row, uproar.

chaîne (ʃɛn) *nf* 1 chain. 2 cable. 3 channel (television). 4 *pl* fetters. **chaîne de montage** assembly line.

chair (ʃɛr) *nf* 1 flesh. 2 meat. 3 pulp. 4 skin (of a person).

chaire (ʃɛr) *nf* 1 pulpit. 2 *educ* chair.

chaise (ʃɛz) *nf* chair, seat. **chaise à bascule** rocking chair. **chaise-longue** *nf* couch.

chaland (ʃa'lã) *nm* barge.

châle (ʃal) *nm* shawl.

chalet (ʃa'lɛ) *nm* chalet, cottage.

chaleur (ʃa'lœr) *nf* 1 heat, warmth. 2 ardour. **chaleureux, -euse** (ʃalœ'rœ, -'rœz) *adj* 1 warm. 2 cordial.

chaloupe (ʃa'lu:p) *nf* launch.

chalumeau, -aux (ʃaly'mo) *nm* 1 straw. 2 *mus* pipe.

chaluter (ʃaly'te:) vi trawl. **chalutier** nm trawler.

se chamailler (ʃama'je:) vr squabble.

chambellan (ʃãbɛ'lã) nm chamberlain.

chambranle (ʃã'brãl) nm 1 frame. 2 mantelpiece.

chambre (ʃãbr) nf 1 room, bedroom. 2 chamber. **chambre d'ami** spare room. **chambre d'enfants** nursery. **Chambre des Communes/Lords** House of Commons/Lords. **Chambre des Députés** French equivalent of the House of Commons.

chameau, -aux (ʃa'mo) nm 1 camel. 2 sl scoundrel.

chamois (ʃa'mwa) nm chamois.

champ (ʃã) nm field. **sur le champ** immediately. **champ d'aviation** airfield. **champ de courses/foire** racecourse/fairground. **champêtre** adj rustic, rural.

champagne (ʃã'paɲ) nf champagne.

champignon (ʃãpi:'ɲɔ̃) nm mushroom.

champion, -ionne (ʃã'pjɔ̃, -'pjɔn) nm,f champion. **championnat** nm championship.

chance (ʃãs) nf 1 luck. 2 chance. **pas de chance!** bad luck! **chanceux, -euse** (ʃã'sœ, -'sœz) adj 1 hazardous. 2 fortunate.

chanceler (ʃã'sle:) vt 1 stagger. 2 totter. **chancelant** adj 1 staggering, unsteady. 2 delicate.

chancelier (ʃãsə'lje:) nm chancellor.

chandail (ʃã'daj) nm sweater.

chandelle (ʃã'dɛl) nf 1 candle. 2 prop, support. 3 sport lob. **chandelier** nm candlestick.

changer (ʃã'ʒe:) vt 1 change, exchange. 2 alter. vi change. **change** nm exchange. **changeant** adj changing, fickle. **changement** nm change, alteration.

chanoine (ʃan'wan) nm rel canon.

chanson (ʃã'sɔ̃) nf 1 song. 2 pl nonsense. **chanson d'enfants** nursery rhyme. **chanson populaire** folksong.

chant (ʃã) nm 1 singing. 2 song. 3 chant. **chant de Noël** carol.

chanter (ʃã'te:) vt 1 sing. 2 chirp. **faire chanter** blackmail. **chantage** nm blackmail. **chanteur, -euse** (ʃã'tœr, -'tœz) nm,f singer.

chantier (ʃã'tje:) nm yard. **chantier naval** shipyard.

chantonner (ʃãtɔ'ne:) vi,vt hum.

chanvre (ʃãvr) nm hemp.

chaos (ka'o) nm chaos. **chaotique** adj chaotic.

chape (ʃap) nf 1 rel cope. 2 covering.

chapeau, -aux (ʃa'po) nm 1 hat. 2 cover.

chapelain (ʃa'plɛ̃) nm chaplain.

chapelet (ʃa'plɛ) nm rosary, beads.

chapelle (ʃa'pɛl) nf chapel.

chapelure (ʃa'plyr) nf breadcrumbs.

chapitre (ʃa'pi:tr) nm 1 chapter. 2 subject.

chaque (ʃak) adj each, every.

char (ʃar) nm 1 chariot. 2 wagon. **char de combat** mil tank. **char funèbre** hearse.

charabia (ʃara'bja) nm gibberish, double dutch.

charbon (ʃar'bɔ̃) nm 1 coal. 2 carbon. **charbon de bois** charcoal.

charcuterie (ʃarky'tri:) nf 1 pork butcher's shop. 2 delicatessen.

chardon (ʃar'dɔ̃) nm thistle.

chardonneret (ʃardɔn'rɛ) nm goldfinch.

charger (ʃar'ʒe:) vt 1 load. 2 charge. 3 instruct. **se charger de** vr undertake. **charge** nf 1 load. 2 burden. 3 responsibility. 4 office. 5 expense. 6 charge. **à charge de** on condition that. **chargement** nm 1 loading. 2 cargo.

chariot (ʃa'rjo) nm 1 wagon. 2 trolley.

charisme (ʃa'ri:sm) nm charisma.

charité (ʃari:'te:) nf charity, alms.

charivari (ʃari:va'ri:) nm inf din, racket.

charlatan (ʃarla'tã) nm quack.

charmer (ʃar'me:) vt 1 charm. 2 delight. **charme** nm 1 charm. 2 spell. 3 attraction.

charnel, -elle (ʃar'nɛl) adj carnal, sensual.

charnière (ʃar'njɛr) nf hinge.

charnu (ʃar'ny) adj fleshy, plump.

charpente (ʃar'pãt) nf framework.

charrette (ʃa'rɛt) nf cart. **charrette à bras** barrow.

charrue (ʃa'ry) nf plough.

charte (ʃart) nf charter.

châsse (ʃas) nf shrine.

chasser (ʃa'se:) vt 1 chase. 2 hunt. 3 shoot. 4 drive out. 5 dismiss. vi hunt. **chasse** nf 1 hunting. 2 shooting. 3 hunt. 4 shoot. 5 chase. **chasse d'eau** flush. **chasse-neige** nm invar snowplough. **chasseur** nm huntsman.

châssis (ʃa'si:) nm 1 frame. 2 chassis.

chaste (ʃast) adj pure, chaste.

chat, chatte (ʃa, ʃat) nm,f cat. **chaton** nm kitten. nm catkin.

châtaigne (ʃa'tɛɲ) nf chestnut. **châtaignier** nm sweet-chestnut tree.

châtain (ʃa'tɛ̃) adj invar auburn, chestnut-brown.

château, -aux (ʃa'to) nm 1 castle. 2 mansion.

châteaubriant (ʃatobri:'ã) nm grilled steak.

châtier (ʃa'tje:) vt 1 punish, chastise. 2 correct. **châtiment** nm punishment, chastisement.

chatouiller (ʃatu:ˈje:) vt tickle. **chatouilleux, -euse** (ʃatu:ˈjœ, -ˈjœz) adj 1 ticklish. 2 sensitive.

chatoyer (ʃatwaˈje:) vi 1 shimmer. 2 sparkle. **chatoiement** nm 1 shimmer. 2 glistening.

châtrer (ʃɑˈtre:) vt castrate.

chaud (ʃo) adj hot, warm. nm warm. **avoir chaud** (of a person) be hot. **tenir au chaud** keep in a warm place. **chaudière** nf boiler.

chauffer (ʃoˈfe:) vt 1 heat, warm. 2 stoke. 3 swot. vi get hot. **chauffage** nm heating. **chauffage central** central heating. **chauffe-assiette** nm, pl **chauffe-assiettes** hotplate. **chauffeur** nm 1 stoker. 2 chauffeur.

chaume (ʃom) nm 1 thatch. 2 stubble. **chaumière** nf thatched cottage.

chaussée (ʃoˈse:) nf 1 causeway. 2 road.

chausser (ʃoˈse:) vt 1 put on (shoes). 2 supply with shoes. **se chausser** vr put on one's shoes. **chaussette** nf sock. **chausson** nm slipper. **chaussure** nf 1 footwear. 2 shoe, boot.

chauve (ʃov) adj bald. **chauve-souris** nf, pl **chauves-souris** zool bat.

chauvinisme (ʃoviˈni:sm) nm chauvinism.

chaux (ʃo) nf lime. **blanchir à la chaux** whitewash. **lait** or **blanc de chaux** nm whitewash.

chavirer (ʃaviˈre:) vi capsize. vt turn upside down, upset.

chef (ʃɛf) nm 1 head. 2 chief. 3 leader. **chef de bande** ringleader. **chef de cuisine** chef. **chef d'équipe** sport captain. **chef de gare** stationmaster. **chef d'orchestre** conductor.

chef-d'œuvre (ʃɛˈdœvr) nm, pl **chefs-d'œuvre** masterpiece.

chef-lieu (ʃɛfˈljœ) nm, pl **chefs-lieux** chief town.

cheik (ʃɛk) nm sheikh.

chelem (ʃlɛm) nm (in bridge, etc.) slam.

chemin (ʃmɛ̃) nm 1 way. 2 road, path. **à moitié chemin** halfway. **chemin de fer** railway. **chemin faisant** on the way. **grand chemin** highway. **se mettre en chemin** set off.

chemineau, -aux (ʃmiˈno) nm tramp.

cheminée (ʃmiˈne:) nf 1 fireplace. 2 mantelpiece. 3 chimney. 4 funnel.

cheminer (ʃmiˈne:) vi tramp, walk.

chemise (ʃmi:z) nf 1 shirt. 2 folder, jacket. **chemise de nuit** nightdress, nightgown.

chêne (ʃɛn) nm oak.

chenille (ʃəˈni:j) nf caterpillar.

chèque (ʃɛk) nm cheque. **chèque de voyage** traveller's cheque.

cher, chère (ʃɛr) adj 1 dear. 2 expensive. adv at a high price, dearly.

chercher (ʃɛrˈʃe:) vt look for, seek. **chercher à** attempt to.

chérir (ʃeˈri:r) vt cherish. **chéri** adj,n dear, darling.

chérubin (ʃeryˈbɛ̃) nm cherub.

chétif, -ive (ʃeˈti:f, -ˈti:v) adj 1 weak, sickly. 2 miserable, poor.

cheval, -aux (ʃaˈval, -ˈvo) nm horse. **à cheval** on horseback. **cheval à bascule** rocking horse. **cheval de course** racehorse. **cheval pur sang** thoroughbred. **chevaux de bois** nm pl merry-go-round.

chevalet (ʃavaˈlɛ) nm 1 support. 2 trestle. **chevalet de peintre** easel.

chevalier (ʃavaˈlje:) nm 1 knight. 2 horseman. **chevalerie** nf chivalry. ·**cheval-vapeur** nm, pl **chevaux-vapeur** horsepower.

chevaucher (ʃavoˈʃe:) vi,vt ride. vt overlap.

chevelu (ʃaˈvly) adj hairy. **chevelure** nf hair, head of hair.

chevet (ʃaˈvɛ) nm bedside.

cheveu, -eux (ʃaˈvœ) nm 1 hair. 2 pl (head of) hair.

cheville (ʃaˈvi:j) nf 1 peg, pin. 2 bolt. 3 ankle.

chèvre (ʃɛvr) nf goat. **chevreau, -aux** (ʃaˈvro) nm zool kid.

chèvrefeuille (ʃɛvraˈfœj) nm honeysuckle.

chevron (ʃaˈvrɔ̃) nm 1 rafter. 2 stripe.

chez (ʃe:) prep 1 at. 2 care of. 3 with. 4 among. 5 in. 6 at the house of. **chez soi** at home.

chic (ʃi:k) nm 1 skill. 2 style. adj invar 1 smart, elegant. 2 first-rate.

chicaner (ʃi:kaˈne:) vi quibble. vt wrangle with.

chiche (ʃi:ʃ) adj 1 poor. 2 mean.

chicorée (ʃi:kɔˈre:) nf **chicorée sauvage** chicory. **chicorée frisée** endive.

chien, chienne (ʃjɛ̃, ʃjɛn) nm,f dog, bitch. **chien de berger/garde** sheepdog/watchdog. **entre chien et loup** in the twilight.

chiffe (ʃi:f) nf rag.

chiffon (ʃi:ˈfɔ̃) nm 1 rag. 2 scrap. 3 duster. 4 chiffon.

chiffonner (ʃi:fɔˈne:) vt 1 crumple. 2 annoy.

chiffrer (ʃi:ˈfre:) vi calculate. vt 1 number. 2 code. 3 work out. **chiffre** nm 1 figure, number. 2 code. **chiffre d'affaires** comm turnover.

chignon (ʃi:ˈɲɔ̃) nm bun, coil of hair.

Chili (ʃiː'liː) nm Chile. **chilien, -ienne** (ʃiː'ljɛ̃, -'ljɛn) adj,n Chilean.

chimère (ʃiː'mɛr) nf illusion. **chimérique** adj fanciful.

chimie (ʃiː'miː) nf chemistry. **chimique** adj chemical. **chimiste** nm,f sci chemist.

chimpanzé (ʃɛ̃pɑ̃'ze:) nm chimpanzee.

Chine (ʃiːn) nf China. **chinois** adj,n Chinese. nm Chinese (language).

chiot (ʃjo) nm puppy.

chiper (ʃiː'pe:) vt inf **1** pinch. **2** scrounge.

chipoter (ʃiːpɔ'te:) vi waste time. vt nibble.

chiquenaude (ʃiːk'nod) nf flick (of fingers).

chiromancie (kiːrɔmɑ̃'siː) nf palmistry.

chiropracteur (kiːrɔprak'tœr) nm osteopath.

chirurgie (ʃiːryr'ʒiː) nf surgery. **chirurgie plastique** plastic surgery. **chirurgien, -ienne** (ʃiːryr'ʒjɛ̃, -'ʒjɛn) nm,f surgeon. **chirurgique** adj surgical.

chlore (klɔr) nm chlorine.

chlorophylle (klɔrɔ'fiːl) nf chlorophyll.

choc (ʃɔk) nm **1** shock. **2** impact. **3** clash.

chocolat (ʃɔkɔ'la) nm chocolate. adj invar chocolate-coloured.

chœur (kœr) nm **1** chorus. **2** choir.

choir* (ʃwar) vi fall.

choisir (ʃwa'ziːr) vt choose, select. **choisi** adj **1** selected. **2** choice.

choix (ʃwa) nm **1** choice. **2** selection. **de tout premier choix** first-class, best quality.

choléra (kɔlɛ'ra) nm cholera.

chômer (ʃo'me:) vi **1** be unemployed. **2** take a holiday. **chômage** nm unemployment. **chômeur** nm unemployed person.

chope (ʃɔp) nf tankard.

chopine (ʃɔ'piːn) nf half-pint.

choquer (ʃɔ'ke:) vt **1** shock. **2** offend. **3** strike. **se choquer** vr **1** be shocked. **2** collide. **se choquer de** take offence at.

choral (kɔ'ral) adj choral.

chorégraphie (kɔre:gra'fiː) nf choreography. **chorégraphe** nm choreographer.

chose (ʃoz) nf **1** thing. **2** matter. **être tout chose** feel queer.

chou, choux (ʃu:) nm **1** cabbage. **2** rosette. **chou de Bruxelles** Brussels sprout. **chou-fleur** nm, pl **choux-fleurs** cauliflower. **mon petit chou** my dear.

choucas (ʃu:'ka) nm jackdaw.

choucroute (ʃu:'kru:t) nf sauerkraut.

chouette (ʃwɛt) nf owl. adj,interj fine, excellent.

choyer (ʃwa'je:) vt **1** pet. **2** cherish.

chrétien, -ienne (kre:'tjɛ̃, -'tjɛn) adj,n Christian. **Christ** (kriːst) nm Christ.

christianisme (kriːstja'niːsm) nm Christianity.

chrome (krom) nm **1** chromium. **2** chrome. **chromatique** adj chromatic. **chromé** adj chrome.

chromo (krɔ'mo) nm inf colour photo.

chromosome (kromo'zom) nm chromosome.

chronique[1] (krɔ'niːk) nf **1** history. **2** report.

chronique[2] (krɔ'niːk) adj chronic.

chronologique (krɔnɔlɔ'ʒiːk) adj chronological.

chronométrer (krɔnɔme:'tre:) vt time, keep the time. **chronomètre** nm stopwatch.

chrysalide (kriːza'liːd) nf chrysalis.

chrysanthème (kriːzɑ̃'tɛm) nm chrysanthemum.

chuchoter (ʃyʃɔ'te:) vi,vt whisper.

chuinter (ʃɥɛ̃'te:) vi (of an owl) hoot.

chut (ʃyt) interj hush!

chute (ʃyt) nf **1** fall. **2** downfall. **chute d'eau** waterfall.

Chypre (ʃiːpr) nf Cyprus. **chypriot** adj,n Cypriot.

ci[1] (si:) adv here.

ci[2] (si:) pron invar this. **ci-après** adv further on. **ci-contre** adv opposite, on the other side. **ci-dessous** adv below. **ci-dessus** adv above. **ci-devant** adv formerly, previously. **ci-inclus** adj enclosed. **ci-joint** adj attached.

cible (siːbl) nf target.

ciboule (siː'bu:l) nf spring onion. **ciboulette** nf chives.

cicatrice (si:ka'triːs) nf scar.

cidre (si:dr) nm cider.

ciel (sjɛl) nm, pl **ciels** or **cieux 1** sky. **2** heaven. **3** climate.

cierge (sjɛrʒ) nm rel candle.

cigale (siː'gal) nf cicada.

cigare (siː'gar) nm cigar. **cigarette** nf cigarette.

cigogne (siː'gɔɲ) nf stork.

cil (si:l) nm eyelash.

cime (si:m) nf summit, top.

ciment (siː'mɑ̃) nm cement.

cimenter (si:mɑ̃'te:) vt cement.

cimetière (sim'tjɛr) nf churchyard, graveyard, cemetery.

cinéaste (si:ne:'ast) nm film producer.

cinéma (si:ne:'ma) nm cinema. **cinématographique** adj film.

cinétique (si:ne:'ti:k) adj kinetic.

cingalais (sɛ̃ga'lɛ) adj,n Ceylonese.

cingler (sɛ̃'gle:) vt whip, lash. **cinglant** adj biting, cutting, scathing.

cinq (sɛ̃k) adj,nm five. **cinquième** adj fifth.

27

cinquante

cinquante (sɛ̃'kɑ̃t) adj,nm fifty. cinquantième adj fiftieth.
cintrer (sɛ̃'tre:) vt 1 arch. 2 bend. cintre nm 1 curve. 2 arch. 3 coat-hanger.
circoncire* (si:rkɔ̃'si:r) vt circumcise. circoncision nf circumcision.
circonférence (si:rkɔ̃fe'rãs) nf circumference, perimeter.
circonflexe (si:rkɔ̃'flɛks) adj circumflex.
circonscrire* (si:rkɔ̃'skri:r) vt 1 circumscribe. 2 encircle. 3 limit. circonscription nf pol division, district. circonscription électorale constituency.
circonstance (si:rkɔ̃'stãs) nf 1 circumstance. 2 event.
circuit (si:r'kɥi:) nm circuit. circuit touristique organized tour.
circuler (si:rky'le:) vi circulate. circulaire adj,nf circular. circulation nf 1 circulation. 2 traffic.
cirer (si:'re:) vt 1 wax. 2 polish. cire nf wax. ciré adj 1 waxed. 2 polished. nm oilskin.
cirque (si:rk) nm circus.
cisaille (si:'zɑj) nf shears.
ciseau, -aux (si:'zo) nm 1 chisel. 2 pl scissors.
ciseler (si:'zle:) vt 1 engrave. 2 chisel.
cité (si:'te:) nf city. cité universitaire student's hall of residence.
citer (si:'te:) vt quote, cite. citation nf quotation.
citerne (si:'tɛrn) nf cistern, tank.
cithare (si:'tar) nf zither.
citoyen, -enne (si:twa'jɛ̃, -'jɛn) nm,f citizen.
citron (si:'trɔ̃) nm 1 bot lemon. 2 citrus. 3 lemon (colour). citron pressé lemon juice. citronnier nm lemon tree.
citrouille (si:'tru:j) nf pumpkin.
civette (si:'vɛt) nf chives.
civière (si:'vjɛr) nf stretcher.
civil (si:'vi:l) adj 1 civil. 2 civilian. 3 polite. nm civilian. en civil in plain clothes.
civiliser (si:vi:li:'ze:) vt civilize. civilisation nf civilization.
civique (si:'vi:k) adj civic.
clair (klɛr) adj 1 clear. 2 obvious, plain. 3 bright. 4 pale. adv clearly, plainly. nm light. clair de lune moonlight.
clairon (klɛ'rɔ̃) nm bugle.
clairsemé (klɛrsə'me:) adj 1 scattered. 2 thinly sown.
clairvoyant (klɛrvwa'jã) adj shrewd.
clameur (kla'mœr) nf clamour, outcry.
clan (klã) nm 1 clan. 2 set.

clandestin (klãdɛ'stɛ̃) adj secret, clandestine, underground.
claquer (kla'ke:) vi 1 clap. 2 bang. 3 snap. 4 sl die. vt smack. claque nf smack, slap.
clarifier (klari:'fje:) vi clarify.
clarinette (klari:'nɛt) nf clarinet.
clarté (klar'te:) nf 1 clarity. 2 light, brightness.
classer (klɑ'se:) vt 1 class. 2 sort out. 3 file. classe nf 1 class. 2 form. aller en classe go to school. de première classe first-class. faire la classe teach. classeur nm 1 rack. 2 filing cabinet.
classifier (klasi:'fje:) vt classify.
classique (kla'si:k) adj 1 classic. 2 classical. 3 academic. nm pl classics.
claustrophobie (klɔstrɔfɔ'bi:) nf claustrophobia.
clavecin (klav'sɛ̃) nm harpsichord.
clavicule (klavi:'kyl) nf collarbone.
clavier (kla'vje:) nm keyboard.
claxon (klak'sɔ̃) nm hooter.
claxonner (klaksɔ'ne:) vi hoot.
clef (kle:) nf also clé 1 key. 2 clue. 3 mus clef. sous clef under lock and key.
clémence (kle'mãs) nf mercy. clément adj 1 lenient, merciful. 2 mild.
cleptomanie (klɛptoma'ni:) nf kleptomania. cleptomane nm,f kleptomaniac.
clerc (klɛr) nm 1 clerk. 2 scholar. faire un pas de clerc make a blunder.
clergé (klɛr'ʒe:) nm clergy, priesthood.
clérical, -aux (kle:ri:'kal, -'ko) adj rel clerical.
cliché (kli:'ʃe:) nm 1 phot negative. 2 stock phrase.
client (kli:'ã) nm client, patient, customer. clientèle nf 1 customers. 2 med practice.
cligner (kli:'ɲe:) vi,vt blink, screw up one's eyes. clignement nm 1 blink. 2 flicker.
clignoter (kli:ɲɔ'te:) vi 1 blink. 2 twitch. 3 twinkle. clignotant nm indicator.
climat (kli:'ma) nm climate. climatisation nf air-conditioning.
clin d'œil (klɛ̃) nm wink.
clinique (kli:'ni:k) adj clinical. nf nursing home.
clinquant (klɛ̃'kã) nm 1 tinsel. 2 glitter. adj flashy.
cliqueter (kli:k'te:) vi rattle, clank.
cliquette (kli:'kɛt) nf pair of castanets.
clitoris (kli:tɔ'ri:s) nm clitoris.
clochard (klɔ'ʃar) nm tramp.
cloche (klɔʃ) nf 1 bell. 2 cover.
clocher¹ (klɔ'ʃe:) nm 1 belfry. 2 steeple.
clocher² (klɔ'ʃe:) vi limp, hobble.

28

cloison (klwa'zɔ̃) *nf* partition.
cloître (klwatr) *nm* 1 cloister. 2 monastery. 3 close.
clopin-clopant (klɔpɛ̃klɔ'pɑ̃) *adv* **aller clopin-clopant** limp along.
clore* (klɔr) *vt* 1 close. 2 end. **clos** *adj* 1 closed. 2 finished. *nm* enclosure.
clôture (klo'tyr) *nf* 1 fence. 2 closing.
clou (klu:) *nm* 1 nail. 2 boil. 3 *Th* main attraction. 4 old car. **clou de girofle** *cul* clove.
clouer (klu:'e:) *vt* 1 nail. 2 hold fast. **être cloué au lit** be bedridden.
clouter (klu:'te:) *vt* stud.
clovisse (klɔ'vi:s) *nf* clam.
clown (klu:n) *nm* clown.
club (klɔb) *nm* 1 club. 2 golf club.
coaguler (koagy'le:) *vt* congeal.
coalition (koali:'sjɔ̃) *nf* coalition, union.
coasser (koa'se:) *vi* croak.
cobaye (kɔ'baj) *nm* guineapig.
cobra (kɔ'bra) *nm* cobra.
cocarde (kɔ'kard) *nf* rosette.
cocasse (kɔ'kas) *adj* funny, humorous.
coccinelle (kɔksi:'nɛl) *nf* ladybird.
cocher[1] (kɔ'ʃe:) *nm* coachman, driver.
cocher[2] (kɔ'ʃe:) *vt* mark off. **coche** *nf* notch.
cochon, -onne (kɔ'ʃɔ̃, -'ʃɔn) *adj* 1 *inf* indecent. 2 dirty. *nm* 1 pig. 2 swine. **cochon d'Inde** guineapig. **cochonnerie** *nf* *inf* 1 filthiness. 2 rubbish. 3 dirty trick.
cocktail (kɔk'tɛl) *nm* 1 cocktail. 2 cocktail party.
coco (kɔ'ko) **noix de coco** *nm* coconut. **cocotier** *nm* coconut palm.
cocon (kɔ'kɔ̃) *nm* cocoon.
cocotte[1] (kɔ'kɔt) *nf* 1 child's word for chicken. 2 *sl* tart.
cocotte[2] (kɔ'kɔt) *nf* stewpan.
code (kɔd) *nm* 1 law. 2 code. **code de la route** highway code.
codéine (kɔde:'i:n) *nf* codeine.
coéducation (koe:dyka'sjɔ̃) *nf* co-education.
cœur (kœr) *nm* 1 heart. 2 mind. 3 courage. 4 middle. 5 *game* hearts. **au cœur léger** light-hearted. **de bon/mauvais cœur** willingly/reluctantly.
coexister (koe:gzi:'ste:) *vi* coexist.
coffre (kɔfr) *nm* 1 chest, box. 2 *mot* boot. **coffre-fort** *nm, pl* **coffres-forts** safe.
cognac (kɔ'ɲak) *nm* brandy.
cogner (kɔ'ɲe:) *vt* hammer, hit. *vi,vt* 1 knock. 2 bump. **cognée** *nf* hatchet, axe.
cohabiter (koabi:'te:) *vi* cohabit, live together.

cohérent (kɔe:'rɑ̃) *adj* coherent.
cohue (kɔ'y) *nf* crowd, mob.
coiffer (kwa'fe:) *vt* 1 cover. 2 put on (a hat). **se coiffer** *vr* 1 put on one's hat. 2 do one's hair. **coiffeur, -euse** (kwa'fœr, -'fœz) *nm,f* hairdresser. *nf* dressing table. **coiffure** *nf* 1 hairdressing. 2 hairstyle.
coin (kwɛ̃) *nm* 1 corner. 2 spot. 3 wedge.
coincer (kwɛ̃'se:) *vt* wedge. *vi* jam, stick.
coïncider (kɔɛ̃si:'de:) *vi* coincide. **coïncidence** *nf* coincidence.
coing (kwɛ̃) *nm* quince.
col (kɔl) *nm* 1 neck. 2 collar. 3 pass (of a mountain).
coléoptère (kɔle:ɔp'tɛr) *nm* beetle.
colère (kɔ'lɛr) *nf* anger. **coléreux, -euse** (kɔle:'rœ, -'rœz) *adj* quick-tempered.
colimaçon (kɔli:ma'sɔ̃) *nm* snail. **en colimaçon** spiral.
colique (kɔ'li:k) *nf* stomach ache.
colis (kɔ'li:) *nm* 1 parcel, package. 2 piece of luggage. **par colis postal** by parcel post.
collaborer (kɔlabɔ're:) *vi* collaborate. **collaborateur** *nm* 1 collaborator. 2 contributor.
collant (kɔ'lɑ̃) *adj* 1 sticky. 2 close-fitting. *nm* tights.
colle (kɔl) *nf* paste, glue.
collectif, -ive (kɔlɛk'ti:f, -'ti:v) *adj* collective. **collectivité** *nf* 1 group. 2 community.
collection (kɔlɛk'sjɔ̃) *nf* collection.
collectionner (kɔlɛksjɔ'ne:) *vt* collect.
collège (kɔ'lɛʒ) *nm* 1 college. 2 school. **collège d'enseignement général** secondary modern school. **collège privé** public school. **collégien, -ienne** (kɔle:'ʒjɛ̃, -'ʒjɛn) *nm,f* schoolboy, schoolgirl.
collègue (kɔl'lɛg) *nm,f* colleague.
coller (kɔ'le:) *vt* paste, glue. *vi* stick, cling. **se coller** *vr* stick or cling close. **colle** *nf* glue, paste.
collet (kɔ'lɛ) *nm* collar. **collet monté** *adj invar* prim, prudish.
collier (kɔ'lje:) *nm* 1 necklace. 2 collar.
colline (kɔ'li:n) *nf* hill.
collision (kɔli:'zjɔ̃) *nf* 1 collision. 2 clash.
colombe (kɔ'lɔ̃b) *nf* pigeon, dove. **colombier** *nm* dovecote.
Colombie (kɔlɔ̃'bi:) *nf* Columbia. **colombien, -ienne** *adj,n* Columbian.
colonel (kɔlɔ'nɛl) *nm* colonel.
colonie (kɔlɔ'ni:) *nf* colony. **colonie de vacances** children's holiday camp. **colonial, -aux** (kɔlɔ'njal, -'njo) *adj,n* colonial.

29

colonne (kɔ'lɔn) nf **1** column. **2** pillar. **colonne vertébrale** backbone.
colorer (kɔlɔ're:) vt **1** colour. **2** stain.
coloris (kɔlɔ'ri:) nm colouring.
colossal, -aux (kɔlɔ'sal, -'so) adj colossal, huge.
colporter (kɔlpɔr'te:) vt **1** peddle. **2** spread (news). **colporteur** nm pedlar.
coma (kɔ'ma) nm coma.
combat (kɔ̃'ba) nm **1** combat, fight. **2** conflict. **hors de combat** disabled.
combattre (kɔ̃'batr) vt fight, combat. vi fight, struggle.
combien (kɔ̃'bjɛ̃) adv how much, how many. **le combien sommes-nous?** what day of the month is it?
combiner (kɔ̃bı'ne:) vt **1** combine. **2** contrive. **combinaison** nf **1** combination. **2** plan.
comble[1] (kɔ̃bl) nm **1** heap. **2** top, summit. **3** roof. **ça, c'est le comble!** that's the limit!
comble[2] (kɔ̃bl) adj **1** heaped. **2** full, crowded.
combler (kɔ̃'ble:) vt **1** fill, fill to overflowing. **2** make good.
combustion (kɔ̃by'stjɔ̃) nf combustion. **combustible** adj combustible. nm fuel.
comédie (kɔme:'di:) nf **1** comedy. **2** play. **jouer la comédie** act a part. **comédien, -ienne** (kɔme:'djɛ̃, -'djɛn) nm,f **1** comedian. **2** actor, actress.
comestible (kɔmɛ'sti:bl) adj edible. nm **1** article of food. **2** pl provisions.
comète (kɔ'mɛt) nf comet.
comique (kɔ'mı:k) adj **1** comic. **2** comical. nm **1** comedy. **2** comedian.
comité (kɔmi:'te:) nm committee, board.
commander (kɔmɑ̃'de:) vt **1** order, command. **2** govern. **3** control. **commandant** nm mil officer in command, major. **commande** nf order. **de commande** forced. **fait sur commande** made to order. **commandement** nm **1** command. **2** commandment.
commanditer (kɔmɑ̃di:'te:) vt finance.
comme (kɔm) adv **1** as, like. **2** in the way of. **3** how. conj as.
commémorer (kɔmme:mɔ're:) vt commemorate.
commencer (kɔmɑ̃'se:) vi,vt begin, commence. **commençant** nm beginner. **commencement** nm beginning.
comment (kɔ'mɑ̃) adv **1** how. **2** what. **3** interj what! why!
commenter (kɔmɑ̃'te:) vi,vt **1** comment. **2** annotate. **commentaire** nm **1** commentary. **2** comment. **commentateur, -trice** (kɔmɑ̃ta-'tœr, -'trı:s) nm,f commentator.

commérage (kɔmɛ'raʒ) nm gossip.
commerce (kɔ'mɛrs) nm commerce, trade. **commerçant** adj business, mercantile. nm tradesman. **commercial, -aux** (kɔmɛr'sjal, -'sjo) adj commercial. **commerciale** nf estate car.
commettre (kɔ'mɛtr) vt **1** commit. **2** entrust.
commis (kɔ'mı:) nm **1** clerk. **2** assistant.
commissaire (kɔmı:'sɛr) nm commissioner. **commissaire de police** police superintendent. **commissaire-priseur** nm, pl **commissaires-priseurs** auctioneer.
commissariat (kɔmı:sa'rja) nm police station.
commission (kɔmı:'sjɔ̃) nf **1** commission. **2** message, errand. **3** board, committee.
commissionnaire (kɔmi:sjɔ'nɛr) nm messenger.
commode (kɔ'mɔd) adj **1** convenient. **2** comfortable. **3** accommodating. nf chest of drawers. **commodité** nf **1** convenience. **2** comfort.
commotion (kɔmo'sjɔ̃) nf **1** commotion. **2** concussion.
commun (kɔ'mœ̃) adj **1** common. **2** general. **3** usual. **4** vulgar. **peu commun** unusual.
commune (kɔ'myn) nf **1** commune. **2** parish. **communal, -aux** (kɔmy'nal, -'no) adj **1** common. **2** communal. **communauté** nf community.
communiant (kɔmy'njɑ̃) nm communicant.
communication (kɔmyni:ka'sjɔ̃) nf **1** communication. **2** connection. **3** telephone call. **4** message.
communion (kɔmy'njɔ̃) nf communion.
communiquer (kɔmynı:'ke:) vt **1** communicate. **2** convey. vi communicate. **se communiquer** vr **1** be communicative. **2** spread.
communisme (kɔmy'ni:sm) nm communism. **communiste** nm,f communist.
compact (kɔ̃'pakt) adj **1** compact. **2** close.
compagnie (kɔ̃pa'ɲi:) nf **1** company. **2** party, group. **compagnon, compagne** nm,f companion.
comparer (kɔ̃pa're:) vt compare. **comparable** adj comparable. **comparaison** nf comparison. **comparatif, -ive** (kɔ̃para'ti:f, -'ti:v) adj comparative. **comparé** adj comparative.
compartiment (kɔ̃parti:'mɑ̃) nm compartment.
compas (kɔ̃'pa) nm **1** pair of compasses. **2** scale.
compassion (kɔ̃pa'sjɔ̃) nf compassion, pity. **avoir compassion de** take pity on.
compatible (kɔ̃pa'ti:bl) adj compatible.
compatir (kɔ̃pa'tı:r) vi **compatir à 1** sympathize

with. **2** be indulgent with. **compatissant** adj
1 soft-hearted. **2** indulgent.

compenser (kɔ̃pɑ̃'se:) vt compensate.

compère (kɔ̃'pɛr) nm **1** accomplice. **2** comrade.

compétent (kɔ̃pe'tɑ̃) adj competent. **avec
compétence** adv competently.

compétition (kɔ̃pe:ti:'sjɔ̃) nf **1** competition. **2**
race.

compiler (kɔ̃pi'le:) vt compile.

complaisance (kɔ̃plɛ'zɑ̃s) nf **1** kindness. **2**
self-satisfaction. **complaisant** adj **1** obliging.
2 self-satisfied, complacent.

complément (kɔ̃ple:'mɑ̃) nm complement.

complet, -ète (kɔ̃'plɛ, -'plɛt) adj **1** complete,
entire. **2** full. nm suit.

compléter (kɔ̃ple:'te:) vt complete.

complexe (kɔ̃'plɛks) adj **1** complex. **2** intricate.
nm complex. **complexité** nf complexity.

complice (kɔ̃'pli:s) adj **1** accessory. **2** accomplice. nm,f accomplice.

compliment (kɔ̃pli:'mɑ̃) nm **1** compliment. **2** pl
compliments. **3** pl congratulations.

complimenter (kɔ̃pli:mɑ̃'te:) vt **1** compliment.
2 congratulate.

compliquer (kɔ̃pli:'ke:) vt complicate.

complot (kɔ̃'plo) nm plot, conspiracy.

comploter (kɔ̃plɔ'te:) vt plot, scheme.

comporter (kɔ̃pɔr'te:) vt **1** allow. **2** require. **3**
comprise. **4** involve. **se comporter** vr behave.

composer (kɔ̃po'ze:) vt **1** compose. **2** arrange.
composer avec come to terms with. **se
composer de** vr consist of. **composé** adj **1**
compound. **2** composed. nm compound.
compositeur, -trice (kɔ̃pɔzi:'tœr, -'tri:s) nm,f
composer. **composition** nf **1** composition. **2**
arrangement.

compote (kɔ̃'pɔt) nf stewed fruit.

compréhensif, -ive (kɔ̃pre:ɑ̃'si:f, -'si:v) adj **1**
comprehensive. **2** intelligent.

comprendre* (kɔ̃'prɑ̃dr) vt **1** include, comprise.
2 understand, comprehend. **se faire comprendre** make oneself understood. **y compris**
including.

comprimer (kɔ̃pri:'me:) vt **1** compress. **2** restrain. **comprimé** adj compressed. nm tablet.

compromettre* (kɔ̃prɔ'mɛtr) vi,vt compromise.
compromis nm compromise.

comptable (kɔ̃'tabl) adj **1** of bookkeeping. **2**
responsible. nm,f accountant. **comptabilité**
nf bookkeeping.

compter (kɔ̃'te:) vt **1** count, reckon. **2** charge. **3**
expect. vi rely. **comptant** nm cash. **compte**
nm **1** account. **2** calculation. **compte à**

rebours countdown. **compte rendu 1** report.
2 review. **en fin de compte** all things considered.

compteur (kɔ̃'tœr) nm **1** counter. **2** meter.
compteur de stationnement parking meter.

comptoir (kɔ̃t'war) nm counter.

comte (kɔ̃t) nm (title) count. **comtesse** nf
countess.

comté (kɔ̃'te:) nm county.

concave (kɔ̃'kav) adj concave.

concéder (kɔ̃se:'de:) vt **1** concede. **2** grant. **3**
admit.

concentrer (kɔ̃sɑ̃'tre:) vt **1** concentrate. **2** focus.
3 repress. **concentration** nf concentration.
concentré adj **1** concentrated. **2** reserved. nm
extract, concentrate.

concentrique adj concentric.

concept (kɔ̃'sɛpt) nm concept.

conception (kɔ̃sɛp'sjɔ̃) nf **1** conception. **2** idea.
conception dirigée birth control.

concerner (kɔ̃sɛr'ne:) vt concern, affect.

concert (kɔ̃'sɛr) nm **1** concert. **2** harmony.

concerto (kɔ̃sɛr'to) nm concerto.

concession (kɔ̃sɛ'sjɔ̃) nf concession.

concevoir* (kɔ̃sə'vwar) vt **1** conceive. **2**
imagine. **3** understand.

concierge (kɔ̃'sjɛrʒ) nm,f **1** caretaker. **2** porter.

concilier (kɔ̃si:'lje:) vt **1** settle. **2** reconcile.

concis (kɔ̃'si:) adj concise.

conclure* (kɔ̃'klyr) vt **1** conclude. **2** finish.
conclusion nf **1** conclusion, decision. **2** end.

concombre (kɔ̃'kɔ̃br) nm cucumber.

concourir* (kɔ̃ku:'ri:r) vi **1** converge. **2** unite. **3**
compete.

concours (kɔ̃'ku:r) nm **1** gathering. **2** assistance. **3** competition. **4** show.

concret, -ète (kɔ̃'krɛ, -'krɛt) adj **1** concrete. **2**
solid.

concurrence (kɔ̃ky'rɑ̃s) nf competition. **concurrent** adj **1** competitive. **2** rival. nm **1**
competitor. **2** candidate. **3** contestant.

condamner (kɔ̃dɑ'ne:) vt **1** condemn. **2**
sentence. **3** reprove. **4** block up. **condamnation** nf **1** condemnation. **2** law sentence.

condenser (kɔ̃dɑ̃'se:) vt condense. **condensation** nf condensation.

condescendre (kɔ̃dɛ'sɑ̃dr) vi condescend.

condition (kɔ̃di:'sjɔ̃) nf **1** condition, proviso. **2**
position. **3** pl terms. **à condition** on approval.
à condition que provided that. **conditionnel,
-elle** adj conditional.

conditionner (kɔ̃di:sjɔ'ne:) vt **1** condition. **2**
comm package.

31

condoléance (kɔ̃dɔle:'ãs) nf condolence.

conducteur, -trice (kɔ̃dyk'tœr, -'trɪ:s) nm,f 1 driver. 2 leader. adj conducting.

conduire* (kɔ̃'dɥi:r) vt 1 conduct. 2 lead. 3 drive. 4 manage. se conduire vr behave. conduit nm 1 passage. 2 pipe. conduite nf 1 behaviour. 2 management. 3 driving. 4 leading. conduite intérieure saloon car.

cône (kon) nm cone.

confectionner (kɔ̃fɛksjɔ'ne:) vt 1 make up. 2 manufacture. confectionné adj ready-made.

confédérer (kɔ̃fe:de:'re:) vt confederate. confédération nf confederation.

conférer (kɔ̃fe:'re:) vt 1 compare. 2 award. vi confer. conférence nf 1 conference. 2 lecture. conférencier, -ière (kɔ̃fe:rã'sje:, -'sjɛr) nm,f lecturer.

confesser (kɔ̃fɛ'se:) vt confess.

confetti (kɔ̃fɛt'ti:) nm pl confetti.

confidentiel, -ielle (kɔ̃fi:dã'sjɛl) adj confidential.

confier (kɔ̃'fje:) vt 1 trust. 2 confide. se confier à vr put one's trust in. confiance nf confidence, trust. digne de confiance reliable, trustworthy. confiant adj 1 confiding. 2 confident, assured.

confire* (kɔ̃'fi:r) vt cul preserve (food).

confirmer (kɔ̃fi:r'me:) vt confirm. confirmation nf confirmation.

confiserie (kɔ̃fi:'zrɪ:) nf 1 confectioner's shop. 2 confectionery. confiseur nm confectioner.

confisquer (kɔ̃fi:'ske:) vt confiscate, seize.

confiture (kɔ̃fi:'tyr) nf jam. confiture d'oranges marmalade.

conflagration (kɔ̃flagra'sjɔ̃) nf blaze, fire.

conflit (kɔ̃'fli:) nm 1 conflict. 2 clash.

confluer (kɔ̃fly'e:) vi join, meet.

confondre (kɔ̃'fɔ̃dr) vt 1 confound, baffle. 2 confuse, mistake. se confondre vr blend. confondu adj 1 overwhelmed. 2 confused.

conforme (kɔ̃'fɔrm) adj conforme à 1 according to. 2 consistent with. conformément adv accordingly.

conformer (kɔ̃fɔr'me:) vt 1 shape. 2 conform. se conformer à vr comply with.

confort (kɔ̃'fɔr) nm comfort. confortable adj comfortable, cosy.

confrère (kɔ̃'frɛr) nm 1 colleague. 2 rel brother.

confus (kɔ̃'fy) adj 1 confused. 2 vague. 3 obscure. confusion nf confusion, muddle.

congé (kɔ̃'ʒe:) nm 1 leave, holiday. 2 notice.

congédier (kɔ̃ʒe:'dje:) vt 1 dismiss. 2 discharge.

congeler (kɔ̃'ʒle:) vt 1 freeze. 2 congeal.

congélateur nm deep-freeze. congélation nf freezing.

congestion (kɔ̃ʒɛs'tjɔ̃) nf congestion. congestion cérébrale med stroke. congestion pulmonaire pneumonia. congestionné adj flushed, red in the face.

congrès (kɔ̃'grɛ) nm congress.

conifère (kɔni:'fɛr) nm conifer.

conique (kɔ'nɪ:k) adj conical.

conjoint (kɔ̃'ʒwɛ̃) adj 1 joined. 2 married. conjoints nm pl husband and wife.

conjonction (kɔ̃ʒɔ̃k'sjɔ̃) nf 1 union. 2 conjunction.

conjugal, -aux (kɔ̃ʒy'gal, -'go) adj conjugal.

conjuguer (kɔ̃ʒy'ge:) vt conjugate. conjugaison nf conjugation.

connaissance (kɔnɛ'sãs) nf 1 knowledge. 2 acquaintance. 3 consciousness. 4 pl learning. sans connaissance unconscious. connaisseur nm connoisseur, expert. adj expert.

connaître* (kɔ'nɛtr) vt 1 know. 2 be acquainted with. 3 have a thorough knowledge of. 4 distinguish. se connaître en vr know all about.

connu (kɔ'ny) v see connaître.

conquérir* (kɔ̃ke:'ri:r) vt 1 conquer. 2 win over.

conquête (kɔ̃'kɛt) nf conquest.

conquis (kɔ̃'kɪ:) v see conquérir.

consacrer (kɔ̃sa'kre:) vt 1 consecrate. 2 devote. consacré adj sacred.

consanguin (kɔ̃sã'gɛ̃) frère consanguin nm half-brother. sœur consanguine nf half-sister.

conscience (kɔ̃'sjãs) nf 1 conscience. 2 consciousness. avoir conscience de be aware of. consciencieux, -euse (kɔ̃sjã'sjœ, -'sjœz) adj conscientious. conscient de adj conscious of.

conscription (kɔ̃skri:p'sjɔ̃) nf conscription.

conscrit (kɔ̃'skri:) nm conscript.

consécutif, -ive (kɔ̃se:ky'ti:f, -'ti:v) adj consecutive.

conseil (kɔ̃'sɛj) nm 1 advice. 2 counsel. 3 council. conseil d'administration board of directors. conseil de guerre court-martial. conseil des ministres pol cabinet. conseil général county council.

conseiller (kɔ̃sɛ'je:) vt advise, counsel.

consentir (kɔ̃sã'ti:r) vi consent, agree. consentement nm consent.

conséquence (kɔsɛ'kãs) nf 1 consequence. 2 importance. conséquent adj 1 consistent. 2 following. par conséquent consequently.

conservatoire (kɔ̃sɛrva'twar) *nm* school, academy (of music).
conserver (kɔ̃sɛr've:) *vt* **1** preserve. **2** keep.
conservateur, -trice (kɔ̃sɛrva'tœr, -'tri:s) *nm,f* **1** curator, warden. **2** *pol* conservative.
considérer (kɔ̃si:de:'re:) *vt* **1** consider. **2** contemplate. **3** regard. **considérable** *adj* **1** considerable. **2** large. **3** eminent, important. **considération** *nf* **1** consideration. **2** reason. **3** respect.
consigner (kɔ̃si:'ɲe:) *vt* **1** deposit. **2** consign. **3** record. **4** confine to barracks. **non consigné** non-returnable. **consignation** *nf* **1** deposit. **2** consignment. **consigne** *nf* **1** order. **2** cloakroom.
consister (kɔ̃si:'ste:) *vi* consist. **consistance** *nf* consistency. **consistant** *adj* firm, solid.
consoler (kɔ̃sɔ'le:) *vt* console, comfort.
consolider (kɔ̃sɔli:'de:) *vt* consolidate. **se consolider** *vr* **1** become firm. **2** heal.
consommer (kɔ̃sɔ'me:) *vt* **1** consume. **2** accomplish. **consommateur, -trice** (kɔ̃sɔma'tœr, -'tri:s) *nm,f* **1** consumer. **2** customer (in restaurant). **consommation** *nf* **1** consumption. **2** accomplishment. **3** drink. **consommé** *nm* clear soup.
consonne (kɔ̃'sɔn) *nf* consonant.
conspirer (kɔ̃spi:'re:) *vi,vt* conspire, plot. **conspiration** *nf* plot.
conspuer (kɔ̃'spɥe:) *vt* to shout down.
constant (kɔ̃'stɑ̃) *adj* **1** constant, steadfast. **2** firm. **constamment** *adv* constantly.
constater (kɔ̃sta'te:) *vt* **1** ascertain. **2** state. **3** certify.
constellation (kɔ̃stɛlla'sjɔ̃) *nf* constellation.
consterner (kɔ̃stɛr'ne:) *vt* dismay.
constipation (kɔ̃sti:pa'sjɔ̃) *nf* constipation.
constituer (kɔ̃sti:'tɥe:) *vt* **1** constitute. **2** form. **3** assign. **4** *comm* incorporate. **constituant** *adj* constituent. *nm* **1** component. **2** constituent. **constitution** *nf* **1** constitution. **2** composition.
construction (kɔ̃stryk'sjɔ̃) *nf* **1** construction. **2** building. **construction mécanique** mechanical engineering.
construire (kɔ̃'strɥi:r) *vt* **1** construct. **2** build.
consul (kɔ̃'syl) *nm* consul.
consulat (kɔ̃sy'la) *nm* consulate.
consulter (kɔ̃syl'te:) *vt* consult. **se consulter** *vr* consider. **consultation** *nf* **1** consultation. **2** advice, opinion.
consumer (kɔ̃sy'me:) *vt* **1** consume. **2** destroy. **3** use up. **se consumer** *vr* burn up.
contact (kɔ̃'takt) *nm* contact, touch.

contagieux, -euse (kɔ̃ta'ʒjœ, -'ʒjœz) *adj* contagious, catching.
contaminer (kɔ̃tamı:'ne:) *vt* **1** contaminate. **2** infect.
conte (kɔ̃t) *nm* story, tale. **conte de fées** fairytale.
contempler (kɔ̃tɑ̃'ple:) *vt* **1** contemplate. **2** meditate. **3** gaze at.
comtemporain (kɔ̃tɑ̃pɔ'rɛ̃) *adj,n* contemporary.
contenance (kɔ̃t'nɑ̃s) *nf* **1** look. **2** content. **faire bonne contenance** put on a brave face.
contenir (kɔ̃t'nı:r) *vt* **1** contain. **2** restrain. **contenu** *adj* **1** restrained. **2** reserved. *nm* **1** contents. **2** subject.
content (kɔ̃'tɑ̃) *adj* **1** content, satisfied. **2** pleased.
contenter (kɔ̃tɑ̃'te:) *vt* **1** content, satisfy. **2** gratify. **contentement** *nm* contentment, satisfaction.
conter (kɔ̃'te:) *vt* tell, relate. **conteur** *nm* narrator.
contester (kɔ̃tɛs'te:) *vi,vt* contest, dispute. **contestable** *adj* debatable. **contestation** *nf* debate.
contexte (kɔ̃'tɛkst) *nm* context.
contigu, -uë (kɔ̃tı:'gy) *adj* adjoining, adjacent.
continent (kɔ̃ti:'nɑ̃) *nm* continent. **continental, -aux** (kɔ̃ti:nɑ̃'tal, -'to) *adj* continental.
contingent (kɔ̃tɛ̃'ʒɑ̃) *nm* quota, allowance.
continuer (kɔ̃tı:'nɥe:) *vi,vt* continue. **continu** *adj* continuous. **continuel, -elle** (kɔ̃tı:'nɥɛl) *adj* continual. **continuité** *nf* continuity.
contour (kɔ̃'tu:r) *nm* **1** outline. **2** contour.
contourner (kɔ̃tu:r'ne:) *vt* **1** shape. **2** skirt. **3** twist. **route de contournement** *nf* bypass.
contraception (kɔ̃trasɛp'sjɔ̃) *nf* contraception.
contracter [1] (kɔ̃trak'te:) *vt* **1** contract, incur. **2** catch.
contracter [2] (kɔ̃trak'te:) *vt* contract, draw together.
contractuel, -elle (kɔ̃trak'tɥɛl) *nm,f* traffic warden.
contradiction (kɔ̃tradi:k'sjɔ̃) *nf* **1** contradiction. **2** discrepancy. **contradictoire** *adj* contradictory, conflicting.
contraindre (kɔ̃'trɛ̃dr) *vt* **1** compel. **2** restrain. **contrainte** *nf* **1** constraint. **2** compulsion.
contraire (kɔ̃'trɛr) *adj* **1** contrary, opposite. **2** adverse. *nm* contrary, reverse.
contrarier (kɔ̃tra'rje:) *vt* **1** oppose. **2** annoy.
contraster (kɔ̃tras'te:) *vi,vt* contrast. **contraste** *nm* contrast.
contrat (kɔ̃'tra) *nm* contract, agreement.

contravention (kɔ̃travɑ̃'sjɔ̃) nf 1 infringement, minor offence. 2 fine.

contre (kɔ̃tr) prep 1 against. 2 for. 3 from. 4 to. 5 by. adv 1 against. 2 close to. **le pour et le contre** the pros and cons.

contre-amiral, -aux nm rear admiral.

contre-attaque nf counterattack.

contre-avion adj anti-aircraft.

contrebande (kɔ̃trə'bɑ̃d) nf 1 contraband. 2 smuggling. **faire la contrebande** smuggle. **contrebandier** nm smuggler.

contrebasse (kɔ̃trə'bas) nf double bass.

contre-boutant nm buttress.

contrecarrer (kɔ̃trəka're:) vt thwart, cross.

contre-cœur (kɔ̃trə'kœr) **à contre-cœur** adv reluctantly.

contre-coup nm 1 repercussion. 2 reaction.

contredire* (kɔ̃trə'di:r) vt contradict.

contrée (kɔ̃'tre:) nf region.

contrefaçon (kɔ̃trəfa'sɔ̃) nf counterfeit, forgery.

contrefaire* (kɔ̃trə'fɛr) vt 1 forge, counterfeit. 2 feign. 3 imitate.

contre-interroger vt cross-question, cross-examine.

contremaître (kɔ̃trə'mɛtr) nm foreman.

contremander (kɔ̃trəmɑ̃'de:) vt 1 cancel. 2 call off.

contre-pied nm opposite view. **à contre-pied** contrary to.

contre-plaqué nm plywood.

contre-poil adv **à contre-poil** the wrong way.

contre-poison nm antidote.

contre-sens nm 1 misunderstanding. 2 wrong way. **à contre-sens** in the wrong direction.

contretemps (kɔ̃trə'tɑ̃) nm 1 mishap. 2 hitch.

contre-torpilleur nm naut destroyer.

contrevenir (kɔ̃trə'vni:r) vt (aux avoir) contravene.

contrevent (kɔ̃trə'vɑ̃) nm shutter.

contre-voie adv **à contre-voie** 1 in the wrong direction. 2 on the wrong side.

contribuer (kɔ̃tri'bɥe:) vi **contribuer à** contribute to. **contribuable** nm,f taxpayer. **contribution** nf 1 contribution. 2 tax.

contrôler (kɔ̃tro'le:) vt 1 inspect. 2 check. 3 control. 4 hallmark. **contrôle** nm 1 inspection, checking. 2 control. 3 list. **contrôleur** nm 1 inspector. 2 ticket collector.

controverse (kɔ̃trə'vɛrs) nf controversy.

contusionner (kɔ̃tyzjɔ'ne:) vt bruise.

convaincre* (kɔ̃'vɛ̃kr) vt 1 convince. 2 convict.

convalescence (kɔ̃valɛs'sɑ̃s) nf convalescence. **convalescent** adj,n convalescent.

convenir* (kɔ̃'vni:r) vi (aux avoir) 1 suit. 2 agree. 3 admit. **convenable** adj 1 suitable, appropriate. 2 proper. **convenance** nf 1 agreement. 2 suitability. 3 convenience. 4 propriety. 5 pl convention. **convenu** adj 1 agreed. 2 appointed.

convention (kɔ̃vɑ̃'sjɔ̃) nf 1 convention. 2 agreement. 3 condition. **conventionnel, -elle** (kɔ̃vɑ̃sjɔ'nɛl) adj conventional.

converger (kɔ̃vɛr'ʒe:) vi converge.

convers (kɔ̃'vɛr) adj 1 rel lay. 2 converse.

conversation (kɔ̃vɛrsa'sjɔ̃) nf conversation, talk.

conversion (kɔ̃vɛr'zjɔ̃) nf conversion.

convertir (kɔ̃vɛr'ti:r) vt convert. **converti** nm convert.

convexe (kɔ̃'vɛks) adj convex.

conviction (kɔ̃vi:k'sjɔ̃) nf conviction.

convier (kɔ̃'vje:) vt 1 invite. 2 urge.

convive (kɔ̃'vi:v) nm,f guest.

convocation (kɔ̃vɔka'sjɔ̃) nf summons.

convoi (kɔ̃'vwa) nm convoy, train.

convoiter (kɔ̃vwa'te:) vt desire.

convoquer (kɔ̃vɔ'ke:) vt summon, call together.

coopérer (kɔɔpe:'re:) vi cooperate. **coopératif, -ive** (kɔɔpe:ra'ti:f, -'ti:v) adj,nf cooperative. **coopération** nf cooperation.

coordonner (kɔɔrdɔ'ne:) vt coordinate.

copain (kɔ'pɛ̃) nm inf friend, pal.

Copenhague (kɔpɛ'nag) nf Copenhagen.

copier (kɔ'pje:) vt 1 copy. 2 imitate. **copie** nf 1 copy. 2 reproduction.

copine (kɔ'pi:n) nf inf friend.

coq (kɔk) nm 1 cock. 2 weathercock. **coq-à-l'âne** nm invar cock-and-bull story.

coque (kɔk) nf 1 shell (of an egg). 2 naut hull. 3 cockle. **coquetier** nm eggcup.

coquelicot (kɔkli:'ko) nm poppy.

coqueluche (kɔ'klyʃ) nf whooping cough.

coquet, -ette (kɔ'kɛ, -'kɛt) adj 1 coy. 2 smart. 3 trim. nf flirt.

coquille (kɔ'ki:j) nf 1 shell. 2 misprint. **coquille d'œuf** nf eggshell. **coquillage** nm 1 shellfish. 2 shell.

coquin (kɔ'kɛ̃) adj naughty. nm rascal.

cor (kɔr) nm 1 mus horn. 2 med corn.

corail, -aux (kɔ'raj, -'ro) nm coral.

corbeau, -aux (kɔr'bo) nm crow.

corbeille (kɔr'bɛj) nf 1 basket. 2 flowerbed. **corbeille à papier** wastepaper basket.

corbillard (kɔrbi'jar) nm hearse.

corder (kɔr'de:) vt 1 twist. 2 rope. 3 string. **cordage** nm naut 1 rope. 2 rigging. **corde** nf 1 rope, cord. 2 mus chord. 3 string. 4 note.

34

corde à linge clothes line. corde de remorque towrope. corde tendue tightrope. cordée nf sport line, group.

cordial, -aux (kɔr'djal, -'djo) adj cordial, hearty. nm cordial.

cordon (kɔr'dɔ̃) nm 1 strand. 2 cord, rope. 3 ribbon. 4 row, cordon. cordonnier nm cobbler.

coriace (kɔ'rjas) adj 1 tough. 2 (of a person) hard.

corne (kɔrn) nf horn. cornet nm 1 small horn. 2 cornet.

corneille (kɔr'nɛj) nf crow.

cornemuse (kɔrnə'myz) nf bagpipes.

cornichon (kɔrni'ʃɔ̃) nm gherkin.

cornu (kɔr'ny) adj horned.

corporation (kɔrpɔra'sjɔ̃) nf 1 corporation. 2 guild.

corporel, -elle (kɔrpɔ'rɛl) adj corporal.

corps (kɔr) nm 1 body. 2 corpse. 3 main part. 4 corps. corps à corps hand to hand.

corpulent (kɔrpy'lɑ̃) adj stout, fat.

correct (kɔ'rɛkt) adj 1 correct. 2 proper. correction nf 1 correction. 2 accuracy. 3 punishment.

correspondre (kɔrɛ'spɔ̃dr) vi 1 agree, tally. 2 correspond, match. correspondance nf 1 correspondence. 2 connection (train, etc.). correspondant adj corresponding. nm 1 correspondent. 2 penfriend.

corrida (kɔri'da) nf bullfight.

corridor (kɔri'dɔr) nm corridor, passage.

corriger (kɔri'ʒe:) vt 1 correct. 2 punish.

corroder (kɔrɔ'de:) vt corrode.

corrompre (kɔ'rɔ̃pr) vt 1 corrupt. 2 bribe. 3 taint. corrompu adj 1 corrupt. 2 tainted.

corsage (kɔr'saʒ) nm bodice.

Corse (kɔrs) nf Corsica. corse adj,n Corsican.

corset (kɔr'sɛ) nm corset.

cortège (kɔr'tɛʒ) nm 1 procession. 2 train.

corvée (kɔr've:) nf drudgery, unpleasant task.

cosmétique (kɔsme'tiːk) adj,nm cosmetic.

cosmique (kɔs'miːk) adj cosmic.

cosmopolite (kɔsmɔpɔ'liːt) adj,n cosmopolitan.

cosmos ('kɔsmɔs) nm cosmos.

cosse (kɔs) nf pod, husk, hull.

cossu (kɔ'sy) adj well-off, rich.

costaud (kɔs'to) adj 1 strong. 2 well-built.

costume (kɔs'tym) nf 1 costume. 2 dress. 3 suit (of clothes).

cote (kɔt) nf 1 share. 2 number. 3 comm quotation.

côte (kot) nf 1 rib. 2 coast. 3 hill. côte à côte side by side. côtier, -ière (ko'tje:, -'tjɛr) adj coastal.

côté (ko'te:) nm 1 side. 2 way. 3 direction. à côté de beside. à côté l'un de l'autre or côte à côte side by side. de côté sideways. de l'autre côté on the other side or hand.

coteau, -aux (kɔ'to) nm hillside.

côtelette (kot'lɛt) nf cutlet, chop.

coter (kɔ'te:) vt 1 assess. 2 classify. 3 comm quote.

se cotiser (kɔti'ze:) vr 1 subscribe. 2 club together. cotisation nf 1 subscription. 2 contribution, share.

coton (kɔ'tɔ̃) nm 1 cotton. 2 cottonwool.

côtoyer (kotwa'je:) vt coast along.

cou (ku:) nm neck. cou-de-pied nm, pl cous-de-pied instep.

coucher (ku:'ʃe:) vt 1 put to bed. 2 lay down. vi sleep. se coucher vr 1 go to bed. 2 lie down. coucher nm setting. coucher du soleil sunset. couchant adj setting. nm 1 west. 2 decline. couche nf 1 couch. 2 pl med labour. 3 nappy. 4 layer. couché sociale social class. fausse couche miscarriage. couché adj 1 lying. 2 in bed. couchette nf 1 cot. 2 berth.

coucou (ku:'ku:) nm cuckoo.

coude (ku:d) nm 1 elbow. 2 bend.

coudre* (ku:dr) vt sew, stitch.

coudrier (ku:'drje:) nm hazel tree.

couenne (kwen) nf rind.

couic (kwi:k) nm 1 chirp. 2 squeak.

couin-couin (kwɛ̃'kwɛ̃) nm quack.

couler (ku:'le:) vt 1 pour. 2 strain. 3 sink. 4 cast. vi 1 flow, run. 2 leak. 3 sink. se couler vr slip, glide. coulant adj running, flowing. coulé adj (of metal) cast. nm mus slur.

couleur (ku:'lœr) nf 1 colour. 2 paint. 3 game suit.

couleuvre (ku:'lœvr) nf grass snake.

coulisse (ku:'liːs) nf 1 slot. 2 pl Th wings. à coulisse sliding.

couloir (ku:l'war) nm 1 corridor, passage. 2 pol lobby.

coup (ku:) nm 1 blow. 2 knock. 3 stroke. 4 attempt. coup de bec peck. coup de coude nudge. coup de feu shot. coup de froid chill. coup d'envoi kick-off. coup de pied kick. coup de soleil sunstroke. coup d'œil glance. coup illicite sport foul. du coup now at last. du premier coup at the first attempt. tout à coup suddenly.

coupable (ku:'pabl) adj guilty. nm culprit.

35

coupe[1] (ku:p) *nf* cup.

coupe[2] (ku:p) *nf* cutting, cut.

couper (ku:'pe:) *vt* 1 cut. 2 cross. 3 interrupt, stop. 4 dilute. **se couper** *vr* 1 cut oneself. 2 intersect. 3 contradict oneself. **coupant** *adj* cutting, sharp. **coupure** *nf* 1 cut, gash. 2 cutting.

couperose (ku:p'roz) *nf* acne.

coupler (ku:'ple:) *vt* 1 couple. 2 connect. **couple** *nm* pair, couple. *nf* couple, brace.

couplet (ku:'plɛ) *nm* verse.

coupon (ku:'pɔ̃) *nm* 1 coupon, warrant. 2 piece cut off or detached. 3 *pl* remnants.

cour (ku:r) *nf* 1 court. 2 courtyard. 3 courtship. 4 playground. **cour de ferme** farmyard.

courage (ku:'raʒ) *nm* courage, pluck. **courageux, -euse** (ku:ra'ʒœ, -'ʒœz) *adj* brave.

couramment (ku:ra'mã) *adv* 1 fluently, easily. 2 generally, currently.

courant (ku:'rã) *v* see **courir**. *adj* 1 running. 2 current, present. *nm* 1 current. 2 stream. 3 course. **courant d'air** draught. **être au courant de** know all about. **mettre au courant** inform.

courbature (ku:rba'tyr) *nf* 1 stiffness. 2 tiredness. **courbaturé** *adj* 1 stiff. 2 aching.

courber (ku:r'be:) *vt* bend, curve. *vi* sag. **se courber** *vr* stoop. **courbe** *nf* curve, bend. **courbé** *adj* curved.

courge (ku:rʒ) *nf* gourd. **courge à la moelle** marrow. **courgette** *nf* courgette.

courir* (ku:'ri:r) *vi* 1 run. 2 race. 3 be current. *vt* 1 run. 2 hunt. 3 roam. **coureur, -euse** (ku:-'rœr, -'rœz) *nm,f* 1 runner. 2 wanderer.

couronner (ku:rɔ'ne:) *vt* 1 crown. 2 cap. 3 award. **couronne** *nf* 1 crown. 2 wreath. **couronnement** *nm* 1 coronation. 2 crowning.

courrier (ku:'rje) *nm* 1 mail, letters. 2 post. 3 messenger. 4 courier.

courroie (ku:r'wa) *nf* strap.

courroux (ku:'ru:) *nm* anger.

cours (ku:r) *nm* 1 course. 2 path. 3 circulation. 4 quotation. 5 lesson. **cours de change** rate of exchange. **en cours** in progress, current.

course (ku:rs) *nf* 1 run. 2 race. 3 journey. 4 errand. 5 path. **faire des courses** 1 go shopping. 2 run errands.

court[1] (ku:r) *adj* short, brief. *adv* short. **à court de** short of. **tout court** simply, merely.

court[2] (ku:r) *nm* tennis court.

courtier (ku:r'tje:) *nm* broker.

courtisan (ku:rti:'zã) *nm* courtier.

courtois (ku:r'twa) *adj* courteous, polite. **courtoisie** *nf* courtesy.

cousant (ku:sã) *v* see **coudre**.

cousin[1] (ku:'zɛ̃) *nm* cousin. **cousin germain** first cousin.

cousin[2] (ku:'zɛ̃) *nm* gnat.

coussin (ku:'sɛ̃) *nm* cushion. **coussinet** *nm* pad.

cousu (ku:'zy) *v* see **coudre**.

coût (ku:) *nm* cost.

couteau, -aux (ku:'to) *nm* knife. **couteau à découper** carving-knife.

coutellerie (ku:tɛl'ri:) *nf* cutlery.

coûter (ku:'te:) *vi* cost. **coûter cher/peu** be expensive/cheap. **coûteux, -euse** (ku:'tœ, -'tœz) *adj* expensive, dear.

coutume (ku:'tym) *nf* custom, habit.

couture (ku:'tyr) *nf* 1 needlework. 2 seam. **couturier, -ière** (ku:ty'rje:, -'rjɛr) *nm,f* dressmaker.

couvent (ku:'vã) *nm* convent.

couver (ku:'ve:) *vt* 1 sit on. 2 hatch. 3 brood. *vi* 1 smoulder. 2 brew, be imminent. **couvée** *nf* clutch, brood. **couveuse artificielle** *nf* incubator.

couvercle (ku:'vɛrkl) *nm* 1 lid. 2 cover.

couvrir* (ku:'vri:r) *vt* 1 cover. 2 conceal. **se couvrir** *vr* 1 put on one's hat. 2 become overcast. **couvert** *adj* 1 covered. 2 overcast. *nm* 1 shelter. 2 place at table. **mettre/ôter le couvert** lay/clear the table. **couverture** *nf* 1 cover. 2 rug. 3 blanket. 4 *pl* bedclothes. **couverture de lit** bedspread. **couvre-feu** *nm invar* curfew. **couvre-lit** *nm, pl* **couvre-lits** bedspread.

crabe (krab) *nm* crab.

crac (krak) *interj,nm* 1 crack. 2 snap.

cracher (kra'ʃe) *vi* spit. *vt* 1 spit out. 2 *sl* cough up. **crachat** *nm* spit.

crachiner (kraʃi:'ne:) *vi* drizzle.

craie (krɛ) *nf* chalk.

craignant (krɛ'ɲã) *v* see **craindre**.

craindre* (krɛdr) *vt* 1 fear, dread. 2 be afraid of.

craint (krɛ̃) *v* see **craindre**.

crainte (krɛ̃t) *nf* fear, dread. **craintif, -ive** (krɛ̃'ti:f, -'ti:v) *adj* 1 timid. 2 afraid.

cramoisi (kramwa'zi:) *adj,nm* crimson.

crampe (krãp) *nf* cramp.

crampon (krã'pɔ̃) *nm* 1 clamp. 2 stud (for a boot).

cramponner (krãpɔ'ne:) *vt* 1 clamp. 2 *inf* buttonhole. **se cramponner à** *vr* hang on to.

cran (krã) *nm* 1 notch. 2 catch. 3 *inf* pluck.

crâner (kraˈne:) vi swagger, swank. **crâne** nf skull. adj 1 swaggering. 2 plucky.

crapaud (kraˈpo) nm toad.

crapuleux, -euse (krapyˈlœ, -ˈlœz) adj 1 lewd. 2 filthy.

craquer (kraˈke:) vi 1 crack. 2 crackle. **craquelure** nf crack.

crasse (kras) adj f gross. nf 1 dirt. 2 meanness. **crasseux, -euse** (kraˈsœ, -ˈsœz) adj 1 filthy. 2 squalid.

cratère (kraˈtɛr) nm crater.

cravate (kraˈvat) nf scarf, necktie.

crayon (krɛˈjɔ̃) nm 1 pencil. 2 stick. 3 sketch. **crayonner** vt 1 make a pencil sketch. 2 note.

créance (kre:ˈɑ̃s) nf 1 belief. 2 trust. 3 credit.

créateur, -trice (kre:aˈtœr, -ˈtri:s) adj creative. nm,f 1 creator. 2 inventor.

création (kre:aˈsjɔ̃) nf creation.

créature (kre:aˈtyr) nf creature.

crèche (krɛʃ) nf 1 crib, manger. 2 day nursery.

crédence (krɛˈdɑ̃s) nf sideboard.

crédit (kre:ˈdi:) nm 1 credit. 2 trust. 3 influence. **créditeur, -trice** (kre:di:ˈtœr, -ˈtri:s) nm,f creditor. adj credit.

créer (kre:ˈe:) vt 1 create. 2 found.

crémaillère (krɛmaˈjɛr) nf **pendre la crémaillère** have a house-warming.

crématoire (krɛmaˈtwar) **four crématoire** nm crematorium.

crème (krɛm) nf 1 cream. 2 custard. 3 best.

crémer (kre:ˈme:) vi cream. **crémerie** nf dairy.

crénelé (krɛnˈle:) adj 1 notched. 2 toothed.

crêpe (krɛp) nf pancake.

crêper (krɛˈpe:) vt fizz. **crépu** adj 1 crisp. 2 crinkled.

crépiter (kre:pi:ˈte:) vi crackle.

crépuscule (kre:pyˈskyl) nm dusk, twilight.

cresson (krəˈsɔ̃) nm cress.

crête (krɛt) nf 1 zool crest. 2 ridge.

creuser (krœˈze:) vt 1 hollow out. 2 excavate. 3 go deeply into.

creux, creuse (krœ, krœz) adj 1 hollow. 2 empty. 3 slack. 4 sunken. nm 1 hollow. 2 pit.

crevaison (krəvɛˈzɔ̃) nf puncture.

crevasser (krəvaˈse:) vt 1 crack. 2 chap. **crevasse** nf 1 crack. 2 crevice.

crever (krəˈve:) vi 1 burst. 2 split. 3 sl die. vt burst, puncture.

crevette (krəˈvɛt) nf 1 shrimp. 2 prawn.

cri (kri:) nm 1 cry. 2 shout. 3 shriek. **le dernier cri** the latest fashion.

criailler (kri:ɑˈje:) vi 1 bawl. 2 whine.

cribler (kri:ˈble:) vt 1 riddle. 2 sift. **crible** nm 1 sieve. 2 riddle.

cric (kri:k) nm jack.

cricri (kri:ˈkri:) nm zool cricket.

cricket (kri:ˈkɛ) nm sport cricket.

criée (kri:ˈe:) nf auction.

crier (kri:ˈe:) vi 1 cry. 2 shout. 3 scream. vt shout. **criant** adj flagrant, gross. **criard** adj 1 crying. 2 shrill. 3 loud, flashy.

crime (kri:m) nm crime. **criminel, -elle** (kri:mi:ˈnɛl) adj 1 guilty. 2 criminal. nm,f criminal. **incendie criminel** nm arson.

crin (krɛ̃) nm horsehair. **crinière** nf mane.

crique (kri:k) nf cove.

criquet (kri:ˈkɛ) nm 1 locust. 2 zool cricket.

crise (kri:z) nf 1 crisis. 2 attack, fit. 3 shortage. **crise cardiaque** heart attack.

crisper (kri:ˈspe:) vt 1 contract. 2 clench. **se crisper** vr 1 contract. 2 shrivel up. **crispé** adj on edge.

crisser (kri:ˈse:) vi,vt 1 grate. 2 grind.

cristal, -aux (kri:ˈstal, -ˈsto) nm crystal. **cristal taillé** cut glass.

cristalliser (kri:staliˈze:) vi,vt crystallize.

critère (kri:ˈtɛr) nm also **critérium** criterion.

critiquer (kri:ti:ˈke:) vt 1 criticize. 2 censure. **critique** adj 1 critical. 2 crucial. nf 1 criticism. 2 censure. nm critic.

croasser (krɔaˈse:) vi croak.

croc (kro) nm 1 hook. 2 fang. 3 tusk. **faire** or **donner un croc-en-jambe** à trip.

croche (krɔʃ) nf mus quaver.

crochet (krɔˈʃɛ) nm 1 hook. 2 crochet. 3 swerve. 4 pl square brackets. **faire du crochet** crochet.

crochu (krɔˈʃy) adj 1 hooked. 2 crooked.

crocodile (krɔkɔˈdi:l) nm crocodile.

crocus (krɔˈkys) nm crocus.

croire* (krwar) vt 1 believe. 2 think. **croire à** or **en** believe in.

croisade (krwaˈzad) nf crusade.

croiser (krwaˈze:) vt 1 cross. 2 pass. vi 1 fold over. 2 cruise. **croisée** nf crossing. **croisement** nm 1 crossing. 2 intersection. **croisière** nf cruise.

croissance (krwaˈsɑ̃s) nf growth.

croissant (krwaˈsɑ̃) v see **croître**. adj 1 growing. 2 increasing. 3 rising. nm 1 crescent. 2 bread roll in a crescent shape.

croître* (krwatr) vi 1 grow. 2 increase. 3 rise.

croix (krwa) nf cross. **croix gammée** swastika.

croquer (krɔˈke:) vt 1 crunch. 2 munch. 3

sketch. **croquant** *adj* crisp. *nm* **1** gristle. **2** crackling.

croquet (krɔ'kɛ) *nm* croquet.

croquis (krɔ'ki:) *nm* sketch.

crosse (krɔs) *nf* **1** crook. **2** *sport* stick, club. **3** butt (of a rifle). **crosse de golf** golf club.

crotter (krɔ'te:) *vt* dirty, soil. **crotte** *nf* **1** dirt. **2** mud. **3** dung. **une crotte de chocolat** a chocolate.

crouler (kru:'le:) *vi* **1** collapse. **2** totter. **3** crumble. **croulement** *nm* collapse.

croupe (kru:p) *nf* **1** rump. **2** ridge. **3** *pl zool* buttocks.

croupir (kru:'pi:r) *vi* **1** wallow. **2** stagnate.

croustiller (kru:sti:'je:) *.vi* crunch. **croustillant** *adj* **1** crisp. **2** spicy.

croûte (kru:t) *nf* **1** crust. **2** rind. **3** scab. **casser une croûte** have a snack. **croûton** *nm* piece of crust.

croyance (krwa'jãs) *nf* belief. **croyable** *adj* **1** credible. **2** trustworthy.

croyant (krwa'jã) *v* see **croire.** *adj* believing. *nm* believer.

cru[1] (kry) *adj* **1** raw. **2** coarse. **3** crude.

cru[2] (kry) *nm* **1** wine-growing district. **2** vintage.

cru[3] (kry) *v* see **croire.**

crû (kry) *v* see **croire.**

cruauté (kryo'te:) *nf* cruelty.

crucifier (krysi:'fje:) *vt* crucify.

crucifix (krysi:'fi:) *nm* crucifix.

crudité (krydi:'te:) *nf* **1** rawness. **2** crudeness. **3** coarseness.

crue (kry) *nf* **1** rising. **2** flood.

cruel, -elle (kry'ɛl) *adj* cruel.

crûment (kry'mã) *adv* **1** crudely. **2** roughly.

crustacés (krysta'se:) *nm pl* shellfish.

crypte (kri:pt) *nf* crypt.

cube (kyb) *nm* cube. **cubique** *adj* cubic.

cueillir (kœ'ji:r) *vt* **1** gather. **2** pick.

cuiller (kyi:'je:) *nf also* **cuillère** spoon. **cuiller à bouche/dessert/pot/thé** tablespoon/dessertspoon/ladle/teaspoon. **cuillerée** *nf* spoonful.

cuir (kyi:r) *nm* **1** leather. **2** hide. **3** skin. **cuir chevelu** scalp. **cuir verni** patent leather.

cuirasse (kyi:'ras) *nf* armour. **cuirassé** *adj* armoured, armour-plated. *nm* battleship.

cuire' (kyi:r) *vt* **1** cook. **2** fire, bake. *vi* **1** cook. **2** smart. **cuire au four** roast, bake. **cuit à point** done to a turn. **cuisant** *adj* **1** burning. **2** smarting. **3** bitter.

cuisine (kyi:'zi:n) *nf* **1** kitchen. **2** cookery. **3** cooking. **faire la cuisine** cook. **cuisinier, -ière** (kyi:zi:'nje:, -'njɛr) *nm,f* cook. *nf* cooker.

cuisse (kyi:s) *nf* thigh. **cuisses de grenouille** *nf pl* frogs' legs.

cuivre (kyi:vr) *nm* copper. **cuivre jaune** brass.

cul (kyl) *nm* **1** bottom. **2** behind. **3** rump. **cul-de-sac** *nm, pl* **culs-de-sac** dead end, blind alley.

culbuter (kylby'te:) *vi* somersault. *vt* **1** overthrow. **2** tip. **culbute** *nf* **1** somersault. **2** tumble.

culinaire (kyli:'nɛr) *adj* culinary.

culminant (kylmi:'nã) *adj* highest.

culot (ky'lo) *nm* **1** bottom, base. **2** *sl* cheek.

culotte (ky'lɔt) *nf* **1** shorts. **2** pants.

culpabilité (kylpabi:li:'te:) *nf* guilt.

culte (kylt) *nm* **1** worship. **2** cult.

cultiver (kylti:'ve:) *vt* **1** farm. **2** cultivate. **cultivateur** *nm* farmer. **cultivé** *adj* **1** cultivated. **2** cultured.

culture (kyl'tyr) *nf* **1** culture. **2** cultivation. **culturel, -elle** (kylty'rɛl) *adj* cultural.

cupide (ky'pi:d) *adj* greedy. **cupidité** *nf* greed.

cure (kyr) *nf* **1** care. **2** cure.

curé (ky're:) *nm* parish priest.

curer (ky're:) *vt* **1** pick. **2** clean out. **cure-dents** *nm invar* toothpick.

curieux, -euse (ky'rjœ, -'rjœz) *adj* **1** curious. **2** interested. **3** inquisitive. **4** odd.

curiosité (kyrjɔzi:'te:) *nf* **1** curiosity. **2** peculiarity.

cuver (ky've:) *vi,vt* ferment. **cuve** *nf* **1** vat. **2** tub. **cuve à lessive** copper. **cuvette** *nf* **1** washbasin. **2** basin.

cycle[1] (si:kl) *nm* cycle.

cycle[2] (si:kl) *nm* bicycle. **cycliste** *nm,f* cyclist.

cyclomoteur (si:klomɔ'tœr) *nm* moped.

cyclone (si:'klon) *nm* cyclone.

cygne (si:ɲ) *nm* swan.

cylindre (si:'lɛ̃dr) *nm* cylinder. **cylindre compresseur** steamroller.

cymbale (sɛ̃'bal) *nf* cymbal.

cynique (si:'ni:k) *adj* **1** cynical. **2** brazen. *nm* cynic.

cyprès (si:'prɛ) *nm* cypress.

cypriote (si:pri:'ɔt) *adj,n* Cypriot.

D

dactylographier (dakti:lɔgra'fje:) *vt* type. **dactylographe** *nm,f* typist.

dague (dag) *nf* dagger.

daigner (dɛ'ɲe) *vt* condescend.
daim (dɛ̃) *nm* 1 deer. 2 buck. 3 suede.
dais (dɛ) *nm* canopy.
daller (da'le:) *vt* pave, flag. **dalle** *nf* tile.
daltonien, -ienne (daltɔ'njɛ̃, -'njɛn) *adj* colour-blind. **daltonisme** *nm* colour-blindness.
damas (da'ma) *nm* damson.
dame¹ (dam) *interj* 1 indeed! 2 rather!
dame² (dam) *nf* 1 lady. 2 *game* queen. 3 *pl* draughts.
damier (da'mje:) *nm* chessboard.
damner (da'ne:) *vt* damn. **damnable** *adj* 1 damnable. 2 frightful.
dandiner (dɑ̃di'ne:) *vi* strut. **se dandiner** *vr* waddle.
Danemark (dan'mark) *nm* Denmark. **danois** *adj* Danish. *nm* 1 Dane. 2 Danish (language).
danger (dɑ̃'ʒe:) *nm* 1 danger, peril. 2 risk. **dangereux, -euse** (dɑ̃ʒ'rœ, -'rœz) *adj* dangerous.
dans (dɑ̃) *prep* 1 in. 2 within. 3 into. 4 during.
danser (dɑ̃'se:) *vi,vt* dance. **danse** *nf* 1 dance. 2 dancing. **danseur, -euse** (dɑ̃'sœr, -'sœz) *nm,f* dancer.
dard (dar) *nm* 1 dart. 2 sting.
darder (dar'de:) *vt* 1 hurl. 2 dart. 3 shoot out.
dater (da'te:) *vi,vt* date. **date** *nf* date.
datte (dat) *nf bot* date. **dattier** *nm* date palm.
daube (dob) *nf* stew.
dauphin (do'fɛ̃) *nm* 1 dolphin. 2 eldest son of the French king.
davantage (davɑ̃'taʒ) *adv* more, any more.
de (də) *prep* 1 from. 2 of. 3 by. 4 with. 5 in. 6 made of. 7 some.
dé (de:) *nm* 1 dice. 2 tee. **dé (à coudre)** thimble.
débâcle (de:'bakl) *nf* 1 collapse, downfall. 2 breaking up.
déballer (de:ba'le:) *vt* unpack.
débander¹ (de:bɑ̃'de:) *vt* 1 relax. 2 unbend.
débander² (de:bɑ̃'de:) *vt* disband. **se débander** *vr* disperse. **débandade** *nf* stampede.
débarbouiller (de:barbu'je:) *vt* wash, clean. **se débarbouiller** *vr* wash one's face.
débarcadère (de:barka'dɛr) *nm* wharf, landing stage.
débardeur (de:bar'dœr) *nm* docker.
débarquer (de:bar'ke:) *vi,vt* 1 land. 2 disembark. *vt* unload. **débarquement** *nm* 1 landing. 2 arrival.
débarras (de:ba'ra) *nm* riddance.
débarrasser (de:bara'se:) *vt* 1 rid. 2 free. 3 clear. **se débarrasser de** *vr* get rid of.

débat (de:'ba) *nm* 1 debate. 2 discussion. 3 dispute.
débattre* (de:'batr) *vt* 1 debate. 2 discuss. **se débattre** *vr* struggle.
débaucher (de:bo'ʃe:) *vt* 1 lead astray. 2 discharge. **se débaucher** *vr* go astray, misbehave.
débile (de:'bi:l) *adj* weak, feeble.
débit¹ (de:'bi:) *nm* 1 sale. 2 retail shop. 3 cutting up. 4 delivery. 5 output. **débit de boissons** public house.
débit² (de:'bi) *nm* debit.
débiter¹ (de:bi:'te:) *vt* 1 retail. 2 cut up. 3 supply. 4 recite.
débiter² (de:bi:'te:) *vt* debit.
déblai (de:'blɛ) *nm* 1 clearing. 2 excavation. 3 rubbish.
déblayer (de:blɛ'je:) *vt* 1 clear. 2 remove.
déboîter (de:bwa'te:) *vt* 1 dislocate. 2 disconnect.
débonnaire (de:bɔ'nɛr) *adj* easygoing.
déborder (de:bɔr'de:) *vi,vt* overflow. *vt* project, protrude. **débordé** *adj* 1 overflowing. 2 busy.
déboucher¹ (de:bu:'ʃe:) *vt* 1 clear. 2 open.
déboucher² (de:bu:'ʃe:) *vi* 1 emerge. 2 come from. **débouché** *nm* 1 outlet. 2 opening.
débourser (de:bu:r'se:) *vt* spend.
debout (də'bu:) *adj* 1 upright. 2 standing.
déboutonner (de:bu:tɔ'ne:) *vt* unbutton.
débraillé (de:bra'je:) *adj* 1 untidy. 2 slovenly. 3 improper.
débrayer (de:brɛ'je:) *vt* disconnect. *vi* declutch. **débrayage** *nm* 1 disconnecting. 2 *mot* clutch.
débris (de:'bri:) *nm pl* 1 remains. 2 rubbish.
débrouiller (de:bru:'je:) *vt* 1 sort-out. 2 extricate. **se débrouiller** *vr* manage.
débuter (de:by'te:) *vi* begin, start. **début** *nm* 1 beginning. 2 first appearance. **débutant** *nm* beginner.
deçà (də'sa) *adv* on this side. **deçà delà** here and there.
décade (dɛ'kad) *nf* decade.
décadent (de:ka'dɑ̃) *adj* 1 decadent. 2 in decay. **décadence** *nf* 1 decline. 2 decay.
décaler (de:ka'le:) *vt* shift, displace. **décalé** *adj* off balance.
décamper (de:kɑ̃'pe:) *vi* 1 *inf* clear off. 2 bolt.
décanter (de:kɑ̃'te:) *vt* decant.
décéder (de:se:'de:) *vi* decease, die.
déceler (de:s'le:) *vt* 1 disclose. 2 reveal.
décembre (de:'sɑ̃br) *nm* December.
décent (de:'sɑ̃) *adj* 1 decent. 2 proper.

déception (de:sɛpˈsjɔ̃) *nf* **1** deception. **2** disappointment.

décerner (de:sɛrˈne:) *vt* **1** award. **2** confer.

décès (de:ˈsɛ) *nm* decease, death.

décevoir* (de:səˈvwar) *vt* **1** deceive. **2** disappoint.

déchaîner (de:ʃɛˈne:) *vt* let loose, loose. **se déchaîner** *vr* break out, rage.

décharger (de:ʃarˈʒe:) *vt* **1** unload. **2** discharge, let off. **décharge** *nf* **1** unloading. **2** discharge. **3** rebate.

décharné (de:ʃarˈne:) *adj* emaciated, skinny.

se déchausser (de:shoˈse:) *vr* take off one's shoes.

déchéance (de:ʃeˈãs) *nf* **1** fall. **2** downfall. **3** loss.

déchet (de:ˈʃɛ) *nm* **1** loss. **2** *pl* waste, scraps.

déchiffrer (de:ʃiˈfre:) *vt* **1** decipher. **2** sightread.

déchiqueter (de:ʃi:kˈte:) *vt* **1** slash. **2** tear. **3** cut.

déchirer (de:ʃi:ˈre:) *vt* tear. **déchirure** *nf* tear, slit.

déchoir* (de:ˈʃwar) *vi* (*aux* être) fall.

décibel (de:si:ˈbɛl) *nm* decibel.

décider (de:si:ˈde:) *vt* **1** decide. **2** settle. **3** persuade. **se décider à** *vr* make up one's mind to.

décimale (de:si:ˈmal) *nf* decimal. **decimal, -aux** (de:si:ˈmal, -ˈmo) *adj* decimal.

décisif, -ive (de:si:ˈsi:f, -ˈsi:v) *adj* **1** decisive. **2** critical.

décision (de:si:ˈzjɔ̃) *nf* **1** decision. **2** determination.

déclarer (de:klaˈre:) *vt* **1** declare. **2** make known. **déclaration** *nf* declaration.

déclencher (de:klãˈʃe:) *vt* **1** release. **2** launch.

déclin (de:ˈklɛ̃) *nm* **1** decline. **2** close. **3** end.

décliner (de:kli:ˈne:) *vi,vt* decline. *vt* refuse. **déclinaison** *nf* declension.

décoiffé (de:kwaˈfe:) *adj* dishevelled.

décoller (de:kɔˈle:) *vt* loosen. *vi* take off. **se décoller** *vr* work loose. **décollage** *nm* take-off. **décolleté** *adj* low-necked. *nm* neckline.

décolorer (de:kɔlɔˈre:) *vt* **1** fade. **2** bleach.

décombres (de:ˈkɔ̃br) *nm pl* **1** rubbish. **2** ruins.

décommander (de:kɔmãˈde:) *vt* cancel.

décomposer (de:kɔ̃poˈze:) *vt* **1** rot. **2** distort.

décompte (de:ˈkɔ̃t) *nm* **1** deduction. **2** disappointment.

déconcerter (de:kɔ̃sɛrˈte:) *vt* **1** confound. **2** baffle.

décongeler (de:kɔ̃ʒˈle:) *vt* thaw.

déconseiller (de:kɔ̃sɛˈje:) *vt* dissuade.

décontracter (de:kɔ̃trakˈte:) *vt* relax.

déconvenue (de:kɔ̃vəˈny) *nf* disappointment.

décor (de:ˈkɔr) *nm* **1** decoration. **2** arrangement. **3** *pl* Th scenery.

décorer (de:kɔˈre:) *vt* decorate. **décoration** *nf* **1** medal. **2** decoration.

découper (de:kuˈpe) *vt* **1** cut up. **2** carve. **3** cut out.

décourager (de:kuːraˈʒe:) *vt* **1** discourage. **2** deter.

décousu (de:kuːˈzy) *adj* **1** undone. **2** disconnected. **3** disjointed.

découverte (de:kuːˈvɛrt) *nf* discovery.

découvrir (de:kuːˈvriːr) *vt* **1** discover. **2** uncover.

décrasser (de:kraˈse:) *vt* **1** clean. **2** scour.

décret (de:ˈkrɛ) *nm* decree.

décrire* (de:ˈkriːr) *vt* describe.

décrocher (de:krɔˈʃe:) *vt* **1** take down. **2** disconnect.

décroître* (de:ˈkrwatr) *vi* **1** decrease. **2** diminish. **décroissance** *nf* **1** decrease. **2** decline.

dédaigner (de:dɛˈɲe:) *vt* scorn. **dédaigneux, -euse** (de:dɛˈɲœ, -ˈɲœz) *adj* scornful.

dédain (de:ˈdɛ̃) *nm* **1** scorn. **2** contempt.

dédale (de:ˈdal) *nm* maze, labyrinth.

dedans (dəˈdã) *adv* inside, within. *nm* **1** inside. **2** interior.

dédier (de:ˈdje:) *vt* dedicate. **dédicace** *nf* dedication.

dédit (de:ˈdi:) *nm* **1** forfeit. **2** retraction.

dédommager (de:dɔmaˈʒe:) *vt* compensate.

déduction (de:dykˈsjɔ̃) *nf* deduction.

déduire* (de:ˈdɥiːr) *vt* **1** deduce. **2** deduct. **3** infer.

déesse (de:ˈɛs) *nf* goddess.

défaillir* (de:faˈjiːr) *vi* **1** grow weak. **2** fail. **3** faint. **défaillance** *nf* **1** lapse. **2** weakness. **3** faint.

défaire* (de:ˈfɛr) *vt* **1** undo. **2** untie. **3** defeat. **défaite** *nf* defeat.

défalquer (de:falˈke:) *vt* deduct.

défaut (de:ˈfo) *nm* **1** defect. **2** fault. **3** lack.

défection (de:fɛkˈsjɔ̃) *nf* defection. **défectueux, -euse** (de:fɛkˈtɥœ, -ˈtɥœz) *adj* **1** defective. **2** deficient.

défendre (de:ˈfãdr) *vt* **1** defend. **2** protect. **3** forbid.

défense (de:ˈfãs) *nf* **1** defence. **2** tusk. **défense de fumer** no smoking.

déférer (de:fɛ're:) *vt* 1 refer. 2 hand over. 3 confer. *vi* defer. **déférent** *adj* deferential.

défi (de:'fi:) *nm* 1 challenge. 2 defiance.

déficeler (de:fi:'sle:) *vt* untie.

déficit (de:fi:'sɪ:) *nm* 1 deficit. 2 shortage.

défier (de:'fje:) *vt* 1 challenge. 2 defy. **se défier** *vr* mistrust. **défiance** *nf* 1 mistrust, distrust. 2 suspicion. **défiant** *adj* 1 wary. 2 suspicious.

défigurer (de:fi:gy're:) *vt* 1 disfigure. 2 distort. 3 deface.

défilé (de:fi:'le:) *nm* 1 pass. 2 procession.

définir (de:fi:'ni:r) *vt* define. **défini** *adj* definite. **définitif, -ive** (de:fi:ni:'ti:f, -'ti:v) *adj* 1 final. 2 permanent. **définition** *nf* 1 definition. 2 clue.

défoncer (de:fɔ̃'se:) *vt* break up. **se défoncer** *vr* collapse.

déformer (de:fɔr'me:) *vt* 1 deform. 2 distort.

défraîchi (de:frɛ'ʃi:) *adj* 1 faded. 2 soiled.

défricher (de:fri:'ʃe:) *vt* 1 clear. 2 reclaim (land).

défunt (de:'fœ̃) *adj* 1 deceased. 2 defunct.

dégager (de:ga'ʒe:) *vt* 1 redeem. 2 clear. 3 release. **dégagé** *adj* 1 free. 2 easy. 3 offhand.

dégarnir (de:gar'ni:r) *vt* strip off.

dégât (de:'gɑ) *nm* damage.

dégel (de:'ʒɛl) *nm* thaw.

dégeler (de:'ʒle:) *vi,vt* thaw.

dégénérer (de:ʒe:ne:'re:) *vi* degenerate. **dégénéré** *adj* degenerate.

dégivrer (de:ʒi:'vre:) *vt* defrost.

dégonfler (de:gɔ̃'fle:) *vt* 1 deflate. 2 reduce. **se dégonfler** *vr* 1 collapse. 2 subside. 3 *inf* back down.

dégorger (de:gɔr'ʒe:) *vt* free, clear. *vi* overflow.

dégourdir (de:gu:r'di:r) *vt* 1 revive. 2 remove stiffness. **dégourdi** *adj* sharp, astute.

dégoûter (de:gu:'te:) *vt* 1 disgust. 2 sicken.

dégrader (de:gra'de:) *vt* 1 degrade. 2 deface. **se dégrader** *vr* lower oneself.

dégrafer (de:gra'fe:) *vt* undo.

dégraisser (de:grɛ'se:) *vt* 1 clean. 2 skim the fat off.

degré (də'gre:) *nm* 1 degree. 2 step.

dégringoler (de:grɛ̃gɔ'le:) *vi,vt* tumble down. **dégringolade** *nf* 1 tumble. 2 collapse.

dégriser (de:gri:'ze:) *vt* sober.

déguenillé (de:gnɪ'je:) *adj* ragged, in rags.

déguerpir (de:gɛr'pi:r) *vi* 1 move out. 2 clear out or off.

déguiser (de:gi:'ze:) *vt* disguise. **déguisement** *nm* 1 disguise. 2 fancy dress.

déguster (de:gy'ste:) *vt* taste, sample.

dehors (də'ɔr) *adv* out, outside, outdoors. *nm* outside, exterior.

déité (de:i:'te:) *nf* deity.

déjà (dɛ'ʒa) *adv* 1 already. 2 before. 3 yet.

déjeuner (de:ʒœ'ne:) *vi* 1 have lunch. 2 breakfast. *nm* lunch. **petit déjeuner** breakfast.

delà (də'la) *prep* beyond. **par delà** beyond. **au delà de** beyond. **par delà** on the other side. **en delà** further away.

délabré (de:la'bre:) *adj* 1 dilapidated. 2 in ruins.

délai (de:'lɛ) *nm* 1 delay. 2 notice.

délaisser (de:lɛ'se:) *vt* 1 forsake, desert. 2 relinquish.

délasser (de:la'se:) *vt* 1 rest. 2 refresh. **délassement** *nm* relaxation.

délateur (dɛla'tœr) *nm* informer.

délavé (de:la've:) *adj* faded, washed out.

délayer (de:lɛ'je:) *vt* 1 mix with water. 2 dilute. 3 spin out.

déléguer (de:le:'ge:) *vt* 1 delegate. 2 assign. **délégation** *nf* delegation. **délégué** *nm* 1 delegate. 2 deputy.

délibérer (de:li:be:'re:) *vi* deliberate, ponder. *vt* discuss. **délibération** *nf* 1 discussion. 2 reflection.

délicat (de:li:'ka) *adj* 1 delicate. 2 dainty. 3 sensitive. 4 tricky. **délicatesse** *nf* delicacy.

délice (de:'li:s) *nm* delight. **délicieux, -euse** (de:li:'sjœ, -'sjœz) *adj* delicious.

délier (de:'lje:) *vt* 1 untie. 2 release. **se délier** *vr* come undone. **délié** *adj* 1 slender. 2 thin.

délinquance (de:lɛ̃'kɑ̃s) *nf* delinquency.

délit (de:'li:) *nm* offence.

délivrer (de:li:'vre:) *vt* 1 deliver. 2 rescue. **délivrance** *nf* rescue.

déloyal, -aux (de:lwa'jal, -'jo) *adj* 1 unfaithful, disloyal. 2 false. 3 unfair.

delta (dɛl'ta) *nm* delta.

déluge (de:'ly3) *nm* 1 flood. 2 downpour.

déluré (de:ly're:) *adj* astute, sharp.

se démailler (de:ma'je:) *vr* (of a stocking) ladder.

demain (də'mɛ̃) *adv,nm* tomorrow. **à demain!** see you tomorrow! **demain en huit** tomorrow week.

demander (dəmɑ̃'de:) *vt* 1 ask. 2 ask for. 3 enquire. 4 want. 5 require. **se demander** *vr* wonder. **demande** *nf* 1 request. 2 question. 3 application. 4 *comm* demand.

démanger (de:mɑ̃'ʒe:) *vi* itch.

démaquiller (de:makɪ'je:) *vt* remove make-up.

démarche (de:'marʃ) *nf* 1 gait, walk. 2 step. 3 proceedings.

démarrer (de:ma're:) vt start (a car). vi drive off.

démêler (de:me:'le:) vt unravel.

démembrer (de:mã'bre:) vt cut up.

déménager (de:mɛna'ʒe:) vi move house. **déménagement** nm removal.

démence (dɛ'mãs) nf lunacy.

se démener (de:m'ne:) vr struggle.

démentir* (de:mã'ti:r) vt 1 contradict. 2 deny. **démenti** nm 1 denial. 2 contradiction.

démesuré (de:mzy're:) adj 1 huge. 2 excessive.

démettre* (de:'mɛtr) vt 1 dislocate. 2 dismiss. **se démettre** vr resign.

demeurer (dəmœ're:) vi (aux être) 1 live. 2 remain, stay. **au demeurant** adv after all. **demeure** nf 1 abode. 2 delay. **à demeure** permanent.

demi (də'mi:) adj,n half. **à demi** half.

demi-arrière nm half-back.

demi-cercle nm semicircle.

demi-douzaine nf half-a-dozen.

demi-finale nf semifinal.

demi-frère nm 1 half-brother. 2 stepbrother.

demi-heure nf half-hour.

demi-sœur nf 1 half-sister. 2 stepsister.

démission (de:mi:'sjɔ̃) nf resignation. **donner sa démission** resign.

demi-teinte nf halftone.

demi-tour nm 1 half-turn. 2 U-turn.

démocratie (de:mɔkra'si:) nf democracy. **démocratique** adj democratic.

démodé (de:mɔ'de:) adj old-fashioned.

demoiselle (dəmwa'zɛl) nf 1 young lady. 2 spinster.

démolir (de:mɔ'li:r) vt 1 demolish. 2 pull down.

démon (de:'mɔ̃) nm demon, fiend.

démonter (de:mɔ̃'te:) vi 1 dismantle. 2 upset. **se démonter** vr 1 come apart. 2 inf get upset.

démontrer (de:mɔ̃'tre:) vt 1 demonstrate. 2 prove.

démoraliser (de:mɔrali:'ze:) vt 1 demoralize. 2 dishearten.

démordre (de:'mɔrdr) vi 1 let go. 2 give up.

démuni (de:my'ni:) adj. **démuni de** short, out of.

dénaturé (de:naty're:) adj unnatural.

dénégation (de:nega'sjɔ̃) nf denial.

dénicher (de:ni:'ʃe:) vt find, discover.

denier (də'nje:) nm small coin, penny.

dénigrer (de:ni:'gre:) vt disparage.

dénombrement (de:nɔ̃brə'mã) nm 1 census. 2 count.

dénominateur (de:nɔmi:na'tœr) nm denominator.

dénomination (de:nɔmi:na'sjɔ̃) nf denomination.

dénommer (de:nɔ'me:) vt name.

dénoncer (de:nɔ̃'se:) vt 1 denounce. 2 declare. 3 betray.

dénoter (de:nɔ'te:) vt denote.

dénouer (de:'nwe:) vt 1 undo, untie. 2 untangle. **se dénouer** vr 1 come undone. 2 end. **dénouement** nm 1 end. 2 outcome.

denrée (dã're:) nf commodity.

densité (dãsi:'te:) nf density.

dent (dã) nf 1 tooth. 2 prong. 3 cog. **avoir une dent contre** bear a grudge against. **dentaire** adj dental. **dental, -aux** (dã'tal, -'to) adj dental.

denteler (dãt'le:) vt 1 notch. 2 indent.

dentelle nf lace.

dentier (dã'tje:) nm denture.

dentifrice (dãti:'fri:s) nm toothpaste.

dentiste (dã'ti:st) nm,f dentist.

dénuder (de:ny'de:) vt 1 strip. 2 lay bare.

dénuer (de:'nɥe:) vt strip. **se dénuer de** vr part with. **dénué** adj 1 devoid. 2 destitute.

dépanner (de:pa'ne:) vt 1 repair. 2 help out.

dépaqueter (de:pak'te:) vt unpack.

dépareillé (de:parɛ'je:) adj 1 odd. 2 ill-assorted.

départ (de:'par) nm 1 departure. 2 start.

département (de:partə'mã) nm department.

départir (de:par'ti:r) vt 1 divide. 2 allot. **se départir de** vr 1 deviate from. 2 part with.

dépasser (de:pa'se:) vt 1 pass beyond. 2 exceed. 3 overtake.

dépaysé (de:pe:i:'ze:) adj 1 lost. 2 bewildered.

dépêcher (de:pe:'ʃe:) vt dispatch. **se dépêcher** vr hurry, make haste. **dépêche** nf 1 dispatch. 2 telegram.

dépeindre* (de:'pɛ̃dr) vt 1 depict. 2 describe.

dépendre[1] (de:'pãdr) vi **dépendre de** 1 depend on. 2 be subject to. 3 belong to.

dépendre[2] (de:'pãdr) vt take down.

dépens (de:'pã) nm pl law costs.

dépenser (de:pã'se:) vt spend. **dépense** nf 1 expense. 2 expenditure. **dépensier, -ière** (de:pã'sje:, -'sjɛr) adj extravagant. nm,f spendthrift.

dépérir (de:pe:'ri:r) vi 1 waste away. 2 decay.

dépêtrer (de:pe:'tre:) vt extricate.

dépister (de:pi:'ste:) vt 1 track down. 2 outwit.

dépit (de:'pi:) nm 1 spite. 2 resentment.

déplacer (de:pla'se:) vt 1 displace. 2 take the

place of. **se déplacer** vr 1 move. 2 travel.
~nm 1 displacement. 2 transfer. 3 travelling.
déplaire* (de:'plɛr) vt 1 displease. 2 offend. **se
déplaire à** vr dislike.
déplantoir (de:plan'twar) nm trowel.
déplier (de:pli:'e:) vt unfold.
déplorer (de:'plɔre:) vt 1 deplore. 2 regret. 3
mourn.
déployer (de:plwa'je:) vt 1 spread out. 2 display.
déplumer (de:ply'me:) vt pluck. **se déplumer**
vr moult.
déporter (de:pɔr'te:) vt deport.
déposer[1] (de:po'ze:) vt 1 lay down. 2 deposit.
déposer[2] (de:po'ze:) vt depose.
dépositaire (de:pozi:'tɛr) nm trustee. **dépositaire de journaux** newsagent.
dépot (de:'po) nm 1 deposit. 2 trust. 3 store,
depot. 4 sediment.
dépouiller (de:pu:'je:) vt 1 skin, strip. 2
deprive. **se dépouiller** vr cast off, shed.
dépouille nf 1 skin, hide. 2 remains.
dépourvu (de:pu:r'vy) adj 1 destitute. 2 devoid.
au dépourvu unawares.
dépraver (de:pra've:) vt deprave.
déprécier (de:pre:'sje:) vt 1 depreciate. 2
underrate. 3 disparage.
dépression (de:prɛ'sjɔ̃) nf 1 depression. 2 fall.
3 hollow. 4 gloom. **dépression nerveuse**
nervous breakdown.
déprimer (de:pri:'me:) vt depress.
depuis (də'pɥi:) prep 1 since. 2 for. 3 from.
depuis lors ever since. **depuis que** since.
députation (de:pyta'sjɔ̃) nf deputation.
député (de:py'te:) nm 1 deputy. 2 member of
parliament.
déraciner (de:rasi:'ne:) vt uproot.
dérailler (de:rɑ'je:) vi become derailed.
déraisonnable (de:rɛzɔ'nabl) adj 1 unreasonable. 2 irrational.
déranger (de:rɑ̃ʒe:) vt 1 disturb. 2 trouble. 3
upset. **se déranger** vr 1 make way. 2 put
oneself out.
déraper (de:rɑ'pe:) vi skid.
derechef (dəre:'ʃɛf) adv a second time, once
more.
dérégler (de:re:'gle:) vt 1 upset. 2 put out of
order. **déréglé** adj 1 out of order. 2 irregular.
3 immoral.
dérision (de:ri:'zjɔ̃) nf ridicule, mockery.
dérisoire adj ridiculous.
dériver[1] (de:ri:'ve:) vt 1 divert. 2 derive. vi be
diverted.

dériver[2] (de:ri:'ve:) vi drift. **dérive** nf drift.
dernier, -ière (dɛr'nje:, -'njɛr) adj 1 last, latest.
2 latter. 3 utmost. 4 extreme.
dérober (de:rɔ'be:) vt 1 steal. 2 hide. **se
dérober** vr 1 escape. 2 evade. 3 give way.
dérobé adj 1 secret. 2 hidden.
dérogatoire (de:rɔga'twar) adj derogatory.
dérouiller (de:ru:'je:) vt rub the rust off. **se
dérouiller** vr brush up.
dérouler (de:ru:'le:) vt 1 unwind. 2 unfold. **se
dérouler** vr 1 unfold. 2 happen.
dérouter (de:ru:'te:) vt 1 lead astray. 2 baffle. 3
divert. **déroute** nf rout, defeat.
derrière (dɛr'jɛr) prep behind. adv behind, at
the back. nm 1 rear. 2 inf behind.
des (de:) contraction of **de les.**
dès (dɛ) prep 1 from. 2 since. **dès lors** ever
since. **dès que** 1 as soon as. 2 when.
désabuser (de:zaby'ze:) vt disillusion.
désaccord (de:za'kɔr) nm 1 disagreement. 2
clash 3 mus discord.
désagréable (de:zagre:'abl) adj 1 disagreeable.
2 unpleasant. 3 offensive.
désagréger (de:zagre:'ʒe:) vt disintegrate.
désagrément (de:zagre:'mɑ̃) nm trouble.
se désaltérer (de:zalte:'re:) vr quench one's
thirst.
désappointer (de:zapwɛ̃'te:) vt disappoint.
désapprobation (de:zaprɔba'sjɔ̃) nf disapproval.
désapprouver (de:zapru:'ve:) vt disapprove of.
désarmer (de:zar'me:) vt disarm.
désarroi (de:za'rwa) nm disorder, confusion.
désassocier (de:zasɔ'sje:) vt dissociate.
désassorti (de:zasɔr'ti:) adj made up of odd
pieces.
désastre (de:'zastr) nm disaster.
désavantage (de:zavɑ̃'taʒ) nm disadvantage,
drawback.
désaveu, -eux (de:za'vœ) nm denial.
désavouer (de:za'vwe:) vt 1 repudiate. 2
disown.
désaxé (de:zak'se:) adj eccentric.
descendre (dɛ'sɑ̃dr) vi (aux être) 1 descend. 2
come or go down. 3 alight. vt 1 go down. 2
take or bring down. **descendant** adj descen-
ding, downward. nm descendant.
descente (dɛ'sɑ̃t) nf 1 descent. 2 slope. 3
raid. **descente de lit** bedside rug.
description (de:skrip'sjɔ̃) nf description.
désembarquer (de:zɑ̃bar'ke:) vi,vt disembark.
désemparer (de:zɑ̃pa're:) vt 1 disable. 2 undo.

43

sans désemparer without stopping. **désemparé** adj 1 in distress. 2 crippled.
désencombrer (de:zãkɔ̃'bre:) vt 1 clear. 2 free.
désenfler (de:zã'fle:) vt deflate. vi go down.
désengager (de:zãga'ʒe:) vt release, free.
désert (de:'zɛr) adj 1 deserted. 2 lonely. nm 1 desert. 2 wilderness.
déserter (de:zɛr'te:) vt desert.
désespérer (de:zɛspe:'re:) vi despair. vt drive to despair. **désespéré** adj 1 desperate. 2 hopeless.
désespoir (de:zɛ'spwar) nm despair.
déshabiller (de:zabı'je:) vt undress.
déshériter (de:ze:ri:'te:) vt disinherit.
déshonnête (de:zɔ'nɛt) adj indecent, improper.
déshonneur (de:zɔ'nœr) nm 1 disgrace. 2 dishonour.
déshonorer (de:zɔnɔ're:) vt 1 dishonour, disgrace. 2 disfigure.
déshydrater (de:zı:dra'te:) vt dehydrate.
désigner (de:zi'ɲe:) vt 1 designate, show. 2 appoint. **désignation** nf 1 designation. 2 description. 3 appointment.
désinfecter (de:zɛ̃fɛk'te:) vt disinfect. **désinfectant** adj,nm disinfectant.
désintégrer (de:zɛ̃te'gre:) vt disintegrate.
désinvolte (de:zɛ̃'vɔlt) adj 1 easy. 2 casual. 2 cheeky.
désir (de:'zı:r) nm desire, wish. **désireux, -euse** (de:zi:'rœ, -'rœz) adj eager, anxious.
désirer (de:zi:'re:) vt desire, wish.
désobéir (de:zɔbe:'i:r) vt disobey. **désobéissant** adj disobedient.
désodorisant (de:zɔdɔrı'zã) nm deodorant.
désœuvré (dezœ'vre:) adj idle.
désoler (de:zɔ'le:) vt 1 distress, grieve. 2 desolate. 3 devastate. **se désoler** vr grieve. **désolé** adj 1 desolate, dreary. 2 grieved, sad, sorry.
désordonné (de:zɔrdɔ'ne:) adj 1 untidy. 2 wild, extravagant.
désordre (de:'zɔrdr) nm 1 disorder. 2 pl riots.
désorganisé (de:zɔrgani:'ze:) adj disorganized.
désorienter (de:zɔrjã'te:) vt bewilder. **se désorienter** vr 1 lose one's bearings. 2 get confused.
désormais (de:zɔr'mɛ) adv from now on.
désosser (de:zo'se:) vt bone.
dessécher (de:se:'ʃe:) vt 1 dry. 2 wither. **se dessécher** vr wither, dry up.
dessein (dɛ'sɛ̃) nm 1 plan, scheme. 2 intention.
desserrer (de:sɛ're:) vt 1 loosen. 2 unscrew.
dessert (de:'sɛr) nm dessert.

desservir (de:sɛr'vi:r) vt 1 clear (the table). 2 do a bad turn. 3 serve, connect.
dessin (de:'sɛ̃) nm 1 drawing. 2 design. **dessin animé** (cinema) cartoon. **dessinateur** nm 1 designer. 2 draughtsman.
dessiner (de:si:'ne:) vt 1 draw, sketch. 2 design. 3 outline. **se dessiner** vr stand out.
dessous (dɔ'su:) prep,adv below, beneath, underneath. nm 1 underneath. 2 lower part. **avoir le dessous** get the worst of it. **dessous de plat** tablemat.
dessus (dɔ'sy) prep,adv 1 above, over. 2 on. **de dessus** from, off. **en dessus** on top. ~nm top. **avoir le dessus** have the upper hand. **dessus de cheminée** mantelpiece.
destin (dɛ'stɛ̃) nm destiny, fate.
destiner (dɛsti:'ne:) vt 1 destine. 2 intend. **destination** nf destination. **destinée** nf destiny.
destituer (dɛsti:'tɥe:) vt dismiss.
destruction (dɛstryk'sjɛ̃) nf destruction.
désuet, -ète (de:'sɥɛ, -'sɥɛt) adj obsolete.
désunir (de:zy'ni:r) vt 1 divide. 2 detach.
détacher[1] (de:ta'ʃe:) vt 1 detach. 2 untie, undo. **se détacher** vr come undone. **se détacher de** vr break away from.
détacher[2] (de:ta'ʃe:) vt remove stains from.
détail (de:'taj) nm 1 detail. 2 retail.
détailler (de:ta'je:) vt 1 cut up. 2 retail. 3 relate in detail.
détective (de:tɛk'ti:v) nm detective.
déteindre (de:'tɛ̃dr) vi lose colour, run.
détendre (de:'tãdr) vt slacken, relax. **se détendre** vr 1 relax. 2 spring out.
détenir (de:t'ni:r) vt 1 hold. 2 detain. 3 withhold. **détenu** nm prisoner.
détente (de:'tãt) nf 1 relaxation. 2 easing (of a political situation). 3 trigger.
détergent (de:tɛr'ʒã) nm detergent.
détériorer (de:te:rjɔ're:) vt damage, spoil. **se détériorer** vr deteriorate.
déterminer (de:tɛrmi:'ne:) vt 1 determine. 2 fix. 3 bring about. **déterminer de** decide to. **se déterminer** vr make up one's mind. **détermination** nf determination. **déterminé** adj 1 resolute. 2 specific.
déterrer (de:te're:) vt 1 dig up. 2 discover.
détester (de:tɛ'ste:) vt detest.
détoner (de:tɔ'ne:) vi detonate. **détonant** adj,nm explosive.
détonner (de:tɔ'ne:) vi 1 be out of tune. 2 clash.
détour (de:'tu:r) nm 1 detour. 2 curve.

détourner (de:tu:r'ne:) *vt* **1** divert. **2** turn away. **3** embezzle. **4** hijack. **détournement** *nm* diversion.

détraqué (de:tra'ke:) *adj* **1** out of order. **2** crazy.

détremper (de:trã'pe:) *vt* **1** moisten. **2** soak.

détresse (de:'trɛs) *nf* distress.

détritus (de:trɪ:'tys) *nm* refuse.

détruire* (de:'trɥi:r) *vt* **1** demolish. **2** destroy. **3** overthrow.

dette (dɛt) *nf* debt.

deuil (dœj) *nm* mourning.

deux (dœ) *adj,nm* two. **tous les deux** both. **tous les deux jours** every other day. **deux-points** *nm* colon. **deuxième** *adj* second.

dévaler (de:va'le:) *vi,vt* rush down. *vi* descend.

dévaliser (de:vali:'ze:) *vt* rob, burgle.

dévaluer (de:va'lɥe:) *vt* devalue.

devancer (dəvã'se:) *vt* precede. **2** leave behind. **3** forestall. **devancier, -ière** (dəvã'sje:, -'sjɛr) *nm,f* predecessor.

devant (də'vã) *prep* before, in front of. *adv* in front, ahead. *nm* front. **devanture** *nf* **1** front. **2** window.

dévaster (de:va'ste:) *vt* devastate.

développer (de:vlɔ'pe:) *vt* **1** develop. **2** spread out. **3** explain.

devenir* (dəv'ni:r) *vi* (*aux* être) become, grow, get.

dévers (de:'vɛr) *nm* **1** slope. **2** warp.

déverser (de:vɛr'se:) *vt* **1** pour. **2** dump.

dévêtir (de:ve:'ti:r) *vt* strip, undress.

dévier (de:'vje:) *vi* **1** deviate. **2** swerve. **déviation** *nf* **1** deviation. **2** diversion. **3** bypass.

deviner (dəvɪ:'ne:) *vt* guess. **devinette** *nf* riddle.

devis (də'vi:) *nm* estimate.

dévisager (de:vi:za'ʒe:) *vt* stare at.

devise (də'vi:z) *nf* **1** motto. **2** slogan. **3** currency.

dévisser (de:vɪ:'se:) *vt* unscrew.

dévoiler (de:vwa'le:) *vt* reveal.

devoir* (də'vwar) *vt* **1** have to, must. **2** owe. *nm* **1** duty. **2** task. **3** exercise. **4** *pl* homework.

dévorer (de:vɔ're:) *vt* devour.

dévot (de:'vo) *adj* devout, religious. *nm* religious person. **faux dévot** hypocrite.

dévouer (de:'vwe:) *vt* **1** dedicate. **2** devote. **dévouement** *nm* devotion.

dextérité (dɛkste:ri:'te:) *nf* skill.

diabète (dja'bɛt) *nm* diabetes.

diable (djabl) *nm* devil. **diablerie** *nf* mischief, fun.

diagonal, -aux (djagɔ'nal, -'no) *adj* diagonal. **diagonale** *nf* diagonal.

dialecte (dja'lɛkt) *nm* dialect.

dialogue (dja'lɔg) *nm* dialogue.

diamant (dja'mã) *nm* diamond.

diamètre (dja'mɛtr) *nm* diameter.

diaphragme (dja'fragm) *nm* diaphragm.

diapositive (djapɔzɪ:'ti:v) *nf phot* slide.

diaprer (dja'pre:) *vt* mottle.

diarrhée (dja're:) *nf* diarrhoea.

dictateur (di:kta'tœr) *nm* dictator. **dictature** *nf* dictatorship.

dicter (di:k'te:) *vt* dictate. **dictée** *nf* dictation.

dictionnaire (di:ksjɔ'nɛr) *nm* dictionary.

dicton (di:k'tɔ̃) *nm* maxim, saying.

dièse (djɛz) *nm mus* sharp.

diète (djɛt) *nm pol* diet.

dieu, dieux (djœ) *nm* god.

diffamer (di:ffa'me:) *vt* **1** slander. **2** libel.

différence (di:fe:'rãs) *nf* difference. **à la différence de** contrary to. **différent** *adj* different.

différencier (di:fɛrã'sje:) *vt* differentiate.

différend (di:fe:'rã) *nm* difference, dispute.

différentiel, -elle (di:fe:rã'sjɛl) *adj,nf* differential.

différer (di:fe:'re:) *vt* **1** defer. **2** put off. *vi* differ.

difficile (di:fi:'si:l) *adj* difficult. **difficulté** *nf* difficulty.

difforme (di:'fɔrm) *adj* deformed.

diffuser (di:fy'ze:) *vt* **1** spread. **2** broadcast.

digérer (di:ʒe:'re:) *vt* **1** digest. **2** assimilate. **digestion** (di:ʒɛs'tjɔ̃) *nf* digestion.

digitale (di:ʒɪ:'tal) **digitale pourprée** *nf* foxglove.

digne (di:ɲ) *adj* **1** worthy. **2** dignified. **digne d'éloges** praiseworthy. **digne de remarque** noteworthy.

dignité (di:ʒi:'te:) *nf* dignity.

digue (di:g) *nf* **1** embankment. **2** dam. **3** jetty. **4** obstacle.

dilapider (di:lapi:'de:) *vt* squander.

dilater (di:la'te:) *vt* expand.

dilemme (di:'lɛm) *nm* dilemma.

diligent (di:li:'ʒã) *adj* **1** diligent. **2** industrious. **3** busy.

diluer (di:'lɥe:) *vt* dilute.

dimanche (di:'mãʃ) *nm* Sunday. **dimanche des rameaux** Palm Sunday.

dimension (dimã'sjɔ̃) *nf* **1** dimension, size. **2** *pl* measurements.

diminuer (di:mi:'nɥe:) *vt* **1** diminish. **2** reduce.

45

vi **1** decrease. **2** abate. **diminutif, -ive** (di:-mɪːny'tiːf, -'tiːv) *adj,nm* diminutive. **diminution** *nf* decrease.

dindon (dɛ̃'dɔ̃) *nm* turkey.

dîner (di:'ne:) *vi* dine, have dinner. *nm* dinner.

dingue (dɛ̃g) *adj* *inf* daft, mad.

dinosaure (di:nɔ'sɔr) *nm* dinosaur.

diocèse (djɔ'sɛz) *nm* diocese.

diphtongue (di:f'tɔ̃g) *nf* diphthong.

diplomatie (di:plɔma'si:) *nf* diplomacy. **diplomate** *nm* diplomat. **diplomatique** *adj* diplomatic.

diplôme (di:'plom) *nm* diploma. **diplômé** *nm* graduate.

dire* (di:r) *vt* **1** say. **2** tell. **c'est à dire** that is to say.

direct (di:rɛkt) *adj* **1** direct. **2** straight.

directeur (di:rɛk'tœr) *nm* **1** director. **2** manager. **3** headmaster. **4** governor.

direction (di:rɛk'sjɔ̃) *nf* **1** direction. **2** management. **3** steering.

diriger (di:ri:'ʒe:) *vt* **1** manage. **2** direct. **3** aim. **se diriger vers** *vr* go towards.

discerner (di:sɛr'ne:) *vt* discern, distinguish.

disciple (di:'si:pl) *nm* disciple.

discipline (di:si'pli:n) *nf* discipline, order.

discontinuer (di:skɔ̃ti:'nɥe:) *vi,vt* discontinue.

discorde (di:s'kɔrd) *nf* discord.

discothèque (diskɔ'tɛk) *nf* **1** discotheque. **2** record library.

discours (di:'skuːr) *nm* **1** talk. **2** speech.

discret, -ète (di'skrɛ, -skrɛt) *adj* **1** discreet. **2** quiet. **discrétion** *nf* discretion.

discriminer (di:skrimi:'ne:) *vt* discriminate.

discussion (di:sky'sjɔ̃) *nf* **1** discussion. **2** debate.

discuter (di:sky'te:) *vt* **1** discuss. **2** question.

disette (di:'zɛt) *nf* scarcity. **disette d'eau** drought.

disgrâce (di:z'grɑs) *nf* disgrace.

disgracieux, -euse (di:zgra'sjœ, -'sjœz) *adj* **1** awkward. **2** uncouth. **3** unsightly.

disloquer (di:slɔ'ke:) *vt* dislocate. **se disloquer** *vr* break up.

disparaître* (di:spa'rɛtr) *vi* (*aux* être or avoir) **1** disappear. **2** vanish. **disparu** *adj* **1** missing. **2** extinct.

disparate (di:spa'rat) *adj* dissimilar.

dispendieux, -euse (di:spɑ̃'djœ, -'djœz) *adj* expensive.

dispenser (di:spɑ̃'se:) *vt* **1** exempt. **2** dispense. **se dispenser de** *vr* get out of, excuse oneself. **dispensaire** *nm* dispensary.

46

disperser (di:spɛr'se:) *vt* scatter, disperse.

disponible (di:spɔ'ni:bl) *adj* **1** available. **2** free. **3** vacant.

dispos (di:'spo) *adj* fit, active.

disposer (di:spo'ze:) *vt* **1** dispose. **2** arrange. **disposer de** have at one's disposal. **se disposer à** *vr* be ready to. **disposition** *nf* **1** disposition. **2** arrangement. **3** disposal. **4** tendency. **5** *pl* provisions.

dispositif (di:spozi:'tiːf) *nm* apparatus, device.

disputer (di:spy'te:) *vt* **1** discuss. **2** dispute, argue. *vi* quarrel. **se disputer** *vr* argue, quarrel. **dispute** *nf* dispute, quarrel.

disqualifier (di:skali:'fje:) *vt* disqualify.

disque (di:sk) *nf* **1** disc. **2** record.

dissemblable (di:sɑ̃'blabl) *adj* dissimilar, different.

disséminer (di:se:mi:'ne:) *vt* scatter, spread.

dissentiment (di:sɑ̃ti:'mɑ̃) *nm* dissent.

disséquer (di:se:'ke:) *vt* dissect.

dissimuler (di:si:my'le:) *vt* **1** conceal. **2** disguise. **se dissimuler** *vr* hide. **dissimulation** *nf* deceit.

dissiper (di:si:'pe:) *vt* **1** waste. **2** dispel.

dissoudre* (di:'suːdr) *vt* dissolve. **se dissoudre** *vr* **1** melt. **2** break up.

dissuader (di:sɥa'de:) *vt* dissuade. **forces de dissuasion** *nf pl mil* deterrent.

distance (di:'stɑs) *nf* distance. **distant** *adj* **1** distant. **2** aloof.

distiller (di:sti:'le:) *vt* distil.

distinct (di:'stɛ̃) *adj* **1** distinct, clear. **2** separate. **distinctif, -ive** (di:stɛ̃k'tiːf, -'tiːv) *adj* distinctive. **distinction** *nf* **1** distinction. **2** honour. **3** rank.

distinguer (di:stɛ̃'ge:) *vt* **1** distinguish. **2** discern. **3** honour. **distingué** *adj* **1** eminent. **2** refined.

distraire* (di:'strɛr) *vt* **1** divert, take out. **2** distract. **3** entertain. **se distraire** *vr* amuse oneself. **distrait** *adj* absent-minded.

distribuer (di:stri:'bɥe:) *vt* **1** distribute. **2** give out. **3** deliver. **distribution** *nf* **1** distribution. **2** delivery.

divaguer (di:va'ge:) *vi* **1** wander. **2** ramble.

divan (di:'vɑ̃) *nm* **1** divan. **2** couch.

diverger (di:vɛr'ʒe:) *vi* diverge.

divers (di:'vɛr) *adj* **1** changing. **2** diverse, sundry. **3** varied.

divertir (di:vɛr'tiːr) *vt* entertain. **divertissement** *nm* entertainment, recreation.

dividende (di:vi:'dɑ̃d) *nm* dividend.

divin (di:'vɛ̃) *adj* divine, holy.

draguer

diviser (di:vi:ˈze:) vt divide. **divisible** adj divisible. **division** nf 1 division. 2 department. 3 discord.

divorcer (di:vɔrˈse:) vi divorce. **divorce** nm divorce.

divulguer (di:vylˈge:) vt divulge, disclose.

dix (di:s, di:) adj,nm ten. **dixième** adj tenth.

dix-huit adj,nm eighteen. **dix-huitième** adj eighteenth.

dix-neuf adj,nm nineteen. **dix-neuvième** adj nineteenth.

dix-sept adj,nm seventeen. **dix-septième** adj seventeenth.

dizaine (di:ˈzɛn) nf about ten.

docile (dɔˈsi:l) adj docile, manageable.

docte (dɔkt) adj learned.

docteur (dɔkˈtœr) nm doctor.

doctrine (dɔkˈtri:n) nf doctrine.

document (dɔkyˈmã) nm document. **documentaire** adj,nm documentary.

documenter (dɔkymãˈte:) vt document.

dodo (dɔˈdo) nm inf sleep. **faire dodo** go to sleep.

dodu (dɔˈdy) adj plump.

dogmatique (dɔgmaˈti:k) adj dogmatic.

dogme (dɔgm) nm dogma.

doigt (dwa) nm 1 finger. 2 digit. **doigt de pied** toe. **doigté** nm 1 inf tact. 2 mus fingering.

dois (dwa) v see **devoir**.

doit (dwa) nm debit.

dol (dɔl) nm fraud.

doléances (dɔleˈãs) nf pl complaints.

dollar (dɔˈlar) nm dollar.

Dolomites (dɔlɔˈmi:t) nf pl Dolomites.

domaine (dɔˈmɛn) nm 1 domain, estate. 2 scope, field.

dôme (dom) nm dome.

domestiquer (dɔmɛstiˈke:) vt domesticate. **domestique** adj domestic. nm,f servant.

domicile (dɔmiˈsi:l) nm residence, abode.

dominer (dɔmiˈne:) vi rule. vt 1 dominate. 2 master. 3 overlook. **dominant** adj 1 ruling. 2 dominant. **domination** nf rule.

dominion (dɔmiˈnjɔ̃) nm dominion.

dommage (dɔˈmaʒ) nm damage, harm. **quel dommage!** what a pity! **dommages-intérêts** nm pl damages.

dompter (dɔ̃ˈte:) vt 1 tame. 2 subdue.

don (dɔ̃) nm 1 gift, present. 2 talent.

donc (dɔ̃k) conj therefore, so. adv 1 well. 2 just.

donner (dɔˈne:) vt 1 give. 2 donate. 3 game deal. 4 provide. **donner contre** run into. **donner dans** fall into. **donner sur** look out

onto. **s'en donner** vr enjoy oneself. **donne** nf game deal. **donnée** nf 1 fundamental idea. 2 pl data.

dont (dɔ̃) pron 1 of whom or which. 2 by, with, from whom or which. 3 whose.

dorénavant (dɔre:naˈvã) adv from now on.

dorer (dɔˈre:) vt 1 gild. 2 brown.

dorloter (dɔrlɔˈte:) vt 1 fondle, cuddle. 2 pamper.

dormir (dɔrˈmi:r) vi sleep, be asleep. **dormant** adj 1 sleeping. 2 dormant. 3 stagnant.

dors (dɔr) v see **dormir**.

dortoir (dɔrˈtwar) nm dormitory.

dorure (dɔˈryr) nf gilt, gilding.

dos (do) nm back.

dose (doz) nf dose. **dosage** nm dosage.

dossier (doˈsje:) nm 1 file. 2 record. 3 back (of a chair).

dot (dɔt) nf dowry.

doter (dɔˈte:) vt endow.

douane (dwan) nf customs.

doubler (du:ˈble:) vt 1 double. 2 line. 3 overtake. 4 quicken. 5 understudy. **double** adj,nm double, duplicate. **doublure** nf 1 lining. 2 understudy.

douceur (du:ˈsœr) nf 1 sweetness. 2 softness. 3 comfort. 4 gentleness.

douche (du:ʃ) nf shower (bath).

douer (dwe:) vt endow. **doué** adj gifted.

douille (du:j) nf 1 socket. 2 case, casing. 3 sleeve.

douillet, -ette (du:ˈjɛ, -ˈjɛt) adj 1 soft. 2 delicate.

douleur (du:ˈlœr) nf 1 pain. 2 sorrow. **douloureux, -euse** (du:lu:ˈrœ, -ˈrœz) adj 1 sore, painful. 2 sad, distressing.

douter (du:ˈte:) vi doubt. **se douter de** vr suspect. **doute** nm 1 doubt. 2 misgiving. **mettre en doute** question. **douteux, -euse** (du:ˈtœ, -ˈtœz) adj 1 uncertain. 2 dubious.

douve (du:v) nf 1 ditch. 2 moat.

Douvres (du:vr) nf Dover.

doux, douce (du:, du:s) adj 1 sweet. 2 soft. 3 gentle. 4 pleasant. 5 mild.

douze (du:z) adj,nm twelve. **douzaine** nf dozen. **douzième** adj twelfth.

doyen, -enne (dwaˈjɛ̃, -ˈjɛn) nm,f 1 dean. 2 senior.

drachme (drakm) nf drachma.

dragée (draˈʒe:) nf 1 sugared almond. 2 lozenge.

dragon (draˈgɔ̃) nm dragon.

draguer (draˈge:) vt dredge, drag.

47

dramatiser

dramatiser (dramati:'ze:) *vt* dramatize. **dramatique** *adj* dramatic.
dramaturge (drama'tyrʒ) *nm,f* dramatist.
drame (dram) *nm* 1 drama. 2 play.
drap (dra) *nm* 1 cloth. 2 sheet. **drapeau, -aux** (dra'po) *nm* 1 flag. 2 *mil* colours.
draper (dra'pe:) *vt* 1 drape. 2 hang. **draperie** *nf* drapery. **drapier, -ière** (dra'pje:, -'pjɛr) *nm,f* draper.
drelin (drə'lɛ̃) *nm* tinkle.
dresser (drɛ'se:) *vt* 1 raise. 2 set, lay. 3 draw up. 4 train. **dresser les oreilles** prick one's ears. **se dresser** *vr* stand up, rise. **dressage** *nm* breaking in, training. **dressoir** *nm* dresser.
drogue (drɔg) *nf* 1 drug. 2 chemical.
droit[1] (drwa) *adj* 1 straight. 2 upright. 3 right (side, etc.). 4 honest. *adv* 1 straight. 2 directly. **tout droit** straight on.
droit[2] (drwa) *nm* 1 right. 2 charge, tax. 3 law. **droit d'auteur** copyright. **droits d'auteur** *nm pl* royalties. **droit de passage** right of way. **exempt de droit** duty-free.
droite (drwat) *nf* right, right-hand side.
drôle (drol) *adj* 1 funny, comic. 2 odd. *nm* rascal.
dromadaire (drɔma'dɛr) *nm* dromedary.
dru (dry) *adj* 1 thick. 2 strong. 3 dense. *adv* 1 thickly. 2 heavily.
du (dy) contraction of **de le.**
dû, due (dy) *v* see **devoir.** *adj* 1 due. 2 owing. 3 proper. *nm* due.
duc (dyk) *nm* duke. **duchesse** (dy'ʃɛs) *nf* duchess.
duel (dɥɛl) *nm* duel.
dûment (dy'mɑ̃) *adv* duly.
dune (dyn) *nf* dune.
Dunkerque (dœ̃'kɛrk) *nf* Dunkirk.
duo (dyo) *nm mus* duet.
duper (dy'pe:) *vt* trick, take in.
dur (dyr) *adj* 1 hard. 2 tough. 3 difficult. 4 harsh. *adv* hard. **durcir** (dyr'si:r) *vi,vt* harden.
durer (dy're:) *vi* 1 last. 2 endure. **durant** *prep* during. **durée** *nf* 1 duration. 2 life, wear.
duvet (dy'vɛ) *nm* 1 down, fluff. 2 quilt.
dynamique (di:na'mi:k) *adj* dynamic.
dynamite (di:na'mi:t) *nf* dynamite.
dynastie (di:na'sti:) *nf* dynasty.
dysenterie (di:sɑ̃'tri:) *nf* dysentery.

E

eau, eaux (o) *nf* water. **eau douce** 1 soft water. 2 freshwater. **eau-de-vie** *nf, pl* **eaux-de-vie** 1 spirits. 2 brandy. **eau minérale** mineral water. **eaux d'égout** *nf pl* sewage. **faire eau** leak.
ébahir (e:ba'i:r) *vt* astound, flabbergast. **s'ébahir de** *vr* be amazed at. **ébahissement** *nm* astonishment.
ébats (e:'ba) *nm pl* sport, frolics.
ébaucher (e:bo'ʃe:) *vt* 1 sketch. 2 outline. **ébauche** *nf* 1 rough sketch. 2 outline.
ébène (e:'bɛn) *nf* ebony. **ébéniste** *nm* cabinet-maker.
éberlué (e:bɛr'lɥe:) *adj* flabbergasted.
éblouir (e:blu:'i:r) *vt* dazzle. **éblouissement** *nm* 1 dazzle. 2 fit of dizziness.
éboulement (e:bu:l'mɑ̃) *nm* landslide.
ébouriffer (e:bu:ri:'fe:) *vt* 1 ruffle. 2 amaze.
ébranler (e:brɑ̃'le:) *vt* 1 shake. 2 loosen. 3 disturb. **s'ébranler** *vr* 1 totter. 2 move off. **ébranlement** *nm* 1 shaking. 2 shock. 3 commotion.
ébrécher (e:bre:'ʃe:) *vt* 1 notch. 2 chip.
ébrouer (e:bru:'e:) *vi* snort. **ébrouement** *nm* snort.
ébullition (e:byli:'sjɔ̃) *nf* 1 boiling. 2 turmoil.
écailler (e:ka'je:) *vt* scale. **s'écailler** *vr* flake off. **écaille** *nf* 1 scale. 2 shell. 3 flake.
écaler (e:ka'le:) *vt* shell, husk. **écale** *nf* shell, pod.
écarlate (e:kar'lat) *adj,nf* scarlet.
écart (e:'kar) *nm* 1 distance apart. 2 deviation, swerve. 3 remote place. **à l'écart** aside, on one side. **faire le grand écart** do the splits. **faire un écart** shy.
écarter (e:kar'te:) *vt* 1 separate. 2 keep off. 3 divert. **s'écarter** *vr* 1 move aside. 2 diverge. **s'écarter de** stray from. **écarté** *adj* 1 isolated, remote. 2 apart.
ecclésiastique (ɛkle:zja'sti:k) *adj* ecclesiastical. *nm* clergyman.
écervelé (e:sɛrvə'le:) *adj* 1 thoughtless. 2 crazy. 3 light-headed.
échafaud (e:ʃa'fo) *nm* scaffold. **échafaudage** *nm* scaffolding.
échalote (e:ʃa'lɔt) *nf* shallot.
échancrer (e:ʃɑ̃'kre:) *vt* 1 cut out. 2 indent.
échanger (e:ʃɑ̃'ʒe:) *vt* exchange.

échantillon (e:ʃɑ̃tɪ'jɔ̃) *nm* 1 sample, specimen. 2 pattern.

échapper (e:ʃa'pe:) *vi* (*aux* être or avoir) escape. **s'échapper** *vr* 1 break free. 2 escape. 3 leak. **échappatoire** *nf* loophole, way out. **échappement** *nm* 1 escape. 2 leakage. 3 exhaust.

écharde (e:'ʃard) *nf* splinter.

écharpe (e:'ʃarp) *nf* 1 scarf. 2 sash. 3 sling.

échasse (e:'ʃɑs) *nf* stilt.

échauder (e:ʃo'de:) *vt* scald.

échauffer (e:ʃo'fe:) *vt* 1 overheat. 2 heat. 3 rouse. **s'échauffer** *vr* 1 get overheated. 2 warm up. **échauffé** *adj* 1 overheated. 2 excited.

échéance (e:ʃe:'ɑ̃s) *nf* 1 date (of payment). 2 maturity. 3 expiration. **échéant** *adj* payable, falling due.

échec (e:'ʃɛk) *nm* 1 check. 2 failure, setback. 3 *pl* chess. **échec et mat** checkmate.

échelle (e:'ʃɛl) *nf* 1 ladder. 2 scale.

échelon (e:ʃ'lɔ̃) *nm* 1 rung. 2 step. 3 level.

échelonner (e:ʃlɔ'ne:) *vt* space out.

échevelé (e:ʃɛv'le:) *adj* 1 dishevelled. 2 wild.

échine (e:'ʃiːn) *nf* spine, backbone.

échiquier (e:ʃi:'kje:) *nm* chessboard.

écho (e:'ko) *nm* echo.

échoir* (e:'ʃwar) 1 fall. 2 mature. 3 expire.

échoppe (e:'ʃɔp) *nf* booth, stall.

échouer (e:'ʃwe:) *vi,vt* ground. *vi* 1 be stranded. 2 fail.

éclabousser (e:klabu'se:) *vt* splash.

éclair (e:'klɛr) *nm* 1 flash. 2 *pl* lightning. 3 eclair.

éclaircir (e:klɛr'siːr) *vt* 1 clear up. 2 lighten. 3 explain. **s'éclaircir** *vr* 1 clear up. 2 thin out. **éclaircie** *nf* 1 break, opening. 2 clearing.

éclairer (e:klɛ're:) *vt* 1 light. 2 enlighten. **s'éclairer** *vr* 1 light up. 2 clear. **éclairage** *nm* 1 lighting. 2 illumination. **éclaireur** *nm* scout.

éclat (e:'kla) *nm* 1 splinter. 2 chip. 3 burst. 4 flash. 5 brightness.

éclater (e:kla'te:) *vi,vt* 1 burst. 2 splinter. *vi* 1 explode. 2 break out. **éclater de rire** burst out laughing. **éclatant** *adj* 1 bright. 2 brilliant. 3 loud.

éclipser (e:kli:p'se:) *vt* 1 eclipse. 2 obscure. **éclipse** *nf* eclipse.

éclisse (e:'kliːs) *nf* 1 wedge. 2 *med* splint.

éclopé (e:klɔ'pe:) *adj* lame. *nm* cripple.

éclore* (e:'klɔr) *vi* (*aux* être) 1 hatch. 2 open, blossom.

écluse (e:'klyz) *nf* 1 sluice. 2 lock.

écœurer (e:kœ're:) *vt* 1 disgust. 2 nauseate.

école (e:'kɔl) *nf* school. **école maternelle/primaire** nursery/primary school.

écologie (e:kɔlɔ'ʒi:) *nf* ecology.

éconduire* (e:kɔ̃'dɥiːr) *vt* 1 show out. 2 reject.

économe (e:kɔ'nɔm) *adj* economical. **économie** *nf* 1 economy. 2 *pl* savings. **faire des économies** save. **économique** *adj* economic.

économiser (e:kɔnɔmi:'ze:) *vt* economize, save.

écoper (e:kɔ'pe:) *vt naut* bail out.

écorcer (e:kɔr'se:) *vt* skin, peel. **écorce** *nf* 1 rind, peel. 2 bark.

écorcher (e:kɔr'ʃe:) *vt* 1 skin. 2 graze. 3 fleece. **écorchure** *nf* 1 graze. 2 scratch.

écornifler (e:kɔrni:'fle:) *vt* scrounge, sponge.

Ecosse (e:'kɔs) *nf* Scotland. **écossais** *adj* Scottish, Scotch, Scots. *nm* Scot.

écot (e:'ko) *nm* share, quota.

écouler (e:ku:'le:) *vt* get rid of. **s'écouler** *vr* 1 flow out. 2 pass, elapse. **écoulement** *nm* 1 flow. 2 discharge. 3 sale.

écouter (e:ku:'te:) *vt* 1 listen to. 2 pay attention to. **écouter à la porte** eavesdrop. **écouteur** *nm* 1 listener. 2 receiver. 3 headphone.

écran (e:'krɑ̃) *nm* screen.

écraser (e:kra'ze:) *vt* 1 crush. 2 overcome. 3 flatten. 4 run over. **se faire écraser** get run over. **s'écraser** *vr* 1 collapse. 2 crash. **écrasant** *adj* 1 crushing. 2 overwhelming.

écrémer (e:kre:'me:) *vt* skim.

écrevisse (e:krə'vi:s) *nf* crayfish.

s'écrier (se:'krje:) *vr* 1 exclaim. 2 cry out.

écrin (e:'krɛ̃) *nm* (jewel) case.

écrire* (e:'kri:r) *vt* 1 write. 2 note down. **s'écrire** *vr* be written. **écrit** *adj* written. *nm* 1 writing. 2 written examination. **écriteau, -aux** (e:kri:'to) *nm* placard. **écriture** *nf* writing.

écrit (e:'kri:) *v* see **écrire.**

écrivain (e:kri:'vɛ̃) *nm* author, writer.

écrivant (e:kri:'vɑ̃) *v* see **écrire.**

écrivasser (e:kri:va'se:) *vt* scribble.

écrou (e:'kru:) *nm tech* nut.

s'écrouler (se:kru:'le:) *vr* collapse, fall in. **écroulement** *nm* 1 collapse. 2 ruin.

écru (e:'kry) *adj* 1 natural. 2 raw.

écu (e:'ky) *nm* 1 shield. 2 crown (money).

écueil (e:'kœj) *nm* 1 reef, rock. 2 snag.

écuelle (e:'kɥɛl) *nf* bowl.

écumer (e:ky'me:) *vi* foam, froth. *vt* skim. **écume** *nf* 1 foam, froth. 2 scum.

écureuil (e:ky'rœj) *nm* squirrel.

écurie (e:ky'ri:) *nf* stable.

écuyer (e:kɥɪ:ˈje:) nm 1 squire. 2 horseman.

édenté (e:dãˈte:) adj toothless.

édifier (e:di:ˈfje:) vt 1 build, erect. 2 enlighten. **édifice** nm 1 building. 2 structure.

Edimbourg (edẽˈbu:r) nm Edinburgh.

édit (e:ˈdi:) nm decree.

éditer (e:di:ˈte:) vt 1 edit. 2 publish. **éditeur** nm 1 editor. 2 publisher. **édition** nf edition, issue. **éditorial, -aux** (e:di:tɔˈrjal, -ˈrjo) adj editorial. nm newspaper leader.

édredon (e:drɔˈdɔ̃) nm eiderdown.

éducation (e:dykaˈsjɔ̃) nf 1 education. 2 upbringing. 3 breeding.

éduquer (e:dyˈke:) vt 1 bring up. 2 train.

effacer (ɛfaˈse:) vt erase, rub out. **s'effacer** vr 1 wear away. 2 fade. 3 stand aside.

effarer (ɛfaˈre:) vt 1 scare. 2 bewilder.

effaroucher (ɛfaruˈʃe:) vt 1 scare away. 2 startle. **s'effaroucher** vr be startled.

effectif, -ive (e:fɛkˈti:f, -ˈti:v) adj 1 effective. 2 actual.

effectuer (e:fɛkˈtɥe:) vt effect, carry out.

efféminé (e:fe:mi:ˈne:) adj effeminate.

effervescence (e:fɛrvɛˈsãs) nf effervescence.

effet (eˈfɛ) nm 1 effect, result. 2 impression. 3 pl bills. 4 pl belongings. **en effet** indeed.

s'effeuiller (e:fœˈje:) vr shed its leaves or petals.

efficace (e:fi:ˈkas) adj 1 effective. 2 efficient.

effigie (e:fi:ˈʒi:) nf effigy.

effiler (e:fi:ˈle:) vt 1 unravel. 2 taper.

effleurer (e:flœˈre:) vt 1 skim, touch lightly. 2 touch on.

effondrer (e:fɔ̃ˈdre:) vt break in. **s'effondrer** vr 1 cave in. 2 collapse. 3 slump. **effondrement** nm 1 collapse. 2 subsidence.

s'efforcer (se:fɔrˈse:) vr **s'efforcer de** strive to.

effort (e:ˈfɔr) nm 1 effort. 2 strain.

effrayer (e:frɛˈje:) vt frighten, scare.

effréné (e:fre:ˈne:) adj frantic.

effroi (e:ˈfrwa) nm fear, dread. **effroyable** adj 1 dreadful. 2 awful.

effronté (e:frɔ̃ˈte:) adj 1 bold. 2 impudent, cheeky. **effronterie** nf impudence, cheek.

égal, -aux (e:ˈgal, -ˈgo) adj 1 equal. 2 level. 3 even. 4 regular. **cela m'est égal** it's all the same to me. **également** adv 1 equally. 2 likewise. 3 also. **égalité** nf 1 equality. 2 regularity.

égaler (e:gaˈle:) vt 1 equal. 2 match.

égaliser (e:galiˈze:) vi,vt equalize. vt smooth.

égard (e:ˈgar) nm 1 respect. 2 regard. 3 consideration.

égarer (e:gaˈre:) vt 1 lead astray. 2 mislay. 3 bewilder. **s'égarer** vr lose one's way. **égaré** adj 1 stray. 2 distracted.

égayer (e:gɛˈje:) vt 1 cheer up. 2 amuse.

Égée (e:ˈʒe:) adj Aegean. **(Mer) Egée** nf Aegean (Sea).

église (e:ˈgli:z) nf church.

ego (ˈe:go) nm ego. **égocentrique** (e:gɔsãˈtri:k) adj self-centred, egocentric. **égoïste** (e:gɔˈi:st) adj selfish. **égoïsme** nm selfishness, egoism.

égorger (e:gɔrˈʒe:) vt 1 cut the throat of. 2 massacre. 3 ruin.

égout (e:ˈgu:) nm 1 drain. 2 sewer. 3 gutter.

égoutter (e:gu:ˈte:) vt 1 drain. 2 drip.

égratigner (e:grati:ˈɲe:) vt scratch. **égratignure** nf scratch.

égrener (e:grɔˈne:) vt 1 shell. 2 pick.

Egypte (ˈe:ʒi:pt) nf Egypt. **égyptien, -ienne** (e:ʒi:pˈsjɛ̃, -ˈsjɛn) adj,n Egyptian.

éjaculer (e:ʒakyˈle:) vt ejaculate.

éjecter (e:ʒɛkˈte:) vt eject.

élaborer (e:labɔˈre:) vt 1 elaborate. 2 work out.

élaguer (e:laˈge:) vt 1 prune. 2 cut down.

élan (e:ˈlã) nm 1 spring, bound. 2 dash. 3 impetus. 4 burst.

s'élancer (se:lãˈse:) vr 1 spring. 2 rush. **élancé** adj slender. **élancement** nm 1 throb. 2 twinge.

élargir (e:larˈʒi:r) vt 1 widen. 2 enlarge. 3 extend. 4 release.

élastique (e:laˈsti:k) adj elastic. nm 1 elastic. 2 rubber band.

élection (e:lɛkˈsjɔ̃) nf 1 election. 2 choice.

électoral, -aux (e:lɛktɔˈral, -ˈro) adj electoral. **électorat** nm electorate.

électricité (e:lɛktri:si:ˈte:) nf electricity.

électrifier (e:lɛktri:ˈfje:) vt electrify.

électrique (e:lɛkˈtri:k) adj electric.

électriser (e:lɛktri:ˈze:) vt 1 electrify. 2 excite.

électrocuter (e:lɛktrɔkyˈte:) vt electrocute.

électrode (e:lɛkˈtrɔd) nf electrode.

électron (e:lɛkˈtrɔ̃) nm electron.

électronique (e:lɛktrɔni:k) adj electronic. nf electronics.

élégant (e:le:ˈgã) adj 1 elegant. 2 smart.

élément (e:le:ˈmã) nm 1 element. 2 unit. 3 pl rudiments. **élémentaire** adj 1 elementary. 2 elemental.

éléphant (e:le:ˈfã) nm elephant.

élevage (ɛlˈvaʒ) nm stockbreeding.

élévation (e:le:vaˈsjɔ̃) nf 1 elevation. 2 rise. 3 raising. 4 height. **élévateur** nm elevator.

élève (eːˈlɛv) *nm,f* pupil. **élevé** *adj* **1** high. **2** raised. **bien/mal élevé** well/ill-bred.

élever (eːlˈveː) *vt* **1** raise. **2** elevate. **3** erect. **4** bring up. **s'élever** *vr* rise up.

elfe (ɛlf) *nm* elf.

éligible (eːliːˈʒiːbl) *adj* eligible.

éliminer (eːliːmiːˈneː) *vt* **1** eliminate. **2** get rid of.

élire* (eːˈliːr) *vt* **1** elect. **2** choose.

élite (eːˈliːt) *nf* **1** elite. **2** cream. **d'élite** crack.

elle (ɛl) *pron 3rd pers fs* **1** she. **2** her. **3** it. **elle-même** *pron 3rd pers fs* **1** herself. **2** itself.

elles (ɛl) *pron 3rd pers f pl* **1** they. **2** them. **elles-mêmes** *pron 3rd pers f pl* themselves.

ellipse (ɛlˈliːps) *nf* ellipse.

élocution (eːlɔkyˈsjɔ̃) *nf* elocution.

éloge (eːˈlɔʒ) *nm* praise.

éloigner (eːlwaˈɲeː) *vt* **1** remove. **2** send away. **3** postpone. **s'éloigner** *vr* **1** go away. **2** stand back. **éloigné** *adj* **1** distant. **2** remote. **éloignement** *nm* **1** removal. **2** distance. **3** absence. **4** aversion.

éloquent (eːlɔˈkã) *adj* eloquent.

élu (eːˈly) *adj* **1** chosen. **2** successful.

élucider (eːlysiːˈdeː) *vt* elucidate.

éluder (eːlyˈdeː) *vt* elude, evade.

émail, -aux (eːˈmaj, -ˈmo) *nm* **1** enamel. **2** glaze.

émailler (eːmaˈjeː) *vt* **1** enamel. **2** glaze. **3** dot.

émanciper (eːmãsiːˈpeː) *vt* emancipate.

émaner (eːmaˈneː) *vi* **émaner de** emanate or come from.

emballer (ãbaˈleː) *vt* **1** pack. **2** wrap up. **3** excite. **s'emballer** *vr* **1** bolt, run away. **2** get carried away. **emballage** *nm* wrapping, packing.

embarcadère (ãbarkaˈdɛr) *nm* **1** quay, wharf. **2** platform.

embargo (ãbarˈgo) *nm* embargo.

embarquer (ãbarˈkeː) *vi,vt* embark. *vt* **1** ship. **2** *inf* arrest. **s'embarquer** *vr* embark.

embarras (ãbaˈrɑ) *nm* **1** obstacle. **2** embarrassment, confusion. **3** difficulty. **4** *pl* fuss.

embarrasser (ãbaraˈseː) *vt* **1** embarrass. **2** encumber. **3** obstruct. **4** perplex. **5** confuse. **s'embarrasser** *vr* burden oneself.

embaucher (ãboˈʃeː) *vt* engage, take on.

embaumer (ãboˈmeː) *vt* **1** embalm. **2** perfume.

embellir (ãbɛˈliːr) *vt* **1** embellish. **2** improve in looks.

embêter (ãbɛˈteː) *vt inf* **1** annoy. **2** bother.

emblée (ãˈbleː) **d'emblée** *adv* straightaway.

emblème (ãˈblɛm) *nm* emblem.

emboîter (ãbwaˈteː) *vt* **1** pack in boxes. **2** fit together.

embouchure (ãbuˈʃyr) *nf* **1** mouthpiece. **2** *geog* mouth.

embouteiller (ãbuːtɛˈjeː) *vt* **1** bottle. **2** block up. **embouteillage** *nm* **1** bottling. **2** traffic jam.

emboutir (ãbuˈtiːr) *vt* collide with.

embrancher (ãbrãˈʃeː) *vt* join up. **embranchement** *nm* **1** branch, fork. **2** junction.

embraser (ãbraˈzeː) *vt* set on fire. **s'embraser** *vr* catch fire.

embrasser (ãbraˈseː) *vt* **1** embrace. **2** hug. **3** kiss. **4** include. **embrassement** *nm* embrace.

embrayer (ãbrɛˈjeː) *vt* **1** connect. **2** let in the clutch. **embrayage** *nm* **1** connecting. **2** *mot* clutch.

embrouiller (ãbruˈjeː) *vt* **1** tangle. **2** confuse, muddle.

embryon (ãˈbrjɔ̃) *nm* embryo.

embuscade (ãbyˈskad) *nf* ambush.

éméché (eːmeːˈʃeː) *adj* tipsy.

émeraude (ɛmˈrod) *adj,nf* emerald.

émerger (eːmɛrˈʒeː) *vi* emerge.

émerveiller (eːmɛrvɛˈjeː) *vt* amaze. **s'émerveiller de** *vr* marvel at.

émettre* (eːˈmɛtr) *vt* **1** emit. **2** utter. **3** broadcast. **4** issue. **émetteur** *nm* transmitter.

émeu (eːˈmœ) *nm* emu.

émeute (eːˈmœt) *nf* riot.

émietter (eːmjɛˈteː) *vt* crumble.

émigrer (eːmiːˈgreː) *vi* **1** emigrate. **2** migrate. **émigrant** *nm* emigrant. **émigré** *nm* refugee.

éminent (eːmiːˈnã) *adj* eminent.

émission (eːmiːˈsjɔ̃) *nf* **1** emission. **2** broadcast. **3** issue.

emmagasiner (ãmagaziːˈneː) *vt* **1** store. **2** store up.

emmancher (ãmãˈʃeː) *vt* **1** put a handle on. **2** fit together. **3** begin.

emmanchure (ãmãˈʃyr) *nf* armhole.

emmêler (ãmɛˈleː) *vt* entangle, mix up.

emménager (ãmeːnaˈʒeː) *vi* move into a new house.

emmener (ãmˈneː) *vt* take or lead away.

emmitoufler (ãmiːtuˈfleː) *vt* muffle up.

émoi (eːmwa) *nm* **1** emotion. **2** agitation.

émonder (eːmɔ̃ˈdeː) *vt* prune.

émotion (eːmoˈsjɔ̃) *nf* **1** emotion. **2** excitement.

émousser (eːmuˈseː) *vt* **1** blunt. **2** deaden.

émouvoir* (eːmuːˈvwar) *vt* **1** move, touch. **2** rouse. **émouvant** *adj* **1** moving. **2** stirring.

empailler (ăpa'je:) vt 1 pack in straw. 2 stuff.

empaqueter (ăpak'te:) vt pack up.

s'emparer (săpa're:) vr **s'emparer de** 1 seize. 2 take possession of.

empâter (ăpɑ'te:) vt 1 paste. 2 make sticky. 3 fatten.

empêcher (ăpe:'ʃe:) vt 1 prevent. 2 hinder. **n'empêche que** nevertheless. **s'empêcher de** vr refrain from.

empereur (ăp'rœr) nm emperor.

empeser (ăpə'ze:) vt starch.

empester (ăpɛ'ste:) vt 1 stink. 2 infect.

empêtrer (ăpɛ'tre:) vt entangle.

empiéter (ăpje:'te:) vi 1 encroach. 2 infringe.

empiffrer (ăpi:'fre:) vt inf stuff.

empiler (ăpi:'le:) vt stack.

empire (ă'pi:r) nm 1 empire. 2 dominion.

empirer (ăpi:'re:) vi worsen. vt make worse, aggravate.

empirique (ăpi:'ri:k) adj empirical.

emplacement (ăplas'mă) nm 1 site. 2 place.

emplâtre (ă'plɑtr) nm plaster.

emplette (ă'plɛt) nf purchase.

emplir (ă'pli:r) vt fill, fill up.

emploi (ă'plwa) nm 1 use. 2 employment.

employer (ăplwa'je:) vt 1 use. 2 employ. **s'employer** vr occupy oneself. **employé** nm clerk, employee. **employeur** nm employer.

empoigner (ăpwa'ɲe:) vt 1 grasp. 2 arrest. 3 grip.

empoisonner (ăpwazɔ'ne:) vt 1 poison. 2 infect. 3 corrupt. 4 bore.

emporter (ăpɔr'te:) vt carry, take away. **l'emporter sur** get the better of. **s'emporter** vr lose one's temper, get very annoyed. **emporté** adj quick-tempered, hot-tempered.

empourpré (ăpu:r'pre:) adj crimson.

empreindre (ă'prɛ̃dr) vt imprint, stamp.

empreinte (ă'prɛ̃t) nf impression, mark. **empreinte de pas** footprint. **empreinte digitale** fingerprint.

s'empresser (săprɛ'se:) vr hurry. **s'empresser à** be eager to. **empressé** adj eager, fervent.

emprisonner (ăpri:zɔ'ne:) vt put in prison.

emprunt (ă'prœ̃) nm loan.

emprunter (ăprœ̃'te:) vt 1 borrow. 2 assume.

ému (e:'my) adj moved, touched.

émulsion (e:myl'sjɔ̃) nf emulsion.

en[1] (ă) prep 1 in. 2 into. 3 to. 4 as. 5 while. 6 by. **en-tête** nm, pl **en-têtes** 1 heading. 2 headline.

en[2] (ă) adv 1 from there. 2 because of that. pron invar 1 of it or them. 2 about it or them. 3 some, any. 4 for that.

encadrer (ăka'dre:) vt frame. **encadrement** nm 1 frame. 2 framework.

encaisser (ăkɛ'se:) vt 1 pack in boxes. 2 collect. 3 cash. **encaisse** nf cash in hand.

enceinte[1] (ă'sɛ̃t) nf 1 surrounding wall. 2 sport ring.

enceinte[2] (ă'sɛ̃t) adj pregnant.

encens (ă'să) nm incense.

encercler (ăsɛr'kle:) vt encircle.

enchaîner (ăʃe'ne:) vt 1 chain up. 2 curb. 3 connect.

enchanter (ăʃă'te:) vt 1 enchant. 2 delight. **enchantement** nm 1 magic. 2 charm. 3 delight.

enchère (ă'ʃɛr) nf 1 bid. 2 auction.

enchérir (ăʃe:'ri:r) vi 1 go up in price. 2 make a higher bid. **enchérissement** nm increase, rise.

enchevêtrer (ăʃvɛ'tre:) vt 1 mix up, confuse. 2 entangle.

enclin (ă'klɛ̃) adj **enclin à** inclined or prone to.

enclore (ă'klɔr) vt enclose, fence in. **enclos** nm 1 enclosure. 2 paddock.

enclume (ă'klym) nf anvil.

encoche (ă'kɔʃ) nf notch.

encoignure (ăkɔ'ɲyr) nf corner.

encolure (ăkɔ'lyr) nf 1 neck. 2 neck size.

encombrer (ăkɔ̃'bre:) vt 1 encumber. 2 crowd. 3 litter. **encombrant** adj 1 cumbersome. 2 clumsy. **sans encombre** adv without a hitch. **encombrement** nm 1 obstruction. 2 litter.

encontre (ă'kɔ̃tr) **à l'encontre** adv to the contrary. **à l'encontre de** 1 against. 2 contrary to.

encore (ă'kɔr) adv 1 still. 2 yet. 3 again. 4 more.

encorner (ăkɔr'ne:) vt gore.

encourager (ăku:ra'ʒe:) vt encourage. **encouragement** nm encouragement.

encourir (ăku:'ri:r) vt 1 incur. 2 bring upon onself.

encrasser (ăkra'se:) vt 1 dirty, soil. 2 clog.

encre (ăkr) nf ink.

encroûter (ăkru:'te:) vt cake.

encyclopédie (ăsi:klɔpe:'di:) nf encyclopedia.

endémique (ăde:'mi:k) adj endemic.

s'endetter (sădɛ'te:) vr get into debt.

endiablé (ădja'ble:) adj 1 reckless. 2 wild.

s'endimancher (ădi:mă'ʃe:) vr dress in one's Sunday best.

endive (ă'di:v) nf endive.

endolori (ādɔlɔ'riː) adj 1 sore. 2 tender.

endommager (ādɔma'ʒe:) vt damage.

endormir* (ādɔr'miːr) vt 1 send to sleep. 2 deaden. **s'endormir** vr fall asleep. **endormi** adj asleep.

endosser (ādo'se:) vt 1 put on. 2 endorse.

endroit (ā'drwa) nm 1 place. 2 spot. 3 part. 4 right side.

enduire* (ā'dɥiːr) vt coat, smear. **enduit** nm layer, coat.

endurcir (ādyr'siːr) vt harden.

endurer (ādy're:) vt endure, bear.

énergie (enɛr'ʒi:) nf 1 energy, drive. 2 force. **énergie atomique** atomic energy.

énerver (enɛr've:) vt get on someone's nerves. **s'énerver** vr get irritable or excited.

enfance (ā'fās) nf 1 childhood. 2 infancy. 3 children. **enfant** nm,f 1 child. 2 infant. **d'enfant** adj childish. **enfant de chœur** choirboy. **enfantin** adj 1 childlike. 2 childish.

enfanter (āfā'te:) vt give birth to.

enfer (ā'fɛr) nm hell.

enfermer (āfɛr'me:) vt 1 shut up. 2 shut in. 3 surround.

enfiler (āfi:'le:) vt 1 thread. 2 string. 3 go along. 4 slip on. **enfilade** nf succession.

enfin (ā'fɛ̃) adv 1 finally. 2 in fact. 3 at last.

enflammer (āfla'me:) vt 1 inflame. 2 ignite. **s'enflammer** vr 1 catch fire. 2 become inflamed.

enfler (ā'fle:) vi,vt swell. vt puff out.

enfoncer (āfɔ̃'se:) vt 1 drive in. 2 break in. vi sink. **s'enfoncer** vr plunge, go deep.

enfouir (ā'fwiːr) vt 1 bury. 2 hide under the ground.

enfreindre* (ā'fɛ̃dr) vt infringe.

s'enfuir* (sā'fɥiːr) vr 1 flee. 2 run away. 3 elope. 4 leak.

engager (āga'ʒe:) vt 1 pledge. 2 engage. 3 begin. 4 urge. **s'engager** vr 1 undertake. 2 enlist. **engagement** nm engagement, commitment.

engelure (āʒ'lyr) nf chilblain.

engendrer (āʒā'dre:) vt 1 breed. 2 produce.

engin (ā'ʒɛ̃) nm 1 engine. 2 device. 3 missile. 4 pl tackle, equipment.

englober (āglɔ'be:) vt 1 include. 2 unite.

engloutir (āglu:'tiːr) vt 1 gulp down. 2 engulf.

engorger (āgɔr'ʒe:) vt block up.

engouffrer (āgu:'fre:) vt 1 engulf. 2 swallow up.

engourdir (āgu:r'diːr) vt 1 numb. 2 dull.

engrais (ā'grɛ) nm 1 manure. 2 fertilizer.

engraisser (āgrɛ'se:) vt 1 fatten. 2 manure.

engrenage (āgrɛ'naʒ) nm 1 gearing. 2 intricacy.

engueuler (āgœ'le:) vt sl 1 blow up, shout at. 2 abuse.

enhardir (āar'diːr) vt encourage. **s'enhardir** vr pluck up courage.

énigme (e:'niːgm) nf 1 enigma. 2 riddle.

enivrer (āni:'vre:) vt intoxicate. **s'enivrer** vr get drunk.

enjamber (āʒā'be:) vt step over.

enjeu, -eux (ā'ʒœ) nm game stake.

enjôler (āʒo'le:) vt coax.

enjoué (ā'ʒwe:) adj 1 lively. 2 cheerful.

enlaidir (āle:'diːr) vt disfigure. vi grow ugly.

enlever (āl've:) vt 1 remove. 2 carry or take off. 3 abduct. 4 kidnap. **s'enlever** vr 1 come off. 2 rise. **enlèvement** (ālɛv'mā) nm 1 removal. 2 kidnapping.

enliser (āli:'ze:) vt suck in. **s'enliser** vr get bogged down.

ennemi (ɛn'mi:) nm enemy, foe. adj hostile.

ennui (ā'nɥi:) nm 1 worry, anxiety. 2 boredom.

ennuyer (ānɥi:'je:) vt 1 worry. 2 annoy. 3 bore. **s'ennuyer** vr be bored. **ennuyant** adj annoying. **ennuyeux, -euse** (ānɥi:'jœ, -'œz) adj tedious, boring.

énoncer (e:nɔ̃'se:) vt 1 state. 2 enunciate.

s'enorgueillir (sānɔrgœ'jiːr) vr become proud.

énorme (e:'nɔrm) adj enormous, huge. **énormément** adj enormously, tremendously.

s'enquérir (sāke:'riːr) vr inquire.

enquête (ā'kɛt) nf 1 inquiry. 2 investigation. 3 inquest.

enraciné (ārasi:'ne:) adj deep-seated.

enrager (āra'ʒe:) vt 1 enrage. 2 excite. **enragé** adj 1 mad. 2 keen. nm fan.

enrayer (ārɛ'je:) vt 1 lock. 2 jam. 3 check.

enregistrer (ārɔʒi:'stre:) vt 1 register. 2 record.

s'enrhumer (āry'me:) vr catch a cold.

enrichir (āri:'ʃiːr) vt enrich.

enrôler (āro'le:) vt 1 enrol. 2 enlist.

enroué (ā'rwe:) adj 1 hoarse. 2 husky.

enseigne[1] (ā'sɛɲ) nf sign, mark.

enseigne[2] (ā'sɛɲ) nf mil ensign.

enseigner (āsɛ'ɲe:) vt teach. **enseignement** nm 1 teaching. 2 education.

ensemble (ā'sābl) adv together. nm 1 whole. 2 general effect. 3 set. **dans l'ensemble** on the whole.

ensemencer (āsmā'se:) vt sow.

ensevelir (āsə'vliːr) vt 1 bury. 2 shroud. **ensevelissement** nm burial.

ensoleillé (ãsɔlɛ'je:) *adj* sunny.
ensorceler (ãsɔrsə'le:) *vt* **1** put a spell on. **2** captivate.
ensuite (ã'sɥi:t) *adv* **1** then. **2** afterwards. **3** next.
s'ensuivre* (sã'sɥi:vr) *vr* follow.
entaille (ã'taj) *nf* **1** notch. **2** slash.
entamer (ãta'me:) *vt* **1** cut into. **2** start.
entasser (ãta'se:) *vt* **1** accumulate. **2** heap up. **3** pack.
entendre (ã'tãdr) *vt* **1** hear. **2** understand. **3** mean. **entendre parler de** hear of. **s'entendre** *vr* **1** agree. **2** understand one another. **entendu** *adj* **1** capable. **2** sensible. **3** agreed. **bien entendu** certainly, of course.
entente (ã'tãt) *nf* **1** understanding. **2** agreement.
enterrer (ãtɛ're:) *vt* bury. **enterrement** *nm* **1** burial. **2** funeral.
entêté (ãtɛ'te:) *adj* **1** obstinate. **2** headstrong.
enthousiasme (ãtu'zjasm) *nm* enthusiasm. **enthousiaste** *nm,f* enthusiast. *adj* enthusiastic.
s'enticher (sãti:'ʃe:) *vr* **s'enticher de** become infatuated with.
entier, -ière (ã'tje:, -'tjɛr) *adj* entire, whole. **en entier** in full.
entité (ãti:'te:) *nf* entity.
entonnoir (ãtɔ'nwar) *nm* funnel.
entorse (ã'tɔrs) *nf* **1** sprain. **2** twist.
entortiller (ãtɔrti:'je:) *vt* **1** twist. **2** wind. **3** get round. **s'entortiller** *vr* coil, twine.
entourer (ãtu:'re:) *vt* surround, encircle. **entourage** *nm* **1** setting. **2** circle of friends.
entracte (ã'trakt) *nm* **1** *Th* interval. **2** interlude.
entrailles (ã'traj) *nf pl* entrails.
entrain (ã'trɛ̃) *nm* spirit, vigour, zest.
entrainer (ãtrɛ'ne:) *vt* **1** drag away. **2** involve. **3** lead astray. **4** bring about. **5** train.
entraver (ãtra've:) *vt* **1** fetter. **2** hinder. **entrave** *nf* **1** fetter. **2** obstacle.
entre (ãtr) *prep* **1** between. **2** among. **entretemps** *adv* in the meantime. *nm* interval.
entrebâillé (ãtrɔbɑ'je:) *adj* ajar.
s'entrechoquer (sãtrəʃɔ'ke:) *vr* collide.
entrecôte (ãtrə'kot) *nf* rib steak.
entrecouper (ãtrəku:'pe:) *vt* **1** intersect. **2** interrupt.
s'entrecroiser (sãtrəkrwa'ze:) *vr* **1** cross each other. **2** intersect.
entrefaite (ãtrə'fɛt) *nf* interval. **sur ces entrefaites 1** at this moment. **2** meanwhile.
entrefilet (ãtrəfi:'lɛ) *nm* paragraph.
entregent (ãtrə'ʒã) *nm* tact.

entremets (ãtrə'mɛ) *nm* dessert, sweet.
s'entremettre* (sãtrə'mɛtr) *vr* intervene.
entrepôt (ãtrə'po) *nm* **1** warehouse. **2** store.
entreprendre* (ãtrə'prãdr) *vt* **1** undertake. **2** attempt. **3** contract for.
entrepreneur (ãtrəprə'nœr) *nm* contractor. **entrepreneur de pompes funèbres** undertaker.
entreprise (ãtrə'pri:z) *nf* **1** enterprise. **2** venture. **3** firm.
entrer (ã'tre:) *vi* (*aux* être) **1** enter. **2** begin. **faire entrer** show in. **entrée** *nf* **1** entrance. **2** entry. **3** admission. **4** beginning. **5** first course.
entretenir* (ãtrət'ni:r) *vt* **1** maintain, keep up. **2** support. **s'entretenir** *vr* converse. **entretien** *nm* **1** upkeep. **2** conversation. **3** interview.
entrevoir* (ãtrə'vwar) *vt* catch a glimpse of.
entrevue (ãtrə'vy) *nf* interview.
entrouvert (ãtru:'vɛr) *adj* ajar.
envahir (ãva'i:r) *vt* **1** invade. **2** overrun.
envelopper (ãvlɔ'pe:) *vt* **1** envelop. **2** wrap up. **3** cover. **4** shroud. **enveloppe** *nf* **1** cover. **2** envelope.
envenimer (ãvni:'me:) *vt* **1** poison. **2** embitter. **s'envenimer** *vr* fester.
envergure (ãvɛr'gyr) *nf* span, spread.
envers[1] (ã'vɛr) *prep* **1** towards. **2** to.
envers[2] (ã'vɛr) *nm* **1** wrong side. **2** reverse. **à l'envers 1** inside out. **2** upside down.
envier (ã'vje:) *vt* **1** envy. **2** begrudge. **envie** *nf* **1** desire. **2** envy. **3** birthmark. **avoir envie de** feel like, fancy.
environ (ãvi:'rɔ̃) *adv* about. **environs** *nm pl* **1** outskirts. **2** neighbourhood.
environnement (ãvi:rɔn'mã) *nm* environment.
envisager (ãviza'ʒe:) *vt* **1** envisage. **2** consider. **3** anticipate.
envoi (ã'vwa) *nm* **1** dispatch, sending. **2** parcel.
s'envoler (sãvɔ'le:) *vr* **1** fly away. **2** take off.
envoyer* (ãvwa'je:) *vt* **1** send. **2** dispatch. **envoyer chercher** send for. **envoyer en chandelle** *lob.* **envoyé** *nm* **1** messenger. **2** envoy. **envoyé spécial** correspondent.
enzyme (ã'zi:m) *nf* enzyme.
épagneul (e:pa'nœl) *nm* spaniel.
épais, -aisse (e:'pɛ, -'pɛs) *adj* **1** thick. **2** dense. **épaisseur** *nf* **1** thickness. **2** density.
épaissir (e:pɛ'si:r) *vt* thicken.
épancher (e:pã'ʃe:) *vt* pour out.
épandre (e:'pãdr) *vt* spread.
s'épanouir (e:pa'nwi:r) *vr* **1** open out. **2** bloom. **3** beam. **épanoui** *adj* in full bloom.

épargner (e:parˈɲeˑ) vt 1 save. 2 economize. 3 spare. **épargne** nf 1 saving. 2 economy.

éparpiller (e:parpiˈjeˑ) vt 1 scatter. 2 disperse.

épars (eˈpar) adj 1 scattered. 2 stray.

épater (e:paˈteˑ) vt stagger, amaze.

épaule (eˈpol) nf shoulder. **épaulette** nf epaulet.

épave (eˈpav) nf 1 wreck. 2 waif. 3 debris.

épée (eˈpeˑ) nf sword.

épeler (eˈpleˑ) vt spell.

éperdu (e:perˈdy) adj 1 distracted, distraught. 2 wild, mad. 3 desperate.

éperon (eˈprɔ̃) nm spur.

éphémère (e:feˈmɛr) adj ephemeral.

épi (eˈpiˑ) nm 1 ear (of corn). 2 cluster.

épice (eˈpiːs) nf spice. **épicerie** nf grocer's shop. **épicier** nm grocer.

épicrâne (e:piˈkrɑn) nm scalp.

épidémie (e:pɪːdeˈmiˑ) nf epidemic.

épier (eˈpjeˑ) vt 1 spy. 2 watch for.

épilepsie (e:pɪːlɛpˈsiˑ) nf epilepsy. **épileptique** adj epileptic.

épilogue (e:pɪːˈlɔg) nm epilogue.

épiloir (e:pɪːˈlwar) nm tweezers.

épinards (e:pɪːˈnar) nm pl spinach.

épine (eˈpiːn) nf thorn. **épine dorsale** spine.

épingler (e:pɛ̃ˈgleˑ) vt pin. **épingle** nf pin. **épingle à cheveux** hairgrip. **épingle de nourrice** or **sûreté** safety pin.

Epiphanie (e:pifaˈniˑ) nf Epiphany.

épique (eˈpiːk) adj epic.

épiscopal, -aux (e:pɪːskɔˈpal, -ˈpo) adj episcopal.

épisode (e:pɪːˈzɔd) nm episode.

épitaphe (e:pɪːˈtaf) nf epitaph.

épitomé (e:pɪːtɔˈmeˑ) nm epitome.

éploré (e:plɔˈreˑ) adj in tears, weeping.

éplucher (e:plyˈʃeˑ) vt 1 clean. 2 peel. 3 examine.

éponger (e:pɔ̃ˈʒeˑ) vt 1 sponge. 2 mop. **éponge** nf sponge.

épopée (e:pɔˈpeˑ) nf epic.

époque (eˈpɔk) nf 1 epoch, age. 2 time, period.

épouser (e:puˈzeˑ) vt marry. **épousée** nf bride.

épousseter (e:puˈsteˑ) vt dust, clean.

épouvanter (e:puːvɑ̃ˈteˑ) vt terrify. **épouvantable** adj dreadful, frightful. **épouvantail** nm scarecrow. **épouvante** nf terror, dread.

époux, -ouse (eˈpuː, -ˈpuːz) nm,f husband, wife.

s'éprendre (seˈprɑ̃dr) vr **s'éprendre de** fall in love with.

épreuve (eˈprœv) nf 1 test. 2 trial. 3 proof. 4 print.

éprouver (e:pruˈveˑ) vt 1 try, test. 2 experience, suffer. **éprouvette** nf test tube.

épuiser (e:pɥiˈzeˑ) vt 1 exhaust. 2 empty. 3 use up. **épuisé** adj 1 exhausted. 2 worn out.

épurer (e:pyˈreˑ) vt 1 purify. 2 refine.

équateur (e:kwaˈtœr) nm 1 equator. 2 cap Ecuador. **équatorial, -aux** (e:kwatɔˈrjal, -ˈrjo) adj equatorial.

équation (e:kwaˈsjɔ̃) nf equation.

équerre (eˈkɛr) nf 1 square. 2 right angle.

équestre (eˈkɛstr) adj equestrian.

équilatéral, -aux (e:kɥiːlateˈral, -ˈro) adj equilateral.

équilibrer (e:kɪːliːˈbreˑ) vt balance. **équilibre** nm 1 balance. 2 equilibrium.

équinoxe (e:kɪːˈnɔks) nm equinox.

équiper (e:kiːˈpeˑ) vt 1 equip. 2 fit out. **équipage** nm 1 crew. 2 equipment. **équipe** nf 1 gang. 2 sport team, side.

équitable (e:kiːˈtabl) adj fair, just.

équitation (e:kɪːtaˈsjɔ̃) nf riding.

équité (e:kiːˈteˑ) nf equity.

équivaloir* (e:kiːvaˈlwar) vi be equivalent or equal. **équivalent** adj,nm equivalent.

équivoque (e:kɪːˈvɔk) adj 1 ambiguous. 2 dubious.

érable (ɛˈrabl) nm maple tree.

érafler (e:rɑˈfleˑ) vt 1 graze. 2 scratch. **éraflure** nf graze.

éraillé (e:ˈraj) adj 1 frayed. 2 scratched. 3 raucous.

ère (ɛr) nf 1 era. 2 epoch.

éreinter (e:rɛ̃ˈteˑ) vt inf 1 exhaust. 2 smash. 3 inf slate, severely criticize. **s'éreinter** vr tire oneself out. **s'éreinter à** slave at.

ériger (e:rɪːˈʒeˑ) vt 1 erect. 2 set up.

ermite (ɛrˈmiːt) nm hermit.

éroder (e:rɔˈdeˑ) vt 1 erode. 2 eat away.

érotique (e:rɔˈtiːk) adj erotic.

errer (ɛˈreˑ) vi 1 wander, roam. 2 stray. 3 err. **erreur** nf 1 error. 2 mistake. 3 fallacy.

éruption (e:rypˈsjɔ̃) nf 1 eruption. 2 med rash.

es (ɛ) v see **être**.

ès (ɛs) prep contraction of **en les. licencié ès lettres/sciences** Bachelor of Arts/Science.

escabeau, -aux (ɛskaˈbo) nm 1 stool. 2 stepladder.

escadre (ɛsˈkadr) nf naut squadron. **escadrille** nf aviat squadron. **escadron** nm mil troop.

escale (ɛsˈkal) nf 1 port of call. 2 stop.

escalier (ɛskaˈljeˑ) nm 1 staircase. 2 stairs.

escalope

escalier roulant escalator. **escalier tournant** spiral staircase.
escalope (ɛska'lɔp) nf escalope.
escamoter (ɛskamɔ'te:) vt 1 make disappear. 2 inf swipe. **escamoteur** nm conjuror.
escarbilles (ɛskar'bi:j) nf pl ashes, cinders.
escargot (ɛskar'go) nm snail.
escarmouche (ɛskar'mu:ʃ) nf skirmish.
escarpé (ɛskar'pe:) adj steep, sheer.
escarpolette (ɛskarpɔ'lɛt) nf swing.
escient (ɛ'sjã) nm knowledge. **à bon escient** deliberately.
esclandre (ɛs'klãdr) nm scandal.
esclave (ɛ'sklav) nm,f slave.
escompter (ɛskɔ̃'te:) vt 1 discount. 2 inf anticipate. **escompte** nm 1 discount. 2 rebate.
escorte (ɛ'skɔrt) nf 1 escort. 2 naut convoy.
escrime (ɛ'skri:m) nf fencing. **faire de l'escrime** fence.
escroc (ɛ'skro) nm crook, swindler.
escroquer (ɛskrɔ'ke:) vt 1 cheat. 2 swindle. **escroquerie** nf swindle.
espace (ɛ'spas) nm space.
espadon (ɛspa'dɔ̃) nm swordfish.
Espagne (ɛ'spaɲ) nf Spain. **espagnol** adj Spanish. nm 1 Spaniard. 2 Spanish (language).
espèce (ɛ'spɛs) nf 1 kind, sort. 2 species.
espérer (ɛspe're:) vt 1 hope. 2 trust. **espérance** nf 1 hope. 2 expectation.
espiègle (ɛ'spjɛgl) adj mischievous.
espion, -onne (ɛ'spjɔ̃, -'spjɔn) nm,f spy.
espionner (ɛspjɔ'ne:) vt spy on. **espionnage** nm espionage.
esplanade (ɛspla'nad) nf esplanade, promenade.
espoir (ɛ'spwar) nm hope.
esprit (ɛ'spri:) nm 1 spirit. 2 ghost. 3 soul. 4 mind. 5 wit. **à l'esprit étroit/large** narrow/broad-minded. **faible d'esprit** weak-minded.
esquimau, -aude, -aux (ɛski:'mo, -'mod, -'mo) adj,n Eskimo.
esquisser (ɛski:'se:) vt 1 sketch. 2 outline. **esquisse** nf 1 sketch. 2 outline. 3 draft.
esquiver (ɛski:'ve:) vt dodge, evade. **s'esquiver** vr slip off.
essai (ɛ'sɛ) nm 1 trial, test. 2 attempt. 3 essay. 4 sport try. **à l'essai** on approval or trial.
essaim (ɛ'sɛ̃) nm swarm.
essaimer (e:sɛ'me:) vi swarm.
essayer (e:sɛ'je:) vt 1 try, test. 2 try on.
essence (ɛ'sãs) nf 1 essence. 2 petrol. 3 extract.

essentiel, -elle (ɛsã'sjɛl) adj essential. nm main point.
essieu, -ieux (e:'sjœ) nm axle.
essor (ɛ'sɔr) nm 1 flight. 2 scope. 3 rise.
essorer (e:sɔ're:) vt wring out. **essoreuse** nf 1 spin-dryer. 2 mangle.
essoufflé (e:su:'fle:) adj out of breath.
essuyer (e:sɥi:'je:) vt 1 wipe. 2 dry. 3 suffer. **essuie-glace** nm, pl **essuie-glaces** windscreen wiper. **essuie-main** nm invar also **essuie-mains** towel. **essuie-pieds** nm invar doormat.
est¹ (ɛst) nm east. adj invar east, eastern. **à l'est** in the east. **d'est** easterly. **vers l'est** eastward, eastwards.
est² (ɛ) v see **être**.
estaminet (ɛstami:'nɛ) nm public house.
estamper (ɛstã'pe:) vt 1 print, engrave. 2 stamp.
estampille (ɛstã'pi:j) nf 1 official stamp. 2 trademark.
esthétique (ɛste:'ti:k) adj aesthetic. nf aesthetics.
estimer (ɛsti:'me:) vt 1 estimate. 2 consider. 3 esteem. **estime** nf esteem.
estivant (ɛsti:'vã) nm holiday-maker.
estomac (ɛstɔ'ma) nm stomach.
estomper (ɛstɔ̃'pe:) vt blur.
estrade (ɛ'strad) nf platform, stage.
estragon (ɛstra'gɔ̃) nm tarragon.
estropier (ɛstrɔ'pje:) vt 1 cripple. 2 maim. 3 ruin.
estuaire (ɛs'tɥɛr) nm estuary.
esturgeon (ɛstyr'ʒɔ̃) nm sturgeon.
et (e:) conj and. **et...et** both...and.
établir (e:ta'bli:r) vt 1 establish. 2 set up. 3 draw up. 4 lay down. **s'établir** vr establish oneself, settle. **établissement** nm 1 establishment. 2 institution.
étage (e:'taʒ) nm floor, storey. **étagère** nf 1 shelf. 2 set of shelves.
étai (e:'tɛ) nm stay, prop.
étain (e:'tɛ̃) nm 1 tin. 2 pewter.
étais (e:'tɛ) v see **être**.
étaler (e:ta'le:) vt 1 display. 2 set out. 3 spread out. 4 inf show off. **s'étaler** vr stretch oneself out. **étalage** nm 1 display. 2 window-dressing. **faire étalage de** show off.
étalon¹ (e:ta'lɔ̃) nm stallion.
étalon² (e:ta'lɔ̃) nm standard.
étancher (e:tã'ʃe:) vt 1 stop, staunch. 2 quench. 3 make watertight or airtight. **étanche** adj 1 watertight. 2 airtight.

56

étang (e:'tã) *nm* pond.
étant (e:'tã) *v* see **être.**
étape (e:'tap) *nf* 1 stage. 2 halt.
état (e:'ta) *nm* 1 state. 2 condition. 3 statement.
4 profession. **faire état de** 1 take into account. 2 depend on. **étatisme** *nm* state control. **état-major** *nm, pl* **états-major** 1 *mil* staff. 2 management.
Etats-Unis *nm pl* United States of America.
étayer (e:tɛ'je:) *vt* 1 prop up. 2 support.
été[1] (e:'te:) *nm* summer.
été[2] (e:'te:) *v* see **être.**
éteindre* (e:'tɛ̃dr) *vi* 1 extinguish, put out. 2 turn off. 3 soften. **s'éteindre** *vr* die out. **éteint** *adj* 1 extinguished. 2 extinct. 3 dim.
étendard (e:tã'dar) *nm* standard, flag.
étendre (e:'tãdr) *vt* 1 stretch. 2 spread. 3 extend, enlarge. **s'étendre** *vr* 1 stretch oneself out. 2 spread. **étendu** *adj* 1 extensive. 2 wide. 3 far-reaching. **étendue** *nf* 1 extent. 2 expanse.
éternel, -elle (e:tɛr'nɛl) *adj* 1 eternal. 2 everlasting.
éternité (e:tɛrni:'te:) *nf* eternity.
éternuer (e:tɛr'nɥe:) *vi* sneeze. **éternuement** *nm* 1 sneeze. 2 sneezing.
êtes (ɛt) *v* see **être.**
éther (e:'tɛr) *nm* ether. **éthéré** *adj* ethereal.
Ethiopie (e:tjɔ'pi:) *nf* Ethiopia. **éthiopien, -ienne** (e:tjɔ'pjɛ̃, -'pjɛn) *adj,n* Ethiopian.
éthique (e:'ti:k) *adj* ethical. *nf* ethics.
ethnique (ɛt'ni:k) *adj* ethnic.
étinceler (e:tɛ̃'sle:) *vi* 1 sparkle. 2 glitter. **étincelle** *nf* spark.
étiquette (e:ti:'kɛt) *nf* 1 label. 2 tag. 3 etiquette. 4 ceremony.
étirer (e:ti:'re:) *vt* 1 stretch. 2 draw out.
étoffe (e:'tɔf) *nf* 1 material, fabric. 2 stuff, potential.
étoile (e:'twal) *nf* 1 star. 2 decoration. 3 fate. **étoile polaire** Pole Star.
étole (e:'tɔl) *nf* stole.
étonner (e:tɔ'ne:) *vt* astonish, amaze. **s'étonner** *vr* 1 be astonished. 2 wonder.
étouffer (e:tu:'fe:) *vi,vt* 1 suffocate. 2 choke. *vt* 1 stifle. 2 smother. 3 hush up. **étouffant** *adj* 1 stifling. 2 stuffy. 3 sultry. **cuire à l'étouffée** braise.
étourdir (e:tu:r'di:r) *vt* 1 stun. 2 daze. 3 make dizzy. 4 deafen. **étourderie** *nf* 1 thoughtlessness. 2 blunder. **étourdi** *adj* 1 giddy. 2 thoughtless. 3 light-headed. **à l'étourdie** thoughtlessly.

étourneau, -aux (e:tu:r'no) *nm* starling.
étrange (e:'trãʒ) *adj* 1 strange. 2 odd. 3 peculiar. 4 weird. **étranger, -ère** (e:trã'ʒe:, -'ʒɛr) *adj* 1 foreign. 2 unfamiliar. 3 irrelevant. *nm,f* 1 stranger. 2 foreigner. **à l'étranger** abroad.
étrangler (e:trãgle:) *vt* 1 strangle. 2 throttle. 3 choke. **étranglé** *adj* 1 choked. 2 narrow.
étrave (e:'trav) *nf naut* bow.
être* (ɛtr) *vi* 1 be. 2 exist. *v aux* be. **être à** 1 belong to. 2 be in or at. **~nm** 1 existence. 2 being. 3 individual. **être humain** human being.
étreindre* (e:'trɛ̃dr) *vt* 1 embrace. 2 grasp. 3 clasp. 4 wring. **étreinte** *nf* 1 grasp. 2 hug.
étrenne (e:'trɛn) *nf* New Year's present.
étrier (e:tri:'e:) *nm* stirrup.
étriqué (e:tri:'ke:) *adj* tight.
étroit (e:'trwa) *adj* 1 narrow. 2 tight. 3 confined. 4 strict. **étroitesse** *nf* 1 narrowness. 2 tightness.
étude (e:'tyd) *nf* 1 study. 2 research. 3 chambers.
étudier (e:ty'dje:) *vt* 1 study. 2 investigate. **s'étudier à** *vr* endeavour to. **étudiant** *nm* 1 student. 2 undergraduate.
étui (e:'tɥi:) *nm* case, box.
étuver (e:ty've:) *vt* 1 dry. 2 heat. 3 steam.
étymologie (e:ti:mɔlɔ'ʒi:) *nf* etymology.
eu (y) *v* see **avoir.**
eucalyptus (œkali:p'tys) *nm* eucalyptus.
eucharistie (œkari:'sti:) *nf* Eucharist.
eunuque (œ'nyk) *nm* eunuch.
euphémisme (œfe:'mi:sm) *nm* euphemism.
euphorie (œfɔ'ri:) *nf* euphoria.
Europe (œ'rɔp) *nf* Europe. **européen, -enne** (œrɔpe:'ɛ̃, -'ɛn) *adj,n* European.
eus (y) *v* see **avoir.**
euthanasie (œtana'zi:) *nf* euthanasia.
eux (œ) *pron 3rd pers m pl* 1 they. 2 them. **eux-mêmes** *pron 3rd pers m pl* themselves.
évacuer (e:va'kɥe:) *vt* 1 evacuate. 2 empty. 3 vacate.
s'évader (se:va'de:) *vr* escape.
évaluer (e:va'lɥe:) *vt* 1 value. 2 assess. 3 estimate.
évangélique (e:vãʒe:'li:k) *adj* 1 Evangelical. 2 Protestant. **évangéliste** *nm* Evangelist.
évangile (e:vã'ʒi:l) *nm* gospel.
s'évanouir (se:va'nwi:r) *vr* 1 vanish. 2 faint. **évanouissement** *nm* 1 disappearance. 2 faint.
évaporer (e:vapɔ're:) *vt* evaporate.
évasion (e:va'zjɔ̃) *nf* escape.

éveil

éveil (e:'vɛj) nm 1 awakening. 2 alert. 3 alarm.
éveiller (e:vɛ'je:) vt 1 wake up, waken. 2 arouse. s'éveiller vr awake, wake up.
événement (e:vɛn'mã) nm 1 event. 2 incident. 3 outcome.
éventail (e:vã'taj) nm fan.
éventer (e:vã'te:) vt 1 air. 2 fan. 3 get wind of. s'éventer vr 1 spoil. 2 go flat or stale. éventé adj stale, flat.
éventrer (e:vã'tre:) vt 1 gut. 2 rip open.
éventuel, -elle (e:vã'tцɛl) adj 1 possible. 2 eventual. éventualité nf contingency.
évêque (e:'vɛk) nm bishop.
s'évertuer (se:vɛr'tцe:) vr do one's utmost.
évidence (e:vi:'dãs) nf 1 obviousness. 2 evidence. évidemment (e:vi:da'mã) adv evidently. évident adj evident, clear.
évider (e:vi:'de:) vt hollow out.
évier (e:'vje:) nm sink.
évincer (e:vɛ̃'se:) vt evict.
éviter (e:vi:'te:) vt 1 avoid. 2 shun.
évoluer (e:vɔ'lцe:) vi 1 manoeuvre. 2 evolve.
évoquer (e:vɔ'ke:) vt 1 evoke. 2 conjure up.
exact (ɛg'zakt) adj 1 exact. 2 accurate. 3 true. 4 punctual. 5 strict.
exagérer (ɛgzaʒe:'re:) vt exaggerate. exagération nf exaggeration.
exalter (ɛgzal'te:) vt 1 exalt. 2 excite.
examen (ɛgza'mɛ̃) nm 1 examination. 2 inspection.
examiner (ɛgzami:'ne:) vt 1 examine. 2 inspect.
exaspérer (ɛgzaspe:'re:) vt 1 aggravate. 2 exasperate.
exaucer (ɛgzo'se:) vt 1 grant. 2 hear. 3 fulfil.
excaver (ɛkska've:) vt excavate.
excédant (ɛkse:'dã) adj surplus, excess.
excellent (ɛksɛ'lã) adj excellent. excellence nf 1 excellence. 2 cap Excellency.
exceller (ɛksɛ'le:) vi excel.
excentrique (ɛksã'tri:k) adj eccentric.
excepter (ɛksɛp'te:) vt exclude. excepté prep except, save, but. exception nf exception. exceptionnel, -elle (e:ksɛpsjɔ'nɛl) adj exceptional.
excès (e:k'sɛ) nm excess. excessif, -ive (e:ksɛ'si:f, -'si:v) adj excessive.
exciter (e:ksi:'te:) vt 1 excite. 2 arouse. 3 animate. 4 inflame. s'exciter vr get excited.
s'exclamer (sɛkskla'me:) vr exclaim. exclamation nf exclamation.
exclure* (ɛks'klyr) vt exclude. exclusif, -ive (ɛkskly'si:f, -'si:v) adj 1 exclusive. 2 sole.

58

excommunier (ɛkskɔmy'nje:) vt excommunicate.
excursion (ɛkskyr'zjɔ̃) nf 1 excursion. 2 tour. 3 trip.
excuser (ɛksky ze:) vt 1 excuse. 2 pardon. s'excuser vr apologize. excuse nf 1 excuse. 2 pl apology.
exécrer (e:gze:'kre:) vt loathe. exécrable (e:gzɛ'krabl) adj abominable.
exécuter (e:gze:ky'te:) vt 1 execute. 2 carry out. 3 perform. exécutif, -ive (e:gze:ky'ti:f, -'ti:v) adj executive.
exemple (e:g'zãpl) nm 1 example. 2 lesson. 3 precedent. par exemple 1 for instance. 2 indeed. exemplaire nm 1 copy. 2 sample.
exempt (e:g'zã) adj exempt, free.
exempter (e:gzã'te:) vt exempt.
exercer (e:gzɛr'se:) vt 1 exercise. 2 train. 3 exert. 4 practise, pursue.
exercice (e:gzɛr'si:s) nm 1 exercise. 2 mil drill. 3 use. 4 practice.
exhaler (e:gza'le:) vt 1 exhale. 2 emit. 3 vent.
exhiber (e:gzi:'be:) vt 1 show. 2 exhibit. exhibition nf exhibition, display.
exiger (egzi:'ʒe:) vt 1 exact. 2 demand. 3 require.
exigu, -uë (e:gzi:'gy) adj 1 tiny. 2 slender.
exil (e:g'zi:l) nm exile.
exiler (e:gzi:'le:) vt 1 exile. 2 banish.
existentialisme (e:gzi:stãsja'li:sm) nm existentialism.
exister (e:gzi:'ste:) vi 1 exist. 2 live.
exorbitant (ɛgzɔrbi:'tã) adj 1 exorbitant. 2 outrageous.
exorciser (ɛgzɔrsi:'ze:) vt exorcize.
exotique (ɛgzɔ'ti:k) adj exotic.
expatrier (ɛkspatri:'e:) vt expatriate. expatrié adj,n expatriate.
expédier (ɛkspe:'dje:) vt 1 dispatch. 2 hurry through. 3 send off. expédient adj,nm expedient. expéditeur nm sender. expédition nf 1 expedition. 2 copy. 3 forwarding. 4 consignment.
expérience (ɛkspe:'rjãs) nf 1 experience. 2 experiment. 3 test.
expérimenter (ɛkspe:ri:mã'te:) vt 1 test. 2 try. vi experiment. expérimenté adj experienced. 2 skilled.
expert (ɛk'spɛr) adj 1 skilled. 2 expert. nm expert.
expier (ɛk'spje:) vt atone for.
expirer (ɛkspi:'re:) vt breathe out. vi 1 die. 2 expire.

explétif, -ive (ɛksple:'tı:f, -'tı:v) *adj,nm* expletive.

explication (ɛkspli:ka'sjɔ̃) *nf* explanation.

explicite (ɛkspli'sı:t) *adj* 1 explicit. 2 clear.

expliquer (ɛkspli'ke:) *vt* 1 explain. 2 account for.

exploit (ɛk'splwa) *nm* 1 exploit. 2 feat. 3 writ.

exploiter (ɛksplwa'te:) *vt* 1 exploit. 2 cultivate. 3 take advantage of.

explorer (ɛksplɔ're:) *vt* explore. **explorateur** *nm* explorer.

exploser (ɛksplo'ze:) *vi* explode. **explosif, -ive** (ɛksplo'sı:f, -'sı:v) *adj,nm* explosive.

exporter (ɛkspɔr'te:) *vt* export. **exportation** *nf* export.

exposer (ɛkspo'ze:) *vt* 1 show. 2 exhibit. 3 explain. 4 expose. **exposé** *nm* 1 account. 2 short talk. **exposition** *nf* 1 exhibition. 2 exposure.

exprès, -esse (ɛk'sprɛ, -'sprɛs) *adj* 1 express. 2 explicit. **exprès** *adv* on purpose.

express (ɛk'sprɛs) *nm* express train.

expression (ɛksprɛ'sjɔ̃) *nf* expression.

exprimer (ɛksprı'me:) *vt* 1 express. 2 squeeze out.

expulser (ɛkspyl'se:) *vt* 1 expel. 2 turn out.

exquis (ɛk'skı:) *adj* exquisite.

extase (ɛk'stɑz) *nf* ecstasy.

extension (ɛkstɑ̃'sjɔ̃) *nf* 1 extension. 2 spread. 3 extent.

exténuer (ɛkste'nɥe:) *vt* exhaust.

extérieur (ɛkste:'rjœr) *adj* 1 exterior. 2 outer. 3 foreign. *nm* 1 exterior. 2 outside. **à l'extérieur** 1 outside. 2 abroad.

exterminer (ɛkstɛrmı:'ne:) *vt* exterminate.

externe (ɛk'stɛrn) *adj* external. *nm* 1 day pupil. 2 outpatient. **externat** *nm* day school.

extirper (ɛkstı:r'pe:) *vt* 1 uproot. 2 eradicate.

extra (ɛk'stra) *nm* invar extra. *adj* invar inf first-class, excellent.

extraire* (ɛk'strɛr) *vt* 1 extract. 2 pull out. **extrait** *nm* 1 extract. 2 excerpt. 3 certificate.

extraordinaire (ɛkstrɔrdi:'nɛr) *adj* 1 extraordinary. 2 unusual.

extravagant (ɛkstrava'gɑ̃) *adj* 1 extravagant. 2 foolish. 3 exorbitant.

extraverti (ɛkstravɛr'tı:) *adj,n* extrovert.

extrême (ɛk'strɛm) *adj* 1 extreme. 2 farthest. 3 utmost. 4 intense. *nm* extreme limit. **extrémité** *nf* 1 extremity. 2 end. 3 tip. 4 limit.

Extrême-Orient *nm* Far East.

exubérant (egzybɛ'rɑ̃) *adj* exuberant.

F

fable (fabl) *nf* 1 fable. 2 story.

fabricant (fabrı:'kɑ̃) *nm* manufacturer.

fabriquer (fabrı:'ke:) *vt* 1 manufacture. 2 make. **fabriquer en série** mass-produce. **fabrique** *nf* 1 manufacture. 2 factory.

fabuleux, -euse (faby'lœ, -'lœz) *adj* fabulous.

façade (fa'sad) *nf* 1 facade. 2 front.

face (fas) *nf* 1 face. 2 front. 3 aspect. **en face** opposite. **face à** facing.

facétie (fase:'sı:) *nf* joke. **facétieux, -euse** (fase:'sjœ, -'sjœz) *adj* facetious.

fâcher (fɑ'ʃe:) *vt* make angry. **se fâcher** *vr* get angry. **fâché** *adj* 1 angry, cross. 2 sorry. **fâcheux, -euse** (fɑ'ʃœ, -'ʃœz) *adj* 1 annoying. 2 unfortunate.

facile (fa'sı:l) *adj* 1 easy. 2 facile, ready. 3 weak.

faciliter (fası:li:'te:) *vt* facilitate. **facilité** *nf* 1 easiness. 2 gift, talent. 3 facility.

façon (fa'sɔ̃) *nf* 1 manner. 2 way. 3 making. 4 make. 5 *pl* fuss. **à façon** made to measure. **de façon à** so as to. **de toute façon** anyway, in any case.

façonner (fasɔ'ne:) *vt* 1 shape. 2 fashion. 3 mould.

fac-similé (faksı:mı:'le:) *nm*, *pl* **fac-similés** facsimile.

facteur (fak'tœr) *nm* 1 postman. 2 factor. 3 agent.

factice (fak'tı:s) *adj* 1 artificial. 2 imitation. 3 dummy.

faction (fak'sjɔ̃) *nf* 1 faction. 2 guard.

facture (fak'tyr) *nf* invoice.

facultatif, -ive (fakylta:'tı:f, -'tı:v) *adj* optional.

faculté (fakyl'te:) *nf* 1 option. 2 right. 3 ability. 4 faculty. 5 *pl* resources.

fadaise (fa'dɛz) *nf* 1 silly remark. 2 *pl* nonsense.

fade (fad) *adj* 1 dull. 2 tasteless.

fagot (fa'go) *nm* bundle.

fagoter (fagɔ'te:) *vt* dress without taste.

faiblir (fɛ'bli:r) *vi* 1 grow weaker. 2 fail. **faible** (fɛbl) *adj* 1 weak. 2 feeble. *nm* failing. **faiblesse** *nf* 1 weakness. 2 failing.

faïence (fa'jɑ̃s) *nf* 1 crockery. 2 earthenware.

faillible (fa'ji:bl) *adj* fallible.

faillir* (fa'ji:r) *vi* fail. **faillir tomber** nearly fall. **failli** *adj,n* bankrupt. **faillite** *nf* bankruptcy. **faire faillite** go bankrupt.

faim (fɛ̃) *nf* hunger. **avoir faim** be hungry.

fainéant (fɛne:'ã) *adj* idle, lazy.
faire* (fɛr) *vt* 1 make. 2 do. 3 matter. 4 be. 5 arrange. 6 cause. 7 *sport* go in for. **ça ne fait rien** that doesn't matter. **faire faire** have made or done. **faire voir** show. **faites attention!** be careful! **il n'y a rien à faire** nothing can be done about it. **que faire?** what is to be done? **se faire** *vr* 1 develop. 2 become. 3 accustom oneself. 4 be. **se faire fort de** undertake to. **faire-part** *nm invar* announcement.
faisable (fə'zabl) *adj* feasible.
faisan (fɛ'zã) *nm* pheasant.
faisant (fɛ'zã) *v* see **faire.**
faisceau, -aux (fɛ'so) *nm* bundle.
fait[1] (fɛ) *v* see **faire.** *adj* 1 done. 2 made. 3 fully grown. 4 ripe.
fait[2] (fɛ) *nm* 1 act. 2 deed. 3 fact. 4 exploit. 5 incident. **au fait** after all. **de** or **en fait** actually, in actual fact. **de son fait** of one's own accord. **fait-divers** *nm* news item.
faîte (fɛt) *nm* 1 top, summit. 2 ridge.
faix (fɛ) *nm* 1 burden. 2 load.
falaise (fa'lɛz) *nf* cliff.
falloir* (fa'lwar) *v imp* 1 need. 2 be necessary. 3 must. **comme il faut** 1 proper. 2 properly. **s'en falloir** *vr* 1 be lacking. 2 be far from.
falsifier (falsi'fje:) *vt* 1 falsify. 2 forge.
famé (fa'me:) *adj* **bien/mal famé** of good/evil repute.
fameux, -euse (fa'mœ, -'mœz) *adj* 1 famous. 2 *inf* great, excellent.
familial, -aux (fami:'ljal, -'ljo) *adj* family.
familier, -ière (fami:'lje:, -'ljɛr) *adj* 1 domestic. 2 of the family. 3 familiar.
famille (fa'mi:j) *nf* 1 family. 2 household. 3 relations. **en famille** informally.
famine (fa'mi:n) *nf* famine.
fanal, -aux (fa'nal, -'no) *nm* lantern.
fanatique (fana'ti:k) *adj* fanatical. *nm,f* fanatic.
faner (fa'ne:) *vt* 1 make hay. 2 cause to fade. **se faner** *vr* 1 droop. 2 wilt. 3 fade.
fanfare (fã'far) *nf* 1 *mus* flourish. 2 brass band.
fange (fãʒ) *nf* 1 mud. 2 filth.
fantaisie (fãtɛ'zi:) *nf* 1 imagination. 2 fantasy. 3 fancy. 4 whim.
fantasmagorique (fãtasmago'ri:k) *adj* 1 weird. 2 fantastic.
fantastique (fãta'sti:k) *adj* 1 fantastic. 2 *inf* incredible.
fantoche (fã'tɔʃ) *nm* puppet.
fantôme (fã'tom) *nm* 1 ghost. 2 phantom.
faon (fã) *nm zool* fawn.

farce (fars) *nf* 1 farce. 2 prank.
farcir (far'si:r) *vt cul* stuff.
fard (far) *nm* 1 make-up. 2 rouge. 3 disguise.
fardeau, -aux (far'do) *nm* burden.
farder (far'de:) *vt* 1 make up. 2 disguise.
farfouiller (farfu:'je:) *vi* rummage.
farine (fa'ri:n) *nf* 1 flour. 2 meal. **farine d'avoine** oatmeal. **farine de maïs** cornflour.
farouche (fa'ru:ʃ) *adj* 1 wild. 2 savage. 3 sullen. 4 shy. 5 cruel.
fart (far) *nm* wax.
fasciner (fassi:'ne:) *vt* fascinate.
fascisme (fa'si:sm) *nm* fascism. **fasciste** *adj,n* fascist.
faste (fast) *nm* 1 pomp. 2 display.
fastidieux, -euse (fasti:'djœ, -'djœz) *adj* 1 tedious. 2 boring.
fastueux, -euse (fa'stɥœ, -'stɥœz) *adj* 1 ostentatious. 2 pompous.
fatal (fa'tal) *adj* 1 fatal. 2 inevitable. **fatalité** *nf* 1 fatality. 2 fate.
fatiguer (fati:'ge:) *vt* 1 tire. 2 overwork. 3 bore. *vi mot* labour. **se fatiguer** *vr* get tired. **fatigue** *nf* fatigue, tiredness.
fatras (fa'tra) *nm* 1 jumble. 2 rubbish.
faubourg (fo'bu:r) *nm* suburb.
faucher (fo'ʃe:) *vt* 1 reap, cut. 2 *inf* pinch, steal. **fauché** *adj* 1 cut. 2 *inf* broke.
faucon (fo'kõ) *nm* 1 falcon. 2 hawk.
faudra (fo:'dra) *v* see **falloir.**
faufiler (fofi:'le:) *vt* 1 (sewing) tack. 2 baste. 3 insert. **se faufiler** *vr* creep.
faune (fon) *nf* fauna.
fausser (fo'se:) *vt* 1 falsify. 2 *mus* put out of tune. 3 pervert. 4 bend.
faut (fo:) *v* see **falloir.**
faute (fot) *nf* 1 fault. 2 error. 3 lack. **faute de** for want of. **sans faute** without fail.
fauteuil (fo'tœj) *nm* 1 armchair. 2 *educ* chair.
fauve (fov) *adj* fawn. *nm* 1 fawn (colour). 2 *pl* wild beasts.
faux[1], **fausse** (fo, fos) *adj* 1 false. 2 untrue. 3 wrong. 4 counterfeit. *nm* 1 falsehood. 2 forgery. **à faux** wrongly. **faux-filet** *nm, pl* **faux-filets** sirloin.
faux[2] (fo) *nf* scythe.
faveur (fa'vœr) *nf* favour. **en faveur de** on behalf of. **favorable** *adj* favourable.
favori, -ite (favɔ'ri:, -'ri:t) *adj,n* favourite.
favoriser (favɔri:'ze:) *vt* 1 favour. 2 assist. 3 patronize. 4 promote.
fébrile (fe:'bri:l) *adj* feverish.
fécond (fe:'kõ) *adj* 1 fertile. 2 prolific.

fédérer (fe:de:'re:) *vt* federate. **fédéral, -aux** (fe:de:'ral, -'ro) *adj* federal.

fée (fe:) *nf* fairy.

feindre* (fēdr) *vt* feign. **feindre de** pretend to. **feinte** *nf* feint, pretence.

fêler (fɛ'le:) *vt* crack. **fêlure** *nf* crack.

féliciter (fe:li:si'te:) *vt* congratulate. **félicitations** *nf pl* congratulations.

félin (fe:'lɛ̃) *adj* feline.

femelle (fə'mɛl) *adj,nf* female, she.

féminin (fe:mi:'nɛ̃) *adj* 1 feminine. 2 female.

femme (fam) *nf* 1 woman. 2 wife. **femme de chambre** 1 chambermaid. 2 housemaid. **femme de charge/ménage** housekeeper/charwoman.

fémur (fe:'myr) *nm* thighbone.

fendre (fādr) *vt* split.

fenêtre (fə'nɛtr) *nf* window.

fenouil (fə'nu:j) *nm* fennel.

fente (fāt) *nf* 1 crack. 2 crevice. 3 split. 4 slit. 5 slot.

féodal, -aux (fe:ɔ'dal, -'do) *adj* feudal.

fer (fɛr) *nm* 1 iron. 2 sword. 3 *pl* chains. **fer à cheval** horseshoe. **fer à repasser** *dom* iron. **fer blanc** tin. **fer forgé** wrought iron.

ferai (fə're) *v* see **faire.**

férié (fe:'rje:) *jour* **férié** *nm* 1 holiday. 2 bank holiday.

férir* (fe:'ri:r) *vt* strike.

ferme¹ (fɛrm) *adj* 1 firm. 2 steady. 3 steadfast. *adv* 1 firmly. 2 hard. **fermeté** *nf* firmness.

ferme² (fɛrm) *nf* 1 farm. 2 farmhouse. **fermier** (fɛr'mje:) *nm* farmer.

fermenter (fɛrmā'te:) *vi* 1 ferment. 2 rise.

fermer (fɛr'me:) *vi,vt* 1 close. 2 shut. *vt* 1 turn or switch off. 2 fasten. **fermer à clef** lock. **fermeture** *nf* 1 closing. 2 shutting. **Fermeture Eclair** *nf Tdmk* zip.

féroce (fe:rɔs) *adj* 1 wild. 2 ferocious.

ferraille (fɛ'rɑj) *nf* scrap iron.

ferré (fɛ're:) *adj* 1 fitted with iron. 2 hobnailed.

ferroviaire (fɛrrɔ'vjɛr) *adj* railway.

fertile (fɛr'ti:l) *adj* 1 fertile. 2 fruitful.

fertiliser (fɛrti:li:'ze:) *vt* fertilize.

fervent (fɛr'vā) *adj* 1 fervent. 2 ardent. *nm* enthusiast.

ferveur (fɛr'vœr) *nf* fervour.

fesser (fɛ'se:) *vt* spank. **fesse** *nf* 1 buttock. 2 *pl inf* bottom. **fessée** *nf* spanking.

festin (fɛ'stɛ̃) *nm* 1 banquet. 2 feast.

feston (fɛ'stɔ̃) *nm* 1 festoon. 2 scallop.

festonner (fɛstɔ'ne:) *vt* 1 festoon. 2 scallop.

fêter (fɛ'te:) *vt* 1 celebrate. 2 keep as a holiday

fête *nf* 1 feast. 2 festival. 3 holiday. 4 entertainment. 5 festivity.

fétiche (fe:'ti:ʃ) *nm* 1 fetish. 2 mascot.

fétide (fe:'ti:d) *adj* fetid.

feu¹, **feux** (fœ) *nm* 1 fire. 2 heat. 3 passion. 4 light. **feu d'artifice** fireworks, firework display. **feu de joie** bonfire. **feu de position** sidelight. **feux de circulation** *n pl* traffic lights.

feu² (fœ) *adj* late, deceased.

feuille (fœj) *nf* 1 leaf. 2 sheet (of paper). **feuillage** *nm* foliage. **feuillet** *nm* leaf (of a book). **feuilleton** *nm* serial story.

feuilleter (fœj'te:) *vt* flip through (a book).

feutre (fœtr) *nm* felt.

fève (fɛv) *nf* bean. **grosse fève** broad bean.

février (fe:vri:'e:) *nm* February.

fiacre (fjakr) *nm* cab.

se fiancer (fjā'se:) *vr* get engaged. **fiançailles** (fjā'saj) *nf pl* engagement. **fiancé** *nm* fiancé.

fiasco (fja'sko) *nm invar* fiasco, wash-out.

fibre (fi:br) *nf* 1 fibre. 2 grain.

ficeler (fi:'sle:) *vt* tie up. **ficelle** *nf* string.

ficher (fi:'ʃe:) *vt* 1 drive in. 2 *sl* stick. 3 give. 4 do. **fiche-moi la paix!** clear off! **se ficher de** *vr* make fun of. **je m'en fiche** I don't care. **fiche** *nf* 1 peg. 2 plug. 3 slip of paper. 4 voucher. 5 form. **fichu** *adj sl* 1 awful. 2 done for.

fiction (fi:k'sjɔ̃) *nf* fiction. **fictif, -ive** (fi:k'ti:f, -'ti:v) *adj* fictitious.

fidèle (fi:'dɛl) *adj* 1 faithful. 2 loyal. **fidélité** *nf* 1 loyalty. 2 fidelity.

fiel (fjɛl) *nm* gall, bile.

fiente (fjāt) *nf* droppings.

fier¹, **fière** (fjɛr) *adj* 1 proud. 2 haughty. **fierté** *nf* pride.

se fier² (fje:) *vr* trust.

fièvre (fjɛvr) *nf* 1 fever, temperature. 2 excitement.

figer (fi:'ʒe:) *vt* 1 congeal, clot. 2 fix.

figue (fi:g) *nf* fig. **figuier** *nm* fig tree.

figurer (fi:gy're:) *vt* 1 represent. 2 appear. **se figurer** *vr* imagine. **figure** *nf* 1 shape. 2 figure. 3 face. **figuré** *adj* 1 figured. 2 figurative.

fil (fi:l) *nm* 1 thread. 2 yarn. 3 edge. 4 grain. 5 current. **fil de fer** wire.

filament (fi:la'mā) *nm* 1 filament. 2 fibre.

filer (fi:'le:) *vt* 1 spin. 2 prolong. 3 shadow. *vi* 1 flow smoothly. 2 slip by. 3 ladder. 4 slip off. **filer à l'anglaise** take French leave. **file** *nf* 1 line. 2 row. **filé** *nm* thread.

filet[1] (fiːˈlɛ) *nm* **1** thin thread. **2** streak. **3** trickle.
filet[2] (fiːˈlɛ) *nm* fillet.
filet[3] (fiːˈlɛ) *nm* net.
filial -aux (fiːˈljal, -ˈljo) *adj* filial. **filiale** *nf* **1** subsidiary company. **2** *comm* branch.
fille (fiːj) *nf* **1** daughter. **2** girl. **jeune fille** young woman or girl. **vieille fille** spinster. **fillette** *nf* little girl.
filleul (fiːˈljœl) *nm* **1** godchild. **2** godson. **filleule** *nf* goddaughter.
film (fiːlm) *nm* film.
filou (fiːˈluː) *nm* **1** pickpocket. **2** cheat.
filouter (fiːluːˈte) *vt* **1** rob. **2** swindle.
fils (fiːs) *nm* **1** son. **2** boy.
filtrer (fiːlˈtre) *vi,vt* **1** filter. **2** strain. *vi* percolate. **filtre** *nm* filter.
fin[1] (fɛ̃) *nf* **1** end. **2** close. **3** aim. **4** purpose. **en fin de compte** finally.
fin[2] (fɛ̃) *adj* **1** fine. **2** choice. **3** delicate. **4** shrewd. **5** expert. **6** slender. **7** semiprecious.
final (fiːˈnal) *adj* **1** final. **2** last. **3** ultimate. **finale** *nf* sport final.
finance (fiːˈnãs) *nf* **1** finance. **2** *pl* resources. **financier, -ière** (fiːnãˈsje:, -ˈsjɛr) *adj* financial. *nm* financier.
finaud (fiːˈno) *adj* cunning, sly.
finesse (fiːˈnɛs) *nf* **1** delicacy. **2** shrewdness.
finir (fiːˈniːr) *vt* **1** finish. **2** end. **3** complete. *vi* come to an end. **fini** *adj* **1** finished. **2** accomplished. **3** finite.
Finlande (fɛ̃ˈlãd) *nf* Finland. **finlandais** *adj* Finnish. **finnois** (fiːˈnwa) *adj* Finnish. *nm* **1** Finn. **2** Finnish (language).
fisc (fiːsk) *nm* **1** treasury. **2** exchequer. **3** Inland Revenue. **fiscal, -aux** (fiːˈskal, -ˈsko) *adj* fiscal.
fission (fiːˈsjɔ̃) *nf* fission.
fissure (fiːˈsyr) *nf* fissure, crack.
fixer (fiːkˈse:) *vt* **1** fix. **2** determine. **3** settle. **fixe** *adj* **1** fixed, immovable. **2** firm. **3** regular. **4** settled.
fjord (fjɔr) *nm also* **fiord** fiord.
flacon (flaˈkɔ̃) *nm* bottle.
flageller (flaʒɛlˈle:) *vt* flog.
flagrant (flaˈgrã) *adj* **1** flagrant. **2** obvious.
flair (flɛr) *nm* **1** scent. **2** gift, flair.
flairer (flɛˈre:) *vt* **1** scent, smell out. **2** sniff.
flamand (flaˈmã) *adj* Flemish. *nm* **1** Fleming. **2** Flemish (language).
flamant (flaˈmã) *nm* flamingo.
flamber (flãˈbe:) *vi* **1** blaze. **2** burn. *vt* singe. **flambeau, -aux** (flãˈbo) *nm* **1** torch. **2** light. **3** candlestick.

flamboyant (flãbwaˈjã) *adj* **1** blazing. **2** gaudy.
flamme (flɑm) *nf* **1** flame. **2** blaze. **3** passion. **flammèche** (flaˈmɛʃ) *nf* spark.
flan (flã) *nm* custard tart.
flanc (flã) *nm* **1** flank. **2** side.
flanelle (flaˈnɛl) *nf* flannel.
flâner (flɑˈne:) *vi* **1** stroll. **2** dawdle.
flanquer (flãˈke:) *vt* **1** flank. **2** chuck, throw.
flaque (flak) *nf* puddle, pool.
flasque (flask) *adj* **1** flabby. **2** limp. **3** weak.
flatter (flaˈte:) *vt* **1** stroke, pat. **2** delude. **3** flatter.
fléau, -aux (fleˈo) *nm* **1** scourge. **2** pest.
flèche (flɛʃ) *nf* **1** arrow. **2** spire.
fléchir (fleˈʃiːr) *vt* **1** bend. **2** move to pity. *vi* **1** give way. **2** sag.
flegme (flɛgm) *nm* calmness.
flet (flɛ) *nm zool* flounder.
flétan (fleˈtã) *nm* halibut.
flétrir[1] (fleˈtriːr) *vt* **1** wither. **2** fade. **3** spoil.
flétrir[2] (fleˈtriːr) *vt* **1** brand: **2** disgrace.
fleur (flœr) *nf* **1** flower. **2** bloom. **3** blossom. **4** prime. **fleuriste** *nm,f* florist.
fleurir (flœˈriːr) *vi* **1** flower, bloom. **2** prosper. *vt* decorate with flowers. **fleuri** *adj* **1** in bloom or flower. **2** flowery.
fleuve (flœv) *nm* river.
flexible (flɛkˈsibl) *adj* flexible.
flibustier (fliːbyˈstje:) *nm* **1** pirate. **2** rogue.
flic (fliːk) *nm inf* copper, policeman.
flirter (flœrˈte:) *vi* flirt.
flocon (flɔˈkɔ̃) *nm* **1** flake. **2** tuft.
flore (flɔr) *nf* flora.
florissant (flɔriːˈsã) *adj* prosperous.
flot (flo) *nm* **1** wave. **2** flood. **3** surge. **à flot** afloat. **à flots** in torrents.
flotter (flɔˈte:) *vi,vt* float. *vi* **1** waft. **2** waver. **3** wander. **flotte** *nf* **1** fleet. **2** float.
flou (fluː) *adj* **1** blurred. **2** woolly.
fluctuer (flykˈtɥe:) *vi* fluctuate.
fluet, -ette (flyˈɛ, -ˈɛt) *adj* thin, slender.
fluide (flyˈiːd) *adj,nm* fluid.
flûte (flyt) *nf* **1** flute. **2** long thin loaf of bread. **3** tall champagne glass.
flux (fly) *nm* **1** flow. **2** flux.
focal, -aux (fɔˈkal, -ˈko) *adj* focal.
fœtus (feˈtys) *nm* foetus.
foi (fwa) *nf* **1** faith. **2** trust. **3** belief.
foie (fwa) *nm* liver.
foin (fwɛ̃) *nm* hay.
foire (fwar) *nf* fair.
fois (fwa) *nf* **1** time. **2** occasion. **à la fois** at the same time. **une fois** once.

foison (fwaˈzɔ̃) nf plenty.
foisonner (fwazɔˈne:) vi 1 abound. 2 increase.
fol (fɔl) adj see **fou.**
folâtre (fɔˈlɑtr) adj 1 playful. 2 lively.
folie (fɔˈliː) nf 1 madness. 2 folly.
folle (fɔl) adj see **fou.**
follet, -ette (fɔˈlɛ, -ˈlɛt) adj merry.
follicule (fɔliːˈkyl) nm follicle.
foncer (fɔ̃ˈse:) vi 1 rush. 2 charge. vt sink. **se foncer** vr get darker. **foncé** adj dark.
foncier, -ière (fɔ̃ˈsje:, -ˈsjɛr) adj 1 of the land. 2 fundamental.
fonction (fɔ̃kˈsjɔ̃) nf 1 function. 2 office. **fonctionnaire** nm 1 official. 2 civil servant.
fonctionner (fɔ̃ksjɔˈne:) vi 1 function. 2 work. 3 run.
fond (fɔ̃) nm 1 bottom. 2 depth. 3 back. 4 background. 5 foundation. **à fond** thoroughly. **de fond** basic, fundamental.
fondamental, -aux (fɔ̃damãˈtal, -ˈto) adj basic, fundamental.
fonder (fɔ̃ˈde:) vt 1 found. 2 establish. 3 base. **se fonder sur** vr 1 be based on. 2 rely on.
fondre (fɔ̃dr) vi,vt 1 melt. 2 dissolve. vt 1 cast. 2 blend. vi pounce.
fondrière (fɔ̃driːˈɛr) nf 1 bog. 2 hollow.
fonds (fɔ̃) nm 1 land. 2 business. 3 fund. 4 funds. 5 pl cash.
font (fɔ̃) v see **faire.**
fontaine (fɔ̃ˈtɛn) nf 1 spring. 2 fountain. 3 cistern.
fonts (fɔ̃) nm pl font.
football (fuːtˈbal) nm football.
for (fɔr) **for intérieur** nm conscience.
forain (fɔˈrɛ̃) adj travelling.
forçat (fɔrˈsa) nm convict.
forcené (fɔrsəˈne:) adj 1 furious. 2 frantic.
forcer (fɔrˈse:) vt 1 force. 2 break open. 3 compel. **force** nf 1 strength. 2 force. 3 power. adj invar a lot of. **à force de** by means of. **forcé** adj 1 forced. 2 compulsory. **forcément** adv 1 necessarily. 2 forcibly.
forer (fɔˈre:) vt 1 drill. 2 bore.
forêt (fɔˈrɛ) nf forest.
forfait[1] (fɔrˈfɛ) nm serious crime.
forfait[2] (fɔrˈfɛ) nm contract.
forfait[3] (fɔrˈfɛ) nm forfeit.
forficule (fɔrfiːˈkyl) nf earwig.
forger (fɔrˈʒe:) vt 1 forge. 2 counterfeit. 3 fabricate. **forge** nf forge.
formaliser (fɔrmaliːˈze:) vt offend. **se formaliser** vr take offence.

former (fɔrˈme:) vt 1 form. 2 create. 3 train. 4 develop. 5 constitute. **se former** vr take shape. **formalité** nf 1 formality. 2 ceremony.
formation nf 1 formation. 2 structure. 3 education, training. 4 development, growth.
forme nf 1 form. 2 figure. 3 method. 4 pl manners. **être en forme** be fit. **formel, -elle** (fɔrˈmɛl) adj 1 formal. 2 explicit. 3 definite.
formidable (fɔrmiːˈdabl) adj 1 formidable. 2 inf tremendous, terrific.
formuler (fɔrmyˈle:) vt 1 formulate. 2 state. 3 express. **formule** nf 1 formula. 2 prescription. 3 form.
fors (fɔr) prep except, but.
fort[1] (fɔr) adj 1 strong. 2 large, stout. 3 loud. 4 clever. 5 thick. 6 violent. nm 1 strong part. 2 height. 3 fort.
fort[2] (fɔr) adv 1 hard. 2 much. 3 very.
forteresse (fɔrtəˈrɛs) nf fortress.
fortifier (fɔrtiːˈfje:) vt 1 strengthen. 2 fortify.
fortuit (fɔrˈtɥi) adj 1 chance. 2 accidental. 3 casual.
fortune (fɔrˈtyn) nf 1 chance. 2 luck. 3 fortune. 4 wealth. **fortuné** adj 1 fortunate. 2 happy. 3 rich.
fosse (fos) nf 1 hole. 2 pit. 3 grave. **fossé** nm 1 ditch. 2 moat. **fossette** nf dimple.
fossile (fɔˈsiːl) adj,nm fossil.
fou, fol, folle (fuː, fɔl, fɔl) adj 1 mad. 2 foolish, silly. 3 insane. nm,f 1 lunatic. 2 fool.
foudre (fuːdr) nm lightning. **coup de foudre** nm 1 flash of lightning. 2 love at first sight.
foudroyer (fuːdrwaˈje:) vt 1 strike by lightning. 2 overwhelm. **foudroyant** adj 1 terrifying. 2 overwhelming. 3 terrific.
fouet (fwɛ) nm 1 whip. 2 lash.
fouetter (fwɛˈte:) vt 1 whip. 2 flog. 3 beat. 4 whisk.
fougère (fuːˈʒɛr) nf fern.
fougue (fuːg) nf 1 ardour. 2 spirit. **fougueux, -euse** (fuːˈgœ, -ˈgœz) adj 1 ardent. 2 fiery. 3 impetuous.
fouiller (fuːˈje:) vt 1 excavate. 2 dig. 3 search. vi rummage. **fouille** nf 1 excavation. 2 search.
fouillis (fuːˈjiː) nm muddle, jumble.
fouir (fwiːr) vt burrow, dig.
foulard (fuːˈlar) nm 1 silk handkerchief. 2 scarf.
fouler (fuːˈle:) vt 1 crush. 2 trample. 3 sprain. **foule** nf crowd, mob. **foulure** nf sprain.
four (fuːr) nm 1 oven. 2 kiln. 3 furnace.
fourbe (fuːrb) adj crafty. nm 1 cheat. 2 rogue. **fourberie** (fuːrbəˈriː) nf 1 swindle. 2 deceit.

63

fourche (fuːrʃ) nf fork, pitchfork. **fourchette** nf cul fork.

fourgon[1] (fuːrˈgɔ̃) nm poker.

fourgon[2] (fuːrˈgɔ̃) nm 1 van. 2 wagon.

fourmi (fuːrˈmiː) nf ant. **avoir des fourmis** have pins and needles.

fourmiller (fuːrmiːˈje:) vi 1 swarm. 2 tingle.

fourneau, -aux (fuːrˈno) nm 1 furnace. 2 stove.

fournir (fuːrˈniːr) vt 1 supply. 2 provide. **fourni** adj 1 thick. 2 bushy. **fournisseur** (fuːrniːˈsœr) nm tradesman. **fourniture** nf pl materials.

fourrer (fuːˈre:) vt 1 stuff, cram. 2 shove. 3 line with fur. **fourreau, -aux** (fuːˈro) nm 1 sheath. 2 case, cover. **fourre-tout** nm invar holdall. **fourreur** nm furrier. **fourrure** nf 1 fur, skin. 2 lining.

foutre' (fuːtr) vt 1 tab have sexual intercourse with. 2 sl do. **je m'en fous** I don't give a damn.

foyer (fwaˈje:) nm 1 hearth, fireplace. 2 centre. 3 home. 4 focus. 5 Th entrance hall.

fracas (fraˈka) nm 1 uproar. 2 din.

fracasser (trakaˈse:) vt 1 smash. 2 shatter.

fraction (frakˈsjɔ̃) nf fraction.

fracturer (fraktyˈre:) vt 1 break. 2 fracture. **fracture** nf fracture.

fragile (fraˈʒiːl) adj 1 fragile. 2 delicate.

fragment (fragˈmã) nm 1 fragment. 2 scrap.

frai (frɛ) nm spawn.

frais[1], **fraîche** (frɛ, frɛʃ) adj 1 fresh. 2 cool. 3 new. **fraîcheur** nf 1 coolness. 2 freshness.

frais[2] (frɛ) nm pl 1 expenses. 2 cost.

fraise[1] (frɛz) nf strawberry.

fraise[2] (frɛz) nf ruff.

framboise (frãˈbwaz) nf raspberry.

franc[1] (frã) nm franc.

franc[2], **franche** (frã, frãʃ) adj 1 free. 2 frank, candid, honest. 3 aboveboard.

France (frãs) nf France. **français** adj French. nm 1 Frenchman. 2 French (language).

franchir (frãˈʃiːr) vt 1 jump over. 2 cross.

franchise (frãˈʃiːz) nf 1 franchise. 2 freedom. 3 exemption. 4 frankness.

franco (frãˈko) adv free of charge.

frange (frãʒ) nf fringe.

frapper (fraˈpe:) vt 1 hit. 2 mint. 3 knock. **frappe** nf 1 striking. 2 stamp, mark.

fraternel, -elle (fratɛrˈnɛl) adj fraternal. **fraternité** nf 1 fraternity. 2 brotherhood.

fraterniser (fratɛrniːˈze:) vi fraternize.

fraude (frod) nf 1 fraud. 2 deceit. 3 false

pretences. **passer en fraude** smuggle through.

frayer (frɛˈje:) vt 1 rub, scrape. 2 clear or open up. vi 1 spawn. 2 associate.

fredaine (fraˈdɛn) nf prank.

fredonner (fradɔˈne:) vt hum.

frein (frɛ̃) nm 1 brake. 2 curb. 3 horse's bit.

freiner (frɛˈne:) vi brake. vt check.

frêle (frɛl) adj 1 frail. 2 delicate.

frelon (fraˈlɔ̃) nm hornet.

frémir (freˈmiːr) vi 1 quiver. 2 rustle. 3 tremble. 4 shudder.

frêne (frɛn) nm ash tree.

frénésie (freneˈziː) nf frenzy. **frénétique** adj frantic.

fréquence (frɛˈkãs) nf 1 frequence. 2 frequency. **fréquent** adj frequent.

fréquenter (frɛkãˈte:) vt 1 visit. 2 associate.

frère (frɛr) nm brother.

fresque (frɛsk) nf fresco.

fret (frɛ) nm freight.

fréter (freˈte:) vt 1 freight. 2 charter.

frétiller (freːtiːˈje:) vi 1 wriggle. 2 wag.

freux (frœ) nm invar rook.

friand (friːˈã) adj 1 fond of delicacies. 2 fond.

fricoter (friːkɔˈte:) vi, vt inf cook.

friction (friːkˈsjɔ̃) nf friction.

frictionner (friːksjɔˈne:) vt rub.

Frigidaire (friːʒiːˈdɛr) nm Tdmk refrigerator. **frigo** (friːˈgo) nm fridge.

frigide (friːˈʒiːd) adj frigid.

frileux, -euse (friːˈlœ, -ˈlœz) adj chilly, sensitive to cold.

frimas (friːˈma) nm frost.

friper (friːˈpe:) vt 1 crumple. 2 crush.

fripon, -onne (friːˈpɔ̃, -ˈpɔn) nm,f rogue, rascal.

frire' (friːr) vi, vt fry.

frise (friːz) nf frieze.

friser (friːˈze:) vi, vt curl. vt skim.

frisson (friːˈsɔ̃) nm shiver.

frissonner (friːsɔˈne:) vi 1 shiver. 2 shudder.

frit (friː) v see **frire.**

frivole (friːˈvɔl) adj 1 frivolous. 2 empty.

froid (frwa) adj 1 cold. 2 cool. 3 indifferent. **avoir froid** feel cold. ~nm cold, coldness. **froideur** nf coldness.

froisser (frwaˈse:) vt 1 crumple. 2 crease. 3 hurt. **se froisser** vr take offence.

frôler (froˈle:) vt touch lightly, brush.

fromage (frɔˈmaʒ) nm cheese.

froment (frɔˈmã) nm wheat.

froncer (frɔ̃ˈse:) vt wrinkle. **froncer les sourcils** frown. **fronce** nf crease.

fronde (frɔ̃d) *nf* sling.
front (frɔ̃) *nm* **1** forehead. **2** front. **3** brow.
  frontal, -aux (frɔ̃'tal, -'to) *adj* front, frontal.
  frontière *nf* frontier.
frotter (frɔ'te:) *vt* **1** rub. **2** strike. **3** scrub.
  frottoir *nm* **1** polisher. **2** scrubbing brush.
fructueux, -euse (fryk'tɥœ, -'tɥœz) *adj* fruitful.
frugal, -aux (fry'gal, -'go) *adj* frugal.
fruit (frɥi:) *nm* fruit.
fruste (fryst) *adj* **1** worn. **2** defaced. **3** rough.
frustrer (fry'stre:) *vt* **1** frustrate. **2** disappoint.
  frustration *nf* frustration.
fuir* (fɥi:r) *vi* **1** flee. **2** recede. **3** leak. *vt* **1** avoid.
  2 shun. **fuite** *nf* **1** flight. **2** leak.
fumer (fy'me:) *vi,vt* smoke. *vi* steam. **fumée** *nf*
  smoke.
fumier (fy'mje:) *nm* manure, dung.
funèbre (fy'nɛbr) *adj* **1** funereal. **2** dismal.
funérailles (fynɛ'rɑj) *nf pl* funeral.
funeste (fy'nɛst) *adj* fatal, deadly.
fur (fyr) **au fur et à mesure** *adv* **1** as. **2**
  gradually.
furet (fy'rɛ) *nm* ferret.
fureter (fyr'te:) *vi* **1** ferret, rummage. **2** pry.
fureur (fy'rœr) *nf* **1** fury, rage. **2** mania. **furibond** *adj* furious. **furie** *nf* fury, rage.
  furieux, -euse (fy'rjœ, -'rjœz) *adj* furious.
furoncle (fy'rɔ̃kl) *nm* boil.
furtif, -ive (fyr'ti:f, -'ti:v) *adj* furtive.
fusée (fy'ze:) *nf* **1** rocket. **2** fuse.
fusil (fy'zi:) *nm* gun. **fusil rayé** rifle.
fusiller (fyzi:'je:) *vt* shoot, execute.
fusion (fy'zjɔ̃) *nf* **1** fusion. **2** melting.
fusionner (fyzjɔ'ne:) *vi,vt* **1** blend. **2** unite.
fustiger (fysti:'ʒe:) *vt* thrash, flog.
fût (fy) *nm* **1** shaft. **2** handle. **3** barrel.
futaie (fy'tɛ) *nf* forest.
futaille (fy'tɑj) *nf* barrel.
futile (fy'ti:l) *adj* **1** futile. **2** trivial.
futur (fy'tyr) *adj,nm* future.
fuyant (fɥi'jɑ̃) *v* see **fuir.**

G

gâche (gɑʃ) *nf tech* staple.
gâcher (gɑ'ʃe:) *vt* **1** spoil. **2** bungle. **3** waste.
  gâchis *nm* **1** mud, slush. **2** mess.
gâchette (gɑ'ʃɛt) *nf* trigger.
gaffe (gaf) *nf* **1** boathook. **2** blunder.
gager (ga'ʒe:) *vt* **1** bet. **2** hire. **gage** *nm* **1**
  pledge. **2** token. **3** forfeit. **4** *pl* wages.

gagner (ga'ɲe:) *vt* **1** earn. **2** gain. **3** win. **4**
  reach. **gagne-pain** *nm invar* breadwinner.
gai (ge:) *adj* **1** gay. **2** merry. **3** bright. **gaieté** *nf*
  gaiety, mirth.
gaillard[1] (ga'jar) *adj* **1** strong. **2** healthy. **3**
  merry. **4** free. *nm* chap, fellow.
gaillard[2] (ga'jar) **gaillard arrière** *nm* quarterdeck.
gain (gɛ̃) *nm* **1** gain. **2** profit.
gaine (gɛn) *nf* **1** sheath. **2** cover. **3** case.
galant (ga'lɑ̃) *adj* **1** gallant. **2** courteous, polite.
  galamment *adv* gallantly.
galaxie (galak'si:) *nf* galaxy.
galbe (galb) *nm* **1** contour. **2** outline. **3** figure.
gale (gal) *nf* mange.
galère (ga'lɛr) *nf* galley.
galerie (gal'ri:) *nf* gallery.
galet (ga'lɛ) *nm* pebble. **gros galet** boulder.
Galles (gal) **pays de Galles** Wales. **gallois**
  (gal'wa) *adj* Welsh. *nm* **1** Welshman. **2** Welsh
  (language).
gallon (ga'lɔ̃) *nm* gallon.
galon (ga'lɔ̃) *nm* **1** braid. **2** stripe.
galop (ga'lo) *nm* gallop. **petit galop** canter.
galoper (galɔ'pe:) *vi* gallop.
galvaniser (galvani:'ze:) *vt* galvanize.
gambade (gɑ̃'bad) *nf* leap, gambol.
gamin (ga'mɛ̃) *n* **1** *inf* rascal. **2** youngster.
gamme (gam) *nf* **1** *mus* scale. **2** range.
gangster (gɑ̃g'stɛr) *nm* gangster.
gant (gɑ̃) *nm* glove. **gant de toilette** facecloth.
garage (ga'raʒ) *nm* **1** garage. **2** shed. **3** storage.
garant (ga'rɑ̃) *nm* **1** guarantor. **2** bail.
garantir (garɑ̃'ti:r) *vt* **1** guarantee. **2** vouch for.
  3 protect. **4** insure. **garantie** *nf* guarantee.
garce (gars) *nf inf* bitch.
garçon (gar'sɔ̃) *nm* **1** boy. **2** lad. **3** bachelor. **4**
  waiter. **garçon d'honneur** best man.
garde-boue (gardə'bu:) *nm invar* mudguard.
garde-chasse (gardə'ʃas) *nm, pl* **gardes-chasse(s)** gamekeeper.
garde-côte (gardə'kot) *nm, pl* **gardes-côte(s)**
  coastguard.
garde-feu (gardə'fœ) *nm invar* fireguard.
garde-malade (gardma'lad) *nm or f,pl* **gardes-malades** nurse.
garde-manger (gardmã'ʒe:) *nm invar* larder,
  pantry.
garder (gar'de:) *vt* **1** guard. **2** take care of. **3**
  watch. **4** keep. **garder les bébés** baby-sit. **se
  garder** *vr* protect oneself. **se garder de**
  beware of. **garde** *nf* **1** care. **2** custody. **3**
  guard. **prendre garde à/de** take care to/not

to. ~*nm* **1** keeper. **2** warder. **garde du corps** bodyguard. **guardien, -ienne** (gar'djĕ, -'djɛn) *nm,f* guardian. **guardien de but** goalkeeper.

garde-robe (gardə'rɔb) *nf, pl* **gardes-robes** wardrobe.

gare[1] (gar) *nf* railway station.

gare[2] (gar) *interj* look out!

garenne (ga'rɛn) *nf* warren.

garer (ga're:) *vt* **1** dock. **2** park. **3** shunt. **se garer** *vr* get out of the way.

se gargariser (gargari:'ze:) *vr* gargle.

gargouiller (gargu:'je:) *vi* **1** gurgle. **2** rumble. **gargouille** *nf* **1** gargoyle. **2** spout.

garnir (gar'ni:r) *vt* **1** strengthen. **2** provide. **3** decorate. **4** garnish. **garnison** *nf* garrison. **garniture** *nf* **1** fittings. **2** *cul* trimmings.

gars (ga) *nm inf* lad.

gaspiller (gaspi:'je:) *vt* **1** waste. **2** squander. **gaspillage** *nm* **1** waste. **2** wastefulness.

gastrique (ga'stri:k) *adj* gastric.

gastronomique (gastrɔnɔ'mi:k) *adj* gastronomic.

gâteau, -aux (ga'to) *nm* cake.

gâter (ga'te:) *vt* **1** spoil. **2** harm. **gâte-tout** *nm invar* spoilsport.

gauche (goʃ) *adj* **1** left. **2** clumsy. gauche. *nf* left. **gaucher, -ère** (go'ʃe:, -'ʃɛr) *adj* left-handed.

gaufre (gofr) *nf* waffle. **gaufrette** (go'fret) *nf* wafer.

gaz (gaz) *nm* gas.

gaze (gaz) *nf* gauze.

gazéifier (gaze:i:'fje:) *vt* aerate.

gazelle (ga'zɛl) *nf* gazelle.

gazon (ga'zɔ̃) *nm* **1** lawn. **2** turf.

gazouiller (gazu:'je:) *vi* **1** twitter. **2** babble.

géant (ʒe:'ã) *nm* giant. *adj* gigantic.

geindre* (ʒɛ̃dr) *vi* **1** whine. **2** whimper.

gel (ʒɛl) *nm* **1** frost. **2** freezing.

gélatine (ʒɛla'ti:n) *nf* gelatine.

geler (ʒə'le:) *vt* freeze. *vi* become frozen. *v imp* freeze. **gelé** *adj* frozen. **gelée** *nf* **1** frost. **2** jelly.

gélignite (ʒe:li:g'ni:t) *nf* gelignite.

Gémeaux (ʒe:'mo) *nm pl* Gemini.

gémir (ʒe:'mi:r) *vi* **1** groan. **2** moan. **3** wail. **gémissement** *nm* **1** groan. **2** moan.

gemme (ʒɛm) *nf* gem.

gencive (ʒã'si:v) *nf anat* gum.

gendarme (ʒã'darm) *nm* policeman.

gendre (ʒãdr) *nm* son-in-law.

gène (ʒɛn) *nm* gene.

généalogie (ʒe:ne:alɔ'ʒi:) *nf* genealogy. **généalogique** *adj* genealogical.

gêner (ʒe:'ne:) *vt* **1** hinder, obstruct. **2** embarrass, inconvenience. **se gêner** *vr* put oneself out. **gênant** (ʒɛ'nã) *adj* **1** awkward. **2** embarrassing. **gêne** (ʒɛn) *nf* **1** difficulty. **2** embarrassment. **3** need.

général, -aux (ʒe:ne:'ral, -'ro) *adj,nm* general. **général de brigade/division** brigadier/ major general.

généraliser (ʒe:ne:rali:'ze:) *vt* generalize.

génération (ʒe:ne:ra'sjɔ̃) *nf* generation.

généreux, -euse (ʒe:ne:'rœ, -'rœz) *adj* generous. **générosité** *nf* generosity.

générique (ʒe:ne:'ri:k) *adj* generic.

génétique (ʒe:ne:'ti:k) *adj* genetic. *nf* genetics.

Genève (ʒə'nɛv) *nf* Geneva.

génie (ʒe:'ni:) *nm* **1** spirit. **2** genius. **génial, -aux** (ʒe:'njal, -'njo) *adj* inspired, brilliant.

genièvre (ʒə'njɛvr) *nf* **1** juniper berry. **2** gin.

génital, -aux (ʒe:ni:'tal, -'to) *adj* genital.

genou, -oux (ʒə'nu:) *nm* knee.

genre (ʒãr) *nm* **1** kind, sort, type. **2** genus, family. **3** gender. **4** style. **genre humain** mankind.

gens (ʒã) *nm,f pl* people, folk.

gentiane (ʒã'sjan) *nf* gentian.

gentil[1]**, -ille** (ʒã'ti:, -'ti:j) *adj* **1** nice. **2** kind. **3** pretty. **4** good. **gentilhomme** *nm* **1** nobleman. **2** gentleman. **gentillesse** *nf* **1** kindness. **2** prettiness. **gentiment** *adv* **1** nicely. **2** kindly. **3** prettily.

gentil[2] (ʒã'ti:) *nm* Gentile.

génuflexion (ʒe:nyflɛk'sjɔ̃) *nf* genuflection.

géographie (ʒe:ɔgra'fi:) *nf* geography. **géographique** *adj* geographic.

geôle (ʒol) *nf* jail, prison.

géométrie (ʒe:ɔme:'tri:) *nf* geometry. **géométrique** *adj* geometric.

géranium (ʒɛra'njɔm) *nm* geranium.

gerbe (ʒɛrb) *nf* **1** sheaf. **2** bunch.

gercer (ʒɛr'se:) *vt* **1** crack. **2** chap. **gerçure** *nf* **1** crack. **2** fissure.

gérer (ʒe:'re:) *vt* manage, run. **gérance** (ʒe:'rãs) *nf* management. **gérant** (ʒe:'rã) *nm* **1** manager. **2** director.

germanique (ʒɛrma'ni:k) *adj* Germanic.

germer (ʒɛr'me:) *vi* **1** germinate. **2** sprout, shoot. **germe** *nm* **1** germ. **2** sprout.

gérondif (ʒe:rɔ̃'di:f) *nm* gerund.

gésir* (ʒe:'zi:r) *vi* lie. **ci-gît** here lies.

geste (ʒɛst) *nm* **1** gesture. **2** movement. **3** sign.

gesticuler (ʒɛsti:ky'le:) *vi* gesticulate.

gestion (ʒɛˈstjɔ̃) *nf* **1** management. **2** administration.

geyser (ʒiːˈzɛr) *nm* geyser.

ghetto (gɛˈto) *nm* ghetto.

gibet (ʒiːˈbɛ) *nm* gallows.

gibier (ʒiːˈbje:) *nm* (hunting) game.

giboulée (ʒiːbuːˈle:) *nf* shower (of rain).

gicler (ʒiːˈkle:) *vi* squirt out. **giclée** *nf* squirt.

gifler (ʒiːˈfle:) *vt* **1** slap. **2** smack. **gifle** *nf* slap.

gigantesque (ʒiːgɑ̃ˈtɛsk) *adj* gigantic, huge.

gigot (ʒiːˈgo) *nm* leg of mutton.

gigue (ʒiːg) *nf* jig.

gilet (ʒiːˈlɛ) *nm* **1** waistcoat. **2** cardigan. **gilet de sauvetage** lifejacket.

gin (dʒiːn) *nm* gin.

gingembre (ʒɛ̃ˈʒɑ̃br) *nm* ginger.

girafe (ʒiːˈraf) *nf* giraffe.

girofle (ʒiːˈrɔfl) *nm* bot clove. **giroflée jaune** *nf* wallflower.

giron (ʒiːˈrɔ̃) *nm* lap.

gisement (ʒiːzˈmɑ̃) *nm* layer, bed. **gisement petrolifère** oilfield.

gît (ʒiː) *v* see **gésir**.

gitan (ʒiːˈtɑ̃) *nm* Gipsy.

gîte (ʒiːt) *nm* **1** shelter, refuge. **2** home.

givre (ʒiːvr) *nm* hoarfrost.

glabre (glabr) *adj* smooth.

glacer (glaˈse:) *vt* **1** freeze. **2** chill. **3** ice. **4** glaze. **glace** *nf* **1** ice. **2** ice-cream. **3** glass. **4** mirror. **glacé** *adj* **1** frozen. **2** icy. **glaçon** *nm* icicle.

glacier (glaˈsje:) *nm* glacier.

glaise (glɛz) *nf* clay.

gland (glɑ̃) *nm* **1** acorn. **2** tassel.

glande (glɑ̃d) *nf* gland.

glaner (glaˈne:) *vt* glean.

glapir (glaˈpiːr) *vi* yelp, yap.

glisser (gliːˈse:) *vi* **1** slide. **2** skid. **3** glide. *vt* slip. **se glisser** *vr* creep. **glissade** *nf* **1** slip. **2** slide. **glissière** *nf* **1** groove. **2** chute.

globe (glɔb) *nm* **1** globe. **2** sphere. **globe de l'œil** eyeball. **global, -aux** (glɔˈbal, -ˈbo) *adj* **1** total. **2** inclusive.

gloire (glwar) *nf* **1** glory. **2** pride. **3** honour. **4** halo. **glorieux, -euse** (glɔˈrjœ, -ˈrjœz) *adj* glorious.

glorifier (glɔriːˈfje:) *vt* **1** glorify. **2** praise. **se glorifier** *vr* boast.

gloser (gloˈze:) *vt* **1** gloss. **2** criticize. **glose** *nf* **1** gloss. **2** comment.

glossaire (glɔsˈsɛr) *nm* glossary.

glouglou (gluːˈgluː) *nm* gurgle.

glouglouter (gluːgluːˈte:) *vi* gurgle.

glouton, -onne (gluːˈtɔ̃, -ˈtɔn) *adj* greedy. *nm,f* glutton.

gluant (glyˈɑ̃) *adj* sticky.

glucose (glyˈkoz) *nm* glucose.

glycine (gliːˈsiːn) *nf* wisteria.

gnome (gnom) *nm* gnome.

go (go) **tout de go** *adv inf* **1** all of a sudden. **2** without a hitch.

gobelet (gɔˈblɛ) *nm* tumbler, mug.

gobelin (gɔˈblɛ̃) *nm* goblin.

gober (gɔˈbe:) *vt* **1** swallow, gulp down. **2** *sl* believe. **se gober** *vr* fancy oneself.

godasse (gɔˈdas) *nf sl* shoe.

godet (gɔˈdɛ) *nm* **1** mug. **2** bowl.

godiche (gɔˈdiːʃ) *adj inf* **1** awkward. **2** simple.

goéland (gɔɛˈlɑ̃) *nm* seagull.

goélette (gɔɛˈlɛt) *nf* schooner.

goémon (gɔɛˈmɔ̃) *nm* seaweed.

gogo (gɔˈgo) **à gogo** *adv inf* galore.

golf (gɔlf) *nm* golf.

golfe (gɔlf) *nm* gulf, bay.

gommer (gɔˈme:) *vt* **1** gum. **2** rub out. **gomme** *nf* **1** gum. **2** eraser.

gond (gɔ̃) *nm* hinge.

gondole (gɔ̃ˈdɔl) *nf* gondola. **gondolier** *nm* gondolier.

gonfler (gɔ̃ˈfle:) *vt* **1** inflate, blow up. **2** swell.

gong (gɔ̃) *nm* gong.

gorge (gɔrʒ) *nf* **1** throat. **2** breast. **3** gorge. **4** (mountain) pass. **5** groove. **gorgée** *nf* mouthful. **petite gorgée** sip.

gorille (gɔˈriːj) *nm* gorilla.

gosier (gɔˈzje:) *nm* **1** gullet. **2** throat.

gosse (gɔs) *nm,f inf* kid, youngster.

gothique (gɔˈtiːk) *adj* Gothic.

goudron (guːˈdrɔ̃) *nm* tar.

gouffre (guːfr) *nm* gulf, abyss.

goulot (guːˈlo) *nm* neck (of a bottle).

goulu (guːˈly) *adj* greedy. *nm* glutton.

gourde (guːrd) *nf* **1** gourd. **2** flask. **3** *inf* fool.

gourmand (guːrˈmɑ̃) *adj* greedy. *nm* glutton.

gousse (guːs) *nf* pod, shell, husk. **gousse d'ail** clove of garlic.

goût (guː) *nm* **1** taste. **2** flavour. **3** liking. **4** style.

goûter (guːˈte:) *vt* **1** taste. **2** enjoy. **goûter à** taste, try. ~*nm* afternoon tea.

goutte (guːt) *nf* **1** drop. **2** spot. **gouttière** *nf* **1** gutter. **2** spout.

gouvernail (guːvɛrˈnaj) *nm* **1** rudder. **2** helm.

gouverner (guːvɛrˈne:) *vt* **1** govern, rule. **2** control. **3** steer. **gouvernante** *nf* governess.

gouvernement (guːvɛrnəˈmã) *nm* government. **gouverneur** *nm* governor.

grâce (grɑs) *nf* 1 grace. 2 charm. 3 favour. 4 pardon. **de bonne grâce** willingly. **grâce à** thanks to. **gracieux, -euse** (graˈsjœ, -ˈsjœz) *adj* 1 gracious. 2 kind. 3 free.

gracile (graˈsiːl) *adj* 1 slender. 2 slim.

grade (grad) *nm* 1 grade. 2 rank. 3 degree. **gradient** *nm* gradient.

gradin (graˈdɛ̃) *nm* 1 tier. 2 step.

graduer (graˈdɥe:) *vt* 1 graduate. 2 grade. **graduel, -elle** (graˈdɥɛl) *adj* gradual.

graffitti (graffiːˈtiː) *nm pl* graffiti.

grain (grɛ̃) *nm* 1 grain. 2 corn. 3 bean. 4 particle. 5 bead. **grain de café** coffee bean. **grain de poivre** peppercorn. **grain de raisin** grape.

graine (grɛn) *nf* seed. **graine de lin** linseed.

graisser (grɛˈse:) *vt* 1 grease. 2 oil. **graisse** *nf* 1 grease. 2 fat. **graisse de porc/rognon** lard/suet.

grammaire (gramˈmɛr) *nf* grammar. **grammatical, -aux** (gramatiːˈkal, -ˈko) *adj* grammatical.

gramme (gram) *nm* gram.

grand (grã) *adj* 1 big. 2 tall. 3 chief, main. 4 great. 5 grand. **grandeur** *nf* 1 size. 2 height. 3 importance. 4 grandeur. 5 *cap* (title) Grace.

grand-chose *nm invar* much.

Grande-Bretagne *nf* Great Britain.

grandiose (grãˈdjoz) *adj* grand, imposing.

grandir (grãˈdiːr) *vi* 1 grow, grow up. 2 increase. *vt* 1 exaggerate. 2 enlarge.

grand-maman *nf, pl* **grands-mamans** granny.

grand-mère *nf, pl* **grands-mères** grandmother.

grand-parent *nm, pl* **grands-parents** grandparent.

grand-père *nm, pl* **grands-pères** grandfather.

grand-route *nf, pl* **grands-routes** highroad.

grand-voile *nf, pl* **grands-voiles** mainsail.

grange (grãʒ) *nf* barn.

granit (graˈniː) *nm* granite.

graphique (graˈfiːk) *adj* graphic. *nm* 1 graph. 2 diagram.

grappe (grap) *nf* 1 bunch. 2 cluster.

gras, grasse (grɑ, grɑs) *adj* 1 fat. 2 rich. 3 thick. *nm* fat. **grassouillet, -ette** (grɑsuːˈjɛ, -ˈjɛt) *adj* plump, chubby.

gratifier (gratiːˈfje:) *vt* 1 confer. 2 give.

gratin (graˈtɛ̃) *nm* burnt part. **au gratin** cooked with breadcrumbs and grated cheese.

gratitude (gratiːˈtyd) *nf* gratitude.

gratter (graˈte:) *vt* 1 scratch. 2 scrape. **gratte-ciel** *nm invar* skyscraper.

gratuit (graˈtɥiː) *adj* free.

grave (grav) *adj* 1 grave, serious. 2 severe. 3 important. 4 *mus* low. **gravité** *nf* gravity.

graver (graˈve:) *vt* 1 engrave. 2 carve. **gravure** *nf* 1 engraving. 2 etching.

gravier (graˈvje:) *nm* gravel.

gravir (graˈviːr) *vt* climb.

gré (gre:) *nm* 1 will. 2 liking.

Grèce (grɛs) *nf* Greece. **grec, grecque** *adj* Greek, Grecian. *nm* 1 Greek. 2 Greek (language).

gredin (graˈdɛ̃) *nm* scoundrel.

gréer (greːˈe:) *vt naut* rig.

greffer (grɛˈfe:) *vt* graft. **greffe** *nf* graft.

greffier (grɛˈfje:) *nm* registrar.

grégaire (greːˈgɛr) *adj* gregarious.

grêle[1] (grɛl) *nf* hail. **grêlon** *nm* hailstone.

grêle[2] (grɛl) *adj* slender, thin.

grêler (grɛˈle:) *v imp* hail.

grelotter (grələˈte:) *vi* 1 tremble, shiver. 2 jingle.

grenade[1] (graˈnad) *nf* 1 pomegranate. **grenadier** *nm* pomegranate tree. **grenadine** *nf* syrup made of pomegranate juice.

grenade[2] (graˈnad) *nf* grenade. **grenade à main** hand grenade.

grenier (graˈnje:) *nm* 1 granary. 2 loft.

grenouille (graˈnuːj) *nf* frog.

grès (grɛ) *nm* grit, sandstone.

grésil (greːˈziː) *nm* sleet.

grésiller[1] (greːziːˈje:) *v imp* sleet.

grésiller[2] (greːziːˈje:) *vi* 1 crackle. 2 sizzle.

grève[1] (grɛv) *nf* bank, shore.

grève[2] (grɛv) *nf* strike. **grève de la faim** hunger-strike. **grève de zèle** work to rule. **se mettre en grève** go on strike.

grever (graˈve:) *vt* 1 mortgage. 2 encumber.

grief (griːˈɛf) *nm* grievance.

griffer (griːˈfe:) *vt* scratch. **griffe** *nf* 1 claw. 2 signature. **griffe à papiers** paperclip.

griffonner (griːfɔˈne:) *vt* scrawl, scribble. **griffonnage** *nm* scrawl, scribble.

grignoter (griːɲɔˈte:) *vt* nibble (at).

gril (griː) *nm* grill.

grille (griːj) *nf* 1 grille. 2 gate.

griller (griːˈje:) *vt* 1 grill. 2 toast. 3 burn. **grille-pain** *nm invar* toaster.

grillon (griːˈjɔ̃) *nm zool* cricket.

grimacer (griːmaˈse:) *vi* 1 grimace. 2 grin. **grimace** *nf* 1 grimace. 2 grin.

grimer (griːˈme:) *vt Th* make up.

grimper (grɛ̃ˈpe:) *vi* climb up. *vt* climb.

grincer (grɛ̃ˈse:) *vi* 1 grate. 2 gnash. 3 creak.

grincheux, -euse (grɛ̃'ʃœ, -'ʃœz) adj 1 bad-tempered. 2 grumpy.

grippe (gri:p) nf influenza.

gris (gri:) adj 1 grey. 2 tipsy. nm grey.

grive (gri:v) nf thrush.

Groenland (grɔɛn'lãd) nm Greenland. **groenlandais** adj of Greenland. nm Greenlander.

grogner (grɔ'ɲe:) vi 1 grunt. 2 growl. 3 grumble. 4 groan.

groin (grwɛ̃) nm snout (of a pig).

grommeler (grɔm'le:) vi grumble. vt mutter.

gronder (grɔ̃'de:) vt scold. vi 1 growl. 2 rumble.

gros, grosse (gro, gros) adj 1 big. 2 stout. 3 thick. 4 coarse. 5 gross. 6 pregnant. **gros** adv much. nm 1 bulk. 2 wholesale. **en gros** 1 wholesale. 2 on the whole. **grosse** nf gross. **grossesse** nf pregnancy. **grosseur** nf 1 size. 2 thickness. **grossier, -ière** (gro'sje:, -'sjɛr) adj 1 coarse, rough. 2 vulgar, rude.

groseille (gro'zɛj) nf currant. **groseille à maquereau** gooseberry. **groseille rouge** redcurrant. **groseillier** nm currant bush.

grossir (gro'si:r) vi 1 increase. 2 grow bigger. vt 1 enlarge. 2 magnify. **grossissant** adj 1 growing. 2 magnifying.

grotesque (grɔ'tɛsk) adj 1 grotesque. 2 absurd, ludicrous. nm grotesque.

grotte (grɔt) nf grotto.

grouiller (gru:'je:) vi crawl.

grouper (gru:'pe:) vt group, arrange. **groupe** nf 1 group, party. 2 clump.

grue (gry) nf zool,tech crane.

grumeau, -aux (gry'mo) nm clot, lump. **se grumeler** (grym'le:) vr clot.

gué (ge:) nm ford.

guenille (gə'ni:j) nf rag.

guépard (ge'par) nm cheetah.

guêpe (gɛp) nf wasp.

guère (gɛr) adv 1 hardly, scarcely. 2 not much or many.

guérilla (ge:rɪ'la) nf band of guerillas.

guérillero (ge:rɪːllɛ'ro) nm guerilla.

guérir (ge:'rɪːr) vt 1 cure. 2 heal. vi recover. **guérison** nf 1 cure. 2 recovery.

Guernesey (gɛrnə'zɛ) nm Guernsey.

guerre (gɛr) nf 1 war. 2 warfare. **guerrier** nm warrior.

guerroyer (gɛrwa'je:) vi war, wage war.

guet (gɛ) nm watch, guard. **guet-apens** nm invar 1 ambush. 2 trap.

guetter (gɛ'te:) vt 1 lie in wait for. 2 watch for.

gueuler (gœ'le:) vi bawl, yell. **gueule** nf 1 mouth (of animals). 2 jaws. 3 sl mouth (of humans). 4 large opening. **avoir la gueule de bois** have a hangover. **ta gueule!** shut up!

gueux, -euse (gœ, gœz) nm,f beggar. adj poor.

gui (gɪ:) nm mistletoe.

guichet (gɪ:'ʃɛ) nm 1 barrier. 2 box office. 3 counter. 4 grille.

guide¹ (gɪ:d) nm 1 guide. 2 guidebook.

guide² (gɪ:d) nf rein.

guider (gɪ:'de:) vt 1 guide. 2 direct. 3 lead.

guidon (gɪ:'dɔ̃) nm handlebar.

guigne (gɪ:ɲ) nf bad luck.

guillemets (gɪ:j'mɛ) nm pl quotation marks. **entre guillemets** in inverted commas.

guilleret, -ette (gɪ:j'rɛ, -'rɛt) adj lively, gay.

guillotine (gɪ:jɔ'tɪ:n) nf guillotine.

guimauve (gɪ:'mo:v) nf marshmallow.

guindé (gɛ̃'de:) adj stiff, formal.

guindeau, -aux (gɛ̃'do) nm windlass.

guinée (gɪ:'ne:) nf guinea.

guingan (gɛ̃'gã) nm gingham.

guingois (gɛ̃'gwa) **de guingois** adv askew, lopsided.

guirlande (gɪ:r'lãd) nf 1 garland. 2 wreath.

guise (gɪ:z) nf manner, way.

guitare (gɪ:'tar) nf guitar.

gymnase (ʒi:m'naz) nm gymnasium. **gymnaste** nm,f gymnast. **gymnastique** adj gymnastic.

gynécologie (ʒi:ne:kɔlɔ'ʒi:) nf gynaecology. **gynécologiste** nm,f also **gynécologue** gynaecologist.

H

(The asterisk denotes that the initial h is aspirate and that there is therefore no liaison or elision.)

habile (a'bɪ:l) adj 1 clever. 2 able. 3 cunning. **habileté** nf 1 ability, skill. 2 cleverness.

habiller (abɪ:'je:) vt 1 dress. 2 clothe. 3 prepare. **s'habiller** vr dress. **habillement** nm 1 clothing. 2 clothes.

habit (a'bɪ:) nm 1 dress. 2 coat. 3 evening dress. 4 pl clothes.

habiter (abɪ:'te:) vi live, reside. vt dwell or live in. **habitable** adj habitable. **habitant** nm 1 inhabitant. 2 resident. **habitation** nf 1 dwelling. 2 abode.

habituer (abɪ:'tɥe:) vt accustom. **s'habituer à** vr get used to. **habitude** nf 1 habit. 2 custom. 3 knack. 4 practice. **comme d'habitude**

as usual. **d'habitude** usually. **habitué** *nm* regular customer. **habituel, -elle** (abɪ:'tɥɛl) *adj* 1 usual. 2 habitual.

*hâbler (ɑ'ble:) *vi* boast, brag.

*hacher (a'ʃe:) *vt* 1 chop. 2 hack. 3 mince. ***hache** *nf* axe. ***hachette** *nf* hatchet. ***hachis** *nm* mince. ***hachoir** *nm* chopper.

*hagard (a'gar) *adj* haggard, drawn.

*haie (ɛ) *nf* 1 hedge. 2 hurdle. 3 line.

*haillon (a'jɔ̃) *nm* rag.

haïr (a'iːr) *vt* hate, detest. ***haine** *nf* 1 hatred, hate. 2 spite.

*halage (ɑ'laʒ) *nm* towing.

*hâle (ɑl) *nm* 1 sunburn. 2 tan.

haleine (a'lɛn) *nf* breath.

*haler (ɑ'le:) *vt* 1 tow. 2 haul.

*haleter (al'te:) *vi* 1 pant. 2 gasp (for breath).

*hall (al) *nm* 1 hall. 2 hotel lounge.

*halle (al) *nf* covered market. **Les Halles** *nf pl* old site of markets in Paris.

hallucination (alysɪna'sjɔ̃) *nf* hallucination.

*halte (alt) *nm* stop, halt. **faire halte** halt.

haltérophilie (alteːrɔfi:'liː) *nf* weight-lifting.

*hamac (a'mak) *nm* hammock.

*hameau, -aux (a'mo) *nm* hamlet.

hameçon (am'sɔ̃) *nm* 1 (fish) hook. 2 bait.

*hampe (ɑ̃p) *nf* 1 shaft. 2 handle. 3 pole.

*hamster (am'stɛr) *nm* hamster.

*hanche (ɑ̃ʃ) *nf* 1 hip. 2 haunch.

*handicap (ɑ̃di:'kap) *nm sport* handicap.

*handicaper (ɑ̃di:ka'pe:) *vt sport* handicap.

*hangar (ɑ̃'gar) *nm* 1 shed. 2 outhouse.

*hanter (ɑ̃'te:) *vt* haunt. ***hantise** *nf* obsession.

*happer (a'pe:) *vt* seize, snatch, snap up. ***happe** *nf* staple.

*haras (a'rɑ) *nm zool* stud.

*harasser (ara'se:) *vt* 1 tire out. 2 harass.

*harceler (arsə'le:) *vt* 1 harass. 2 worry. 3 pester.

*harde (ard) *nf* herd, flock.

*hardes (ard) *nf pl inf* clothes.

*hardi (ar'di:) *adj* 1 bold. 2 daring. 3 rash. 4 impudent. *interj* courage! ***hardiesse** *nf* 1 daring. 2 pluck.

*hareng (a'rɑ̃) *nm* herring. **hareng salé et fumé** kipper. **hareng saur** red herring.

*hargneux, -euse (ar'ɲœ, -'ɲœz) *adj* 1 peevish. 2 cross. 3 surly.

*haricot (arɪ:'ko) *nm* kidney bean. **haricot vert** French bean.

harmonica (armɔnɪ:'ka) *nm* harmonica.

harmoniser (armɔnɪ:'ze:) *vt* 1 *mus* harmonize. 2 match. **s'harmoniser avec** *vr* 1 be in keeping

with. 2 tone in with. **harmonie** *nf* 1 harmony. 2 agreement. **harmonieux, -euse** (armɔ'njœ, -'njœz) *adj* harmonious. **harmonique** *adj,nm mus* harmonic.

*harnais (ar'nɛ) *nm* harness.

*harpe (arp) *nf* harp.

*harpon (ar'pɔ̃) *nm* harpoon.

*hasard (a'zar) *nm* 1 chance. 2 luck. 3 accident. 4 risk. 5 hazard.

*hasarder (azar'de:) *vt* 1 risk. 2 venture.

*haschich (a'ʃiːʃ) *nm* hashish.

*hâter (ɑ'te:) *vt* hasten, quicken. ***hâte** *nf* haste, hurry.

*hausser (o'se:) *vt* 1 raise. 2 lift. *vi* rise. **hausser les épaules** shrug one's shoulders. ***hausse** *nf* rise.

*haut (o) *adj* 1 high. 2 tall. 3 lofty. 4 loud. 5 upper. *nm* 1 height. 2 top. 3 head. **de haut en bas** 1 downwards. 2 from top to bottom. **en haut** 1 upstairs. 2 above.

*haut-de-forme *nm, pl* **hauts-de-forme** top-hat.

*haut-parleur *nm, pl* **haut-parleurs** loud-speaker.

*hautain (o'tɛ̃) *adj* haughty.

*hautbois (o'bwa) *nm* oboe.

*hâve (ɑv) *adj* 1 haggard. 2 hollow. 3 sunken.

*hâvre (ɑvr) *nm* 1 harbour. 2 haven.

*havresac (ɑvrə'sak) *nm* haversack.

*Haye, La (ɛ) *nf* The Hague.

hebdomadaire (ɛbdɔma'dɛr) *adj* weekly.

héberger (e:bɛr'ʒe:) *vt* 1 lodge. 2 shelter.

hébéter (e:be:'te:) *vt* 1 dull. 2 daze.

hébraïque (e:bra'i:k) *adj* Hebrew.

hébreu, -eux (e:'brœ) *adj* Hebrew. *nm* 1 Hebrew. 2 Hebrew (language).

hectare (ɛk'tar) *nm* French measurement equivalent to 2.47 acres.

hélas (e:'las) *interj* alas!

*héler (e:'le:) *vt* hail, call.

hélice (e:'li:s) *nf* screw, propeller.

hélicoptère (e:li:kɔp'tɛr) *nm* helicopter.

helvétique (ɛlve:'ti:k) *adj* Swiss.

hémisphère (e:mi:'sfɛr) *nm* hemisphere.

hémorragie (e:mɔra'ʒi:) *nf* haemorrhage.

hémorroïde (e:mɔrɔ'i:d) *nf med* pile.

*henné (ɛn'ne:) *nm* henna.

*hennir (ɛ'ni:r) *vi* neigh.

*héraut (e:'ro) *nm* herald.

herbe (ɛrb) *nf* 1 grass. 2 herb. 3 plant. **fines herbes** *nf pl* herbs used for seasoning. **mauvaise herbe** weed. **herbicide** *nm* weedkiller.

hérédité (e:re:di:'te:) *nf* heredity. **héréditaire** *adj* hereditary.

hérésie (e:re:'zı:) *nf* heresy.

*hérisser (e:rı:'se:) *vt* 1 bristle up. 2 ruffle. **se hérisser** *vr* 1 bristle. 2 (of hair) stand on end. ***hérisson** *nm* hedgehog.

hériter (e:rı:'te:) *vt* inherit. **héritage** *nm* 1 inheritance, heritage. 2 legacy. **héritier, -ière** (e:rı:'tje:, -'tjɛr) *nm,f* heir, heiress.

hermétique (ɛrme:'tı:k) *adj* 1 airtight. 2 watertight.

hermine (ɛr'mı:n) *nf* 1 stoat. 2 ermine.

héroïne[1] (e:rɔ'i:n) *nf* heroine.

héroïne[2] (e:rɔ'i:n) *nf* heroin.

*héron (e:'rɔ̃) *nm* heron.

*héros (e:'ro) *nm* hero. **héroïque** *adj* heroic. **héroïsme** *nm* heroism.

hésiter (e:zı:'te) *vi* 1 hesitate. 2 falter. 3 waver.

hétéroclite (e:te:rɔ'kli:t) *adj* 1 irregular. 2 strange, odd.

*hêtre (ɛtr) *nm* beech tree. **hêtre rouge** copper beech tree.

heure (œr) *nf* 1 hour. 2 time. 3 o'clock. **à tout à l'heure** see you later. **de bonne heure** early. **dernière heure** latest news. **être à l'heure** be punctual. **heures d'affluence** or **de pointes** *nf pl* rush hour. **heures supplémentaires** *nf pl* overtime. **tout à l'heure** just now.

heureux, -euse (œ'rœ, -'rœz) *adj* 1 happy. 2 lucky, fortunate. 3 successful.

*heurt (œr) *nm* 1 shock. 2 bump. **sans heurt** smoothly.

*heurter (œr'te:) *vi,vt* 1 knock (against). 2 run (into). *vt* 1 shock. 2 offend. **se heurter** *vr* collide. **heurtoir** *nm* doorknocker.

hexagone (ɛgza'gɔn) *nm* hexagon. *adj* hexagonal.

hiberner (i:bɛr'ne:) *vi* hibernate.

*hibou, -oux (i:'bu:) *nm* owl.

*hideux, -euse (i:'dœ, -'dœz) *adj* hideous.

hier (i:'ɛr) *adv,nm* yesterday.

*hiérarchie (jɛrar'ʃi:) *nf* hierarchy.

hippique (i:p'pı:k) *adj* of horses.

hippodrome (i:pɔ'drɔm) *nm* racecourse.

hippopotame (i:pɔpɔ'tam) *nm* hippopotamus.

hirondelle (i:rɔ̃'dɛl) *nf* swallow.

*hisser (i:'se:) *vt* hoist. **se hisser** *vr* pull oneself up.

histoire (i:'stwar) *nf* 1 history. 2 story; tale. **faire des histoires** make a fuss. **historien, -ienne** (i:stɔ'rjɛ̃, -'rjɛn) *nm,f* historian.

hiver (i:'vɛr) *nm* winter.

hiverner (i:vɛr'ne:) *vi* hibernate.

*hocher (ɔ'ʃe:) *vt* 1 shake. 2 toss. 3 nod.

*hockey (ɔ'kɛ) *nm* hockey. **hockey sur glace** ice hockey.

*Hollande (ɔ'lɑ̃d) *nf* Holland. ***hollandais** *adj* Dutch. *nm* 1 Dutchman. 2 Dutch (language).

*homard (ɔ'mar) *nm* lobster.

hommage (ɔ'maʒ) *nm* 1 homage. 2 token. 3 *pl* respects.

homme (ɔm) *nm* 1 man. 2 mankind. **homme de loi** lawyer. **homme d'état** statesman. **homme politique** politician.

homonyme (ɔmɔ'nı:m) *nm* 1 homonym. 2 namesake.

homosexuel, -elle (ɔmɔsɛk'sɥɛl) *adj,n* homosexual.

*Hongrie (ɔ̃'grı:) *nf* Hungary. ***hongrois** *adj,n* Hungarian. *nm* Hungarian (language).

honnête (ɔ'nɛt) *adj* 1 honest, upright. 2 honourable. 3 decent. 4 well-bred. 5 reasonable. **honnêteté** *nf* 1 honesty. 2 fairness.

honneur (ɔ'nœr) *nm* 1 honour. 2 credit.

honoraire (ɔnɔ'rɛr) *adj* honorary.

honorer (ɔnɔ're:) *vt* 1 honour. 2 respect. **honorable** *adj* 1 honourable. 2 respectable.

*honte (ɔ̃t) *nf* 1 shame. 2 disgrace. **avoir honte** be ashamed. **faire honte à** put to shame. ***honteux, -euse** (ɔ'tœ, -'tœz) *adj* 1 ashamed. 2 shamefaced. 3 shameful.

hôpital, -aux (ɔpı:'tal, -'to) *nm* hospital.

*hoquet (ɔ'kɛ) *nm* 1 hiccup. 2 gasp.

horaire (ɔ'rɛr) *nm* timetable.

*horde (ɔrd) *nf* horde.

*horizon (ɔrı:'zɔ̃) *nm* horizon.

horizontal, -aux (ɔrı:zɔ̃'tal, -'to) *adj* horizontal.

horloge (ɔr'lɔʒ) *nf* clock.

*hormis (ɔr'mı:) *prep* except, but, save.

hormone (ɔr'mɔn) *nf* hormone.

horoscope (ɔrɔ'skɔp) *nm* horoscope.

horreur (ɔr'rœr) *nf* 1 horror. 2 disgust. 3 *pl* atrocities. **avoir en horreur** 1 hate. 2 have a horror of.

horrible (ɔr'rı:bl) *adj* 1 horrible. 2 awful.

horrifier (ɔrrı:'fje:) *vt* horrify.

*hors (ɔr) *prep* 1 outside. 2 out of. 3 beyond. 4 except. **hors de** outside, out of. **être hors de soi** be beside oneself. ***hors-bord** *nm invar* speedboat. **hors de combat** out of action, disabled. ***hors-d'œuvre** *nm invar* a dish served as the first course of a meal. ***hors-jeu** *adj invar* offside. ***hors-la-loi** *nm invar* outlaw.

horticulture (ɔrtːkylˈtyr) *nf* horticulture. **horti-culteur** *nm* horticulturist.
hospice (ɔˈspiːs) *nm* 1 home, institution. 2 asylum.
hospitalier, -ière (ɔspiːtaˈlje:, -ˈljɛr) *adj* hospitable. **hospitalité** *nf* hospitality.
hostile (ɔˈstiːl) *adj* 1 hostile. 2 adverse.
hôte, hôtesse (ot, oˈtɛs) *nm,f* 1 host, hostess. 2 landlord, landlady. 3 guest. **hôtesse de l'air** air-hostess.
hôtel (oˈtɛl) *nm* 1 hotel. 2 mansion. **hôtel de ville** town hall. **hôtel des Postes** General Post Office.
*****houblon** (uːˈblɔ̃) *nm* *bot* hop.
*****houer** (uːˈeː) *vt* hoe. *****houe** *nf* hoe.
*****houille** (uːj) *nf* coal. *****houille blanche** hydro-electric power. *****houillère** *nf* coalmine. *****houilleur** *nm* coal-miner.
*****houle** (uːl) *nf* swell (of the sea). **houleux, -euse** (uːˈlœ, -ˈlœz) *adj* rough.
*****houppe** (uːp) *nf* 1 tuft. 2 bunch. 3 crest.
*****hourra** (uːˈrɑ) *interj,nm* hurrah.
*****houspiller** (uːspiːˈjeː) *vt* 1 hustle. 2 jostle. 3 abuse. 4 reprimand.
*****houx** (uː) *nm* holly.
*****hublot** (hyˈblo) *nm* porthole.
*****huer** (yˈeː) *vi* 1 shout, boo. 2 (of an owl) hoot.
huiler (ɥiːˈleː) *vt* oil, grease. **huile** (ɥiːl) *nf* oil.
huis (ɥiː) **à huis clos** *adv* behind closed doors, in camera.
huissier (ɥiːˈsjeː) *nm* bailiff.
*****huit** (ɥiːt) *adj,nm* eight. *****huitaine** *nf* 1 about eight. 2 week. *****huitième** *adj* eighth.
huître (ɥiːtr) *nf* oyster.
humain (yˈmɛ̃) *adj* 1 human. 2 humane. **humanisme** *nm* humanism. **humanitaire** *adj* 1 humanitarian. 2 humane. **humanité** *nf* 1 humanity. 2 mankind. 3 kindness.
humble (œ̃bl) *adj* 1 humble. 2 lowly.
humecter (ymɛkˈteː) *vt* dampen, moisten.
humer (yˈmeː) *vt* breathe in, sniff.
humeur (yˈmœr) *nf* humour, mood. **avoir l'humeur vive** be quick-tempered. **de mauvaise humeur** bad-tempered. **d'humeur égale** even-tempered.
humide (yˈmiːd) *adj* 1 humid. 2 damp. 3 watery. **humidité** *nf* 1 moisture. 2 dampness. 3 humidity.
humilier (ymiːˈljeː) *vt* humiliate. **humilité** *nf* humility.
humour (yˈmuːr) *nm* humour. **humoriste** *adj* humorous. *nm* humorist. **humoristique** *adj* humorous.

*****huppe** (yp) *nf* *zool* crest.
*****hurler** (yrˈleː) *vi* 1 yell. 2 howl. *****hurlement** (yrləˈmɑ̃) *nm* 1 yell. 2 howl.
*****hussard** (yˈsar) *nm* hussar.
*****hutte** (yt) *nf* hut, shed.
hybride (iːˈbriːd) *adj,nm* hybrid.
hydrate (iːˈdrat) **hydrate de carbone** *nm* carbohydrate.
hydraulique (iːdroˈliːk) *adj* hydraulic. *nf* hydraulics.
hydro-électrique (iːdrɔeːlɛkˈtriːk) *adj* hydroelectric.
hydrofuge (iːdrɔˈfyʒ) *adj* waterproof.
hydrogène (iːdrɔˈʒɛn) *nm* hydrogen.
hydrophile (iːdrɔˈfiːl) *adj* absorbent.
hyène (jɛn) *nf* hyena.
hygiène (iːˈʒjɛ̃) *nf* hygiene. **hygiénique** *adj* 1 hygienic. 2 healthy. 3 sanitary.
hymne (iːm) *nm* 1 song, anthem. **hymne national** national anthem. ~*nf* hymn. **hymnaire** *nm* hymnbook.
hypnose (iːpˈnoz) *nf* hypnosis. **hypnotisme** *nm* hypnotism.
hypocondrie (iːpɔkɔ̃ˈdriː) *nf* hypochondria. **hypocondriaque** *adj,n* hypochondriac.
hypocrisie (iːpɔkriːˈziː) *nf* hypocrisy. **hypocrite** *adj* hypocritical. *nm,f* hypocrite.
hypodermique (iːpɔdɛrˈmiːk) *adj* hypodermic.
hypothéquer (iːpɔteːˈkeː) *vt* mortgage. **hypothèque** *nf* mortgage.
hypothèse (iːpɔˈtɛz) *nf* hypothesis. **hypothétique** *adj* hypothetical.
hystérectomie (iːsteːrɛktɔˈmiː) *nf* hysterectomy.
hystérie (iːsteːˈriː) *nf* hysteria. **hystérique** *adj* hysterical.

I

Ibérie (iːbeːˈriː) *nf* Iberia. **ibère** *adj,n* Iberian.
iceberg (iːsˈbɛrk) *nm* iceberg.
ici (iːˈsiː) *adv* 1 there. 2 now. **d'ici là** between now and then. **d'ici peu** before long. **ici et là** here and there.
icône (iːˈkon) *nf* icon.
idéal, -als or **-aux** (iːdeːˈal, -ˈal, -ˈo) *adj,nm* ideal. **idéaliste** *adj* idealistic. *nm,f* idealist.
idéaliser (iːdeːaliːˈzeː) *vt* idealize.
idée (iːˈdeː) *nf* 1 idea. 2 thought, notion. 3 opinion. 4 mind. **idée fixe/lumineuse** obsession/brainwave.

identifier (i:dāti:'fje:) vt ıdentify. identique adj identical. identité nf identity.

idéologie (i:de:ɔlɔ'ʒi:) nf ıdeology. idéologique adj ideological.

idiome (i:'djom) nm 1 idiom. 2 dialect.

idiosyncrasie (i:djɔsɛ̃kra'zı:) nf idiosyncrasy.

idiot (i:'djo) adj 1 idiotıc. 2 absurd. nm ıdiot.

idiotisme (i:djɔ'ti:sm) nm idiom.

idolâtrer (i:dɔla'tre:) vt idolize. idolâtrie nf idolatry.

idole (i:'dɔl) nf idol.

idyllique (i:di:'li:k) adj idyllic.

if (i:f) nm yew.

igloo (i:'glu:) nm ıgloo.

ignorer (i:ɲɔ're:) vt not to know, be unaware of.

il (i:l) pron 3rd pers ms 1 he. 2 it. 3 there. il y a there is or are.

île (i:l) nf island, isle. îles Anglo-Normandes nf pl Channel Islands.

illégal, -aux (i:llɛ'gal, -'go) adj illegal, unlawful.

illégitime (i:lle:ʒi:'ti:m) adj illegitimate.

illettré (i:llɛ'tre:) adj illiterate.

illicite (i:lli:'sı:t) adj illicit, unlawful.

illimité (i:lli:mi:'te:) adj 1 boundless. 2 indefinite.

illisible (i:lli:'zi:bl) adj illegible.

illuminer (i:lymi:'ne:) vt 1 illumınate. 2 enlighten. illumination nf illumination, lighting.

illusion (i:lly'zjɔ̃) nf illusion.

illustrer (i:lly'stre:) vt illustrate. illustration nf illustration. illustre adj famous.

ils (i:l) pron 3rd pers m pl they.

image (i:maʒ) nf 1 ımage. 2 pıcture. 3 likeness. 4 reflection. 5 simile, metaphor. imagé (i:ma-'ʒe:) adj vivid. imagerie nf imagery.

imaginer (i:maʒi:'ne:) vt 1 imagine. 2 conceıve. 3 invent. 4 suppose. s'imaginer vr think, fancy. imaginaire adj imaginary. imaginatif, -ive (i:maʒi:na'ti:f, -'ti:v) adj imaginative. imagination nf 1 ımagination. 2 fancy.

imbécile (ɛ̃be:'si:l) adj silly. nm,f idiot, halfwit.

imbiber (ɛ̃bi:'be:) vt 1 soak. 2 steep. 3 absorb. s'imbiber vr 1 absorb. 2 become saturated.

imbrisable (ɛ̃bri:'sabl) adj unbreakable.

imiter (i:mi:'te:) vt 1 ımitate. 2 mimic. 3 copy. 4 forge.

immaculé (i:mmaky'le:) adj immaculate.

immanquable (ɛ̃mã'kabl) adj 1 inevitable. 2 infallible.

immatriculer (i:mmatri:ky'le:) vt register.

immaturité (i:mmatyri:'te:) nf immaturity.

immédiat (i:mme:'djat) adj 1 ımmediate. 2 near. 3 urgent.

immense (i:m'mãs) adj huge, vast, ımmense.

immerger (i:mmɛr'ʒe:) vt 1 immerse. 2 plunge.

immeuble (i:m'mœbl) adj law real, fixed. nm block of flats.

immigrer (i:mmi:'gre:) vi ımmıgrate. immigrant nm immıgrant. immigration nf immigration.

imminent (i:mmi:'nã) adj immınent.

immiscer (i:mmı:'se:) vt involve. s'immiscer dans vr interfere wıth.

immobile (i:mmɔ'bı:l) adj ımmobile, still. immobilier, -ière (i:mmɔbi:'lje:, -'ljɛr) adj of land, property.

immobiliser (i:mmɔbi:li:'ze:) vt ımmobilize.

immonde (i:m'mɔ̃d) adj 1 filthy. 2 foul.

immortel, -elle (i:mmɔr'tɛl) adj ımmortal, everlastıng. immortalité nf immortality.

immuniser (i:mmynı:'ze:) vt immunıze.

impair (ɛ̃'pɛr) adj odd, uneven.

imparfait (ɛ̃par'fɛ) adj ımperfect. nm ımperfect tense.

impartial, -aux (ɛ̃par'sjal, -'sjo) adj impartıal.

impasse (ɛ̃'pas) nf 1 deadlock. 2 dead end.

impassible (ɛ̃pa'sı:bl) adj unmoved. 2 callous.

impatience (ɛ̃pa'sjãs) nf impatience. impatient adj 1 ımpatient. 2 eager.

impatienter (ɛ̃pasjã'te:) vt annoy. s'impatienter vr lose one's patience.

impeccable (ɛ̃pɛ'kabl) adj faultless, ımpeccable.

imper (ɛ̃'pɛr) nm inf mac.

impératif, -ive (ɛ̃pɛra'ti:f, -'tı:v) adj,nm imperative.

impératrice (ɛ̃pɛra'trı:s) nf empress.

impérial, -aux (ɛ̃pɛ'rjal, -'ro) adj ımperial. impériale nf top deck (of a bus).

imperméable (ɛ̃pɛrme:'abl) adj waterproof. nm mackıntosh.

impersonnel, -elle (ɛ̃pɛrsɔ'nɛl) adj impersonal.

impétueux, -euse (ɛ̃pe:'tyœ, -'tyœz) adj ımpetuous.

impitoyable (ɛ̃pi:twa'jabl) adj 1 ruthless. 2 cruel.

implicite (ɛ̃pli:'sı:t) adj 1 ımplicıt. 2 absolute.

impliquer (ɛ̃pli:'ke:) vt 1 involve. 2 ımply.

impopulaire (ɛ̃pɔpy'lɛr) adj unpopular.

implorer (ɛ̃plɔ're:) vt ımplore, entreat.

importer¹ (ɛ̃pɔr'te:) vt import.

importer*² (ɛ̃pɔr'te:) vı matter, be important. n'importe never mınd. n'importe comment/ quand/qui/quoi anyhow/anytıme/anyone/

anything. **importance** nf importance. **important** adj 1 important. 2 large. 3 considerable.
importuner (ɛpɔrty'ne:) vt 1 pester. 2 trouble, inconvenience.
imposer (ɛpo'ze:) vt 1 impose. 2 inflict. 3 tax. **imposant** adj imposing, grand.
impossible (ɛpɔ'si:bl) adj impossible.
imposteur (ɛpɔ'stœr) nm imposter.
impôt (ɛ'po) nm tax, duty.
impotent (ɛpɔ'tã) adj 1 helpless. 2 infirm. nm cripple.
imprécis (ɛpre:'si:) adj 1 vague, indefinite. 2 inaccurate.
impression (ɛprɛ'sjɔ̃) nf 1 impression. 2 printing. 3 print.
impressionner (ɛprɛsjɔ'ne:) vt 1 impress. 2 move. **impressionnant** adj 1 impressive. 2 sensational.
imprévu (ɛpre:'vy) adj unexpected.
imprimer (ɛpri:'me:) vt 1 print. 2 imprint. 3 publish. 4 stamp. **imprimé** nm 1 printed matter. 2 form. **imprimeur** nm printer.
improbable (ɛprɔ'babl) adj improbable, unlikely.
impromptu (ɛprɔ̃'ty) adj,adv without preparation, impromptu.
improviser (ɛprɔvi:'ze:) vt 1 improvise. 2 ad-lib. **à l'improviste** adv unexpectedly, without warning.
imprudent (ɛpry'dã) adj imprudent, rash.
impudent (ɛpy'dã) adj cheeky, impudent.
impuissant (ɛpɥi:'sã) adj 1 impotent. 2 helpless. 3 incapable.
impulsion (ɛpyl'sjɔ̃) nf 1 impulse. 2 impetus. **impulsif, -ive** (ɛpyl'si:f, -'si:v) adj impulsive.
impur (ɛ'pyr) adj 1 impure. 2 indecent, lewd.
imputer (ɛpy'te:) vt 1 attribute. 2 charge.
inadapté (i:nadap'te:) nm (social) misfit.
inadéquat (i:nade:'kwa) adj inadequate.
inadvertance (i:nadvɛr'tãs) nf oversight.
inalliable (i:na'ljabl) adj incompatible.
inappréciable (i:napre:'sjabl) adj 1 not perceptible. 2 invaluable.
inapte (i:'napt) adj unfit, not suited.
inarticulé (i:narti:ky'le:) adj inarticulate.
inaugurer (i:nogy're:) vt inaugurate, open. **inaugural, -aux** (i:nogy'ral, -'ro) adj 1 opening. 2 maiden.
incapable (ɛka'pabl) adj 1 incapable, unable. 2 unfit.
incapacité (ɛkapasi:'te:) nf inability.
incendier (ɛsã'dje:) vt set fire to. **incendiaire**

adj incendiary. **incendie** nm fire. **incendie volontaire** arson.
incertain (ɛsɛr'tɛ̃) adj 1 uncertain, unsettled. 2 doubtful. **incertitude** nf uncertainty, doubt.
incessant (ɛsɛ'sã) adj ceaseless, incessant. **incessamment** adv immediately.
inceste (ɛ'sɛst) nm incest.
incident (ɛsi:'dã) nm 1 incident. 2 hitch, difficulty. adj incidental. **incidemment** (ɛsi:da-'mã) adv incidentally. **incidentel, -elle** (ɛsi:-dã'tɛl) adj incidental.
incinérer (ɛsi:ne:'re:) vt cremate. **incinération** (ɛsi:nɛra'sjɔ̃) nf cremation.
inciter (ɛsi:'te:) vt incite, urge.
incliner (ɛkli:'ne:) vt 1 slope, slant. 2 tilt. 3 bend. **incliner à** be inclined to. **s'incliner** vr bow. **inclinaison** nf 1 slope. 2 nod.
inclure (ɛ'klyr) vt include. **inclusif, -ive** (ɛkly-'zi:f, -'zi:v) adj inclusive.
incohérent (ɛkɔe:'rã) adj incoherent.
incolore (ɛkɔ'lɔr) adj colourless.
incommoder (ɛkɔmɔ'de:) vt 1 inconvenience. 2 annoy. 3 upset. **incommode** adj 1 inconvenient. 2 uncomfortable. **incommodité** nf inconvenience.
incompatible (ɛkɔ̃pa'ti:bl) adj incompatible, inconsistent.
incompétent (ɛkɔ̃pe:'tã) adj incompetent.
inconnu (ɛkɔ'ny) adj unknown. nm stranger.
inconscience (ɛkɔ̃'sjãs) nf unconsciousness. **inconscient** adj,nm unconscious.
inconséquent (ɛkɔ̃se:'kã) adj 1 inconsistent. 2 irresponsible.
inconstant (ɛkɔ̃'stã) adj 1 fickle. 2 erratic.
incontestable (ɛkɔ̃tɛ'stabl) adj undeniable.
inconvenant (ɛkɔ̃v'nã) adj improper, indecent.
inconvénient (ɛkɔ̃ve:'njã) nm drawback, disadvantage.
incorporer (ɛkɔrpɔ're:) vt incorporate.
incriminer (ɛkri:mi:'ne:) vt 1 incriminate. 2 accuse.
incroyable (ɛkrwa'jabl) adj incredible, unbelievable.
incuber (ɛky'be:) vt 1 incubate. 2 hatch. **incubateur** nm incubator.
inculper (ɛkyl'pe:) vt law charge.
inculte (ɛ'kylt) adj 1 wild. 2 untidy.
Inde (ɛd) nf India. **indien, -ienne** (ɛ'djɛ̃, -'djɛn) adj,n Indian.
indéchiffrable (ɛde:ʃi:'frabl) adj illegible.
indécis (ɛde:'si:) adj 1 undecided. 2 vague. 3 uncertain.
indéfini (ɛde:fi:'ni:) adj indefinite.

indemne (ɛ̃'dɛmn) *adj* unhurt. indemnité *nf* 1 compensation. 2 allowance.

indemniser (ɛ̃dɛmnɪ'ze:) *vt* compensate.

indépendant (ɛ̃de:pã'dã) *adj* 1 independent. 2 free. 3 self-contained. indépendance *nf* independence.

index (ɛ̃'dɛks) *nm* 1 forefinger, index finger. 2 index.

indication (ɛ̃di:ka'sjɔ̃) *nf* 1 indication. 2 information. 3 sign. 4 *pl* instructions. indicateur, -trice (ɛ̃di:ka'tœr, -'trɪ:s) *adj* indicating. *nm* 1 indicator. 2 timetable. 3 gauge. indicatif, -ive (ɛ̃di:ka'tɪ:f, -'tɪ:v) *adj* indicative. *nm* indicative mood.

indice (ɛ̃'di:s) *nm* 1 sign. 2 indication. 3 index.

indifférent (ɛ̃di:fɛ'rã) *adj* indifferent.

indigence (ɛ̃di:'ʒãs) *nf* poverty. indigent *adj* poor, needy.

indigène (ɛ̃di:'ʒɛn) *adj,n* native.

indigestion (ɛ̃di:ʒɛ'stjɔ̃) *nf* indigestion.

indigner (ɛ̃di:'ɲe) *vt* make indignant. s'indigner *vr* become indignant. indigné *adj* indignant.

indiquer (ɛ̃di:'ke:) *vt* 1 indicate. 2 point out. 3 show.

indiscipliné (ɛ̃di:sɪ:pli:'ne:) *adj* unruly.

indispensable (ɛ̃di:spã'sabl) *adj* essential.

indisposé (ɛ̃di:spo'ze:) *adj* unwell.

individu (ɛ̃di:vɪ:'dy) *nm* 1 individual. 2 *inf* fellow. individuel, -elle (ɛ̃di:vɪ:'dɥɛl) *adj* 1 individual. 2 personal, private.

indolent (ɛ̃dɔ'lã) *adj* indolent, lazy.

indolore (ɛ̃dɔ'lɔr) *adj* painless.

induire* (ɛ̃'dɥɪːr) *vt* 1 induce. 2 infer.

indulgence (ɛ̃dyl'ʒãs) *nf* indulgence. indulgent *adj* 1 indulgent. 2 lenient.

industrie (ɛ̃dy'strɪ:) *nf* 1 industry. 2 trade. 3 activity. industriel, -elle (ɛ̃dystrɪ:'ɛl) *adj* industrial. industrieux, -euse (ɛ̃dy'strɥœ, -'strɥœz) *adj* industrious.

inébranlable (i:ne:brã'labl) *adj* 1 firm, solid. 2 resolute, steadfast.

inégal, -aux (i:ne:'gal, -'go) *adj* 1 unequal. 2 uneven. 3 irregular. inégalité *nf* inequality.

inéluctable (i:ne:lyk'tabl) *adj* inevitable.

inepte (i:'nɛpt) *adj* inane, idiotic.

inestimable (i:nɛstɪ:'mabl) *adj* invaluable.

inévitable (i:ne:vɪ:'tabl) *adj* unavoidable, inevitable.

inexact (i:nɛg'zakt) *adj* 1 incorrect. 2 inaccurate. 3 unreliable.

infaillible (ɛ̃fa'ji:bl) *adj* 1 infallible. 2 sure.

infâme (ɛ̃'fɑm) *adj* 1 infamous. 2 vile, foul.

infanterie (ɛ̃fã'trɪ:) *nf* infantry.

infatuer (ɛ̃fa'tɥe:) *vt* infatuate. s'infatuer *vr* become infatuated.

infécond (ɛ̃fe:'kɔ̃) *adj* barren, sterile.

infect (ɛ̃'fɛkt) *adj* foul, putrid.

infecter (ɛ̃fɛk'te:) *vt* 1 infect. 2 pollute. s'infecter *vr* turn septic. infectieux, -euse (ɛ̃fɛk-'sjœ, -'sjœz) *adj* infectious. infection *nf* 1 infection. 2 stink.

inférieur (ɛ̃fe:'rjœr) *adj* 1 inferior. 2 lower. 3 poor. *nm* inferior.

infester (ɛ̃fɛ'ste:) *vt* 1 infest. 2 overrun.

infidèle (ɛ̃fi:'dɛl) *adj* 1 unfaithful, disloyal. 2 false. 3 faithless. infidélité *nf* infidelity.

s'infiltrer (ɛ̃fi:l'tre:) *vr* 1 infiltrate, seep. 2 filter in.

infime (ɛ̃fi:m) *adj* minute.

infini (ɛ̃fi:'ni:) *adj* infinite. infinité *nf* infinity. infinitif, -ive (ɛ̃fi:ni:'tɪ:f, -'tɪ:v) *adj,nm* infinitive.

infirme (ɛ̃'fi:rm) *adj* 1 disabled. 2 crippled. 3 infirm. infirmier, -ière (ɛ̃fi:r'mjɛ:, -'mjɛr) *nm,f* nurse. infirmité *nf* disability.

inflammable (ɛ̃fla'mabl) *adj* inflammable.

inflation (ɛ̃fla'sjɔ̃) *nf* inflation.

inflexion (ɛ̃flɛk'sjɔ̃) *nf* inflection.

infliger (ɛ̃fli:'ʒe:) *vt* inflict.

influencer (ɛ̃flyã'se:) *vt* influence. influence *nf* influence.

influenza (ɛ̃flyã'za) *nf* influenza.

influer (ɛ̃fly'e:) *vi* influer sur influence, have an effect upon.

informer (ɛ̃fɔr'me:) *vt* inform. s'informer *vr* make enquiries. information *nf* 1 information. 2 inquiry. 3 *pl* news.

infortune (ɛ̃fɔr'tyn) *nf* misfortune. infortuné *adj* unfortunate.

infraction (ɛ̃frak'sjɔ̃) *nf* 1 infringement. 2 breach.

infroissable (ɛ̃frwa'sabl) *adj* crease-resistant.

ingénieur (ɛ̃ʒe:'njœr) *nm* engineer.

ingénieux, -euse (ɛ̃ʒe:'njœ, -'njœz) *adj* ingenious.

ingénu (ɛ̃ʒe:'ny) *adj* 1 simple, naïve. 2 candid.

s'ingérer (sɛ̃ʒe:'re:) *vr* 1 interfere. 2 meddle.

ingrat (ɛ̃'gra) *adj* 1 ungrateful. 2 thankless. 3 unpleasant.

ingrédient (ɛ̃gre:'djã) *nm* ingredient.

inhabile (i:na'bi:l) *adj* 1 clumsy. 2 unfit. 3 incompetent.

inhaler (i:na'le:) *vt* inhale.

inhérent (i:nɛ'rã) *adj* inherent.

75

inhiber (i:ni:'be:) *vt* inhibit. **inhibition** *nf* inhibition.

inhumain (i:ny'mɛ̃) *adj* inhuman.

initial, -aux (i:ni:'sjal, -'sjo) *adj* initial, starting. *nf* initial.

initier (i:ni:'sje:) *vt* initiate. **initiative** *nf* initiative.

injecter (ɛ̃ʒɛk'te:) *vt* inject. **injection** *nf* injection.

injurier (ɛ̃ʒy'rje:) *vt* insult, abuse. **injure** *nf* 1 insult. 2 *pl* abuse. 3 wrong. **injurieux, -euse** (ɛ̃ʒy'rjœ, -'rjœz) *adj* 1 abusive. 2 offensive.

injuste (ɛ̃'ʒyst) *adj* unfair. **injustice** *nf* 1 injustice. 2 wrong.

inné (i:n'ne:) *adj* innate.

innocent (i:nɔ'sɑ̃) *adj* 1 innocent, pure. 2 simple. 3 harmless. *nm* idiot. **innocence** *nf* innocence.

innovation (i:nnɔva'sjɔ̃) *nf* innovation.

inoccupé (i:nɔky'pe:) *adj* 1 idle. 2 vacant.

inoculer (i:nɔky'le:) *vt* 1 inoculate. 2 inject.

inonder (i:nɔ̃'de:) *vt* 1 flood. 2 inundate. **inondation** *nf* flood.

inopiné (i:nɔpi:'ne:) *adj* 1 sudden. 2 unexpected.

inouï (i:'nwi:) *adj* 1 extraordinary, incredible. 2 outrageous.

inquiet, -iète (ɛ̃'kjɛ, -'kjɛt) *adj* anxious, worried.

inquiéter (ɛ̃kje:'te:) *vt* 1 alarm. 2 disturb, trouble. **s'inquiéter** *vr* worry. **inquiétude** *nf* 1 anxiety. 2 concern.

inquisition (ɛ̃ki:zi:'sjɔ̃) *nf* inquisition, inquiry.

insciemment (ɛ̃sja'mɑ̃) *adv* unconsciously.

inscription (ɛ̃skri:'psjɔ̃) *nf* 1 registration. 2 inscription.

inscrire (ɛ̃'skri:r) *vt* 1 inscribe, write down. 2 enrol. 3 register. 4 inscribe. **s'inscrire** *vr* 1 enrol. 2 register.

insecte (ɛ̃'sɛkt) *nm* insect. **insecticide** *nm* insecticide.

inséminer (ɛ̃se:mi:'ne:) *vt* inseminate.

insensé (ɛ̃sɑ̃'se:) *adj* 1 mad, insane. 2 wild. 3 ridiculous.

insensible (ɛ̃sɑ̃'si:bl) *adj* 1 insensitive. 2 indifferent. 3 callous.

insérer (ɛ̃se:'re:) *vt* insert.

insidieux, -euse (ɛ̃si:'djœ, -'djœz) *adj* insidious.

insigne (ɛ̃'si:ɲ) *adj* 1 remarkable. 2 notorious. *nm* 1 badge. 2 emblem. 3 medal.

insinuer (ɛ̃si:'nɥe:) *vt* 1 insinuate. 2 hint at, suggest. **s'insinuer** *vr* 1 creep in. 2 slip in.

insister (ɛ̃si:'ste:) *vi* insist. **insister sur** lay stress on.

insolation (ɛ̃sɔla'sjɔ̃) *nf* sunstroke.

insolent (ɛ̃sɔ'lɑ̃) *adj* insolent, cheeky.

insomnie (ɛ̃sɔm'ni:) *nf* insomnia.

insonore (ɛ̃sɔ'nɔr) *adj* soundproof.

insouciant (ɛ̃su:'sjɑ̃) *adj* carefree. **insoucieux, -euse** (ɛ̃su:'sjœ, -'sjœz) *adj* heedless.

inspecter (ɛ̃spɛk'te:) *vt* inspect, examine. **inspecteur, -trice** (ɛ̃spɛk'tœr, -'tri:s) *nm,f* inspector.

inspirer (ɛ̃spi:'re:) *vt* 1 inspire. 2 breathe in. **inspiration** *nf* 1 inspiration. 2 suggestion.

instabilité (ɛ̃stabi:li:'te:) *nf* instability.

installer (ɛ̃sta'le:) *vt* 1 install. 2 equip. **s'installer** *vr* 1 settle down. 2 move in. **installation** *nf* 1 installation. 2 fittings. 3 *tech* plant.

instant (ɛ̃'stɑ̃) *adj* 1 urgent. 2 imminent. *nm* moment, instant. **à l'instant** a moment ago. 2 at once. **par instants** on and off. **instantané** *adj* instantaneous. *nm* snapshot.

instar (ɛ̃'star) **à l'instar de** *prep* like, after the fashion of.

instiller (ɛ̃sti:'le:) *vt* instil.

instinct (ɛ̃'stɛ̃) *nm* instinct. **instinctif, -ive** (ɛ̃stɛ̃k'ti:f, -'ti:v) *adj* instinctive.

instituer (ɛ̃sti:'tɥe:) *vt* 1 set up, institute. 2 appoint. **institut** *nm* 1 institute. 2 institution. **instituteur, -trice** (ɛ̃sti:ty'tœr, -'tri:s) *nm,f* 1 primary school teacher. 2 founder. **institution** *nf* 1 establishment, institution. 2 boarding school.

instruire (ɛ̃'strɥi:r) *vt* 1 inform. 2 teach, instruct. 3 train. **instruction** *nf* 1 instruction. 2 education. 3 *pl* directions.

instrument (ɛ̃stry'mɑ̃) *nm* 1 instrument. 2 tool, implement. **instrumental, -aux** (ɛ̃strymɑ̃'tal, -'to) *adj* instrumental.

insu (ɛ̃'sy) **à l'insu de** *prep* unknown to.

insubordonné (ɛ̃sybɔrdɔ'ne:) *adj* insubordinate.

insuccès (ɛ̃syk'sɛ) *nm* failure.

insuffisant (ɛ̃syfi:'zɑ̃) *adj* 1 inadequate. 2 incompetent.

insulaire (ɛ̃sy'lɛr) *adj* insular.

insuline (ɛ̃sy'li:n) *nf* insulin.

insulter (ɛ̃syl'te:) *vt* insult. **insulte** *nf* insult.

insupportable (ɛ̃sypɔr'tabl) *adj* unbearable.

s'insurger (sɛ̃syr'ʒe:) *vr* 1 rebel. 2 revolt. **insurgé** *nm* rebel.

intact (ɛ̃'takt) *adj* whole, intact.

intégrer (ɛ̃te:'gre:) *vt* integrate. **intégral, -aux** (ɛ̃te:'gral, -'gro) *adj* entire, whole, integral. **intégrant** (ɛ̃te:'grɑ̃) *adj* integral. **intègre** *adj* honest, upright. **intégrité** *nf* 1 integrity, honesty. 2 entirety.

intellect (ɛ̃tɛl'lɛkt) *nm* intellect. **intellectuel, -elle** (ɛ̃tɛlɛk'tɥɛl) *adj,n* intellectual.

intelligence (ɛ̃tɛli:'ʒãs) *nf* 1 intelligence, intellect. 2 understanding. **intelligent** *adj* clever, intelligent. **intelligible** *adj* intelligible, clear.

intendant (ɛ̃tã'dã) *nm* 1 steward. 2 administrator.

intensifier (ɛ̃tãsi:'fje:) *vt* intensify. **intense** *adj* intense, severe. **intensif, -ive** (ɛ̃tã'si:f, -'si:v) *adj* intensive. **intensité** *nf* intensity, strength.

intention (ɛ̃tã'sjɔ̃) *nf* intention, purpose. **à l'intention de** for, in honour of. **avoir l'intention de** intend to.

intercepter (ɛ̃tɛrsɛp'te:) *vt* intercept.

interdire* (ɛ̃tɛr'di:r) *vt* 1 forbid, prohibit. 2 bewilder

intéresser (ɛ̃te:rɛ'se:) *vt* 1 interest. 2 concern. **s'intéresser à** *vr* be interested in.

intérêt (ɛ̃te:'rɛ) *nm* 1 interest. 2 advantage. 3 profit. 4 share. **avoir intérêt à** be in one's interest to.

intérieur (ɛ̃te:'rjœr) *adj* 1 interior. 2 inner. 3 internal. 4 domestic. *nm* interior, inside. **à l'intérieur** inside.

intérim (ɛ̃te:'ri:m) *nm* interim.

interjection (ɛ̃tɛrʒɛk'sjɔ̃) *nf* interjection.

interloquer (ɛ̃tɛrlɔke:) *vt* disconcert.

intermède (ɛ̃tɛr'mɛd) *nm* interlude. **intermédiaire** *adj* intermediate. *nm* intermediary.

intermission (ɛ̃tɛrmi:'sjɔ̃) *nf* intermission.

intermittent (ɛ̃tɛrmi:t'tã) *adj* irregular, intermittent.

international, -aux (ɛ̃tɛrnasjɔ'nal, -'no) *adj* international.

interner (ɛ̃tɛr'ne:) *vt* intern, confine. **internat** *nm* boarding school. **interne** *adj* 1 internal. 2 interior. *nm* 1 boarder. 2 medical student.

interpeller (ɛ̃tɛrpɛ'le:) *vt* 1 challenge. 2 heckle. **interpellation** *nf* 1 question. 2 challenge.

interposer (ɛ̃tɛrpo'ze:) *vt* interpose. **s'interposer** *vr* intervene.

interpréter (ɛ̃tɛrpre:'te:) *vt* interpret. **interprétation** (ɛ̃tɛrpreta'sjɔ̃) *nf* interpretation. **interprète** *nm,f* interpreter.

interroger (ɛ̃tɛrɔ'ʒe:) *vt* question, examine, interrogate. **interrogatif, -ive** (ɛ̃tɛrɔga'ti:f, -'ti:v) *adj* interrogative. **interrogation** *nf* 1 interrogation, questioning. 2 question.

interrompre (ɛ̃tɛ'rɔ̃pr) *vt* 1 interrupt. 2 stop. 3 break, cut short.

interruption (ɛ̃tɛryp'sjɔ̃) *nf* interruption. **interrupteur** *nm* switch.

intervalle (ɛ̃tɛr'val) *nm* 1 interval. 2 gap. 3 period. **dans l'intervalle** in the meantime.

intervenir* (ɛ̃tɛrvə'ni:r) *vi* (aux être) 1 intervene. 2 interfere. 3 happen.

intervertir (ɛ̃tɛrvɛr'ti:r) *vt* invert.

interview (ɛ̃tɛr'vju:) *nm,f* interview.

intestin (ɛ̃tɛ'stɛ̃) *adj* internal. *nm* 1 intestine. 2 gut. 3 *pl* bowels.

intime (ɛ̃'ti:m) *adj* 1 intimate, close. 2 private. 3 interior.

intimider (ɛ̃ti:mi:'de:) *vt* intimidate, frighten.

intituler (ɛ̃ti:ty'le:) *vt* 1 entitle, give a title to. **intitulé** *nm* title.

intolérable (ɛ̃tɔlɛ'rabl) *adj* intolerable, unbearable.

intonation (ɛ̃tɔna'sjɔ̃) *nf* intonation.

intoxiquer (ɛ̃tɔksi:'ke:) *vt* poison.

intransitif, -ive (ɛ̃trãzi:'ti:f, -'ti:v) *adj* intransitive.

intrépide (ɛ̃tre:'pi:d) *adj* bold, daring.

intriguer (ɛ̃tri:'ge:) *vt* 1 puzzle. 2 intrigue. *vi* plot. **intrigue** *nf* plot, scheme.

intrinsèque* (ɛ̃trɛ̃'sɛk) *adj* intrinsic.

introduire* (ɛ̃trɔ'dɥi:r) *vt* 1 introduce. 2 insert. 3 show in. **s'introduire** *vr* get in, enter. **introduction** *nf* 1 introduction. 2 admission. 3 preface.

introverti (ɛ̃trɔvɛr'ti:) *nm* introvert.

intrusion (ɛ̃try'zjɔ̃) *nf* intrusion. **faire intrusion** intrude.

intuition (ɛ̃tɥi:'sjɔ̃) *nf* intuition. **intuitif, -ive** (ɛ̃tɥi:'ti:f, -'ti:v) *adj* intuitive.

inutile (i:ny'ti:l) *adj* 1 useless. 2 unnecessary. 3 vain.

invaincu (ɛ̃vɛ̃'ky) *adj* unbeaten.

invalide (ɛ̃va'li:d) *adj* 1 infirm, invalid. 2 *law* invalid, null. *nm,f med* invalid.

invariable (ɛ̃va'rjabl) *adj* invariable.

invasion (ɛ̃va'zjɔ̃) *nf* invasion.

inventer (ɛ̃vã'te:) *vt* 1 invent. 2 discover. **inventaire** *nm* 1 inventory. 2 stocktaking. **invention** *nf* 1 invention. 2 device.

inverser (ɛ̃vɛr'se:) *vt* reverse. **inverse** *adj* 1 opposite. 2 reverse. 3 inverted. *nm* opposite, reverse.

invertébré (ɛ̃vɛrte:'bre:) *adj* invertebrate.

invertir (ɛ̃vɛr'ti:r) *vt* invert, reverse.

investir (ɛ̃vɛ'sti:r) *vt* invest. **investissement** *nm* investment.

invisible (ɛ̃vi:'zi:bl) *adj* invisible.

inviter (ɛ̃vi:'te:) *vt* 1 invite. 2 ask, request. **invitation** *nf* invitation. **invité** *nm* guest.

invoquer (ẽvɔ'ke:) vt 1 plead, call upon. 2 bring forward.

invraisemblable (ẽvrɛsã'blabl) adj 1 unlikely, improbable. 2 unbelievable.

iode (i:'ɔd) nm iodine.

ion (i:'ɔ̃) nm ion.

iouler (ju:'le:) vi yodel.

irai (i:'rɛ) v see aller.

Irak (i:'rak) nm Iraq. irakien, -ienne (i:ra'kjẽ, -'kjɛn) adj,n Iraqi.

Iran (i:'rɑ̃) nm Iran. iranien, -ienne (i:ra'njẽ, -'njɛn) adj,n Iranian.

iris (i:'ri:s) nm anat,bot iris.

Irlande (i:r'lɑ̃d) nf Ireland. irlandais adj Irish. nm Irishman.

ironie (i:rɔ'ni:) nf irony. ironique adj ironic.

irrationnel, -elle (irrasjɔ'nɛl) adj irrational.

irréfléchi (irre:fle:'ʃi:) adj 1 thoughtless. 2 rash.

irrégulier, -ière (i:rre:gy'lje:, -'ljɛr) adj irregular.

irrésistible (i:rre:zi:'stabl) adj irresistible.

irrespect (i:rrɛ'spɛ) nm disrespect. irrespectueux, -euse (i:rrɛspɛk'tɥœ, -'tɥœz) adj disrespectful.

irresponsable (i:rrɛspɔ̃'sabl) adj irresponsible.

irrévocable (i:rre:vɔ'kabl) adj irrevocable.

irriguer (i:rri:'ge:) vt irrigate. irrigation nf irrigation.

irriter (i:rri:'te:) vt 1 annoy, provoke. 2 irritate. s'irriter vr 1 get angry. 2 become inflamed.

irruption (i:rryp'sjɔ̃) nf 1 raid, attack. 2 flood. faire irruption dans burst or rush into.

Islam (i:'slam) nm Islam. islamique adj Islamic.

Islande (i:'slɑ̃d) nf Iceland. islandais adj Icelandic. nm 1 Icelander. 2 Icelandic (language).

isoler (i:zɔ'le:) vt 1 isolate. 2 insulate. isolé adj 1 isolated, remote. 2 lonely. 3 detached.

Isorel (i:zɔ'rɛl) nm Tdmk hardboard.

Israël (i:zra'ɛl) nm Israel. israélien, -ienne (i:zrae:'ljẽ, -'ljɛn) adj,n Israeli.

issu (i:'sy) issu de adj descended from.

issue (i:'sy) nf 1 exit. 2 escape. 3 end, result.

Italie (i:ta'li:) nf Italy. italien, -ienne (i:ta'ljẽ, -'ljɛn) adj Italian. nm Italian (language).

italique (i:ta'li:k) adj italic. nm italics.

itinéraire (i:ti:ne:'rɛr) nm 1 route, itinerary. 2 guidebook.

ivoire (i:'vwar) nm ivory.

ivre (i:vr) adj drunk, drunken. ivrogne nm drunkard.

J

jabot (ʒa'bo) nm 1 zool crop. 2 frill.

jacasser (ʒaka'se:) vt chatter. jacasse nf inf 1 magpie. 2 chatterbox.

jachère (ʒa'ʃɛr) nf fallow.

jacinthe (ʒa'sẽt) nf hyacinth. jacinthe des bois or près nf bluebell.

jade (ʒad) nm jade.

jadis (ʒa'di:s) adv 1 formerly. 2 once.

jaguar (ʒa'gwar) nm jaguar.

jaillir (ʒa'ji:r) vi 1 squirt, gush out. 2 run, spread. 3 flash. 4 spring up.

jais (ʒɛ) nm min jet.

jalonner (ʒalɔ'ne:) vt 1 mark out. 2 set out.

jaloux, -ouse (ʒa'lu:, -'lu:z) adj 1 jealous. 2 anxious, keen. jalousie nf jealousy.

Jamaïque (ʒama'i:k) nf Jamaica. jamaïquain adj,n Jamaican.

jamais (ʒa'mɛ) adv ever. à tout jamais for ever and ever. ne...jamais never.

jambe (ʒɑ̃b) nf 1 leg. 2 prop, stay.

jambon (ʒɑ̃'bɔ̃) nm ham.

janséniste (ʒɑ̃se:'ni:st) adj,n Jansenist.

jante (ʒɑ̃t) nf rim (of a wheel).

janvier (ʒɑ̃'vje:) nm January.

Japon (ʒa'pɔ̃) nm Japan. japonais adj,n Japanese. nm Japanese (language).

japper (ʒa'pe:) vi yap, yelp.

jaquette (ʒa'kɛt) nf 1 (lady's) jacket. 2 morning coat.

jardin (ʒar'dẽ) nm garden. jardin d'enfants kindergarten. jardin maraîcher market garden.

jardiner (ʒardi:'ne:) vi garden. jardinage nm gardening. jardinier, -ière (ʒardi:'nje:, -'njɛr) adj garden. nm,f gardener. nf window box. jardiniste nm landscape gardener.

jargon (ʒar'gɔ̃) nm 1 jargon. 2 slang.

jarret (ʒa'rɛ) nm 1 bend of the knee. 2 zool hock. 3 cul knuckle, shin.

jars (ʒar) nm gander.

jaser (ʒa'ze:) vi 1 chatter. 2 gossip.

jasmin (ʒa'smẽ) nm jasmine.

jatte (ʒat) nf bowl, basin.

jauger (ʒɔ'ʒe:) vt 1 gauge. 2 measure. jauge nf gauge.

jaune (ʒon) adj yellow. nm 1 yellow. 2 yolk (of an egg). 3 blackleg. jaunir vt make or turn yellow. vi turn yellow. jaunisse nf jaundice.

javelot (ʒa'vlo) nm javelin.

jazz (ʒaz) nm jazz.
je, j' (ʒə) pron 1st pers m,f s I.
jeep (dʒiːp) nf jeep.
jersey (ʒɛrˈzɛ) nm jersey, jumper.
Jersey (ʒɛrˈzɛ) nm Jersey.
Jérusalem (ʒɛryzaˈlɛm) nf Jerusalem.
jésuite (ʒeˈzɥiːt) nm Jesuit. **jésuitique** adj 1 Jesuit. 2 hypocritical.
Jésus (ʒeˈzy) nm Jesus.
jet (ʒɛ) nm 1 throw. 2 cast. 3 jet, stream, ray, spurt.
jeter (ʒəˈteː) vt throw, fling. **jetée** nf jetty. **jeton** nm 1 counter. 2 token.
jeu, jeux (ʒœ) nm 1 game. 2 play. 3 set. 4 gambling. **jeu de cartes** pack of cards. **jeu de mots** pun. **prendre du jeu** work loose.
jeudi (ʒœˈdi) nm Thursday. **jeudi saint** Maundy Thursday.
jeun (ʒœ̃) **à jeun** adv fasting.
jeune (ʒœn) adj 1 young. 2 juvenile. 3 junior, younger. **jeunesse** nf 1 youth. 2 childhood, boyhood, girlhood. 3 young people.
jeûner (ʒœˈne:) vi fast. **jeûne** nm fast.
joaillier, -ière (ʒwaˈje:, -ˈjɛr) nm,f jeweller. **joaillerie** nf 1 jewellery. 2 jeweller's shop.
jockey (ʒɔˈkɛ) nm jockey.
joie (ʒwa) nf joy, delight.
joindre* (ʒwɛ̃dr) vt 1 join. 2 combine. 3 add. 4 clasp. vi fit. **se joindre** vr join, unite. **joint** adj joined, united. nm join, joint. **jointure** nf joint. **jointure du doigt** knuckle.
joli (ʒɔˈli:) adj 1 pretty. 2 good-looking. 3 pleasant, nice. **joliment** adv 1 prettily. 2 nicely. 3 inf very, awfully.
jonc (ʒɔ̃) nm bot rush. **jonc à balais** reed.
joncher (ʒɔ̃ˈʃe:) vt scatter, litter.
jonction (ʒɔ̃kˈsjɔ̃) nf junction.
jongler (ʒɔ̃ˈgle:) vi juggle. **jongleur** nm juggler.
jonquille (ʒɔ̃ˈkiːj) nf daffodil.
Jordanie (ʒɔrdaˈni:) nf Jordan. **jordanien, -ienne** (ʒɔrdaˈnjɛ̃, -ˈnjɛn) adj,n Jordanian.
joue (ʒu:) nf anat cheek.
jouer (ʒwe:) vi 1 play. 2 gamble. 3 be loose. vt 1 stake. 2 play. 3 perform. 4 trick. **se jouer de** vr make fun of. **jouet** nm toy. **joueur, -euse** (ʒwœr, ʒwœz) nm,f 1 player. 2 gambler. **joujou, -oux** (ʒu:ˈʒu:) nm inf toy.
joufflu (ʒu:ˈfly) adj chubby.
joug (ʒu:g) nm yoke.
jouir (ʒwiːr) vi **jouir de** enjoy. **jouissance** nf 1 enjoyment. 2 possession.
jour (ʒu:r) nm 1 day. 2 daylight. 3 light. 4 hole, gap. **au jour le jour** 1 from day to day. 2

from hand to mouth. **de nos jours** nowadays. **jour de semaine** weekday. **journée** nf 1 day. 2 day's work. **toute la journée** all day long.
journal, -aux (ʒu:rˈnal, -ˈno) nm 1 newspaper. 2 diary. 3 journal. **journalier, -ière** (ʒu:rnaˈlje:, -ˈljɛr) adj daily. **journalisme** nm journalism. **journaliste** nm,f journalist.
jovial, -aux (ʒɔˈvjal, -ˈvjo) adj jolly, jovial.
joyau, -aux (ʒwaˈjo) nm jewel.
joyeux, -euse (ʒwaˈjœ, -ˈjœz) adj 1 merry. 2 glad.
jubilé (ʒybiːˈle:) nm jubilee.
jucher (ʒyˈʃe:) vi 1 perch. 2 roost.
judaïsme (ʒydaˈiːsm) nm Judaism.
judiciaire (ʒydiːˈsjɛr) adj 1 judicial. 2 legal.
judicieux, -euse (ʒydiːˈsjœ, -ˈsjœz) adj judicious.
juger (ʒyˈʒe:) vt 1 judge. 2 law try. 3 adjudicate. 4 consider, think. **au jugé** adv 1 by guesswork. 2 at random. **juge** nm 1 judge. 2 umpire. **jugement** nm 1 judgment. 2 law trial.
juif, juive (ʒɥiːf, ʒɥiːv) nm,f Jew. adj Jewish.
juillet (ʒɥiːˈjɛ) nm July.
juin (ʒɥɛ̃) nm June.
jumeler (ʒymˈle:) vt pair, arrange in pairs. **jumeau, -elle, -aux, -elles** (ʒyˈmo:, -ˈmɛl, -ˈmo, -ˈmɛl) adj,n twin. **jumelles** nf pl binoculars.
jument (zyˈmɑ̃) nf mare.
jungle (ʒɔ̃gl) nf jungle.
junte (ʒɔ̃t) nf junta.
jupe (ʒyp) nf skirt. **jupon** nm petticoat.
Jupiter (ʒypiːˈtɛr) nm Jupiter.
jurer (ʒyˈre:) vt swear, vow. vi 1 curse, use bad language. 2 clash. **juré** adj sworn. nm 1 juror. 2 pl jury. **juron** nm 1 oath. 2 swearword. **jury** nm jury.
juridique (ʒyriːˈdi:k) adj 1 judicial. 2 legal.
jus (ʒy) nm 1 juice. 2 gravy.
jusant (ʒyˈzɑ̃) nm ebb.
jusque (ʒysk) prep 1 as far as. 2 up to. 3 till, until. 4 even. **jusqu'à ce que** until. **jusqu'ici** so far, up to now. **jusqu'où?** how far?
juste (ʒyst) adj 1 just, fair. 2 right, exact. 3 upright. 4 tight. adv 1 just. 2 exactly. 3 barely. **justesse** nf 1 accuracy. 2 correctness.
justice (ʒyˈstiːs) nf 1 justice. 2 law.
justifier (ʒystiːˈfje:) vt 1 justify. 2 clear.
jute (ʒyt) nm jute.
juteux, -euse (ʒyˈtœ, -ˈtœz) adj juicy.
juvénile (ʒyveˈniːl) adj juvenile.

juxtaposer (ʒykstapo'ze:) vt juxtapose, put side by side.

K

kaki (ka'kı:) adj ınvar,nm khaki.
kaléidoscope (kale:ı:dɔ'skɔp) nm kaleidoscope.
kangourou (kãgu:'ru:) nm kangaroo.
karaté (kara'te:) nm karate.
képi (ke:'pı:) nm mil cap.
kermesse (kɛr'mɛs) nf village fair.
kérosène (ke:rɔ'zɛn) nm paraffin oil.
kibboutz (kı:'bu:ts) nm kibbutz.
kilo (ki:'lo) nm ınf kilo.
kilogramme (kı:lɔ'gram) nm kilogram.
kilomètre (kı:lɔ'mɛtr) nm kilometre. **kilométrique** adj kilometric.
kilowatt (kı:lɔ'wat) nm kilowatt.
kimono (ki:mɔ'no) nm kimono.
kiosque (kjɔsk) nm 1 kiosk. 2 newspaper stall. 3 summerhouse.
kiwi (ki:'wi:) nm kiwı.
klaxon (klak'sɔ̃) nm hooter, horn.
klaxonner (klaksɔ'ne:) vi blow one's horn, hoot.
kleptomanie (klɛptɔma'ni:) nf kle omania. **kleptomane** adj,n kleptomanıac.

L

l' def art see **le** and **la.**
la, l' (la) def art f 1 the. 2 a. pron 3rd pers fs 1 her. 2 it.
là (la) adv 1 there. 2 then. 3 that. **là-bas** adv 1 over there, yonder. 2 down there. **là-dedans** adv 1 ın there. 2 wıthın, in it or there. **là-dessous** adv 1 under there. 2 under ıt, that, or them. 3 underneath. **là-dessus** adv 1 on that. 2 thereupon. **là-haut** adv up there.
laboratoire (labɔra'twar) nm laboratory.
labourer (labu:'re:) vt till, plough. **laborieux, -euse** (labɔ'rjœ, -'rjœz) adj 1 hard-workıng. 2 arduous. **labourable** adj arable.
labyrinthe (labi:'rɛ̃t) nm labyrinth, maze.
lac (lak) nm lake, loch.
lacer (la'se:) vt lace (up). **lacet** nm 1 lace, shoelace. 2 noose. **en lacet** windıng.
lacérer (lase're:) vt 1 slash. 2 tear.
lâcher (la'ʃe:) vt 1 let go, release. 2 drop. 3 slacken. 4 divulge. **lâcher pied** give way. **lâche** adj 1 cowardly, faint-hearted. 2 loose, slack. nm coward. **lâcheté** nf cowardice.

lacrymogène (lakri:mɔ'ʒɛn) **gaz lacrymogène** nm tear-gas.
lacté (lak'te:) adj milky.
lacune (la'kyn) nf 1 gap. 2 break. 3 blank.
ladre (ladr) adj mean. nm mıser.
laid (lɛ) adj 1 ugly, plain. 2 unsightly. **laideur** nf ugliness.
laine (lɛn) nf wool. **de laine** 1 woollen. 2 woolly. **laine filée** yarn. **laineux, -euse** (lɛ'nœ, -'nœz) adj woolly.
laïque (la'i:k) adj lay, secular. nm 1 layman. 2 pl laity.
laisser (lɛ'se:) vt 1 let, allow. 2 leave. **laisse** nf lead, leash. **laisser-aller** nm ınvar 1 carefreeness. 2 neglect. **laisser-passer** nm invar pass, permıt.
lait (lɛ) nm milk. **laiterie** nf dairy. **laitier, -ière** (lɛ'tje:, -'tjɛr) adj daıry. nm milkman.
laiton (lɛ'tɔ̃) nm brass.
laitue (lɛ'ty) nf lettuce.
lama (la'ma) nm llama.
lambeau, -aux (lã'bo) nm 1 scrap. 2 shred.
lambrequin (lãbrə'kɛ̃) nm pelmet.
lame (lam) nf 1 blade. 2 strıp, sheet. 3 naut wave.
se lamenter (lamã'te:) vr wail, lament, bewail. **lamentation** nf lament.
lampe (lãp) nf lamp.
lamper (lã'pe:) vt inf swıg. **lampée** nf swıg, gulp.
lancer (lã'se:) vt 1 throw, fling, hurl. 2 start, set goıng. 3 launch. **se lancer** vr rush, dash. **lance** (lãs) nf spear. **lance-pierre** nm ınvar catapult.
lanciner (lãsı:'ne:) vi throb.
landau (lã'do) nm pram.
lande (lãd) nf heath.
landier (lã'dje:) nm gorse.
langage (lã'gaʒ) nm 1 language. 2 speech. 3 talk.
langouste (lã'gu:st) nf crayfish. **langoustines** nf pl scampi.
langue (lãg) nf 1 anat tongue. 2 language. **langue maternelle** mother tongue.
languir (lã'gı:r) vi pıne, yearn. **languissant** adj 1 listless. 2 dull.
lanterne (lã'tɛrn) nf lantern.
laper (la'pe:) vt lap.
lapin (la'pɛ̃) nm rabbıt.
Laponie (lapɔ'ni:) nf Lapland. **lapon** adj,n Lapp.
laque (lak) nm lacquer. **laquer** vt lacquer.
larcin (lar'sɛ̃) nm larceny.

lard (lar) *nm* bacon.
larder (lar'de:) *vt* 1 lard. 2 cover.
large (larʒ) *adj* 1 broad. 2 wide. 3 ample. 4 generous. 5 big. *nm* 1 width. 2 room, space. 3 sea. *adv* 1 largely. 2 broadly. 3 loosely. **largeur** *nf* breadth, width.
larme (larm) *nf* tear, teardrop.
larmoyer (larmwa'je:) *vi* 1 weep. 2 snivel. **larmoyant** *adj* tearful.
larron (la'rɔ̃) *nm* thief.
larve (larv) *nf* larva, grub.
laryngite (larɛ̃'ʒi:t) *nf* laryngitis.
larynx (la'rɛ̃ks) *nm* larynx.
las, lasse (lɑ, lɑs) *adj* tired, weary.
lascif, -ive (la'si:f, -'si:v) *adj* lewd.
lasser (lɑ'se:) *vt* 1 tire. 2 exhaust. **se lasser** *vr* grow, get tired.
lasso (la'so) *nm* lasso. **prendre au lasso** lasso.
latent (la'tɑ̃) *adj* latent, hidden.
latin (la'tɛ̃) *adj,nm* Latin.
latitude (latı'tyd) *nf* 1 latitude. 2 scope.
laurier (lɔ'rje:) *nm* laurel.
lavabo (lava'bo) *nm* 1 washbasin. 2 lavatory.
lavande (la'vɑ̃d) *nf* lavender.
lave (lav) *nf* lava.
laver (la've:) *vt* 1 wash. 2 bathe. **se laver** *vr* wash oneself, have a wash. **laverie** *nf* laundry. **lavette** *nf* dishcloth.
laxatif, -ive (laksa'ti:f, -'ti:v) *adj,nm* laxative.
le, l' (lə) *def art m* 1 the. 2 a. *pron 3rd pers ms* 1 him. 2 it. *pron* so.
lécher (le:'ʃe:) *vt* 1 lick. 2 polish, refine. **lèche-vitrines** *nm* windowshopping. **faire du lèche-vitrines** windowshop.
leçon (lə'sɔ̃) *nf* lesson.
lecteur, -trice (lɛk'tœr, -'tri:s) *nm,f* 1 reader. 2 foreign language assistant (in a university). **lecture** *nf* reading.
ledit, ladite (lə'di:, la'di:t) *adj, pl* **lesdits, lesdites** aforesaid.
légal, -aux (le'gal, -'go) *adj* 1 legal, lawful. 2 statutory.
légaliser (le:gali:'ze:) *vt* 1 legalize. 2 certify
légataire (leːga'tɛr) *nm,f* heir.
légende (leʒɑ̃d) *nf* legend, myth, fable. **légendaire** *adj* legendary.
léger, -ère (le:'ʒe:, -'ʒɛr) *adj* 1 light. 2 slight. 3 agile. 4 loose, fast. 5 mild. 6 weak. **à la légère** lightly. **légèreté** *nf* lightness.
légiférer (le:ʒiːfe:'re:) *vi* legislate.
légion (le:'ʒjɔ̃) *nf* 1 legion. 2 crowd, host.
légitime (le:ʒiː'ti:m) *adj* legitimate, lawful.
legs (lɛ) *nm* legacy.

léguer (le:'ge:) *vt* leave, bequeath.
légume (le:'gym) *nm* vegetable.
lendemain (lɑ̃d'mɛ̃) *nm* next day, day after.
lent (lɑ̃) *adj* slow. **lenteur** *nf* slowness.
lentille (lɑ̃'ti:j) *nf* 1 lentil. 2 lens. 3 freckle. **lentilles de contact** *nf pl* contact lenses.
léopard (le:ɔ'par) *nm* leopard.
lèpre (lɛpr) *nf* leprosy. **lépreux, -euse** (le:'prœ, -'prœz) *nm,f* leper.
lequel, laquelle (lə'kɛl, la'kɛl) *pron, pl* **lesquels, lesquelles** 1 who, whom. 2 which.
les (lɛ) *def art m,f pl* the. *pron 3rd pers m,f pl* them.
lesbien (lɛs'bjɛ̃) *adj* lesbian. **lesbienne** (lɛs-'bjɛn) *nf* lesbian.
léser (le:'ze:) *vt* 1 wrong, wound. 2 injure.
lésiner (le:ziː'ne:) *vi* 1 be mean. 2 haggle.
lessive (lɛ'si:v) *nf* 1 washing. 2 detergent.
lest (lɛst) *nm* ballast.
leste (lɛst) *adj* 1 lively, nimble, agile. 2 sharp, smart. 3 free, brazen.
léthargie (lɛtar'ʒi:) *nf* 1 lethargy. 2 apathy. **léthargique** *adj* lethargic.
lettre (lɛtr) *nf* 1 letter (of the alphabet). 2 letter, note. 3 *pl* literature, letters. 4 *pl* arts. **lettré** *adj* 1 literate. 2 learned. *nm* scholar.
leu (lœ) **à la queue leu leu** *adv* in single file.
leucémie (lœse:'mi:) *nf* leukaemia.
leur (lœr) *poss adj 3rd pers pl* their. *poss pron 3rd pers m,f pl* **le** or **la leur** 1 theirs. 2 their own. 3 to them.
leurrer (lœ're:) *vt* 1 lure. 2 bait. 3 entice. **se leurrer** *vr* delude oneself. **leurre** *nm* 1 lure. 2 bait. 3 decoy.
lever (lə've:) *vt* 1 lift, raise. 2 collect. 3 levy. 4 adjourn. **se lever** *vr* 1 rise. 2 get up. 3 stand up. *~nm* rising. **lever du soleil** *nm* sunrise. **levant** *adj* rising. *nm* east. **levé** *adj* raised. *nm* survey. **levée** *nf* 1 lifting. 2 levy. 3 collection. 4 embankment. 5 *game* trick.
levier *nm* lever.
lèvre (lɛvr) *nf* lip.
lévrier (le:vriː'e:) *nm* greyhound.
levure (lə'vyr) *nf* yeast.
lézard (le:'zar) *nm* lizard.
lézarder (le:zar'de:) *vt* crack, split. *vi inf* 1 bask in the sun. 2 lounge. **lézarde** *nf* 1 crack. 2 crevice.
liaison (ljɛ'zɔ̃) *nf* 1 joining, liaison. 2 connection. 3 relationship. 4 *mus* slur.
liasse (ljas) *nf* 1 bundle, wad. 2 file.
Liban (li:'bɑ̃) *nm* Lebanon. **libanais** *adj,n* Lebanese.

libelle (liːˈbɛl) *nf* libel.
libellule (liːbɛlˈlyl) *nf* dragonfly.
libérer (liːbeˈreː) *vt* 1 free, liberate. 2 release. 3 discharge. **libéral, -aux** (liːbɛˈral, -ˈro) *adj* 1 broad, wide. 2 free. 3 generous. 4 *pol* liberal. **liberté** *nf* liberty, freedom.
librairie (liːbrɛˈriː) *nf* 1 bookshop. 2 publishing house. **libraire** *nm,f* bookseller.
libre (liːbr) *adj* 1 free. 2 clear, open. 3 independent. 4 exempt. 5 vacant. **libre-service** *nm, pl* **libres-services** self-service (shop or restaurant, etc.).
Libye (liːˈbɪ) *nf* Libya. **libyen, -enne** (liːˈbjɛ̃, -ˈbjɛn) *adj,n* Libyan.
licence (liːˈsãs) *nf* 1 licence. 2 leave, permission. 3 *educ* degree. 4 excessive liberty. **licencié** *nm* 1 graduate. 2 licensee.
licorne (liːˈkɔrn) *nf* unicorn.
licou (liːˈkuː) *nm* halter.
lie (liː) *nf* dregs.
liège (ljɛʒ) *nm* cork.
lier (lje:) *vt* 1 fasten, bind. 2 link, connect. 3 *cul* thicken. **lien** *nm* 1 tie, bond. 2 link. 3 fetter. 4 strap.
lierre (ljɛr) *nm* ivy.
lieu, -eux (ljœ) *nm* 1 place. 2 spot. 3 reason. 4 *pl* premises. **au lieu de** instead of. **au lieu que** whereas. **avoir lieu** take place. **donner lieu à** give rise to. **lieux d'aisances** *nm pl* lavatory.
lieutenant (ljœtˈnã) *nm* lieutenant. **lieutenant-colonel** *nm, pl* **lieutenants-colonels** 1 lieutenant colonel. 2 wing commander.
lièvre (ljɛvr) *nm* hare.
ligne (liɲ) *nf* 1 line. 2 row. 3 cord. 4 formation. **à la ligne** new paragraph. **hors ligne** outstanding. **soigner sa ligne** watch one's figure.
ligoter (liːɡɔˈteː) *vt* bind, tie.
ligue (liːɡ) *nf* league, alliance.
lilas (liːˈla) *nm* lilac. *adj invar* lilac.
limace (liːˈmas) *nf* slug. **limaçon** (liːmaˈsɔ̃) *nm* snail.
limaille (liːˈmaj) *nf* filings.
limer (liːˈmeː) *vt* file. **lime** *nf* file. **lime à ongles** nailfile.
limiter (liːmɪˈteː) *vt* 1 limit, restrict. 2 mark the bounds of. **limite** (liːˈmɪːt) *nf* 1 boundary. 2 limit. 3 *pl* bounds.
limon[1] (liːˈmɔ̃) *nm* silt, mud.
limon[2] (liːˈmɔ̃) *nm* lime.
limonade (liːmɔˈnad) *nf* lemonade.
lin (lɛ̃) *nm* 1 flax. 2 linen.

linceul (lɛ̃ˈsœj) *nm* shroud.
linéaire (liːneˈɛr) *adj* linear.
linge (lɛ̃ʒ) *nm* 1 linen. 2 household linen. **linge de corps** underwear. **lingerie** *nf* lingerie, underwear.
linguiste (lɛ̃ˈɡɥiːst) *nm,f* linguist. **linguistique** *adj* linguistic. *nf* linguistics.
lino (liːˈno) *nm inf* lino.
linoléum (liːnɔleˈɔm) *nm* linoleum.
lion (ljɔ̃) *nm* 1 lion. 2 *cap* Leo.
liqueur (liːˈkœr) *nf* 1 liquor. 2 liqueur. 3 drink.
liquider (liːkiˈdeː) *vt* 1 liquidate. 2 settle. 3 realize. **liquide** *adj,nm* liquid.
lire*[1] (liːr) *vt* read. **lire à vue** sightread. **lisible** *adj* legible.
lire[2] (liːr) *nf* lira.
lis[1] (liː) *v see* **lire**[1].
lis[2] (liːs) *nm* lily.
lisière (liːˈzjɛr) *nf* edge, border.
lisser (liːˈseː) *vt* 1 smooth, gloss. 2 polish.
liste (liːst) *nf* 1 list. 2 register. **liste des abonnés** mailing list.
lit (liː) *nm* 1 bed. 2 layer. 3 bottom. **lit d'enfant** cot, crib. **lit de camp** *or* **de sangle** camp bed.
litanies (liːtaˈniː) *nf pl* litany.
litée (liːˈteː) *nf* litter.
litre (liːtr) *nm* litre.
littéraire (liːteˈrɛr) *adj* literary.
littéral, -aux (liːteˈral, -ˈro) *adj* literal.
littérature (liːteraˈtyr) *nf* literature.
littoral, -aux (liːtɔˈral, -ˈro) *adj* coastal. *nm* coastline.
livide (liːˈviːd) *adj* 1 livid. 2 ghastly, pale.
livre[1] (liːvr) *nm* book. **livre à succès** *or* **à fort tirage** bestseller. **livre de poche** paperback. **livret** *nm* 1 booklet. 2 handbook.
livre[2] (liːvr) *nf* 1 pound (weight). 2 pound (money). **livre sterling** pound sterling.
livrer (liːˈvreː) *vt* 1 surrender, give up. 2 deliver. 3 confide. **se livrer** *vr* give oneself up. **se livrer à** give way to, indulge in. **livraison** *nf* 1 delivery. 2 instalment.
lobe (lɔb) *nm* lobe.
local, -aux (lɔˈkal, -ˈko) *adj* local. *nm* 1 building. 2 premises. **localité** *nf* 1 place. 2 area.
localiser (lɔkaliˈzeː) *vt* 1 localize. 2 locate.
locataire (lɔkaˈtɛr) *nm,f* tenant.
location (lɔkaˈsjɔ̃) *nf* 1 hiring. 2 renting. 3 booking. **en location** on hire.
locomotive (lɔkɔmɔˈtiːv) *nf* locomotive, engine.
locuste (lɔˈkyst) *nf* locust.
locution (lɔkyˈsjɔ̃) *nf* expression, saying.

logarithme (lɔgaˈriːtm) *nm* logarithm.
loger (lɔˈʒe:) *vi* **1** lodge, stay. **2** live. *vt* **1** accommodate, house. **2** put, plant. **loge** *nf* **1** hut. **2** lodge. **3** cabin. **4** *Th* box. **5** dressing-room. **logement** *nm* **1** accommodation, housing. **2** lodgings. **logeur, -euse** (lɔˈʒœr, -ˈʒœz) *nm,f* landlord, landlady. **logis** *nm* dwelling.
logique (lɔˈʒiːk) *nf* logic. *adj* logical.
loi (lwa) *nf* **1** law. **2** authority. **3** *pol* act.
loin (lwɛ̃) *adv* **1** far. **2** distant. **au loin** in the distance. **de loin 1** by far. **2** from afar. **plus loin** further. **lointain** *adj* distant, remote. *nm* **1** distance. **2** background.
loir (lwar) *nm* dormouse.
loisir (lwaˈziːr) *nm* leisure.
lombric (lɔ̃ˈbriːk) *nm* earthworm.
Londres (lɔ̃dr) *nm* London.
long, longue (lɔ̃, lɔ̃g) *adj* **1** long. **2** lengthy. **3** slow. **longue-vue** *nf, pl* **longues-vues** telescope. ~*nm* length. **de long en large** up and down, to and fro. **le long de** along, alongside. **tout au long de** throughout. **tout le long du jour** all day long. **longueur** *nf* length. **longueur d'onde** wavelength.
longer (lɔ̃ˈʒe:) *vt* **1** walk along. **2** skirt round.
longévité (lɔ̃ʒeːviˈte:) *nf* longevity.
longitude (lɔ̃ʒiˈtyd) *nf* longitude.
longtemps (lɔ̃ˈtɑ̃) *adv* long, a long time.
loque (lɔk) *nf* rag.
loquet (lɔˈkɛ) *nm* latch.
lorgner (lɔrˈɲe:) *vt* **1** make eyes at. **2** leer at.
lors (lɔr) *adv* **1** even. **2** at the time, when.
lorsque (lɔrsk) *conj* when.
lot (lo) *nm* **1** share, portion. **2** batch, lot. **3** prize.
loterie (lɔˈtri:) *nf* **1** lottery. **2** raffle.
lotion (lɔˈsjɔ̃) *nf* lotion.
lotus (lɔˈtys) *nm* lotus.
louche[1] (luːʃ) *adj* **1** cross-eyed. **2** suspicious.
louche[2] (luːʃ) *nf* ladle.
loucher (luːˈʃe:) *vi* squint.
louer[1] (lwe:) *vt* praise, commend. **louable** *adj* praiseworthy. **louange** *nf* praise.
louer[2] (lwe:) *vt* **1** let. **2** rent, hire. **3** reserve.
loufoque (luːˈfɔk) *adj* mad, eccentric.
loup (lu:) *nm* wolf. **loup-cervier** *nm, pl* **loups-cerviers** lynx.
loupe (luːp) *nf* magnifying glass.
louper (luːˈpe:) *vt inf* **1** bungle, fluff. **2** fail. **3** miss.
lourd (lu:r) *adj* **1** heavy. **2** clumsy. **3** stupid, dull. **4** close, sultry. **lourdeur** *nf* **1** heaviness. **2** clumsiness. **3** dullness.
loutre (luːtr) *nm* **1** otter. **2** sealskin.

loyal, -aux (lwaˈjal, -ˈjo) *adj* **1** loyal, faithful. **2** honest. **3** fair. **loyauté** *nf* **1** loyalty. **2** honesty.
loyer (lwaˈje:) *nm* rent.
lu (ly) *v* see **lire**[1].
lubie (lyˈbi:) *nf* whim.
lucarne (lyˈkarn) *nf* attic window.
lucide (lyˈsiːd) *adj* lucid, clear.
lucratif, -ive (lykraˈtiːf, -ˈtiːv) *adj* lucrative.
lueur (lɥœr) *nf* **1** glimmer. **2** flash.
luge (lyʒ) *nf* toboggan.
lugubre (lyˈgybr) *adj* dismal, gloomy.
lui (lɥi:) *pron 3rd pers ms* **1** he. **2** it. **3** him. **4** to him, her, or it. **lui-même** *pron 3rd pers ms* himself.
luire* (lɥi:r) *vi* **1** shine. **2** glimmer, glitter. **luisant** *adj* **1** shining, bright. **2** glossy. *nm* **1** shine. **2** gloss.
lumière (lyˈmjɛr) *nf* **1** light. **2** *pl* knowledge. **lumineux, -euse** (lymiːˈnœ, -ˈnœz) *adj* **1** luminous. **2** lucid.
lundi (lœ̃ˈdi:) *nm* Monday.
lune (lyn) *nf* moon. **lune de miel** honeymoon. **lunaire** *adj* lunar.
lunette (lyˈnɛt) *nf* **1** telescope. **2** *pl* spectacles. **lunettes protectrices** *nf pl* goggles. **lunettes de soleil** *nf pl* sunglasses.
luron (lyˈrɔ̃) *nm inf* jolly fellow.
lustrer (lyˈstre:) *vt* **1** polish. **2** gloss. **lustre** *nm* **1** lustre, polish. **2** chandelier.
luth (lyt) *nm* lute.
lutin (lyˈtɛ̃) *nm* **1** imp. **2** *inf* mischievous child. *adj* mischievous.
lutrin (lyˈtrɛ̃) *nm* lectern.
lutter (lyˈte:) *vi* **1** struggle, fight. **2** compete. **3** wrestle. **lutte** *nf* **1** struggle, fight. **2** contest. **3** wrestling.
luxe (lyks) *nm* luxury. **luxueux, -euse** (lykˈsɥœ, -ˈsɥœz) *adj* luxurious.
Luxembourg (lyksɑ̃ˈbuːr) *nm* Luxembourg.
lycée (liːˈse:) *nm* grammar school.
lyncher (lɛ̃ˈʃe:) *vt* lynch.
lynx (lɛ̃ks) *nm* lynx.
Lyon (ljɔ̃) *nm* Lyons.
lyre (liːr) *nf* lyre.
lyrique (liːˈriːk) *adj* lyrical.

M

ma (ma) *poss adj* see **mon.**
macabre (maˈkɑbr) *adj* gruesome, macabre.

macédoine (mase:'dwan) *nf* 1 salad. 2 miscellany.

mâcher (mɑ'ʃe:) *vt* 1 chew. 2 munch. **mâchoire** (mɑ'ʃwar) *nf* jaw.

machin (ma'ʃɛ̃) *nm inf* gadget, thing.

machine (ma'ʃiːn) *nf* 1 machine. 2 engine. 3 device, apparatus. 4 *pl* machinery. **machine á calculer** calculator **machine à coudre** sewing machine. **machine à écrire** typewriter. **machine à sous** fruit machine. **machinal, -aux** (maʃi:'nal, -'no) *adj* mechanical, unconscious.

macis (ma'si:) *nm cul* mace.

maçon (ma'sɔ̃) *nm* mason.

maçonner (masɔ'ne:) *vt* build. **maçonnerie** *nf* masonry.

maculer (maky'le:) *vt* stain, spot. **macule** *nf* 1 stain, spot. 2 blemish.

madame (ma'dam) *nf, pl* **mesdames** 1 madam. 2 *cap* Mrs.

mademoiselle (madmwa'zɛl) *nf, pl* **mesdemoiselles** 1 miss. 2 young lady. 3 *cap* Miss.

madone (ma'dɔn) *nf* madonna.

madrier (madri:'e) *nm* 1 beam. 2 joist.

magasin (maga'zɛ̃) *nm* 1 shop. 2 warehouse. 3 stock. **grand magasin** store. **magasin à succursales multiples** chain-store.

magazine (maga'ziːn) *nm* magazine.

magie (ma'ʒiː) *nf* magic. **magicien** *nm* magician, wizard. **magique** *adj* magic.

magistrat (maʒi:'stra) *nm* magistrate. **magistral, -aux** (maʒi:'stral, -'stro) *adj* 1 authoritative, magisterial. 2 brilliant.

magnat (mag'na) *nm* magnate, tycoon.

magnétiser (maɲe:ti:'ze:) *vt* 1 magnetize. 2 mesmerize. **magnétique** *adj* magnetic. **magnétisme** (maɲe:'tiːsm) *nm* 1 magnetism. 2 mesmerism. 3 attraction.

Magnétophone (maɲe:tɔ'fɔn) *nm Tdmk* tape-recorder.

magnifique (maɲi:'fiːk) *adj* magnificent, splendid.

magnitude (magni:'tyd) *nf* magnitude.

mai (mɛ) *nm* 1 May. 2 Maypole. **le premier mai** May Day.

maigrir (mɛ'griːr) *vi* slim, lose weight. **maigre** *adj* 1 thin, skinny. 2 lean. 3 meagre. 4 frugal. **maigreur** *nf* thinness.

maille (maj) *nf* 1 mesh. 2 (knitting) stitch. 3 link.

maillet (ma'jɛ) *nm* mallet.

maillot (ma'jo) *nm* 1 *sport* vest. 2 tights. **maillot de bain** swimming costume.

main (mɛ̃) *nf* 1 hand. 2 handwriting. 3 *game* deal. **à main** by hand. **main-d'œuvre** *nf* manpower, labour. **sous la main** to or at hand.

maint (mɛ̃) *adj* many a.

maintenant (mɛ̃t'nɑ̃) *adv* now.

maintenir* (mɛ̃t'niːr) *vt* 1 uphold. 2 support. 3 maintain, hold. **se maintenir** *vr* 1 hold one's own. 2 continue. **maintien** *nm* 1 maintenance. 2 deportment.

maire (mɛr) *nm* mayor. **mairie** *nf* town hall.

mais (mɛ) *conj* 1 but. 2 why.

maïs (ma'iːs) *nm* maize.

maison (mɛ'zɔ̃) *nf* 1 house. 2 home. 3 household. **maison de commerce** firm. **maison de santé** nursing home.

maître, -esse (mɛtr, mɛ'trɛs) *nm,f* master, mistress. **maître de chapelle** choirmaster. **maître d'hôtel** 1 butler. 2 head waiter. ~*adj* chief, principal.

maîtriser (mɛtri:'ze:) *vt* 1 master. 2 control. **maîtrise** *nf* command, control.

majesté (maʒe'ste:) *nf* 1 majesty. 2 dignity. 3 grandeur. **majestueux, -euse** (maʒe'stɥœ, -'stɥœz) *adj* majestic.

majeur (ma'ʒœr) *adj* 1 major, greater. 2 chief, main. 3 *law* of age.

majorer (maʒɔ're:) *vt* raise or increase the price of. **majorité** *nf* 1 majority. 2 coming of age.

majuscule (maʒy'skyl) *adj* large, capital. *nf* capital letter.

mal[1], **maux** (mal, mo) *nm* 1 evil. 2 wrong, ill. 3 harm. 4 pain, ache. 5 difficulty. **avoir le mal de mer** be seasick. **avoir le mal du pays** be homesick. **avoir mal à l'oreille** have earache. **mal de dents** toothache. **mal de tête** headache. **se donner du mal à** take pains to.

mal[2] (mal) *adv* 1 badly. 2 ill. 3 amiss. 4 uncomfortably. **pas mal de** a good many, a lot of.

malade (ma'lad) *adj* ill, unwell, sick. *nm* invalid. **maladie** *nf* 1 illness. 2 disease. 3 ailment.

maladresse (mala'drɛs) *nf* 1 awkwardness. 2 blunder.

maladroit (mala'drwa) *adj* 1 clumsy, awkward. 2 tactless.

malaise (ma'lɛz) *nm* 1 uneasiness. 2 indisposition.

Malaisie (malɛ'ziː) *nf* 1 Malaya. 2 Malaysia. **malais** (ma'lɛ) *adj,n* Malay. *nm* Malay (language).

malappris (mala'pri:) adj 1 ill-bred. 2 uncouth.

malavisé (malavi:'ze:) adj rash, unwise.

malchance (mal'ʃãs) nf bad luck. malchanceux, -euse (malʃã'sœ, -'sœz) adj unfortunate, unlucky.

malcommode (malkɔ'mɔd) adj inconvenient.

mâle (mɑl) nm male. adj 1 male, cock, dog. 2 virile.

malédiction (male:di:k'sjɔ̃) nf curse.

malentendu (malãtã'dy) nm misunderstanding.

malfaisant (malfə'zã) adj 1 harmful. 2 evil.

malgré (mal'gre:) prep in spite of.

malheur (ma'lœr) nm 1 misfortune. 2 accident. malheureux, -euse (malœ'rœ, -'rœz) adj 1 unfortunate. 2 unhappy, wretched. 3 poor.

malhonnête (malɔ'nɛt) adj 1 dishonest. 2 rude. 3 improper.

malice (ma'li:s) nf 1 mischievousness. 2 prank. 3 spite, malice.

malin, -igne (ma'lɛ̃, -'li:ɲ) adj 1 mischievous. 2 shrewd, sly. 3 malignant.

malingre (ma'lɛ̃gr) adj sickly.

malle (mal) nf 1 (luggage) trunk. 2 mot boot.

malmener (malmə'ne:) vt maltreat, manhandle.

malotru (malɔ'try) adj 1 vulgar. 2 uncouth.

malpropre (mal'prɔpr) adj 1 grubby, dirty. 2 immoral. 3 dishonest.

malsain (mal'sɛ̃) adj unhealthy.

malséant (malse:'ã) adj improper.

malt (malt) nm malt.

Malte (malt) nf Malta. maltais adj,n Maltese. nm Maltese (language).

maltraiter (maltrɛ'te:) vt 1 ill-treat. 2 misuse.

maman (ma'mã) nf inf mummy.

mamelle (ma'mɛl) nf 1 breast. 2 udder. mamelon nm 1 nipple. 2 teat.

mammifère (mammi:'fɛr) nm mammal.

mammouth (mam'mu:t) nm mammoth.

manche¹ (mãʃ) nf 1 sleeve. 2 cap English Channel. manchette nf 1 cuff. 2 headline. manchon nm muff.

manche² (mãʃ) nm handle.

manchot (mã'ʃo) adj one-armed. nm penguin.

mandarine (mãda'ri:n) nf mandarin, tangerine.

mander (mã'de:) vt 1 order. 2 summon. 3 report. mandat nm 1 mandate. 2 warrant. mandat-poste nm, pl mandats-postes postal or money order.

mandoline (mãdɔ'li:n) nf mandolin.

manège (ma'nɛʒ) nm 1 horsemanship. 2 inf trick. 3 behaviour. manège (de chevaux de bois) roundabout, merry-go-round.

manette (ma'nɛt) nf handle.

manger (mã'ʒe:) vt 1 eat. 2 squander. nm food. mangeable adj edible.

mangue (mãg) nf mango. manguier nm mango tree.

manie (ma'ni:) nf 1 mania. 2 craze.

manier (ma'nje:) vt 1 feel. 2 handle. 3 control.

manière (ma'njɛr) nf 1 manner, way. 2 style. 3 kind, sort. 4 pl manners. d'une manière ou d'une autre somehow or other. maniéré adj affected. maniérisme nm mannerism.

manifeste¹ (mani:'fɛst) adj evident, obvious, manifest.

manifeste² (mani:'fɛst) nm manifesto.

manifester (mani:fɛ'ste:) vt 1 reveal, manifest. 2 demonstrate. manifestation nf 1 demonstration. 2 manifestation.

manipuler (mani:py'le:) vt 1 manipulate. 2 handle. 3 operate.

manivelle (mani:'vɛl) nf crank, handle.

manne (man) nf hamper, basket.

manœuvrer (manœ'vre:) vt operate, work. vi 1 manoeuvre. 2 inf scheme. manœuvre nf 1 working. 2 mil drill. 3 manoeuvre. nm labourer.

manoir (ma'nwar) nm manor.

manquer (mã'ke:) vi 1 lack. 2 fail. 3 be missing. vt miss. elle a manqué (de) tomber she nearly fell. ne pas manquer de be sure to. manque (mãk) nm lack, want.

mansarde (mã'sard) nf attic.

manteau, -aux (mã'to) nm 1 coat. 2 cloak.

manuel, -elle (ma'nɥɛl) adj manual. nm manual, handbook.

manuscrit (many'skri:) nm manuscript.

manutention (manytã'sjɔ̃) nf 1 administration. 2 handling.

manxois (mãk'swa) adj Manx.

maori (maɔ'ri:) adj,n Maori.

maquereau, -aux¹ (ma'kro) nm mackerel.

maquereau, -aux² (ma'kro) nm pimp.

maquette (ma'kɛt) nf Art model.

maquiller (maki:'je:) vt 1 make up (the face). 2 fake. maquillage nm make-up.

maquis (ma'ki:) nm scrub, bush.

maraîcher (marɛ'ʃe:) nm market gardener.

marais (ma'rɛ) nm marsh, bog.

marathon (mara'tɔ̃) nm marathon.

marâtre (ma'ratr) nf stepmother.

marbre (marbr) nm marble.

marchand (mar'ʃã) nm 1 shopkeeper. 2 dealer. 3 merchant. 4 tradesman. marchand de poisson fishmonger. marchand en détail retailer. **marchand en gros** wholesaler. ~*adj* commercial, market.

marchander (marʃɑ̃'de:) *vt* haggle, bargain. **marchandise** *nf* merchandise, goods.

marché (mar'ʃe:) *nm* 1 market. 2 deal, contract. **bon marché** cheap. **marché commun** Common Market.

marcher (mar'ʃe:) *vi* 1 walk. 2 tread. 3 go, move. 4 work, run. 5 march. **marche** *nf* 1 step, stair. 2 walk. 3 march. 4 progress, development. **marche arrière** *mot* reverse. **mettre en marche** start, set going. **marchepied** *nm* 1 step. 2 step-ladder.

mardi (mar'di:) *nm* Tuesday. **mardi gras** Shrove Tuesday.

mare (mar) *nf* 1 pool. 2 pond.

marécage (marɛ'kaʒ) *nm* 1 bog, swamp. 2 marsh.

maréchal, -aux (marɛ'ʃal, -'ʃo) *nm* 1 marshal. 2 field marshal. **maréchal-ferrant** *nm, pl* **maréchaux-ferrants** blacksmith.

marée (ma're:) *nf* tide.

margarine (marga'ri:n) *nf* margarine.

marge (marʒ) *nf* 1 margin. 2 edge, border.

marguerite (margə'ri:t) *nf* daisy.

mari (ma'ri:) *nm* husband.

marier (mar'je:) *vt* 1 marry. 2 blend. **se marier** *vr* marry, get married. **mariage** (mar'jaʒ) *nm* 1 marriage. 2 wedding. **nouveau marié** *nm* bridegroom. **nouvelle mariée** *nf* bride.

marihuana (mariwa'na) *nf* marijuana.

marin (ma'rɛ̃) *adj* 1 marine. 2 nautical. *nm* sailor, seaman.

marine (ma'ri:n) *nf* seamanship. **marine de guerre** navy. **marine marchande** merchant navy.

mariner (mari:'ne:) *vt* pickle. *vi* marinate. **marinade** *nf* 1 pickle. 2 marinade.

marionnette (marjɔ'nɛt) *nf* puppet.

marital, -aux (mari:'tal, -'to) *adj* marital.

maritime (mari:'ti:m) *adj* maritime.

marjolaine (marʒɔ'lɛn) *nf* marjoram.

mark (mark) *nm* comm mark.

marmite (mar'mi:t) *nf* saucepan, pot.

marmonner (marmɔ'ne:) *vt* mumble.

marmot (mar'mo) *nm inf* child, brat.

marmotter (marmɔ'te:) *vt* mumble, mutter.

Maroc (ma'rɔk) *nm* Morocco. **marocain** (marɔ'kɛ̃) *adj,n* Moroccan.

marotte (ma'rɔt) *nf* hobby.

marquer (mar'ke:) *vt* 1 mark. 2 note down. 3 score. 4 indicate. *vi* stand out. **marque** *nf* 1 mark. 2 brand, make. 3 score. 4 token.

marque de fabrique trademark. **marque de standing** status symbol.

marquis (mar'ki) *nm* marquess.

marquise (mar'ki:z) *nf* 1 marchioness. 2 marquee. 3 porch.

marraine (ma'rɛn) *nf* godmother.

marrant (ma'rɑ̃) *adj inf* 1 funny. 2 strange, odd.

marron (ma'rɔ̃) *nm* chestnut. **marron d'Inde** horse chestnut. ~*adj* maroon. **marronnier** *nm* chestnut tree. **marronnier d'Inde** horse chestnut tree.

mars (mars) *nm* 1 March. 2 *cap* Mars.

Marseille (mar'sɛj) *nf* Marseilles. **marseillaise** *nf* French national anthem.

marsouin (mar'swɛ̃) *nm* porpoise.

marsupial, -aux (marsy'pjal, -'pjo) *adj,nm* marsupial.

marteau, -aux (mar'to) *nm* 1 hammer. 2 door-knocker. **marteau pneumatique** pneumatic drill.

marteler (martə'le:) *vt* hammer.

martial, -aux (mar'sjal, -'sjo) *adj* martial.

martinet (marti:'nɛ) *nm* swift.

martin-pêcheur (martɛ̃pɛ'ʃœr) *nm, pl* **martins-pêcheurs** kingfisher.

martre (martr) *nf* **martre du Canada** mink. **martre zibeline** sable.

martyr (mar'ti:r) *nm* martyr. **martyre** *nm* martyrdom.

marxisme (mark'si:sm) *nm* Marxism. **marxiste** *adj,n* Marxist.

mascara (maska'ra) *nm* mascara.

mascarade (maska'rad) *nf* masquerade.

mascotte (ma'skɔt) *nf* mascot.

masculin (masky'lɛ̃) *adj* masculine, male. *nm* masculine gender.

masochisme (mazɔ'ʃi:sm) *nm* masochism. **masochiste** *adj,n,f* masochist.

masquer (mas'ke:) *vt* 1 mask. 2 hide. 3 disguise. **masque** *nm* 1 mask. 2 expression. 3 pretence. **masque anti-rides** *nm* face-pack.

massacrer (masa'kre:) *vt* 1 massacre. 2 spoil. **massacre** *nm* massacre.

masse[1] (mas) *nf* 1 mass. 2 bulk.

masse[2] (mas) *nf* 1 sledge-hammer. 2 mace.

massepain (mas'pɛ̃) *nm* marzipan.

masser[1] (ma'se:) *vt* mass. **se masser** *vr* mass together.

masser[2] (ma'se:) *vt* massage. **massage** *nm* massage.

massif, -ive (ma'si:f, -'si:v) *adj* 1 massive. 2 solid. 3 heavy. *nm* 1 clump, bed (of flowers). 2 mountain range.

massue (maˈsy) *nf* club.
mastic (maˈstɪːk) *nm* putty.
mastiquer[1] (mastiːˈke:) *vt* chew, masticate.
mastiquer[2] (mastiːˈke:) *vt* fill with cement.
se masturber (mastyrˈbe:) *vr* masturbate.
mat[1] (mat) *adj invar* checkmated. *nm* checkmate.
mat[2] (mat) *adj* 1 dull, matt. 2 heavy.
mât (mɑ) *nm* 1 mast. 2 pole.
matelas (matˈlɑ) *nm* mattress.
matelot (matˈlo) *nm* sailor, seaman.
matérialiser (mate:rjaliːˈze:) *vt* materialize. **matérialiste** *nm,f* materialist. *adj* materialistic.
matériaux (mate:ˈrjo) *nm pl tech* materials.
matériel, -elle (mate:ˈrjɛl) *adj* 1 material. 2 physical. *nm* 1 *tech* plant. 2 equipment.
maternel, -elle (matɛrˈnɛl) *adj* maternal. **maternité** *nf* maternity, motherhood.
mathématique (mate:maˈtiːk) *adj* mathematical. *nf* mathematics.
matière (maˈtjɛr) *nf* 1 matter, substance. 2 material. 3 subject. **matières grasses** *nf pl* fats. **matières premières** *nf pl* raw materials.
matin (maˈtɛ̃) *nm* morning. **de bon matin** early in the morning. **le matin** in the morning. **matinal, -aux** (matiːˈnal, -ˈno) *adj* 1 morning. 2 early. **matinée** *nf* 1 morning. 2 *Th* afternoon performance.
matois (maˈtwa) *adj* sly, crafty.
matriarcal, -aux (matriːarˈkal, -ˈko) *adj* matriarchal.
matrice (maˈtriːs) *nf* 1 matrix. 2 womb.
matriculer (matriːkyˈle:) *vt* register.
matrimonial, -aux (matriːmɔˈnjal, -ˈnjo) *adj* matrimonial.
maturité (matyriːˈte:) *nf* maturity.
maudire* (moˈdiːr) *vt* curse.
maure (mɔr) *nm,f* Moor. *adj* Moorish.
Maurice (mɔˈriːs) **île Maurice** *nm* Mauritius.
mausolée (mozɔˈle:) *nm* mausoleum.
maussade (moˈsad) *adj* 1 sullen. 2 surly. 3 dismal.
mauvais (mɔˈvɛ) *adj* 1 evil, wicked. 2 bad. 3 poor. 4 unpleasant. *adv* bad.
mauve (mov) *adj, nm* mauve.
maxime (makˈsiːm) *nf* maxim.
maximum (maksiːˈmɔm) *adj,nm* maximum.
mayonnaise (majɔˈnɛz) *nf* mayonnaise.
mazout (maˈzu) *nm* fuel oil.
me, m' (mə) *pron 1st pers m,f s* 1 me. 2 to me. 3 myself. 4 to myself.
méandre (me:ˈɑ̃dr) *nm* meander, bend.
mec (mɛk) *nm sl* bloke, fellow.

mécaniser (mɛkanɪːˈze:) *vt* mechanize. **mécanicien** *nm* 1 mechanic. 2 engineer. **mécanique** *adj* mechanical. *nf* mechanics.
mécanisme (mɛkaˈnɪːsm) *nm* 1 mechanism. 2 machinery.
méchant (mɛˈʃɑ̃) *adj* 1 wicked, evil. 2 naughty. 3 spiteful. 4 vicious. 5 miserable. **méchanceté** *nf* 1 wickedness. 2 spite, malice.
mèche (mɛʃ) *nf* 1 lock (of hair). 2 wisp. **être de mèche avec** be in league with.
mécompte (me:ˈkɔ̃t) *nm* 1 error. 2 disappointment.
mécontent (me:kɔ̃ˈtã) *adj* dissatisfied.
mécontenter (me:kɔ̃tãˈte:) *vt* displease.
médaille (me:ˈdaj) *nf* medal.
médecin (mɛtˈsɛ̃) *nm* doctor, physician. **médecin chirurgien** surgeon. **médecin de médecine générale** general practitioner. **médecine** *nf* medicine.
médial, -aux (me:ˈdjal, -ˈdjo) *adj* medial.
médian (me:ˈdjã) *adj* median.
médical, -aux (me:diːˈkal, -ˈko) *adj* medical.
médicament (me:diːkaˈmã) *nm* medicine.
médication (me:diːkaˈsjɔ̃) *nf* medication.
médiéval, -aux (me:dje:ˈval, -ˈvo) *adj* medieval.
médiocre (me:ˈdjɔkr) *adj* 1 moderate, mediocre. 2 second-rate, indifferent.
médire* (me:ˈdiːr) *vi* slander.
méditer (me:diːˈte:) *vt* contemplate, have in mind. *vi* 1 meditate. 2 muse.
méditerrané (me:diːtɛraˈne:) **(Mer) Méditerranée** *nf* Mediterranean (Sea). **méditerranéen, -enne** (me:diːtɛrane:ˈɛ̃, -ˈɛn) *adj* Mediterranean.
méduse (me:dyz) *nf* jellyfish.
méfait (me:ˈfɛ) *nm* 1 misdeed. 2 *pl* damage.
se méfier (me:ˈfje:) *vr* **se méfier de** 1 distrust, mistrust. 2 beware of. **méfiance** *nf* distrust, mistrust. **méfiant** *adj* 1 suspicious. 2 timid.
mégaphone (mɛgaˈfɔn) *nm* megaphone.
mégarde (me:ˈgard) **par mégarde** *adv* inadvertently.
mégère (me:ˈʒɛr) *nf* shrew.
mégot (me:ˈgo) *nm- sl* fag-end, stub (of a cigarette).
meilleur (mɛˈjœr) *adj* better. **le meilleur** best. ~*adv* better.
mélancolie (me:lãkɔˈliː) *nf* melancholy, gloom.
mélanger (me:lãˈʒe:) *vt* mix, mingle, blend. **mélange** *nm* 1 mixture, blend. 2 jumble. 3 miscellany.
mélasse (me:ˈlas) *nf* treacle.

mêler

mêler (me:'le:) *vt* **1** mix. **2** tangle. **3** involve. **4** shuffle. **mêlée** *nf* fray, scuffle.
mélèze (me:'lɛz) *nm* larch.
mélodie (me:lɔ'di:) *nf* melody, tune.
mélodrame (me:lɔ'dram) *nm* melodrama. **mélodramatique** *adj* melodramatic.
melon (mɔ'lɔ̃) *nm* **1** melon. **2** bowler hat.
membrane (mã'bran) *nf* **1** membrane. **2** web.
membre (mãbr) *nm* **1** member. **2** limb.
même (mɛm) *adj* **1** same. **2** very. **3** self. *pron* same thing. *adv* even. **de même** in the same way. **tout de même** all the same.
mémento (me:mɛ̃'to) *nm* **1** note, memento. **2** notebook.
mémoire¹ (me:'mwar) *nf* **1** memory. **2** recollection.
mémoire² (me:'mwar) *nm* **1** statement. **2** bill, account. **3** thesis. **4** *pl* memoirs.
mémorable (me:mɔ'rabl) *adj* **1** memorable. **2** eventful.
mémorandum (me:mɔrã'dɔm) *nm* **1** memorandum. **2** notebook.
menacer (mɔna'se:) *vt* threaten. **menace** *nf* threat, menace.
ménager (me:na'ʒe:) *vt* **1** save. **2** be sparing. **3** manage. **4** arrange. **ménage** *nm* **1** housekeeping. **2** household. **3** married couple. **faire le ménage** do the housework. **ménagement** *nm* **1** consideration. **2** tact. **3** care. **ménager, -ère** (mena'ʒe:, -'ʒɛr) *adj* **1** domestic. **2** thrifty. *nf* housewife.
mendier (mãdje:) *vi* beg. *vt* beg for. **mendiant** *nm* beggar.
mener (mɔ'ne:) *vt* **1** lead. **2** conduct. **3** drive. **4** manage. **menée** *nf* intrigue, plot. **meneur** *nm* **1** leader. **2** ringleader.
ménestrel (me:nɛ'strɛl) *nm* minstrel.
ménopause (me:nɔ'poz) *nf* menopause.
menottes (mɔ'nɔt) *nf pl* handcuffs.
mensonge (mã'sɔ̃ʒ) *nm* lie, falsehood. **petit mensonge** fib.
menstruel, -elle (mãstry'ɛl) *adj* menstrual.
mensuel, -elle (mã'syɛl) *adj* monthly.
mensurer (mãsy're:) *vt* measure. **mensuration** (mãsyra'sjɔ̃) *nf* measurement.
mental, -aux (mã'tal, -'to) *adj* mental. **mentalité** *nf* mentality.
menthe (mãt) *nf* mint. **menthe anglaise** or **poivrée** peppermint.
menthol (mɛ̃'tɔl) *nm* menthol.
mention (mã'sjɔ̃) *nf* **1** mention. **2** (on a letter) reference. **faire mention de** refer to.
mentionner (mãsjɔ'ne:) *vt* mention.

mentir (mã'ti:r) *vi* lie, tell lies. **menteur, -euse** (mã'tœr, -'tœz) *nm,f* liar. *adj* **1** false. **2** deceptive.
menton (mã'tɔ̃) *nm* chin.
menu (mɔ'ny) *adj* **1** small, fine. **2** slender, slight. **3** petty. *adv* small, finely. *nm cul* menu.
menuisier (mɔnɥi:'zje:) *nm* carpenter, joiner. **menuiserie** *nf* woodwork, carpentry.
se méprendre (me:'prãdr) *vr* make a mistake.
mépris (me:'pri:) *nm* scorn, contempt.
méprise (me:'pri:z) *nf* mistake, error.
mépriser (me:pri:'ze:) *vt* despise, scorn.
mer (mɛr) *nf* sea. **en/sur mer** at sea/afloat.
mercantile (mɛrkã'ti:l) *adj* commercial.
mercenaire (mɛrsɔ'nɛr) *adj* mercenary. *nm* mercenary.
merci (mɛr'si:) *nf* mercy. *nm* thanks. *adv* **1** thank you. **2** no thank you. **merci bien** thank you very much.
mercier, -ière (mɛr'sje:, -'sjɛr) *nm,f* haberdasher. **mercerie** *nf* haberdashery.
mercredi (mɛrkrɔ'di:) *nm* Wednesday. **mercredi des cendres** Ash Wednesday.
mercure (mɛr'kyr) *nm* mercury.
mère (mɛr) *nf* **1** mother. **2** *zool* dam. **3** source. **mère nourricière** fostermother. **mère supérieure** mother superior.
méridien (me:ri:'djɛ̃) *nm* meridian. **méridienne** *nf* **1** meridian line. **2** *inf* siesta.
méridional, -aux (me:ri:djɔ'nal, -'no) *adj* southern.
meringue (mɔ'rɛ̃g) *nf* meringue.
mériter (me:ri:'te:) *vt* **1** deserve, merit. **2** earn, gain. **mérite** *nm* **1** merit, credit. **2** worth. **3** talent.
merlan (mɛr'lã) *nm* whiting.
merle (mɛrl) *nm* blackbird.
merveille (mɛr'vɛj) *nf* marvel, wonder. **à merveille** excellently. **merveilleux, -euse** (mɛrvɛ'jœ, -'jœz) *adj* marvellous, wonderful.
mes (mɛ) *poss adj* see **mon.**
mésaventure (me:zavã'tyr) *nf* mishap.
mesquin (mɛ'skɛ̃) *adj* **1** shabby. **2** petty. **3** mean.
message (mɛ'saʒ) *nm* message. **messager, -ère** (mɛsa'ʒe:, -'ʒɛr) *nm, f* messenger. **messagerie** (mɛsaʒ'ri:) *nf* **1** parcels office. **2** goods department.
messe (mɛs) *nf rel* mass.
messeoir (me:'swar) *vi* be unbecoming.
mesurer (mɔzy're:) *vt* **1** measure. **2** calculate. **3** distribute. **mesure** *nf* **1** measure. **2** measurement. **3** gauge. **4** limit. **5** size. **6** *mus* time. **à**

mesure que (in proportion) as. **dépasser la mesure** overstep the mark. **fait sur mesure** made to measure. **mesuré** adj 1 measured. 2 moderate, restrained.

mésuser (me:zy'ze:) vt **mésuser de** 1 misuse. 2 abuse. **mésusage** nm misuse.

métabolisme (mɛtabɔ'li:sm) nm metabolism.

métal, -aux (me:'tal, -'to) nm metal.

métallurgie (me:tallyr'ʒi:) nf metallurgy.

métamorphose (mɛtamɔr'foz) nf metamorphosis.

métaphore (mɛta'fɔr) nf metaphor. **métaphorique** adj metaphorical.

métaphysique (mɛtafi:'zi:k) adj metaphysical. nf metaphysics.

météore (me:te:'ɔr) nm meteor.

météorologie (me:te:ɔrɔlɔ'ʒi:) nf meteorology. **météorologique** adj meteorological. **météorologiste** nm meteorologist.

méthane (mɛ'tan) nm methane.

méthode (me:'tɔd) nf 1 method, system. 2 way. **méthodique** adj methodical, systematic. **méthodologie** nf methodology.

méthodiste (me:tɔ'di:st) adj,n Methodist.

méticuleux, -euse (me:ti:ky'lœ, -'lœz) adj meticulous, particular.

métier (me:'tje:) nm trade, profession, craft. **métier à tisser** loom.

métis, -isse (me:'ti:, -'ti:s) adj,n half-breed, hybrid, mongrel.

métrage (mɛ'traʒ) nm 1 measure. 2 length.

mètre (mɛtr) nm 1 metre. 2 rule. **mètre à ruban** tape-measure. **métrique** adj metric.

métro (me:'tro) nm underground, tube.

métropole (me:trɔ'pɔl) nf 1 metropolis. 2 capital. **métropolitain** (me:trɔpɔli:'tɛ̃) adj metropolitan.

mets (mɛ) nm 1 dish (of food). 2 food.

mettre* (mɛtr) vt 1 put, set, place. 2 wear. 3 contribute. **mettre les pieds dans le plat** put one's foot in it. **se mettre** vr 1 go. 2 dress. **se mettre à** begin, set about. **metteur en scène** nm 1 Th producer. 2 director (of films).

meubler (mœ'ble:) vt 1 furnish. 2 stock. **meuble** adj movable. nm 1 piece of furniture. 2 pl furniture.

meugler (mœ'gle:) vi low, moo. **meuglement** nm lowing.

meule (mœl) nf 1 millstone. 2 stack, pile. **meule de foin** haystack.

meurs (mœr) v see **mourir.**

meurtre (mœrtr) nm murder. **meurtrier, -ière**

(mœrtri:'e:, -'ɛr) nm, f murderer, murderess. adj deadly, murderous.

meurtrir (mœr'tri:r) vt bruise. **meurtrissure** nf bruise.

meute (mœt) nf 1 zool pack. 2 inf mob.

Mexique (mɛk'si:k) nm Mexico. **mexicain** adj,n Mexican.

mi (mi:) pref 1 half. 2 mid. 3 semi. **à mi-chemin** adv halfway. **à mi-corps** adv to the waist. **à mi-côte** adv halfway up or down. **mi-matin** nf midmorning. **mi-temps** nf half-time, interval. **à mi-temps** part-time.

miaou (mjau) nm miaow.

miauler (mjo'le:) vi miaow.

miche (mi:ʃ) nf round loaf.

micro (mi:'kro) nm inf microphone, mike.

microbe (mi:'krɔb) nm 1 microbe. 2 germ.

microphone (mi:krɔ'fɔn) nm microphone.

microscope (mi:krɔ'skɔp) nm microscope. **microscopique** adj microscopic.

microsillon (mi:krɔsi:'jɔ̃) nm long-playing record.

midi (mi:'di:) nm 1 midday, noon. 2 south. 3 cap South of France.

mie (mi:) nf crumb.

miel (mjɛl) nm honey.

mien, mienne (mjɛ̃, mjɛn) poss pron 1st pers s **le mien, la mienne** 1 mine. 2 my own.

miette (mjɛt) nf soft part of bread.

mieux (mjœ) adj,adv better. **le mieux** best.

mièvre (mjɛvr) adj 1 affected. 2 delicate.

mignard (mi:'ɲar) adj affected, mincing.

mignon, -onne (mi:'ɲɔ̃, -'ɲɔn) adj 1 dainty, delicate. 2 sweet. nm, f darling.

migraine (mi:'grɛn) nf migraine.

mijoter (mi:ʒɔ'te:) vi,vt 1 stew. 2 simmer. vt plot.

mil (mi:l) adj thousand.

milieu, -eux (mi:'ljœ) nm 1 middle, midst. 2 environment. 3 class, circle. 4 mean. **au (beau) milieu de** (right) in the middle of. **juste milieu** happy medium.

militaire (mi:li:'tɛr) adj military. nm soldier. **militant** adj militant.

mille¹ (mi:l) adj,nm thousand. **millénium** nm millennium. **millième** adj thousandth. **millier** nm about a thousand.

mille² (mi:l) nm mile. **mille-feuille** nf pastry filled with cream and jam. **mille-pattes** nm invar centipede.

milligramme (mi:lli:'gram) nm milligram.

millilitre (mi:lli:'li:tr) nm millilitre.

millimètre (mi:lli:'mɛtr) nm millimetre.

89

million (mɪ:'ljɔ̃) *nm* million. **milliard** *nm* **1** one thousand million. **2** *US* billion. **millionième** *adj* millionth.

mimer (mɪ:'me:) *vt* **1** mimic. **2** imitate. **mime** *nm* **1** mime. **2** mimic.

minable (mɪ:'nabl) *adj* **1** shabby. **2** miserable, wretched.

minauder (mɪ:no'de:) *vi* smirk.

mince (mɛ̃s) *adj* **1** thin. **2** slim. **3** scanty. *interj* blast! **minceur** *nf* thinness.

mine[1] (mi:n) *nf* **1** appearance, look. **2** expression. **avoir bonne/mauvaise mine** look well/ill.

mine[2] (mi:n) *nf* **1** mine, pit. **2** *mil* mine. **3** lead (of a pencil). **mine de houille** coalmine. **mine d'or** goldmine.

minérai (mɪ:n'rɛ) *nm* ore.

minéral, -aux (mɪ:ne:'ral, -'ro) *adj,nm* mineral.

mineur[1] (mɪ:'nœr) *adj* **1** minor. **2** under age. *nm law* minor, infant.

mineur[2] (mɪ:'nœr) *nm* miner.

miniature (mɪ:nja'tyr) *nf* miniature.

minimiser (mɪ:nɪ:mi'ze:) *vt* minimize. **minime** *adj* **1** very small. **2** trivial. **minimum** *adj,nm* minimum.

ministère (mɪ:nɪ:'stɛr) *nm* **1** ministry. **2** agency. **3** government office, department. **ministre** *nm* **1** *pol* minister, secretary. **2** clergyman. **premier ministre** prime minister.

minorité (mɪ:nɔrɪ:'te:) *nf* minority.

Minorque (mɪ:'nɔrk) *nf* Minorca. **minorquin** *adj,n* Minorcan.

minuit (mɪ:'nɥɪ:) *nm* midnight.

minuscule (mɪ:nɪ:'skyl) *adj* **1** minute, tiny. **2** small.

minute (mɪ:'nyt) *nf* **1** minute. **2** moment. **3** record, draft.

minutieux, -euse (mɪ:ny'sjœ, -'sjœz) *adj* **1** scrupulous, extremely careful. **2** thorough, detailed.

mioche (mjɔʃ) *nm,f inf* brat, small child.

miracle (mɪ:'rakl) *nm* miracle. **miraculeux, -euse** (mɪ:raky'lœ, -'lœz) *adj* miraculous, marvellous.

mirage (mɪ:'raʒ) *nm* mirage.

mirer (mɪ:'re:) *vt* aim at. **se mirer** *vr* look at oneself.

miroir (mɪ:r'war) *nm* mirror.

miroiter (mɪ:rwa'te:) *vi* **1** gleam, shimmer. **2** flash.

mis (mɪ:) *v see* **mettre.**

miscellanées (mɪ:sɛlla'ne:) *nf pl* miscellany.

mise (mɪ:z) *nf* **1** placing. **2** dress, appearance. **3**

game stake. **4** bid. **être de mise** be the done thing. **mise en scène** *Th* production.

miser (mɪ:'ze:) *vt* **1** *game* stake. **2** bid.

misérable (mɪ:zɛ'rabl) *adj* **1** miserable, unhappy. **2** wretched, destitute. *nm* wretch, rogue.

misère (mɪ:'zɛr) *nf* **1** misery, distress. **2** poverty. **3** *inf* trifle. **crier misère** plead poverty. **dans la misère** poverty-stricken. **faire des misères à 1** tease. **2** worry.

miséricorde (mɪ:ze:rɪ:'kɔrd) *nf* mercy.

mission (mɪ:'sjɔ̃) *nf* mission. **missionnaire** *nm* missionary.

mistral (mɪ:'stral) *nm* cold north wind.

mitaine (mɪ:'tɛn) *nf* mitten.

mite (mɪ:t) *nf* moth. **mité** *adj* moth-eaten. **miteux, -euse** (mɪ:'tœ, -'tœz) *adj* shabby.

mitoyen, -enne (mɪ:twa'jɛ̃, -'jɛn) *adj* intermediate, middle, dividing.

mitrailleuse (mɪ:tra'jœz) *nf* machine-gun. **mitraillette** *nf* submachine gun.

mitre (mɪ:tr) *nf* **1** mitre. **2** chimneypot.

mixte (mɪ:kst) *adj* mixed.

mobile (mɔ'bi:l) *adj* **1** mobile, movable. **2** changeable. **3** detachable. *nm* **1** motive. **2** mobile. **mobilier, -ière** (mɔbɪ:'lje:, -'ljɛr) *adj* **1** personal. **2** movable. *nm* furniture.

mobiliser (mɔbɪ:li:'ze:) *vt* mobilize.

moche (mɔʃ) *adj sl* **1** ugly. **2** rotten, lousy.

mode[1] (mɔd) *nf* **1** fashion. **2** manner. **à la mode** in fashion.

mode[2] (mɔd) *nm* **1** *gram* mood. **2** method, mode. **mode d'emploi** directions for use.

modeler (mɔd'le:) *vt* model, mould. **modèle** *nm* **1** model. **2** pattern.

modérer (mɔde:'re:) *vt* moderate, restrain. **se modérer** *vr* control oneself. **modéré** *adj* **1** moderate. **2** temperate.

moderne (mɔ'dɛrn) *adj* modern.

moderniser (mɔdɛrnɪ:'ze:) *vt* modernize.

modeste (mɔ'dɛst) *adj* unassuming, humble.

modifier (mɔdi:'fje:) *vt* **1** modify. **2** alter.

modique (mɔ'di:k) *adj* **1** modest, slender. **2** moderate, reasonable.

module (mɔ'dyl) *nm* **1** module. **2** unit.

moduler (mɔdy'le:) *vt* modulate.

moelle (mwal) *nf* **1** *anat* marrow. **2** pith. **moelleux, -euse** (mwa'lœ, -'lœz) *adj* **1** mellow. **2** soft.

mœurs (mœrs) *nf pl* **1** customs. **2** manners. **3** morals.

mohair (mɔ'ɛr) *nm* mohair.

moi (mwa) *pron 1st pers m,f s* **1** I. **2** me. *nm*

ego, self. **moi-même** *pron 1st pers m,f s* myself.

moindre (mwɛ̃dr) *adj* **1** less, minor. **2** least.

moine (mwan) *nm* monk, friar.

moineau, -aux (mwa'no) *nm* sparrow.

moins (mwɛ̃) *adv* **1** less. **2** under. **3** least. **à moins de** unless, barring. **à moins que** unless. **au moins** at least, not less than. **de moins en moins** less and less. **du moins** at least. **moins de** less than. ~*prep* minus.

mois (mwa) *nm* month.

moisir (mwa'zi:r) *vi* go mouldy. **moisissure** *nf* mildew, mould.

moisson (mwa'sɔ̃) *nf* **1** harvest. **2** crop.

moissonner (mwasɔ'ne:) *vt* harvest, reap. **moissonneuse-batteuse** *nf, pl* **moissonneuses-batteuses** combine harvester.

moite (mwat) *adj* moist, clammy.

moitié (mwa'tje:) *nf* half. **à moitié** half. **moitié moitié** half-and-half.

molécule (mole:'kyl) *nf* molecule.

molester (mɔlɛ'ste:) *vt* molest.

mollasse (mɔ'las) *adj* **1** flabby. **2** apathetic, lazy.

mollesse (mɔ'lɛs) *nf* **1** softness. **2** slackness. **3** apathy.

mollet, -ette (mɔ'lɛ, -'lɛt) *adj* soft. *nm anat* calf.

mollir (mɔ'li:r) *vt* slacken. *vi* **1** soften. **2** abate. **3** slacken.

mollusque (mɔ'lysk) *nm* mollusc.

môme (mom) *nm,f sl* kid.

moment (mɔ'mɑ̃) *nm* **1** moment. **2** time, instant. **3** occasion.

momie (mɔ'mi:) *nf* mummy (dead body).

mon, ma, mes (mɔ̃, ma, mɛ) *poss adj 1st pers s* my.

monarque (mɔ'nark) *nm* monarch.

monastère (mɔna'stɛr) *nm* monastery. **monastique** *adj* monastic.

monceau, -aux (mɔ̃'so) *nm* pile, heap.

monde (mɔ̃d) *nm* **1** world. **2** people. **3** society. **tout le monde** everybody, everyone. **mondain** *adj* **1** worldly. **2** mundane. **mondial, -aux** (mɔ̃'djal, -'djo) *adj* worldwide.

monétaire (mone:'tɛr) *adj* monetary.

moniteur, -trice (mɔni:'tœr, -'tri:s) *nm,f* **1** monitor. **2** instructor. **3** *sport* coach.

monnayer (mɔnɛ'je:) *vt* **1** coin, mint. **2** *inf* cash in on. **monnaie** *nf* **1** money. **2** currency. **3** change. **petite monnaie** small change.

monogamie (mɔnɔga'mi:) *nf* monogamy.

monologue (mɔnɔ'lɔg) *nm* monologue.

monopole (mɔnɔ'pɔl) *nm* monopoly.

monopoliser (mɔnɔpɔli:'ze:) *vt* monopolize.

monosyllabe (mɔnɔsi:l'lab) *adj* monosyllabic. *nm* monosyllable.

monotone (mɔnɔ'tɔn) *adj* monotonous.

monseigneur (mɔ̃sɛ'ɲœr) *nm* **1** *pl* **nosseigneurs** His or Your Royal Highness, His Grace. **2** *pl* **messeigneurs** Your Grace, His or Your Lordship.

monsieur (mɔ'sjœ) *nm, pl* **messieurs** **1** sir. **2** master. **3** gentleman. **4** *cap* Mr.

monstre (mɔ̃str) *nm* monster. *adj* huge, enormous. **monstrueux, -euse** (mɔ̃stry'œ, -'œz) *adj* **1** monstrous. **2** huge. **3** scandalous.

mont (mɔ̃) *nm* mount, mountain.

montagne (mɔ̃'taɲ) *nf* mountain. **montagnard** *adj* mountain, highland. *nm* highlander, person living in the mountains. **montagneux, -euse** (mɔ̃ta'ɲœ, -'ɲœz) *adj* mountainous.

monter (mɔ̃'te:) *vi (aux usu* être) **1** climb. **2** go up. **3** ride. **4** mount. **5** rise. *vt* **1** climb, ascend. **2** carry or take up. **3** erect. **4** *Th* produce. **monter à cheval** ride. **montant** *adj* **1** rising. **2** uphill. *nm* **1** upright. **2** rise. **3** (total) amount. **monté** *adj* **1** mounted. **2** equipped. **montée** *nf* **1** rise. **2** step. **monture** *nf* **1** mount (a horse, etc.). **2** setting. **3** frame. **4** handle.

montrer (mɔ̃'tre:) *vt* **1** show. **2** display. **3** point out. **4** teach. **se montrer** *vr* appear. **montre** *nf* **1** watch. **2** show, display. **montre-bracelet** *nf, pl* **montres-bracelets** wristwatch.

monument (mɔny'mɑ̃) *nm* monument.

se moquer (mɔ'ke:) *vr* **se moquer de** mock, make fun of. **moquerie** *nf* mockery, ridicule.

moral, -aux (mɔ'ral, -'ro) *adj* **1** moral. **2** ethical. **3** mental. **morale** *nf* **1** morals. **2** ethics. **3** moral. **moralité** *nf* **1** morality. **2** moral.

moraliser (mɔrali:'ze:) *vi* moralize. *vt* lecture.

morbide (mɔr'bi:d) *adj* morbid.

morceau, -aux (mɔr'so) *nm* **1** piece. **2** bit, scrap.

mordre (mɔrdr) *vt* **1** bite. **2** nip. **mordant** *adj* **1** biting, caustic. **2** sarcastic. **mordu** *adj sl* mad, keen.

morgue (mɔrg) *nf* **1** mortuary. **2** pride.

moribond (mɔri:'bɔ̃) *adj* dying.

morne (mɔrn) *adj* **1** gloomy. **2** dreary, dull.

morose (mɔ'roz) *adj* morose, sullen.

morphine (mɔr'fi:n) *nf* morphine.

mors (mɔr) *nm* bit (of a bridle).

morse [1] (mɔrs) *nm* walrus.

morse [2] (mɔrs) *nm* morse code.

morsure (mɔr'syr) *nf* bite.

mort¹ (mɔr) v see **mourir**. adj 1 dead. 2 stagnant. 3 neutral. **mort-né** adj, pl **mort-nés** stillborn. **morte-saison** nf, pl **mortes-saisons** off-season.

mort² (mɔr) nf death.

mortalité (mɔrtali:'te:) nf 1 mortality. 2 death rate.

mortel, -elle (mɔr'tɛl) adj 1 mortal. 2 fatal. 3 deadly.

mortier (mɔr'tje:) nm mortar.

mortifier (mɔrtı:'fje:) vt 1 mortify, hurt. 2 cul hang.

mortuaire (mɔr'tɥɛr) adj mortuary.

morue (mɔ'ry) nf cod.

morveux, -euse (mɔr'vœ, -'vœz) nm,f brat, child.

mosaïque (mɔza'i:k) adj,nf mosaic.

mosquée (mɔ'ske:) nf mosque.

mot (mo) nm 1 word. 2 saying. 3 hint. **gros mot** swearword. **mots croisés** crossword.

motel (mɔ'tɛl) nm motel.

moteur, -trice (mɔ'tœr, -'trı:s) adj motive, driving. nm motor, engine. **moteur-fusée** nm, pl **moteurs-fusées** rocket.

motif (mɔ'tı:f) nm 1 motive, reason. 2 pattern. 3 mus theme.

motion (mɔ'sjɔ̃) nf motion, proposal.

motiver (mɔtı:'ve:) vt 1 give the reason for. 2 warrant.

motocyclette (mɔtɔsı:'klɛt) nf motorcycle.

motte (mɔt) nf 1 mound. 2 lump. 3 cul pat, roll.

mou, mol, molle (mu:, mɔl, mɔl) adj 1 soft. 2 weak. 3 slack. 4 limp. nm 1 slack. 2 zool lungs.

mouche (mu:ʃ) nf 1 fly. 2 spot, stain.

moucher (mu:'ʃe:) vt 1 wipe (the nose of). 2 snuff. **se moucher** vr blow one's nose.

moucheter (mu:ʃ'te:) vt speckle, spot. **moucheture** nf speckle, fleck, spot.

mouchoir (mu:'ʃwar) nm handkerchief.

moudre* (mu:dr) vt grind.

moue (mu:) nf pout. **faire la moue** pout, sulk.

mouette (mwɛt) nf gull.

moufette (mu:'fɛt) nf skunk.

moufle (mu:fl) nf mitten.

mouiller (mu:'je:) vt 1 dampen, moisten. 2 anchor. **se mouiller** vr get wet.

moule¹ (mu:l) nm mould.

moule² (mu:l) nf mussel.

mouler (mu:'le:) vt 1 cast. 2 mould.

moulin (mu:'lɛ̃) nm mill. **moulin à eau** watermill. **moulin à poivre** peppermill. **moulin à vent** windmill. **moulinet** nm sport reel.

moulu (mu:'ly) v see **moudre**. adj ground.

mourir* (mu:'rı:r) vi (aux être) die. **se mourir** vr 1 be dying. 2 die out.

mousse¹ (mu:s) nf 1 moss. 2 foam, froth. 3 lather. 4 mousse.

mousse² (mu:s) nm cabin boy.

mousseline (mu:s'li:n) nf muslin.

mousser (mu:'se:) vi 1 froth, foam. 2 lather. 3 sparkle.

mousson (mu:'sɔ̃) nf monsoon.

moustache (mu:'staʃ) nf 1 moustache. 2 zool whiskers.

moustique (mu:'stı:k) nm mosquito.

moutarde (mu:'tard) nf mustard.

mouton (mu:'tɔ̃) nm 1 sheep. 2 mutton.

mouvoir* (mu:'vwar) vt 1 move. 2 drive. 3 prompt, activate. **se mouvoir** vr move. **mouvant** adj 1 moving. 2 mobile. 3 fickle. **mouvement** nm 1 movement. 2 change. 3 impulse. 4 emotion. **mouvementé** adj 1 lively. 2 thrilling.

moyen¹, **-enne** (mwa'jɛ̃, -'jɛn) adj 1 middle. 2 average. 3 medium. **moyen âge** Middle Ages. ~nf average.

moyen² (mwa'jɛ̃) nm 1 means. 2 way. 3 pl ability.

moyennant (mwajɛ'nã) prep for, at (a price). **moyennant que** on condition that.

Moyen Orient nm Middle East.

moyeu, -eux (mwa'jœ) nm hub.

muer (mɥe:) vi 1 moult. 2 (of the voice) break.

muet, -ette (mɥɛ, mɥɛt) adj 1 dumb, mute. 2 silent.

mufle (myfl) nm 1 muzzle. 2 sl mug, face. 3 sl swine.

muge (myʒ) nm mullet.

mugir (my'ʒı:r) vi 1 moo. 2 bellow. 3 roar.

muguet (my'gɛ) nm lily-of-the-valley.

mule¹ (myl) nf mule.

mule² (myl) nf slipper.

multiplier (myltı:pli:'e:) vi,vt multiply. **multiple** adj multiple, manifold. nm multiple.

multitude (myltı:'tyd) nf multitude, crowd.

municipal, -aux (mynı:sı:'pal; -'po) adj municipal. **municipalité** nf 1 municipality. 2 town hall. 3 town council.

munir (my'nı:r) vt **munir de** 1 provide, supply. 2 equip. **munitions** nf pl 1 ammunition. 2 supplies.

mur (myr) nm wall.

mûr (myr) adj 1 ripe. 2 mature. 3 mellow.

mural, -aux (my'ral, -'ro) adj mural.

mûre (myr) *nf* mulberry. **mûre sauvage** blackberry. **mûrier** *nm* mulberry tree or bush.

mûrir (my'riːr) *vi,vt* 1 ripen. 2 mature.

murmurer (myrmy're:) *vi* 1 murmur. 2 grumble. *vt* whisper. **murmure** *nm* murmur.

musc (mysk) *nm* musk.

muscade (my'skad) *nf* nutmeg.

muscle (myskl) *nm* muscle. **musclé** *adj* muscular.

museau, -aux (my'zo) *nm* muzzle, snout.

musée (my'ze:) *nm* museum. **musée de peinture** or **beaux arts** art gallery.

museler (my'zle:) *vt* muzzle. **muselière** *nf* muzzle.

muser (my'ze:) *vi* dawdle, loiter.

muséum (myze:'ɔm) *nm* natural history museum.

musique (my'ziːk) *nf* 1 music. 2 *mil* band. **musique de chambre** chamber music. **musical, -aux** (myzi'kal, -'ko) *adj* musical. **musicien, -ienne** (myzi:'sjɛ̃, -'sjɛn) *nm,f* musician. *adj* musical.

musulman (myzyl'mã) *adj,n* Muslim.

mutiler (myti:'le:) *vt* 1 maim. 2 mutilate, deface. **mutilé** *adj* maimed, disabled.

mutin (my'tɛ̃) *adj* insubordinate, disobedient.

se mutiner (myti:'ne:) *vr* mutiny, revolt. **mutinerie** *nf* mutiny, rebellion.

mutisme (my'ti:sm) *nm* dumbness.

mutuel, -elle (my'tɥɛl) *adj* mutual.

myope (mjɔp) *adj* short-sighted. **myopie** *nf* short-sightedness.

myrrhe (myr) *nf* myrrh.

myrte (mi:rt) *nm* myrtle.

myrtille (mi:r'ti:j) *nf* bilberry.

mystère (mi:'stɛr) *nm* mystery. **mystérieux, -euse** (mi:ste:'rjœ, -'rjœz) *adj* mysterious.

mystifier (mi:sti:'fje:) *vt* 1 hoax, fool. 2 mystify.

mystique (mi:'sti:k) *adj,n* mystic. *nf* mystique.

mythe (mi:t) *nm* myth, legend.

mythologie (mi:tɔlɔ'ʒi:) *nf* mythology. **mythologique** *adj* mythological.

N

nabot (na'bo) *nm* dwarf, midget.

nacré (na'kre:) *adj* pearly.

nager (na'ʒe:) *vi* 1 swim. 2 float. 3 row. **nager debout** tread water. **nage** *nf* 1 rowing. 2 swimming. 3 stroke. **nageoire** *nf* fin.

naguère (na'gɛr) *adv* not long ago.

naïf, -ïve (na'i:f, -'i:v) *adj* 1 naive, simple. 2 innocent.

nain (nɛ̃) *adj,n* dwarf.

naissance (nɛ'sɑ̃s) *nf* 1 birth. 2 descent. 3 source.

naître° (nɛtr) *vi (aux être)* 1 be born. 2 originate, rise. **faire naître** provoke, arouse.

nappe (nap) *nf* 1 tablecloth. 2 cloth. 3 cover. 4 sheet.

naquis (na'ki:) *v* see **naître**.

narcotique (narkɔ'ti:k) *adj,nm* narcotic.

narine (na'ri:n) *nf* nostril.

narquois (nar'kwa) *adj* sneering, mocking.

narrer (na're:) *vt* narrate, relate. **narratif, -ive** (narra'ti:f, -'ti:v) *adj* narrative. **narration** *nf* 1 narration. 2 narrative.

nasal, -aux (na'zal, -'zo) *adj* nasal. **naseau, -aux** (na'zo) *nm zool* nostril.

natal (na'tal) *adj* native (country, town, etc.). **natalité** *nf* birthrate.

natation (nata'sjɔ̃) *nf* swimming.

natif, -ive (na'ti:f, -'ti:v) *adj* 1 native. 2 natural.

nation (na'sjɔ̃) *nf* nation. **national, -aux** (nasjɔ'nal, -'no) *adj* national. **nationalité** *nf* nationality.

nationaliser (nasjɔnali:'ze:) *vt* nationalize.

nativité (nati:vi:'te:) *nf* nativity.

natter (na'te:) *vt* plait. **natte** *nf* 1 mat. 2 plait.

naturaliser (natyrali:'ze:) *vt* naturalize.

nature (na'tyr) *nf* 1 nature. 2 character. 3 temperament. 4 kind. **nature morte** still life. ~*adj invar* plain, natural. **naturaliste** *nm,f* naturalist.

naturel, -elle (naty'rɛl) *adj* 1 natural. 2 unaffected. 3 illegitimate. *nm* disposition.

naufrage (no'fraʒ) *nm* shipwreck.

nauséabond (noze:a'bɔ̃) *adj* 1 nauseating. 2 foul. **nausée** *nf* nausea.

nautique (no'ti:k) *adj* nautical.

naval (na'val) *adj* naval, nautical.

navet (na'vɛ) *nm* 1 turnip. 2 *inf* rubbish.

naviguer (navi:'ge:) *vi* 1 sail. 2 navigate. **navigateur** *nm* navigator.

navire (na'vi:r) *nm* ship, vessel.

navrer (na'vre:) *vt* grieve. **navré** *adj* sad, distressed, sorry.

ne, n' (nə) *adv* not.

né (ne:) *v* see **naître**. *adj* born.

néanmoins (ne:ɑ̃'mwɛ̃) *adv* nevertheless, yet.

néant (ne:'ɑ̃) *nm* nought, nothing.

nébuleux, -euse (ne:by'lœ, -'lœz) *adj* 1 nebulous. 2 cloudy. 3 vague, obscure.

nécessité (ne:sɛsi:'te:) *nf* 1 necessity. 2 need,

want. **nécessaire** adj 1 necessary. 2 essential.

nécrologie (ne:krɔlɔ'ʒi) nf obituary notice, deaths column.

néerlandais (ne:ɛrlã'dɛ) adj Dutch. nm Dutchman.

nef (nɛf) nf nave. **nef latérale** aisle.

néfaste (ne:'fast) adj 1 baneful. 2 evil.

nèfle (nɛfl) nf medlar. **néflier** nm medlar tree.

négatif, -ive (ne:ga'tɪːf, -'tɪːv) adj negative. nm phot negative. nf negative, refusal.

négliger (ne:gli:'ʒe:) vt 1 neglect. 2 disregard. **négligé** adj 1 neglected. 2 careless. **négligence** nf 1 carelessness. 2 neglect. **négligent** adj negligent, careless.

négocier (ne:gɔ'sje:) vt negotiate. **négoce** nm trade. **négociant** nm merchant. **négociateur** nm negotiator. **négotiation** nf 1 negotiation. 2 transaction.

nègre, négresse (nɛgr, ne:'grɛs) nm,f Negro, Negress. **parler petit nègre** speak pidgin French. ~adj Negro.

neiger (ne:'ʒe:) v imp snow. **neige** (nɛʒ) nf snow.

nénuphar (ne:ny'far) nm waterlily.

néon (ne:'ɔ̃) nm neon.

néo-Zélandais (ne:oze:lã'dɛ) adj New Zealand. nm New Zealander.

nerf (nɛrf) nm 1 nerve. 2 energy. 3 sinew. **nerveux, -euse** (nɛr'vœ, -'vœz) adj 1 med nervous. 2 vigorous. 3 excitable, hysterical. **nervosité** (nɛrvozi:'te:) nf nerves, irritability.

net, nette (nɛt) adj 1 clean. 2 clear. 3 distinct. 4 net. adv 1 plainly. 2 clearly. 3 outright. **netteté** nf 1 cleanness. 2 clearness.

nettoyer (nɛtwa'je:) vt 1 clean. 2 scour. 3 wipe. 4 clear out. **nettoyer à fond** spring-clean. **nettoyer à sec** dry-clean. **nettoiement** nm also **nettoyage** 1 cleaning. 2 clearing.

neuf[1] (nœf) adj,nm nine. **neuvième** adj ninth.

neuf[2], **neuve** (nœf, nœv) adj new. **à neuf** again.

neutraliser (nœtrali:'ze:) vt neutralize.

neutralité (nœtrali:'te:) nf neutrality.

neutre (nœtr) adj 1 neutral. 2 neuter. nm neuter.

neveu, -eux (nə'vœ) nm nephew.

névrose (ne:'vroz) nf neurosis. **névrosé** adj,n neurotic.

nez (ne:) nm 1 nose. 2 scent.

ni (ni:) conj nor, or. **ni...ni** neither...nor.

niais (ni:'ɛ) adj 1 simple, foolish. 2 inane. nm fool.

nicher (ni:'ʃe:) vi 1 nest. 2 lodge. **se nicher** vr nestle. **niche** nf 1 recess. 2 kennel.

nickel (ni:'kɛl) nm nickel.

nicotine (ni:kɔ'ti:n) nf nicotine.

nid (ni:) nm nest.

nièce (njɛs) nf niece.

nier (ni:'e:) vt deny.

nigaud (ni:'go) adj simple, stupid. nm idiot.

Nigéria (ni:ʒe:'rja) nf Nigeria. **nigérien, -ienne** (ni:ʒe:'rjɛ̃, -'rjɛn) adj,n Nigerian.

Nil (ni:l) nm Nile.

nimbe (nɛ̃b) nm halo.

nitouche (ni:'tu:ʃ) **sainte nitouche** nf inf little hypocrite.

niveau, -aux (ni:'vo) nm 1 level. 2 standard.

niveler (ni:v'le:) vt level.

noble (nɔbl) adj 1 noble. 2 lofty. nm nobleman. **noblesse** nf nobility.

noce (nɔs) nf wedding.

nocif, -ive (nɔ'si:f, -'si:v) adj harmful.

nocturne (nɔk'tyrn) adj nocturnal.

Noël (nɔ'ɛl) nm Christmas.

nœud (nœ) nm 1 knot. 2 bow. 3 bond. **nœud coulant** noose.

noir (nwar) adj 1 black. 2 dark. 3 gloomy. 4 dirty. 5 base. nm 1 black. 2 cap Black. nf mus crotchet. **noirceur** nf 1 blackness. 2 darkness. 3 baseness. **noircir** vi turn black, darken. vt blacken.

noisette (nwa'zɛt) nf hazelnut. adj invar hazel. **noisetier** nm hazel tree.

noix (nwa) nf 1 nut. 2 walnut. **noix de coco** coconut.

nom (nɔ̃) nm 1 name. 2 noun. **nom de famille** surname. **nom de jeune fille** maiden name.

nomade (nɔ'mad) adj nomadic. nm nomad.

nombre (nɔ̃br) nm number. **nombreux, -euse** (nɔ̃'brœ, -'brœz) adj 1 numerous. 2 many.

nombril (nɔ̃'bri:) nm navel.

nominal, -aux (nɔmi:'nal, -'no) adj nominal.

nommer (nɔ'me:) vt 1 call, name. 2 mention by name. 3 appoint.

non (nɔ̃) adv 1 no. 2 non- nm invar no. **non-être** nm nonentity.

nonne (nɔn) nf nun.

nonobstant (nɔnɔp'stã) prep notwithstanding. adv nevertheless.

nord (nɔr) nm north. adj invar north, northern. **au nord** in the north. **du nord** 1 northern. 2 northerly. **vers le nord** northward, northwards. **nord-est** nm north-east. adj invar north-east. **du nord-est** 1 north-eastern. 2 north-easterly. **nord-ouest** nm north-west. adj

ınvar north-west. **du nord-ouest 1** north-western. **2** north-westerly.
normal, -aux (nɔr'mal, -'mo) *adj* **1** normal. **2** standard. **école normale** *nf* teacher-training college.
Normandie (nɔrmã'diː) *nf* Normandy. **normand** *adj, n* Norman.
norme (nɔrm) *nf* norm, standard.
Norvège (nɔr'vɛʒ) *nf* Norway. **norvégien, -ienne** (nɔrve'ʒjɛ̃, -'ʒjɛn) *adj,n* Norwegian. *nm* Norwegian (language).
nos (no) *poss adj* see **notre.**
nostalgie (nɔstal'ʒiː) *nf* nostalgia, homesickness. **nostalgique** (nɔstal'ʒiːk) *adj* homesick.
notable (nɔ'tabl) *adj* **1** notable, considerable. **2** eminent.
notaire (nɔ'tɛr) *nm* lawyer.
notamment (nɔta'mã) *adv* in particular.
notation (nɔta'sjɔ̃) *nf* notation.
noter (nɔ'te:) *vt* **1** note, observe. **2** make a note of. **note** *nf* **1** note. **2** notice. **3** *educ* mark. **4** bill. **5** *mus* note.
notice (nɔ'tiːs) *nf* **1** account. **2** *lit* review. **3** directions (for use).
notifier (nɔtiːˈfje:) *vt* notify, inform.
notion (no'sjɔ̃) *nf* notion, idea.
notoire (nɔ'twar) *adj* **1** well-known. **2** evident. **notoriété** *nf* **1** notoriety. **2** repute. **notoriété publique** common knowledge.
notre, nos (nɔtr, no) *poss adj 1st pers pl* our.
nôtre (notr) *poss pron 1st pers pl* **le** *or* **la nôtre 1** ours. **2** our own.
nouer (nu:'e:) *vt* **1** tie. **2** knot. **3** establish. **noueux, -euse** (nu:'œ, -'œz) *adj* **1** knotted. **2** gnarled.
nouilles (nu:j) *nf pl* noodles.
nounou (nu:'nu:) *nf inf* nanny.
nounours (nu:'nu:rs) *nm inf* teddy.
nourrice (nu:'riːs) *nf* nurse. **nourricier, -ière** (nu:riːˈsje:, -'sjer) *adj* **1** nutritious. **2** foster.
nourrir (nu:'riːr) *vt* **1** nourish, feed. **2** rear. **3** foster, harbour. **nourrisson, -onne** (nu:riːˈsɔ̃, -'sɔn) *nm,f* fosterchild. **nourriture** *nf* **1** food. **2** board, keep.
nous (nu) *pron 1st pers m,f pl* **1** we. **2** us. **3** to us. **4** ourselves. **5** each other. **nous-mêmes** *pron 1st pers m,f pl* ourselves.
nouveau, -el, -elle, -aux (nu:'vo, -'vɛl, -'vɛl, -'vo) *adj* **1** new. **2** recent. **3** fresh. **4** another. **à/de nouveau** afresh/again. **nouvel an** *nm* New Year. **nouveauté** *nf* **1** novelty. **2** change.
nouvelle[1] (nu:'vɛl) *adj* see **nouveau.**

nouvelle[2] (nu:'vɛl) *nf* **1** piece of news. **2** news. **3** short story.
Nouvelle-Zélande (ze:'lãd) *nf* New Zealand.
novateur, -trice (nɔva'tœr, -'triːs) *nm,f* innovator. *adj* innovating.
novembre (nɔ'vãbr) *nm* November.
novice (nɔ'viːs) *nm,f* novice.
noyau, -aux (nwa'jo) *nm* **1** stone (of fruit). **2** kernel. **3** nucleus.
noyer[1] (nwa'je:) *vt* **1** drown. **2** swamp. **3** flood. **noyade** *nf* drowning.
noyer[2] (nwa'je:) *nm* walnut tree.
nu (ny) *adj* **1** naked, nude. **2** bare. **3** plain. *nm* nude. **à nu** bare, exposed.
nuage (nɥaʒ) *nm* **1** cloud. **2** haze. **nuageux, -euse** (nɥa'ʒœ, -ʒœz) *adj* cloudy.
nuancer (nɥã'se:) *vt* **1** blend. **2** vary. **nuance** *nf* **1** shade. **2** nuance.
nucléaire (nykle:'ɛr) *adj* nuclear.
nuée (nɥe:) *nf* **1** cloud. **2** swarm. **3** host, crowd.
nuire* (nɥiːr) *vt* **nuire à 1** harm. **2** prejudice. **nuisible** *adj* harmful.
nuit (nɥi) *nf* **1** night. **2** darkness. **bonne nuit!** good night! **cette nuit 1** tonight. **2** last night.
nul, nulle (nyl) *adj* **1** no, not one. **2** worthless. **nul et non avenu** null and void. **nulle part** nowhere.
numéral, -aux (nyme:'ral, -'ro) *adj, nm* numeral.
numéro (nyme:'ro) *nm* **1** number. **2** *lit* issue.
numéroter (nyme:rɔ'te:) *vt* number.
nuptial, -aux (nyp'sjal, -'sjo) *adj* bridal.
nutrition (nytri:'sjɔ̃) *nf* nutrition.
nylon (niː'lɔ̃) *nm* nylon.
nymphe (nɛ̃f) *nf* nymph.

O

oasis (oa'ziːs) *nf* oasis.
obéir (ɔbe:'iːr) *vi* **obéir à 1** obey. **2** yield. **obéissance** *nf* **1** obedience. **2** submission. **obéissant** *adj* **1** obedient. **2** docile. **3** dutiful.
obèse (ɔ'bɛz) *adj* obese, fat.
obituaire (ɔbiː'tɥɛr) *nm* obituary.
objecter (ɔbʒɛk'te:) *vt* object.
objectif (ɔbʒɛk'tiːf) *adj* objective. *nm* **1** aim, objective. **2** target. **3** lens.
objection (ɔbʒɛk'sjɔ̃) *nf* objection.
objet (ɔb'ʒɛ) *nm* **1** object, thing. **2** aim, purpose. **3** *gram* object. **objet d'art** work of art. **objets trouvés** *pl* lost property.
obliger (ɔbliː'ʒe:) *vt* **1** oblige, compel. **2** help. **obligation** *nf* **1** obligation, duty. **2** *law*

agreement. **3** *comm* bond. **obligatoire** *adj* obligatory.

oblique (ɔ'bliːk) *adj* **1** oblique. **2** underhand.

oblitérer (ɔbliːteːˈreː) *vt* **1** obliterate. **2** cancel.

oblong, -ongue (ɔbˈlɔ̃, -ˈlɔ̃g) *adj* oblong.

obscène (ɔpˈsɛn) *adj* obscene.

obscur (ɔpˈskyr) *adj* **1** dark, gloomy. **2** obscure. **3** humble. **obscurité** *nf* obscurity.

obscurcir (ɔpskyrˈsiːr) *vt* **1** darken. **2** dim. **3** obscure.

obséder (ɔpseːˈdeː) *vt* **1** haunt. **2** obsess. **3** worry.

obsèques (ɔpˈsɛk) *nf pl* funeral.

observer (ɔpsɛrˈveː) *vt* **1** observe, comply with. **2** watch. **3** note. **s'observer** *vr* be careful. **observance** *nf* observance. **observateur, -trice** (ɔpsɛrvaˈtœr, -ˈtriːs) *nm,f* observer. *adj* observant. **observatoire** *nm* observatory.

obsession (ɔpsɛˈsjɔ̃) *nf* obsession.

obstacle (ɔpˈstakl) *nm* obstacle, hindrance.

s'obstiner (sɔpstiːˈneː) *vr* **s'obstiner à** persist in. **obstination** *nf* obstinacy. **obstiné** *adj* obstinate, stubborn.

obstruer (ɔpstryˈeː) *vt* obstruct, block.

obtenir* (ɔptəˈniːr) *vt* **1** obtain, get. **2** achieve.

obtus (ɔpˈty) *adj* **1** obtuse. **2** blunt. **3** dull.

obus (ɔˈbys) *nm mil* shell.

occasion (ɔkaˈzjɔ̃) *nf* **1** opportunity. **2** bargain. **3** cause. **d'occasion** second-hand. **occasionnel, -elle** (ɔkazjɔˈnɛl) *adj* occasional.

occident (ɔksiːˈdɑ̃) *nm* **1** west. **2** Occident. **occidental, -aux** (ɔksiːdɑ̃ˈtal, -ˈto) *adj* western.

occulte (ɔˈkylt) *adj* **1** occult. **2** hidden.

occuper (ɔkyˈpeː) *vt* **1** occupy. **2** live in. **3** take up. **s'occuper de** *vr* attend to. **occupant** *nm* occupant. **occupation** *nf* **1** occupation. **2** employment. **3** profession. **occupé** *adj* **1** busy. **2** engaged, taken.

océan (ɔseːˈɑ̃) *nm* ocean.

ocre (ɔkr) *nf* ochre.

octane (ɔkˈtan) *nm* octane.

octave (ɔkˈtav) *nf* octave.

octobre (ɔkˈtɔbr) *nm* October.

octogone (ɔktoˈgɔn) *nm* octagon. **octogonal, -aux** (ɔktɔgɔˈnal, -ˈno) *adj* octagonal.

octroi (ɔkˈtrwa) *nm* concession.

octroyer (ɔktrwaˈjeː) *vt* grant, concede.

oculiste (ɔkyˈliːst) *nm* oculist. **oculaire** *adj* ocular. **témoin oculaire** *nm* eyewitness.

ode (ɔd) *nf* ode.

odeur (oˈdœr) *nf* **1** smell, odour. **2** scent.

odorant *adj* fragrant. **odorat** *nm* sense of smell.

odieux, -euse (ɔˈdjœ, -ˈdjœz) *adj* **1** odious. **2** hateful.

œil (œj) *nm, pl* **yeux 1** eye. **2** sight. **3** look. **œil poché** black eye. **œillade** *nf* **1** glance. **2** leer. **œillet** *nm* **1** eyelet. **2** *bot* pink, carnation.

œstre (ɛstr) *nm* oestrus.

œuf (œf) *nm* **1** egg. **2** *pl* roe, spawn. **œuf à la coque** boiled egg. **œuf dur/poché** hard-boiled/poached egg. **œufs brouillés** scrambled eggs. **œuf sur le plat** fried egg.

œuvre (œvr) *nf* **1** work. **2** act. *nm* works (of an artist, etc.).

offenser (ɔfɑ̃ˈseː) *vt* **1** offend. **2** shock. **offensant** *adj* offensive. **offense** *nf* **1** offence. **2** sin. **offensif, -ive** (ɔfɑ̃ˈsiːf, -ˈsiːv) *adj* offensive. *nf mil* offensive.

offert (ɔˈfɛr) *v* see **offrir.**

office (ɔˈfiːs) *nm* **1** office, duty. **2** help. **3** *rel* service. **4** office. *nf* pantry. **officiel, -elle** (ɔfiːˈsjɛl) *adj* **1** official. **2** formal. *nm* official. **officier** *nm* officer.

officieux, -euse (ɔfiːˈsjœ, -ˈsjœz) *adj* **1** officious. **2** unofficial.

officine (ɔfiːˈsiːn) *nf* dispensary.

offrir* (ɔˈfriːr) *vt* **1** offer. **2** give. **3** bid. **4** afford, present. **offrande** *nf* **1** offering. **2** present. **offre** *nf* **1** offer. **2** proposal. **3** tender. **4** bid.

offusquer (ɔfyˈskeː) *vt* **1** veil, obscure. **2** shock.

ogre, ogresse (ɔgr, ɔˈgrɛs) *nm,f* ogre, ogress.

oie (wa) *nf* goose.

oignon (ɔˈɲɔ̃) *nm* **1** onion. **2** *bot* bulb.

oindre* (wɛ̃dr) *vt* **1** oil. **2** anoint.

oiseau, -aux (waˈzo) *nm* bird.

oisif, -ive (waˈziːf, -ˈziːv) *adj* **1** idle. **2** lazy.

oison (waˈzɔ̃) *nm* gosling.

olive (ɔˈliːv) *nf* olive. **olivier** *nm* olive tree.

ombrage (ɔ̃ˈbraʒ) *nm* **1** shade. **2** offence.

ombre (ɔ̃br) *nf* **1** shadow. **2** shade. **3** darkness.

omettre* (ɔˈmɛtr) *vt* **1** omit, fail. **2** leave out. **omission** *nf* omission.

omnibus (ɔmniːˈbys) *nm* **1** omnibus. **2** slow train. *adj invar* general, blanket.

omnipotent (ɔmniːpɔˈtɑ̃) *adj* omnipotent, almighty.

omoplate (ɔmɔˈplat) *nf* shoulder-blade.

on (ɔ̃) *indef pron s* one, people, they, we, you. **on demande** wanted. **on dit** it is said. **on y va?** shall we go?

once (ɔ̃s) *nf* ounce.

oncle (ɔ̃kl) *nm* uncle.

onde (ɔ̃d) *nf* wave. **grande onde** long wave. **onde courte** short wave. **ondée** *nf* heavy shower.

on-dit *nm invar* rumour.

ondoyer (ɔ̃dwa'je:) *vi* wave, ripple.

onduler (ɔ̃dy'le:) *vi* ripple. *vt* wave, curl.

ongle (ɔ̃gl) *nm* 1 fingernail. 2 claw. 3 talon.

onguent (ɔ̃'gɑ̃) *nm* ointment.

ont (ɔ̃) *v* see **avoir.**

onze (ɔ̃z) *adj,nm* eleven. **onzième** *adj* eleventh.

opale (ɔ'pal) *nf* opal.

opaque (ɔ'pak) *adj* opaque.

opéra (ɔpe'ra) *nm* 1 opera. 2 opera house.

opérer (ɔpe:re:) *vt* 1 operate. 2 work. 3 effect. **se faire opérer** undergo an operation. **opération** *nf* 1 operation. 2 process. 3 transaction.

s'opiniâtrer (sɔpɪːnjɑ'tre:) *vr* be stubborn, obstinate. **opiniâtre** *adj* 1 stubborn, obstinate. 2 headstrong. 3 persistent.

opinion (ɔpɪːˈnjɔ̃) *nf* opinion, view.

opportun (ɔpɔr'tœ̃) *adj* 1 opportune, favourable. 2 expedient. **opportunité** *nf* 1 timeliness. 2 favourable occasion. 3 expediency.

opposer (ɔpo'ze:) *vt* 1 oppose. 2 place opposite. **opposer à** compare with. **s'opposer à** *vr* oppose, be opposed to. **opposé** *adj* 1 opposed. 2 opposite. 3 contrary. **opposite** *nm* opposite, contrary. **opposition** *nf* 1 opposition. 2 contrast.

opprimer (ɔprɪːˈme:) *vt* oppress.

opprobre (ɔ'prɔbr) *nm* shame, disgrace.

opter (ɔp'te:) *vi* opt, choose. **option** *nf* option, choice.

opticien (ɔptɪːˈsjɛ̃) *nm* optician.

optimisme (ɔptɪːˈmɪːsm) *nm* optimism. **optimiste** *adj* optimistic. *nm,f* optimist.

optique (ɔp'tɪːk) *adj* 1 optical. 2 optic. *nf* optics.

opulent (ɔpy'lɑ̃) *adj* 1 opulent. 2 abundant.

or¹ (ɔr) *nm* gold. **d'or** *adj* golden.

or² (ɔr) *conj* 1 now. 2 well. 3 but.

orage (ɔ'raʒ) *nm* thunderstorm. **orageux, -euse** (ɔra'ʒœ, -'ʒœz) *adj* stormy.

oraison (ɔre'zɔ̃) *nf* 1 oration. 2 prayer.

oral, -aux (ɔ'ral, -'ro) *adj* 1 oral. 2 verbal. *nm* oral examination.

orange (ɔ'rɑ̃ʒ) *nf* 1 *bot* orange. 2 orange (colour). *adj invar* orange. **oranger** *nm* orange tree.

orateur (ɔra'tœr) *nm* orator.

orbite (ɔr'bɪːt) *nf* orbit.

Orcades (ɔr'kad) *nf pl* Orkneys.

orchestrer (ɔrkɛ'stre:) *vt* orchestrate. **orchestre** *nm* orchestra.

orchidée (ɔrki:'de:) *nf* orchid.

ordinaire (ɔrdi:'nɛr) *adj* 1 ordinary. 2 usual. 3 common. *nm* habit.

ordinal, -aux (ɔrdi:'nal, -'no) *adj* ordinal.

ordinateur (ɔrdi:na'tœr) *nm* computer.

ordonner (ɔrdɔ'ne:) *vt* 1 arrange. 2 order. 3 ordain. **ordonnance** *nf* 1 arrangement. 2 order. 3 prescription. **ordonné** *adj* 1 orderly. 2 tidy.

ordre (ɔrdr) *nm* 1 order. 2 discipline. 3 sequence. 4 class, category. 5 *pl* holy orders. **ordre du jour** agenda.

ordure (ɔr'dyr) *nf* 1 filth, dirt. 2 filthiness. 3 *pl* refuse.

oreille (ɔ'rɛj) *nf* ear. **oreiller** *nm* pillow. **oreillons** *nm pl* mumps.

ores (ɔr) *adv* **d'ores et déjà** here and now.

orfèvre (ɔr'fɛvr) *nm* goldsmith.

organe (ɔr'gan) *nm* 1 organ. 2 voice. 3 agency, means. 4 mouthpiece.

organique (ɔrga'ni:k) *adj* organic.

organiser (ɔrganɪː'ze:) *vt* 1 organize. 2 arrange. 3 set up. **organisation** *nf* 1 organization. 2 structure. 3 system. **organisé** *adj* 1 organic. 2 organized. **organisme** *nm* organism.

orge (ɔrʒ) *nf* barley.

orgie (ɔr'zɪː) *nf* orgy.

orgue (ɔrg) *nm mus* organ.

orgueil (ɔr'gœj) *nm* pride. **orgueilleux, -euse** (ɔrgœ'jœ, -'jœz) *adj* 1 proud. 2 arrogant.

orient (ɔ'rjɑ̃) *nm* 1 Orient. 2 east. **oriental, -aux** (ɔrjɑ̃'tal, -'to) *adj* 1 eastern. 2 oriental.

orienter (ɔrjɑ̃'te:) *vt* 1 orientate. 2 direct.

origan (ɔrɪː'gɑ̃) *nm* oregano.

originaire (ɔrɪːʒɪːˈnɛr) *adj* 1 native. 2 original.

origine (ɔrɪːˈʒɪːn) *nf* 1 origin. 2 beginning. 3 source. 4 descent. **à l'origine** originally. **original, -aux** (ɔrɪːʒɪːˈnal, -'no) *adj* 1 original. 2 novel. 3 eccentric. **originalité** *nf* 1 originality. 2 eccentricty.

orme (ɔrm) *nm* elm tree.

ornement (ɔrnə'mɑ̃) *nm* ornament. **ornemental, -aux** (ɔrnəmɑ̃tal, -'to) *adj* ornamental.

orner (ɔr'ne:) *vt* 1 decorate. 2 adorn.

ornière (ɔr'njɛr) *nf* 1 rut. 2 groove.

ornithologie (ɔrnɪːtɔlɔ'ʒɪː) *nf* ornithology.

orphelin (ɔrfə'lɛ̃) *nm* orphan. **orphelinat** *nm* ophanage.

orteil (ɔr'tɛj) *nm* toe.

orthodoxe (ɔrtɔ'dɔks) *adj* orthodox, conventional.

orthographe (ɔrtɔ'graf) *nf* orthography, spelling.

orthopédique (ɔrtɔpe:'di:k) *adj* orthopaedic.
ortie (ɔr'ti:) *nf* nettle.
os (ɔs) *nm* bone. **os à moelle** marrowbone.
osciller (ɔsı:'je:) *vi* **1** sway. **2** waver. **3** fluctuate.
oser (o'ze:) *vt* dare. **osé** *adj* bold.
ossature (ɔssa'tyr) *nf* **1** skeleton. **2** framework.
ostentation (ɔstāta'sjɔ̃) *nf* ostentation, show.
ostraciser (ɔstrası:'ze:) *vt* ostracize.
otage (ɔ'taʒ) *nm* hostage.
ôter (o'te:) *vt* **1** remove. **2** take away.
ou (u:) *conj* **1** or. **2** either. **3** else. **ou bien** or else. **ou...ou** either...or.
où (u:) *adv* **1** where. **2** when.
ouater (wa'te:) *vt* pad, wad. **ouate** *nf* **1** cottonwool. **2** wadding.
oubli (u:'bli:) *nm* **1** forgetfulness. **2** oblivion. **3** oversight. **oublie** *nf* wafer.
oublier (u:bli:'e:) *vt* **1** forget. **2** overlook. **oublieux, -euse** (u:bli:'œ, -'œz) *adj* **1** forgetful. **2** oblivious.
ouest (wɛst) *nm* west. *adj invar* west, western. **à l'ouest** westward. **de l'ouest** westerly. **vers l'ouest** westward, westwards.
oui (wı:) *adv,nm invar* yes.
ouïr (wı:r) *vt* hear. **ouï-dire** *nm invar* hearsay. **ouïe** *nf* **1** sense of hearing. **2** *pl zool* gill.
ouragan (u:ra'gā) *nm* hurricane.
ourler (u:r'le:) *vt* hem. **ourlet** *nm* hem.
ours (u:rs) *nm* bear. **ours blanc** polar bear.
outil (u:'tı:) *nm* **1** tool. **2** implement. **outillage** *nm* **1** set of tools. **2** equipment. **3** *tech* plant.
outiller (u:tı:'je:) *vt* equip with tools.
outrager (u:tra'ʒe:) *vt* **1** insult. **2** outrage. **outrage** *nm* **1** outrage. **2** insult, affront.
outrance (u:'trãs) *nf* excess.
outre (u:tr) *prep* **1** beyond. **2** in addition to. *adv* further. **en outre 1** besides. **2** moreover. **outre-mer** *adv* abroad, overseas.
outrer (u:'tre:) *vt* **1** carry to excess, overdo. **2** exaggerate. **3** exasperate.
ouvert (u:'vɛr) *v* see **ouvrir**. *adj* **1** open. **2** frank. **3** exposed. **ouverture** *nf* **1** opening. **2** hole. **3** overture.
ouvrable (u:'vrabl) **jour ouvrable** *nm* weekday.
ouvrage (u:'vraʒ) *nm* **1** work. **2** piece of work. **3** workmanship.
ouvrier, -ière (u:vrı:'e:, -'ɛr) *adj* **1** working. **2** labour, industrial. *nm* **1** worker. **2** workman.
ouvrir (u:'vrı:r) *vt* **1** open. **2** turn on. **3** cut through. **4** begin, start. *vi* open. **ouvre-boîte** *nm invar* tin-opener. **ouvre-bouteille** *nm, pl* **ouvre-bouteilles** bottle-opener.
ovaire (ɔ'vɛr) *nm* ovary.

ovale (ɔ'val) *adj,nm* oval.
ovation (ɔva'sjɔ̃) *nf* ovation.
oxygène (oksı:'ʒɛn) *nm* oxygen.

P

pacage (pa'kaʒ) *nm* **1** pasture. **2** grazing.
pacifier (pası:'fje:) *vt* **1** pacify. **2** appease. **se pacifier** *vr* calm down. **pacifisme** *nm* pacifism.
pacifique (pası:'fi:k) *adj* peaceful. (**Océan**) **Pacifique** *nm* Pacific (Ocean).
pacte (pakt) *nm* pact, agreement.
pagaie (pa'gɛ) *nf* paddle (for a canoe).
pagaïe (pa'gaj) *nf* disorder, confusion, chaos.
pagayer (pagɛ'je:) *vi,vt* paddle (a boat).
page¹ (paʒ) *nf* page.
page² (paʒ) *nm* page (boy).
pagode (pa'gɔd) *nf* **1** pagoda. **2** temple.
paie (pɛ) *nf* **1** pay. **2** wages. **paiement** *nm* payment.
païen, -ienne (pa'jɛ̃, -jɛn) *adj,n* pagan.
paillasson (paja'sɔ̃) *nm* **1** mat. **2** doormat.
paille (pɑj) *nf* **1** straw. **2** flaw. **paillette** *nf* **1** grain. **2** flake. **3** flaw.
pain (pɛ̃) *nm* **1** bread. **2** loaf. **pain d'épice** gingerbread. **pain de savon** cake of soap. **pain grillé** toast. **petit pain** roll.
pair¹ (pɛr) *adj* **1** equal. **2** even.
pair² (pɛr) *nm* peer. **pairesse** *nf* peeress.
paire (pɛr) *nf* pair, brace.
paisible (pɛ'zı:bl) *adj* **1** peaceful, calm. **2** quiet.
paître (pɛtr) *vt* **1** graze (cattle). **2** feed upon. *vi* **1** graze. **2** feed.
paix (pɛ) *nf* **1** peace. **2** quiet.
Pakistan (pakı:'stā) *nm* Pakistan. **pakistanais** *adj,n* Pakistani.
palace (pa'las) *nm* luxury hotel.
palais¹ (pa'lɛ) *nm* palace. **palais de justice** law courts.
palais² (pa'lɛ) *nm* **1** palate. **2** sense of taste.
pâle (pɑl) *adj* **1** pale. **2** faint. **pâleur** *nf* paleness.
palefrenier (palfrə'nje:) *nm* groom.
Palestine (palɛ'stı:n) *nf* Palestine. **palestinien, -ienne** *adj,n* Palestinian.
palette (pa'lɛt) *nf* **1** bat. **2** blade (of an oar). **3** palette.
palier (pal'je:) *nm* (of stairs) landing.
pâlir (pa'lı:r) *vi* **1** turn or grow pale. **2** grow dim. **3** fade. *vt* make pale.

palissader (pali:saˈde:) *vt* enclose, fence in. **palissade** *nf* fence.

palmarès (palmaˈrɛs) *nm* prize list.

palme (palm) *nf* 1 palm (branch). 2 victory. **palmier** *nm* palm tree.

palombe (paˈlɔ̃b) *nf* woodpigeon.

palourde (paˈlu:rd) *nf* clam.

palper (palˈpe:) *vt* 1 feel. 2 finger.

palpiter (palpɪ:ˈte:) *vi* 1 quiver. 2 throb.

paludisme (palyˈdi:sm) *nm* malaria.

pâmer (pɑˈme:) *vi* faint. **se pâmer de** *vr* be overcome with.

pamphlet (pɑ̃ˈflɛ) *nm* pamphlet.

pamplemousse (pɑ̃plɔˈmu:s) *nm* grapefruit.

pan (pɑ̃) *nm* 1 flap (of a garment). 2 section. 3 side.

panache (paˈnaʃ) *nm* 1 plume. 2 tuft. **avoir du panache** have style or dash. **panaché** *adj* 1 mixed. 2 plumed. *nm* shandy.

panais (paˈnɛ) *nm* parsnip.

pancarte (pɑ̃ˈkart) *nf* 1 placard. 2 poster, bill.

pancréas (pɑ̃kreˈas) *nm* pancreas.

panda (pɑ̃ˈda) *nm* panda.

panier (paˈnje:) *nm* basket. **gros panier** hamper.

panique (paˈni:k) *adj,nf* panic.

panne (pan) *nf* 1 breakdown. 2 failure.

panneau, -aux (paˈno) *nm* 1 snare. 2 trap. 3 panel. 4 board. **panneau-réclame** *nm, pl* **panneaux-réclames** hoarding.

panorama (panɔraˈma) *nm* panorama. **panoramique** *adj* panoramic.

panse (pɑ̃s) *nf* 1 *inf* belly. 2 paunch.

panser (pɑ̃ˈse:) *vt* 1 *med* dress. 2 groom (a horse). **pansement** *nm med* dressing.

pantalon (pɑ̃taˈlɔ̃) *nm* trousers.

panteler (pɑ̃tˈle:) *vi* 1 pant. 2 gasp.

panthère (pɑ̃ˈtɛr) *nf* panther.

pantomime (pɑ̃tɔˈmi:m) *nf* 1 pantomime. 2 mime.

pantoufle (pɑ̃ˈtu:fl) *nf* slipper.

paon (pɑ̃) *nm* peacock.

papa (paˈpa) *nm inf* dad.

pape (pap) *nm* pope. **papal, -aux** (paˈpal, -ˈpo) *adj* papal. **papauté** *nf* papacy.

papeterie (papˈtri:) *nf* 1 stationer's shop. 2 stationery. **papetier** *nm* stationer.

papier (paˈpje:) *nm* 1 paper. 2 document. **papier à écrire** notepaper. **papier buvard** blotting paper. **papier de verre** sandpaper. **papier ministre** foolscap. **papier teint** wallpaper.

papillon (papɪ:ˈjɔ̃) *nm* 1 butterfly. 2 moth. 3 leaflet. 4 ticket.

paquebot (pakˈbo) *nm* 1 liner. 2 steamer.

pâquerette (pɑkˈrɛt) *nf* daisy.

Pâques (pak) *nf pl* Easter. **pâque** *nf* Passover.

paquet (paˈkɛ) *nm* 1 parcel. 2 packet. 3 bundle.

paqueter (pakˈte:) *vt* parcel up.

par (par) *prep* 1 by. 2 through. 3 in. 4 out of, for the sake of. **par-ci par-là** here and there. **par-dessous** *prep,adv* under, underneath. **par-dessus** *prep,adv* over. **par ici/là** this/that way.

parabole (paraˈbɔl) *nf* parable.

parachuter (paraʃyˈte:) *vt* parachute. **parachute** *nm* parachute. **parachutiste** *nm* 1 parachutist. 2 paratrooper.

parade (paˈrad) *nf* 1 parade. 2 show, display.

paradigme (paraˈdi:gm) *nm* paradigm.

paradis (paraˈdi:) *nm* 1 paradise. 2 *inf Th* gallery.

paradoxe (paraˈdɔks) *nm* paradox. **paradoxal, -aux** (paradɔkˈsal, -ˈso) *adj* paradoxical.

paraffine (paraˈfi:n) *nf* paraffin.

parages (paˈraʒ) *nm pl* district, area.

paragraphe (paraˈgraf) *nm* paragraph.

paraître* (paˈrɛtr) *vi* 1 appear. 2 show, be visible. 3 seem. 4 be published. *v imp* seem. **faire paraître** publish.

parallèle (paralˈlɛl) *adj* parallel.

paralyser (paraliˈze:) *vt* paralyse. **paralysie** *nf* paralysis.

paraphraser (parafraˈze:) *vt* paraphrase. **paraphrase** *nf* paraphrase.

parapluie (paraˈplɥi:) *nm* umbrella.

parasite (paraˈzi:t) *nm* 1 parasite. 2 *pl tech* interference. *adj* parasitic.

parc (park) *nm* 1 park. 2 pen. **parc de stationnement** car park.

parcelle (parˈsɛl) *nf* 1 particle. 2 plot, patch.

parce que (pars kə) *conj* because.

parchemin (parʃəˈmɛ̃) *nm* parchment.

parcomètre (parkɔˈmɛtr) *nm* parking meter.

parcourir* (parkuːˈriːr) *vt* 1 travel through. 2 wander. 3 glance through.

parcours (parˈkuːr) *nm* 1 distance. 2 route. 3 course.

pardessus (pardəˈsy) *nm* overcoat.

pardon (parˈdɔ̃) *nm* 1 forgiveness. 2 pardon. **pardonner** (pardɔˈne:) *vt* 1 pardon. 2 forgive. 3 excuse.

pareil, -eille (paˈrɛj) *adj* 1 like, similar. 2 same. 3 such.

parement (par'mã) *nm* 1 ornament. 2 facing. 3 cuff (of a coat, etc.).

parent (pa'rã) *nm* 1 parent. 2 relative.

parenthèse (parã'tɛz) *nf* 1 parenthesis. 2 bracket.

parer[1] (pa're:) *vt* 1 decorate. 2 adorn. 3 prepare. **se parer de** *vr* dress oneself in.

parer[2] (pa're:) *vt* 1 ward off. 2 avoid. **pare-boue** *nm invar* mudguard. **pare-brise** *nm invar* windscreen. **pare-choc** *nm invar* bumper.

paresseux, -euse (parɛ'sœ, -'sœz) *adj* lazy.

parfait (par'fɛ) *adj* 1 perfect. 2 complete.

parfois (par'fwa) *adv* sometimes, occasionally.

parfum (par'fœ̃) *nm* 1 perfume. 2 scent. 3 flavour.

parfumer (parfy'me:) *vt* 1 scent, perfume. 2 flavour.

pari (pa'rı:) *nm* bet. **parier** *vt* bet.

Paris (pa'rı:) *nm* Paris. **parisien, -ienne** (parı-'zjɛ̃, -'zjɛn) *adj,n* Parisian.

parité (parı:'te:) *nf* parity, equality.

parjure (par'ʒyr) *nm* perjury.

parking (par'kı:ŋ) *nm* car park.

parlement (parlə'mã) *nm* parliament.

parler (par'le:) *vi* 1 speak. 2 talk. **tu parles!** you can say that again! ~*nm* speech. **parleur, -euse** ((par'lœr,-'lœz) *nm,f* speaker. **parloir** *nm* parlour.

parmi (par'mı:) *prep* among, amid.

parodie (parɔ'dı:) *nf* parody.

paroi (par'wa) *nf* 1 partition. 2 wall. 3 lining.

paroisse (par'was) *nf* parish.

parole (pa'rɔl) *nf* 1 word. 2 remark. 3 parole. 4 speech.

parquet (par'kɛ) *nm* 1 floor. 2 *cap* magistrate.

parrain (pa'rɛ̃) *nm* 1 godfather. 2 patron.

parrainer (parɛ'ne:) *vt* sponsor.

pars (par) *v* see **partir.**

parsemer (parsə'me:) *vt* sprinkle, scatter.

part (par) *nf* 1 share, portion. 2 participation. 3 part. **à part** apart. **autre/nulle/quelque part** elsewhere/nowhere/somewhere. **d'autre part** moreover.

partager (parta'ʒe:) *vt* 1 divide. 2 share. **partage** *nm* 1 division. 2 sharing. 3 share.

partance (par'tãs) *nf* departure. **en partance pour** bound for.

partenaire (partə'nɛr) *nm,f* partner.

parterre (par'tɛr) *nm* 1 flowerbed. 2 *Th* stalls.

parti (par'tı:) *nm* 1 party. 2 side, part. 3 decision. 4 advantage. **parti pris** bias.

100

partial, -aux (par'sjal, -'sjo) *adj* partial, biased. **partialité** *nf* partiality, bias.

participe (partı:'sı:p) *nm* participle. **participe passé** past participle.

participer (partı:sı:'pe:) *vi* **participer à** 1 participate in. 2 take part in. **participer de** partake of. **participant** *nm* participant. **participation** *nf* 1 participation. 2 interest, share.

particulariser (partı:kyları:'ze:) *vt* specify.

particule (partı:'kyl) *nf* particle.

particulier, -ière (partı:ky'lje:, -'ljɛr) *adj* 1 particular. 2 special. 3 characteristic. 4 private. *nm* private individual.

partie (par'tı:) *nf* 1 part. 2 party. 3 game. 4 client. **partie carrée** foursome. **partie nulle** *sport* draw. **partiel, -elle** (par'sjɛl) *adj* partial, part.

partir* (par'tı:r) *vi* (*aux* être) 1 depart. 2 leave. set off. 4 start. **à partir de** as from.

partisan (partı:'zã) *nm* partisan, supporter.

partout (par'tu:) *adv* everywhere. **partout où** wherever. **un peu partout** all over the place.

paru (pa'ry) *v* see **paraître.**

parure (pa'ryr) *nf* 1 ornament. 2 dress. 3 set (of clothing, etc.).

parvenir* (parvə'nı:r) *vi* (*aux* être) **parvenir à** 1 reach. 2 succeed. **parvenu** *nm* self-made man.

pas[1] (pɑ) *nm* 1 pace, stride. 2 step. 3 footstep. 4 doorstep. 5 pass. **à pas de loup** slyly.

pas[2] (pɑ) *adv* not. **ne...pas** not. **pas du tout** not at all.

passage (pɑ'saʒ) *nm* 1 passage. 2 crossing. 3 way. **passage à niveau** level crossing. **passage clouté** pedestrian crossing. **passage interdit** no thoroughfare. **passage souterrain** subway. **passager, -ère** (pɑsa'ʒe:, -'ʒɛr) *adj* 1 migratory. 2 momentary. 3 busy. *nm,f* passenger. **passager clandestin** stowaway.

passer (pɑ'se:) *vi* (*aux* avoir or être) 1 go by or through. 2 pass. 3 call. 4 cease. 5 become. *vt* 1 cross. 2 pass. 3 show. 4 spend. 5 surpass. 6 filter, strain. **en passant** by the way. **passer un examen** sit an exam. **se passer** *vr* 1 happen. 2 decay. **se passer de** do without. **passe** *nf* 1 passing. 2 permit. 3 pass. **passé** *adj,nm* past. *prep* after, beyond.

passeport (pɑs'pɔr) *nm* passport.

passerelle (pɑs'rɛl) *nf* footbridge. **passerelle de service** *naut* gangway.

passe-temps *nm invar* pastime.

passif, -ive (pɑ'sı:f, -'sı:v) *adj* passive.

passion (pɑ'sjɔ̃) *nf* passion.

passionner (pasjɔ'ne:) vt 1 interest greatly. 2 thrill, exite. **se passionner pour** vr become very fond of. **passionnant** (pasjɔ'nã) adj thrilling. **passionné** adj 1 passionate. 2 ardent. nm enthusiast.
pastel (pa'stɛl) nm 1 crayon. 2 pastel.
pastèque (pa'stɛk) nf watermelon.
pasteuriser (pastœri:'ze:) vt pasteurize.
pastille (pa'sti:j) nf pastille.
pastis (pa'sti:s) nm 1 aniseed aperitif. 2 inf muddle.
pat (pat) nm invar stalemate.
pataud (pa'to) adj clumsy.
patauger (pato'ʒe:) vi 1 paddle. 2 flounder.
pâte (pat) nf 1 paste. 2 dough. 3 pl pasta. **pâte à modeler** Plasticine Tdmk. **pâte dentifrice** toothpaste. **pâte lisse** batter.
pâté (pa'te:) nm 1 meat paste. 2 blot. 3 block (of houses). **pâté en croûte** pie.
patelin (pat'lɛ̃) adj 1 glib. 2 wheedling. nm inf place, locality.
patelle (pa'tɛl) nf limpet.
patenôtre (pat'notr) nf Lord's Prayer.
patent (pa'tã) adj 1 patent. 2 obvious.
patenter (patã'te:) vt license. **patente** nf 1 licence. 2 tax.
patère (pa'tɛr) nf peg (for coats, etc.).
paterne (pa'tɛrn) adj benevolent, kind.
paternel, -elle (patɛr'nɛl) adj paternal.
pâteux, -euse (pa'tœ, -'tœz) adj 1 pasty. 2 thick. 3 dull.
pathétique (pate:'ti:k) adj 1 pathetic. 2 touching. nm pathos.
pathologie (patɔlɔ'ʒi:) nf pathology. **pathologique** adj pathological. **pathologiste** nm,f pathologist.
patience (pa'sjãs) nf patience. **patiemment** adv patiently. **patient** adj 1 patient. 2 long-suffering. nm med patient.
patin (pa'tɛ̃) nm skate. **patin à roulette** roller-skate.
patiner (pati:'ne:) vi 1 skate. 2 skid. **patinage** nm skating. **patinoire** nf skating rink.
pâtir (pa'ti:r) vi suffer.
pâtisserie (patı:s'rı:) nf 1 pastry. 2 cake. 3 cake shop.
patois (pa'twa) nm 1 dialect. 2 jargon.
patouiller (patu:'je:) vi splash, flounder. vt 1 finger. 2 meddle with.
patrie (pa'tri:) nf fatherland, native country.
patrimoine (patri:'mwan) nm heritage.
patriote (patri:'ɔt) nm,f patriot. adj patriotic.

patriotique adj patriotic. **patriotisme** nm patriotism.
patron (pa'trɔ̃) nm 1 patron. 2 proprietor. 3 patron saint. 4 employer. 5 skipper. 6 inf boss. 7 pattern (for a dress). **patronage** nm 1 patronage. 2 club. **patronat** nm 1 body of employers. 2 management.
patrouiller (patru:'je:) vi patrol. **patrouille** nf patrol.
patte (pat) nf 1 zool paw, foot, leg. 2 flap. **patte de derrière** hindleg. **patte de devant** foreleg. **patte de mouche** scrawl.
pâture (pa'tyr) nf 1 pasture. 2 food.
paume (pom) nf anat palm.
paupière (po'pjɛr) nf eyelid.
pause (poz) nf 1 pause. 2 rest. **pause café** tea-break.
pauvre (povr) adj 1 poor. 2 unfortunate. 3 wretched. **pauvreté** nf poverty.
se pavaner (pava'ne:) vr strut about.
paver (pa've:) vt pave. **pavé** nm 1 pavement. 2 highway. 3 slab,flagstone.
pavillon (pavi:'jɔ̃) nm 1 pavilion. 2 tent. 3 flag.
pavot (pa'vo) nm poppy.
payer (pa'je:) vt pay.
pays (pe:'i:) nm 1 land, country. 2 district. 3 nation. 4 home. **pays chauds** nm pl tropics. **paysage** nm 1 landscape. 2 scenery. **paysan, -anne** (pe:i:'zã, -'zan) adj,n 1 peasant. 2 rustic.
Pays-Bas nm pl Netherlands.
péage (pe:'aʒ) nm toll.
peau, peaux (po) nf 1 anat skin. 2 zool fur, hide, pelt. 3 peel. **peau de mouton** sheepskin. **peau-rouge** nm, pl **peaux-rouges** Red Indian.
pêche[1] (pɛʃ) nf peach.
pêche[2] (pɛʃ) nf 1 fishing. 2 catch (of fish). **aller à la pêche** go fishing.
pécher (pe:'ʃe:) vi sin. **péché** nm sin. **pécheur, -eresse** (pe:'ʃœr, pɛʃ'rɛs) nm,f 1 sinner. 2 offender. adj sinful.
pêcher[1] (pe:'ʃe:) nm peach tree.
pêcher[2] (pe:'ʃe:) vt fish for. **pêcher à la ligne** angle. **pêcheur** nm fisherman.
pédaler (pɛda'le:) vi 1 pedal. 2 inf cycle. **pédale** nf pedal.
pédéraste (pe:de:'rast) nm homosexual.
pédicure (pe:di:'kyr) nm,f chiropodist.
peignant (pɛ'ɲã) v see **peindre**.
peigner (pɛ'ɲe:) vt comb. **peigne** nm 1 comb. 2 zool scallop. **bien/mal peigné** trim/slovenly. **peignoir** nm dressing-gown.
peindre* (pɛ̃dr) vt 1 paint. 2 depict. 3 describe.

peine (pɛn) *nf* 1 punishment. 2 sorrow. 3 trouble. 4 difficulty. **à peine** hardly, scarcely.

peiner (pɛ'ne:) *vt* 1 grieve. 2 tire. *vi* toil.

peint (pɛ̃) *v* see **peindre**.

peintre (pɛ̃tr) *nm* 1 painter. 2 decorator. **peinture** *nf* 1 painting. 2 picture. 3 paint.

péjoratif, -ive (pe:ʒɔra'ti:f, -'ti:v) *adj* pejorative, disparaging.

pelage (pə'laʒ) *nm* coat, fur (of an animal).

pêle-mêle (pɛl'mɛl) *adv* pell-mell. *nm invar* jumble.

peler (pə'le:) *vi,vt* peel. *vt* skin.

pèlerin (pɛl'rɛ̃) *nm* pilgrim. **pèlerinage** *nm* pilgrimage. **pèlerine** *nf* cloak.

pélican (pe:li:'kã) *nm* pelican.

pelle (pɛl) *nf* 1 shovel. 2 scoop. **pelle à poussière** dustpan.

pelleter (pɛl'te:) *vt* shovel.

pelletier (pɛl'tje:) *nm* furrier.

pellicule (pɛlli:'kyl) *nf* 1 film, layer. 2 *phot* film. 3 *pl* dandruff.

pelote (plɔt) *nf* 1 ball (of wool). 2 wad. **pelote à épingles** pincushion.

peloton (plɔ'tɔ̃) *nm* 1 ball (of wool). 2 group. 3 squad.

pelotonner (plɔtɔ'ne:) *vt* wind into a ball. **se pelotonner** *vr* 1 curl up. 2 crowd together.

pelouse (plu:z) *nf* lawn.

pelu (pə'ly) *adj* hairy.

pelure (plyr) *nf* 1 peel. 2 rind.

pénal, -aux (pe:'nal, -'no) *adj* penal.

pénaliser (pe:nali:'ze:) *vt* penalize. **pénalité** *nf* penalty.

penaud (pə'no) *adj* shamefaced.

pencher (pã'ʃe:) *vi* 1 lean. 2 slope. 3 incline. *vt* tilt. **se pencher** *vr* 1 bend. 2 lean. **penchant** *adj* sloping. *nm* 1 slope. 2 tendency. 3 taste.

pendant[1] (pã'dã) *adj* 1 hanging. 2 flabby. *nm* 1 pendant. 2 pair, match.

pendant[2] (pã'dã) *prep,adv* during. **pendant que** *conj* whilst.

pendiller (pãdi:'je:) *vi* dangle.

pendre (pãdr) *vt* hang (up). *vi* 1 hang. 2 sag. **se pendre à** *vr* cling to. **pendule** *nm* pendulum.

pêne (pɛn) *nm* bolt, latch.

pénétrer (pe:ne:'tre:) *vi* 1 enter. 2 break into. *vt* 1 penetrate. 2 fathom. **pénétrant** *adj* 1 penetrating. 2 sharp. 3 keen.

pénible (pe:'ni:bl) *adj* 1 hard. 2 laborious. 3 painful. 4 *inf* annoying.

péniche (pe:'ni:ʃ) *nf* barge.

pénicilline (pe:ni:si:'li:n) *nf* penicillin.

péninsule (pe:nɛ̃'syl) *nf* peninsula.

pénis (pe:'ni:s) *nm* penis.

pénitent (pe:ni:'tã) *adj,n* penitent. **pénitence** *nf* 1 repentance. 2 penance.

penser (pã'se:) *vi,vt* think. *vt* 1 imagine. 2 believe. **penser à** think about. **penser de** think of, have an opinion of. **penser faire** expect to do. ~*nm* thought. **pensée** *nf* 1 thought. 2 *bot* pansy.

pension (pã'sjɔ̃) *nf* 1 pension. 2 board and lodging. 3 boarding school. **pension de famille** boarding house. **pensionnat** *nm* boarding school.

pentagone (pɛ̃ta'gɔn) *nm* pentagon. *adj* pentagonal.

pente (pãt) *nf* 1 slope. 2 gradient.

Pentecôte (pãt'kot) *nf* 1 Whitsun. 2 Pentecost.

pénurie (pe:ny'ri:) *nf* 1 scarcity. 2 lack. 3 poverty.

pépier (pe:'pje:) *vi* chirp.

pépin (pe:'pɛ̃) *nm* 1 pip. 2 *bot* stone. 3 *inf* hitch. **pépinière** *nf bot* nursery.

pépite (pe:'pi:t) *nf* nugget.

perception (pɛrsɛp'sjɔ̃) *nf* 1 collection. 2 tax-office. 3 perception. **percepteur, -trice** (pɛrsɛp'tœr, -'tri:s) *adj* discerning. *nm* tax-collector. **perceptible (à l'oreille)** *adj* audible. **perceptif, -ive** (pɛrsɛp'ti:f, -'ti:v) *adj* perceptive.

percer (pɛr'se:) *vt* 1 pierce. 2 break through. 3 penetrate. *vi* come through. **perçant** *adj* 1 piercing. 2 sharp. 3 shrill. **perce-neige** *nm invar* snowdrop. **perce-oreille** *nm, pl* **perce-oreilles** earwig.

percevoir* (pɛrsə'vwar) *vt* 1 perceive. 2 collect.

perche[1] (pɛrʃ) *nf zool* perch.

perche[2] (pɛrʃ) *nf* pole.

percher (pɛr'ʃe:) *vi* 1 perch. 2 roost. **perchoir** *nm* 1 perch. 2 roost.

perclus (pɛr'kly) *adj* 1 crippled. 2 stiff.

percussion (pɛrky'sjɔ̃) *nf* 1 impact. 2 *mus* percussion.

perdre (pɛrdr) *vt* 1 lose. 2 ruin. 3 waste. 4 leak. *vi* 1 deteriorate. 2 leak. **se perdre** *vr* 1 get lost. 2 disappear.

perdrix (pɛr'dri:) *nf* partridge.

père (pɛr) *nm* father.

perfection (pɛrfɛk'sjɔ̃) *nf* perfection.

perfide (pɛr'fi:d) *adj* treacherous.

perforer (pɛrfɔ're:) *vt* 1 perforate. 2 punch. 3 drill. 4 puncture. **perforation** *nf* 1 perforation. 2 hole.

péril (pe:'ri:l) *nm* peril, danger.

périmé (pe:rɪ:'me:) *adj* out-of-date.
périmètre (pe:rɪ:'mɛtr) *nm* **1** perimeter. **2** area.
période (pe:'rjɔd) *nf* **1** period. **2** era. **périodique** *adj* periodical. *nm* periodical (magazine).
périphérie (pe:rɪ:fe:'rɪ:) *nf* **1** periphery. **2** outskirts. **boulevard périphérique** *nm* ringroad.
périr (pe:'rɪ:r) *vi* **1** perish. **2** be destroyed. **3** die. **périssable** *adj* perishable.
périscope (pe:rɪ:'skɔp) *nm* periscope.
périssoire (pe:rɪ:'swar) *nf* canoe.
perle (pɛrl) *nf* **1** pearl. **2** bead.
permanent (pɛrma'nã) *adj* **1** permanent. **2** continuous. **permanence** *nf* permanence.
perméable (pɛrme:'abl) *adj* porous.
permettre* (pɛr'mɛtr) *vt* **1** permit. **2** allow. **3** enable.
permis (pɛr'mɪ:) *adj* **1** allowed. **2** permissible. *nm* **1** permit. **2** licence. **permis de conduire** *nm* driving licence.
permission (pɛrmɪ:'sjɔ̃) *nf* **1** permission. **2** *mil* leave.
permutation (pɛrmyta'sjɔ̃) *nf* **1** exchange. **2** permutation.
pernicieux, -euse (pɛrnɪ:'sjœ, -'sjœz) *adj* **1** injurious. **2** harmful.
peroxyde (pɛrɔk'sɪ:d) *nm* peroxide.
perpendiculaire (pɛrpãdi:ky'lɛr) *adj,nf* perpendicular.
perpétuer (pɛrpe:'tɥe:) *vt* perpetuate. **se perpétuer** *vr* **1** endure. **2** survive. **perpétuel, -elle** (pɛrpe:'tɥɛl) *adj* **1** perpetual. **2** constant. **perpétuité** *nf* endlessness. **à perpétuité** for ever, for life.
perplexe (pɛr'plɛks) *adj* perplexed, puzzled.
perquisition (pɛrkɪ:zɪ:'sjɔ̃) *nf* house search.
perron (pɛ'rɔ̃) *nm* flight of steps.
perroquet (pɛrɔ'kɛ) *nm* parrot.
perruque (pɛ'ryk) *nf* wig.
persécuter (pɛrse:ky'te:) *vt* **1** persecute. **2** harass. **persécution** *nf* persecution.
persévérer (pɛrse:ve:'re:) *vi* **1** persevere. **2** persist. **persévérance** (pɛrse:vɛ'rãs) *nf* perseverance. **persévérant** (pɛrse:vɛ'rã) *adj* **1** persevering. **2** steadfast.
persienne (pɛr'sjɛn) *nf* shutter.
persifler (pɛrsɪ:'fle:) *vt* mock.
persil (pɛr'sɪ:l) *nm* parsley.
persister (pɛrsɪ:'ste:) *vi* **persister à** persist in. **persistance** *nf* persistance. **persistant** *adj* **1** persistent. **2** lasting.
personne (pɛr'sɔn) *nf* **1** person. **2** individual. *pron* anyone, anybody. **ne...personne** no one, nobody. **personnage** *nm* **1** person. **2** *lit* character. **personnalité** *nf* **1** personality. **2** important person. **3** personal remark. **personnel, -elle** (pɛrsɔ'nɛl) *adj* personal. *nm* personnel, staff.
personnifier (pɛrsɔnɪ:'fje:) *vt* **1** personify. **2** impersonate.
perspective (pɛrspɛk'tɪ:v) *nf* **1** outlook. **2** prospect. **3** perspective.
perspicace (pɛrspɪ:'kas) *adj* shrewd. **perspicacité** *nf* **1** insight. **2** shrewdness.
persuader (pɛrsɥa'de:) *vt* **1** persuade. **2** convince. **3** induce. **persuasif, -ive** (pɛrsɥa'zɪ:f, -'zɪ:v) *adj* **1** persuasive. **2** convincing. **persuasion** *nf* **1** persuasion. **2** belief.
perte (pɛrt) *nf* **1** loss. **2** waste. **3** ruin. **4** death. **à perte de vue** as far as the eye can see.
pertinent (pɛrtɪ:'nã) *adj* pertinent, relevant. **pertinemment** (pɛrtɪ:na'mã) *adv* pertinently. **pertinence** *nf* relevance.
perturbateur, -trice (pɛrtyrba'tœr, -'trɪ:s) *adj* disturbing. *nm,f* agitator. **perturbation** *nf* disturbance.
pervers (pɛr'vɛr) *adj* **1** perverse. **2** depraved.
pervertir (pɛrvɛr'tɪ:r) *vt* **1** pervert. **2** corrupt. **perverti** *nm* pervert.
peser (pə'ze:) *vt* weigh. *vi* be heavy. **pesage** *nm* **1** weighing. **2** *sport* paddock. **pesant** *adj* **1** heavy. **2** clumsy. *nm* weight. **pesanteur** *nf* **1** weight. **2** *sci* gravity. **3** heaviness. **4** dullness.
pessimisme (pɛsɪ:'mɪ:sm) *nm* pessimism. **pessimiste** *adj* pessimistic. *nm,f* pessimist.
peste (pɛst) *nf* **1** plague. **2** *inf* pest.
pet (pɛ) *nm* *sl* fart.
pétale (pe'tal) *nm* petal.
pétanque (pe:'tãk) *nf* game of bowls.
pétarader (pe:tara'de:) *vi* backfire.
pétard (pe:'tar) *nm* **1** blast. **2** firework, banger. **3** *inf* row, noise.
pet-de-nonne (pɛdə'nɔn) *nm, pl* **pets-de-nonne** *cul* fritter.
pétiller (pe:tɪ:'je:) *vi* **1** crackle. **2** sparkle.
petit (pə'tɪ:) *adj* **1** small, little. **2** petty, insignificant. **en petit** in miniature. **petit-enfant** *nm, pl* **petits-enfants** grandchild. **petite-fille** *nf, pl* **petites-filles** granddaughter. **petit-fils** *nm, pl* **petits-fils** grandson. **petitesse** *nf* **1** smallness. **2** pettiness.
pétition (pe:tɪ:'sjɔ̃) *nf* petition.
pétrifier (pe:trɪ:'fje:) *vt* petrify.
pétrir (pe:'trɪ:r) *vt* **1** knead. **2** mould.

103

pétrole (pe:'trɔl) *nm* petroleum. **pétrole brut** crude oil. **pétrolier, -ière** (pe:trɔ'lje:, -'ljɛr) *adj* oil. *nm* tanker. **pétrolifère** *adj* oil-producing.

pétulant (pe:ty'lã) *adj* lively.

peu (pœ) *adv* 1 little. 2 few. 3 not very. *nm* little, bit. **à peu près** almost, more or less.

peupler (pœ'ple:) *vt* people, populate. **peuple** *nm* 1 people. 2 nation. 3 masses.

peuplier (pœpli:'e:) *nm* poplar tree.

peur (pœr) *nf* 1 fear. 2 fright. 3 dread. **peureux, -euse** (pœ'rœ, -'rœz) *adj* 1 timid. 2 shy. 3 nervous.

peut (pœ) *v* see **pouvoir**.

peut-être (pœ'tɛtr) *adv* 1 perhaps. 2 maybe. 3 possibly.

peux (pœ) *v* see **pouvoir**.

phallus (fal'lys) *nm* phallus.

phare (far) *nm* 1 lighthouse. 2 headlamp.

pharmacie (farma'si:) *nf* 1 pharmacy. 2 chemist's shop. **pharmacien, -ienne** (farma-'sjɛ̃, -'sjɛn) *nm,f* 1 chemist. 2 pharmacist.

pharynx (fa'rɛ̃ks) *nm* pharynx.

phase (fɑz) *nf* 1 phase. 2 stage.

phénix (fe:'nɪ:ks) *nm* 1 phoenix. 2 paragon.

phénomène (fe:nɔ'mɛn) *nm* 1 phenomenon. 2 *inf* freak. **phénoménal, -aux** (fe:nɔmɛ'nal, -'no) *adj* 1 phenomenal. 2 extraordinary.

philanthropie (fi:lãtrɔ'pi:) *nf* philanthropy. **philanthrope** *nm,f* philanthropist.

philatélie (fi:late:'li:) *nf* philately. **philatéliste** *nm,f* philatelist.

philistin (fi:li:'stɛ̃) *adj,nm* Philistine.

philosophie (fi:lɔzɔ'fi:) *nf* philosophy. **philosophe** *nm,f* philosopher. *adj* philosophical. **philosophique** *adj* philosophical.

phobie (fɔ'bi:) *nf* phobia.

phonétique (fɔne:'ti:k) *adj* phonetic. *nf* phonetics.

phonographe (fɔnɔ'graf) *nm* gramophone.

phoque (fɔk) *nm* seal.

phosphate (fɔs'fat) *nm* phosphate.

phosphore (fɔs'fɔr) *nm* phosphorus.

photo (fɔ'to) *nf* photo.

photocopier (fɔtɔkɔ'pje:) *vt* photocopy. **photocopie** *nf* photocopy.

photographier (fɔtɔgra'fje:) *vt* photograph. **photographe** *nm,f* photographer. **photographie** *nf* 1 photography. 2 photograph. **photographique** *adj* photographic.

phrase (frɑz) *nf* 1 sentence. 2 phrase.

physiologie (fi:zjɔlɔ'ʒi:) *nf* physiology. **physiologique** *adj* physiological. **physiologiste** *nm,f* physiologist.

physiothérapie (fi:zjɔte:ra'pi:) *nf* physiotherapy. **physiothérapiste** *nm,f* physiotherapist.

physique[1] (fi:'zi:k) *adj* physical. *nm* physique.

physique[2] (fi:'zi:k) *nf* physics. **physicien, -ienne** (fi:zi:'sjɛ̃, -'sjɛn) *nm,f* physicist.

piaffer (pja'fe:) *vi* 1 prance. 2 paw the ground.

piailler (pja'je:) *vi* 1 chirp. 2 squeal.

piano (pja'no) *nm* piano. **piano à queue** grand piano. **pianiste** *nm,f* pianist.

piauler (pjo'le:) *vi* whine.

pic[1] (pi:k) *nm* woodpecker.

pic[2] (pi:k) *nm* pick.

pic[3] (pi:k) *nm* peak. **à pic** sheer. **tomber à pic** 1 fall sheer. 2 happen just in time.

picoter (pi:kɔ'te:) *vt* 1 peck (at). 2 prick. 3 sting. *vi* 1 smart. 2 tingle.

pie (pi:) *nf* magpie.

pièce (pjɛs) *nf* 1 piece. 2 part. 3 room (in a house). 4 fragment. 5 chessman. **à la pièce** separately. **pièce de monnaie** coin. **pièce de théâtre** play.

pied (pje:) *nm* 1 foot. 2 leg (of a chair, etc.). 3 stem. **à pied** on foot. **en pied** full-length. **mettre sur pied** establish, start. **pied bot** club foot. **pied-noir** *nm*, *pl* **pieds-noirs** Algerian of French origin. **pied plat** flat-footed.

piédestal, -aux (pje:dɛ'stal, -'sto) *nm* pedestal.

piéger (pje:'ʒe:) *vt* trap. **piège** *nm* trap.

pierre (pjɛr) *nf* stone. **pierre à briquet** flint. **pierre à chaux** limestone. **pierre précieuse** gem. **pierres de gué** *nf pl* stepping stones.

piété (pje:'te:) *nf* 1 piety. 2 devotion.

piétiner (pje:ti:'ne:) *vt* 1 trample. 2 tread under foot. 3 stamp.

piéton (pje:'tɔ̃) *nm* pedestrian.

pieu, pieux (pjœ) *nm* stake, pole.

pieuvre (pjœvr) *nf* octopus.

pieux, pieuse (pjœ, pjœz) *adj* pious, devout.

pigeon (pi:'ʒɔ̃) *nm* pigeon.

pigment (pi:g'mã) *nm* pigment.

pignon (pi:'ɲɔ̃) *nm* 1 gable. 2 pinion.

pile[1] (pi:l) *nf* 1 pile, heap. 2 battery.

pile[2] (pi:l) *nf* reverse (of a coin). **pile ou face** heads or tails.

piler (pi:'le:) *vt* 1 pound. 2 crush. 3 grind.

pilier (pi:l'je:) *nm* 1 pillar. 2 column.

piller (pi:'je:) *vt* plunder, pillage. **pillage** *nm* pillage, looting.

piloter (pi:lɔ'te:) *vt* **1** pilot. **2** fly. **pilote** *nm* pilot.

pilule (pi:'lyl) *nf* **1** pill. **2** contraceptive pill.

piment (pi:'mã) *nm* **1** pimento. **2** capsicum.

pimenter (pi:mã'te:) *vt* season with spices.

pimpant (pɛ̃'pã) *adj* smart.

pin (pɛ̃) *nm* pine.

pinacle (pi:'nakl) *nm* pinnacle.

pinceau, -aux (pɛ̃'so) *nm* paintbrush.

pincer (pɛ̃'se:) *vt* **1** pinch. **2** nip. **3** *mus* pluck. **4** catch (a thief). **pince** *nf* **1** grip. **2** pincers. **3** forceps. **4** clip. **5** claw. **6** dart (in clothes). **pince à épiler** tweezers. **pince à linge** clothes peg. **pincé** *adj* **1** affected. **2** prim. **pincée** *nf* pinch.

pingouin (pɛ̃'gwɛ̃) *nm* penguin.

Ping-pong (pi:ɲ'pɔŋ) *nm invar Tdmk* table-tennis.

pinson (pɛ̃'sɔ̃) *nm* chaffinch.

piocher (pjɔ'ʃe:) *vt* **1** dig (with a pick). **2** *sl* swot. **3** *game* pick up (a card, etc.). **pioche** *nf* pick.

pion (pjɔ̃) *nm* **1** *educ* junior master. **2** *game* pawn.

pionnier (pjɔ'nje:) *nm* pioneer.

pipe (pi:p) *nf* **1** pipe. **2** tube.

pipette (pi:'pɛt) *nf* pipette.

piquant (pi:'kã) *adj* **1** stinging. **2** cutting. **3** tart. **4** piquant. *nm* **1** point, pith. **2** sting. **3** quill.

pique¹ (pi:k) *nf mil* pike. *nm game* spade.

pique² (pi:k) *nf* pique, spite.

piquer (pi:'ke:) *vt* **1** prick. **2** sting. **3** offend. **4** excite. **5** stitch. **piqué** *adj* **1** quilted. **2** padded. **3** spotted. **4** vertical. **piqûre** *nf* **1** sting, bite. **2** prick. **3** small hole. **4** injection. **pique-nique** *nm, pl* **pique-niques** picnic.

piquet (pi:'kɛ) *nm* **1** peg. **2** stake. **3** picket.

pirate (pi:'rat) *nm* pirate.

pire (pi:r) *adj* worse. **le pire** worst.

pis¹ (pi:) *nm* udder.

pis² (pi:) *adv* worse. **de pis en pis** worse and worse. **le pis** worst. **tant pis!** too bad! it can't be helped! **pis-aller** *nm invar* makeshift.

piscine (pi:s'si:n) *nf* swimming pool.

pissenlit (pi:sã'li:) *nm* dandelion.

pistache (pi:'staʃ) *nf* pistachio.

piste (pi:st) *nf* **1** track. **2** trail. **3** scent. **piste cavalière** bridlepath. **piste d'envol** runway.

pistolet (pi:stɔ'lɛ) *nm* pistol.

piston (pi:'stɔ̃) *nm* **1** piston. **2** influence.

pitié (pi:'tje:) *nf* **1** pity. **2** compassion. **piteux, -euse** (pi:'tœ, -'tœz) *adj* pitiful, sorry. **pitoyable** *adj* **1** wretched. **2** pitiful. **3** contemptible.

pitre (pi:tr) *nm* clown.

pittoresque (pi:ttɔ'rɛsk) *adj* picturesque.

pivot (pi:'vo) *nm* **1** pivot. **2** axis. **3** centre.

pivoter (pi:vɔ'te:) *vi* **1** pivot. **2** revolve. **3** swivel. **pivoter sur** hinge on.

plaçage (pla'saʒ) *nm* veneer.

placard (pla'kar) *nm* **1** poster. **2** placard. **3** wall cupboard.

placer (pla'se:) *vt* **1** place. **2** invest. **3** sell. **4** find a job for. **se placer** *vr* **1** take one's place. **2** sit. **3** find a job. **place** *nf* **1** place. **2** seat. **3** room. **4** job. **5** spot. **6** square. **rester sur place** stay put.

placide (pla'si:d) *adj* placid, calm.

plafond (pla'fɔ̃) *nm* ceiling.

plage (plaʒ) *nf* **1** beach. **2** shore. **3** seaside resort.

plagier (pla'ʒje:) *vt* plagiarize. **plagiaire** *nm,f* plagiarist. **plagiat** *nm* plagiarism.

plaider (plɛ'de:) *vi,vt* plead.

plaie (plɛ) *nf* **1** wound. **2** sore. **3** evil, misfortune.

plaignant (plɛ'ɲã) *v* see **plaindre**.

plaindre° (plɛ̃dr) *vt* pity. **se plaindre de** *vr* complain about.

plaine (plɛn) *nf geog* plain.

plain-pied (plɛ̃'pje:) **de plain-pied** *adv* **1** on a level. **2** easily.

plaint (plɛ̃) *v* see **plaindre**.

plainte (plɛ̃t) *nf* **1** complaint. **2** groan.

plaire° (plɛr) *vt* **plaire à 1** please. **2** suit. **s'il vous plaît** please. **se plaire** *vr* be happy. **se plaire à** enjoy.

plaisance (plɛ'zãs) *nf* pleasure. **plaisancier** *nm* **1** yacht. **2** yachtsman.

plaisant (plɛ'zã) *adj* **1** attractive. **2** agreeable. **3** amusing.

plaisanter (plɛzã'te:) *vi* joke, jest. *vt* tease. **plaisanterie** *nf* joke, jest.

plaisir (plɛ'zi:r) *nm* **1** pleasure. **2** delight. **3** amusement.

plan¹ (plã) *adj* **1** flat. **2** level. **3** even. *nm* **1** plane. **2** sphere. **premier plan** *nm* foreground.

plan² (plã) *nm* **1** plan. **2** project. **3** draft. **4** model.

planche (plãʃ) *nf* **1** board. **2** plank. **3** shelf. **faire la planche** float on one's back.

plancher (plã'ʃe:) *nm* floor.

plancton (plãk'tɔ̃) *nm* plankton.

planer¹ (pla'ne:) *vt* plane, smooth.

planer² (pla'ne:) *vi* **1** soar. **2** hover. **3** *aviat* glide. **planeur** *nm* glider.

planète (pla'nɛt) *nf* planet.
plant (plā) *nm* **1** plantation. **2** sapling. **jeune plant** *nm* seedling.
plantation (plăta'sjɔ̃) *nf* **1** plantation. **2** planting.
plante[1] (plãt) *nf anat* sole.
plante[2] (plãt) *nf* plant. **plante verte** evergreen.
planter (plā'te:) *vt* **1** plant. **2** set, place. **planter là** jilt. **se planter** *vr* stand.
planton (plā'tɔ̃) *nm* **1** *mil* orderly. **2** usher.
plaque (plak) *nf* **1** sheet (of metal). **2** slab. **3** plaque. **4** badge. **plaque chauffante** hotplate. **plaque tournante** turntable.
plaquer (pla'ke:) *vt* **1** veneer. **2** plate. **3** plaster. **4** *sport* tackle. **5** *inf* abandon. **se plaquer** *vr* lie flat.
plastique (pla'sti:k) *adj,nm* plastic.
plat (pla) *adj* **1** flat. **2** level. **3** dull. *nm* **1** flat (of the hand). **2** dish. **3** course. **à plat** **1** flat. **2** *inf* exhausted. **plate-bande** *nf, pl* **plates-bandes** flowerbed. **plate-forme** *nf, pl* **plates-formes** platform.
plateau, -aux (pla'to) *nm* **1** tray. **2** plateau. **3** platform. **4** stage. **plateau à thé** teatray.
platine (pla'ti:n) *nm* platinum.
platonique (platɔ'ni:k) *adj* **1** platonic. **2** futile.
plâtrer (plɑ'tre:) *vt* **1** plaster. **2** patch up. **plâtre** *nm* **1** plaster. **2** plaster cast. **plâtre de moulage** plaster of Paris. **plâtrier** *nm* plasterer.
plausible (plo'zi:bl) *adj* likely, probable.
plectre (plɛktr) *nm* plectrum.
plein (plɛ̃) *adj* **1** full. **2** complete. **3** solid. **4** (of animals) with young. *adv* full. **en plein air/jour** in the open air/in broad daylight. **faire le plein** fill up.
pleurer (plœ're:) *vi* **1** cry, weep. **2** water. **3** drip. *vt* mourn for. **pleurard** *adj* tearful.
pleurnicher (plœrni:'ʃe:) *vi* **1** whine. **2** snivel.
pleuvoir* (plœ'vwar) *v imp* rain.
pli (pli:) *nm* **1** fold. **2** pleat. **3** crease. **4** bend. **5** envelope. **6** note. **petit pli** tuck.
plie (pli:) *nf* plaice.
plier (pli:'e:) *vt* **1** fold. **2** bend. *vi* **1** bend. **2** submit. **pliant** *adj* **1** flexible. **2** collapsible. *nm* folding chair.
plisser (pli:'se:) *vt* **1** crease. **2** pleat.
plomb (plɔ̃) *nm* lead. **à plomb** vertically. **plombier** *nm* plumber.
plomber (plɔ̃'be:) *vt* **1** cover with lead. **2** stop, fill (a tooth). **3** seal.
plonger (plɔ̃'ʒe:) *vi* **1** dive. **2** plunge. *vt* **1** immerse. **2** thrust. **plonge** *nf* washing-up. **plongée** *nf* **1** dive. **2** plunge. **3** slope.
plongée autonome skin diving. **plongeoir** *nm* diving board. **plongeur, -euse** (plɔ̃'ʒœr, -'ʒœz) *nm,f* **1** diver. **2** washer-up.
ployer (plwa'je:) *vt* bend. *vi* bow, give way.
plu[1] (ply) *v* see **plaire.**
plu[2] (ply) *v* see **pleuvoir.**
pluie (plɥi:) *nf* rain. **pluie battante** downpour.
plumer (ply'me:) *vt* **1** pluck. **2** *sl* fleece. **plume** *nf* **1** feather. **2** pen. **3** nib.
plupart (ply'par) *nf* **1** most. **2** the greater part. **pour la plupart** mostly.
pluriel, -elle (ply'rjɛl) *adj,nm* plural.
plus (ply) *adv* **1** more. **2** most. **3** plus, in addition. *nm* **1** more. **2** most. **de plus 1** more. **2** besides. **en plus** in addition. (**tout**) **au plus** at most or best. **plus-que-parfait** *nm* pluperfect.
plusieurs (ply'zjœr) *adj,pron pl* several.
Pluton (ply'tɔ̃) *nm* Pluto.
plutôt (ply'to) *adv* **1** rather. **2** on the whole.
pluvieux, -euse (ply'vjœ, -'vjœz) *adj* rainy, wet.
pneu (pnœ) *nm* tyre.
pneumatique (pnœma'ti:k) *adj* pneumatic. *nm* **1** tyre. **2** express letter (in Paris).
pneumonie (pnœmɔ'ni:) *nf* pneumonia.
pochard (pɔ'ʃar) *nm* drunkard.
poche (pɔʃ) *nf* **1** pocket. **2** bag. **pochette** *nf* **1** small pocket. **2** handbag. **3** fancy handkerchief.
pocher (pɔ'ʃe:) *vt* **1** *cul* poach. **2** sketch. **pochade** *nf* sketch.
poêle[1] (pwal) *nm* stove, cooker.
poêle[2] (pwal) *nf* frying pan.
poème (pɔ'ɛm) *nm* poem. **poésie** *nf* **1** poetry. **2** poem. **poète** *nm* poet. **poétique** *adj* poetic.
poids (pwa) *nm* **1** weight. **2** importance. **3** burden. **poids léger** lightweight. **poids lourd 1** heavyweight. **2** heavy goods vehicle.
poignant (pwa'ɲā) *adj* poignant, gripping.
poignard (pwa'ɲar) *nm* dagger.
poignarder (pwaɲar'de:) *vt* stab.
poigne (pwaɲ) *nf* **1** grip. **2** energy. **3** will. **poignée** *nf* **1** handful. **2** handle. **poignée de main** handshake. **poignet** *nm* **1** wrist. **2** cuff (of a garment).
poil (pwal) *nm* **1** hair, fur (of animals). **2** hair (of humans). **3** nap (of material). **4** *inf* mood. **à poil 1** hairy. **2** *inf* naked. **poilu** *adj* hairy.
poinçon (pwɛ̃'sɔ̃) *nm* **1** *tech* punch. **2** stamp, mark. **3** hallmark.
poinçonner (pwɛ̃sɔ'ne:) *vt* **1** stamp. **2** hallmark. **3** punch, clip.

poindre* (pwɛ̃dr) vi **1** dawn. **2** sprout.

poing (pwɛ̃) nm fist.

point¹ (pwɛ̃) nm **1** point. **2** stitch. **3** dot. **4** extent. **5** full stop. **6** score, mark. **à point** perfect, to a turn. **mettre au point 1** focus. **2** perfect. **deux points** colon. **point d'exclamation** exclamation mark. **point d'interrogation** question mark. **point du jour** daybreak. **point-virgule** nm semicolon.

point² (pwɛ̃) adv **1** not. **2** no. **3** not at all. **ne...point** not any.

pointe (pwɛ̃t) nf **1** point. **2** tip. **3** touch, hint. **4** peak.

pointer¹ (pwɛ̃'te:) vt **1** check. **2** tick off. **3** aim, train.

pointer² (pwɛ̃'te:) vt **1** prick. **2** stab. **3** point. vi **1** appear. **2** sprout. **3** rise. **4** soar. **pointu** adj pointed.

pointiller¹ (pwɛ̃tɪ'je:) vt dot. **pointillé** adj dotted. nm dotted line.

pointiller² (pwɛ̃tɪ'je:) vi bicker.

pointilleux, -euse (pwɛ̃tɪ'jœ, -'jœz) adj **1** touchy. **2** fastidious.

pointure (pwɛ̃'tyr) nf size (in clothes).

poire (pwar) nf **1** pear. **2** sl mug, face. **3** sl fool, dupe. **poirier** nm pear tree.

poireau, -aux (pwɑ'ro) nm leek.

pois (pwɑ) nm **1** pea. **2** spot. **petits pois** nm pl green peas. **pois de senteur** sweet pea.

poison (pwɑ'zɔ̃) nm poison.

poisson (pwɑ'sɔ̃) nm **1** fish. **2** cap pl Pisces. **poisson d'avril** April fool. **poisson rouge** goldfish. **poissonnerie** nf fish shop. **poissonnier, -ière** (pwɑsɔn'je:, -'jɛr) nm,f fishmonger.

poitrine (pwɑ'trɪn) nf **1** chest. **2** breast, bosom.

poivrer (pwɑ'vre:) vt season with pepper. **poivre** nm pepper. **poivre de Cayenne** Cayenne pepper. **poivré** adj **1** peppery. **2** spicy. **poivron** nm sweet pepper.

poix (pwɑ) nf pitch. **poix liquide** tar.

polaire (pɔ'lɛr) adj polar.

polariser (pɔlarɪ'ze:) vt polarize.

pôle (po!) nm pole. **pôle nord** North Pole. **pôle sud** South Pole.

polémique (pɔle'mɪːk) adj,nf polemic.

poli¹ (pɔ'li:) adj **1** polite. **2** courteous. **poliment** adv politely.

poli² (pɔ'li:) adj **1** polished. **2** glossy. nm **1** polish. **2** gloss.

police¹ (pɔ'li:s) nf police. **faire la police** keep order. **policier, -ière** (pɔli'sje:, -'sjɛr) adj **1** police. **2** detective. nm policeman.

police² (pɔ'li:s) nf comm policy.

polir (pɔ'li:r) vt **1** polish. **2** perfect.

polisson, -onne (pɔli:'sɔ̃, -'sɔn) adj **1** naughty. **2** depraved. nm,f rascal, rogue. **polissonnerie** nf **1** mischievousness. **2** depravity.

politesse (pɔli:'tɛs) nf **1** politeness. **2** courtesy.

politique (pɔli:'tɪːk) adj **1** political. **2** diplomatic. nf **1** politics. **2** policy. **politicien, -ienne** (pɔli:tɪ:'sjɛ̃, -'sjɛn) nm,f politician.

pollen (pɔl'lɛn) nm pollen.

polliniser (pɔli:nɪ'ze:) vt pollinate.

polluer (pɔl'lɥe:) vt pollute. **pollution** nf pollution.

Pologne (pɔ'lɔɲ) nf Poland. **polonais** adj Polish. nm **1** Pole. **2** Polish (language).

poltron, -onne (pɔl'trɔ̃, -'trɔn) adj **1** timid. **2** cowardly. **poltronnerie** nf cowardice.

polygamie (pɔli:ga'mi:) nf polygamy. **polygame** adj polygamous. nm,f polygamist.

polygone (pɔli:'gɔn) nm polygon. **polygonal, -aux** (pɔl:gɔn'al, -'no) adj polygonal.

polytechnique (pɔli:tɛk'ni:k) adj polytechnic.

polythène (pɔli:'tɛn) nm polythene.

pommade (pɔ'mad) nf ointment.

pomme (pɔm) nf apple. **pomme d'Adam** Adam's apple. **pomme de pin** pine cone. **pomme de terre** potato. **pommé** adj **1** rounded. **2** inf utter, complete. **pommelé** adj mottled. **pommier** nm apple tree.

pommeau, -aux (pɔ'mo) nm pommel.

pommette (pɔ'mɛt) nf cheekbone.

pompe¹ (pɔ̃p) nf pomp, ceremony. **pompeux, -euse** (pɔ̃'pœ, -'pœz) adj **1** pompous. **2** stately.

pompe² (pɔ̃p) nf pump. **pompe à incendie** fire-engine. **pompier** nm fireman.

pomper (pɔ̃'pe:) vt **1** pump. **2** suck up.

ponce (pɔ̃s) nf pumice stone.

ponctuel, -elle (pɔ̃k'tɥɛl) adj punctual. **ponctualité** nf punctuality.

ponctuer (pɔ̃k'tɥe:) vt **1** punctuate. **2** emphasize. **ponctuation** nf punctuation.

pondéré (pɔ̃de:'re:) adj **1** level-headed. **2** calm.

pondre (pɔ̃dr) vt **1** lay (eggs). **2** produce. **pondaison** nf laying (of eggs).

poney (pɔ'ni:) nm pony.

pont (pɔ̃) nm **1** bridge. **2** naut deck. **3** axle. **4** public holiday. **pont à bascule** weighbridge. **pont aérien** airlift. **pont-levis** nm, pl **ponts-levis** drawbridge. **pont suspendu** suspension bridge.

populace (pɔpy'las) nf rabble.

populaire (pɔpy'lɛr) adj **1** popular. **2** pol peo-

ple's. **popularité** nf popularity. **populeux,
-euse** (pɔpy'lœ, -'lœz) adj densely populated.
population (pɔpyla'sjɔ̃) nf population.
porc (pɔr) nm **1** pig. **2** pork. **3** sl swine.
porc-épic nm, pl **porcs-épics** porcupine.
porcelaine (pɔrsə'lɛn) nf **1** porcelain. **2** china.
porche (pɔrʃ) nm porch.
porcherie (pɔrʃə'riː) nf pigsty.
pore (pɔr) nm pore. **poreux, -euse** (pɔ'rœ,
-'rœz) adj porous.
pornographie (pɔrnɔgra'fiː) nf pornography.
pornographique adj pornographic.
port[1] (pɔr) nm **1** port. **2** harbour.
port[2] (pɔr) nm **1** carriage. **2** transport. **3**
bearing.
porte (pɔrt) nf **1** door. **2** doorway. **3** entrance. **4**
gate. **5** pl geog pass.
porte-affiches nm invar notice board.
porte-bagages nm invar luggage rack.
porte-bébé nm invar carrycot.
porte-bonheur nm invar **1** mascot. **2** charm.
porte-clefs nm invar keyring.
porte-fenêtre nf, pl **portes-fenêtres** French
window.
portefeuille (pɔrtə'fœj) nm **1** portfolio. **2** wallet.
porte-monnaie nm invar purse.
porte-parole nm invar spokesman.
porter (pɔr'te:) vt **1** carry. **2** wear. **3** bear. **4**
enter. **5** induce. vi **1** rest. **2** hit, strike home.
se porter vr proceed. **se porter bien/mal** be
in good/bad health. **portable** adj wearable.
portatif, -ive (pɔrta'tiːf, -'tiːv) adj portable.
porté adj inclined, prone. **portée** nf **1** span. **2**
litter. **3** reach, range. **4** significance. **5** mus
scale. **porteur, -euse** (pɔr'tœr, -'tœz) nm, f
porter, carrier, bearer.
porte-vêtements nm invar coat-hanger.
porte-voix nm invar megaphone.
portière (pɔr'tjɛr) nf door (of a car, train, etc.).
portion (pɔr'sjɔ̃) nf **1** portion, helping. **2** part.
portique (pɔr'tiːk) nm porch.
porto (pɔr'to) nm port (wine).
portrait (pɔr'trɛ) nm **1** portrait. **2** likeness.
Portugal (pɔrty'gal) nm Portugal. **portugais**
adj,n Portuguese. nm Portuguese (language).
poser (po'ze:) vt **1** set, put. **2** place. **3** fix up. **4**
suppose. vi **1** rest, lie. **2** pose. **se poser** vr
alight. **se poser en** set oneself up as. **pose**
nf **1** pose. **2** attitude. **3** affectation. **4** laying.
posé adj **1** sedate. **2** steady. **3** staid.
positif, -ive (pɔziː'tiːf, -'tiːv) adj **1** positive. **2**
certain. **3** actual. **4** practical.

108

position (pɔziː'sjɔ̃) nf **1** position. **2** posture. **3**
status. **4** job.
posséder (pose:'de:) vt possess, own. **possédé**
adj possessed. nm madman.
possessif, -ive (pɔsɛ'siːf, -'siːv) adj possessive.
possession nf possession.
possible (pɔ'siːbl) adj possible. **possibilité** nf
possibility.
poste[1] (pɔst) nf **1** post. **2** post office. **mettre à**
la poste post (a letter). **postal, -aux** (pɔ'stal,
-'sto) adj postal.
poste[2] (pɔst) nm **1** post, station. **2** position. **3**
inf television set. **4** (telephone) extension.
poste de police local police station. **poste**
d'incendie fire station.
poster (pɔ'ste:) vt post, station.
postérieur (pɔsteː'rjœr) adj **1** subsequent. **2**
hind. nm inf bottom, posterior. **postérité** nf
posterity.
posthume (pɔ'stym) adj posthumous.
postiche (pɔ'stiːʃ) adj **1** false. **2** imitation. nm
wig.
postscolaire (pɔstskɔ'lɛr) adj after-school.
post-scriptum (pɔstskriːp'tɔm) nm invar postscript.
postuler (pɔsty'le:) vt **1** apply for. **2** postulate.
postulant nm applicant.
posture (pɔ'styr) nf **1** posture. **2** position.
pot (po) nm **1** pot. **2** jug. **3** can. **pot-au-feu**
nm invar beef and vegetable stew. **pot-de-vin**
nm, pl **pots-de-vin** inf bribe. **pot en étain**
tankard. **prendre un pot** inf have a drink.
potable (pɔ'tabl) adj drinkable.
potage (pɔ'taʒ) nm soup.
potager, -ère (pɔta'ʒe:, -'ʒɛr) adj for cooking.
nm kitchen garden.
poteau, -aux (pɔ'to) nm stake, post.
potelé (pɔt'le:) adj **1** plump. **2** chubby.
potence (pɔ'tɑ̃s) nf **1** gallows. **2** support.
potentiel, -elle (pɔtɑ̃'sjɛl) adj,nm potential.
poterie (pɔ'triː) nf pottery. **potier, -ière**
(pɔ'tjeː, -'tjɛr) nm,f potter.
potin (pɔ'tɛ̃) nm **1** pl gossip. **2** row, noise.
potiner (pɔtiː'ne:) vi gossip.
potion (pɔ'sjɔ̃) nf med potion, mixture.
potiron (pɔtiː'rɔ̃) nm pumpkin.
pou, poux (puː) nm louse.
poubelle (puː'bɛl) nf dustbin.
pouce (puːs) nm **1** thumb. **2** big toe. **3** inch.
manger sur le pouce have a snack.
poudrer (puː'dre:) vt powder. **poudre** nf **1**
powder. **2** explosive. **poudre à canon** gun-

powder. **poudreux, -euse** (puːˈdrœ, -ˈdrœz) *adj* dusty.
pouffer (puːˈfe:) *vi* burst out laughing.
poulain (puːˈlɛ̃) *nm* 1 foal. 2 colt.
poule (puːl) *nf* 1 hen. 2 fowl. 3 *sl* tart. **poulet** *nm* 1 chicken. 2 *inf* cop, policeman.
pouliche (puːˈliːʃ) *nf* filly.
poulie (puːˈliː) *nf* pulley.
poulpe (puːlp) *nm* octopus.
pouls (pu) *nm* pulse.
poumon (puːˈmɔ̃) *nm* lung.
poupe (puːp) *nf naut* stern.
poupée (puːˈpe:) *nf* 1 doll. 2 puppet.
pour (puːr) *prep* 1 for. 2 instead of. 3 for the sake of. 4 as to. 5 to. **pour que** in order that.
pourboire (puːrˈbwar) *nm* tip, gratuity.
pourceau, -aux (puːrˈso) *nm* swine, pig.
pour-cent *nm invar* per cent. **pourcentage** *nm* percentage.
pourchasser (puːrʃaˈse:) *vt* pursue.
pourpre (puːrpr) *nf* purple. *adj,nm* crimson.
pourquoi (puːrˈkwa) *adv,conj* why. **pourquoi faire?** what for?
pourrai (puːˈrɛ) *v* see **pouvoir.**
pourrir (puːˈriːr) *vi,vt* rot. *vi* 1 decay. 2 go bad. **pourriture** *nf* 1 rot. 2 decay.
poursuivre (puːrˈsɥiːvr) *vt* 1 pursue, chase. 2 *law* prosecute. 3 continue. **poursuite** *nf* 1 pursuit. 2 chase. 3 *pl law* proceedings.
pourtant (puːrˈtã) *adv* 1 however. 2 yet. 3 still.
pourtour (puːrˈtuːr) *nm* 1 circumference. 2 precincts.
pourvoir* (puːrˈvwar) *vt* 1 supply. 2 equip. **pourvoir à** provide.
pourvu (puːrˈvy) *v* see **pouvoir.**
pourvu que (puːrˈvy) *conj* provided that.
pousser (puːˈse:) *vt* 1 push. 2 thrust. 3 urge. 4 utter. 5 shoot out. *vi* 1 grow. 2 push forward or on. **pousser du coude** nudge. **pousse** *nf* 1 growth. 2 *bot* shoot. **poussé** *adj* 1 elaborate. 2 thorough. **poussée** *nf* 1 push, shove. 2 thrust. 3 growth. **poussette** *nf* pushchair.
poussière (puːˈsjɛr) *nf* 1 dust. 2 powder. 3 spray. **poussiéreux, -euse** (puːsjeˈrœ, -ˈrœz) *adj* dusty.
poussin (puːˈsɛ̃) *nm* chick.
poutre (puːtr) *nf* 1 beam. 2 girder.
pouvoir* (puːˈvwar) *vt* 1 be able. 2 be allowed. *v imp* be possible. **n'en plus pouvoir** be tired out. **on n'y peut rien** nothing can be done about it. ~*nm* 1 power. 2 command.
pragmatique (pragmaˈtiːk) *adj* pragmatic.

prairie (prɛˈriː) *nf* 1 meadow. 2 prairie.
praticable (pratiˈkabl) *adj* 1 practicable. 2 feasible. 3 passable.
pratique[1] (praˈtiːk) *nf* 1 practice. 2 application. 3 custom. 4 habit.
pratique[2] (praˈtiːk) *adj* 1 practical. 2 useful.
pratiquer (pratiˈke:) *vt* 1 practise. 2 employ. 3 do.
pré (pre:) *nm* meadow.
préalable (preaˈlabl) *adj* 1 previous. 2 preliminary. **au préalable** to begin with.
préavis (preaˈviː) *nm* (previous) notice.
précaire (preˈkɛr) *adj* 1 precarious. 2 uncertain. 3 delicate. **précarité** *nf* precariousness.
précaution (prekoˈsjɔ̃) *nf* 1 precaution. 2 care.
précéder (preseˈde:) *vt* precede. **précédement** *adv* previously, already. **précédence** *nf* precedence, priority. **précédent** *adj* 1 preceding, previous. 2 former. *nm* precedent.
précepteur, -trice (presɛpˈtœr, -ˈtriːs) *nm,f* tutor, governess.
prêcher (preːˈʃe:) *vt* preach. **prêche** (prɛʃ) *nm* sermon.
précieux, -euse (preˈsjœ, -ˈsjœz) *adj* 1 precious. 2 valuable. 3 affected.
précipiter (presiːpiˈte:) *vt* 1 precipitate. 2 rush. 3 throw down. **précipitamment** *adv* 1 headlong. 2 in a hurry. **précipité** *adj* 1 precipitate. 2 hasty. 3 headlong.
précis (preˈsiː) *adj* 1 precise. 2 accurate. 3 clear. *nm* summary, precis.
préciser (presiːˈze:) *vt* 1 state precisely. 2 specify. **se préciser** *vr* become clear. **précisément** *adv* precisely, just. **précision** *nf* 1 precision. 2 accuracy. 3 *pl* full details.
précoce (preˈkɔs) *adj* 1 precocious. 2 early. 3 advanced, forward.
préconcevoir* (prekɔ̃səˈvwar) *vt* preconceive.
préconiser (prekɔniˈze:) *vt* 1 recommend. 2 praise.
prédateur, -trice (predaˈtœr, -ˈtriːs) *adj* predatory. *nm* beast of prey.
prédécesseur (predeseˈsœr) *nm* predecessor.
prédestiner (predɛstiˈne:) *vt* predestine.
prédicat (prediˈka) *nm* predicate.
prédicateur (predikaˈtœr) *nm* preacher.
prédire* (preˈdiːr) *vt* predict, foretell.
prédominer (predɔmiˈne:) *vi* 1 predominate, prevail. **prédominance** *nf* predominance. **prédominant** *adj* 1 predominant. 2 prevalent.
prééminent (preemiˈnã) *adj* pre-eminent.
préfabriquer (prefabriˈke:) *vt* prefabricate.
préface (prɛˈfas) *nf* preface.

préfecture

préfecture (pre:fɛk'tyr) *nf* headquarters of the prefect of a French department. **préfecture de police** headquarters of the Paris police.

préférer (pre:fe:'re:) *vt* prefer. **préféré** *adj,n* favourite. **préférence** *nf* preference. **préférentiel, -elle** (pre:fɛrɑ̃'sjɛl) *adj* preferential.

préfet (pre:'fɛ) *nm* prefect. **préfet de police** chief commissioner of Paris police.

préfixe (pre:'fi:ks) *nm* prefix.

préhistorique (pre:ɪ:stɔ'ri:k) *adj* prehistoric.

préjudice (pre:ʒy'di:s) *nm* 1 wrong. 2 detriment. 3 prejudice.

préjugé (pre:ʒy'ʒe:) *nm* prejudice, bias.

prélever (pre:l've:) *vt* levy. **prélèvement** *nm* levy, tax.

préliminaire (pre:li:mi:'nɛr) *adj* preliminary.

prélude (pre:'lyd) *nm* prelude.

prématuré (pre:maty're:) *adj* premature.

préméditer (pre:me:di:'te:) *vt* premeditate. **préméditation** *nf* premeditation. **prémédité** *adj* deliberate.

premier, -ière (prə'mje:, -'mjɛr) *adj* 1 first. 2 original. 3 foremost. 4 maiden (voyage, speech, etc.). *nf* first class.

prémisse (pre:'mi:s) *nf* premise.

prenant (prə'nɑ̃) *v* see **prendre.**

prénatal (pre:na'tal) *adj* antenatal.

prendre* (prɑ̃dr) *vt* 1 take. 2 seize. 3 assume. *vi* 1 set, congeal. 2 take, catch on. **se prendre** *vr* catch, get caught. **s'en prendre à** blame. **se prendre à** 1 cling to. 2 begin. **s'y prendre** set about.

prénom (pre:'nɔ̃) *nm* Christian name.

prénuptial, -aux (pre:nyp'sjal) *adj* premarital.

préoccupé (pre:ɔky'pe:) *adj* 1 preoccupied. 2 engrossed. 3 anxious. **préoccupation** *nf* 1 preoccupation. 2 anxiety. 3 obsession.

préparer (pre:pa're:) *vt* 1 prepare. 2 get ready. **se préparer à** *vr* get ready for. **préparatifs** *nm pl* preparations. **préparation** *nf* preparation. **préparatoire** *adj* preparatory.

préposition (pre:pɔzi:'sjɔ̃) *nf* preposition.

prérogative (pre:rɔga'ti:v) *nf* prerogative.

près (prɛ) *adv* near. **à cela près** with that exception. **à peu près** 1 approximately. 2 nearly. **de près** closely, near to. **près de** *prep* near to.

présager (pre:za'ʒe:) *vt* 1 predict. 2 foresee. 3 signify. **présage** *nm* omen.

presbyte (prɛz'bi:t) *adj* long-sighted.

presbytère (prɛzbi:'tɛr) *nm* vicarage.

prescrire* (prɛ'skri:r) *vt* 1 prescribe. 2 order. 3 110

demand. **prescription** *nf* 1 prescription. 2 instruction. 3 *med* directions for use.

préséance (pre:se:'ɑ̃s) *nf* 1 precedence. 2 priority.

présence (pre:'zɑ̃s) *nf* presence.

présent¹ (pre:'zɑ̃) *adj* present. *nm* present (time or tense). **à présent** now. **jusqu'à présent** as yet, up to now.

présent² (pre:'zɑ̃) *nm* present, gift.

présenter (pre:zɑ̃'te:) *vt* 1 present. 2 offer. 3 introduce. **se présenter** *vr* 1 present oneself. 2 occur. **présentateur, -trice** (pre:zɑ̃ta'tœr, -'tri:s) *nm,f* 1 presenter. 2 disc jockey. **présentation** (pre:zɑ̃ta'sjɔ̃) *nf* 1 presentation. 2 introduction.

préserver (pre:zɛr've:) *vt* 1 preserve. 2 protect. **préservateur, -trice** (pre:zɛrva'tœr, -'tri:s) *adj* preserving. **préservatif, -ive** (pre:zɛrva'ti:f, -'ti:v) *adj* 1 preservative. 2 protective. *nm* contraceptive sheath.

présider (pre:zi:'de:) *vt* preside over. *vi* be in the chair. **président** *nm* 1 president. 2 chairman. **présidentiel, -elle** (pre:zi:dɑ̃'sjɛl) *adj* presidential.

presque (prɛsk) *adv* 1 almost, nearly. 2 hardly.

presqu'île (prɛ'ski:l) *nf* peninsula.

presser (prɛ'se:) *vt* 1 press. 2 squeeze. 3 hurry. **se presser** *vr* 1 hurry. 2 crowd. **pressant** *adj* urgent. **presse** *nf* 1 press. 2 press, newspapers. 3 pressure. 4 crowd. **pressé** *adj* 1 crowded. 2 hurried. 3 urgent. **pression** *nf* pressure.

preste (prɛst) *adj* 1 quick. 2 nimble. 3 alert.

prestidigitateur (prɛsti:di:ʒi:ta'tœr) *nm* conjurer. **prestidigitation** *nf* conjuring.

prestige (prɛs'ti:ʒ) *nm* 1 prestige. 2 attraction. **prestigieux, -euse** (prɛsti:'ʒjœ, -'ʒjœz) *adj* marvellous.

présumer (pre:zy'me:) *vt* presume, assume.

prêt¹ (prɛ) *adj* 1 ready. 2 prepared. **prêt à porter** ready-made (clothes).

prêt² (prɛ) *nm* loan.

prétendre (pre:'tɑ̃dr) *vt* 1 claim. 2 require. 3 maintain. **prétendant** (prɛtɑ̃'dɑ̃) *nm* 1 applicant. 2 candidate. **prétendu** (prɛtɑ̃'dy) *adj* 1 alleged. 2 so-called.

prétention (pre:tɑ̃'sjɔ̃) *nf* 1 pretension. 2 claim. **prétentieux, -euse** (pre:tɑ̃'sjœ, -'sjœz) *adj* 1 pretentious. 2 conceited.

prêter (prɛ'te:) *vt* 1 lend. 2 attribute. *vi* stretch. **prête-nom** *nm, pl* **prête-noms** figurehead. **prêter attention** pay attention. **prêteur,**

-euse (prɛˈtœr, -ˈtœz) *nm,f* lender. **prêteur sur gages** *nm* pawnbroker.

prétexte (preˈtɛkst) *nm* pretext, excuse.

prêtre (prɛtr) *nm* priest. **prêtrise** *nf* priesthood.

preuve (prœv) *nf* 1 proof. 2 evidence.

prévaloirˈ (prɛvalˈwar) *vi* prevail. **se prévaloir de** *vr* take advantage of.

prévenirˈ (preːvˈniːr) *vt* 1 warn. 2 forestall. 3 prevent. 4 prejudice. **prévenance** *nf* 1 attention. 2 kindness. **prévenant** *adj* 1 attentive. 2 considerate. 3 pleasing.

préventif, -ive (preːvãˈtiːf, -ˈtiːv) *adj* preventive. **prévention** *nf* 1 prejudice. 2 imprisonment. 3 prevention.

prévenu (preːvˈny) *adj* prejudiced. *nm* law accused.

prévision (preːviˈzjɔ̃) *nf* 1 forecast. 2 expectation.

prévoirˈ (preːˈvwar) *vt* 1 foresee. 2 provide for. **prévoyance** *nf* 1 foresight. 2 precaution.

prévu (preːˈvy) *v* see **prévoir.**

prier (priːˈeː) *vt* 1 pray. 2 ask. 3 invite. **je vous en prie** don't mention it. **prière** *nf* 1 prayer. 2 request.

prieuré (priːœˈreː) *nm* priory.

primaire (priːˈmɛr) *adj* primary.

prime[1] (priːm) *adj* first. **de prime abord** at first.

prime[2] (priːm) *nf* 1 premium. 2 bonus.

primer[1] (priːˈmeː) *vt* excel.

primer[2] (priːˈmeː) *vt* award a prize to. **primé** *adj* 1 prized. 2 subsidized.

primerose (priːmˈroz) *nf* hollyhock.

primesautier, -ière (priːmsoˈtjeː, -ˈtjɛr) *adj* 1 impulsive. 2 spontaneous.

primeur (priːˈmœr) *nf* 1 newness. 2 freshness. 3 *pl* early vegetables.

primevère (priːmˈvɛr) *nf* primrose.

primitif, -ive (priːmiːˈtiːf, -ˈtiːv) *adj* 1 primitive. 2 original.

primordial, -aux (priːmɔrˈdjal, -ˈdjo) *adj* 1 prime. 2 primeval.

prince (prɛ̃s) *nm* prince.

princesse (prɛ̃ˈsɛs) *nf* princess.

principal, -aux (prɛ̃siːˈpal, -ˈpo) *adj* principal, chief, main. *nm* 1 chief. 2 headmaster. 3 main thing. **principauté** *nf* principality.

principe (prɛ̃ˈsiːp) *nm* principle.

printanier, -ière (prɛ̃taˈnjeː, -ˈnjɛr) *adj* spring.

printemps (prɛ̃ˈtã) *nm* spring, springtime.

priorité (priːɔriːˈteː) *nf* priority.

pris (priː) *v* see **prendre.** *adj* 1 engaged, occupied. 2 busy.

prise (priːz) *nf* 1 hold. 2 grip. 3 solidification. 4 capture. 5 pinch. **en prise** in gear. **lâcner prise** let go. **prise de courant** 1 (electric) socket. 2 plug.

priser (priːˈzeː) *vt* 1 value. 2 prize.

prisme (priːsm) *nm* prism.

prison (priːˈzɔ̃) *nf* 1 prison, jail. 2 imprisonment. **prisonnier, -ière** (priːzɔˈnjeː, -ˈnjɛr) *nm,f* prisoner.

privé (priːˈveː) *adj* 1 private. 2 privy.

priver (priːˈveː) *vt* deprive. **se priver** *vr* deny oneself. **privation** *nf* deprivation.

privilège (priːviːˈlɛʒ) *nm* 1 privilege. 2 licence. **privilégié** *adj* 1 privileged. 2 licensed.

prix (priː) *nm* 1 price. 2 cost. 3 worth. 4 prize. **à tout prix** at all costs.

prix-courant *nm, pl* **prix-courants** price-list.

probable (prɔˈbabl) *adj* probable, likely. **probabilité** *nf* probability, likelihood.

probe (prɔb) *adj* honest. **probité** *nf* integrity.

problème (prɔˈblɛm) *nm* problem.

procéder (prɔseːˈdeː) *vi* 1 proceed. 2 originate. **procédé** *nm* 1 dealing. 2 process. 3 behaviour. **procédure** *nf* law procedure.

procès (prɔˈsɛ) *nm* law 1 case. 2 trial. **procès-verbal** *nm, pl* **procès-verbaux** 1 official report. 2 minutes. 3 *law* particulars.

procession (prɔsɛˈsjɔ̃) *nf* procession.

processus (prɔsɛsˈsys) *nm* 1 process. 2 method.

prochain (prɔˈʃɛ̃) *adj* 1 next. 2 nearest. 3 immediate. *nm* neighbour. **prochainement** *adv* soon.

proche (prɔʃ) *adv* near. *adj* near, close. **Proche Orient** *nm* Near East.

proclamer (prɔklaˈmeː) *vt* 1 proclaim. 2 announce. 3 declare. **proclamation** *nf* proclamation.

procréer (prɔkreːˈeː) *vt* procreate.

procurer (prɔkyˈreː) *vt* 1 procure, get. 2 obtain. **procuration** (prɔkyraˈsjɔ̃) *nf* power of attorney. **procureur** *nm* attorney. **procureur général** Attorney General.

prodige (prɔˈdiːʒ) *nm* prodigy, marvel.

produireˈ (prɔˈdɥiːr) *vt* 1 produce. 2 bring about. 3 yield. **productif, -ive** (prɔdykˈtiːf, -ˈtiːv) *adj* productive. **production** *nf* 1 production. 2 product. **produit** *nm* product.

proéminence (prɔeːmiːˈnãs) *nf* prominence. **proéminent** *adj* protruding.

profane (prɔˈfan) *adj* 1 profane. 2 secular. *nm* layman.

professer (prɔfɛˈseː) *vt* 1 profess. 2 teach.

111

professeur *nm* 1 professor. 2 teacher. 3 instructor.

profession (prɔfɛ'sjɔ̃) *nf* profession, trade. **professionnel, -elle** (prɔfɛsjɔ'nɛl) *adj* 1 professional. 2 vocational. *nm,f* professional.

profil (prɔ'fi:l) *nm* profile.

profit (prɔ'fi:) *nm* 1 profit, gain. 2 advantage.

profiter (prɔfi:'te:) *vi* 1 profit. 2 make a profit. **profiter de** take advantage of.

profond (prɔ'fɔ̃) *adj* 1 deep. 2 profound. 3 deep-seated. **profondeur** *nf* depth.

profus (prɔ'fy) *adj* profuse, abundant.

programme (prɔ'gram) *nm* 1 programme. 2 syllabus. 3 plan.

progrès (prɔ'grɛ) *nm* 1 progress. 2 improvement.

progressif, -ive (prɔgrɛ'si:f, -'si:v) *adj* 1 progressive. 2 gradual.

prohiber (prɔi:'be:) *vt* prohibit, forbid.

proie (prwa) *nf* prey.

projecteur (prɔʒɛk'tœr) *nm* 1 projector. 2 searchlight. 3 floodlight. **projectile** *nm* 1 missile. 2 projectile. **projection** *nf* 1 projection. 2 slide, film.

projet (prɔ'ʒɛ) *nm* 1 project, scheme. 2 (rough) plan. **projet de loi** *pol* bill.

prolétariat (prɔlɛta'rja) *nm* proletariat.

prolifique (prɔli:'fi:k) *adj* prolific.

prolonger (prɔlɔ̃'ʒe:) *vt* prolong, extend.

promener (prɔm'ne:) *vt* take for a walk. **se promener** *vr* 1 go for a walk. 2 wander. **promenade** *nf* 1 walk. 2 walking. 3 outing. 4 promenade.

promesse (prɔ'mɛs) *nf* promise.

promettre (prɔ'mɛtr) *vt* 1 promise. 2 make a promise.

promouvoir (prɔmu:'vwar) *vt* promote. **promotion** *nf* promotion.

prompt (prɔ̃) *adj* 1 quick, prompt. 2 hasty.

prône (pron) *nm* sermon.

pronom (prɔ'nɔ̃) *nm* pronoun.

prononcer (prɔnɔ̃'se:) *vt* 1 pronounce. 2 deliver (a speech). **se prononcer** *vr* express one's opinion. **prononciation** *nf* pronunciation.

propagande (prɔpa'gɑ̃d) *nf* 1 propaganda. 2 publicity. **faire de la propagande** advertise.

propager (prɔpa'ʒe:) *vt* 1 propagate. 2 spread.

prophète, prophétesse (prɔ'fɛt, prɔfe:'tɛs) *nm,f* prophet, prophetess. **prophétie** (prɔfe:-'si:) *nf* prophecy. **prophétique** *adj* prophetic.

prophétiser (prɔfe:ti:'ze:) *vt* prophesy.

propice (prɔ'pi:s) *adj* favourable.

proportion (prɔpɔr'sjɔ̃) *nf* 1 proportion. 2 ratio.

3 *pl* size. **proportionnel, -elle** (prɔpɔrsjɔ'nɛl) *adj* proportional.

propos (prɔ'po) *nm* 1 purpose. 2 subject. 3 remark. 4 *pl* gossip. **à propos** 1 by the way. 2 at the right moment. **à propos de** with regard to, concerning.

proposer (prɔpo'ze:) *vt* propose. **se proposer** *vr* 1 offer oneself. 2 intend. **proposition** *nf* 1 proposal. 2 proposition.

propre (prɔpr) *adj* 1 proper. 2 own. 3 appropriate. 4 clean. **propre à** 1 suitable to. 2 peculiar to. **propreté** *nf* 1 cleanness. 2 tidiness.

propriétaire (prɔpri:e:'tɛr) *nm,f* 1 proprietor, proprietress. 2 landlord, landlady. **propriété** *nf* 1 property. 2 ownership. 3 propriety.

propulser (prɔpyl'se:) *vt* propel. **propulseur** *nm* propeller. **propulsion** *nf* propulsion, drive.

proscrire (prɔ'skri:r) *vt* banish. **proscrit** *nm* outlaw.

prose (proz) *nf* prose.

prospectif, -ive (prɔspɛk'ti:f, -'ti:v) *adj* prospective.

prospérer (prɔspe:'re:) *vi* prosper, do well. **prospère** *adj* 1 prosperous. 2 thriving. **prospérité** *nf* prosperity.

se prosterner (prɔstɛr'ne:) *vr* 1 bow down. 2 *inf* grovel. **prosterné** *adj* prostrate.

prostituée (prɔsti:'ty'e:) *nf* prostitute. **prostitution** *nf* prostitution.

protagoniste (prɔtagɔ'ni:st) *nm* protagonist.

protecteur, -trice (prɔtɛk'tœr, -'tri:s) *nm,f* 1 protector. 2 patron, patroness. *adj* protective. **protection** *nf* 1 protection. 2 patronage.

protéger (prɔte:'ʒe:) *vt* 1 protect. 2 shelter. 3 patronize. **protégé** *nm* dependant.

protéine (prɔte:'i:n) *nf* protein.

protester (prɔtɛ'ste:) *vt* declare. *vi* protest. **protestant** *adj,n* Protestant. **protestation** *nf* protest.

protocole (prɔtɔ'kɔl) *nm* protocol.

proton (prɔ'tɔ̃) *nm* proton.

proue (pru:) *nf naut* bow, prow.

prouesse (pru:'ɛs) *nf* prowess, bravery.

prouver (pru:'ve:) *vt* prove.

provençal, -aux (prɔvɑ̃'sal, -'so) *adj,nm* Provençal.

provenir (prɔv'ni:r) *vi* **provenir de** 1 arise from. 2 originate in or from. **provenance** *nf* 1 source. 2 origin. **en provenance de** coming from.

proverbe (prɔ'vɛrb) *nm* proverb. **proverbial, -aux** (prɔvɛr'bjal, -'bjo) *adj* proverbial.
province (prɔ'vɛ̃s) *nf* province. **provincial, -aux** (prɔvɛ̃'sjal, -'sjo) *adj* provincial.
proviseur (prɔvi:'zœr) *nm* headmaster.
provision (prɔvi:'zjɔ̃) *nf* 1 provision. 2 stock. 3 funds.
provisoire (prɔvi:'zwar) *adj* 1 provisional. 2 temporary. **à titre provisoire** provisionally.
provoquer (prɔvɔ'ke:) *vt* 1 provoke. 2 challenge. 3 arouse. 4 cause. **provocant** *adj* 1 provocative. 2 aggressive. **provocateur, -trice** (prɔvɔka'tœr, -'tri:s) *adj* provocative. **provocation** *nf* provocation.
proximité (prɔksi:mi:'te:) *nf* proximity.
prude (pryd) *nf* prude. *adj* prudish.
prudent (pry'dã) *adj* 1 prudent, wise. 2 discreet. **prudemment** (prydaˈmã) *adv* prudently. **prudence** *nf* prudence, carefulness.
prune (pryn) *nf* plum. **prune de damas** damson. **pruneau, -aux** (pry'no) *nm* prune. **prunelle** *nf* 1 *anat* pupil. 2 sloe. **prunier** *nm* plum tree.
psaume (psom) *nm* psalm.
pseudonyme (psœdɔ'ni:m) *nm* pseudonym.
psychanalyse (psi:kana'li:z) *nf* psychoanalysis.
psychédélique (psi:ke:de:'li:k) *adj* psychedelic.
psychiatrie (psi:kja'tri:) *nf* psychiatry. **psychiatre** *nm,f* psychiatrist. **psychiatrique** *adj* psychiatric.
psychique (psi:'ʃi:k) *adj* psychic.
psychologie (psi:kɔlɔ'ʒi:) *nf* psychology. **psychologique** *adj* psychological. **psychologue** *nm,f* psychologist.
psychopathique (psi:kɔpa'ti:k) *adj* psychopathic.
psychosomatique (psi:kosɔma'ti:k) *adj* psychosomatic.
pu (py) *v* see **pouvoir.**
puanteur (pɥã'tœr) *nf* stink.
puberté (pybɛr'te:) *nf* puberty.
public, -ique (py'bli:k) *adj* 1 public. 2 common. *nm* public. **grand public** general public.
publicité (pybli:si:'te:) *nf* 1 publicity. 2 advertising. **publicitaire** *adj* advertising.
publier (pybli:'e:) *vt* 1 publish. 2 proclaim. **publication** *nf* 1 publication. 2 publishing.
puce (pys) *nf* flea. **puceron** *nm* greenfly.
pudeur (py'dœr) *nf* modesty, decency.
pudique (py'di:k) *adj* 1 modest. 2 chaste.
puer (pɥe:) *vi* stink.
puéril (pɥe:'ri:l) *adj* childish.

pugilat (pyʒi:'la) *nm* boxing. **pugiliste** *nm* boxer.
puîné (pɥi:'ne:) *adj* younger.
puis[1] (pɥi:) *adv* 1 then. 2 afterwards. 3 besides.
puis[2] (pɥi:) *v* see **pouvoir.**
puiser (pɥi:'ze:) *vt* 1 draw (water). 2 derive.
puisque (pɥi:sk) *conj* since, as.
puissance (pɥi:'sãs) *nf* 1 power. 2 authority. **puissant** *adj* 1 powerful. 2 strong. 3 potent.
puits (pɥi:) *nm* 1 well. 2 shaft.
pull-over (pu:lo'vɛr) *nm* pullover.
pulluler (pylly'le:) *vi* swarm.
pulpe (pylp) *nf* pulp.
pulsation (pylsa'sjɔ̃) *nf* throb. **pulsation du cœur** heartbeat.
pulvériser (pylve:ri:'ze:) *vt* 1 pulverize. 2 grind.
punaise (py'nɛz) *nf* 1 bug. 2 drawing pin.
punch[1] (pɔ̃ʃ) *nm* (drink) punch.
punch[2] (pœnʃ) *nm sport* punch.
punir (py'ni:r) *vt* punish. **punition** *nf* 1 punishment. 2 forfeit.
pupille[1] (py'pi:l) *nm,f law* ward.
pupille[2] (py'pi:l) *nf anat* pupil.
pupitre (py'pi:tr) *nm* desk.
pur (pyr) *adj* 1 pure. 2 genuine. 3 clear. 4 innocent. **pur-sang** *nm invar* thoroughbred. **pureté** *nf* purity.
purée (py're:) *nf* 1 mash. 2 thick soup.
purgatoire (pyrga'twar) *nm* purgatory.
purger (pyr'ʒe:) *vt* 1 purge. 2 cleanse. 3 clear. **purge** *nf* 1 purge. 2 cleaning.
purifier (pyri:'fje:) *vt* 1 purify. 2 refine.
puritain (pyri:'tɛ̃) *nm* Puritan.
pus (py) *nm med* pus.
pusillanime (pyzi:lla'ni:m) *adj* faint-hearted.
pustule (py'styl) *nf* pimple.
putain (py'tɛ̃) *nf sl* prostitute.
putride (py'tri:d) *adj* putrid.
puzzle (pyzl) *nm* jigsaw.
pygmée (pi:g'me:) *adj,n* pygmy.
pyjama (pi:ʒa'ma) *nm* pyjamas.
pyramide (pi:ra'mi:d) *nf* pyramid.
Pyrénées (pi:re:'ne:) *nf pl* Pyrenees.

Q

quadrant (ka'drã) *nm* quadrant.
quadrilatéral, -aux (kwadri:latɛ'ral, -'ro) *adj* quadrilateral.
quadrilatère (kwadri:la'tɛr) *nm* 1 quadrilateral. 2 quadrangle.
quadrillé (kadri:'je:) *adj* squared, checked.

quadrupède (kwadry'pɛd) *nm* quadruped.
quadrupler (kwadry'ple:) *vi,vt* quadruple. **quadruplés** *nm pl* quadruplets.
quai (ke:) *nm* **1** quay, wharf. **2** platform. **3** embankment. **Quai d'Orsay** French Foreign Office.
quaker, -eresse (kwa'kɛr, -'krɛs) *nm,f* Quaker.
qualifier (kali:'fje:) *vt* **1** call, term. **2** qualify. **qualification** *nf* **1** qualification. **2** title.
qualité (kali:'te:) *nf* **1** quality. **2** excellence. **3** property. **4** qualification. **5** title. **6** rank. **en qualité de** as, in the capacity of.
quand (kã) *conj, adv* when. **quand même 1** all the same. **2** even if.
quant (kãt) *prep* **quant à** with regard to.
quantifier (kãti:'fje:) *vt* quantify.
quantité (kãti:'te:) *nf* quantity, amount.
quarante (ka'rãt) *adj,nm* forty. **quarantaine** *nf* **1** about forty. **2** quarantine. **faire quarantaine** be in quarantine. **quarantième** *adj* fortieth.
quart (kar) *nm* quarter, fourth part. **quart de finale** quarterfinal. **quart d'heure** quarter of an hour. **trois quarts** *nm pl* threequarters.
quartier (kar'tje:) *nm* **1** quarter. **2** piece. **3** district. **bas quartier** slum. **quartier général** *mil* headquarters.
quartz (kwarts) *nm* quartz.
quasi (ka'zi:) *adv* almost.
quatorze (ka'tɔrz) *adj,nm* fourteen. **quatorzième** *adj* fourteenth.
quatre (katr) *adj,nm* four. **à quatre pattes** on all fours. **quatrième** *adj* fourth.
quatre-vingt-dix *adj,nm* ninety. **quatre-vingt-dixième** *adj* ninetieth.
quatre-vingts *adj,nm* eighty. **quatre-vingtième** *adj* eightieth.
quatuor (kwa'tɥɔr) *nm* quartet.
que[1] (kə) *conj* **1** that. **2** lest, in case. **3** but. **4** as. **5** than. **à ce que** or **de ce que** that. **ne...que** only. **que...ou non** whether...or not. **que...que** whether...or.
que[2] (kə) *adv* **1** how. **2** how much or many.
que[3] (kə) *pron* **1** that. **2** whom. **3** which. **4** what. **qu'est-ce que** or **qui?** what?
quel, quelle (kɛl) *adj,pron* **1** what. **2** which. **quel que 1** whatever. **2** whoever. **quelconque** *adj* **1** any (whatever). **2** some kind of. **3** ordinary, commonplace. **quelque** *adj* **1** some. **2** *pl* some, a few. *adv* **1** about. **2** some. **quelque chose** *pron m invar* something, anything. **quelquefois** *adv* sometimes. **quelque part** *adv* somewhere. **quelque...que** or

114

qui 1 whatever, whatsoever. **2** however. **quelqu'un, quelqu'une** (kɛl'kœ̃, kɛl'kyn) *pron, pl* **quelques-uns, quelques-unes** one.
quémander (ke:mã'de:) *vi* beg. *vt* beg for.
quenelle (kə'nɛl) *nf* fish or mincemeat ball.
quereller (kɔrɛ'le:) *vt* quarrel with. **se quereller** *vr* quarrel. **querelle** *nf* quarrel. **querelleur, -euse** (kɔrɛ'lœr, -'løz) *adj* quarrelsome.
quérir (ke:'ri:r) *vt* **1** fetch. **2** send for.
question (kɛ'stjɔ̃) *nf* **1** question, query. **2** matter, issue. **question pour la forme** rhetorical question. **questionnaire** *nm* questionnaire.
questionner (kɛstjɔ'ne:) *vt* **1** question. **2** ask questions.
quêter (kɛte:) *vt* **1** collect (money, etc.). **2** look for. **quête** (kɛt) *nf* **1** search, quest. **2** *rel* collection.
queue (kœ) *nf* **1** tail. **2** end. **3** queue. **4** *sport* cue. **faire la queue** queue up.
qui (ki:) *pron* **1** who. **2** whom. **3** which. **4** that. **qui est-ce qui/que?** who/whom? **qui...que** whoever. **quiconque** *pron* **1** whoever. **2** anyone.
quiche (ki:ʃ) *nf* flan filled with cheese, eggs, cream, and bacon, etc.
quignon (ki:'ɲɔ̃) *nm* hunk (of bread, etc.).
quille[1] (ki:j) *nf* **1** skittle. **2** *pl sl* pins, legs.
quille[2] (ki:j) *nf* keel.
quincaillerie (kɛ̃kaj'ri:) *nf* **1** ironmongery. **2** hardware shop. **quincaillier** *nm* ironmonger.
quintal, -aux (kɛ̃'tal, -'to) *nm* (approx.) hundredweight.
quinte (kɛ̃t) *nf* **1** fit, bout. **2** *mus* fifth.
quintessence (kɛ̃tɛs'sãs) *nf* quintessence.
quintette (kɛ̃'tɛt) *nm* quintet.
quinze (kɛ̃z) *adj,nm* fifteen. **quinze jours** *nm pl* fortnight. **quinzaine** *nf* **1** fortnight. **2** about fifteen. **quinzième** *adj* fifteenth.
quiproquo (ki:prɔ'ko) *nm* **1** mistake. **2** misunderstanding.
quittance (ki:'tãs) *nf* receipt.
quitter (ki:'te:) *vt* leave, quit. **quitte** *adj* **1** quit. **2** free, rid. **quitte à quitte** quits.
quoi (kwa) *pron* **1** what. **2** which. **à quoi bon?** what's the use? **avoir de quoi** be well-off. **quoi que** or **qui** whatever. **sans quoi** otherwise. **quoique** *conj* although, though.
quote-part (kot'par) *nf* quota.
quotidien, -ienne (kɔti:'djɛ̃, -'djɛn) *adj* **1** daily. **2** everyday. *nm* daily newspaper.

R

rabâcher (rabɑ'ʃe:) vi keep repeating the same thing.

rabais (ra'bɛ) nm **1** reduction. **2** discount.

rabaisser (rabɛ'se:) vt **1** lower. **2** disparage.

rabattre* (ra'batr) vt **1** fold back. **2** lower, bring down. **3** reduce. **4** sport beat. vi turn off. **rabat-joie** nm,f invar spoil-sport.

rabbin (ra'bɛ̃) nm rabbi.

rabot (ra'bo) nm tech plane.

raboter (rabɔ'te:) vt **1** plane. **2** file down. **raboteux, -euse** (rabɔ'tœ, -'tœz) adj **1** uneven, rough. **2** rugged.

rabougrir (rabu'gri:r) vt stunt.

racaille (ra'kɑj) nf rabble.

raccommoder (rakɔmɔ'de:) vt **1** mend, repair. **2** darn. **3** reconcile. **raccommodage** nm **1** mending. **2** mend.

raccorder (rakɔr'de:) vt join, connect.

raccourcir (raku:r'si:r) vt **1** shorten. **2** abridge. vi grow shorter, shorten. **raccourci** nm **1** abridgment. **2** short cut.

raccrocher (rakrɔ'ʃe:) vt **1** hang up again. **2** ring off. **3** get hold of again. **se raccrocher à** vr clutch, cling to.

race (ras) nf **1** race. **2** breed. **3** descent. **racial, -aux** (ra'sjal, -'sjo) adj racial. **racisme** nm racialism.

rachat (ra'ʃa) nm **1** repurchase. **2** atonement. **3** ransom.

racheter (raʃ'te:) vt **1** buy back. **2** atone for. **3** redeem. **4** ransom.

racine (ra'si:n) nf root.

racler (rɑ'kle:) vt scrape. **se racler la gorge** clear one's throat. **raclée** nf inf thrashing, hiding. **raclure** nf scrapings.

racoler (rakɔ'le:) vt recruit.

raconter (rakɔ̃'te:) vt tell, relate. **racontar** nm inf gossip. **raconteur, -euse** (rakɔ̃'tœr, -'tœz) nm,f narrator, storyteller.

radar (ra'dar) nm radar.

radeau, -aux (ra'do) nm raft.

radial, -aux (ra'djal, -'djo) adj radial.

radiateur (radja'tœr) nm radiator.

radiation[1] (radja'sjɔ̃) nf **1** crossing out. **2** cancellation.

radiation[2] (radja'sjɔ̃) nf radiation.

radical, -aux (radi'kal, -'ko) adj radical.

radier (ra'dje:) vt **1** erase. **2** cross out.

radieux, -euse (ra'djœ, -'djœz) adj **1** radiant. **2** brilliant.

radin (ra'dɛ̃) adj inf mean, miserly.

radio (ra'djo) nf **1** radio. **2** X-ray. **passer à radio** X-ray. **radioactif, -ive** (radjoak'ti:f, -'ti:v) adj radioactive. **radioactivité** nf radioactivity.

radiodiffuser (radjodi:ffy'ze:) vt broadcast.

radis (ra'di:) nm radish.

radium (ra'djɔm) nm radium.

radoter (radɔ'te:) vi talk nonsense, ramble. **radotage** nm nonsense.

radoucir (radu:'si:r) vt **1** calm down. **2** soften. **se radoucir** vr grow softer or milder.

rafale (ra'fal) nf gust, blast (of wind).

raffermir (rafɛr'mi:r) vt **1** harden. **2** strengthen. **3** restore. **se raffermir** vr **1** improve. **2** recover.

raffiner (rafi:'ne:) vt refine. **raffinage** nm refining. **raffiné** adj **1** refined. **2** subtle. **3** delicate.

raffoler (rafɔ'le:) vi **raffoler de** rave about, love madly.

raffut (ra'fy) nm inf din, uproar.

rafistoler (rafi:stɔ'le:) vt inf patch up, mend.

rafle (rafl) nf raid (by police).

rafraîchir (rafrɛ'ʃi:r) vt **1** cool. **2** refresh. **3** revive. **rafraîchissement** nm **1** cooling. **2** refreshing, brushing up. **3** pl refreshments.

rager (ra'ʒe:) vi be in a rage. **rage** (raʒ) nf **1** rage, fury. **2** mania. **3** rabies. **rageur, -euse** (ra'ʒœr, -'ʒœz) adj **1** passionate. **2** hot-tempered.

ragot (ra'go) nm gossip, scandal.

ragoût (ra'gu:) nm stew.

raidir (rɛ'di:r) vt **1** stiffen. **2** tighten. **se raidir** vr **1** stiffen. **2** brace oneself. **raide** adj **1** stiff, rigid. **2** taut. **3** steep. **4** inf hard. adv hard. **raideur** nf **1** stiffness. **2** steepness.

raie[1] (rɛ) nf **1** line. **2** streak, stripe. **3** parting (of hair).

raie[2] (rɛ) nf zool skate.

raifort (rɛ'fɔr) nm horseradish.

rail (rɑj) nm rail (of a railway track).

railler (rɑ'je:) vt **1** jeer at. **2** tease. **raillerie** (rɑj'ri:) nf jest, joke.

rainure (rɛ'nyr) nf groove, channel.

raisin (rɛ'zɛ̃) nm grape. **raisin de Corinthe/ Smyrne** currant/sultana. **raisin sec** raisin.

raison (rɛ'zɔ̃) nf **1** reason. **2** reasoning. **3** satisfaction. **4** ratio. **avoir raison** be right. **raisonnable** adj **1** reasonable. **2** rational.

raisonner (rɛzɔ'ne:) vi **1** reason. **2** argue. vt **1**

115

rajeunir

consider. **2** reason with. **raisonnement** *nm* **1** reasoning. **2** argument.

rajeunir (raʒœˈniːr) *vt* **1** rejuvenate. **2** renovate. *vi* get younger.

rajuster (raʒyˈste:) *vt* **1** readjust. **2** put straight.

ralentir (ralãˈtiːr) *vt,vi* slow down, slacken. **ralenti** *adj* slow.

rallier (ralˈje:) *vt* **1** rally, assemble. **2** win over.

rallonger (ralɔˈʒe:) *vt* lengthen, let down. *vi* draw out. **rallonge** *nf* extension.

ramas (raˈmo) *nm* **1** heap. **2** collection

ramasser (ramoˈse:) *vt* **1** gather together. **2** collect. **3** pick up. **se ramasser** *vr* pick oneself up. **ramassé** *adj* **1** thickset. **2** squat. **3** concise. **ramasse-poussière** *nm* invar dustpan.

rame¹ (ram) *nf* oar.

rame² (ram) *nf* stick, prop. **rameau, -aux** (raˈmo) *nm* branch.

rame³ (ram) *nf* train.

ramener (ramˈne:) *vt* **1** bring back or round. **2** restore.

ramer (raˈme:) *vi* row. **rameur** *nm* oarsman.

ramier (raˈmje:) *nm* woodpigeon.

se ramifier (ramiˈfje:) *vr* branch out.

ramollir (ramɔˈliːr) *vt* **1** soften. **2** weaken.

ramoner (ramɔˈne:) *vt* sweep (a chimney). **ramoneur** *nm* chimneysweep.

ramper (rãˈpe:) *vi* **1** creep. **2** trail. **3** grovel. **rampe** *nf* **1** slope. **2** banister, handrail. **3** Th footlights.

rancart (rãˈkar) *nm* **mettre au rancart** cast aside.

rance (rãs) *adj* **1** rancid. **2** rank.

rançon (rãˈsɔ̃) *nf* ransom.

rançonner (rãsɔˈne:) *vt* ransom, hold to ransom.

rancune (rãˈkyn) *nf* **1** spite. **2** malice. **3** grudge.

rang (rã) *nm* **1** row, line. **2** rank. **3** status. **de premier rang** first-rate.

ranger (rãˈʒe:) *vt* **1** arrange. **2** put away. **3** tidy. **se ranger** *vr* **1** draw up. **2** settle down. **rangé** *adj* **1** tidy, orderly. **2** staid. **rangée** *nf* row, line.

ranimer (raniˈme:) *vt* **1** revive. **2** stir up.

rapace (raˈpas) *adj* **1** rapacious. **2** predatory.

rapatrier (rapatriˈe:) *vt* repatriate. **rapatrié** *nm* repatriate.

râper (rɑˈpe:) *vt* **1** *cul* grate. **2** grind. **3** wear out. **râpé** *adj* **1** shabby. **2** grated.

rapetisser (raptiˈse:) *vt* **1** make smaller. **2** shrink. *vi* **1** shorten. **2** become smaller.

raphia (raˈfja) *nm* raffia.

rapide (raˈpiːd) *adj* rapid, swift. *nm* express train. **rapidité** *nf* rapidity.

rapiécer (rapjeˈse:) *vt* patch (a garment).

rapin (raˈpɛ̃) *nm* inf art student.

rappel (raˈpɛl) *nm* **1** recall. **2** repeal. **3** reminder.

rappeler (raˈple:) *vt* **1** recall. **2** remind. **3** repeal. **se rappeler** *vr* remember.

rapport (raˈpɔr) *nm* **1** return, yield. **2** report. **3** connection. **4** relations, relationship. **par rapport à 1** with regard to. **2** in comparison with.

rapporter (rapɔrˈte:) *vt* **1** bring back. **2** yield. **3** report. **4** inf tell tales. **se rapporter** *vr* **1** tally. **2** refer. **s'en rapporter à** rely on. **rapporteur, -euse** (rapɔrˈtœr, -ˈtœz) *nm,f* sneak. *nm* **1** reporter. **2** chairman.

rapprocher (raprɔˈʃe:) *vt* **1** bring nearer. **2** bring together. **3** compare. **se rapprocher de** *vr* **1** draw nearer to. **2** reconcile with. **rapprochement** *nm* **1** nearness. **2** comparison. **3** reconciliation.

raquette (raˈkɛt) *nf* sport racket.

rare (rɑr) *adj* **1** rare. **2** unusual. **3** exceptional. **4** sparse.

ras (rɑ) *adj* **1** short, cropped. **2** smooth, level. **3** bare. **au ras de** on a level with. **avoir ras le bol de** be sick of. **faire table rase** make a clean sweep.

raser (rɑˈze:) *vt* **1** shave. **2** brush, skim. **3** *sl* bore. **rasoir** *nm* **1** razor. **2** inf bore.

rassasier (rasaˈzje:) *vt* satisfy (hunger). **se rassasier** *vr* eat one's fill.

rassembler (rasãˈble:) *vt* assemble.

se rasséréner (rase:re:ˈne:) *vr* **1** (of weather) clear up. **2** brighten up.

rassir (raˈsiːr) *vi* get stale. **rassis** *adj* **1** stale. **2** staid. **3** sedate.

rassurer (rasyˈre:) *vt* **1** reassure. **2** strengthen.

rat (ra) *nm* rat.

ratatiner (ratatiˈne:) *vt* **1** shrivel up. **2** shrink.

râteau, -aux (rɑˈto) *nm* rake.

râteler (rɑtˈle:) *vt* rake up. **râtelier** *nm* **1** rack. **2** denture.

rater (raˈte:) *vi* **1** misfire. **2** fail. *vt* miss.

ration (raˈsjɔ̃) *nf* ration, allowance.

rationaliser (rasjɔnaliˈze:) *vt* rationalize. **rationnel, -elle** (rasjɔˈnɛl) *adj* rational.

rationner (rasjɔˈne:) *vt* ration.

ratisser (ratiˈse:) *vt* **1** rake. **2** inf raid. **ratissoire** *nm* hoe.

rattacher (rataˈʃe:) *vt* **1** fasten. **2** bind. **3** link. **se rattacher à** *vr* **1** be fastened to. **2** be connected with.

rattraper (ratra'pe:) *vt* **1** catch again. **2** catch up. **3** recover. **se rattraper** *vr* save oneself.

rauque (rok) *adj* raucous, hoarse.

ravager (rava'ʒe:) *vt* **1** devastate. **2** ruin. **3** ravage. **ravages** *nm pl* havoc.

ravauder (ravo'de:) *vt* mend, patch.

ravir (ra'vi:r) *vt* **1** ravish, delight. **2** carry off. **ravi de** *adj* **1** overjoyed at. **2** delighted to. **ravissant** *adj* lovely. **ravisseur** *nm* kidnapper.

se raviser (ravi:'ze:) *vr* change one's mind.

rayer (rɛ'je:) *vt* **1** rule. **2** stripe. **3** scratch. **4** delete.

rayon[1] (rɛ'jɔ̃) *nm* **1** ray. **2** beam. **3** radius. **4** spoke (of a wheel). **rayon X** X-ray.

rayon[2] (rɛ'jɔ̃) *nm* **1** shelf. **2** department (in a shop). **3** counter (of a shop). **rayon de miel** honeycomb.

rayon[3] (rɛ'jɔ̃) *nm* **1** drill (for seed). **2** row.

rayonne (rɛ'jɔn) *nf* rayon.

rayonner (rɛjɔ'ne:) *vi* **1** radiate. **2** beam. **rayonnant** *adj* **1** radiant. **2** beaming. **rayonnement** *nm* **1** radiation. **2** radiance. **3** influence.

rayure (rɛ'jyr) *nf* **1** stripe, streak. **2** scratch. **3** deletion.

razzia (rad'zja) *nf* raid.

réaction (re:ak'sjɔ̃) *nf* reaction. **réacteur** *nm* reactor. **réactionnaire** *adj* reactionary.

réagir (re:a'ʒi:r) *vi* react.

réaliser (re:ali:'ze:) *vt* **1** realize. **2** carry out. **3** sell out.

réalité (re:ali:'te:) *nf* reality. **en réalité** really. **réalisme** *nm* realism. **réaliste** *adj* realistic. *nm,f* realist.

rébarbatif, -ive (re:barba'ti:f, -'ti:v) *adj* **1** grim. **2** surly.

rebattu (rəba'ty) *adj* hackneyed, trite.

rebelle (rə'bɛl) *adj* **1** rebellious. **2** stubborn. **3** opposed. *nm,f* rebel. **rébellion** *nf* rebellion, revolt.

rebondir (rəbɔ̃'di:r) *vi* **1** rebound. **2** bounce.

rebord (rə'bɔr) *nm* **1** edge. **2** rim. **3** hem.

rebours (rə'bu:r) *nm* **1** wrong way. **2** reverse. **à rebours 1** the wrong way. **2** against the grain.

rebrousser (rəbru:'se:) *vt* brush up (hair or nap). *vi* turn back. **rebrousser chemin** retrace one's steps. **à rebrousse-poil** *adv* the wrong way. **à rebrousse-poil** *adv* the wrong way.

rebuffade (rəby'fad) *nf* snub.

rebut (rə'by) *nm* **1** waste. **2** scrap. **3** *pl* rejects.

rebutant (rəby'tã) *adj* **1** tedious. **2** repulsive.

recéler (rase:'le:) *vt* **1** receive. **2** contain.

récemment (re:sa'mã) *adv* recently.

recensement (rəsãs'mã) *nm* census.

récent (re:'sã) *adj* recent, fresh.

récepteur, -trice (re:sɛp'tœr, -'tri:s) *adj* receiving. *nm* receiver. **réception** *nf* **1** receipt. **2** welcome. **3** reception.

récession (re:sɛ'sjɔ̃) *nf* recession, slump.

recette (rə'sɛt) *nf* **1** takings. **2** receipt. **3** recipe.

recevable (rəsə'vabl) *adj* allowable.

receveur, -euse (rəsə'vœr, -'vœz) *nm,f* **1** receiver. **2** collector. **3** (bus) conductor.

recevoir* (rəsə'vwar) *vt* **1** receive. **2** entertain. **3** accept. **être reçu à un examen** pass an exam.

rechange (rə'ʃãʒ) *nm* replacement, refill, spare. **de rechange** *adj* spare.

réchapper (re:ʃa'pe:) *vi* (*aux* être *or* avoir) **réchapper de 1** escape from. **2** recover from.

recharge (rə'ʃarʒ) *nf* refill.

réchaud (re:'ʃo) *nm* **1** portable stove. **2** hot-plate.

réchauffer (re:ʃo'fe:) *vt* **1** reheat. **2** warm up.

rêche (rɛʃ) *adj* **1** harsh. **2** rough.

rechercher (rəʃɛr'ʃe:) *vt* **1** search for. **2** inquire into. **recherche** *nf* **1** search. **2** research. **3** affectation. **recherché** *adj* **1** in demand. **2** choice. **3** affected.

rechute (rə'ʃyt) *nf* relapse.

récif (re:'si:f) *nm* reef.

récipient (re:si:'pjã) *nm* container, receptacle.

réciproque (re:si:'prɔk) *adj* reciprocal, mutual.

récit (re:'si:) *nm* **1** narrative, story. **2** account.

réciter (re:si:'te:) *vt* recite. **récital** *nm mus* recital. **récitant** *adj,n mus* solo.

réclame (re:'klam) *nf* **1** publicity, advertising. **2** advertisement. **3** sign. **en réclame** on offer. **faire de la réclame** advertise. **réclamation** *nf* complaint.

recoin (rə'kwɛ̃) *nm* recess.

reçois (rə'swa) *v see* **recevoir.**

récolter (re:kɔl'te:) *vt* **1** harvest. **2** gather. **récolte** *nf* **1** crop. **2** harvest. **3** harvesting.

recommander (rəkɔmã'de:) *vt* **1** recommend. **2** advise. **3** register (mail).

recommencer (rəkɔmã'se:) *vt,vi* begin again.

récompenser (re:kɔ̃pã'se:) *vt* recompense, reward. **récompense** *nf* reward.

réconcilier (re:kɔ̃si:'lje:) *vt* reconcile.

reconduire (rəkɔ̃'dɥi:r) *vt* **1** accompany back. **2** escort home. **3** see out.

réconforter (re:kɔ̃fɔr'te:) *vt* **1** cheer up. **2** fortify.

reconnaissant (rəkɔnɛ'sã) *adj* **1** grateful. **2**

117

thankful. **reconnaissance** nf **1** recognition. **2** acknowledgment. **3** gratitude. **4** thankfulness.

reconnaître (rəkɔ'nɛtr) vt **1** recognize. **2** acknowledge, admit. **3** explore.

reconstituer (rəkɔ̃sti'tɥe:) vt restore.

record (rə'kɔr) nm record.

recours (rə'ku:r) nm recourse, resort.

récréation (re:kre:a'sjɔ̃) nf **1** recreation, amusement. **2** educ break.

recrue (rə'kry) nf recruit.

recruter (rəkry'te:) vt **1** recruit. **2** enlist.

rectangle (rɛk'tɑ̃g) adj right-angled. nm rectangle. **rectangulaire** adj rectangular.

recteur (rɛk'tœr) nm **1** educ vice-chancellor. **2** rector.

rectifier (rɛkti:'fje:) vt **1** straighten. **2** rectify. **3** correct. **4** adjust.

rectitude (rɛkti:'tyd) nf **1** straightness. **2** correctness. **3** integrity.

reçu (rə'sy) v see **recevoir**. adj **1** received. **2** recognized. nm **1** receipt. **2** voucher.

recueil (rə'kœj) nm **1** collection. **2** selection. **recueil d'expressions** phrasebook.

recueillir (rəkœ'ji:r) vt **1** gather. **2** pick up, obtain. **3** take in. **se recueillir** vr collect one's thoughts. **recueillement** nm **1** meditation. **2** composure. **recueilli** adj meditative.

recul (rə'kyl) nm **1** retreat. **2** setback.

reculer (rəky'le:) vi **1** move back. **2** draw back. vt **1** move back. **2** postpone. **reculé** adj remote. **à reculons** adv backwards.

récupérer (re:kype:'re:) vt **1** recover. **2** retrieve. **3** make up. **4** inf scrounge.

récurer (re:ky're:) vt scour, clean.

récurrent (re:kyr'rɑ̃) adj recurrent.

rédacteur, -trice (re:dak'tœr, -'tri:s) nm,f **1** writer. **2** editor. **rédacteur en chef** editor (of a newspaper, etc.). **rédaction** nf **1** writing. **2** editing. **3** editorial staff.

rédiger (re:di:'ʒe:) vt **1** draft. **2** write. **3** edit.

redire (rə'di:r) vt repeat. **trouver à redire à** find fault with.

redondant (rədɔ̃'dɑ̃) adj superfluous. **redondance** nf superfluity.

redouter (rədu:'te:) vt fear, dread. **redoutable** adj **1** formidable. **2** dangerous.

redresser (rədrɛ'se:) vt **1** set upright again. **2** straighten. **3** rectify.

réduire (re:'dɥi:r) vt reduce. **se réduire à** vr **1** amount to. **2** confine oneself to. **réduction** nf reduction, cut. **réduit** nm **1** retreat. **2** nook.

réel, réelle (re:'ɛl) adj **1** real. **2** actual. **3** true. nm reality.

refaire (rə'fɛr) vt **1** do or make again. **2** repair. **se refaire** vr recover.

réfectoire (re:fɛk'twar) nm refectory.

référendum (re:fe:rɛ̃'dɔm) nm referendum.

référer (re:fe:'re:) vt **1** refer. **2** ascribe. **se référer à** vr refer to. **référence** nf reference.

réfléchir (re:fle:'ʃi:r) vt reflect. vi think, ponder. **réfléchir à** consider. **réfléchi** adj **1** thoughtful. **2** deliberate. **3** reflexive.

réflecteur (re:flɛk'tœr) nm reflector.

reflet (rə'flɛ) nm reflection.

refléter (rəfle:'te:) vt reflect.

réflexe (re:'flɛks) adj,nm reflex.

réflexion (re:flɛk'sjɔ̃) nf **1** reflection. **2** thought.

reflux (rə'fly) nm ebb (tide).

réformer (re:fɔr'me:) vt **1** reform. **2** discharge. **réformation** nf reformation. **réforme** nf **1** reform. **2** discharge.

refouler (rəfu:'le:) vt **1** drive back. **2** repress.

refrain (rə'frɛ̃) nm **1** refrain. **2** chorus.

réfrigérer (re:fri:ʒe:'re:) vt refrigerate. **réfrigérateur** nm refrigerator.

refroidir (rəfrwa'di:r) vt cool, chill. vi cool down. **refroidissement** nm **1** cooling. **2** med chill.

refuge (rə'fyʒ) nm refuge, shelter.

se réfugier (re:fy'ʒje:) vr take refuge. **réfugié** nm refugee.

refus (rə'fy) nm refusal.

refuser (rəfy'ze:) vt **1** refuse. **2** decline. **3** deny. **4** reject. **être refusé** fail.

réfuter (re:fy'te:) vt refute, disprove.

regagner (rəga'ɲe:) vt **1** recover, regain. **2** catch up. **3** return to.

regain (rə'gɛ̃) nm **1** aftermath. **2** renewal.

régal (re:'gal) nm **1** feast. **2** treat.

régaler (re:ga'le:) vt **1** entertain. **2** treat.

regard (rə'gar) nm **1** look. **2** gaze. **3** glance. **4** manhole. **regard fixe** stare.

regarder (rəgar'de:) vt **1** look at. **2** consider. **3** concern. **regarder fixement** stare at.

régent (re:'ʒɑ̃) nm regent. **régence** (re:'ʒɑ̃s) nf regency.

régie (re:'ʒi:) nf administration.

régime (re:'ʒi:m) nm **1** regime. **2** system. **3** diet.

régiment (re:ʒi:'mɑ̃) nm regiment. **régimentaire** adj regimental.

région (re:'ʒjɔ̃) nf **1** region. **2** territory. **régional, -aux** (re:ʒjɔ'nal, -'no) adj **1** regional. **2** local.

régir (re:'ʒi:r) vt **1** govern. **2** manage. **régisseur** nm **1** manager. **2** agent. **3** stage manager.

registre (rə'ʒi:str) nm register.

régler (re:'gle:) *vt* **1** rule (paper, etc.). **2** regulate. **3** adjust. **4** settle. **règle** *nf* **1** rule. **2** ruler. **3** *pl med* period. **en règle** in order. **règle à calcul** *nf* slide rule. **réglé** *adj* **1** ruled. **2** regular. **3** methodical. **règlement** *nm* **1** regulation. **2** settlement. **réglementaire** (rɛglǝmãˈtɛr) *adj* **1** regulation. **2** compulsory, statutory.

réglisse (re:ˈgli:s) *nf* liquorice.

régner (rɛˈɲe:) *vi* reign. **règne** *nm* **1** reign. **2** kingdom.

regret (rǝˈgrɛ) *nm* regret.

regretter (rǝgrɛˈte:) *vt* regret, be sorry.

régulier, -ière (re:gyˈlje:, -ˈljɛr) *adj* **1** regular. **2** steady. **3** even. **régularité** *nf* regularity.

réhabiliter (re:abi:li:ˈte:) *vt* rehabilitate.

rehausser (re:oˈze:) *vt* **1** raise. **2** accentuate. **3** enhance.

rein (rɛ̃) *nm* **1** kidney. **2** *pl* back.

réincarnation (re:ɛ̃karnaˈsjɔ̃) *nf* reincarnation.

reine (rɛn) *nf* queen. **reine-claude** *nf, pl* **reines-claude** greengage.

réintégrer (re:ɛ̃te:ˈgre:) *vt* **1** reinstate. **2** resume.

rejeter (rǝʒǝˈte:) *vt* **1** throw back. **2** cast aside. **3** reject. **se rejeter sur** *vr* fall back on.

rejoindre* (rǝˈʒwɛ̃dr) *vt* **1** rejoin. **2** connect. **3** catch up. **se rejoindre** *vr* meet.

réjouir (re:ˈʒwi:r) *vt* **1** amuse. **2** please. **se réjouir** *vr* **1** be delighted. **2** rejoice.

relâcher (rǝlaˈʃe:) *vt* **1** slacken. **2** relax. **3** release. **se relâcher** *vr* **1** become slack. **2** abate. **relâche** *nm* **1** relaxation. **2** respite. *nf* port of call.

relais (rǝˈlɛ) *nm* **1** relay. **2** shift (in a factory, etc.). **relais d'essence** filling station.

relatif, -ive (rǝlaˈti:f, -ˈti:v) *adj* relative.

relation (rǝlaˈsjɔ̃) *nf* **1** relation. **2** communication, contact. **3** statement.

relativité (rǝlati:vi:ˈte:) *nf* relativity.

relayer (rǝlɛˈje:) *vt* **1** relay. **2** relieve.

relever (rǝlˈve:) *vt* **1** raise. **2** pick up. **3** point out. **4** relieve. **relever de** be dependent on. **relève** *nf* **1** relief. **2** changing of the guard. **relevé** *adj* **1** raised. **2** high. *nm* **1** abstract. **2** summary. **relevé de compte** bank statement.

relief (rǝˈljɛf) *nm Art* relief.

religion (rǝli:ˈʒjɔ̃) *nf* religion. **religieux, -euse** (rǝli:ˈʒjœ, -ˈʒjœz) *adj* **1** religious. **2** sacred. *nm* monk. *nf* nun.

relique (rǝˈli:k) *nf* relic.

relire* (rǝˈli:r) *vt* re-read.

reluire (rǝˈlɥi:r) *vi* **1** shine. **2** glitter.

remanier (rǝmaˈnje:) *vt* adapt, alter.

remarquer (rǝmarˈke:) *vt* notice. **faire remarquer** point out. **se faire remarquer** attract attention. **remarque** *nf* remark.

remblai (rãˈblɛ) *nm* embankment.

rembourrer (rãbu:ˈre:) *vt* stuff, pad.

rembourser (rãbu:rˈse:) *vt* reimburse, refund. (rãbu:rsǝˈmã) *nm* repayment.

remédier (rǝme:ˈdje:) *vi* **remédier à** remedy. **remède** *nm* remedy, cure.

remercier (rǝmɛrˈsje:) *vt* **1** thank. **2** dismiss. **remerciement** *nm* thanks.

remettre* (rǝˈmɛtr) *vt* **1** put back. **2** hand over. **3** recollect. **4** postpone.

remise (rǝˈmi:z) *nf* **1** delivery. **2** remittance. **3** discount. **4** garage.

rémission (re:mi:ˈsjɔ̃) *nf* remission.

remonter (rǝmɔ̃ˈte:) *vi* (*aux être*) **1** go up again. **2** go back. *vt* **1** climb up again. **2** carry or pull up, raise. **3** wind up. **remontant** *nm* tonic. **remontée** *nf* climb. **remontée du visage** facelift.

remords (rǝˈmɔr) *nm* remorse.

remorquer (rǝmɔrˈke:) *vt* tow. **remorque** *nf* **1** towing. **2** towrope. **3** trailer.

remous (rǝˈmu:) *nm naut* swirl, wash.

rempart (rãˈpar) *nm* rampart.

remplacer (rãplaˈse:) *vt* **1** replace. **2** substitute. **3** succeed. **remplaçant** *nm* substitute.

rempli (rãˈpli:) *nm* tuck (in a dress).

remplir (rãˈpli:r) *vt* **1** refill. **2** fill up or in. **3** fulfil.

remporter (rãpɔrˈte:) *vt* **1** take away. **2** carry off. **3** win.

remuer (rǝˈmɥe:) *vt* **1** move. **2** stir. *vi* fidget.

rémunérer (re:myne:ˈre:) *vt* **1** remunerate. **2** reward. **rémunérateur, -trice** (re:myne:raˈtœr, -ˈtri:s) *adj* remunerative.

renâcler (rǝnãˈkle:) *vi* snort.

renaissance (rǝnɛˈsãs) *nf* renaissance.

renard (rǝˈnar) *nm* fox.

renchérir (rãʃe:ˈri:r) *vi* increase in price.

rencontrer (rãkɔ̃ˈtre:) *vt* **1** meet. **2** encounter. **se rencontrer** *vr* **1** meet. **2** collide. **3** agree. **rencontre** *nf* **1** meeting. **2** encounter. **3** occasion.

se rendormir (rãdɔrˈmi:r) *vr* go back to sleep.

rendre (rãdr) *vt* **1** give back. **2** render. **3** restore. **4** yield. **5** deliver. **6** surrender. **7** make. **se rendre** *vr* **1** go. **2** surrender. **rendez-vous** *nm invar* **1** appointment. **2** meeting place.

rêne (rɛn) *nf* rein.

renfermer (rãfɛrˈme:) *vt* **1** shut up. **2** contain, comprise. **renfermé** *adj* uncommunicative, reserved.

renforcer (rãfɔr'se:) *vt* **1** reinforce. **2** strengthen. **3** intensify. *vi* grow stronger.

renfort (rã'fɔr) *nm* reinforcement(s).

se renfrogner (rãfrɔ'ɲe:) *vr* **1** scowl. **2** frown. **renfrogné** *adj* sullen.

rengaine (rã'gɛn) *nf* hackneyed story.

renier (rə'nje:) *vt* **1** disown. **2** repudiate, deny. **reniement** *nm* **1** repudiation, denial.

renifler (rənı:'fle:) *vi,vt* sniff.

renne (rɛn) *nm* reindeer.

renommée (rənɔ'me:) *nf* renown, fame. **renommé** *adj* famous.

renoncer (rənɔ̃'se:) *vt* **1** renounce. **2** give up.

renoncule (rənɔ̃'kyl) *nf* buttercup.

renouer (rə'nwe:) *vt* **1** tie up again. **2** resume.

renouveler (rənu:'vle:) *vt* renew. **se renouveler** *vr* recur.

rénover (re:nɔ've:) *vt* **1** renovate. **2** restore.

renseigner (rãsɛ'ɲe:) *vt* inform. **se renseigner sur** *vr* make enquiries about. **renseignement** *nm* information.

rente (rãt) *nf* **1** private income. **2** pension. **3** rent.

rentrer (rã'tre:) *vi (aux être)* **1** return. **2** come in again. **3** go home. *vt* take or bring in. **rentrée** *nf* **1** return. **2** reopening. **3** beginning of school term.

renverser (rãvɛr'se:) *vt* **1** turn upside down. **2** knock over. **3** invert. **4** *inf* amaze. **se renverser** *vr* overturn. **renverse** *nf* **1** turn. **2** change. **renversement** *nm* **1** reversal, inversion. **2** overthrow.

renvoi (rã'vwa) *nm* **1** return. **2** dismissal. **3** postponement.

renvoyer (rãvwa'je:) *vt* **1** send back. **2** dismiss. **3** postpone. **4** refer.

réorganiser (re:ɔrganı:'ze:) *vt* reorganize.

repaire (rə'pɛr) *nm* **1** den. **2** refuge.

répandre (re:'pãdr) *vt* **1** spill. **2** spread. **3** scatter. **se répandre** *vr* be spread. **répandu** *adj* **1** widespread. **2** well-known.

reparaitre (rəpa'rɛtr) *vi* reappear.

réparer (re:pa're:) *vt* **1** repair. **2** make amends. **réparation** *nf* **1** repair. **2** amends.

repartie (rəpar'ti:) *nf* **1** repartee. **2** retort.

répartir (re:par'ti:r) *vt* **1** distribute. **2** divide. **3** allocate. **répartition** *nf* **1** distribution. **2** allocation.

repas (rə'pa) *nm* meal.

repasser (rəpa'se:) *vi (aux être)* pass again. *vt* **1** pass over. **2** go over. **3** sharpen. **4** iron. **repassage** *nm* **1** sharpening. **2** ironing.

se repentir (rəpã'ti:r) *vr* repent, be sorry. **repenti** *adj* repentant. **repentir** *nm* repentance.

répercussion (re:pɛrky'sjɔ̃) *nf* repercussion.

répercuter (re:pɛrky'te:) *vt* **1** reverberate. **2** reflect.

repérer (rəpe:'re:) *vt* spot, locate. **repère** *nm* reference. **point de repère** *nm* landmark.

répertoire (re:pɛr'twar) *nm* **1** index, catalogue. **2** repertoire. **3** repertory.

répéter (re:pe:'te:) *vt* **1** repeat. **2** rehearse. **répétiteur, -trice** (re:pe:ti:'tœr, -'tri:s) *nm,f* tutor. **répétition** *nf* **1** repetition. **2** rehearsal. **répétition générale** dress rehearsal.

répit (re:'pi:) *nm* respite.

replacer (rəpla'se:) *vt* **1** put back. **2** reassign.

repli (rə'pli:) *nm* **1** fold, crease. **2** coil.

replier (rəpli:'e:) *vt* **1** fold up. **2** turn back.

répliquer (re:pli:'ke:) *vi* retort. **réplique** *nf* **1** retort. **2** *Th* cue. **3** *Art* replica.

répondre (re:'pɔ̃dr) *vt* **1** reply, answer. **2** respond. **répondre de** answer for.

réponse (re:'pɔ̃s) *nf* **1** answer, reply. **2** response.

reporter[1] (rəpɔr'te:) *vt* **1** carry back. **2** defer. **se reporter** *vr* refer.

reporter[2] (rəpɔr'te:) *nm* reporter. **reportage** *nm* **1** report. **2** reporting.

repos (rə'po) *nm* **1** rest. **2** peace.

reposer[1] (rəpo'ze:) *vt* put back, replace.

reposer[2] (rəpo'ze:) *vt* rest. *vi* **1** lie. **2** be based. **se reposer** *vr* **1** rest. **2** settle. **3** rely.

repousser (rəpu:'se:) *vt* **1** push back. **2** repulse. **3** reject.

reprendre (rə'prɛdr) *vt* **1** take back. **2** resume. **3** reply. **4** reprimand. *vi* recommence. **se reprendre** *vr* **1** pull oneself together. **2** correct oneself.

représailles (rəpre'zaj) *nf pl* retaliation, reprisal. **user de représailles** retaliate.

représenter (rəpre:zã'te:) *vt* **1** represent. **2** depict. **3** act for. **4** *Th* perform. **représentant** *adj,n* representative. **représentation** *nf* **1** representation. **2** agency. **3** *Th* performance.

répressif, -ive (re:prɛ'si:f, -'si:v) *adj* repressive. **répression** *nf* repression.

réprimander (re:prı:mã'de:) *vt* reprimand, censure. **réprimande** *nf* reprimand.

réprimer (re:'prı:'me:) *vt* **1** repress. **2** quell.

reprise (rə'pri:z) *nf* **1** renewal. **2** revival. **3**

repetition. **4** darning. **5** *sport* round. **à plu-sieurs reprises** again and again.
reprocher (rəprɔ'ʃe:) *vt* **1** reproach. **2** grudge. **reproche** *nm* reproach.
reproduction (rəprɔdyk'sjɔ̃) *nf* reproduction.
reproduire (rəprɔ'dɥi:r) *vt* reproduce. **se repro-duire** *vr* recur.
reptile (rɛp'ti:l) *adj,nm* reptile.
répu (re:'py) *adj* well fed, sated.
républicain (re:pybli:'kɛ̃) *adj,n* republican.
république (re:py'bli:k) *nf* republic.
répudier (re:py'dje:) *vt* repudiate.
répulsif, -ive (re:pyl'si:f, -'si:v) *adj* repulsive. **répulsion** *nf* repulsion.
réputation (re:pyta'sjɔ̃) *nf* reputation, repute. **réputé** *adj* famous, well-known.
requérir* (rəke:'ri:r) *vt* **1** ask, request. **2** demand.
requête (rə'kɛt) *nf* **1** request. **2** petition.
requiem (re:kɥi:'ɛm) *nm* invar requiem.
requin (rə'kɛ̃) *nm* shark.
requis (rə'ki:) *adj* necessary.
rescapé (rɛska'pe:) *nm* survivor.
réseau, -aux (re:'zo) *nm* network, system.
réserver (re:zɛr've:) *vt* reserve. **réserve** *nf* **1** reservation. **2** reserve. **3** caution. **4** store. **réservé** *adj* **1** reserved. **2** cautious. **3** secretive. **réservoir** *nm* **1** reservoir. **2** tank.
résider (re:zi:'de:) *vi* **1** reside, live. **2** consist. **résidence** *nf* residence. **résident** *nm* resident. **résidentiel, -elle** (re:zi:dɑ̃'sjɛl) *adj* residential.
résidu (re:si:'dy) *nm* residue.
se résigner (re:zi:'ɲe:) *vr* resign oneself.
résilier (re:zi:'lje:) *vt* cancel, annul.
résille (re:'zi:j) *nf* hairnet.
résine (re:'zi:n) *nf* resin.
résister (re:zi:'ste:) *vi* (of colours) be fast. **résister à 1** resist. **2** withstand. **3** oppose. **résistance** *nf* **1** resistance. **2** strength.
résolu (re:zɔ'ly) *v* see **résoudre.** *adj* determined, resolute. **résolution** *nf* **1** solution (of a problem). **2** resolution. **3** resolve.
résolvant (re:zɔl'vɑ̃) *v* see **résoudre.**
résonner (re:zɔ'ne:) *vi* resound, reverberate.
résoudre* (re:'zu:dr) *vt* **1** dissolve. **2** solve, settle. **3** resolve.
respect (rɛ'spɛ) *nm* respect. **respect de soi** self-respect.
respecter (rɛspɛk'te:) *vt* **1** respect. **2** abide by. **respectable** *adj* respectable. **respectueux, -euse** (rɛspɛk'tɥœ, -'tɥœz) *adj* respectful. **respectueux des lois** law-abiding.

respectif, -ive (rɛspɛk'ti:f, -'ti:v) *adj* respective.
respirer (rɛspi:'re:) *vi,vt* breathe. **respiration** *nf* breathing. **respiration artificielle** artifical respiration.
resplendir (rɛsplɑ̃'di:r) *vi* **1** glitter. **2** glow.
responsable (rɛspɔ̃'sabl) *adj* responsible. **responsabilité** *nf* responsibility.
resquiller (rɛski:'je:) *vi* gatecrash. *vt* inf wangle.
ressaisir (rəsɛ'zi:r) *vt* seize again. **se ressaisir** *vr* pull oneself together.
ressembler (rəsɑ̃'ble:) *vt* resemble. **se res-sembler** *vr* be alike. **ressemblance** *nf* resemblance.
ressentir* (rəsɑ̃'ti:r) *vt* feel. **ressentiment** *nm* resentment.
ressort[1] (rə'sɔr) *nm* **1** spring. **2** energy. **3** elasticity.
ressort[2] (rə'sɔr) *nm* scope, province.
ressortir* (rəsɔr'ti:r) *vi* (aux être) **1** come or go out again. **2** stand out. *vt* bring out again. **ressortir de** follow from.
ressource (rə'su:rs) *nf* **1** resource. **2** expedient. **3** *pl* means.
ressusciter (re:sysi:'te:) *vt* restore to life. *vt,vi* revive.
restaurer (rɛstɔ're:) *vt* **1** restore. **2** refresh. **restauration** *nf* restoration.
rester (rɛ'ste:) *vi* (aux être) **1** remain, stay. **2** be left. **restant** *adj* remaining. *nm* remainder. **reste** *nm* **1** remainder. **2** *pl* remains. **du reste** moreover.
restituer (rɛsti:'tɥe:) *vt* **1** restore. **2** return.
restreindre* (rɛ'strɛ̃dr) *vt* restrict, limit.
restriction (rɛstri:k'sjɔ̃) *nf* restriction.
résulter (re:zyl'te:) *vi* (aux être) result, follow. **résultat** *nm* **1** result. **2** outcome.
résumer (re:zy'me:) *vt* summarize. **résumé** *nm* summary, résumé.
résurrection (re:zyrɛk'sjɔ̃) *nf* resurrection.
rétablir (re:ta'bli:r) *vt* **1** re-establish. **2** restore. **3** reinstate. **rétablissement** *nm* **1** restoration. **2** recovery.
retard (rə'tar) *nm* delay. **en retard 1** late, behindhand. **2** backward.
retarder (rətar'de:) *vt* retard, delay. *vi* be late. **retardataire** *adj* **1** late. **2** backward.
retenir* (rət'ni:r) *vt* **1** hold back. **2** detain. **3** secure. **4** retain. **5** book, reserve. **se retenir** *vr* **1** restrain oneself. **2** cling.
retentir (rətɑ̃'ti:r) *vi* **1** resound. **2** reverberate. **3** echo. **retentissement** *nm* **1** repercussion. **2** reverberation.

retenue (rət'ny) nf 1 discretion. 2 withholding. 3 detention. **retenu** adj prudent.

réticent (re:ti:'sã) adj reticent, reserved.

rétif, -ive (re:'ti:f, -'ti:v) adj obstinate.

rétine (re:'ti:n) nf retina.

retirer (rəti:'re:) vt 1 withdraw. 2 pull out. 3 remove. **se retirer** vr retire, withdraw.

retomber (rətɔ̃'be:) vi (aux être) 1 fall back. 2 hang down.

retors (rə'tɔr) adj 1 twisted. 2 cunning.

retoucher (rətu:'ʃe:) vt touch up, improve. **retouche** nf small alteration.

retour (rə'tu:r) nm return. **être de retour** be back.

retourner (rətu:r'ne:) vt 1 turn (inside out). 2 turn round or back. 3 return. vi (aux être) go back. **se retourner** vr turn round or back.

rétracter¹ (re:trak'te:) vt retract, withdraw.

rétracter² (re:trak'te:) vt retract, draw in.

retraite (rə'trɛt) nf 1 retreat. 2 mil tattoo. 3 retirement. 4 refuge. **prendre sa retraite** retire. **retraité** nm pensioner.

retrancher (rətrã'ʃe:) vt 1 cut off or down. 2 entrench.

rétrécir (re:tre:'si:r) vi,vt 1 narrow. 2 contract, shrink. **rétrécissement** nm shrinkage.

rétribuer (re:tri:'bɥe:) vt remunerate, pay.

rétroaction (re:troak'sjɔ̃) nf feedback.

rétrograder (re:trɔgra'de:) vi retrogress, go backwards. **rétrograde** adj retrograde, backward.

rétrospectif, -ive (re:trɔspɛk'ti:f, -'ti:v) adj retrospective.

retrousser (rətru:'se:) vt 1 turn up. 2 tuck up. 3 roll up.

retrouver (rətru:'ve:) vt 1 find again. 2 regain.

rétroviseur (re:trɔvi:'zœr) nm driving mirror.

réunir (re:y'ni:r) vt reunite. **se réunir** vr gather together. **réunion** nf reunion, meeting.

réussir (re:y'si:r) vi succeed. **réussi** adj successful. **réussite** nf 1 success. 2 pl game patience.

revanche (rə'vãʃ) nf 1 revenge. 2 return match. **en revanche** 1 in return. 2 on the other hand.

rêvasser (rɛva'se:) vi daydream.

rêve (rɛv) nm dream.

revêche (rə'vɛʃ) adj 1 perverse, difficult. 2 harsh, churlish.

réveiller (re:vɛ'je:) vt wake, awaken. **se réveiller** vr awake, wake up. **réveille-matin** nm invar alarm clock.

révéler (re:ve:'le:) vt 1 reveal, disclose. 2

show. **révélateur, -trice** (re:ve:la'tœr, -'tri:s) adj revealing, telltale.

revendiquer (rəvãdi:'ke:) vt 1 claim, demand. 2 assume. **revendication** nf demand.

revenir* (rəv'ni:r) vi (aux être) 1 return, come back. 2 go back on. 3 cost. 4 amount. **revenir de** recover. **en revenir** get over it. **revenant** adj pleasing. nm ghost. **revenu** nm revenue, income.

rêver (rɛ've:) vi 1 dream. 2 muse.

réverbérer (re:vɛrbe:'re:) vt reflect. vi reverberate. **réverbère** nm 1 streetlamp. 2 reflector.

révérence (re:vɛ'rãs) nf 1 reverence. 2 bow, curtsy.

revers (rə'vɛr) nm 1 reverse. 2 wrong side. 3 lapel.

revêtir* (rəvɛ'ti:r) vt 1 clothe, dress. 2 coat, case.

revirement (rəvi:r'mã) nm sudden change.

reviser (rəvi:'ze:) vt revise, modify. **revision** nf 1 revision. 2 inspection.

revivre* (rə'vi:vr) vi relive. **faire revivre** revive.

revoir* (rə'vwar) vt 1 see again. 2 revise. **au revoir!** interj goodbye!

révolter (re:vɔl'te:) vt 1 rouse, stir up. 2 disgust. **révolte** nf revolt. **révolté** nm rebel.

révolution (re:vɔly'sjɔ̃) nf revolution. **révolutionnaire** adj revolutionary.

revolver (re:vɔl'vɛr) nm revolver.

révoquer (re:vɔ'ke:) vt 1 revoke. 2 dismiss.

revue (rə'vy) nf 1 inspection. 2 review. 3 revue.

rez-de-chaussé (re:dʃo'se:) nm invar ground floor.

rhétorique (re:tɔ'ri:k) nf rhetoric.

Rhin (rɛ̃) nm Rhine.

rhinocéros (rinɔse:'rɔs) nm rhinoceros.

Rhodésie (rɔde:'zi:) nf Rhodesia. **rhodésien, -ienne** (rɔde:'zjɛ̃, -'zjɛn) adj,n Rhodesian.

Rhône (ron) nm Rhone.

rhubarbe (ry'barb) nf rhubarb.

rhum (rɔm) nm rum.

rhumatisme (ryma'ti:sm) nm rheumatism.

rhume (rym) nm med cold. **rhume des foins** hayfever.

ri (ri:) v see **rire**.

riant (ri:'ã) v see **rire**.

ricaner (ri:ka'ne:) vi sneer.

riche (ri:ʃ) adj 1 rich, wealthy. 2 valuable. 3 fertile. **richesse** nf 1 wealth. 2 richness.

rider (ri:'de:) vt 1 wrinkle. 2 shrivel. **se rider** vr 1 wrinkle. 2 shrivel. 3 ripple. **ride** nf 1 wrinkle. 2 ripple. **ridé** adj 1 wrinkled. 2 corrugated.

rideau, -aux (rı:'do) nm 1 curtain. 2 screen. **Rideau de Fer** Iron Curtain.

ridectomie (rı:dɛktɔ'mı:) nf facelift.

ridicule (rı:di:'kyl) adj ridiculous. nm 1 absurdity. 2 ridicule.

rien (rjɛ̃) pron anything. **ne...rien** nothing. **cela ne fait rien** that doesn't matter. **il n'y a rien à faire** it can't be helped. ~nm trifle, trivial thing or affair.

rigide (rı:'ʒı:d) adj 1 rigid. 2 stiff. 3 tense. **rigidité** nf rigidity.

rigole (rı:'gɔl) nf drain, gutter.

rigoler (rı:gɔ'le:) vi inf 1 laugh. 2 enjoy oneself. 3 joke. **rigolo, -ote** adj funny, comical.

rigoureux, -euse (rı:gu:'rœ, -'rœz) adj 1 rigorous. 2 harsh. 3 strict.

rigueur (rı:'gœr) nf 1 rigour, strictness. 2 severity. 3 hardship. **à la rigueur** 1 strictly. 2 if need be. **de rigueur** compulsory.

rimer (rı:'me:) vi rhyme. **rime** nf rhyme.

rincer (rɛ̃'se:) vt rinse.

riposter (rı:pɔ'ste:) vi retort. **riposte** nf retort.

rire* (rı:r) vi 1 laugh. 2 joke. **rire nerveusement** giggle. **rire tout bas** chuckle. **se rire de** vr laugh at. ~nm 1 laughter. 2 laugh. **petit rire nerveux** giggle. **rire étouffé** chuckle.

ris (rı:) **ris de veau** nm sweetbread.

risquer (rı:'ske:) vt risk. **se risquer** vr take a risk. **risque** nm risk.

ristourne (rı:'stu:rn) nf 1 refund, rebate. 2 discount.

rite (rı:t) nm rite. **rituel, -elle** (rı:'tɥɛl) adj,nm ritual.

rival, -aux (rı:'val, -'vo) adj,n rival.

rivaliser (rı:vali:'ze:) vi 1 rival. 2 compete. **rivalité** nf rivalry.

rive (rı:v) nf 1 bank (of a river). 2 shore. 3 riverside. 4 edge. **rivage** nm 1 bank (of a river). 2 shore.

river (rı:'ve:) vt rivet. **rivet** nm rivet.

rivière (rı:'vjɛr) nf 1 river. 2 stream.

rixe (rı:ks) nf brawl, scuffle.

riz (rı:) nm rice.

robe (rɔb) nf 1 dress. 2 gown. 3 robe. 4 skin (of an onion, etc.). **robe de chambre** dressing-gown. **robe du soir** evening dress.

robinet (rɔbı:'nɛ) nm tap.

robot (ro'bo) nm robot.

robuste (rɔ'byst) adj 1 robust. 2 sturdy. 3 hardy.

roche (rɔʃ) nf rock, boulder. **rocher** nm rock.

rôder (ro'de:) vi prowl.

rogner (rɔ'ɲe:) vt clip, trim.

rognon (rɔ'ɲɔ̃) nm cul kidney.

rogue (rɔg) adj arrogant.

roi (rwa) nm king.

roitelet (rwat'lɛ) nm wren.

rôle (rol) nm 1 roll. 2 part, role.

romain (rɔ'mɛ̃) adj,n Roman.

roman¹ (rɔ'mã) nm 1 novel. 2 pl fiction. **roman policier** detective novel. **romancier, -ière** (rɔmã'sje:, -'sjɛr) nm,f novelist.

roman² (rɔ'mã) adj 1 romance. 2 Romanesque.

romanesque (rɔma'nɛsk) adj romantic.

romantique (rɔmã'tı:k) adj romantic.

romarin (rɔma'rɛ̃) nm rosemary.

Rome (rɔm) nf Rome.

rompre (rõpr) vt 1 break. 2 snap. 3 break off or up. vi break. **rompu** adj broken.

ronce (rõs) nf 1 blackberry bush. 2 pl thorns.

rond (rõ) adj 1 round. 2 plump. 3 sl drunk. nm 1 ring, circle. 2 washer. 3 disc. **rond-de-cuir** nm, pl **ronds-de-cuir** inf 1 clerk. 2 bureaucrat. **rond-point** nm, pl **ronds-points** roundabout. **ronde** nf 1 round, inspection. 2 semibreve.

ronfler (rõ'fle:) vi 1 snore. 2 (of a fire) roar. 3 hum. **ronflement** nm 1 snore. 2 snoring. 3 buzzing.

ronger (rõ'ʒe:) vt 1 gnaw. 2 corrode. 3 erode. **rongeur, -euse** (rõ'ʒœr, -'ʒœz) adj gnawing. nm rodent.

ronron (rõ'rõ) nm purr.

ronronner (rõrɔ'ne:) vi purr.

roquet (rɔ'kɛ) nm mongrel.

roquette (rɔ'kɛt) nf rocket.

rosaire (ro'zɛr) nm rosary.

rosbif (rɔs'bi:f) nm roast beef.

rose (roz) nf rose. **rose trémière** hollyhock. adj pink, rosy. nm pink. **rosé** adj pink. nm rosé wine. **rosier** nm rose bush or tree.

roseau, -aux (ro'zo) nm reed.

rosée (ro'ze:) nf dew.

roselet (ro'zlɛ) nm ermine.

rosette (ro'zɛt) nf 1 bow (of ribbon). 2 rosette.

rosser (ro'se:) vt give a beating. **rossée** nf inf thrashing.

rossignol (rɔsı:'ɲɔl) nm 1 nightingale. 2 inf piece of junk.

rotatif, -ive (rɔta'tı:f, -'tı:v) adj rotary. **rotation** nf rotation.

rôtir (ro'tı:r) vt,vi 1 roast. 2 toast. 3 scorch. **rôti** nm roast (meat). **rôtisserie** nf grillroom.

rotor (rɔ'tɔr) nm rotor.

rotule (rɔ'tyl) *nf* kneecap.

rouage (rwaʒ) *nm* 1 works, machinery. 2 wheel.

roublard (ru:'blar) *adj inf* sly, artful.

rouble (ru:bl) *nm* rouble.

roue (ru:) *nf* wheel. **faire la roue** 1 strut. 2 do a cartwheel.

roué (rwe:) *adj* cunning.

rouelle (rwɛl) *nf* round slice, round.

rougeole (ru:'ʒɔl) *nf* measles.

rougir (ru:'ʒi:r) *vt* redden. *vi* 1 turn red. 2 blush. **rouge** *adj* red. **rouge-gorge** *nm, pl* **rouges-gorges** robin. *nm* 1 red. 2 rouge. **rougeur** *nf* 1 redness. 2 blush, flush.

rouiller (ru:'je:) *vi* 1 rust. 2 mildew. **rouille** *nf* 1 rust. 2 mildew.

rouler (ru:'le:) *vt* 1 roll. 2 *inf* take in, swindle. 3 turn over. *vi* 1 roll (over or down). 2 rumble. 3 roam. 4 turn. **se rouler** *vr* roll. **roulage** *nm* carriage, haulage. **roulant** *adj* 1 sliding, moving. 2 smooth. 3 *sl* hilarious. **rouleau, -aux** (ru:'lo) *nm* 1 roller. 2 roll. 3 spool. 4 rolling pin. **rouleau compresseur** steamroller. **rouleau de papier hygiénique** toilet roll. **roulette** *nf* 1 castor, small wheel. 2 roulette.

roulotte (ru:'lɔt) *nf* (gipsy) caravan.

roupiller (ru:pi:'je:) *vi inf* sleep, snooze. **roupillon** *nm* snooze.

rouquin (ru:'kɛ̃) *adj inf* red-haired, ginger.

rouspéter (ru:spe:'te:) *vi* 1 protest. 2 grumble.

roussir (ru:'si:r) *vi,vt* turn brown. *vi* singe, get scorched. **rousseur** *nf* redness (of hair).

route (ru:t) *nf* 1 road, track. 2 route. **route nationale** main road, trunk road.

routine (ru:'ti:n) *nf* routine.

roux, rousse (ru:, ru:s) *adj* 1 red-haired. 2 reddish.

royal, -aux (rwa'jal, -'jo) *adj* royal, regal.

royaume (rwa'jom) *nm* 1 kingdom. 2 realm. **royauté** (rwajo'te:) *nf* royalty.

Royaume-Uni *nm* United Kingdom.

ruban (ry'bɑ̃) *nm* 1 ribbon. 2 band.

rubéole (rybe:'ɔl) *nf* German measles.

rubis (ry'bi:) *nm* ruby.

rubrique (ry'bri:k) *nf* heading, title.

ruche (ryʃ) *nf* beehive.

rude (ryd) *adj* 1 hard. 2 rough. 3 harsh. 4 uncouth. 5 gruff. **rudement** *adv inf* very. **rudesse** *nf* 1 harshness. 2 severity. 3 roughness.

rudiment (rydi:'mɑ̃) *nm* rudiment.

rudoyer (rydwa'je:) *vt* 1 treat roughly. 2 bully.

rue (ry) *nf* street, thoroughfare. **rue à sens unique** one-way street. **ruelle** *nf* alley, lane.

ruer (rɥe:) *vi* (of a horse, etc.) kick (out). **se ruer** *vr* 1 fling oneself. 2 rush. **ruée** *nf* rush.

rugir (ry'ʒi:r) *vi* 1 roar. 2 howl. **rugissement** *nm* 1 roar. 2 roaring.

rugueux, -euse (ry'gœ, -'gœz) *adj* 1 rough. 2 rugged. 3 wrinkled.

ruiner (rɥi:'ne:) *vt* ruin. **se ruiner** *vr* 1 go to ruin. 2 ruin oneself. **ruine** *nf* 1 ruin. 2 downfall. 3 destruction.

ruisseau, -aux (rɥi:'so) *nm* 1 gutter. 2 brook. 3 stream.

ruisseler (rɥi:'sle:) *vi* 1 trickle, drip. 2 stream, flow.

rumeur (ry'mœr) *nf* 1 murmur, distant noise. 2 din. 3 rumour.

rupture (ryp'tyr) *nf* 1 breaking. 2 rupture.

rural, -aux (ry'ral, -'ro) *adj* rural.

ruse (ryz) *nf* trick, stratagem. **rusé** *adj* sly.

Russie (ry'si:) *nf* Russia. **russe** *adj,n* Russian. *nm* Russian (language).

rustique (ry'sti:k) *adj* 1 rustic. 2 rural.

rutabaga (rytaba'ga) *nm* swede.

rythme (ri:tm) *nm* 1 rhythm. 2 *mus* beat. **rythmique** *adj* rhythmical.

S

sa (sa) *poss adj* see **son.**

sabbat (sa'ba) *nm* Sabbath.

sable [1] (sɑbl) *nm* sand. **sables mouvants** *nm pl* quicksand. **sableux, -euse** (sa'blœ, -'blœz) *adj* sandy. **sablière** (sɑbli:'ɛr) *nf* sandpit.

sable [2] (sɑbl) *nm* sable.

sabot (sa'bo) *nm* 1 clog. 2 hoof.

sabotage (sabɔ'taʒ) *nm* sabotage.

sabre (sabr) *nm* 1 sabre. 2 swordfish.

sac (sak) *nm* 1 sack. 2 bag. **sac à dos** rucksack. **sac à main** handbag. **sac de couchage** sleeping-bag.

saccade (sa'kad) *nf* jolt, jerk. **par saccades** by fits and starts.

saccager (saka'ʒe:) *vt* 1 pillage. 2 ransack, cause havoc.

saccharine (sakka'ri:n) *nf* saccharin.

sacerdoce (sasɛr'dɔs) *nm* priesthood.

sachant (sa'ʃɑ̃) *v* see **savoir.**

sachet (sa'ʃɛ) *nm* 1 small bag. 2 sachet.

sacoche (sa'kɔʃ) *nf* 1 saddlebag. 2 satchel.

sacrement (sakrə'mɑ̃) *nm* sacrament.

sacrer (sa'kre:) *vt* anoint, crown. *vi* swear.

sacre nm 1 coronation. 2 consecration. **sacré** adj 1 holy, sacred. 2 sl damned, cursed.

sacrifier (sakrı:ˈfje:) vt 1 sacrifice. 2 give up. **sacrifice** nm sacrifice.

sacrilège (sakrı:ˈlɛʒ) nm sacrilege. adj sacrilegious.

sacristie (sakrı:ˈstı:) nf vestry.

sadisme (saˈdi:sm) nm sadism. **sadique** adj sadistic. nm,f sadist.

safran (saˈfrã) nm 1 saffron. 2 crocus.

sagace (saˈgas) adj shrewd.

sage (saʒ) adj 1 wise. 2 discreet. 3 well-behaved. 4 chaste. **sois sage!** be good! **sage-femme** nf, pl **sages-femmes** midwife. **sagesse** nf 1 wisdom. 2 prudence.

Sagittaire (saʒi:tˈtɛr) nm Sagittarius.

sagou (saˈgu:) nm sago.

saigner (sɛˈɲe:) vi,vt bleed. **saignant** adj 1 bleeding. 2 cul underdone, rare.

saillir (saˈji:r) vi 1 gush out. 2 protrude. 3 stand out. **saillant** adj 1 prominent, protruding. 2 outstanding. **saillie** nf 1 spurt. 2 bound. 3 flash of wit. 4 ledge.

sain (sɛ̃) adj 1 healthy. 2 sound. 3 wholesome. **sain et sauf** safe and sound.

saindoux (sɛ̃ˈdu:) nm lard.

saint (sɛ̃) adj 1 holy. 2 saintly. 3 hallowed. nm saint. **sainteté** nf holiness.

Saint-Esprit nf Holy Ghost.

sais (sɛ) v see **savoir**.

saisir (sɛˈzi:r) vt 1 seize, grab. 2 understand. **se saisir de** vr 1 seize upon. 2 lay hands on. **saisie** nf seizure. **saisissant** adj 1 striking. 2 piercing. 3 thrilling. **saisissement** nm 1 shock. 2 shiver.

saison (sɛˈzõ) nf season. **de saison** in season. **saisonnier, -ière** (sɛzɔˈnje:, -ˈnjɛr) adj seasonal.

salade (saˈlad) nf 1 salad. 2 lettuce. 3 sl mess.

salaire (saˈlɛr) nm 1 wages, salary. 2 reward.

salamandre (salaˈmãdr) nf salamander. **salamandre aquatique** newt.

sale (sal) adj 1 dirty, filthy. 2 offensive, obscene. **saleté** nf 1 dirt. 2 trash. 3 obscenity. 4 dirty trick.

saler (saˈle:) vt 1 salt. 2 cul cure. 3 inf overcharge. **salaison** nf cul curing. **salé** adj 1 salted. 2 inf spicy. 3 sl exorbitant. **salière** nf salt-cellar.

salir (saˈli:r) vt 1 dirty, soil. 2 sully. **saliver** (saliːˈve:) vi salivate. **salive** nf saliva.

salle (sal) nf 1 room. 2 Th house. 3 pol lobby. **salle à manger** dining room. **salle**

d'attente waiting room. **salle de bain** bathroom. **salle de bal** ballroom. **salle de classe** classroom. **salle de séjour** living room. **salle de spectacle** theatre. **salle d'hôpital** med ward. **salle d'opérations** med theatre.

salon (saˈlõ) nm 1 drawing room. 2 saloon. 3 salon.

saloperie (salɔˈpri:) nf 1 filthiness. 2 inf rubbish. 3 dirty trick.

salopette (salɔˈpɛt) nf 1 overalls. 2 dungarees.

saltimbanque (saltɛ̃ˈbãk) nm 1 showman. 2 charlatan.

salubre (saˈlybr) adj 1 healthy. 2 wholesome.

saluer (salˈɥe:) vt 1 greet. 2 salute. 3 bow.

salut (saˈly) nm 1 safety. 2 salvation. 3 bow. 4 greeting. 5 salute. interj hello! **salutation** nf 1 greeting. 2 bow.

salutaire (salyˈtɛr) adj 1 beneficial. 2 healthy.

samedi (samˈdi:) nm Saturday.

sanctifier (sãktı:ˈfje:) vt hallow.

sanction (sãkˈsjõ) nf 1 sanction, approval. 2 law penalty.

sanctionner (sãksjɔˈne:) vt 1 sanction, approve. 2 penalize.

sanctuaire (sãkˈtɥɛr) nm sanctuary.

sandale (sãˈdal) nf sandal.

sandwich (sãˈdwi:tʃ) nm sandwich.

sang (sã) nm 1 blood. 2 relationship. **à sang chaud/froid** warm/cold-blooded. **sang-froid** nm composure, coolness. **sang-mêlé** nm invar half-caste.

sanglant (sãˈglã) adj 1 covered in blood. 2 scathing.

sangler (sãˈgle:) vt 1 strap, tie up. 2 thrash. **sangle** nf 1 strap. 2 girth.

sanglier (sãgliːˈe:) nm wild boar.

sanglot (sãˈglo) nm sob. **sangloter** vi sob.

sangsue (sãˈsy) nf leech.

sanguin (sãˈgɛ̃) adj blood. **sanguinaire** adj bloodthirsty.

sanitaire (sanı:ˈtɛr) adj sanitary.

sans (sã) prep 1 without. 2 but for. **sans que** without. **sans-abri** nm invar homeless person. **sans-façon** adj homely. nm straightforwardness. **sans-gêne** adj offhand, blunt. nm inf cheek. **sans-souci** adj invar carefree, easygoing.

sansonnet (sãsɔˈnɛ) nm starling.

santé (sãˈte:) nf health. **à votre santé!** cheers!

saper (saˈpe:) vt undermine.

sapeur (saˈpœr) nm mil pioneer, scout. **sapeur-**

125

pompier *nm, pl* **sapeurs-pompiers** 1 fireman. 2 *pl* fire brigade.

saphir (sa'fi:r) *nm* sapphire.

sapin (sa'pɛ̃) *nm* fir.

sarcasme (sar'kasm) *nm* sarcasm. **sarcastique** *adj* sarcastic.

sarcler (sar'kle:) *vt* 1 weed. 2 hoe.

Sardaigne (sar'dɛɲ) *nf* Sardinia. **sarde** *adj,n* Sardinian.

sardine (sar'di:n) *nf* 1 pilchard. 2 sardine.

sardonique (sardɔ'ni:k)'*adj* sardonic.

Satan (sa'tã) *nm* Satan.

satin (sa'tɛ̃) *nm* satin.

satire (sa'ti:r) *nf* satire. **satirique** *adj* satirical.

satisfaction (satɪ:sfak'sjɔ̃) *nf* satisfaction.

satisfaire° (satɪ:s'fɛr) *vt* 1 satisfy, content. 2 meet, fulfil. **satisfaisant** *adj* satisfactory.

saturer (saty're:) *vt* saturate.

Saturne (sa'tyrn) *nm* Saturn.

sauce (sos) *nf* 1 sauce. 2 gravy.

saucée (so'se:) *nf sl* 1 downpour. 2 telling-off

saucisse (so'sɪ:s) *nf* sausage. **saucisson** *nm* large dry sausage.

sauf, sauve (sof, sov) *adj* safe, intact. **sauf** *prep* save, except, but.

sauge (soʒ) *nf bot* sage.

saugrenu (sogrə'ny) *adj* absurd, ridiculous.

saule (sol) *nm* willow.

saumon (so'mɔ̃) *nm* salmon.

saumure (so'myr) *nf* pickle.

sauna (so'na) *nm* sauna.

saupoudrer (sopu'dre:) *vt* sprinkle, dust.

saurai (so:'rɛ) *v* see **savoir.**

saut (so) *nm* leap, jump. **saut-de-lit** *nm, pl* **sauts-de-lit** bedside rug. **saut-de-mouton** *nm, pl* **sauts-de-mouton** *mot* flyover. **saute-mouton** *nm* leapfrog. **saut périlleux** somersault.

sauter (so'te:) *vi* 1 jump, leap. 2 skip. 3 explode. 4 (of a fuse) blow. *vt* jump over. **sauterelle** *nf* grasshopper. **sauterie** *nf* 1 jumping. 2 private party.

sautiller (sotɪ:'je:) *vt* 1 hop. 2 skip.

sauvage (so'vaʒ) *adj* 1 savage, wild. 2 primitive. 3 shy. *nm,f* savage. **sauvagerie** *nf* 1 brutality. 2 unsociability.

sauvegarder (sovgar'de:) *vt* safeguard, protect. **sauvegarde** *nf* 1 safeguard, protection. 2 bodyguard.

sauver (so've:) *vt* 1 save, rescue. 2 protect. **se sauver** *vr* 1 escape. 2 run away. **sauve-qui-peut** *nm invar* stampede, panic. **sauve-**

tage *nm* 1 rescue. 2 salvage. **sauveur** *nm* 1 saviour. 2 rescuer.

savant (sa'vã) *adj* 1 learned, scholarly. 2 able. 3 skilful. *nm* 1 scientist. 2 scholar. **savamment** *adv* 1 knowingly. 2 skilfully.

savate (sa'vat) *nf* 1 old shoe. 2 French boxing. **savetier** *nm* cobbler.

saveur (sa'vœr) *nf* 1 taste, flavour. 2 piquancy.

savoir° (sa'vwar) *vt* 1 know. 2 be aware of. 3 be able. **c'est à savoir** that remains to be seen. **faire savoir à** inform. **savoir-faire** *nm invar* 1 ability. 2 tact. **savoir-vivre** *nm invar* breeding, good manners. ~*nm* knowledge.

savon (sa'vɔ̃) *nm* soap. **savon en poudre** soap powder.

savonner (savɔ'ne:) *vt* soap, lather.

savourer (savu:'re:) *vt* 1 relish. 2 enjoy. **savoureux, -euse** (savu:'rœ, -'rœz) *adj* 1 tasty. 2 *inf* juicy.

scabreux, -euse (ska'brœ, -'brœz) *adj* 1 difficult, ticklish. 2 indecent.

scandale (skã'dal) *nm* 1 scandal. 2 disgrace. **scandaliser** (skãdali:'ze:) *vt* shock, offend.

Scandinavie (skãdi:na'vi:) *nf* Scandinavia. **scandinave** *adj,n* Scandinavian.

scaphandrier (skafã'dri:'e:) *nm* diver.

sceau, sceaux (so) *nm* 1 seal. 2 stamp, mark.

scélérat (ske:le'ra) *adj* wicked, criminal. *nm* 1 scoundrel. 2 villain.

sceller (sɛ'le:) *vt* 1 seal. 2 confirm. **scellé** *nm* seal.

scène (sɛn) *nf* 1 stage. 2 scene. 3 *inf* quarrel, scene.

sceptique (sɛp'ti:k) *nm,f* sceptic. *adj* sceptical. **scepticisme** *nm* scepticism.

schéma (skɛ'ma) *nm* diagram.

schizophrénie (skɪ:zɔfre:'ni:) *nf* schizophrenia. **schizophrène** *adj* schizophrenic.

scie (si:) *nf* 1 saw. 2 *inf* bore.

sciemment (sja'mã) *adv* knowingly.

science (sjãs) *nf* 1 knowledge, learning. 2 science. **sciences naturelles** *nf pl* natural science.

scientifique (sjãti:'fi:k) *adj* scientific. *nm,f* scientist.

scier (sje:) *vt* 1 saw (off). 2 *inf* bore. **scierie** *nf* sawmill. **sciure de bois** *nf* sawdust.

scintiller (sɛ̃tɪ:'je:) *vi* 1 sparkle. 2 twinkle. 3 flicker.

scolaire (skɔ'lɛr) *adj* scholastic.

scooter (sku:'tɛr) *nm* scooter.

scorpion (skɔr'pjɔ̃) *nm* 1 scorpion. 2 *cap* Scorpio.

scrupuleux, -euse (skrypy'lœ, -'lœz) *adj* scrupulous.

scruter (skry'te:) *vt* scrutinize.

scrutin (skry'tɛ̃) *nm* **1** poll. **2** ballot. **3** voting.

sculpter (skyl'te:) *vt* **1** sculpt. **2** carve. **sculpteur** *nm* sculptor. **sculpture** *nf* sculpture.

se, s' (sə) *pron 3rd pers m,f s,pl* **1** oneself, himself, herself, itself, themselves. **2** each other, one another.

séance (se:'ɑ̃s) *nf* **1** meeting. **2** *pol* session. **3** sitting. **4** *Th* performance.

séant (se:'ɑ̃) *adj* fitting, seemly. *nm inf* bottom.

seau, sceaux (so) *nm* bucket.

sec, sèche (sɛk, sɛʃ) *adj* **1** dry. **2** dried. **3** curt. **4** harsh. *nf sl* fag, cigarette.

sécher (se:'ʃe:) *vt,vi* dry. **sécheresse** (se:ʃ'rɛs) *nf* **1** dryness. **2** drought. **3** harshness.

second (sə'gɔ̃) *adj* second. *nm* second in command. **en second** in second place. **seconde** *nf* **1** second, moment. **2** second class. **secondaire** *adj* secondary, subordinate.

secouer (sə'kwe:) *vt* **1** shake. **2** jolt. **3** shake off.

secourir* (səku:'ri:r) *vt* help. **secours** *nm* help, assistance. **au secours!** help! **premiers secours** *nm pl* first aid.

secousse (sə'ku:s) *nf* **1** jolt, jerk. **2** shock.

secret¹, -ète (sə'krɛ, -'krɛt) *adj* **1** secret, confidential. **2** hidden.

secret² (sə'krɛ) *nm* **1** secret. **2** secrecy.

secrétaire (səkre:'tɛr) *nm,f* **1** secretary. **2** clerk. *nm* bureau, desk.

sécréter (se:kre:'te:) *vt* secrete.

secte (sɛkt) *nf* sect, group. **sectaire** *adj,n* sectarian.

secteur (sɛk'tœr) *nm* **1** sector. **2** area, district.

section (sɛk'sjɔ̃) *nf* **1** section. **2** branch, division. **3** stage (on a bus route).

séculaire (se:ky'lɛr) *adj* **1** occurring once in a century. **2** venerated.

séculier, -ière (se:ky'lje:, -'ljɛr) *adj* secular. *nm* layman.

sécurité (se:kyri:'te:) *nf* **1** security. **2** safety.

sédatif, -ive (sɛda'ti:f, 'ti:v) *adj,nm* sedative.

sédiment (se:di:'mɑ̃) *nm* sediment.

séduire* (se:'dɥi:r) *vt* **1** seduce. **2** lead astray. **3** charm. **séduisant** *adj* **1** seductive. **2** attractive.

segment (sɛg'mɑ̃) *nm* segment.

ségrégation (se:grega'sjɔ̃) *nf* segregation.

seigle (sɛgl) *nm* rye.

seigneur (sɛ'ɲœr) *nm* lord.

sein (sɛ̃) *nm* breast, bosom.

séisme (se:'i:sm) *nm* earthquake.

seize (sɛz) *adj,nm* sixteen. **seizième** *adj* sixteenth.

séjour (se:'ʒu:r) *nm* **1** stay. **2** residence.

séjourner (se:ʒu:r'ne:) *vi* **1** stay. **2** reside.

sel (sɛl) *nm* **1** salt. **2** wit.

sélection (se:lɛk'sjɔ̃) *nf* selection, choice. **sélectif, -ive** (se:lɛk'ti:f, -'ti:v) *adj* selective. **sélectionner** (se:lɛksjɔ'ne:) *vt* select, choose.

selle (sɛl) *nf* **1** saddle. **2** stool. **sellier** *nm* saddler.

selon (sə'lɔ̃) *prep* according to.

Seltz (sɛls) **eau de Seltz** *nm Tdmk* soda-water.

semaine (sə'mɛn) *nf* week.

sémantique (se:mɑ̃'ti:k) *adj* semantic. *nf* semantics.

sémaphore (sɛma'fɔr) *nm* semaphore.

sembler (sɑ̃'ble:) *vi* seem, appear. **semblable** *adj* **1** similar, alike. **2** such. **semblant** *nm* appearance, show. **faire semblant de** pretend.

semelle (sə'mɛl) *nf* sole (of a shoe).

semence (sə'mɑ̃s) *nf* seed.

semer (sə'me:) *vt* **1** sow. **2** scatter.

semestre (sə'mɛstr) *nm* **1** term. **2** half-year.

séminaire (se:mi:'nɛr) *nm* **1** seminary. **2** seminar.

semi-voyelle (səmi:vwa'jɛl) *nf* semivowel.

semoule (sə'mu:l) *nf* semolina.

sénat (se:'na) *nm* senate. **sénateur** *nm* senator.

sénile (se:'ni:l) *adj* senile.

sens (sɑ̃s) *nm* **1** sense. **2** judgment. **3** meaning. **4** direction. **bon sens** commonsense. **dans le sens des aiguilles d'une montre** clockwise. **sens dessus dessous** upside down. **sens interdit** no entry.

sensation (sɑ̃sa'sjɔ̃) *nf* **1** sensation. **2** feeling. **sensationnel, -elle** (sɑ̃sasjɔ'nɛl) *adj* **1** sensational. **2** *inf* superb.

sensé (sɑ̃'se:) *adj* sensible.

sensible (sɑ̃'si:bl) *adj* **1** sensitive. **2** susceptible. **3** sympathetic. **4** tender. **5** apparent. **sensibilité** *nf* **1** sensibility. **2** sensitivity. **3** feeling. **4** tenderness.

sensuel, -elle (sɑ̃'sɥɛl) *adj* sensual, sensuous.

sentence (sɑ̃'tɑ̃s) *nf* **1** *law* sentence. **2** maxim.

sentier (sɑ̃'tje:) *nm* path, footpath.

sentiment (sɑ̃ti:'mɑ̃) *nm* **1** feeling. **2** sensation. **3** opinion. **4** sentiment. **sentimental, -aux** *adj* sentimental.

sentinelle (sɑ̃ti:'nɛl) *nf* sentry.

sentir* (sɑ̃'ti:r) *vt* **1** feel. **2** be conscious of. **3** smell. *vi* **1** smell of. **2** taste of. **sentir mauvais** stink.

seoir* (swar) *vi* suit, become.
séparer (sɛpaˈre:) *vt* **1** separate. **2** divide. **séparation** *nf* separation. **séparé** *adj* **1** separate. **2** apart.
sept (sɛt) *adj,nm* seven. **septième** (sɛˈtjɛm) *adj* seventh.
septembre (sɛpˈtãbr) *nm* September.
septentrional, -aux (sɛptãriːɔˈnal, -ˈno) *adj* north, northern.
septique (sɛpˈtiːk) *adj* septic.
séquence (sɛˈkãs) *nf* sequence.
sequin (səˈkɛ̃) *nm* sequin.
serai (səˈrɛ) *v* see **être.**
serais (səˈrɛ) *v* see **être.**
serein (səˈrɛ̃) *adj* serene, calm.
sérénade (se:rɛˈnad) *nf* serenade.
serf, serve (sɛrf, sɛrv) *nm,f* serf.
sergent (sɛrˈʒã) *nm* sergeant.
série (se:ˈriː) *nf* **1** series, succession. **2** range. **3** set. **hors série 1** specially made. **2** outsize.
sérieux, -euse (se:ˈrjœ, -ˈrjœz) *adj* **1** serious. **2** grave. **3** earnest. **4** important. *nm* gravity.
serin (səˈrɛ̃) *nm* canary.
seringue (səˈrɛ̃g) *nf* syringe.
serment (sɛrˈmã) *nm* oath.
sermon (sɛrˈmɔ̃) *nm* sermon.
serpent (sɛrˈpã) *nm* snake, serpent.
serpenter (sɛrpãˈte:) *vi* meander, wind.
serrer (sɛˈre:) *vt* **1** squeeze, clench. **2** put away. **3** tighten. **4** close (up). **serrer la main à** shake hands with. **se serrer** *vr* group together. **serre** *nf* **1** greenhouse, conservatory. **2** claw. **3** grip. **serre chaude** hothouse. **serré** *adj* **1** close. **2** tight. **3** concise. **4** *inf* mean. **serre-tête** *nm invar* crash-helmet.
serrure (sɛˈryr) *nf* lock.
sers (sɛr) *v* see **servir.**
servante (sɛrˈvãt) *nf* maid.
serveur, -euse (sɛrˈvœr, -ˈvœz) *nm,f* **1** barman, barmaid. **2** waiter, waitress.
service (sɛrˈviːs) *nm* **1** service. **2** attendance. **3** department. **4** duty. **5** set.
serviette (sɛrvˈjɛt) *nf* **1** napkin. **2** towel. **3** briefcase. **serviette hygiénique** sanitary towel.
servir* (sɛrˈviːr) *vt* **1** serve. **2** attend to. **3** help. *vi* be useful. **servir de** be used as. **se servir de** *vr* use. **serviteur** *nm* servant.
ses (se:) *poss adj* see **son.**
session (sɛˈsjɔ̃) *nf* session, sitting.
seuil (sœj) *nm* **1** threshold. **2** doorstep.
seul (sœl) *adj* **1** only. **2** single, sole. **3** alone. **seulement** *adv* only.

sève (sɛv) *nf* sap.
sévère (se:ˈvɛr) *adj* **1** harsh, hard. **2** strict. **3** severe. **sévérité** *nf* **1** severity. **2** strictness.
sévir (se:ˈviːr) *vi* **1** punish severely. **2** rage.
sexe (sɛks) *nm* sex. **sexualité** *nf* sexuality. **sexuel, -elle** (sɛkˈsɥɛl) *adj* sexual.
sextuor (sɛkˈstɥɔr) *nm* sextet.
shampooing (ʃãpuːˈiːɲ) *nm* shampoo.
shérif (ʃɛˈriːf) *nm* sheriff.
si[1] (siː) *conj* **1** if. **2** whether.
si[2] (si:) *adv* **1** so, so much. **2** such. **3** as. **4** yes. **si...que** however.
Sicile (si:ˈsi:l) *nf* Sicily. **sicilien, -ienne** (si:si:ˈljɛ̃, -ˈljɛn) *adj,n* Sicilian.
siècle (sjɛkl) *nm* **1** century. **2** age, time.
siéger (sjeˈʒe:) *vi* **1** *pol* sit. **2** be centred. **siège** *nm* **1** seat. **2** chair. **3** siege. **4** see. **siège central** *comm* head office.
sien, sienne (sjɛ̃, sjɛn) *poss pron 3rd pers s* **le sien, la sienne 1** his, hers, one's. **2** his, hers, one's or its own.
sieste (sjɛst) *nf* **1** siesta. **2** *inf* nap.
siffler (si:ˈfle:) *vi,vt* whistle, hiss. **sifflet** *nm* whistle.
signal, -aux (si:ˈɲal, -ˈɲo) *nm* signal.
signaler (si:ɲaˈle:) *vt* **1** point out. **2** signal. **3** report. **4** give a description of. **se signaler** *vr* distinguish oneself. **signalement** *nm* description, particulars. **signalisateur anti-vol** *nm* burglar alarm.
signature (si:ɲaˈtyr) *nf* **1** signature. **2** signing.
signe (si:ɲ) *nm* **1** sign. **2** mark. **3** gesture. **faire signe à** beckon. **signet** *nm* bookmark.
signer (si:ˈɲe) *vt* sign.
signifier (si:ɲi:ˈfje:) *vt* signify, mean. **significatif, -ive** (si:ɲi:fi:kaˈti:f, -ˈti:v) *adj* significant. **signification** *nf* meaning.
silence (si:ˈlãs) *nm* silence. **silencieux, -euse** (si:lãˈsjœ, -ˈsjœz) *adj* silent.
silex (si:ˈlɛks) *nm* flint.
silhouette (si:lˈwɛt) *nf* silhouette, outline.
sillon (si:ˈjɔ̃) *nm* **1** furrow. **2** trail. **3** groove.
sillonner (si:jɔˈne:) *vt* **1** furrow. **2** streak. **3** wrinkle.
simagrée (si:maˈgre:) *nf* **1** pretence. **2** *pl* grimaces. **3** *pl* affectation.
simple (sɛ̃pl) *adj* **1** simple. **2** single. **3** ordinary. **4** plain. **simplicité** *nf* simplicity.
simplifier (sɛ̃pli:ˈfje:) *vt* simplify.
simulacre (si:myˈlakr) *nm* **1** pretence, show. **2** image.
simuler (si:myˈle:) *vt* feign, counterfeit.

simultané (si:mylta'ne:) *adj* simultaneous. **simultanément** *adv* simultaneously.

sincère (sɛ̃'sɛr) *adj* **1** sincere. **2** genuine. **3** true. **sincérité** *nf* **1** sincerity. **2** honesty. **3** candour.

singe (sɛ̃ʒ) *nm* monkey, ape.

singer (sɛ̃'ʒe:) *vt* ape, mimic. **singerie** *nf* grimace.

singulier, -ière (sɛ̃gu'lje:, -'ljɛr) *adj* **1** singular. **2** peculiar. **3** strange. *nm* singular. **singularité** *nf* **1** singularity. **2** peculiarity. **3** eccentricity.

sinistre (si:'ni:str) *adj* **1** sinister, ominous. **2** dangerous. **3** gloomy. *nm* disaster.

sinon (si:'nɔ̃) *conj* **1** otherwise, or else. **2** except.

sinueux, -euse (si:'nɥœ, -'nɥœz) *adj* winding.

sionisme (sjɔ'ni:sm) *nm* Zionism. **sioniste** *adj,n* Zionist.

siphon (si:'fɔ̃) *nm* siphon.

sirène (si:'rɛn) *nf* **1** siren, hooter. **2** mermaid.

sirop (si:'ro) *nm* syrup.

siroter (si:rɔ'te:) *vt inf* sip.

site (si:t) *nm* **1** beauty spot. **2** site.

sitôt (si:'to) *adv* as soon. **sitôt que** as soon as.

situer (si:'tɥe:) *vt* situate, place. **situation** *nf* **1** situation. **2** position. **3** condition. **4** appointment, job. **situation difficile** predicament.

six (si:s) *adj,nm* six. **sixième** *adj* sixth.

ski (ski:) *nm* **1** ski. **2** skiing. **faire du ski** ski. **ski-nautique** *nm* water-skiing.

slip (sli:p) *nm* underpants, briefs.

slogan (slɔ'gã) *nm* slogan.

smoking (smɔ'ki:ɲ) *nm* dinner jacket.

snob (snɔb) *adj invar* **1** *inf* smart. **2** snobbish. *nm* snob.

sobre (sɔbr) *adj* **1** temperate. **2** sober. **3** economical. **sobriété** *nf* **1** sobriety. **2** moderation.

sobriquet (sɔbri:'kɛ) *nm* nickname.

sociable (sɔ'sjabl) *adj* sociable.

social, -aux (sɔ'sjal, -'sjo) *adj* social. **socialisme** *nm* socialism. **socialiste** *adj,n* socialist.

société (sɔsje:'te:) *nf* **1** society. **2** community. **3** club. **4** company. **5** companionship. **sociétaire** *nm,f* **1** member. **2** shareholder.

sociologie (sɔsjɔlɔ'ʒi:) *nf* sociology. **sociologique** *adj* sociological. **sociologue** *nm,f* sociologist.

socle (sɔkl) *nm* **1** pedestal. **2** base.

socquette (sɔ'kɛt) *nf* ankle-sock.

sœur (sœr) *nf* **1** sister. **2** nun.

soi (swa) *pron 3rd pers m,f s* oneself, himself, herself, itself. **soi-disant** *adj invar* so-called.

adv supposedly. **soi-même** *pron 3rd pers m,f s* oneself.

soie (swa) *nf* **1** silk. **2** bristle (of a badger, etc.). **soie artificielle** rayon.

soif (swaf) *nf* thirst. **avoir soif** be thirsty.

soigner (swa'ɲe) *vt* **1** look after. **2** nurse. **3** do carefully. **se soigner** *vr* look after oneself. **soigné** (swa'ɲe:) *adj* **1** neat, tidy. **2** carefully done. **soigneux, -euse** (swa'ɲœ, -'ɲœz) *adj* **1** careful. **2** painstaking. **3** tidy.

soin (swɛ̃) *nm* care.

soir (swar) *nm* **1** evening. **2** night. **ce soir** tonight. **hier soir** last night. **soirée** *nf* **1** evening. **2** party.

sois (swa) *v* see **être**.

soit (swa) *interj* agreed!. *conj* whether. **soit... soit** either...or.

soixante (swa'sãt) *adj,nm* sixty. **soixantième** *adj* sixtieth.

soixante-dix *adj,nm* seventy. **soixante-dixième** *adj* seventieth.

soja (sɔʒa) *nm* soya bean.

sol (sɔl) *nm* **1** ground, earth. **2** soil.

solaire (sɔ'lɛr) *adj* **1** solar. **2** sun.

soldat (sɔl'da) *nm* soldier.

solde[1] (sɔld) *nf mil* pay.

solde[2] (sɔld) *nm* **1** *comm* balance. **2** surplus stock. **3** (clearance) sale.

sole (sɔl) *nf cul* sole.

soleil (sɔ'lɛj) *nm* **1** sun. **2** sunshine.

solennel, -elle (sɔla'nɛl) *adj* **1** solemn. **2** state, official.

solidarité (sɔli:dari:'te:) *nf* **1** solidarity. **2** fellowship.

solide (sɔ'li:d) *adj* **1** solid. **2** strong. **3** sound.

solidifier (sɔli:di:'fje:) *vt* solidify.

soliste (sɔ'li:st) *nm,f* soloist.

solitaire (sɔli:'tɛr) *adj* solitary, lonely. *nm* hermit.

solitude (sɔli:'tyd) *nf* solitude.

solive (sɔ'li:v) *nf* **1** joist. **2** beam.

solliciter (sɔlli:si:'te:) *vt* **1** request. **2** incite.

solo (sɔ'lo) *adj invar,nm* solo.

soluble (sɔ'lybl) *adj* soluble.

solution (sɔly'sjɔ̃) *nf* **1** solution. **2** answer, explanation.

solvable (sɔl'vabl) *adj* solvent.

sombre (sɔ̃br) *adj* **1** sombre, gloomy. **2** dark. **3** dejected.

sombrer (sɔ̃'bre:) *vi* sink.

sommaire (sɔm'mɛr) *adj* **1** concise. **2** elementary. **3** rapid. *nm* summary.

sommation (sɔma'sjɔ̃) *nf law* summons.

somme[1] (sɔm) *nm* nap, snooze.

somme[2] (sɔm) *nf* sum, amount. **en somme 1** on the whole. **2** in short.

somme[3] (sɔm) **bête de somme** *nf* beast of burden.

sommeil (sɔ'mɛj) *nm* **1** sleep. **2** sleepiness. **avoir sommeil** be sleepy.

sommeiller (sɔmɛ'je:) *vi* doze, sleep lightly.

sommelier (sɔmə'lje:) *nm* wine waiter.

sommer (sɔ'me:) *vt law* summon.

sommes (sɔm) *v* see **être**.

sommet (sɔ'mɛ) *nm* summit, top.

somnambule (sɔmnã'byl) *nm,f* sleepwalker. **somnambulisme** *nm* sleepwalking. **somnifère** *nm* sleeping-pill.

somnoler (sɔmnɔ'le:) *vi* doze, drowse. **somnolent** *adj* sleepy.

son[1], **sa**, **ses** (sɔ̃, sa, se:) *poss adj 3rd pers s* his, her, its, one's.

son[2] (sɔ̃) *nm* sound.

son[3] (sɔ̃) *nm* bran.

sonate (sɔ'nat) *nf* sonata.

sonder (sɔ̃'de:) *vt* **1** sound. **2** probe, examine. **3** fathom. **sondage** *nm* **1** sounding. **2** *min* boring. **3** opinion poll.

songer (sɔ̃'ʒe:) *vi* **1** dream. **2** imagine. **3** muse. **songer à** think about. **songe** *nm* dream. **songerie** *nf* dreaming. **songeur, -euse** (sɔ̃'ʒœr, -'ʒœz) *nm,f* dreamer. *adj* pensive.

sonique (sɔ'ni:k) *adj* sonic.

sonner (sɔ'ne:) *vi,vt* **1** ring. **2** toll. *vi* **1** sound. **2** strike. **sonnerie** *nf* **1** ringing. **2** chimes. **3** bell. **4** trumpet call. **sonnette** *nf* **1** small bell. **2** doorbell.

sonnet (sɔ'nɛ) *nm* sonnet.

sonore (sɔ'nɔr) *adj* **1** resonant. **2** loud.

sont (sɔ̃) *v* see **être**.

soprano (sɔpra'no) *nm,f* soprano.

sorcier, -ière (sɔr'sje:, -'sjɛr) *nm,f* wizard, witch. **sorcellerie** *nf* witchcraft.

sordide (sɔr'di:d) *adj* **1** sordid, squalid. **2** base.

sors (sɔr) *v* see **sortir**.

sort (sɔr) *nm* **1** fate. **2** lot. **3** spell.

sorte (sɔrt) *nf* **1** sort, kind. **2** manner. **de sorte que** so that.

sortir* (sɔr'ti:r) *vi* **1** go out. **2** come up. **3** leave. *vt* take or bring out. **sortie** *nf* **1** way out, exit. **2** leaving. **3** outing. **4** *inf* outburst. **sortie de secours** emergency exit.

sot, sotte (so, sɔt) *adj* **1** stupid. **2** ridiculous. **3** sheepish. *nm,f* fool, idiot. **sottise** (sɔ'ti:z) *nf* **1** stupidity. **2** silly remark or action.

sou (su:) *nm* penny. **sans le sou** penniless.

soubresaut (su:brə'so) *nm* sudden start, jerk.

souche (su:ʃ) *nf* **1** stump. **2** stub. **3** counterfoil.

souci[1] (su:'si:) *nm* **1** worry. **2** anxiety. **3** care. **sans souci** carefree.

souci[2] (su:'si:) *nm* marigold.

se soucier (su:'sje:) *vr* **1** care, concern oneself. **2** be anxious. **soucieux, -euse** (su:'sjœ, -'sjœz) *adj* **1** anxious. **2** thoughtful. **3** preoccupied.

soucoupe (su:'ku:p) *nf* saucer.

soudain (su:'dɛ̃) *adj* **1** sudden. **2** unexpected. *adv* suddenly.

soude (su:d) *nf* soda.

souder (su:'de:) *vt* **1** solder. **2** weld. **se souder** *vr* **1** weld. **2** join together.

soudoyer (su:dwa'je:) *vt* **1** hire. **2** bribe.

souffler (su:'fle:) *vi* **1** blow. **2** pant. **3** breathe. *vt* **1** blow out or up. **2** utter. **3** *inf* trick. **souffler son rôle à** prompt. **souffle** *nm* **1** breath. **2** puff. **3** blast. **4** inspiration. **soufflet** *nm* **1** bellows. **2** box (the ears). **3** *inf* insult.

souffleter (su:flə'te:) *vt* **1** slap. **2** insult.

souffrir* (su:'fri:r) *vt* **1** endure. **2** permit. *vi* suffer, be in pain. **souffrance** *nf* **1** suspense. **2** pain. **souffrant** *adj* **1** suffering. **2** unwell. **souffre-douleur** *nm invar* **1** drudge. **2** butt (of jokes, etc.).

soufre (su:fr) *nm* sulphur.

souhait (swɛ) *nm* wish. **souhaiter** *vt* wish, desire.

souiller (su:'je:) *vt* **1** soil. **2** pollute. **3** tarnish. **souillure** *nf* **1** spot, stain. **2** blemish.

soûl (su:) *adj inf* **1** drunk. **2** full.

soulager (su:la'ʒe:) *vt* **1** relieve, ease. **2** soothe. **soulagement** *nm* **1** relief. **2** comfort.

se soûler (su:'le:) *vr* **1** get drunk. **2** gorge oneself. **soûlard** *nm sl* drunkard.

soulever (su:l've:) *vt* **1** lift. **2** raise. **3** rouse. **4** provoke. **soulèvement** *nm* **1** raising. **2** revolt. **3** protest.

soulier (su:'lje:) *nm* shoe.

souligner (su:li:'ɲe:) *vt* **1** underline. **2** emphasize.

soumettre* (su:'mɛtr) *vt* **1** subdue. **2** subject. **3** submit, refer. **se soumettre** *vr* submit, yield. **soumis** *adj* obedient.

soumission (su:mi:'sjɔ̃) *nf* **1** submission. **2** obedience. **3** *comm* tender.

soupape (su:'pap) *nf* **1** valve. **2** plug.

soupçon (su:p'sɔ̃) *nm* **1** suspicion. **2** slight flavour, dash.

soupçonner (su:psɔ'ne:) *vt* **1** suspect. **2** guess.

soupçonneux, -euse (su:psɔ'nœ, -'nœz) *adj* suspicious.

soupe (su:p) *nf* soup.

soupente (su:'pãt) *nf* loft.

souper (su:'pe:) *vi* have supper. *nm* supper.

soupir (su:'pi:r) *nm* sigh. **soupirer** *vi* sigh.

soupirail, -aux (su:pi:'raj, -'ro) *nm* ventilator.

souple (su:pl) *adj* 1 supple. 2 flexible. 3 adaptable. **souplesse** *nf* 1 suppleness. 2 flexibility.

source (su:rs) *nf* 1 source. 2 spring, well. 3 origin.

sourcil (su:r'si:) *nm* eyebrow.

sourd (su:r) *adj* 1 deaf. 2 dull, muffled. 3 hollow. 4 secret. *nm* deaf person. **sourd-muet, sourde-muette** *adj,pl* **sourds-muets, sourdes-muettes** deaf-and-dumb. *nm,f* deaf-mute.

souricière (su:ri:'sjɛr) *nf* 1 mousetrap. 2 trap.

sourire* (su:'ri:r) *vi* smile. **sourire à belles dents** grin. ~*nm* smile. **large sourire** grin. **sourire affecté** smirk.

souris (su:'ri:) *nf* mouse.

sournois (su:r'nwa) *adj* 1 sly. 2 cunning. 3 underhand. *nm* sneak.

sous (su:) *prep* 1 under. 2 below. 3 within (time). **sous la pluie** in the rain. **sous terre** underground.

sous-alimentation *nf* malnutrition.

souscrire* (su:'skri:r) *vt* 1 subscribe. 2 sign. **souscription** *nf* 1 subscription. 2 signature. 3 contribution.

sous-développé *adj* underdeveloped.

sous-entendre *vt* 1 imply. 2 understand. **sous-entendu** *nm* implication.

sous-estimer *vt* underestimate.

sous-marin *adj* underwater.

sous-sol *nm* basement.

sous-titrer *vt* subtitle. **sous-titre** *nm* subtitle.

soustraire* (su:'strɛr) *vt* 1 take away. 2 withdraw. 3 subtract. 4 protect. **se soustraire** *vr* escape. **soustraction** *nf* 1 removal. 2 subtraction.

sous-traiter *vt* subcontract.

soutane (su:'tan) *nf* cassock.

soutenir* (su:t'ni:r) *vt* 1 support. 2 prop up. 3 maintain. 4 encourage. 5 withstand. 6 sustain. **se soutenir** *vr* 1 support oneself. 2 continue. **soutenu** *adj* 1 sustained. 2 elevated. 3 constant.

souterrain (su:tɛ'rɛ̃) *adj* underground. *nm* 1 underground passage. 2 vault.

soutien (su:'tjɛ̃) *nm* 1 support, prop. 2 supporter. **soutien-gorge** *nm invar* brassiere, bra.

souvenir* (su:v'ni:r) *v imp* come to mind. **se souvenir de** *vr* remember, recall. ~*nm* 1 memory. 2 remembrance, recollection. 3 memento. 4 souvenir.

souvent (su:'vã) *adv* often. **peu souvent** seldom.

souverain (su:v'rɛ̃) *adj* 1 sovereign. 2 supreme. *nm* sovereign. **souveraineté** *nf* sovereignty.

soyez (swa'je:) *v* see **être.**

soyons (swa'jɔ̃) *v* see **être.**

spacieux, -euse (spa'sjœ, -'sjœz) *adj* spacious.

spasme (spasm) *nm* spasm. **spasmodique** *adj* spasmodic.

spatial, -aux (spa'sjal, -'sjo) *adj* spatial.

spatule (spa'tyl) *nf* spatula.

spécial, -aux (spe:'sjal, -'sjo) *adj* 1 special. 2 especial. 3 particular.

spécialiser (spe:sjali:'ze:) *vt* specialize. **se spécialiser dans** *vr* specialize in. **spécialiste** *nm,f* 1 expert. 2 *med* specialist. **spécialité** *nf* speciality.

spécieux, -euse (spe:'sjœ, -'sjœz) *adj* plausible.

spécifier (spe:si:'fje:) *vt* specify. **spécifique** *adj* specific.

spécimen (spe:si:'mɛn) *nm* specimen.

spectacle (spɛk'takl) *nm* 1 sight, spectacle. 2 *Th* play. 3 show. **spectaculaire** *adj* spectacular.

spectateur, -trice (spɛkta'tœr, -'tri:s) *nm,f* 1 onlooker, spectator. 2 *pl* audience.

spectre (spɛktr) *nm* 1 ghost, apparition. 2 spectrum.

spéculer (spe:ky'le:) *vi* speculate. **spéculateur, -trice** (spe:kyla'tœr, -'tri:s) *nm,f* speculator. **spéculation** *nf* speculation.

spéléologie (spe:le:ɔlɔ'ʒi:) *nf* potholing. **spéléologue** *nm* potholer.

sperme (spɛrm) *nm* sperm.

sphère (sfɛr) *nf* 1 sphere. 2 globe. 3 field, area.

spiral, -aux (spi:'ral, -'ro) *adj* spiral. **spirale** *nf* spiral.

spirituel, -elle (spi:ri:'tɥɛl) *adj* 1 spiritual. 2 witty.

splendeur (splã'dœr) *nf* 1 splendour. 2 magnificence. 3 pomp. **splendide** *adj* 1 splendid, magnificent. 2 superb.

spolier (spɔ'lje:) *vt* rob, plunder.

spontané (spɔ̃ta'ne:) *adj* spontaneous.

sport (spɔr) *nm* sport, games. **sportif, -ive** (spɔr'ti:f, -'ti:v) *adj* sporting.

131

square (skwar) *nm* small square with a (public) garden.
squelette (skə'lɛt) *nm* 1 skeleton. 2 framework.
stabiliser (stabi:li:'ze:) *vt* stabilize, steady.
stable (stabl) *adj* stable, steady, firm.
stade (stad) *nm* 1 stadium. 2 stage, phase.
stage (staʒ) *nm* 1 probationary period. 2 training course.
stagnant (stag'nã) *adj* stagnant.
stalle (stal) *nf* stall, seat.
standard (stã'dar) *nm* 1 switchboard. 2 standard.
station (sta'sjɔ̃) *nf* 1 stop. 2 (tube) station. 3 standing. **station-service** *nf, pl* **stations-service** service station.
stationner (stasjɔ'ne:) *vi* 1 stop. 2 park. **stationnaire** *adj* stationary. **stationnement** *nm* parking.
statique (sta'ti:k) *adj* static.
statistique (stati:'sti:k) *nf* statistics. *adj* statistical.
statue (sta'ty) *nf* statue.
statuer (sta'tчe:) *vi* decide. *vt* decree.
stature (sta'tyr) *nf* stature.
statut (sta'ty) *nm* 1 statute, rule. 2 status.
sténodactylographe (ste:nɔdakti:lɔ'graf) *nm,f* shorthand typist.
sténographie (ste:nɔgra'fi:) *nf* shorthand.
stéréophonique (ste:re:ɔfɔ'ni:k) *adj* stereophonic.
stéréotype (ste:re:ɔ'ti:p) *adj* stereotype.
stérile (ste:'ri:l) *adj* 1 sterile. 2 barren. 3 fruitless. **stérilité** *nf* sterility.
stériliser (ste:ri:li:'ze:) *vt* sterilize.
sterling (stɛr'lɛ̃) *adj invar* sterling.
stéthoscope (ste:tɔ'skɔp) *nm* stethoscope.
stigmate (sti:g'mat) *nm* 1 stigma. 2 scar. 3 brand, mark. 4 stain.
stimuler (sti:my'le:) *vt* 1 stimulate. 2 incite. **stimulant** *adj* stimulating. *nm* 1 stimulus. 2 tonic.
stipuler (sti:py'le:) *vt* stipulate.
stock (stɔk) *nm* stock (of goods, etc.).
stocker (stɔ'ke:) *vt* 1 stock. 2 stockpile.
stoïque (stɔ'i:k) *adj* stoical.
stop (stɔp) *nm* **faire du stop** hitch-hike.
store (stɔr) *nm* blind.
strabisme (stra'bi:sm) *nm* squint.
strapontin (strapɔ̃'tɛ̃) *nm* folding seat.
stratégie (strate:'ʒi:) *nf* strategy. **stratégique** *adj* strategic.
strict (stri:kt) *adj* 1 strict, severe. 2 exact.
strident (stri:'dã) *adj* 1 shrill. 2 piercing.

strié (stri:'e:) *adj* 1 streaked. 2 scratched.
strophe (strɔf) *nf* verse.
structure (stryk'tyr) *nf* structure.
studieux, -euse (sty'djœ, -'djœz) *adj* studious.
studio (sty'djo) *nm* 1 studio. 2 small or one-room flat.
stupéfier (stype:'fje:) *vt* astound, dumbfound. **stupéfaction** (stypɛfak'sjɔ̃) *nf* amazement. **stupéfait** *adj* astounded. **stupéfiant** *adj* amazing. *nm* narcotic, drug.
stupide (sty'pi:d) *adj* stupid, silly. **stupidité** *nf* stupidity.
style (sti:l) *nm* style.
stylo (sti:'lo) *nm* fountain pen. **stylo à bille** ball-point pen.
su (sy) *v see* **savoir.**
suaire (sчɛr) *nm* shroud.
suant (sчã) *adj* sweating, sweaty.
suave (sчav) *adj* 1 sweet, mellow. 2 soft, delicate.
subconscient (sybkɔ̃'sjã) *adj,nm* subconscious.
subir (sy'bi:r) *vt* 1 undergo. 2 endure. 3 suffer.
subit (sy'bi:) *adj* sudden. **subitement** *adv also inf* **subito** suddenly.
subjectif, -ive (sybʒɛk'ti:f, -'ti:v) *adj* subjective.
subjonctif, -ive (sybʒɔ̃k'ti:f, -'ti:v) *adj,nm* subjunctive.
subjuguer (sybʒy'ge:) *vt* 1 subdue. 2 captivate.
sublime (sy'bli:m) *adj* sublime, exalted.
submerger (sybmɛr'ʒe:) *vt* 1 submerge. 2 immerse. 3 swamp.
subordonner (sybɔrdɔ'ne:) *vt* subordinate. **subordonné** *adj,n* subordinate.
subséquent (sybsɛ'kã) *adj* subsequent. **subséquemment** (sybsɛka'mã) *adv* subsequently.
subsister (sybsi:'ste:) *vi* remain, subsist.
substance (syb'stãs) *nf* 1 substance. 2 matter. 3 stuff. **substantiel, -elle** (sybstã'sjɛl) *adj* substantial. **substantif** *nm* substantive.
substituer (sybsti:'tчe:) *vt* substitute. **substitut** *nm* substitute.
subtil (syp'ti:l) *adj* 1 subtle. 2 sharp, penetrating. 3 fine. **subtilité** *nf* subtlety.
suburbain (sybyr'bɛ̃) *adj* suburban.
subvenir* (sybvə'ni:r) *vt* provide, supply.
subvention (sybvã'sjɔ̃) *nv* subsidy, grant.
subventionner (sybvãsjɔ'ne:) *vt* subsidize.
suc (syk) *nm* 1 juice. 2 quintessence.
succédané (syksɛda'ne:) *nm* substitute.
succéder (sykse:'de:) *vt* 1 succeed, inherit. 2 follow. **succès** (syk'sɛ) *nm* 1 success. 2 result, issue. **succession** (syksɛ'sjɔ̃) *nf* suc-

cession. **successeur** *nm* successor. **successif, -ive** (syksɛ'siːf, -'siːv) *adj* successive.
succomber (sykɔ̃'be:) *vi* 1 succumb. 2 die.
succulent (syky'lɑ̃) *adj* succulent, tasty.
succursale (sykyr'sal) *nf comm* branch.
sucer (sy'se:) *vt* suck. **sucette** *nf* lollipop.
sucrer (sy'kre:) *vt* sugar, sweeten. **sucre** *nm* sugar. **sucre d'orge** 1 barley-sugar. 2 lollipop.
sud (syd) *nm* south. *adj invar* south, southerly, southern. **au sud** in the south. **du sud** southern, southerly. **vers le sud** southward, southwards. **sud-est** *nm,adj invar* south-east. **du sud-est** 1 south-eastern. 2 south-easterly. **sud-ouest** *nm,adj invar* south-west. **du sud-ouest** south-western, south-westerly.
Suède (sɥɛd) *nf* Sweden. **suède** *nf* suede. **suédois** *adj,n* Swedish. *nm* Swedish (language).
suer (sɥe:) *vi* sweat, perspire. **sueur** *nf* sweat, perspiration.
suffire* (sy'fiːr) *vi* be sufficient. **suffisant** *adj* 1 sufficient, adequate. 2 conceited.
suffixe (syf'fiːks) *nm* suffix.
suffoquer (syfɔ'ke:) *vt* suffocate, stifle. *vi* choke.
suffrage (sy'fraʒ) *nm* 1 franchise. 2 vote.
suggérer (sygʒe:'re:) *vt* suggest. **suggestion** *nf* suggestion.
se suicider (sɥiːsi:'de:) *vr* commit suicide. **suicide** *nm* suicide.
suie (sɥiː) *nf* soot.
suinter (sɥɛ̃'te:) *vi* 1 ooze, seep. 2 leak.
suis[1] (sɥiː) *v* see **être.**
suis[2] (sɥiː) *v* see **suivre.**
Suisse (sɥiːs) *nf* Switzerland. **suisse** *adj,n* Swiss.
suite (sɥiːt) *nf* 1 continuation. 2 sequel. 3 consistency. 4 sequence. 5 suite, train. **de suite** in succession. **par la suite** 1 later on. 2 consequently. **tout de suite** immediately.
suivre* (sɥiːvr) *vt* 1 follow. 2 attend. 3 accompany. *v imp* result. **faire suivre** forward (a letter). **suivant** *adj* next, following. *prep* according to. **suivi** *adj* 1 consistent. 2 steady. 3 coherent.
sujet, -ette (sy'ʒɛ, -'ʒɛt) *adj* 1 subject. 2 dependent. 3 exposed. 4 liable. *nm,f* subject (person). *nm* 1 subject. 2 cause. 3 theme.
sultan (syl'tɑ̃) *nm* sultan.
superbe (sy'pɛrb) *adj* 1 superb, splendid. 2 stately. 3 arrogant.

supercherie (sypɛrʃə'riː) *nf* 1 deceit. 2 fraud. 3 hoax.
superficie (sypɛrfi:'siː) *nf* 1 surface. 2 *math* area.
superficiel, -elle (sypɛrfi:'sjɛl) *adj* superficial.
superflu (sypɛr'fly) *adj* 1 superfluous. 2 useless.
supérieur (sype:'rjœr) *adj* 1 upper. 2 superior. 3 higher. *nm* superior. **supériorité** *nf* superiority.
superlatif, -ive (sypɛrla'tiːf, -'tiːv) *adj,nm* superlative.
supermarché (sypɛrmar'ʃe:) *nm* supermarket.
supersonique (sypɛrsɔ'niːk) *adj* supersonic.
superstition (sypɛrstiː'sjɔ̃) *nf* superstition. **superstitieux, -euse** (sypɛrstiː'sjœ, -'sjœz) *adj* superstitious.
suppléer (syple:'e:) *vt* 1 make up or good. 2 deputize. **suppléer à** 1 make up for. 2 fill. **suppléant** *adj* temporary. *nm* 1 substitute. 2 deputy. **supplément** *nm* 1 supplement. 2 addition. 3 extra charge. **supplémentaire** *adj* 1 supplementary. 2 additional.
supplice (sy'pliːs) *nm* 1 corporal punishment. 2 torture. 3 torment. **dernier supplice** death penalty.
supplier (sypli:'e:) *vt* implore, entreat.
support (sy'pɔr) *nm* 1 support, prop. 2 stand, rest.
supporter (sypɔr'te:) *vt* 1 support, prop up. 2 endure. 3 tolerate.
supposer (sypo'ze:) *vt* 1 suppose, imagine. 2 imply.
supprimer (sypri:'me:) *vt* 1 suppress. 2 abolish. 3 omit. 4 *inf* kill.
suprême (sy'prɛm) *adj* 1 supreme, highest. 2 last. **suprématie** (syprɛma'siː) *nf* supremacy.
sur (syr) *prep* 1 on. 2 upon. 3 after. 4 about. 5 out of. 6 by. **sur ce** whereupon. **sur-le-champ** *adv* immediately.
sûr (syr) *adj* 1 sure. 2 trustworthy. 3 certain. **à coup sûr** for certain. **bien sûr!** of course!
surabondance (syrabɔ̃'dɑ̃s) *nf* surfeit.
suranné (syra'ne:) *adj* 1 out of date. 2 old-fashioned.
surcharger (syrʃar'ʒe:) *vt* 1 overload. 2 overwork. **surcharge** *nf* 1 overload. 2 surcharge.
surchauffer (syrʃo'fe:) *vt* overheat.
surcroît (syr'krwa) *nm* increase. **par surcroît** in addition.
surdité (syrdi:'te:) *nf* deafness.
sureau, -aux (sy'ro) *nm* elder tree.
surélever (syre:l've:) *vt* 1 heighten. 2 raise.

133

surenchère (syrã'ʃɛr) nf higher bid.

surestimer (syrɛsti:'me:) vt overestimate.

sûreté (syr'te:) nf 1 safety, protection. 2 sureness. 3 guarantee.

surface (syr'fas) nf 1 surface. 2 outside.

surfaire* (syr'fɛr) vt 1 overcharge. 2 overestimate.

surgeler (syrʒə'le:) vt deep-freeze.

surgir (syr'ʒi:r) vt 1 rise. 2 loom, crop up.

surhumain (syry'mɛ̃) adj superhuman.

surimposer (syrɛ̃po'ze:) vt 1 superimpose. 2 increase the tax on.

surlendemain (syrlãd'mɛ̃) nm next day but one, two days later.

surmener (syrmə'ne:) vt overwork. **surmenage** nm overworking.

surmonter (syrmɔ̃'te) vt 1 surmount. 2 dominate, overcome.

surnaturel, -elle (syrnaty'rɛl) adj supernatural.

surnom (syr'nɔ̃) nm nickname.

surnombre (syr'nɔ̃br) nm excess.

surpasser (syrpa'se:) vt surpass, transcend.

surplomb (syr'plɔ̃) nm overhang.

surplomber (syrplɔ̃'be:) vi,vt overhang.

surplus (syr'ply) nm surplus, excess. **au surplus** besides.

surprendre* (syr'prãdr) vt 1 surprise, astonish. 2 catch in the act. **surprise** nf surprise.

surréalisme (syre:a'li:sm) nm surrealism. **surréaliste** adj,n surrealist.

sursaut (syr'so) nm start, jump.

surseoir* (syr'swar) vt suspend, put off. **sursis** nm 1 delay. 2 reprieve.

surtout (syr'tu:) adv 1 above all. 2 especially, particularly. **surtout que** especially as.

surveiller (syrvɛ'je:) vt 1 supervise. 2 inspect. 3 observe, watch. 4 look after. **surveillance** nf supervision. **surveillant** nm 1 supervisor. 2 superintendent. 3 master on duty.

survenir* (syrvə'ni:r) vi 1 happen, occur. 2 crop up.

survêtement (syrvɛt'mã) nm tracksuit.

survivre* (syr'vi:vr) vi **survivre à** outlive. **survivance** nf survival. **survivant** nm survivor.

sus (sys) **en sus** adv in addition.

susceptible (sysɛp'ti:bl) adj 1 susceptible. 2 capable. 3 sensitive. 4 thin-skinned. **peu susceptible** thick-skinned.

susciter (syssi:'te:) vt 1 rouse. 2 create.

susdit (syz'di:) adj aforesaid.

suspect (sy'spɛ) adj suspicious, dubious. nm suspect.

134

suspendre (sy'spãdr) vt 1 suspend. 2 hang up. **suspension** nf suspension.

suspens (sy'spã) **en suspens** adv 1 in suspense. 2 undecided.

susurrer (sysy're:) vi murmur, rustle.

suture (sy'tyr) nf join. **point de suture** nm med stitch.

svastika (svasti:'ka) nm swastika.

svelte (svɛlt) adj slim, slender.

sycomore (sikɔ'mɔr) nm sycamore.

syllabe (si:l'lab) nf syllable.

sylvestre (si:l'vɛstr) adj woodland.

symbole (sɛ̃'bɔl) nm symbol. **symbolique** adj symbolic.

symboliser (sɛ̃bɔli:'ze:) vt symbolize. **symbolisme** nm symbolism.

symétrie (si:me:'tri:) nf symmetry. **symétrique** adj symmetrical.

sympathie (sɛ̃pa'ti:) nf 1 liking, attraction. 2 sympathy. **sympathique** adj likeable, attractive.

symphonie (sɛ̃fɔ'ni:) nf symphony.

symposium (sɛ̃po'zjɔm) nm symposium.

symptôme (sɛ̃p'tom) nm 1 symptom. 2 sign.

synagogue (si:na'gɔg) nf synagogue.

synchroniser (sɛ̃krɔni:'ze:) vt synchronize.

syndicat (sɛ̃di:'ka) nm 1 syndicate. 2 association. 3 trade union. **syndicat d'initiative** tourist information bureau. **syndical, -aux** (sɛ̃di:'kal, -'ko) adj trade-union. **syndicaliste** nm,f trade unionist. **syndiqué** nm trade-union member.

syndrome (sɛ̃'drom) nm syndrome.

synonyme (si:nɔ'ni:m) adj synonymous. nm synonym.

syntaxe (sɛ̃'taks) nf syntax.

synthèse (sɛ̃'tɛz) nf synthesis.

synthétique (sɛ̃te:'ti:k) adj synthetic.

syphilis (si:fi:'li:s) nf syphilis.

Syrie (si:'ri:) nf Syria. **syrien, -ienne** (si:'rjɛ̃, -'rjɛn) adj,n Syrian.

système (si:'stɛm) nm 1 system. 2 network. 3 device. **systématique** adj systematic.

T

ta (ta) poss adj see **ton**.

tabac (ta'ba) nm tobacco. **tabac à priser** snuff.

table (tabl) nf 1 table. 2 tablet, slab. 3 list. **table roulante** trolley. **tableau, -aux** (ta'blo) nm 1 picture. 2 board. 3 list. **tableau d'annonces** notice board. **tableau noir** black-

teinter

board. **tablette** nf 1 shelf. 2 slab. **tablier** nm apron.
tabou (ta'bu:) adj,nm taboo.
tabouret (tabu:'rɛ) nm stool.
tacher (ta'ʃe:) vt 1 stain, spot. 2 impair. **tache** nf 1 stain, spot. 2 blot. **tache de rousseur** freckle.
tâcher (tɑ'ʃe:) vi try, strive. **tâche** nf task, job.
tacheté (taʃ'te:) adj flecked, mottled.
tact (takt) nm 1 sense of touch. 2 tact. **avoir du tact** be tactful.
tactique (tak'ti:k) adj tactical. nf tactics.
taffetas (taf'tɑ) nm taffeta.
taie (tɛ) nf **taie d'oreiller** pillowcase.
tailler (ta'je:) vt 1 cut. 2 prune. 3 trim. 4 sharpen. **taillade** nf 1 slash. 2 gash. **taille** nf 1 cutting. 2 cut. 3 stature. 4 waist. **taille-crayon** nm invar pencil-sharpener. **taille de cheveux** haircut. **tailleur** nm 1 tailor. 2 cutter. 3 (woman's) suit.
tain (tɛ̃) nm tinfoil.
taire* (tɛr) vt conceal, hide. **faire taire** silence. **se taire** vr be quiet, hold one's tongue.
talc (talk) nm talcum powder.
talent (ta'lɑ̃) nm 1 talent, gift. 2 ability.
talon (ta'lɔ̃) nm 1 heel. 2 stock. 3 remainder. 4 voucher.
talonner (talɔ'ne:) vt 1 follow closely. 2 spur on.
tambour (tɑ̃'bu:r) nm 1 drum. 2 barrel. **tambour de basque** tambourine.
tamis (ta'mi:) nm sieve.
tamiser (tami:'ze:) vt 1 sieve. 2 strain, filter.
tampon (tɑ̃'pɔ̃) nm 1 plug. 2 med wad. 3 stamp, mark. 4 buffer.
tamponner (tɑ̃pɔ'ne:) vt 1 plug. 2 dab. 3 collide with. **tamponnement** nm 1 plugging. 2 collision.
tancer (tɑ̃'se:) vt inf scold.
tandis que (tɑ̃'di: kə) conj 1 whereas. 2 whilst.
tangent (tɑ̃'ʒɑ̃) nf tangent.
Tanger (tɑ̃'ʒe:) nm Tangier.
tanguer (tɑ̃'ge:) vi naut pitch.
tanière (ta'njɛr) nf den, earth, hole.
tan-sad (tɑ̃'sad) nm mot pillion.
tant (tɑ̃) adv 1 so much. 2 so many. 3 as much. 4 as many. 5 so. **en tant que** in so far as. **tant mieux/pis!** so much the better/too bad! **tant s'en faut** far from it.
tante (tɑ̃t) nf aunt.
tantôt (tɑ̃'to) adv 1 soon. 2 a little while ago. **tantôt...tantôt** sometimes....sometimes.
taon (tɑ̃) nm horsefly.
tapage (ta'paʒ) nm din, racket. **tapageur,**

-euse (tapa'ʒœr, -'ʒœz) adj 1 rowdy, noisy. 2 showy.
taper (ta'pe:) vt 1 tap. 2 hit. 3 beat. 4 inf borrow. **ça tape** it's hot. **taper à la machine** type. **taper sur les nerfs** get on one's nerves. **tape** nf tap, pat.
se tapir (ta'pi:r) vr crouch.
tapis (ta'pi:) nm 1 carpet. 2 rug. 3 cover. **tapis de sol** groundsheet.
tapisser (tapi:'se:) vt paper (a room). **tapisserie** nf 1 tapestry. 2 wallpaper. **tapissier** nm upholsterer.
tapoter (tapɔ'te:) vt inf 1 pat. 2 strum.
taquin (ta'kɛ̃) adj teasing. **taquiner** vt tease. **taquinerie** nf teasing.
tard (tar) adv late.
tarder (tar'de:) vi delay. **tardif, -ive** (tar'di:f, -'di:v) adj 1 late. 2 backward.
tarif (ta'ri:f) nm 1 price-list. 2 tariff. 3 fare.
tarir (ta'ri:r) vt,vi dry up.
tarte (tart) nf 1 tart. 2 flan. **tartine** nf slice of bread and butter.
tas (tɑ) nm 1 pile. 2 inf group, crew. 3 inf lot.
tasse (tɑs) nf cup. **tasse à thé** teacup. **tassée** nf cupful.
tasser (tɑ'se:) vt 1 cram together. 2 press down. **se tasser** vr 1 settle. 2 huddle together.
tâter (tɑ'te:) vt 1 feel, handle. 2 sound. 3 try.
tâtonner (tɑtɔ'ne:) vi 1 grope. 2 feel one's way.
tâtons (tɑ'tɔ̃) **à tâtons** adv warily.
tatouer (ta'twe:) vt tattoo.
taudis (to'di:) nm slum.
taupe (top) nf zool mole.
taureau, -aux (tɔ'ro) nm 1 bull. 2 cap Taurus.
taux (to) nm rate, scale.
taverne (ta'vɛrn) nf 1 tavern. 2 restaurant.
taxer (tak'se:) vt 1 tax. 2 regulate the price. 3 accuse. **taxe** nf 1 fixed price. 2 charge. 3 tax.
taxi (tak'si:) nm taxi.
Tchécoslovaquie (tʃekɔslɔva'ki:) nf Czechoslovakia. **tchèque** (tʃɛk) adj,n Czech. nm Czech (language).
te, t' (tə) pron 2nd pers m,f s fam 1 you. 2 to you.
technique (tɛk'ni:k) adj technical. nf technique. **technicien** nm technician. **technologie** nf technology. **technologique** adj technological.
teck (tɛk) nm also **tek** teak.
teindre* (tɛ̃dr) vt 1 dye. 2 tinge. 3 colour.
teint (tɛ̃) nm 1 dye. 2 complexion.
teinter (tɛ̃'te:) vt tint. **teinte** nf 1 tint. 2 tinge. **teinture** nf 1 dyeing. 2 colour. 3 dye.

135

tel

tel, telle (tɛl) *adj* 1 such. 2 as. 3 like. **tel que** such as. *pron* 1 such a one. 2 many a.

télégramme (te:le:'gram) *nm* telegram.

télégraphier (te:le:gra'fje:) *vt* telegraph. **télégraphe** *nm* telegraph.

téléphérique (te:le:fe:'ri:k) *nm* cable car.

téléphoner (te:le:fɔ'ne:) *vt,vi* telephone. **téléphone** *nm* telephone. **téléphoniste** *nm,f* operator.

télésiège (te:le:'sjɛʒ) *nm* chair-lift.

téléski (te:le:'ski:) *nm* ski-lift.

téléviser (te:le:vi:'ze:) *vt* televise. **télévision** *nf* television.

tellement (tɛl'mã) *adv* 1 so. 2 in such a way.

téméraire (te:me:'rɛr) *adj* 1 rash. 2 reckless.

témoigner (te:mwa'ɲe:) *vi* give evidence. *vt* 1 testify. 2 show. 3 prove. **témoignage** *nm* 1 evidence. 2 *law* statement. 3 token, mark. **témoin** *nm* 1 witness. 2 *sport* baton.

tempe (tãp) *nf anat* temple.

tempérament (tãpɛra'mã) *nm* 1 temperament. 2 *med* constitution. 3 *comm* instalment.

tempérant (tãpɛ'rã) *adj* temperate.

température (tãpɛra'tyr) *nf* temperature.

tempérer (tãpe:'re:) *vt* moderate.

tempête (tã'pɛt) *nf* storm. **tempétueux, -euse** (tãpe:'tɥœ, -'tɥœz) *adj* stormy, tempestuous.

temple (tãpl) *nm* 1 *rel* temple. 2 church.

tempo (tɛ'po) *nm* tempo.

temporaire (tãpɔ'rɛr) *adj* 1 temporary. 2 provisional.

temporel, -elle (tãpɔ'rɛl) *adj* temporal.

temps (tã) *nm* 1 time. 2 age, period. 3 weather. 4 tense. 5 *mus* beat. **à temps** on time. **de temps en temps** now and again. **quel temps fait-il?** what's the weather like?

tenace (tə'nas) *adj* 1 tenacious. 2 tough. 3 stubborn. **ténacité** *nf* tenacity.

tenailles (tə'nɑj) *nf pl* pincers.

tendance (tã'dãs) *nf* tendency, trend.

tendon (tã'dɔ̃) *nm* 1 tendon. 2 sinew.

tendre[1] (tãdr) *adj* 1 tender. 2 affectionate. 3 delicate. **tendresse** *nf* 1 affection. 2 tenderness. 3 *pl* caress. **tendreté** *nf cul* tenderness.

tendre[2] (tãdr) *vt* 1 stretch. 2 strain. 3 tighten. 4 hold out. 5 set. **tendre à** 1 tend to. 2 aim at. **se tendre** *vr* become taut or strained. **tendu** *adj* 1 taut. 2 strained. 3 tense.

ténèbres (te:'nɛbr) *nf pl* darkness, gloom. **ténébreux, -euse** (te:ne:'brœ, -'brœz) *adj* 1 dark, gloomy. 2 sinister. 3 mysterious.

tenir (tə'ni:r) *vt* 1 hold. 2 keep. 3 run. 4 restrain. 5 occupy. *vi* 1 hold. 2 stick. 3 remain.

136

4 last. **tenir à** 1 value. 2 result from. **tenir bon** hold out. **tenir compte de** take into consideration. **tenir de** take after. **se tenir** *vr* 1 keep. 2 remain. 3 contain oneself. **se tenir à** 1 hold on to. 2 abide by. **se tenir bien** behave.

tennis (tɛ'ni:s) *nm* 1 tennis. 2 tennis court.

ténor (te:'nɔr) *nm* tenor.

tension (tã'sjɔ̃) *nf* 1 tension. 2 pressure. 3 voltage. **tension artérielle** blood pressure.

tente (tãt) *nf* 1 tent. 2 awning.

tenter (tã'te:) *vt* 1 tempt. 2 try. 3 attempt. **tentant** *adj* tempting. **tentation** *nf* temptation. **tentative** *nf* attempt.

tenture (tã'tyr) *nf* 1 tapestry. 2 wallpaper.

tenu (tə'ny) *v* see **tenir**. *adj* **bien tenu** neat, tidy. **être tenu à** be bound to. **mal tenu** 1 neglected. 2 untidy. **tenue** *nf* 1 holding. 2 bearing. 3 behaviour. 4 dress. **tenue de soirée** evening dress. **tenue des livres** bookkeeping.

ténu (te:'ny) *adj* 1 fine. 2 thin. 3 tenuous. 4 subtle.

tenure (tə'nyr) **tenure à bail** *nf* leasehold.

térébenthine (te:re:bã'ti:n) *nf* turpentine.

tergiverser (tɛrʒi:vɛr'se:) *vi* 1 beat about the bush. 2 hesitate.

terme (tɛrm) *nm* 1 limit. 2 term, expression. 3 quarter's rent. **avant terme** prematurely. **mettre terme à** put an end to.

terminer (tɛrmi:'ne:) *vt* end, terminate. **terminaison** *nf* ending.

terminologie (tɛrmi:nɔlɔ'ʒi:) *nf* terminology.

terminus (tɛrmi:'nys) *nm* terminus, terminal.

ternir (tɛr'ni:r) *vt* 1 tarnish. 2 dull. **terne** *adj* 1 dull. 2 lifeless.

terrain (tɛ'rɛ̃) *nm* 1 ground. 2 plot of land. **terrain de jeux** playing field.

terrasse (tɛ'ras) *nf* 1 terrace. 2 bank.

terre (tɛr) *nf* 1 earth. 2 world. 3 land, soil. 4 estate. **descendre à terre** go ashore. **par terre** on the ground. **basses terres** *nf pl* lowlands. **hautes terres** *nf pl* highlands.

terrestre (tɛ'rɛstr) *adj* 1 terrestrial. 2 worldly.

terreur (tɛ'rœr) *nf* terror, fear.

terrible (tɛ'ri:bl) *adj* 1 terrible, awful. 2 *inf* terrific.

terrier (tɛ'rje:) *nm* hole, burrow.

terrifier (tɛri:'fje:) *vt* terrify.

terrine (tɛ'ri:n) *nf* 1 earthenware dish. 2 potted meat.

territoire (tɛri:'twar) *nm* territory. **territorial, -aux** (tɛri:tɔ'rjal, -'rjo) *adj* territorial.

terroir (tɛr'war) *nm* soil.

terroriser (tɛrɔri:'ze:) *vt* terrorize. **terrorisme** *nm* terrorism. **terroriste** *nm,f* terrorist.

Térylène (te:ri:'lɛn) *nm Tdmk* Terylene.

tes (te:) *poss adj* see **ton.**

tesson (tɛ'sɔ̃) *nm* broken fragment (of glass, etc.).

testament (tɛsta'mã) *nm* **1** *law* will. **2** testament. **ancien Testament** Old Testament. **nouveau Testament** New Testament.

testicule (tɛstiː'kyl) *nm* testicle.

têtard (tɛ'tar) *nm* tadpole.

tête (tɛt) *nf* **1** head. **2** brains. **3** front. **4** top. **en tête** in front, ahead. **forte tête** strong-minded. **tenir tête à** resist. **tête-à-tête** *nm invar* private interview. **têtu** *adj* stubborn.

tétin (te:'tɛ̃) *nm* nipple, teat.

tétras (te:'trɑ) *nm zool* grouse.

texte (tɛkst) *nm* **1** text. **2** passage. **3** subject.

textile (tɛk'stiːl) *adj,nm* textile.

texture (tɛk'styr) *nf* texture.

thé (te:) *nm* tea. **théière** *nf* teapot.

théâtre (te:'ɑtr) *nm* **1** theatre. **2** stage. **3** drama. **théâtral, -aux** (te:ɑ'tral, -'tro) *adj* theatrical.

thème (tɛm) *nm* **1** theme, subject. **2** *educ* prose.

théologie (te:ɔlɔ'ʒi:) *nf* theology. **théologien** *nm* theologian. **théologique** *adj* theological.

théorème (te:ɔ'rɛm) *nm* theorem.

théorie (te:ɔ'ri:) *nf* theory. **théorique** *adj* theoretical.

théoriser (te:ɔri:'ze:) *vi* theorize.

thérapeutique (tɛrapœ'tiːk) *adj* therapeutic.

thérapie (te:ra'piː) *nf* therapy.

thermal, -aux (tɛr'mal, -'mo) *adj* thermal.

thermodynamique (tɛrmɔdiːna'miːk) *nf* thermodynamics.

thermomètre (tɛrmɔ'mɛtr) *nm* thermometer.

thermonucléaire (tɛrmonykle:'ɛr) *adj* thermonuclear.

thermoplongeur (tɛrmɔplɔ̃'ʒœr) *nm* immersion heater.

Thermos (tɛr'mɔs) *nm Tdmk* Thermos flask.

thermostat (tɛrmɔ'sta) *nm* thermostat.

thésauriser (te:zɔri:'ze:) *vt,vi* hoard.

thèse (tɛz) *nf* **1** proposition. **2** theory. **3** thesis.

thon (tɔ̃) *nm* tunny, tuna fish.

thym (tɛ̃) *nm* thyme.

tiare (tjar) *nf* tiara.

tic (tiːk) *nm* **1** *med* twitch. **2** mannerism.

ticket (tiː'kɛ) *nm* **1** ticket. **2** slip.

tiède (tjɛd) *adj* tepid, lukewarm.

tien, tienne (tjɛ̃, tjɛn) **le tien, la tienne** *poss pron 2nd pers s fam* **1** yours. **2** your own.

tiens[1] (tjɛ̃) *v* see **tenir.**

tiens[2] (tjɛ̃) *interj* **1** hello! **2** look!

tiers, tierce (tjɛr, tjɛrs) *adj* third. *nm* **1** third. **2** third person or party.

tige (tiːʒ) *nf* **1** stem, stalk. **2** *bot* trunk. **3** rod.

tigre (tiːgr) *nm* tiger. **tigré** *adj* **1** spotted. **2** striped.

tilleul (tiː'jœl) *nm* linden or lime tree.

timbale (tɛ̃'bal) *nf* **1** kettledrum. **2** *pl* timpani. **3** metal mug.

timbrer (tɛ̃'bre:) *vt* **1** stamp. **2** postmark. **timbre** *nm* **1** stamp. **2** bell.

timide (tiː'miːd) *adj* **1** timid. **2** shy.

tintamarre (tɛ̃ta'mar) *nm* din, racket.

tinter (tɛ̃'te:) *vt* ring, toll (a bell). *vi* **1** tinkle. **2** jingle. **3** clink.

tir (tiːr) *nm* **1** shooting. **2** firing. **tir à l'arc** archery.

tirelire (tiːr'liːr)·*nf* moneybox.

tirer (tiː're:) *vt* **1** pull. **2** draw (out). **3** drag. **4** take out. **5** shoot. *vi* **1** pull. **2** incline. **se tirer** *vr* extricate oneself. **tirage** *nm* **1** pulling. **2** draw (of a lottery). **3** *comm* circulation. **tire** *nf* pull. **tire-bouchon** *nm, pl* **tire-bouchons** corkscrew.

tiret (tiː'rɛ) *nm* **1** hyphen. **2** dash.

tiroir (tiː'rwar) *nm, pl* drawer. **tiroir-caisse** *nm, pl* **tiroirs-caisses** till.

tisane (tiː'zan) *nf* infusion.

tisonner (tiːzɔ'ne:) *vt* poke, stir. **tisonnier** *nm* poker.

tisser (tiː'se:) *vt* weave. **tissu** *nm* **1** material. **2** fabric. **3** *zool* tissue.

titre (tiːtr) *nm* **1** title. **2** diploma. **3** claim. **4** *comm* bond. **à titre de** by virtue of.

tituber (tiː'ty'be:) *vi* stagger, lurch.

toast (tɔst) *nm* toast (drink).

toi (twa) *pron 2nd pers m,f s fam* you. **toi-même** *pron 2nd pers m,f s fam* yourself.

toile (twal) *nf* **1** linen. **2** canvas. **3** oil painting. **4** *Th* curtain. **toile cirée** oilskin. **toile d'araignée** cobweb.

toilette (twa'lɛt) *nf* **1** washing, toilet. **2** dressing-table. **3** lavatory. **4** dress.

toise (twaz) *nf* fathom.

toison (twa'zɔ̃) *nf* fleece.

toit (twa) *nm* **1** roof. **2** *inf* home.

tôle (to:l) *mf* metal sheet.

tolérer (tɔle:'re:) *vt* tolerate. **tolérance** *nf* tolerance. **tolérant** *adj* tolerant.

tomate (tɔ'mat) *nf* tomato.

tombe

tombe (tɔ̃b) nf **1** tomb. **2** tombstone. **tombeau, -aux** (tɔ̃'bo) nm **1** tomb. **2** monument (over a grave).

tomber (tɔ̃'be:) vi (aux être) **1** fall. **2** hang. **3** subside. **laisser tomber** drop. **tomber juste 1** happen at the right moment. **2** guess right. **tombée** nf fall.

tome (tom) nm volume (of a book).

ton[1], **ta**, **tes** (tɔ̃, ta, te:) poss adj 2nd pers s fam your.

ton[2] (tɔ̃) nm **1** tone. **2** colour. **3** mus pitch. **4** mus key.

tondre (tɔ̃dr) vt shear, clip, mow. **tondeuse** nf **1** shears. **2** lawn-mower.

tonifier (tɔnɪ'fje:) vt invigorate, brace.

tonique (tɔ'niːk) nm tonic.

tonne (tɔn) nf ton.

tonneau, -aux (tɔ'no) nm barrel.

tonner (tɔ'ne:) vi thunder. **tonnerre** nm thunder.

topaze (tɔ'paz) nf topaz.

toper (tɔ'pe:) vi inf agree. **tope!** interj done!

torche (tɔrʃ) nf torch.

torchon (tɔr'ʃɔ̃) nm **1** duster. **2** dishcloth.

tordre (tɔrdr) vt **1** twist. **2** wring. **3** distort. **se tordre** vr writhe.

tornade (tɔr'nad) nf tornado.

torpille (tɔr'piːj) nf torpedo.

torréfier (tɔrre'fje:) vt **1** roast. **2** scorch.

torrent (tɔ'rã) nm torrent. **torrentiel, -elle** (tɔrã'sjɛl) adj torrential.

tors (tɔr) adj **1** twisted. **2** crooked.

torse (tɔrs) nm torso.

tort (tɔr) nm **1** wrong. **2** fault. **3** harm. **avoir tort** be wrong.

torticolis (tɔrtikɔ'li:) nm stiff neck.

tortiller (tɔrtɪ'je:) vt **1** twist. **2** twiddle. vi **1** wriggle. **2** quibble. **se tortiller** vr **1** writhe. **2** squirm.

tortu (tɔr'ty) adj crooked.

tortue (tɔr'ty) nf tortoise. **tortue de mer** turtle.

tortueux, -euse (tɔr'tɥœ, -'tɥœz) adj **1** winding. **2** underhand.

torturer (tɔrty're:) vt torture. **torture** nf torture.

Tory (tɔ'ri:) adj or nm, pl **Tories** Tory.

tôt (to) adv **1** soon. **2** early. **tôt ou tard** sooner or later.

total, -aux (tɔ'tal, -'to) adj **1** total, whole. **2** complete, absolute. nm total. **au total** on the whole. **totalitaire** adj totalitarian. **totalité** nf whole.

toucher (tu:'ʃe:) vt **1** touch. **2** hit. **3** cash. **4** receive. **5** move. **6** concern. **toucher à 1** be

near to. **2** affect. **3** meddle with. **se toucher** vr adjoin. ~nm touch, feel. **touche** nf **1** touch. **2** mus key.

touffu (tu:'fy) adj **1** bushy. **2** thick. **3** complicated.

toujours (tu:'ʒu:r) adv **1** always, ever, forever. **2** still. **3** all the same.

toupet (tu:'pɛ) nm **1** tuft (of hair). **2** forelock. **3** sl cheek, nerve.

toupie (tu:'piː) nf top (toy).

tour[1] (tu:r) nf tower.

tour[2] (tu:r) nm **1** turn. **2** revolution. **3** circumference. **4** lathe. **5** stroll. **6** trick. **à tour de rôle** in turn. **tour de main** knack.

tourbe (tu:rb) nf peat, turf.

tourbillon (tu:rbi:'jɔ̃) nm whirlwind.

tourelle (tu:'rɛl) nf turret.

tourisme (tu:'ri:sm) nm tourism. **touriste** nm,f tourist.

tourment (tu:r'mã) nm **1** torment. **2** anguish. **tourmenter** vt **1** torture. **2** harass. **3** pester.

tourmente (tu:r'mã) nf **1** storm. **2** upheaval.

tournedos (tu:rnə'do) nm fillet steak.

tourner (tu:r'ne:) vt **1** turn. **2** rotate. **3** dodge. **4** wind. vi **1** revolve. **2** result. **3** curdle. **tourner un film** shoot a film. **tournant** adj **1** turning. **2** winding. nm **1** bend, turning. **2** turning point. **tourne-disques** nm invar record-player. **tournée** nf **1** round, circuit. **2** tour. **tournevis** nm screwdriver.

tournesol (tu:rnə'sɔl) nm sunflower.

tourniquet (tu:rni:'kɛ) nm **1** turnstile. **2** tourniquet.

tournoi (tu:r'nwa) nm tournament.

tournoyer (tu:rnwa'je:) vi whirl.

tournure (tu:r'nyr) nf **1** shape, appearance. **2** form, figure.

tourte (tu:rt) nf **1** pie. **2** inf idiot.

tourterelle (tu:rtə'rɛl) nf turtle dove.

Toussaint (tu:'sɛ̃) nf All Saints' Day.

tousser (tu:'se:) vi cough.

tout (tu:) adj, pl **tous, toutes 1** all. **2** every. **3** any. **de toute importance** of utmost importance. **tous les deux** both. **toutes les fois que** whenever. ~pron **1** all. **2** anything. **3** everything. nm **1** whole. **2** total. adv **1** quite, completely. **2** while. **3** though. **tout à fait** completely. **tout au plus** at the very most. **tout fait** ready-made. **tout neuf** brand new. **toutefois** adv however, yet. **tout-puissant** adj omnipotent.

toux (tu:) nf cough.

toxique (tɔk'si:k) *adj* **1** toxic **2** poisonous *nm* poison

trac (trak) *nm sl* fright

tracas (tra'ka) *nm* **1** worry **2** bother

tracasser (traka'sje:) *vt* **1** worry **2** plague **3** annoy

tracer (tra'se:) *vt* **1** trace **2** outline **3** mark out **4** plot **trace** *nf* trace, trail, track

tract (trakt) *nm pol* leaflet

tracteur (trak'tœr) *nm* tractor

tradition (tradi:'sjɔ̃) *nf* **1** tradition **2** legend **tradition populaire** folklore **traditionnel, -elle** (tradi:sjɔ'nɛl) *adj* traditional

traduire° (tra'dɥi:r) *vt* **1** translate **2** interpret **traducteur, -trice** (tradyk'tœr, -'tri:s) *nm,f* translator **traduction** *nf* translation

trafiquer (trafi:'ke:) *vi* **trafiquer en** traffic or deal in

tragédie (traʒe:'di:) *nf* tragedy **tragique** *adj* tragic

trahir (tra'i:r) *vt* **1** betray **2** reveal **trahison** *nf* **1** betrayal **2** treachery

train (trɛ̃) *nm* **1** train **2** line **3** movement **4** pace **5** mood **être en train de** be in the middle of **mettre en train** start, set going **train de marchandises** goods train **train-train** *nm inf* routine

traîner (trɛ'ne:) *vt* **1** drag **2** trail **3** drawl **4** drag on or out *vi* **1** trail **2** linger **3** languish **se traîner** *vr* crawl **traînant** *adj* **1** dragging **2** listless **traîneau, -aux** (trɛ'no) *nm* sledge **traînée** *nf* **1** train **2** trail

traire° (trɛr) *vt* milk

trait (trɛ) *nm* **1** gulp **2** dart **3** flash **4** line **5** stroke **6** *anat* feature **d'un trait** at a stretch **trait d'union** hyphen

traiter (trɛ'te) *vt* **1** treat **2** call **3** discuss **4** handle *vi* negotiate **traité** *nm* **1** treatise **2** treaty **traitement** *nm* **1** treatment **2** salary

traître, traîtresse (trɛtr, trɛ'trɛs) *adj* treacherous *nm* traitor

trajet (tra'ʒɛ) *nm* **1** journey **2** passage

trame (tram) *nf* **1** thread **2** conspiracy

tramway (tram'wɛ) *nm* tram

trancher (trɑ̃'ʃe:) *vt* **1** cut **2** break off **3** solve *vi* contrast **tranche** *nf* **1** slice, portion **2** slab **3** edge. **tranchée** *nf* trench

tranquille (trɑ̃'ki:l) *adj* **1** tranquil **2** calm **3** peaceful **tranquillisant** *nm* tranquillizer **tranquillité** *nf* **1** quiet. **2** calm **3** stillness

transaction (trɑ̃zak'sjɔ̃) *nf* **1** transaction **2** compromise

transatlantique (trɑ̃zatlɑ̃'ti:k) *adj* transatlantic *nm* **1** liner **2** deckchair

transcrire° (trɑ̃'skri:r) *vt* transcribe

transe (trɑ̃s) *nf* **1** trance **2** fear

transférer (trɑ̃sfe:'re:) *vt* **1** transfer **2** remove **3** convey **transfert** *nm* transfer

transformer (trɑ̃sfɔr'me:) *vt* **1** transform **2** convert **transformateur** *nm* transformer

transfuge (trɑ̃s'fyʒ) *nm* deserter

transfuser (trɑ̃sfy'ze:) *vt* transfuse **transfusion** *nf* transfusion

transiger (trɑ̃zi:'ʒe:) *vi* come to a compromise

transir (trɑ̃'si:r) *vt* **1** chill **2** seize (with fear)

transistor (trɑ̃zi:'stɔr) *nm* transistor

transition (trɑ̃zi:'sjɔ̃) *nf* transition

transmettre° (trɑ̃s'mɛtr) *vt* **1** transmit **2** *law* transfer **3** hand down

transparent (trɑ̃spa'rɑ̃) *adj* transparent

transpirer (trɑ̃spi:'re:) *vi* perspire **transpiration** *nf* perspiration

transplanter (trɑ̃splɑ̃'te:) *vt* transplant

transport (trɑ̃'spɔr) *nm* **1** transport, carriage **2** outburst

transporter (trɑ̃spɔr'te:) *vt* **1** transport, convey **2** carry away, delight

transposer (trɑ̃spo'ze:) *vt* transpose

transvaser (trɑ̃svo'ze:) *vt* decant

trapèze (tra'pɛz) *nm* trapeze

trappe (trap) *nf* **1** pitfall **2** trapdoor

trapu (tra'py) *adj* **1** stocky **2** squat

traquer (tra'ke:) *vt* **1** surround **2** track down **traquenard** *nm* trap

trauma (tro'ma) *nm* trauma **traumatique** *adj* traumatic

travail, -aux (tra'vaj, -'vo) *nm* work **travail à l'aiguille** needlework

travailler (trava'je:) *vt* **1** work **2** work on *vi* **1** work, toil **2** ferment **travaillé** *adj* **1** elaborate **2** wrought **travailleur, -euse** (trava'jœr, -'jœz) *nm* workman *adj* industrious **travailliste** *nm,f* member of the Labour Party *adj pol* Labour

travers (tra'vɛr) *nm* **1** breadth **2** fault, defect **à travers** across **au travers de** across **de travers** amiss, the wrong way

traverser (travɛr'se:) *vt* **1** cross **2** go through **traverse** *nf* **1** short cut **2** *tech* sleeper **3** hitch **traversée** *nf* passage, crossing

traversin (travɛr'sɛ̃) *nm* bolster

travestir (travɛ'sti:r) *vt* disguise, dress up **travesti** *adj* disguised *nm* fancy dress

trébucher (tre:by'ʃe:) *vi* **1** stumble **2** trip **faire trébucher** trip up

trèfle (trɛfl) nm 1 clover. 2 game club.

treillis (trɛ'jiː) nm trellis, lattice.

treize (trɛz) adj,nm thirteen. **treizième** adj thirteenth.

trembler (trɑ̃'ble:) vi 1 tremble. 2 flicker. 3 shake. 4 quake. **tremblement** nm 1 trembling. 2 tremor. **tremblement de terre** earthquake.

trémière (tre:'mjɛr) **rose trémière** nf hollyhock.

se trémousser (tre:muːˈse:) vr 1 fidget. 2 flutter.

tremper (trɑ̃'pe:) vt,vi soak, steep. vt 1 drench. 2 dip. 3 mix.

tremplin (trɑ̃'plɛ̃) nm 1 springboard. 2 diving board.

trente (trɑ̃t) adj,nm thirty. **trentième** adj thirtieth.

trépas (tre:'pɑ) nm death.

trépider (tre:piːˈde:) vi vibrate.

trépied (tre:'pje:) nm tripod.

trépigner (tre:piːˈɲe:) vi stamp, prance.

très (trɛ) adv 1 very. 2 most. 3 very much.

trésor (tre:'zɔr) nm 1 treasure. 2 pl riches. 3 treasury. **trésorerie** (tre:zɔrˈriː) nf treasury. **trésorier, -ière** (tre:zɔˈrje:, -ˈrjɛr) nm,f treasurer.

tressaillir* (trɛsaˈjiːr) vi 1 start, jump. 2 quiver. 3 shudder. **tressaillir de douleur** wince. **tressaillement** nm 1 start, jump. 2 shudder. 3 wince.

tresser (trɛ'se:) vt 1 plait. 2 weave. **tresse** nf plait.

tréteau, -aux (tre:'to) nm 1 trestle. 2 support. 3 stage.

treuil (trœj) nm 1 winch. 2 windlass.

trêve (trɛv) nf truce.

tri (triː) nm sorting. **triage** nm sorting.

triangle (triːˈɑ̃gl) nm triangle. **triangulaire** adj triangular.

tribord (triːˈbɔr) nm starboard.

tribu (triːˈby) nf tribe.

tribunal, -aux (triːbyˈnal, -ˈno) nm 1 tribunal. 2 law court. **tribune** nf 1 platform. 2 grandstand. 3 forum.

tribut (triːˈby) nm tribute.

tributaire (triːbyˈtɛr) adj,nm tributary.

tricher (triːˈʃe:) vt,vi 1 cheat. 2 trick.

tricolore (triːkɔˈlɔr) nm inf French national flag, tricolour.

tricot (triːˈko) nm 1 knitting. 2 jersey, jumper.

tricoter (triːkɔˈte:) vi knit.

tricycle (triːˈsiːkl) nm tricycle.

trier (triːˈe:) vt sort. **trier à la main** hand-pick.

trille (triː'j) nm mus trill.

trimestre (triːˈmɛstr) nm 1 educ term. 2 quarter, three months. **trimestriel, -elle** (triː-mɛstriːˈɛl) adj quarterly.

tringle (trɛ̃gl) nf rod, bar.

trinquer (trɛ̃'ke:) vi clink glasses.

trio (triːˈo) nm trio.

triompher (triːɔ̃ˈfe:) vi 1 triumph. 2 overcome. **triomphant** adj triumphant. **triomphe** nm triumph.

tripaille (triːˈpɑj) nf inf offal.

tripe (triːp) nf 1 tripe. 2 sl guts.

tripler (triːˈple:) vt,vi triple, treble. **triple** adj triple, treble. **triplés** nm triplets.

tripoter (triːpɔˈte:) vt inf 1 meddle with. 2 deal dishonestly with. vi 1 mess about. 2 tamper with.

triste (triːst) adj 1 sad. 2 melancholy. 3 dismal. 4 unfortunate. **tristesse** nf 1 sadness. 2 gloom. 3 bleakness.

triton (triːˈtɔ̃) nm newt.

trivial (triːˈvjal) adj 1 trite. 2 trivial. 3 vulgar. 4 obscene. **trivialité** nf 1 obscenity. 2 triviality.

troc (trɔk) nm 1 swop. 2 barter.

trognon (trɔˈɲɔ̃) nm 1 core (of an apple, etc.). 2 stump.

trois (trwa) adj,nm three. **troisième** adj third. **trois-quarts** nm invar three-quarters.

trombe (trɔ̃b) nf 1 waterspout. 2 whirlwind.

trombone (trɔ̃'bɔn) nm 1 trombone. 2 paper-clip.

tromper (trɔ̃'pe:) vt 1 deceive. 2 cheat. 3 mislead. 4 baffle. **se tromper** vr be mistaken, make a mistake. **tromperie** nf deceit.

trompette (trɔ̃'pɛt) nf trumpet.

tronc (trɔ̃) nm bot trunk.

tronçon (trɔ̃'sɔ̃) nm 1 fragment. 2 stump, stub.

trône (tron) nm throne.

tronquer (trɔ̃'ke:) vt cut up, mutilate.

trop (tro) adv 1 too. 2 too much. nm too much or many. **de trop** too much or many. **trop-plein** nm, pl **trop-pleins** overflow.

trophée (trɔ'fe:) nm trophy.

tropique (trɔ'piːk) nm tropic. adj tropical. **tropical, -aux** (trɔpiːˈkal, -ˈko) adj tropical.

troquer (trɔ'ke:) vt 1 swop. 2 barter.

trot (tro) nm trot.

trotter (trɔ'te:) vi trot.

trottoir (trɔ'twar) nm pavement.

trou (truː) nm 1 hole. 2 inf pothole. **trou de serrure** keyhole. **trou d'homme** manhole.

trouble [1] (truːbl) adj 1 cloudy. 2 confused.

trouble [2] (truːbl) nm 1 disorder. 2 agitation.

troubler (tru:'ble:) *vt* **1** disturb. **2** confuse. **3** agitate. **4** make muddy. **se troubler** *vr* **1** become cloudy or overcast. **2** get confused.

trouer (tru:'e:) *vt* make a hole in, pierce. **trouée** *nf* **1** gap. **2** *mil* breakthrough.

troupe (tru:p) *nf* **1** troop, gang. **2** troupe. **3** herd. **4** *pl* troops. **troupeau, -aux** *nm* herd, flock.

trousser (tru:'se:) *vt* **1** turn up. **2** *inf* get through. **3** *inf* turn out. **trousse** *nf* **1** bundle. **2** kit. **trousseau, -aux** *nm* **1** bunch. **2** bride's outfit.

trouver (tru:'ve:) *vt* **1** find. **2** discover. **3** think. **se trouver** *vr* **1** be. **2** feel. **3** happen. **trouvaille** *nf* **1** find. **2** discovery. **3** windfall.

truc (tryk) *nm* *inf* **1** thing, gadget. **2** knack.

truelle (try'ɛl) *nf* trowel.

truffe (tryf) *nf* truffle.

truie (trɥi:) *nf* sow.

truite (trɥi:t) *nf* trout.

trumeau, -aux (try'mo) *nm* *arch* pier.

truquer (try'ke:) *vt* fake.

tsar (tsar) *nm* tsar.

tu[1] (tu) *pron 2nd pers m,f s fam* you.

tu[2] (ty) *v* see **taire.**

tuba (ty'ba) *nm* tuba.

tube (tyb) *nm* **1** tube. **2** pipe.

tuberculose (tybɛrky'loz) *nf* tuberculosis.

tuer (tɥe:) *vt* **1** kill. **2** slaughter. **à tue-tête** at the top of one's voice. **tuerie** *nf* slaughter.

tuile (tɥi:l) *nf* **1** tile. **2** *inf* bother, trouble.

tulipe (ty'li:p) *nf* tulip.

tumeur (ty'mœr) *nf* tumour, growth.

tumulte (ty'mylt) *nm* tumult, uproar. **tumultueux, -euse** (tymyl'tɥœ, -'tɥœz) *adj* noisy, riotous.

tunique (ty'ni:k) *nf* tunic.

Tunisie (tyni:'zi:) *nf* Tunisia. **tunisien, -ienne** (tyni:'zjɛ̃, -'zjɛn) *adj,n* Tunisian.

tunnel (ty'nɛl) *nm* tunnel.

turbulent (tyrby'lɑ̃) *adj* **1** turbulent, restless. **2** unruly.

turf (tyrf) *nm* **1** racecourse. **2** racing.

Turquie (tyr'ki:) *nf* Turkey. **turc, turque** (tyrk) *adj* Turkish. *nm,f* Turk. *nm* Turkish (language).

turquoise (tyr'kwaz) *nf* turquoise. *nm* turquoise (colour). *adj invar* turquoise.

tutelle (ty'tɛl) *nf* **1** guardianship. **2** protection.

tuteur, -trice (ty'tœr, -'tri:s) *nm,f* guardian. *nm* prop.

tutoyer (tytwa'je:) *vt* address as **tu,** be on familiar terms with.

tuyau, -aux (tɥi:'jo) *nm* **1** pipe, hose. **2** *inf* tip, hint.

tympan (tɛ̃'pɑ̃) *nm* eardrum.

type (ti:p) *nm* **1** type, pattern. **2** *inf* chap, bloke.

typhoïde (ti:fɔ'i:d) *adj,nf* typhoid.

typhon (ti:'fɔ̃) *nm* typhoon.

typique (ti:'pi:k) *adj* typical.

tyran (ti:'rɑ̃) *nm* tyrant. **tyrannie** *nf* tyranny. **tyrannique** *adj* tyrannical.

U

ulcérer (ylse:'re:) *vt* **1** ulcerate. **2** wound, embitter. **ulcère** *nm* ulcer.

ultérieur (ylte:'rjœr) *adj* **1** ulterior. **2** subsequent.

ultimatum (yltima'tɔm) *nm* ultimatum.

ultime (yl'ti:m) *adj* ultimate, final.

ultrasonique (yltrasɔ'ni:k) *adj* supersonic.

ultra-violet, -ette (yltravjɔle, -'lɛt) *adj, pl* **ultra-violets, -ettes** ultraviolet.

un, une (œ̃, yn) *indef art* a, an. *indef pron* one. *nm,f* one. **les uns...les autres** some...others. ~*adj* **1** one. **2** first. **unième** *adj* first.

unanime (yna'ni:m) *adj* unanimous.

uni (y'ni:) *adj* **1** united. **2** smooth. **3** plain.

unifier (yni:'fje:) *vt* **1** unify. **2** amalgamate. **3** standardize.

uniforme (yni:'fɔrm) *adj* uniform, unvarying. *nm* uniform. **uniformité** *nf* uniformity.

union (y'njɔ̃) *nf* **1** union. **2** society, association. **3** harmony, agreement.

unique (y'ni:k) *adj* **1** sole, only. **2** unique.

unir (y'ni:r) *vt* unite, join. **unité** *nf* **1** unity. **2** unit.

unisson (yni:'sɔ̃) *nf* unison.

univers (yni:'vɛr) *nm* universe. **universel, -elle** (yni:vɛr'sɛl) *adj* universal, worldwide.

université (yni:vɛrsi:'te:) *nf* university.

urbain (yr'bɛ̃) *adj* urban, town. **urbanisme** *nm* town-planning.

urgent (yr'ʒɑ̃) *adj* urgent, pressing. **urgence** *nf* **1** urgency. **2** emergency.

uriner (yri:'ne:) *vi* urinate. **urine** *nf* urine. **urinoir** *nm* urinal.

urne (yrn) *nf* **1** urn. **2** ballot-box.

user (y'ze:) *vt* **1** use, consume. **2** wear out. **user de** make use of. **s'user** *vr* wear away. **usage** *nm* **1** use. **2** custom. **3** practice. **4** wear. **5** breeding, manners. **usagé** *adj* second-hand. **usé** *adj* **1** worn. **2** threadbare. **3** hackneyed. **usité** *adj* current, in use.

usine (yˈziːn) *nf* factory, works.
ustensile (ytɑˈsiːl) *nm* utensil, implement.
usuel, -elle (yˈzɥɛl) *adj* 1 usual, customary. 2 current.
usurper (yzyrˈpeː) *vt* usurp. **usurpateur, -trice** (yzyrpaˈtœr, -ˈtriːs) *n* usurper.
utérus (yteˈrys) *nm* uterus.
utiliser (ytiːliːˈzeː) *vt* use, make use of. **utile** *adj* 1 useful, handy. 2 effective. 3 necessary. **utilité** *nf* use, utility.

V

va (va) *v see* **aller.**
vacance (vaˈkɑ̃s) *nf* 1 vacancy. 2 *pl* holidays. **vacant** *adj* vacant, empty.
vacarme (vaˈkarm) *nm* din, racket.
vaccin (vakˈsɛ̃) *nm* vaccine.
vacciner (vaksiːˈneː) *vt* vaccinate, inoculate. **vaccination** *nf* vaccination.
vache (vaʃ) *nf* 1 cow. 2 *sl* bitch. **vachement** *adv sl* terribly, very.
vaciller (vasiːˈjeː) *vi* 1 waver. 2 flicker. 3 wobble. **vacillant** *adj* 1 wobbly. 2 undecided.
va-et-vient *nm invar* 1 coming and going. 2 shuttle.
vagabond (vagaˈbɔ̃) *adj* wandering. *nm* tramp, vagrant.
vagabonder (vagabɔ̃ˈdeː) *vi* 1 roam. 2 wander.
vagin (vaˈʒɛ̃) *nm* vagina.
vague [1] (vag) *nf* 1 wave. 2 generation, age-group. **vague de chaleur** heatwave.
vague [2] (vag) *adj* vague, hazy. *nm* vagueness.
vague [3] (vag) *adj* vacant, empty. *nm* empty space.
vaillant (vaˈjɑ̃) *adj* valiant, brave.
vain (vɛ̃) *adj* 1 vain, conceited. 2 empty, futile.
vaincre° (vɛ̃kr) *vt* 1 conquer. 2 beat, defeat. **vainqueur** *nm* 1 conqueror. 2 winner. *adj* victorious.
vaincu (vɛ̃ˈky) *v see* **vaincre.**
vainquant (vɛ̃ˈkɑ̃) *v see* **vaincre.**
vais (vɛ) *v see* **aller.**
vaisseau, -aux (vɛˈso) *nm* 1 ship. 2 container.
vaisselle (vɛˈsɛl) *nf* crockery, plates and dishes. **faire la vaisselle** do the washing up.
val (val) *nm* valley.
valable (vaˈlabl) *adj* valid.
valet (vaˈlɛ) *nm* 1 valet, servant. 2 *game* jack.
valeur (vaˈlœr) *nf* 1 value, worth. 2 courage. 3 *comm* assets.
valide (vaˈliːd) *adj* valid.

valise (vaˈliːz) *nf* suitcase.
vallée (vaˈle:) *nf* valley.
valoir° (valˈwar) *vt,vi* 1 be worth. 2 deserve. 3 yield. **faire valoir** 1 make the most of. 2 put forward. **il vaut mieux** it is better.
valse (vals) *nf* waltz.
vandale (vɑ̃ˈdal) *nm* vandal. **vandalisme** *nm* vandalism.
vanille (vaˈniːj) *nf* vanilla.
vanité (vaniːˈte:) *nf* 1 vanity, pride. 2 conceit. **vaniteux, -euse** (vaniːˈtœ, -ˈtœz) *adj* 1 vain. 2 conceited.
vantail, -aux (vɑ̃taj, -ˈto) *nm* leaf (of a table, etc.).
vanter (vɑ̃ˈte:) *vt* praise. **se vanter** *vr* boast. **se vanter de** pride oneself on.
vanterie (vɑ̃ˈtriː) *nf* 1 boasting. 2 boast.
vapeur (vaˈpœr) *nf* 1 vapour. 2 steam. *nm* steamer.
varicelle (variːˈsɛl) *nf* chickenpox.
varier (vaˈrje:) *vt,vi* vary. **variation** *nf* variation. **varié** *adj* 1 varied. 2 miscellaneous. **variété** *nf* variety.
variole (vaˈrjɔl) *nf* smallpox.
vase [1] (vaz) *nm* 1 vase. 2 vessel.
vase [2] (vaz) *nf* mud, slime.
vaste (vast) *adj* 1 vast, huge. 2 wide, spacious.
vau (vo) **à vau l'eau** *adv* 1 downstream. 2 to rack and ruin.
vaudou (voˈduː) *nm* voodoo.
vaudra (voːˈdra) *v see* **valoir.**
vaurien, -ienne (voˈrjɛ̃, -ˈrjɛn) *nm,f inf* scoundrel.
vautour (voˈtuːr) *nm* vulture.
vaux (vo:) *v see* **valoir.**
veau, veaux (vo) *nm* 1 *zool* calf. 2 veal. 3 calfskin.
vécu (ve:ˈky) *v see* **vivre.**
vedette (vɔˈdɛt) *nf* 1 motor boat. 2 *Th* star. **vedette de l'écran** filmstar.
végétal, -aux (ve:ʒɛˈtal, -ˈto) *adj* plant, vegetable. *nm* plant.
végétarien, -enne (ve:ʒɛtaˈrjɛ̃, -ˈrjɛn) *adj,n* vegetarian.
végétation (ve:zɛtaˈsjɔ̃) *nf* 1 vegetation. 2 *pl inf* adenoids.
véhément (ve:ɛˈmɑ̃) *adj* vehement, passionate, eager.
véhicule (ve:iːˈkyl) *nm* vehicle.
veiller (vɛˈje:) *vi* 1 stay up. 2 watch. *vt* look after. **veiller à** see to. **veille** *nf* 1 wakefulness. 2 watch. 3 eve, day before. **veillée** *nf* 1 vigil. 2 party.

veine (vɛn) nf 1 vein. 2 ınf luck.
vélo (ve:'lo:) nm ınf bike.
vélocité (ve:lɔsı:'te:) nf speed, velocıty.
velours (və'lu:r) nm 1 velvet. 2 corduroy.
velu (və'ly) adj haıry.
venaison (vənɛ'zɔ̃) nf venıson.
vendange (vã'dãʒ) nf 1 grape harvest. 2 vın-
tage.
vendre (vãdr) vt 1 sell. 2 betray. **vendeur,**
-euse (vã'dœr, -'dœz) nm,f 1 seller. 2 shop
assıstant.
vendredi (vãdrə'di:) nm Frıday. **vendredi saint**
Good Frıday.
vénéneux, -euse (ve:ne:'nœ, -'nœz) adj
poisonous.
vénérer (ve:ne:'re:) vt 1 venerate. 2 worshıp.
vénérien, -ienne (ve:ne:'rjɛ̃, -'rjɛn) adj venereal.
venger (vã'ʒe:) vt avenge. **se venger** vr have
one's revenge. **vengeance** nf revenge.
venin (və'nɛ̃) nm 1 poıson. 2 spite. **venimeux,**
-euse (vənı:'mœ, -'mœz) adj poısonous.
venir (və'ni:r) vı (aux être) 1 come. 2 result. 3
occur. 4 grow. **venir de** have ʝust.
vent (vã) nm 1 wınd, breeze. 2 scent. **il fait du**
vent it ıs wındy.
vente (vɛ̃t) nf sale.
ventiler (vɛ̃tı:'le:) vt ventilate, aır. **ventilateur**
nm 1 ventilator. 2 fan.
ventre (vɛ̃tr) nm 1 abdomen. 2 stomach, belly.
3 paunch.
ventriloque (vãtrı:'lɔk) nm ventriloquıst.
venu (və'ny) v see **venir.**
venue (və'ny) nf 1 comıng, arrıval. 2 advent. 3
growth.
Vénus (ve:'nys) nf Venus.
ver (vɛr) nm 1 worm. 2 maggot. **ver à soie**
silkworm.
véranda (verã'da) nf veranda.
verbe (vɛrb) nm verb. **verbal, -aux** (vɛr'bal,
-'bo) adj verbal.
verdir (vɛr'di:r) vı turn green. vt make green.
verdeur nf 1 greenness. 2 tartness, sourness.
3 heartıness. **verdure** nf 1 greenness. 2
greenery.
verge (vɛrʒ) nf 1 rod, cane. 2 penıs.
verger (vɛr'ʒe:) nm orchard.
verglas (vɛr'gla) nm black ıce.
vergogne (vɛr'gɔɲ) nf shame.
véridique (ve:rı:'di:k) adj truthful.
vérifier (ve:rı:'fje) vt 1 verify, check. 2 overhaul.
3 audit.
vérité (ve:rı:'te:) nf truth. **véritable** adj 1 true.
2 real, genuıne.

vermeil, -eille (vɛr'mɛj) adj brıght red, rosy.
vermine (vɛr'mi:n) nf vermın.
vermout (vɛr'mu:t) nm vermouth.
vernir (vɛr'ni:r) vt 1 varnısh. 2 polish. **vernis**
nm 1 varnısh. 2 polish. 3 glaze.
vérole (ve:'rɔl) nf **petite vérole** smallpox.
verrai (vɛre) v see **voir.**
verre (vɛr) nm glass. **verre (de lunettes)** lens.
verrou, -oux (vɛ'ru:) nm bolt, bar.
verrouiller (vɛru:'je:) vt bolt, fasten.
verrue (vɛ'ru:) nf wart.
vers[1] (vɛr) nm 1 line. 2 pl poetry, verse.
vers[2] (vɛr) prep 1 towards, to. 2 about.
versant (vɛr'sã) nm 1 slope. 2 sıde, bank.
Verseau (vɛr'so) nm Aquarıus.
verser (vɛr'se:) vt 1 pour. 2 shed. 3 pay ın. 4
overturn. **à verse** ın torrents. **versé** adj
experıenced. **versement** nm 1 payment. 2
comm ınstalment.
version (vɛr'sjɔ̃) nf 1 version, account. 2 educ
translation, unseen.
verso (vɛr'so) nm back, reverse sıde.
vert (vɛr) adj 1 green. 2 unrıpe. 3 sharp, stern. 4
ınf spıcy. nm green (colour).
vertébré (vɛrte:'bre:) adj,nm vertebrate.
vertical, -aux (vɛrtı:'kal, -'ko) adj vertıcal,
uprıght.
vertige (vɛr'ti:ʒ) nm dizzıness. **avoir le vertige**
feel dizzy. **vertigineux, -euse** (vɛrtı:ʒı:'nœ,
-'nœz) adj dizzy, gıddy.
vertu (vɛr'ty) nf 1 vırtue. 2 chastıty. 3 quality,
property. **vertueux, -euse** (vɛr'tɥœ, -'tɥœz)
adj vırtuous.
verve (vɛrv) nf zest, vıgour, go.
vessie (vɛ'si:) nf bladder.
veste (vɛst) nf jacket. **veston** nm ʝacket.
vestiaire (vɛ'stjɛr) nm 1 cloakroom. 2 changıng
room.
vestibule (vɛstı:'byl) nm 1 hall. 2 lobby.
vestige (vɛ'sti:ʒ) nm 1 mark, trace. 2 remnant,
remaıns.
vêtement (vɛt'mã) nm 1 garment. 2 pl clothıng.
3 pl clothes.
vétéran (ve:tɛ'rã) nm veteran.
vétérinaire (ve:te:rı:'nɛr) nm veterınary surgeon. adj veterınary.
vêtir (vɛ'ti:r) vt 1 clothe. 2 dress.
veto (ve:'to) nm veto. **mettre son veto à** veto.
vêtu (vɛ'ty) v see **vêtir.**
vétusté (ve:ty'ste:) nf decay.
veuf, veuve (vœf, vœv) nm,f wıdower, wıdow.
adj wıdowed.
veule (vœl) adj 1 weak, soft. 2 flabby. 3 drab.

143

veulent (vœl) v see **vouloir.**
veux (vœ) v see **vouloir.**
vexer (vɛk'se:) vt **1** vex, annoy. **2** harass.
viable[1] (vjabl) adj strong enough to live.
viable[2] (vjabl) adj fit for traffic.
viaduc (vja'dyk) nm viaduct.
viager, -ère (vja'ʒe:, -'ʒɛr) adj for life.
viande (vjɑ̃d) nf meat.
vibrer (vi:'bre:) vi vibrate. **vibrant** adj **1** vibrating. **2** resonant. **vibration** nf **1** vibration. **2** resonance.
vicaire (vi:'kɛr) nm curate.
vice (vi:s) nm **1** vice, corruption. **2** fault, flaw. **vice-président** nm, pl **vice-présidents 1** vice-president. **2** vice-chairman.
vicié (vi:'sje:) adj corrupt.
vicieux, -euse (vi:'sjœ, -'sjœz) adj **1** vicious. **2** faulty. **3** perverted.
vicomte, -esse (vi:'kɔ̃t, -kɔ̃'tɛs) nm,f viscount, viscountess.
victime (vi:k'ti:m) nf victim.
victoire (vi:k'twar) nf victory. **victorieux, -euse** (vi:ktɔ'rjœ, -'rjœz) adj victorious.
vidange (vi:'dɑ̃ʒ) nf **1** emptying. **2** draining. **3** mot oil change.
vider (vi:'de:) vt **1** empty. **2** clear out. **3** drain. **4** settle (an argument). **vide** adj **1** empty. **2** vacant. nm **1** gap. **2** vacuum.
vie (vi:) nf **1** life. **2** existence. **3** living, livelihood.
vieillir (vjɛ'ji:r) vi grow old, age. **vieillard** nm old man. **vieillesse** nf old age.
viens (vjɛ̃) v see **venir.**
vierge (vjɛrʒ) nf **1** virgin. **2** cap Virgo. adj **1** virgin. **2** pure. **3** blank.
Viet-nam (vjɛt'nam) nm Vietnam. **vietnamien, -ienne** (vjɛtna'mjɛ̃, -'mjɛn) adj,n Vietnamese.
vieux, vieil, vieille (vjœ, vjɛj, vjɛj) adj old. **vieux** nm old man. **vieille** nf old woman.
vif, vive (vi:f, vi:v) adj **1** alive. **2** lively, vivacious. **3** brisk. **4** sharp, keen. **5** quick-tempered. **6** vivid. **7** bright. nm quick, core.
vigile (vi:'ʒi:l) nf vigil.
vigne (viɲ) nf **1** vine. **2** vineyard. **vigneron** nm vine-grower. **vignoble** nm vineyard.
vignette (vi:ɲɛt) nf **1** car tax label. **2** cigarette card.
vigoureux, -euse (vi:gu:'rœ, -'rœz) adj vigorous, strong.
vigueur (vi:'gœr) nf **1** vigour, strength. **2** effect, force.
vil (vi:l) adj **1** base, low, vile. **2** cheap.

vilain (vi:'lɛ̃) adj **1** unpleasant, nasty. **2** mean. **3** ugly. nm villain.
villa (vi:'la) nf villa, house.
village (vi:'laʒ) nm village.
ville (vi:l) nf town. **grande ville** city. **ville d'eau** spa.
villégiateur (vi:le:ʒja'tœr) nm holiday-maker.
vin (vɛ̃) nm wine. **vin du Rhin** hock. **vin ordinaire** table wine.
vinaigre (vi:'nɛgr) nm vinegar. **vinaigrette** nf French dressing.
vindicatif, -ive (vɛ̃di:ka'ti:f, -'ti:v) adj spiteful.
vingt (vɛ̃) adj,nm twenty. **vingtaine** nf about twenty, a score. **vingtième** adj twentieth.
viol (vjɔl) nm rape.
violence (vjɔ'lɑ̃s) nf violence, force. **violent** adj **1** violent. **2** intense. **3** strong.
violer (vjœ'le:) vt **1** violate, break. **2** rape.
violet, -ette (vjɔ'lɛ, -'lɛt) adj,nm violet (colour). nf bot violet.
violon (vjɔ'lɔ̃) nm **1** violin. **2** sl (prison) cell. **violoncelle** nm cello.
vipère (vi:'pɛr) nf adder, viper.
virage (vi:'raʒ) nm **1** turning. **2** sharp turn, bend.
virer (vi:'re:) vi turn. vt comm transfer.
virgule (vi:r'gyl) nf comma.
viril (vi:'ri:l) adj virile, manly. **virilité** nf **1** manliness. **2** manhood.
virtuel, -elle (vi:r'tɥɛl) adj virtual.
virus (vi:'rys) nm virus.
vis[1] (vi:) v see **vivre.**
vis[2] (vi:s) nf screw.
visa (vi:'za) nm **1** visa. **2** signature.
visage (vi:'zaʒ) nm **1** face. **2** countenance.
vis-à-vis (vi:za'vi:) adv opposite. **vis-à-vis de 1** opposite. **2** with regard to.
viser (vi:'ze:) vt **1** aim. **2** relate to. **3** allude to. **visée** nf **1** aim. **2** design, plan.
visible (vi:'zi:bl) adj **1** visible. **2** obvious, evident. **visibilité** nf visibility.
visière (vi:'zjɛr) nf **1** visor. **2** peak (of a cap).
vision (vi:'zjɔ̃) nf **1** vision, sight. **2** eyesight. **3** apparition, phantom.
visiter (vi:zi:'te:) vt **1** visit. **2** examine. **3** search. **visite** nf **1** visit. **2** inspection. **3** search. **rendre visite à** call on. **visiteur, -euse** (vi:zi:'tœr, -'tœz) nm,f visitor.
vison (vi:'zɔ̃) nm mink.
visser (vi:'se:) vt screw in or up.
visuel, -elle (vi:'zɥɛl) adj visual.
vital, -aux (vi:'tal, -'to) adj vital. **vitalité** nf vitality.

vitamine (vɪ:taˈmɪ:n) *nf* vitamin.
vite (vɪːt) *adj* quick, rapid, fast. *adv* 1 quickly, fast. 2 soon. **au plus vite** as quickly as possible. **vitesse** *nf* 1 speed. 2 quickness.
vitrer (vɪːˈtre:) *vt* glaze (a window, etc.). **vitrail, -aux** (vɪːˈtraj, -ˈtro) *nm* stained-glass window. **vitre** *nf* pane of glass. **vitrine** *nf* 1 shopwindow. 2 showcase. 3 glass case.
vivace (vɪːˈvas) *adj* 1 hardy. 2 perennial. **vivacité** *nf* 1 vivacity. 2 outburst of temper.
vivier (vɪːˈvje:) *nm* fishpond.
vivifier (vɪːvɪːˈfje:) *vt* enliven, invigorate.
vivre (vɪːvr) *vi* 1 live. 2 be alive. *nm* 1 food. 2 *pl* provisions. **vivant** *adj* 1 living, alive. 2 lively.
vocabulaire (vɔkabyˈlɛr) *nm* vocabulary.
vocal, -aux (vɔˈkal, -ˈko) *adj* vocal.
vocation (vɔkaˈsjɔ̃) *nf* 1 vocation. 2 bent, inclination.
vœu, vœux (vœ) *nm* 1 wish. 2 vow.
voguer (vɔˈge:) *vi* sail. **vogue** *nf* vogue, fashion.
voici (vwaˈsɪː) *prep* here is or are.
voie (vwa) *nf* way, road, track. **voie d'eau** 1 *naut* leak. 2 canal. **voie ferrée** railway line. **voie publique** public highway.
voilà (vwaˈla) *prep* there is or are.
voile[1] (vwal) *nf* sail. **voilier** *nm* sailing vessel.
voile[2] (vwal) *nm* veil.
voiler (vwaˈle:) *vt* 1 veil. 2 obscure, dim. 3 muffle. **se voiler** *vr* cloud over.
voir (vwar) *vt* 1 see. 2 visit. 3 understand. 4 notice. **faire voir** show. **n'avoir rien à voir avec** have nothing to do with.
voire (vwar) *adv* indeed. **voire même** and even.
voirie (vwaˈrɪː) *nf* 1 highways. 2 refuse dump.
voisin (vwaˈzɛ̃) *adj* neighbouring, near. *nm* neighbour. **voisinage** *nm* 1 neighbourhood, district. 2 proximity.
voiture (vwaˈtyr) *nf* 1 car. 2 van. **voiture d'enfant** pram.
voix (vwa) *nf* 1 voice. 2 vote. **à haute voix** aloud. **voix publique** public opinion.
vol[1] (vɔl) *nm* 1 flight. 2 flying. 3 flock, swarm. **vol à voile** *aviat* gliding.
vol[2] (vɔl) *nm* theft. **vol à l'étalage** shoplifting. **vol avec effraction** burglary.
volaille (vɔˈlaj) *nf* poultry.
volatil (vɔlaˈtɪːl) *adj* volatile.
volcan (vɔlˈkɑ̃) *nm* volcano. **volcanique** *adj* volcanic.
voler[1] (vɔˈle:) *vi* fly. **volant** *nm* 1 steering

wheel. 2 shuttlecock. **volée** *nf* 1 flight. 2 volley.
voler[2] (vɔˈle:) *vt* 1 steal. 2 rob. **voleur, -euse** (vɔˈlœr, -ˈlœz) *nm,f* thief, robber. **voleur à tire** *nm* pickpocket. ~*adj* thieving.
volet (vɔˈlɛ) *nm* shutter.
volière (vɔˈljɛr) *nf* aviary.
volontaire (vɔlɔ̃ˈtɛr) *adj* 1 voluntary. 2 deliberate. 3 headstrong. *nm* volunteer.
volonté (vɔlɔ̃ˈte:) *nf* 1 will. 2 *pl* whims. **bonne volonté** goodwill. **volontiers** *adv* willingly, with pleasure.
volt (vɔlt) *nm* volt. **voltage** *nm* voltage.
volte-face *nf invar* about turn.
voltiger (vɔltɪːˈʒe:) *vi* flit.
volume (vɔˈlym) *nm* 1 volume. 2 bulk, mass. 3 capacity.
volupté (vɔlypˈte:) *nf* sensual pleasure.
vomir (vɔˈmɪːr) *vt* vomit.
vont (vɔ̃) *v* see **aller.**
vorace (vɔˈras) *adj* ravenous.
vos (vo) *poss adj* see **votre.**
voter (vɔˈte:) *vi* vote. *vt* 1 pass. 2 vote (money). **vote** *nm* vote.
votre, vos (vɔtr, vo) *poss adj* 2nd *pers s,pl* your.
vôtre (votr) *poss pron* 2nd *pers s,pl* **le** or **la vôtre** 1 yours. 2 your own.
voudrai (vuːˈdrɛ) *v* see **vouloir.**
vouer (vwe:) *vt* devote, consecrate.
vouloir (vuːˈlwar) *vt* 1 be willing. 2 want. 3 mean. 4 consent. 5 need. 6 try. **en vouloir à** have a grudge against. ~*nm* will.
vous (vuː) *pron* 2nd *pers m,f* 1 *s fml* you. 2 *pl* you. **vous-même** *pron* 2nd *pers m,f s fml* yourself. **vous-mêmes** *pron* 2nd *pers m,f pl* yourselves.
voûter (vuːˈte:) *vt* arch. **voûte** *nf* arch, vault.
vouvoyer (vuːvwaˈje:) *vt* address as **vous.**
voyager (vwajaˈʒe:) *vi* travel. **voyage** *nm* journey, trip, tour. **voyageur, -euse** (vwajaˈʒœr, -ˈʒœz) *nm,f* 1 traveller. 2 passenger. *adj* travelling.
voyant (vwaˈjɑ̃) *adj* 1 gaudy. 2 conspicuous.
voyelle (vwaˈjɛl) *nf* vowel.
voyou, -oux (vwaˈjuː) *nm inf* hooligan.
vrai (vrɛ) *adj* 1 true. 2 real, genuine. 3 downright. *adv* really, truly. **à vrai dire** as a matter of fact. ~*nm* truth. **vraiment** *adv* 1 really. 2 indeed.
vraisemblable (vrɛsɑ̃ˈblabl) *adj* 1 probable. 2 credible. **vraisemblance** *nf* 1 probability, likelihood. 2 credibility.

vrille

vrille (vrɪːj) *nf* tendril.
vrombir (vrɔ̃'biːr) *vi* hum, throb. **vrombissement** *nm* 1 humming. 2 drone.
vu (vy) *v* see **voir**. *adj* 1 seen. 2 considered. *prep* considering, in view of. **vu que** *conj* seeing that. ~*nm* sight. **vue** *nf* 1 sight. 2 view. 3 intention, design.
vulgaire (vyl'gɛr) *adj* 1 vulgar 2 common.
vulnérable (vylnɛ'rabl) *adj* vulnerable.

zinc (zɛ̃g) *nm* 1 zinc. 2 *sl* bar, counter (in a pub).
zodiaque (zɔ'djak) *nm* zodiac.
zone (zon) *nm* zone, area.
zoo (zo) *nm* zoo. **zoologie** (zɔɔlɔ'ʒiː) *nf* zoology. **zoologique** (zɔɔlɔ'ʒiːk) *adj* zoological. **zoologiste** (zɔɔlɔ'ʒiːst) *nm* zoologist.

W

wagon (va'gɔ̃) *nm* 1 (railway) carriage or coach. 2 waggon, truck. **wagon-lit** *nm, pl* **wagons-lits** sleeping-car.
watt (wat) *nm* watt. **wattage** *nm* wattage.
week-end (wiːk'ɛnd) *nm* weekend.
whist (wiːst) *nm* whist.

X

xénophobie (kseːnɔfɔ'biː) *nf* xenophobia.
xérès (gze:'rɛs) *nm* sherry.

Y

y (iː) *adv* 1 there. 2 here. **ça y est!** that's it! **j'y suis** I've got it, I understand. **n'y être pour rien** have nothing to do with it. ~*pron invar* 1 at, by, or in it. 2 of them.
yacht (jɔt) *nm* yacht.
yaourt (ja'uːrt) *nm* yoghurt.
yeux (jœ) *nm pl* eyes.
yiddish (jiː'diːʃ) *nm* Yiddish.
yoga (jɔ'ga) *nm* yoga.
Yougoslavie (juːgɔ'slaˈviː) *nf* Yugoslavia. **yougoslave** *adj,n* Yugoslav.
youyou (juː'juː) *nm* dinghy.

Z

zèbre (zɛbr) *nm* zebra. **zébré** *adj* striped.
zèle (zɛl) *nm* zeal, ardour. **zélé** *adj* zealous.
zéro (ze:'ro) *nm* zero, nought.
zeste (zɛst) *nm cul* zest, outer skin.
zézayer (ze:zɛ'je:) *vi,vt* lisp. **zézaiement** *nm* 1 lisp. 2 lisping.
zigzag (ziːg'zag) *nm* zigzag. **zigzaguer** *vi* zigzag.

146

A

a, an (ə, ən; *stressed* eı, æn) *ındef art* un *m*. une *f*.

aback (ə'bæk) *adv* en arrière. **be taken aback** être déconcerté.

abandon (ə'bændən) *vt* 1 abandonner. 2 délaisser. 3 renoncer à. **abandoned** *adj* 1 abandonné. 2 dévergondé, dépravé. **abandonment** *n* 1 abandon *m*. 2 délaissement *m*.

abash (ə'bæʃ) *vt* confondre, déconcerter.

abate (ə'beıt) *vt* diminuer, affaiblir. *vi* 1 s'affaiblir. 2 se calmer.

abattoir ('æbətwɑ:) *n* abattoir *m*.

abbess ('æbıs) *n* abesse *f*.

abbey ('æbi) *n* abbaye *f*.

abbot ('æbət) *n* abbé *m*.

abbreviate (ə'bri:vıeıt) *vt* abréger, raccourcir. **abbreviation** *n* abréviation *f*.

abdicate ('æbdikeıt) *vt,vi* abdiquer. *vt* renoncer à. **abdication** *n* abdication *f*.

abdomen ('æbdəmən) *n* abdomen *m*.

abduct (æb'dʌkt) *vt* enlever. **abduction** *n* enlèvement *m*. **abductor** *n* ravisseur *m*.

abet (ə'bet) *vt* encourager. **abettor** *n* complice *m,f*.

abhor (əb'hɔ:) *vt* abhorrer, avoir horreur de. **abhorrent** *adj* 1 répugnant. 2 contraire.

abide* (ə'baıd) *vi* 1 demeurer. 2 *inf* supporter. **abide by** 1 rester fidèle à. 2 se conformer à.

ability (ə'biliti) *n* 1 capacité *f*. 2 pouvoir *m*. intelligence *f*. **to the best of one's ability** de son mieux.

abject ('æbdʒekt) *adj* 1 abject, misérable. 2 vil. **abjection** *n* 1 abjection *f*. 2 misère *f*.

ablaze (ə'bleız) *adv,adj* en flammes. *adj* enflammé.

able ('eibəl) *adj* capable, compétent, habile. **be able** 1 pouvoir. 2 savoir. **able-bodied** *adj* fort, robuste.

abnormal (æb'nɔ:məl) *adj* anormal, -aux. **abnormality** *n* 1 anomalie *f*. 2 malformation *f*.

aboard (ə'bɔ:d) *adv* à bord. **all aboard!** embarquez! **go aboard** s'embarquer. ~*prep* à bord de.

abode (ə'boud) *n* 1 demeure, habitation *f*. 2 *law* domicile *m*.

abolish (ə'bɔliʃ) *vt* abolir, supprimer. **abolition** *n* abolition *f*.

abominable (ə'bɔminəbəl) *adj* 1 abominable, odieux, -euse. 2 exécrable.

Aborigine (æbə'ridʒini) *n* aborigène, indigène *m*. **aboriginal** *adj* 1 aborigène, indigène. 2 primitif, -ive.

abort (ə'bɔ:t) *vi* avorter. **abortion** *n* 1 avortement *m*. 2 avorton *m*.

abound (ə'baund) *vi* abonder.

about (ə'baut) *adv, prep* 1 autour (de). 2 de ci de là. 3 environ. 4 au sujet de. **be about to** être sur le point de. **what is it about?** de quoi s'agit-il?

above (ə'bʌv) *prep* 1 au-dessus (de). 2 plus de. **above all** surtout. ~*adv* 1 en haut. 2 ci-dessus. 3 au-dessus. **aboveboard** *adj* loyal, -aux.

abrasion (ə'breıʒən) *n* 1 frottement *m*. 2 *med* écorchure *f*. **abrasive** *adj,n* abrasif, -ive *m*.

abreast (ə'brest) *adv* de front, sur la même ligne.

abridge (ə'bridʒ) *vt* 1 abréger. 2 restreindre.

abroad (ə'brɔ:d) *adv* 1 à l'étranger. 2 au loin.

abrupt (ə'brʌpt) *adj* 1 abrupt. 2 brusque. **abruptly** *adv* 1 à pic. 2 brusquement.

abscess ('æbses) *n* abcès *m*.

abscond (əb'skɔnd) *vi* 1 s'évader. 2 *law* se soustraire à.

absent (*adj* 'æbsənt; *v* ab'sent) *adj* 1 absent. 2 manquant. **absent-minded** *adj* distrait. **absent-mindedness** *n* distraction *f*. ~*v* **absent oneself** s'absenter. **absence** *n* 1 absence *f*. 2 manque *m*. **absentee** *n* absent *m*.

absolute ('æbsəlu:t) *adj* 1 absolu. 2 parfait. 3 catégorique. **absolutely** *adv* 1 absolument. 2 complètement.

absolve (əb'zɔlv) *vt* 1 absoudre. 2 *law* acquitter.

147

absorb (əb'zɔːb) vt absorber. **absorbent** adj absorbant. **absorption** n 1 absorption f. 2 concentration f.

abstain (əb'steɪn) vi s'abstenir. **abstention** n abstention f. **abstinence** n abstinence f.

abstract (adj,n 'æbstrækt; v əb'strækt) adj,n abstrait m. n résumé m. vt 1 soustraire. 2 extraire. **abstraction** n abstraction f.

absurd (əb'sɔːd) adj absurde.

abundance (ə'bʌndəns) n abondance f. **abundant** adj abondant, copieux, -euse. **abundantly** adv abondamment.

abuse (v ə'bjuːz; n ə'bjuːs) vt 1 abuser de. 2 médire. 3 injurier. n 1 abus m. 2 insultes f pl. **abusive** adj 1 abusif, -ive. 2 injurieux, -euse.

abyss (ə'bɪs) n abîme m. **abysmal** adj 1 sans fond. 2 profond.

academy (ə'kædəmi) n académie f. **academic** adj 1 académique. 2 universitaire. 3 théorique.

accelerate (æk'seləreɪt) vt accélérer. vi s'accélérer. **acceleration** n accélération f. **accelerator** n accélérateur m.

accent ('æksənt) n 1 accent m. 2 ton m. **accentuate** vt accentuer.

accept (ək'sept) vt 1 accepter. 2 admettre. **acceptance** n 1 acceptation f. 2 réception f.

access ('ækses) n 1 accès m. 2 entrée f. **accessible** adj accessible, abordable. **accession** n 1 accès m. 2 accession f. 3 accroissement m.

accessory (æk'sesəri) adj accessoire, subsidiaire. n 1 accessoire m. 2 pl équipement m. 3 law complice m,f.

accident ('æksɪdnt) n accident m. **by accident** par hasard. **accidental** adj 1 accidentel, -elle. 2 accessoire.

acclaim (ə'kleɪm) vt acclamer.

acclimatize (ə'klaɪmətaɪz) vt acclimater. **get acclimatized** s'acclimater, s'habituer.

accommodate (ə'kɔmədeɪt) vt 1 accommoder. 2 rendre service à. 3 loger. **accomodating** adj complaisant. **accommodation** n 1 adaptation f. 2 arrangement m. 3 logement m.

accompany (ə'kʌmpəni) vt accompagner. **accompaniment** n accompagnement m. **accompanist** n mus accompagnateur, -trice.

accomplice (ə'kʌmplɪs) n complice m,f.

accomplish (ə'kʌmplɪʃ) vt 1 accomplir, aboutir. 2 achever. **accomplishment** n 1 accomplissement, achèvement m. 2 talent m. 3 pl arts d'agrément m pl.

accord (ə'kɔːd) n accord m. **of one's own**

accord de son plein gré. ~vt accorder. vi s'accorder. **accordance** n conformité f. **according to** suivant, d'après.

accordion (ə'kɔːdɪən) n accordéon m.

accost (ə'kɔst) vt accoster, aborder.

account (ə'kaunt) n 1 compte m. 2 valeur f. profit m. 3 récit m. description f. **take into account** tenir compte de. ~v **account for** expliquer **accountant** n comptable m. **chartered accountant** expert comptable m.

accumulate (ə'kjuːmjuleɪt) vt accumuler. vi s'accumuler. **accumulation** n accumulation f.

accurate ('ækjurət) adj 1 exact, juste. 2 fidèle. **accuracy** n exactitude, précision f.

accuse (ə'kjuːz) vt accuser. **accusation** n accusation f.

accustom (ə'kʌstəm) vt accoutumer, habituer.

ace (eɪs) n 1 game as m. 2 atout m.

ache (eɪk) n mal m. douleur f. vi faire mal.

achieve (ə'tʃiːv) vt 1 accomplir. 2 acquérir. 3 atteindre. **achievement** n 1 accomplissement m. 2 exploit m.

acid ('æsɪd) adj 1 acide. 2 aigre. n acide m.

acknowledge (ək'nɔlidʒ) vt reconnaître. **acknowledgement** n 1 reconnaissance f. 2 aveu, -eux m.

acne ('ækni) n acné f.

acorn ('eikɔːn) n gland m.

acoustic (ə'kuːstik) adj acoustique. **acoustics** n acoustique f.

acquaint (ə'kweɪnt) vt informer, faire savoir. **be acquainted with** connaître. **acquaintance** n connaissance f.

acquiesce (ækwi'es) vi acquiescer.

acquire (ə'kwaɪə) vt acquérir. **acquisition** n acquisition f. **acquisitive** adj âpre au gain.

acquit (ə'kwit) vt acquitter. **acquittal** n 1 acquittement m. 2 exécution f.

acre ('eikə) n arpent m.

acrimony ('ækrɪməni) n acrimonie f. **acrimonious** adj acrimonieux, -euse.

acrobat ('ækrəbæt) n acrobate m,f. **acrobatic** adj acrobatique. **acrobatics** n pl acrobatie f.

across (ə'krɔs) adv,prep à or en travers. adv de l'autre côté.

acrylic (ə'krilik) adj acrylique.

act (ækt) n 1 acte m. action f. 2 décret m. 3 Th acte m. vt jouer. vi agir.

action ('ækʃən) n action f.

active ('æktiv) adj,n actif, -ive m. **activate** vt activer. **activity** n 1 activité f. 2 pl occupations f pl.

actor ('æktə) n 1 acteur m. 2 comédien m.

actress ('æktrıs) *n* 1 actrice *f*. 2 comédienne *f*.

actual ('æktʃuəl) *adj* 1 réel, -elle. 2 actuel, -elle. **in actual fact** en fait. **actually** *adv* 1 réellement. 2 à l'heure actuelle, maintenant.

actuary ('æktʃuəri) *n* actuaire *m*.

acupuncture ('ækjupʌŋktʃə) *n* acuponcture *f*.

acute (ə'kjuːt) *adj* 1 aigu, -uë. 2 perspicace.

adamant ('ædəmənt) *adj* insensible.

Adam's apple ('ædəmz) *n* pomme d'Adam *f*.

adapt (ə'dæpt) *vt* adapter.

add (æd) *vt* 1 ajouter. 2 additionner. **add up** 1 totaliser. 2 *inf* s'accorder. **addition** *n* addition *f*. **in addition** en outre. **additional** *adj* additionel, -elle, supplémentaire.

addendum (ə'dendəm) *n*, *pl* **addenda** addendum *m* *invar*. supplément *m*.

adder ('ædə) *n* vipère *f*.

addict (*n* 'ædikt; *v* ə'dikt) *n* **drug addict** toxicomane *m,f*. *v* **be addicted to** s'adonner à.

address (ə'dres) *n* 1 adresse *f*. 2 discours *m*. *vt* 1 adresser. 2 aborder.

adenoids ('ædinɔidz) *n pl* adénoïdes *f pl*.

adept ('ædept) *adj* habile, expert. *n* 1 adepte *m*. 2 expert *m*.

adequate ('ædikwət) *adj* 1 adéquat, suffisant. 2 proportionné.

adhere (əd'hiə) *vi* adhérer. **adherent** *adj,n* adhérent *m*. **adhesion** *n* 1 adhésion *f*. 2 approbation *f*. **adhesive** *adj,n* adhésif, -ive *m*.

adjacent (ə'dʒeisənt) *adj* adjacent, contigu, -uë.

adjective ('ædʒiktiv) *n* adjectif *m*.

adjoin (ə'dʒɔin) *vt* être contigu à, avoisiner.

adjourn (ə'dʒəːn) *vt* ajourner, différer. *vi* 1 s'ajourner. 2 lever la séance.

adjudicate (ə'dʒuːdikeit) *vt,vi* juger. **adjudication** *n* jugement *m*. **adjudicator** *n* arbitre *m*.

adjust (ə'dʒʌst) *vt* 1 concilier. 2 ajuster.

ad-lib (æd'lib) *adv* à volonté. *vt inf* improviser.

administer (əd'ministə) *vt* 1 administrer. 2 rendre. **administration** *n* administration *f*. **administrative** *adj* administratif, -ive. **administrator** *n* administrateur, gestionnaire *m*.

admiral ('ædmərəl) *n* amiral, -aux, *m*. **admiralty** *n* 1 amirauté *f*. 2 ministère de la marine *m*.

admire (əd'maiə) *vt* admirer. **admiration** *n* admiration *f*. **admirer** *n* soupirant *m*. **admiring** *adj* admiratif, -ive.

admission (əd'miʃən) *n* 1 admission *f*. 2 entrée *f*. 3 aveu, -eux *m*.

admit (əd'mit) *vt* 1 admettre. 2 laisser entrer. 3 avouer. **admittance** *n* admission *f*. **no admittance** entrée interdite.

adolescence (ædə'lesəns) *n* adolescence *f*. **adolescent** *adj,n* adolescent *m*.

adopt (ə'dɔpt) *vt* adopter. **adopted child** *n* enfant adoptif *m*. **adoption** *n* adoption *f*.

adore (ə'dɔː) *vt* adorer. **adoration** *n* adoration *f*.

adorn (ə'dɔːn) *vt* orner.

adrenaline (ə'drenəlin) *n* adrénaline *f*.

Adriatic (eidri'ætik) *adj* adriatique. **Adriatic (Sea)** *n* (Mer) Adriatique *f*.

adrift (ə'drift) *adv* à la dérive.

adroit (ə'drɔit) *adj* adroit, habile.

adulation (ædju'leiʃən) *n* flatterie *f*.

adult ('ædʌlt) *adj,n* adulte.

adulterate (ə'dʌltəreit) *vt* adultérer, falsifier. **adulteration** *n* adultération, falsification *f*.

adultery (ə'dʌltəri) *n* adultère *m*. **adulterer** *n* adultère *m,f*.

advance (əd'vaːns) *vt* 1 avancer. 2 faire progresser. 3 augmenter. *vi* (s')avancer. *n* 1 avance *f*. 2 progrès *m*. 3 hausse *f*.

advantage (əd'vaːntidʒ) *n* avantage *m*. **take advantage of** profiter de.

advent ('ædvent) *n* 1 venue *f*. 2 *cap rel* Avent *m*.

adventure (əd'ventʃə) *n* aventure *f*. **adventurer** *n* aventurier *m*. **adventurous** *adj* 1 aventureux, -euse. 2 entreprenant.

adverb ('ædvəːb) *n* adverbe *m*.

adverse ('ædvəːs) *adj* 1 adverse, opposé. 2 hostile. 3 défavorable. **adversary** *n* adversaire *m,f*. **adversity** *n* adversité *f*.

advertise ('ædvətaiz) *vi* 1 faire de la publicité. 2 insérer une annonce. *vt* annoncer. **advertisement** *n* 1 publicité *f*. 2 annonce *f*. **advertising** *n* publicité *f*.

advise (əd'vaiz) *vt* 1 conseiller. 2 avertir. **advise with** (se) consulter avec. **advice** *n* avis, conseil *m*. **advisable** *adj* 1 recommandable, judicieux, -euse. 2 convenable.

advocate (*n* 'ædvəkət; *v* 'ædvəkeit) *n* 1 avocat *m*. 2 défenseur *m*. *vt* 1 préconiser. 2 défendre.

Aegean (i'dʒiːən) *adj* égée. **Aegean (Sea)** (Mer) Egée *f*.

aerate ('ɛəreit) *vt* 1 aérer. 2 gazéifier. **aerated** *adj* 1 aéré. 2 gazeux, -euse.

aerial ('ɛəriəl) *adj* aérien, -ienne. *n* antenne *f*.

aerodynamics (ɛəroudai'næmiks) *n* aérodynamique *f*.

aeronautics (ɛərə'nɔːtiks) *n* aéronautique *f*.

aeroplane ('ɛərəplein) *n* avion *m*.

aerosol ('ɛərəsɔl) n aérosol m
aesthetic (is'θetik) adj esthétique **aesthetics** n esthétique f
afar (ə'fɑ) adv **from afar** de loin
affable ('æfəbəl) adj affable
affair (ə'fɛə) n affaire f
affect[1] (ə'fekt) vt **1** atteindre, affecter **2** influer sur **3** émouvoir **affection** n affection f **affectionate** adj affectueux, -euse
affect[2] (ə'fekt) vt affecter, feindre **affected** adj **1** affecté, maniéré **2** simulé
affiliate (ə'filieit) vt affilier **affiliated firm** n filiale f **affiliation** n affiliation f
affinity (ə'finiti) n affinité f
affirm (ə'fə:m) vt affirmer **affirmative** adj affirmatif, -ive
affix (v ə'fiks, n 'æfiks) vt apposer n **1** addition f **2** gram affixe m
afflict (ə'flikt) vt affliger **affliction** n **1** affliction f **2** infirmité f
affluent ('æfluənt) adj **1** abondant **2** riche **affluence** n richesse f
afford (ə'fɔ:d) vt **1** avoir les moyens **2** pouvoir **3** fournir
affront (ə'frʌnt) n affront m vt **1** insulter **2** faire honte à
Afghanistan (æf'gænistɑn, -stæn) n Afghanistan m **Afghan** adj,n afghan
afield (ə'fi:ld) adv **far afield** très loin
afloat (ə'flout) adv à flot
afoot (ə'fut) adv à pied **there's something afoot** il se prépare quelque chose
aforesaid (ə'fɔ:sed) adj susdit
afraid (ə'freid) adj **be afraid 1** avoir peur **2** ne pas oser
afresh (ə'freʃ) adv de or à nouveau
Africa ('æfrikə) n Afrique f **African** adj,n africain
aft (ɑ:ft) adv à or sur l'arrière
after ('ɑ:ftə) adv après, ensuite, d'après prep **1** après **2** suivant, selon **after all** après tout ~conj après que **after-care** n surveillance f **after-effects** n pl **1** suites f pl **2** med reliquat m **aftermath** n regain m **afternoon** n après-midi m **afterthought** n réflexion après coup, arrière-pensée f **afterwards** adv ensuite, après
again (ə'gen) adv de nouveau, encore **again and again** à plusieurs reprises
against (ə'genst) prep **1** contre **2** vis-à-vis **3** à l'encontre de
age (eidʒ) n **1** âge m **2** époque f **age-group** n
150

classe f **be of age** être majeur ~vt,vi vieillir **aged** adj vieux, vieille, âgé
agency ('eidʒənsi) n **1** comm agence f bureau, -aux m **2** action f
agenda (ə'dʒendə) n ordre du jour m
agent ('eidʒənt) n agent, représentant m
aggravate ('ægrəveit) vt **1** aggraver **2** inf exaspérer, agacer
aggregate (adj,n 'ægrigit, v 'ægrigeit) n ensemble, total, -aux m adj global, -aux, collectif, -ive vt rassembler
aggression (ə'greʃən) n agression f **aggressive** adj agressif, -ive
aghast (ə'gɑ:st) adj épouvanté, ébahi
agile ('ædʒail) adj agile, leste **agility** n agilité f
agitate ('ædʒiteit) vt **1** agiter **2** troubler **agitated** adj ému, troublé **agitation** n agitation f **agitator** n agitateur, -trice
agnostic (æg'nɔstik) adj,n agnostique
ago (ə'gou) adj,adv il y a **long ago** il y a longtemps
agog (ə'gɔg) adj impatient **be all agog** brûler d'envie
agony ('ægəni) n **1** angoisse f **2** med agonie f
agrarian (ə'grɛəriən) adj agraire
agree (ə'gri) vi **1** consentir **2** s'accorder **3** être d'accord **4** convenir **agreeable** adj **1** plaisant, agréable **2** consentant **agreement** n **1** accord m **2** contrat m
agriculture ('ægrikʌltʃə) n agriculture f **agricultural** adj agricole
ahead (ə'hed) adv en avant, devant
aid (eid) vt aider, assister **aid and abet** être le complice de ~n **1** aide f **2** secours m assistance f
ailment ('eilmənt) n mal m indisposition f
aim (eim) vt,vi viser n **1** but m **2** objet m **aimless** adj sans but
air (ɛə) n **1** air m **2** brise f **3** apparence f vt aérer
airborne ('ɛəbɔ:n) adj aéroporté
air-conditioning n climatisation f **air-conditioned** adj climatisé
aircraft ('ɛəkrɑ:ft) n avion m **aircraft carrier** n porte-avions m invar
airfield ('ɛəfi:ld) n terrain d'aviation m
airforce ('ɛəfɔ:s) n armée de l'air f
airhostess ('ɛəhoustis) n hôtesse de l'air f
air lift n pont aérien m
airline ('ɛəlain) n ligne aérienne f
airmail ('ɛəmeil) n poste aérienne f **by airmail** par avion

airman (´ɛəmən) n aviateur m

airport (´ɛapɔ t) n aéroport m

air-raid n raid aérien m

airtight (´ɛatait) adj hermétique

airy (´ɛari) adj 1 aéré 2 léger, -ère 3 sans consistance

aisle (ail) n 1 rel nef latérale f bas-côté m 2 passage m

ajar (ə´dʒɑ) adj,adv entrouvert

alabaster (´ælabɑ stə) n albâtre m

alarm (ə´lɑ m) n alarme, alerte f **alarm clock** n réveille-matin m invar ~vt 1 alarmer 2 effrayer

alas (ə´læs) interj hélas!

albatross (´ælbɔtros) n albatros m

albeit (ɔ´lbi it) conj quoique, bien que

album (´ælbəm) n album m

alchemy (´ælkəmi) n alchimie f

alcohol (´ælkəhɔl) n alcool m **alcoholic** adj,n alcoolique **alcoholism** n alcoolisme m

alcove (´ælkouv) n 1 alcôve f 2 niche f

alderman (´ɔ ldəmən) n conseiller municipal m

ale (eil) n bière f

alert (ə´lɔ t) adj,n alerte f

algebra (´ældʒibrə) n algèbre f

Algeria (æl´dʒiəriə) n Algérie f **Algerian** adj,n algérien, -ienne

alias (´eiliəs) adv autrement dit

alibi (´ælibai) n alibi m

alien (´eiliən) adj,n étranger, -ère **alienate** vt aliéner **alienation** n aliénation f

alight[1] (ə´lait) adj en feu, allumé

alight[2] (ə´lait) vi 1 descendre 2 se poser

align (ə´lain) vt aligner vi s´aligner

alike (ə´laik) adj semblable adv pareillement, également

alimentary (æli´mentəri) adj alimentaire

alimony (´æliməni) n pension alimentaire f

alive (ə´laiv) adj 1 vivant 2 éveillé **be alive with** grouiller de

alkali (´ælkəlai) n alcali m

all (ɔ l) pron,adj tout, tous **all of us** nous tous ~adv tout, entièrement **all but** presque **all right** ça va ~n totalité f tout m

allay (ə´lei) vt soulager, apaiser

allege (ə´ledʒ) vt alléguer **allegation** n allégation f

allegiance (ə´li dʒəns) n fidélité f

allegory (´æligəri) n allégorie f **allegorical** adj allégorique

allergy (´ælədʒi) n allergie f **allergic** adj allergique

alleviate (ə´li vieit) vt soulager

alley (´æli) n 1 allée f 2 passage m

alliance (ə´laiəns) n alliance f **allied** adj 1 allié 2 apparenté

alligator (´æligeitə) n alligator m

alliteration (əlitə´reiʃən) n allitération f

allocate (´æləkeit) vt allouer **allocation** n allocation f

allot (ə´lɔt) vt 1 attribuer 2 distribuer **allotment** n 1 répartition f 2 jardin ouvrier m

allow (ə´lau) vt 1 permettre 2 admettre 3 accorder **allow for** tenir compte de **allowance** n 1 allocation f 2 pension f 3 indemnité f 4 comm remise f 5 ration f

alloy (´ælɔi) n alliage m vt allier

All Saints' Day n Toussaint f

allude (ə´lu d) vi faire allusion **allusion** n allusion f

allure (ə´luə) vt attirer, séduire **alluring** adj attrayant

ally (n ´ælai, v ə´lai) n allié m vt allier vi s´allier

almanac (´ɔ lmənæk) n almanach m

almighty (ɔ´lmaiti) adj tout-puissant

almond (´ɑ mənd) n amande f

almost (´ɔ lmoust) adv presque, à peu près

alms (ɑ mz) n pl aumône f

aloft (ə´lɔft) adv en haut

alone (ə´loun) adj seul, solitaire **leave alone** laisser tranquille

along (ə´lɔŋ) prep le long de **all along** tout le temps **alongside** adv bord à bord

aloof (ə´lu f) adv à l´écart adj 1 éloigné 2 distant

aloud (ə´laud) adv à haute voix, haut

alphabet (´ælfəbet) n alphabet m **alphabetical** adj alphabétique

alpine (´ælpain) adj alpin, alpestre

Alps (ælps) n pl Alpes f pl

already (ɔ l´redi) adv déjà

Alsatian (æl´seiʃən) n chien-loup m

also (´ɔ lsou) adv aussi

altar (´ɔ ltə) n autel m

alter (´ɔ ltə) vt vi changer **alteration** n 1 changement m 2 modification f

alternate (v ´ɔ ltəneit, adj ɔ l´tə nit) vt,vi alterner adj alternatif, -ive **alternative** n alternative f choix m

although (ɔ l´ðou) conj quoique, bien que

altitude (´æltitju d) n altitude f

alto (´æltou) n alto m

altogether (ɔ ltə´geðə) adv 1 entièrement, tout à fait 2 tout compris

aluminium (ælju´miniəm) n aluminium m

always ('ɔ lweiz) *adv* toujours
am (əm, *stressed* æm) *v* see **be.**
amalgamate (ə'mælgəmeit) *vt* amalgamer,
 fusionner *vi* s'amalgamer **amalgamation** *n*
 1 amalgamation *f* **2** fusion *f*
amass (ə'mæs) *vt* amasser
amateur ('æmətə) *n* amateur *m*
amaze (ə'meiz) *vt* stupéfier, étonner **amazement** *n* stupéfaction *f* étonnement *m*
ambassador (æm'bæsədə) *n* ambassadeur *m*
amber ('æmbə) *n* ambre *m*
ambidextrous (æmbi'dekstrəs) *adj* ambidextre
ambiguous (æm'bigjuəs) *adj* ambigu, -ue,
 équivoque **ambiguity** *n* ambiguité *f*
ambition (æm'biʃən) *n* ambition *f* **ambitious**
 adj ambitieux, -euse
ambivalent (æm'bivələnt) *adj* ambivalent
amble ('æmbəl) *vi* **1** aller l'amble **2** flâner *n* **1**
 (of horse) amble *m* **2** pas tranquille *m*
ambulance ('æmbjuləns) *n* ambulance *f*
ambush ('æmbuʃ) *n* embuscade *f* *vt* attirer
 dans un piège
amenable (ə'mi nəbəl) *adj* **1** responsable **2**
 soumis
amend (ə'mend) *vt* amender, corriger *vi*
 s'amender **amendment** *n* **1** modification *f* **2**
 pol amendement *m*
amenity (ə'mi niti) *n* **1** aménité *f* agrément *m*
 2 *pl* commodités *f pl*
America (ə'merikə) *n* Amérique *f* **American**
 adj,n américain
amethyst ('æmiθist) *n* améthyste *f*
amiable ('eimiəbəl) *adj* aimable
amicable ('æmikəbəl) *adj* **1** amical, -aux **2** *law*
 à l'amiable
amid (ə'mid) *prep also* **amidst** parmi, au milieu
 de
amiss (ə'mis) *adv* **1** mal, de travers **2** mal à
 propos *adj* de travers, qui cloche
ammonia (ə'mouniə) *n* ammoniaque *f*
ammunition (æmju'niʃən) *n* munitions *f pl*
amnesty ('æmnəsti) *n* amnistie *f*
amoeba (ə'mi bə) *n, pl* **-bae** *or* **-bas** amibe *f*
among (ə'mʌŋ) *prep also* **amongst** parmi, entre
amoral (ei'mɔrəl) *adj* amoral, -aux
amorous ('æmərəs) *adj* amoureux, -euse
amorphous (ə'mɔ fəs) *adj* amorphe
amount (ə'maunt) *n* **1** montant *m* **2** quantité *f*
 vi **1** s'élever **2** revenir
ampere ('æmpɛə) *n* ampère *m*
amphetamine (æm'fetəmi n) *n* amphétamine *f*
amphibian (æm'fibiən) *n* amphibie *m*
 amphibious *adj* amphibie

amphitheatre ('æmfiθiətə) *n* amphithéâtre *m*
ample ('æmpəl) *adj* **1** ample, vaste **2** abondant
amplify ('æmplifai) *vt* amplifier **amplifier** *n*
 amplificateur *m*
amputate ('æmpjuteit) *vt* amputer **amputation** *n* amputation *f*
amuse (ə'mju z) *vt* amuser, divertir **amusement** *n* divertissement *m*
an (ən, *stressed* æn) *indef art* see **a.**
anachronism (ə'nækrənizəm) *n* anachronisme
 m
anaemia (ə'ni miə) *n* anémie *f* **anaemic** *adj*
 anémique
anaesthetic (ænis'θetik) *adj,n* anesthésique
 m **anaesthetist** *n* anesthésiste *m,f* **anaesthetize** *vt* anesthésier
anagram ('ænəgræm) *n* anagramme *f*
anal ('einl) *adj* anal, -aux
analogy (ə'nælədʒi) *n* analogie *f*
analysis (ə'næləsis) *n, pl* **analyses** analyse
 f **analyse** *vt* analyser
anarchy ('ænəki) *n* anarchie *f* **anarchism** *n*
 anarchisme *m* **anarchist** *n* anarchiste *m,f*
anatomy (ə'nætəmi) *n* anatomie *f*
ancestor ('ænsəstə) *n* ancêtre, aieul, -eux
 m **ancestral** *adj* héréditaire, de famille
anchor ('æŋkə) *n* ancre *f* *vt* ancrer *vi* jeter
 l'ancre
anchovy ('æntʃəvi) *n* anchois *m*
ancient ('einʃənt) *adj* ancien, -ienne, antique
ancillary (æn'siləri) *adj* **1** subordonné **2**
 auxiliaire
and (ən, ənd, *stressed* ænd) *conj* et **and so on**
 et ainsi de suite
Andorra (æn'dɔ rə) *n* Andorre *f*
anemone (ə'neməni) *n* anémone *f*
anew (ə'nju) *adv* de nouveau
angel ('eindʒəl) *n* ange *m* **angelic** *adj* angélique
angelica (æn'dʒelikə) *n* angélique *f*
anger ('æŋgə) *n* colère *f* *vt* irriter, mettre en
 colère **angry** *adj* fâché, en colère
angle[1] ('æŋgəl) *n* angle *m*
angle[2] ('æŋgəl) *vi* pêcher à la ligne **angler** *n*
 pêcheur à la ligne *m*
Anglican ('æŋglikən) *adj,n* anglican
anguish ('æŋgwiʃ) *n* angoisse *f*
angular ('æŋgjulə) *adj* **1** angulaire **2** anguleux,
 -euse **3** maigre
animal ('æniməl) *adj,n* animal, -aux *m*
animate (*adj* ænimət, *v* 'ænimeit) *adj* animé *vt*
 animer **animation** *n* animation, vivacité *f*
aniseed ('ænisi d) *n* graine d'anis *f*

ankle ('æŋkəl) *n* cheville *f.*
annals ('ænļz) *n pl* annales *f pl.*
annex (ə'neks) *vt* annexer. **annexe** *n* annexe *f.*
annihilate (ə'naɪəleɪt) *vt* anéantir. **annihilation** *n* anéantissement *m.*
anniversary (æni'vəːsəri) *n* anniversaire *m.*
annotate ('ænəteɪt) *vt* annoter.
announce (ə'nauns) *vt* annoncer. **announcement** *n* annonce *f.* avis *m.* **announcer** *n* 1 annonceur *m.* 2 speaker *m.*
annoy (ə'nɔi) *vt* 1 gêner, ennuyer. 2 contrarier. **annoyance** *n* désagrément, ennui *m.*
annual ('ænjuəl) *adj* annuel, -elle. *n* 1 annuaire *m.* 2 *bot* plante annuelle *f.*
annul (ə'nʌl) *vt* annuler.
anode ('ænoud) *n* anode *f.*
anoint (ə'nɔint) *vt* oindre.
anomaly (ə'nɔməli) *n* anomalie *f.* **anomalous** *adj* anormal, -aux, irregulier, -ière.
anonymous (ə'nɔniməs) *adj* anonyme.
another (ə'nʌðə) *pron,adj* 1 encore un. 2 un autre. **one another** l'un l'autre, les uns les autres.
answer ('aːnsə) *n* 1 réponse *f.* 2 solution *f.* *vt,vi* répondre. **answerable** *adj* responsable.
ant (ænt) *n* fourmi *f.*
antagonize (æn'tægənaiz) *vt* contrarier. **antagonism** *n* antagonisme *m.* **antagonist** *n* antagoniste, adversaire *m,f.*
Antarctic (æn'taːktik) *adj,n* antarctique *m.*
antelope ('æntiloup) *n* antilope *f.*
antenatal (ænti'neitļ) *adj* prénatal, -aux.
antenna (æn'tenə) *n, pl* **antennae** antenne *f.*
anthem ('ænθəm) *n* hymne *m.*
anthology (æn'θɔlədʒi) *n* anthologie *f.*
anthropology (ænθrə'pɔlədʒi) *n* anthropologie *f.* **anthropologist** *n* anthropologiste *m,f.*
anti-aircraft *adj* antiaérien, -ienne.
antibiotic (æntibai'ɔtik) *n* antibiotique *m.*
antibody ('æntibɔdi) *n* anticorps *m.*
antic ('æntik) *n* singerie *f.*
anticipate (æn'tisipeit) *vt* 1 anticiper. 2 prévoir. **anticipation** *n* 1 anticipation *f.* 2 prévision *f.* 3 attente *f.*
anticlimax (ænti'klaimæks) *n* anticlimax *m.* chute, culbute *f.*
anticlockwise (ænti'klɔkwaiz) *adj* en sens inverse des aiguilles d'une montre.
anticyclone (ænti'saikloun) *n* anticyclone *m.*
antidote ('æntidout) *n* antidote *f.*
antifreeze ('æntifriːz) *n* antigel *m invar.*
antique (æn'tiːk) *adj* antique. *n* objet antique *m.* antiquité *f.* **antique dealer** *n* antiquaire

m. **antique shop** *n* magasin d'antiquités
m. **antiquated** *adj* 1 vieilli. 2 démodé.
antiquity *n* antiquité *f.*
anti-Semitic *adj* antisémitique.
antiseptic (ænti'septik) *adj,n* antiseptique *m.*
antisocial (ænti'souʃəl) *adj* antisocial, -aux.
antithesis (æn'tiθəsis) *n, pl* **antitheses** antithèse *f.*
antler ('æntlə) *n* 1 andouiller *m.* 2 *pl* bois *m pl.*
antonym ('æntənim) *n* antonyme *m.*
anus ('einəs) *n* anus *m.*
anvil ('ænvil) *n* enclume *f.*
anxious ('æŋkʃəs) *adj* 1 soucieux, -euse. 2 désireux, -euse. **anxiety** *n* anxiété, angoisse *f.*
any ('eni) *adj,pron* 1 du, de la. 2 en. 3 aucun. 4 n'importe (le)quel. 5 tout. **any further** plus loin. **any more** encore. **anybody** *pron also* **anyone** n'importe qui, quelqu'un. **not anybody** personne. **anyhow** *conj also* **anyway** de toute façon. *adv* n'importe comment. **anything** *pron* 1 quelque chose. 2 n'importe quoi. **not anything** rien. **anywhere** *adv* n'importe où. **not anywhere** nulle part.
apart (ə'paːt) *adv* de côté. **apart from** en dehors de. **apart from the fact that** hormis que.
apartheid (ə'paːtait) *n* ségrégation *f.*
apartment (ə'paːtmənt) *n* 1 pièce *f.* 2 appartement *m.* 3 *pl* logement *m.*
apathy ('æpəθi) *n* apathie *f.* **apathetic** *adj* apathique.
ape (eip) *n* singe *m.* *vt* singer.
aperitive (ə'peritiv) *n* apéritif *m.*
aperture ('æpətʃə) *n* ouverture *f.*
apex ('eipeks) *n* sommet *m.* apogée *f.*
apiece (ə'piːs) *adv* chacun.
apology (ə'pɔlədʒi) *n* 1 excuses *f pl.* 2 apologie *f.* **apologetic** *adj* 1 d'excuse. 2 apologétique. **apologize** *vi* s'excuser, demander pardon.
apostle (ə'pɔsəl) *n* apôtre *m.*
apostrophe (ə'pɔstrəfi) *n* apostrophe *f.*
appal (ə'pɔːl) *vt* épouvanter. **appalling** *adj* effroyable.
apparatus (æpə'reitəs) *n, pl* **-tus** or **-tuses** appareil *m.*
apparent (ə'pærənt) *adj* apparent, manifeste. **apparently** *adv* apparemment. **apparition** *n* apparition *f.*
appeal (ə'piːl) *n* appel *m.* *vi* faire appel. **appeal to** 1 plaire à. 2 s'adresser à.
appear (ə'piə) *vi* 1 paraître, sembler. 2 apparaître. **appearance** *n* 1 apparition *f.* 2 apparence *f.*

153

appease (ə'pi:z) *vt* apaiser.

appendix (ə'pendiks) *n*, *pl* **appendices** appendice *m*. **appendicitis** *n* appendicite *f*.

appetite ('æpətait) *n* **1** appétit *m*. **2** désir *m*. **appetizer** *n* apéritif *m*. **appetizing** *adj* appétissant.

applaud (ə'plɔ:d) *vt,vi* applaudir. **applause** *n* applaudissements *m pl*.

apple ('æpəl) *n* pomme *f*.

apply (ə'plai) *vt* appliquer. *vi* s'adresser. **appliance** *n* **1** dispositif *m*. **2** *pl* accessoires *m pl*. **applicable** *adj* applicable. **applicant** *n* candidat *m*. **application** *n* **1** application *f*. **2** demande *f*.

appoint (ə'pɔint) *vt* **1** nommer. **2** fixer. **3** équiper. **appointment** *n* **1** rendez-vous *m*. **2** désignation *f*.

appraise (ə'preiz) *vt* estimer, apprécier. **appraisal** *n* évaluation *f*.

appreciate (ə'pri:ʃieit) *vt* apprécier. *vi* augmenter de valeur. **appreciation** *n* **1** appréciation *f*. **2** hausse de valeur *f*.

apprehend (æpri'hend) *vt* **1** appréhender. **2** comprendre. **apprehension** *n* **1** appréhension *f*. **2** crainte *f*. **3** arrestation *f*. **apprehensive** *adj* anxieux, -euse.

apprentice (ə'prentis) *n* apprenti *m*. *vt* mettre en apprentissage. **apprenticeship** *n* apprentissage *m*.

approach (ə'proutʃ) *vi* (s')approcher *vt* (s')approcher de. *n* **1** approche *f*. **2** accès *m*.

appropriate (*adj* ə'proupriət; *v* ə'prouprieit) *adj* approprié, convenable. *vt* (s')approprier.

approve (ə'pru:v) *vt* approuver. **approval** *n* approbation *f*.

approximate (*adj* ə'prɔksimət; *v* ə'prɔksimeit) *adj* approximatif, -ive. *vt* rapprocher.

apricot ('eiprikɔt) *n* abricot *m*. **apricot tree** *n* abricotier *m*.

April ('eiprəl) *n* avril *m*. **April Fools' Day** *n* premier avril *m*.

apron ('eiprən) *n* tablier *m*.

apse (æps) *n* abside *f*.

apt (æpt) *adj* **1** porté à. **2** juste. **3** doué. **aptly** *adv* à propos.

aptitude ('æptitju:d) *n* **1** tendance *f*. **2** aptitude, disposition *f*.

aquarium (ə'kwɛəriəm) *n* aquarium *m*.

Aquarius (ə'kwɛəriəs) *n* Verseau *m*.

aquatic (ə'kwætik) *adj* aquatique. **aquatics** *n pl* sports nautiques *m pl*.

Arabia (ə'reibiə) *n* Arabie *f*. **Arab** *adj,n* arabe.

154

Arabian *adj* arabe. **Arabic** *adj* arabique, arabe. **Arabic** (language) *n* arabe *m*.

arable ('ærəbəl) *adj* arable.

arbitrary ('ɑːbitrəri) *adj* arbitraire.

arbitrate ('ɑːbitreit) *vt,vi* arbitrer. **arbitration** *n* arbitrage *m*.

arc (ɑːk) *n* arc *m*.

arcade (ɑː'keid) *n* **1** arcade *f*. **2** passage *m*.

arch (ɑːtʃ) *n* **1** arche *f*. **2** arc *m*. **3** voûte *f*. *vt* arquer. *vi* former voûte.

archaeology (ɑːki'ɔlədʒi) *n* archéologie *f*. **archaeological** *adj* archéologique. **archaeologist** *n* archéologue *m,f*.

archaic (ɑː'keiik) *adj* archaïque.

archbishop (ɑːtʃ'biʃəp) *n* archevêque *m*.

archduke (ɑːtʃ'dju:k) *n* archiduc *m*. **archduchess** *n* archiduchesse *f*.

archery ('ɑːtʃəri) *n* tir à l'arc *m*.

archetype ('ɑːkitaip) *n* archétype *m*.

archipelago (ɑːki'peləgou) *n* archipel *m*.

architect ('ɑːkitekt) *n* architecte *m*. **architecture** *n* architecture *f*.

archives ('ɑːkaivz) *n pl* archives *f pl*.

Arctic ('ɑːktik) *adj* arctique. **Arctic (Ocean)** *n* (Océan) Arctique *m*.

ardent ('ɑːdnt) *adj* ardent.

ardour ('ɑːdə) *n* ardeur *f*.

arduous ('ɑːdjuəs) *adj* **1** ardu. **2** acharné.

are (ə; *stressed* ɑː) *v* see **be**.

area ('ɛəriə) *n* **1** aire, surface *f*. **2** territoire *m*. région *f*.

arena (ə'ri:nə) *n* arène *f*.

argue ('ɑːgjuː) *vi* **1** discuter. **2** se disputer. *vt* **1** prouver. **2** soutenir. **argument** *n* **1** argument *m*. **2** discussion *f*. **argumentative** *adj* raisonneur, -euse.

arid ('ærid) *adj* aride.

Aries ('ɛəriːz) *n* Bélier *m*.

arise (ə'raiz) *vi* **1** s'élever. **2** se lever. **3** provenir.

aristocracy (æri'stɔkrəsi) *n* aristocratie *f*. **aristocrat** *n* aristocrate *m,f*. **aristocratic** *adj* aristocratique.

arithmetic (ə'riθmətik) *n* arithmétique *f*.

arm[1] (ɑːm) *n anat* bras *m*. **at arm's length** à distance. **armchair** *n* fauteuil *m*. **armhole** *n* emmanchure *f*. **armpit** *n* aisselle *f*. **armful** *n* brassée *f*.

arm[2] (ɑːm) *n* **1** *mil* arme *f*. **2** *pl* armoiries *f pl*. **be up in arms** se gendarmer. ~*vt* armer. *vi* s'armer. **armament** *n* armement *m*.

armour ('ɑːmə) *n* **1** armure *f*. **2** blindage *f*. *vt*

cuirasser, blinder. **armour-plated** adj cuirassé, blindé. **armoury** n arsenal, -aux m.
army (ˈɑːmi) n armée f.
aroma (əˈroumə) n arome m. **aromatic** adj aromatique.
arose (əˈrouz) v see **arise.**
around (əˈraund) prep autour de. adv autour, à l'entour.
arouse (əˈrauz) vt 1 réveiller. 2 provoquer.
arrange (əˈreindʒ) vt 1 arranger, organiser. 2 ranger. vi s'arranger. **arrangement** n disposition f. arrangement m.
array (əˈrei) vt 1 ranger. 2 orner. n 1 ordre m. 2 atours m pl.
arrears (əˈriəz) n pl arrérages m pl. **in arrears** en retard.
arrest (əˈrest) vt arrêter. n 1 arrestation f. 2 arrêt m.
arrive (əˈraiv) vi arriver. **arrival** n arrivée f.
arrogance (ˈærəgəns) n arrogance f. **arrogant** adj arrogant.
arrow (ˈærou) n flèche f.
arsenic (ˈɑːsnik) n arsenic m.
arson (ˈɑːsən) n crime d'incendie m.
art (ɑːt) n 1 art m. 2 habileté f. 3 artifice m. **art gallery** n musée d'art m. **art school** n école de beaux arts f. **artful** adj 1 astucieux, -euse, rusé. 2 adroit.
artery (ˈɑːtəri) n artère f. **arterial** adj artériel, -elle.
arthritis (ɑːˈθraitis) n arthrite f.
artichoke (ˈɑːtitʃouk) n artichaut m.
article (ˈɑːtikəl) n 1 article m. 2 pl law contrat m. vt engager par contrat.
articulate (v ɑːˈtikjuleit; adj ɑːˈtikjulət) vt articuler, énoncer. vi s'articuler. adj 1 articulé. 2 distinct. **articulation** n articulation f.
artificial (ɑːtiˈfiʃəl) adj artificiel, -elle.
artillery (ɑːˈtiləri) n artillerie f.
artist (ˈɑːtist) n artiste m,f. **artistic** adj artistique.
as (əz; stressed æz) adv 1 aussi, si. 2 comme, en. conj 1 comme. 2 puisque. 3 au moment où. 4 à mesure que. 5 que. **as for** quant à. **as if** comme si. **as well** aussi.
asbestos (æsˈbestəs) n amiante m.
ascend (əˈsend) vt,vi monter. vi remonter. **ascension** n ascension f. **ascent** n montée f.
ascertain (æsəˈtein) vt 1 constater. 2 vérifier.
ash¹ (æʃ) n cendre f. **ashtray** n cendrier m.
ash² (æʃ) n bot frêne m.
ashamed (əˈʃeimd) adj honteux, -euse. **be ashamed of** avoir honte de.

ashore (əˈʃɔː) adv à terre. **go ashore** débarquer.
Asia (ˈeiʃə) n Asie f. **Asian** adj,n also **Asiatic** asiatique.
aside (əˈsaid) adv 1 de côté. 2 à l'écart. n aparté m.
ask (ɑːsk) vt 1 demander, prier. 2 inviter. **ask about** se renseigner sur. **ask a question** poser une question. **ask for** demander.
askew (əˈskjuː) adv de côté.
asleep (əˈsliːp) adv endormi. **be asleep** dormir. **fall asleep** s'endormir.
asparagus (əˈspærəgəs) n asperge f.
aspect (ˈæspekt) n aspect m. point de vue f.
asphalt (ˈæsfælt) n asphalte m. vt asphalter.
aspire (əˈspaiə) vi aspirer. **aspiring** adj ambitieux, -euse.
aspirin (ˈæsprin) n aspirine f.
ass (æs) n 1 âne, ânesse. 2 sot, sotte.
assassin (əˈsæsin) n assassin m. **assassinate** vt assassiner. **assassination** n assassinat m.
assault (əˈsɔːlt) n attaque f. assaut m. vt attaquer.
assemble (əˈsembəl) vt assembler. vi s'assembler. **assembly** n 1 assemblée f. 2 montage m. **assembly line** n chaîne de montage f.
assent (əˈsent) n assentiment m. vi consentir.
assert (əˈsɔːt) vt 1 affirmer. 2 revendiquer. **assertion** n 1 assertion f. 2 revendication f.
assess (əˈses) vt 1 estimer. 2 imposer. **assessment** n 1 estimation f. 2 impôt m.
asset (ˈæset) n 1 avantage m. 2 pl comm actif m. 3 pl biens m pl.
assign (əˈsain) vt assigner. **assignment** n assignation f. 2 law transfert m.
assimilate (əˈsimileit) vt assimiler.
assist (əˈsist) vt,vi assister. **assistance** n aide f. **assistant** adj auxiliaire. n 1 assistant m,f. adjoint m. 2 comm commis m.
assizes (əˈsaiziz) n pl assises f pl.
associate (əˈsouʃieit) adj,n associé. n collègue m. vt associer. vi s'associer. **association** n association f.
assort (əˈsɔːt) vt assortir. vi s'associer. **assortment** n assortiment m.
assume (əˈsjuːm) vt 1 supposer. 2 assumer. 3 affecter. **assumption** n supposition, présomption f.
assure (əˈʃuə) vt assurer. **assurance** n assurance f.
asterisk (ˈæstərisk) n astérisque m.

155

asthma (ˈæsmə) n asthme m. **asthmatic** adj,n asthmatique.

astonish (əˈstɔniʃ) vt étonner. **astonishment** n étonnement m.

astound (əˈstaund) vt ébahır.

astray (əˈstrei) adv égaré.

astride (əˈstraid) adv à califourchon.

astrology (əˈstrɔlədʒi) n astrologie f. **astrologer** n astrologue m. **astrological** adj astrologique.

astronaut (ˈæstrənɔːt) n astronaute m. **astronautics** n astronautique f.

astronomy (əˈstrɔnəmi) n astronomie f. **astronomer** n astronome m. **astronomical** adj astronomique.

astute (əˈstjuːt) adj astucieux, -euse, avisé.

asunder (əˈsʌndə) adv en deux, à part.

asylum (əˈsailəm) n 1 asile m. 2 med hospice m.

at (ət; stressed æt) prep 1 à. 2 chez. **at first** d'abord. **at hand** sous la main. **at last** enfin. **at least** du moins. **at once** tout de suite.

ate (eit, et) v see **eat**.

atheism (ˈeiθiizəm) n athéisme m. **atheist** n athée m,f. **atheistic** adj athée.

Athens (ˈæθinz) n Athènes f.

athlete (ˈæθliːt) n athlète m. **athletic** adj athlétique. **athletics** n athlétisme m.

Atlantic (ətˈlæntik) adj atlantique. **Atlantic (Ocean)** n (Océan) Atlantique m.

atlas (ˈætləs) n atlas m.

atmosphere (ˈætməsfiə) n atmosphère f. **atmospheric** adj atmosphérique. **atmospherics** n pl parasites m pl.

atom (ˈætəm) n atome m. **atom bomb** n bombe atomique f. **atomic** adj atomique.

atone (əˈtoun) vi expier. **atonement** n expiation f.

atrocious (əˈtrouʃəs) adj atroce. **atrocity** n atrocité f.

attach (əˈtætʃ) vt attacher, lier. vi s'attacher. **attachment** n 1 attache f. 2 attachement m.

attaché (əˈtæʃei) n attaché m.

attack (əˈtæk) vt attaquer. n 1 attaque f. 2 med crise f. accès m.

attain (əˈtein) vt,vi atteindre, parvenir à.

attempt (əˈtempt) n 1 tentative f. 2 law attentat m. vt tenter, tâcher.

attend (əˈtend) vt 1 assister à. 2 servir, accompagner. 3 s'occuper de. vi faire attention. **attend to** s'occuper de. **attendance** n 1 assistance f. 2 fréquentation f. 3 service m. **attendant** n 1 serviteur m. 2 employé

m. **attention** n attention f. **attentive** adj 1 attentif, -ive. 2 prévenant.

attic (ˈætik) n mansarde f. grenier m.

attire (əˈtaiə) vt vêtir. n vêtements m pl.

attitude (ˈætitjuːd) n attitude f.

attorney (əˈtəːni) n 1 avoué m. 2 mandataire m. **attorney general** n procureur général m.

attract (əˈtrækt) vt attirer. **attraction** n 1 attraction f. 2 pl attraits m pl. **attractive** adj attrayant, séduisant.

attribute (v əˈtribjuːt; n ˈætribjuːt) vt attribuer, imputer. n attribut m.

aubergine (ˈoubəʒiːn) n aubergine f.

auburn (ˈɔːbən) adj châtain, roux, rousse.

auction (ˈɔːkʃən) n vente aux enchères f. **auctioneer** n commissaire-priseur m.

audacious (ɔːˈdeiʃəs) adj audacieux, -euse. **audacity** n audace f.

audible (ˈɔːdibəl) adj 1 audible. 2 intelligible. **audibly** adv distinctement.

audience (ˈɔːdiəns) n 1 audience f. 2 public m. spectateurs m pl.

audiovisual (ɔːdiouˈviʒuəl) adj audio-visuel, -elle.

audit (ˈɔːdit) n vérification f. vt vérifier. **auditor** n expert comptable m.

audition (ɔːˈdiʃən) n audition f.

auditorium (ɔːdiˈtɔːriəm) n, pl **auditoria** or **auditoriums** auditorium m.

August (ˈɔːgəst) n août m.

aunt (ɑːnt) n tante f.

au pair (ou ˈpɛə) n (jeune fille) au pair f.

aura (ˈɔːrə) n aura f.

austere (ɔːˈstiə) adj austère. **austerity** n austérité f.

Australia (ɔːˈstreiliə) n Australie f. **Australian** adj,n australien, -ienne.

Austria (ˈɔːstriə) n Autriche f. **Austrian** adj,n autrichien, -ienne.

authentic (ɔːˈθentik) adj authentique. **authenticity** authenticité f.

author (ˈɔːθə) n auteur m. **authoress** n femme auteur f.

authority (ɔːˈθɔriti) n autorité f. **authoritarian** adj autoritaire. **authoritative** adj 1 autoritaire. 2 impérieux, -ieuse. 3 autorisé.

authorize (ˈɔːθəraiz) vt autoriser. **authorization** n autorisation f.

autistic (ɔːˈtistik) adj autistique.

autobiography (ɔːtəbaiˈɔgrəfi) n autobiographie f. **autobiographical** adj autobiographique.

autograph (ˈɔːtəgrɑːf) n autographe m. vt signer, dédicacer.

automatic (ɔ:tə'mætik) *adj* automatique.
automation (ɔ:tə'meiʃən) *n* automatisation *f*.
autonomous (ɔ:'tɔnəməs) *adj* autonome.
  autonomy *n* autonomie *f*.
autumn ('ɔ:təm) *n* automne *m*.
auxiliary (ɔ:g'ziliəri) *adj,n* auxiliaire *m*.
available (ə'veiləbəl) *adj* 1 disponible. 2 valable.
avalanche ('ævəlɑ:nʃ) *n* avalanche *f*.
avenge (ə'vendʒ) *vt* venger.
avenue ('ævənju:) *n* avenue *f*.
average ('ævridʒ) *n* moyenne *f*. *adj* moyen,
  -enne. *vt* prendre la moyenne de. *vi* donner
  une moyenne.
aversion (ə'vɔ:ʃən) *n* aversion *f*. **pet aversion**
  bête noire *f*.
aviary ('eiviəri) *n* volière *f*.
aviation (eivi'eiʃən) *n* aviation *f*.
avid ('ævid) *adj* avide. **avidity** *n* avidité *f*.
avocado (ævə'kɑ:dou) *n* avocat *m*.
avoid (ə'vɔid) *vt* éviter.
await (ə'weit) *vt* attendre.
awake* (ə'weik) *vt* 1 éveiller. 2 réveiller. *vi*
  s'éveiller, se réveiller. **awaken** *vt* 1 éveiller. 2
  réveiller.
award (ə'wɔ:d) *n* 1 récompense *f*. 2 adjudication *f*. *vt* 1 décerner. 2 accorder.
aware (ə'wɛə) *adj* 1 conscient. 2 avisé. **be
  aware** savoir. **not be aware of** ignorer.
  awareness *n* conscience *f*.
away (ə'wei) *adv* 1 au loin, loin. 2 absent.
  right away tout de suite.
awe (ɔ:) *n* crainte *f*. **awe-inspiring** *adj*
  impressionnant. **awe-struck** *adj* trés impres-
  sionné.
awful ('ɔ:fəl) *adj* 1 redoutable. 2 imposant. 3
  épouvantable.
awkward ('ɔ:kwəd) *adj* 1 maladroit. 2 gêné. 3
  embarrassant. 4 incommode. **awkwardness**
  n 1 maladresse *f*. 2 embarras *m*. 3 inconvénient *m*.
awoke (ə'wouk) *v see* **awake.**
axe (æks) *n* hache *f*.
axis ('æksis) *n, pl* **axes** axe *m*.
axle ('æksəl) *n* essieu, -eux *m*.
azalea (ə'zeiliə) *n* azaleé *f*.

B

babble ('bæbəl) *vi* babiller. *n* babil, bavardage
  m.
baboon (bə'bu:n) *n* babouin *m*.
baby ('beibi) *n* bébé *m*. *adj* puéril. **baby-sit** *vi*

garder des enfants. **baby-sitter** *n* garde
  d'enfants *m,f*.
baccarat ('bækərɑ:) *n* baccara *m*.
bachelor ('bætʃələ) *n* célibataire *m*. **bachelor
  of Arts/Science** licencié ès lettres/sciences
  m. **bachelorhood** *n* célibat *m*.
back (bæk) *n* 1 dos *m*. reins *m pl*. 2 arrière,
  derrière *m*. 3 verso *m*. 4 fond *m*. 5 dossier *m*.
  adj arrière. *adv* en arrière. **be back** être de
  retour. **come back** revenir.
backache ('bækeik) *n* maux de reins *m pl*.
  courbature *f*.
backbone ('bækboun) *n* épine dorsale *f*.
backdate ('bækdeit) *vt* antidater.
backfire ('bækfaiə) *n* retour de flamme *m*. *vi* 1
  mot pétarader. 2 *sl* echouer.
backgammon ('bækgæmən) *n* jacquet *m*.
background ('bækgraund) *n* arrière-plan, fond
  m.
backhand ('bækhænd) *n* sport revers *m*.
  backhanded *adj* injuste, équivoque. **back-
  hander** *n sl* pot-de-vin *m*.
backlash ('bæklæʃ) *n* 1 battement *m*. 2 contre-
  coup *m*.
backlog ('bæklɔg) *n* arriéré *m*.
backstage (bæk'steidʒ) *adv* dans les coulisses.
backstroke ('bækstrouk) *n* brasse sur le dos *f*.
backward ('bækwəd) *adj* arriéré, rétrograde,
  lent. **backwardness** *n* 1 retard *m*. 2 arriéra-
  tion mentale *f*. **backwards** *adv* en arrière, à
  reculons, à rebours.
backwater ('bækwɔtə) *n* eau stagnante *f*.
bacon ('beikən) *n* lard, bacon *m*.
bacteria (bæk'tiəriə) *n pl* bactéries *f pl*.
  bacterial *adj* bactérien, -ienne.
bad (bæd) *adj* 1 mauvais, mal. 2 méchant.
  bad-tempered *adj* acariâtre, de mauvaise
  humeur. **badly** *adv* 1 mal. 2 grièvement.
bade (bæd) *v see* **bid.**
badge (bædʒ) *n* 1 insigne *m*. 2 symbole *m*.
badger ('bædʒə) *n* blaireau, -aux *m*. *vt* harceler.
badminton ('bædmintən) *n* badminton, volant
  m.
baffle ('bæfəl) *vt* 1 déconcerter. 2 déjouer.
bag (bæg) *n* sac, sachet *m*. *vt* 1 mettre en sac. 2
  sl chiper. **baggage** *n* bagages *m pl*. **baggy**
  adj bouffant. **bagpipes** *n pl* cornemuse *f*.
bail (beil) *n* 1 caution *f*. 2 répondant *m*. *vt* porter
  garant de.
bailiff ('beilif) *n* 1 huissier *m*. 2 régisseur *m*. 3
  bailli *m*.
bait (beit) *n* 1 amorce *f*. 2 appât, leurre *m*. *vt* 1
  amorcer. 2 *inf* harceler.

bake (beik) *vt,vi* cuire au four. **baker** *n* boulanger *m*. **bakery** *n* boulangerie *f*.

balance ('bæləns) *n* **1** balance *f*. **2** équilibre *m*. **3** solde *m*. *vt* **1** balancer, équilibrer. **2** solder. *vi* **1** se balancer, s'équilibrer. **2** se solder. **balance sheet** *n* bilan *m*.

balcony ('bælkəni) *n* balcon *m*.

bald (bɔːld) *adj* **1** chauve. **2** sec, sèche, plat.

bale[1] (beil) *vt* **bale out** écoper.

bale[2] (beil) *vt* empaqueter.

baleful ('beilfəl) *adj* sinistre, funeste.

ball[1] (bɔːl) *n* **1** boule *f*. **2** balle *f*. ballon *m*. **3** boulet *m*. **4** pelote *f*. **5** *cul* boulette *f*. **ball-bearing** *n* roulement à bille *m*.

ball[2] (bɔːl) *n* bal *m*. **ballroom** *n* salle de bal *or* de danse *f*.

ballad ('bæləd) *n* **1** *mus* romance *f*. **2** *lit* ballade *f*.

ballast ('bæləst) *n* **1** *naut* lest *m*. **2** ballast *m*. *vt* **1** lester. **2** empierrer, ballaster.

ballet ('bælei) *n* **1** ballet *m*. **2** corps de ballet *m*.

ballistic (bə'listik) *adj* balistique.

balloon (bə'luːn) *n* **1** ballon à air *m*. **2** *aviat* ballon, aérostat *m*. *vi* se gonfler.

ballot ('bælət) *n* scrutin, vote *m*. *vi* voter au scrutin. **ballot-box** *n* urne électorale *f*.

Baltic ('bɔːltik) *adj* balte. **Baltic (Sea)** *n* (Mer) Baltique *f*.

bamboo (bæm'buː) *n* bambou *m*.

ban (bæn) *n* **1** ban *m*. proscription *f*. **2** *rel* interdit *m*. *vt* interdire.

banal (bə'nɑːl) *adj* banal, -aux.

banana (bə'nɑːnə) *n* banane *f*.

band[1] (bænd) *n* **1** bande, troupe *f*. **2** orchestre *m*. *vt* liguer. *vi* se liguer.

band[2] (bænd) *n* **1** lien *m*. **2** bande *f*. **bandage** *n* bandage, pansement *m*. *vt* bander, panser.

bandit ('bændit) *n* bandit, brigand *m*.

bandy ('bændi) *vt* échanger. *adj* arqué. **bandy-legged** *adj* bancal.

bang (bæŋ) *n* **1** coup *m*. **2** détonation *f*. *interj* pan! *vi,vt* frapper. **bang the door** claquer la porte.

bangle ('bæŋgəl) *n* bracelet *m*.

banish ('bæniʃ) *vt* bannir, exiler. **banishment** *n* bannissement, exil *m*.

banister ('bænistə) *n* rampe *f*.

banjo ('bændʒou) *n* banjo *m*.

bank[1] (bæŋk) *n* **1** talus, remblai *m*. **2** *geog* berge, rive *f*. *vt* endiguer. **bank up** remblayer.

bank[2] (bæŋk) *n* *comm* banque *f*. **bank account** *n* compte en banque *m*. **bankbook** *n* carnet de banque *m*. **bank holiday** *n* jour

férié légal *m*. **banknote** *n* billet de banque *m*. ~*vt* déposer en banque. **bank on** compter sur.

bankrupt ('bæŋkrʌpt) *n* banqueroutier *m*. *adj* en faillite, ruiné. **go bankrupt** faire faillite. ~*vt* mettre en faillite.

banner ('bænə) *n* bannière *f*.

banquet ('bæŋkwit) *n* banquet, festin *m*.

baptize (bæp'taiz) *vt* baptiser, surnommer. **baptism** *n* baptême *m*.

bar (bɑː) *n* **1** bar *m*. **2** barre *f*. **3** *law* barreau, -aux *m*. **4** obstacle *m*. **5** *mus* mesure *f*. **6** tablette *f*. *vt* **1** barrer. **2** interdire. **barmaid** *n* serveuse *f*.

barbarian (bɑː'bɛəriən) *adj,n* barbare. **barbaric** *adj* barbare, primitif, -ive. **barbarity** *n* barbarie, cruauté *f*. **barbarous** *adj* barbare.

barbecue ('bɑːbikjuː) *n* gril *m*. *vt* rôtir à la broche.

barbed wire (bɑːbd) *n* fil de fer barbelé *m*.

barber ('bɑːbə) *n* coiffeur *m*.

barbiturate (bɑː'bitjurət) *n* barbiturique *m*.

bare (bɛə) *adj* **1** nu, dégarni. **2** sec, sèche, simple. *vt* mettre à nu, révéler. **barefoot** *adv* nu-pieds. **barely** *adv* à peine, tout juste.

bargain ('bɑːgin) *n* affaire, occasion *f*.

barge (bɑːdʒ) *n* péniche *f*. chaland *m*. *v* **barge into** bousculer, entrer en coup de vent.

baritone ('bæritoun) *n* baryton *m*.

bark[1] (bɑːk) *n* aboiement *m*. *vi* aboyer.

bark[2] (bɑːk) *n* *bot* écorce *f*.

barley ('bɑːli) *n* orge *f*. **barley-sugar** *n* sucre d'orge *m*. **barley-water** *n* orgeat *m*.

barn (bɑːn) *n* grange *f*.

barometer (bə'rɔmitə) *n* baromètre *m*.

baron ('bærən) *n* baron *m*. **baroness** *n* baronne *f*. **baronet** *n* baronnet *m*.

barracks ('bærəks) *n pl* caserne *f*.

barrel ('bærəl) *n* **1** tonneau, -aux *m*. **2** caque *f*. **3** cylindre *m*. **4** (of a gun) canon *m*.

barren ('bærən) *adj* stérile, aride.

barricade ('bærikeid) *n* barricade *f*. *vt* barricader.

barrier ('bæriə) *n* **1** barrière *f*. **2** obstacle *m*.

barrister ('bæristə) *n* avocat *m*.

barrow ('bærou) *n* brouette *f*.

barter ('bɑːtə) *n* troc *m*. *vt* troquer.

base[1] (beis) *n* base *f*. fondement *m*. *vt* fonder. **baseball** *n* base-ball *m*. **basement** *n* **1** sous-sol *m*. **2** soubassement *m*.

base[2] (beis) *adj* vil, bas, basse.

bash (bæʃ) *n* coup *m*. *vt* *inf* taper sur, cogner.

bashful ('bæʃfəl) *adj* timide.

basic ('beisik) *adj* **1** fondamental, -aux. **2** basique.

basil ('bæzəl) *n* basilic *m*.

basin ('beisən) *n* **1** cuvette *f.* **2** *cul* bol *m.* **3** *geog* bassin *m*.

basis ('beisis) *n, pl* **bases** base *f.* fondement *m*.

bask (bɑ:sk) *vi* se chauffer.

basket ('bɑ:skit) *n* panier *m.* corbeille *f.* **basketball** *n* basket-ball *m*.

bass[1] (beis) *n mus* basse *f*.

bass[2] (bæs) *n zool* perche *f*.

bassoon (bə'su:n) *n* basson *m*.

bastard ('bɑ:stəd) *n* bâtard *m. adj* bâtard, faux, fausse.

baste ('beist) *vt* **1** arroser. **2** faufiler, bâtir.

bat[1] (bæt) *n* batte *f.* battoir *m.* **batsman** *n* batteur *m*.

bat[2] (bæt) *n zool* chauve-souris *f*.

batch (bætʃ) *n* **1** fournée *f.* **2** tas *m*.

bath (bɑ:θ) *n* **1** bain *m.* **2** baignoire *f. vt* baigner. *vi* prendre un bain. **bathrobe** *n* peignoir de bain *m.* **bathroom** *n* salle de bain *f*.

bathe (beið) *vt* baigner. *vi* se baigner. **bathing costume** *n* maillot de bain *m.* **bathing trunks** *n* caleçon de bain *m*.

baton ('bætən) *n* **1** bâton *m.* **2** matraque *f*.

battalion (bə'tæliən) *n* bataillon *m*.

batter[1] ('bætə) *vt* **1** battre, rouer de coups. **2** démolir. **battered** *adj* délabré.

batter[2] ('bætə) *n* pâte lisse *f*.

battery ('bætəri) *n* **1** pile *f.* **2** *mil* batterie *f*.

battle ('bætl) *n* bataille *f.* combat *m. vi* se battre, lutter. **battlefield** *n* champ de bataille *m.* **battleship** *n* cuirassé *m*.

bawl (bɔ:l) *vi,vt* brailler.

bay[1] (bei) *n geog* baie *f*.

bay[2] (bei) *n arch* travée *f.* **bay window** *n* fenêtre en saillie *f*.

bay[3] (bei) *n* abois *m pl.* **keep at bay** tenir en échec. ~*vi* aboyer.

bay[4] (bei) *n bot* laurier *m*.

bayonet ('beiənit) *n* baïonnette *f*.

be* (bi:) *vi* **1** être. **2** se trouver. **3** exister. *v aux* être. **there is** *or* **are** il y a.

beach (bi:tʃ) *n* plage *f*.

beacon ('bi:kən) *n* **1** feu, feux *m.* **2** balise *f*.

bead (bi:d) *n* **1** perle *f.* **2** grain *m.* **3** *pl* chapelet *m*.

beak (bi:k) *n* bec *m*.

beaker ('bi:kə) *n* gobelet *m*.

beam (bi:m) *n* **1** poutre *f.* **2** rayon, faisceau,

-aux *m. vi* rayonner. **beaming** *adj* radieux, -euse.

bean (bi:n) *n* **1** grain *m.* **2** haricot *m*.

bear*[1] (bɛə) *vt* **1** porter, supporter. **2** produire. **3** donner naissance à. *vi* **1** souffrir. **2** peser. **3** avoir rapport. **bearable** *adj* supportable. **bearing** *n* **1** port, maintien *m.* conduite *f.* **2** rapport *m.* **lose one's bearings** perdre le nord.

bear[2] (bɛə) *n* ours *m*.

beard (biəd) *n* barbe *f*.

beast (bi:st) *n* **1** bête *f.* **2** animal, -aux *m.* brute *f*.

beat* (bi:t) *vt* **1** battre. **2** frapper. *n* **1** battement *m.* **2** ronde *f.* **3** *mus* mesure *f.* **beating** *n* **1** battement *m.* **2** *inf* rossée *f*.

beauty ('bju:ti) *n* beauté *f.* **beautiful** *adj* **1** beau, belle, beaux, magnifique. **2** admirable. **beauty queen** *n* reine de beauté *f*.

beaver ('bi:və) *n* castor *m*.

became (bi'keim) *v see* **become.**

because (bi'kɔ:z) *conj* parce que, car. **because of** à cause de.

beckon ('bekən) *vt* faire signe à. *vi* faire signe.

become* (bi'kʌm) *vi* devenir, se faire. *vt* convenir. **becoming** *adj* **1** convenable. **2** seyant.

bed (bed) *n* **1** lit *m.* **2** parterre *m.* **3** couche *f.* **go to bed** se coucher. **bedclothes** *n pl* couvertures et draps de lit. **bedding** *n* literie *f.* **bedridden** *adj* alité, cloué au lit. **bedroom** *n* chambre (à coucher) *f.* **bedside** *n* chevet *m.* **bed-sitter** *n* chambre-studio *f.* **bedspread** *n* dessus de lit *m*.

bedraggled (bi'drægəld) *adj* dépenaillé.

bee (bi:) *n* abeille *f.* **beehive** *n* ruche *f.* **beekeeper** *n* apiculteur *m.* **beeline** *n* ligne droite *f*.

beech (bi:tʃ) *n* hêtre *m*.

beef (bi:f) *n* bœuf *m.* **roast beef** rosbif *m*.

been (bi:n) *v see* **be.**

beer (biə) *n* bière *f*.

beet (bi:t) *n* betterave *f.* **beetroot** *n* betterave *f*.

beetle ('bi:tl) *n* scarabée, coléoptère *m*.

befall* (bi'fɔ:l) *vt* survenir, arriver.

before (bi'fɔ:) *adv* **1** avant, auparavant. **2** devant. *prep* **1** devant. **2** avant. *conj* avant que. **beforehand** *adv* au préalable.

befriend (bi'frend) *vt* venir en aide à.

beg (beg) *vt* demander, prier. *vt,vi* mendier. **I beg your pardon 1** plaît-il? **2** *inf* comment? **beggar** *n* mendiant *m.* **poor beggar!** pauvre type!

begin* (bi'gin) *vt* commencer, entamer. **begin**

159

to se mettre à. **beginner** n débutant, novice m. **beginning** n commencement, début m.

begrudge (bi'grʌdʒ) vt envier. **begrudge doing something** faire quelque chose à contre-cœur.

behalf (bi'hɑ:f) n 1 sujet m. 2 faveur f. **on behalf of** au nom de, pour le compte de.

behave (bi'heɪv) vi se comporter. **behave yourself!** inf tiens-toi bien! **badly-behaved** mal élevé. **well-behaved** sage. **behaviour** n 1 conduite f. 2 tenue f. 3 manières f pl.

behind (bi'haɪnd) adv derrière, en arrière. prep derrière, en arrière de. n 1 derrière m. 2 inf cul m. **behindhand** adj,adv en retard, en arrière.

behold° (bi'hould) vt contempler, regarder.

beige (beɪʒ) adj,n beige m.

being ('bi:ɪŋ) n 1 être m. 2 existence f. **for the time being** pour le moment.

belfry ('belfri) n beffroi m.

Belgium ('beldʒəm) n Belgique f. **Belgian** adj,n belge.

believe (bi'li:v) vt,vi croire. **I believe so** je crois que oui. **make believe** faire semblant. **belief** n 1 croyance f. 2 confiance f. **believable** adj croyable. **believer** n croyant m.

bell (bel) n 1 cloche f. 2 sonnette f. **bellringer** n sonneur, carillonneur m.

bellow ('belou) vt,vi 1 beugler, mugir. 2 vociférer. n 1 mugissement m. 2 hurlement m.

bellows ('belouz) n pl soufflet m.

belly ('beli) n 1 ventre m. 2 panse f.

belong (bi'lɔŋ) vi 1 appartenir. 2 être propre. **belongings** n pl effets m pl. affaires f pl.

below (bi'lou) adv 1 en bas, (au-)dessous, ci-dessous. prep au-dessous de, sous.

belt (belt) n 1 ceinture f. 2 tech courroie f. 3 zone m.

bench (bentʃ) n 1 banc m. 2 établi m. 3 law tribunal, -aux m.

bend° (bend) vt plier, courber, fléchir. vi 1 se pencher. 2 se soumettre à. n 1 virage, tournant m. 2 coude m. courbe f.

beneath (bi'ni:θ) adv au-dessous, en bas. prep sous, au-dessous de.

benefit ('benifit) n 1 profit, avantage m. 2 bienfait m. 3 allocation f. vt profiter à, faire du bien à. **benefit by** profiter de. **beneficial** adj profitable, avantageux, -euse.

benevolent (bi'nevələnt) adj 1 bienveillant. 2 charitable.

bent (bent) v see **bend**. adj 1 courbé. 2 déterminé.

bequeath (bi'kwi:ð) vt léguer.

bereave° (bi'ri:v) vt priver. **bereavement** n deuil m. perte f.

berry ('beri) n baie f.

berth (bə:θ) n 1 couchette f. 2 naut emplacement m. vt amarrer. vi mouiller.

beside (bi'said) prep 1 à côté de. 2 hors de. **besides** adv en outre, de plus.

besiege (bi'si:dʒ) vt assiéger.

best (best) adj,pron le meilleur m. adv,n le mieux m. **best man** n garçon d'honneur m. **best-seller** n livre à succès m. **do one's best** faire de son mieux. **make the best of** tirer le meilleur parti de.

bestow (bi'stou) vt accorder.

bet° (bet) vt parier. n pari m. **betting shop** n bureau de pari m.

betray (bi'trei) vt 1 trahir. 2 révéler. **betrayal** n trahison f.

better ('betə) adj meilleur. adv mieux. **be better** 1 aller mieux. 2 valoir mieux. **get better** 1 s'améliorer. 2 guérir. **so much the better!** tant mieux! **think better of** se raviser.

between (bi'twi:n) prep entre.

beverage ('bevridʒ) n boisson f.

beware° (bi'wɛə) vi prendre garde. **beware of** se méfier de.

bewilder (bi'wildə) vt désorienter. **bewildered** adj 1 ahuri. 2 abasourdi.

beyond (bi'jɔnd) adv au-delà, plus loin. prep au-delà de, par-delà, outre. **that is beyond me** cela me dépasse.

bias ('baiəs) n 1 parti pris m. 2 penchant m. 3 biais m. vt prédisposer. **biased** adj partial, -aux.

bib (bib) n bavette f.

Bible ('baibəl) n Bible f. **biblical** adj biblique.

bibliography (bibli'ɔgrəfi) n bibliographie f. **bibliographer** n bibliographe m. **bibliographical** adj bibliographique.

biceps ('baiseps) n biceps m.

bicker ('bikə) vi se chamailler, se quereller. **bickering** n prise de bec f. querelles f pl.

bicycle ('baisikəl) n 1 bicyclette f. 2 inf vélo m.

bid° (bid) n 1 offre, soumission f. 2 enchère f. vt 1 ordonner. 2 inviter à. 3 souhaiter. vi faire une offre.

biennial (bai'eniəl) adj biennal, -aux.

big (big) adj grand, gros, grosse.

bigamy ('bigəmi) n bigamie f.

bigot ('bigət) n fanatique m,f. **bigoted** adj à l'esprit étroit.

bikini (bi'ki:ni) *n* bikini *m*.
bilingual (bai'liŋgwəl) *adj* bilingue.
bilious ('biliəs) *adj* **1** bilieux, -euse. **2** colérique.
bill[1] (bil) *n* **1** facture, note, addition *f*. **2** effet *m*. **3** affiche *f*. **4** *pol* projet de loi *m*. **bill-board** *n* panneau d'affichage *m*.
bill[2] (bil) *n zool* bec *m*.
billiards ('biliədz) *n pl* billard *m*.
billion ('biliən) *n* **1** billion *m*. **2** *US* milliard *m*.
bin (bin) *n* coffre *m*. poubelle *f*.
binary ('bainəri) *adj* binaire.
bind* (baind) *vt* **1** lier. **2** attacher. **3** relier. **binding** *n* **1** reliure *f*. **2** ligature *f*. **3** fixation *f*. *adj* obligatoire.
binoculars (bi'nɔkjuləz) *n pl* jumelles *f pl*.
biography (bai'ɔgrəfi) *n* biographie *f*. **biographer** *n* biographe *m*. **biographical** *adj* biographique.
biology (bai'ɔlədʒi) *n* biologie *f*. **biological** *adj* biologique. **biologist** *n* biologiste *m*.
birch (bə:tʃ) *n* bouleau, -aux *m*.
bird (bə:d) *n* **1** oiseau, -aux *m*. **2** *inf* fille *f*. **birdcage** *n* volière, cage d'oiseau *f*. **bird's-eye view** vue à vol d'oiseau *f*.
birth (bə:θ) *n* **1** naissance *f*. **2** *zool* mise bas *f*. **3** origine *f*. **birth certificate** *n* acte de naissance *m*. **birth control** *n* limitation des naissances *f*. **birthday** *n* anniversaire *m*. **birthmark** *n* tache de naissance *f*. **birth rate** *n* natalité *f*.
biscuit ('biskit) *n* biscuit *m*.
bishop ('biʃəp) *n* **1** évêque *m*. **2** *game* fou *m*.
bit[1] (bit) *n* **1** (of a bridle) mors *m*. **2** mèche *f*.
bit[2] (bit) *n* morceau, -aux, bout *m*. *adv* un peu. **bit by bit** petit à petit.
bitch (bitʃ) *n* **1** chienne *f*. **2** femelle *f*. **3** *sl* garce *f*.
bite* (bait) *n* **1** morsure, piqûre *f*. **2** bouchée *f*. *vt* mordre, piquer. **biting** *adj* **1** mordant. **2** perçant.
bitter ('bitə) *adj* amer, -ère, aigre. *n* bière amère *f*. **bitterness** *n* **1** amertume *f*. **2** rancune, rancœur *f*.
bizarre (bi'zɑ:) *adj* bizarre.
black (blæk) *adj,n* noir *m*. *n cap* Noir *m*. **blacken** *vt* noircir *vi* se noircir. **blackness** *n* **1** noirceur *f*. **2** obscurité *f*.
blackberry ('blækbəri) *n* mûre *f*. **blackberry bush** *n* ronce *f*. mûrier *m*.
blackbird ('blækbə:d) *n* merle *m*.
blackboard ('blækbɔ:d) *n* tableau noir *m*.
blackcurrant (blæk'kʌrənt) *n* cassis *m*.
black eye *n* œil poché *m*.

blackleg ('blæklɛg) *n* jaune *m*.
blackmail ('blækmeil) *n* chantage *m*. *vt* faire chanter.
black market *n* marché noir *m*.
blackout ('blækaut) *n* **1** blackout *m*. **2** panne d'électricité *f*. **3** *med* évanouissement *m*. *vt* obscurcir. *vi* s'évanouir.
black pudding *n* boudin noir *m*.
blacksmith ('blæksmiθ) *n* forgeron, maréchal ferrant *m*.
bladder ('blædə) *n* vessie *f*. **gall-bladder** *n* vésicule biliaire *f*.
blade (bleid) *n* **1** brin *m*. **2** lame *f*. **3** pale *f*.
blame (bleim) *n* **1** reproches *m pl*. **2** faute *f*. *vt* blâmer.
blancmange (blə'mɔnʒ) *n* blanc-manger *m*.
blank (blæŋk) *adj* **1** blanc, -che, vierge. **2** vide. *n* vide *m*. lacune *f*.
blanket ('blæŋkit) *n* couverture *f*. **wet blanket** trouble-fête *m invar*.
blare (blɛə) *vi* sonner. *n* **1** sonnerie *f*. **2** fracas *m*.
blaspheme (blæs'fi:m) *vi,vt* blasphémer **blasphemy** *n* blasphème *m*.
blast (blɑ:st) *n* **1** bouffée *f*. coup de vent *m*. **2** explosion *f*. **3** coup *m*. *vt* **1** faire sauter. **2** détruire.
blatant ('bleitnt) *adj* **1** criard. **2** criant, flagrant.
blaze (bleiz) *n* **1** feu *m*. flamme *f*. **2** éclat *m*. *vi* **1** flamber. **2** étinceler.
bleach (bli:tʃ) *vt,vi* blanchir. *n* eau de javel *f*.
bleak (bli:k) *adj* **1** désolé, nu. **2** triste, morne.
bleat (bli:t) *vi* bêler. *n* bêlement *m*.
bleed* (bli:d) *vi,vt* saigner. **bleeding** *n* **1** écoulement de sang *m*. **2** *med* saignée *f*.
blemish ('blemiʃ) *n* **1** imperfection *f*. **2** souillure, tache *f*. *vt* **1** tacher. **2** abîmer.
blend (blend) *n* mélange *m*. *vt* mélanger, mêler. *vi* **1** se fondre. **2** aller bien ensemble.
bless (bles) *vt* bénir, consacrer. **blessed** *adj* bienheureux, -euse, saint. **blessing** *n* **1** *rel* bénédiction *f*. **2** bienfait *m*.
blew (blu:) *v see* **blow**[2].
blind (blaind) *adj* **1** aveugle. **2** sans issue. *n* store *m*. abat-jour *m invar*. *vt* aveugler, éblouir. **blindfold** *adj,adv* les yeux bandés. *vt* bander les yeux à. **blindness** *n* cécité *f*.
blink (bliŋk) *vi* clignoter. *n* battement de paupières *m*. **blinker** *n* œillère *f*.
bliss (blis) *n* félicité *f*. **blissful** *adj* heureux, -euse, serein.
blister ('blistə) *n* **1** *med* ampoule *f*. vésicatoire

161

m. **2** cloque *f. vi* **1** se couvrir d'ampoules. **2** se cloquer.

blizzard ('blizəd) *n* tempête de neige *f.*

blob (blɔb) *n* tache *f.* pâté *m.*

bloc (blɔk) *n* bloc *m.*

block (blɔk) *n* **1** bloc *m.* **2** billot *m.* **3** obstacle *m.* **block of flats** immeuble *m.* ~*vt* obstruer, bloquer. **block up** boucher.

blockade (blɔ'keid) *n* blocus *m. vt* bloquer.

bloke (blouk) *n inf* type, mec *m.*

blond (blɔnd) *adj* blond. **blonde** *adj,n* blonde *f.*

blood (blʌd) *n* sang *m.* **bloodcurdling** *adj* à vous figer le sang. **blood pressure** *n* tension artérielle *f.* **bloodshot** *adj* injecté de sang. **bloodstream** *n* sang, flot sanguin *m.* **bloodthirsty** *adj* sanguinaire, avide de sang. **bloody** *adj* **1** ensanglanté. **2** *sl* sacré.

bloom (blu:m) *n* fleur, floraison *f. vi* **1** fleurir. **2** resplendir. **blooming** *adj* **1** en fleur. **2** florissant.

blossom ('blɔsəm) *n* fleur *f. vi* fleurir.

blot (blɔt) *n* **1** tache *f.* **2** pâté *m. vt* **1** tacher. **2** sécher. **blotting paper** *n* papier buvard *m.*

blouse (blauz) *n* blouse *f.* chemisier *m.*

blow[1] (blou) *n* coup *m.*

blow[2] (blou) *vt,vi* souffler. *vt* sonner. **blow away** emporter. **blow one's nose** se moucher. **blow up** **1** éclater. **2** faire sauter. **3** gonfler.

blubber ('blʌbə) *n* graisse de baleine *f.*

blue (blu:) *adj* **1** bleu. **2** triste. **3** grivois. *n* bleu *m.* **bluebell** *n* jacinthe des prés *f.*

bluff (blʌf) *n* bluff *m. vt* bluffer.

blunder ('blʌndə) *n* bévue *f. vi* gaffer, faire une gaffe.

blunt (blʌnt) *adj* **1** émoussé. **2** épointé. **3** obtus. **4** brusque. *vt* émousser.

blur (blə:) *vt* **1** brouiller. **2** obscurcir. *n* **1** tache *f.* **2** brouillard *m.* **blurred** *adj* flou, confus.

blush (blʌʃ) *n* rougeur *f. vi* rougir.

boar (bɔ:) *n* verrat *m.* **wild boar** *n* sanglier *m.*

board (bɔ:d) *n* **1** planche *f.* **2** tableau, -aux *m.* **3** table, pension *f.* **4** *naut* bord *m.* **5** conseil *m.* **6** carton *m. vi* être en pension. *vt* monter dans, aborder. **boarder** *n* pensionnaire *m,f.* **boarding house** *n* pension de famille *f.* **boarding school** *n* pensionnat *m.*

boast (boust) *vi* se vanter. *n* vanterie *f.*

boat (bout) *n* bateau, -aux *m.* barque *f.* navire *m.*

bob (bɔb) *vt* **1** écourter. **2** secouer. *vi* s'agiter.

bodice ('bɔdis) *n* corsage *m.*

body ('bɔdi) *n* **1** corps *m.* **2** carrosserie *f.* **3**

organisme *m.* **4** consistance *f.* **bodyguard** *n* gorille, garde du corps *m.*

bog (bɔg) *n* marais *m.* fondrière *f.* **boggy** *adj* marécageux, -euse.

bohemian (bə'hi:miən) *adj,n* **1** bohémien, -ienne. **2** bohème.

boil[1] (bɔil) *vi* bouillir. *vt* **1** faire bouillir. **2** cuire à l'eau. **boil down** se réduire. **boil over** déborder. **boiler** *n* chaudière *f.* **boiling** *adj* bouillant, en ébullition.

boil[2] (bɔil) *n med* furoncle *m.*

boisterous ('bɔistərəs) *adj* **1** turbulent. **2** tumultueux, -euse.

bold (bould) *adj* **1** hardi, audacieux, -euse. **2** effronté. **boldness** *n* **1** hardiesse, audace *f.* **2** impudence *f.*

bolster ('boulstə) *n* traversin *m. vt* **1** rembourrer. **2** soutenir, étayer.

bolt (boult) *n* **1** verrou, -oux *m.* **2** boulon *m. vt* **1** verrouiller. **2** avaler. *vi* décamper.

bomb (bɔm) *n* bombe *f. vt* bombarder. **bombshell** *n* **1** obus *m.* **2** grande surprise *f.* **bombard** *vt* **1** bombarder. **2** assaillir.

bond (bɔnd) *n* **1** lien *m.* attache *f.* **2** obligation *f.* bon *m.* **3** dépôt, entrepôt douanier *m.* **bondage** *n* servitude *f.*

bone (boun) *n* **1** os *m.* **2** (of fish) arête *f.* **3** *pl* ossements *m pl. vt* désosser. **bone-dry** *adj* archisec, archisèche. **bony** *adj* **1** osseux, -euse. **2** plein d'os.

bonfire ('bɔnfaiə) *n* feu de joie *m.*

bonnet ('bɔnit) *n* **1** bonnet, béret *m.* **2** capot *m.*

bonus ('bounəs) *n* gratification, prime, indemnité *f.*

booby trap ('bu:bi) *n* attrape-nigaud *f.*

book (buk) *n* **1** livre *m.* **2** *inf* bouquin *m.* **3** registre *m.* **4** (of tickets) carnet *m. vt* **1** inscrire. **2** retenir. **3** *sl law* dresser procès-verbal. **bookcase** *n* bibliothèque *f.* **bookkeeping** comptabilité *f.* **bookmaker** *n* bookmaker *m.* **bookseller** *n* libraire *m.* **bookshop** *n* librairie *f.* **bookstall** *n* **1** étalage de librairie *m.* **2** kiosque à livres *m.* **booking** *n* **1** réservation *f.* **2** enregistrement *m.* **booking office** *n* **1** guichet *m.* **2** bureau de location *m.* **booklet** *n* livret, fascicule *m.*

boom (bu:m) *n* **1** grondement *m.* **2** *comm* essor *m.* hausse *f. vi* **1** gronder. **2** *comm* être en hausse.

boost (bu:st) *vt* **1** faire de la réclame. **2** augmenter. **3** survolter. *n* poussée *f.* coup de pouce *m.*

boot (bu:t) n **1** botte f. **2** bottine, chaussure f. **3** mot coffre m.

booth (bu:θ) n **1** loge f. **2** cabine f.

booze (bu:z) n inf boisson alcoolique f. vi inf picoler.

border ('bɔ:də) n **1** bordure f. bord m. **2** frontière f. vt border. **border on** confiner à. **borderline** n ligne de démarcation f. **borderline case** n cas limite m.

bore[1] (bɔ:) vt **1** forer, percer. **2** sonder. n **1** calibre m. **2** sondage m.

bore[2] (bɔ:) vt ennuyer. n **1** raseur m. **2** ennui m. **boredom** n ennui m. **boring** adj ennuyeux, -euse, assommant.

bore[3] (bɔ:) v see **bear.**

born (bɔ:n) adj né, de naissance. **be born** naître.

borough ('bʌrə) n **1** circonscription électorale f. **2** ville f.

borrow ('bɔrou) vt emprunter.

bosom ('buzəm) n **1** sein m. **2** giron, cœur m. **bosom friend** n ami intime m.

boss (bɔs) n patron, chef m. vt diriger, mener. **bossy** adj autoritaire.

botany ('bɔtəni) n botanique f. **botanical** adj botanique. **botanist** n botaniste m,f.

botch (bɔtʃ) vt bousiller, saboter. **botch up** rafistoler.

both (bouθ) adj,pron tous les deux, tous deux. conj à la fois.

bother ('bɔðə) n ennui, tracas m. vt **1** gêner, ennuyer. **2** soucier. vi se tracasser.

bottle ('bɔtl) n bouteille f. flacon m. **bottleneck** n **1** goulot d'étranglement m. **2** embouteillage m. ~vt mettre en bouteilles. **bottle up** ravaler, étouffer.

bottom ('bɔtəm) n **1** fond m. **2** bas m. **3** derrière m. **4** base f. adj **1** inférieur. **2** du bas. **bottomless** adj **1** insondable. **2** sans fond.

bought (bɔ:t) v see **buy.**

boulder ('bouldə) n galet m. grosse pierre f.

bounce (bauns) vi rebondir. vt faire rebondir. n bond m. **bouncing** adj rebondissant.

bound[1] (baund) v see **bind.**

bound[2] (baund) n bond, saut m. vi bondir.

bound[3] (baund) n limite, borne f. vt borner. **boundary** n bornes f pl. frontière f.

bound[4] (baund) adj **bound for** en partance pour, à destination de.

boundary ('baundri) n bornes f pl. frontière f.

bouquet (bu'kei) n bouquet m.

bourgeois ('buəʒwa:) adj,n bourgeois.

bout (baut) n **1** med accès m. attaque f. **2** coup m. **3** partie f. **4** assaut m.

bow[1] (bau) vt courber, incliner. vi s'incliner, baisser la tête. n salut m.

bow[2] (bou) n **1** sport arc m. **2** mus archet m. **3** nœud m. **bow-legged** adj bancal.

bow[3] (bau) n naut avant m. proue f.

bowels ('bauəlz) n pl **1** intestins m pl. **2** inf entrailles f pl.

bowl[1] (boul) n **1** bol m. **2** bassin m. **bowler hat** n chapeau melon m.

bowl[2] (boul) vt rouler. vi servir la balle. n **1** boule f. **2** pl boules f pl. pétanque f.

box[1] (bɔks) n **1** boîte, caisse f. coffret m. **2** Th cabine, loge f. **box number** n boîte postale f. **box office** n **1** bureau de location m. **2** guichet m.

box[2] (bɔks) vt gifler, boxer. n gifle f. **boxer** n boxeur, pugiliste m. **boxing** n boxe f.

Boxing Day n lendemain de Noël m.

boy (bɔi) n **1** garçon, fils m. **2** inf gars m. **3** élève m. **boyfriend** n (petit) ami m. **boyhood** n enfance, adolescence f.

boycott ('bɔikɔt) vt boycotter. n boycottage m.

bra (bra:) n soutien-gorge m invar.

brace (breis) n **1** paire, couple f. **2** attache f. **3** pl bretelles f pl. **4** tech vilebrequin m. vt **1** fortifier. **2** lier.

bracelet ('breislət) n bracelet m.

bracket ('brækit) n **1** support m. **2** applique f. **3** gram parenthèse f. vt **1** mettre entre parenthèses. **2** accolader.

brag (bræg) vi se vanter.

braid (breid) n tresse f. galon m.

Braille (breil) n Braille m.

brain (brein) n **1** cerveau, -aux m. **2** cervelle f. **brainwash** vt endoctriner. **brainwave** n idée lumineuse f. **brainy** adj inf intelligent.

braise (breiz) vt braiser.

brake (breik) n frein m. vt freiner, ralentir.

branch (bra:ntʃ) n **1** branche f. **2** embranchement * m. **3** comm succursale f. **4** secteur m. v **branch off** bifurquer. **branch out** se ramifier, se diversifier.

brand (brænd) n **1** brandon m. **2** fer chaud m. **3** stigmate m. **4** comm marque f. vt **1** marquer. **2** graver. **3** stigmatiser. **brand-new** adj tout neuf.

brandish ('brændiʃ) vt brandir.

brandy ('brændi) n eau-de-vie f. cognac m.

brass (bra:s) n cuivre jaune, laiton m. adj de cuivre. **brass band** n fanfare f.

brassiere ('bræziə) n soutien-gorge m invar.

163

brat (bræt) n *sl* gosse, môme m,f.
brave (breiv) courageux, -euse, brave. vt braver, affronter.
brawl (brɔ:l) n rixe f. tapage m. vi 1 chamailler. 2 brailler.
bray (brei) vi braire. n braiment m.
brazen ('breizən) adj 1 d'airain. 2 *inf* effronté, impudent.
Brazil (brə'zil) n Brésil m. **Brazilian** adj,n brésilien, -ienne.
breach (bri:tʃ) n 1 infraction f. manque m. 2 rupture f. 3 brèche f. **breach of the peace** attentat contre l'ordre public m.
bread (bred) n 1 pain m. 2 *sl* du fric **breadcrumb** n chapelure f. **breadknife** n couteau à pain m. **breadwinner** n chef de famille m. gagne-pain m invar. **loaf of bread** pain m. **wholemeal bread** pain complet.
breadth (bredθ) n largeur f.
break* (breik) vt 1 casser, rompre, briser. 2 amortir. 3 violer, manquer à. 4 ruiner. **break into** s'introduire par effraction. **break out 1** se déclarer 2 s'échapper. **break up 1** se disperser. 2 morceler. ~n 1 rupture f. 2 brèche f. 3 altération f. 4 interruption f. 5 répit m. **breakage** n 1 casse f. 2 rupture f. **breakdown** n 1 *mot* panne f. 2 rupture f. 3 effondrement m. 4 *med* dépression nerveuse f. **breakthrough** n 1 découverte f pas en avant m. 2 *mil* percée f.
breakfast ('brekfəst) n petit déjeuner m vi prendre le petit déjeuner.
breast (brest) n sein m. poitrine f. **breastbone** n sternum, bréchet m. **breaststroke** n brasse f.
breath (breθ) n haleine f. souffle m. **out of breath** essoufflé. **breathtaking** adj 1 à vous couper le souffle 2 ahurissant.
breathe (bri:ð) vt,vi respirer vi souffler **breathe in/out** aspirer/exhaler. **breathing** n respiration f. **breathing space** n répit m.
breed* (bri:d) n race, espèce f. vt 1 produire, engendrer. 2 élever vi se reproduire.
breeze (bri:z) n brise f
Breton ('bretn̩) adj,n breton, -onne. **Breton** (language) n breton m.
brew (bru:) vt 1 brasser. 2 faire infuser vi 1 s'infuser. 2 se préparer. n 1 infusion f 2 brassage m. **brewery** n brasserie f
bribe (braib) n 1 paiement illicite. 2 *inf* pot-de-vin m. vt corrompre, acheter. **bribery** n corruption f.

brick (brik) n 1 brique f. 2 *inf* chic type m. **bricklayer** n maçon m.
bride (braid) n fiancée, mariée f. **bridegroom** n nouveau marié m. **bridesmaid** n demoiselle d'honneur f.
bridge[1] (bridʒ) n 1 pont m. 2 *naut* passerelle f. 3 *anat* dos m. arête f. v **bridge a gap** combler une lacune.
bridge[2] (bridʒ) n *game* bridge m. **game of bridge** partie de bridge f.
bridle ('braidl̩) n bridle f. **bridlepath** n sentier pour cavaliers m. piste cavalière f.
brief (bri:f) adj bref, brève, succinct. n 1 dossier m. 2 résumé m. vt documenter. **briefing** n instructions f pl. **briefcase** n serviette f.
brigade (bri'geid) n brigade f. **brigadier** n général de brigade m.
bright (brait) adj 1 lumineux, -euse, brillant. 2 vif, vive, éveillé. 3 intelligent **brighten** vt faire briller. vi 1 s'éclaircir. 2 s'épanouir. **brightness** n 1 éclat m 2 clarté f 3 vivacité f.
brilliant ('briliənt) adj brillant. **brilliance** n éclat, lustre m
brim (brim) n bord m. **to the brim** à ras bord. ~v **brim over** déborder.
bring* (briŋ) vt 1 amener, apporter. 2 mettre. 3 porter. **bring about** occasionner, aménager. **bring back** rapporter. **bring in 1** faire entrer. 2 *comm* rapporter **bring out 1** faire sortir 2 mettre en évidence, faire valoir. **bring round 1** ranimer. 2 rallier. **bring together** réunir. **bring up 1** élever 2 soulever. 3 apporter. 4 vomir.
brink (briŋk) n bord m
brisk (brisk) adj vif, vive, alerte, animé.
bristle ('brisəl) n soie f. poil m. vt hérisser
Britain ('britn̩) n Grande-Bretagne f. **British** adj britannique. **British Isles** n pl Iles Britanniques m pl **Briton** n anglais m.
Brittany ('britəni) n Bretagne f.
brittle ('britl̩) adj cassant, fragile.
broad (brɔ:d) adj 1 large. 2 (of an accent) prononcé 3 hardi **broad bean** n fève f **broadcast** n émission, transmission radiodiffusée f vt 1 radiodiffuser 2 annoncer à la radio. **broad-minded** adj tolérant. **broaden** vt élargir. vi s'élargir. **broadness** n largeur f.
broccoli ('brɔkəli) n brocoli m.
brochure ('brouʃə) n brochure f.
broke (brouk) v see **break.** adj *inf* fauché, sans le sou.
broken ('broukən) v see **break.**

broker ('broukə) n courtier m **stock-broker** n agent de change m.

bronchitis (broŋ'kaitis) n bronchite f.

bronze (bronz) n bronze m. adj de bronze. vt bronzer. vi se bronzer

brooch (broutʃ) n broche f

brood (bru:d) n 1 couvée f 2 inf marmaille vi couver. **brood over** ressasser, ruminer.

brook (bruk) n ruisseau, -aux m.

broom (bru:m) n 1 balai m. 2 bot genêt m

brothel ('broθəl) n bordel m

brother ('brʌðə) n frère m. **brother-in-law** n beau-frère m **brotherhood** n 1 fraternité f 2 rel confrèrie f.

brow (brau) n 1 sourcil m 2 front m 3 geog sommet m

brown (braun) adj 1 brun, marron 2 bronzé vt 1 brunir 2 cul faire roussir vi (se) brunir **be browned off** avoir le cafard.

browse (brauz) vt brouter. vi bouquiner

bruise (bru:z) n contusion f. bleu m. vt meurtrir.

brunette (bru:'net) n brunette f.

brush (brʌʃ) n 1 brosse f 2 Art pinceau, -aux m 3 coup de brosse m. 4 escarmouche f. vt 1 brosser. 2 effleurer, frôler **brush up 1** brosser. 2 rafraîchir, dérouiller

brusque (bru:sk) adj brusque, bourru

Brussels ('brʌsəlz) n Bruxelles f **Brussels sprout** n chou de Bruxelles m.

brute (bru:t) n brute f animal, -aux m adj brut, brutal, -aux. **brutal** adj brutal, -aux, animal, -aux.

bubble ('bʌbəl) n bulle f vi 1 bouillonner 2 pétiller

buck[1] (bʌk) n 1 daim, chevreuil m 2 mâle m

buck[2] (bʌk) vi se cabrer **buck someone off** désarçonner quelqu'un

bucket ('bʌkit) n 1 seau, -aux m 2 godet m

buckle ('bʌkəl) n boucle f vt 1 boucler 2 tech déjeter, voiler. vi se déformer.

bud (bʌd) n 1 bourgeon m. 2 bouton m vi bourgeonner. **budding** adj 1 en bouton 2 en herbe.

Buddhism ('budizəm) n bouddhisme m **Buddhist** n bouddhiste m,f adj bouddhique

budget ('bʌdʒit) n budget m.

buffalo ('bʌfəlou) n pl -os or -oes buffle m

buffer ('bʌfə) n 1 tampon. 2 amortisseur m

buffet[1] ('bʌfit) n coup m vt souffleter. vi se battre à coups de poing

buffet[2] ('bufei)) n buffet m.

bug (bʌg) n punaise f.

bugle ('bju:gəl) n clairon m

build[*] (bild) vt 1 bâtir, construire 2 échafauder 3 fonder n carrure, stature f **builder** n entrepreneur m **building** n 1 construction f 2 bâtiment m adj de construction, à bâtir. **building society** n société immobilière f.

bulb (bʌlb) n 1 bot bulbe, oignon m 2 ampoule, lampe f

Bulgaria (bʌl'gɛəriə) n Bulgarie f **Bulgarian** adj,n bulgare

bulge (bʌldʒ) n renflement m bosse f vi faire saillie, ballonner.

bulk (bʌlk) n 1 charge f 2 grosseur f volume m **in bulk** en gros, en vrac.

bull (bul) n 1 taureau, -aux m 2 mâle m **bulldog** n bouledogue m **bulldoze** vt 1 intimider, menacer 2 passer au bulldozer **bulldozer** n bulldozer m **bullfight** n corrida f **bullring** n arène f **bull's eye** n mouche f noir m

bullet ('bulit) n balle f **bullet-proof** adj à l'épreuve des balles, blindé

bulletin ('bulətin) n bulletin, communiqué m. **news bulletin** informations f pl

bully ('buli) n 1 brute f. tyran m 2 bravache m vt malmener

bumble bee ('bʌmbəl) n bourdon m

bump (bʌmp) n 1 choc m secousse f. 2 bosse f vt cogner **bump into 1** entrer en collision avec 2 inf rencontrer **bumper** n pare-chocs m invar adj inf magnifique, comble

bun (bʌn) n 1 cul petit pain m. brioche f 2 chignon m.

bunch (bʌntʃ) n 1 bouquet m grappe f 2 touffe f 3 groupe m vt réunir

bundle ('bʌndl) n 1 ballot, paquet m 2 liasse f vt botteler, entasser

bungalow ('bʌŋgəlou) n bungalow m

bungle ('bʌŋgəl) n gâchis m vt bousiller, gâcher **bungling** adj maladroit

bunk (bʌŋk) n couchette f

bunker ('bʌŋkə) n 1 soute f 2 sport banquette f

buoy (bɔi) n bouée, balise flottante f **buoyancy** n 1 flottabilité f 2 inf entrain m **buoyant** adj 1 flottable, léger, -ère 2 vif, vive

burden ('bə:dn) n fardeau, -aux m charge f vt 1 charger 2 être un fardeau pour

bureau ('bjuərou) n 1 bureau, -aux m 2 secrétaire m

bureaucracy (bju'rɔkrəsi) n bureaucratie f **bureaucrat** n 1 bureaucrate m,f 2 inf rond-de-cuir m

burglar ('bə:glə) n cambrioleur m **burglar**

165

alarm n sonnerie d'alarme f. **burglary** n vol avec effraction, cambriolage m. **burgle** vt cambrioler, dévaliser.

burn* (bə:n) vt **1** brûler. **2** incendier. vi flamber. n brûlure f. **burning** adj brûlant, ardent.

burrow ('bʌrou) n terrier m. vt creuser. vi se terrer.

burst* (bə:st) vi éclater, crever. vt faire éclater, fendre. **burst in** faire irruption. ~n **1** éclatement m. explosion f. **2** élan m. **bursting** adj **1** sur le point d'éclater. **2** débordant.

bury ('beri) vt enterrer. **burial** n enterrement m. **burial ground** n cimetière m.

bus (bʌs) n autobus, bus, car m. **bus-stop** n arrêt du bus m.

bush (buʃ) n **1** buisson m. **2** arbuste m. **3** brousse f.

bushy ('buʃi:) adj **1** touffu. **2** broussailleux, -euse.

business ('biznis) n **1** affaire, occupation f. **2** affaires f pl. **3** commerce m. **set up in business** s'établir. **businessman** n homme d'affaires m.

bust[1] (bʌst) n **1** Art buste m. **2** anat poitrine f.

bust[2] (bʌst) vi inf éclater. **go bust** faire faillite.

bustle ('bʌsəl) n agitation f. mouvement m. vi se remuer, s'affairer. vt faire dépêcher.

busy ('bizi) adj affairé, occupé. **busybody** n officieux, -euse. **busy oneself with** s'occuper à.

but (bət; stressed bʌt) conj **1** mais. **2** sauf que. adv ne...que, seulement. prep excepté, sinon. **but for** sans.

butcher ('butʃə) n boucher m. vt égorger. **butcher's shop** n boucherie f. **butchery** n carnage m.

butler ('bʌtlə) n **1** maître d'hôtel m. **2** sommelier m.

butt[1] (bʌt) n **1** bout m. **2** crosse f. **3** mégot m.

butt[2] (bʌt) n souffre-douleur m invar.

butt[3] (bʌt) vt donner des coups de corne à, buter. **butt in** inf intervenir sans façon, s'ingérer. ~n coup de tête or corne m.

butter ('bʌtə) n beurre m. vt beurrer. **buttercup** n **1** renoncule f. **2** inf bouton d'or m. **butter-fingers** n inf maladroit. **butterfly** n papillon m. **butterscotch** n caramel dur au beurre m.

buttocks ('bʌtəks) n pl **1** anat derrière m. fesses f pl. **2** zool croupe f.

button ('bʌtn̩) n bouton m. vt boutonner. **buttonhole** n boutonnière f. vt inf attraper, cramponner.

166

buttress ('bʌtrəs) n arc-boutant m.

buy* (bai) vt acheter. **buy up** accaparer. ~n affaire f. achat m. **buyer** n **1** acheteur, -euse. **2** comm chef de rayon m.

buzz (bʌz) n **1** bourdonnement, vrombissement m. **2** bruit confus, brouhaha m. vi bourdonner.

by (bai) prep **1** près de, à côté de. **2** au bord de. **3** par. **4** de. **5** à. **6** sur. adv **1** près. **2** de côté. **by and by** tout à l'heure. **by-election** n élection partielle f. **bylaw** n arrêté municipal, -aux m. **bypass** n route d'évitement f. détour m. vt contourner, éviter. **bystander** n spectateur, -trice.

Byzantine (bi'zæntain, bai-) adj,n byzantin.

C

cab (kæb) **1** fiacre m. **2** taxi m. **3** (of a lorry, etc.) cabine f.

cabaret ('kæbərei) n **1** cabaret, café-concert m. **2** spectacle au cabaret m.

cabbage ('kæbidʒ) n chou, choux m.

cabin ('kæbin) n **1** cabine f. **2** cabane f. **cabin cruiser** n yacht à moteur m.

cabinet ('kæbinət) n cabinet m. **cabinet-maker** n ébéniste m. **cabinet minister** n ministre d'état.

cable ('keibəl) n câble m. vt câbler.

cackle ('kækəl) n caquet m. vt **1** caqueter. **2** ricaner.

cactus ('kæktəs) n, pl **-ti** or **-tuses** cactus m.

cadence ('keidn̩s) n cadence f.

cadet (kə'det) n cadet m.

cafe ('kæfei) n café(-restaurant) m.

cafeteria (kæfi'tiəriə) n cafétéria f. libre-service m.

caffeine ('kæfi:n) n caféine f.

cage (keidʒ) n cage f.

cake (keik) n **1** cul gâteau, -aux m. **2** pain, bloc, morceau, -aux m. vi se cailler.

calamity (kə'læməti) n calamité f. désastre m.

calcium ('kælsiəm) n calcium m.

calculate ('kælkjuleit) vt,vi calculer. vt combiner. vi compter. **calculation** n calcul m. **calculator** n machine à calculer f.

calendar ('kælində) n calendrier m.

calf[1] (kɑ:f) n, pl **calves** zool veau, -aux m.

calf[2] (kɑ:f) n, pl **calves** anat mollet m.

calibre ('kælibə) n calibre m.

call (kɔ:l) vt **1** appeler. **2** convoquer. **call for** demander. **call on** passer chez. **call off** décommander. **call out** appeler. ~n **1** appel, cri *m*. **2** visite *f*. **3** demande *f*. **4** *naut* escale *f*. **callbox** *n* taxiphone *m*. cabine téléphonique *f*.

callous (ˈkæləs) *adj* endurci, insensible.

calm (kɑːm) *adj,n* calme *m*. *vt* calmer. **calm down** se calmer.

calorie (ˈkæləri) *n* calorie *f*.

Cambodia (kæmˈboudiə) *n* Cambodge *m*. **Cambodian** *adj,n* cambodgien, -ienne.

came (keim) *v see* **come.**

camel (ˈkæməl) *n* chameau, -aux *m*. chamelle *f*. **camelhair** *n* poil de chameau *m*.

camera (ˈkæmrə) *n* appareil photographique *m*. **cameraman** *n* **1** photographe *m*. **2** opérateur *m*.

camouflage (ˈkæməflɑːʒ) *n* camouflage *m*. *vt* camoufler.

camp[1] (kæmp) *vt,vi* camper. *n* camp *m*. **campbed** *n* lit de camp *m*. **camping** *n* camping *m*. **camping site** *n* terrain de camping *m*.

camp[2] (kæmp) *adj* **1** exagéré, affecté. **2** efféminé. **3** *inf* homosexuel, -elle.

campaign (kæmˈpein) *n* campagne *f*. *vi* faire campagne.

campus (ˈkæmpəs) *n* campus *m*.

can[1] (kæn) *v mod aux* **1** pouvoir. **2** savoir.

can[2] (kæn) *n* **1** bidon, pot *m*. **2** boîte *f*. *vt* mettre en boîte.

Canada (ˈkænədə) *n* Canada *m*. **Canadian** *adj,n* canadien, -ienne.

canal (kəˈnæl) *n* canal, -aux *m*.

canary (kəˈnɛəri) *n* serin *m*.

Canary Islands *n* îles Canaries *f pl*.

cancel (ˈkænsəl) *vt* annuler. **cancellation** *n* **1** annulation *f*. **2** contre-ordre *m*.

cancer (ˈkænsə) *n* **1** cancer *m*. **2** *cap* Cancer *m*.

candid (ˈkændid) *adj* **1** franc, franche. **2** impartial, -aux.

candidate (ˈkændidət) *n* candidat *m*.

candle (ˈkændl) *n* bougie *f*. **candlelight** *n* lumière d'une chandelle *f*. **candlestick** *n* chandelier, bougeoir *m*.

candour (ˈkændə) *n* **1** franchise *f*. **2** impartialité *f*.

cane (kein) *n* canne *f*. *vt* **1** fouetter. **2** canner.

canine (ˈkeinain) *adj* canin. *n* (tooth) canine *f*.

cannabis (ˈkænəbis) *n* chanvre indien *m*.

cannibal (ˈkænəbəl) *adj,n* cannibale. **cannibalism** *n* cannibalisme *m*.

cannon (ˈkænən) *n* canon *m*. **cannonball** *n* boulet de canon *m*.

cannot (ˈkænət) contraction of **can not.**

canoe (kəˈnuː) *n* canoë *m*. périssoire *f*.

canon[1] (ˈkænən) *n* (law) canon *m*. règle *f*. **canonical** *adj* canonique, canonial, -aux. **canonize** *vt* canoniser. **canonization** *n* canonisation *f*.

canon[2] (ˈkænən) *n* (title) chanoine *m*.

canopy (ˈkænəpi) *n* dais *m*.

canteen (kænˈtiːn) *n* **1** cantine *f*. **2** *mil* bidon *m*. **canteen (of cutlery)** ménagère *f*.

canter (ˈkæntə) *n* petit galop *m*. *vi* aller au petit galop.

canton (ˈkæntən) *n* canton *m*.

canvas (ˈkænvəs) *n* toile *f*.

canvass (ˈkænvəs) *vi* faire une campagne électorale. *vt* **1** solliciter. **2** discuter. **canvasser** *n* **1** *pol* agent électoral *m*. **2** *comm* demarcheur *m*.

canyon (ˈkænjən) *n* cañon *m*.

cap (kæp) *n* bonnet *m*. toque, casquette *f*. *vt* **1** coiffer. **2** couvrir. **3** surpasser.

capable (ˈkeipəbəl) *adj* **1** capable, compétent. **2** susceptible. **capability** *n* **1** capacité *f*. **2** faculté *f*.

capacity (kəˈpæsiti) *n* capacité *f*.

cape[1] (keip) *n* cape, pèlerine *f*.

cape[2] (keip) *n* *geog* cap *m*.

caper (ˈkeipə) *n* *cul* câpre *f*.

capital (ˈkæpitl) *n* **1** capitale *f*. **2** *comm* capital, -aux *m*. *adj* **1** capital, -aux. **2** essentiel, -elle. **capital letter** *n* lettre majuscule *f*. **capitalism** *n* capitalisme *m*. **capitalist** *adj,n* capitaliste. **capitalize** *vt* **1** capitaliser. **2** exploiter.

capricious (kəˈpriʃəs) *adj* capricieux, -euse.

Capricorn (ˈkæprikɔːn) *n* Capricorne *m*.

capsicum (ˈkæpsikəm) *n* piment *m*.

capsize (ˈkæpsaiz) *vi* chavirer. *vt* faire chavirer.

capsule (ˈkæpsjuːl) *n* capsule *f*.

captain (ˈkæptin) *n* capitaine *m*.

caption (ˈkæpʃən) *n* **1** rubrique *f*. **2** légende *f*. **3** sous-titre *m*.

captivate (ˈkæptiveit) *vt* captiver.

captive (ˈkæptiv) *adj,n* captif, -ive. **captivity** *n* captivité *f*.

capture (ˈkæptʃə) *n* capture, prise *f*. *vt* capturer, prendre.

car (kɑː) *n* **1** automobile, voiture *f*. **2** (of a train) wagon *m*. **car park** *n* parking *m*.

caramel (ˈkærəməl) *n* caramel *m*.

carat (ˈkærət) *n* carat *m*.

caravan (ˈkærəvæn) *n* caravane *f*.

caraway (ˈkærəwei) *n* cumin *m*.

carbohydrate (kɑːbouˈhaidreit) *n* hydrate de carbone *m*.

carbon (ˈkɑːbən) *n* carbone *m*. **carbon dioxide**

167

n anhydride carbonique *m*. **carbon paper** *n* papier carbone *m*.

carburettor (ka:bju'retə) *n* carburateur *m*.

carcass ('ka:kəs) *n* cadavre *m*. carcasse *f*.

card (ka:d) *n* carte *f*. **cardboard** *n* carton *m*.

cardigan ('ka:digən) *n* cardigan, gilet de tricot *m*.

cardinal ('ka:dinļ) *adj,n* cardinal, -aux *m*.

care (kɛə) *n* 1 soin *m*. 2 attention *f*. 3 souci *m*. **care of** chez. **take care** prendre garde. ~*vi* se soucier. **care for** 1 aimer. 2 soigner. **carefree** *adj* insouciant. **careful** *adj* 1 soigneux, -euse. 2 attentif, -ive. 3 prudent. 4 économe. **careless** *adj* 1 insouciant. 2 négligent. **caretaker** *n* gardien, -ienne, concierge *m,f*.

career (kə'riə) *n* carrière, course *f*. *vi* courir rapidement.

caress (kə'res) *n* caresse *f*. *vt* caresser, câliner.

cargo ('ka:gou) *n, pl* **cargoes** cargaison *f*.

Caribbean (kæri'biən) *adj* des Caraïbes. **Caribbean Islands** *n* Antilles *f pl*. **Caribbean (Sea)** *n* Mer des Antilles *f*.

caricature ('kærikətjuə) *n* caricature *f*. *vt* caricaturer. **caricaturist** *n* caricaturiste *m*.

carnal ('ka:nļ) *adj* charnel, -elle.

carnation (ka:'neiʃən) *n* œillet *m*.

carnival ('ka:nivəl) *n* carnaval *m*.

carnivorous (ka:'nivərəs) *adj* carnivore.

carol ('kærəl) *n* chant *m*. **Christmas carol** *n* noël *m*.

carpenter ('ka:pintə) *n* charpentier, menuisier *m*. **carpentry** *n* charpenterie *f*.

carpet ('ka:pit) *n* tapis *m*. **carpet-sweeper** *n* balai mécanique *m*.

carriage ('kæridʒ) *n* 1 voiture *f*. 2 port, transport *m*. 3 maintien *m*. **dual carriageway** *n* route à double voie *f*.

carrier ('kæriə) *n* porteur, -euse. **carrier bag** *n* (grand) sac *m*.

carrot ('kærət) *n* carotte *f*.

carry ('kæri) *vt* 1 porter. 2 transporter. 3 entraîner. 4 adopter. 5 retenir. *vi* porter. **carry on** continuer. **carry out** exercer. **carrycot** *n* porte-bébé *m invar*.

cart (ka:t) *n* charrette *f*. *vt* transporter. **carthorse** *n* cheval de trait *m*. **cartwheel** *n* roue de charrette *f*. **turn cartwheels** faire la roue.

cartilage ('ka:tlidʒ) *n* cartilage *m*.

carton ('ka:tn) *n* carton *m*.

cartoon (ka:'tu:n) *n* 1 carton *m*. caricature *f*. 2 dessin animé *m*.

cartridge ('ka:tridʒ) *n* cartouche *f*.

carve (ka:v) *vt* 1 *Art* sculpter. 2 découper. **carving** *n* sculpture *f*. **carving-knife** *n* couteau à découper *m*.

cascade (kæ'skeid) *n* cascade *f*.

case[1] (keis) *n* 1 cas *m*. 2 *law* affaire *f*.

case[2] (keis) *n* 1 caisse *f*. 2 boîte *f*. 3 étui *m*. *vt* envelopper, encaisser.

cash (kæʃ) *n* espèces *f pl*. monnaie *f*. *vt* toucher. **cash desk** *n* caisse *f*. **cash register** *n* caisse enregistreuse *f*.

cashier[1] (kæ'ʃiə) *n* caissier, -ière.

cashier[2] (kæ'ʃiə) *vt* casser.

cashmere (kæʃ'miə) *n* cachemire *m*.

casino (kə'si:nou) *n* casino *m*.

casket ('ka:skit) *n* coffret *m*.

casserole ('kæsəroul) *n* 1 cocotte en terre *f*. 2 ragoût *m*.

cassette (kə'set) *n* cassette *f*. chargeur *m*.

cassock ('kæsək) *n* soutane *f*.

cast ' (ka:st) *vt* 1 lancer. 2 projeter. 3 *tech* couler. **cast off** rejeter ~*n* 1 coup *m*. 2 *Th* distribution *f*. 3 moule *m*.

castanets (kæstə'nets) *n pl* castagnettes *f pl*.

caste (ka:st) *n* caste *f*.

castle ('ka:səl) *n* 1 château, -aux *m*. 2 *game* tour *f*.

castrate (kæ'streit) *vt* châtrer. **castration** *n* castration *f*.

casual ('kæʒuəl) *adj* 1 fortuit. 2 insouciant. **casualty** *n* 1 accident *m*. 2 *pl* pertes *f pl*.

cat (kæt) *n* chat, chatte. **cat's eye** *n* mot cataphote *m*.

catalogue ('kætəlɔg) *n* catalogue *m*. *vt* cataloguer.

catamaran (kætəmə'ræn) *n* catamaran *m*.

catapult ('kætəpʌlt) *n* lance-pierre *m invar*. catapulte *f*. *vt* catapulter, lancer.

cataract ('kætərækt) *n* cataracte *f*.

catarrh (kə'ta:) *n* catarrhe *m*.

catastrophe (kə'tæstrəfi) *n* catastrophe *f*. **catastrophic** *adj* désastreux, -euse.

catch' (kætʃ) *vt* 1 attraper. 2 surprendre. 3 accrocher. 4 comprendre. *vi* s'accrocher. **catch up** rattraper ~*n* 1 prise *f*. 2 loquet *m*. 3 attrape *f*.

catechism ('kætikizəm) *n* catéchisme *m*.

category ('kætigəri) *n* catégorie *f*. **categorical** *adj* catégorique. **categorize** *vt* classer.

cater ('keitə) *vi* **cater for** 1 approvisionner. 2 pourvoir à. **caterer** *n* fournisseur, traiteur *m*.

caterpillar ('kætəpilə) *n* chenille *f*.

cathedral (kə'θi:drəl) *n* cathédrale *f*.

cathode ('kæθoud) n cathode f.
catholic ('kæθlik) n catholique m,f. adj 1 universel, -elle. 2 catholique. **catholicism** n catholicisme m.
catkin ('kætkin) n chaton m.
cattle ('kætl) n bétail, bestiaux m.
caught (kɔ:t) v see **catch**.
cauliflower ('kɔliflauə) n chou-fleur m.
cause (kɔ:z) n 1 cause f. 2 motif m. vt causer, occasionner.
causeway ('kɔ:zwei) n chaussée f.
caustic ('kɔ:stik) adj caustique.
caution ('kɔ:ʃən) n 1 prudence f. 2 law caution f. 3 avis m. vt avertir. **cautious** adj prudent.
cavalry ('kævəlri) n cavalerie f.
cave (keiv) n caverne, grotte f. v **cave in** 1 s'effondrer. 2 céder.
caviar ('kævia:) n caviar m.
cavity ('kæviti) n cavité f.
cayenne (kei'en) n also **cayenne pepper** cayenne, poivre de Cayenne m.
cease (si:s) vt,vi cesser. **cease-fire** n cessez-le-feu m. **ceaseless** adj incessant.
cedar ('si:də) n cèdre m.
cedilla (si'dilə) n cédille f.
ceiling ('si:liŋ) n plafond m.
celebrate ('seləbreit) vt célébrer. **celebration** n célébration f. **celebrity** n célébrité f.
celery ('seləri) n céleri m.
celestial (si'lestiəl) adj céleste.
celibate ('selibət) adj,n célibataire. **celibacy** n célibat m.
cell (sel) n 1 cellule f. 2 (of a prison) cachot m.
cellar ('selə) n cave f.
cello ('tʃelou) n violoncelle m.
Cellophane ('seləfein) n Tdmk Cellophane f.
Celt (kelt) n Celte m,f. **Celtic** adj,n celtique. **Celtic** (language) n celtique m.
cement (si'ment) n ciment m. vt cimenter.
cemetery ('semətri) n cimetière m.
censor ('sensə) n censeur m. vt censurer, interdire. **censorship** n censure f.
censure ('senʃə) n blâme m. vt blâmer, censurer.
census ('sensəs) n recensement m.
cent (sent) n 1 cent m. 2 inf sou m. **per cent** pour cent.
centenary (sen'ti:nəri) adj,n centenaire m.
centigrade ('sentigreid) adj centigrade.
centime (sɔn'ti:m) n centime m.
centimetre ('sentimi:tə) n centimètre m.
centipede ('sentipi:d) n mille-pattes m.
centre ('sentə) n centre m. vt placer au centre.

vi se concentrer. **centre-forward** n avant-centre m. **centre-half** n demi-centre m. **central** adj central, -aux. **central heating** n chaffage central m. **centralization** n centralisation f. **centralize** vt centraliser.
century ('sentʃəri) n siècle m.
ceramic (si'ræmik) adj céramique. n pl céramique f.
cereal ('siəriəl) adj,n céréale f.
ceremony ('serəməni) n cérémonie f. **without ceremony** sans façon. **ceremonial** adj de cérémonie. n cérémonial, -aux m. **ceremonious** adj cérémonieux, -euse.
certain ('sə:tn) adj certain, sûr. **make certain** s'assurer. **certainly** adv assurément. **certainty** n certitude f.
certify ('sə:tifai) vt certifier, attester. **certificate** n 1 certificat m. 2 acte m.
Ceylon (si'lon) n Ceylan m. **Ceylonese** adj,n cingalais.
chaffinch ('tʃæfintʃ) n pinson m.
chain (tʃein) n chaîne f. **chain-smoke** vi fumer des cigarettes à la file. **chain-store** n succursale de grand magasin f.
chair (tʃɛə) n 1 chaise f. 2 educ chaire f. **chair-lift** n télésiège m. **chairman** n président m.
chalet ('ʃælei) n chalet m.
chalk (tʃɔ:k) n 1 craie f. 2 calcaire m. **chalky** adj 1 crayeux, -euse. 2 calcaire.
challenge ('tʃæləndʒ) n défi m. vt 1 défier. 2 contester.
chamber ('tʃeimbə) n 1 chambre f. 2 pl cabinet m. étude f. **chambermaid** n femme de chambre f. **chamber music** n musique de chambre f.
chamberlain ('tʃeimbəlin) n chambellan m.
chameleon (kə'mi:liən) n caméléon m.
chamois ('ʃæmwa:) n chamois m.
champagne (ʃæm'pein) n champagne m.
champion ('tʃæmpiən) n champion, -ionne. vt défendre. **championship** n championnat m.
chance (tʃa:ns) n 1 chance f. hasard m. 2 occasion f. vt risquer. vi arriver par hasard. adj fortuit.
chancellor ('tʃa:nsələ) n chancelier m.
chandelier (ʃændə'liə) n lustre m.
change (tʃeindʒ) n 1 changement m. 2 monnaie f. 3 comm change m. vt changer. vi se changer.
channel ('tʃænl) n 1 canal, -aux m. 2 voie f. 3 (television) chaîne f. 4 cap Manche f. vt 1 creuser. 2 diriger.

Channel Islands n pl îles Anglo-Normandes f pl.

chant (tʃɑːnt) n chant m. vt psalmodier.

chaos ('keɪɔs) n chaos m ınvar. **chaotic** adj chaotique.

chap[1] (tʃæp) n gerçure f. vt gercer, crevasser. vı se gercer.

chap[2] (tʃæp) n inf garçon, type m.

chapel ('tʃæpəl) n chapelle f.

chaperon ('ʃæpəroun) n chaperon m. vt chaperonner.

chaplain ('tʃæplin) n aumônıer m.

chapter ('tʃæptə) n chapitre m.

char[1] (tʃɑː) vt carboniser. vı se carbonıser.

char[2] (tʃɑː) vı faire des ménages. **charwoman** n femme de ménage f.

character ('kærıktə) n 1 caractère m. 2 réputation f. 3 Th personnage m. **characteristic** adj,n caractéristique f. **characterize** vt caractériser.

charcoal ('tʃɑːkoul) n charbon (de boıs) m.

charge (tʃɑːdʒ) n 1 charge f. 2 devoır m. 3 prıx m. frais m pl. 4 recommandatıon f. vt,vı charger. vt 1 ordonner de faire. 2 payer. 3 law accuser.

chariot ('tʃærıət) n char m.

charisma (kə'rızmə) n charısme m.

charity ('tʃærıti) n 1 charité f. 2 œuvre de bienfaisance f. **charitable** adj charıtable.

charm (tʃɑːm) n 1 charme m. 2 porte-bonheur m invar. vt charmer, enchanter. **charming** adj ravissant, charmant.

chart (tʃɑːt) n 1 naut carte f. 2 tableau, -aux m. vt porter sur une carte.

charter ('tʃɑːtə) n 1 charte f. 2 comm affrètement m. vt affréter.

chase (tʃeɪs) n chasse f. vt chasser, poursuıvre.

chasm ('kæzəm) n abîme m.

chassis ('ʃæsi) n châssıs m.

chaste (tʃeist) adj 1 chaste. 2 pur. **chastity** n 1 chasteté f. 2 pureté f.

chastise (tʃæ'staız) vt châtıer, corrıger. **chastisement** n châtıment m.

chat (tʃæt) n inf causerıe f. vi bavarder, causer.

chatter ('tʃætə) n bavardage m. vı 1 bavarder. 2 (of teeth) claquer. **chatterbox** n inf jacasse f. moulin à paroles m.

chauffeur ('ʃoufə) n chauffeur m.

chauvinism ('ʃouvınızəm) n chauvınısme m. **chauvinist** adj,n chauvin m.

cheap (tʃiːp) adj 1 bon marché ınvar. 2 sans grande valeur. **cheapen** vt rabaisser le prıx de.

cheat (tʃiːt) vt 1 tromper. 2 tricher. n 1 trıcheur, escroc m. 2 fraude f.

check (tʃek) vt 1 vérifier. 2 retenır. 3 game faire échec à. n 1 contrôle m. 2 freın m. 3 game échec m. 4 chèque m. 5 carreau, -aux m. **checkmate** n échec et mat m. vt faire échec et mat. **checkpoint** n contrôle routier m. **check-up** n 1 vérification f. 2 examen medical, -aux m.

cheek (tʃiːk) n 1 anat joue f. 2 ımpudence f. **cheekbone** n pommette f. **cheeky** adj effronté.

cheer (tʃıə) n 1 gaieté f. 2 pl acclamations f. **cheers!** ınterj à la vôtre! ~vt 1 réconforter. 2 acclamer. **cheer up** prendre courage. **cheerful** adj gaı, joyeux, -euse.

cheese (tʃiːz) n fromage m. **cheesecake** n tarte à la frangıpane f.

cheetah ('tʃiːtə) n guépard m.

chef (ʃef) n chef de cuısine m.

chemical ('kemikəl) adj chimique. **chemicals** n pl produıts chımıques m pl.

chemist ('kemist) n 1 med pharmacıen, -ıenne. 2 scı chımıste m. **chemist's shop** n pharmacıe f.

chemistry ('kemistri) n chimıe f.

cheque (tʃek) n chèque m. **chequebook** n carnet de chèques m. **cheque card** n carte bancaıre f.

cherish ('tʃerıʃ) vt 1 soıgner tendrement. 2 caresser.

cherry ('tʃeri) n cerıse f. **cherry tree** n cerisier m.

cherub ('tʃerəb) n chérubın m.

chess (tʃes) n échecs m pl. **chess-board** n échiquıer m. **chess set** n échecs m pl.

chest (tʃest) n poıtrıne f. **chest of drawers** n commode f.

chestnut ('tʃesnʌt) n châtaıgne f. marron m. adj châtaın, marron. **chestnut tree** n châtaıgnıer m.

chew (tʃuː) vt mâcher. **chew over** rumıner. **chewing gum** n chewing-gum m.

chick (tʃik) n poussin m.

chicken ('tʃikən) n poulet m. **chickenpox** n varıcelle f.

chicory ('tʃikəri) n chıcorée f.

chief (tʃiːf) n chef m. adj prıncipal, -aux, premıer, -ière. **chiefly** adv surtout.

chilblain ('tʃilblein) n engelure f.

child (tʃaild) n, pl **children** enfant m,f. **childbirth** n accouchement m. **childhood** n

enfance f. **childish** adj **1** enfantin. **2** puéril.
childlike adj enfantin, candide.
Chile ('tʃili) n Chili m. **Chilean** adj,n chilien,
-ienne.
chill (tʃil) n **1** froid m. **2** frisson m. **catch a
chill** prendre froid. ~adj froid. vt refroidir,
réfrigérer. vi se refroidir.
chilli ('tʃili) n piment m.
chilly adj **1** frais, fraîche. **2** (of a person) frileux,
-euse.
chime (tʃaim) n carillon m. vt,vi carillonner.
chimney ('tʃimni) n cheminée f. **chimneypot** n
mitre f. pot de cheminée m. **chimneysweep**
n ramoneur m.
chimpanzee (tʃimpæn'zi:) n chimpanzé m.
chin (tʃin) n menton m.
china ('tʃainə) n porcelaine f.
China ('tʃainə) n Chine f. **Chinese** adj,n
chinois. **Chinese** (language) n chinois m.
chink[1] (tʃiŋk) n fissure, lézarde f. vi se fendiller.
chink[2] (tʃiŋk) n tintement m. vt tinter. vi faire
tinter.
chip (tʃip) n **1** éclat, fragment m. **2** pl frites f pl.
vt ébrécher. vi s'ébrécher, s'écailler.
chiropody (ki'rɔpədi) n soins du pédicure m
pl. **chiropodist** n pédicure m,f.
chirp (tʃə:p) n gazouillement m. vi gazouiller.
chisel ('tʃizəl) n ciseau, -aux. vt ciseler.
chivalry ('ʃivəlri) n **1** chevalerie f. **2** courtoisie
f. **chivalrous** adj chevaleresque.
chive (tʃaiv) n ciboulette f.
chlorine ('klɔ:ri:n) n chlore m.
chlorophyll ('klɔrəfil) n chlorophylle f.
chocolate ('tʃɔklit) n chocolat m.
choice (tʃɔis) n choix m invar. adj (bien) choisi,
de choix invar.
choir (kwaiə) n chœur m. **choirboy** n enfant de
chœur m. **choirmaster** n maître de chapelle
m.
choke (tʃouk) vt **1** étouffer. **2** boucher. vi **1**
s'étrangler. **2** se boucher. n mot starter m.
cholera ('kɔlərə) n choléra m.
choose' (tʃu:z) vt **1** choisir. **2** élire. vi vouloir.
chop[1] (tʃɔp) vt couper, hacher. n **1** coup de
hache m. **2** cul côtelette f.
chop[2] (tʃɔp) vi changer. **chop and change**
changer à chaque instant.
chopstick ('tʃɔpstik) n baguette f.
chord (kɔ:d) n **1** corde f. **2** mus accord m.
chore (tʃɔ:) n corvée f.
choreography (kɔri'ɔgrəfi) n chorégraphie
f. **choreographer** n chorégraphe m,f.

chorus ('kɔ:rəs) n **1** chœur m. **2** refrain
m. **choral** adj choral.
chose (tʃouz) v see **choose.**
chosen ('tʃouzən) v see **choose.**
Christ (kraist) n Christ m.
christen ('krisən) vt baptiser. **christening** n
baptême m.
Christian ('kristʃən) adj,n chrétien, -ienne.
Christian name n prénom m. **Christianity** n
christianisme m.
Christmas ('krisməs) n Noël m. **Christmas
tree** n arbre de Noël m.
chromatic (krə'mætik) adj chromatique.
chrome (kroum) n chrome m. adj chromé. vt
chromer.
chromium ('kroumiəm) n chrome m.
chromosome ('krouməsoum) n chromosome m.
chronic ('krɔnik) adj chronique.
chronicle ('krɔnikəl) n chronique f.
chronological (krɔnə'lɔdʒikəl) adj chronologique.
chrysalis ('krisəlis) n chrysalide f.
chrysanthemum (kri'zænθiməm) n chrysanthème m.
chubby ('tʃʌbi) adj potelé, joufflu.
chuck (tʃʌk) vt **1** lancer. **2** lâcher. **chuck out**
expulser.
chuckle ('tʃʌkəl) n rire étouffé m. vi rire tout
bas.
chunk (tʃʌŋk) n **1** gros morceau, -aux m. **2** (of
bread) quignon m.
church (tʃə:tʃ) n **1** église f. **2** temple m.
churchyard n cimetière m.
churn (tʃə:n) n baratte f. vt baratter.
chute (ʃu:t) n glissière, piste f.
chutney ('tʃʌtni) n chutney m.
cicada (si'ka:də) n cigale f.
cider ('saidə) n cidre m.
cigar (si'ga:) n cigare m. **cigarette** n cigarette
f.
cinder ('sində) n **1** cendre f. **2** pl escarbilles f pl.
cinecamera ('sinikæmrə) n caméra f.
cinema ('sinəmə) n cinéma m.
cinnamon ('sinəmən) n cannelle f.
circle ('sə:kəl) n **1** cercle m. **2** milieu, -eux m. vt
1 entourer. **2** faire le tour de. vi tourner.
circular adj,n circulaire f. **circulate** vi circuler. vt faire circuler, répandre. **circulation** n
1 circulation f. **2** (of a newspaper) tirage m.
circuit ('sə:kit) n **1** circuit m. **2** law tournée
f. **circuitous** adj indirect, détourné.
circumcise ('sə:kəmsaiz) vt circoncire. **circumcision** n circoncision f.

171

circumference (sə'kʌmfərəns) *n* circonférence *f*.

circumflex ('sə:kəmfleks) *n* accent circonflexe *m. adj* circonflexe.

circumscribe ('sə:kəmskraib) *vt* circonscrire. **circumscription** *n* circonscription *f*.

circumstance ('sə:kəmstæns) *n* **1** circonstance *f*. **2** *pl* moyens *m pl*.

circus ('sə:kəs) *n* cirque *m*.

cistern ('sistən) *n* réservoir *m*. citerne *f*.

cite (sait) *vt* citer.

citizen ('sitizən) *n* **1** citoyen, -enne. **2** bourgeois, habitant *m*. **citizenship** *n* nationalité *f*.

citrus ('sitrəs) *n* citron *m*. **citrus fruits** agrumes *m pl*.

city ('siti) *n* ville, cité *f*.

civic ('sivik) *adj* civique.

civil ('sivəl) *adj* civil. **civil engineering** *n* génie civil *m*. **civil servant** *n* fonctionnaire *m*. **civil service** *n* administration *f*. **civil war** *n* guerre civile *f*.

civilian (si'viliən) *adj,n* civil *m*.

civilization (sivilai'zeiʃən) *n* civilization *f*. **civilize** *vt* civiliser.

claim (kleim) *n* **1** demande, réclamation *f*. **2** droit *m*. *vt* **1** réclamer, revendiquer. **2** prétendre à.

clam (klæm) *n* palourde *f*.

clamber ('klæmbə) *vt* grimper.

clammy ('klæmi) *adj* moite, humide, pâteux, -euse.

clamour ('klæmə) *n* clameur *f*. *vi* vociférer.

clamp (klæmp) *n* **1** serre-joint *m*. **2** crampon *m*. *vt* **1** cramponner. **2** presser.

clan (klæn) *n* clan *m*.

clandestine (klæn'destin) *adj* clandestin.

clang (klæŋ) *n* bruit métallique *m*. *vi* retentir.

clank (klæŋk) *n* cliquetis *m*. *vi* résonner. *vt* faire résonner.

clap (klæp) *n* **1** battement (of hands) *m*. **2** coup (of thunder) *m*. *vt,vi* applaudir.

claret ('klærət) *n* bordeaux *m*.

clarify ('klærifai) *vt* clarifier, éclaircir. *vi* se clarifier. **clarity** *n* clarté *f*.

clarinet (klæri'net) *n* clarinette *f*.

clash (klæʃ) *n* **1** choc *m*. **2** conflit *m*. **3** cliquetis *m*. *vi* **1** s'entre-choquer. **2** (of colours) jurer. *vt* heurter.

clasp (klɑ:sp) *n* **1** agrafe *f*. **2** fermoir *m*. **3** étreinte *f*. *vt* **1** agrafer. **2** étreindre.

class (klɑ:s) *n* **1** classe *f*. **2** *educ* cours *m*. **3** catégorie *f*. *vt* classer. **classification** *n* classi-

fication *m*. **classify** *vt* classifier. **classroom** *n* salle de classe *f*.

classic ('klæsik) *adj,n* classique *m*. **classical** *adj* classique.

clatter ('klætə) *n* vacarme, bruit *m*. *vi* claquer. *vt* faire résonner.

clause (klɔ:z) *n* **1** clause *f*. **2** *gram* membre de phrase *m*. proposition *f*.

claustrophobia (klɔstrə'foubiə) *n* claustrophobie *f*.

claw (klɔ:) *n* griffe, serre, pince *f*. *vt* griffer.

clay (klei) *n* argile *f*.

clean (kli:n) *adj* **1** propre. **2** net, nette. *vt* nettoyer. **cleaning** *n* nettoyage *m*. **cleanliness** *n* propreté *f*.

cleanse (klenz) *vt* **1** nettoyer. **2** démaquiller.

clear (kliə) *adj* **1** clair. **2** net, nette. **3** libre. **4** certain. *vt* **1** débarrasser, déblayer. **2** évacuer. **3** franchir. **4** acquitter. **5** desservir. *vi* s'éclaircir. **clear up 1** ranger. **2** éclaircir. **clearance** *n* **1** dégagement *m*. **2** *comm* (sale) solde *m*. **clear-headed** *adj* lucide. **clearing** *n* **1** défrichement *m*. **2** acquittement *m*. **3** éclaircie *f*. **clearness** *n* clarté *f*.

clef (klef) *n* clef *f*.

clench (klentʃ) *vt* serrer.

clergy ('klɔ:dʒi) *n* clergé *m*. **clergyman** *n* pasteur, prêtre *m*.

clerical ('klerikəl) *adj* **1** *rel* ecclésiastique. **2** *comm* de bureau, -aux.

clerk (klɑ:k) *n* **1** employé *m*. **2** clerc *m*.

clever ('klevə) *adj* **1** habile. **2** intelligent.

cliché ('kliʃei) *n* cliché *m*.

click (klik) *n* bruit sec *m*. *vt,vi* cliqueter.

client ('klaiənt) *n* client *m*.

cliff (klif) *n* falaise *f*.

climate ('klaimit) *n* climat *m*.

climax ('klaimæks) *n* **1** apogée, comble *m*. **2** gradation *f*.

climb (klaim) *vt,vi* **1** monter. **2** grimper. *vt* gravir, franchir. *n* **1** montée *f*. **2** ascension *f*.

cling * (kliŋ) *vi* s'accrocher, adhérer. **clinging** *adj* collant.

clinic ('klinik) *n* clinique *f*. **clinical** *adj* clinique.

clip [1] (klip) *vt* tondre, couper.

clip [2] (klip) *n* pince, attache *f*. *vt* pincer.

clitoris ('klitəris) *n* clitoris *m*.

cloak (klouk) *n* manteau, -aux *m*. *vt* masquer. **cloakroom** *n* vestiaire *m*. consigne *f*.

clock (klɔk) *n* horloge *f*. **it is two o'clock** il est deux heures. **clocktower** *n* tour d'horloge *f*. **clockwise** *adj* dans le sens des aiguilles d'une montre. **clockwork** *n* mouvement

d'horlogerie m. **like clockwork** comme sur des roulettes.
clog (klɔg) n 1 sabot m. 2 entrave f. vt 1 entraver. 2 boucher. vi se boucher, s'obstruer.
cloister ('klɔistə) n cloître m. vt cloîtrer.
close (adj,adv klous; v klouz) adj 1 proche. 2 lourd. 3 serré. 4 fermé. **close fitting** adj ajusté. ~n 1 (klous) enclos m. 2 (klous) cul-de-sac m. 3 (klouz) fin f. vt 1 fermer. 2 conclure. 3 serrer. vi 1 se fermer. 2 se terminer. adv (de) près. **closing** n fermeture f.
closet ('klɔzit) n 1 cabinet m. 2 placard m.
clot (klɔt) n caillot m. vi se cailler, se figer.
cloth (klɔθ) n 1 étoffe f. 2 toile f. 3 nappe f.
clothe (klouð) vt vêtir, habiller. **clothes** n pl vêtements m pl. **clothes brush** n brosse à habits f. **clothes line** n corde à linge f. **clothes peg** n pince à linge f. **clothing** n habillement m.
cloud (klaud) n nuage m. vt couvrir. **cloudburst** n rafale de pluie f. **cloudy** adj nuageux, -euse.
clove[1] (klouv) n (of garlic, etc.) gousse f.
clove[2] (klouv) n clou de girofle m.
clover ('klouvə) n trèfle m.
clown (klaun) n clown, pitre, rustre m.
club (klʌb) n 1 club m. 2 game trèfle m. 3 sport crosse f. **club foot** n pied bot m.
clue (klu:) n fil, indice m.
clump (klʌmp) n 1 masse f. 2 bouquet, massif m.
clumsy ('klʌmzi) adj maladroit, gauche.
clung (klʌŋ) v see cling.
cluster ('klʌstə) n groupe, bouquet m. vi se grouper.
clutch (klʌtʃ) vt empoigner, saisir n 1 griffe f. 2 étreinte f. 3 mot embrayage m.
clutter ('klʌtə) n encombrement m. v **clutter up** encombrer.
coach (koutʃ) n 1 mot (auto)car m. 2 (railway) wagon m. 3 educ répétiteur m. 4 sport entraîneur m. vt 1 préparer. 2 entraîner. **coaching** n 1 répétitions f pl. 2 entraînement m.
coal (koul) n charbon m. houille f. **coalmine** n mine de charbon f. houillère f.
coalition (kouə'liʃən) n coalition f.
coarse (kɔ:s) adj 1 grossier, -ière. 2 rude.
coast (koust) n côte f. vi naut côtoyer. **coastguard** n garde-côte, gardes-côte m. **coastline** n littoral, -aux m.
coat (kout) n 1 habit, manteau, -aux m. 2 (of an

animal) pelage m. 3 robe f. 4 (of paint) couche f. vt couvrir, enduire. **coat-hanger** n cintre m.
coax (kouks) vt cajoler.
cobble ('kɔbəl) n galet m. vt carreler.
cobbler ('kɔblə) n cordonnier m.
cobra ('koubrə) n cobra m.
cobweb ('kɔbweb) n toile d'araignée f.
cock[1] (kɔk) n 1 coq m. 2 mâle m.
cock[2] (kɔk) vt 1 dresser. 2 retrousser.
cockle ('kɔkəl) n 1 zool clovisse f. 2 bot ivraie f.
cockpit ('kɔkpit) n carlingue f.
cockroach ('kɔkroutʃ) n blatte f.
cocktail ('kɔkteil) n cocktail m. **cocktail party** n cocktail m.
cocky ('kɔki) adj inf impertinent.
cocoa ('koukou) n cacao m.
coconut ('koukənʌt) n noix de coco f. **coconut palm** n cocotier m.
cocoon (kə'ku:n) n cocon m.
cod (kɔd) n morue f.
code (koud) n code m. vt chiffrer.
codeine ('koudi:n) n codéine f.
co-education (kouedju'keiʃən) n enseignement mixte m. **co-educational** adj mixte.
coerce (kou'ə:s) vt contraindre. **coercion** n contrainte f.
coexist (kouig'zist) vi coexister.
coffee ('kɔfi) n café m. **coffee bar** n café m. **coffee bean** n grain de café m. **coffee table** n table de salon f.
coffin ('kɔfin) n cercueil m. bière f.
cog (kɔg) n dent f.
cognac ('kɔnjæk) n cognac m.
cohabit (kou'hæbit) vi cohabiter.
cohere (kou'hiə) vi 1 adhérer. 2 s'agglomérer. 3 se tenir. **coherence** n cohérence f. **coherent** adj cohérent.
coil (kɔil) n 1 rouleau, -aux m. 2 (electric) bobine f. vt enrouler. vi s'enrouler.
coin (kɔin) n pièce de monnaie f. vt 1 frapper. 2 inventer.
coincide (kouin'said) vi coïncider. **coincidence** n coïncidence f.
colander ('kʌləndə) n passoire f.
cold (kould) adj froid. **be cold** 1 (of a person) avoir froid. 2 (of the weather) faire froid. ~n 1 froid m. 2 med rhume m. **have a cold** être enrhumé. **cold-blooded** adj 1 (of a person) insensible. 2 (of an animal) à sang froid.
collaborate (kə'læbəreit) vi collaborer. **collaboration** n collaboration f.
collapse (kə'læps) vi s'effondrer. n effon-

drement, écroulement *m.* **collapsible** *adj*
pliant.

collar ('kɔlə) *n* **1** (of a shirt, etc.) col *m.* **2** collier
m. **collarbone** *n* clavicule *f.*

colleague ('kɔliːg) *n* collègue *m,f.*

collect (kə'lekt) *vt* **1** rassembler. **2** collectionner.
3 percevoir. *vi* se grouper. **collected** *adj*
calme. **collection** *n* **1** collection *f.* **2** quête *f.*
3 levée *f.* **collective** *adj* collectif, -ive.

college ('kɔlidʒ) *n* collège *m.*

collide (kə'laid) *vi* se heurter, entrer en collision. **collision** *n* collision *f.* choc *m.*

colloquial (kə'loukwiəl) *adj* familier, -ière, parlé.

colon ('koulən) *n gram* deux points *m pl.*

colonel ('kəːnl) *n* colonel *m.*

colony ('kɔləni) *n* colonie *f.* **colonial** *adj*
colonial, -aux. **colonization** *n* colonisation
f. **colonize** *vt* coloniser.

colossal (kə'lɔsəl) *adj* colossal, -aux.

colour ('kʌlə) *n* **1** couleur *f.* **2** *mil* drapeau, -aux
m. vt colorer. *vi* **1** se colorer. **2** rougir.
colour-bar *n* ségrégation raciale *f.* **colour-
blind** *adj* daltonien, -ienne. **coloured** *adj* de
couleur, coloré. **colourless** *adj* incolore.

column ('kɔləm) *n* colonne *f.*

coma ('koumə) *n* coma *m.*

comb (koum) *n* **1** peigne *m.* **2** *zool* crête *f. vt*
peigner.

combat ('kɔmbæt) *n* combat *m.* lutte *f. vt,vi*
combattre. **combatant** *n* combattant *m.*

combine (*v* kəm'bain; *n* 'kɔmbain) *vt* combiner.
vi s'unir. *n* cartel *m.* **combination** *n* combinaison *f.*

combustion (kəm'bʌstʃən) *n* combustion *f.*

come* (kʌm) *vi* venir, arriver. **come about**
arriver. **come across** recontrer. **come back**
revenir, rentrer. **comeback** *n* retour
m. **come down** descendre. **come in** entrer.
come off se détacher. **come out** sortir.

comedy ('kɔmədi) *n* comédie *f.* **comedian** *n*
comédien, -ienne. **comic** *adj* comique, drôle.
n **1** comique *m.* **2** journal de bandes illustrées
m. **comical** *adj* comique.

comet ('kɔmit) *n* comète *f.*

comfort ('kʌmfət) *n* réconfort *m.* consolation *f.
vt* réconforter. **comfortable** *adj* **1** confortable,
commode. **2** à l'aise.

comical ('kɔmikəl) *adj* comique.

comma ('kɔmə) *n* virgule *f.* **inverted commas**
n pl guillemets *m pl.*

command (kə'mɑːnd) *vt* **1** ordonner, commander. **2** posséder. *n* **1** commandement, ordre *m.*

2 maîtrise *f.* **commandment** *n* commandement *m.*

commemorate (kə'meməreit) *vt* commémorer.
commemoration *n* commémoration *f.* **com-
memorative** *adj* commémoratif, -ive.

commence (kə'mens) *vt,vi* commencer. **commencement** *n* commencement, début *m.*

commend (kə'mend) *vt* **1** recommander. **2**
louer. **3** confier. **commendation** *n* louange *f.*
éloge *m.*

comment ('kɔment) *n* commentaire *m.* observation *f. vi* commenter. **commentary** *n* commentaire *m.* **commentator** *n* commentateur,
-trice.

commerce ('kɔməːs) *n* commerce *m.* affaires *f
pl.* **commercial** *adj* commercial, -aux. **commercial vehicle** *n* véhicule utilitaire *m.*

commission (kə'miʃən) *n* **1** commission *f.* **2** *mil*
brevet *m. vt* **1** charger. **2** déléguer. **commissioner** *n* commissaire *m.*

commit (kə'mit) *vt* **1** commettre. **2** confier. **3**
engager. **commitment** *n* engagement *m.*

committee (kə'miti) *n* **1** comité *m.* **2** *pol*
commission *f.*

commodity (kə'mɔditi) *n* marchandise, denrée
f.

common ('kɔmən) *adj* **1** commun, ordinaire. **2**
vulgaire. **3** public. *n* lieu commun *m.* **commonplace** *adj* banal, -aux, terre à terre. *n*
banalité *f.* **commonsense** *n* sens commun
m. **commonwealth** *n* **1** fédération, république *f.* **2** *cap* Commonwealth *m.*

Common Market *n* Marché Commun *m.*

commotion (kə'mouʃən) *n* tumulte *m.* commotion *f.*

commune[1] (kə'mjuːn) *vi* converser intimement.
communion *n* communion *f.*

commune[2] ('kɔmjuːn) *n* commune *f.* **communal** *adj* communal, -aux.

communicant (kə'mjuːnikənt) *n* communiant
m.

communicate (kə'mjuːnikeit) *vt,vi* communiquer. **communication** *n* communication
f. **communicative** *adj* communicatif, -ive.

communism ('kɔmjunizəm) *n* communisme
m. **communist** *adj,n* communiste.

community (kə'mjuːniti) *n* communauté *f.*

commute (kə'mjuːt) *vt* échanger. *vi* faire un
trajet journalier de sa résidence à son lieu de
travail et vice-versa. **commuter** *n* abonné *m.*

compact[1] (kəm'pækt) *adj* compact, serré. *vt*
condenser.

compact[2] ('kɔmpækt) *n* contrat *m.*

companion (kəm'pænıən) *n* compagnon *m.* compagne *f.* **companionship** *n* camaraderie *f.*

company ('kʌmpəni) *n* **1** compagnie *f.* **2** société *f.* **3** *naut* équipage *m.* **4** *Th* troupe *f.*

compare (kəm'pɛə) *vt* comparer. *vi* se comparer. **compared with** par rapport à, auprès de. **comparable** *adj* comparable. **comparative** *adj* comparatif, -ive, relatif, -ive. *n* comparatif *m.* **comparison** *n* comparaison *f.*

compartment (kəm'pɑːtmənt) *n* compartiment *m.*

compass ('kʌmpəs) *n* boussole *f.* (**pair of**) **compasses** *n* compas *m.*

compassion (kəm'pæʃən) *n* compassion *f.* **compassionate** *adj* compatissant.

compatible (kəm'pætibəl) *adj* compatible.

compel (kəm'pel) *vt* contraindre, obliger.

compensate ('kɔmpənseıt) *vt* dédommager, rémunérer. *vi* compenser. **compensation** *n* compensation *f.*

compete (kəm'piːt) *vi* concourir, rivaliser. **competition** *n* **1** compétition *f.* concours *m.* **2** concurrence *f.* **competitive** *adj* compétitif, -ive. **competitor** *n* **1** concurrent *m.* **2** compétiteur *m.*

competent ('kɔmpitənt) *adj* compétent, capable.

compile (kəm'pail) *vt* compiler.

complacent (kəm'pleisənt) *adj* satisfait de soi. **complacency** *n* suffisance *f.*

complain (kəm'plein) *vi* se plaindre. **complaint** *n* **1** plainte *f.* **2** *med* maladie *f.*

complement ('kɔmplimənt) *n* complément *m.* **complementary** *adj* complémentaire.

complete (kəm'pliːt) *adj* **1** complet, -ète. **2** achevé. *vt* **1** achever. **2** accomplir. **completion** *n* achèvement *m.*

complex ('kɔmpleks) *adj,n* complexe *m.* **complexity** *n* complexité *f.*

complexion (kəm'plekʃən) *n* **1** teint *m.* **2** aspect *m.*

complicate ('kɔmplikeit) *vt* compliquer. **complication** *n* complication *f.*

compliment ('kɔmplimənt) *n* compliment *m.* *vt* complimenter. **complimentary** *adj* **1** flatteur, -euse. **2** gracieux, -euse, gratuit.

comply (kəm'plai) *vi* se conformer, accéder.

component (kəm'pounənt) *adj* constituant. *n* composant *m.*

compose (kəm'pouz) *vt* **1** composer. **2** apaiser. **composed** *adj* calme. **composer** *n* compo-

siteur *m.* **composition** *n* **1** composition *f.* arrangement *m.* **2** *educ* rédaction *f.*

composure (kəm'pouʒə) *n* calme, sang-froid *m.*

compound[1] (*adj,n* 'kɔmpaund; *v* kəm'paund) *n* composé *m.* *adj* composé. *vt* composer, mélanger. *vi* s'arranger.

compound[2] ('kɔmpaund) *n* enclos fortifié *m.*

comprehend (kɔmpri'hend) *vt* comprendre. **comprehensible** *adj* compréhensible. **comprehension** *n* compréhension *f.* **comprehensive** *adj* compréhensif, -ive, étendu. **comprehensive school** *n* centre d'études secondaires *m.*

compress (*v* kəm'pres; *n* 'kɔmpres) *vt* comprimer. *n* compresse *f.*

comprise (kəm'praiz) *vt* comprendre, contenir.

compromise ('kɔmprəmaiz) *n* compromis *m.* *vt,vi* compromettre.

compulsion (kəm'pʌlʃən) *n* contrainte *f.* **compulsive** *adj* forcé. **compulsory** *adj* obligatoire.

computer (kəm'pjuːtə) *n* ordinateur *m.*

comrade ('kɔmrəd, -reid) *n* camarade *m,f.*

concave ('kɔŋkeiv) *adj* concave.

conceal (kən'siːl) *vt* **1** cacher. **2** dissimuler. **concealment** *n* dissimulation *f.*

concede (kən'siːd) *vt* **1** accorder. **2** admettre. *vi* faire des concessions.

conceit (kən'siːt) *n* vanité *f.* **conceited** *adj* prétentieux, -euse, suffisant.

conceive (kən'siːv) *vt,vi* concevoir. *vt* comprendre. **conceivable** *adj* concevable.

concentrate ('kɔnsəntreit) *vt* concentrer. *vi* se concentrer. **concentration** *n* concentration *f.* **concentration camp** *n* camp de concentration *m.*

concentric (kən'sentrik) *adj* concentrique.

concept ('kɔnsept) *n* concept *m.* **conception** *n* conception, idée *f.*

concern (kən'səːn) *vt* **1** concerner, regarder. **2** inquiéter. *n* **1** rapport *m.* **2** intérêt *m.* **3** inquiétude *f.* **4** *comm* entreprise *f.* **concerning** *prep* en ce qui concerne.

concert ('kɔnsət) *n* concert *m.*

concertina (kɔnsə'tiːnə) *n* concertina *f.*

concerto (kən'tʃɛətou) *n* concerto *m.*

concession (kən'seʃən) *n* concession *f.*

concise (kən'sais) *adj* concis.

conclude (kən'kluːd) *vt,vi* conclure. **conclusion** *n* conclusion *f.*

concoct (kən'kɔkt) *vt* **1** *cul* préparer. **2** inventer. **concoction** *n* **1** confectionnement *m.* **2** machination *f.*

concrete (ˈkɔŋkriːt) n béton m. adj concret. vt bétonner. vi se solidifier.

concussion (kənˈkʌʃən) n 1 choc m. 2 med commotion (cérébrale) f.

condemn (kənˈdem) vt condamner. **condemnation** n condamnation, censure f.

condense (kənˈdens) vt 1 condenser. 2 abréger. vi se condenser. **condensation** n condensation f.

condescend (kɔndiˈsend) vi condescendre, daigner. **condescension** n condescendance f.

condition (kənˈdiʃən) n condition f. état m. vt conditionner. **conditional** adj,n conditionnel, -elle m.

condolence (kənˈdoulɑns) n condoléance f.

condone (kənˈdoun) vt pardonner.

conduct (v kənˈdʌkt; n ˈkɔndʌkt) vt 1 conduire. 2 mus diriger. n conduite f.

conductor (kənˈdʌktə) n 1 conducteur m. 2 (on a bus) receveur m. 3 chef d'orchestre m.

cone (koun) n cône m.

confectioner (kənˈfekʃənə) n confiseur m. **confectionery** n confiserie f.

confederate (adj,n kənˈfedərət; v kənˈfedəreit) adj,n confédéré m. vt confédérer. vi se confédérer. **confederation** n confédération f.

confer (kənˈfəː) vt,vi conférer. **conference** n conférence f.

confess (kənˈfes) vt confesser, avouer. vi se confesser. **confession** n confession f. aveu, -eux m.

confetti (kənˈfeti) n pl confetti m.

confide (kənˈfaid) vt confier. vi se fier. **confidence** n 1 confiance f. 2 confidence f. **confident** adj sûr, confiant, assuré. **confidently** adv avec confiance. **confidential** adj confidentiel, -elle, de confiance. **confidentially** adv de confiance.

confine (kənˈfain) vt 1 limiter, restreindre. 2 enfermer. **confinement** n 1 emprisonnement m. 2 med accouchement m. couches f pl.

confirm (kənˈfəːm) vt confirmer. **confirmation** n confirmation f.

confiscate (ˈkɔnfiskeit) vt confisquer. **confiscation** n confiscation f.

conflict (n ˈkɔnflikt; v kənˈflikt) n conflit m. vi s'opposer. **conflicting** adj incompatible, contradictoire.

conform (kənˈfɔːm) vt conformer. vi se conformer. **conformity** n conformité f.

confound (kənˈfaund) vt 1 confondre. 2 embarrasser.

confront (kənˈfrʌnt) vt 1 affronter. 2 confronter. **confrontation** n confrontation f.

confuse (kənˈfjuːz) vt 1 embrouiller. 2 confondre, déconcerter. **confusion** n 1 confusion f. 2 désordre m.

congeal (kənˈdʒiːl) vt congeler, figer. vi se congeler.

congenial (kənˈdʒiːniəl) adj 1 approprié. 2 agréable, sympathique.

congested (kənˈdʒestid) adj congestionné, embouteillé. **congestion** n 1 med congestion f. 2 encombrement m.

congratulate (kənˈgrætjuleit) vt féliciter. **congratulation** n félicitation f.

congregate (ˈkɔŋgrigeit) vt rassembler. vi s'assembler. **congregation** n assemblée f.

congress (ˈkɔŋgres) n congrès m.

conical (ˈkɔnikəl) adj conique.

conifer (ˈkɔnifə) n conifère m.

conjugal (ˈkɔndʒugəl) adj conjugal, -aux.

conjugate (ˈkɔndʒugeit) vt conjuguer. **conjugation** n conjugaison f.

conjunction (kənˈdʒʌŋkʃən) n conjonction f.

conjure (ˈkʌndʒə) vt,vi conjurer. vt faire apparaître. **conjurer** n prestidigitateur m.

connect (kəˈnekt) vt relier, joindre. vi se lier, se joindre. **connection** n 1 rapport m. liaison f. 2 (train, bus, etc.) correspondance f.

connoisseur (kɔnəˈsəː) n connaisseur m.

connotation (kɔnəˈteiʃən) n signification f.

conquer (ˈkɔŋkə) vt conquérir, vaincre. **conqueror** n conquérant, vainqueur m. **conquest** n conquête f.

conscience (ˈkɔnʃəns) n conscience f. **conscientious** adj consciencieux, -euse.

conscious (ˈkɔnʃəs) adj conscient. **consciously** adv sciemment. **consciousness** n 1 conscience f. 2 med connaissance f.

conscript (ˈkɔnskript) n conscrit m. **conscription** n conscription f.

consecrate (ˈkɔnsikreit) vt consacrer. **consecration** n consécration f.

consecutive (kənˈsekjutiv) adj consécutif, -ive.

consent (kənˈsent) n consentement m. vi consentir.

consequence (ˈkɔnsikwəns) n 1 conséquence, suite f. 2 importance f. **consequent** adj résultant.

conserve (kənˈsəːv) vt conserver. **conservation** n conservation f. **conservative** adj,n conservateur, -trice. n cap Conservateur, -trice. **conservatory** n serre f.

consider (kənˈsidə) vt 1 considérer. 2 regarder.

considerable adj considérable. **considerate** adj attentionné, attentif, -ive. **consideration** n 1 considération f. 2 rémunération f. 3 importance f.
consign (kən'saın) vt 1 consigner. 2 expédier. **consignment** n envoi, expédition m.
consist (kən'sıst) vi **consist of** consister en, se composer de. **consistency** n 1 consistance f. 2 logique f. **consistent** adj 1 conséquent. 2 en accord.
console (kən'soul) vt consoler.
consolidate (kən'sɔlideıt) vt consolider. vi se consolider.
consonant ('kɔnsənənt) n consonne f.
conspicuous (kən'spikjuəs) adj en vue, remarquable.
conspire (kən'spaıə) vt comploter. vı conspirer. **conspiracy** n conspiration f.
constable ('kɔnstəbəl) n agent de police m. **constabulary** n police, gendarmerie f.
constant ('kɔnstənt) adj 1 constant. 2 continuel. n constante f.
constellation (kɔnstə'leıʃən) n constellation f.
constipation (kɔnsti'peıʃən) n constipation f.
constitute ('kɔnstıtjuːt) vt constituer. **constituency** n circonscription électorale f. **constituent** n électeur, -trice. adj constituant, essentiel, -elle. **constitution** n constitution f. **constitutional** adj constitutionnel, -elle.
constraint (kən'streınt) n contrainte f.
constrict (kən'strıkt) vt resserrer.
construct (kən'strʌkt) vt construire. **construction** n construction f. **constructive** adj constructif, -ive.
consul ('kɔnsəl) n consul m. **consular** adj consulaire. **consulate** n consulat m.
consult (kən'sʌlt) vt consulter. vi délibérer. **consultant** n médecin consultant m.
consume (kən'sjuːm) vt 1 consumer. 2 consommer, épuiser. **consumer** n consommateur, -trice. **consumption** n consommation f.
contact ('kɔntækt) vt contacter. n contact, rapport m. **contact lenses** n verres de contact m pl.
contagious (kən'teıdʒəs) adj contagieux, -euse.
contain (kən'teın) vt contenir. **container** n récipient m.
contaminate (kən'tæmıneıt) vt contaminer.
contemplate ('kɔntəmpleıt) vt 1 contempler. 2 envisager. vi réfléchir. **contemplation** n 1 contemplation f. 2 projet m.
contemporary (kən'temprəri) adj,n contemporain.

contempt (kən'tempt) n mépris m. **contemptible** adj méprisable.
content[1] ('kɔntent) n contenu m.
content[2] (kən'tent) adj satisfait. vt satisfaire. **be content with** se contenter de.
contest (n 'kɔntest; v kən'test) n 1 conflict m. 2 compétition f. vt contester. **contestant** n contestant, concurrent m.
context ('kɔntekst) n contexte m.
continent ('kɔntınənt) n continent m. **continental** adj continental, -aux.
contingency (kən'tındʒənsi) n éventualité f. **contingent** adj contingent, fortuit.
continue (kən'tınjuː) vt continuer. **continual** adj continuel, -elle. **continuation** n 1 continuation f. 2 suite f. **continuity** n continuité f. **continuous** adj continu.
contour ('kɔntuə) n contour, profil m.
contraband ('kɔntrəbænd) n contrebande f.
contraception (kɔntrə'sepʃən) n contraception f. **contraceptive** adj anticonceptionnel, -elle. n 1 contraceptif m. 2 préservatif m.
contract (n 'kɔntrækt; v kən'trækt) n contrat m. entreprise f. vt contracter. vi 1 se contracter. 2 s'engager. **contraction** n contraction f. **contractor** n entrepreneur m.
contradict (kɔntrə'dıkt) vt contredire. **contradiction** n contradiction f. **contradictory** adj contradictoire.
contralto (kən'træltou) n contralto m.
contraption (kən'træpʃən) n machin, truc m.
contrary ('kɔntrəri) adj,n contraire m.
contrast (n 'kɔntraːst; v kən'traːst) n contraste m. vt mettre en contraste. vi contraster.
contravene (kɔntrə'viːn) vt 1 transgresser, enfreindre. 2 s'opposer à.
contribute (kən'tribjuːt) vt,vi contribuer. **contribution** n contribution f. **contributor** n 1 collaborateur, -trice. 2 souscripteur m.
contrive (kən'traıv) vt 1 inventer. 2 arranger. vı s'arranger.
control (kən'troul) n 1 autorité, maîtrise f. 2 contrôle m. vt 1 contrôler. 2 diriger.
controversy ('kɔntrəvəːsi, kən'trɔvəsi) n controverse f. **controversial** adj controversable.
convalesce (kɔnvə'les) vı relever de maladie. **convalescence** n convalescence f. **convalescent** adj,n convalescent.
convenience (kən'viːniəns) n commodité, convenance f. **convenient** adj commode, approprié.
convent ('kɔnvənt) n couvent m.
convention (kən'venʃən) n 1 convention f. 2

177

assemblée f. **conventional** adj conventionnel, -elle.

converge (kən'vəːdʒ) vi converger.

converse[1] (kən'vəːs) vi causer. **conversation** n conversation f. entretien m.

converse[2] ('kɔnvəːs) adj 1 contraire. 2 math réciproque.

convert (v kən'vəːt; n 'kɔnvəːt) vt convertir, transformer. n converti m.

convex ('kɔnveks) adj convexe.

convey (kən'vei) vt 1 transporter. 2 transmettre. **conveyor belt** n chaîne de montage f.

convict (n 'kɔnvikt; v kən'vikt) n forçat m. vt condamner, convaincre.

conviction (kən'vikʃən) n 1 condamnation f. 2 conviction f.

convince (kən'vins) vt convaincre.

convoy ('kɔnvɔi) n convoi m.

cook (kuk) vt 1 faire cuire. 2 comm inf falsifier. vi cuire. n cuisinier, -ière. **cooker** n cuisinière f. **cookery** n cuisine f. **cookery book** n livre de cuisine m. **cooking** n cuisine f.

cool (kuːl) adj 1 frais, fraîche. 2 calme. vt rafraîchir, refroidir. vi se refroidir. **cool down** s'apaiser. **coolness** n 1 fraîcheur f. 2 sang-froid m.

coop (kuːp) n mue f.

cooperate (kou'ɔpəreit) vi coopérer. **cooperation** n coopération f. **cooperative** adj coopératif, -ive.

coordinate (v kouˈɔːdineit; adj kouˈɔːdinət) vt coordonner. adj coordonné.

cope[1] (koup) vi venir à bout, se débrouiller.

cope[2] (koup) n chape f.

Copenhagen (koupənˈheigən) n Copenhague f.

copper[1] ('kɔpə) n cuivre m. adj de cuivre. **copper beech** n hêtre rouge m.

copper[2] ('kɔpə) n inf flic m.

copy ('kɔpi) n 1 copie f. 2 exemplaire m. vt copier. **copyright** n droit d'auteur m.

coral ('kɔrəl) n corail, -aux m.

cord (kɔːd) n corde f. vt corder.

cordial ('kɔːdiəl) adj,n cordial, -aux m.

cordon ('kɔːdn̩) n cordon m.

corduroy ('kɔːdərɔi) n velours côtelé m.

core (kɔː) n 1 centre m. 2 (of an apple, etc.)trognon m.

cork (kɔːk) n 1 liège m. 2 bouchon m. vt boucher. **corkscrew** n tire-bouchon m.

corn[1] (kɔːn) n blé, grain m. **cornflour** n farine de maïs f. **cornflower** n bleuet m.

corn[2] (kɔːn) n med cor m.

corner ('kɔːnə) n 1 coin, angle m. 2 virage m. vt

1 inf mettre au pied du mur. 2 comm accaparer.

cornet ('kɔːnit) n cornet (à piston) m.

coronary ('kɔrənəri) adj coronaire f. **coronary thrombosis** n infarctus m.

coronation (kɔrəˈneiʃən) n couronnement m.

corporal[1] ('kɔːprəl) adj corporel, -elle.

corporal[2] ('kɔːprəl) n caporal, -aux m.

corporation (kɔːpəˈreiʃən) n 1 corporation f. 2 conseil municipal, -aux m.

corps (kɔː) n invar corps m invar.

corpse (kɔːps) n cadavre m.

correct (kəˈrekt) adj correct, exact. vt corriger.

correction n correction f.

correlate ('kɔrəleit) vi correspondre. vt mettre en corrélation. **correlation** n corrélation f.

correspond (kɔriˈspɔnd) vi correspondre. **correspondence** n correspondance f. courrier m. **correspondent** n correspondant m.

corridor ('kɔridɔː) n corridor m.

corrode (kəˈroud) vt corroder. vi se corroder. **corrosion** n corrosion f. **corrosive** adj,n corrosif, -ive m.

corrupt (kəˈrʌpt) vt corrompre, altérer. vi se corrompre. adj corrompu. **corruption** n corruption f.

corset ('kɔːsit) n corset m.

Corsica ('kɔːsikə) n Corse f. **Corsican** adj,n corse.

cosmetic (kɔzˈmetik) adj,n cosmétique m.

cosmopolitan (kɔzməˈpɔlitən) adj,n cosmopolite.

cosmos ('kɔzmɔs) n cosmos m. **cosmic** adj cosmique.

cost[*] (kɔst) n coût m. frais m pl. vi coûter. **costly** adj coûteux, -euse.

costume ('kɔstjuːm) n costume m.

cosy ('kouzi) adj confortable.

cot (kɔt) n lit d'enfant m.

cottage ('kɔtidʒ) n 1 chaumière f. 2 villa f.

cotton ('kɔtn̩) n coton m. **cotton-wool** n ouate f. coton hydrophile m.

couch (kautʃ) n canapé m. vt coucher.

cough (kɔf) n toux f. vi tousser.

council ('kaunsəl) n conseil m. **councillor** n conseiller m.

counsel ('kaunsəl) n conseil, avis m. vt conseiller.

count[1] (kaunt) vt,vi compter. n compte, calcul m. **countdown** n compte à rebours m.

count[2] (kaunt) n (title) comte m.

counter[1] ('kauntə) n 1 comptoir, guichet m. 2 game jeton m.

counter[2] ('kauntə) *adj* contraire. *adv* en sens inverse, contre.
counterattack ('kauntərətæk) *n* contre-attaque f.
counterfeit ('kauntəfit) *adj* faux, fausse. *n* contrefaçon f. *vt* contrefaire.
counterfoil ('kauntəfɔil) *n* souche f. talon *m*.
counterpart ('kauntəpɑ:t) *n* contrepartie f.
countess ('kauntis) *n* comtesse f.
country ('kʌntri) *n* **1** pays *m*. **2** campagne f. **countryside** *n* campagne f.
county ('kaunti) *n* comté *m*. **county council** *n* conseil général *m*.
coup (ku:) *n* coup *m*.
couple ('kʌpəl) *n* couple *m*. *vt* coupler.
coupon ('ku:pɔn) *n* coupon *m*.
courage ('kʌridʒ) *n* courage *m*. **courageous** *adj* courageux, -euse.
courgette (kuə'ʒet) *n* courgette f.
courier ('kuriə) *n* **1** courrier *m*. **2** guide *m*.
course (kɔ:s) *n* **1** cours *m*. **2** route f. **3** *cul* plat *m*. **4** champ de courses *m*. **of course** bien entendu.
court (kɔ:t) *n* **1** cour f. **2** *law* tribunal, -aux *m*. *vt* **1** courtiser. **2** solliciter. **court martial** *n* conseil de guerre *m*. **courtship** *n* cour f. **courtyard** *n* cour f.
courteous ('kə:tiəs) *adj* courtois. **courtesy** *n* courtoisie f.
cousin ('kʌzən) *n* cousin *m*.
cove (kouv) *n* crique f.
covenant ('kʌvənənt) *n* contrat, pacte *m*. *vt* accorder. *vi* convenir de.
cover ('kʌvə) *vt* couvrir. *n* **1** couverture f. **2** couvercle *m*. **3** abri *m*.
cow (kau) *n* vache f. **cowboy** *n* cowboy *m*.
coward ('kauəd) *adj,n* lâche *m*. **cowardice** *n* lâcheté f.
cower ('kauə) *vi* se blottir.
coy (kɔi) *adj* farouche, timide.
crab (kræb) *n* crabe *m*. **crab-apple** pomme sauvage f.
crack (kræk) *n* **1** craquement *m*. **2** fissure f. *adj* de premier ordre. *vt* **1** faire claquer. **2** fêler. **3** casser. *vi* **1** claquer. **2** se fêler. **3** se casser.
cracker ('krækə) *n* pétard *m*.
crackle ('krækəl) *n* crépitement *m*. *vi* crépiter.
cradle ('kreidl) *n* berceau, -aux *m*.
craft (krɑ:ft) *n* **1** métier (manuel) *m*. **2** ruse f. **3** bateau, -aux *m*. **craftsman** *n* artisan *m*. **craftsmanship** *n* habileté d'exécution f. **crafty** *adj* rusé.
cram (kræm) *vt* bourrer. *vi* s'entasser.

cramp[1] (kræmp) *n med* crampe f.
cramp[2] (kræmp) *n* crampon *m*.
crane (krein) *n* grue f.
crash (kræʃ) *n* **1** fracas *m*. **2** catastrophe f. *vt* fracasser. *vi* **1** retentir. **2** se tamponner. **crash-helmet** *n* casque protecteur *m*.
crate (kreit) *n* caisse à claire-voie f.
crater ('kreitə) *n* cratère *m*.
crave (kreiv) *vt* **1** implorer. **2** demander. **crave for** désirer ardemment.
crawl (krɔ:l) *vi* **1** ramper. **2** se traîner. *n sport* crawl *m*.
crayfish ('kreifiʃ) *n* écrevisse f.
crayon ('kreiən) *n* pastel *m*. *vt* crayonner.
craze (kreiz) *n inf* manie f. **crazy** *adj* fou, folle, insensé.
creak (kri:k) *n* grincement *m*. *vi* grincer.
cream (kri:m) *n* crème f. **creamy** *adj* crémeux, -euse.
crease (kri:s) *n* (faux) pli *m*. *vt* froisser. *vi* se plisser. **crease-resistant** *adj* infroissable.
create (kri'eit) *vt* créer. **creation** *n* création f. **creative** *adj* créateur, -trice.
creature ('kri:tʃə) *n* créature f.
creche (kreʃ) *n* crèche f.
credible ('kredibəl) *adj* croyable. **credibility** *n* crédibilité f.
credit ('kredit) *n* **1** crédit *m*. **2** mérite *m*. **3** croyance f. **credit card** *n* carte de crédit f. ~*vt* **1** croire. **2** reconnaître. **3** *comm* créditer. **creditable** *adj* estimable. **creditor** *n* créancier *m*.
creep[*] (kri:p) *vi* ramper, se glisser, grimper.
cremate (kri'meit) *vt* incinérer. **cremation** *n* incinération f. **crematorium** *n* four crématoire *m*.
crept (krept) *v* see **creep**.
crescent ('kresənt) *n* croissant *m*.
cress (kres) *n* cresson *m*.
crest (krest) *n* crête f.
crevice ('krevis) *n* fissure f.
crew (kru:) *n* équipage *m*. équipe f.
crib (krib) *n* **1** mangeoire f. **2** berceau, -aux *m*.
cricket[1] ('krikit) *n zool* grillon *m*.
cricket[2] ('krikit) *n sport* cricket *m*.
crime (kraim) *n* crime *m*. **criminal** *adj,n* criminel, -elle.
crimson ('krimzən) *adj,n* pourpre *m*.
cringe (krindʒ) *vi* **1** se faire tout petit. **2** s'humilier. *n* courbette servile f.
crinkle ('kriŋkəl) *vt* froisser. *vi* se chiffonner. *n* fronce, ride f.
cripple ('kripəl) *n* infirme *m,f*. *vt* estropier.

crisis (ˈkraisis) *n, pl* **crises** crise *f.*

crisp (krisp) *adj* **1** croquant, croustillant. **2** vif, vive. **3** tranchant, net, nette.

criterion (kraiˈtiəriən) *n, pl* **criteria** *or* **criterions** critérium, critère *m.*

criticize (ˈkritisaiz) *vt* **1** critiquer. **2** blâmer, censurer. **critic** *n* **1** critique. **2** censeur *m.* **critical** *adj* critique. **criticism** *n* critique *f.*

croak (krouk) *n* coassement, croassement *m. vi* **1** coasser, croasser. **2** *inf* grogner.

crochet (ˈkrouʃei) *n* crochet *m. vt* faire au crochet. *vi* faire du crochet.

crockery (ˈkrɔkəri) *n* faïence, poterie *f.*

crocodile (ˈkrɔkədail) *n* crocodile *m.*

crocus (ˈkroukəs) *n* crocus *m.*

crook (kruk) *n* **1** croc, crochet *m.* **2** angle *m.* **3** *inf* escroc *m.*

crooked (ˈkrukid) *adj* **1** courbé, tordu. **2** tortueux, -euse. **3** malhonnête.

crop (krɔp) *n* **1** récolte, moisson *f.* **2** (of hair) coupe *f. vt* couper, tondre.

croquet (ˈkroukei) *n* croquet *m.*

cross (krɔs) *n* **1** croix *f.* **2** contrariété *f.* **3** croisement *m. adj* **1** en colère, fâché. **2** transversal, -aux, oblique. *vt* **1** croiser. **2** traverser. **3** (a cheque) barrer. **cross-examine** *vt* contre-interroger. **cross-examination** *n* contre-interrogatoire. *m.* **cross-eyed** *adj* louche. **cross-fire** *n* feu croisé *m.* **crossing** *n* **1** croisement *m.* **2** traversée *f.* passage *m.* **cross-question** *vt* interroger contradictoirement. **cross-reference** *n* renvoi *m.* **crossroads** *n* carrefour *m.* **crossword** *n* mots croisés *m pl.*

crotchet (ˈkrɔtʃit) *n mus* noire *f.*

crouch (krautʃ) *vi* se blottir, s'accroupir.

crow[1] (krou) *n* corbeau, -aux *m.*

crow[2] (krou) *n* chant du coq, coquerico *m. vi* chanter.

crowd (kraud) *n* foule, bande *f.* rassemblement *m. vt* **1** serrer, entasser. **2** remplir. **crowded** *adj* bondé, encombré.

crown (kraun) *n* **1** couronne *f.* **2** sommet *m. vt* couronner. **crown prince** *n* prince héritier *m.*

crucial (ˈkruːʃəl) *adj* critique, décisif, -ive.

crucify (ˈkruːsifai) *vt* crucifier, mettre en croix. **crucifix** *n* crucifix *m.* **crucifixion** *n* crucifixion *f.*

crude (kruːd) *adj* **1** brut. **2** cru. **3** grossier, -ère. **crude oil** *n* mazout *m.* **crudely** *adv* crûment, grossièrement.

cruel (ˈkruəl) *adj* cruel, -elle. **cruelty** *n* cruauté *f.*

cruise (kruːz) *n* croisière *f. vi* croiser.

crumb (krʌm) *n* miette *f.*

crumble (ˈkrʌmbəl) *vt* émietter, effriter. *vi* **1** s'émietter. **2** s'écrouler.

crumple (ˈkrʌmpəl) *vt* friper, froisser. **crumple up** se friper, se froisser.

crunch (krʌntʃ) *vt* croquer. *vi* craquer. *n* bruit de broiement *m.*

crusade (kruːˈseid) *n* croisade *f.*

crush (krʌʃ) *n* presse, foule *f. vt* **1** écraser. **2** froisser. *vi* se presser en foule.

crust (krʌst) *n* croûte *f. vt* encroûter.

crustacean (krʌsˈteiʃən) *n* crustacé *m.*

crutch (krʌtʃ) *n* béquille *f.*

cry[*] (krai) *n* cri *m. vt,vi* **1** crier. **2** pleurer. **cry off** se récuser. **cry out** s'écrier.

crypt (kript) *n* crypte *f.*

crystal (ˈkristl) *n* cristal, -aux *m.* **crystallize** *vt* cristalliser. *vi* se cristalliser.

cub (kʌb) *n* petit *m.*

cube (kjuːb) *n* cube *m. vt* cuber. **cubic** *adj* cubique. **cubicle** *n* **1** alcôve *f.* **2** cabine *f.*

cuckoo (ˈkuːkuː) *n* coucou *m.*

cucumber (ˈkjuːkʌmbə) *n* concombre *m.*

cuddle (ˈkʌdl) *vt* serrer dans les bras. *vi* se pelotonner. *n* étreinte, embrassade *f.*

cue[1] (kjuː) *n* **1** *Th* réplique *f.* **2** avis *m.* indication *f.*

cue[2] (kjuː) *n* queue (de billard) *f.*

cuff[1] (kʌf) *n* manchette *f.* **cufflink** *n* bouton de manchette *f.*

cuff[2] (kʌf) *n* taloche *f. vt* talocher.

culinary (ˈkʌlinri) *adj* culinaire.

culprit (ˈkʌlprit) *n* **1** coupable *m,f.* **2** *law* accusé, prévenu *m.*

cult (kʌlt) *n* culte *m.*

cultivate (ˈkʌltiveit) *vt* cultiver. **cultivation** *n* culture *f.*

culture (ˈkʌltʃə) *n* culture *f.* **cultural** *adj* culturel, -elle. **cultured** *adj* cultivé, instruit.

cumbersome (ˈkʌmbəsəm) *adj* encombrant, incommode.

cunning (ˈkʌniŋ) *adj* malin, -igne, rusé. *n* ruse, fourberie *f.*

cup (kʌp) *n* **1** tasse *f.* **2** *sport* coupe *f.* **cupful** *n* pleine coupe *f.*

cupboard (ˈkʌbəd) *n* armoire *f.* placard *m.*

curate (ˈkjuəreit) *n* vicaire *m.*

curator (kjuˈreitə) *n* conservateur *m.*

curb (kəːb) *n* **1** bordure *f.* **2** frein *m. vt* réprimer, brider.

curdle ('kɔ:dl) vt **1** cailler. **2** glacer. vi **1** se cailler. **2** se figer.

cure (kjuə) n **1** med guérison f. **2** remède m. vt **1** guérir. **2** cul saler, fumer.

curfew ('kɔ:fju:) n couvre-feu m invar.

curious ('kjuəriəs) adj **1** curieux, -euse. **2** singulier, -ière. **curiosity** n curiosité f.

curl (kɔ:l) n boucle f. vt,vi **1** boucler, friser. **2** enrouler. **curly** adj bouclé.

currant ('kʌrənt) n **1** groseille f. **2** raisin de Corinthe m. **currant bush** n groseillier m.

current ('kʌrənt) adj courant, en cours. n courant m. **currency** n **1** circulation f. cours m. **2** unité monétaire f. **currently** adv couramment. **current account** n compte courant m.

curry ('kʌri) n cari m. **curry powder** n cari m.

curse (kɔ:s) n **1** malédiction f. **2** juron. **3** fléau, -aux m. vt maudire. vi blasphémer.

curt (kɔ:t) adj brusque, sec, sèche.

curtail (kɔ:'teil) vt **1** raccourcir. **2** diminuer.

curtain ('kɔ:tn) n rideau, -aux m.

curtsy ('kɔ:tsi) n révérence f. vi faire une révérence.

curve (kɔ:v) n **1** courbe f. **2** tournant m. vt courber, cintrer. vi se courber.

cushion ('kuʃən) n coussin m. vt amortir.

custard ('kʌstəd) n crème anglaise f.

custody ('kʌstədi) n **1** garde f. **2** emprisonnement m.

custom ('kʌstəm) n **1** coutume, habitude f. **2** clientèle f. **3** pl douane f. **customary** adj habituel, -elle, d'usage. **customer** n **1** client m. **2** inf type m.

cut* (kʌt) vt,vi couper. **cut down** réduire. **cut off** trancher. **cut out 1** enlever. **2** supprimer. **cut glass** n cristal taillé m. **cut-price** adj à prix réduit. ~n **1** coupe f. **2** coupure f. **3** tranche. f. **4** réduction f. **cutting** n **1** coupage m. **2** coupure f. adj mordant.

cute (kju:t) adj inf **1** mignon, -onne. **2** rusé.

cuticle ('kju:tikəl) n cuticule f.

cutlery ('kʌtləri) n coutellerie f.

cutlet ('kʌtlit) n côtelette f.

cycle ('saikəl) n **1** cycle m. **2** vélo m. vi faire de la bicyclette, aller à bicyclette. **cycling** n cyclisme m. **cyclist** n cycliste m,f.

cyclone ('saikloun) n cyclone m.

cygnet ('signit) n jeune cygne m.

cylinder ('silində) n cylindre m. **cylindrical** adj cylindrique.

cymbal ('simbəl) n cymbale f.

cynic ('sinik) n sceptique, cynique m. **cynical** adj sceptique, cynique.

cypress ('saiprəs) n cyprès m.

Cyprus ('saiprəs) n Chypre f. **Cypriot** adj,n cypriote.

czar (zɑ:) n tsar m.

Czechoslovakia (tʃekəslə'vækiə) n Tchécoslovaquie f. **Czech** adj,n tchèque. **Czechoslovakian** adj tchécoslovaque.

D

dab (dæb) n **1** coup léger m. **2** tache f. vt tamponner, tapoter.

dabble ('dæbəl) vt mouiller. vi barboter. **dabble in** se mêler de.

dad (dæd) n inf papa m.

daffodil ('dæfədil) n narcisse des bois m. jonquille f.

daft (dɑ:ft) adj écervelé, toqué.

dagger ('dægə) n poignard m. dague f.

daily ('deili) adj quotidien, -ienne, journalier, -ière. n **1** (newspaper) quotidien m. **2** inf femme de ménage f. adv tous les jours.

dainty ('deinti) adj délicat, friand.

dairy ('dɛəri) n laiterie f. ferme laitière f.

daisy ('deizi) n marguerite, pâquerette f.

dam¹ (dæm) n barrage. vt contenir, endiguer.

dam² (dæm) n zool mère f.

damage ('dæmidʒ) n **1** dégâts, dommages m pl. **2** préjudice m. **3** law dommages-intérêts m pl. vt **1** abîmer, endommager. **2** nuire à.

damn (dæm) vt **1** condamner. **2** ruiner. **3** damner. interj zut! **damnable** adj maudit. **damnation** n damnation f.

damp (dæmp) adj humide, moite. n humidité f. vt **1** mouiller. **2** étouffer. **3** décourager. **dampen** vt humidifier.

damson ('dæmzən) n prune de Damas f.

dance (dɑ:ns) n **1** danse f. **2** bal m. vt,vi danser. **dancing** n danse f.

dandelion ('dændilaiən) n pissenlit m.

dandruff ('dændrʌf) n pellicules f pl.

Dane (dein) n danois m. **Danish** adj,n danois. **Danish** (language) n danois m.

danger ('deindʒə) n danger, péril m. **dangerous** adj dangereux, -euse, périlleux, -euse.

dangle ('dæŋgəl) vi pendiller, se balancer. vt faire pendiller.

dare* (dɛə) vt **1** oser, risquer. **2** défier. **daring** adj hardi, audacieux, -euse. n témérité, audace f.

dark (dɑ:k) adj **1** noir, obscur. **2** foncé. **3** brun. **4** secret, -ète. n also **darkness** obscurité f.

ténèbres f pl. **darken** vt obscurcir, assombrir. vi s'obscurcir, s'assombrir.

darling ('da:liŋ) adj,n chéri.

darn (da:n) vt repriser, raccommoder. n reprise f. **darning** n reprise f.

dart (da:t) n **1** dard m. **2** sport fléchette f. **3** (in sewing) pince f. vi s'élancer, se précipiter. **dartboard** n cible f.

dash (dæʃ) n **1** coup m. **2** goutte f. **3** trait m. **4** élan m. vt **1** jeter. **2** anéantir. vi s'élancer. **dashboard** n tablier m. **dashing** adj plein d'élan.

data ('deitə) n données f pl. **data processing** n traitement d'informatique m.

date[1] (deit) n **1** date f. **2** rendez-vous m. **date line** n ligne de changement de date f. **out of date** démodé. **up to date** à la page.

date[2] (deit) n bot datte f. **date palm** n dattier m.

daughter ('dɔ:tə) n fille f. **daughter-in-law** n belle-fille, bru f.

dawdle ('dɔ:dl) vi flâner, lambiner.

dawn (dɔ:n) n aube f. **at dawn** au point du jour.

day (dei) n jour m. journée f. **day after** lendemain m. **day before** veille f. **in those days** à ce moment-là. **daybreak** n point du jour m. **daydream** n rêverie f. vi rêvasser. **daylight** n jour m.

daze (deiz) vt **1** hébéter. **2** étourdir. n étourdissement m.

dazzle ('dæzəl) vt éblouir, aveugler. n éblouissement m.

dead (ded) adj mort, décédé. **deadline** n date limite f. **deadlock** n impasse f. **deaden** vt amortir, assourdir, assoupir. **deadly** adj mortel, -elle.

deaf (def) adj sourd. **deaf-aid** n appareil de correction auditive pour sourds m. **deaf-mute** n sourd-muet, sourde-muette. **deafness** n surdité f. **deafen** vt assourdir.

deal* (di:l) n **1** comm affaire f. **2** quantité f. **3** game donne f. vt distribuer, donner. vi **1** s'occuper. **2** faire des affaires. **dealer** n **1** fournisseur, marchand m. **2** game donneur m.

dean (di:n) n doyen m.

dear (diə) adj **1** cher, chère. **2** coûteux, -euse. n cher, chère. **dearly** adv cher, chèrement.

death (deθ) n mort f. **death certificate** n acte de décès m. **death rate** n mortalité f.

debate (di'beit) n débat m. discussion f. vt discuter, débattre. vi disputer.

debit ('debit) n débit m. vt débiter.

debris ('deibri) n débris m pl.

debt (det) n dette f. créance f. **debtor** n débiteur m.

decade ('dekeid) n décade f.

decadent ('dekədənt) adj décadent. **decadence** n décadence f.

decant (di'kænt) vt décanter. **decanter** n carafe f.

decay (di'kei) n **1** pourriture f. **2** décadence f. vi **1** pourrir. **2** tomber en ruine.

decease (di'si:s) n décès m. vi décéder.

deceit (di'si:t) n tromperie f. **deceitful** adj trompeur, -euse, fourbe. **deceitfulness** n fausseté f.

deceive (di'si:v) vt tromper, décevoir.

December (di'sembə) n décembre m.

decent ('di:sənt) adj **1** honnête, bienséant. **2** assez bon. **decency** n décence f.

deceptive (di'septiv) adj trompeur, -euse.

decibel ('desibel) n décibel m.

decide (di'said) vt décider. vi se décider. **decided** adj décidé, arrêté. **decidedly** adv résolument. **deciding** adj décisif, -ive.

deciduous (di'sidjuəs) adj caduc, caduque.

decimal ('desiməl) adj décimal, -aux. n décimale f. **decimalization** n décimalisation f.

decipher (di'saifə) vt déchiffrer.

decision (di'siʒən) n **1** décision f. **2** résolution f. **decisive** adj décisif, -ive.

deck (dek) n **1** naut pont m. **2** (of a bus) impériale f. vt orner. **deckchair** n transatlantique m.

declaration (deklə'reiʃən) n déclaration, annonce f.

declare (di'kleə) vt déclarer, annoncer. vi se déclarer. **declared** adj avoué, ouvert.

decline (di'klain) n **1** déclin m. **2** baisse f. **3** pente f. vt,vi décliner. vt refuser poliment. vi **1** décliner, repousser. **2** baisser. **declension** n déclinaison f.

decorate ('dekəreit) vt décorer, orner. **decoration** n **1** décoration f. **2** décor m. **decorative** adj décoratif, -ive. **decorator** n décorateur m.

decoy (n 'di:kɔi; v di'kɔi) n appât, leurre m. amorce f. vt **1** piper. **2** leurrer.

decrease (di'kri:s) n diminution f. vt,vi diminuer. vt amoindrir. vi décroître.

decree (di'kri:) n décret, édit m. vt ordonner, décréter.

decrepit (di'krepit) adj décrépit m.

dedicate ('dedikeit) vt dédier. **dedication** n dedicace f.

deduce (di'dju:s) vt déduire, conclure.

deduct (di'dʌkt) vt déduire, retrancher. **deduction** n déduction f.

deed (di:d) n **1** action f. acte m. **2** exploit m.

deep (di:p) adj **1** profond. **2** (of colour) foncé. n **1** profondeur f. **2** abîme m. **deepen** vt approfondir. vi devenir plus profond. **deeply** adv profondément. **deep-freeze**° n congélateur m. vt congeler. **deep-seated** adj profond, enraciné.

deer (diə) n cerf, daim m.

deface (di'feis) vt mutiler, défigurer, lacérer.

default (di'fɔ:lt) n défaut m. contumace f. vi faire défaut.

defeat (di'fi:t) n défaite f. vt **1** vaincre. **2** renverser.

defect (n 'di:fekt; v di'fekt) n défaut m. vi déserter. **defection** n défection f. **defective** adj **1** défectueux, -euse. **2** gram défectif, -ive.

defence (di'fens) n défense, protection, justification f. **defend** vt défendre. **defendant** n défendeur, -eresse. **defensive** adj défensif, -ive.

defer (di'fə:) vt ajourner, différer. vi déférer. **deference** n déférence f. **deferential** adj déférent.

defiant (di'faiənt) adj rebelle, provocant. **defiance** n défi m. **defiantly** adv d'un air de défi.

deficient (di'fiʃənt) adj insuffisant, défectueux, -euse. **deficiency** n **1** manque m. **2** défaut m.

deficit ('defisit) n déficit m.

define (di'fain) vt **1** définir. **2** déterminer. **definition** n définition f.

definite ('defənit) adj **1** défini. **2** bien déterminé. adv décidément.

deflate (di'fleit) vt dégonfler. **deflation** n **1** dégonflement m. **2** comm déflation f.

deform (di'fɔ:m) vt déformer. **deformed** adj difforme. **deformity** n difformité f.

defraud (di'frɔ:d) vt frauder.

defrost (di'frɔst) vt déglacer, décongeler.

deft (deft) adj habile, adroit. **deftness** n habileté, dextérité f.

defunct (di'fʌŋkt) adj défunt, décédé.

defy (di'fai) vt défier.

degenerate (adj,n di'dʒenərit; v di'dʒenəreit) adj,n dégénéré. vi dégénérer.

degrade (di'greid) vt dégrader, avilir. **degradation** n dégradation f.

degree (di'gri:) n **1** degré m. **2** educ licence f. **by degrees** petit à petit. **in some degree** dans une certaine mesure. **to some degree** à un certain degré.

dehydrate (di'haidreit) vt déshydrater. **dehydration** n déshydratation f.

deity ('deiiti) n **1** dieu m. déesse f. **2** déité f.

dejected (di'dʒektid) adj triste, abattu.

delay (di'lei) n délai, retard m. vt traîner, retarder, arriérer. vi s'attarder.

delegate (n 'deligət; v 'deligeit) n délégué m. vt déléguer. **delegation** n délégation f.

delete (di'li:t) vt effacer, rayer.

deliberate (adj di'libərət; v di'libəreit) adj **1** intentionnel, -elle, prémédité. **2** réfléchi. vt,vi délibérer. **deliberately** adv exprès.

delicate ('delikət) adj délicat. **delicacy** n **1** délicatesse. **2** cul friandise f.

delicatessen (delikə'tesən) n charcuterie f.

delicious (di'liʃəs) adj délicieux, -euse, exquis.

delight (di'lait) n délices f pl. joie f. vt enchanter, réjouir. **delightful** adv délicieux, -euse, ravissant.

delinquency (di'liŋkwənsi) n **1** délinquance f. **2** délit m. **delinquent** n délinquant m.

deliver (di'livə) vt **1** livrer, distribuer. **2** (a speech) faire. **delivery** n **1** livraison f. **2** distribution f.

delta ('deltə) n delta m.

delude (di'lu:d) vt tromper, abuser, duper. **delusion** n erreur, illusion f.

delve (delv) vt fouiller.

demand (di'ma:nd) vt exiger, demander, réclamer. n demande f.

democracy (di'mɔkrəsi) n démocratie f. **democratic** adj démocratique.

demolish (di'mɔliʃ) vt démolir. **demolition** n démolition f.

demon ('di:mən) n démon m.

demonstrate ('demənstreit) vt **1** démontrer. **2** pol manifester. **demonstration** n **1** démonstration f. **2** pol manifestation f. **demonstrator** n **1** démonstrateur m. **2** manifestant m. **demonstrative** adj démonstratif, -ive.

demoralize (di'mɔrəlaiz) vt démoraliser.

demure (di'mjuə) adj réservé, composé.

den (den) n **1** tanière f. **2** repaire m.

denial (di'naiəl) n déni m. dénégation f.

denim ('denim) n **1** serge de coton f. **2** pl blue-jean m.

Denmark ('denma:k) n Danemark m.

denomination (dinɔmi'neiʃən) n **1** dénomination f. **2** rel secte f. **denominator** n dénominateur m.

denote (di'nout) vt **1** dénoter. **2** signifier.

denounce (di'nauns) vt dénoncer.

dense (dens) adj **1** dense, épais, -aisse. **2** inf

stupide, bête. **density** n 1 densité f. 2 inf
stupidité f.

dent (dent) n bosselure f. renfoncement m. vt
bosseler.

dental ('dentl) adj dentaire. **dentist** n dentiste
m. **dentistry** n art dentaire m. **denture** n
dentier m.

deny (di'nai) vt 1 nier, démentir. 2 refuser.

deodorant (di'oudərənt) n déodorant m.

depart (di'pa:t) vi partir, s'en aller. vt quitter.
departed adj passé, mort. **departure** n
départ m.

department (di'pa:tmənt) n 1 département m. 2
(of a shop) rayon m.

depend (di'pend) vi dépendre. **depend on**
compter sur. **dependant** n charge de famille
f. **dependence** n dépendance f.

depict (di'pikt) vt peindre.

deplete (di'pli:t) vt épuiser.

deplore (di'plɔ:) vi déplorer, regretter fort.

deport (di'pɔ:t) vt déporter. **deportment** n
tenue f.

depose (di'pouz) vt déposer.

deposit (di'pɔzit) n 1 comm dépôt, versement
m. 2 sédiment m. vt déposer.

depot ('depou) n dépôt, entrepôt m.

deprave (di'preiv) vt dépraver, corrompre.

depreciate (di'pri:ʃieit) vt déprécier. vi se
déprécier, baisser.

depress (di'pres) vt 1 abaisser. 2 décourager. 3
comm faire languir. **depressed** adj 1 abattu.
2 comm languissant. **depression** n 1 abat-
tement m. 2 dépression f. **depressive** adj
déprimant.

deprive (di'praiv) vt priver.

depth (depθ) n profondeur f.

deputize ('depjutaiz) vi remplacer. **deputation**
n délégation f. **deputy** n délégué, suppléant
m.

derail (di'reil) vt faire dérailler.

derelict ('derəlikt) adj abandonné, délaissé.

deride (di'raid) vt se moquer de, railler.
derision n dérision f. **derisive** adj railleur,
-euse.

derive (di'raiv) vt,vi tirer. vi provenir.
derivation n dérivation f.

derogatory (di'rɔgətri) adj dérogatoire.

descend (di'send) vt,vi descendre. **descendant**
n descendant m.

descent (di'sent) n descente f.

describe (di'skraib) vt décrire. **description** n
description f.

desert[1] ('dezət) n désert m.

desert[2] (di'zə:t) vt abandonner, laisser. vi
déserter. **deserter** n déserteur m.

deserve (di'zə:v) vt mériter.

design (di'zain) n 1 dessein m. 2 dessin m. 3
intention f. 4 modèle m. vt 1 projeter. 2 créer.
3 destiner. **designing** adj intrigant.

designate ('dezigneit) vt désigner, nommer. 2
indiquer.

desire (di'zaiə) n désir, souhait m. vt désirer,
vouloir.

desk (desk) n 1 (school) pupitre m. 2 (office)
bureau, -aux m. 3 caisse f.

desolate ('desələt) adj 1 désert, abandonné. 2
affligé.

despair (di'spɛə) n désespoir m.

desperate ('desprət) adj désespéré. **despera-
tion** n désespoir m.

despise (di'spaiz) vt mépriser.

despite (di'spait) prep malgré.

despondent (di'spɔndənt) adj découragé, abattu.

dessert (di'zə:t) n dessert m. **dessertspoon** n
cuiller à dessert f.

destine ('destin) vt destiner. **destination** n
destination f. **destiny** n destin, sort m.

destitute ('destitju:t) adj 1 dépourvu, dénué. 2
sans ressources.

destroy (di'strɔi) vt 1 détruire, anéantir. 2
tuer. **destruction** n destruction f. **destruc-
tive** adj destructeur, -trice, destructif, -ive.
destroyer n contre-torpilleur m.

detach (di'tætʃ) vt détacher, séparer. **detach-
ment** n 1 détachement m. 2 indifférence f.

detail ('di:teil) n détail m. vt 1 détailler. 2
affecter.

detain (di'tein) vt 1 law détenir. 2 retenir.
detention n 1 détention f. 2 educ retenue f.

detect (di'tekt) vt 1 découvrir. 2 apercevoir.
detective n détective m. **detective story**
roman policier m.

deter (di'tə:) vt décourager, détourner. **deterrent** n force préventive f.

detergent (di'tə:dʒənt) n détergent m.

deteriorate (di'tiəriəreit) vi se détériorer.
deterioration n détérioration f.

determine (di'tə:min) vt,vi déterminer, décider.
determination n détermination, résolution
f. **determined** adj résolu.

detest (di'test) vt détester.

detonate ('detəneit) vt faire détoner. vi détoner.
detonator n amorce f.

detour ('di:tuə) n détour m.

detract (di'trækt) vi **detract from** diminuer de, déprécier de.

devalue (di'vælju:) vt dévaluer. **devaluation** n dévaluation f.

devastate ('devəsteit) vt ravager, dévaster.

develop (di'veləp) vt développer. vi se développer, se manifester. **development** n 1 développement m. 2 exploitation f. 3 fait m.

deviate ('di:vieit) vi dévier, s'écarter. **deviation** n déviation f. **devious** adj tortueux, -euse, détourné.

device (di'vais) n 1 moyen m. 2 ruse f. 3 truc m.

devil ('devəl) n diable m.

devise (di'vaiz) vt inventer, combiner.

devoid (di'vɔid) adj dépourvu, dénué.

devote (di'vout) vt consacrer, vouer, accorder.

devotion (di'vouʃən) n dévouement m.

devour (di'vauə) vt dévorer.

devout (di'vaut) adj pieux, -euse, dévot.

dew (dju:) n rosée f.

dexterous ('dekstrəs) adj habile, adroit. **dexterity** n dextérité, habileté f.

diabetes (daiə'bi:tiz) n diabète m. **diabetic** adj,n diabétique.

diagonal (dai'agənl) adj diagonal, -aux. n diagonale f.

diagram ('daiəgræm) n diagramme, schéma m.

dial (dail) n cadran m. vt 1 appeler. 2 (a number) composer.

dialect ('daiəlekt) n dialecte, patois m.

dialogue ('daiələg) n dialogue m.

diameter (dai'æmitə) n diamètre m.

diamond ('daiəmənd) n 1 diamant m. 2 game carreau, -aux m.

diaphragm ('daiəfræm) n diaphragme m.

diarrhoea (daiə'riə) n diarrhée f.

diary ('daiəri) n 1 (personal) journal, -aux m. 2 agenda m.

dice (dais) n pl or s dé m. vt couper en cubes.

dictate (v dik'teit; n 'dikteit) vt dicter. vi faire la loi. n commandement m. **dictation** n dictée f. **dictator** n dictateur m. **dictatorship** n dictature f.

dictionary ('dikʃənri) n dictionnaire m.

did (did) v see **do**.

die (dai) vi mourir. **die down** s'apaiser.

diesel ('di:zəl) n diesel m.

diet ('daiət) n régime m. vi être au régime.

differ ('difə) vi différer. **difference** n 1 différence f. 2 dispute f. **different** adj différent, divers, autre. **differential** adj différentiel,

-elle. n 1 mot différentiel m. 2 différentielle f. **differentiate** vt différencier.

difficult ('difikəlt) adj difficile. **difficulty** n 1 difficulté f. 2 obstacle, ennui m.

dig (dig) vt bêcher, creuser. n 1 fouille f. 2 inf coup de patte m.

digest (dai'dʒest) vt digérer. vi se digérer. **digestion** n digestion f.

digit ('didʒit) n 1 chiffre m. 2 anat doigt m.

dignity ('digniti) n dignité f. **dignified** adj digne.

dilapidated (di'læpideitid) adj délabré, décrépit.

dilemma (di'lemə) n dilemme f.

diligent ('dilidʒənt) adj diligent, assidu. **diligently** adv diligemment.

dilute (dai'lu:t) vt diluer, arroser.

dim (dim) adj faible, pâle. vt obscurcir, ternir. vi s'effacer, baisser.

dimension (di'menʃən) n dimension f.

diminish (di'miniʃ) vt,vi diminuer, réduire.

diminutive (di'minjutiv) adj,n diminutif, -ive m.

dimple ('dimpəl) n fossette f.

din (din) n fracas, tapage m.

dine (dain) vt dîner. **dining car** n wagon-restaurant. **dining room** n salle à manger f.

dinghy ('diŋgi) n canot m.

dingy ('dindʒi) adj terne, sombre.

dinner ('dinə) n dîner m. **dinner jacket** n smoking m.

dinosaur ('dainəsɔ:) n dinosaure m.

diocese ('daiəsis) n diocèse m.

dip (dip) vt,vi 1 plonger. 2 baisser. vi incliner. n 1 plongée f. 2 inf baignade f.

diphthong ('difθɔŋ) n diphtongue f.

diploma (di'ploumə) n diplôme m.

diplomacy (di'ploumsi) n diplomatie f. n diplomate m. **diplomatic** adj 1 diplomatique. 2 prudent.

direct (di'rekt) vt 1 diriger. 2 ordonner. 3 indiquer. adj 1 direct. 2 franc, -che. 3 absolu. **direct object** n objet direct m. **direction** n 1 direction f. sens m. 2 pl instructions f pl. **director** n administrateur, directeur m. **directory** n annuaire. **directly** adv tout de suite.

dirt (də:t) n 1 saleté f. 2 ordure f. **dirty** adj 1 sale, crasseux, -euse. 2 inf vulgaire. 3 inf vilain. vt salir, crotter.

disability (disə'biliti) n 1 incapacité f. 2 infirmité f. **disabled** adj invalide, estropié.

disadvantage (disəd'va:ntidʒ) n désavantage, inconvénient m.

disagree (disə'gri:) vi 1 être en désaccord. 2 se

brouiller. **disagreeable** adj désagréable. **disagreement** n 1 différence f. 2 querelle f.

disappear (disə'pɪə) vi disparaître. **disappearance** n disparition f.

disappoint (disə'pɔint) vt désappointer, décevoir. **disappointment** n déception f.

disapprove (disə'pru:v) vi désapprouver. **disapproval** n désapprobation f. **disapproving** adj désapprobateur, -trice.

disarm (dis'ɑ:m) vt,vi désarmer. **disarmament** n désarmement m.

disaster (di'zɑ:stə) n désastre m. **disastrous** adj désastreux, -euse.

disband (dis'bænd) vt licencier. vi se débander.

disc (disk) n disque m. **disc jockey** n présentateur de disques m.

discard (di'skɑ:d) vt rejeter, se défausser de.

discern (di'sə:n) vt discerner, distinguer. **discerning** adj judicieux, -euse.

discharge (dis'tʃɑːdʒ) vt 1 décharger. 2 congédier. 3 renvoyer. 4 law libérer, acquitter. n 1 décharge f. 2 renvoi m. 3 acquittement m.

disciple (di'saipəl) n disciple m.

discipline ('disəplin) n discipline f. vt discipliner.

disclose (dis'klouz) vt révéler, divulguer.

disconnect (diskə'nekt) vt couper, décrocher, disjoindre.

disconsolate (dis'kɔnsələt) adj désolé, triste.

discontinue (diskən'tinju:) vt discontinuer. vi cesser.

discord ('diskɔ:d) n 1 discorde f. 2 mus dissonance f. **discordant** adj 1 discordant. 2 mus dissonant.

discotheque ('diskətek) n discothèque f.

discount (n 'diskaunt; v dis'kaunt) n rabais m. remise f. vt ne pas tenir compte de.

discourage (dis'kʌridʒ) vt décourager, abattre.

discover (dis'kʌvə) vt découvrir. **discovery** n découverte f.

discreet (dis'kri:t) adj discret, -ète, prudent. **discretion** n 1 discrétion f. 2 jugement m.

discrepancy (dis'krepənsi) n désaccord m.

discrete (dis'kri:t) adj discret, -ète.

discriminate (dis'krimineit) vt distinguer, discerner. vi faire des distinctions. **discrimination** n 1 discernement m. 2 jugement m. 3 distinction f.

discus ('diskəs) n disque m.

discuss (dis'kʌs) vt discuter, débattre. **discussion** n discussion f. débat m.

disease (di'zi:z) n maladie f. mal m.

186

disembark (disim'bɑ:k) vt,vi débarquer. **disembarkation** n débarquement m.

disfigure (dis'figə) vt défigurer. **disfigurement** n défiguration f.

disgrace (dis'greis) n 1 disgrâce f. 2 honte f. vt déshonorer. **disgraceful** adj honteux, -euse.

disgruntled (dis'grʌntəld) adj mécontent, contrarié.

disguise (dis'gaiz) vt déguiser, travestir. n déguisement m.

disgust (dis'gʌst) n dégoût m. vt dégoûter, écœurer.

dish (diʃ) n 1 plat m. 2 cul mets m. **dishcloth** n torchon m.

dishearten (dis'hɑ:tn) vt décourager.

dishevelled (di'ʃevəld) adj échevelé, en désordre.

dishonest (dis'ɔnist) adj malhonnête. **dishonesty** n malhonnêteté f.

dishonour (dis'ɔnə) n déshonneur m. vt déshonorer. **dishonourable** adj déshonorant, honteux, -euse.

disillusion (disi'lu:ʒən) n désillusion f. désenchantement m.

disinfect (disin'fekt) vt désinfecter. **disinfectant** adj,n désinfectant m.

disinherit (disin'herit) vt déshériter.

disintegrate (dis'intigreit) vt désintégrer, désagréger. vi se désintégrer, se désagréger. **disintegration** n désagrégation f.

disinterested (dis'intrəstid) adj désintéressé, impartial, -aux.

disjointed (dis'dʒɔintid) adj 1 désarticulé. 2 décousu, sans suite.

dislike (dis'laik) vt détester, avoir de l'aversion pour. n aversion f. dégoût m. **take a dislike to** prendre en aversion.

dislocate ('disləkeit) vt 1 disloquer. 2 med déboîter.

disloyal (dis'lɔiəl) adj infidèle, déloyal, -aux.

dismal ('dizməl) adj 1 sombre. 2 lugubre. 3 triste.

dismantle (dis'mæntl) vt 1 démonter. 2 dégarnir.

dismay (dismei) vt effrayer, consterner. n consternation f.

dismiss (dis'mis) vt 1 renvoyer, congédier. 2 écarter (a thought, etc.).

dismount (dis'maunt) vi descendre. vt désarçonner, démonter.

disobey (disə'bei) vt désobéir à. **disobedience** n désobéissance f. **disobedient** adj désobéissant.

disorder (dis'ɔːdə) *n* désordre *m*. confusion *f*.
disorganized (dis'ɔːgənaizd) *adj* désorganisé.
disown (dis'oun) *vt* **1** renier. **2** désavouer.
disparage (dis'pærɪdʒ) *vt* **1** dénigrer. **2** discréditer.
dispassionate (dis'pæʃənət) *adj* **1** impassible. **2** impartial, -aux. **dispassionately** *adv* **1** sans parti pris. **2** avec calme.
dispatch (dis'pætʃ) *vt* expédier. *n* **1** envoi *m*. **2** expédition *f*.
dispel (dis'pel) *vt* dissiper.
dispense (dis'pens) *vt* **1** distribuer, dispenser. **2** *law* administrer. **3** *med* préparer. **dispense with** se passer de. **dispensary** *n* **1** dispensaire *m*. **2** pharmacie *f*.
disperse (dis'pəːs) *vt* **1** disperser, éparpiller. **2** dissiper. *vi* **1** se disperser, s'éparpiller. **dispersal** *n* dispersion *f*.
displace (dis'pleis) *vt* déplacer.
display (dis'plei) *vt* **1** exposer, exhiber. **2** manifester. *n* **1** exposition. **2** *comm* étalage *m*.
displease (dis'pliːz) *vt* **1** déplaire à. **2** contrarier.
dispose (dis'pouz) *vt* disposer, arranger. *vi* disposer, se débarrasser. **be ill-/well-disposed** être mal/bien disposé. **disposal** *n* **1** disposition *f*. **2** *comm* vente *f*. **disposition** *n* **1** disposition *f*. **2** tempérament, caractère *m*. **3** penchant *m*.
disprove (dis'pruːv) *vt* réfuter.
dispute (dis'pjuːt) *vi* **1** discuter. **2** se disputer. *vt* **1** débattre. **2** contester. *n* **1** dispute *f*. **2** contestation *f*. **beyond dispute** incontestable.
disqualify (dis'kwɔlifai) *vt* disqualifier.
disregard (disri'gɑːd) *vt* négliger, ne pas faire attention à. *n* indifférence, insouciance *f*.
disreputable (dis'repjutəbəl) *adj* **1** de mauvaise réputation. **2** louche. **3** minable.
disrespect (disri'spekt) *n* manque de respect *m*. irrévérence *f*. **disrespectful** *adj* irrespectueux, -euse.
disrupt (dis'rʌpt) *vt* rompre, briser.
dissatisfy (di'sætisfai) *vt* mécontenter. **dissatisfied** *adj* mécontent.
dissect (di'sekt) *vt* disséquer. **dissection** *n* dissection *f*.
dissent (di'sent) *vi* différer. *n* dissentiment *m*. **dissenting** *adj* dissident.
dissimilar (di'similə) *adj* dissemblable, différent.
dissociate (di'souʃieit) *vt* désassocier.
dissolve (di'zɔlv) *vt* dissoudre. *vi* **1** se dissoudre. **2** fondre.
dissuade (di'sweid) *vt* dissuader.
distance ('distəns) *n* **1** distance *f*. **2** éloignement *m*. **3** lointain *m*. **in the distance** au loin. **distant** *adj* **1** éloigné, lointain. **2** distant, froid.
distaste (dis'teist) *n* dégoût *m*. **distasteful** *adj* déplaisant.
distil (dis'til) *vt* distiller.
distinct (dis'tiŋkt) *adj* **1** distinct, différent. **2** net, clair. **3** bien défini, marqué. **distinction** *n* distinction *f*. **distinctive** *adj* distinctif, -ive.
distinguish (dis'tiŋgwiʃ) *vt* **1** distinguer. **2** caractériser. *vi* faire une distinction. **distinguished** *adj* distingué.
distort (dis'tɔːt) *vt* **1** déformer. **2** fausser.
distract (dis'trækt) *vt* **1** distraire, détourner. **2** troubler. **distraction** *n* **1** distraction *f*. **2** folie *f*.
distraught (dis'trɔːt) *adj* affolé, fou, folle.
distress (dis'tres) *n* **1** détresse, angoisse *f*. **2** (poverty) misère *f*. *vt* désoler. **distressing** *adj* **1** affligeant. **2** douloureux, -euse.
distribute (dis'tribjuːt) *vt* distribuer. **distribution** *n* distribution, répartition *f*.
district ('distrikt) *n* **1** région. **2** (of a town) quartier *m*. **3** arrondissement *m*.
distrust (dis'trʌst) *vi* se méfier de. *n* méfiance *f*.
disturb (dis'təːb) *vt* **1** déranger. **2** troubler. **disturbance** *n* **1** dérangement *m*. **2** tapage *m*. **3** agitation *f*.
ditch (ditʃ) *n* fossé *m*.
ditto ('ditou) *adv* idem, de même.
divan (di'væn) *n* divan *m*.
dive (daiv) *vi* plonger. *n* **1** plongeon *m*. **2** *sl* cabaret *m*. **diving board** *n* plongeoir *m*.
diverge (dai'vəːdʒ) *vi* **1** diverger, s'écarter.
diverse (dai'vəːs) *adj* divers, varié.
divert (dai'vəːt) *vt* **1** détourner, dévier. **2** distraire. **diversion** *n* **1** (of a road, etc.) déviation *f*. **2** distraction *f*.
divide (di'vaid) *vt* **1** diviser, séparer. **2** répartir. **3** désunir. *vi* se diviser. **divisible** *adj* divisible. **division** *n* **1** division *f*. **2** partage *m*. discorde *f*.
dividend ('dividend) *n* dividende *m*.
divine (di'vain) *adj* divin, sacré. **divinity** *n* **1** divinité *f*. **2** théologie *f*.
divorce (di'vɔːs) *n* divorce *m*. *vi* divorcer. *vt* divorcer d'avec.
divulge (di'vʌldʒ) *vt* divulguer, révéler.
dizzy ('dizi) *adj* **1** étourdi. **2** vertigineux, -euse. **dizziness** *n* vertige, étourdissement *m*.
do[a] (duː) *vt* **1** faire. **2** rendre. **3** finir. **4** *sl* duper. **do again 1** refaire. **2** recommencer. **do one's best** faire de son mieux. **do up 1**

empaqueter. **2** *inf* réparer. **do without** se passer de. **how do you do?** comment allez-vous? **that will do** cela suffit.

docile ('dousail) *adj* docile.

dock[1] (dɔk) *n naut* bassin *m.* **dockyard** *n* chantier de constructions navales *m.*

dock[2] (dɔk) *vt* **1** retrancher. **2** couper la queue à.

dock[3] (dɔk) *n law* banc des accusés *m.*

doctor ('dɔktə) *n* **1** *med* médecin *m.* **2** *educ* docteur *m.*

doctrine ('dɔktrin) *n* doctrine *f.*

document ('dɔkjumənt) *n* document *m.* pièce *f.* *vt* documenter. **documentary** *adj,n* documentaire *m.*

dodge (dɔdʒ) *vi* **1** s'esquiver. **2** biaiser. *vt* **1** esquiver. **2** éviter. *n* **1** détour *m.* **2** esquive *f.* **3** *inf* ruse *f.* **dodgy** *adj inf* roublard.

dog (dɔg) *n* chien *m.* *vt* **1** suivre à la piste. **2** harceler. **dogged** *adj* tenace. **dog-collar** *n* **1** collier de chien *m.* **2** *rel* col droit *m.* **dogfish** *n* roussette *f.*

dogma ('dɔgmə) *n* dogme *m.* **dogmatic** *adj* **1** dogmatique. **2** autoritaire.

dole (doul) *n* allocation de chômage *f.*

doll (dɔl) *n* poupée *f.*

dollar ('dɔlə) *n* dollar *m.*

dolphin ('dɔlfin) *n* dauphin *m.*

domain (də'mein) *n* domaine *m.*

dome (doum) *n* dôme *m.*

domestic (də'mestik) *adj* **1** domestique. **2** de famille. **3** *comm* intérieur. *n* domestique *m,f.* **domesticate** *vt* domestiquer.

dominate ('dɔmineit) *vt,vi* dominer. **dominant** *adj* dominant.

domineer (dɔmi'niə) *vi* dominer. **domineering** *adj* autoritaire.

dominion (də'miniən) *n* **1** dominion *m.* **2** autorité *f.*

domino ('dɔminou) *n, pl* **dominoes** domino *m.*

donate (dou'neit) *vt* faire don de. **donation** *n* donation *f.*

done (dʌn) *v see* **do.**

donkey ('dɔŋki) *n* âne *m.*

donor ('dounə) *n* donateur, -trice.

doom (du:m) *n* destin *m.* *vt* **1** condamner. **2** vouer.

door (dɔ:) *n* **1** porte *f.* **2** *mot* portière *f.* **out of doors** dehors. **doorbell** *n* sonnette *f.* **doorhandle** *n* poignée de porte *f.* **doorknob** *n* bouton de porte *m.* **doorknocker** *n* marteau, -aux *m.* **doormat** *n* paillasson

m. **doorstep** *n* pas, seuil *m.* **doorway** *n* encadrement de la porte *m.*

dope (doup) *vt* doper, droguer. *n* **1** *inf* drogue, narcotique *f.* **2** *inf* imbécile *m,f.*

dormant ('dɔ:mənt) *adj* assoupi, endormi.

dormitory ('dɔ:mitri) *n* dortoir *m.*

dormouse ('dɔ:maus) *n* loir *m.*

dose (dous) *n* dose *f.* *vt* médicamenter. **dosage** *n* dosage *m.*

dot (dɔt) *n* point *m.* *vt* **1** mettre un point sur. **2** *Art* pointiller.

dote (dout) *vi* **dote on** raffoler de.

double ('dʌbəl) *adj* double, en deux. *n* **1** double *m.* **2** sosie *m.* *vt* **1** doubler. **2** plier en deux. *vi* (se) doubler. **double back** revenir sur ses pas. **double bass** *n* contrebasse *f.* **double bed** *n* grand lit *m.* **double-cross** *vt inf* duper, tromper. **double-decker bus** *n* autobus à impériale *m.* **double-dutch** *n* chinois, hébreu *m.* **talk double-dutch** baragouiner. **double glazing** *n* double vitrage *m.*

doubt (daut) *n* doute *m.* *vt,vi* douter. *vi* **1** soupçonner. **2** hésiter. **doubtful** *adj* **1** douteux, -euse. **2** incertain. **3** *inf* louche.

dough (dou) *n* **1** pâte *f.* **2** *sl* galette *f.* **doughnut** *n* beignet *m.*

dove (dʌv) *n* colombe *f.* **dovecote** *n* colombier *m.*

Dover ('douvə) *n* Douvres *m.*

dowdy ('daudi) *adj* mal vêtu.

down[1] (daun) *adv* **1** en bas. **2** par terre. **3** à bas. *prep* **1** en bas de. **2** le long de. **down there** là-bas.

down[2] (daun) *n* duvet *m.*

downcast ('daunkɑ:st) *adj* abattu, découragé.

downfall ('daunfɔ:l) *n* chute *f.*

downhearted (daun'hɑ:tid) *adj* découragé.

downhill ('daunhil) *adj* en pente. *adv* en descendant.

downpour ('daunpɔ:) *n* pluie torrentielle *f.* déluge *m.*

downright ('daunrait) *adj* **1** franc. **2** véritable. *adv* **1** tout à fait. **2** carrément.

downstairs (daun'stɛəz) *adv* en bas.

downstream (daun'stri:m) *adv* en aval, à l'aval.

downtrodden ('dauntrɔdn) *adj* opprimé.

downward ('daunwəd) *adj* descendant.

downwards ('daunwədz) *adv* **1** en bas. **2** en descendant. **3** en aval.

dowry ('dauəri) *n* dot *f.*

doze (douz) *vi* somnoler, sommeiller. *n* petit somme *m.*

dozen ('dʌzən) n douzaine f.

drab (dræb) adj terne.

drachma ('drækmə) n drachme m.

draft (drɑːft) n 1 mil détachement m. 2 Art dessin m. 3 brouillon m. 4 comm traite f. vt 1 mil détacher. 2 rédiger.

drag (dræg) vt 1 traîner. 2 naut draguer. vi se traîner. n 1 drague f. 2 inf obstacle m.

dragon ('drægən) n dragon m. **dragonfly** n libellule f.

drain (drein) n égoût m. vt 1 assécher. 2 faire écouler. 3 vider. vi s'écouler. **drainage** n système d'égouts m. **draining board** n égouttoir m. **drainpipe** n tuyau d'écoulement m.

drake (dreik) n canard m.

dram (dræm) n goutte f.

drama ('drɑːmə) n drame m. **dramatic** adj dramatique. **dramatist** n dramaturge m. **dramatize** vt dramatiser.

drank (dræŋk) v see **drink**.

drape (dreip) n rideau m. vt draper. **draper** n drapier m. **draper's shop** n magasin de nouveautés m. mercerie f. **drapery** n draperie f.

drastic ('dræstik) adj 1 énergique. 2 rigoureux, -euse.

draught (drɑːft) n 1 courant d'air m. 2 tirage m. 3 med potion f. 4 coup m. 5 pl jeu de dames m. **draught beer** n bière à la pression f. **draughtboard** n damier m. **draughtsman** n dessinateur m.

draw* (drɔː) vt 1 tirer. 2 dessiner. 3 attirer. vi tirer. **draw back** reculer. **draw near** se rapprocher. ~n 1 loterie f. tirage m. 2 partie nulle f. 3 attraction f. **drawback** n obstacle, inconvénient m. **drawbridge** n pont-levis m. **drawer** n tiroir m. **drawing** n dessin m. **drawing board** n planche à dessin f. **drawing pin** n punaise f. **drawing room** n salon m.

drawl (drɔːl) vi parler d'une voix traînante. n voix traînante f.

dread (dred) n crainte, terreur f. vt redouter. **dreadful** adj affreux, -euse. **dreadfully** adv terriblement.

dream* (driːm) n rêve, songe m. vi 1 rêver. 2 rêvasser. vt 1 rêver. 2 imaginer. **dreamy** adj 1 rêveur, -euse. 2 chimérique.

dreary ('driəri) adj morne, lugubre.

dredge (dredʒ) n drague f. vt 1 draguer. 2 cul saupoudrer.

dregs (dregz) n pl 1 lie f. 2 rebut m.

drench (drentʃ) vt 1 tremper, mouiller. 2 (an animal) purger.

dress (dres) vt 1 habiller, vêtir. 2 parer, orner. 3 med panser. 4 cul apprêter. vi s'habiller. n 1 vêtement m. 2 robe f. 3 tenue f. 4 toilette f. **dress circle** n premier balcon m. **dressmaker** n couturière f. **dress rehearsal** n répétition générale f. **dressing** n 1 toilette f. 2 cul assaisonnement m. 3 med pansement m. **dressing-gown** n robe de chambre f. peignoir m. **dressing-room** n 1 cabinet de toilette m. 2 Th loge. **dressing-table** n coiffeuse f. **dressy** adj élégant.

dresser[1] ('dresə) n habilleur, -euse.

dresser[2] ('dresə) n dressoir, buffet m.

drew (druː) v see **draw**.

dribble ('dribəl) vi 1 dégoutter. 2 (of a child) baver. vt sport dribbler. n 1 goutte f. 2 bave f.

drier ('draiə) n séchoir m.

drift (drift) n 1 (of snow) monceau, -aux m. 2 naut dérive f. 3 portée f. vi 1 dériver, aller à la derive. 2 se laisser aller.

drill (dril) n 1 foret m. foreuse f. 2 mil exercice m. vt 1 percer, forer. 2 instruire.

drink* (driŋk) n boisson f. vt boire. **drinking water** n eau potable f.

drip (drip) n 1 égouttement m. 2 goutte f. 3 inf nouille f. vi dégoutter. **drip-dry** adj ne nécessitant aucun repassage. **dripping** n 1 cul graisse de rôti f. 2 égouttement m.

drive* (draiv) vt 1 conduire. 2 enfoncer. 3 pousser. 4 forcer. vi 1 se promener. 2 conduire. n 1 promenade en voiture f. 2 énergie f. 3 allée f. **driver** n chauffeur, conducteur m. **driving licence** n permis de conduire m. **driving school** n auto-école f. **driving test** n examen de permis de conduire m.

drivel ('drivəl) vi 1 baver. 2 inf radoter. n 1 bave f. 2 radotage m.

drizzle ('drizəl) v imp bruiner. n bruine f.

dromedary ('drʌmədəri) n dromadaire m.

drone[1] (droun) n zool faux-bourdon m.

drone[2] (droun) n bourdonnement m. vi bourdonner.

droop (druːp) vi 1 languir. 2 s'affaiblir. 3 se pencher.

drop (drop) vt 1 laisser tomber. 2 abandonner. vi tomber. **drop in** entrer en passant. n 1 goutte f. 2 chute f. 3 baisse f. **dropout** n raté m.

drought (draut) n sécheresse f.

drove (drouv) v see **drive**.

drown (draun) vt noyer. vi se noyer.

drowsy (drauzi) adj somnolent, assoupi.

189

drudge (drʌdʒ) vi peiner, trimer. n souffre-douleur m,f. **drudgery** n corvée f.

drug (drʌg) vt droguer. n **1** drogue f. **2** inf stupéfiant m. **drug addict** n toxicomane m,f.

drum (drʌm) n **1** mus tambour m. **2** tonneau, -aux m. vi tambouriner. **drummer** n tambour m. **drumstick** n baguette de tambour f.

drunk (drʌŋk) v see **drink.** adj ivre, soûl. **drunkard** n ivrogne m. **drunken** adj ivre.

dry (drai) vt **1** sécher, essuyer. vi (se) sécher. adj sec, sèche. **dry-clean** vt nettoyer à sec. **dry-cleaning** n nettoyage à sec m.

dual ('djuəl) adj double. **dual carriageway** n route à double voie f.

dubious ('dju:biəs) adj douteux, -euse.

duchess ('dʌtʃis) n duchesse f.

duck[1] (dʌk) n canard m. **duckling** n caneton m.

duck[2] (dʌk) vi **1** plonger. **2** baisser la tête.

duct (dʌkt) n conduit m.

dud (dʌd) adj **1** raté. **2** inf moche.

due (dju:) adj **1** dû. **2** voulu. **3** attendu. n **1** dû m. **2** pl droits m pl. adv droit. **due to** à cause de, par suite à.

duel ('djuəl) n duel m. vi se battre en duel.

duet (dju'et) n duo m.

dug (dʌg) v see **dig.**

duke (dju:k) n duc m.

dulcimer ('dʌlsimə) n tympanon m.

dull (dʌl) adj **1** sombre. **2** ennuyeux, -euse. **3** terne, stupide. vt **1** émousser. **2** amortir.

duly ('dju:li) adv **1** dûment. **2** en temps voulu.

dumb (dʌm) adj **1** muet, -ette. **2** inf stupide. **dumbfound** vi abasourdir, confondre.

dummy ('dʌmi) n **1** mannequin m. **2** game mort. **3** (for a baby) sucette f. **4** comm simulacre m.

dump (dʌmp) vt décharger, vider. **2** inf trou m. n dépôt m.

dumpling ('dʌmpliŋ) n chausson m.

dunce (dʌns) n ignorant, âne m.

dune (dju:n) n dune f.

dung (dʌŋ) n fiente, crotte f. fumier m.

dungeon ('dʌndʒən) m cachot m.

Dunkirk (dʌn'kə:k) n Dunkerque m.

duplicate (adj,n 'dju:plikət; v 'dju:plikeit) adj,n double m. vt faire en double, copier.

durable ('djuərəbəl) adj durable. **duration** n durée f.

during ('djuəriŋ) prep pendant.

dusk (dʌsk) n crépuscule m. **dusky** adj **1** sombre. **2** noirâtre.

dust (dʌst) n poussière f. vt épousseter.

dustbin n poubelle f. **dustman** n boueur m. **dustpan** n pelle à poussière f. **duster** n torchon m. **dusty** adj poussiéreux, -euse.

Dutch (dʌtʃ) adj hollandais. **Dutchman** n hollandais m.

duty ('dju:ti) n **1** devoir m. **2** comm droit m. **3** fonction f. **on duty** de service. **duty-free** adj **1** exempt de droits. **2** en franchise. **dutiful** adj obéissant, soumis.

duvet ('dju:vei) n duvet m.

dwarf (dwɔ:f) adj,n nain. vt rapetisser.

dwell* (dwel) vi habiter, demeurer. **dwell on** s'étendre sur. **dwelling** n demeure, résidence f.

dwindle ('dwindl) vi **1** diminuer. **2** se réduire.

dye (dai) n teinte f. vt teindre.

dyke (daik) n digue f.

dynamic (dai'næmik) adj dynamique.

dynamite ('dainəmait) n dynamite f.

dynasty ('dinəsti) n dynastie f.

dysentery ('disəntri) n dysenterie f.

dyslexia (dis'leksiə) n dyslexie f.

E

each (i:tʃ) adj chaque. pron chacun. **each other** l'un l'autre, les uns les autres.

eager ('i:gə) adj **1** passionné, ardent. **2** avide. **3** impatient. **eagerness** n **1** ardeur f. **2** avidité. **3** empressement m.

eagle ('i:gəl) n aigle m.

ear[1] (iə) n anat oreille f. **earache** n mal d'oreille m. **eardrum** n tympan m. **earmark** n marque distinctive f. vt mettre de côté. **earphone** n casque m. **earring** n boucle d'oreille f. **earwig** n perce-oreille m.

ear[2] (iə) n bot épi m.

earl (ə:l) n comte m.

early ('ə:li) adv de bonne heure, tôt. adj **1** matinal, -aux. **2** précoce.

earn (ə:n) vt **1** gagner. **2** mériter.

earnest ('ə:nist) adj **1** sérieux, -euse. **2** sincère.

earth (ə:θ) n **1** terre f. **2** (of animal) terrier m. **down to earth** terre à terre, réaliste. **earthenware** n poterie, faïence f. **earthquake** n tremblement de terre m. **earthworm** n ver de terre, lombric m.

ease (i:z) n **1** aise f. **2** tranquillité f. **3** facilité f. vt **1** adoucir. **2** soulager. **easy** adj **1** facile. **2** tranquille. **3** libre. adv doucement.

easel ('i:zəl) n chevalet m.

east (i:st) n **1** est m. **2** cap Orient m. adj est

invar. adv à *or* vers l'est. **easterly** *adj* d'est.
eastern *adj* de l'est, oriental, -aux. **eastward**
adj à l'est, dans l'est. **eastwards** *adv* vers
l'est.

Easter ('i:stə) *n* Pâques *f pl.*

eat* (i:t) *vt* manger. **eatable** *adj* mangeable.

eavesdrop ('i:vzdrɔp) *vi* écouter aux portes.

ebb (eb) *n* **1** reflux *m.* **2** déclin *m.*

ebony ('ebəni) *n* ébène *f.*

eccentric (ik'sentrik) *adj* excentrique.

ecclesiastical (ikli:zi'æstikəl) *adj* ecclésiastique.

echo ('ekou) *n, pl* **echoes** écho *m. vi* **1** faire
écho. **2** retentir. *vt* répéter (en écho).

eclair (ei'klɛə) *n* éclair *m.*

eclipse (i'klips) *n* éclipse *f. vt* éclipser.

ecology (i:'kɔlədʒi) *n* écologie *f.*

economize (i'kɔnəmaiz) *vt* économiser.

economy (i'kɔnəmi) *n* économie *f.* **economic**
adj économique. **economical** *adj* **1** économe.
2 économique. **economics** *n* sciences écono-
miques *f pl.*

ecstasy ('ekstəsi) *n* **1** extase *f.* **2** ravissement
m. **ecstatic** *adj* extatique.

edelweiss ('eidlvais) *n* edelweiss *m.*

edge (edʒ) *n* **1** bord *m.* **2** lisière, bordure *f.* **3** (of
a blade) tranchant *m.* **on edge** énervé. ~*vt*
border.

edible ('edibəl) *adj* comestible.

Edinburgh ('edinbərə) *n* Edimbourg *m.*

edit ('edit) *vt* **1** éditer. **2** rédiger. **edition** *n*
édition *f.* **editor** *n* **1** éditeur *m.* **2** (of a paper)
rédacteur en chef *m.* **editorial** *adj* éditorial,
-aux. *n* article de fond *m.*

educate ('edjukeit) *vt* **1** élever. **2** instruire.
educated *adj* instruit, cultivé. **education** *n*
éducation *f.* enseignement *m.* instruction *f.*

eel (i:l) *n* anguille *f.*

eerie ('iəri) *adj* étrange, mystérieux, -euse.

effect (i'fekt) *n* **1** effet *m.* influence *f.* **2** *pl* biens
m pl. **in effect** en réalité. ~*vt* effectuer.
effective *adj* efficace. **effectiveness** *n* efficacité *f.*

effeminate (i'feminət) *adj* efféminé.

effervesce (efə'ves) *vi* **1** être en effervescence.
2 mousser. **effervescence** *n* effervescence
f. **effervescent** *adj* effervescent.

efficient (i'fiʃənt) *adj* **1** capable, compétent. **2**
efficace. **efficiency** *n* efficacité *f.*

effigy ('efidʒi) *n* effigie *f.*

effort ('efət) *n* effort *m.*

egg[1] (eg) *n* œuf *m.* **boiled egg** œuf à la coque.
fried egg œuf sur le plat. **hard-boiled/
poached egg** œuf dur/poché. **scrambled**
eggs œufs brouillés. **egg-cup** *n* coquetier *m.*
egg-shell *n* coquille d'œuf *f.* **egg-whisk** *n*
batteur *or* fouet à œufs *m.*

egg[2] (eg) *vt* **egg on** encourager, inciter.

ego ('i:gou) *n* moi *m.* **egocentric** *adj* égocentrique. **egoism** *n* égoïsme *m.*

Egypt ('i:dʒipt) *n* Egypte *f.* **Egyptian** *adj,n*
égyptien, -ienne.

eiderdown ('aidədaun) *n* édredon *m.*

eight (eit) *adj,n* huit *m.* **eighth** *adj* huitième.

eighteen (ei'ti:n) *adj,n* dix-huit *m.* **eighteenth**
adj dix-huitième.

eighty ('eiti) *adj,n* quatre-vingts *m.* **eightieth**
adj quatre-vingtième.

either ('aiðə) *adj,pron* **1** l'un et *or* ou l'autre. **2**
chaque. **3** chacun. *conj* ou, soit. **either...or**
ou...ou, soit...soit. ~*adv* non plus.

ejaculate (i'dʒækjuleit) *vt* **1** éjaculer. **2** pousser.

eject (i'dʒekt) *vt* expulser, émettre.

eke (i:k) *vt* **1** allonger, suppléer. **2** faire durer.

elaborate (*adj* i'læbrət; *v* i'læbəreit) *adj* **1**
compliqué. **2** soigné. *vt* élaborer.

elapse (i'læps) *vi* s'écouler.

elastic (i'læstik) *adj* élastique. **elastic band** *n*
élastique *m.* **elasticity** élasticité *f.*

elated (i'leitid) *adj* transporté, exalté.

elbow ('elbou) *n* coude *m. vt* coudoyer.

elder[1] ('eldə) *adj,n* aîné. **elderly** *adj* d'un
certain âge, âgé.

elder[2] ('eldə) *n bot* sureau *m.* **elderberry** *n*
baie de sureau *f.*

eldest ('eldist) *adj,n* aîné.

elect (i'lekt) *vt* élire, choisir. **election** *n* élection
f. **electoral** *adj* électoral, -aux. **electorate** *n*
corps électoral *m.*

electricity (ilek'trisiti) *n* électricité *f.* **electric**
adj électrique. **electrician** *n* électricien
m. **electrify** *vt* électrifier, électriser. **electrocute** *vt* électrocuter. **electrode** *n* électrode
f. **electron** *n* électron *m.* **electronic** *adj*
électronique. **electronics** *n pl* électronique *f.*

elegant ('eligənt) *adj* **1** élégant. **2** *inf* chic.
elegance *n* élégance *f.*

element ('eləmənt) *n* élément *m.* **elemental**
adj **1** des éléments. **2** élémentaire. **elementary** *adj* élémentaire.

elephant ('eləfənt) *n* éléphant *m.*

elevate ('eləveit) *vt* **1** élever, hausser. **2** exalter.
elevation *n* élévation *m.* **elevator** *n* ascenseur, élévateur, monte-charge *m.*

eleven (i'levən) *adj,n* onze *m.* **eleventh** *adj*
onzième.

elf (elf) *n, pl* **elves** elfe, lutin *m.*

eligible ('elidʒəbəl) adj éligible.
eliminate (i'limineit) vt 1 éliminer. 2 supprimer. **elimination** n élimination f.
elite (ei'liːt) n élite f.
ellipse (i'lips) n ellipse f.
elm (elm) n orme m.
elocution (elə'kjuːʃən) n élocution, diction f.
elope (i'loup) vi s'enfuir.
eloquent ('eləkwənt) adj éloquent.
else (els) adv autrement, ou bien. adj autre. **elsewhere** adv ailleurs.
elucidate (i'luːsideit) vt élucider, éclaircir.
elude (i'luːd) vt éluder, échapper à.
emaciate (i'meiʃieit) vt amaigrir. **emaciated** adj émacié, étique.
emanate ('eməneit) vi émaner.
emancipate (i'mænsipeit) vt émanciper. **emancipation** n émancipation f.
embalm (im'baːm) vt embaumer.
embankment (im'bæŋkmənt) n 1 levée f. 2 (of a river) quai m. 3 (of a road) remblai m.
embargo (im'baːgou) n, pl **embargoes** embargo m.
embark (im'baːk) vt embarquer. vi s'embarquer.
embarrass (im'bærəs) vt embarrasser, gêner. **embarrassment** n embarras m.
embassy ('embəsi) n ambassade f.
embellish (im'beliʃ) vt embellir, orner.
ember ('embə) n braise f.
embezzle (im'bezəl) vt détourner. **embezzlement** n détournement de fonds m.
embitter (im'bitə) vt 1 aigrir. 2 envenimer.
emblem ('embləm) n emblème, insigne m.
embody (im'bɔdi) vt 1 incarner. 2 personnifier. **embodiment** n personnification f.
emboss (im'bɔs) vt 1 graver en relief. 2 repousser.
embrace (im'breis) vt embrasser, étreindre. n étreinte f.
embroider (im'brɔidə) vt broder. **embroidery** n broderie f.
embryo ('embriou) n embryon m.
emerald ('emrəld) n émeraude f.
emerge (i'məːdʒ) vi émerger, sortir.
emergency (i'məːdʒənsi) n 1 circonstance critique f. cas urgent m. 2 med urgence f. **emergency exit** n sortie de secours f.
emigrate ('emigreit) vi émigrer. **emigrant** adj,n émigrant. **emigration** n émigration f.
eminent ('eminənt) adj éminent. **eminence** n éminence f.
emit (i'mit) vt 1 émettre. 2 dégager.

emotion (i'mouʃən) n émotion f. **emotional** adj émotif, -ive.
empathy ('empəθi) n identification f.
emperor ('empərə) n empereur m.
emphasis ('emfəsis) n, pl **emphases** emphase f. **emphasize** vt accentuer, souligner. **emphatic** adj emphatique, énergique.
empire ('empaiə) n empire m.
empirical (im'pirikəl) adj empirique.
employ (im'plɔi) vt employer. **employee** n employé. **employer** n patron, employeur m. **employment** n emploi m. **employment agency** n bureau de placement m.
empower (im'pauə) vt autoriser.
empress ('emprəs) n impératrice f.
empty ('empti) adj vide. vt vider. **empty-handed** adj bredouille.
emu ('iːmjuː) n émeu m.
emulate ('emjuleit) vt rivaliser avec, imiter. **emulation** n émulation f.
emulsion (i'mʌlʃən) n émulsion f.
enable (i'neibəl) vt permettre, rendre capable.
enact (i'nækt) vt décréter, ordonner.
enamel (i'næməl) vt émailler. n émail, -aux m.
encapsulate (in'kæpsjuleit) vt incorporer.
enchant (in'tʃaːnt) vt enchanter. **enchantment** n enchantement m.
encircle (in'səːkəl) vt entourer, cerner.
enclose (in'klouz) vt 1 enclore. 2 enfermer, joindre. **enclosed** adj ci-inclus, ci-joint.
encore ('ɔŋkɔː) interj,n bis m. vt bisser.
encounter (in'kauntə) vt rencontrer. n rencontre f.
encourage (in'kʌridʒ) vt encourager. **encouragement** n encouragement m.
encroach (in'kroutʃ) vi **encroach on 1** empiéter sur. 2 abuser de. **encroachment** n empiétement m.
encumber (in'kʌmbə) vt encombrer. **encumbrance** n embarras m. charge f.
encyclopedia (insaklə'piːdiə) n encyclopédie f.
end (end) n fin f. bout m. **make ends meet** joindre les deux bouts. ~vt terminer, finir, achever. vi finir, se terminer. **ending** n 1 fin f. 2 gram terminaison f. 3 dénouement m. **endless** adj sans fin, incessant.
endanger (in'deindʒə) vt 1 mettre en danger. 2 risquer.
endeavour (in'devə) vi s'efforcer, tâcher. n effort m.
endemic (en'demik) adj endémique. n endémie f.
endive ('endaiv) n chicorée f.

endorse (in'dɔ:s) vt **1** endosser, viser. **2** appuyer. **endorsement** n **1** endossement m. **2** sanction f.

endow (in'dau) vt doter.

endure (in'djuə) vt supporter. vi durer. **endurance** n résistance f.

enemy ('enəmi) adj,n ennemi.

energy ('enədʒi) n énergie f. **energetic** adj énergique.

enfold (in'fould) vt envelopper.

enforce (in'fɔ:s) vt **1** faire observer. **2** imposer.

engage (in'geidʒ) vt **1** engager. **2** embaucher. vi **1** s'engager. **2** s'embarquer. **engaged** adj **1** occupé, pris. **2** fiancé. **engaging** adj attirant. **engagement** n **1** engagement m. promesse f. **2** fiançailles f pl. **3** mil combat m.

engine ('endʒin) n **1** machine f. **2** moteur m.

engineer (endʒi'niə) n ingénieur m. vt inf machiner. **engineering** n technique de l'ingénieur f. **civil engineering** n génie civil m.

England ('iŋglənd) n Angleterre f. **English** adj,n anglais. **English** (language) n anglais m.

engrave (in'greiv) vt graver.

engross (in'grous) vt **1** rédiger. **2** absorber.

engulf (in'gʌlf) vt engouffrer.

enhance (in'ha:ns) vt **1** rehausser. **2** mettre en valeur.

enigma (i'nigmə) n énigme f. **enigmatic** adj énigmatique.

enjoy (in'dʒɔi) vt **1** aimer, prendre plaisir à. **2** jouir de. **enjoy oneself** s'amuser. **enjoyable** adj agréable. **enjoyment** n plaisir m.

enlarge (in'la:dʒ) vt **1** agrandir. **2** élargir. **enlargement** n agrandissement m.

enlighten (in'laitṇ) vt éclairer.

enlist (in'list) vt enrôler, recruter. vi s'enrôler, s'engager.

enormous (i'nɔ:məs) adj énorme. **enormously** adv énormément.

enough (i'nʌf) adv,adj assez. **be enough** suffire.

enquire (in'kwaiə) vi se renseigner, s'informer. **enquiry** n **1** enquête f. **2** demande de de renseignements f.

enrage (in'reidʒ) vt faire enrager, exaspérer.

enrich (in'ritʃ) vt enrichir.

enrol (in'roul) vt enrôler, immatriculer. vi se faire inscrire.

ensign ('ensain) n **1** (flag) enseigne f. **2** naut pavillon m. **3** (rank) enseigne m.

enslave (in'sleiv) vt asservir.

ensure (in'ʃuə) vt assurer.

entail (in'teil) vt **1** substituer. **2** occasionner.

entangle (in'tæŋgəl) vt empêtrer, emmêler.

enter ('entə) vt **1** entrer dans. **2** prendre part à. **3** inscrire. vi entrer.

enterprise ('entəpraiz) n entreprise f. **enterprising** adj entreprenant.

entertain (entə'tein) vt **1** amuser, divertir. **2** (guests) recevoir. **3** (an idea) concevoir. vi recevoir. **entertaining** adj amusant. **entertainment** n divertissement m.

enthral (in'θrɔ:l) vt captiver.

enthusiasm (in'θju:ziæzəm) n enthousiasme m. **enthusiast** n enthousiaste m,f. **enthusiastic** adj enthousiaste.

entice (in'tais) vt attirer, séduire.

entire (in'taiə) adj entier, -ière, complet, -ète.

entitle (in'taitḷ) vt **1** intituler. **2** donner droit à.

entity ('entiti) n entité f.

entrails ('entreilz) n pl entrailles f pl.

entrance[1] ('entrəns) n entreé f.

entrance[2] (in'tra:ns) vt extasier, ravir.

entreat (in'tri:t) vt supplier. **entreaty** n supplication f.

entrench (in'trentʃ) vt retrancher.

entrepreneur (ɔntrəprə'nə:) n entrepreneur m.

entrust (in'trʌst) vt confier, charger.

entry ('entri) n entrée f. **no entry 1** mot sens interdit. **2** interdit au public.

entwine (in'twain) vt entrelacer. vi s'entrelacer.

enunciate (i'nʌnsieit) vt **1** énoncer. **2** articuler.

envelop (in'veləp) vt envelopper.

envelope ('envəloup) n enveloppe f.

environment (in'vaiərənmənt) n milieu, -eux, environnement m.

envisage (in'vizidʒ) vt envisager.

envoy ('envɔi) n envoyé m.

envy ('envi) n envie f. vt envier.

enzyme ('enzaim) n enzyme f.

epaulet ('epəlet) n épaulette f.

ephemeral (i'femərəl) adj éphémère.

epic ('epik) adj épique. n poème épique m. épopée f.

epidemic (epi'demik) n épidémie f. adj épidémique.

epilepsy ('epilepsi) n épilepsie f. **epileptic** adj,n épileptique.

epilogue ('epilɔg) n épilogue m.

Epiphany (i'pifəni) n Epiphanie f. la fête des Rois.

episcopal (i'piskəpəl) adj épiscopal, -aux.

episode ('episoud) n épisode m.

epitaph ('epita:f) n épitaphe f.

epitome (i'pɪtəmi) n 1 épitomé, abrégé m. 2 quintessence f.
epoch ('iːpɔk) n époque f.
equable ('ekwəbəl) adj uniforme, egal, -aux.
equal ('iːkwəl) adj,n égal, -aux. vt égaler. **equality** n égalité f. **equalize** vt 1 égaliser. 2 compenser. vi s'égaliser.
equate (i'kweɪt) vt égaler. **equation** n équation f. **equator** n équateur m. **equatorial** adj équatorial, -aux.
equestrian (i'kwestrɪən) adj équestre.
equilateral (iːkwi'lætərəl) adj équilatéral, -aux.
equilibrium (iːkwi'lɪbrɪəm) n équilibre m.
equinox ('iːkwɪnɔks) n équinoxe m.
equip (i'kwɪp) vt 1 équiper, munir. 2 tech outiller. **equipment** n 1 équipement m. 2 outillage m. 3 matériel m.
equity ('ekwɪti) n équité f.
equivalent (i'kwɪvələnt) adj,n équivalent m.
era ('ɪərə) n ère f.
eradicate (i'rædɪkeɪt) vt déraciner, extirper.
erase (i'reɪz) vt 1 effacer, gommer. 2 rayer.
erect (i'rekt) vt 1 dresser. 2 ériger. adj droit, debout. **erection** n construction f.
ermine ('əːmɪn) n hermine f.
erode (i'roud) vt éroder, corroder. **erosion** n érosion f.
erotic (i'rɔtik) adj érotique.
err (əː) vi 1 s'égarer, errer. 2 se tromper.
errand ('erənd) n commission, course f.
erratic (i'rætik) adj 1 irrégulier, -ière. 2 fantasque.
error ('erə) n erreur, faute f.
erupt (i'rʌpt) vi faire éruption. **eruption** n éruption f.
escalate ('eskəleɪt) vt (a war) élargir. **escalator** n escalier roulant m.
escalope (i'skæləp) n escalope f.
escape (i'skeɪp) vt échapper à. vi s'échapper. n fuite, évasion f.
escort ('eskɔːt) n escorte f. vt escorter.
Eskimo ('eskɪmou) n esquimau, -aude, -aux.
esoteric (esə'terik) adj ésotérique.
especial (i'speʃəl) adj spécial, -aux. **especially** adv surtout.
espionage ('espɪənɑːʒ) n espionnage m.
esplanade ('espləneɪd) n esplanade f.
essay ('esei) n 1 tentative, épreuve f. 2 lit essai m. 3 educ dissertation f.
essence ('esəns) n essence f. **essential** adj essentiel, -elle, indispensable.
establish (i'stæbliʃ) vt fonder. **establishment**
194

n 1 établissement m. fondation f. 2 maison (de commerce) f. 3 cap ordre établi m.
estate (i'steɪt) n 1 état m. 2 law biens m pl. **estate car** n break m.
esteem (i'stiːm) n estime f. vt estimer.
estimate (n 'estɪmət; v 'estɪmeɪt) n 1 évaluation f. 2 devis m. vt estimer, évaluer, apprécier.
estuary ('estʃuəri) n estuaire m.
etching ('etʃiŋ) n gravure à l'eau-forte f.
eternal (i'təːnl) adj éternel, -elle. **eternity** n éternité f.
ether ('iːθə) n éther m.
ethereal (i'θɪərɪəl) adj éthéré.
ethical ('eθɪkəl) adj moral, -aux. **ethics** n pl éthique, morale f.
ethnic ('eθnik) adj ethnique.
etiquette ('etikɪt) n étiquette f. convenances f pl. protocole m.
etymology (eti'mɔlədʒi) n étymologie f.
eucalyptus (juːkə'liptəs) n eucalyptus m.
Eucharist ('juːkərɪst) n Eucharistie f.
eunuch ('juːnək) n eunuque m.
euphemism ('juːfəmɪzəm) n euphémisme m. **euphemistic** adj euphémique.
euphoria (juː'fɔːriə) n euphorie f.
Europe ('juərəp) n Europe f. **European** adj,n européen, -enne.
European Economic Community n Communauté Economique Européenne f.
euthanasia (juːθə'neɪziə) n euthanasie f.
evacuate (i'vækjueit) vt évacuer. **evacuation** n évacuation f.
evade (i'veid) vt éviter, esquiver. **evasive** adj évasif, -ive.
evaluate (i'væljueit) vt évaluer.
evangelical (iːvæn'dʒelikəl) adj évangélique. **evangelist** n évangéliste m.
evaporate (i'væpəreit) vt faire évaporer. vi s'évaporer, se volatiliser. **evaporation** n évaporation f.
evasive (i'veisiv) adj evasif, -ive.
eve (iːv) n veille f.
even ('iːvən) adj 1 égal, -aux. 2 uni. 3 pair. 4 quitte. adv 1 même. 2 encore. **even so** quand même. ∼vt aplanir, égaliser. **even-tempered** adj d'humeur égale, placide.
evening ('iːvəniŋ) n soir m. soirée f. **evening class** n cours du soir m. **evening dress** n tenue de soirée f.
event (i'vent) n 1 événement m. 2 cas m. in the event of au cas où. **eventful** adj mouvementé. **eventual** adj 1 éventuel, -elle. 2 définitif, -ive. **eventually** adv finalement.

ever ('evə) *adv* **1** toujours. **2** jamais. **evergreen** *adj* toujours vert. *n* arbre vert *m*. **everlasting** *adj* éternel, -elle.

every ('evri) *adj* **1** chaque. **2** tout. **everybody** *pron* tout le monde, chacun. **everyday** *adj* quotidien, -enne. *adv* tous les jours. **everyone** *pron* tout le monde, chacun. **every other day** tous les deux jours, un jour sur deux. **everything** *pron* tout. **everywhere** *adv* partout.

evict (i'vikt) *vt* expulser.

evidence ('evidəns) *n* **1** évidence *f*. **2** témoignage *m*. **jive évidence** témoigner. **evident** *adj* évident. **evidently** *adv* évidemment.

evil ('i:vəl) *adj* mauvais, méchant. *n* mal, maux *m*.

evoke (i'vouk) *vt* évoquer.

evolution (i:və'lu:ʃən) *n* **1** développement *m*. **2** évolution *f*.

evolve (i'vɔlv) *vt* développer, dérouler. *vi* se dérouler, évoluer. **evolution** *n* évolution *f*.

ewe (ju:) *n* brebis *f*.

exact (ig'zækt) *adj* exact, précis. *vt* exiger. **exacting** *adj* exigeant. **exactly** précisément, justement, tout juste.

exaggerate (ig'zædʒəreit) *vt* exagérer. **exaggeration** *n* exagération *f*.

exalt (ig'zɔ:lt) *vt* **1** exalter. **2** louer.

examine (ig'zæmin) *vt* examiner, inspecter. **examination** *n* examen *m*. **fail/pass an examination** échouer/réussir à un examen. **take an examination** passer un examen.

example (ig'zɑ:mpəl) *n* exemple *m*. **for example** par exemple.

exasperate (ig'zɑ:spəreit) *vt* exaspérer, irriter.

excavate ('ekskəveit) *vt* creuser, fouiller. **excavation** *n* fouille, excavation *f*.

exceed (ik'si:d) *vt* excéder, dépasser.

excel (ik'sel) *vt,vi* surpasser. **excellence** *n* excellence *f*. **excellent** *adj* excellent.

Excellency ('eksələnsi) *n* Excellence *f*.

except (ik'sept) *prep* excepté, sauf. **except that** sauf que. **exception** *n* exception *f*. **exceptional** *adj* exceptionnel, -elle.

excerpt ('eksə:pt) *n* extrait *m*.

excess (ik'ses) *n* excès, excédent *m*. **excessive** *adj* excessif, -ive.

exchange (iks'tʃeindʒ) *vt* échanger. *vi* faire un échange. *n* **1** échange *m*. **2** *comm* change *m*.

exchequer (eks'tʃekə) *n* trésorerie *f*.

excise ('eksaiz) *n* **1** contributions indirectes *f pl*. **2** régie *f*.

excite (ik'sait) *vt* exciter. **excited** *adj* excité,

agité. **excitement** *n* surexcitation, émotion *f*. **exciting** *adj* captivant, passionnant.

exclaim (ik'skleim) *vi* s'écrier, s'exclamer.

exclamation (eksklə'meiʃən) *n* exclamation *f*. **exclamation mark** *n* point d'exclamation *m*.

exclude (ik'sklu:d) *vt* exclure. **exclusive** *adj* exclusif, -ive.

excommunicate (ekskə'mju:nikeit) *vt* excommunier. **excommunication** *n* excommunication *f*.

excruciating (ik'skru:ʃieitiŋ) *adj* atroce, affreux, -euse.

excursion (ik'skə:ʒən) *n* excursion, partie de plaisir *f*.

excuse (*n* ik'skju:s; *v* ik'skju:z) *n* excuse *f*. prétexte *m*. *vt* excuser, pardonner. **excuse me!** pardon!

execute ('eksikju:t) *vt* exécuter. **execution** *n* exécution *f*. **executioner** *n* bourreau, -aux *m*.

executive (ig'zekjutiv) *n* cadre (supérieur) *m*.

exempt (ig'zempt) *vt* exempter, dispenser. *adj* exempt, dispensé. **exemption** *n* exemption *f*.

exercise ('eksəsaiz) *n* exercice *m*. *vt* exercer, pratiquer. *vi* s'entraîner. **exercise book** *n* cahier *m*.

exert (ig'zə:t) *vt* employer, exercer. **exertion** *n* effort, emploi *m*.

exhale (eks'heil) *vt* exhaler.

exhaust (ig'zɔ:st) *vt* épuiser. *n* échappement *m*. **exhaust pipe** *n* tuyau d'échappement *m*.

exhibit (ig'zibit) *vt* exhiber, montrer, exposer. *n* objet exposé *m*. **exhibition** *n* exposition *f*. **exhibitionism** *n* exhibitionisme *m*.

exhilarate (ig'ziləreit) *vt* rejouir, ranimer. **exhilaration** *n* joie de vivre *f*.

exile ('egzail) *n* **1** exil *m*. **2** exilé, banni *m*. *vt* exiler, bannir.

exist (ig'zist) *vi* exister, être. **existence** *n* existence *f*. **existentialism** *n* existentialisme *m*. **existing** *adj* actuel, -elle.

exit ('eksit) *n* sortie *f*.

exorbitant (ig'zɔ:bitənt) *adj* exorbitant, excessif, -ive.

exorcize ('eksɔ:saiz) *vt* exorciser.

exotic (ig'zɔtik) *adj* exotique.

expand (ik'spænd) *vt* élargir, dilater, développer. *vi* se développer, se dilater. **expanding** *adj* extensible. **expansion** *n* développement *m*. dilatation *f*.

expanse (ik'spæns) *n* étendue *f*.

expatriate (*v* iks'peitrieit; *n* iks'peitriit) *vt* expatrier. *n* expatrié *m*.

195

expect (ik'spekt) *vt* attendre, s'attendre à. **expectation** *n* espérance, attente *f.*

expedient (ik'spi:diənt) *n* expédient, moyen *m. adj* expédient, convenable.

expedition (ekspi'diʃən) *n* expédition, excursion *f.*

expel (ik'spel) *vt* expulser, bannir.

expenditure (ik'spenditʃə) *n* dépense *f.*

expense (ik'spens) *n* **1** dépense *f.* frais *m pl.* **2** dépens *m.* **expensive** *adj* cher, chère, coûteux, -euse.

experience (ik'spiəriəns) *n* **1** expérience *f.* **2** épreuve *f. vt* éprouver. **experienced** *adj* expérimenté.

experiment (ik'sperimənt) *n* expérience *f.* essai *m. vi* faire une expérience, expérimenter. **experimental** *adj* expérimental, -aux.

expert ('ekspə:t) *n* expert, spécialiste *m. adj* habile, expert. **expertise** *n* expertise *f.*

expire (ik'spaiə) *vi* expirer.

explain (ik'splein) *vt* expliquer, éclaircir. **explanation** *n* explication *f.*

expletive (ik'spli:tiv) *adj,n* explétif, -ive.

explicit (ik'splisit) *adj* explicite, catégorique.

explode (ik'sploud) *vt* faire sauter. *vi* sauter, éclater. **explosive** *adj,n* explosif, -ive *m.*

exploit[1] ('eksplɔit) *n* exploit *m.*

exploit[2] (ik'splɔit) *vt* exploiter.

explore (ik'splɔ:) *vt* explorer. **explorer** *n* explorateur *m.*

exponent (ik'spounənt) *n* interprète *m,f.*

export (*v* ik'spɔ:t, 'ekspɔ:t; *n* 'ekspɔ:t) *vt* exporter. *n* exportation *f.*

expose (ik'spouz) *vt* **1** exposer. **2** révéler. **exposure** *n* **1** exposition *f.* **2** dévoilement *m.*

express (ik'spres) *vt* exprimer. *n* rapide *m. adj* exprès. **expression** *n* expression *f.*

exquisite (ek'skwizit) *adj* **1** exquis. **2** vif, vive.

extend (ik'stend) *vt* étendre, prolonger. *vi* s'étendre. **extension** *n* extension *f.* prolongement *m.* **extensive** *adj* **1** vaste, ample. **2** approfondi.

extent (ik'stent) *n* **1** étendue *f.* **2** point *m.* mesure *f.*

exterior (ek'stiəriə) *adj,n* extérieur *m.*

exterminate (ik'stə:mineit) *vt* exterminer.

external (ek'stə:nl) *adj* externe, extérieur.

extinct (ik'stiŋkt) *adj* disparu, éteint.

extinguish (ik'stiŋgwiʃ) *vt* éteindre.

extra ('ekstrə) *adj* de plus, en sus, supplémentaire. *n* **1** supplément *m* **2** *pl inf* à-côtés *m pl.*

extract (*n* 'ekstrakt; *v* ik'strækt) *n* extrait *m. vt* extraire.

extramural (ekstrə'mjuərəl) *adj* extramuros invar.

extraordinary (ik'strɔ:dənri) *adj* extraordinaire, remarquable.

extravagant (ik'strævəgənt) *adj* extravagant, dépensier, -ière. **extravagance** *n* extravagance *f.*

extreme (ik'stri:m) *adj,n* extrême *m.* **extremity** *n* extrémité *f.*

extricate ('ekstrikeit) *vt* dégager.

extrovert ('ekstrəvə:t) *n* extroverti *m.*

exuberant (ig'zju:bərənt) *adj* exubérant.

eye (ai) *n* œil *m pl* yeux. *vt* regarder, lorgner.

eyeball ('aibɔ:l) *n* globe de l'oeil *m.*

eyebrow ('aibrau) *n* sourcil *m.*

eye-catching *adj* accrocheur, -euse.

eyelash ('ailæʃ) *n* cil *m.*

eyelid ('ailid) *n* paupière *f.*

eye-opener *n* révélation *f.*

eye shadow *n* fard à paupières *m.*

eyesight ('aisait) *n* vue *f.*

eyestrain ('aistrein) *n* mal aux yeux *m.*

eye-witness (ai'witnis) *n* témoin oculaire *m.*

F

fable ('feibəl) *n* conte *m.* fable *f.*

fabric ('fæbrik) *n* **1** tissu *m.* étoffe *f.* **2** fabrique *f.* **fabricate** *vt* fabriquer, inventer.

fabulous ('fæbjuləs) *adj* fabuleux, -euse.

facade (fə'sɑ:d) *n* façade *f.*

face (feis) *n* **1** *anat* visage *m.* figure *f.* **2** face *f.* **3** *inf* toupet *m.* **4** mine *f. vt* faire face à. **facecloth** *n* gant de toilette *m.* **facelift** *n* ridectomie *f.* **face-pack** *n* masque anti-rides *m.* **face value** *n* valeur nominale *f.*

facet ('fæsit) *n* aspect *m.*

facetious (fə'si:ʃəs) *adj* plaisant, facétieux, -euse.

facile ('fæsail) *adj* facile. **facilitate** *vt* faciliter. **facility** *n* facilité *f.*

facing ('feisiŋ) *n* parement *m.*

facsimile (fæk'siməli) *n* fac-similé *m.*

fact (fækt) *n* fait *m.* **as a matter of fact** à vrai dire. **factual** *adj* positif, -ive.

faction ('fækʃən) *n* faction *f.*

factor ('fæktə) *n* **1** facteur, diviseur *m.* **2** élément *m.*

factory ('fæktri) *n* usine, fabrique *f.*

faculty ('fækəlti) *n* **1** faculté *f.* **2** talent *m.*

fad (fæd) *n* dada *m.* manie *f.*

fade (feid) *vi* se faner, se déteindre, passer. *vt* décolorer. **fade away** s´évanouir.

fag (fæg) *n* 1 corvée *f.* 2 *sl* sèche *f.*

Fahrenheit ('færənhait) *adj* Fahrenheit.

fail (feil) *vi* 1 manquer. 2 échouer. 3 baisser. *vt* refuser. **failing** *n* défaut *m. prep* faute de. **failure** *n* 1 défaut *m.* 2 échec *m.* 3 raté *m.*

faint (feint) *vi* s´évanouir. *n* évanouissement *m. adj* faible, pâle, léger, -ère. **faint-hearted** *adj* timide, pusillanime.

fair[1] (fɛə) *adj* 1 juste. 2 passable. 3 beau, belle. 4 blond. **fair-minded** *adj* impartial, -aux. **fairly** *adv* 1 honnêtement. 2 assez. **fairness** *n* 1 justice *f.* 2 blondeur *f.*

fair[2] (fɛə) *n* foire *f.* **fairground** *n* champ de foire *m.*

fairy ('fɛəri) *n* fée *f. adj* féerique. **fairytale** *n* conte de fées *m.*

faith (feiθ) *n* 1 foi *f.* 2 confiance *f.* **faithful** *adj* fidèle, loyal, -aux. **faithfulness** *n* fidélité *f.*

fake (feik) *n* article truqué *m. vt* truquer.

falcon ('fɔːlkən) *n* faucon *m.*

fall* (fɔːl) *n* 1 chute, tombée *f.* 2 baisse *f. vi* 1 tomber. 2 baisser.

fallacy ('fæləsi) *n* erreur *f.* **fallacious** *adj* trompeur, -euse.

fallible ('fæləbəl) *adj* faillible.

fallow ('fælou) *adj* en friche.

false (fɔːls) *adj* 1 faux, fausse. 2 artificiel, -elle. 3 perfide. **false alarm** *n* fausse alerte *f.* **falsehood** *n* mensonge *m.* **false pretences** *n pl* faux semblant *m.* **under false pretences** par fraude. **false teeth** *n pl* fausses dents *f pl.* **falseness** *n* 1 fausseté *f.* 2 infidélité *f.* **falsify** *vt* fausser, dénaturer.

falter ('fɔːltə) *vi* 1 vaciller, chanceler. 2 hésiter.

fame (feim) *n* renommée *f.*

familiar (fə'miliə) *adj* intime, familier, -ière. **familiarize** *vt* familiariser.

family ('fæmili) *n* famille *f.*

famine ('fæmin) *n* famine *f.* **famished** *adj* affamé.

famous ('feiməs) *adj* célèbre, fameux, -euse.

fan[1] (fæn) *n* 1 éventail *m.* 2 ventilateur *m. vt* éventer, vanner. **fanbelt** *n* courroie de ventilateur *m.*

fan[2] (fæn) *n* passionné, fervent, fan *m.* **fan club** *n* club de fans *m.*

fanatic (fə'nætik) *n* fanatique *m,f.*

fancy ('fænsi) *n* 1 imagination *f.* 2 caprice *f.* 3 envie *f. vt* 1 imaginer. 2 avoir envie de. **fancy oneself** se gober. ~*adj* de fantaisie. **fancy dress** *n* déguisement, travesti *m.*

fanfare ('fænfɛə) *n* fanfare *f.*

fang (fæŋ) *n* croc, crochet *m.*

fantastic (fæn'tæstik) *adj* 1 *inf* fantastique. 2 bizarre, excentrique.

fantasy ('fæntəsi) *n* fantaisie *f.*

far (fɑː) *adj* éloigné. *adv* 1 loin. 2 beaucoup. **far and wide** partout. **so far** jusqu'ici. **faraway** *adj* lointain, éloigné. **far-fetched** *adj* outré, tiré par les cheveux. **far-off** *adj* éloigné. **far-reaching** *adj* d'une grande portée.

farce (fɑːs) *n* farce *f.* **farcical** *adj* risible.

fare (fɛə) *n* prix du voyage *m.*

Far East *n* Extrême-Orient *m.*

farewell (fɛə'wel) *interj* adieu! *n* au revoir, adieu, -eux *m.*

farm (fɑːm) *n* ferme *f. vt* exploiter, cultiver. *vi* être cultivateur. **farmer** *n* agriculteur *m.* **farmhouse** *n* ferme *f.* **farming** *n* exploitation agricole *f.* **farmland** *n* ferme *f.* **farmyard** *n* basse-cour *f.*

farther ('fɑːðə) *adv* plus loin. *adj* 1 plus lointain. 2 supplémentaire. **farthest** *adj* 1 le plus éloigné. 2 le plus long. *adv* le plus loin.

fascinate ('fæsineit) *vt* fasciner, charmer. **fascinating** *adj* séduisant. **fascination** *n* fascination *f.* charme *m.*

fascism ('fæʃizəm) *n* fascisme *m.* **fascist** *adj,n* fasciste.

fashion ('fæʃən) *n* 1 mode *f.* 2 façon *f.* 3 manière *f.* **in fashion** à la mode. ~*vt* façonner, former. **fashionable** *adj* à la mode.

fast[1] (fɑːst) *adj* 1 vite, rapide. 2 (of colour) bon teint *invar.* 3 ferme. 4 en avance. *adv* 1 fort, ferme. 2 vite.

fast[2] (fɑːst) *vi* jeûner. *n* jeûne *m.*

fasten ('fɑːsən) *vt* 1 attacher. 2 fermer. *vi* s'attacher. **fastener** *n* attache *f.*

fastidious (fə'stidiəs) *adj* 1 difficile. 2 délicat.

fat (fæt) *n* graisse *f.* gras *m. adj* gras, grasse, gros, grosse. **get fat** grossir. **fatten** *vi,vt* engraisser.

fatal ('feitl) *adj* fatal. **fatality** *n* fatalité *f.*

fate (feit) *n* destin, sort *m.*

father ('fɑːðə) *n* père *m. vt* engendrer. **father-in-law** *n* beau-père *m.* **fatherland** *n* patrie *f.*

fathom ('fæðəm) *n* brasse *f. vt* sonder.

fatigue (fə'tiːg) *n* fatigue *f. vt* fatiguer.

fatuous ('fætjuəs) *adj* imbécile, sot, sotte.

fault (fɔːlt) *n* 1 défaut *m.* 2 faute *f.* **faultless** *adj* impeccable. **faulty** *adj* défectueux, -euse.

fauna ('fɔːnə) *n* faune *f.*

favour ('feivə) *n* faveur *f. vt* favoriser.

197

favourable adj favorable, avantageux, -euse.
favourite adj,n préféré, favori, -ite.
fawn¹ (fɔːn) n faon m. adj fauve.
fawn² (fɔːn) vt se coucher servilement.
fear (fiə) n peur, crainte f. vt craindre, redouter.
fearful adj craintif, -ive, effroyable. **fearless**
adj intrépide.
feasible ('fiːzibəl) adj 1 faisable, possible. 2
probable.
feast (fiːst) n fête f. banquet m.
feat (fiːt) n 1 exploit m. 2 tour de force m.
feather ('feðə) n plume f. vt emplumer.
featherbed n lit de plume m. **featherweight**
n poids plume m.
feature ('fiːtʃə) n trait m. caractéristique f. vt 1
caractériser. 2 mettre en manchette.
February ('februəri) n février m.
feckless ('fekləs) adj incapable.
fed (fed) v see **feed**.
federal ('fedərəl) adj fédéral, -aux. **federate** vt
fédérer. vi se fédérer. adj fédéré. **federation**
n fédération f.
fee (fiː) n honoraires m pl. droit m.
feeble ('fiːbəl) adj faible.
feed* (fiːd) vt nourrir, alimenter. vi manger, se
nourrir. **be fed up** en avoir assez. n nourriture f. fourrage m. **feedback** n rétroaction f.
feel* (fiːl) n 1 toucher m. 2 sensation f. vt 1
toucher, palper. 2 sentir. vi 1 tâtonner. 2 se
sentir. **feeler** n antenne f. **feeling** n 1 sensation f. 2 sentiment m. 3 impression f. 4
toucher m. adj sensible.
feign (fein) vt simuler, affecter.
feint¹ (feint) vi feindre. n feinte f.
feint² (feint) **feint-ruled paper** n papier réglé
m.
feline ('fiːlain) adj félin.
fell¹ (fel) v see **fall**.
fell² (fel) vt abattre, assommer.
fellow ('felou) n 1 compagnon m. 2 membre m.
3 type m. 4 pareil m. **fellowship** n 1 amitié f.
2 association f. 3 fraternité f.
felony ('feləni) n crime m.
felt¹ (felt) v see **feel**.
felt² (felt) n feutre m.
female ('fiːmeil) adj féminin. n femelle, femme
f.
feminine ('feminin) adj féminin.
fence (fens) n clôture, palissade f. vi faire de
l'escrime. vt renfermer. **fencing** n 1 sport
escrime f. 2 clôture, barrière f.
fend (fend) vt **fend off** parer. **fend for oneself**
se débrouiller. **fender** n garde-feu m invar.

fennel ('fenl) n fenouil m.
ferment (n 'fɔːment; v fɔ'ment) n 1 ferment m.
2 agitation f. vi fermenter.
fern (fɔːn) n fougère f.
ferocious (fə'rouʃəs) adj féroce.
ferret ('ferit) n furet m. vi fureter.
ferry ('feri) n bac m. vt transborder. **ferryboat**
n navire transporteur m.
fertile ('fɔːtail) adj fécond, fertile. **fertility** n
fertilité, fécondité f. **fertilize** vt fertiliser,
féconder. **fertilizer** n engrais m.
fervent ('fɔːvənt) adj fervent.
fervour ('fɔːvə) n ferveur, passion f.
fester ('festə) vi suppurer, pourrir.
festival ('festivəl) n fête f. festival m.
fetch (fetʃ) vt aller chercher, apporter. **fetching**
adj séduisant.
fete (feit) n fête f.
fetid ('fetid) adj fétide.
fetish ('fetiʃ) n fétiche m.
fetlock ('fetlɔk) n fanon m.
fetter ('fetə) n 1 lien m. entrave f. 2 pl chaînes f
pl. vt enchaîner, entraver.
feud (fjuːd) n inimitié, vendetta f. **feudal** adj
féodal, -aux.
fever ('fiːvə) n fièvre f. **feverish** adj fiévreux,
-euse.
few (fjuː) adj peu de. **a few** quelques, quelques-uns, quelques-unes.
fiancé (fi'ɔnsei) n fiancé m.
fiasco (fi'æskou) n fiasco m.
fib (fib) n petit mensonge m. vi en conter.
fibre ('faibə) n fibre f. **fibreglass** n fibre de
verre f.
fickle ('fikəl) adj inconstant.
fiction ('fikʃən) n fiction f. **fictitious** adj 1
fictif, -ive. 2 simulé.
fiddle ('fidl) n 1 violon m. 2 inf combine f. vi 1
jouer du violon. 2 tripoter. vt truquer.
fidelity (fi'deliti) n fidélité, loyauté f.
fidget ('fidʒit) vi se trémousser. vt agacer.
field (fiːld) n 1 champ m. 2 sport terrain m. 3
domaine m. vi tenir le champ. vt arrêter.
fiend (fiːnd) n démon m. **fiendish** adj diabo-
lique.
fierce (fiəs) adj féroce, acharné, ardent.
fiery ('faiəri) adj 1 brûlant, ardent. 2 emporté,
irascible.
fifteen (fif'tiːn) adj,n quinze m. **fifteenth** adj
quinzième.
fifth (fifθ) adj cinquième.
fifty ('fifti) adj,n cinquante m. **fifty-fifty**
moitié-moitié. **fiftieth** adj cinquantième.

fig (fig) n figue f. **fig tree** figuier m.
fight (fait) n bataille, lutte f. combat m. vi se battre. vt,vi combattre.
figment ('figmənt) n invention f.
figure ('figə) n 1 figure f. 2 forme f. 3 taille f. 4 chiffre m. vt 1 figurer, représenter. 2 inf estimer. vi calculer. **figurehead** n prête-nom m. **figurative** adj 1 figuratif, -ive. 2 gram figuré.
filament ('filəmənt) n filament, fil m.
file[1] (fail) n 1 (in an office) classeur m. 2 dossier m. vt classer, ranger. **filing cabinet** n classeur m.
file[2] (fail) n lime f. vt limer. **filing** n 1 limage m. 2 pl limaille f.
filial ('filiəl) adj filial, -aux.
fill (fil) vt 1 remplir, combler. 2 (a tooth) plomber. vi se remplir. **fill up** faire le plein. ~n 1 plein m. 2 suffisance f. **filling** n plombage m. **filling station** n poste d'essence m.
fillet ('filit) n filet m. vt détacher les filets.
filly ('fili) n pouliche f.
film (film) n 1 film m. 2 phot pellicule f. 3 couche f. vt filmer, tourner. **film star** n vedette de cinéma f.
filter ('filtə) n filtre m. vt filtrer, épurer. vi s'infiltrer.
filth (filθ) n ordure, saleté f. **filthy** adj sale, infecte.
fin (fin) n nageoire f. aileron m.
final ('fainl) adj 1 final, dernier, -ière. 2 définitif, -ive. **finalize** vt finaliser.
finance ('fainæns) n 1 finance f. 2 fonds m. vt financer. **financial** adj financier, -ière. **financier** n financier m.
finch (fintʃ) n pinson m.
find (faind) n 1 découverte f. 2 trouvaille f. vt trouver, découvrir. **find out** découvrir.
fine[1] (fain) adj 1 fin, raffiné. 2 beau, belle. 3 excellent. 4 menu. **fine arts** n pl beaux arts m pl. **finery** n parure f.
fine[2] (fain) n amende f. vt condamner à une amende.
finger ('fiŋgə) n doigt m. vt tâter, manier. **fingermark** n empreinte digitale f. **fingernail** n ongle m. **fingerprint** n empreinte digitale f. **fingertip** n bout du doigt m.
finish ('finiʃ) vt finir, terminer, achever. vi se terminer. n 1 fin f. 2 arrivée f.
finite ('fainait) adj fini. **finite verb** n verbe à un mode fini m.
Finland ('finlənd) n Finlande f. **Finn** n finlan-

dais, finnois. m. **Finnish** adj finlandais. **Finnish** (language) n finnois m.
fiord (fjɔːd) n also **fjord** fiord m.
fir (fəː) n sapin m. **fir cone** n pomme de pin f.
fire (faiə) n 1 feu m pl feux. 2 incendie m. vt 1 mettre le feu à. 2 enflammer. 3 tirer. **fire alarm** n avertisseur d'incendie m. **fire brigade** n corps de sapeurs-pompiers m. **fire drill** n exercices de sauvetage m pl. **fire engine** n pompe à incendie f. **fire-escape** n échelle de sauvetage f. **fireguard** ('faiəgɑːd) n garde-feu m invar. **firelight** ('faiəlait) n lumière du feu f. **fireman** ('faiəmən) n (sapeur-)pompier m. **fireplace** ('faiəpleis) n cheminée f. foyer m. **fireside** ('faiəsaid) n coin du feu m. **fire station** n caserne de pompiers f. poste d'incendie m. **firework** ('faiəwəːk) n 1 pièce d'artifice f. 2 pl feu d'artifice m.
firing squad n peloton d'exécution m.
firm[1] (fəːm) adj 1 ferme, solide, constant. 2 résolu. **firmness** n fermeté f.
firm[2] (fəːm) n maison de commerce f.
first (fəːst) adj,n premier, -ière. adv première-ment. **at first** d'abord. **first aid** n premiers secours m pl. **first-class** adj 1 de première classe. 2 de premier ordre. **first-hand** adj de première main. **first name** n prénom m. **first person** n première personne f. **first-rate** adj excellent, de première classe.
fiscal ('fiskəl) adj fiscal, -aux.
fish (fiʃ) n,pl **fish** or **fishes** poisson m. vt,vi pêcher. **fisherman** n pêcheur m. **fish finger** n carré de poisson pané m. **fishing** n pêche f. **go fishing** aller à la pêche. **fishing rod** n canne à pêche f. **fishmonger** n marchand de poisson m. **fishslice** n truelle à poisson f.
fission ('fiʃən) n fission f.
fist (fist) n poing m.
fit[1] (fit) adj 1 propre, convenable. 2 capable. 3 en forme. vt 1 ajuster. 2 aller à. 3 garnir. n ajustement m. **fitting** n 1 essayage, ajustage m. 2 pl accessoires m pl. **fitness** 1 aptitude f. 2 bonne forme f.
fit[2] (fit) n accès m. attaque f.
five (faiv) adj,n cinq m.
fix (fiks) vt fixer. n inf difficulté f. embarras m. **fixation** n fixation f. **fixture** n 1 appareil fixe m. 2 sport engagement m. **fixture list** n programme m.
fizz (fiz) vi pétiller, siffler. n pétillement, sif-flement m. **fizzy** adj gaseux, -euse.

199

flabbergast (ˈflæbəgɑːst) vt épater, ahurir.
flabby (ˈflæbi) adj mou, molle, flasque.
flag[1] (flæg) n drapeau, -aux m. **flagpole** n mât m.
flag[2] (flæg) vi languir, pendre.
flagon (ˈflægən) n flacon m.
flagrant (ˈfleigrənt) adj flagrant, scandaleux, -euse.
flair (ˈflɛə) n flair m.
flake (fleik) n flocon m. écaille, paillette f. vi tomber en flocons. **flake off** écailler. **flaky** adj 1 écailleux, -euse. 2 feuilleté.
flamboyant (flæmˈbɔiənt) adj flamboyant.
flame (fleim) n flamme f. vi flamber.
flamingo (fləˈmiŋgou) n, pl **-gos** or **-goes** flamant m.
flan (flæn) n flan m. tarte f.
flank (flæŋk) n flanc m. vt flanquer.
flannel (ˈflænļ) n 1 flanelle f. 2 gant de toilette m.
flap (flæp) n 1 rabat m. 2 battement m. 3 battant m. 4 affolement m. vt battre. vi 1 claquer. 2 s'affoler. 3 battre.
flare (flɛə) n 1 feu de signal m. 2 godet m. vi 1 flamboyer. 2 s'évaser. **flare up** s'emporter.
flash (flæʃ) n éclair, éclat m. vi jeter des éclairs. vt projeter. **flashback** n retour en arrière m. **flashbulb** n ampoule flash f. **flashlight** n flash m. **flashy** adj tapageur, -euse.
flask (flɑːsk) n flacon m.
flat[1] (flæt) adj 1 plat. 2 catégorique. 3 fade. 4 mus faux. n mus bémol m. **flatfish** n poisson plat m. **flat-footed** adj à pied plat, aux pieds plats. **flatten** vt aplatir. vi s'aplatir.
flat[2] (flæt) n appartement m.
flatter (ˈflætə) vt flatter. **flattering** adj flatteur, -euse. **flattery** n flatterie f.
flaunt (flɔːnt) vi s'afficher. vt faire étalage de.
flautist (ˈflɔːtist) n flûtiste m,f.
flavour (ˈfleivə) n 1 saveur m. 2 parfum m. vt assaisonner. **flavouring** n assaisonnement m.
flaw (flɔː) n défaut m. **flawed** adj défectueux, -euse.
flax (flæks) n lin m.
flea (fliː) n puce f. **fleabite** n 1 morsure de puce f. 2 rien m.
fleck (flek) n 1 petite tache f. 2 particule f. vt tacheter.
fled (fled) v see **flee.**
flee' (fliː) vt fuir. vi s'enfuir, fuire.
fleece (fliːs) n toison f. vt inf tondre, rouler.
fleet (fliːt) n flotte f.
fleeting (ˈfliːtiŋ) adj fugace, passager, -ère.

Fleming (ˈflemiŋ) n flamand m.
Flemish (ˈflemiʃ) adj flamand. **Flemish** (language) n flamand m.
flesh (fleʃ) n chair f.
flew (fluː) v see **fly.**
flex (fleks) n câble souple m. vt fléchir. **flexible** adj flexible, souple.
flick (flik) n 1 petit coup m. 2 pl inf ciné m. vt effleurer.
flicker (ˈflikə) n battement, clignement m. vi trembloter, vaciller.
flight[1] (flait) n 1 vol m. volée f. 2 trajectoire m.
flight[2] (flait) n fuite f.
flimsy (ˈflimzi) adj peu solide, léger, -ère.
flinch (flintʃ) vi 1 reculer. 2 tressaillir. **without flinching** sans broncher.
fling' (fliŋ) vi jeter. n 1 jet m. 2 tentative f.
flint (flint) n 1 silex m. 2 pierre à briquet f.
flip (flip) n secousse, chiquenaude f. vt tapoter. **flip through** feuilleter. **flipper** n nageoire m.
flippant (ˈflipənt) adj désinvolte. **flippantly** adv légèrement.
flirt (fləːt) n coquette f. vi flirter.
flit (flit) vi 1 passer légèrement. 2 voleter. 3 déménager. n déménagement m.
float (flout) vi 1 flotter, nager. 2 faire la planche. vt flotter. n flotteur m.
flock[1] (flɔk) n (of sheep, etc.) troupeau, -aux m. troupe f. vi s'attrouper.
flock[2] (flɔk) n bourre de laine f.
flog (flɔg) vt flageller, fouetter.
flood (flʌd) n inondation f. déluge m. vt inonder. vi déborder. **floodlight** n phare d'éclairage m. vt illuminer par projecteurs.
floor (flɔː) n 1 plancher m. 2 (of a building) étage m. vt terrasser. **floorboard** n planche f.
flop (flɔp) vi 1 faire faillite. 2 se laisser tomber. n fiasco m.
flora (ˈflɔːrə) n flore f.
floral (ˈflɔːrəl) adj floral, -aux. **florist** n fleuriste m,f.
flounce[1] (flauns) n mouvement vif m. vi se démener.
flounce[2] (flauns) n (of a dress) volant m.
flounder[1] (ˈflaundə) vi patauger.
flounder[2] (ˈflaundə) n flet m.
flour (ˈflauə) n farine f.
flourish (ˈflʌriʃ) n trait de plume m. vt brandir. vi prospérer.
flout (flaut) vt railler, narguer.
flow (flou) n écoulement, flot m. vi couler.
flower (ˈflauə) n fleur f. vi fleurir. **flowerbed** n plate-bande f. **flowery** adj fleuri.

flown (floun) v see **fly.**
fluctuate ('flʌktʃueɪt) vi fluctuer, vaciller. **fluctuation** n fluctuation f.
flue (fluː) n tuyau de cheminée m.
fluent ('fluːənt) adj coulant. **fluently** adv couramment.
fluff (flʌf) n peluches f pl. duvet m.
fluid ('fluːɪd) adj,n fluide m.
flung (flʌŋ) v see **fling.**
fluorescent (flu'resənt) adj fluorescent. **fluorescence** n fluorescence f.
fluoride ('fluəraɪd) n fluorure f.
flush[1] (flʌʃ) vi rougir. vt inonder, balayer à grande eau. n 1 éclat m. 2 accès m. 3 rougeur f.
flush[2] (flʌʃ) adj 1 ras, de niveau. 2 abondant.
fluster ('flʌstə) n agitation f. vt agiter. vi s'énerver.
flute (fluːt) n flûte f.
flutter ('flʌtə) n 1 battement m. 2 trouble m. vi trembler, s'agiter. vt agiter.
flux (flʌks) n flux m.
fly[*1] (flaɪ) vi voler. **fly away** s'envoler. **flyover** n mot saut-de-mouton m.
fly[2] (flaɪ) n mouche f.
foal (foul) n poulain m.
foam (foum) n écume f. vi écumer.
focal ('foukəl) adj focal, -aux. **focus** n, pl **-ci** or **-cuses** foyer m. vt concentrer. vi converger.
fodder ('fɔdə) n fourrage m.
foe (fou) n ennemi m.
foetus ('fiːtəs) n fœtus m.
fog (fɔg) n 1 brouillard m. 2 brume f. **foggy** adj brumeux, -euse. **foghorn** n sirène de brume f.
foible ('fɔɪbəl) n faible m. faiblesse f.
foil[1] (fɔɪl) vt faire échouer.
foil[2] (fɔɪl) n tain m.
foil[3] (fɔɪl) n sport fleuret m.
foist (fɔɪst) vt refiler.
fold[1] (fould) n pli m. vt,vi plier. **fold one's arms** se croiser les bras. **folder** n classeur m.
fold[2] (fould) n parc à moutons m.
foliage ('fouliidʒ) n feuillage m.
folk (fouk) n pl gens m,f pl. **folkdance** n danse rustique f. **folklore** n folklore m. **folksong** n chanson populaire or folklorique f. **folktale** n histoire traditionnelle f.
follicle ('fɔlikəl) n follicule m.
follow ('fɔlou) vt 1 suivre. 2 poursuivre. 3 succéder à. vi 1 suivre. 2 s'ensuivre. **following** n suite f. adj suivant. **follower** n disciple m.
folly ('fɔli) n folie, sottise f.

fond (fɔnd) adj affectueux, -euse, aimant.
fondant ('fɔndənt) n fondant m.
fondle ('fɔndl) vt caresser, câliner.
font (fɔnt) n fonts baptismaux m pl.
food (fuːd) n 1 nourriture f. aliments, vivres m pl. 2 pâture f. **food poisoning** n intoxication alimentaire f.
fool (fuːl) n imbécile m,f. vt berner, mystifier. vi faire l'idiot. **foolhardy** adj téméraire. **foolish** adj sot, sotte. **foolproof** adj indéréglable, indétraquable.
foolscap ('fuːlzkæp) n papier ministre m.
foot (fut) n, pl **feet** 1 pied m. 2 zool patte f. 3 base f. **put one's foot in it** mettre les pieds dans le plat. **football** n 1 football m. 2 ballon m. **footbridge** n passerelle f. **foothold** n 1 prise pour le pied f. 2 position f. **footing** n pied m. **footlights** n pl rampe f. **footnote** n note (au bas de la page) f. renvoi m. **footprint** n empreinte de pas f. **footstep** n pas m. **footwear** n chaussures f pl.
for (fə; stressed fɔː) prep pour, comme, pendant. conj car.
forage ('fɔridʒ) vi fourrager, fouiller. vt saccager. n fourrage m.
forbear*** (fɔ'bɛə) vt s'abstenir de. vi s'abstenir.
forbid*** (fə'bɪd) vt défendre, interdire. **forbidding** adj rébarbatif, -ive.
force (fɔːs) n 1 force, violence f. 2 puissance f. 3 corps m. vt 1 forcer. 2 contraindre. **forcefeed** vt alimenter de force. **forceful** adj vigoureux, -euse, fort.
forceps ('fɔːseps) n pl pince f. forceps m.
ford (fɔːd) n gué m. vt passer à gué.
fore (fɔː) adj de devant, antérieur. n avant, premier plan m. adv à l'avant.
forearm[1] ('fɔːrɑːm) n anat avant-bras m invar.
forearm[2] (fɔː'rɑːm) vt prévenir, avertir.
forecast*** ('fɔːkɑːst) n prévision f. vt prévoir.
forecourt ('fɔːkɔːt) n avant-cour f.
forefather ('fɔːfɑːðə) n aïeul, -eux, ancêtre m.
forefinger ('fɔːfiŋgə) n index m.
forefront ('fɔːfrʌnt) n premier plan or rang m.
foreground ('fɔːgraund) n premier plan, avant-plan m.
forehand ('fɔːhænd) adj d'avant-main. **forehand stroke** n coup droit m.
forehead ('fɔrid) n front m.
foreign ('fɔrin) adj étranger, -ère. **foreigner** n étranger, -ère.
foreleg ('fɔːleg) n jambe or patte de devant f.
forelock ('fɔːlɔk) n mèche f. toupet m.

201

foreman ('fɔ:mən) *n* contremaître, chef d'équipe *m.*

foremost ('fɔ:moust) *adj* premier, en tête. *adv* en premier.

forensic (fə'rensik) *adj* judiciaire, légale.

forerunner ('fɔ:rʌnə) *n* précurseur *m.*

foresee* (fɔ:'si:) *vt* prévoir, entrevoir. **fore-seeable** *adj* prévisible.

foresight ('fɔ:sait) *n* prévoyance *f.*

forest ('fɔrist) *n* forêt *f.* **forestry** *n* sylviculture *f.*

forestall (fɔ:'stɔ:l) *vt* anticiper, devancer.

foretaste ('fɔ:teist) *n* avant-goût *m.*

foretell* (fɔ:'tel) *vt* prédire, présager.

forethought ('fɔ:θɔ:t) *n* **1** préméditation *f.* **2** prévoyance *f.*

forfeit ('fɔ:fit) *n* **1** amende *f.* **2** *sport* gage *m.* punition *f. vt* perdre, forfaire.

forge¹ (fɔ:dʒ) *vt* **1** forger. **2** contrefaire. *n* forge *f.*

forge² (fɔ:dʒ) *vi* **forge ahead** pousser de l'avant.

forgery ('fɔ:dʒəri) *n* contrefaçon *f.* faux *m.*

forget* (fə'get) *vt* **1** oublier. **2** omettre. **forgetful** *adj* oublieux, -euse.

forgive* (fə'giv) *vt* pardonner. **forgiving** *adj* indulgent. **forgiveness** *n* **1** pardon *m.* **2** clémence *f.*

forgo* (fɔ:'gou) *vt* renoncer à, s'abstenir de.

fork (fɔ:k) *n* **1** fourche *f.* **2** *cul* fourchette *f.* **3** (of a road) bifurcation. *vi* bifurquer, fourcher.

forlorn (fə'lɔ:n) *adj* **1** abandonné. **2** désespéré.

form (fɔ:m) *n* **1** forme *f.* **2** figure *f.* **3** formule *f.* **4** *educ* classe *f.* **5** banc *m. vt* former, façonner. *vi* se former, se faire. **formal** *adj* formel, -elle. **formality** *n* formalité *f.* **formation** *n* formation *f.* **formative** *adj* formatif, -ive, de formation.

former ('fɔ:mə) *adj* précédent, ancien, -enne, premier, -ière. *pron* celui-là, celle-là. **formerly** *adv* autrefois, jadis.

formidable ('fɔ:midəbəl) *adj* formidable, redoutable.

formula ('fɔ:mjulə) *n, pl* **-las** *or* **-lae** formule *f.*

formulate ('fɔ:mjuleit) *vt* formuler.

forsake* (fə'seik) *vt* abandonner, délaisser.

fort (fɔ:t) *n* fort *m.*

forth (fɔ:θ) *adv* en avant. **and so forth** et ainsi de suite. **forthcoming** *adj* **1** à venir. **2** (of a person) ouvert.

fortify ('fɔ:tifai) *vt* **1** fortifier. **2** affermir. **fortification** *n* fortification *f.* **fortitude** *n* courage *m.*

fortnight ('fɔ:tnait) *n* quinzaine *f.* **fortnightly** *adj* bimensuel, -elle. *adv* tous les quinze jours.

fortress ('fɔ:trəs) *n* forteresse *f.*

fortune ('fɔ:tʃən) *n* **1** hasard *m.* chance *f.* **2** fortune, richesse *f.* **fortune-teller** *n* diseur de bonne aventure *m.* **fortune-telling** *n* bonne aventure *f.* **fortunate** *adj* **1** heureux, -euse, fortuné. **2** propice. **fortunately** *adv* **1** heureusement. **2** par bonheur.

forty ('fɔ:ti) *adj,n* quarante *m.* **fortieth** *adj* quarantième.

forum ('fɔ:rəm) *n* forum *m.*

forward ('fɔ:wəd) *adj* **1** de devant. **2** avancé. **3** précoce. *adv* en avant. *n sport* avant *m. vt* **1** avancer. **2** expédier. **please forward** prière de faire suivre. **forwardness** *n* précocité *f.* **forwards** *adv* en avant.

fossil ('fɔsəl) *adj,n* fossile *m.*

foster ('fɔstə) *vt* **1** nourrir. **2** encourager. **fosterchild** *n* enfant adoptif *m.* **fostermother** *n* mère adoptive.

fought (fɔ:t) *v* see **fight.**

foul (faul) *adj* **1** infect, nauséabond. **2** sale. **3** obscène. **4** déloyal, -aux. *n* coup déloyal *m. vt* **1** salir. **2** enchevêtrer. *vi* s'encrasser. *adv* déloyalement. **foul play** *n* **1** *sport* jeu déloyal *m.* **2** malveillance *f.*

found¹ (faund) *v* see **find.**

found² (faund) *vt* fonder. **foundation** *n* **1** fondation *f.* **2** institution *f.* **3** fondement *m.* **founder** *n* fondateur *m.*

foundry ('faundri) *n* fonderie *f.*

fountain ('fauntin) *n* **1** fontaine *f.* **2** source *f.*

four (fɔ:) *adj,n* quatre *m.* **four-poster** *n* lit à colonnes *m.* **fourth** *adj* quatrième. **foursome** *n* partie double *f. adj* à quatre.

fourteen (fɔ:'ti:n) *adj,n* quatorze *m.* **fourteenth** *adj* quatorzième.

fowl (faul) *n* **1** oiseau, -aux *m.* volaille *f.* **2** *cul* poule *f.*

fox (fɔks) *n* renard *m. vt inf* mystifier. **foxglove** *n* digitale *f.* **foxhound** *n* chien courant *m.* **foxhunting** *n* chasse au renard *f.*

foyer ('fɔiei) *n* foyer *m.*

fraction ('frækʃən) *n* **1** fragment *m.* **2** fraction *f.*

fracture ('fræktʃə) *n* fracture *f. vt* casser, fracturer. *vi* se casser, se fracturer.

fragile ('frædʒail) *adj* fragile.

fragment ('frægmənt) *n* fragment, morceau, -aux *m.*

fragrant ('freigrənt) *adj* embaumé, parfumé. **fragrance** *n* parfum *m.*

frail (freil) *adj* fragile, frêle.

frame (freɪm) n **1** cadre m. **2** structure f. **3** charpente f. **4** châssis m. **5** monture f. vt **1** former. **2** encadrer. **framework** n **1** construction, charpente f. **2** cadre m.

franc (fræŋk) n franc m.

France (frɑːns) n France f.

franchise ('fræntʃaɪz) n franchise f. droit de vote m.

frank (fræŋk) adj franc, franche, sincère. **frankness** n sincérité f.

frantic ('fræntɪk) adj frénétique, forcené.

fraternal (frə'tɜːnl̩) adj fraternel, -elle. **fraternity** n fraternité, confrérie f. **fraternize** vi fraterniser.

fraud (frɔːd) n **1** supercherie, fraude f. **2** imposteur m.

fraught (frɔːt) adj **fraught with** plein de.

fray¹ (freɪ) n bagarre, rixe f.

fray² (freɪ) vt érailler, effiler. vi s'érailler, s'effiler.

freak (friːk) n **1** fantaisie f. **2** curiosité f. phénomène m. adj extraordinaire.

freckle ('frekl) n tache de rousseur f.

free (friː) adj **1** libre. **2** gratuit. **free and easy** sans façons. ~vt **1** libérer, affranchir. **2** dégager. **freedom** n liberté f. **freehand** adj à main levée. **freehold** n propriété libre f. **freelance** adj indépendant. **freemason** n franc-maçon m. **free will** n libre arbitre m.

freeze* (friːz) v imp geler. vt **1** congeler, glacer. **2** bloquer. vi se congeler. n gel m. **freezing** n congélation f.

freight (freɪt) n **1** fret, transport m. **2** cargaison f. vt fréter, affréter. **freight train** n train de marchandises m.

French (frentʃ) adj français. **French** (language) n français m. **French bean** n haricot vert m. **French dressing** n vinaigrette f. **French horn** n cor d'harmonie m. **Frenchman** n français m. **French window** n porte-fenêtre f.

frenzy ('frenzi) n frénésie f.

frequency ('friːkwənsi) n fréquence f. **frequent** adj fréquent. vt fréquenter, hanter. **frequently** adv fréquemment.

fresco ('freskou) n, pl **-oes** or **-os** fresque f.

fresh (freʃ) adj **1** frais, fraîche, nouveau, -elle. **2** novice. **3** alerte. **freshness** n fraîcheur f. **freshwater** n eau douce f.

fret (fret) vi se tourmenter, se tracasser. vt ronger.

friar ('fraɪə) n moine m. **friary** n monastère m.

friction ('frikʃən) n **1** friction f. **2** frottement m. **3** conflit m.

Friday ('fraɪdi) n vendredi m.

fridge (frɪdʒ) n inf réfrigérateur, frigo m.

friend (frend) n ami m. **make friends with** se lier d'amitié avec. **friendliness** n bienveillance f. bonté f. **friendly** adj amical, -aux, sympathique. **friendship** n amitié f.

frieze (friːz) n frise f.

fright (fraɪt) n peur f. effroi m. **frighten** vt effrayer, faire peur. **frightful** adj terrible, épouvantable.

frigid ('frɪdʒid) adj **1** glacial, froid. **2** med frigide.

frill (fril) n volant m. ruche f. vt plisser, froncer.

fringe ('frindʒ) n **1** frange f. **2** bord m. bordure f.

frisk (frisk) vi gambader. **frisky** adj folâtre.

fritter¹ ('frɪtə) vt morceler. **fritter away** gaspiller.

fritter² ('frɪtə) n beignet m.

frivolity (fri'vɒliti) n frivolité f. **frivolous** adj frivole, futile.

frizz (friz) vt friser, crêper. vi se friser. **frizzy** adj crépu.

frizzle¹ ('frizl̩) vt (hair) friser.

frizzle² ('frizl) vt grésiller, crépiter.

fro (fro) adv **to and fro** de long en large.

frock (frɒk) n robe f.

frog (frɒg) n grenouille f. **frogs' legs** n pl cuisses de grenouille f pl.

frolic ('frɒlik) n cabriole f. ébats m pl. vi batifoler, folâtrer.

from (frəm; stressed frɒm) prep **1** de. **2** à partir de. **3** à. **4** d'après. **5** de la part de.

front (frʌnt) n front, devant m. façade f. **in front of** devant. ~adj de devant, d'avant. **frontal** adj de devant.

frontier ('frʌntiə) n frontière f.

frost (frɒst) n gelée f. vt geler, givrer. **frosty** adj gelé, glacial. **frostbite** n gelure f.

froth (frɒθ) n écume, mousse f. **frothy** adj mousseux, -euse.

frown (fraun) vi froncer les sourcils. **frown upon** regarder de travers. ~n froncement de sourcils m.

froze (frouz) v see **freeze.**

frozen ('frouzn̩) v see **freeze.** adj gelé, glacé.

frugal ('fruːgəl) adj frugal, -aux.

fruit (fruːt) n fruit m. **fruit machine** n machine à sous f. **fruitful** adj fructueux, -euse, fécond. **fruition** n **1** jouissance f. **2** réalisation f. **fruitless** adj stérile.

frustrate (frʌs'treit) vt frustrer.

fry (frai) vt faire frire. vi frire. **frying pan** n poêle (à frire) f.

fudge (fʌdʒ) n fondant m.

fuel ('fju:əl) n combustible, carburant m.

fugitive ('fju:dʒitiv) adj,n fugitif, -ive.

fulcrum ('fʌlkrəm) n, pl **-crums** or **-cra 1** tech point d'appui m. **2** centre m.

fulfil (ful'fil) vt **1** accomplir. **2** satisfaire. **3** achever. **fulfilment** n **1** accomplissement m. **2** achèvement m.

full (ful) adj **1** plein, rempli, complet, -ète. **2** ample. **full-length** adj **1** Art en pied. **2** long, longue. **full moon** n pleine lune f. **full stop** n point m. **full-time** adj à temps complet. **fullness** n **1** plénitude f. **2** ampleur f. **fully** adv pleinement, entièrement.

fumble ('fʌmbəl) vi fouiller, farfouiller.

fume (fju:m) n fumée, vapeur f. vi fumer.

fun (fʌn) n **1** amusement m. **2** plaisanterie f. **for fun** pour rire. **make fun of** se moquer de. **funfair** n fête foraine f.

function ('fʌŋkʃən) n **1** fonction f. **2** réception f. vi fonctionner, marcher.

fund (fʌnd) n fonds m. caisse f.

fundamental (fʌndə'mentl) adj fondamental, -aux, essentiel, -elle.

funeral ('fju:nərəl) n funérailles, obsèques f pl. adj funéraire, funèbre.

fungus ('fʌŋgəs) n, pl **-gi** or **-guses** champignon (vénéneux) m.

funnel ('fʌnl) n **1** entonnoir m. **2** cheminée f.

funny ('fʌni) adj **1** drôle, comique, marrant. **2** étrange, bizarre.

fur (fə:) n **1** fourrure f. poil m. **2** tartre m. vt· incruster. vi s'incruster. **furrier** n fourreur m.

furious ('fjuəriəs) adj furieux, -euse, furibond.

furnace ('fə:nis) n fourneau, -aux, four m.

furnish ('fə:niʃ) vt **1** fournir, munir. **2** (a room, etc.) meubler.

furniture ('fə:nitʃə) n meubles m pl. mobilier m. **antique furniture** meubles d'époque. **piece of furniture** meuble m.

furrow ('fʌrou) n **1** sillon m. **2** rainure f. vt sillonner.

further ('fə:ðə) adv **1** plus loin. **2** d'avantage. adj supplémentaire. vt avancer, favoriser. **furthermore** adv en outre. **furthest** adj **1** le plus éloigné. **2** le plus long. adv le plus loin.

furtive ('fə:tiv) adj furtif, -ive, sournois.

fury ('fjuəri) n furie, fureur f.

fuse[1] (fju:z) n fusible, plomb m.

fuse[2] (fju:z) vt,vi **1** fondre. **2** fusionner.

fuselage ('fju:zəla:ʒ) n fuselage m.

fusion ('fju:ʒən) n fusion f.

fuss (fʌs) n **1** bruit exagéré m. **2** embarras m pl. vi faire des histoires. vt tracasser. **fussy** adj tatillon, -onne, méticuleux, -euse.

futile ('fju:tail) adj futile, vain.

future ('fju:tʃə) adj future, à venir. n **1** avenir m. **2** gram futur m.

fuzz (fʌz) n peluches m pl. vt faire bouffer. vi bouffer, frisotter. **fuzzy** adj **1** frisotté. **2** flou.

G

gabble ('gæbəl) n bredouillement m. jacasserie f. vi bredouiller, jacasser. vt débiter très vite.

gable ('geibəl) n pignon m.

gadget ('gædʒit) n inf dispositif, truc m.

gag[1] (gæg) n bâillon m. vt bâillonner.

gag[2] (gæg) inf vt tromper. vi blaguer. n blague f.

gaiety ('geiəti) n gaieté f.

gaily ('geili) adv gaiement, allègrement.

gain (gein) vt **1** gagner, acquérir. **2** (of a clock) avancer. n gain, profit m.

gait (geit) n allure, démarche f.

gala ('gɑ:lə) n fête f. gala m.

galaxy ('gæləksi) n galaxie f.

gale (geil) n tempête f. coup de vent m.

gallant ('gælənt) adj **1** brave, vaillant. **2** galant. **gallantly** adv **1** bravement. **2** galamment. **gallantry** n **1** vaillance f. **2** galanterie f.

gallery ('gæləri) n **1** galerie f. **2** pol tribune f. **3** Art musée m.

galley ('gæli) n naut cuisine f.

gallon ('gælən) n gallon m.

gallop ('gæləp) n galop m. vi galoper. vt faire galoper.

gallows ('gælouz) n potence f. gibet m.

galore (gə'lɔ:) adv en abondance, à gogo.

galvanize ('gælvənaiz) vt galvaniser.

gamble ('gæmbəl) vt,vi jouer, miser. vt risquer. n jeu, jeux m. spéculation f. **gambling** n jeu, jeux m.

game (geim) n **1** amusement, jeu, jeux m. **2** (hunting) gibier m. **gamekeeper** n garde-chasse m.

gammon ('gæmən) n **1** quartier de lard fumé m. **2** jambon fumé m.

gander ('gændə) n jars m.

gang (gæŋ) n troupe, bande f. v **gang up**

s'allier. **gangster** n bandit, gangster m.
gangway n 1 passage m. 2 naut passerelle f.
gangrene (ˈgæŋˈgrɪːn) n gangrène f.
gap (gæp) n 1 trou m. ouverture, brèche f. 2
écart m.
gape (geip) vi 1 regarder bouche bée. 2 bâiller.
gaping adj 1 bouche bée. 2 béant.
garage (ˈgærɑːʒ) n garage m.
garble (ˈgɑːbəl) vt fausser, mutiler.
garden (ˈgɑːdn̩) n jardin m. vi jardiner.
gardening n jardinage m.
gargle (ˈgɑːgəl) vt se gargariser. n gargarisme
m.
gargoyle (ˈgɑːgɔil) n gargouille f.
garland (ˈgɑːlənd) n guirlande f. vt enguirlander.
garlic (ˈgɑːlik) n ail m,pl aulx. **clove of garlic** n
gousse d'ail f.
garment (ˈgɑːmənt) n vêtement m.
garnish (ˈgɑːniʃ) n garniture f. vt garnir, orner.
garrison (ˈgærisən) n garnison f. vt mettre en
garnison.
garter (ˈgɑːtə) n jarretière f.
gas (gæs) n gaz m invar. vt asphyxier.
gash (gæʃ) n coupure, entaille f. vt entailler,
couper, balafrer.
gasket (ˈgæskit) n joint m.
gasp (gɑːsp) n hoquet, sursaut m. vi 1 haleter,
suffoquer. 2 sursauter.
gastric (ˈgæstrik) adj gastrique. **gastronomic**
adj gastronomique.
gate (geit) n porte, grille, barrière f. **gatecrash**
vi resquiller.
gateau (ˈgætou) n,pl **-teaux** gâteau, -aux m.
gather (ˈgæðə) vt 1 rassembler, recueillir. 2
prendre. 3 comprendre, déduire. vi se
rassembler. **gathering** n rassemblement m.
gauche (gouʃ) adj gauche.
gaudy (ˈgɔːdi) adj voyant, criard. **gaudily** adv
de manière voyante.
gauge (geidʒ) n calibre, indicateur m. jauge f. vt
calibrer, jauger, mesurer.
gaunt (gɔːnt) adj maigre, décharné.
gauze (gɔːz) n gaze f.
gave (geiv) v see **give.**
gay (gei) adj 1 gai, allègre. 2 sl homosexuel,
-elle.
gaze (geiz) n regard fixe m. vi regarder
fixement.
gazelle (gəˈzel) n gazelle f.
gear (giə) n 1 équipement m. effets m pl. 2 mot
vitesse f. **put into/out of gear** embrayer/
débrayer. **gearbox** n boîte de vitesses

f. **gear lever** n levier de changement de
vitesse m.
gelatine (ˈdʒelətiːn) n gélatine f.
gelignite (ˈdʒelignait) n gélignite f.
gem (dʒem) n pierre précieuse, gemme f. joyau,
-aux m.
Gemini (ˈdʒɛminai) n pl Gémeaux m pl.
gender (ˈdʒendə) n 1 gram genre m. 2 sexe m.
gene (dʒiːn) n gène m.
genealogy (dʒiniˈælədʒi) n généalogie f.
general (ˈdʒenərəl) adj,n général, -aux
m. **general practitioner** n médecin généra-
liste m. **generalization** n généralisation
f. **generalize** vt généraliser.
generate (ˈdʒenəreit) vt engendrer, produire.
generation n génération f. **generator** n
générateur m.
generic (dʒiˈnerik) adj générique.
generous (ˈdʒenərəs) adj généreux, -euse,
magnanime. **generosity** n générosité f.
genetic (dʒiˈnetik) adj génétique. **genetics** n
génétique f.
Geneva (dʒiˈniːvə) n Genève f. **Lake Geneva**
lac Léman m.
genial (ˈdʒiːniəl) adj doux, clément, bienveillant.
genital (ˈdʒenitl) adj génital, -aux. **genitals** n pl
organes génitaux m pl.
genius (ˈdʒiːniəs) n 1 génie m. 2 démon m. 3
aptitude f.
genteel (dʒenˈtiːl) adj de bon ton.
gentile (ˈdʒentail) adj,n gentil.
gentle (ˈdʒentl̩) adj doux, douce. **gentleman** n
1 monsieur m. 2 homme comme il faut m.
gentleness n douceur f.
genuflect (ˈdʒenjuflekt) vi faire une génuflexion.
genuine (ˈdʒenjuin) adj 1 authentique, véritable. 2 sincère.
genus (ˈdʒiːnəs) n, pl **genera** genre m.
geography (dʒiˈɔgrəfi) n géographie f. **geographic** adj also **geographical** géographique.
geology (dʒiˈɔlədʒi) n géologie f. **geological**
adj géologique. **geologist** n géologue m.
geometry (dʒiˈɔmətri) n géométrie f. **geometric** adj also **geometrical** géométrique.
geriatrics (dʒeriˈætriks) n gériatrie f.
germ (dʒəːm) n germe, microbe m.
Germany (ˈdʒəːməni) n Allemagne f. **German**
adj,n allemand. **German** (language) n
allemand m. **German measles** n rubéole
f. **Germanic** adj germanique.
germinate (ˈdʒəːmineit) vi germer. vt faire
germer.

gerund ('dʒerənd) n gérondif m.

gesticulate (dʒɪs'tɪkuleɪt) vt gesticuler.

gesture ('dʒestʃə) n geste, signe m.

get* (get) vt **1** obtenir. **2** gagner. **3** aller chercher. **4** inf comprendre. **5** faire. **6** avoir. vi **1** devenir. **2** arriver. **get back** revenir. **get down** descendre. **get in 1** entrer. **2** arriver. **get off** descendre. **get on** monter. **get out** sortir. **get up** se lever.

geyser ('gɪːzə) n geyser m.

ghastly ('gɑːstli) adj **1** horrible, effroyable. **2** blême. adv horriblement, effroyablement.

gherkin ('gəːkɪn) n cornichon m.

ghetto ('getou) n, pl **-os** or **-oes** ghetto m.

ghost (goust) n fantôme f. spectre m.

giant ('dʒaɪənt) adj,n géant.

giddy ('gɪdi) adj **1** étourdi, vertigineux, -euse. **2** frivole. **giddiness** n vertige m.

gift (gift) n don, cadeau, -aux m. **gifted** adj doué.

gigantic (dʒaɪ'gæntik) adj gigantesque, géant.

giggle ('gɪgəl) n petit rire, gloussement m. vi rire nerveusement, glousser.

gild (gild) vt dorer. **gilded** adj doré.

gill (gil) n zool branchie f.

gilt (gilt) n dorure f.

gimmick ('gimik) n machin, truc m. trouvaille f.

gin (dʒin) n gin, genièvre m.

ginger ('dʒɪndʒə) n gingembre m. adj roux, rousse. **gingerbread** n pain d'épice m. **gingerly** adv avec précaution.

gingham ('gɪŋəm) n guingan m.

Gipsy ('dʒɪpsi) n bohémien, -ienne.

giraffe (dʒɪ'rɑːf) n girafe f.

girder ('gəːdə) n support m. poutre f.

girdle ('gəːdl) n ceinture, cordelière f. vt ceindre.

girl (gəːl) n (jeune) fille f. **girlfriend** n (petite) amie f. **girlhood** n jeunesse f.

girth (gəːθ) n sangle f.

give* (gɪv) vt,vi donner. vt faire. **give away 1** donner. **2** inf trahir. **give in** céder. **give out 1** distribuer. **2** annoncer. **give up** renoncer, abandonner. **give way 1** céder. **2** s'affaisser.

glacier ('glæsɪə) n glacier m.

glad (glæd) adj heureux, -euse, content. **gladly** adv avec plaisir, volontiers.

glamour ('glæmə) n **1** charme m. **2** fascination f. prestige m. **glamorize** vt donner un prestige factice. **glamorous** adj enchanteur, -eresse.

glance (glɑːns) n regard, coup d'œil m. vi jeter un coup d'œil. **glance through** feuilleter.

gland (glænd) n glande f.

glare (glɛə) n **1** lumière aveuglante f. éclat m. **2** regard farouche m. vi éblouir. **glare at** regarder d'un air furieux.

glass (glɑːs) n **1** verre m. **2** pl lunettes f pl. **pane of glass** vitre f.

glaze (gleɪz) n glace f. lustre, vernis m. vi **1** vitrer. **2** vernir. **3** cul glacer.

gleam (gliːm) n lueur f. rayon m. vi luire, miroiter.

glean (gliːn) vt glaner.

glee (gliː) n joie, allégresse f. adj joyeux, -euse, allègre.

glib (glib) adj spécieux, -euse.

glide (glaɪd) vi **1** glisser, couler. **2** aviat planer. n **1** glissement m. **2** vol plané m. **glider** n planeur m.

glimmer ('glimə) n lueur (faible) f. vi luire faiblement.

glimpse (glimps) n aperçu m. **catch a glimpse** entrevoir, apercevoir.

glint (glint) n trait de lumière m. vi étinceler.

glisten ('glisən) vi étinceler, reluire.

glitter ('glitə) n étincellement m. vi étinceler.

gloat (glout) vi **gloat over** couver du regard, se réjouir.

globe (gloub) n globe m. sphère f.

gloom[1] (gluːm) n (darkness) obscurité f. ténèbres f pl. **gloomy** adj sombre, ténébreux, -euse.

gloom[2] (gluːm) n mélancolie f. **gloomy** adj lugubre, morne.

glory ('glɔːri) n gloire f. honneur m. v **glory in** se glorifier de, se faire gloire de. **glorify** vt glorifier. **glorious** adj glorieux, -euse.

gloss[1] (glɔs) n (shine) lustre m. vt lustrer, glacer. **gloss over** farder. **glossy** adj lustré, brillant.

gloss[2] (glɔs) n glose f. commentaire m. vt gloser.

glossary ('glɔsəri) n glossaire, lexique m.

glove (glʌv) n gant m.

glow (glou) n rougeur, ardeur f. vi briller, rayonner. **glowing** adj **1** rayonnant. **2** chaleureux, -euse.

glower ('glauə) vi **glower at** regarder d'un air fâché.

glucose ('gluːkous) n glucose m.

glue (gluː) n colle f. vt coller.

glum (glʌm) adj renfrogné, maussade.

glut (glʌt) n surabondance f. **glutton** n gourmand m. **gluttony** n gloutonnerie f.

gnarled (nɑːld) adj noueux, -euse, tordu.

gnash (næʃ) vt grincer.

gnat (næt) n moustique, cousin m.

gnaw (nɔ:) vt ronger. **gnawing** n rongement m.

gnome (noum) n gnome m.

go* (gou) vi 1 aller, partir. 2 (of a machine) marcher. 3 passer. **go away** s'en aller. **go back** retourner. **go down** descendre. **go on** continuer. **go out** sortir. **go through** traverser. **go up** monter. **go without** se passer de. ~n, pl **goes** 1 coup m. 2 entrain m.

goad (goud) vt aiguillonner. n aiguillon m.

goal (goul) n 1 but m. 2 objectif m. **goalkeeper** n gardien de but m. **goalpost** n montant de but m.

goat (gout) n chèvre f. **he-goat** n bouc m.

gobble ('gɔbəl) vt avaler goulûment.

goblin ('gɔblin) n lutin m.

god (gɔd) n dieu, -eux m. **godchild** n filleul m. **goddaughter** n filleule f. **godfather** n parrain m. **godmother** n marraine f. **godson** n filleul m. **goddess** n déesse f.

goggles ('gɔgəlz) n lunettes protectrices f pl.

gold (gould) n or m. adj doré, d'or. **golden** adj doré, d'or. **golden syrup** n mélasse raffinée f. **goldfinch** n chardonneret m. **goldfish** n poisson rouge m. **goldmine** n 1 mine d'or f. 2 inf affaire d'or f. **goldsmith** n orfèvre m.

golf (gɔlf) n golf m. **golfcourse** n terrain de golf m.

gondola ('gɔndələ) n gondole f. **gondolier** n gondolier m.

gone (gɔn) v see **go.**

gong (gɔŋ) n gong m.

good (gud) adj 1 bon, bonne. 2 sage. **good for nothing** bon à rien. ~n 1 bien m. 2 pl effets m pl. marchandises f pl. **for good** pour de bon. **good afternoon** interj bonjour! **goodbye** interj,n au revoir, adieu, -eux m. **good evening** interj bonsoir! **good-looking** adj beau, belle. **good morning** interj bonjour! **good night** interj bonne nuit! **goods train** n train de marchandises m. **good will** n bonne volonté, bienveillance f.

Good Friday n vendredi saint m.

goose (gu:s) n, pl **geese** oie f. **gooseberry** n groseille à maquereau f. **gooseberry bush** groseillier (à maquereau) m.

gore¹ (gɔ:) n sang caillé m.

gore² (gɔ:) vt encorner.

gorge (gɔ:dʒ) n gorge f. vi se gorger, s'empiffrer. vt gorger, rassasier.

gorgeous ('gɔ:dʒəs) adj magnifique, splendide.

gorilla (gə'rilə) n gorille m.

gorse (gɔ:s) n ajonc m.

gory ('gɔ:ri) adj ensanglanté.

gosh (gɔʃ) interj sapristi!

gosling ('gɔzliŋ) n oison m.

gospel ('gɔspəl) n évangile m.

gossip ('gɔsip) vi bavarder, faire des cancans. n 1 commérage m. 2 commère, bavarde f.

got (gɔt) v see **get.**

Gothic ('gɔθik) adj gothique.

goulash ('gu:læʃ) n gulache m.

gourd (guəd) n courge, gourde f.

gourmet (guə'mei) n gourmet, gastronome m.

govern ('gʌvən) vt gouverner, régir, administrer. **government** n gouvernement m. **governor** n 1 gouverneur m. 2 inf patron m.

gown (gaun) n robe f.

grab (græb) n mouvement vif pour saisir m. étreinte f. vi saisir brusquement, empoigner.

grace (greis) n 1 grâce f. 2 bénédicité m. **Her/His Grace** Madame/Monseigneur. **Your Grace** votre Grandeur. **graceful** adj gracieux, -euse. **gracefully** adv avec grâce. **gracious** adj bienveillant.

grade (greid) n grade, rang, degré m. vt 1 grader, classer. 2 graduer. **gradient** n dénivellation, pente, rampe f. **gradual** adj graduel, -elle. **graduate** n diplômé. vi recevoir ses diplômes. vt graduer.

graffiti (grə'fi:ti) n pl graffiti n pl.

graft (grɑ:ft) n greffe f. vt greffer.

grain (grein) n 1 grain m. 2 texture f.

gram (græm) n gramme m.

grammar ('græmə) n grammaire f. **grammar school** n lycée m. **grammatical** adj grammatical, -aux.

gramophone ('græməfoun) n phonographe m.

granary ('grænəri) n grenier m.

grand (grænd) adj grandiose, magnifique. **grandeur** n grandeur, splendeur f.

grandad ('grændæd) n inf also **grandpa** n grand-papa m.

grandchild ('græntʃaild) n petit-enfant m.

granddaughter ('grændɔ:tə) n petite-fille f.

grandfather ('grænfɑ:ðə) n grand-père m.

grandma ('grænmɑ:) n inf also **granny** bonnemaman, mémé f.

grandmother ('grændmʌðə) n grand-mère f.

grandparent ('grænpɛərənt) n grand-parent m.

grand piano n piano à queue m.

grandson (grænsʌn) n petit-fils m.

grandstand ('grændstænd) n tribune (d'honneur) f.

granite ('grænɪt) *n* granit *m.*

grant (grɑːnt) *n* subvention, bourse *f. vt* accorder, concéder.

grape (greɪp) *n* raisin *m.* **bunch of grapes** grappe de raisins *f.* **grapefruit** *n* pamplemousse *m.* **grapevine** *n* 1 vigne *f.* 2 source d'informations *f.*

graph (grɑːf) *n* graphique *n.* courbe *f.*

grapple ('græpəl) *vi* **grapple with** en venir aux prises avec.

grasp (grɑːsp) *n* prise, étreinte *f. vt* 1 saisir, empoigner. 2 comprendre. **grasping** *adj* rapace, avide.

grass (grɑːs) *n* herbe *f.* **grassroots** *n* base, source *f.*

grate[1] (greɪt) *n* grille *f.*

grate[2] (greɪt) *vt* râper. *vi* grincer.

grateful ('greɪtfəl) *adj* reconnaissant. **gratify** *vt* 1 faire plaisir. 2 satisfaire. **gratifying** *adj* agréable.

gratitude ('grætɪtjuːd) *n* gratitude, reconnaissance *f.*

grave[1] (greɪv) *n* tombe *f.* tombeau, -aux *m.* **gravestone** *n* pierre tombale *f.* **graveyard** *n* cimetière *m.*

grave[2] (greɪv) *adj* sérieux, -euse, grave.

gravel ('grævəl) *n* gravier *m.*

gravity ('grævitɪ) *n* gravité *f.*

gravy ('greɪvɪ) *n* jus *m.* sauce *f.*

graze[1] (greɪz) *vi* (of animals) paître, brouter. *vt* faire paître.

graze[2] (greɪz) *n* éraflure, écorchure *f. vt* 1 érafler, écorcher. 2 frôler.

grease (griːs) *n* graisse *f. vt* graisser. **greasepaint** *n* fard *m.* **greaseproof** *adj* sulfurisé, parcheminé. **greasy** *adj* graisseux, -euse.

great (greɪt) *adj* grand, fort. **greatly** *adv* beaucoup. **greatness** *n* grandeur *f.*

Great Britain *n* Grande-Bretagne *f.*

Greece (griːs) *n* Grèce *f.* **Grecian** *adj* grec, grecque. **Greek** *adj,n* grec, grecque. **Greek** (language) *n* grec *m.*

greed (griːd) *n* cupidité, avidité *f.* **greedy** *adj* 1 gourmand. 2 avide. **greedily** *adv* avidement, goulûment.

green (griːn) *adj* 1 vert. 2 *inf* naif, naïve. *n* 1 vert *m.* 2 *pl* légumes verts *m pl.* **greenery** *n* verdure *f.* feuillage *m.* **greenfly** *n* puceron *m.* **greengage** *n* reine-claude *f.* **greengrocer** *n* marchand de légumes *m.* fruitier, -ière. **greenhouse** *n* serre *f.*

Greenland ('griːnlənd) *n* Groenland *m.* **Greenlander** *n* groenlandais *m.*

greet (griːt) *vt* saluer, accueillir. **greeting** *n* salutation *f.*

gregarious (griˈgɛərɪəs) *adj* grégaire.

grenade (griˈneɪd) *n* grenade *f.*

grew (gruː) *v see* **grow.**

grey (greɪ) *adj,n* gris *m.* **greyhound** *n* lévrier *m.*

grid (grɪd) *n* grille *f.* grillage *m.*

grief (griːf) *n* chagrin *m.* douleur *f.*

grieve (griːv) *vt* chagriner, peiner. *vi* se chagriner, s'affliger. **grievance** *n* grief *m.* injustice *f.* **grieved** *adj* désolé. **grievous** *adj* douloureux, -euse, pénible.

grill (grɪl) *n* 1 *cul* grillade *f.* 2 gril *m. vt cul* griller.

grille (grɪl) *n* grille *f.*

grim (grɪm) *adj* 1 menaçant, sinistre. 2 sévère.

grimace (griˈmeɪs) *n* grimace *f. vi* grimacer.

grime (graɪm) *n* saleté, crasse *f.* **grimy** *adj* crasseux, -euse.

grin (grɪn) *n* large sourire *m. vi* sourire à belles dents.

grind* (graɪnd) *vt* 1 moudre, broyer. 2 aiguiser. *vi* grincer. *n* 1 grincement *m.* 2 *sl* corvée *f.*

grip (grɪp) *n* prise, étreinte *f.* **come to grips with** en venir aux mains avec. ~*vt* 1 saisir. 2 serrer. **gripping** *adj inf* passionnant.

gripe (graɪp) *vt* affliger. *vi inf* rouspéter. *n* colique *f.*

gristle ('grɪsəl) *n* cartilage *m.*

grit (grɪt) *n* 1 grès *m.* 2 *sl* cran, courage *m. vi,vt* grincer. *vt* sabler.

groan (groun) *n* gémissement *m. vi* gémir, se plaindre.

grocer ('grousə) *n* épicier, -ière. **grocery** *n* épicerie *f.*

groin (groɪn) *n anat* aine *f.*

groom (gruːm) *n* palefrenier *m. vt* panser.

groove (gruːv) *n* rainure, cannelure *f. vt* rayer, canneler.

grope (group) *vi* tâtonner. **grope for** chercher à tâtons.

gross (grous) *adj* 1 gros, grosse. 2 grossier, -ière. 3 flagrant. *n* grosse *f.*

grotesque (grouˈtesk) *adj,n* grotesque *m.*

grotto ('grɒtou) *n, pl* **-os** *or* **-oes** grotte *f.*

ground[1] (graund) *n* 1 sol, terrain *m.* 2 raison *f.* 3 fond *m. vt* fonder, baser. *vi* s'échouer. **ground floor** *n* rez-de-chaussée *m.* **groundsheet** *n* tapis de sol *m.* **groundsman** *n* préposé à l'entretien d'un terrain de jeux *m*. **groundwork** *n* assise *f*. plan *m*.

ground[2] (graund) *v* see **grind**.

group (gru:p) *n* groupe *m*. *vt* grouper. *vi* se grouper.

grouse[1] (graus) *n zool* tétras *m*.

grouse[2] (graus) *vi inf* grogner, rouspéter.

grove (grouv) *n* bocage *m*.

grovel ('grɔvəl) *vi* ramper.

grow* (grou) *vi* pousser, grandir, croître. *vt* cultiver. **grown-up** *n* adulte *m,f*. **growth** *n* croissance *f*.

growl (graul) *vi* grogner, gronder. *n* grognement *m*.

grub (grʌb) *n* 1 larve *f*. 2 *sl* boustifaille *f*.

grubby ('grʌbi) *adj* sale, malpropre.

grudge (grʌdʒ) *n* rancune *f*. *vt* donner à contre-cœur. **grudgingly** *adv* à contre-cœur.

gruelling ('gru:əliŋ) *adj* épuisant, éreintant.

gruesome ('gru:səm) *adj* macabre.

gruff (grʌf) *adj* bourru, brusque.

grumble ('grʌmbəl) *vt,vi* grommeler, grogner. *n* grognement *m*.

grumpy ('grʌmpi) *adj* maussade, grincheux, -euse.

grunt (grʌnt) *n* grognement *m*. *vi* grogner.

guarantee (gærən'ti:) *n* garantie *f*. *vt* garantir, cautionner. **guarantor** *n* garant *m*.

guard (gɑ:d) *n* 1 garde *f*. 2 chef de train *m*. *vi* garder, protéger. **guard's van** *n* fourgon *m*. **guarded** *adj* prudent, mesuré. **guardian** *n* 1 gardien, -ienne. 2 *law* tuteur, -trice. **guardianship** *n* tutelle *f*.

Guernsey ('gə:nzi) *n* Guernesey *m*.

guerrilla (gə'rilə) *n* guérillero *m*.

guess (ges) *vt,vi* deviner, conjecturer. *n* conjecture *f*. **at a guess** au jugé. **guesswork** *n* conjecture, hypothèse *f*.

guest (gest) *n* 1 invité *m*. 2 (in a hotel, etc.) pensionnaire *m,f*. **guesthouse** *n* pension de famille *f*.

guide (gaid) *n* guide *m*. *vt* guider, diriger. **guidebook** *n* guide *m*. **guide-dog** *n* chien d'aveugles *m*. **guidance** *n* direction, conduite *f*.

guild (gild) *n* corporation, confrérie *f*.

guillotine (gilə'ti:n) *n* guillotine *f*. *vt* guillotiner.

guilt (gilt) *n* culpabilité *f*. **guilty** *adj* coupable.

guinea ('gini) *n* guinée *f*. **guinea pig** *n* cobaye, cochon d'Inde *m*.

guitar (gi'tɑ:) *n* guitare *f*.

gulf (gʌlf) *n* 1 *geog* golfe *m*. 2 abîme *m*.

gull (gʌl) *n* mouette *f*. goéland *m*.

gullet ('gʌlit) *n* 1 œsophage *m*. 2 *inf* gosier *m*.

gulp (gʌlp) *n* trait *m*. lampée *f*. *vt* avaler.

gum[1] (gʌm) *n* gomme *f*. *vt* gommer.

gum[2] (gʌm) *n anat* gencive *f*.

gun (gʌn) *n* fusil, canon *m*. **gunman** *n* bandit (armé) *m*. **gunpowder** *n* poudre (à canon) *f*. **gunrunning** *n* trafic d'armes *m*. **gunshot** *n* coup de fusil *m*.

gurgle ('gə:gəl) *n* glouglou, gloussement *m*. *vi* gargouiller.

gush (gʌʃ) *n* jet, flot *m*. *vi* jaillir, déborder.

gust (gʌst) *n* ondée, giboulée, rafale *f*.

gut (gʌt) *n* 1 *anat* boyau, -aux, intestin *m*. 2 *pl inf* cran *m*. *vt* étriper, vider.

gutter ('gʌtə) *n* 1 gouttière *f*. 2 ruisseau, -aux *m*.

guy[1] (gai) *n* 1 épouvantail *m*. 2 type *m*.

guy[2] (gai) *n* cable, hauban *m*.

gymnasium (dʒim'neiziəm) *n* gymnase *m*. **gymnast** *n* gymnaste *m,f*. **gymnastic** *adj* gymnastique. **gymnastics** *n* gymnastique *f*.

gynaecology (gaini'kɔlədʒi) *n* gynécologie *f*. **gynaecologist** *n* gynécologue *m,f*.

gypsum ('dʒipsəm) *n* gypse *m*.

H

haberdasher ('hæbədæʃə) *n* mercier *m*. **haberdashery** *n* mercerie *f*.

habit ('hæbit) *n* 1 coutume, habitude *f*. 2 habit *m*. 3 *pl* mœurs *f pl*. **habitable** *adj* habitable. **habitual** *adj* habituel, -elle.

hack[1] (hæk) *vt* hacher, taillader. *vi* toussoter. *n* entaille *f*. **hacksaw** *n* scie à métaux *f*.

hack[2] (hæk) *n* 1 cheval de louage *m*. 2 *inf* rosse *f*. 3 homme de peine *m*.

hackneyed ('hæknid) *adj* banal, -aux, rebattu.

had (hæd) *v* see **have**.

haddock ('hædək) *n* aiglefin *m*.

haemorrhage ('heməridʒ) *n* hémorragie *f*.

hag (hæg) *n* sorcière *f*.

haggard ('hægəd) *adj* hagard, hâve.

haggle ('hægl) *vi* 1 marchander. 2 chicaner.

Hague, The (heig) *n* La Haye *f*.

hail[1] (heil) *n* grêle *f*. *v imp* grêler. **hailstone** *n* grêlon *m*. **hailstorm** *n* averse de grêle *f*.

hail[2] (heil) *interj* salut! *vt* 1 saluer, acclamer. 2 héler.

hair (hɛə) *n* 1 (of the head) cheveu, -eux *m*. 2 (of the head) chevelure *f*. 3 poil *m*. 4 (of a horse) crin *m*. **hairbrush** *n* brosse à cheveux *f*. **haircut** *n* coupe de cheveux *f*. **hairdresser**

n coiffeur *m.* **hairdressing** *n* coiffure *f.* **hair-grip** *n* épingle à cheveux *f.* **hairnet** *n* résille *f.* **hairpiece** *n* postiche *m.* **hair-raising** *adj* horripilant. **hairstyle** *n* coiffure *f.*

half (hɑːf) *n, pl* **halves** moitié *f.* demi *m.* demie *f. adj* demi. *adv* à moitié, à demi.

half-a-dozen *n* demi-douzaine *f.*

half-and-half *adv* moitié l'un moitié l'autre.

half-back *n* demi *m.*

half-baked *adj inf* **1** qui ne tient pas debout, bâclé. **2** niais.

half-breed *n* **1** métis, -isse. **2** cheval demi-sang *m.*

half-brother *n* demi-frère *m.*

half-caste *n* métis, -isse.

half-hearted *adj* peu enthousiaste, tiède.

half-hour *n* demi-heure *f.*

half-mast *adv* **at half-mast** en berne.

halfpenny ('heipni) *n* **1** *pl* **halfpence** demi-penny *m.* **2** *pl* **halfpennies** pièce d'un demi-penny *f.*

half-pint *n* demi-pinte, chopine *f.*

half-sister *n* demi-sœur *f.*

half-term *n* congé de mi-trimestre *m.*

half-time *n* mi-temps *f.*

halftone ('hɑːftoun) *n* **1** *Art* demi-teinte *f.* **2** *mus* demi-ton *m.*

halfway (hɑːf'wei) *adv* à mi-chemin.

halfwit ('hɑːfwit) *n* faible d'esprit, idiot *m.*

half-year *n* semestre *m.*

halibut ('hælibət) *n* flétan *m.*

hall (hɔːl) *n* salle *f.* vestibule, hall *m.*

hallelujah (hæli'luːjə) *interj, n* alléluia *m.*

hallmark ('hɔːlmɑːk) *n* **1** poinçon *m.* **2** empreinte *f.* cachet *m. vt* poinçonner.

hallo (hə'lou) *interj* see **hello.**

hallowed ('hæloud) *adj* saint, sanctifié.

Hallowe'en (hælou'iːn) *n* veille de la Toussaint *f.*

hallucination (həluːsi'neiʃən) *n* hallucination *f.*

halo ('heilou) *n, pl* **-os** *or* **oes** halo *m.* auréole *f.*

halt (hɔːlt) *n* arrêt *m.* halte *f. vi* faire halte, s'arrêter. *vt* arrêter.

halter ('hɔːltə) *n* licou *m.*

halve (hɑːv) *vt* partager en deux, réduire de moitié.

ham (hæm) *n* jambon *m.*

hamburger ('hæmbəːgə) *n* steak haché grillé *m.*

hammer ('hæmə) *n* marteau, -aux *m. vt* marteler.

hammock ('hæmək) *n* hamac *m.*

hamper[1] ('hæmpə) *vt* gêner.

hamper[2] ('hæmpə) *n* manne *f.* panier *m.*

hamster ('hæmstə) *n* hamster *m.*

hand (hænd) *n* **1** main *f.* **2** (of a clock) aiguille *f.* **3** *game* jeu *m.* **4** *inf* coup de main *m. vt* remettre, passer. **handful** *n* poignée *f.*

handbag ('hændbæg) *n* sac à main *m.*

handbook ('hændbuk) *n* **1** manuel *m.* **2** guide *m.*

handbrake ('hændbreik) *n* frein à main *m.*

handcart ('hændkɑːt) *n* charrette à bras *f.*

handcuffs ('hændkʌfs) *n pl* menottes *f pl.*

hand grenade *n* grenade à main *f.*

handicap ('hændikæp) *n* handicap, désavantage *m. vt* handicaper.

handicraft ('hændikrɑːft) *n* **1** travail manuel *m.* **2** artisanat *m.*

handiwork ('hændiwəːk) *n* ouvrage *m.*

handkerchief ('hæŋkətʃif) *n* mouchoir *m.*

handle ('hændl) *n* manche *m.* poignée, anse, manivelle *f. vt* manipuler, manier. **handlebars** *n pl* guidon *m.*

handmade (hænd'meid) *adj* fait à la main.

hand-out *n* communiqué *m.*

hand-pick *vt* trier à la main.

handrail ('hændreil) *n* balustrade, rampe *f.*

handshake ('hændʃeik) *n* poignée de main *f.*

handsome ('hænsəm) *adj* **1** beau, belle. **2** généreux, -euse.

handstand ('hændstænd) *m* poirier *m.* **do a handstand** faire l'arbre droit.

handwriting ('hændraitiŋ) *n* écriture *f.*

handy ('hændi) *adj* **1** adroit. **2** commode. **3** sous la main.

hang[*] (hæŋ) *vt* pendre, suspendre. *vi* **1** pendre. **2** peser. **hang around** flâner. **hang up** accrocher. **hanger** *n* cintre *m.* **hangman** *n* bourreau, -aux *m.* **hangover** *n* gueule de bois *f.*

hanker ('hæŋkə) *vi* **hanker after** désirer ardemment. **hankering** *n* aspiration, grande envie *f.*

haphazard (hæp'hæzəd) *adj* fortuit. *adv* au hasard.

happen ('hæpən) *vi* arriver, se passer.

happy ('hæpi) *adj* heureux, -euse. **happiness** *n* bonheur *m.*

harass ('hærəs) *vt* **1** *mil* harceler. **2** tourmenter.

harbour ('hɑːbə) *n* port *m. vt* héberger, receler.

hard (hɑːd) *adj* **1** dur. **2** difficile. **3** sévère. **hard up** à court d'argent. ∼*adv* **1** fort. **2** difficilement. **hardback** *n* livre relié *m.* **hard-boiled** *adj* dur. **hard-headed** *adj* positif, -ive, pratique. **hard-hearted** *adj* insensible, impitoyable. **hardware** *n* quincaillerie *f.* **harden**

vt,vi durcir. **hardness** *n* 1 dureté *f.* 2 difficulté *f.* **hardship** *n* épreuve, privation *f.*

hardly (ˈhɑːdli) *adv* à peine, ne...guère. **hardly ever** presque jamais.

hardy (ˈhɑːdi) *adj* 1 hardi. 2 robuste. 3 *bot* vivace.

hare (ˈhɛə) *n* lièvre *m.*

haricot (ˈhærikou) *n* haricot blanc *m.*

hark (hɑːk) *vi* écouter.

harm (hɑːm) *n* mal, tort *m. vt* faire du mal à, nuire à. **harmful** *adj* nuisible. **harmless** *adj* inoffensif, -ive, anodin.

harmonic (hɑːˈmɔnik) *adj,n* harmonique *m.* **harmonica** *n* harmonica *m.* **harmonize** *vt* harmoniser. *vi* s'assortir. **harmony** *n* 1 *mus* harmonie *f.* 2 entente *f.* accord *m.*

harness (ˈhɑːnis) *n* harnais *m. vt* 1 harnacher. 2 aménager.

harp (hɑːp) *n* harp *f. v* **harp on about** rabâcher.

harpoon (hɑːˈpuːn) *n* harpon *m. vt* harponner.

harpsichord (ˈhɑːpsikɔːd) *n* clavecin *m.*

harsh (hɑːʃ) *adj* 1 dur. 2 âpre. 3 aigre. **harshly** *adv* rudement, sévèrement.

harvest (ˈhɑːvist) *n* récolte *f. vt* récolter.

has (hæz) *v see* **have.**

hashish (ˈhæʃiʃ) *n* hachisch *m.*

haste (heist) *n* hâte *f.* **hasten** *vi* se presser, s'empresser. *vt* accélérer, hâter, presser.

hat (hæt) *n* chapeau, -aux *m.*

hatch¹ (hætʃ) *n* couvée *f. vt* faire éclore, incuber. **hatch out** éclore.

hatch² (hætʃ) *n* 1 *naut* écoutille *f.* 2 trappe *f.* passe-plats *m.*

hatchet (ˈhætʃit) *n* cognée, hachette *f.*

hate (heit) *vt* haïr, détester. *n* haine *f.* **hateful** *adj* odieux, -euse.

haughty (ˈhɔːti) *adj* hautain, arrogant.

haul (hɔːl) *vt* 1 traîner. 2 transporter. *vt,vi* haler. *n* 1 coup de filet *m.* 2 charge *f.* **haulage** *n* 1 roulage *m.* 2 remorquage *m.*

haunch (hɔːntʃ) *n* 1 hanche *f.* 2 *cul* cuissot *m.*

haunt (hɔːnt) *vt* hanter, obséder. *n* repaire *m.*

have (hæv) *vt* 1 avoir, posséder. 2 obtenir. 3 prendre. 4 faire. *v aux* avoir. **have to** devoir.

haven (ˈheivən) *n* 1 havre *m.* 2 abri *m.*

haversack (ˈhævəsæk) *n* haversac *m.*

havoc (ˈhævək) *n* ravage *m.*

hawk (hɔːk) *n* faucon, épervier *m.*

hawthorn (ˈhɔːθɔːn) *n* aubépine *f.*

hay (hei) *n* foin *m.* **hayfever** *n* rhume des foins *m.* **haystack** *n* meule de foin *f.* **haywire** *adj* loupé.

hazard (ˈhæzəd) *n* hasard, risque *m. vt* hasarder. **hazardous** *adj* périlleux, -euse.

haze (heiz) *n* 1 brume *f.* 2 incertitude *f. vt* embrumer. **hazy** *adj* 1 brumeux, -euse. 2 nébuleux, -euse.

hazel (ˈheizəl) *n* noisetier *m.* **hazelnut** *n* noisette *f.*

he (hiː) *pron 3rd pers s* 1 il. 2 lui. **he who** celui qui.

head (hed) *n* 1 tête *f.* 2 chef, directeur *m.* 3 principal, -aux *m. adj* principal, -aux, premier, -ière. *vt* 1 conduire. 2 intituler. **heading** *n* titre, en-tête *m.*

headache (ˈhedeik) *n* mal de tête *m.*

headfirst (hedˈfəːst) *adv* la tête la première.

headlight (ˈhedlait) *n* phare *m.*

headline (ˈhedlain) *n* manchette *f.*

headlong (ˈhedlɔŋ) *adv* 1 la tête la première. 2 téméraire.

headmaster (hedˈmɑːstə) *n* directeur (d'école) *m.* **headmistress** *n* directrice (d'école) *f.*

headphone (ˈhedfoun) *n* écouteur, casque *m.*

headquarters (ˈhedkwɔːtəz) *n pl* 1 siège social *m.* 2 *mil* quartier général *m.*

headscarf (ˈhedskɑːf) *n* foulard *m.*

headstrong (ˈhedstrɔŋ) *adj* têtu, obstiné.

headway (ˈhedwei) *n* avance *f.* progrès *m.*

heal (hiːl) *vt,vi* guérir.

health (helθ) *n* santé *f.* **healthy** *adj* 1 en bonne santé. 2 robuste.

heap (hiːp) *n* tas *m. vt* entasser, amasser, combler.

hear* (hiə) *vi* entendre. *vt* 1 entendre. 2 écouter. 3 apprendre. **hear from** recevoir des nouvelles de. **hear of** entendre parler de. **hearing** *n* 1 ouïe *f.* 2 audience *f.* 3 audition *f.* **hearing aid** *n* appareil auditif *m.* **hearsay** *n* ouï-dire *m invar.*

hearse (həːs) *n* corbillard *m.*

heart (hɑːt) *n* 1 cœur *m.* 2 courage *m.* **heart attack** *n* crise cardiaque *f.* **heartbeat** *n* battement de cœur *m.* **heartbroken** *adj* accablé, navré. **heartily** *adv* 1 de bon cœur. 2 avec appétit. **heartless** *adj* insensible, cruel, -elle. **hearty** *adj* 1 chaleureux, -euse. 2 robuste.

hearth (hɑːθ) *n* âtre *m.*

heat (hiːt) *n* 1 chaleur *f.* 2 épreuve *f. vt* chauffer. **heater** *n* appareil de chauffage, radiateur *m.* **heatwave** *n* vague de chaleur *f.*

heath (hiːθ) *n* bruyère, lande *f.*

heathen (ˈhiːðən) *adj,n* païen, -enne.

heather (ˈheðə) *n* bruyère *f.*

heave

heave (hi:v) vt 1 lever 2 porter 3 pousser vi 1 se soulever. 2 avoir des haut-le-cœur. n 1 effort m. 2 soulèvement m.

heaven ('hevən) n ciel, cieux m. **heavenly** adj céleste.

heavy ('hevi) adj 1 lourd, gros, grosse 2 profond 3 pénible. **heaviness** n 1 lourdeur f 2 lassitude f **heavyweight** n poids lourd m. adj lourd.

Hebrew ('hi:bru:) n hébreu, -eux m adj hébreu, -eux, hébraïque **Hebrew** (language) n hébreu m

heckle ('hekəl) vt interpeller

hectic ('hektik) adj agité

hedge (hedʒ) n 1 haie f 2 protection f vt entourer d'une haie vi chercher des faux-fuyants **hedgehog** n hérisson m

heed (hi:d) n attention f. vt faire attention à. **heedless** adj étourdi, peu soucieux, -euse

heel (hi:l) n talon m

hefty ('hefti) adj solide, costaud.

height (hait) n 1 hauteur f 2 élévation f 3 apogée f **heighten** vt 1 surélever 2 accroître, rehausser

heir (ɛə) n héritier m **heiress** n héritière f. **heirloom** n meuble or bijou de famille m

held (held) v see **hold.**

helicopter ('helikɔptə) n hélicoptère m

hell (hel) n enfer m **hellish** adj infernal, -aux

hello (hə'lou) interj 1 bonjour! 2 salut! 3 allô! holà!

helm (helm) n naut barre f gouvernail m

helmet ('helmit) n casque m.

help (help) n 1 aide f secours m 2 inf domestique f interj au secours! vt 1 secourir, aider 2 servir **it can't be helped!** tant pis! **helpful** adj utile **helpless** adj impuissant.

hem (hem) n ourlet, bord m

hemisphere ('hemisfiə) n hémisphère m

hemp (hemp) n chanvre m

hen (hen) n 1 poule f 2 femelle f **henpecked** adj mené par le bout du nez

hence (hens) adv 1 en conséquence 2 dorénavant 3 d'ici **henceforth** adv désormais

henna ('henə) n henné m

her (hə:) pron 3rd pers s 1 elle 2 la 3 lui poss adj 3rd pers s son, sa, ses

herald ('herəld) n 1 héraut m 2 avant-coureur m. vt annoncer **heraldry** n blason m

herb (hə:b) n herbe f

herd (hə:d) n troupeau, -aux m bande f vi s'attrouper **herdsman** m gardien m

here (hiə) adv ici **here and there** par-ci par-là **here, there, and everywhere** un peu partout **hereafter** adv 1 ci-après. 2 désormais **hereby** adv par là **herein** adv ci-inclus.

hereditary (hi'reditri) adj héréditaire.

heredity (hi'rediti) n hérédité f.

heresy ('herəsi) n hérésie f **heretic** n hérétique m,f

heritage ('heritidʒ) n héritage m

hermit ('hə:mit) n ermite m.

hero ('hiərou) n, pl **-oes** héros m **heroine** n héroïne f

heroin ('herouin) n héroïne f.

heron ('herən) n héron m

herring ('heriŋ) n hareng m. **red herring** n inf diversion f

hers (hə:z) poss pron 3rd pers s 1 le sien, la sienne 2 à elle **herself** pron 3rd pers s 1 elle-même. 2 se **by herself** toute seule

hesitate ('heziteit) vi hésiter. **hesitation** n hésitation f

hexagon ('heksəgən) n hexagone m **hexagonal** adj hexagone.

hibernate ('haibəneit) vi hiberner

hiccup ('hikʌp) n hoquet m. vi avoir le hoquet.

hide[1] (haid) vt cacher vi se cacher. **hide-and-seek** n cache-cache m

hide[2] (haid) n peau, peaux f cuir m

hideous ('hidiəs) adj hideux, -euse.

hiding[1] ('haidiŋ) n 1 cachette f 2 dissimulation f

hiding[2] ('haidiŋ) n inf raclée f

hierarchy ('haiəra:ki) n hiérarchie f

high (hai) adj 1 haut. 2 élevé 3 grand. 4 faisandé 5 sl parti **highbrow** adj intellectuel, -elle **high frequency** adj à haute fréquence **highland** adj montagnard. n 1 haute terre f 2 cap pl Haute Ecosse f **highlight** vt mettre en évidence n point culminant m **highly** adv 1 hautement 2 fort, très **highpitched** adj aigu, -uë, criard **high-rise** adj élevé. **high-rise block** n tour f **high-spirited** adj 1 exubérant. 2 fougueux, -euse **highway** n 1 grand-route f 2 voie publique f

Highness ('hainəs) n Altesse f

hijack ('haidʒæk) vt détourner

hike (haik) n excursion à pied f vi faire de la marche

hilarious (hi'lɛəriəs) adj hilare. **hilarity** n hilarité f

hill (hil) n 1 colline f 2 côte f **hillside** n versant, flanc de coteau m **hilltop** n cime f

him (him) pron 3rd pers s 1 le 2 lui **himself**

212

pron 3rd pers s **1** lui-même **2** se **by himself** tout seul.

hind (haind) *adj* de derrierè, postérieur. **hindleg** *n* patte de derrière *f*. **hindsight** *n* sagesse d'après coup *f*.

hinder ('hində) *vt* **1** gêner. **2** empêcher **hindrance** *n* empêchement *m*

Hindu ('hindu:) *adj,n* hindou.

hinge (hindʒ) *n* **1** gond *m* **2** pivot *m*. **3** charnière *f*. *v* **hinge on** être axé sur, dépendre de.

hint (hint) *n* **1** insinuation, allusion *f* **2** conseil *m*. *vi* insinuer.

hip (hip) *n* hanche *f*.

hippopotamus (hipə'pɔtəməs) *n pl* **-mi** *or* **-muses** hippopotame *m*.

hire (haiə) *vt* louer, engager. **hire out** donner en location. ~*n* location *f*. louage *m* **hire-purchase** *n* vente à tempérament *f*.

his (hiz) *poss adj 3rd pers s* son, sa, ses. *poss pron 3rd pers s* **1** le sien, la sienne. **2** à lui.

hiss (his) *vi* siffler. *n* sifflement *m*.

history ('histri) *n* histoire *f*. **historian** *n* historien *m*. **historic** *adj* historique

hit (hit) *vt* **1** frapper. **2** atteindre, toucher *n* coup *m*.

hitch *n* **1** saccade, secousse *f* **2** contretemps *m*. *vt* **1** accrocher **2** remuer par saccades. **hitch-hike** *vi* faire du stop.

hive (haiv) *n* ruche *f*.

hoard (hɔ:d) *vt* amasser, accumuler *vi* thésauriser. *n* **1** amas *m*. **2** trésor *m*.

hoarding ('hɔ:diŋ) *n* **1** palissade *f* panneauréclame *m*. **2** resserre, cache *f*

hoarfrost ('hɔ:frɔst) *n* givre *m*

hoarse (hɔ:s) *adj* enroué, rauque

hoax (houks) *n* mystification *f* mauvais tour *m*

hobble ('hɔbəl) *vi* boitiller *vt* entraver *n* boitillement *m*.

hobby ('hɔbi) *n* passe-temps *m*.

hock¹ (hɔk) *n* jarret *m*.

hock² (hɔk) *n* vin du Rhin *m*.

hockey ('hɔki) *n* hockey *m*.

hoe (hou) *n* houe *f* *vt* sarcler.

hog (hɔg) *n* **1** porc *m*. **2** *inf* goinfre *m* *vt inf* monopoliser

hoist (hɔist) *n* treuil *m* *vt* hisser.

hold¹ (hould) *vt,vi* tenir *vt* **1** contenir **2** avoir, posséder. **3** retenir **hold back** retenir. **hold on** tenir ferme, s'accrocher **hold out** tendre ~*n* prise *f* **holdall** *n* fourre-tout *m invar* **holder** *n* **1** détenteur *m* **2** propriétaire *m* **3** récipient *m*

hold² (hould) *n naut* cale *f*.

hole (houl) *n* **1** trou, creux *m*. **2** orifice *m* *vt* trouer. *vi* se trouer.

holiday ('hɔlidi) *n* **1** jour férié, congé *m*. **2** *pl* vacances *f pl*. **holiday-maker** *n* estivant *m*.

Holland ('hɔlənd) *n* Hollande *f*.

hollow ('hɔlou) *adj* **1** creux, creuse **2** sourd *adv* creux *n* **1** creux *m* **2** vallon *m*. *vt* creuser

holly ('hɔli) *n* houx *m* **hollyhock** *n* rose trémière *f*.

holster ('houlstə) *n* étui *m*.

holy ('houli) *adj* saint, sacré.

Holy Ghost *n* Saint-Esprit *m*.

homage ('hɔmidʒ) *n* hommage *m*.

home (houm) *n* **1** logis, foyer *m* maison *f* **2** patrie *f* **3** hospice *m* *adv* à la maison, de retour *adj* **1** familial, -aux, domestique **2** *pol* intérieur. **homecoming** *n* retour *m* **home help** *n* aide ménagère *f* **homeland** *n* patrie *f*. **homesick** *adj* nostalgique **homesickness** *n* mal du pays *m* nostalgie *f* **homework** *n* devoirs (du soir) *m pl*.

homonym ('hɔmənim) *n* homonyme *m*

homosexual (houmə'sekʃuəl) *adj,n* homosexuel, -elle.

honest ('ɔnist) *adj* **1** honnête **2** sincère **honesty** *n* honnêteté, probité *f*.

honey ('hʌni) *n* miel *m* **honeycomb** *n* rayon de miel *m* **honeymoon** *n* lune de miel *f* **honeysuckle** *n* chèvrefeuille *m*.

honour ('ɔnə) *vt* **1** honorer. **2** faire honneur à *n* **1** honneur *m*. **2** distinction *f* **His** *or* **Your Honour** Monsieur le juge, Monsieur le président **honorary** *adj* **1** honoraire **2** honorifique

hood (hud) *n* **1** capuchon *m* **2** *mot* capote *f*

hoof (hu:f) *n, pl* **hooves** sabot *m*

hook (huk) *n* **1** crochet, croc *m* agrafe *f* **2** (in angling) hameçon *m* *vt* **1** accrocher **2** agrafer **3** attraper

hooligan ('hu:ligən) *n* voyou *m*

hoop (hu:p) *n* **1** cercle, cerceau, -aux *m* **2** *sport* arceau, -aux *m*

hoot (hu:t) *vi* **1** huer **2** *mot* klaxonner *n* **1** huée *f*. **2** klaxonnement *m* **hooter** *n* klaxon *m*.

hop¹ (hɔp) *n* saut, sautillement *m* *vi* sautiller, sauter

hop² (hɔp) *n bot* houblon *m*

hope (houp) *n* **1** espérance *f*. **2** espoir *m* *vi,vt* espérer *vt* s'attendre à. **hopeful** *adj* plein d'espoir **hopeless** *adj* **1** sans espoir **2** vain

horde (hɔ:d) *n* horde *f*

horizon (hə'raɪzən) n horizon m. **horizontal** adj horizontal, -aux.

hormone ('hɔːmoun) n hormone f.

horn (hɔːn) n **1** corne f. **2** mus cor m. trompe f.

hornet ('hɔːnit) n frelon m.

horoscope ('hɔrəskoup) n horoscope m.

horrible ('hɔrəbl) adj horrible, épouvantable.

horrid ('hɔrid) adj horrible, affreux, -euse.

horrify ('hɔrifai) vt horrifier.

horror ('hɔrə) n horreur f.

hors d'oeuvres (ɔː 'dəːv) n pl hors d'œuvre m invar.

horse (hɔːs) n cheval, -aux m. adj hippique. **on horseback** adv à cheval. **horse chestnut** n marron d'Inde m. **horse chestnut tree** n marronnier d'Inde m. **horsefly** n taon m. **horseman** n cavalier, chevalier m. **horsepower** n cheval-vapeur m. **horseradish** n raifort m. **horseshoe** n fer à cheval m.

horticulture ('hɔːtikʌltʃə) n horticulture f. **horticultural** adj horticole.

hose (houz) n **1** tuyau, -aux m. **2** bas m.

hosiery ('houziəri) n bonneterie f.

hospitable ('hɔspitəbəl) adj accueillant, hospitalier, -ière.

hospital ('hɔspitl) n hôpital, -aux m.

hospitality (hɔspi'tæliti) n hospitalité f.

host [1] (houst) n **1** hôte m. **2** hôtelier m.

host [2] (houst) n foule, armée f.

hostage ('hɔstidʒ) n otage m.

hostel ('hɔstl) n pension f. foyer m.

hostess ('houstis) n hôtesse f.

hostile ('hɔstail) adj hostile, opposé. **hostility** n hostilité, animosité f.

hot (hɔt) adj **1** chaud. **2** ardent. **3** violent. **4** cul épicé. **5** inf intenable. **hotplate** n chauffe-plat m. **hotpot** n ragoût m. **hot-tempered** adj emporté, vif, vive. **hot-water bottle** n bouillotte f.

hotel (hou'tel) n hôtel m.

hound (haund) n **1** chien de chasse m. **2** pl meute f. équipage m. vt chasser, poursuivre.

hour (auə) n heure f. **hourly** adj à chaque heure. adv toutes les heures.

house (n haus; v hauz) n **1** maison f. **2** Th salle f. vt loger, héberger.

houseboat ('hausbout) n péniche (aménagée en habitation) f.

housebound ('hausbaund) adj reclus.

household ('haushould) n famille f. ménage m. adj domestique.

housekeeper ('hauskiːpə) n concierge, ménagère f. **housekeeping** n ménage m.

housemaid ('hausmeid) n bonne f.

House of Commons n Chambre des Communes f.

House of Lords n Chambre des Lords f.

houseproud ('hauspraud) adj fier de son intérieur.

housewife ('hauswaif) n ménagère f.

housework ('hauswəːk) n travaux domestiques m pl.

housing (hauziŋ) n logement m. **housing estate** n cité f.

hover ('hɔvə) vi **1** planer. **2** rôder. **hovercraft** n aéroglisseur m.

how (hau) adv comment, comme. **how do you do?** comment allez-vous? **how much** or **many?** combien? **however** conj cependant. adv de quelque manière que.

howl (haul) n hurlement m. vi hurler.

hub (hʌb) n **1** moyeu, -eux m. **2** centre m.

huddle ('hʌdl) n ramassis m. vt **1** entasser, fourrer. **2** confondre. vi se presser.

huff (hʌf) vt souffler. **be in a huff** être fâché.

hug (hʌg) n étreinte f. vt embrasser.

huge (hjuːdʒ) adj énorme, vaste.

hulk (hʌlk) n **1** naut carcasse f. **2** inf lourdaud m. **hulking** adj lourd, gros, grosse.

hull [1] (hʌl) n cosse, gousse f. vt écosser.

hull [2] (hʌl) n naut coque f.

hullo (hə'lou) interj see **hello.**

hum (hʌm) n bourdonnement m. vi bourdonner. vt fredonner.

human ('hjuːmən) n être humain m. adj humain. **human nature** n nature humaine f. **humane** adj humain, compatissant. **humanism** n humanisme m.

humanity (hjuː'mæniti) n humanité f. **humanitarian** adj,n humanitaire.

humble ('hʌmbəl) adj **1** humble. **2** modeste. vt humilier. **humbly** adv avec humilité, pauvrement.

humdrum ('hʌmdrʌm) adj monotone.

humid ('hjuːmid) adj humide.

humiliate (hjuː'milieit) vt humilier. **humiliation** n affront m.

humility (hjuː'militi) n humilité f.

humour ('hjuːmə) n **1** humeur, disposition f. **2** humour m. vt ménager. **humorist** n comique, humoriste m. **humorous** adj humoristique, comique.

hump (hʌmp) n bosse f. vt arquer.

hunch (hʌntʃ) n **1** bosse f. **2** inf pressentiment m. vt arrondir. **hunchback** n bossu m.

hundred ('hʌndrəd) adj cent. n **1** cent m. **2**

centaine f. **hundredth** adj centième. **hundredweight** n quintal, -aux m.

hung (hʌŋ) v see **hang.**

Hungary (ˈhʌŋgəri) n Hongrie f. **Hungarian** adj,n hongrois. **Hungarian** (language) n hongrois m.

hunger (ˈhʌŋgə) n faim f. vi avoir faim. **hunger for** désirer. **hunger-strike** n grève de la faim f. **hungrily** adv voracement. **hungry** adj 1 affamé. 2 avide. **be hungry** avoir faim.

hunt (hʌnt) n 1 chasse f. 2 recherche f. vt chasser. **hunting** n chasse f. **huntsman** n chasseur, veneur m.

hurdle (ˈhəːdl) n 1 sport claie f. 2 obstacle m. vt,vi sauter.

hurl (həːl) vt jeter, lancer.

hurrah (huˈrɑː) interj hourra!

hurricane (ˈhʌrikein) n ouragan m.

hurry (ˈhʌri) vi se dépêcher. se hâter. vt presser. n hâte. **be in a hurry** être pressé. **hurried** adj précipité.

hurt (həːt) vt 1 faire mal à. 2 blesser. vi faire mal. n 1 mal m. 2 tort m.

husband (ˈhʌzbənd) n mari m.

hush (hʌʃ) vt 1 calmer. 2 étouffer. vi se taire. interj chut! n calme m.

husk (hʌsk) n cosse, gousse f. vt décortiquer.

husky (ˈhʌski) adj enroué.

hussar (huˈzɑː) n hussard m.

hustle (ˈhʌsəl) vt bousculer. vi se dépêcher. n 1 activité f. 2 bousculade f.

hut (hʌt) n hutte f.

hutch (hʌtʃ) n 1 huche f. 2 clapier m.

hyacinth (ˈhaiəsinθ) n jacinthe f.

hybrid (ˈhaibrid) adj,n hybride m.

hydraulic (haiˈdrɔːlik) adj hydraulique.

hydro-electric (haidrouiˈlektrik) adj hydroélectrique. **hydro-electric power** n énergie hydroélectrique f.

hydrogen (ˈhaidrədʒən) n hydrogène m.

hyena (haiˈiːnə) n hyène f.

hygiene (ˈhaidʒiːn) n hygiène f. **hygienic** adj hygiénique.

hymn (him) n hymne f. cantique m. **hymnbook** n hymnaire m.

hyphen (ˈhaifən) n trait d'union m.

hypnosis (hipˈnousis) n, pl **-ses** hypnose f. **hypnotism** n hypnotisme m.

hypochondria (haipəˈkɔndriə) n hypocondrie f. **hypochondriac** adj,n hypocondriaque.

hypocrisy (hiˈpɔkrəsi) n hypocrisie f. **hypocrite** n hypocrite m,f. **hypocritical** adj hypocrite.

hypodermic (haipəˈdəːmik) adj hypodermique.

hypothesis (haiˈpɔθəsis) n, pl **-ses** hypothese f. **hypothetical** adj hypothétique.

hysterectomy (histəˈrektəmi) n hystérectomie f.

hysteria (hisˈtiəriə) n hystérie f. **hysterical** adj 1 med hystérique. 2 énervé. **hysterics** n pl crise de nerfs f.

I

I (ai) pron 1st pers s 1 je. 2 moi.

Iberia (aiˈbiəriə) n Ibérie f. **Iberian** adj,n ibérien, -ienne.

ice (ais) n glace f. vt 1 geler. 2 cul glacer. 3 (champagne, etc.) frapper. **iceberg** n iceberg m. **ice-cream** n glace f. **ice-cube** n glaçon m. **ice hockey** n hockey sur glace m. **ice rink** n patinoire f. **ice-skate** n patin (à glace) m. **icicle** n glaçon m. **icing** n 1 cul glacé m. 2 glaçage m. **icy** adj 1 glacial. 2 verglacé.

Iceland (ˈaislənd) n Islande f. **Icelander** n islandais m. **Icelandic** adj islandais. **Icelandic** (language) n islandais m.

icon (ˈaikɔn) n icone f.

idea (aiˈdiə) n idée f.

ideal (aiˈdiəl) adj,n idéal, -aux m. **idealistic** adj idéaliste. **idealize** vt idéaliser.

identify (aiˈdentifai) vt identifier.

identity (aiˈdentiti) n identité f. **identity card** n carte d'identité f. **identical** adj identique. **identical twins** n pl vrais jumeaux m pl.

ideology (aidiˈɔlədʒi) n idéologie f.

idiom (ˈidiəm) n idiome m.

idiosyncrasy (idiəˈsiŋkrəsi) n idiosyncrasie f.

idiot (ˈidiət) n idiot m. **idiotic** adj idiot, bête.

idle (ˈaidl) adj 1 oisif, -ive, paresseux, -euse. 2 futile. vi fainéanter. **idleness** n oisiveté f.

idol (ˈaidl) n idole f. **idolatry** n idolâtrie f. **idolize** vt idolâtrer.

idyllic (iˈdilik) adj idyllique.

if (if) conj si. **as if** comme si. **if not** sinon.

ignite (igˈnait) vt allumer. vi prendre feu. **ignition** n 1 allumage m. 2 mot contact m.

ignorant (ˈignərənt) adj ignorant.

ignore (igˈnɔː) vt ne tenir aucun compte de.

ill (il) adj 1 malade. 2 mauvais. n 1 mal, maux m. 2 tort m. adv mal. **ill-bred** adj mal élevé. **illness** n maladie f.

illegal (iˈliːgəl) adj illégal, -aux.

illegible (iˈledʒəbəl) adj illisible.

illegitimate (iliˈdʒitimət) adj illégitime.

illicit (iˈlisit) adj illicite.

illiterate (iˈlitərət) adj,n illettré, analphabète.

illogical (i'lɔdʒikəl) *adj* illogique.
illuminate (i'luːmineit) *vt* **1** illuminer. **2** éclaircir. **illumination** *n* illumination *f*. éclairage *m*.
illusion (i'luːʒən) *n* illusion *f*.
illustrate ('iləstreit) *vt* **1** illustrer. **2** expliquer. **illustration** *n* **1** illustration *f*. **2** exemple *m*.
illustrious (i'lʌstriəs) *adj* illustre.
image ('imidʒ) *n* image *f*. **imagery** ·*n* images *f pl.*
imagine (i'mædʒin) *vt* **1** s'imaginer. **2** croire. **imaginary** *adj* imaginaire. **imagination** *n* imagination *f*. **imaginative** *adj* imaginatif, -ive.
imitate ('imiteit) *vt* imiter. **imitation** *n* **1** imitation *f*. **2** *comm* contrefaçon *f*.
immaculate (i'mækjulət) *adj* **1** immaculé. **2** impeccable.
immature (imə'tjuə) *adj* **1** pas mûr. **2** prématuré.
immediate (i'miːdiət) *adj* immédiat, direct, proche.
immense (i'mens) *adj* immense, énorme.
immerse (i'məːs) *vt* immerger.
immigrate ('imigreit) *vi* immigrer. **immigrant** *adj,n* immigrant. **immigration** *n* immigration *f*.
imminent ('iminənt) *adj* imminent.
immobile (i'moubail) *adj* **1** immobile. **2** fixe.
immoral (i'mɔrəl) *adj* **1** immoral, -aux. **2** (of a person) dissolu. **immorality** *n* **1** immoralité *f*. **2** débauche *f*.
immortal (i'mɔːtl) *adj* immortel, -elle. **immortality** *n* immortalité *f*.
immovable (i'muːvəbəl) *adj* **1** fixe. **2** immuable.
immune (i'mjuːn) *adj* immunisé, vacciné. **immune from** à l'abri de. **immunity** *n* **1** exemption *f*. **2** immunité *f*. **immunization** *n* immunisation *f*. **immunize** *vt* immuniser.
imp (imp) *n* diablotin *m*.
impact ('impækt) *n* **1** impact, choc *m*. **2** effet *m*.
impair (im'pɛə) *vt* affaiblir, abîmer.
impart (im'pɑːt) *vt* **1** communiquer. **2** faire part de.
impartial (im'pɑːʃəl) *adj* impartial, -aux.
impatient (im'peiʃənt) *adj* impatient. **get impatient** s'impatienter.
impeach (im'piːtʃ) *vt* **1** accuser. **2** contester. **impeachment** *n* accusation *f*.
impediment (im'pedimənt) *n* empêchement *m*.
impel (im'pel) *vt* pousser, forcer.
imperative (im'perativ) *adj* **1** impérieux, -euse. **2** urgent. *n gram* impératif *m*.
imperfect (im'pəːfikt) *adj,n* imparfait *m*.

imperial (im'piəriəl) *adj* impérial, -aux. **imperialism** *n* impérialisme *m*.
impersonal (im'pəːsənl) *adj* impersonnel, -elle.
impersonate (im'pəːsəneit) *vt* **1** personnifier. **2** *Th* représenter.
impertinent (im'pəːtinənt) *adj* impertinent, insolent. **impertinence** *n* impertinence *f*.
impetuous (im'petʃuəs) *adj* impétueux, -euse, fougueux, -euse.
impetus ('impitəs) *n* élan *m*. impulsion *f*.
impinge (im'pindʒ) ·*vi* **impinge on** empiéter sur.
implement (*n* 'impləmənt; *v* 'impləment) *n* instrument, outil *m*. *vt* exécuter.
implicit (im'plisit) *adj* **1** implicite. **2** sans réserve.
implore (im'plɔː) *vt* implorer.
imply (im'plai) *vt* **1** impliquer, supposer. **2** insinuer. **implied** *adj* tacite, sous-entendu.
import (*v* im'pɔːt; *n* 'impɔːt) *vt* **1** *comm* importer. **2** signifier. *n* **1** sens *m*. **2** importance *f*. **3** *pl* importations *f pl.*
importance (im'pɔːtns) *n* importance *f*. **important** *adj* important.
impose (im'pouz) *vt* imposer. **impose upon** en imposer à. **imposing** *adj* imposant. **imposition** *n* **1** imposition *f*. **2** abus *m*.
impossible (im'posəbəl) *adj* impossible.
impostor (im'postə) *n* imposteur *m*.
impotent ('impətənt) *adj* impuissant. **impotence** *n* impuissance *f*.
impound (im'paund) *vt* **1** enfermer. **2** confisquer.
impoverish (im'povəriʃ) *vt* appauvrir.
impress (im'pres) *vt* **1** imprimer. **2** impressionner. *n* empreinte *f*. **impression** *n* impression *f*. **impressive** *adj* impressionnant.
imprint (*n* 'imprint; *v* im'print) *n* empreinte *f*. *vt* imprimer.
imprison (im'prizən) *vt* emprisonner. **imprisonment** *n* emprisonnement *m*.
improbable (im'probabəl) *adj* invraisemblable.
impromptu (im'promptjuː) *adj* improvisé. *adv* impromptu.
improper (im'propə) *adj* **1** malséant. **2** impropre.
improve (im'pruːv) *vt* améliorer, perfectionner. *vi* s'améliorer, se perfectionner. **improvement** *n* amélioration *f*. progrès *m*.
improvise ('imprəvaiz) *vt,vi* improviser. **improvisation** *n* improvisation *f*.
impudent ('impjudənt) *adj* insolent, impudent. **impudence** *n* impudence *f*.

impulse (´impʌls) n 1 impulsion f. 2 poussée f. **impulsive** adj impulsif, -ive.

impure (im´pjuə) adj impur. **impurity** n impureté f.

in (in) prep 1 en, à, dans, de. 2 sur, par. adv 1 chez soi, y, là. 2 dedans.

inability (inə´biliti) n incapacité f.

inaccurate (in´ækjurət) adj inexact, incorrect.

inadequate (in´ædikwit) adj inadéquat, insuffisant. **inadequacy** n insuffisance f.

inadvertent (inəd´və:tnt) adj 1 involontaire. 2 inattentif, -ive. **inadvertently** adv par inadvertance.

inane (i´nein) adj inepte, niais.

inarticulate (ina:´tikjulət) adj inarticulé.

inasmuch (inəz´mʌtʃ) conj **inasmuch as** attendu or vu que.

inaudible (in´ɔ:dəbəl) adj imperceptible.

inaugurate (i´nɔ:gjureit) vt inaugurer. **inauguration** n inauguration f.

incapable (in´keipəbəl) adj incapable, incompétent.

incendiary (in´sendiəri) adj incendiaire.

incense[1] (´insens) n encens m. vt encenser.

incense[2] (in´sens) vt exaspérer, courroucer.

incessant (in´sesənt) adj incessant.

incest (´insest) n inceste m. **incestuous** adj incestueux, -euse.

inch (intʃ) n pouce m. **inch by inch** petit à petit. ~vi avancer petit à petit.

incident (´insidənt) n incident m. **incidental** adj 1 fortuit. 2 accessoire.

incite (in´sait) vt inciter.

incline (in´klain) vt incliner, pencher. vi s´incliner. n pente f. **inclination** n 1 pente f. 2 penchant m. tendance f.

include (in´klu:d) vt inclure, comprendre. **inclusive** adj 1 global, -aux. 2 inclus.

incognito (inkɔg´ni:tou) adv incognito.

incoherent (inkou´hiərənt) adj incohérent.

income (´inkʌm) n revenu m. **income tax** n impôt sur le revenu m. **income tax return** déclaration de revenu f. **private income** rente f.

incompatible (inkəm´pætibəl) adj incompatible.

incompetent (in´kɔmpətənt) adj incompétent.

incomprehensible (inkɔmpr´hensibəl) adj incompréhensible.

inconclusive (inkən´klu:siv) adj peu concluant.

incongruous (in´kɔŋgruəs) adj incongru, déplacé.

inconsiderate (inkən´sidərit) adj 1 irréfléchi. 2 sans égards.

inconsistent (inkən´sistənt) adj 1 incompatible. 2 illogique. 3 incongru. **inconsistency** n 1 disparité f. 2 contradiction f.

inconspicuous (inkənspikjuəs) adj effacé, discret, -ète.

inconvenient (inkən´vi:niənt) adj incommode, inopportun.

incorporate (in´kɔ:pəreit) vt 1 incorporer. 2 comm réunir. vi s´incorporer.

incorrect (inkə´rekt) adj inexact, incorrect.

increase (v in´kri:s; n ´inkri:s) vi 1 augmenter. 2 s´accroître. vt accroître, augmenter. n augmentation f. **increasing** adj croissant.

incredible (in´kredəbəl) adj incroyable.

incubate (´inkjubeit) vt,vi couver. **incubator** n couveuse f.

incur (in´kə:) vt 1 (expenses) courir, faire. 2 encourir.

indecent (in´di:sənt) adj indécent.

indeed (in´di:d) adv en effet, vraiment, à vrai dire.

indefinite (in´defənit) adj 1 indéfini. 2 illimité.

indent (in´dent) vt denteler.

independent (indi´pendənt) adj indépendant. **independence** n indépendance f.

index (´indeks) n pl **-dexes** or **-dices** 1 (of a book) répertoire m. 2 indice, signe m. vt classer. **index finger** n index m.

India (´indiə) n Inde f. **Indian** adj,n indien, -ienne.

indicate (´indikeit) vt indiquer. **indication** n signe m. **indicator** n indicateur m.

indifferent (in´difrənt) adj 1 indifférent. 2 médiocre.

indigestion (indi´dʒestʃən) n indigestion f.

indignant (in´dignənt) adj indigné. **be indignant** s´indigner.

indirect (indi´rekt) adj 1 indirect. 2 détourné.

indiscriminate (indi´skriminit) adj aveugle.

individual (indi´vidʒuəl) n individu m. adj 1 particulier, -ière. 2 original, -aux.

indoctrinate (in´dɔktrineit) vt endoctriner.

indolent (´indələnt) adj indolent, paresseux, -euse.

indoor (´indɔ:) adj 1 d´intérieur. 2 de société. **indoors** adv à la maison, à l´intérieur.

induce (in´dju:s) vt 1 induire. 2 causer. 3 provoquer. **inducement** n encouragement m.

indulge (in´dʌldʒ) vt satisfaire. **indulge in** s´adonner à. **indulgence** n indulgence f.

industry (´indəstri) n 1 industrie f. 2 diligence f. **industrial** adj industriel, -elle. **industrious** adj assidu, industrieux, -euse.

inefficient (ini'fiʃənt) *adj* 1 inefficace. 2 incapable.

inept (i'nept) *adj* 1 inepte. 2 déplacé.

inequality (ini'kwɔliti) *n* inégalité *f*.

inert (i'nɔːt) *adj* inerte. **inertia** *n* inertie *f*.

inevitable (in'evitəbəl) *adj* inévitable, fatal.

infallible (in'fæləbəl) *adj* infaillible.

infamous ('infəməs) *adj* infâme.

infancy ('infənsi) *n* 1 enfance *f*. bas âge *m*. 2 débuts *m pl*.

infant ('infənt) *n* 1 enfant (en bas âge) *m,f*. 2 *law* mineur *m*. **infantile** *adj* enfantin.

infantry ('infəntri) *n* infanterie *f*.

infatuate (in'fætʃueit) *vt* 1 enticher. 2 affoler. **be infatuated with** s'enticher de. **infatuation** *n* engouement *m*.

infect (in'fekt) *vt* 1 *med* contaminer. 2 infecter. **infection** *n* 1 *med* contamination *f*. 2 infection *f*.

infer (in'fɔː) *vt* 1 impliquer. 2 déduire.

inferior (in'fiəriə) *adj,n* inférieur *m*. **inferiority** *n* infériorité *f*.

infernal (in'fɔːnļ) *adj* infernal, -aux.

infest (in'fest) *vt* infester.

infidelity (infi'deliti) *n* infidélité, déloyauté *f*.

infiltrate ('infiltreit) *vt* infiltrer. *vi* s'infiltrer.

infinite ('infinit) *adj* infini. **infinitely** *adv* infiniment. **infinity** *n* infinité *f*.

infinitive (in'finitiv) *adj,n* infinitif, -ive *m*.

infirm (in'fɔːm) *adj* infirme.

inflame (in'fleim) *vt* enflammer. *vi* s'enflammer.

inflammable (in'flæməbəl) *adj* inflammable.

inflate (in'fleit) *vt* 1 gonfler. 2 *comm* faire monter. **inflation** *n* inflation *f*.

inflection (in'flekʃən) *n* inflexion *f*.

inflict (in'flikt) *vt* 1 infliger. 2 occasionner.

influence ('influəns) *n* influence *f*. *vt* 1 influencer. 2 influer sur. **influential** *adj* influent.

influenza (influ'enzə) *n* grippe *f*.

influx ('inflʌks) *n* affluence *f*.

inform (in'fɔːm) *vt* informer, renseigner. **information** *n* renseignements *m pl*. avis *m*. **piece of information** renseignement *m*. **informer** *n* mouchard, dénonciateur *m*.

informal (in'fɔːməl) *adj* sans cérémonie, familier, -ère.

infringe (in'frindʒ) *vt* enfreindre. *vi* empiéter. **infringement** *n* infraction *f*.

infuriate (in'fjuərieit) *vt* rendre furieux, exaspérer.

ingenious (in'dʒiːniəs) *adj* ingénieux, -euse.

ingredient (in'griːdiənt) *n* ingrédient, élément *m*.

inhabit (in'hæbit) *vt* habiter. **inhabitant** *n* habitant *m*.

inhale (in'heil) *vt* 1 inhaler. 2 inspirer.

inherent (in'hiərənt) *adj* inhérent, propre.

inherit (in'herit) *vt* hériter de. **inheritance** *n* 1 héritage *m*. 2 succession *f*.

inhibit (in'hibit) *vt* 1 inhiber, empêcher. 2 prohiber. **inhibition** *n* 1 inhibition *f*. 2 prohibition *f*.

inhuman (in'hjuːmən) *adj* inhumain. **inhumanity** *n* cruauté *f*.

initial (i'niʃəl) *adj* premier, initial, -aux. *n* initiale *f*. *vt* parafer.

initiate (i'niʃieit) *vt* 1 commencer, lancer. 2 initier. **initiation** *n* 1 début *m*. 2 initiation *f*.

initiative (i'niʃətiv) *n* initiative *f*.

inject (in'dʒekt) *vt* injecter. **injection** *n* injection, piqûre *f*.

injure ('indʒə) *vt* 1 blesser. 2 endommager. **injury** *n* 1 blessure *f*. 2 tort *m*.

injustice (in'dʒʌstis) *n* injustice *f*.

ink (iŋk) *n* encre *f*.

inkling ('iŋkliŋ) *n* soupçon *m*.

inland (*adj* 'inlənd; *n,adv* 'inlænd) *adj,n* intérieur *m*. *adv* à l'intérieur. **Inland Revenue** *n* fisc *m*.

inmate ('inmeit) *n* 1 pensionnaire *m*. 2 prisonnier, -ière.

inn (in) *n* auberge *f*.

innate (i'neit) *adj* inné.

inner ('inə) *adj* intérieur, interne.

innocent ('inəsənt) *adj* 1 innocent. 2 naïf, -ive. **innocence** *n* 1 innocence *f*. 2 naïveté *f*.

innocuous (i'nɔkjuəs) *adj* inoffensif, -ive.

innovation (inə'veiʃən) *n* innovation *f*.

innuendo (inju'endou) *n* insinuation *f*.

inoculate (i'nɔkjuleit) *vt* inoculer, vacciner. **inoculation** *n* inoculation *f*.

input ('input) *n* entrée, consommation *f*.

inquest ('inkwest) *n* enquête *f*.

inquire (in'kwaiə) *vt* demander. *vi* s'enquérir, se renseigner. **inquiry** *n* 1 demande de renseignements *f*. 2 enquête *f*.

inquisition (inkwi'ziʃən) *n* 1 investigation *f*. 2 *cap* Inquisition *f*.

inquisitive (in'kwizitiv) *adj* curieux, -euse.

insane (in'sein) *adj* 1 fou, folle. 2 insensé. **insanity** *n* folie, démence *f*.

insatiable (in'seiʃəbəl) *adj* insatiable.

inscribe (in'skraib) *vt* inscrire, graver. **inscription** *n* inscription *f*.

insect ('insekt) *n* insecte *m*.
insecure (insi'kjuə) *adj* **1** incertain. **2** peu solide.
inseminate (in'semineit) *vt* inséminer. **insemination** *n* insémination *f*.
insert (in'sə:t) *vt* **1** insérer. **2** introduire. **insertion** *n* insertion *f*.
inside (in'said) *adj* intérieur. *adv* à l'intérieur. *prep* à l'intérieur de. *n* dedans, intérieur *m*. **on the inside** au dedans.
insidious (in'sidiəs) *adj* insidieux, -euse.
insight ('insait) *n* **1** perspicacité *f*. **2** aperçu *m*.
insinuate (in'sinjueit) *vt* insinuer.
insist (in'sist) *vi* insister. **insistence** *n* insistance *f*.
insolent ('insələnt) *adj* insolent.
insomnia (in'sɔmniə) *n* insomnie *f*.
inspect (in'spekt) *vt* inspecter, examiner. **inspection** *n* inspection *f*. contrôle *m*. **inspector** *n* inspecteur *m*.
inspire (in'spaiə) *vt* inspirer. **inspiration** *n* inspiration *f*.
instability (instə'biliti) *n* instabilité *f*.
install (in'stɔ:l) *vt* installer.
instalment (in'stɔ:lmənt) *n* **1** versement partiel *m*. **2** (of a serial) épisode *m*.
instance ('instəns) *n* **1** exemple, cas *m*. **2** instance *f*. **for instance** par exemple. **instant** *n* instant *m*. *adj* **1** immédiat. **2** courant. **3** urgent. **instantaneous** *adj* instantané.
instead (in'sted) **instead of** *prep* au lieu de. *adv* à la place.
instep ('instep) *n* **1** *anat* cou-de-pied *m*. **2** cambrure *f*.
instigate ('instigeit) *vt* inciter, provoquer.
instil (in'stil) *vt* inculquer.
instinct ('instiŋkt) *n* instinct *m*. **instinctive** *adj* instinctif, -ive.
institute ('institju:t) *n* institut *m*. *vt* instituer. **institution** *n* institution *f*. établissement *m*.
instruct (in'strʌkt) *vt* **1** instruire. **2** charger. **instruction** *n* **1** instruction *f*. **2** *pl* ordres *m pl*.
instrument ('instrumənt) *n* instrument *m*. **instrumental** *adj* **1** contributif, -ive. **2** *mus* instrumental, -aux.
insubordinate (insə'bɔ:dinət) *adj* insubordonné.
insular ('insjulə) *adj* **1** insulaire. **2** borné.
insulate ('insjuleit) *vt* **1** isoler. **2** calorifuger. **insulation** *n* isolement *m*.
insulin ('insjulin) *n* insuline *f*.
insult (*v* in'sʌlt; *n* 'insʌlt) *vt* insulter. *n* insulte *f*. affront *m*.
insure (in'ʃuə) *vt* assurer. **insurance** *n* assurance *f*.

intact (in'tækt) *adj* intact, indemne.
intake ('inteik) *n* **1** consommation *f*. **2** prise *f*. **3** admission *f*.
integral ('intigrəl) *adj* intégrant.
integrate ('intigreit) *vt* intégrer, compléter.
integrity (in'tegriti) *n* intégrité *f*.
intellect ('intəlekt) *n* intelligence *f*. esprit *m*. **intellectual** *adj,n* intellectuel, -elle.
intelligent (in'telidʒənt) *adj* intelligent. **intelligence** *n* **1** intelligence *f*. **2** renseignements *m pl*.
intelligible (in'telidʒəbəl) *adj* intelligible.
intend (in'tend) *vt* **1** avoir l'intention. **2** destiner.
intense (in'tens) *adj* intense, profond. **intensify** *vt* intensifier. *vi* s'accroître. **intensity** *n* intensité *f*. **intensive** *adj* intensif, -ive.
intent[1] (in'tent) *n* intention *f*. dessein *m*.
intent[2] (in'tent) *adj* **1** absorbé. **2** résolu. **3** acharné. **4** sérieux, -euse.
intention (in'tenʃən) *n* intention *f*. **intentional** *adj* voulu. **intentionally** *adv* exprès.
inter (in'tə:) *vt* enterrer.
interact (intə'rækt) *vi* agir l'un sur l'autre.
intercept (intə'sept) *vt* intercepter, arrêter en passage.
interchange (intə'tʃeindʒ) *vt* échanger. *vi* s'interchanger. *n* **1** échange *m*. **2** succession *f*.
intercourse ('intəkɔ:s) *n* commerce *m*. rapports *m pl*.
interest ('intrəst) *n* **1** intérêt *m*. **2** avantage *m*. *vt* intéresser. **be interested in** s'intéresser à.
interfere (intə'fiə) *vi* s'ingérer, s'immiscer. **interference** *n* **1** intervention *f*. **2** *tech* parasites *m pl*. **interfering** *adj* importun.
interim ('intərim) *adj* intérimaire. *n* intérim *m*.
interior (in'tiəriə) *adj,n* intérieur *m*.
interjection (intə'dʒekʃn) *n* interjection *f*.
interlude ('intəlu:d) *n* intermède *m*.
intermediate (intə'mi:diət) *adj* intermédiaire. **intermediary** *adj,n* intermédiaire *m*.
intermission (intə'miʃən) *n* **1** interruption *f*. **2** (cinema) entracte *m*.
intermittent (intə'mitnt) *adj* intermittent.
intern (in'tə:n) *vt* interner.
internal (in'tə:nl) *adj,n* intérieur, interne.
international (intə'næʃnl) *adj* international, -aux.
internment (in'tə:nmənt) *n* internement *m*.
interpose (intə'pouz) *vt* interposer. *vi* s'interposer.
interpret (in'tə:prit) *vt* interpréter. **interpretation** *n* interprétation *f*. **interpreter** *n* interprète *m,f*.

interrogate (in'terəgeit) *vt* questionner, interroger. **interrogation** *n* **1** interrogation *f*. **2** *law* interrogatoire *m*. **interrogative** *adj* **1** interrogateur, -trice. **2** *gram* interrogatif, -ive.

interrupt (intə'rʌpt) *vt* interrompre. **interruption** *n* interruption *f*.

intersect (intə'sekt) *vt* entrecouper. *vi* se couper. **intersection 1** intersection *f*. **2** *mot* carrefour *m*.

interval ('intəvəl) *n* **1** intervalle *m*. **2** *Th* entracte *m*.

intervene (intə'vi:n) *vi* **1** intervenir. **2** survenir. **intervention** *n* intervention *f*.

interview ('intəvju:) *n* entrevue, interview *f*. *vt* interviewer.

intestine (in'testin) *n* intestin *m*.

intimate[1] ('intimit) *adj* intime. **intimacy** *n* intimité *f*.

intimate[2] ('intimeit) *vt* suggérer, intimer.

intimidate (in'timideit) *vt* intimider. **intimidation** *n* **1** intimidation *f*. **2** *law* menaces *f pl*.

into ('intə; *stressed* 'intu:) *prep* dans, en, à.

intolerable (in'tɔlərəbəl) *adj* intolérable, insupportable. **intolerant** *adj* intolérant.

intonation (intə'neiʃən) *n* **1** intonation *f*. **2** ton *m*.

intoxicate (in'tɔksikeit) *vt* enivrer. **intoxicated** *adj* ivre. **intoxication** *n* **1** intoxication *f*. **2** ivresse *f*.

intransitive (in'trænsitiv) *adj* intransitif, -ive.

intrepid (in'trepid) *adj* intrépide.

intricate ('intrikət) *adj* **1** compliqué. **2** confus. **intricacy** *n* complexité *f*.

intrigue (in'tri:g) *n* intrigue *f*. *vt, vi* intriguer.

intrinsic (in'trinsik) *adj* intrinsèque.

introduce (intrə'dju:s) *vt* **1** introduire. **2** présenter. **introduction** *n* **1** introduction *f*. **2** présentation *f*. **3** *lit* avant-propos *m invar*.

introspective (intrə'spektiv) *adj* introspectif, -ive.

introvert ('intrəvə:t) *n* introverti *m*.

intrude (in'tru:d) *vi* faire intrusion. **intruder** *n* intrus *m*.

intuition (intju'iʃən) *n* intuition *f*. **intuitive** *adj* intuitif, -ive.

inundate ('inʌndeit) *vt* inonder.

invade (in'veid) *vt* envahir.

invalid[1] ('invəli:d) *adj,n* infirme, malade.

invalid[2] (in'vælid) *adj* nul et non avenu, périmé.

invaluable (in'væljuəbəl) *adj* inestimable.

invariable (in'vɛəriəbəl) *adj* invariable. **invariably** *adv* immanquablement.

invent (in'vent) *vt* inventer. **invention** *n* invention *f*. **inventor** *n* inventeur *m*.

inventory ('invəntəri) *n* inventaire *m*.

invert (in'və:t) *vt* **1** renverser. **2** intervertir. **inverted commas** *n pl* guillemets *m pl*.

invertebrate (in'və:təbreit) *adj,n* invertébré *m*.

invest (in'vest) *vt* **1** investir. **2** revêtir. **investment** *n* placement *m*.

investigate (in'vestigeit) *vt* **1** examiner. **2** enquêter sur.

invincible (in'vinsəbəl) *adj* invincible.

invisible (in'vizəbəl) *adj* invisible.

invite (in'vait) *vt* inviter. **invitation** *n* invitation *f*. **inviting** *adj* tentant, engageant.

invoice ('invɔis) *n* facture *f*. *vt* facturer.

invoke (in'vouk) *vt* **1** invoquer. **2** évoquer.

involve (in'vɔlv) *vt* **1** impliquer. **2** comporter. **involved** *adj* compliqué. **involvement** *n* implication *f*.

inward ('inwəd) *adj* **1** intérieur, interne. **2** vers l'intérieur. **inwards** *adv* vers l'intérieur.

iodine ('aiədi:n) *n* iode *m*.

Iran (i'ra:n) *n* Iran *m*. **Iranian** *adj,n* iranien, -ienne.

Iraq (i'ra:k) *n* Irak *m*. **Iraqi** *adj,n* irakien, -ienne.

Ireland ('aiələnd) *n* Irlande *f*. **Irish** *adj* irlandais. **Irishman** *n* irlandais *m*.

iris ('airis) *n* *anat, bot* iris *m*.

iron ('aiən) *n* **1** fer *m*. **2** *dom* fer à repasser *m*. *adj* de fer. *vt* repasser. **ironing board** *n* planche à repasser *f*. **ironmonger** *n* quincaillier *m*. **Iron Curtain** *n* Rideau de Fer *m*.

irony ('airəni) *n* ironie *f*. **ironic** *adj* ironique.

irrational (i'ræʃən|) *adj* absurde, déraisonnable.

irregular (i'regjulə) *adj* irrégulier, -ière.

irrelevant (i'reləvənt) *adj* hors de propos.

irresistible (iri'zistəbəl) *adj* irrésistible.

irrespective (iri'spektiv) *adj* indépendant. *adv* indépendamment.

irresponsible (iri'spɔnsəbəl) *adj* irresponsable.

irrevocable (i'revəkəbəl) *adj* irrévocable.

irrigate ('irigeit) *vt* irriguer. **irrigation** *n* irrigation *f*.

irritate ('iriteit) *vt* irriter. **irritating** *adj* irritant, agaçant. **irritation** *n* irritation *f*.

is (iz) *v* see **be.**

Islam ('izla:m) *n* Islam *m*. **Islamic** *adj* Islamique.

island ('ailənd) *n* **1** île *f*. **2** îlot *m*.

isle (ail) *n* île *f*.

isolate ('aisəleit) *vt* isoler. **isolation** *n* isolement *m*.

Israel (ˈizreiəl) *n* Israël *m*. **Israeli** *adj,n* israélien, -ienne.
issue (ˈiʃuː) *n* **1** sortie *f*. **2** résultat *m*. **3** (of a book, etc.) numéro *m*. **4** progéniture *f*. *vt* **1** émettre. **2** publier. **3** distribuer. *vi* sortir.
it (it) *pron 3rd pers s* **1** il *m*. elle *f*. **2** le *m*. la *f*. **3** lui *m,f*. **4** il, cela *m*.
italic (iˈtælik) *adj,n* italique *m*.
Italy (ˈitəli) *n* Italie *f*. **Italian** *adj,n* italien, -ienne. **Italian** (language) *n* italien *m*.
itch (itʃ) *n* démangeaison *f*. *vi* **1** démanger. **2** *sl* brûler.
item (ˈaitəm) *n comm* article, détail *m*. **item of news** *n* nouvelle *f*.
itinerary (aiˈtinərəri) *n* itinéraire *m*.
its (its) *poss adj 3rd pers s* son, sa, ses. **itself** *pron 3rd pers s* **1** lui-même *m*. elle-même *f*. soi-même *m,f*. **2** se *m,f*. **by itself** tout seul.
ivory (ˈaivəri) *n* ivoire *m*. *adj* en ivoire.
ivy (ˈaivi) *n* lierre *m*.

J

jab (dʒæb) *n* **1** coup de pointe *m*. **2** *inf med* piqûre *f*. *vt* **1** piquer. **2** faire une piqûre à.
jack (dʒæk) *n* **1** cric, vérin *m*. **2** *game* valet *m*.
jackal (ˈdʒækəl) *n* chacal *m*.
jackdaw (ˈdʒækdɔː) *n* choucas *m*.
jacket (ˈdʒækit) *n* **1** veste *f*. gilet *m*. **2** (for a woman) jaquette *f*. **3** (of a book) chemise *f*.
jackpot (ˈdʒækpɔt) *n* gros lot *m*.
jade (dʒeid) *n* jade *m*.
jaded (ˈdʒeidid) *adj* excédé, éreinté.
jagged (ˈdʒægid) *adj* déchiqueté, dentelé.
jaguar (ˈdʒægjuə) *n* jaguar *m*.
jail (dʒeil) *n* prison *f*. *vt* emprisonner.
jam[1] (dʒæm) *n* **1** embouteillage *m*. **2** foule *f*. *vt* bloquer, coincer. *vi* se coincer, se caler.
jam[2] (dʒæm) *n cul* confiture *f*.
Jamaica (dʒəˈmeikə) *n* Jamaïque *f*. **Jamaican** *adj,n* jamaïquain.
Jansenist (ˈdʒænsənist) *n* janséniste *m,f*.
January (ˈdʒænjuəri) *n* janvier.
Japan (dʒəˈpæn) *n* Japon *m*. **Japanese** *adj,n* japonais. **Japanese** (language) *n* japonais *m*.
jar[1] (dʒɑː) *n* pot *m*. **glass jar** bocal, -aux *m*.
jar[2] (dʒɑː) *n* **1** son discordant *m*. **2** choc *m*. secousse *f*. *vt* ébranler. *vi* **1** grincer. **2** agacer.
jargon (ˈdʒɑːgən) *n* jargon *m*.
jaundice (ˈdʒɔːndis) *n* jaunisse *f*.
jaunt (dʒɔːnt) *n* petite promenade *f*. *vi* se balader.

javelin (ˈdʒævlin) *n* javelot *m*.
jaw (dʒɔː) *n* mâchoire *f*. **jawbone** *n* mâchoire *f*.
jazz (dʒæz) *n* jazz *m*.
jealous (ˈdʒeləs) *adj* jaloux, -ouse. **jealousy** *n* jalousie *f*.
jeans (dʒiːnz) *n pl* blue-jean *m*.
jeep (dʒiːp) *n* jeep *f*.
jeer (dʒiə) *n* **1** raillerie *f*. **2** huée *f*. *vi* railler. **jeer at** se moquer de, huer. **jeering** *adj* railleur, -euse.
jelly (ˈdʒeli) *n cul* gelée *f*. **jellyfish** *n* méduse *f*.
jeopardize (ˈdʒepədaiz) *vt* mettre en danger, compromettre. **jeopardy** *n* danger *m*.
jerk (dʒəːk) *n* secousse *f*. *vt* secouer. *vi* se mouvoir brusquement.
jersey (ˈdʒəːzi) *n* jersey *m*.
Jersey (ˈdʒəːzi) *n geog* Jersey *m*.
Jerusalem (dʒəˈruːsələm) *n* Jérusalem *f*.
jest (dʒest) *n* raillerie *f*. *vi* plaisanter.
Jesus (ˈdʒiːzəs) *n* Jésus *m*.
jet[1] (dʒet) *n* **1** *aviat* avion à réaction *m*. **2** jet, gicleur *m*.
jet[2] (dʒet) *n* jais *m*.
jetty (ˈdʒeti) *n* jetée, digue *f*.
Jew (dʒuː) *n* juif, juive. **Jewish** *adj* juif, juive.
jewel (ˈdʒuːəl) *n* bijou, -oux, joyau, -aux *m*. **jeweller** *n* bijoutier *m*. **jewellery** *n* bijouterie *f*.
jig[1] (dʒig) *n tech* gabarit *m*.
jig[2] (dʒig) *n mus* gigue.
jiggle (ˈdʒigəl) *vi* sautiller.
jigsaw (ˈdʒigsɔː) *n* puzzle *m*.
jilt (dʒilt) *vt* délaisser, plaquer.
jingle (ˈdʒiŋgəl) *n* tintement *m*. *vi* tinter, cliqueter. *vt* faire tinter.
job (dʒɔb) *n* **1** besogne *f*. travail, -aux *m*. **2** emploi *m*. situation *f*.
jockey (ˈdʒɔki) *n* jockey *m*. *vt* tromper. *vi* manœuvrer.
jodhpurs (ˈdʒɔdpəz) *n pl* pantalon d'équitation *m*.
jog (dʒɔg) *n* **1** coup *m*. secousse *f*. **2** petit trot *m*. *vt* secouer. **jog along** trottiner.
join (dʒɔin) *vt* **1** joindre, unir. **2** rejoindre. **3** adhérer à. **join in** prendre part à. **join up** **1** assembler. **2** s'enrôler. ~*n* joint *m*. jointure *f*. **joint** *n* **1** joint *m*. jointure *f*. **2** *anat* articulation *f*. **3** *cul* rôti *m*. **4** *sl* boîte *f*. *adj* **1** commun. **2** solidaire, concerté. **jointly** *adv* ensemble, conjointement.
joist (dʒɔist) *n* solive *f*.
joke (dʒouk) *n* plaisanterie *f*. **practical joke** *n* mauvais tour *m*. ~*vi* plaisanter.

jolly ('dʒɔli) *adj* enjoué, gaillard. *adv* inf rudement.

jolt (dʒoult) *vt,vi* cahoter. *n* **1** secousse *f.* **2** surprise *f.* choc *m.*

Jordan ('dʒɔ:dn̥) *n* Jordanie *f.* (**River**) **Jordan** Jourdain *m.* **Jordanian** *adj,n* jordanien, -ienne.

jostle ('dʒɔsəl) *vt* bousculer, coudoyer. *n* bousculade *f.*

journal ('dʒə:nl̩) *n* journal, -aux *m.* **journalism** *n* journalisme *m.* **journalist** *n* journaliste *m,f.*

journey ('dʒə:ni) *n* voyage, trajet *m.* *vi* voyager.

jovial ('dʒouviəl) *adj* jovial, -aux.

joy (dʒɔi) *n* joie *f.* **joyful** *adj* heureux, -euse.

jubilee ('dʒu:bili:) *n* jubilé *m.*

Judaism ('dʒu:deiizəm) *n* judaïsme *m.*

judge (dʒʌdʒ) *n* **1** juge *m.* **2** connaisseur *m.* *vt* **1** juger. **2** estimer. **judgment** *n* **1** jugement *m.* **2** opinion *f.* **3** discernement *m.*

judicial (dʒu:'diʃəl) *adj* **1** judiciaire. **2** juridique.

judicious (dʒu:'diʃəs) *adj* judicieux, -euse.

judo ('dʒu:dou) *n* judo *m.*

jug (dʒʌg) *n* **1** cruche *f.* pot, pichet *m.* **2** *sl* violon *m.* prison *f.*

juggernaut ('dʒʌgənɔ:t) *n* camion poids lourd *m.*

juggle ('dʒʌgəl) *vi* jongler. *vt* escamoter. **juggler** *n* jongleur *m.* **jugglery** *n* jonglerie *f.* tours de passe-passe *m pl.*

juice (dʒu:s) *n* jus *m.* **juicy** *adj* juteux, -euse.

jukebox ('dʒu:kbɔks) *n* phonographe à sous, juke-box *m.*

July (dʒu'lai) *n* juillet *m.*

jumble ('dʒʌmbəl) *n* méli-mélo, fouillis *m.* *vt* mêler. **jumble sale** *n* vente d'objets usagés *f.*

jump (dʒʌmp) *vi,vt* sauter. *n* **1** saut *m.* **2** sursaut *m.* **3** *sport* obstacle *m.*

jumper ('dʒʌmpə) *n* pull, tricot *m.*

junction ('dʒʌŋkʃən) *n* **1** jonction *f.* **2** (of a road, etc.) embranchement *m.*

June (dʒu:n) *n* juin *m.*

jungle ('dʒʌŋgəl) *n* jungle *f.*

junior ('dʒu:niə) *adj* **1** cadet, -ette. **2** jeune. *n* cadet, -ette.

juniper ('dʒu:nipə) *n* genévrier, genièvre *m.*

junk (dʒʌŋk) *n* rebut *m.* étoupe *f.* **piece of junk** rossignol *m.*

junta ('dʒʌntə) *n* junte *f.*

Jupiter ('dʒu:pitə) *n* Jupiter *m.*

jurisdiction (dʒuəris'dikʃən) *n* juridiction *f.*

jury ('dʒuəri) *n* jury *m.* **juror** *n* juré *m.*

just (dʒʌst) *adj* juste, équitable. *adv* **1**

222

justement, juste. **2** seulement, simplement. **3** à l'instant.

justice ('dʒʌstis) *n* justice *f.*

justify ('dʒʌstifai) *vt* justifier. **justification** *n* justification *f.*

jut (dʒʌt) *vi* **jut out** faire saillie.

jute (dʒu:t) *n* jute *m.*

juvenile ('dʒu:vənail) *adj* **1** juvénile. **2** *law* mineur *f.*

juxtapose (dʒʌkstə'pouz) *vt* juxtaposer. **juxtaposition** *n* juxtaposition *f.*

K

kaftan ('kæftŋ) *n* kaftan *m.*

kaleidoscope (kə'laidəskoup) *n* kaléidoscope *m.*

kangaroo (kæŋgə'ru:) *n* kangourou *m.*

karate (kə'rɑ:ti) *n* karaté *m.*

kebab (kə'bæb) *n* brochette *f.*

keel (ki:l) *n* quille *f.* *v* **keel over** chavirer.

keen (ki:n) *adj* **1** (of an object) tranchant, affilé. **2** vif, vive. **3** ardent. **4** enragé. **5** fin.

keenness *n* **1** finesse *f.* **2** ardeur *f.* **3** empressement *m.*

keep* (ki:p) *vt* **1** garder. **2** tenir, observer. **3** célébrer. *vi* **1** rester. **2** continuer. **3** se conserver. **keep back** retenir. **keep on** continuer de *or* à. **keep to** tenir. **keepsake** *n* souvenir *m.*

keg (keg) *n* barillet, tonnelet *m.*

kennel ('kenl̩) *n* chenil *m.* niche *f.*

Kenya ('kenjə) *n* Kenya *m.* **Kenyan** *adj,n* kenien, -ienne.

kept (kept) *v* see **keep.**

kerb (kə:b) *n* bordure de trottoir *f.*

kernel ('kə:nl̩) *n* amande, graine *f.*

kettle ('ketl̩) *n* bouilloire *f.* **kettledrum** *n* timbale *f.*

key (ki:) *n* **1** clef *f.* **2** (of a book, etc.) corrigé *m.* **3** touche *f.* **4** *mus* ton *m.* *adj* clef, essentiel, -elle. *vt* accorder. **keyboard** *n* clavier *m.* **keyhole** *n* trou de serrure *m.* **keyring** *n* porte-clefs *m invar.*

khaki ('kɑ:ki) *n* kaki *m.* *adj* kaki *invar.*

kibbutz (ki'buts) *n* kibboutz *m.*

kick (kik) *n* **1** coup de pied *m.* **2** (of a gun) recul *m.* réaction *f.* *vi* donner un coup de pied, ruer. *vt* donner un coup de pied à. **kick-off** *n* coup d'envoi *m.*

kid¹ (kid) *n* **1** *zool* chevreau, -aux *m.* **2** *inf* mioche, gosse *m,f.* *adj* de chevreau, -aux.

kid[2] (kid) *vt inf* faire marcher. **kid oneself** se faire accroire, se leurrer.

kidnap ('kidnæp) *vt* enlever, kidnapper. **kidnapper** *n* ravisseur *m*. **kidnapping** *n* enlèvement *m*.

kidney ('kidni) *n* 1 *anat* rein *m*. 2 (of animals) rognon *m*. **kidney bean** *n* haricot nain *m*.

kill (kil) *vt* 1 tuer. 2 (an animal) abattre. **killing** *adj* 1 meurtrier, -ière. 2 *inf* crevant. *n* tuerie *f*.

kiln (kiln) *n* four *m*.

kilo ('ki:lou) *n* kilo *m*.

kilogram ('kiləgræm) *n* kilogramme *m*.

kilometre (ki'lɔmitə) *n* kilomètre *m*.

kilowatt ('kiləwɔt) *n* kilowatt *m*.

kilt (kilt) *n* kilt *m*.

kin (kin) *n* 1 parenté *f*. 2 parents *m pl*.

kind[1] (kaind) *adj* bon, bonne, aimable, gentil, -ille, bienveillant. **kindness** *n* bonté, bienveillance *f*.

kind[2] (kaind) *n* espèce, sorte *f*. genre *m*.

kindergarten ('kindəgɑ:tn) *n* école maternelle *f*.

kindle ('kindl) *vt* 1 allumer, enflammer. 2 éveiller, exciter. *vi* 1 s'allumer. 2 s'éveiller.

kinetic (ki'netik) *adj* cinétique.

king (kiŋ) *n* 1 roi *m*. 2 (draughts) dame *f*. **kingdom** *n* 1 royaume *m*. 2 règne *m*. **kingfisher** *n* martin-pêcheur *m*.

kink (kiŋk) *n* nœud, tortillement *m*. *vi* se nouer, se tortiller.

kiosk ('kiɔsk) *n* kiosque *m*.

kipper ('kipə) *n* hareng fumé *m*.

kiss (kis) *n* baiser *m*. *vt* embrasser.

kit (kit) *n* 1 trousse *f*. fourniment *m*. 2 *inf* effets *m pl*.

kitchen ('kitʃin) *n* cuisine *f*. *adj* de cuisine, cuisinier, -ière. **kitchen garden** *n* jardin potager *m*.

kite (kait) *n* 1 cerf-volant *m*. 2 *zool* milan *m*.

kitten ('kitn) *n* chaton *m*.

kitty ('kiti) *n* cagnotte *f*.

kiwi ('ki:wi) *n* kiwi, aptéryx *m*.

kleptomania (kleptə'meiniə) *n* kleptomanie *f*. **kleptomaniac** *adj,n* kleptomane.

knack (næk) *n* tour de main, truc *m*.

knave (neiv) *n* 1 coquin *m*. 2 *game* valet *m*.

knead (ni:d) *vt* pétrir, travailler.

knee (ni:) *n* genou, -oux *m*. **kneecap** *n* rotule *f*.

kneel[*] (ni:l) *vi* s'agenouiller.

knew (nu:) *v see* **know.**

knickers ('nikəz) *n pl* culotte *f*.

knife (naif) *n, pl* **knives** couteau, -aux *m*. *vt* donner un coup de couteau à, poignarder.

knight (nait) *n* 1 chevalier *m*. 2 *game* cavalier *m*. *vt* créer chevalier.

knit[*] (nit) *vt* 1 tricoter. 2 joindre. *vi* se souder. **knitting** *n* tricot *m*. **knitting needle** aiguille à tricoter *f*. **knitwear** *n* tricot *m*.

knob (nɔb) *n* 1 bouton *m*. bosse *f*. 2 morceau, -aux *m*.

knock (nɔk) *n* coup, heurt *m*. *vt,vi* frapper, heurter. **knock down** renverser. **knock over** renverser. **knocker** *n* marteau, -aux *m*.

knot (nɔt) *n* nœud *m*. *vt* nouer.

know[*] (nou) *vt* 1 savoir, connaître. 2 reconnaître. **get to know** 1 apprendre. 2 faire la connaissance de. **knowing** *adj* fin, rusé.

knowledge ('nɔlidʒ) *n* 1 connaissance *f*. 2 savoir *m*. science *f*.

knuckle ('nʌkəl) *n* articulation, jointure *f*.

Korea (kə'riə) *n* Corée *f*. **Korean** *adj,n* coréen, -enne.

kosher ('kouʃə) *adj* cachir *invar*.

L

label ('leibəl) *n* étiquette *f*. *vt* étiqueter.

laboratory (lə'bɔrətri) *n* laboratoire *m*.

labour ('leibə) *n* 1 travail, -aux, labeur *m*. 2 main-d'œuvre *f*. *vi* travailler, peiner. **laboursaving** *adj* qui allège le travail. **laborious** *adj* laborieux, -euse, pénible. **Labour Party** *n* parti travailliste *m*.

laburnum (lə'bə:nəm) *n* cytise *m*.

labyrinth ('læbərinθ) *n* labyrinthe, dédaie *m*.

lace (leis) *n* 1 dentelle *f*. 2 (of a shoe, etc.) lacet *m*. *vt* lacer.

lack (læk) *n* manque, défaut *m*. **for lack of** faute de. ~*vt,vi* manquer.

lacquer ('lækə) *n* vernis *m*. laque *f*. *vt* laquer.

lad (læd) *n* gars, garçon *m*.

ladder ('lædə) *n* 1 échelle *f*. 2 (in a stocking) maille filée *f*.

laden ('leidn) *adj* chargé.

ladle ('leidl) *n* louche *f*.

lady ('leidi) *n* dame *f*. **ladies and gentlemen** mesdames, mesdemoiselles, messieurs. **ladybird** *n* coccinelle *f*. *inf* bête à bon Dieu *f*.

lag[1] (læg) *vi* traîner, rester en arrière. *n* retard *m*.

lag[2] (læg) *vt* calorifuger. **lagging** *n* revêtement calorifuge *m*.

lager ('lɑ:gə) *n* bière blonde allemande *f*.

laid (leid) *v see* **lay.**

lain (lein) *v see* **lie.**

laity (ˈleiəti) n laïques m pl.
lake (leik) n lac m.
lamb (læm) n agneau, -aux m.
lame (leim) adj 1 boiteux, -euse, estropié. 2 pauvre, faible. vt estropier.
lament (ləˈment) n lamentation f. vt pleurer. vi se lamenter.
lamp (læmp) n lampe f. **standard lamp** lampadaire m. **lamppost** n réverbère m. **lampshade** n abat-jour m invar.
lance (lɑːns) n lance f.
land (lænd) n 1 terre f. 2 pays m. vt,vi 1 naut débarquer. 2 aviat atterrir. **landing** n 1 palier m. 2 aviat atterrissage m. 3 naut débarquement m. **landlady** n propriétaire, patronne f. **landlord** n propriétaire, patron m. **landmark** n 1 point de repère m. 2 événement marquant m. **landscape** n paysage m.
lane (lein) n 1 chemin, sentier m. ruelle f. 2 (on a motorway) voie f.
language (ˈlæŋgwidʒ) n 1 (of a people) langue f. 2 langage m.
lanky (ˈlæŋki) adj maigre, décharné.
lantern (ˈlæntən) n lanterne f. fanal, -aux m.
lap[1] (læp) n anat genoux m pl. giron m.
lap[2] (læp) n sport tour, circuit m. vt 1 assembler. 2 ourler.
lap[3] (læp) vt laper. vi (of waves) clapoter. n clapotement m.
lapel (ləˈpel) n revers m.
Lapland (ˈlæplænd) n Laponie f. **Lapp** adj,n lapon. **Lapp** (language) n lapon m.
lapse (læps) n 1 cours m. 2 faute, erreur f. vi s'écouler. 2 manquer.
larceny (ˈlɑːsəni) n larcin m.
larch (lɑːtʃ) n mélèze m.
lard (lɑːd) n saindoux m.
larder (ˈlɑːdə) n garde-manger m invar.
large (lɑːdʒ) adj grand, fort, gros, grosse. **at large** en liberté.
lark[1] (lɑːk) n zool alouette f.
lark[2] (lɑːk) n inf farce, blague f.
larva (ˈlɑːvə) n, pl **larvae** larve f.
larynx (ˈlæriŋks) n larynx m. **laryngitis** n laryngite f.
laser (ˈleizə) n laser m.
lash (læʃ) n 1 coup de fouet m. 2 lanière f. 3 cil m. vt,vi fouetter, cingler. **lash out** 1 lâcher un coup. 2 ruer.
lass (læs) n jeune fille f.
lasso (læˈsuː) n lasso m.
last[1] (lɑːst) adj dernier, -ière. **at last** enfin. **last but one** avant-dernier. **last night** cette nuit f.

last[2] (lɑːst) vi durer. **lasting** adj durable.
latch (lætʃ) n loquet m. clenche f. vt fermer au loquet.
late (leit) adv 1 tard. 2 en retard. adj 1 tard. 2 tardif, -ive. 3 feu. 4 dernier, -ière. 5 ancien, -ienne. **lately** adv dernièrement, récemment. **latecomer** n retardataire m,f. **later** adv plus tard. adj ultérieur.
latent (ˈleitnt) adj latent, caché.
lateral (ˈlætərəl) adj latéral, -aux.
latest (ˈleitist) adj récent, dernier, -ière. **at the latest** au plus tard.
lathe (leið) n tour m.
lather (ˈlɑːðə) n mousse f. vt savonner. vi mousser.
Latin (ˈlætin) adj,n latin m. **Latin America** n Amérique latine f.
latitude (ˈlætitjuːd) n 1 latitude f. 2 largeur, étendue f.
latter (ˈlætə) adj 1 dernier, -ière. 2 celui-ci, celle-ci.
lattice (ˈlætis) n treillage, treillis m.
laugh (lɑːf) n rire m. vi rire. **laugh at** se moquer de. **laughter** n rire m.
launch[1] (lɔːntʃ) n chaloupe f.
launch[2] (lɔːntʃ) vt lancer. **launch out** se lancer. **launching** n lancement m.
launder (ˈlɔːndə) vt blanchir. **launderette** n laverie f. **laundry** n 1 blanchisserie f. 2 linge m.
laurel (ˈlɔrəl) n laurier m.
lava (ˈlɑːvə) n lave f.
lavatory (ˈlævətri) n lavabo m. toilette f. cabinets m pl.
lavender (ˈlævində) n lavande f.
lavish (ˈlæviʃ) adj 1 prodigue. 2 somptueux, -euse, abondant. vt prodiguer.
law (lɔː) n 1 loi f. 2 droit m. **law-abiding** adj respectueux des lois. **lawful** adj 1 légal, -aux. 2 légitime. **lawyer** n avocat, avoué m.
lawn (lɔːn) n pelouse f. gazon m. **lawn-mower** n tondeuse à gazon f.
lax (læks) adj 1 mou, molle, lâche. 2 vague.
laxative (ˈlæksətiv) adj,n laxatif, -ive m.
lay*[1] (lei) vt 1 placer, mettre, poser. 2 (an egg) pondre. 3 coucher. **lay down** 1 déposer. 2 stipuler. **lay out** étaler. **lay the table** mettre le couvert. **layer** n couche f.
lay[2] (lei) v see **lie.**
lay[3] (lei) adj rel lai, laie, laïque. **layman** n laïque m.
laze (leiz) vi **laze about** fainéanter. **lazy** adj paresseux, -euse. **laziness** n paresse f.

lead* [1] (li:d) vt **1** mener, conduire. **2** diriger. **3** *game* jouer. vi mener, conduire. n **1** exemple m. **2** laisse f. **3** *game* main f. **4** *Th* premier rôle m. **5** câble m. adj principal, -aux. **leader** n **1** directeur, -trice, chef m. **2** guide m. **3** article de fond m. **leadership** n conduite f. commandement m.

lead[2] (led) n **1** plomb m. **2** (of a pencil) mine f. vt plomber.

leaf (li:f) n, pl **leaves 1** bot feuille f. **2** rallonge f. **leaflet** n tract, prospectus m.

league (li:g) n ligue f.

leak (li:k) n fuite f. écoulement m. vi **1** fuir. **2** faire eau. **leak out** s'ébruiter.

lean* [1] (li:n) vi s'appuyer, s'incliner. vt incliner, appuyer. **lean out** se pencher. ~n inclinaison f.

lean[2] (li:n) adj maigre.

leap* (li:p) n saut, bond m. vi sauter, bondir. vt franchir. **leapfrog** n saute-mouton m. **leap year** n année bissextile f.

learn* (lə:n) vi,vt apprendre. **learned** adj savant, érudit. **learner** n débutant.

lease (li:s) n bail m, pl baulx. vt louer, donner à bail. **leasehold** n location à bail f.

leash (li:ʃ) n laisse, attache f. vt attacher.

least (li:st) adj le or la moindre. n moins m. **at least** au moins. ~adv le moins.

leather ('leðə) n cuir m.

leave* [1] (li:v) vt **1** laisser. **2** quitter. **3** abandonner. **4** léguer. vi partir, s'en aller. **leave out** omettre, oublier.

leave[2] (li:v) n **1** permission f. **2** congé m.

Lebanon ('lebənən) n Liban m. **Lebanese** adj,n libanais.

lecherous ('letʃərəs) adj lascif -ive, débauché.

lectern ('lektən) n lutrin m.

lecture ('lektʃə) n **1** conférence f. cours m. **2** inf semonce f. vi donner une conférence. vt réprimander. **lecturer** n conférencier, chargé de cours m.

led (led) v see **lead.**

ledge (ledʒ) n rebord m. saillie f.

ledger ('ledʒə) n grand livre m.

lee (li:) n **1** abri m. **2** naut côté sous le vent m.

leech (li:tʃ) n sangsue f.

leek (li:k) n poireau, -aux m.

leer (liə) n œillade (en dessous) f. regard polisson m. vi lorgner, guigner.

left [1] (left) adj,n gauche f. **left-hand** adj à gauche. **left-handed** adj gaucher, -ère. **left-wing** adj gauchiste, de gauche.

left[2] (left) v see **leave. left-luggage office** n consigne m.

leg (leg) n **1** jambe f. **2** (of an animal) patte f. **3** (of furniture) pied m. **4** cul cuisse f. gigot m.

legacy ('legəsi) n legs m.

legal ('li:gəl) adj licite, judiciaire, légal, -aux. **legalize** vt légaliser.

legend ('ledʒənd) n légende, fable f. **legendary** adj légendaire.

legible ('ledʒibl) adj lisible.

legion ('li:dʒən) n légion f.

legislate ('ledʒisleit) vi faire les lois, légiférer. **legislation** n législation f.

legitimate (li'dʒitimət) adj légitime.

leisure ('leʒə) n loisir m.

lemon ('lemən) n citron m. **lemonade** n limonade f. **lemon tree** n citronnier m.

lend* (lend) vt prêter.

length (lenθ) n **1** longueur f. **2** durée f. **3** morceau, -aux m. **lengthen** vt allonger. vi s'allonger. **lengthy** adj long, longue.

lenient ('li:niənt) adj clément, indulgent. **leniently** adv avec clémence.

lens (lenz) n **1** lentille f. verre m. **2** phot objectif m.

lent (lent) v see **lend.**

Lent (lent) n Carême m.

lentil ('lentl) n lentille f.

Leo ('li:ou) n Lion m.

leopard ('lepəd) n léopard m.

leper ('lepə) n lépreux, -euse. **leprosy** n lèpre f. **leprous** adj lépreux, -euse.

lesbian ('lezbiən) n lesbienne f.

less (les) adj moindre. adv,prep moins. **less and less** de moins en moins. ~n moins m. **lessen** vi s'amoindrir. vt diminuer.

lesson ('lesən) n leçon f.

lest (lest) conj de peur que.

let* (let) vt **1** permettre, laisser. **2** louer. **let down** vt baisser. **2** allonger. **let in** laisser entrer. **let out** laisser sortir.

lethal ('li:θəl) adj mortel, -elle.

lethargy ('leθədʒi) n léthargie f.

letter ('letə) n lettre f. **letterbox** n boîte aux lettres f.

lettuce ('letis) n laitue f.

leukaemia (lu:'ki:miə) n leucémie f.

level ('levəl) n niveau, -aux m. adj de niveau, égal, -aux, en palier. vt **1** niveler, aplanir. **2** viser. **level crossing** n passage à niveau m. **level-headed** adj d'aplomb, pondéré.

lever ('li:və) n levier m.

levy ('levi) n impôt m. vt lever, imposer.

225

lewd (lu:d) *adj* impudique.
liable ('laiǝbǝl) *adj* 1 *law* responsable. 2 sujet, -ette, exposé. **liability** *n* 1 responsabilité. 2 *pl* engagements *m pl*.
liaison (li'eizɔn) *n* liaison *f*.
liar ('laiǝ) *n* menteur, -euse.
libel ('laibǝl) *n* diffamation, libelle *f*.
liberal ('libǝrǝl) *adj,n* libéral -aux.
liberate ('libǝreit) *vt* libérer.
liberty ('libǝti) *n* liberté *f*.
Libra ('li:brǝ) *n* Balance *f*.
library ('laibrǝri) *n* bibliothèque *f*. **librarian** *n* bibliothécaire *m,f*.
libretto (li'bretou) *n, pl* **-tos** *or* **-ti** *n* libretto, livret *m*.
Libya ('libiǝ) *n* Libye *f*. **Libyan** *adj,n* libyen, -enne.
licence ('laisǝns) *n* 1 permis *m*. 2 autorisation *f*. **license** *vt* autoriser, patenter. **licensee** *n* patenté, gérant *m*.
lick (lik) *vt* lécher. **lick into shape** dégrossir. ~*n* coup de langue *m*.
lid (lid) *n* couvercle *m*.
lie[1] (lai) *n* mensonge *m*. *vi* mentir.
lie[2] (lai) *vi* 1 être couché. 2 se trouver. **lie down** se coucher.
lieutenant (lef'tenǝnt) *n* lieutenant *m*. **lieutenant colonel** *n* lieutenant-colonel *m*.
life (laif) *n, pl* **lives** 1 vie *f*. 2 vivacité *f*. entrain *m*. **lifebelt** *n* ceinture de sauvetage *f*. **lifeboat** *n* canot de sauvetage *m*. **lifebuoy** *n* bouée de sauvetage *f*. **lifeguard** *n* garde du corps *m*. **lifeline** *n* ligne de sauvetage, sauvegarde *f*. **lifetime** *n* vie *f*.
lift (lift) *vt* 1 lever, soulever. 2 voler. *vi* se lever. *n* ascenseur *m*. **give someone a lift** emmener quelqu'un dans sa voiture.
light[1] (lait) *n* lumière, clarté *f*. jour *m*. *vt* 1 allumer. 2 éclairer. **lighthouse** *n* phare *m*. **lighting** *n* éclairage *m*.
light[2] (lait) *adj* 1 léger, -ère. 2 (of colour, etc.) clair. **light-hearted** *adj* allègre. **lightweight** *n* poids léger *m*. *adj* léger, -ère.
light[3] (lait) *vi* **light upon** tomber sur.
lighten[1] ('laitņ) *vt* éclairer. *vi* s'éclairer, s'illuminer.
lighten[2] ('laitņ) *vt* alléger, réduire.
lightning ('laitniŋ) *n* éclair *m*. foudre *f*.
like[1] (laik) *adj* pareil, -eille, semblable. *prep* comme. **likelihood** *n* probabilité *f*. **likewise** *adv* également, de même.
like[2] (laik) *vt* 1 aimer. 2 vouloir. **liking** *n* goût, gré *m*.

likely ('laikli) *adj* 1 probable. 2 susceptible. *adv* probablement.
lilac ('lailǝk) *n* lilas *m*.
lily ('lili) *n* lis *m*. **lily-of-the-valley** *n* muguet *m*.
limb (lim) *n* membre *m*.
limbo ('limbou) *n* limbes *m pl*.
lime[1] (laim) *n* chaux *f*. **in the limelight** *adv* en vedette. **limestone** *n* pierre à chaux *f*.
lime[2] (laim) *n bot* limon. **lime tree** *n* 1 limonier *m*. 2 tilleul *m*.
limerick ('limǝrik) *n* poème comique *m*.
limit ('limit) *n* limite, borne *f*. **that's the limit!** ça c'est le comble! ~*vt* limiter, borner, restreindre. **limitation** *n* limitation, restriction *f*.
limp[1] (limp) *vi* boiter. *n* boitement *m*.
limp[2] (limp) *adj* flasque, mou, molle.
limpet ('limpit) *n* patelle, bernique *f*.
linden ('lindņ) *n* tilleul *m*.
line[1] (lain) *n* 1 ligne *f*. 2 corde *f*. 3 trait *m*. 4 compagnie *f*. 5 (railway) voie *f*. *vt* ligner, régler. **lineage** *n* lignée *f*. **linear** *adj* linéaire.
line[2] (lain) *vt* (of clothes, etc.) doubler.
linen ('linin) *n* 1 toile *f*. 2 linge *m*. **linen basket** *n* panier à linge, corbeille *f*.
liner ('lainǝ) *n* paquebot, transatlantique *m*.
linger ('liŋgǝ) *vi* traîner, lambiner.
lingerie ('lɔnʒǝri:) *n* lingerie *f*.
linguist ('liŋgwist) *n* linguiste *m,f*. **linguistic** *adj* linguistique. **linguistics** *n* linguistique *f*.
lining ('lainiŋ) *n* doublure *f*.
link (liŋk) *n* 1 chaînon, maillon *m*. 2 lien *m*. *vt* 1 attacher. 2 lier.
linoleum (li'nouliǝm) *n* linoléum *m*. **lino** *n inf* lino *m*.
linseed ('linsi:d) *n* graine de lin *f*. **linseed oil** *n* huile de lin *f*.
lion ('laiǝn) *n* lion *m*.
lip (lip) *n* 1 *anat* lèvre *f*. 2 (of animals) babine *f*. 3 bord *m*. **lip-read** *vi* lire sur les lèvres. **lipstick** *n* rouge à lèvres *m*.
liqueur (li'kjuǝ) *n* liqueur *f*.
liquid ('likwid) *adj,n* liquide *m*. **liquidate** *vt* liquider. **liquidize** *vt* liquéfier.
liquor ('likǝ) *n* boisson alcoolique *f*.
liquorice ('likǝris) *n* réglisse *f*.
lira ('liǝrǝ) *n* lire *f*.
lisp (lisp) *n* zézaiement *m*. *vi,vt* zézayer.
list[1] (list) *n* liste *f*. *vt* cataloguer.
list[2] (list) *n naut* bande *f*. faux bord *m*. *vi* donner de la bande.
listen ('lisǝn) *vi* écouter.
listless ('listlǝs) *adj* nonchalant, apathique.
lit (lit) *v see* **light**.

litany ('lɪtənɪ) n litanies f pl.
literal ('lɪtərəl) adj littéral, -aux.
literary ('lɪtərərɪ) adj littéraire.
literate ('lɪtərət) adj qui sait lire et écrire.
literature ('lɪtərətʃə) n littérature f.
litre ('liːtə) n litre m.
litter ('lɪtə) n 1 fouillis m. 2 zool portée f. vt mettre en désordre. **litter-bin** n poubelle f.
little ('lɪtl) adj 1 petit. 2 peu de. n peu m. **little by little** petit à petit. ~adv peu. **little finger** n petit doigt m. **little toe** n petit orteil m.
liturgy ('lɪtədʒɪ) n liturgie f.
live[1] (lɪv) vi 1 vivre. 2 demeurer, habiter. vt mener. **live down** faire oublier.
live[2] (laɪv) adj 1 vivant. 2 (of a wire, etc.) en charge. **livestock** n bétail m, pl bestiaux.
livelihood ('laɪvlɪhud) n vie f. gagne-pain m invar.
lively ('laɪvlɪ) adj animé, plein d'entrain. **liveliness** n vivacité f. entrain m.
liver ('lɪvə) n foie m.
livid ('lɪvɪd) adj 1 blême. 2 enragé, emporté.
living ('lɪvɪŋ) n 1 vie f. 2 rel bénéfice m. adj vivant. **living room** n salle de séjour f.
lizard ('lɪzəd) n lézard m.
llama ('lɑːmə) n lama m.
load (loud) n 1 charge f. 2 inf quantité f. tas m. vt charger.
loaf[1] (louf) n, pl **loaves** pain m. miche f.
loaf[2] (louf) vi **loaf about** flâner, fainéanter.
loan (loun) n 1 prêt m. avance f. 2 emprunt m. vt prêter.
loathe (louð) vt haïr, détester.
lob (lɔb) n chandelle f. vt envoyer en chandelle.
lobby ('lɔbɪ) n 1 vestibule m. 2 groupe de pression m. 3 pol couloirs m pl. vi faire les couloirs.
lobe (loub) n lobe m.
lobster ('lɔbstə) n homard m.
local ('loukəl) adj local, -aux, du pays. **locals** n pl gens du pays m pl. **locality** n localité f. parages m pl. **localize** vt localiser. **locate** vt situer, localiser. **location** n emplacement, repérage m.
loch (lɔx) n lac m.
lock[1] (lɔk) n 1 serrure f. 2 (of a canal) écluse f. vt fermer à clef.
lock[2] (lɔk) n (of hair) mèche, boucle f.
locker ('lɔkə) n armoire f. coffre m.
locket ('lɔkɪt) n médaillon m.
locomotive (loukə'moutɪv) adj,n locomotif, -ive m.
locust ('loukəst) n criquet m. sauterelle f.

lodge (lɔdʒ) n loge f. vt 1 loger. 2 déposer. vi se loger. **lodger** n pensionnaire m,f. **lodgings** n pl logis, logement m.
loft (lɔft) n grenier m. soupente f. **lofty** adj 1 haut. 2 élevé.
log (lɔg) n bûche f. **logbook** n 1 naut journal de bord m. 2 mot carnet de route m. vt enregistrer.
logarithm ('lɔgəriðəm) n logarithme m.
logic ('lɔdʒik) n logique f. **logical** adj logique.
loins (lɔɪnz) n pl reins m pl.
loiter ('lɔɪtə) vi flâner, traîner.
lollipop ('lɔlɪpɔp) n sucette f.
London ('lʌndən) n Londres m.
lonely ('lounlɪ) adj solitaire, isolé. **loneliness** n solitude f. isolement m.
long[1] (lɔŋ) adj long, longue. adv longtemps. **long-distance** adj 1 à longue distance. 2 (of a telephone) interurbain. **long-playing record** n microsillon m. **long-range** adj à longue portée. **long-sighted** adj 1 presbyte, hypermétrope. 2 prévoyant. **longstanding** adj de longue date. **long wave** n onde longue f. **longwinded** adj 1 interminable. 2 verbeux, -euse.
long[2] (lɔŋ) vi **long for** désirer ardemment. **longing** n désir ardent m.
longevity (lɔn'dʒevɪtɪ) n longévité f.
longitude ('lɔndʒɪtjuːd) n longitude f.
loo (luː) n inf cabinets m pl.
look (luk) n 1 regard m. 2 apparence, mine f. vi 1 regarder. 2 avoir l'air. **look after** soigner, s'occuper de. **look for** chercher. **look forward** to s'attendre à. **look out** faire attention. **look out of** regarder par.
loom[1] (luːm) n métier à tisser m.
loom[2] (luːm) vi apparaître indistinctement, se dessiner.
loop (luːp) n boucle f. vt,vi boucler.
loophole ('luːphoul) n 1 trou m. ouverture f. 2 échappatoire f.
loose (luːs) vt détacher, délier. 2 relâcher. adj 1 lâche. 2 branlant. 3 détaché. 4 dissolu. **loosen** vt 1 relâcher. 2 desserrer. 3 défaire. vi 1 se défaire. 2 se délier.
loot (luːt) vt piller, saccager. n butin m.
lop (lɔp) vt élaguer. **lop off** couper.
lopsided (lɔp'saɪdɪd) adj de guingois, déjeté.
lord (lɔːd) n 1 maître m. 2 cap rel Seigneur m. 3 cap (title) Lord m. v **lord it** faire l'important. **lordship** n 1 suzeraineté f. 2 cap Seigneurie f. Monseigneur m.
lorry ('lɔrɪ) n camion m.

lose* (luːz) *vt, vi* perdre.
loss (lɔs) *n* perte *f*. **be at a loss** être désorienté.
lost (lɔst) *v* see **lose.**
lot (lɔt) *n* **1** sort *m*. **2** tas *m*. **3** tout *m*. **a lot (of)** beaucoup (de).
lotion (ˈloʊʃən) *n* lotion *f*.
lottery (ˈlɔtəri) *n* loterie *f*.
loud (laʊd) *adj* **1** haut, fort. **2** (of a person, etc.) bruyant. **3** *inf* (of a colour) criard. **loud-mouthed** *adj inf* fort en gueule, braillard. **loudspeaker** *n* haut-parleur *m*.
lounge (laʊndʒ) *n* salon *m*. *vi* **1** flâner. **2** s'étendre.
louse (laʊs) *n, pl* **lice** pou, poux *m*. **lousy** *adj* **1** pouilleux, -euse. **2** *inf* sale. **3** *inf* moche.
love (lʌv) *n* **1** amour *m*. affection *f*. **2** *sport* rien *m*. **fall in love with** s'éprendre de. ~*vt* aimer. **lover** *n* amant *m*. **lovely** *adj* beau, belle. **loveliness** *n* **1** beauté *f*. **2** charme *m*.
low[1] (loʊ) *adj* **1** bas, basse, peu élevé. **2** vulgaire. **3** vil. **4** abattu. *adv* bas. **lowbrow** *adj* terre à terre *invar*. **lower-case** *adj* minuscule, bas de casse. **low-grade** *adj* de qualité inférieure. **lowland** *n* plaine basse *f*. **low-necked** *adj* décolleté. **low-pitched** *adj* grave.
low[2] (loʊ) *vi* meugler. *n* meuglement *m*.
lower (ˈloʊə) *vt* baisser, abaisser.
loyal (ˈlɔɪəl) *adj* fidèle, loyal, -aux. **loyalty** *n* fidélité *f*.
lozenge (ˈlɔzɪndʒ) *n med* pastille *f*.
LSD *n* LSD, drogue hallucinogène *f*.
lubricate (ˈluːbrɪkeɪt) *vt* lubrifier, graisser.
lucid (ˈluːsɪd) *adj* lucide, clair.
luck (lʌk) *n* **1** hasard *m*. **2** bonheur *m*. chance *f*. **lucky** *adj* heureux, -euse, fortuné.
lucrative (ˈluːkrətɪv) *adj* lucratif, -ive.
ludicrous (ˈluːdɪkrəs) *adj* risible, grotesque.
lug (lʌg) *vt* traîner, tirer.
luggage (ˈlʌgɪdʒ) *n* bagages *m pl*. **luggage rack** *n* porte-bagages *m invar*.
lukewarm (luːkˈwɔːm) *adj* tiède.
lull (lʌl) *n* calme *m*. trève *f*. *vt* **1** bercer. **2** endormir. *vi* se calmer. **lullaby** *n* berceuse *f*.
lumbago (lʌmˈbeɪgoʊ) *n* lumbago *m*.
lumber[1] (ˈlʌmbə) *n* **1** bois de charpente *m*. **2** fatras *m*. *vt* encombrer. **lumberjack** *n* bûcheron *m*.
lumber[2] (ˈlʌmbə) *vi* se traîner lourdement.
luminous (ˈluːmɪnəs) *adj* lumineux, -euse.
lump (lʌmp) *n* **1** bloc *m*. **2** grumeau, -aux *m*. **3** bosse *f*. **4** *sl* pataud *m*. *vt* mettre en tas. **lumpy** *adj* grumeleux, -euse.
lunacy (ˈluːnəsi) *n* folie, démence *f*.

lunar (ˈluːnə) *adj* lunaire.
lunatic (ˈluːnətɪk) *n* fou, folle. *adj* aliéné.
lunch (lʌntʃ) *n* déjeuner *m*. *vi* déjeuner.
lung (lʌŋ) *n* poumon *m*.
lunge (lʌndʒ) *n* **1** *sport* botte *f*. **2** ruée *f*. *v* **lunge forward** se jeter en avant.
lurch[1] (lɜːtʃ) *n* **1** embardée *f*. **2** cahot *m*. *vi* **1** faire une embardée. **2** tituber.
lurch[2] (lɜːtʃ) *n* **leave in the lurch** laisser le bec dans l'eau.
lure (lʊə) *n* **1** leurre *m*. **2** piège *m*. *vt* **1** leurrer. **2** attirer, séduire.
lurid (ˈlʊərɪd) *adj* blafard.
lurk (lɜːk) *vi* se cacher, rester tapis.
luscious (ˈlʌʃəs) *adj* succulent.
lush (lʌʃ) *adj* plein de sève.
lust (lʌst) *n* désir *m*. convoitise *f*.
lustre (ˈlʌstə) *n* lustre, éclat *m*. *vt* lustrer.
lute (luːt) *n* luth *m*.
Luxembourg (ˈlʌksəmbɜːg) *n* Luxembourg *m*.
luxury (ˈlʌkʃəri) *n* luxe *m*. **luxurious** *adj* somptueux, -euse.
lynch (lɪntʃ) *vt* lyncher.
lynx (lɪŋks) *n* lynx, loup-cervier *m*.
Lyons (ˈlaɪənz) *n* Lyon *m*.
lyre (ˈlaɪə) *n* lyre *f*.
lyrics (ˈlɪrɪks) *n* paroles *m pl*. **lyrical** *adj* lyrique.

M

mac (mæk) *n inf* imper *m*.
macabre (məˈkɑːb) *adj* macabre.
mace[1] (meɪs) *n* masse *f*.
mace[2] (meɪs) *n cul* muscade *f*.
machine (məˈʃiːn) *n* machine *f*. appareil *m*. **machine-gun** *n* mitrailleuse *f*. **machinery** *n* machines *f pl*. mécanisme *m*. **machinist** *n* **1** machiniste *m*. **2** mécanicienne *f*.
mackerel (ˈmækrəl) *n* maquereau, -aux *m*.
mackintosh (ˈmækɪntɔʃ) *n* imperméable *m*.
mad (mæd) *adj* fou, folle. **madness** *n* folie, démence *f*.
madam (ˈmædəm) *n* madame, mesdames *f*.
made (meɪd) *v* see **make.**
Madonna (məˈdɔnə) *n* Madone *f*.
madrigal (ˈmædrɪgəl) *n* madrigal, -aux *m*.
magazine (mægəˈziːn) *n* **1** magazine *m*. revue *f*. **2** *mil* magasin *m*.
maggot (ˈmægət) *n* ver, asticot *m*.
magic (ˈmædʒɪk) *n* magie *f*. *adj* magique, enchanté. **magician** *n* magicien, -ienne *f*.

magistrate (ˈmædʒɪstreɪt) n magistrat m.
magnanimous (mægˈnænɪməs) adj magnanime.
magnate (ˈmægneɪt) n magnat m.
magnet (ˈmægnɪt) n aimant m. **magnetic** adj magnétique. **magnetism** n 1 magnétisme m. 2 aimantation f. **magnetize** vt 1 magnétiser. 2 aimanter.
magnificent (mægˈnifisənt) adj magnifique.
magnify (ˈmægnifai) vt grossir, agrandir. **magnifying glass** n loupe f.
magnitude (ˈmægnitjuːd) n 1 grandeur f. 2 importance f.
magpie (ˈmægpai) n pie f.
mahogany (məˈhɔgəni) n acajou m.
maid (meid) n 1 domestique f. 2 jeune fille f. **maiden** n jeune fille f. adj 1 non mariée. 2 premier, -ière, inaugural, -aux. **maiden name** n nom de jeune fille m.
mail (meil) n courrier m. poste f. vt envoyer par la poste, expédier. **mail order** n commande par correspondance f. **mailing list** n liste des abonnés f.
maim (meim) vt mutiler.
main (mein) adj principal, -aux, essentiel, -elle. n (pipe, wire, etc.) conduite principale f. **mainland** n continent m. **mainly** adv surtout. **mainsail** n grand-voile f.
maintain (meinˈtein) vt 1 maintenir. 2 soutenir. 3 garder. **maintenance** n 1 entretien m. 2 law pension alimentaire f.
maize (meiz) n maïs m.
majesty (ˈmædʒɪsti) n majesté f. **majestic** adj majestueux, -euse.
major (ˈmeidʒə) adj majeur, principal, -aux. n mil commandant m. **major general** n général de division m. **majority** n majorité f.
Majorca (məˈdʒɔːkə) n Majorque f.
make (meik) n 1 marque f. 2 fabrication f. vt 1 faire. 2 fabriquer, confectionner. 3 rendre. **make for** se diriger vers. **make off** filer. **make over** céder. **make up 1** compléter. 2 rattraper. 3 inventer. 4 se maquiller. **make-up** n maquillage m. **make up one's mind** se décider. **make-believe** n semblant m. feinte f. adj fictif, -ive. **maker** n fabricant m. **makeshift** n pis-aller m invar. adj de fortune.
maladjusted (mælə'dʒʌstid) adj inadapté.
malaria (mə'lɛəriə) n malaria f.
Malaya (mə'leiə) n Malaisie f. **Malay** adj,n malais. **Malay** (language) n malais m.
Malaysia (mə'leiziə) n Malaysia f. **Malaysian** adj,n malais.

male (meil) adj,n mâle m.
malice (ˈmælis) n malveillance, rancune f. **malicious** adj malveillant, malicieux, -euse.
malignant (məˈlignənt) adj 1 malin, maligne. 2 méchant.
mallet (ˈmælət) n maillet m.
malt (mɔːlt) n malt m.
Malta (ˈmɔːltə) n Malte f. **Maltese** adj,n maltais.
maltreat (mælˈtriːt) vt maltraiter.
mammal (ˈmæməl) n mammifère m.
mammoth (ˈmæməθ) n mammouth m. adj énorme.
man (mæn) n, pl **men** 1 homme m. 2 employé m. 3 game pièce f. pion m. vt armer, garnir. **manhandle** vt 1 manutentionner. 2 maltraiter. **manhole** n regard m. **manhood** n maturité, virilité f. **man-made** adj artificiel, -elle. **manpower** n main-d'œuvre f. **manslaughter** n homicide m.
Man, Isle of (mæn) n île de Man f.
manage (ˈmænidʒ) vt 1 diriger, administrer, gérer. 2 venir à bout de. 3 manœuvrer. vi se débrouiller. **manageable** adj maniable. **management** n 1 direction, gestion f. 2 administration f. **manager** n directeur, gérant m. **manageress** n directrice, gérante f. **managing director** n administrateur gérant m.
mandarin (ˈmændərin) n 1 mandarin m. 2 bot mandarine f.
mandate (ˈmændeit) n mandat m. **mandatory** adj obligatoire.
mandolin (ˈmændəlin) n mandoline f.
mane (mein) n crinière f.
mange (meindʒ) n gale f. **mangy** adj galeux, -euse.
mangle[1] (ˈmæŋgəl) vt 1 taillader. 2 dénaturer.
mangle[2] (ˈmæŋgəl) n calandre f. vt calandrer.
mango (ˈmæŋgou) n, pl **-oes** or **-os** mangue f.
mania (ˈmeiniə) n 1 manie, passion f. 2 med folie f. **maniac** adj,n fou, folle, furieux, -euse. **manic** adj qui tient de la folie.
manicure (ˈmænikjuə) n soins des mains m pl. vt soigner les mains.
manifest (ˈmænifest) vt,vi manifester. adj manifeste, évident.
manifesto (mæniˈfestou) n manifeste m.
manifold (ˈmænifould) adj multiple, varié.
manipulate (məˈnipjuleit) vt manipuler, actionner. **manipulation** n manipulation f.
mankind (ˈmænkaind) n genre humain m.
manner (ˈmænə) n 1 manière, façon f. 2 pl

229

mœurs f pl. **3** pl manières f pl. savoir-vivre m. **mannerism** n maniérisme m.

manoeuvre (mɔ'nu:vɔ) vt,vi manœuvrer. n manœuvre f.

manor ('mænɔ) n manoir m.

mansion ('mænʃən) n château, -aux, hôtel particulier m.

mantelpiece ('mæntɔlpɪ:s) n dessus de cheminée m.

mantle ('mænt|) n **1** cape f. **2** manteau, -aux m. vt couvrir.

manual ('mænjuɔl) adj,n manuel, -elle m.

manufacture (mænju'fæktʃɔ) vt manufacturer, fabriquer. n **1** fabrication f. **2** produit manufacturé m. **manufacturer** n fabricant, industriel m.

manure (mɔ'njuɔ) n fumier m. vt fumer.

manuscript ('mænjuskript) adj,n manuscrit m.

Manx (mæŋks) adj de l'île de Man.

many ('meni) adj beaucoup (de), bien des, nombreux, -euse. n multitude, foule f. **as many as** autant que. **how many?** combien? **many a** maint. **so many** tant (de). **too many** trop (de).

Maori ('mauri) adj,n maori.

map (mæp) n **1** carte f. **2** (of a town) plan m.

maple ('meipɔl) n érable m.

mar (ma:) vt gâcher, troubler.

marathon ('mærɔθɔn) n marathon m.

marble ('ma:bɔl) n **1** marbre m. **2** game bille f.

march (ma:tʃ) n marche f. vi marcher. vt faire marcher. **march past** défiler.

March (ma:tʃ) n mars m.

marchioness ('ma:ʃɔnis) n marquise f.

mare (mɛɔ) n jument f.

margarine (ma:dʒɔ'ri:n) n margarine f.

margin ('ma:dʒin) n **1** marge f. **2** bord m. **marginal** adj marginal, -aux.

marigold ('mærigould) n souci m.

marijuana (mæri'wa:nɔ) n marijuana f.

marinade (mæri'neid) n marinade f. **marinate** vt mariner.

marine (mɔ'ri:n) adj **1** marin, maritime. **2** de marine. n marine f.

marital ('mæritl) adj **1** marital, -aux. **2** matrimonial, -aux.

maritime ('mæritaim) adj maritime.

marjoram ('ma:dʒɔrɔm) n marjolaine f.

mark[1] (ma:k) n **1** marque f. **2** but m. **3** note f. vt **1** marquer. **2** noter. **3** corriger. **markedly** adv nettement. **marksman** n tireur d'élite m.

mark[2] (ma:k) n comm mark m.

market ('ma:kit) n **1** marché m. **2** débouché m.

230

vt lancer sur le marché. **market garden** n jardin maraîcher m. **marketplace** n marché m. **market research** n étude du marché f. **market town** n bourg m.

marmalade ('ma:mɔleid) n confiture d'oranges f.

maroon[1] (mɔ'ru:n) adj,n marron m.

maroon[2] (mɔ'ru:n) vt abandonner.

marquee (ma:'ki:) n marquise, grande tente f.

marquess ('ma:kwis) n marquis m.

marriage ('mæridʒ) n mariage m. **marriage certificate** n acte de mariage m.

marrow ('mærou) n **1** moelle f. **2** bot courge f. **marrowbone** n os à moelle m.

marry ('mæri) vt marier, épouser. vi se marier avec.

Mars (ma:z) n Mars m.

Marseillaise (ma:sɔ'leiz) n Marseillaise f.

Marseilles (ma:'sei) n Marseille f.

marsh (ma:ʃ) n marécage, marais m. **marshy** adj marécageux, -euse. **marshmallow** n guimauve f.

marshal ('ma:ʃɔl) n **1** maréchal, -aux m. **2** maître des cérémonies m. vt ranger.

marsupial (ma:'sju:piɔl) adj,n marsupial, -aux m.

martial ('ma:ʃɔl) adj martial, -aux.

martin ('ma:tin) n martinet m.

martini (ma:'ti:ni) n martini m.

martyr ('ma:tɔ) n martyr m. vt martyriser. **martyrdom** n martyre m.

marvel ('ma:vɔl) n merveille f. vi s'étonner. **marvellous** adj merveilleux, -euse.

Marxism ('ma:ksizɔm) n marxisme m. **marxist** adj,n marxiste.

marzipan ('ma:zipæn) n massepain m.

mascara (mæ'ska:rɔ) n mascara m.

mascot ('mæskɔt) n mascotte f. porte-bonheur m invar.

masculine ('mæskjulin) adj masculin, mâle. n masculin m.

mash (mæʃ) n **1** pâtée f. **2** cul purée f. vt écraser.

mask (ma:sk) n masque m. vt **1** masquer. **2** cacher, voiler.

masochism ('mæsɔkizɔm) n masochisme m. **masochist** adj,n masochiste.

mason ('meisɔn) n maçon m. **masonry** n maçonnerie f.

masquerade (mæskɔ'reid) n mascarade f. vi se déguiser.

mass[1] (mæs) n **1** masse f. **2** foule f. vt masser. vi se masser. **mass media** n pl moyens publicitaires de masse *m pl*. **mass-produce** *vt* fabriquer en série.

mass[2] (mæs) *n rel* messe *f*.

massacre ('mæsəkə) *n* massacre *m*. *vt* massacrer.

massage ('mæsɑːʒ) *n* massage *m*. *vt* masser.

massive ('mæsiv) *adj* massif, -ive.

mast (mɑːst) *n* 1 *naut* mât *m*. 2 pylône *m*. **masthead** *n* tête de mât *f*.

mastectomy (mæs'tektəmi) *n* mastectomie *f*.

master ('mɑːstə) *n* 1 maître *m*. 2 patron, chef *m*. 3 professeur *m*. **Master of Arts/Science** licencié ès lettres/sciences *m*. ~*vt* 1 maîtriser. 2 surmonter. *adj* 1 principal, -aux. 2 de maître. **masterful** *adj* autoritaire. **mastermind** *n* esprit supérieur *m*. **masterpiece** *n* chef-d'œuvre *m*.

masturbate ('mæstəbeit) *vi* se masturber. **masturbation** *n* masturbation *f*.

mat (mæt) *n* 1 natte *f*. 2 tapis *m*. 3 dessous de plat *m*. *vt* emmêler, tresser. *vi* s'emmêler.

match[1] (mætʃ) *n* allumette *f*. **matchbox** *n* boîte d'allumettes *f*. **matchstick** *n* allumette *f*.

match[2] (mætʃ) *n* 1 match *m*. lutte, partie *f*. 2 égal, -aux *m*. 3 mariage *m*. 4 assortiment *m*. *vt* 1 égaler. 2 assortir. *vi* s'assortir, s'harmoniser. **matchless** *adj* incomparable.

mate (meit) *n* 1 compagnon, compagne. 2 *naut* officier *m*. *vt* accoupler. *vi* s'accoupler.

material (mə'tiəriəl) *n* 1 matière *f*. 2 (for building, etc.) matériaux *m pl*. 3 étoffe, tissu *m*. *adj* 1 matériel, -aux. 2 essentiel, -elle. **raw material** *n* matière première *f*. **materialism** *n* matérialisme *m*. **materialist** *n* matérialiste *m,f*. **materialistic** *adj* matérialiste. **materialize** *vi* se réaliser.

maternal (mə'təːnl) *adj* maternel, -elle. **maternity** *n* maternité *f*.

mathematics (mæθə'mætiks) *n* mathématiques *f pl*. **mathematical** *adj* mathématique.

matins ('mætinz) *n pl* matines *f pl*.

matinee ('mætinei) *n* matinée *f*.

matriarchal ('meitriɑːkəl) *adj* matriarcal, -aux.

matrimony ('mætriməni) *n* mariage *m*. **matrimonial** *adj* matrimonial, -aux.

matrix ('meitriks) *n, pl* **-rices** matrice *f*.

matron ('meitrən) *n* 1 intendante *f*. 2 infirmière en chef *f*. 3 matrone *f*.

matter ('mætə) *n* 1 matière *f*. 2 affaire *f*. 3 sujet *m*. 4 *med* pus *m*. **what's the matter?** qu'y a-t-il? ~*vi* importer. **matter-of-fact** *adj* pratique.

Matterhorn ('mætəhɔːn) *n* Mont Cervin *m*.

mattress ('mætrəs) *n* matelas *m*.

mature (mə'tjuə) *adj* 1 mûr. 2 *comm* échu. *vt,vi* mûrir. **maturity** *n* 1 maturité *f*. 2 *comm* échéance *f*.

maudlin ('mɔːdlin) *adj* larmoyant, pleurard.

maul (mɔːl) *vt* malmener, meurtrir.

Maundy Thursday ('mɔːndi) *n* jeudi saint *m*.

mausoleum (mɔːsə'liəm) *n* mausolée *m*.

mauve (mouv) *adj,n* mauve *m*.

maxim ('mæksim) *n* maxime *f*. dicton *m*.

maximum ('mæksiməm) *adj* maximum, limite. *n, pl* **-ums** *or* **-a** maximum *m*. **maximize** *vt* maximiser.

may* (mei) *v mod aux* pouvoir. **that may be** cela se peut. **maybe** *adv* peut-être.

May (mei) *n* mai *m*. **May Day** *n* premier mai *m*. **maypole** *n* mai *m*.

mayonnaise (meiə'neiz) *n* mayonnaise *f*.

mayor ('mɛə) *n* maire *m*. **mayoress** *n* mairesse *f*.

maze (meiz) *n* labyrinthe *m*.

me (miː) *pron 1st pers s* 1 me. 2 moi.

meadow ('medou) *n* prairie *f*.

meagre ('miːgə) *adj* maigre.

meal[1] (miːl) *n* repas *m*.

meal[2] (miːl) *n* farine *f*. **mealy** *adj* farineux, -euse.

mean*[1] (miːn) *vt* 1 vouloir dire, signifier. 2 avoir l'intention de. **meaning** *n* signification *f*. sens *m*. **meaningful** *adj* significatif, -ive.

mean[2] (miːn) *adj* 1 avare, mesquin. 2 méprisable.

meander (mi'ændə) *n* méandre *m*. *vi* serpenter.

means (miːnz) *n pl* 1 moyen *m*. 2 ressources *f pl*. moyens *m pl*. **by means of** au moyen de.

meantime ('miːntaim) *adv* **in the meantime** dans l'intervalle.

meanwhile ('miːnwail) *adv* dans l'intervalle.

measles ('miːzəlz) *n pl* rougeole *f*.

measure ('meʒə) *n* mesure *f*. *vt* mesurer. **measurement** *n* mesure, dimension *f*.

meat (miːt) *n* viande *f*.

mechanic (mi'kænik) *n* mécanicien *m*. **mechanical** *adj* mécanique. **mechanical engineering** *n* construction mécanique *f*. **mechanics** *n* 1 mécanique *f*. 2 *pl* mécanisme *m*. **mechanism** *n* mécanisme *m*. **mechanize** *vt* mécaniser. **mechanization** *n* mécanisation *f*.

medal ('medl) *n* médaille *f*. **medallion** *n* médaillon *m*.

meddle ('medl) *vi* **meddle in** s'immiscer dans.

media ('miːdiə) *n pl* voie f. moyen *m.*
medial ('miːdiəl) *adj* moyen, -enne, intermédiaire.
median ('miːdiən) *adj* médian. *n math* médiane f.
mediate ('miːdieit) *vi* s'entremettre, intervenir. **mediation** *n* médiation f. **mediator** *n* médiateur m.
medical ('medikəl) *adj* médical, -aux. **medication** *n* médication f. **medicine** *n* 1 (science) médecine f. 2 médicament *m.*
medieval (medi'iːvəl) *adj* médiéval, -aux.
mediocre (miːdi'oukə) *adj* médiocre.
meditate ('mediteit) *vt,vi* méditer. **meditation** *n* méditation f. **meditative** *adj* méditatif, -ive.
Mediterranean (meditə'reiniən) *adj* méditerranéen, -enne. **Mediterranean (Sea)** *n* (Mer) Mediterranée f.
medium ('miːdiəm) *n, pl* **media** 1 moyen *m.* 2 milieu, -eux *m.* 3 intermédiaire *m.* 4 médium *m.* **happy medium** juste milieu. ~*adj* moyen, -enne.
meek (miːk) *adj* doux, douce, humble. **meekly** *adv* avec douceur.
meet* (miːt) *vt* 1 rencontrer. 2 faire la connaissance de. 3 satisfaire. *vt* 1 se rencontrer. 2 se réunir. **meet with** éprouver, trouver. **meeting** *n* 1 rencontre f. 2 assemblée, réunion f.
megaphone ('megəfoun) *n* porte-voix *m invar.*
melancholy ('melənkəli) *n* mélancolie f. *adj* mélancolique.
mellow ('melou) *adj* 1 doux, douce. 2 moelleux, -euse. *vt,vi* mûrir.
melodrama ('melədraːmə) *n* mélodrame *m.* **melodramatic** *adj* mélodramatique.
melody ('melədi) *n* mélodie f. air *m.* **melodious** *adj* mélodieux, -euse.
melon ('melən) *n* melon *m.*
melt (melt) *vt,vi* fondre. *vt* attendrir. **melting** *n* fusion f.
member ('membə) *n* membre *m.* **member of Parliament** député *m.* **membership** *n* 1 cotisation f. 2 qualité de membre f.
membrane ('membrein) *n* membrane f.
memento (mə'mentou) *n, pl* **-os** *or* **-oes** mémento, souvenir *m.*
memo ('memou) *n* mémo *m.* note f.
memoir ('memwaː) *n* mémoire *m.*
memorandum (memə'rændəm) *n, pl* **-dums** *or* **-da** mémorandum *m.*
memory ('meməri) *n* 1 mémoire f. 2 souvenir *m.* **memorable** *adj* mémorable. **memorial** *n*

monument commémoratif *m. adj* commémoratif, -ive. **memorize** *vt* apprendre par cœur.
menace ('menəs) *n* menace f. *vt* menacer.
menagerie (mə'nædʒəri) *n* ménagerie f.
mend (mend) *vt* 1 raccommoder. 2 réparer. 3 arranger. *vi* s'améliorer. *n* reprise f. **mending** *n* raccommodage *m.*
menial ('miːniəl) *adj* servile.
menopause ('menəpoːz) *n* ménopause f.
menstrual ('menstruəl) *adj* menstruel, -elle. **menstruate** *vi* avoir ses règles.
mental ('mentl) *adj* 1 mental, -aux. 2 *inf* fou, folle. **mental hospital** *n* hôpital psychiatrique *m.* **mentality** *n* mentalité f.
menthol ('menθol) *n* menthol *m.*
mention ('menʃən) *n* mention f. *vt* mentionner.
menu ('menjuː) *n* menu *m.*
mercantile ('məːkəntail) *adj* commercial, -aux.
mercenary ('məːsənəri) *adj,n* mercenaire *m.*
merchant ('məːtʃənt) *n* négociant, commerçant *m. adj* marchand, de commerce. **merchant bank** *n* banque commerciale f. **merchant navy** *n* marine marchande f. **merchandise** *n* marchandise f.
mercury ('məːkjuri) *n* 1 mercure *m.* 2 *cap* Mercure *m.*
mercy ('məːsi) *n* 1 grâce, pitié f. 2 bienfait *m.* **merciful** *adj* clément. **merciless** *adj* impitoyable.
mere (miə) *adj* simple, pur.
merge (məːdʒ) *vt* fusionner, fondre. *vi* 1 se fondre. 2 *comm* fusionner. **merger** *n* fusion f.
meridian (mə'ridiən) *adj,n* méridien, -ienne *m.*
meringue (mə'ræŋ) *n* meringue f.
merit ('merit) *n* 1 mérite *m.* 2 valeur f. *vt* mériter.
mermaid ('məːmeid) *n* sirène f.
merry ('meri) *adj* 1 joyeux, -euse, gai. 2 *inf* gris. **merry-go-round** *n* manège (de chevaux de bois) *m.*
mesh (meʃ) *n* maille f. *vt* engrener. *vi* être en prise.
mesmerize ('mezməraiz) *vt* hypnotiser.
mess (mes) *n* 1 saleté f. 2 gâchis *m.* confusion f. 3 *mil* mess *m.* **make a mess of** gâcher. ~*v* **mess up** 1 gâcher. 2 salir.
message ('mesidʒ) *n* message *m.* **messenger** *n* messager, -ère.
met (met) *v see* **meet.**
metabolism (mi'tæbəlizəm) *n* métabolisme *m.*
metal ('metl) *n* métal, -aux *m.* **metallic** *adj* métallique. **metallurgy** *n* métallurgie f. **metallurgical** *adj* métallurgique.

metamorphosis (metə'mɔ:fəsis) *n*, *pl* **-ses** métamorphose *f*.

metaphor ('metəfə) *n* métaphore *f*. **metaphorical** *adj* métaphorique.

metaphysics (metə'fiziks) *n* métaphysique *f*. **metaphysical** *adj* métaphysique.

meteor ('mi:tiə) *n* météore *m*. **meteorological** *adj* météorologique. **meteorologist** *n* météorologiste, météorologue *m,f*. **meteorology** *n* météorologie *f*.

meter ('mi:tə) *n* compteur *m*.

methane ('mi:θein) *n* méthane *m*.

method ('meθəd) *n* méthode *f*. procédé *m*. **methodical** *adj* méthodique.

Methodist ('meθədist) *adj,n* méthodiste.

meticulous (mi'tikjuləs) *adj* méticuleux, -euse.

metre ('mi:tə) *n* mètre *m*. **metric** *adj* métrique.

metropolis (mə'trɔpəlis) *n* métropole *f*. **metropolitan** *adj* métropolitain.

miaow (mi'au) *vi* miauler. *n* miaulement *m*.

microbe ('maikróub) *n* microbe *m*.

microphone ('maikrəfoun) *n* microphone *m*.

microscope ('maikrəskoup) *n* microscope *m*. **microscopic** *adj* microscopique.

mid (mid) *adj* mi, moyen, -enne. **midday** *n* midi *m*. **midland** *adj* du centre. **midmorning** *n* mi-matin *m*. **midnight** *n* minuit *m*. **in midstream** *adv* au milieu de la rivière. **midsummer** *n* cœur de l'été *m*. **midway** *adv,adj* à mi-chemin. **midweek** *adj* du milieu de la semaine.

middle ('midl) *n* centre, milieu, -eux *m*. *adj* du milieu, moyen -enne. **middle-aged** *adj* d'un certain âge. **middle class** *n* bourgeoisie *f*. **middle-class** *adj* bourgeois. **middleman** *n* intermédiaire *m*.

Middle Ages *n* moyen âge *m*.

Middle East *n* Moyen Orient *m*.

midget ('midʒit) *n* nain *m*.

midst (midst) **in the midst of** *prep* parmi, au milieu de.

midwife ('midwaif) *n* sage-femme *f*.

might[1] (mait) *v* see **may**.

might[2] (mait) *n* force, puissance *f*. **mighty** *adj* 1 puissant. 2 vaste, énorme.

migraine ('mi:grein) *n* migraine *f*.

migrate (mai'greit) *vi* émigrer. **migration** *n* 1 migration *f*. 2 émigration *f*. **migratory** *adj* migrateur, -trice.

mike (maik) *n inf* micro *m*.

mild (maild) *adj* doux, douce. **mildness** *n* douceur *f*.

mildew ('mildju:) *n* 1 (on a plant) rouille *f*. 2 moisissure *f*.

mile (mail) *n* mille *m*. **mileage** *n* distance en milles *f*. **mileometer** *n* compteur kilométrique *m*. **milestone** *n* borne kilométrique *f*.

militant ('militənt) *adj,n* militant *m*. **military** *adj* militaire.

milk (milk) *n* lait *m*. *vt* traire. **milking** *n* traite *f*. **milkman** *n* laitier *m*.

Milky Way *n* Voie lactée *f*.

mill (mil) *n* 1 moulin *m*. 2 usine, fabrique *f*. *vt* moudre. *vi* fourmiller. **millstone** *n* meule *f*.

millennium (mi'leniəm) *n*, *pl* **-niums** *or* **-nia** millénaire *m*.

millet ('milit) *n* millet *m*.

milligram ('miligræm) *n* milligramme *m*.

millilitre ('mili:tə) *n* millilitre *m*.

millimetre ('milimi:tə) *n* millimètre *m*.

million ('miliən) *adj,n* million *m*. **millionaire** *n* millionnaire *m,f*. **millionth** *adj* millionième.

mime (maim) *n* mime *m*. *vt* mimer. *vi* imiter par gestes. **mimic** *n* mime *m*. *adj* 1 imitateur, -trice. 2 mimique. *vt* imiter, singer. **mimicry** *n* mimique, imitation *f*.

mince (mins) *vt* hacher. *vi* minauder. *n* hachis *m*. **mincer** *n* hachoir *m*.

mind (maind) *n* 1 esprit *m*. 2 mémoire *f*. 3 avis *m*. 4 envie *f*. *vt* 1 faire attention à. 2 surveiller. **I don't mind** 1 cela m'est égal. 2 je veux bien. **never mind!** peu importe!

mine[1] (main) *poss pron 1st pers s* 1 le mien, la mienne. 2 à moi.

mine[2] (main) *n* mine *f*. *vt* 1 exploiter. 2 *mil* miner. **miner** *n* mineur *m*.

mineral ('minərəl) *adj* minéral, -aux. *n* 1 minéral, -aux *m*. 2 *min* minerai *m*. **mineral water** *n* eau minérale *f*.

mingle ('miŋgəl) *vt* mêler. *vi* se mêler.

miniature ('miniətʃə) *n* miniature *f*. *adj* minuscule, en miniature.

minim ('minim) *n* blanche *f*.

minimum ('miniməm) *n*, *pl* **-mums** *or* **-ma** minimum *m*. **minimal** *adj* minimal, -aux, minime.

mining ('mainiŋ) *n* exploitation des mines *f*.

minister ('ministə) *n* ministre *m*. **ministerial** *adj* ministériel, -elle. **ministry** *n* ministère *m*.

mink (miŋk) *n* vison *m*.

minor ('mainə) *adj,n* mineur. **minority** *n* minorité *f*.

Minorca (mi'nɔ:kə) *n* Minorque *f*.

minstrel ('minstrəl) *n* ménestrel *m*.

mint[1] (mint) *n bot* menthe *f*.

mint² (mɪnt) *n* Hôtel de la Monnaie *m*. *vt* **1** (a coin, etc.) battre, frapper. **2** forger.

minuet (mɪnju'et) *n* menuet *m*.

minus ('maɪnəs) *prep* moins, sans. *adj* **1** moins. **2** négatif, -ive.

minute¹ ('mɪnɪt) *n* **1** minute *f*. **2** instant *m*. **3** *pl* procès-verbal *m*.

minute² (mai'nju:t) *adj* **1** menu, minuscule. **2** minutieux, -euse.

miracle ('mɪrəkəl) *n* miracle *m*. **miraculous** *adj* miraculeux, -euse.

mirage ('mɪrɑ:ʒ) *n* mirage *m*.

mirror ('mɪrə) *n* miroir *m*.

mirth (mə:θ) *n* gaieté *f*.

misbehave (mɪsbi'heɪv) *vi* se conduire mal.

miscarriage (mɪs'kærɪdʒ) *n* **1** echec, insuccès *m*. **2** *med* fausse couche *f*. **miscarry** *vi* **1** échouer. **2** *med* avorter.

miscellaneous (mɪsə'leɪnɪəs) *adj* divers, varié. **miscellany** *n* mélange *m*.

mischance (mɪs'tʃɑ:ns) *n* malheur *m*. mésaventure *f*.

mischief ('mɪstʃif) *n* **1** mal *m,pl* maux. **2** malice *f*. **3** sottises *f pl*. **mischievous** *adj* **1** malfaisant. **2** espiègle.

misconceive (mɪskən'si:v) *vt* mal comprendre. **misconception** *n* **1** idée fausse *f*. **2** malentendu *m*.

misconduct (*n* mɪs'kɔndʌkt; *v* mɪskən'dʌkt) *n* **1** (of a person) inconduite *f*. **2** mauvaise gestion *f*. *vt* mal gérer.

misdeed (mɪs'di:d) *n* méfait *m*.

miser ('maɪzə) *n* avare *m,f*. **miserly** *adj* avare. **miserliness** *n* avarice *f*.

miserable ('mɪzərəbəl) *adj* **1** triste, malheureux, -euse. **2** misérable, pitoyable.

misery ('mɪzəri) *n* **1** souffrance *f*. **2** misère, détresse *f*.

misfire (mɪs'faɪə) *vi* **1** rater. **2** tomber à plat.

misfit ('mɪsfit) *n* **1** malfaçon *f*. **2** inadapté *m*.

misfortune (mɪs'fɔ:tʃən) *n* malheur *m*.

misgiving (mɪs'gɪvɪŋ) *n* doute, pressentiment *m*. crainte *f*.

misguided (mɪs'gaɪdid) *adj* **1** égaré. **2** hors de propos.

mishap ('mɪshæp) *n* mésaventure *f*.

mislay* (mɪs'leɪ) *vt* égarer.

mislead* (mɪs'li:d) *vt* **1** tromper. **2** fourvoyer.

misprint ('mɪsprɪnt) *n* faute d'impression *f*.

miss¹ (mɪs) *vt,vi* manquer, rater. **miss out** passer, omettre. *n* coup manqué *m*. **missing** *adj* **1** manquant, absent. **2** perdu.

234

miss² (mɪs) *n* **1** mademoiselle *f*. **2** *cap* (title of address) Mlle.

missile ('mɪsail) *n* projectile *m*.

mission ('mɪʃən) *n* mission *f*. **missionary** *adj,n* missionnaire *m*.

mist (mɪst) *n* brume *f*.

mistake* (mɪs'teik) *n* erreur, faute *f*. **by mistake** par mégarde. ~*vt* **1** se méprendre (sur), se tromper de. **2** prendre. **mistaken** *adj* faux, fausse. **be mistaken** se tromper.

mister ('mɪstə) *n* monsieur *m*.

mistletoe ('mɪsəltou) *n* gui *m*.

mistress ('mɪstrəs) *n* **1** maîtresse *f*. **2** *educ* professeur *m*.

mistrust (mɪs'trʌst) *vt* se méfier de. *n* méfiance *f*. **mistrustful** *adj* méfiant.

misunderstand* (mɪsʌndə'stænd) *vt* mal comprendre. **misunderstanding** *n* **1** malentendu *m*. **2** mésentente *f*.

misuse (*v* mɪs'ju:z; *n* mɪs'ju:s) *vt* **1** faire mauvais usage de. **2** maltraiter. *n* abus, mauvais usage *m*.

mitre ('maɪtə) *n* mitre *f*.

mitten ('mɪtn̩) *n* mitaine *f*.

mix (mɪks) *vt* mélanger, mêler. *vi* se mélanger. **mix up 1** embrouiller. **2** confondre. **mixed** *adj* mixte. **mixed grill** *n* grillade variée *f*. **mixture** *n* **1** mélange *m*. **2** *med* potion *f*.

moan (moun) *vi* gémir. *n* plainte *f*.

moat (mout) *n* fossé *m*. douve *f*.

mob (mɔb) *n* cohue, foule *f*. *vt* **1** molester. **2** s'attrouper.

mobile ('moubail) *adj* mobile. **mobility** *n* mobilité *f*. **mobilize** *vt* mobiliser.

mock (mɔk) *vt,vi* se moquer de. *vt* imiter. *adj* simulé, faux, fausse. **mockery** *n* raillerie, moquerie *f*.

mode (moud) *n* **1** manière *f*. **2** mode *f*.

model ('mɔdl̩) *adj* modèle. *n* **1** modèle *m*. **2** (fashion) mannequin *m*. *vt* modeler. *vi* être mannequin.

moderate ('mɔdərət) *adj* **1** modéré, raisonnable. **2** médiocre. **3** moyen, -enne. *vt* modérer. *vi* se modérer. **moderation** *n* modération *f*. **in moderation** modérément.

modern ('mɔdən) *adj* moderne. **modernity** *n* modernité *f*. **modernize** *vt* moderniser.

modest ('mɔdist) *adj* **1** modeste. **2** pudique. **modesty** *n* **1** modestie *f*. **2** pudeur *f*. **3** modération *f*.

modify ('mɔdifai) *vt* modifier. **modification** *n* modification *f*. **modifier** *n* modificateur *m*.

modulate ('mɔdjuleɪt) *vt,vi* moduler.

module ('mɔdju:l) *n* module *m.*
mohair ('mouhɛə) *n* mohair *m.*
moist (mɔist) *adj* **1** humide. **2** moite. **moisten**
vt humecter, mouiller.
moisture ('mɔistʃə) *n* humidité *f.* **moisturize**
vt humidifier.
mole[1] (moul) *n* grain de beauté *m.*
mole[2] (moul) *n zool* taupe *f.*
molecule ('mɔlikju:l) *n* molécule *f.* **molecular**
adj moléculaire.
molest (mə'lest) *vt* molester, rudoyer.
mollusc ('mɔləsk) *n* mollusque *m.*
molten ('moultən) *adj* fondu.
moment ('moumənt) *n* moment, instant
m. **momentary** *adj* momentané. **momen-
tous** *adj* important, capital, -aux. **momentum**
n, pl **-ta 1** *sci* force vive *f.* **2** vitesse acquise *f.*
monarch ('mɔnək) *n* monarque *m.* **monar-
chism** *n* monarchisme *m.* **monarchist** *n*
monarchiste *m,f.* **monarchy** *n* monarchie *f.*
monastery ('mɔnəstri) *n* monastère *m.*
monastic *adj* monastique.
Monday ('mʌndi) *n* lundi *m.*
money ('mʌni) *n* **1** argent *m.* **2** (coin) monnaie
f. **ready money** argent comptant. **moneybox** *n* tirelire *f.* **money order** *n* mandat-poste
m. **monetary** *adj* monétaire.
mongrel ('mʌngrəl) *n* métis, -isse. *adj* métis,
-isse, hybride.
monitor ('mɔnitə) *n* moniteur, -trice. *vt*
contrôler.
monk (mʌŋk) *n* moine *m.*
monkey ('mʌŋki) *n* **1** singe *m.* **2** *inf* polisson,
-onne.
monochrome ('mɔnəkroum) *adj,n* monochrome
m.
monogamy (mə'nɔgəmi) *n* monogamie *f.* **mo-
nogamist** *n* monogame *m,f.* **monogamous**
adj monogame.
monologue ('mɔnəlɔg) *n* monologue *m.*
monopoly (mə'nɔpəli) *n* monopole *m.* **monopolize** *vt* **1** monopoliser. **2** accaparer.
monosyllable ('mɔnəsiləbəl) *n* monosyllabe
m. **monosyllabic** *adj* monosyllabique.
monotone ('mɔnətoun) *n* voix monotone *f.*
monotonous *adj* monotone. **monotony** *n*
monotonie *f.*
monsoon (mɔn'su:n) *n* mousson *f.*
monster ('mɔnstə) *n* monstre *m.* **monstrous**
adj monstrueux, -euse. **monstrosity** *n*
monstruosité *f.*
month (mʌnθ) *n* mois *m.* **monthly** *adj*

mensuel, -elle. *adv* mensuellement. *n* publication mensuelle *f.*
monument ('mɔnjumənt) *n* monument *m.*
monumental *adj* monumental, -aux.
moo (mu:) *vi* meugler. *n* meuglement *m.*
mood[1] (mu:d) *n* humeur *f.* **moody** *adj*
d'humeur changeante, maussade.
mood[2] (mu:d) *n gram* mode *m.*
moon (mu:n) *n* lune *f.* **moonlight** *n* clair de
lune *m.*
moor[1] (muə) *n* lande *f.* **moorhen** *n* poule d'eau
f.
moor[2] (muə) *vt* amarrer. **moorings** *n pl* amar-
res *f pl.*
Moor (muə) *n* maure *m.* mauresque *f.* **Moorish**
adj mauresque.
mop (mɔp) *n* balai à laver *m.* **mop of hair**
tignasse *f.* ~ *vt* éponger.
mope (moup) *vi* s'ennuyer, avoir le cafard.
moped ('mouped) *n* cyclomoteur *m.*
moral ('mɔrəl) *adj* moral, -aux. *n* **1** morale *f.* **2** *pl*
mœurs *f pl.* **moralist** *n* moraliste *m.* **morale**
n moral *m.* **morality** *n* moralité *f.* **moralize**
vi,vt moraliser.
morbid ('mɔ:bid) *adj* morbide, malsain.
more (mɔ:) *adj* plus. *adv* **1** plus. **2** davantage,
encore. **more and more** de plus en plus.
once more encore une fois. **more than** plus
que, plus de. **some more** encore, davantage.
moreover *adv* de plus, en outre.
morgue (mɔ:g) *n* morgue *f.*
morning ('mɔ:niŋ) *n* matin *m.* matinée *f.* **morning coat** *n* jaquette *f.*
Morocco (mə'rɔkou) *n* Maroc *m.* **Moroccan**
adj,n marocain.
moron ('mɔ:rɔn) *n* **1** *med* arriéré *m.* **2** *sl* idiot,
moron *m.*
morose (mə'rous) *adj* morose, maussade.
morphine ('mɔ:fi:n) *n* morphine *f.*
morse code (mɔ:s) *n* (alphabet) morse *m.*
mortal ('mɔ:tl) *adj,n* mortel, -elle. **mortality** *n*
mortalité *f.*
mortar[1] ('mɔ:tə) *n cul,mil* mortier *m.*
mortar[2] ('mɔ:tə) *n* (for building) mortier *m.*
mortgage ('mɔ:gidʒ) *n* hypothèque *f. vt* hypothéquer.
mortify ('mɔ:tifai) *vt* mortifier.
mortuary ('mɔ:tjuəri) *n* **1** morgue *f.* **2** salle
mortuaire *f. adj* mortuaire.
mosaic (mou'zeiik) *n* mosaïque *f.*
mosque (mɔsk) *n* mosquée *f.*
mosquito (mə'ski:tou) *n, pl* **-oes** *or* **-os** moustique *m.*

235

moss (mɔs) n mousse f. **mossy** adj moussu.
most (moust) adj le or la plus, la plupart. n plus
m. plupart f. **at most** au maximum. ∼adv 1
très, fort. 2 plus. **mostly** adv 1 princi-
palement. 2 le plus souvent.
motel (mou'tel) n motel m.
moth (mɔθ) n papillon de nuit m. **clothes
moth** n mite f.
mother ('mʌðə) n mère f. vt dorloter.
motherhood n maternité f. **mother-in-law** n
belle-mère f. **mother superior** n mère supérieure f. **mother tongue** n langue maternelle f. **motherly** adj maternel, -elle.
motion ('mouʃən) n 1 mouvement m. 2 signe
m. 3 pol motion f. vt faire signe. **motionless**
adj immobile.
motive ('moutiv) n motif m. adj moteur, -trice.
motivate vt motiver.
motor ('moutə) n moteur m. adj moteur, -trice.
motor car n automobile f. **motor cycle** n
motocyclette f. **motorist** n automobiliste
m,f. **motorway** n autoroute f.
mottle ('mɔtļ) vt tacheter, moucheter.
motto ('mɔtou) n, pl **-oes** or **-os** devise f.
mould[1] (mould) n moule m. vt mouler, pétrir.
mould[2] (mould) n (mildew) moisi m. moissure
f. vi se moisir. **mouldy** adj moisi.
moult (moult) vi muer. **moulting** n mue f.
mound (maund) n tertre m.
mount[1] (maunt) vt,vi monter. **mount up** augmenter. ∼n monture f.
mount[2] (maunt) n geog mont m.
mountain ('mauntin) n montagne f. **mountainous** adj montagneux, -euse. **mountaineer**
n alpiniste m,f. **mountaineering** n alpinisme
m.
mourn (mɔːn) vt,vi pleurer. **mournful** adj lugubre, funèbre. **mourning** n deuil m.
mouse (maus) n, pl **mice** souris f. **mousetrap**
n souricière f. **mousy** adj (of hair) terne.
mousse (muːs) n mousse f.
moustache (mə'stɑːʃ) n moustache f.
mouth (mauθ) n 1 anat bouche f. 2 (of animals) geule f. 3 ouverture f. 4 (of rivers)
embouchure f. **mouthful** n bouchée f. **mouthpiece** n 1 embouchure f. 2 porte-parole m
invar.
move (muːv) vt 1 déplacer. 2 animer. 3 émouvoir. 4 proposer. vi 1 se déplacer, bouger. 2
agir. **move in** emménager. **move on**
s'avancer, circuler. **move out** déménager.
∼n 1 mouvement m. 2 game tour, coup m. 3
déménagement m. **movable** adj mobile.

movement n mouvement m. **moving** adj 1
en marche. 2 émouvant.
mow* (mou) vt 1 faucher. 2 tondre.
Mr ('mistə) (title of address) M.
Mrs ('misiz) (title of address) Mme.
much (mʌtʃ) adj beaucoup (de). adv 1 beaucoup. 2 bien. **as much** autant. **how much?**
combien de? **much more** bien plus. **very
much** beaucoup.
muck (mʌk) n 1 fumier m. 2 saleté f. v **muck
up** gâcher. **mucky** adj sale.
mud (mʌd) n boue f. **mudguard** n garde-boue
m invar. **muddy** adj boueux, -euse.
muddle ('mʌdļ) n confusion f. vt embrouiller.
muff (mʌf) n manchon m.
muffle ('mʌfəl) vt 1 emmitoufler. 2 assourdir. n
mufle m.
mug (mʌg) n timbale f. pot m.
muggy ('mʌgi) adj lourd.
mulberry ('mʌlbəri) n mûre f. **mulberry bush** n
mûrier m.
mule[1] (mjuːl) n zool mule f. mulet m.
mule[2] (mjuːl) n mule f.
mullet ('mʌlit) n muge m.
multiple ('mʌltipəl) adj,n multiple m.
multiply ('mʌltiplai) vt multiplier. vi se multiplier. **multiplication** n multiplication f.
multitude ('mʌltitjuːd) n multitude f.
mum (mʌm) n inf maman f.
mumble ('mʌmbəl) vt,vi marmonner.
mummy[1] ('mʌmi) n momie f. **mummify** vt
momifier.
mummy[2] ('mʌmi) n inf maman f.
mumps (mʌmps) n oreillons m pl.
munch (mʌntʃ) vt mâcher, mâchonner.
mundane ('mʌndein) adj mondain.
municipal (mjuː'nisipəl) adj municipal, -aux.
mural ('mjuərəl) adj mural, -aux.
murder ('mɔːdə) n meurtre m. vt assassiner.
murderer n assassin, meurtrier m. **murderous** adj meurtrier, -ière.
murmur ('mɔːmə) vi,vt murmurer. n murmure
m.
muscle ('mʌsəl) n muscle m. **muscular** adj 1
musculaire. 2 musclé.
muse (mjuːz) n muse f. vi méditer, rêver.
museum (mjuː'ziəm) n musée m.
mushroom ('mʌʃrum) n champignon m.
music ('muːzik) n musique f. **musical** adj 1
musical, -aux. 2 (of a person) musicien,
-ienne. **musician** n musicien, -ienne.
musk (mʌsk) n musc m.

musket (´mʌskit) *n* mousquet *m.* **musketeer** *n* mousquetaire *m.*

Muslim (´muzlim) *adj,n* musulman.

muslin (´mʌzlin) *n* mousseline *f.*

mussel (´mʌsəl) *n* moule *f.*

must¹ (mʌst) *v mod aux* falloir, devoir. *n* nécessité *f.*

mustard (´mʌstəd) *n* moutarde *f.*

mute (mju:t) *adj,n* muet, -ette. *vt* amortir, assourdir. **muteness** *n* mutisme *m.*

mutilate (´mju:tileit) *vt* mutiler. **mutilation** *n* mutilation *f.*

mutiny (´mju:tini) *n* mutinerie, révolte *f. vi* se révolter. **mutinous** *adj* rebelle.

mutter (´mʌtə) *vi* marmotter.

mutton (´mʌtn̩) *n* mouton *m.* **leg of mutton** *n* gigot *m.*

mutual (´mju:tjuəl) *adj* mutuel, -elle, commun.

muzzle (´mʌzəl) *n* 1 *zool* mouseau, -aux *m.* 2 *mil* gueule *f.* 3 muselière *f. vt* museler.

my (mai) *poss adj 1st pers s* mon, ma, mes. **myself** *pron 1st pers s* 1 moi-même. 2 me. **by myself** tout seul.

myrrh (mə:) *n* myrrhe *f.*

myrtle (´mə:tl̩) *n* myrte *m.*

mystery (´mistəri) *n* mystère *m.* **mysterious** *adj* mystérieux, -euse.

mystic (´mistik) *adj,n* mystique. **mysticism** *n* mysticisme *m.* **mystified** *adj* intrigué. **mystify** *vt* 1 mystifier. 2 désorienter.

mystique (mi´sti:k) *n* mystique *f.*

myth (miθ) *n* mythe *m.* **mythical** *adj* mythique. **mythological** *adj* mythologique. **mythology** *n* mythologie.

N

nag¹ (næg) *vt* gronder, criailler. *vi* être toujours après.

nag² (næg) *n inf* bidet *m.*

nail (neil) *n* 1 *anat* ongle *m.* 2 clou *m. vt* clouer. **nailbrush** *n* brosse à ongles *f.* **nailfile** *n* lime à ongles *f.* **nail varnish** *n* vernis à ongles *m.*

naive (nai´i:v) *adj* naïf, -ïve, ingénu.

naked (´neikid) *adj* nu. **nakedness** *n* nudité *f.*

name (neim) *n* 1 nom *m.* 2 réputation *f. vt* nommer. **namely** *adv* à savoir, c´est-à-dire.

nanny (´næni) *n* 1 bonne d´enfant *f.* 2 *inf* nounou *f.*

nap (næp) *n* somme *m.* sieste *f. vi* sommeiller.

napalm (´neipɑ:m) *n* napalm *m.*

napkin (´næpkin) *n* serviette *f.*

nappy (´næpi) *n* couche *f.*

narcotic (nɑ:´kɔtik) *adj,n* narcotique *m.*

narrate (nə´reit) *vt* raconter. **narration** *n* narration *f.* **narrative** *n* récit *m. adj* narratif, -ive. **narrator** *n* narrateur, -trice.

narrow (´nærou) *adj* étroit, serré. *vt* restreindre. *vi* se rétrécir. **narrow-minded** *adj* borné. **narrowness** *n* étroitesse *f.*

nasal (´neizəl) *adj* nasal, -aux.

nasturtium (nə´stə:ʃəm) *n* capucine *f.*

nasty (´nɑ:sti) *adj* 1 mauvais, méchant. 2 désagréable. 3 dangereux, -euse. **nastiness** *n* 1 méchanceté *f.* 2 saleté *f.*

nation (´neiʃən) *n* nation *f.* **national** *adj* national, -aux. **national anthem** *n* hymne national *m.* **national insurance** *n* assurances sociales *f pl.* **national service** *n* service militaire *m.* **nationality** *n* nationalité *f.* **nationalization** *n* nationalisation *f.* **nationalize** *vt* nationaliser. **nationwide** *adj* sur le plan national.

native (´neitiv) *n* originaire, indigène *m,f. adj* 1 natal. 2 naturel, -elle.

nativity (nə´tiviti) *n* nativité *f.*

natural (´nætʃərəl) *adj* naturel, -elle. **natural gas** *n* gaz naturel *m.* **natural history** *n* histoire naturelle *f.* **natural science** *n* sciences naturelles *f pl.* **naturalization** *n* naturalisation *f.* **naturalize** *vt* naturaliser.

nature (´neitʃə) *n* 1 nature *f.* 2 sorte *f.*

naughty (´nɔ:ti) *adj* méchant, vilain.

nausea (´nɔ:siə, -ziə) *n* nausée *f.* **nauseate** *vt* dégoûter. **nauseating** *adj* ecœurant.

nautical (´nɔ:tikəl) *adj* nautique, marin.

naval (´neivəl) *adj* de marine, maritime.

nave (neiv) *n* nef *f.*

navel (´neivəl) *n* nombril *m.*

navigate (´nævigeit) *vi* naviguer. *vt* diriger, gouverner. **navigation** *n* navigation *f.* **navigator** *n* navigateur *m.*

navy (´neivi) *n* marine de guerre *f.* **navy blue** *n* bleu marine *m.*

near (niə) *adj* proche. *adv* près. *prep* près *or* auprès de. *vt* approcher de. **nearby** *adv* tout près (de). *adj* avoisinant. **nearly** *adv* presque, à peu près. **nearside** *n* côté gauche *m. adj* gauche.

Near East *n* Proche Orient *m.*

neat (ni:t) *adj* 1 net, nette, soigné. 2 élégant. 3 pur. **neatness** *n* 1 netteté *f.* 2 ordre *m.*

nebulous (´nebjuləs) *adj* nébuleux, -euse.

necessary (´nesəsəri) *adj* nécessaire. **if**

237

necessary au besoin. **necessity** n nécessité f.

neck (nek) n **1** anat cou m. **2** (of a bottle) goulot m. **3** (of clothing) col m. encolure f. **neckband** n encolure f. **necklace** n collier m. **neckline** n encolure f.

nectar ('nektə) n nectar m.

need (niːd) vt **1** avoir besoin de. **2** exiger, demander. vi **1** être obligé. **2** falloir. **needy** adj indigent.

needle ('niːdļ) n aiguille f. **needlework** n travail à l'aiguille m.

negate (ni'geit) vt nier. **negation** n négation f. **negative** adj négatif, -ive. n **1** négative f. **2** phot négatif m.

neglect (ni'glekt) vt négliger. n négligence f.

negligent ('neglidʒənt) adj négligent. **negligence** n négligence f.

negotiate (ni'gouʃieit) vi,vt négocier. vt franchir, surmonter. **negotiation** n négociation f.

Negro ('niːgrou) n, pl **-oes** nègre m. **Negress** n négresse f.

neigh (nei) vi hennir. n hennissement m.

neighbour ('neibə) n voisin m. **neighbourhood** n voisinage m. alentours m pl. **neighbourly** adj (de) bon voisin.

neither ('naiðə) adj,pron ni l'un ni l'autre. conj ni, non plus. **neither...nor** ni...ni.

neon ('niːən) n néon m.

nephew ('nevjuː) n neveu, -eux m.

Neptune ('neptjuːn) n Neptune m.

nerve (nəːv) n **1** anat nerf m. **2** inf aplomb, toupet m. **3** courage m.**nerve-racking** adj énervant. **nervous** adj **1** nerveux, -euse. **2** intimidé. **nervous breakdown** n crise de nerfs f. **nervousness** n nervosité f.

nest (nest) n nid m. vi nicher.

nestle ('nesəl) vi se nicher.

net[1] (net) n filet m. **netball** n netball m. **network** n réseau, -aux m.

net[2] (net) adj net, nette. vt toucher or rapporter net.

Netherlands ('neðələndz) n pl Pays Bas m pl.

nettle ('netļ) n ortie f. vt agacer, piquer. **nettle rash** n urticaire f.

neurosis (njuə'rousis) n pl **-ses** névrose f. **neurotic** adj,n névrosé.

neuter ('njuːtə) adj,n neutre m.

neutral ('njuːtrəl) adj neutre. **neutrality** n neutralité f. **neutralize** vt neutraliser.

neutron ('njuːtrɔn) n neutron m.

never ('nevə) adv (ne...)jamais. interj pas possible! **never mind!** peu importe! **nevertheless** adv pourtant, quand-même.

new (njuː) adj **1** neuf, neuve. **2** nouveau, -elle. **3** frais, fraîche. **newcomer** n nouveau venu m. **news** n pl **1** nouvelle f pl. **2** (radio, etc.) informations f pl. **newsagent** n marchand de journaux m. **newspaper** n journal, -aux m. **newsreel** n bande d'actualités f.

newt (njuːt) n salamandre f.

New Testament n Nouveau Testament m.

New Year n Nouvel An m. **New Year's Day** n jour de l'an m.

New Zealand ('ziːlənd) n Nouvelle-Zélande f. **New Zealander** n néo-zélandais m.

next (nekst) adj **1** prochain. **2** suivant. **3** voisin. adv ensuite. **next to** à côté de. **next-door** adj d'à côté. adv à côté.

nib (nib) n plume f.

nibble ('nibəl) vt,vi grignoter.

nice (nais) adj **1** agréable, bon, bonne. **2** gentil, -ille. **3** délicat. **nicety** n **1** délicatesse f. **2** précision f.

niche (nitʃ) n niche f.

nick (nik) n **1** encoche f. **2** sl prison f.

nickel ('nikəl) n nickel m.

nickname ('nikneim) n sobriquet m. vt surnommer.

nicotine ('nikətiːn) n nicotine f.

niece (niːs) n nièce f.

Nigeria (nai'dʒiəriə) n Nigéria m. **Nigerian** adj,n nigérien, -ienne.

nigger ('nigə) n derog nègre m. négresse f.

niggle ('nigəl) vi tatillonner.

night (nait) n **1** nuit f. **2** soir m. **nightclub** n boîte de nuit f. **nightdress** n also **nightgown** chemise de nuit f. **nightmare** n cauchemar m. **night-time** n nuit f. **night-watchman** n veilleur de nuit m.

nightingale ('naitiŋgeil) n rossignol m.

nil (nil) n zéro, rien m.

Nile (nail) n Nil m.

nimble ('nimbəl) adj agile. **nimbleness** n agileté f.

nine (nain) adj,n neuf m. **ninth** adj neuvième.

nineteen (nain'tiːn) adj,n dix-neuf m. **nineteenth** adj dix-neuvième.

ninety ('nainti) adj,n quatre-vingt-dix m. **ninetieth** adj quatre-vingt-dixième.

nip[1] (nip) vt pincer. **nip off** filer. ~n pincement m.

nip[2] (nip) n goutte f. doigt m.

nipple ('nipəl) n anat mamelon m.

nit (nit) n **1** lente f. **2** inf crétin m.

nitrogen ('naitrədʒən) n azote m.
no¹ (nou) adv 1 non. 2 ne... pas. n, pl noes non
m invar.
no² (nou) adj 1 pas un, pas de, aucun, nul,
nulle. 2 peu, ne...pas. no longer ne...plus.
no more ne...plus. no smoking défense de
fumer.
noble ('noubəl) adj,n noble m. nobility n
noblesse f. nobleman n noble m.
nobody ('noubədi) pron personne. n inf zéro,
rien m.
nocturnal (nɔk'tɔ:nl) adj nocturne.
nod (nɔd) n signe de tête m. vi 1 faire un signe
de tête. 2 somnoler.
node (noud) n nœud m.
noise (nɔiz) n 1 bruit m. 2 tapage, fracas
m. noisily adv bruyamment. noisy adj tumultueux, -euse.
nomad ('noumæd) n nomade m,f. nomadic adj
nomade.
nominal ('nɔminl) adj nominal, -aux.
nominate ('nɔmineit) vt désigner, nommer.
nomination n nomination f.
non- pref 1 non- 2 in- 3 sans.
nonchalant ('nɔnʃələnt) adj nonchalant. nonchalance n nonchalance f.
nondescript ('nɔndiskript) adj 1 indéfinissable.
2 quelconque.
none (nʌn) pron 1 aucun. 2 personne. adv pas,
point.
nonentity (nɔn'entiti) n non-être m. nullité f.
nonsense ('nɔnsəns) n absurdité f.
noodles ('nu:dlz) n pl nouilles f pl.
noon (nu:n) n midi m.
no-one pron personne.
noose (nu:s) n nœud coulant, collet m.
nor (nɔ:) conj ni, ni...ne.
norm (nɔ:m) n norme f. normal adj normal,
-aux.
Norman ('nɔ:mən) adj,n normand.
Normandy ('nɔ:məndi) n Normandie f.
Norse (nɔ:s) adj nordique. Norse (language) n
norvégien m.
north (nɔ:θ) n nord m. adj septentrional, -aux,
nord invar. adv au or vers le nord. northeast
n nord-est m. adv vers le nord-est. adj du
nord-est. northeasterly adj du nord-est. north-
eastern adj du nord-est. northerly adj du
nord. northern adj du nord. northwards
vers le nord. northwest n nord-ouest m. adv
vers le nord-ouest. adj du nord-ouest. north-
westerly adj du nord-ouest. northwestern
adj du nord-ouest.

North America n Amérique du Nord f.
Northern Ireland n Irlande du Nord f.
Norway ('nɔ:wei) n Norvège f. Norwegian
adj,n norvégien, -ienne. Norwegian (language) n norvégien m.
nose (nouz) n 1 nez m. 2 (of animals) museau,
-aux m. vt flairer. nosy adj inf fouinard,
indiscret, -ète.
nostalgia (nɔ'stældʒiə) n nostalgie f. nostalgic
adj nostalgique.
nostril ('nɔstril) n 1 narine f. 2 (of an animal)
naseau, -aux m.
not (nɔt) adv ne...pas, ne...point, pas.
notch (nɔtʃ) n encoche f. cran m. vt entailler,
encocher.
note (nout) n 1 note f. 2 remarque f. 3 comm
billet m. vt noter, remarquer. notable adj
notable. notation n notation f. notebook n
carnet m. notepaper n papier à lettres
m. noteworthy adj remarquable.
nothing ('nʌθiŋ) pron,n rien m. for nothing
en vain. ~adv pas du tout. nothingness n
néant m.
notice ('noutis) n 1 avis m. notification f. 2
affiche f. 3 congé m. vt remarquer, apercevoir.
noticeable adj perceptible. notice board n
tableau d'affichage m.
notify ('noutifai) vt notifier, aviser. notification
n avis m.
notion ('nouʃən) n notion, idée f.
notorious (nou'tɔ:riəs) adj notoire, mal famé.
notoriety n notoriété f.
notwithstanding (nɔtwiθ'stændiŋ) prep malgré. adv néanmoins. conj bien que.
nougat ('nu:gɑ:) n nougat m.
nought (nɔ:t) n zéro, rien m.
noun (naun) n nom m.
nourish ('nʌriʃ) vt nourrir. nourishment n
nourriture f.
novel¹ ('nɔvəl) n roman m. novelist n
romancier, -ière.
novel² ('nɔvəl) adj original, -aux, singulier,
-ière. novelty n nouveauté f.
November (nou'vembə) n novembre m.
novice ('nɔvis) n novice m,f.
now (nau) adv 1 maintenant, à l'heure actuelle.
2 tout de suite. now and then de temps en
temps. nowadays adv de nos jours.
nowhere ('nouwɛə) adv nulle part.
noxious ('nɔkʃəs) adj nuisible.
nozzle ('nɔzəl) n lance f.
nuance ('nju:əns) n nuance f.

nucleus ('nju:kliəs) *n, pl* **-clei** noyau, -aux *m.* **nuclear** *adj* nucléaire.
nude (nju:d) *adj,n* nu *m.* **nudity** *n* nudité *f.*
nudge (nʌdʒ) *vt* pousser du coude. *n* coup de coude *m.*
nugget ('nʌgit) *n* pépite *f.*
nuisance ('nju:səns) *n* **1** ennui *m.* **2** *inf* peste *f.*
null (nʌl) *adj* nul, nulle. **null and void** nul et non avenu. **nullify** *vt* annuler.
numb (nʌm) *adj* engourdi. *vt* engourdir.
number ('nʌmbə) *n* **1** nombre *m.* **2** (of a house, etc.) numéro *m.* **3** quantité *f.* *vt* **1** compter. **2** numéroter. **numeral** *n* chiffre *m. adj* numéral, -aux. **numerate** *adj* possédant les mathématiques de base. **numerical** *adj* numérique. **numerous** *adj* nombreux, -euse.
nun (nʌn) *n* religieuse *f.* **nunnery** *n* couvent *m.*
nurse (nə:s) *n* **1** infirmière *f.* **2** nourrice *f.* **3** (for children) bonne *f.* **nursing home** *n* clinique *f.*
nursery ('nə:səri) *n* **1** chambre d'enfants *f.* **2** garderie *f.* **3** *bot* pépinière *f.* **nursery man** *n* pépiniériste *m.* **nursery rhyme** *n* chanson enfantine *f.* **nursery school** *n* école maternelle *f.*
nurture ('nə:tʃə) *vt* **1** élever. **2** nourrir. *n* **1** éducation *f.* **2** nourriture *f.*
nut (nʌt) *n* **1** noix *f.* **2** *tech* écrou *m.* **nutcrackers** *n pl* casse-noisettes *m invar.* **nutmeg** *n* muscade *f.* **nutshell** *n* coquille de noix *f.* **in a nutshell** en un mot.
nutrition (nju:'triʃən) *n* nutrition *f.* **nutritious** *adj* nourrissant.
nuzzle ('nʌzəl) *vi* fouiller. *vt* fourrer son nez contre.
nylon ('nailən) *n* **1** nylon *m.* **2** *pl inf* bas *m pl.*
nymph (nimf) *n* nymphe *f.*

O

oak (ouk) *n* chêne *m.*
oar (ɔ:) *n* rame *f.* aviron *m.* **oarsman** *n* rameur *m.*
oasis (ou'eisis) *n, pl* **oases** oasis *f.*
oath (ouθ) *n* **1** serment *m.* **2** juron *m.*
oats (outs) *n pl* avoine *f.*
oatmeal ('outmi:l) *n* farine d'avoine *f.*
obedient (ə'bi:diənt) *adj* obéissant. **obedience** *n* obéissance *f.*
obese (ou'bi:s) *adj* obèse. **obesity** *n* obésité *f.*
obey (ə'bei) *vt* obéir à. *vi* obéir.
obituary (ə'bitjuəri) *n* nécrologie *f. adj* nécrologique.

object (*n* 'ɔbdʒikt; *v* əb'dʒekt) *n* **1** objet *m.* **2** but *m.* **3** *gram* complément *m.* *vt* objecter. **object to** trouver à redire à, s'opposer à. **objection** *n* **1** objection *f.* **2** inconvénient *m.* **objectionable** *adj* **1** répréhensible. **2** désagréable. **objective** *adj,n* objectif, -ive *m.* **objectivity** *n* objectivité *f.*
oblige (ə'blaidʒ) *vt* **1** obliger, contraindre. **2** rendre service à. **obligation** *n.* obligation *f.* **obligatory** *adj* obligatoire, de rigueur.
oblique (ə'bli:k) *adj* oblique, indirect.
obliterate (ə'blitəreit) *vt* **1** effacer. **2** oblitérer.
oblivion (ə'bliviən) *n* oubli *m.* **oblivious** *adj* oublieux, -euse.
oblong ('ɔblɔŋ) *n* rectangle *m. adj* oblong, -gue.
obnoxious (əb'nɔkʃəs) *adj* exécrable, odieux, -euse.
oboe ('oubou) *n* hautbois *m.*
obscene (əb'si:n) *adj* obscène. **obscenity** *n* obscénité *f.*
obscure (əb'skjuə) *adj* obscur. *vt* obscurcir. **obscurity** *n* obscurité *f.*
observe (əb'zə:v) *vt* **1** observer. **2** remarquer. **3** faire remarquer. **observance** *n* observance *f.* **observant** *adj* observateur, -trice. **observation** *n* observation *f.* **observatory** *n* observatoire *m.*
obsess (əb'ses) *vt* obséder. **obsession** *n* obsession, idée fixe *f.*
obsolete ('ɔbsəli:t) *adj* hors d'usage, suranné.
obstacle ('ɔbstəkəl) *n* obstacle *m.*
obstinate ('ɔbstinət) *adj* opiniâtre, têtu. **obstinacy** *n* obstination *f.*
obstruct (əb'strʌkt) *vt* **1** obstruer, boucher. **2** gêner. **obstruction** *n* **1** obstruction *f.* **2** obstacle *m.*
obtain (əb'tein) *vt* obtenir, se procurer.
obtrusive (əb'tru:siv) *adj* importun.
obtuse (əb'tju:s) *adj* obtus.
obverse ('ɔbvə:s) *n* face *f.*
obvious ('ɔbviəs) *adj* évident, manifeste. **obviously** *adv* évidemment.
occasion (ə'keiʒən) *n* occasion *f.* *vt* occasionner. **occasional** *adj* **1** occasionel, -elle. **2** de circonstance. **occasionally** *adv* de temps en temps.
Occident ('ɔksidənt) *n* Occident *m.* **occidental** *adj* occidental, -aux.
occult (ɔ'kʌlt) *adj* occulte. **occultism** *n* occultisme *m.*
occupy ('ɔkjupai) *vt* **1** occuper. **2** habiter. **occupant** *n* locataire *m,f.* **occupation** *n* **1**

occupation f. 2 métier m. **occupational** adj professionnel, -elle. **occupier** n occupant m.

occur (ə'kə:) vi 1 arriver. 2 se trouver. 3 venir à l'esprit. **occurrence** n fait, événement m.

ocean ('ouʃən) n océan m. **oceanic** adj océanique.

ochre ('oukə) n ocre f.

octagon ('ɔktəgən) n octogone m. **octagonal** adj octogonal, -aux.

octane ('ɔktein) n octane m.

octave ('ɔktiv) n octave f.

October (ɔk'toubə) n octobre m.

octopus ('ɔktəpəs) n, pl **-puses** or **-pi** pieuvre f.

oculist ('ɔkjulist) n oculiste m,f.

odd (ɔd) adj 1 (of a number) impair. 2 dépareillé. 3 quelconque. 4 étrange. **oddity** n 1 étrangeté f. 2 (of a person) original, -aux m. **oddly** adv singulièrement. **oddment** n article dépareillé m. fin de série f. **odds** n pl 1 chances f pl. 2 inégalités f pl. **odds and ends** restes m pl.

ode (oud) n ode f.

odious ('oudiəs) adj odieux, -euse.

odour ('oudə) n odeur f. **odourless** adj inodore.

oesophagus (i:'sɔfəgəs) n œsophage m.

oestrogen ('i:strədʒən) n œstrogène m.

oestrus ('i:strəs) n œstre m.

of (əv; stressed ɔv) prep 1 de. 2 parmi, d'entre. 3 à, en. 4 par.

off (ɔf) adv 1 au loin. 2 fermé. prep de.

offal ('ɔfəl) n abats m pl.

offend (ə'fend) vt offenser, froisser. **offence** n 1 offense f. 2 law délit m. **take offence** s'offenser. **offender** n coupable m,f. **offensive** adj désagréable. n offensive f.

offer ('ɔfə) n offre f. **on offer** en vente. ~vt 1 offrir. 2 tenter. vi se présenter. **offering** n offre f.

offhand (ɔf'hænd) adj 1 improvisé. 2 désinvolte.

office ('ɔfis) n 1 bureau, -aux m. 2 pol ministère m. 3 fonction f. **officer** n 1 officier m. 2 agent m. **official** adj officiel, -elle. n fonctionnaire m.

officious (ə'fiʃəs) adj 1 empressé. 2 officieux, -euse. **officiousness** n excès de zèle m.

offing ('ɔfiŋ) **in the offing** adv au large.

off-licence n débit de boissons à emporter m.

off-peak adj 1 creux, creuse. 2 de nuit.

off-putting adj inf déconcertant.

off-season n morte-saison f.

offset ('ɔfset) vt compenser.

offshore (ɔf'ʃɔ:) adv au large. adj éloigné de la côte.

offside (ɔf'said) n 1 côté droit m. 2 sport hors-jeu m invar. adj droit.

offspring ('ɔfspriŋ) n rejeton m.

offstage (ɔf'steidʒ) adv à la cantonade.

often ('ɔfən) adv souvent. **how often?** combien de fois? **more often than not** le plus souvent.

ogre ('ougə) n ogre m.

oil (ɔil) n huile f. vt graisser. **oilfield** n gisement pétrolifère m. **oil painting** n peinture à l'huile f. **oilskin** n ciré m.

ointment ('ɔintmənt) n onguent m. pommade f.

old (ould) adj 1 vieux, vieil, vieille. 2 ancien, -ienne. **how old are you?** quel âge avez-vous? **I am twelve years old** j'ai douze ans. **old-fashioned** adj démodé.

Old Testament n Ancien Testament m.

olive ('ɔliv) n olive f. **olive oil** n huile d'olive f. **olive tree** n olivier m.

omelette ('ɔmlət) n omelette f.

omen ('oumen) n augure m.

ominous ('ɔminəs) adj de mauvais augure, inquiétant. **ominously** adv d'une façon menaçante.

omit (ə'mit) vt omettre. **omission** n omission f.

omnibus ('ɔmnibəs) adj,n omnibus m.

omnipotent (ɔm'nipətənt) adj tout puissant.

on (ɔn) prep 1 sur. 2 à. 3 de. 4 en. adv 1 en avant. 2 dessus. 3 ouvert.

once (wʌns) adv 1 une fois. 2 autrefois. **at once** immédiatement.

one (wʌn) adj 1 un. 2 seul, unique. 3 certain. n un m. pron 3rd pers s on. **one another** l'un, l'autre. **one's** poss adj 3rd pers s son, sa, ses. **oneself** pron 3rd pers s 1 soi-même. 2 se. **one-sided** adj 1 unilatéral, -aux. 2 injuste. **one-sidedness** n partialité f. **one-way** adj 1 à sens unique. 2 (of a ticket) simple.

onion ('ʌnien) n oignon m.

onlooker ('ɔnlukə) n spectateur, -trice.

only ('ounli) adj seul, unique. adv seulement, ne...que. conj mais.

onset ('ɔnset) n attaque f. **at the onset** d'emblée.

onslaught ('ɔnslɔ:t) n attaque f.

onus ('ounəs) n responsabilité f.

onwards ('ɔnwədz) adv also **onwards** 1 en avant. 2 à partir de.

ooze (u:z) vi,vt suinter, filtrer.

opal ('oupəl) n opale f.

opaque (ou'peik) adj opaque.

241

open ('oupən) *adj* ouvert. *vt* ouvrir. *vi* s'ouvrir.
open air *adj* en plein air. **open-ended** *adj*
pendant. **open-handed** *adj* généreux, -euse.
open-hearted *adj* franc, franche. **open minded** *adj* sans parti pris. **open-mouthed** *adj*
bouche bée. **open-plan** *adj* sans cloisons.
opening *n* ouverture *f.*

opera ('oprə) *n* opéra *m.* **opera house** *m* opéra
m. **operetta** *n* opérette *f.*

operate ('opəreit) *vt,vi* opérer. *vt tech* faire
manœuvrer. **operation** *n* opération *f.* **come
into operation** entrer en vigueur. **operative**
adj actif, -ive.

opinion (ə'pinjən) *n* opinion *f.* avis *m.* **opinion
poll** *n* sondage *m.*

opium ('oupiəm) *n* opium *m.*

opponent (ə'pounənt) *n* adversaire *m,f.*

opportune (opə'tju:n) *adj* opportun.

opportunity (opə'tju:niti) *n* occasion *f.* **take
the opportunity** profiter de l'occasion.

oppose (ə'pouz) *vt* 1 opposer. 2 s'opposer à,
contrecarrer. **opposed** *adj* hostile. **as opposed to** par opposition à.

opposite ('opəzit) *adj* 1 opposé, en face. 2
inverse. *n* contraire *m.* *adv* vis-à-vis. *prep* en
face de. **opposition** *n* 1 opposition *f.* 2
résistance *f.* 3 obstacle *m.*

oppress (ə'pres) *vt* opprimer. **oppression** *n*
oppression *f.* **oppressive** *adj* 1 opprimant. 2
étouffant, accablant.

opt (opt) *vi* opter.

optical ('optikəl) *adj* 1 optique. 2 d'optique.
optician *n* opticien, -ienne.

optimism ('optimizəm) *n* optimisme *m.* **optimist** *n* optimiste *m,f.* **optimistic** *adj* optimiste. **optimistically** *adv* avec optimisme.

option ('opʃən) *n* option *f.* choix *m.* **optional**
adj facultatif, -ive.

opulent ('opjulənt) *adj* opulent, abondant.

or (o:) *conj* ou. **or else** sinon. **or so** environ.

oral ('o:rəl) *adj* 1 oral, -aux. 2 *anat* buccal.
orally *adv* de vive voix.

orange ('orind3) *n* 1 *bot* orange *f.* 2 (colour)
orange, orangé *m.* *adj* orangé, orange. **orange
tree** *n* oranger *m.*

oration (o:'reiʃən) *n* allocution *f.* discours
m. **orator** *n* orateur *m.*

orbit ('o:bit) *n* orbite *f.* *vt* tourner autour de.

orchard ('o:tʃəd) *n* verger *m.*

orchestra ('o:kistrə) *n* orchestre *m.* **orchestral**
adj orchestral, -aux. **orchestrate** *vt* orchestrer.

orchid ('o:kid) *n* orchidée *f.*

ordain (o:'dein) *vt* 1 *rel* ordonner. 2 décréter.

ordeal (o:'di:l) *n* épreuve *f.*

order ('o:də) *n* 1 ordre *m.* 2 *comm* commande
f. **in order to** afin de, pour. **in order that**
afin *or* pour que. **out of order** en panne. ~*vt*
1 ordonner. 2 commander. **orderly** *adj* 1
ordonné. 2 posé. *n* planton *m.*

ordinal ('o:dinl) *adj* ordinal, -aux.

ordinary ('o:dənri) *adj* 1 ordinaire, normal, -aux.
2 quelconque. **out of the ordinary** exceptionnel, -elle.

ore (o:) *n* minerai *m.*

oregano (ori'ga:nou) *n* marjolaine *f.*

organ ('o:gən) *n* 1 *mus* orgue *m.* 2 organe
m. **organist** *n* organiste *m,f.*

organism ('o:gənizəm) *n* organisme *m.* **organic**
adj organique.

organize ('o:gənaiz) *vt* 1 organiser. 2 arranger.
organization *n* 1 organisation *f.* 2 organisme,
mouvement *m.* **organizer** *n* organisateur,
-trice. **organizing** *n* organisation *f.* aménagement *m.*

orgasm ('o:gæzəm) *n* orgasme *m.*

orgy ('o:d3i) *n* orgie *f.*

Orient ('o:riənt) *n* Orient *m.* **oriental** *adj,n*
oriental, -aux.

orientate ('o:rienteit) *vt* orienter.

origin ('oridʒin) *n* origine *f.* **original** *adj,n*
original, -aux *m.* **originality** *n* originalité
f. **originate** *vi* prendre naissance, provenir. *vt*
créer, amorcer. **origination** *n* source *f.*

Orkneys ('o:kniz) *n* Orcades *f.*

Orlon ('o:lon) *n Tdmk* Orlon *m.*

ornament ('o:nəmənt) *n* ornement *m.* parure *f.*
vt orner, agrémenter. **ornamental** *adj*
ornemental, -aux.

ornate (o:'neit) *adj* orné, surchargé.

ornithology (o:ni'θolədʒi) *n* ornithologie *f.*

orphan ('o:fən) *n* orphelin *m.* **orphanage** *n*.
orphelinat *m.*

orthodox ('o:θədoks) *adj* orthodoxe. **orthodoxy** *n* orthodoxie *f.*

orthography (o:'θogrəfi) *n* orthographe *f.*

orthopaedic (o:θə'pi:dik) *adj* orthopédique.

oscillate ('osəleit) *vi* osciller.

ostensible (o'stensəbəl) *adj* prétendu, soi-
distant. **ostensibly** *adv* censément.

ostentatious (osten'teiʃəs) *adj* ostentatoire.

osteopath ('ostiəpæθ) *n* chiropracteur *m.*
osteopathy *n* ostéopathie *f.*

ostracize ('ostrəsaiz) *vt* ostraciser, exiler.
ostracism *n* ostracisme *m.*

ostrich ('ostritʃ) *n* autruche *f.*

other (ˈʌðə) adj autre. **every other day** tous les deux jours. ~pron autre, autrui. adv autrement. **otherwise** adv autrement.

otter (ˈɔtə) n loutre f.

ought° (ɔːt) v mod aux devoir, falloir.

ounce (auns) n once f.

our (auə) poss adj 1st pers pl notre, nos. **ours** poss pron 1st pers pl le or la nôtre. **ourselves** pron 1st pers pl 1 nous-mêmes. 2 nous.

oust (aust) vt 1 supplanter. 2 law déposséder.

out (aut) adv 1 hors, dehors. 2 sorti. 3 éteint. 4 sport hors jeu. **out of 1** hors de, au dehors de. 2 dans. 3 par. 4 parmi.

outboard (ˈautbɔːd) adj extérieur.

outbreak (ˈautbreik) n éruption, ouverture f.

outburst (ˈautbəːst) n accès, éclat m.

outcast (ˈautkɑːst) adj,n proscrit.

outcome (ˈautkʌm) n résultat m. issue f.

outcry (ˈautkrai) n cri m. clameur f.

outdo° (autˈduː) vt surpasser.

outdoor (ˈautdɔː) adj extérieur, de plein air. **outdoors** adv dehors, en plein air.

outer (ˈautə) adj extérieur, externe.

outfit (ˈautfit) n 1 attirail, équipement m. 2 costume m.

outgoing (ˈautgouiŋ) adj 1 ouvert. 2 sortant. 3 démissionnaire.

outgrow° (autˈgrou) vt 1 dépasser. 2 devenir trop grand pour.

outhouse (ˈauthaus) n dépendance f.

outing (ˈautiŋ) n sortie f.

outlandish (autˈlændiʃ) adj extravagant, bizarre.

outlaw (ˈautlɔː) n hors-la-loi m invar. vt proscrire.

outlay (ˈautlei) n débours m pl. mise de fonds f.

outlet (ˈautlet) n 1 sortie f. 2 débouché m.

outline (ˈautlain) n 1 contour m. 2 ébauche f. vt 1 esquisser. 2 silhouetter.

outlive (autˈliv) vt survivre à.

outlook (ˈautluk) n perspective f. point de vue m.

outlying (ˈautlaiiŋ) adj isolé, écarté.

outnumber (autˈnʌmbə) vt surpasser en nombre.

outpatient (ˈautpeiʃənt) n malade venant consulter à l'hôpital m.

outpost (ˈautpoust) n avant-poste m.

output (ˈautput) n production f. rendement m.

outrage (autˈreidʒ) n outrage m. vt outrager, violenter. **outrageous** adj 1 outrageux, -euse. 2 indigne, exorbitant.

outright (ˈautrait) adv 1 franchement. 2 complètement. 3 du premier coup. adj 1 carré. 2 pur et simple.

outside (autˈsaid) adj extérieur, externe. prep en dehors de. adv dehors, à l'extérieur. n dehors, extérieur m. **on the outside** à l'extérieur. **outsider** n 1 étranger m. 2 sport ailier m.

outsize (ˈautsaiz) n taille hors série f. adj 1 de taille hors série. 2 énorme.

outskirts (ˈautskəːts) n pl banlieue f. abords m pl.

outspoken (autˈspoukən) adj franc, franche. **outspokenness** n franc-parler m invar.

outstanding (autˈstændiŋ) adj 1 saillant, marquant. 2 excellent. 3 comm en souffrance, arriéré.

outstrip (autˈstrip) vt 1 devancer. 2 surpasser.

outward (ˈautwəd) adj 1 extérieur, externe. 2 apparent. adv au dehors. **outwards** adv au dehors, vers l'extérieur.

outweigh (autˈwei) vt 1 peser plus que. 2 l'emporter sur.

outwit (autˈwit) vt 1 circonvenir. 2 dépister.

oval (ˈouvəl) adj,n ovale m.

ovary (ˈouvəri) n ovaire m.

ovation (ouˈveiʃən) n ovation f.

oven (ˈʌvən) n four m.

over (ˈouvə) prep 1 sur, au-dessus de. 2 au cours de. 3 de l'autre côté de. **over and above** en outre. **over there** là-bas.

overall (ˈouvərɔːl) adj global, -aux. n 1 blouse f. 2 pl salopette f.

overbalance (ouvəˈbæləns) vt renverser. vi tomber.

overboard (ˈouvəbɔːd) adv par-dessus bord.

overcast (ouvəˈkɑːst) adj couvert, assombri.

overcharge (ouvəˈtʃɑːdʒ) vt surcharger.

overcoat (ˈouvəkout) n pardessus m.

overcome° (ouvəˈkʌm) vt surmonter, triompher de. **be overcome by** être accablé de, succomber à.

overdo° (ouvəˈduː) vt 1 exagérer. 2 surmener. 3 cul trop cuire.

overdose (ˈouvədous) n dose mortelle f.

overdraft (ˈouvədrɑːft) n découvert m.

overdraw° (ouvəˈdrɔː) vt tirer à découvert.

overdue (ouvəˈdjuː) adj échu, en retard.

overestimate (ouvərˈestimeit) vt surestimer.

overfill (ouvəˈfil) vt remplir trop.

overflow (v ouvəˈflou; n ˈouvəflou) vi déborder. n trop-plein m invar.

overhang° (v ouvəˈhæŋ; n ˈouvəhæŋ) vt surplomber, faire saillie. n porte-à-faux m. saillie f. **overhanging** adj en porte-à-faux.

overhaul (ouvə'hɔ:l) n révisıon f. vt examiner, réviser.

overhead (adv ouvə'hed; adj, n 'ouvəhed) adv en haut, en l'aır. adj aérien, -ienne. **overheads** n pl frais généraux m pl.

overhear (ouvə'hıə) vt surprendre.

overheat (ouvə'hi:t) vt surchauffer. vi chauffer.

overjoyed (ouvə'dʒɔid) adj transporté de joie.

overland (ouvə'lænd) adv par voie de terre.

overlap (v ouvə'læp; n 'ouvəlæp) vt recouvrir, chevaucher. n recouvrement, chevauchement m.

overlay (v ouvə'lei; n 'ouvəlei) vt recouvrir. n matelas m.

overleaf (ouvə'li:f) adv au verso.

overload (v ouvə'loud; n 'ouvəloud) vt 1 surcharger. 2 surmener. n surcharge f.

overlook (ouvə'luk) vt 1 oublier. 2 donner sur. 3 laisser passer.

overnight (adv ouvə'naıt; adj œuvənait) adv 1 la nuit, jusqu'au lendemain. 2 du jour au lendemain. adj de nuit.

overpower (ouvə'pauə) vt maîtriser. **overpowering** adj 1 accablant. 2 écrasant.

overrate (ouvə'reit) vt surestimer, surfaıre.

overreach (ouvə'ri:tʃ) vt dépasser.

overrule (ouvə'ru:l) vt 1 diriger. 2 rejeter.

overrun* (ouvə'rʌn) vt 1 envahir, se répandre. 2 dépasser.

overseas (ouvə'sı:z) adv outre-mer. adj d'outre-mer.

overshadow (ouvə'ʃædou) vt 1 ombrager. 2 éclipser.

overshoot* (ouvə'ʃu:t) vt dépasser.

oversight ('ouvəsait) n oubli m. **through an oversight** par inadvertance.

oversleep* (ouvə'sli:p) vı dormir trop longtemps.

overspill* (v ouvə'spil; n 'ouvəspil) vi déborder. n déversement de population m.

overt ('ouvə:t) adj manifeste, évident.

overtake* (ouvə'teik) vt 1 rattraper. 2 (a car, etc.) doubler.

overthrow* (v ouvə'θrou; n 'ouvəθrou) vt vaincre. n chute f.

overtime ('ouvətaim) n heures supplémentaires f pl.

overtone ('ouvətoun) n nuance f.

overture ('ouvətʃə) n ouverture f.

overturn (ouvə'tə:n) vt renverser. vi verser, se retourner.

overweight (n 'ouvəweit; adj ouvə'weit) n surpoids m. adj trop lourd.

overwhelm (ouvə'welm) vt 1 écraser, accabler. 2 combler.

overwork (v ouvə'wə:k; n 'ouvəwə:k) vt surmener. n surmenage m.

overwrought (ouvə'rɔ:t) adj excédé.

ovulate ('ɔvjuleit) vi ovuler. **ovulation** n ovulation f.

owe (ou) vt devoir. **owing** adj dû, due. **owing to** en raison de.

owl (aul) n hibou, -oux m.

own (oun) vt posséder. **own up to** avouer. ~adj propre. **owner** n propriétaire m,f. **ownership** n propriété, possession f.

ox (ɔks) n, pl **oxen** bœuf m. **oxtail** n queue de bœuf f.

oxygen ('ɔksidʒən) n oxygène m.

oyster ('ɔistə) n huître f. **oyster-bed** n banc d'huîtres m.

P

pace (peis) n 1 pas m. 2 allure f. vt arpenter. **pace up and down** faire les cent pas.

Pacific (pə'sifik) adj pacifique. **Pacific (Ocean)** n (Océan) Pacifique m.

pacify ('pæsifai) vt pacifier, apaiser. **pacifism** n pacifisme m.

pack (pæk) n 1 paquet m. 2 bande f. 3 game jeu, jeux m. 4 (of hounds) meute f. vt 1 emballer. 2 tasser, empiler. 3 bourrer. **package** n 1 paquet m. 2 emballage m. **packet** n 1 paquet m. 2 colis m. **packhorse** n cheval de somme m.

pact (pækt) n pacte m. convention f.

pad[1] (pæd) n 1 coussinet m. 2 tampon m. 3 (of paper) bloc m. vt 1 rembourrer, matelasser. 2 délayer. **padding** n rembourrage m.

pad[2] (pæd) n bruit de pas feutrés m.

paddle[1] ('pædļ) n 1 pagaie f. 2 aube f. vt pagayer.

paddle[2] ('pædļ) vi patauger.

paddock ('pædɔk) n 1 enclos m. 2 paddock m.

paddyfield ('pædifi:ld) n champ de riz m.

padlock ('pædlɔk) n cadenas m. vt cadenasser.

paediatric (pi:di'ætrik) adj pédiatrique. **paediatrician** n pédiatre m.

pagan ('peigən) adj,n païen, -ienne.

page[1] (peidʒ) n (of a book) page f.

page[2] (peidʒ) n (boy) page m.

pageant ('pædʒənt) n cortège historique m.

pagoda (pə'goudə) n pagode f.

paid (peid) v see **pay**.

pain (pein) n 1 douleur, souffrance f. 2 pl peine f. **painful** adj douloureux, -euse. **painless** adj sans douleur. **painstaking** adj soigneux, -euse, appliqué.

paint (peint) n 1 peinture f. 2 Art couleur f. vt 1 peindre. 2 dépeindre. vi faire de la peinture. **paintbrush** n pinceau, -aux m. **painter** n peintre m. **painting** n 1 peinture f. 2 tableau, -aux m.

pair (pɛə) n 1 paire f. 2 couple m. vt assortir. **pair off** 1 disposer deux par deux. 2 s'en aller à deux.

Pakistan (pɑːkiˈstɑːn) n Pakistan m. **Pakistani** adj,n pakistanais.

pal (pæl) n inf camarade m.

palace (ˈpælis) n palais m.

palate (ˈpælət) n palais m. **palatable** adj savoureux, -euse.

pale (peil) adj pâle, blême. **turn pale** pâlir. **paleness** n pâleur f.

Palestine (ˈpælistain) n Palestine f. **Palestinian** adj,n palestinien, -ienne.

palette (ˈpælit) n palette f.

palm¹ (pɑːm) n anat paume f. v **palm off** refiler. **palmist** n chiromancien m. **palmistry** n chiromancie f.

palm² (pɑːm) n bot palmier m.

Palm Sunday n dimanche des Rameaux m.

pamper (ˈpæmpə) vt dorloter.

pamphlet (ˈpæmflət) n 1 brochure f. 2 pamphlet m. **pamphleteer** n 1 auteur de brochures m. 2 pamphlétaire m.

pan (pæn) n 1 casserole f. 2 bac m. **pancake** n crêpe f.

Panama (ˈpænəmɑː) n Panama m.

pancreas (ˈpæŋkriəs) n pancréas m.

panda (ˈpændə) n panda m.

pander (ˈpændə) vi **pander to** encourager.

pane (pein) n vitre f. carreau, -aux m.

panel (ˈpænl) n 1 panneau, -aux m. 2 (of people) liste f. jury m. vt lambrisser.

pang (pæŋ) n angoisse f.

panic* (ˈpænik) n panique f. vi paniquer. **panic-stricken** adj pris de panique.

pannier (ˈpæniə) n panier m. hotte f.

panorama (pænəˈrɑːmə) n panorama m. **panoramic** adj panoramique.

pansy (ˈpænzi) n bot pensée f.

pant (pænt) vi panteler, haleter. n halètement m.

panther (ˈpænθə) n panthère f.

pantomime (ˈpæntəmaim) n pantomime f.

pantry (ˈpæntri) n garde-manger m invar.

pants (pænts) n pl caleçon, slip m.

papal (ˈpeipəl) adj papal, -aux.

paper (ˈpeipə) n 1 papier m. 2 document, rapport m. 3 journal, -aux m. 4 épreuve f. adj de papier. vt tapisser. **paperback** n livre de poche m. **paperclip** n attache-papiers m invar. trombone f. **paperwork** n écritures f pl.

papier-mâché (ˌpæpieiˈmæʃei) n carton-pâte m.

papist (ˈpeipist) n papiste m,f.

paprika (ˈpæprikə) n paprika m.

par (pɑː) n pair m. moyenne f. **be on a par with** être au niveau de.

parable (ˈpærəbəl) n parabole f.

parachute (ˈpærəʃuːt) n parachute m. vi descendre en parachute. **parachutist** n parachutiste m,f.

parade (pəˈreid) n 1 parade f. 2 mil exercice, rassemblement m. 3 défilé m. vt faire parade de. vi 1 mil parader. 2 se pavaner.

paradise (ˈpærədais) n paradis m.

paradox (ˈpærədɔks) n paradoxe m. **paradoxical** adj paradoxal, -aux.

paraffin (ˈpærəfin) n 1 paraffine f. 2 comm pétrole m.

paragraph (ˈpærəgrɑːf) n paragraphe m.

parallel (ˈpærəlel) adj 1 parallèle. 2 semblable. n parallèle f. vt 1 placer parellèlement. 2 comparer. 3 égaler.

paralyse (ˈpærəlaiz) vt paralyser. **paralysed** adj 1 med paralysé. 2 transi. **paralysis** n paralysie f. **paralytic** adj 1 paralytique. 2 sl soûl.

paramount (ˈpærəmaunt) adj 1 éminent. 2 suprême.

paranoia (pærəˈnɔiə) n paranoïa f.

parapet (ˈpærəpit) n parapet m.

paraphernalia (pærəfəˈneiliə) n pl attirail m.

paraphrase (ˈpærəfreiz) n paraphrase f. vt paraphraser.

parasite (ˈpærəsait) n 1 parasite m. 2 (person) pique-assiette m,f invar.

paratrooper (ˈpærətruːpə) n parachutiste m.

parcel (ˈpɑːsəl) n 1 colis m. 2 portion, parcelle f. vt 1 empaqueter. 2 morceler.

parch (pɑːtʃ) vt 1 rôtir. 2 dessécher. vi se dessécher. **parched** adj sec, aride.

parchment (ˈpɑːtʃmənt) n parchemin m.

pardon (ˈpɑːdn) vt 1 excuser. 2 absoudre. 3 gracier. **pardon me!** excusez-moi! ~n 1 pardon m. 2 grâce f. **I beg your pardon** 1 excusez-moi! 2 pardon? comment?

245

pare (pɛə) vt **1** rogner. **2** éplucher. **paring** n **1** ébarbage m. **2** épluchures f pl.

parent ('pɛərənt) n **1** père m. mère f. **2** pl parents m pl. adj mère. **parenthood** n paternité, maternité f.

parenthesis (pə'renθəsis) n pl **-eses** parenthèse f.

Paris ('pæris) n Paris m. **Parisian** adj,n parisien, -ienne.

parish ('pæriʃ) n **1** paroisse f. **2** commune f. **parishioner** n paroissien, -ienne.

parity ('pæriti) n **1** égalité f. **2** comm parité f. pair m.

park (pɑːk) n parc m. vt garer. vi stationner. **parking** n stationnement m. **parking meter** n parcomètre m.

parliament ('pɑːləmənt) n parlement m. **parliamentary** adj parlementaire.

parlour ('pɑːlə) n salon m.

parochial (pə'roukiəl) adj **1** paroissial, -aux. **2** de clocher. **parochialism** n esprit de clocher m.

parody ('pærədi) n parodie f. vt parodier.

parole (pə'roul) n parole, foi f.

parquet ('pɑːkei) n parquet m.

parrot ('pærət) n perroquet m.

parsley ('pɑːsli) n persil m.

parsnip ('pɑːsnip) n panais m.

parson ('pɑːsən) n pasteur m. **parsonage** n presbytère m.

part (pɑːt) n **1** partie f. **2** part f. **3** pièce f. **4** région f. **5** Th rôle m. vt **1** diviser. **2** séparer. vi **1** se quitter. **2** se diviser. **part with** céder.

partake* (pɑː'teik) vt partager. vi **1** prendre part. **2** manger.

partial ('pɑːʃəl) adj **1** partial, -aux. **2** partiel, -elle. **be partial to** avoir un faible pour. **partiality** n **1** partialité f. **2** prédilection f.

participate (pɑː'tisipeit) vi participer. **participant** n participant m. **participation** n participation f.

participle ('pɑːtisəpəl) n participe m. **present/past participle** participe présent/passé.

particle ('pɑːtikəl) n particule f.

particular (pə'tikjulə) adj **1** particulier, -ière, spécial, -aux. **2** détaillé. **3** méticuleux, -euse. **4** exigeant. n détail m.

parting ('pɑːtiŋ) n **1** séparation f. **2** (of the hair) raie f.

partisan (pɑːti'zæn) n partisan m.

partition (pɑː'tiʃən) n **1** partage m. **2** cloison f. vt **1** morceler. **2** partager. **3** cloisonner.

partner ('pɑːtnə) n **1** comm associé m. **2** sport

partenaire m,f. **3** danseur m. vt être associé à. **partnership** n **1** association f. **2** comm société f. **go into partnership with** s'associer avec.

partridge ('pɑːtridʒ) n **1** perdrix f. **2** cul perdreau, -aux.

part-time adj,adv à mi-temps.

party ('pɑːti) n **1** parti m. **2** groupe m. **3** réception, soirée f. **4** law partie f. **party line** n **1** ligne à poste groupés f. **2** pol ligne du parti f.

pass* (pɑːs) n **1** col, défilé m. **2** educ réussite sans mention f. **3** permis m. laissez-passer m invar. vt **1** passer devant. **2** transmettre. **3** educ être reçu à. **4** approuver. **5** law voter. vi passer. **pass out** s'évanouir. **password** n mot de passe m.

passage ('pæsidʒ) n **1** passage m. **2** couloir m. **3** traversée f. **passageway** n ruelle f.

passenger ('pæsindʒə) n voyageur, -euse, passager, -ère.

passion ('pæʃən) n passion f. **passionate** adj **1** passionné. **2** emporté.

passive ('pæsiv) adj,n passif, -ive m.

Passover ('pɑːsouvə) n Pâque f.

passport ('pɑːspɔːt) n passeport m.

past (pɑːst) adj,n passé m. **in the past** autrefois. ~prep au delà de. **twenty past two** deux heures vingt. ~adv **go past** passer.

pasta ('pæstə) n pâtes f pl.

paste (peist) n **1** pâte f. **2** colle f. vt coller.

pastel ('pæstəl) n pastel m.

pasteurize ('pæstəraiz) vt pasteuriser.

pastime ('pɑːstaim) n passe-temps m invar. délassement m.

pastoral ('pæstərəl) adj pastoral, -aux.

pastry ('peistri) n **1** pâtisserie f. **2** pâte f. **puff pastry** n pâte feuilletée f.

pasture ('pɑːstʃə) n pâturage m. vt,vi paître.

pasty[1] ('peisti) adj **1** pâteux, -euse. **2** terreux, -euse.

pasty[2] ('pæsti) n pâté (en croûte) m.

pat[1] (pæt) n **1** caresse f. **2** (of butter) rondelle f. vt **1** tapoter. **2** caresser.

pat[2] (pæt) adv à propos. **off pat** par cœur. ~adj apte.

patch (pætʃ) n **1** pièce f. **2** tache f. **3** lopin m. **4** emplâtre f. vt rapiécer. **patch up** ravauder. **patchwork** n rapiéçage m.

patent ('peitnt) n brevet m. patente f. vt breveter. adj **1** manifeste. **2** breveté. **patent leather** n cuir verni m.

paternal (pə'tɜːnl) adj paternel, -elle. **paternity** n paternité f.

path (pɑ:θ) *n* 1 chemin, sentier *m*. 2 cours *m*.
pathetic (pə'θetik) *adj* pathétique.
pathology (pə'θɔlədʒi) *n* pathologie *f*. **pathologist** *n* pathologiste *m,f*.
patience ('peiʃəns) *n* 1 patience *f*. 2 *game* réussite *f*. **patient** *adj* patient. *n* malade *m,f*.
patio ('pætiou) *n* patio *m*.
patriarchal (peitri'ɑ:kəl) *adj* patriarcal, -aux.
patriot ('peitriət) *n* patriote *m,f*. **patriotic** *adj* 1 patriote. 2 patriotique. **patriotism** *n* patriotisme *m*.
patrol (pə'troul) *vi* patrouiller. *vt* faire la patrouille dans. *n* patrouille *f*.
patron ('peitrən) *n* 1 protecteur *m*. 2 client *m*. **patronage** *n* 1 protection *f*. patronage *m*. 2 clientèle *f*. **patronize** *vt* 1 patronner. 2 fréquenter.
patter[1] ('pætə) *n* tapotement *m*. *vi* 1 trottiner. 2 crépiter.
patter[2] ('pætə) *n* boniment, bavardage *m*.
pattern ('pætən) *n* 1 modèle *m*. 2 motif *m*. 3 patron *m*. 4 échantillon *m*.
paunch (pɔ:ntʃ) *n* panse *f*. ventre *m*.
pauper ('pɔ:pə) *n* indigent, mendiant *m*.
pause (pɔ:z) *n* 1 pause *f*. 2 silence *m*. *vi* 1 s'arrêter un instant. 2 hésiter.
pave (peiv) *vt* paver. **pave the way** préparer le terrain. **pavement** *n* trottoir *m*. **paving** *n* dallage *m*.
pavilion (pə'viliən) *n* pavillon *m*.
paw (pɔ:) *n* patte *f*. *vt* donner des coups de patte à.
pawn[1] (pɔ:n) *n* gage *m*. *vt* mettre en gage. **pawnbroker** *n* prêteur sur gage *m*.
pawn[2] (pɔ:n) *n game* pion *m*.
pay (pei) *n* paie *f*. traitement *m*. *vt* 1 payer, verser. 2 rétribuer. **payroll** *n* état des paiements *m*.
pea (pi:) *n* 1 pois *m*. 2 *cul* petit pois *m*.
peace (pi:s) *n* 1 paix *f*. 2 tranquillité *f*. **peaceful** *adj* 1 paisible. 2 pacifique. **peacemaker** *n* pacificateur, -trice *f*.
peach (pi:tʃ) *n* pêche *f*. **peach tree** *n* pêcher *m*.
peacock ('pi:kɔk) *n* paon *m*.
peak (pi:k) *n* 1 cime *f*. 2 pointe *f*. 3 visière *f*.
peal (pi:l) *n* 1 carillon *m*. 2 grondement *m*. *vi* 1 carillonner. 2 gronder. *vt* sonner.
peanut ('pi:nʌt) *n* arachide, cacahuète *f*.
pear (pɛə) *n* poire *f*. **pear tree** *n* poirier *m*.
pearl ('pə:l) *n* perle *f*. **mother of pearl** *n* nacre *f*. **pearly** *adj* perlé, nacré.
peasant ('pezənt) *n* paysan, -anne.

peat (pi:t) *n* tourbe *f*.
pebble ('pebəl) *n* caillou, -oux, galet *m*. **pebbly** *adj* cailouteux, -euse.
peck (pek) *n* 1 coup de bec *m*. 2 *inf* bécot *m*. *vt* 1 becqueter. 2 bécoter. *vi inf* manger du bout des dents.
peckish ('pekiʃ) *adj* **feel peckish** avoir le ventre creux.
peculiar (pi'kju:liə) *adj* 1 particulier, -ière. 2 bizarre. **peculiarity** *n* 1 particularité *f*. 2 singularité *f*.
pedal ('pedl) *n* pédale *f*. *vi* pédaler.
peddle ('pedl) *vt* colporter.
pedestal ('pedistəl) *n* 1 piédestal, -aux *m*. 2 socle *m*.
pedestrian (pi'destriən) *n* piéton *m*. **pedestrian crossing** passage clouté *m*. ~*adj* 1 à pied. 2 prosaïque.
pedigree ('pedigri:) *n* 1 pedigree *m*. 2 ascendance *f*.
peel (pi:l) *n* 1 pelure, écorce *f*. 2 *cul* zeste *m*. *vt* 1 éplucher, peler. 2 dépouiller. *vi* 1 se peler. 2 se décrépir.
peep (pi:p) *n* coup d'œil *m*. *v* **peep at** regarder à la dérobée. **peep out** se montrer.
peer[1] (piə) *n* 1 (title) pair *m*. 2 égal, -aux *m*. **peerage** *n* pairie *f*.
peer[2] (piə) *vi* risquer un coup d'œil. **peer at** scruter.
peevish ('pi:viʃ) *adj* maussade.
peg (peg) *n* 1 cheville *f*. 2 fiche *f*. 3 patère *f*. *vt* 1 cheviller, accrocher. 2 *game* marquer.
pejorative (pi'dʒɔrətiv) *adj* péjoratif, -ive.
pelican ('pelikən) *n* pélican *m*.
pellet ('pelit) *n* 1 boulette *f*. 2 plomb *m*.
pelmet ('pelmit) *n* lambrequin *m*.
pelt[1] (pelt) *vt* 1 assaillir. 2 cribler. *vi* tomber à verse. **at full pelt** à toute vitesse.
pelt[2] (pelt) *n* peau, -aux *f*.
pelvis ('pelvis) *n* bassin *m*.
pen[1] (pen) *n* plume *f*. **penfriend** *n* correspondant *m*. **penknife** *n* canif *m*. **pen-nib** *n* bec de plume *m*.
pen[2] (pen) *n* enclos *m*. *v* **pen in** parquer.
penal ('pi:nl) *adj* pénal, -aux. **penalize** *vt* 1 sanctionner. 2 *sport* pénaliser. **penalty** *n* 1 peine *f*. 2 *sport* pénalisation *f*.
penance ('penəns) *n* pénitence *f*.
pencil ('pensəl) *n* crayon *m*. **pencil-sharpener** *n* taille-crayon *m*.
pendant ('pendənt) *n* pendentif *m*.
pending ('pendiŋ) *prep* 1 en attendant. 2 durant. *adj* pendant.

pendulum ('pendjuləm) *n* pendule *m.*

penetrate ('penitreit) *vt,vi* pénétrer. **penetrating** *adj* 1 pénétrant. 2 perspicace. **penetration** *n* pénétration *f.*

penguin ('peŋgwin) *n* manchot, pingouin *m.*

penicillin (peni'silin) *n* pénicilline *f.*

peninsula (pə'ninsjulə) *n* péninsule *f.* **peninsular** *adj* péninsulaire.

penis ('piːnis) *n* pénis *m.*

penitent ('penitənt) *adj,n* pénitent.

pennant ('penənt) *n* banderole *f.*

penny ('peni) *n* 1 *pl* **pence** British unit of currency. 2 *pl* **pennies** sou *m.* **penniless** *adj* sans le sou.

pension ('penʃən) *n* 1 pension *f.* 2 pension de famille *f.* **old age pension** retraite *f.* ~*vt* pensionner. **pension off** mettre à la retraite. **pensioner** *n* retraité *m.*

pensive ('pensiv) *adj* pensif, -ive.

pent (pent) *adj* **pent up** 1 renfermé. 2 refoulé.

pentagon ('pentəgən) *n* pentagone *m.*

Pentecost ('pentikɔst) *n* Pentecôte *f.*

penthouse ('penthaus) *n* appentis *m.*

people ('piːpəl) *n* 1 peuple *m.* 2 nation *f.* 3 gens *m or f pl.* 4 *inf* parents *m pl. vt* peupler.

pepper ('pepə) *n* poivre *m. vt* 1 poivrer. 2 cribler. **peppercorn** *n* grain de poivre *m.* **peppermill** *n* moulin à poivre *m.* **peppermint** *n* menthe poivrée *f.* **pepper-pot** *n* poivrière *f.*

per (pəː) *prep* par. **as per** selon.

perambulator (pə'ræmbjuleitə) *n* voiture d'enfant *f.*

perceive (pə'siːv) *vt* 1 percevoir. 2 s'apercevoir de. 3 apercevoir. **perceivable** *adj* perceptible, sensible.

per cent (pə'sent) *n* pour cent *m.*

percentage (pə'sentidʒ) *n* 1 pourcentage *m.* 2 proportion *f.*

perception (pə'sepʃən) *n* 1 perception *f.* 2 sensibilité *f.* **perceptive** *adj* perceptif, -ive.

perch (pəːtʃ) *n* perchoir *m. vi* (se) percher. *vt* jucher.

percolate ('pəːkəleit) *vi* s'infiltrer, filtrer. *vt* passer. **percolator** *n* percolateur *m.*

percussion (pə'kʌʃən) *n* percussion *f.*

perennial (pə'reniəl) *adj* 1 éternel, -elle. 2 *bot* vivace. *n* plante vivace *f.*

perfect (*adj,n* 'pəːfikt; *v* pə'fekt) *adj* 1 parfait. 2 complet, -ète. *n* parfait *m. vt* 1 achever. 2 perfectionner, mettre au point. **perfection** *n* 1 perfection *f.* 2 achèvement *m.*

perforate ('pəːfəreit) *vt,vi* perforer. **perforation** *n* perforation *f.*

perform (pə'fɔːm) *vt* 1 exécuter. 2 *Th* jouer. **performance** *n* 1 exécution *f.* 2 exploit *m.* 3 *Th* représentation *f.*

perfume (pə'fjuːm) *n* parfum *m.* odeur *f. vt* parfumer.

perhaps (pə'hæps) *adv* peut-être.

peril ('perəl) *n* péril *m.* **perilous** *adj* périlleux, -euse.

perimeter (pə'rimitə) *n* périmètre *m.*

period ('piəriəd) *n* 1 période *f.* 2 durée *f.* 3 époque *f.* 4 *med* règles *f pl.* **periodical** *adj,n* périodique *m.*

peripheral (pə'rifərəl) *adj* périphérique.

periscope ('periskoup) *n* périscope *m.*

perish ('periʃ) *vi* 1 périr. 2 se détériorer. *vt* altérer, gâter. **perishable** *adj* périssable.

perjury ('pəːdʒəri) *n* 1 parjure *m.* 2 *law* faux témoignage *m.*

perk (pəːk) **perk up** *vi* se ranimer. *vt* redresser.

perm (pəːm) *n also* **permanent wave** permanente *f.*

permanent ('pəːmənənt) *adj* permanent. **permanence** *n* permanence *f.* **permanently** *adv* en permanence, à titre définitif.

permeate ('pəːmieit) *vt* s'infiltrer.

permit (*v* pə'mit; *n* 'pəːmit) *vt* 1 permettre. 2 autoriser. *n* 1 permis *m.* 2 autorisation *f.* **permission** *n* 1 permission *f.* 2 permis *m.* **permissible** *adj* admissible. **permissive** *adj* 1 libertin. 2 toléré.

permutation (pəːmju'teiʃən) *n* permutation *f.*

peroxide (pə'rɔksaid) *n* peroxyde *m. vt inf* décolorer.

perpendicular (pəːpən'dikjulə) *adj,n* perpendiculaire *f.*

perpetual (pə'petʃuəl) *adj* 1 perpétuel, -elle. 2 incessant.

perpetuate (pə'petʃueit) *vt* perpétuer.

perplex (pə'pleks) *vt* embarrasser, troubler. **perplexed** *adj* perplexe. **perplexity** *n* perplexité *f.*

persecute ('pəːsikjuːt) *vt* 1 persécuter. 2 tourmenter. **persecution** *n* persécution *f.*

persevere (pəːsi'viə) *vi* persévérer. **perseverance** *n* persévérance *f.*

Persia ('pəːʃə) *n* Perse *f.* **Persian** *adj,n* persan. **Persian** (language) *n* persan *m.*

persist (pə'sist) *vi* 1 persister, s'obstiner. 2 continuer. **persistence** *n* persistance *f.* **persistent** *adj* 1 persistant, tenace. 2 continu.

person ('pəːsən) *n* personne *f.* **personal** *adj*

personnel, -elle. **personality** n 1 personnalité f. 2 caractère personnel m.

personify (pə'sɔnifai) vt personnifier. **personification** n personnification f.

personnel (pə:sə'nel) n personnel m.

perspective (pə'spektiv) n perspective f.

Perspex ('pə:speks) n Tdmk Perspex m.

perspire (pə'spaiə) vi transpirer. **perspiration** n transpiration, sueur f. **perspiring** adj en sueur.

persuade (pə'sweid) vt persuader. **persuasion** n persuasion f. **persuasive** adj persuasif, -ive.

pert (pə:t) adj mutin, effronté.

pertain (pə'tein) vi appartenir, se rapporter. **pertinent** adj pertinent, à propos.

perturb (pə'tə:b) vt perturber, troubler.

Peru (pə'ru:) n Pérou m. **Peruvian** adj,n péruvien, -ienne.

pervade (pə'veid) vt s'infiltrer or pénétrer dans. **pervading** adj dominant.

perverse (pə'və:s) adj 1 pervers. 2 contrariant. **perversity** n perversité f.

pervert (v pə'və:t n 'pə:və:t) vt 1 pervertir. 2 détourner. n perverti m.

peseta (pə'seitə) n peseta f.

peso ('peisou) n peso m.

pessimism ('pesimizəm) n pessimisme m. **pessimist** n pessimiste m,f. **pessimistic** adj pessimiste.

pest (pest) n peste f. fléau, -aux m. **pesticide** n pesticide m.

pester ('pestə) vt importuner.

pet[1] (pet) n 1 animal familier m. 2 inf chouchou m. adj favori, -ite. vt choyer.

pet[2] (pet) n accès de mauvaise humeur m.

petal ('petl) n pétale m.

peter (pi:tə) vi **peter out** 1 s'épuiser. 2 flancher, s'arrêter.

petition (pi'tiʃən) n 1 pétition, requête f. 2 law recours m. vt 1 adresser une pétition. 2 réclamer.

petrify ('petrifai) vt pétrifier. vi se pétrifier.

petroleum (pi'trouliəm) n pétrole m. **petrol** n essence f.

petticoat ('petikout) n jupon m.

petty ('peti) adj 1 insignifiant. 2 mesquin. **petty cash** n petite caisse f. **petty officer** n sous-officier m.

petulant ('petjulənt) adj irritable. **petulance** n irritabilité f.

pew (pju:) n banc d'église m.

pewter ('pju:tə) n étain m.

phantom ('fæntəm) n fantôme m.

pharmacy ('fɑ:məsi) n pharmacie f.

pharynx ('færiŋks) n pharynx m.

phase (feiz) n phase f.

pheasant ('fezənt) n faisan m.

phenomenon (fi'nɔminən) n pl **-ena** phénomène m. **phenomenal** adj phénoménal, -aux.

philanthropy (fi'lænθrəpi) n philanthropie f. **philanthropist** n philanthrope m,f.

philately (fi'lætəli) n philatélie f. **philatelist** n philatéliste m,f.

Philippines ('filipi:nz) n pl Philippines f pl.

Philistine ('filistain) adj,n philistin.

philosophy (fi'lɔsəfi) n philosophie f. **philosopher** n philosophe m. **philosophical** adj 1 philosophique. 2 philosophe.

phlegm (flem) n flegme m.

phlegmatic (fleg'mætik) adj flegmatique.

phobia ('foubiə) n phobie f.

phoenix ('fi:niks) n phénix m.

phone (foun) n inf téléphone m. vt téléphoner à. **phone for** appeler.

phonetic (fə'netik) adj phonétique. **phonetics** n phonétique f.

phoney ('founi) adj faux, fausse.

phosphate ('fɔsfeit) n phosphate m.

phosphorescence (fɔsfə'resəns) n phosphorescence f. **phosphorescent** adj phosphorescent.

phosphorus ('fɔsfərəs) n phosphore m. **phosphorous** adj phosphoreux, -euse.

photo ('foutou) n inf photo f.

photocopy ('foutoukɔpi) vt photocopier. n photocopie f.

photogenic (foutə'dʒenik) adj photogénique.

photograph ('foutəgrɑ:f) n photographie f. vt photographier. **photographer** n photographe m,f. **photography** n photographie f.

phrase (freiz) n locution, expression f. vt exprimer. **phrasebook** n recueil de locutions m.

physical ('fizikəl) adj physique. **physical education** n culture physique f.

physician (fi'ziʃən) n médecin m.

physics ('fiziks) n physique f.

physiology (fizi'ɔlədʒi) n physiologie f.

physiotherapy (fiziou'θerəpi) n physiothérapie f. **physiotherapist** n physiothérapeute m,f.

physique (fi'zi:k) n physique m.

piano (pi'ænou) n piano m. **grand piano** n piano à queue m. **pianist** n pianiste m,f.

pick[1] (pik) vt 1 choisir. 2 cueillir. 3 (a lock) crocheter. **pick a quarrel with** chercher querelle. **pick out** faire le tri de, choisir. **pick**

over trier. **pick up 1** ramasser. **2** apprendre. **3** prendre. **pick-up** n **1** reprise f. **2** pick-up m. **3** connaissance de rencontre f. ~n choix m. élite f. **pickpocket** n voleur à la tire m.

pick² (pik) n pic m.

picket ('pikit) n piquet m. vi se tenir en faction. vt piqueter.

pickle ('pikəl) n **1** marinade f. **2** pl conserves au vinaigre f pl. vt **1** mariner. **2** conserver au vinaigre.

picnic* ('piknik) n pique-nique m. vi pique-niquer.

pictorial (pik'tɔ:riəl) adj **1** en images. **2** illustré.

picture ('piktʃə) n **1** image f. **2** tableau, -aux m. **3** pl inf ciné m. vt représenter, dépeindre.

picturesque (piktʃə'resk) adj pittoresque.

pidgin ('pidʒən) n pidgin m. **speak pidgin** parler petit nègre.

pie (pai) n **1** pâté (en croûte) m. **2** tourte f.

piece (pi:s) n **1** morceau, -aux m. **2** pièce f. **3** partie f. **piecemeal** adv par morceaux. adj fragmentaire. **piecework** n travail à la pièce m. ~vt joindre, assembler. **piece together** rassembler.

pied (paid) adj bigarré.

pier (piə) n **1** jetée f. **2** arch pilier m.

pierce (piəs) vt percer, transpercer. **piercing** adj **1** perçant. **2** (of cold) pénétrant.

piety ('paiəti) n piété f.

pig (pig) n porc, cochon m. **pig-headed** adj têtu, buté. **pig-iron** n gueuse de fer f. **piglet** n porcelet m. **pigskin** n cuir de porc m. **pigsty** n porcherie f. **pigtail** n queue, natte f.

pigeon ('pidʒən) n pigeon m. **pigeonhole** n alvéole f. casier m. vt caser.

piggyback ('pigibæk) n **give someone a piggyback** porter quelqu'un sur le dos.

pigment ('pigmənt) n **1** sci pigment m. **2** matière colorante f. **pigmentation** n pigmentation f.

pike (paik) n zool brochet m.

pilchard ('piltʃəd) n pilchard m.

pile¹ (pail) n tas, monceau, -aux. v **pile up 1** entasser. **2** amasser.

pile² (pail) n pieu, pieux m. vt soutenir avec des pieux.

pile³ (pail) n (of carpet, etc.) poil m.

pile⁴ (pail) n med hémorroïde f.

pilfer ('pilfə) vt dérober, chaparder. **pilferage** n larcins m pl.

pilgrim ('pilgrim) n pèlerin m. **pilgrimage** n pèlerinage m.

pill (pil) n pilule f.

pillage ('pilidʒ) n pillage m. vt piller, saccager.

pillar ('pilə) n pilier m. colonne f. **pillar-box** n boîte aux lettres f.

pillion ('piliən) n siège arrière m. **ride pillion** monter en croupe.

pillow ('pilou) n oreiller m. **pillowcase** n taie d'oreiller f.

pilot ('pailət) n pilote m. vt piloter, guider.

pimento (pi'mentou) n piment m.

pimple ('pimpəl) n bouton m. adj boutonneux, -euse.

pin (pin) n épingle f. **pins and needles** fourmillements m. **pinball** n billard automatique m. **pincushion** n pelote à épingles f. **pinpoint** vt indiquer. **pinstripe** n rayure f. **pin-up** n pin-up f invar. ~vt **1** épingler. **2** clouer. **pin down** engager.

pinafore ('pinəfɔ:) n tablier m.

pincers ('pinsəz) n pl tenaille, pince f.

pinch (pintʃ) vt **1** pincer. **2** inf chiper. n **1** pincée f. **2** pincement m. **at a pinch** au besoin.

pine¹ (pain) n pin m.

pine² (pain) vi languir.

pineapple ('painæpəl) n ananas m.

Ping-pong ('piŋpɔŋ) n Tdmk Ping-pong m.

pinion ('piniən) n aileron m. vt **1** rogner les ailes à. **2** lier, ligoter.

pink (piŋk) n **1** rose m. **2** bot œillet m. adj rose.

pinnacle ('pinəkəl) n **1** arch pinacle m. **2** cime f. **3** apogée f.

pint (paint) n pinte f.

pioneer (paiə'niə) n **1** pionnier m. **2** précurseur m. vt défricher. vi frayer le chemin.

pious ('paiəs) adj pieux, -euse.

pip (pip) n pépin m.

pipe (paip) n **1** tuyau, -aux m. **2** pipe f. **pipedream** n rêvasserie f. **pipeline** n canalisation, conduite f. **pipette** n pipette f. compte-gouttes m invar.

piquant ('pi:kənt) adj piquant. **piquancy** n **1** piquant m. **2** goût relevé m.

pique (pi:k) n pique f. vt piquer, vexer.

pirate ('pairət) n pirate m. vt **1** contrefaire. **2** s'approprier de.

pirouette (piru'et) n pirouette f. vi pirouetter.

Pisces ('pisi:z) n pl Poissons m pl.

piss (pis) tab vi uriner. n urine f.

pistachio (pis'tæʃiou) n pistache f.

pistol ('pistəl) n pistolet m.

piston ('pɪstən) *n* pɪston *m*.
pit (pɪt) *n* 1 fosse *f*. 2 puits *m*. **pitfall** *n* embûche *f*. piège *m*.
pitch[1] (pɪtʃ) *vt* 1 dresser. 2 placer. 3 lancer. *n* 1 niveau, -aux *m*. 2 *mus* diapason *m*. 3 *sport* terrain *m*. **pitchfork** *n* fourche *f*.
pitch[2] (pɪtʃ) *n* poix *f*. *vt* enduire de poix.
pith (pɪθ) *n* 1 moelle *f*. 2 sève, vigueur *f*.
pittance ('pɪtns) *n* pitance *f*.
pity ('pɪti) *n* pitié, compassion *f*. **what a pity!** quel dommage! ~*vt* plaindre.
pivot ('pɪvət) *n* pɪvot *m*. *vi* pivoter.
pizza ('pi:tsə) *n* pɪzza *f*.
placard ('plækɑ:d) *n* affiche *f*. *vt* afficher.
placate (plə'keɪt) *vt* apaiser.
place (pleɪs) *n* 1 lieu, -eux *m*. 2 localité *f*. 3 place *f*. **out of place** hors de propos. **placename** *n* nom de lieu *m*. **take place** se passer. ~*vt* 1 mettre. 2 situer. **place an order** passer commande.
placenta (plə'sentə) *n* placenta *m*.
placid ('plæsid) *adj* placide.
plagiarize ('pleidʒəraɪz) *vt* plagier. **plagiarist** *n* plagiaire *m*.
plague (pleɪg) *n* 1 peste *f*. 2 fléau, -aux *m*. *vt* harceler.
plaice (pleɪs) *n* plie *f*.
plaid (plæd) *n* 1 plaɪd *m*. 2 tartan *m*.
plain (pleɪn) *adj* 1 clair. 2 simple. 3 plat. 4 quelconque. *n* plaine *f*. **plain-clothes** *adj* en civil.
plaintiff ('pleintif) *n law* demandeur, plaignant *m*.
plaintive ('pleintɪv) *adj* plaintif, -ive.
plait (plæt) *n* natte, tresse *f*. *vt* tresser.
plan (plæn) *n* 1 plan *m*. 2 projet *m*. *vt* 1 projeter. 2 planifier. **planning** *n* 1 conception *f*. 2 planification *f*.
plane[1] (pleɪn) *n* 1 plan *m*. 2 *inf* avion *m*. 3 niveau, -aux *m*. *adj* plat.
plane[2] (pleɪn) *n* rabot *m*. *vt* raboter.
planet ('plænit) *n* planète *f*.
plank (plæŋk) *n* planche *f*.
plankton ('plæŋktən) *n* plancton, plankton *m*.
plant (plɑ:nt) *n* 1 *bot* plante *f*. 2 *tech* usine *f*. *vt* 1 planter. 2 poser, asséner. **plantation** *n* plantation *f*.
plaque (plɑ:k) *n* plaque *f*.
plasma ('plæzmə) *n* plasma *m*.
plaster ('plɑ:stə) *n* 1 *med* emplâtre *m*. 2 plâtre *m*. **plaster of Paris** plâtre de moulage *m*. **sticking plaster** sparadrap *m*. ~*vt* 1 plâtrer. 2 couvrir.

plastic ('plæstik) *adj,n* plastique *m*. **plastic surgery** *n* chirurgie esthétique *f*.
Plasticine ('plæstisi:n) *n Tdmk* pâte à modeler *f*.
plate (pleɪt) *n* 1 plaque *f*. 2 assiette *f*. 3 *Art* gravure, estampe *f*. **dinner/soup plate** assiette plate/creuse *f*. **number plate** plaque d'immatriculation *f*. **platelayer** *n* poseur de rails *m*. ~*vt* plaquer.
plateau ('plætou) *n* plateau, -aux *m*.
platform ('plætfɔ:m) *n* 1 estrade, tribune *f*. 2 (railway) quai *m*. 3 plate-forme *f*.
platinum ('plætnəm) *n* platine *m*.
platonic (plə'tɒnik) *adj* platonique.
plausible ('plɔ:zəbəl) *adj* 1 plausible, vraisemblable. 2 enjoleur, -euse.
play (pleɪ) *vi,vt* jouer *n* 1 *Th* pièce *f*. 2 jeu *m*. **playboy** *n* gaillard *m*. **player** *n* jouer *m*. **playful** *adj* folâtre, enjoué. **playfulness** *n* badinage *m*. **playground** *n* cour de récréation *f*. **playhouse** *n* théâtre *m*. **playing card** *n* carte à jouer *f*. **playing field** *n* terrain de jeux *m*. **playmate** *n* camarade (de jeu) *m,f*. **playschool** *n* jardin d'enfants *m*. **playwright** *n* dramaturge *m*.
plea (pli:) *n* 1 prétexte *m*. 2 appel *m*.
plead (pli:d) *vi,vt* plaider. *vt* prétexter, alléguer. **plead guilty** s'avouer coupable. **plead not guilty** nier sa culpabilité.
please (pli:z) *vt* plaire à, faire plaisir à. *vi* plaire. *adv* s'il vous plaît. **please do!** je vous en prie! **pleasant** *adj* 1 agréable, charmant. 2 aimable. **pleased** *adj* satisfait, content. **pleasing** *adj* agréable. **pleasure** *n* 1 plaisir *m*. 2 gré *m*.
pleat (pli:t) *n* pli *m*. *vt* plisser.
plectrum ('plektrəm) *n* médiator *m*.
pledge (pledʒ) *n* 1 gage *m*. 2 promesse *f*. *vt* 1 mettre en gage. 2 engager.
plenty ('plenti) *n* abondance *f*. *adv inf* largement, bien. **plentiful** *adj* abondant, copieux, -euse.
pliable ('plaiəbəl) *adj* 1 flexible, souple. 2 docile.
pliers ('plaiəz) *n pl* pince, tenaille *f*.
plight (plait) *n* état *m*. condition *f*.
plimsoll ('plimsəl) *n* sandale de gymnastique *f*.
plod (plɒd) *vi* marcher lourdement. **plod on** persévérer. **plodder** *n* bûcheur, -euse.
plonk (plɒŋk) *n* bruit sourd *m*. *v* **plonk down** poser sans façons.
plot[1] (plɒt) *n* 1 *lit* intrigue *f*. 2 complot *m*. conspiration *f*. *vt,vi* comploter, conspirer.
plot[2] (plɒt) *n* terrain *m*. **building plot** lotissement *m*.

plough

plough (plau) *n* charrue *f*. *vt* labourer. **plough through** avancer péniblement dans.
pluck (plʌk) *vt* 1 arracher, cueillir. 2 plumer. **pluck up courage** prendre courage. ~*n* courage, cran *m*.
plug (plʌg) *n* 1 boucher *m*. 2 (electric) prise *f*. *vt* boucher, tamponner.
plum (plʌm) *n* prune *f*. **plum tree** prunier *m*.
plumage (ˈpluːmidʒ) *n* plumage *f*.
plumb (plʌm) *n* plomb *m*. *adj* d'aplomb, vertical, -aux. *adv* 1 d'aplomb. 2 juste. *vt* sonder. **plumber** *n* plombier *m*. **plumbing** *n* plomberie *f*.
plume (pluːm) *n* plume *f*. *vt* orner de plumes.
plump[1] (plʌmp) *adj* grassouillet, -ette, dodu.
plump[2] (plʌmp) *vi* tomber lourdement. *vt* jeter brusquement. **plump for** choisir.
plunder (ˈplʌndə) *n* 1 pillage *m*. 2 butin *m*. *vt* piller.
plunge (plʌndʒ) *n* plongeon *m*. *vt* plonger, immerger. *vi* 1 jeter. 2 tanguer.
pluperfect (pluːˈpəːfikt) *n* plus-que-parfait *m*.
plural (ˈpluərəl) *adj,n* pluriel, -elle *m*.
plus (plʌs) *prep* plus. *adj* positif, -ive.
plush (plʌʃ) *n* peluche *f*.
Pluto (ˈpluːtou) *n* Pluton *f*.
ply[1] (plai) *vt* 1 manier. 2 exercer. 3 assaillir. *vi* faire la navette.
ply[2] (plai) *n* 1 épaisseur *f*. 2 pli *m*. **plywood** *n* contre-plaqué *m*.
pneumatic (njuːˈmætik) *adj* pneumatique. **pneumatic drill** *n* marteau piqueur *m*.
pneumonia (njuːˈmouniə) *n* pneumonie *f*.
poach[1] (poutʃ) *vi* braconner. **poacher** *n* braconnier *m*.
poach[2] (poutʃ) *vt* cul pocher.
pocket (ˈpɔkit) *n* poche *f*. *vt* empocher. **pocket-knife** *n* couteau de poche, canif *m*. **pocket-money** *n* argent de poche *m*.
pod (pɔd) *n* cosse, gousse *f*. *vt* écosser.
poem (ˈpouim) *n* poème *m*. poésie *f*.
poet (ˈpouit) *n* poète *m*. **poetic** *adj* poétique. **poetry** *n* poésie *f*.
poignant (ˈpɔinjənt) *adj* 1 poignant. 2 vif, vive.
point (pɔint) *n* 1 point *m*. 2 question *f*. sujet *m*. 3 idée *f*. 4 pointe *f*. **beside the point** hors de propos. **come to the point** en venir au fait. **point-blank** *adj* 1 à bout portant. 2 direct, catégorique. *adv* 1 à bout portant. 2 catégoriquement. ~*vt* 1 indiquer, signaler. 2 aiguiser. **point out** faire remarquer. **point to** annoncer. **pointed** *adj* 1 pointu. 2 mordant.

poise (pɔiz) *n* 1 équilibre *m*. 2 port *m*. *vt* équilibrer, balancer.
poison (ˈpɔizən) *n* poison *m*. *vt* empoisonner. **poisonous** *adj* 1 empoisonné. 2 (of an animal) venimeux, -euse. 3 (of a plant) vénéneux, -euse.
poke (pouk) *vt* 1 pousser du coude. 2 attiser. 3 passer. **poke fun at** se moquer de. ~*n* 1 coup de coude *m*. 2 coup de tisonnier *m*.
poker[1] (ˈpoukə) *n* tisonnier *m*.
poker[2] (ˈpoukə) *n* game poker *m*.
Poland (ˈpoulənd) *n* Pologne *f*.
polar (ˈpoulə) *adj* polaire. **polar bear** *n* ours blanc *m*. **polarize** *vt* polariser. *vi* se polariser.
pole[1] (poul) *n* perche *f*. mât *m*. **pole-vault** *vi* sauter à la perche. **pole-vaulting** *n* saut à la perche *m*.
pole[2] (poul) *n geog* pôle *m*.
Pole (poul) *n* polonais *m*.
polemic (pəˈlemik) *adj,n* polémique *f*.
Pole Star *n* étoile polaire *f*.
police (pəˈliːs) *n* police *f*. **policeman** *n* agent de police, gendarme *m*. **police station** *n* commissariat de police *m*.
policy[1] (ˈpɔlisi) *n* politique, ligne de conduite *f*.
policy[2] (ˈpɔlisi) *n* police *f*. **insurance policy** police d'assurance.
polish (ˈpɔliʃ) *n* 1 poli, lustre *m*. 2 cire *f*. cirage *m*. 3 raffinement *m*. *vt* 1 polir. 2 cirer.
Polish (ˈpouliʃ) *adj* polonais. **Polish** (language) *n* polonais *m*.
polite (pəˈlait) *adj* poli, courtois. **politeness** *n* politesse, courtoisie *f*.
politics (ˈpɔlitiks) *n* politique *f*. **political** *adj* politique. **politician** *n* homme politique *m*.
polka (ˈpɔlkə) *n* polka *f*.
poll (poul) *n* vote, scrutin *m*. *vi* voter. **polling booth** isoloir *m*.
pollen (ˈpɔlən) *n* pollen *m*. **pollinate** *vt* polliniser.
pollute (pəˈluːt) *vt* polluer, souiller. **pollution** *n* pollution *f*.
polygamy (pəˈligəmi) *n* polygamie *f*.
polygon (ˈpɔligən) *n* polygone *m*.
polytechnic (pɔliˈteknik) *adj* polytechnique. *n* institut de technologie *m*.
polythene (ˈpɔliθiːn) *n* polyéthylène *m*.
pomegranate (ˈpɔmigrænət) *n* grenade *f*. **pomegranate tree** *n* grenadier *m*.
pommel (ˈpʌməl) *n* pommeau, -aux *m*. *vt* rouer de coups.
pomp (pɔmp) *n* faste, apparat *m*. pompe *f*.

252

pompous adj **1** fastueux, -euse. **2** suffisant. **3** ampoulé.

pond (pɔnd) n étang m. mare f.

ponder ('pɔndə) vi méditer. vt considérer, peser, ruminer.

pony ('pouni) n poney m.

poodle ('puːdļ) n caniche m.

pool[1] (puːl) n flaque, mare f.

pool[2] (puːl) n **1** game cagnotte, poule f. **2** fonds commun m. vt mettre en commun.

poor (puə, pɔː) adj **1** pauvre. **2** de mauvaise qualité, médiocre.

pop[1] (pɔp) n bruit sec m. vi **1** éclater, sauter. **2** crever. vt **1** faire sauter. **2** inf mettre au clou. **3** fourrer. **pop in** entrer en passant. ~interj crac! **popcorn** n maïs grillé m.

pop[2] (pɔp) adj pop. **pop music** n musique pop f.

pope (poup) n pape m.

poplar ('pɔplə) n peuplier m.

poppy ('pɔpi) n coquelicot, pavot m.

popular ('pɔpjulə) adj **1** populaire. **2** à la mode. **3** courant. **popularity** n popularité f.

population (pɔpju'leiʃən) n population f.

porcelain ('pɔːslin) n porcelaine f.

porch (pɔːtʃ) n porche m. marquise f.

porcupine ('pɔːkjupain) n porc-épic m.

pore[1] (pɔː) vi **pore over** s'absorber dans, méditer.

pore[2] (pɔː) n pore m.

pork (pɔːk) n porc m.

pornography (pɔː'nɔgrəfi) n pornographie f. **pornographic** adj pornographique.

porous ('pɔːrəs) adj poreux, -euse, perméable.

porpoise ('pɔːpəs) n marsouin m.

porridge ('pɔridʒ) n porridge m.

port[1] (pɔːt) n (harbour) port m.

port[2] (pɔːt) n naut bâbord m.

port[3] (pɔːt) n (wine) porto m.

portable ('pɔːtəbəl) adj portatif, -ive.

porter[1] ('pɔːtə) n (luggage) porteur, garçon m.

porter[2] ('pɔːtə) n concierge, portier m.

portfolio (pɔːt'fouliou) n **1** serviette f. porte-documents m. **2** Art chemise f. **3** pol portefeuille f.

porthole ('pɔːthoul) n hublot m.

portion ('pɔːʃən) n **1** partie, part f. **2** portion, ration f.

portrait ('pɔːtrit) n portrait m.

portray (pɔː'trei) vt **1** peindre. **2** dépeindre.

Portugal ('pɔːtjugəl) n Portugal m. **Portuguese** adj,n portugais invar. **Portuguese** (language) n portugais m.

pose (pouz) vt,vi poser. **pose as** se faire passer pour. ~n pose f.

posh (pɔʃ) adj chic.

position (pə'ziʃən) n **1** position f. **2** situation f. **3** place f. **4** rang m. **position closed** guichet fermé. ~vt **1** situer. **2** orienter.

positive ('pɔzitiv) adj **1** positif, -ive. **2** convaincu, assuré. n positif m.

possess (pə'zes) vt **1** posséder. **2** s'approprier. **possession** n possession, jouissance f. **possessive** adj possessif, -ive.

possible ('pɔsəbəl) adj possible. **it is possible that** il se peut que. **possibility** n possibilité f. **2** éventualité f. **possibly** adv peut-être.

post[1] (poust) n poteau, -aux m. vt afficher, placarder.

post[2] (poust) n **1** mil poste m. **2** situation f. emploi m. vt mettre en faction, affecter.

post[3] (poust) n **1** courrier m. **2** poste f. vt mettre à la poste. **postage** n affranchissement, port m. **postal order** n mandat-poste m. **postbox** n boîte aux lettres f. **postcard** n carte postale f. **postcode** n code postal m. **postman** n facteur m. **postmark** n cachet de la poste m. **post office** n bureau de poste m.

poster ('poustə) n affiche f.

posterior (pɔs'tiəriə) adj postérieur. n inf postérieur, derrière m.

posterity (pɔs'teriti) n postérité f.

postgraduate (poust'grædjuət) adj de troisième cycle. n étudiant de troisième cycle m.

posthumous ('pɔstjuməs) adj posthume.

post-mortem (poust'mɔːtəm) n autopsie f.

postpone (pəs'poun) vt ajourner, différer. **postponement** n ajournement m.

postscript ('pousskript) n post-scriptum m invar.

postulate (v 'pɔstjuleit; n 'pɔstjulət) vt **1** postuler, demander. **2** supposer. n postulat m.

posture ('pɔstʃə) n **1** posture, attitude f. **2** état m.

pot (pɔt) n **1** pot m. **2** marmite f. **pots and pans** batterie de cuisine f.

potato (pə'teitou) n, pl **-oes** pomme de terre f.

potent ('poutnt) adj fort, puissant.

potential (pə'tenʃəl) adj **1** possible, latent. **2** potentiel, -elle. n potentiel m.

pothole ('pɔthoul) n **1** (in a road) trou, nid de poule m. **2** marmite torrentielle f. **potholer** n spéléologue m,f. **potholing** n spéléologie f.

potion ('pouʃən) n potion f.

potter

---

potter ('pɔtə) *n* potier *m*. *vi* s'occuper de bagatelles. **potter about** bricoler.
pottery ('pɔtəri) *n* poterie *f*.
pouch (pautʃ) *n* 1 poche *f*. petit sac *m*. 2 *zool* poche ventrale *f*. 3 {for tobacco} blague *f*.
poultice ('poultɪs) *n* cataplasme *m*.
poultry ('poultri) *n* volaille *f*.
pounce (pauns) *vi* **pounce on** fondre *or* s'abattre sur. ∼*n* attaque, griffe *f*.
pound[1] (paund) *vt* 1 cogner, battre. 2 piler, broyer.
pound[2] (paund) *n, pl* **pounds** *or* **pound** 1 (currency) livre sterling *f*. 2 (weight) livre *f*.
pour (pɔ:) *vt* verser, couler. *vi* tomber à verse. **pour in** entrer à flots. **pour out** 1 verser. 2 sortir en foule.
pout (paut) *vi* faire la moue, bouder. *n* moue *f*.
poverty ('pɔvəti) *n* 1 misère, pauvreté *f*. 2 manque *m*. **poverty-stricken** *adj* indigent.
powder ('paudə) *n* poudre *f*. *vt* 1 pulvériser. 2 saupoudrer. 3 poudrer. **powder room** *n* toilette pour dames *f*.
power ('pauə) *n* 1 pouvoir *m*. 2 faculté *f*. 3 puissance *f*. 4 force *f*. **power station** *n* centrale électrique *f*. **powerful** *adj* puissant, fort. **powerless** *adj* impuissant.
practicable ('præktikəbəl) *adj* faisable, praticable.
practical ('præktikəl) *adj* pratique. **practical joke** *n* mauvaise plaisanterie *f*.
practice ('præktɪs) *n* 1 pratique *f*. 2 coutume *f*. 3 clientèle *f*. 4 *sport* exercice *m*. **out of practice** rouillé.
practise ('præktɪs) *vt* 1 pratiquer, exercer. 2 étudier, s'exercer. *vi* s'entraîner, faire des exercices.
practitioner (præk'tiʃənə) *n* praticien *m*.
pragmatic (præg'mætik) *adj* pragmatique.
prairie ('prɛəri) *n* prairie *f*.
praise (preiz) *n* éloge *m*. louange *f*. *vt* faire l'éloge de, louer. **praiseworthy** *adj* louable, méritoire.
pram (præm) *n* landau *m*. voiture d'enfant *f*.
prance (prɑ:ns) *vi* 1 piaffer. 2 se pavaner.
prank (præŋk) *n* 1 escapade, fredaine *f*. 2 tour *m*. farce *f*.
prattle ('prætl) *vi* babiller, bavarder. *n* babillage *m*.
prawn (prɔ:n) *n* crevette *f*.
pray (prei) *vi,vt* 1 prier. 2 implorer. **prayer** *n* prière *f*. **prayerbook** *n* livre de prières *m*.
preach (pri:tʃ) *vi,vt* prêcher.
precarious (pri'kɛəriəs) *adj* 1 précaire. 2 incertain. **precariousness** *n* 1 précarité *f*. 2 incertitude *f*.
precaution (pri'kɔ:ʃən) *n* précaution *f*.
precede (pri'si:d) *vt* précéder. **precedence** *n* préséance, priorité *f*. **precedent** *n* précédent *m*.
precinct ('pri:siŋkt) *n* enceinte *f*. **pedestrian precinct** zone piétonnière *f*.
precious ('preʃəs) *adj* 1 précieux, -euse. 2 recherché, affecté.
precipice ('presipis) *n* précipice *m*.
precipitate (prə'sipiteit) *vt* 1 hâter. 2 précipiter. *vi* (se) précipiter. *adj* 1 précipité. 2 irréfléchi. **precipitation** *n* précipitation *f*.
precis ('preisi) *n* résumé, précis *m*.
precise (pri'sais) *adj* 1 précis, exact. 2 méticuleux, -euse. **precision** *n* précision *f*.
precocious (pri'kouʃəs) *adj* précoce. **precociousness** *n* précocité *f*.
preconceive (pri:kən'si:v) *vt* préconcevoir. **preconception** *n* 1 idée préconçue. 2 préjugé *m*.
predatory ('predətəri) *adj* prédateur, -trice, rapace.
predecessor ('pri:disesə) *n* prédécesseur *m*.
predestine (pri:'destin) *vt* prédestiner. **predestination** *n* prédestination *f*.
predicament (pri'dikəmənt) *n* situation difficile, mauvaise passe *f*.
predicate (*n* 'predikit; *v* 'predikeit) *n* prédicat *m*. *vt* affirmer.
predict (pri'dikt) *vt* prédire. **predictable** *adj* prévisible. **prediction** *n* prédiction *f*.
predominate (pri'dɔmineit) *vi* prédominer. **predominance** *n* prédominance *f*. **predominant** *adj* prédominant.
pre-eminent *adj* 1 prééminent. 2 remarquable.
preen (pri:n) *vt* lisser, nettoyer. **preen oneself** se bichonner, faire des grâces.
prefabricate (pri'fæbrikeit) *vt* préfabriquer.
preface ('prefis) *n* 1 *lit* préface *f*. avant-propos *m invar*. 2 préambule *m*. *vt* 1 *lit* préfacer. 2 préluder à.
prefect ('pri:fekt) *n* préfet *m*.
prefer (pri'fə:) *vt* préférer, aimer mieux. **preference** *n* préférence *f*. **preferential** *adj* préférentiel, -elle.
prefix ('pri:fiks) *n* préfixe *m*. *vt* mettre en tête.
pregnant ('pregnənt) *adj* 1 (of a woman) enceinte, grosse. 2 (of an animal) pleine. 3 chargé, lourd.
prehistoric (pri:his'tɔrik) *adj* préhistorique.
prejudice ('predʒədis) *n* 1 préjugé, parti pris *m*. 2 tort *m*. *vt* 1 prévenir, prédisposer. 2 nuire à.

254

preliminary (pri'limɪnəri) *adj* préliminaire, préalable.
prelude ('prelju:d) *n* prélude *m*.
premarital (prɪ:'mærɪt|) *adj* prénuptial.
premature ('premətʃuə) *adj* prématuré.
premeditate (prɪ:'mediteɪt) *vt* préméditer.
premise ('premɪs) *n* 1 prémisse *f*. 2 *pl* lieux *m pl*. *vt* poser en prémisse.
premium ('pri:mɪəm) *n* 1 prime *f*. 2 prix, récompense *f*. **premium bond** *n* bon du trésor *m*.
preoccupied (prɪ:'ɔkjupaɪd) *adj* préoccupé. **preoccupation** *n* préoccupation *f*.
prepare (pri'pɛə) *vt* préparer. *vi* se préparer, s'apprêter. **preparation** *n* 1 préparation *f*. 2 *pl* préparatifs *m pl*. **preparatory** *adj* préparatoire.
preposition (prepə'ziʃən) *n* préposition *f*.
preposterous (pri'pɔstərəs) *adj* absurde.
prerogative (pri'rɔgətɪv) *n* prérogative *f*. privilège *m*.
prescribe (pri'skraɪb) *vt* prescrire, ordonner. **prescription** *n* 1 *med* ordonnance *f*. 2 prescription *f*.
presence ('prezəns) *n* 1 présence *f*. 2 prestance *f*. air *m*. **presence of mind** sang-froid *m*.
present[1] ('prezənt) *adj* présent, actuel, -elle. *n* présent *m*. **presently** *adv* dans un instant, tout à l'heure.
present[2] (*v* pri'zent; *n* 'prezənt) *vt* 1 présenter. 2 offrir. *n* cadeau, -aux *m*. **presentable** *adj* présentable, portable. **presentation** *n* 1 présentation *f*. 2 remise *f*.
preserve (pri'zə:v) *vt* 1 conserver. 2 préserver. **preserves** *n pl* conserves *f pl*.
preside (pri'zaɪd) *vi* présider.
president ('prezɪdənt) *n* président *m*. **presidency** *n* présidence *f*. **presidential** *adj* présidentiel, -elle.
press (pres) *vt* 1 appuyer sur. 2 presser. 3 repasser. *vi* se serrer, se presser. *n* presse *f*. **press conference** *n* conférence de presse *f*. **press-gang** *n* presse *f*. **press-stud** *n* bouton pression *m*. **press-up** *n* exercice musculaire *m*. **pressing** *adj* urgent.
pressure ('preʃə) *n* 1 pression *f*. 2 urgence *f*. **pressure cooker** *n* marmite à pression, cocotte minute *f*. **pressurize** *vt* pressuriser.
prestige (pres'ti:ʒ) *n* prestige *m*.
presume (pri'zju:m) *vt,vi* présumer, supposer. *vt* oser.
pretend (pri'tend) *vt* 1 feindre, simuler. 2 prétendre. *vi* faire semblant. **pretence** *n* 1

simulation *f*. prétexte *m*. 2 prétention *f*. **pretension** *n* prétention *f*. **pretentious** *adj* prétentieux, -euse.
pretext ('pri:tekst) *n* prétexte *m*.
pretty ('prɪti) *adj* joli, beau, belle. *adv* *inf* assez, passablement.
prevail (pri'veil) *vi* 1 prévaloir. 2 régner. **prevail upon** persuader. **prevalent** *adj* prédominant, répandu.
prevent (pri'vent) *vt* 1 empêcher. 2 détourner. **prevention** *n* prévention *f*. empêchement *m*. **preventive** *adj* préventif, -ive.
preview ('pri:vju:) *n* 1 exhibition préalable. 2 (cinema, etc.) avant-première *f*.
previous ('pri:vɪəs) *adj* précédent, antérieur, préalable. **previously** *adv* auparavant.
prey (prei) *n* proie *f*. *v* **prey on** tourmenter, ronger.
price (praɪs) *n* prix *m*. *vt* mettre un prix à. **price-list** *n* tarif *m*.
prick (prik) *n* piqûre *f*. *vt* piquer, crever. *vi* picoter. **prick up one's ears** dresser l'oreille. **prickle** *n* piquant *m*. épine *f*. *vi* picoter, fourmiller. *vt* piquer. **prickly** *adj* épineux, -euse.
pride (praɪd) *n* orgueil *m*. fierté *f*. **pride oneself on** se vanter de.
priest (pri:st) *n* prêtre *m*. **priesthood** *n* prêtrise *f*.
prim (prim) *adj* guindé, pincé, collet monté *invar*.
primary ('praɪməri) *adj* 1 premier, -ière. 2 originel, -elle. 3 primaire. **primary school** *n* école primaire *f*.
primate *n* 1 ('praɪmɪt) *rel* primat *m*. 2 ('praɪmeɪt) *zool* primate *m*.
prime (praɪm) *adj* 1 premier, -ière. 2 de premier ordre. 3 principal, -aux. *vt* préparer. **prime minister** *n* premier ministre *m*.
primitive ('primitɪv) *adj* primitif, -ive.
primrose ('primrouz) *n* primevère *f*.
prince (prins) *n* prince *m*.
princess (prin'ses) *n* princesse *f*.
principal ('prinsəpəl) *adj* principal, -aux. *n* directeur, patron *m*.
principality (prinsi'pæliti) *n* principauté *f*.
principle ('prinsəpəl) *n* principe *m*.
print (print) *n* 1 empreinte, trace *f*. 2 impression *f*. 3 *phot* épreuve *f*. **in/out of print** disponible/épuisé. ~*vt* imprimer, tirer. **printed matter** *n* imprimés *m pl*. **printing** *n* impression *f*.

255

prior

prior (ˈpraɪə) *adj* précédent, antérieur. **priority** *n* priorité *f.*
prise (praɪz) *vt* **prise open** ouvrir de force.
prism (ˈprɪzəm) *n* prisme *m.*
prison (ˈprɪzən) *n* prison *f.* **prisoner** *n* prisonnier, -ière.
private (ˈpraɪvɪt) *adj* **1** privé, particulier, -ière. **2** intime, confidentiel, -elle. *n* simple soldat *m.* **privacy** *n* intimité *f.* **privately** *adv* en particulier.
privet (ˈprɪvɪt) *n* troène *m.*
privilege (ˈprɪvɪlɪdʒ) *n* privilège *m.* prérogative *f.* *vt* privilégier.
prize[1] (praɪz) *n* prix *m.*
prize[2] (praɪz) *vt* évaluer, estimer.
probable (ˈprɒbəbəl) *adj* probable, vraisemblable. **probability** *n* probabilité *f.*
probation (prəˈbeɪʃən) *n* **1** épreuve *f.* **2** *law* liberté surveillée *f.* **probation officer** *n* délégué à la liberté surveillée *m.* **probationer** *n* stagiaire *m,f.*
probe (proub) *vt* sonder.
problem (ˈprɒbləm) *n* problème *m.* **problematic** *adj* problématique, douteux, -euse.
proceed (prəˈsiːd) *vi* **1** continuer. **2** procéder. **3** provenir. **proceedings** *n pl* **1** débats *m pl.* **2** *law* poursuites *f pl.* **procedure** *n* **1** procédé *m.* **2** *law* procédure *f.*
process (ˈprouses) *n* **1** processus *m.* **2** cours *m.* **3** procédé *m.* méthode *f.* *vt* traiter. **procession** *n* cortège, défilé *m.*
proclaim (prəˈkleɪm) *vt* proclamer, annoncer. **proclamation** *n* proclamation, déclaration *f.*
procreate (ˈproukrɪeɪt) *vt* procréer, engendrer.
procure (prəˈkjuə) *vt* procurer.
prod (prɒd) *vt* **1** pousser du doigt. **2** aiguillonner. *n* coup de pointe *m.*
prodigal (ˈprɒdɪgəl) *adj* prodigue.
prodigy (ˈprɒdɪdʒɪ) *n* prodige *m.*
produce (*v* prəˈdjuːs; *n* ˈprɒdjuːs) *vt* **1** produire. **2** présenter, montrer. **3** *Th* mettre en scène. *n* produit *m.* denrées *f pl.* **producer** *n* **1** producteur, -trice. **2** *Th* metteur en scène *m.* **product** *n* **1** produit *m.* **2** résultat *m.* **production** *n* **1** production *f.* **2** *comm* fabrique *f.* **3** *Th* mise en scène *f.* **productive** *adj* productif, -ive.
profane (prəˈfeɪn) *adj* profane. *vt* profaner.
profess (prəˈfes) *vt* **1** professer. **2** prétendre. **profession** *n* **1** profession *f.* **2** métier *m.* **professional** *adj* professionnel, -elle. **professor** *n* professeur *m.*

proficient (prəˈfɪʃənt) *adj* compétent, capable. **proficiency** *n* compétence *f.*
profile (ˈproufaɪl) *n* profil *m.* silhouette *f.*
profit (ˈprɒfɪt) *n* bénéfice, profit *m.* *vi* bénéficier *or* profiter de. *vt* bénéficier *or* profiter à.
profound (prəˈfaund) *adj* **1** profond. **2** approfondi. **profoundly** *adv* profondément.
profuse (prəˈfjuːs) *adj* abondant, excessif, -ive.
programme (ˈprougræm) *n* **1** programme *m.* **2** (radio, etc.) émission *f.* **program** (in computers) *n* programme *m.* *vt* programmer.
progress (*n* ˈprougres; *v* prəˈgres) *n* **1** progrès *m.* **2** cours *m.* marche *f.* **make progress** faire des progrès. ∼*vi* s'avancer, progresser. **progression** *n* progression *f.* **progressive** *adj* progressif, -ive.
prohibit (prəˈhɪbɪt) *vt* défendre, interdire. **smoking prohibited** défense de fumer. **prohibition** *n* interdiction, défense *f.*
project (*n* ˈprɒdʒekt; *v* prəˈdʒekt) *n* projet *m.* *vi* dépasser, faire saillie. *vt* projeter. **projectile** *n* projectile *m.* **projection** *n* **1** projection *f.* **2** lancement *m.* **3** saillie *f.* **projector** *n* projecteur *m.*
proletariat (prouliˈtɛərɪət) *n* prolétariat *m.*
proliferate (prəˈlɪfəreɪt) *vi,vt* proliférer.
prolific (prəˈlɪfɪk) *adj* prolifique, fécond.
prologue (ˈproulɒg) *n* prologue *m.*
prolong (prəˈlɒŋ) *vt* prolonger.
promenade (prɒməˈnɑːd) *n* promenade, esplanade *f.* *vi* se promener.
prominent (ˈprɒmɪnənt) *adj* **1** éminent, remarquable. **2** saillant, proéminent. **prominence** *n* **1** proéminence *f.* **2** importance *f.*
promiscuous (prəˈmɪskjuəs) *adj* **1** casuel, -elle. **2** confus. **promiscuity** *n* promiscuité *f.*
promise (ˈprɒmɪs) *n* promesse *f.* **break one's promise** manquer de parole. ∼*vt,vi* promettre. **promising** *adj* plein de promesses.
promote (prəˈmout) *vt* **1** donner de l'avancement à. **2** encourager. **be promoted** monter en grade. **promotion** *n* promotion *f.*
prompt (prɒmpt) *adj* prompt. *vt* **1** *Th* souffler. **2** suggérer à, inciter. **prompter** *n* souffleur, -euse.
prone (proun) *adj* enclin, porté.
prong (prɒŋ) *n* **1** fourche *f.* **2** dent de fourche *f.*
pronoun (ˈprounaun) *n* pronom *m.*
pronounce (prəˈnauns) *vt* **1** articuler. **2** déclarer. **pronounced** *adj* marqué. **pronunciation** *n* prononciation *f.*
proof (pruːf) *n* **1** preuve *f.* **2** épreuve *f.* *adj* à

l'épreuve de, résistant. **proofread** vt faire des corrections sur épreuves.
prop[1] (prɔp) n appui, soutien m. vt soutenir, appuyer.
prop[2] (prɔp) n Th accessoire m.
propaganda (prɔpə'gændə) n propagande f.
propagate ('prɔpəgeit) vt propager.
propel (prə'pel) vt propulser. **propeller** n hélice f.
proper ('prɔpə) adj 1 propre. 2 approprié, juste. 3 convenable, comme il faut. **properly** adv 1 correctement. 2 comme il faut. **proper noun** n nom propre m.
property ('prɔpəti) n 1 propriété f. 2 biens m pl. 3 immeuble m. 4 qualité f. **lost property** objets trouvés m pl.
prophecy ('prɔfisi) n prophétie f. **prophesy** vt prophétiser, prédire. vi parler en prophète.
prophet ('prɔfit) n prophète m. **prophetic** adj prophétique.
proportion (prə'pɔ:ʃən) n 1 part, partie f. 2 rapport m. proportion f. **out of proportion** mal proportionné. ~vt proportionner. **proportional** adj proportionnel, -elle, proportionné à.
propose (prə'pouz) vt proposer. vi faire une demande en mariage. **proposal** n 1 proposition f. 2 projet m. 3 demande en mariage f. **proposition** n 1 proposition f. 2 affaire f.
proprietor (prə'praiətə) n propriétaire m,f.
propriety (prə'praiəti) n 1 bienséance f. convenances f pl. 2 propriété f.
propulsion (prə'pʌlʃən) n propulsion f.
prose (prouz) n 1 prose f. 2 educ thème m.
prosecute ('prɔsikju:t) vt poursuivre. **prosecution** n poursuites f pl. **prosecutor** n plaignant m.
prospect ('prɔspekt) n 1 perspective f. 2 vue f. 3 pl avenir m. vt prospecter. **prospective** adj à venir, futur. **prospectus** n prospectus m.
prosper ('prɔspə) vi prospérer, réussir. **prosperity** n prospérité f. **prosperous** adj prospère.
prostitute ('prɔstitju:t) n prostituée f. vt prostituer. **prostitution** n prostitution f.
prostrate (v prɔs'treit; adj 'prɔstreit) vt coucher, étendre. **prostrate oneself** se prosterner. ~adj 1 prosterné, étendu. 2 accablé.
protagonist (prə'tægənist) n protagoniste m.
protect (prə'tekt) vt 1 protéger. 2 sauvegarder. **protection** n 1 protection, défense f. 2 abri m. **protective** adj protecteur, -trice.
protein ('prouti:n) n protéine f.

protest (n 'proutest; v prə'test) n protestation f. vt,vi protester.
Protestant ('prɔtistənt) adj,n protestant.
protocol ('proutəkɔl) n protocole m.
proton ('proutɔn) n proton m.
prototype ('proutətaip) n prototype m.
protrude (prə'tru:d) vi déborder, faire saillie. **protruding** adj saillant.
proud (praud) adj orgueilleux, -euse, fier, -ère.
prove (pru:v) vt démontrer, prouver. vi se montrer, se trouver. **proven** adj avéré.
proverb ('prɔvə:b) n proverbe m. **proverbial** adj proverbial, -aux.
provide (prə'vaid) vt fournir, munir, pourvoir. **provide for** pourvoir à. **provided** conj pourvu que. **provision** n 1 provision f. 2 stipulation f. 3 pl comestibles m pl. **make provision for** pourvoir à. **provisional** adj provisoire.
province ('prɔvins) n 1 province f. 2 ressort, domaine m. **provincial** adj provincial, -aux.
proviso (prə'vaizou) n condition, clause conditionnelle f.
provoke (prə'vouk) vt 1 provoquer, exaspérer. 2 exciter. **provocation** n provocation f. **provocative** adj provocateur, -trice.
prow (prau) n proue f.
prowess ('prauis) n prouesse f.
prowl (praul) vi rôder.
proximity (prɔk'simiti) n proximité f.
prude (pru:d) n prude f. **prudish** adj prude, bégueule.
prudent ('pru:dnt) adj prudent, sage. **prudence** n prudence f.
prune[1] (pru:n) n pruneau, -aux m.
prune[2] (pru:n) vt tailler, émonder.
pry (prai) vt fureter, fourrer le nez.
psalm (sɑ:m) n psaume m.
pseudonym ('sju:dənim) n pseudonyme m.
psychedelic (saiki'delik) adj psychédélique.
psychiatry (sai'kaiətri) n psychiatrie f. **psychiatric** adj psychiatrique. **psychiatrist** n psychiatre m.
psychic ('saikik) adj psychique, métaphysique.
psychoanalysis (saikouə'nælisis) n psychanalyse f. **psychoanalysist** n psychanalyste m.
psychology (sai'kɔlədʒi) n psychologie f. **psychological** adj psychologique. **psychologist** n psychologue m.
psychopathic (saikə'pæθik) adj psychopathe.
psychosomatic (saikousə'mætik) adj psychosomatique.
pub (pʌb) n inf bistrot, bar m. **pub crawl** n tournée des bistrots f.

puberty

puberty ('pjuːbəti) *n* puberté *f.*
public ('pʌblik) *adj,n* public, -ique *m.* **general public** grand public. **public house** *n* auberge *f.* **public relations** *n* rapports extérieurs *m pl.* **public school** *n* grande école privée d'enseignement secondaire *f.* **publican** *n* propriétaire de bistrot *m.*
publication (pʌbliˈkeiʃən) *n* publication *f.*
publicity (pʌbˈlisiti) *n* publicité, réclame *f.*
publicize ('pʌblisaiz) *vt* faire connaître au public.
publish ('pʌbliʃ) *vt* publier, faire paraître. **publisher** *n* éditeur *m.* **publishing** *n* publication *f.* **publishing house** *n* maison d'édition *f.*
pucker ('pʌkə) *vt* **1** rider. **2** froncer. *vi* faire des plis, se froncer. *n* **1** ride *f.* **2** fronce *f.*
pudding ('pudiŋ) *n* pouding, pudding *m.*
puddle ('pʌdl) *n* flaque d'eau *f.*
puff (pʌf) *n* souffle *m.* bouffée *f.* *vi* souffler, haleter. *vt* gonfler. **puff pastry** *n* pâte feuilletée *f.* **puffy** *adj* boursouflé.
pull (pul) *n* coup *m.* *vt,vi* tirer. **pull a face** faire une grimace. **pull down** démolir. **pull off** enlever. **pull oneself together** se reprendre. **pull out 1** arracher. **2** sortir. **pull up 1** remonter. **2** arrêter. **pullover** *n* pull *m.*
pulley ('puli) *n* poulie *f.*
pulp (pʌlp) *n* pulpe *f.* *vt* réduire en pulpe, décortiquer.
pulpit ('pʌlpit) *n* chaire *f.*
pulsate (pʌlˈseit) *vi* **1** (of the heart) battre. **2** palpiter.
pulse (pʌls) *n* pouls *m.* *vi* battre, vibrer.
pulverize ('pʌlvəraiz) *vt* pulvériser.
pump (pʌmp) *n* pompe *f.* *vt* **1** pomper. **2** *sl* tirer les vers du nez de.
pumpkin ('pʌmpkin) *n* citrouille *f.*
pun (pʌn) *n* jeu de mots *m.*
punch¹ (pʌntʃ) *n* coup de poing *m.* *vt* donner un coup de poing à.
punch² (pʌntʃ) *n* (drink) punch *m.*
punch³ (pʌntʃ) *vt* percer. *n* poinçon *m.*
punctual ('pʌŋktʃuəl) *adj* ponctuel, -elle, exact. **punctuality** *n* ponctualité *f.*
punctuate ('pʌŋktʃueit) *vt* ponctuer. **punctuation** *n* ponctuation *f.*
puncture ('pʌŋktʃə) *n* crevaison, perforation *f.* *vt* **1** crever. **2** ponctionner.
pungent ('pʌndʒənt) *adj* **1** âcre, fort. **2** mordant. **pungency** *n* **1** aigreur *f.* **2** saveur *f.*
punish ('pʌniʃ) *vt* punir, châtier. **punishment** *n*

258

punition *f.* châtiment *m.* **capital punishment** *n* peine capitale *f.*
punt¹ (pʌnt) *n* bateau plat *m.* *vt* conduire à la perche.
punt² (pʌnt) *vi* game ponter. **punter** *n* joueur *m.*
pupil¹ ('pjuːpəl) *n* élève *m,f.* écolier, -ière.
pupil² ('pjuːpəl) *n* anat pupille *f.*
puppet ('pʌpit) *n* **1** marionnette *f.* **2** (person) pantin *m.*
puppy ('pʌpi) *n* jeune chien, chiot *m.*
purchase ('pəːtʃis) *vt* acheter. *n* achat *m.*
pure (pjuə) *adj* pur. **purity** *n* pureté *f.*
purgatory ('pəːgətri) *n* purgatoire *m.*
purge (pəːdʒ) *vt* purger, purifier. *n* purge *f.*
purify ('pjuərifai) *vt* purifier, épurer.
Puritan ('pjuəritən) *adj,n* puritain.
purl (pəːl) *vt* faire des mailles à l'envers.
purple ('pəːpəl) *adj,n* pourpre *f.*
purpose ('pəːpəs) *n* dessein, but *m.* fin *f.* **on purpose** exprès. **purposely** *adv* **1** à dessein. **2** exprès.
purr (pəː) *vi* ronronner. *n* ronron *m.*
purse (pəːs) *n* porte-monnaie *m invar.* bourse *f.*
pursue (pəˈsjuː) *vt,vi* poursuivre. **pursuit** *n* **1** poursuite *f.* **2** recherche *f.*
pus (pʌs) *n* pus *m.* sanie *f.*
push (puʃ) *vt,vi* pousser. *vt* **1** appuyer. **2** bousculer. *n* poussée *f.* **at a push** au besoin. **pushchair** *n* poussette *f.*
pussy ('pusi) *n* minet, chaton *m.*
put⁎ (put) *vt* mettre, poser, placer. **put back 1** remettre. **2** retarder. **put down 1** déposer. **2** noter. **3** attribuer. **put forward** avancer. **put off** différer. **put on** mettre. **put out 1** éteindre. **2** déconcerter. **3** tendre. **put up 1** construire. **2** hausser. **put up with** supporter.
putrid ('pjuːtrid) *adj* putride.
putt (pʌt) *n* coup roulé *m.* *vt* poter. **putting green** *n* vert *m.*
putty ('pʌti) *n* mastic *m.*
puzzle ('pʌzəl) *n* **1** devinette, énigme *f.* **2** puzzle *m.* *vt* intriguer.
PVC *n* PCV *m.*
Pygmy ('pigmi) *n* pygmée *m.*
pyjamas (pəˈdʒɑːməz) *n pl* pyjama *m.*
pylon ('pailən) *n* pylône *m.*
pyramid ('pirəmid) *n* pyramide *f.*
Pyrenees (pirəˈniːz) *n pl* Pyrénées *f pl.*
Pyrex ('paireks) *n Tdmk* pyrex *m.*
python ('paiθən) *n* python *m.*

Q

quack[1] (kwæk) *n* couin-couin *m. vi* faire couin-couin.

quack[2] (kwæk) *n* charlatan *m.*

quadrangle ('kwɔdræŋgəl) *n* **1** *math* quadrilatère *m.* **2** cour *f.*

quadrant ('kwɔdrənt) *n* quadrant *m.*

quadrilateral (kwɔdri'lætərəl) *adj,n* quadrilatère *m.*

quadruped ('kwɔdruped) *adj,n* quadrupède *m.*

quadruple ('kwɔdrupəl) *adj* quadruple. *vt* quadrupler.

quadruplet ('kwɔdruplit) *n* quadruplé *m.*

quail[1] (kweil) *n* caille *f.*

quail[2] (kweil) *vi* fléchir, faiblir.

quaint (kweint) *adj* **1** étrange, bizarre. **2** pittoresque, de l'ancienne mode.

quake (kweik) *vi* **1** trembler. **2** frémir.

Quaker ('kweikə) *n* quaker *m.*

qualify ('kwɔlifai) *vt* **1** qualifier. **2** modifier. *vi* se qualifier, acquérir les connaissances nécessaires. **qualification** *n* **1** capacité *f.* **2** restriction *f.* **3** *pl* titres *m pl.*

quality ('kwɔliti) *n* qualité *f.*

qualm (kwɑːm) *n* remords, scrupule *m.*

quandary ('kwɔndəri) *n* embarras *m.* **be in a quandary** se trouver dans une impasse.

quantify ('kwɔntifai) *vt* quantifier.

quantity ('kwɔntiti) *n* quantité *f.*

quarantine ('kwɔrəntiːn) *n* quarantaine *f.* *vt* mettre en quarantaine.

quarrel ('kwɔrəl) *vi* se disputer. *n* querelle, dispute *f.* **quarrelsome** *adj* querelleur, -euse.

quarry[1] ('kwɔri) *n* *min* carrière *f.* *vt* extraire.

quarry[2] ('kwɔri) *n* proie *f.* gibier *m.*

quart (kwɔːt) *n* quart de gallon *m.*

quarter ('kwɔːtə) *n* **1** quart *m.* **2** quartier *m.* **3** trimestre *m.* **quarter past four** quatre heures et quart. **quarter to four** quatre heures moins le quart. ~*vt* **1** diviser en quatre. **2** *mil* caserner. **quarterdeck** *n* gaillard d'arrière *m.* **quartermaster** *n* maître de timonerie *m.* **quarterly** *adj* trimestriel, -elle.

quartet (kwɔː'tet) *n* quatuor *m.*

quartz (kwɔːts) *n* quartz *m.*

quash[1] (kwɔʃ) *vt* étouffer.

quash[2] (kwɔʃ) *vt* *law* annuler.

quaver ('kweivə) *n* **1** *mus* croche *f.* **2** tremblement *m.* *vi* trembloter.

quay (kiː) *n* quai *m.*

queasy ('kwiːzi) *adj* délicat, barbouillé.

queen (kwiːn) *n* **1** reine *f.* **2** *game* dame *f.* **queen mother** *n* reine-mère *f.*

queer (kwiə) *adj* **1** bizarre, singulier, -ière. **2** suspect. **3** *sl* homosexuel, -elle. *n* *sl* homosexuel *m.*

quell (kwel) *vt* **1** étouffer. **2** vaincre. **3** calmer.

quench (kwentʃ) *vt* apaiser, éteindre.

query ('kwiəri) *n* **1** question *f.* **2** point d'interrogation *m.* *vt* mettre en question. **query whether** s'informer si.

quest (kwest) *n* quête, recherche *f.*

question ('kwestʃən) *n* question *f.* *vt* questionner. **question mark** *n* point d'interrogation *m.* **questionable** *adj* discutable. **questionnaire** *n* questionnaire *m.*

queue (kjuː) *n* queue *f.* *vi* faire la queue.

quibble ('kwibəl) *n* chicane. *vi* chicaner.

quick (kwik) *adj* **1** vite, rapide. **2** vif, vive. *n* vif *m.* **quicksand** *n* sable mouvant *m.* **quicksilver** *n* mercure, vif-argent *m.* **quickstep** *n* pas redoublé *m.* **quick-tempered** *adj* emporté, prompt à la colère. **quick-witted** *adj* d'un esprit vif. **quicken** *vt* **1** stimuler. **2** accélerer. *vi* s'animer. **quickly** *adv* vite, rapidement.

quid (kwid) *n* *invar* *inf* livre sterling *f.*

quiet[1] ('kwaiət) *n* tranquillité *f.* repos *m.*

quiet[2] ('kwaiət) *adj* **1** tranquille. **2** (of behaviour, etc.) discret, -ète. **quieten** *vt* **1** apaiser, calmer. **2** faire taire. **quieten down** se calmer. **quietly** *adv* silencieusement, doucement. **quietness** *n* tranquillité *f.*

quill (kwil) *n* tuyau, -aux *m.* plume *f.*

quilt (kwilt) *n* couverture piquée *f.* *vt* piquer, ouater. **quilting** *n* piquage *m.*

quince (kwins) *n* coing *m.*

quinine (kwi'niːn) *n* quinine *f.*

quintessence (kwin'tesəns) *n* quintessence *f.*

quintet (kwin'tet) *n* quintette *m.*

quirk (kwɔːk) *n* faux-fuyant *m.*

quit* (kwit) *vt* **1** quitter. **2** cesser. *vi* **1** démissionner. **2** s'en aller. **quits** *adj* quitte.

quite (kwait) *adv* **1** tout à fait, bien. **2** assez.

quiver[1] ('kwivə) *vi* trembler, tressaillir. *n* tremblement, frisson *m.*

quiver[2] ('kwivə) *n* (for arrows) carquois *m.*

quiz (kwiz) *n,* *pl* **quizzes** devinette *f.* *vt* interroger, poser des colles à.

quizzical ('kwizikəl) *adj* railleur, -euse.

quoit (kɔit) *n* palet *m.*

quota ('kwoutə) *n* quote-part, quotité *f.*

quote (kwout) *vt* **1** citer. **2** *comm* établir. *n*

259

citation f. **quotation** n citation f. **quotation marks** n pl guillemets m pl.

R

rabbi ('ræbai) n rabbin m.

rabbit ('ræbɪt) n lapin m.

rabble ('ræbəl) n cohue, foule f.

rabies ('reibiːz) n rage f. **rabid** adj enragé, féroce.

race[1] (reis) n course f. vt faire courir. vi faire une course. **racecourse** n champ de courses m. **racehorse** n cheval de course m.

race[2] (reis) n (of people) race f. **race relations** n pl relations raciales f pl. **racial** adj de race. **racialism** n racisme m.

rack (ræk) n 1 râtelier m. 2 classeur m. 3 filet m. 4 roue f. **be on the rack** être au supplice. ~vt tourmenter. **rack one's brains** se creuser la tête.

racket[1] ('rækɪt) n inf 1 vacarme, tapage m. 2 combine, escroquerie f.

racket[2] ('rækɪt) n sport raquette f.

radar ('reidɑː) n radar m.

radial ('reidiəl) adj radial, -aux.

radiant ('reidiənt) adj rayonnant, radieux, -euse. **radiance** n rayonnement m. splendeur f.

radiate ('reidieit) vt,vi émettre. vi rayonner. **radiation** n irradiation f. **radiator** n radiateur m.

radical ('rædikəl) adj,n radical, -aux.

radio ('reidiou) n radio f. vt envoyer par radio. **radioactivity** (reidiouæk'tiviti) n radio-activité f. **radioactive** adj radio-actif, -ive.

radish ('rædiʃ) n radis m.

radium ('reidiəm) n radium m.

radius ('reidiəs) n pl -dii or -diuses rayon m.

raffia ('ræfiə) n raphia m.

raffle ('ræfəl) n loterie f. vt mettre en loterie.

raft (rɑːft) n radeau, -aux m.

rafter ('rɑːftə) n chevron m.

rag[1] (ræg) n 1 chiffon, lambeau, -aux m. 2 pl haillons m pl. **ragged** adj en lambeaux, en loques.

rag[2] (ræg) vt inf chahuter, brimer.

rage (reidʒ) n 1 rage, fureur f. 2 manie f. **be all the rage** être du dernier cri. ~vi rager, être furieux.

raid (reid) n rafle f. vt faire une rafle, marauder.

rail (reil) n 1 barre, rampe f. barreau, -aux m. 2 (railway) rail m. **railing** n grille f. garde-fou

m. **railway** n chemin de fer m. **railway station** n gare f.

rain (rein) n pluie f. vt,vi pleuvoir. **rainbow** n arc-en-ciel m. **raindrop** n goutte de pluie f. **rainfall** n chute de pluie, précipitation f.

raise (reiz) vt 1 dresser. 2 lever. 3 hausser. 4 soulever.

raisin ('reizən) n raisin sec m.

rajah ('rɑːdʒə) n raja m.

rake (reik) n râteau, -aux m. vt ratisser, râteler.

rally ('ræli) n 1 ralliement m. 2 mot rallye m. vt rallier. vi se rallier, se reprendre.

ram (ræm) n bélier m. vt pilonner, battre. éperonner.

ramble ('ræmbəl) vi 1 flâner, errer. 2 parler sans suite. n 1 promenade f. 2 randonnée f.

ramp (ræmp) n rampe f.

rampage ('ræmpeidʒ) n **be on the rampage** en avoir après tout le monde.

rampant ('ræmpənt) adj rampant, forcené.. **be rampant** sévir.

rampart ('ræmpɑːt) n rempart m.

ramshackle ('ræmʃækəl) adj délabré.

ran (ræn) v see **run**.

ranch (rɑːntʃ) n ranch m. ferme d'élevage f.

rancid ('rænsid) adj rance. **turn rancid** rancir.

rancour ('ræŋkə) n rancune f.

random ('rændəm) adj fait au hasard. **at random** au hasard, à tort et à travers.

rang (ræŋ) v see **ring**[2].

range (reindʒ) n 1 gamme f. 2 étendue f. 3 distance f. 4 geog chaîne f. 5 champ de tir m. 6 cul fourneau, -aux m. vt ranger. vi 1 parcourir. 2 s'étendre.

rank[1] (ræŋk) n rang m. vt compter. vi se classer, se ranger. **rank and file** n hommes de troupe m pl.

rank[2] (ræŋk) adj 1 (trop) luxuriant. 2 rance, fétide.

rankle ('ræŋkəl) vi s'envenimer, s'irriter.

ransack ('rænsæk) vt 1 fouiller. 2 saccager.

ransom ('rænsəm) n rançon f. vt racheter, rançonner.

rap (ræp) vt,vi frapper. n petit coup sec m.

rape (reip) n viol m. vt violer.

rapid ('ræpid) adj,n rapide m. **rapidity** n rapidité f.

rapier ('reipiə) n rapière f.

rapture ('ræptʃə) n extase m.

rare[1] (rɛə) adj rare, peu commun. **rareness** n rareté f.

rare[2] (rɛə) adj cul saignant.

rascal ('rɑːskəl) n polisson m.

rash[1] (ræʃ) *adj* téméraire. **rashness** *n* témérité f.
rash[2] (ræʃ) *n med* éruption f.
rasher ('ræʃə) *n* tranche f.
raspberry ('rɑːzbrɪ) *n* framboise f. **raspberry cane** *n* framboisier m.
rat (ræt) *n* rat m.
rate (reit) *n* 1 taux f. 2 cours m. 3 proportion f. 4 vitesse f. 5 *pl* impôts locaux m *pl.* **at any rate** en tout cas. ~*vt* évaluer, classer. **ratepayer** *n* contribuable m.
rather ('rɑːðə) *adv* 1 plutôt. 2 un peu, assez.
ratio ('reiʃiou) *n* rapport m. proportion f.
ration ('ræʃən) *n* ration f. *vt* rationner. **rationing** *n* rationnement m.
rational ('ræʃənəl) *adj* raisonnable, raisonné. **rationalize** *vt* rationaliser.
rattle ('rætl) *vi* cliqueter, faire du bruit. *vt* agiter, faire cliqueter. *n* 1 fracas, cliquetis m. 2 (toy) hochet m.
raucous ('rɔːkəs) *adj* rauque.
ravage ('rævidʒ) *vt* ravager, dévaster.
rave (reiv) *vi* être en délire. **rave about** s'extasier sur. **raving** *adj* furieux, -euse. *n* délire m.
raven ('reivən) *n* corbeau, -aux m.
ravenous ('rævənəs) *adj* vorace.
ravine (rə'viːn) *n* ravin m. ravine f.
ravish ('ræviʃ) *vt* ravir, enlever.
raw (rɔː) *adj* 1 cru, brut. 2 sans expérience. 3 *med* à vif.
ray (rei) *n* rayon m. lueur f.
rayon ('reiɔn) *n* rayonne f.
razor ('reizə) *n* rasoir m. **razor blade** *n* lame de rasoir f.
reach (riːtʃ) *vt* 1 arriver à. 2 atteindre. 3 tendre. *vi* s'élever. **reach out** s'étendre. ~*n* 1 portée f. 2 *sport* allonge f.
react (ri'ækt) *vi* réagir. **reaction** *n* réaction f. **reactionary** *adj,n* réactionnaire.
read[2] (riːd) *vt* 1 lire. 2 *educ* étudier. **reading** *n* lecture f.
readjust (riːə'dʒʌst) *vt* rajuster. **readjustment** *n* rajustement m. rectification f.
ready ('redi) *adj* 1 prêt. 2 prompt. **get ready** se préparer. **ready-made** *adj* tout fait. **readily** *adv* volontiers.
real (riəl) *adj* 1 réel, -elle. 2 authentique. **realism** *n* réalisme m. **realist** *n* réaliste m,f. **realistic** *adj* réaliste. **reality** *n* réalité f. **really** *adv* vraiment.
realize ('riəlaiz) *vi* se rendre compte de. *vt* réaliser.
realm (relm) *n* royaume m.

reap (riːp) *vt* moissonner, recueillir.
reappear (riːə'piə) *vi* reparaître. **reappearance** *n* réapparition f.
rear[1] (riə) *adj* d'arrière, postérieur. *n* arrière, derrière m. **rear admiral** *n* contre-amiral m. **rearguard** *n* arrière-garde f.
rear[2] (riə) *vt* élever, cultiver. *vi* se cabrer.
rearrange (riːə'reindʒ) *vt* arranger de nouveau.
reason ('riːzən) *n* 1 raison f. 2 cause f. *vi* raisonner. **reasonable** *adj* 1 raisonnable. 2 modéré, abordable. **reasoning** *n* raisonnement m.
reassure (riːə'ʃuə) *vt* rassurer.
rebate ('riːbeit) *n* 1 *comm* rabais m. 2 ristourne f.
rebel (*adj,n* 'rebəl; *v* ri'bel) *adj,n* rebelle. *vi* se révolter. **rebellion** *n* révolte f. **rebellious** *adj* rebelle.
rebuff (ri'bʌf) *n* rebuffade f. échec m. *vt* repousser.
rebuild[*] (riː'bild) *vt* rebâtir, reconstruire.
rebuke (ri'bjuːk) *vt* réprimander. *n* réprimande f.
recall (ri'kɔːl) *vt* 1 rappeler. 2 se souvenir de. *n* 1 mémoire m. 2 rappel m.
recede (ri'siːd) *vi* 1 reculer, s'éloigner. 2 fuir.
receipt (ri'siːt) *n* 1 *comm* quittance f. 2 reçu m. *vt* acquitter.
receive (ri'siːv) *vt* recevoir. **receiver** *n* 1 destinataire m,f. 2 *law* administrateur judiciaire m. 3 (of a telephone) récepteur m.
recent ('riːsənt) *adj* récent. **recently** *adv* récemment.
receptacle (ri'septəkəl) *n* récipient m.
reception (ri'sepʃən) *n* 1 réception f. 2 accueil m. 3 soirée f. **receptionist** *n* préposée à la réception f. **receptive** *adj* réceptif, -ive.
recess (ri'ses) *n* 1 recoin, renfoncement m. 2 alcôve f. 3 *pol* vacances f *pl.*
recession (ri'seʃən) *n* 1 recul m. régression f. 2 *pol* récession f.
recipe ('resipi) *n* recette f.
recipient (ri'sipiənt) *n* bénéficiaire m,f.
reciprocate (ri'siprəkeit) *vt* 1 rendre. 2 payer de retour. *vi* rendre la pareille. **reciprocal** *adj* 1 réciproque, mutuel, -elle. 2 *math* inverse.
recite (ri'sait) *vt* réciter, réclamer. **recital** *n* 1 *mus* audition f. récital m. 2 narration f.
reckless ('rekləs) *adj* insouciant, téméraire, imprudent.
reckon ('rekən) *vt,vi* compter, calculer.
reclaim (ri'kleim) *vt* 1 récupérer. 2 défricher, assécher. 3 corriger.

recline

recline (riˈklaɪn) *vt* reposer, appuyer. *vi* être couché, se reposer.
recluse (riˈkluːs) *n* reclus *m*.
recognize (ˈrekəgnaɪz) *vt* **1** reconnaître. **2** avouer, admettre. **recognition** *n* reconnaissance *f*.
recoil (riˈkɔɪl) *vi* **1** reculer. **2** se détendre. *n* **1** recul *m*. **2** mouvement de dégoût *m*.
recollect (rekəˈlekt) *vt* se rappeler, se souvenir de. **recollection** *n* souvenir *m*. mémoire *f*.
recommence (riːkəˈmens) *vt,vi* recommencer.
recommend (rekəˈmend) *vt* recommander, conseiller. **recommendation** *n* recommandation *f*.
recompense (ˈrekəmpəns) *n* **1** récompense *f*. **2** dédommagement *m* *vt* **1** récompenser. **2** réparer. **3** dédommager.
reconcile (ˈrekənsail) *vt* **1** réconcilier. **2** concilier.
reconstruct (riːkənˈstrʌkt) *vt* reconstruire.
record (*n* ˈrekɔːd; *v* riˈkɔːd) *n* **1** registre *m*. **2** dossier *m*. **3** disque *m*. **4** *sport* record *m*. *vt* **1** enregistrer. **2** rapporter. **record-player** *n* électrophone *m*. tourne-disques *m invar*.
recount (riˈkaunt) *vt* raconter.
recover (riˈkʌvə) *vt* **1** recouvrer, retrouver. **2** rattraper. **3** récupérer. *vi* se rétablir, se remettre. **recovery** *n* **1** guérison *f*. **2** redressement *m*. **3** recouvrement *m*.
recreation (rekriˈeiʃən) *n* récréation *f*. divertissement *m*.
recruit (riˈkruːt) *vt* recruter. *n* recrue *f*. conscrit *m*.
rectangle (ˈrektæŋgəl) *n* rectangle *m*. **rectangular** *adj* rectangulaire.
rectify (ˈrektifai) *vt* rectifier, réparer.
recuperate (riˈkjuːpəreit) *vt* remettre, récupérer. *vi* se remettre.
recur (riˈkə) *vi* revenir. **recurrence** *n* **1** réapparition *f*. **2** *med* récidive *f*. **recurring** *adj* récidive.
red (red) *adj,n* rouge *m*. **turn red** rougir. **red-currant** *n* groseille rouge *f*. **red-handed** *adj* sur le fait, en flagrant délit. **red herring** *n* **1** hareng saur *m*. **2** diversion *f*.
redeem (riˈdiːm) *vt* **1** racheter. **2** rembourser. **3** dégager.
redevelop (riːdiˈveləp) *vt* redévelopper.
Red Indian *n* peau rouge *m*.
redress (riˈdres) *n* redressement *m*. réparation *f*. *vt* **1** rétablir. **2** réparer.
reduce (riˈdjuːs) *vt* **1** réduire. **2** rabaisser.

reduction *n* **1** réduction *f*. **2** baisse *f*. **3** rabais *m*.
redundant (riˈdʌndənt) *adj* **1** surabondant, superflu. **2** en surnombre.
reed (riːd) *n* roseau, -aux *m*.
reef (riːf) *n* récif, banc *m*.
reek (riːk) *vt* exhaler une mauvaise odeur, puer. *n* odeur âcre *f*.
reel[1] (riːl) *n* **1** bobine *f*. **2** moulinet *m*.
reel[2] (riːl) *vi* chanceler, tituber.
re-establish (riːiˈstæbliʃ) *vt* rétablir.
refectory (riˈfektəri) *n* réfectoire *m*.
refer (riˈfəː) *vt* **1** rapporter. **2** renvoyer. **3** s'en référer. *vi* **1** s'en rapporter. **2** se référer, faire allusion. **referee** *n* arbitre *m*. **reference** *n* **1** renvoi *m*. référence *f*. **2** rapport *m*. **3** allusion *f*. **4** recommandation *f*. **referendum** *n* référendum *m*.
refill (*v* riːˈfil; *n* ˈriːfil) *vt* remplir, regarnir. *n* recharge, cartouche *f*.
refine (riˈfain) *vt* raffiner, affiner. *vi* se raffiner. **refinement** *n* **1** affinage, raffinage *m*. **2** raffinement *m*. **refinery** *n* raffinerie *f*.
reflation (riˈfleiʃən) *n* *pol* nouvelle inflation, reprise *f*.
reflect (riˈflekt) *vt* réfléchir, refléter. *vi* méditer. **reflection** *n* **1** réflexion *f*. **2** reflet *m*. **reflector** *n* réflecteur *m*.
reflex (ˈriːfleks) *n* **1** reflet *m*. **2** réflexe *m*. **reflexive** *adj* réfléchi.
reform (riˈfɔːm) *n* réforme *f*. *vt* réformer. *vi* se réformer. **reformation** *n* réformation, réforme *f*.
refract (riˈfrækt) *vt* réfracter.
refrain[1] (riˈfrein) *vi* s'abstenir, s'empêcher.
refrain[2] (riˈfrein) *n* refrain *m*.
refresh (riˈfreʃ) *vt* rafraîchir. *vi* se rafraîchir, se restaurer. **refreshment** *n* rafraîchissement *m*.
refrigerator (riˈfridʒəreitə) *n* réfrigérateur *m*.
refuel (riːˈfjuːəl) *vi* se réapprovisionner, faire le plein d'essence.
refuge (ˈrefjuːdʒ) *n* **1** refuge, abri *m*. **2** asile *m*. **take refuge** se réfugier. **refugee** *n* réfugié *m*.
refund (*v* riˈfʌnd; *n* ˈriːfʌnd) *vt* rembourser, rendre. *n* remboursement *m*.
refuse[1] (riˈfjuːz) *vt* **1** refuser. **2** rejeter. **refusal** *n* refus *m*.
refuse[2] (ˈrefjuːs) *n* déchets *m pl*. ordures *f pl*. rebut *m*. *adj* de rebut.
refute (riˈfjuːt) *vt* réfuter.
regain (riˈgein) *vt* **1** regagner, reconquérir. **2** reprendre.

regal ('ri:gǝl) adj royal, -aux.
regard (ri'ga:d) n 1 égard m. 2 considération f. respect m. 3 pl amitiés f pl. vt 1 considérer. 2 concerner. **regarding** prep quant à. **regardless** adj 1 insouciant. 2 inattentif,-ive. **regardless of** sans regarder à.
regatta (ri'gɑ:tǝ) n régates f pl.
regent ('ri:dʒǝnt) adj,n régent m.
regime (rei'ʒi:m) n régime m.
regiment ('redʒimǝnt) n régiment m. vt 1 enrégimenter. 2 organiser. **regimental** adj régimentaire.
region ('ri:dʒǝn) n région f.
register ('redʒistǝ) n 1 registre m. 2 compteur m. vt 1 enregistrer, inscrire. 2 (a letter) recommander. **registrar** n 1 officier d'etat civil m. 2 educ secrétaire m. **registration** n enregistrement m. inscription, immatriculation f.
regress (ri'gres) vi régresser. n retour en arrière m. **regression** n retour m.
regret (ri'gret) n regret m. vt regretter.
regular ('regjulǝ) adj 1 régulier, -ière. 2 rangé. 3 réglementaire. 4 habituel, -elle. 5 véritable. **regularity** n régularité f.
regulate ('regjuleit) vt régler. **regulation** n règlement m. adj réglementaire.
rehabilitate (ri:ǝ'biliteit) vt 1 réhabiliter. 2 réadapter. **rehabilitation** n 1 réhabilitation f. 2 rééducation f.
rehearse (ri'hǝ:s) vt répéter. **rehearsal** n répétition f.
reheat (ri:'hi:t) vt réchauffer.
reign (rein) vi régner. n règne m.
reimburse (ri:im'bǝ:s) vt rembourser.
rein (rein) n rêne, guide f.
reincarnation (ri:inka:'neiʃǝn) n réincarnation f.
reindeer ('reindiǝ) n renne m.
reinforce (ri:in'fɔ:s) vt 1 renforcer. 2 consolider. **reinforcement** n 1 renforcement m. 2 pl renforts m pl.
reinstate (ri:in'steit) vt 1 réintégrer. 2 rétablir.
reinvest (ri:in'vest) vt replacer.
reissue (ri:'iʃu:) n 1 nouvelle émission f. 2 (of a book) nouvelle édition f. vt 1 émettre de nouveau. 2 donner une nouvelle édition.
reject (v ri'dʒekt; n 'ri:dʒekt) n pièce de rebut f. vt 1 rejeter, repousser. 2 refuser. **rejection** n 1 rejet m. 2 refus m.
rejoice (ri'dʒɔis) vt réjouir. vi se réjouir.
rejuvenate (ri'dʒu:vǝneit) vt rajeunir.
relapse (ri'læps) n 1 récidive f. 2 med rechute f.

vi 1 retomber, récidiver. 2 med faire une rechute.
relate (ri'leit) vt raconter. vi se rapporter, avoir rapport. **related** adj apparenté.
relation (ri'leiʃǝn) n 1 relation f. récit m. 2 rapport m. 3 parent m. **relationship** n 1 parenté f. 2 rapport m.
relative ('relǝtiv) adj relatif, -ive. n parent m. **relativity** n relativité f.
relax (ri'læks) vt 1 relâcher, détendre. 2 mitiger. vi se relâcher, se décontracter. **relaxation** n 1 relâchement m. 2 mitigation f. 3 détente f.
relay (n 'ri:lei; v ri'lei) n relais m. vt 1 relayer. 2 transmettre.
release (ri'li:s) n 1 décharge, libération f. 2 échappement, dégagement m. 3 relâche f. vt 1 acquitter, libérer. 2 dégager, émettre.
relent (ri'lent) vi se radoucir, céder.
relevant ('relǝvǝnt) adj pertinent, à propos, en rapport. **relevance** n pertinence f. rapport m.
reliable (ri'laiǝbǝl) adj 1 sûr, sérieux, -euse. 2 solide. **reliability** n sûreté, régularité f.
relic ('relik) n 1 relique f. 2 pl vestiges, restes m pl.
relief (ri'li:f) n 1 soulagement m. 2 secours m. 3 Art relief m.
relieve (ri'li:v) vt 1 soulager, alléger. 2 secourir, aider. 3 débarrasser. 4 faire ressortir.
religion (ri'lidʒǝn) n religion f. culte m. **religious** adj 1 religieux, -euse. 2 scrupuleux, -euse.
relinquish (ri'liŋkwiʃ) vt 1 abandonner, renoncer. 2 lâcher.
relish ('reliʃ) n goût m. saveur f. vt 1 relever. 2 savourer, aimer.
relive (ri:'liv) vt revivre.
reluctant (ri'lʌktǝnt) adj peu disposé. **reluctance** n répugnance f. **reluctantly** adv à contre-cœur.
rely (ri'lai) vi **rely on** compter sur, se fier à.
remain (ri'mein) vi 1 rester. 2 demeurer. **remainder** n reste, restant m. **remains** n pl restes, vestiges m pl.
remand (ri'ma:nd) vt renvoyer à une autre audience. n renvoi m.
remark (ri'ma:k) n 1 observation f. commentaire m. 2 remarque f. vt observer, remarquer. vi faire une remarque. **remarkable** adj remarquable, frappant.
remarry (ri:'mæri) vi se remarier.
remedy ('remǝdi) n remède m. vt remédier à.
remember (ri'membǝ) vt se rappeler, se sou-

venir de. **remembrance** n souvenir m. mémoire f.

remind (ri'maind) vt rappeler, faire penser. **reminder** n 1 mémento m. 2 comm rappel m.

reminiscence (remi'nisəns) n réminiscence f. souvenir m. **reminiscent** adj 1 qui se souvient. 2 qui rapelle.

remiss (ri'mis) adj 1 négligent, insouciant. 2 inexact, lâche.

remission (ri'miʃən) n pardon m. rémission f.

remit (ri'mit) vt remettre. **remittance** n remise f. envoi de fonds m.

remnant ('remnənt) n 1 reste, restant m. 2 (of material) coupon m.

remorse (ri'mɔːs) n remords m.

remote (ri'mout) adj 1 éloigné, reculé. 2 loin, lointain. 3 vague. 4 distant.

remove (ri'muːv) vt 1 enlever, écarter. 2 déplacer. 3 déménager. **removal** n 1 enlèvement m. 2 déplacement m. 3 déménagement m.

remunerate (ri'mjuːnəreit) vt rémunérer. **remuneration** n rémunération f. **remunerative** adj rémunérateur, -trice.

renaissance (ri'neisəns) n renaissance f.

rename (riː'neim) vt débaptiser.

render ('rendə) vt 1 rendre. 2 remettre. 3 cul fondre.

renew (ri'njuː) vt 1 renouveler. 2 remplacer. vi se renouveler. **renewal** n 1 renouvellement m. 2 remplacement m.

renounce (ri'nauns) vt 1 renoncer. 2 renier, dénoncer. **renunciation** n renoncement m. renonciation f.

renovate ('renəveit) vt rénover, remettre à neuf. **renovation** n rénovation f.

renown (ri'naun) n renommée f. renom m. **renowned** adj célèbre.

rent (rent) n loyer m. location f. vt louer, affermer. **rental** n loyer m. location f.

reopen (riː'oupən) vt 1 rouvrir. 2 reprendre. vi 1 se rouvrir. 2 rentrer.

reorganize (riː'ɔːgənaiz) vt réorganiser. vi se réorganiser. **reorganization** n réorganisation f.

repair (ri'pɛə) vt réparer, réfectionner. n réparation f. rétablissement m.

repartee (repɑ'tiː) n répartie, riposte f.

repatriate (ri'pætrieit) vt rapatrier. n rapatrié m. **repatriation** n rapatriement m.

repay* (ri'pei) vt 1 rendre, rembourser. 2 récompenser, s'acquitter envers. **repayment** n 1 remboursement m. 2 récompense f.

repeal (ri'piːl) vt 1 rapporter, abroger. 2 révoquer. n abrogation, révocation f.

repeat (ri'piːt) vt répéter, réitérer. vi 1 se répéter. 2 donner des renvois. n 1 répétition f. 2 mus reprise f.

repel (ri'pel) vt 1 repousser. 2 répugner à. **repellent** adj 1 répulsif, -ive. 2 repoussant.

repent (ri'pent) vi se repentir. vt se repentir de. **repentance** n repentir m.

repercussion (riːpə'kʌʃən) n 1 répercussion f. 2 résonnance f.

repertoire ('repətwɑː) n répertoire m.

repertory ('repətri) n répertoire m. **repertory theatre** n théâtre de province m.

repetition (repə'tiʃən) n répétition f.

replace (ri'pleis) vt 1 replacer, remettre. 2 remplacer.

replay (v riː'plei; n 'riːplei) v rejouer. n match rejoué m.

replenish (ri'pleniʃ) vt remplir, se réapprovisionner.

replica ('replikə) n 1 reproduction, copie f. 2 double m.

reply (ri'plai) n réponse f. vt,vi répondre.

report (re'pɔːt) n 1 rapport, compte rendu m. 2 nouvelle f. 3 educ bulletin m. 4 mil détonation f. vt 1 rapporter, rendre compte de. 2 signaler. **reporter** n journaliste m,f.

repose (ri'pouz) n repos, calme m. vi se délasser.

represent (repri'zent) vt représenter. **representation** n représentation f. **representative** adj représentatif, -ive. n représentant m.

repress (ri'pres) vt 1 réprimer. 2 étouffer. **repression** n répression f.

reprieve (ri'priːv) vt 1 grâcier. 2 donner un répit à. n 1 grâce f. 2 sursis, répit m.

reprimand ('reprimɑːnd) n réprimande f. vt réprimander.

reprint (v riː'print; n 'riːprint) vt réimprimer. n réimpression f. nouveau tirage m.

reprisal (ri'praizəl) n représaille f.

reproach (ri'proutʃ) n reproche, blâme m. vt reprocher à.

reproduce (riːprə'djuːs) vt reproduire. vi se reproduire. **reproduction** n 1 reproduction f. 2 copie, imitation f.

reptile ('reptail) n reptile m.

republic (ri'pʌblik) n république f. **republican** adj,n républicain.

repudiate (ri'pjuːdieit) vt répudier. **repudiation** n répudiation f.

repugnant (ri'pʌgnənt) adj répugnant.

repulsion (ri'pʌlʃən) n répulsion, répugnance f. **repulsive** adj repoussant, répugnant.

repute (ri'pju:t) n réputation, renommée f. vt estimer. **reputable** adj honorable, estimable. **reputation** n réputation f. renom m. **reputed** adj censé, supposé.

request (ri'kwest) n demande, requête f. vt demander, prier.

requiem ('rekwiəm) n 1 requiem m. 2 chant funèbre m.

require (ri'kwaiə) vt 1 demander, exiger. 2 avoir besoin de, falloir. **requirement** n 1 besoin m. 2 demande f.

re-read (ri:'ri:d) vt relire.

re-run (ri:'rʌn) vt 1 recourir. 2 recommencer. n répétition d'un film f.

resale ('ri:seil) n revente f.

rescue ('reskju:) n délivrance f. sauvetage m. vt sauver, delivrer, secourir.

research (ri'sə:tʃ) n recherche f. vi faire des recherches.

resell* (ri:'sel) vt revendre.

resemble (ri'zembəl) vt ressembler à. **resemblance** n ressemblance, similarité f.

resent (ri'zent) vt s'offenser de, ressentir. **resentful** adj rancunier, -ière. **resentment** n ressentiment m.

reserve (ri'zə:v) n 1 réserve f. 2 prix minimum m. 3 terrain réservé m. vt réserver. **reservation** n 1 réserve f. 2 location, place retenue f. **reserved** adj 1 réservé. 2 renfermé.

reservoir ('rezəvwɑ:) n réservoir m.

reside (ri'zaid) vi résider. **residence** n résidence, demeure f. **resident** n 1 pensionnaire m,f. habitant m. 2 résident m. adj résidant.

residue ('rezidju:) n résidu m.

resign (ri'zain) vt donner sa démission de, résigner. vi démissionner. **resignation** n 1 démission f. 2 résignation f.

resilient (ri'ziliənt) adj 1 rebondissant, élastique. 2 qui a du ressort. **resilience** n 1 élasticité f. 2 ressort m.

resin ('rezin) n résine f. vt résiner.

resist (ri'zist) vt résister à. **resistance** n résistance f.

resit (ri:'sit) vi doubler, retenter.

resolute ('rezəlu:t) adj résolu, déterminé, ferme. **resolutely** adv résolument. **resolution** n 1 résolution f. 2 fermeté f.

resolve (ri'zɔlv) vt 1 résoudre. 2 décider. vi se résoudre. n résolution f.

resonant ('rezənənt) adj résonnant, sonore.

resort (ri'zɔ:t) n 1 station f. séjour m. 2 ressource f. recours m. vi avoir recours, user.

resound (ri'zaund) vi résonner, retentir.

resource (ri'zɔ:s) n ressource f.

respect (ri'spekt) n 1 respect m. 2 rapport, égard m. 3 pl respects, hommages m pl. vt respecter. **respectable** adj 1 convenable. 2 honnête. 3 passable. **respectful** adj respectueux, -euse. **respective** adj respectif, -ive.

respite ('respit) n répit m. relâche f.

respond (ri'spɔnd) vi répondre. **response** n réponse f. **responsibility** n responsabilité f. **responsible** adj 1 responsable, chargé. 2 compétent, capable. **responsive** adj impressionnable, sensible.

rest[1] (rest) n 1 repos m. 2 support m. 3 mus pause f. vi 1 se reposer. 2 se poser, s'appuyer. vt 1 reposer. 2 appuyer. **restful** adj calme, tranquille. **restive** adj 1 rétif, -ive, quinteux, -euse. 2 inquiet, -ète.

rest[2] (rest) n 1 reste, restant m. 2 autres m,f pl. vi rester. **restive** adj rétif, -ive.

restaurant ('restərɔnt) n restaurant m.

restless ('restləs) adj agité, inquiet, ète.

restore (ri'stɔ:) vt 1 restituer. 2 restaurer, réparer. 3 rétablir. **restoration** n 1 restitution f. 2 restauration f.

restrain (ri'strein) vt 1 retenir, empêcher. 2 contenir. **restrain oneself** se contraindre. **restraint** n 1 contrainte, entrave f. 2 réserve f.

restrict (ri'strikt) vt restreindre, limiter. **restriction** n restriction f. **restrictive** adj restrictif, -ive.

result (ri'zʌlt) n 1 résultat m. 2 conséquence f. vi 1 résulter, s'ensuivre. 2 aboutir.

resume (ri'zju:m) vt reprendre. **resumption** n reprise f.

resurrect (rezə'rekt) vt ressusciter. **resurrection** n résurrection f.

retail ('ri:teil) n détail m. vt détailler, vendre au détail.

retain (ri'tein) vt 1 retenir, maintenir. 2 conserver. 3 garder.

retaliate (ri'tælieit) vi user de représailles. **retaliation** n revanche f. représailles f. pl.

retard (ri'tɑ:d) vt retarder. **retarded** adj attardé, arriéré.

reticent ('retisənt) adj réticent, taciturne.

retina ('retinə) n rétine f.

retire (ri'taiə) vi 1 se retirer. 2 prendre sa retraite. 3 reculer. vt mettre à la retraite. **retirement** n 1 retraite f. 2 retrait m.

retort [1] (ri'tɔ:t) n réplique, riposte f. vt répliquer, riposter.

retort [2] (ri'tɔ:t) n sci cornue f.

retrace (ri'treis) vt 1 reconstituer. 2 revenir sur.

retract (ri'trækt) vt 1 rétracter. 2 rentrer. vi se rétracter.

retreat (ri'tri:t) n retraite f. vi 1 se retirer, s'éloigner. 2 mil battre en retraite.

retrieve (ri'tri:v) vt 1 rapporter, retrouver. 2 relever.

retrograde ('retrəgreid) adj 1 rétrograde. 2 inverse.

retrogress (retrə'gres) vi rétrograder.

retrospect ('retrəspekt) n coup d'œil rétrospectif m.

return (ri'tə:n) vi 1 revenir, rentrer. 2 retourner. vt 1 rendre. 2 renvoyer. 3 pol élire. n 1 retour m. 2 renvoi m. 3 récompense f. 4 échange f. 5 profit m. 6 pl recettes f pl. **return ticket** n billet d'aller et retour m.

reunite (ri:ju:'nait) vt réunir. vi se réunir.

reveal (ri'vi:l) vt 1 révéler. 2 déceler. **revealing** adj révélateur, -trice. **revelation** n révélation f.

revel ('revəl) vi se réjouir, se délecter.

revenge (ri'vendʒ) vt venger. n vengeance f.

revenue ('revənju:) n revenu, rapport m.

reverberate (ri'və:bəreit) vt renvoyer, répercuter. vi résonner, retentir. **reverberation** n 1 renvoi m. 2 réverbération f.

reverence ('revərəns) n révérence, vénération f.

reverse (ri'və:s) adj inverse, contraire. n 1 inverse m. 2 revers m. 3 marche arrière f. vt renverser, invertir. vi faire marche arrière.

revert (ri'və:t) vi revenir, retourner.

review (ri'vju:) n 1 revue f. 2 examen m. 3 revue périodique f. 4 critique f. vt 1 passer en revue. 2 faire la critique de.

revise (ri'vaiz) vt 1 revoir, corriger. 2 réviser. **revision** n révision f.

revive (ri'vaiv) vi ressusciter, se ranimer, reprendre. vt faire revivre, ranimer. **revival** n reprise f.

revoke (ri'vouk) vt révoquer, retirer.

revolt (ri'voult) n révolte f. vi se révolter, se soulever. vt révolter. **revolting** adj écœurant, dégoûtant. **revolution** n révolution f. **revolutionary** adj révolutionnaire.

revolve (ri'vɔlv) vt tourner. vt faire tourner. **revolver** n revolver m.

revue (ri'vju:) n revue f.

revulsion (ri'vʌlʃən) n 1 revirement m. 2 écœurement m.

266

reward (ri'wɔ:d) n récompense f. vt récompenser.

rhetoric ('retərik) n rhétorique f. **rhetorical** adj 1 de rhétorique. 2 ampoulé. **rhetorical question** n question pour la forme f.

rheumatism ('ru:mətizəm) n rhumatisme m.

Rhine (rain) n Rhin m.

rhinoceros (rai'nɔsərəs) n rhinocéros m.

Rhodesia (rou'di:ʃə) n Rhodésie f. **Rhodesian** adj,n rhodésien, -ienne.

rhododendron (roudə'dendrən) n rhododendron m.

Rhone (roun) n Rhône m.

rhubarb ('ru:ba:b) n rhubarbe f.

rhyme (raim) n rime f. vi rimer.

rhythm ('riðəm) n rythme m.

rib (rib) n côte f.

ribbon ('ribən) n ruban m.

rice (rais) n riz m. **rice pudding** riz au lait m.

rich (ritʃ) adj 1 riche. 2 fertile. 3 somptueux, -euse. **richness** n 1 richesse f. 2 somptuosité f.

rickety ('rikiti) adj branlant, chancelant.

rickshaw ('rikʃɔ:) n pousse-pousse m invar.

rid* (rid) vt débarrasser, délivrer. **get rid of** se débarrasser de. **riddance** n débarras m.

riddle [1] ('ridl) n (puzzle) énigme f.

riddle [2] ('ridl) n crible m. claie f. vt cribler, tamiser.

ride* (raid) vi 1 monter à cheval. 2 voguer. vt 1 monter. 2 diriger. n promenade, course f. **rider** n cavalier, -ière.

ridge (ridʒ) n 1 crête, cime f. 2 faîte m. 3 strie f.

ridicule ('ridikju:l) vt se moquer de. n moquerie, raillerie f. **ridiculous** adj ridicule.

rife (raif) adj abondant, répandu. **be rife** régner.

rifle [1] ('raifəl) n fusil m. carabine f.

rifle [2] ('raifəl) vt piller, vider.

rift (rift) n 1 fente, dechirure f. 2 fissure f.

rig (rig) n 1 naut gréement m. 2 équipement m. vt gréer. **rig out** accoutrer, equiper. **rigging** n gréement m. agrès m pl.

right (rait) adj 1 droit. 2 bon, bonne. 3 juste. **be right** avoir raison. ~adv droit, juste, bien. n 1 droit m. 2 droite f. **right of way** priorité f. droit de passage m. ~vt 1 redresser, remettre. 2 rectifier. **right angle** n angle droit m. **right-hand** adj de or à droite. **right handed** adj droitier, -ière. **right-wing** adj de droite.

righteous ('raitʃəs) adj droit, vertueux, -euse.

rigid ('ridʒid) adj 1 rigide, raide. 2 sévère, strict.

rigour ('rigə) n rigueur f. **rigorous** adj rigoureux, -euse.

rim (rim) n 1 bord m. 2 (of a wheel) jante f.

rind (raind) n peau, -aux, croûte, couenne f.

ring[1] (riŋ) n 1 cercle m. 2 bague f. 3 anneau, -aux m. 4 arène f. **ringleader** n meneur m. **ring-road** n boulevard périphérique m. **ringside** adj au premier rang.

ring[2] (riŋ) n 1 tintement m. 2 coup de sonnette m. vt sonner, faire sonner. vi 1 sonner. 2 retentir. **ring off** raccrocher. **ring up** téléphoner.

rink (riŋk) n patinoire f.

rinse (rins) vt rincer. n rinçage m.

riot ('raiət) n émeute, bagarre f. vi s'ameuter.

rip (rip) n déchirure, fente f. vt déchirer, fendre. vi se déchirer. **rip out** arracher.

ripe (raip) adj 1 mûr. 2 prêt, à point. **ripen** vt,vi mûrir.

ripple ('ripəl) n 1 ride, ondulation f. 2 murmure m. vi se rider, onduler.

rise* (raiz) vi 1 se lever. 2 monter, s'élever. 3 hausser. 4 se soulever. n 1 lever m. 2 montée f. 3 hausse f. 4 avancement m. **give rise to** occasionner.

risk (risk) n risque, péril m. vt risquer, hasarder. **risky** adj hasardeux, -euse.

rissole ('risoul) n croquette f.

rite (rait) n rite m.

ritual ('ritjuəl) adj,n rituel, -elle m.

rival ('raivəl) n 1 rival, -aux m. 2 comm concurrent m. adj rival, -aux. vt rivaliser avec. **rivalry** n rivalité f.

river ('rivə) n fleuve m. rivière f. **riverbed** n lit de rivière m. **riverside** n bord de l'eau m. adj situé au bord de la rivière.

rivet ('rivit) n rivet, clou m. vt 1 river. 2 capter, fixer.

road (roud) n route, voie f. chemin m. **roadblock** n barrage m. **roadside** n bord de la route m. adj situé au bord de la route.

roam (roum) vi errer, rôder. vt parcourir.

roar (rɔ:) n hurlement, rugissement m. vi hurler, rugir.

roast (roust) vt,vi rôtir. adj,n rôti m.

rob (rɔb) vt voler, dérober. **robber** n voleur, -euse. **robbery** n vol m.

robe (roub) n robe f. vt,vi revêtir.

robin ('rɔbin) n rouge-gorge m.

robot ('roubɔt) n robot m.

robust (rou'bʌst) adj robuste, vigoureux, -euse.

rock[1] (rɔk) n rocher, roc m. **rock-bottom** adj le plus bas. **rockery** n jardin de rocaille m.

rock[2] (rɔk) vt bercer, balancer, basculer. vi (se) balancer, osciller. **rocker** n bascule f. **rocking-chair** n fauteuil à bascule m. **rocking-horse** n cheval à bascule m.

rocket ('rɔkit) n fusée f.

rod (rɔd) n 1 baguette, verge f. 2 tringle f.

rode (roud) v see **ride.**

rodent ('roudnt) adj,n rongeur, -euse m.

roe (rou) n œufs de poisson m pl. laitance f.

rogue (roug) n coquin, fripon m.

role (roul) n rôle m.

roll (roul) n 1 rouleau, -aux m. 2 petit pain m. 3 roulement m. vt,vi rouler. **roll over** se retourner. **roll up** s'enrouler. **rollcall** n appel m. **roller** n 1 rouleau, -aux m. 2 cylindre m. **roller-skate** vi patiner sur roulettes. n patin à roulettes m. **rolling pin** n rouleau, -aux m.

Roman Catholic adj,n catholique.

romance (n,adj 'roumæns; v rə'mæns) n 1 idylle f. 2 romanesque m. adj roman. vi exagérer, broder.

romantic (rə'mæntik) adj 1 romantique. 2 romanesque.

romanticize (rə'mæntisaiz) vt romancer. vi donner dans le romantique.

romp (rɔmp) vi s'ébattre. n gambades f pl. **rompers** n pl barboteuse f.

roof (ru:f) n 1 toit m. 2 anat palais m.

rook (ruk) n zool corneille f. vt sl filouter, rouler.

room (ru:m) n 1 salle, pièce f. 2 place f.

roost (ru:st) n juchoir, perchoir m. vi se jucher, se percher.

root[1] (ru:t) n 1 racine f. 2 source f. vt enraciner. vi s'enraciner.

root[2] (ru:t) vi 1 fouiller avec le groin. 2 fouiller.

rope (roup) n corde f. cordage m. vt corder, lier.

rosary ('rouzəri) n rosaire m.

rose[1] (rouz) n rose f. **rose bush** n rosier m. **rosette** n 1 cocarde f. 2 arch rosace f. **rosy** adj rose, rosé, vermeil, -eille.

rose[2] (rouz) v see **rise.**

rosemary ('rouzməri) n romarin m.

rot (rɔt) n 1 pourriture, carie f. 2 démoralisation f. 3 sl bêtises f pl. vi,vt pourrir. vi se décomposer. **rotten** adj 1 pourri, carié. 2 fichu, patraque.

rota ('routə) n liste de roulement f. **rotary** adj rotatoire, rotatif, -ive. **rotate** vi tourner, pivoter. vt 1 faire tourner. 2 alterner, varier. **rotation** n 1 succession f. 2 rotation f. **in rotation** à tour de rôle.

rotor ('routə) n rotor m.

rouble ('ru:bəl) n rouble m.

rouge

rouge (ruːʒ) n rouge, fard m.
rough (rʌf) adj 1 rugueux, -euse, rude. 2 grossier, -ière. 3 tempêtueux, -euse. 4 approximatif, -ive. 5 rauque. **roughly** adv 1 brutalement. 2 à peu près. **roughness** 1 rudesse f. 2 grossièreté f.
roulette (ruːˈlet) n roulette f.
round (raund) adj rond, circulaire. n 1 rond, cercle m. 2 tour, circuit m. 3 tournée f. prep autour de. vt arrondir. **roundabout** n rond-point m. adj détourné, indirect.
rouse (rauz) vt 1 réveiller. 2 susciter.
route (ruːt) n itinéraire, chemin m. route f.
routine (ruːˈtiːn) n routine f. adj routinier, -ière.
rove (rouv) vi rôder. vt parcourir.
row[1] (rou) n rang m. ligne f.
row[2] (rou) vi naut ramer. vt naut conduire à l'aviron. n promenade en bateau f. **rowing** n canotage m.
row[3] (rau) n 1 querelle, dispute f. 2 chahut, tapage m.
rowdy (ˈraudi) adj tapageur, -euse.
royal (ˈrɔiəl) adj royal, -aux. **royal blue** n bleu roi m. **royalty** n 1 royauté f. 2 pl droits d'auteur m pl.
rub (rʌb) vt,vi frotter. vt enduire, frictionner. **rub in** faire pénétrer. **rub out** effacer. ~n 1 frottement m. 2 friction f.
rubber (ˈrʌbə) n 1 gomme f. 2 caoutchouc m. **rubber band** n élastique m.
rubbish (ˈrʌbiʃ) n 1 détritus m. déchets m pl. 2 inf camelote f. 3 inf bêtises f pl.
rubble (ˈrʌbəl) n 1 moellon m. 2 décombres m pl.
ruby (ˈruːbi) n rubis m.
rucksack (ˈrʌksæk) n sac à dos m.
rudder (ˈrʌdə) n gouvernail m.
rude (ruːd) adj 1 impoli, grossier, -ière. 2 primitif, -ive. 3 violent. 4 brut. **rudeness** n impolitesse f.
rudiment (ˈruːdimənt) n rudiment m. **rudimentary** adj rudimentaire.
rueful (ˈruːfəl) adj triste, lugubre.
ruff (rʌf) n fraise f.
ruffian (ˈrʌfiən) n bandit, polisson m.
ruffle (ˈrʌfəl) n 1 agitation f. 2 volant m. vt 1 troubler. 2 plisser.
rug (rʌg) n 1 couverture f. 2 (mat) tapis m.
rugby (ˈrʌgbi) n rugby m.
rugged (ˈrʌgid) adj 1 accidenté, rugueux, -euse. 2 bourru, rude.
ruin (ˈruːin) n ruine f. vt ruiner.
rule (ruːl) n 1 règle f. 2 autorité f. vt 1

gouverner. 2 rayer, régler. **rule out** 1 écarter. 2 biffer. **ruler** n 1 souverain m. 2 règle f. **ruling** adj dominant. n ordonnance f.
rum (rʌm) n rhum m.
Rumania (ruːˈmeiniə) n Roumanie f. **Rumanian** adj,n roumain.
rumble (ˈrʌmbəl) n grondement, roulement m. vi gronder.
rummage (ˈrʌmidʒ) vi fouiller.
rumour (ˈruːmə) n rumeur f. bruit m.
rump (rʌmp) n croupe f.
run[*] (rʌn) vi 1 courir. 2 fuir. 3 marcher, circuler. 4 couler. 5 déteindre. vt 1 tenir, diriger, gerer. 2 courir. 3 entretenir. 4 promener. **run away** s'enfuir. **run out** 1 expirer. 2 s'épuiser. ~n 1 course f. 2 tour m. promenade f. 3 suite f. 4 vogue f. 5 enclos m. **in the long run** à la longue. **runner** n coureur, -euse. **runner bean** n haricot vert m. **runner-up** n second m. **running** adj 1 courant. 2 continu. 3 de suite. n 1 course f. 2 marche f. fonctionnement m. 3 direction f. **runway** n piste d'envol f.
rung[1] (rʌŋ) v see **ring**.
rung[2] (rʌŋ) n échelon, barreau, -aux m.
rupee (ruːˈpiː) n roupie f.
rupture (ˈrʌptʃə) n rupture f. vt rompre. vi se rompre.
rural (ˈruərəl) adj rural, -aux, champêtre.
rush[1] (rʌʃ) vi 1 se dépêcher. se précipiter. 2 faire irruption. vt bousculer, dépêcher, précipiter. n hâte, course précipitée f.
rush[2] (rʌʃ) n bot jonc m. paille f.
Russia (ˈrʌʃə) n Russie f. **Russian** adj,n russe. **Russian** (language) n russe m.
rust (rʌst) n rouille f. vi se rouiller. **rusty** adj rouillé.
rustic (ˈrʌstik) adj rustique.
rustle (ˈrʌsəl) vi bruire. vt froisser. n bruissement m.
rut (rʌt) n ornière f. **get into a rut** s'encroûter.
ruthless (ˈruːθləs) adj impitoyable, sans pitié.
rye (rai) n seigle m.

S

Sabbath (ˈsæbəθ) n sabbat m.
sable (ˈseibəl) n zibeline f.
sabotage (ˈsæbətaːʒ) n sabotage m. vt saboter.
sabre (ˈseibə) n sabre m.
saccharin (ˈsækərin) n saccharine f.
sachet (ˈsæʃei) n sachet m.

sack (sæk) *n* sac *m*. **get the sack** recevoir son congé. ~ *vt inf* congédier.

sacrament ('sækrəmənt) *n* sacrement *m*.

sacred ('seikrid) *adj* sacré, saint.

sacrifice ('sækrifais) *n* sacrifice *m*. *vt* sacrifier, immoler.

sacrilege ('sækrilidʒ) *n* sacrilège *m*. **sacrilegious** *adj* sacrilège.

sad (sæd) *adj* **1** triste. **2** cruel, -elle. **3** déplorable. **sadden** *vt* attrister, affliger. *vi* s'attrister. **sadness** *n* tristesse *f*.

saddle ('sædl) *n* selle *f*. *vt* **1** seller. **2** *inf* encombrer. **saddler** *n* sellier *m*.

sadism ('seidizəm) *n* sadisme *m*. **sadist** *n* sadique *m,f*. **sadistic** *adj* sadique.

safari (sə'fɑːri) *n* safari *m*.

safe (seif) *adj* **1** en sûreté, à l'abri, sauf, sauve. **2** solide, sûr. **3** prudent. **safe and sound** sain et sauf. ~ *n* coffre-fort *m*. **safeguard** *n* sauvegarde *f*. *vt* sauvegarder, protéger. **safety** *n* sûreté, sécurité *f*. **safety belt** *n* ceinture de sécurité *f*. **safety pin** *n* épingle de sûreté *f*. **safety valve** *n* soupape de sûreté *f*.

saffron ('sæfrən) *n* safran *m*.

sag (sæg) *vi* s'affaisser, fléchir. *n* affaissement *m*.

saga ('sɑːgə) *n* saga *f*.

sage[1] (seidʒ) *adj,n* sage.

sage[2] (seidʒ) *n bot* sauge *f*.

Sagittarius (sædʒi'tɛəriəs) *n* Sagittaire *m*.

sago ('seigou) *n* sagou *m*.

said (sed) *v* see **say.**

sail (seil) *n* **1** voile *f*. **2** promenade en bateau *f*. *vi* **1** naviguer. **2** faire de la voile. **sailing** *n* navigation *f*. **sailor** *n* matelot, marin *m*.

saint (seint) *n* saint *m*.

sake (seik) *n* **for the sake of 1** pour, par égard pour. **2** à cause de. **3** pour l'amour de.

salad ('sæləd) *n* salade *f*. **salad dressing** *n* vinaigrette *f*. assaisonnement *m*.

salamander ('sæləmændə) *n* salamandre *f*.

salami (sə'lɑːmi) *n* salami *m*.

salary ('sæləri) *n* traitement, salaire *m*. appointements *m pl*.

sale (seil) *n* **1** vente *f*. **2** solde *f*. **salesman** *n* vendeur *m*. **travelling salesman** commis voyageur *m*. **salesmanship** *n* art de vendre *m*.

saliva (sə'laivə) *n* salive *f*. **salivate** *vi* saliver.

sallow ('sælou) *adj* jaunâtre, blême.

salmon ('sæmən) *n* saumon *m*.

salon ('sælɔn) *n* salon *m*.

saloon (sə'luːn) *n* salle *f*. salon *m*. **saloon car** *n* conduite intérieure *f*.

salt (sɔːlt) *n* sel *m*. *adj* salé. *vt* saler. **saltcellar** *n* salière *f*. **salty** *adj* salé.

salute (sə'luːt) *n* **1** salut *m*. salutation *f*. **2** (of guns) salve *f*. *vt* saluer.

salvage ('sælvidʒ) *n* sauvetage *m*. récupération *f*. *vt* sauver.

salvation (sæl'veiʃən) *n* salut *m*.

salve (sælv) *n* onguent *m*. pommade *f*.

same (seim) *adj,pron* même. **all the same** tout de même.

sample ('sɑːmpəl) *n* échantillon *m*. *vt* goûter, essayer.

sanatorium (sænə'tɔːriəm) *n, pl* **-oriums** *or* **-oria** sanatorium *m*.

sanction ('sæŋkʃən) *n* **1** sanction *f*. **2** consentement *m*. *vt* **1** sanctionner. **2** approuver.

sanctity ('sæŋktiti) *n* **1** sainteté *f*. **2** inviolabilité *f*.

sanctuary ('sæŋktʃuəri) *n* **1** sanctuaire *m*. **2** asile, refuge *m*.

sand (sænd) *n* sable *m*. *vt* sabler. **sandpaper** *n* papier de verre *m*. **sandpit** *n* sablière *f*. **sandy** *adj* sablonneux, -euse.

sandal ('sændl) *n* sandale *f*.

sandwich ('sænwidʒ) *n* sandwich *m*.

sane (sein) *adj* sain d'esprit, sensé. **sanity** *n* santé d'esprit, raison *f*.

sang (sæŋ) *v* see **sing.**

sanitary ('sænitri) *adj* sanitaire, hygiénique. **sanitary towel** *n* serviette hygiénique *f*.

sank (sæŋk) *v* see **sink.**

sap (sæp) *n* sève *f*.

sapphire ('sæfaiə) *n* saphir *m*.

sarcasm ('sɑːkæzəm) *n* sarcasme *m*. ironie *f*. **sarcastic** *adj* sarcastique, mordant.

sardine (sɑː'diːn) *n* sardine *f*.

Sardinia (sɑː'diniə) *n* Sardaigne *f*. **Sardinian** *adj,n* sarde.

sardonic (sɑː'dɔnik) *adj* sardonique.

sari ('sɑːri) *n* sari *m*.

sash[1] (sæʃ) *n* écharpe, ceinture *f*.

sash[2] (sæʃ) *n arch* châssis, cadre *m*. **sash-window** *n* fenêtre à guillotine *f*.

sat (sæt) *v* see **sit.**

Satan ('seitn) *n* Satan *m*.

satchel ('sætʃəl) *n* cartable *m*. sacoche *f*.

satellite ('sætəlait) *n* satellite *m*.

satin ('sætin) *n* satin *m*.

satire ('sætaiə) *n* satire *f*. **satirical** *adj* satirique.

satisfy ('sætisfai) *vt* **1** satisfaire, contenter. **2**

convaincre. **satisfaction** *n* satisfaction *f*. **satisfactory** *adj* satisfaisant.
saturate ('sætʃəreit) *vt* saturer, imprégner.
Saturday ('sætədi) *n* samedi *m*.
Saturn ('sætən) *n* Saturne *m*.
sauce (sɔ:s) *n* sauce *f*. **saucepan** *n* casserole *f*. **saucer** *n* soucoupe *f*. **saucy** *adj* impertinent, effronté.
Saudi Arabia ('saudi) *n* Arabie Séoudite *f*.
sauerkraut ('sauəkraut) *n* choucroute *f*.
sauna ('sɔ:nə) *n* sauna *m*.
saunter ('sɔ:ntə) *vi* flâner, se balader.
sausage ('sɔsidʒ) *n* saucisse *f*. **sausage meat** *n* chair à saucisse *f*.
savage ('sævidʒ) *adj* sauvage, féroce. *n* sauvage *m,f*. *vt* attaquer.
save[1] (seiv) *vt* **1** sauver. **2** économiser, épargner. **3** éviter. **4** garder. **savings** *n pl* économies *f pl*. épargne *f*.
save[2] (seiv) *prep* sauf.
saviour ('seiviə) *n* sauveur *m*.
savoury ('seivəri) *adj* savoureux -euse, appétissant. *n* entremets non sucré *m*.
saw[*1] (sɔ:) *n* scie *f*. *vt* scier. **sawdust** *n* sciure *f*.
saw[2] (sɔ:) *v* see **see**[1].
Saxon ('sæksən) *adj,n* saxon, -onne.
saxophone ('sæksəfoun) *n* saxophone *m*.
say* (sei) *vt,vi* dire. **saying** *n* proverbe, dicton *m*.
scab (skæb) *n* croûte *f*. *vi* se cicatriser, former une croûte.
scaffold ('skæfəld) *n* échafaud *m*. **scaffolding** *n* échafaudage *m*.
scald (skɔ:ld) *vt* échauder, ébouillanter. *n* échaudure *f*.
scale[1] (skeil) *n* (of a fish, etc.) écaille *f*. *vt* écailler. *vi* s'écailler.
scale[2] (skeil) *n* **1** plateau, -aux *m*. **2** *pl* balance *f*.
scale[3] (skeil). *n* échelle, graduation *f*. *vt* escalader.
scallop ('skɔləp) *n* **1** coquille Saint-Jacques *f*. **2** (in sewing) feston *m*.
scalp (skælp) *n* épicrâne, cuir chevelu *m*. *vt* scalper.
scalpel ('skælpəl) *n* scalpel *m*.
scampi ('skæmpi) *n pl* langoustines *f pl*.
scan (skæn) *vt* **1** examiner, scruter. **2** parcourir. **3** *lit* scander. *n* regard scrutateur *m*.
scandal ('skændl) *n* scandale *m*. médisance *f*. **scandalous** *adj* scandaleux, -euse.

Scandinavia (skændi'neiviə) *n* Scandinavie *f*. **Scandinavian** *adj,n* scandinave.
scant (skænt) *adj* insuffisant, sommaire.
scapegoat ('skeipgout) *n* bouc émissaire *m*.
scar (ska:) *n* cicatrice *f*. *vt* balafrer. *vi* se cicatriser.
scarce (skɛəs) *adj* rare. **scarcely** *adv* à peine, ne...guère.
scare (skɛə) *vt* effrayer. *n* panique, alarme *f*. **scarecrow** *n* épouvantail *m*.
scarf (ska:f) *n, pl* **scarfs** *or* **scarves** écharpe *f*.
scarlet ('ska:lit) *adj,n* écarlate *f*. **scarlet fever** *n* fièvre scarlatine *f*.
scathing ('skeiðiŋ) *adj* acerbe, cinglant.
scatter ('skætə) *vt* éparpiller, semer. *vi* se disperser.
scavenge ('skævindʒ) *vt* **1** nettoyer. **2** balayer.
scene (si:n) *n* scène *f*.
scenery ('si:nəri) *n* **1** paysage *m*. **2** *Th* décors *m pl*.
scent (sent) *n* **1** parfum *m*. odeur *f*. **2** odorat, flair *m*. *vt* **1** parfumer. **2** flairer.
sceptic ('skeptik) *n* sceptique *m,f*. **sceptical** *adj* sceptique. **scepticism** *adj* sceptique.
sceptre ('septə) *n* sceptre *m*.
schedule ('ʃedju:l) *n* plan *m*. *vt* ajouter.
scheme (ski:m) *n* **1** arrangement *m*. **2** projet *m*. *vi* comploter, intriguer.
schizophrenia (skitsou'fri:niə) *n* schizophrénie *f*. **schizophrenic** *adj,n* schizophrène.
scholar ('skɔlə) *n* **1** savant *m*. **2** écolier, -ière. **scholarship** *n* **1** érudition *f*. **2** bourse *f*.
scholastic (skə'læstik) *adj* **1** scolastique. **2** scolaire.
school[1] (sku:l) *n* école *f*. *vt* instruire, entraîner. **schoolboy** *n* élève, écolier *m*. **schoolgirl** *n* élève, écolière *f*. **schoolmaster** *n* instituteur *m*. **schoolmistress** *n* institutrice *f*. **schoolteacher** *n* professeur *m,f*.
school[2] (sku:l) *n* bande *f*.
schooner ('sku:nə) *n* schooner *m*. goélette *f*.
science ('saiəns) *n* science *f*. **science fiction** *n* science-fiction *f*. **scientific** *adj* scientifique. **scientist** *n* homme de science *m*.
scissors ('sizəz) *n pl* ciseaux *m pl*.
scoff[1] (skɔf) *vi* railler.
scoff[2] (skɔf) *vt inf* manger gloutonnement; bouffer.
scold (skould) *vt* gronder.
scone (skoun) *n* pain au lait *m*.
scoop (sku:p) *n* **1** pelle, écope *f*. **2** *tech* cuiller *f*. *vt* creuser, écoper.
scooter ('sku:tə) *n* scooter *m*.

scope ('skoup) *n* **1** portée *f.* **2** étendue *f.*

scorch (skɔ:tʃ) *vt* roussir, dessécher. *n* brûlure *f.*

score (skɔ:) *n* **1** *sport* marque *f.* **2** sujet *m.* **3** vingtaine *f. vt* **1** marquer, compter. **2** entailler. **scoreboard** *n* tableau, -aux *m.*

scorn (skɔ:n) *n* mépris, dédain *m. vt* mépriser.

Scorpio ('skɔ:piou) *n* Scorpion *m.*

scorpion ('skɔ:piən) *n* scorpion *m.*

Scotland ('skɔtlənd) *n* Écosse *f.* **Scot** *n* écossais *m.* **Scotch** *adj* écossais. *n* whisky *m.* **Scots** *adj,n* écossais. **Scottish** *adj* écossais.

scoundrel ('skaundrəl) *n* scélérat, gredin *m.*

scour[1] ('skauə) *vt* (clean) récurer.

scour[2] ('skauə) *vt* parcourir, battre.

scout (skaut) *n* éclaireur *m.*

scowl (skaul) *n* froncement des sourcils *m. vi* se renfrogner.

scramble ('skræmbəl) *vt* brouiller. *vi* se bousculer.

scrap (skræp) *n* **1** bout, fragment *m.* **2** *pl* restes *m pl. vt* mettre au rebut. **scrapbook** *n* album de découpures *m.* **scrap iron** *n* ferraille *f.*

scrape (skreip) *vt* **1** érafler. **2** racler. *vi* gratter. *n* **1** grincement *m.* **2** *inf* embarras *m.*

scratch (skrætʃ) *vt* **1** égratigner, griffer. **2** gratter. *vi* **1** se gratter, griffer. **2** *sport inf* se retirer. *n* **1** égratignure *f.* **2** grincement *m.*

scrawl (skrɔ:l) *vt* griffonner. *n* griffonnage *m.*

scream (skri:m) *vi* crier. *n* cri perçant *m.*

screech (skri:tʃ) *vi* pousser un cri rauque. *n* cri rauque *m.*

screen (skri:n) *n* écran *m. vt* protéger, cacher.

screw (skru:) *n* vis *f. vt* visser. *vi* tourner. **screwdriver** *n* tournevis *m.*

scribble ('skribəl) *n* griffonnage *m. vt* griffonner.

script (skript) *n* manuscrit *m.*

Scripture ('skriptʃə) *n* Ecriture sainte *f.*

scroll (skroul) *n* rouleau, -aux *m.*

scrounge (skraundʒ) *vt* *inf* chiper, écornifler.

scrub[1] (skrʌb) *vt* frotter, récurer. *n* friction *f.* nettoyage *m.* **scrubbing brush** *n* brosse dure *f.*

scrub[2] (skrʌb) *n* *bot* brousse *f.* broussailles *m pl.*

scruffy ('skrʌfi) *adj inf* peu soigné.

scrunch (skrʌntʃ) *vt* **1** croquer. **2** écraser.

scruple ('skru:pəl) *n* scrupule *m.* **scrupulous** *adj* **1** scrupuleux, -euse. **2** méticuleux, -euse.

scrutiny ('skru:tini) *n* examen minutieux *m.* **scrutinize** *vt* scruter.

scuffle ('skʌfəl) *n* mêlée *f. vi* se bousculer.

scullery ('skʌləri) *n* arrière-cuisine *f.*

sculpt (skʌlpt) *vt* sculpter. **sculptor** *n* sculpteur *m.* **sculpture** *n* sculpture *f.*

scum (skʌm) *n* **1** écume, mousse *f.* **2** rebut *m.*

scurf (skə:f) *n* pellicule *f.*

scythe (saið) *n* faux *f. vt* faucher.

sea (si:) *n* mer *f.* **by the sea** au bord de la mer. **~adj** marin, maritime.

seabed ('si:bed) *n* fond marin *m.*

seafaring ('si:fɛəriŋ) *adj* marin, de mer.

seafront ('si:frʌnt) *n* esplanade de mer *f.*

seagull ('si:gʌl) *n* mouette *f.*

seahorse ('si:hɔ:s) *n* hippocampe *m.*

seal[1] (si:l) *n* sceau, -aux, cachet *m. vt* sceller, cacheter.

seal[2] (si:l) *n* *zool* phoque *m.* **sealskin** *n* peau de phoque *f.*

sea-level *n* niveau de la mer *m.*

sea-lion *n* otarie *f.*

seam (si:m) *n* **1** couture *f.* **2** *min* veine *f.*

seaman ('si:mən) *n* marin *m.* **seamanship** *n* matelotage *m.*

search (sə:tʃ) *vt* **1** fouiller. **2** chercher. *n* recherche *f.* **searchlight** *n* projecteur *m.*

seashore ('si:ʃɔ:) *n* **1** rivage *m.* **2** plage *f.*

seasick ('si:sik) *adj* **be seasick** avoir le mal de mer.

seaside ('si:said) *n* bord de la mer *m.* **seaside resort** *n* station balnéaire *f.*

season ('si:zən) *n* **1** saison *f.* **2** période *f. vt* assaisonner. *vi* sécher. **seasoning** *n* assaisonnement *f.* **season ticket** *n* carte d'abonnement *f.*

seat (si:t) *n* **1** siège *m.* **2** place *f. vt* (faire) asseoir. **seat-belt** *n* ceinture de sécurité *f.*

seaweed ('si:wi:d) *n* algue *f.*

secluded (si'klu:did) *adj* retiré, écarté.

second[1] ('sekənd) *adj* second, deuxième. *n* deuxième *m,f. vt* seconder, appuyer. **second-best** *adj* numéro deux. **second-class** *adj* de qualité inférieure. **second-hand** *adj* d'occasion. **second nature** *n* seconde nature *f.* **second-rate** *adj* médiocre, inférieur. **secondary** *adj* secondaire. **secondary school** *n* école secondaire *f.* lycée *m.*

second[2] ('sekənd) *n* seconde *f.*

secret ('si:krət) *n* secret *m. adj* secret, -ète, caché. **secrecy** *n* discrétion *f.* **secretive** *adj* réservé, cachottier, -ière.

secretary ('sekrətri) *n* **1** secrétaire *m,f.* **2** *pol* ministre *m.*

secrete (si'kri:t) *vt* **1** sécréter. **2** cacher.

sect (sekt) *n* secte *f.* **sectarian** *adj* sectaire.

section ('sekʃən) n section f.
sector ('sektə) n secteur m.
secular ('sekjulə) adj 1 séculier, -ère, laïque. 2 séculaire.
secure (si'kjuə) adj 1 sûr, assuré. 2 en sûreté. 3 ferme, solide. vt 1 mettre en sûreté. 2 assujettir, maintenir. 3 obtenir, se procurer. **security** n sécurité, sûreté f.
sedate (si'deit) adj posé. **sedation** n sédation f. **sedative** adj,n sédatif, -ive m.
sediment ('sedimənt) n sédiment m. lie f.
seduce (si'dju:s) vt séduire. **seduction** n séduction f.
see°¹ (si:) vt 1 voir. 2 comprendre. 3 examiner. **see to** s'occuper de.
see² (si:) n rel siège m.
seed (si:d) n graine, semence f.
seedy ('si:di) adj 1 minable, râpé. 2 patraque.
seek° (si:k) vt 1 chercher, rechercher. 2 demander.
seem (si:m) vi sembler, paraître, avoir l'air. **seeming** adj apparent, soi -disant. **seemingly** adv apparemment.
seep (si:p) vi suinter, s'infiltrer.
seesaw ('si:sɔ:) n balançoire f. vi osciller.
seethe (si:ð) vi grouiller, bouillonner.
segment ('segmənt) n segment m. tranche f.
segregate ('segrigeit) vt isoler, séparer. **segregation** n ségrégation f.
seize (si:z) vt 1 saisir. 2 s'emparer de.
seldom ('seldəm) adv rarement.
select (si'lekt) vt choisir, trier. adj choisi. **selection** n sélection f. choix m. **selective** adj sélectif, -ive.
self (self) n, pl **selves** moi m. pron soi-même, se.
self-assured adj sûr de soi.
self-aware adj conscient de soi.
self-centred adj égocentrique.
self-confident adj plein d'assurance.
self-conscious adj intimidé, gêné.
self-contained adj 1 indépendant. 2 renfermé.
self-defence n légitime défense f.
self-discipline n maîtrise de soi f.
self-employed adj indépendant.
self-expression n expression personnelle f.
self-government n autonomie f.
self-indulgent adj sybarite, qui se dorlote.
self-interest n intérêt personnel, égoïsme m.
selfish ('selfiʃ) adj égoïste. **selfishness** n égoïsme m.
self-made adj arrivé par soi-même.
self-pity n pitié de soi-même f.

self-portrait n autoportrait m.
self-respect n respect de soi, amour propre m.
self-righteous adj pharisaïque.
self-sacrifice n abnégation f.
selfsame ('selfseim) adj identique.
self-satisfied adj content de soi.
self-service n libre-service m.
self-sufficient adj indépendant, suffisant.
self-will n obstination f. entêtement m.
sell° (sel) vt vendre. **sell off** solder, liquider. **sell up** vendre.
Sellotape ('seləteip) n Tdmk Scotch Tdmk m.
semantic (si'mæntik) adj sémantique. **semantics** n sémantique f.
semaphore ('seməfɔ:) n sémaphore m.
semibreve ('semibri:v) n ronde f.
semicircle ('semisə:kəl) n demi-cercle m.
semicolon (semi'koulən) n point-virgule m.
semidetached (semidi'tætʃt) adj accolé, jumeau, -elle.
semifinal (semi'fainl) n demi-finale f.
seminar ('seminɑ:) n séminaire m.
semiprecious (semi'preʃəs) adj fin.
semiquaver (semi'kweivə) n double croche f.
semivowel ('semivauəl) n semi-voyelle f.
semolina (seməli:nə) n semoule f.
senate ('senət) n sénat m. **senator** n sénateur m.
send° (send) vt envoyer. **send back** renvoyer. **send for** envoyer chercher.
Senegal (seni'gɔ:l) n Sénégal m. **Senegalese** adj,n sénégalais.
senile ('si:nail) adj sénile.
senior ('si:niə) adj,n aîné, doyen, -enne.
sensation (sen'seiʃən) n sensation f. **sensational** adj sensationnel, -elle.
sense (sens) n 1 sens m. 2 bon sens m. vt sentir, pressentir. **senseless** adj 1 déraisonnable. 2 inanimé.
sensible ('sensəbəl) adj 1 sensé. 2 sensible. 3 conscient. **sensibility** n sensibilité, émotivité f.
sensitive ('sensitiv) adj sensible, susceptible.
sensual ('senʃuəl) adj sensuel, -elle.
sensuous ('senʃuəs) adj voluptueux, -euse, susceptible. **sensual** adj sensuel, -elle. **sensuous** adj voluptueux, -euse.
sentence ('sentəns) n 1 gram phrase f. 2 jugement m. sentence f. vt condamner.
sentiment ('sentimənt) n sentiment m. opinion f. **sentimental** adj sentimental, -aux.
sentry ('sentri) n sentinelle f.
separate ('sepəreit) vt séparer, détacher. vi se

séparer, se désunir. *adj* séparé, distinct, indépendant. **separation** *n* séparation *f.*
September (sep'tembə) *n* septembre *m.*
septet (sep'tet) *n* septuor *m.*
septic ('septik) *adj* septique.
sequel ('si:kwəl) *n* **1** suite *f.* **2** conséquence *f.*
sequence ('si:kwəns) *n* **1** succession *f.* **2** séquence *f.*
sequin ('si:kwin) *n* sequin *m.*
serenade (serə'neid) *n* sérénade *f.*
serene (si'ri:n) *adj* serein. **serenity** *n* sérénité *f.*
serf (sə:f) *n* serf, serve.
sergeant ('sa:dʒənt) *n* sergent *m.* **sergeant major** *n* sergent-major, adjudant *m.*
serial ('siəriəl) *adj* de série. *n* feuilleton *m.* **serialize** *vt* publier *or* présenter en feuilleton.
series ('siəri:z) *n invar* série, suite *f.*
serious ('siəriəs) *adj* grave, sérieux, -euse. **seriousness** *n* gravité *f.*
sermon ('sə:mən) *n* sermon *m.*
serpent ('sə:pənt) *n* serpent *m.*
serrated (sə'reitid) *adj* dentelé.
serve (sə:v) *vt* **1** servir. **2** être utile à. **3** desservir. *vi* servir. **serve out** distribuer. **servant** *n* domestique *m,f.*
service ('sə:vis) *n* **1** service *m.* **2** entretien *m.* **3** *rel* office *m.* *vt* entretenir, réparer. **service station** *n* station-service *f.*
serviette (sə:vi'et) *n* serviette *f.*
servile ('sə:vail) *adj* servile.
session ('seʃən) *n* session, séance *f.*
set (set) *n* **1** ensemble, jeu, jeux *m.* **2** collection *f.* **3** groupe *f.* **4** mise en pli *f.* **5** *Th* décors *m pl. adj* **1** figé, immobile. **2** fixe. *vt* **1** mettre, poser. **2** régler. **3** composer. **4** donner. **5** poser. **6** sertir. **7** fixer. **8** dresser. *vi* **1** se coucher. **2** se coaguler, prendre. **3** *med* se ressouder. **set about** se mettre à. **set off** partir. **set out 1** arranger. **2** se mettre en route. **set up 1** établir. **2** ériger. **setback** *n* revers de fortune *m.* **setting** *n* **1** montage *m.* **2** monture *f.* cadre *m.* **3** disposition *f.* **4** coucher *m.*
settee (se'ti:) *n* canapé *m.*
settle ('setl) *vt* **1** installer. **2** conclure, résoudre. **3** régler. **4** déterminer. *vi* **1** s'installer. **2** s'arranger. **settlement** *n* **1** établissement *m.* colonie *f.* **2** règlement *m.*
seven ('sevən) *adj,n* sept *m.* **seventh** *adj* septième.
seventeen (sevən'ti:n) *adj,n* dix-sept *m.* **seventeenth** *adj* dix-septième.

seventy ('sevənti) *adj,n* soixante-dix *m.* **seventieth** *adj* soixante-dixième.
several ('sevrəl) *adj* **1** plusieurs, quelques. **2** différent.
severe (si'viə) *adj* **1** sévère, rigoureux, -euse. **2** dur. **severity** *n* sévérité, rigueur *f.*
sew (sou) *vt* coudre. **sewing machine** *n* machine à coudre *f.*
sewage ('su:idʒ) *n* eau d'égout *f.*
sewer ('su:ə) *n* égout *m.* **sewerage** *n* système d'égout *m.*
sex (seks) *n* sexe *m.* **sexual** *adj* sexuel, -elle. **sexual intercourse** *n* rapports sexuels *m pl.* **sexuality** *n* sexualité *f.* **sexy** *adj* excitant, affriolant.
sextet (seks'tet) *n* sextuor *m.*
shabby ('ʃæbi) *adj* râpé, usé, minable.
shack (ʃæk) *n* cabane *f.*
shade (ʃeid) *n* **1** ombre *f.* **2** nuance *f.* *vt* **1** ombrager. **2** nuancer.
shadow ('ʃædou) *n* ombre *f.* *vt* filer. **shadow cabinet** *n* cabinet fantôme *m.*
shaft (ʃɑ:ft) *n* **1** hampe *f.* **2** flèche *f.* trait *m.*
shaggy ('ʃægi) *adj* hirsute.
shake (ʃeik) *vt* **1** secouer, agiter. **2** hocher. *vi* trembler, chanceler. **shake hands** serrer la main. ~*n* **1** secousse *f.* **2** hochement *m.*
shall (ʃəl; *stressed* ʃæl) *v mod aux* **1** devoir. **2** vouloir.
shallot (ʃə'lɔt) *n* échalote *f.*
shallow ('ʃælou) *adj* **1** peu profond. **2** frivole.
sham (ʃæm) *adj* simulé, feint. *n* feinte *f.* *vt* feindre, simuler.
shame (ʃeim) *n* honte *f.* *vt* faire honte à. **shamefaced** *adj* penaud, timide.
shampoo (ʃæm'pu:) *n* shampooing *m.* *vt* se laver la tête.
shamrock ('ʃæmrɔk) *n* trèfle d'Irlande *m.*
shandy ('ʃændi) *n* panaché *m.*
shanty[1] ('ʃænti) *n* cabane, baraque *f.* **shanty-town** *n* bidonville *m.*
shanty[2] ('ʃænti) *n* chanson de marin *f.*
shape (ʃeip) *n* **1** forme *f.* **2** coupe, tournure *f.* *vt* modeler, former.
share (ʃɛə) *n* **1** part, portion *f.* **2** *comm* action *f.* *vt,vi* partager. **shareholder** *n* actionnaire *m,f.*
shark (ʃɑ:k) *n* requin *m.*
sharp (ʃɑ:p) *adj* **1** aigu, -uë, pointu. **2** fin. **3** aigre. **4** *sl* rusé. *n mus* dièse *m.* **sharp-sighted** *adj* à la vue perçante. **sharpen** *vt* aiguiser, affûter. *vi* s'aiguiser. **sharpness** *n* acuité *f.*

shatter ('ʃætə) vt fracasser, briser. vi se fracasser, se briser.
shave (ʃeiv) vt raser. vi se raser.
shawl (ʃɔːl) n châle m.
she (ʃiː) pron 3rd pers s elle.
sheaf (ʃiːf) n, pl **sheaves** gerbe f.
shear* (ʃiə) vt tondre. **shears** n pl cisailles f pl.
sheath (ʃiːθ) n fourreau, -aux, étui m. **sheathe** vt rengainer, recouvrir.
shed [1] (ʃed) n hangar m. remise f.
shed* [2] (ʃed) vt jeter, répandre.
sheen (ʃiːn) n lustre, chatoiement m.
sheep (ʃiːp) n invar mouton m. **sheepdog** n chien de berger m. **sheepskin** n peau de mouton f.
sheer [1] (ʃiə) adj 1 pur, véritable. 2 perpendiculaire, à pic. 3 transparent.
sheer [2] (ʃiə) vi embarder.
sheet (ʃiːt) n 1 drap m. 2 (of paper, etc.) feuille f.
sheikh (ʃeik) n cheik m.
shelf (ʃelf) n, pl **shelves** rayon m. étagère f.
shell (ʃel) n 1 coquille, carapace, écaille f. 2 mil obus m. vt 1 écosser. 2 mil bombarder. **shellfish** n coquillage m. fruits de mer m pl.
shelter ('ʃeltə) n 1 abri m. 2 refuge m. vt abriter, protéger. vi s'abriter.
shelve (ʃelv) vt 1 mettre sur un rayon. 2 mettre au rancart. 3 ajourner.
shepherd ('ʃepəd) n berger m.
sherbet ('ʃɔːbət) n sorbet m.
sheriff ('ʃerif) n sherif m.
sherry ('ʃeri) n xérès m.
shield (ʃiːld) n bouclier m. carapace f. vt protéger, couvrir.
shift (ʃift) n 1 changement de place m. 2 équipe f. poste m. vt 1 remuer. 2 changer. vi se changer, se déplacer. **shiftwork** n travail par équipes m.
shilling ('ʃiliŋ) n shilling m.
shimmer ('ʃimə) vi luire, miroiter. n lueur f. chatoiement m.
shin (ʃin) n tibia m.
shine* (ʃain) vi briller, reluire, rayonner. vt polir. n 1 éclat m. 2 brillant m.
ship (ʃip) n bateau, -aux, navire m. vt embarquer, expédier. vi s'embarquer. **shipwreck** n naufrage m. vt faire naufrager. **be shipwrecked** faire naufrage. **shipyard** n chantier naval m.
shirk (ʃɔːk) vt se dérober à, esquiver. **shirker** n carotteur, -euse.
shirt (ʃɔːt) n chemise f.

shiver ('ʃivə) vi frissonner, grelotter. n frisson m.
shock [1] (ʃɔk) n 1 choc, heurt, coup m. 2 secousse f. vt choquer, scandaliser. **shock absorber** n amortisseur m. **shocking** adj 1 choquant. 2 abominable.
shock [2] (ʃɔk) n (of hair) tignasse f.
shoddy ('ʃɔdi) adj de camelote.
shoe* (ʃuː) n soulier m. chaussure f. vt 1 chausser. 2 ferrer. **shoelace** n lacet m. **shoemaker** n cordonnier m.
shone (ʃɔn) v see **shine.**
shook (ʃuk) v see **shake.**
shoot* (ʃuːt) vi 1 s'élancer, se précipiter. 2 pousser, jaillir. 3 tirer. vt 1 précipiter, lancer. 2 fusiller. 3 abattre. n 1 bot pousse f. 2 goulotte f. 3 sport chasse f. **shooting** n 1 tir m. 2 chasse f.
shop (ʃɔp) n magasin m. boutique f. vi faire des achats. **shop assistant** n vendeur, -euse. **shop floor** n 1 atelier m. 2 ouvriers m pl. **shopkeeper** n commerçant m. **shoplifter** n voleur à l'étalage m. **shopping** n achats m pl. emplettes f pl. **shop steward** n délégué syndicale m. **shopwindow** n vitrine f.
shore [1] (ʃɔː) n rivage, littoral, -aux m.
shore [2] (ʃɔː) vt **shore up** étayer, étançonner.
shorn (ʃɔːn) v see **shear.**
short (ʃɔːt) adj 1 court, bref, brève. 2 petit. 3 insuffisant. 4 à court de. **shortage** n insuffisance, crise f. **shorten** vt raccourcir, rapetisser, abréger.
shortbread ('ʃɔːtbred) n sablé m.
shortcoming ('ʃɔːtkʌmiŋ) n défaut m. imperfection f.
short cut n raccourci m.
shorthand ('ʃɔːthænd) n sténographie f. **shorthand typist** n sténodactylographe m,f.
shortlived ('ʃɔːtlivd) adj de courte durée, éphémère.
short-sighted adj myope.
short-term adj à court terme.
short wave n onde courte f.
shot [1] (ʃɔt) n 1 coup de feu m. 2 boulet m. 3 inf coup m. 4 phot prise de vue f.
shot [2] (ʃɔt) v see **shoot.** adj 1 chatoyant. 2 moiré.
should (ʃəd; stressed ʃud) v see **shall.**
shoulder ('ʃouldə) n épaule f. vt endosser. **shoulder-blade** n omoplate f.
shout (ʃaut) vi,vt crier. n cri m.

shove (ʃʌv) n coup d'épaule m. poussée f. vt,vi pousser.

shovel ('ʃʌvəl) n pelle f. vt entasser à la pelle.

show* (ʃou) vt 1 montrer, exhiber. 2 indiquer. 3 témoigner. vi apparaître, se montrer. **show off** parader, se pavaner. ~n 1 exposition f. spectacle m. 2 étalage m. 3 apparence f. **show business** n monde du spectacle m. **showcase** n vitrine f. **showdown** n règlement de compte m. **show-jumping** n saut à cheval m. **showmanship** n art de la mise en scène m. **showroom** n salle d'exposition f.

shower ('ʃauə) n 1 averse f. 2 (bath) douche f. vt 1 verser. 2 accabler, combler. **showerproof** adj caoutchouté, imperméable.

shrank (ʃræŋk) v see **shrink.**

shred (ʃred) n brin, lambeau, -aux m. vt déchiqueter.

shrew (ʃru:) n mégère f.

shrewd (ʃru:d) adj sagace, perspicace.

shriek (ʃri:k) vi pousser des cris perçants. n cri perçant m.

shrill (ʃril) adj aigu, -uë, strident.

shrimp (ʃrimp) n crevette f.

shrine (ʃrain) n 1 châsse f. 2 tombeau, -aux m. 3 sanctuaire m.

shrink* (ʃriŋk) vi se rétrécir, se contracter. vt rétrécir, faire se contracter.

shrivel ('ʃrivəl) vt rider. vi se rider, se ratatiner.

shroud (ʃraud) n linceul m. vt ensevelir, voiler.

Shrove Tuesday (ʃrouv) n mardi gras m.

shrub (ʃrʌb) n arbuste m. **shrubbery** n bosquet m.

shrug (ʃrʌg) vt hausser. vi hausser les épaules. n haussement d'épaules m.

shrunk (ʃrʌŋk) v see **shrink.**

shudder ('ʃʌdə) vi frissonner, frémir. n frisson, frémissement m.

shuffle ('ʃʌfəl) vt 1 game battre. 2 traîner. vi traîner les pieds. n 1 traînement de pieds m. 2 game mélange m.

shun (ʃʌn) vt fuir, éviter.

shunt (ʃʌnt) vt manœuvrer, garer. n manœuvre f.

shut* (ʃʌt) vt,vi fermer. **shut down** fermer. **shut in** enfermer. **shut off** 1 couper. 2 isoler. **shut out** exclure. **shut up!** ta gueule!

shutter ('ʃʌtə) n 1 volet m. 2 phot obturateur m.

shuttlecock ('ʃʌtəlkɔk) n volant m.

shy (ʃai) adj timide, farouche.

Sicily ('sisəli) n Sicile f. **Sicilian** adj,n sicilien, -ienne.

sick (sik) adj malade. **be sick** vomir. **be sick of** en avoir marre de. **sicken** vi tomber malade. vt dégoûter. **sickening** adj navrant, écœurant. **sickness** n maladie f.

side (said) n 1 côté m. 2 flanc m. 3 versant m. 4 parti, camp m. 5 face f. 6 bord m. adj 1 de côté, latéral, -aux. 2 secondaire. **sideboard** n buffet m. **side effect** n répercussion f. **sidelight** n feu de position m. **sideline** n violon d'Ingres m. **sideshow** n spectacle forain m. **sidestep** n pas de côté m. vi faire un pas de côté. vt éviter. **sidetrack** vt détourner l'attention de. **sideways** adv de côté, latéralement. adj latéral, -aux. **siding** n voie de garage f.

sidle ('saidl) vi **sidle up to** s'approcher de biais.

siege (si:dʒ) n siège m.

siesta (si'estə) n sieste f.

sieve (siv) n crible, tamis m. vt tamiser.

sift (sift) vt 1 tamiser, cribler. 2 dégager, démêler.

sigh (sai) n soupir m. vi soupirer.

sight (sait) n 1 vue, vision f. 2 spectacle m. vt apercevoir, aviser. **sightread** vt déchiffrer à vue. **sightseeing** n visite touristique f.

sign (sain) n 1 signe, indice m. trace f. 2 enseigne f. vt signer. **signpost** n poteau indicateur m.

signal ('signl) n signal, -aux m. vi,vt signaler.

signature ('signətʃə) n signature f.

signify ('signifai) vt signifier. vi importer. **significance** n 1 signification f. 2 conséquence f. **significant** adj 1 significatif, -ive. 2 important.

silence ('sailəns) n silence m. vt faire taire, réduire au silence. **silencer** n silencieux, pot d'échappement m. **silent** adj silencieux, -euse.

silhouette (silu:'et) n silhouette f. vt silhouetter.

silk (silk) n soie f. **silkworm** n vers à soie m.

sill (sil) n 1 seuil m. 2 appui m.

silly ('sili) adj sot, sotte, stupide.

silt (silt) n vase f. v **silt up** envaser.

silver ('silvə) n argent m. adj argenté, d'argent. vt argenter.

similar ('similə) adj semblable. **similarity** n ressemblance f.

simile ('simili) n image, comparaison f.

simmer ('simə) vi mijoter, cuire à petit feu. vt faire mijoter.

275

simple ('sɪmpəl) *adj* **1** simple. **2** niais. **simplicity** *n* simplicité *f*. **simplify** *vt* simplifier.

simultaneous (sɪməl'teɪnɪəs) *adj* simultané.

sin (sɪn) *n* péché *m*. *vi* pécher.

since (sɪns) *adv,prep* depuis. *conj* **1** depuis que. **2** puisque.

sincere (sɪn'sɪə) *adj* sincère. **sincerity** *n* sincérité *f*.

sinew ('sɪnju:) *n* tendon *m*.

sing* (sɪŋ) *vt,vi* chanter. **singer** *n* chanteur, -euse.

singe (sɪndʒ) *vt* brûler légèrement, roussir. *n* légère brûlure *f*.

single ('sɪŋgəl) *adj* **1** seul, unique. **2** célibataire. **3** simple. **single-handed** *adj* seul. **single-minded** *adj* sincère, loyal, -aux.

singular ('sɪŋgjulə) *adj* singulier, -ère. **2** unique. *n* singulier *m*.

sinister ('sɪnɪstə) *adj* sinistre.

sink* (sɪŋk) *vi* **1** couler, sombrer. **2** s'enfoncer. **3** baisser. *vt* **1** faire sombrer. **2** creuser. *n* évier *m*.

sinner ('sɪnə) *n* pécheur, -eresse.

sinus ('saɪnəs) *n* **1** sinus *m*. **2** *med* fistule *f*.

sip (sɪp) *vt* boire à petites gorgées. *n* petite gorgée *f*.

siphon ('saɪfən) *n* siphon *m*. *vt* siphonner.

sir (sə:) *n* **1** monsieur *m*. **2** *cap* Sir *m*.

siren ('saɪrən) *n* sirène *f*.

sirloin ('sə:lɔɪn) *n* aloyau, -aux, faux-filet *m*.

sister ('sɪstə) *n* **1** sœur *f*. **2** *rel* religieuse *f*. **sisterhood** *n* communauté religieuse *f*. **sister-in-law** *n* belle-sœur *f*.

sit* (sɪt) *vi* **1** s'asseoir, se tenir. **2** siéger. **3** couver. *vt* asseoir. **sit down** s'asseoir. **sit up** se redresser. **sit-in** *n* occupation *f*. **sitting** *n* séance *f*. *adj* assis. **sitting room** *n* salle de séjour *f*.

site (saɪt) *n* site, emplacement *m*.

situation (sɪtju'eɪʃən) *n* **1** situation *f*. **2** emploi *m*.

six (sɪks) *adj,n* six *m*. **sixth** *adj* sixième.

sixteen (sɪks'tɪːn) *adj,n* seize *m*. **sixteenth** *adj* seizième.

sixty ('sɪksti) *adj,n* soixante *m*. **sixtieth** *adj* soixantième.

size (saɪz) *n* **1** grandeur, dimension *f*. **2** taille, pointure *f*.

sizzle ('sɪzəl) *vi* grésiller. *n* grésillement *m*.

skate[1] (skeɪt) *n* patin *m*. *vi* patiner.

skate[2] (skeɪt) *n* zool raie *f*.

skeleton ('skelətn̩) *n* squelette *m*.

sketch (sketʃ) *n* croquis *m*. esquisse *f*. *vt* esquisser.

skewer ('skjuə) *n* brochette *f*.

ski (ski:) *n* ski *m*. *vi* faire du ski. **ski-lift** *n* remonte-pente *m invar*. téléski *m*.

skid (skɪd) *vi* déraper, glisser. *n* dérapage *m*.

skill (skɪl) *n* habileté, adresse *f*. **skilful** *adj* adroit, habile. **skilled** *adj* qualifié.

skim (skɪm) *vt,vi* **1** écumer. **2** raser, effleurer. **skim through** parcourir rapidement.

skimp (skɪmp) *vt* **1** mesurer, lésiner sur. **2** bâcler. **skimpy** *adj* étriqué.

skin (skɪn) *n* **1** peau, -aux *f*. **2** (of an animal) dépouille *f*. cuir *m*. **3** écorce, pelure *f*. *vt* **1** peler. **2** écorcher. **3** *sl* plumer. **skin-diving** *n* plongée autonome *f*. **skin-tight** *adj* collant. **skinny** *adj inf* maigre.

skip (skɪp) *n* petit saut *m*. gambade *f*. *vi* **1** sauter, gambader. **2** sauter à la corde.

skipper ('skɪpə) *n* patron (de bateau) *m*.

skirmish ('skə:mɪʃ) *n* escarmouche *f*.

skirt (skə:t) *n* jupe *f*. *vt* contourner, longer.

skittle ('skɪtl̩) *n* **1** quille *f*. **2** *pl* jeu de quilles *m*.

skull (skʌl) *n* crâne *m*.

skunk (skʌŋk) *n* mouffette *f*.

sky (skaɪ) *n* ciel, cieux *m*. **sky-high** *adv* jusqu'aux nues. **skylark** *n* alouette *f*. **skyline** *n* ligne d'horizon *f*. **skyscraper** *n* gratte-ciel *m invar*.

slab (slæb) *n* **1** plaque, dalle *f*. **2** tablette *f*.

slack (slæk) *adj* **1** lâche, flasque. **2** négligent. **3** faible. *n* mou *m*. **slacken** *vt* **1** ralentir. **2** détendre. *vi* se relâcher.

slacks (slæks) *n pl* pantalon *m*.

slalom ('slɑ:ləm) *n* slalom *m*.

slam (slæm) *vt,vi* claquer.

slander ('slɑːndə) *n* calomnie *f*. *vt* **1** calomnier. **2** *law* diffamer.

slang (slæŋ) *n* argot *m*. *vt* **1** injurier. **2** engueuler.

slant (slɑ:nt) *n* **1** pente, inclinaison *f*. **2** biais *m*. *vt* incliner. *vi* s'incliner. **slanting** *adj* oblique.

slap (slæp) *n* claque, gifle *f*. *vt* claquer, gifler. **slapdash** *adj* sans soin, bâclé. *adv* sans soin. **slapstick** *n* bouffonnerie *f*.

slash (slæʃ) *vt* entailler, balafrer, taillader. *n* entaille, balafre *f*.

slat (slæt) *n* lame *f*.

slate (sleɪt) *n* ardoise *f*. *vt* ardoiser.

slaughter ('slɔːtə) *n* **1** abattage *m*. **2** carnage *m*. *vt* **1** abattre. **2** massacrer.

slave (sleɪv) *n* esclave *m,f*. **slavery** *n* esclavage *m*.

sledge (sledʒ) n traîneau, -aux m.
sledgehammer ('sledʒhæmə) n marteau de forgeron m.
sleek (sli:k) adj lisse, luisant.
sleep* (sli:p) vi dormir, coucher. n sommeil m. **go to sleep** s'endormir. **sleeper** n (railway) poutre horizontale f. **sleeping-bag** n sac de couchage m. **sleeping car** n wagon-lit m. **sleeping-pill** n somnifère m. **sleepwalk** vi être noctambule.
sleet (sli:t) n grésil m. v imp grésiller.
sleeve (sli:v) n manche f.
sleigh (slei) n traîneau, -aux m.
slender ('slendə) adj **1** svelte. **2** mince.
slept (slept) v see **sleep.**
slice (slais) n tranche f. rond m. vt découper en tranches.
slick (slik) adj **1** habile, adroit. **2** lisse.
slide* (slaid) n **1** glissade f. **2** phot diapositive f. vi, vt glisser. **slide-rule** n règle à calculer f.
slight (slait) adj **1** mince, ténu. **2** léger, -ère. vt manquer d'égards envers. n affront m.
slim (slim) adj svelte, mince. vt amincir. vi suivre un régime.
slime (slaim) n vase f. limon m.
sling* (slin) n **1** med écharpe f. **2** fronde f. vt **1** lancer, jeter. **2** suspendre.
slink* (slink) vi **slink off** partir furtivement.
slip[1] (slip) vi glisser. vt **1** échapper. **2** filer. **3** décrocher. n **1** glissade f. **2** erreur f. faux-pas m. **slippery** adj **1** glissant. **2** incertain.
slip[2] (slip) n bout m. bande f.
slipper ('slipə) n pantoufle f.
slit* (slit) n fente, fissure f. vt fendre, couper.
sloe (slou) n prunelle f.
slog (slɔg) vt inf **1** cogner violemment. **2** bûcher. n coup violent m.
slogan ('slougən) n slogan m.
slop (slɔp) vt répandre.
slope (sloup) n pente f. vi incliner, pencher.
sloppy ('slɔpi) adj inf **1** bâclé. **2** flasque. **3** mal ajusté.
slot (slɔt) vt mettre. n **1** entaille, encoche f. **2** fente f. **3** ouverture f. **slot machine** n distributeur automatique m.
slouch (slautʃ) vi pencher, se tenir mal.
slovenly ('slʌvənli) adj mal peigné or soigné.
slow (slou) adj **1** lent. **2** en retard. v **slow down** ralentir.
slug[1] (slʌg) n limace f. **sluggish** adj **1** paresseux, -euse. **2** lent. **3** lourd.
slug[2] (slʌg) vt cogner(violemment).
sluice (slu:s) n écluse f.

slum (slʌm) n taudis m.
slumber (slʌmbə) vi sommeiller, être assoupi. n assoupissement m.
slump (slʌmp) n dépression économique, baisse des cours f. vi tomber lourdement.
slung (slʌŋ) v see **sling.**
slur (slə:) n **1** affront m. flétrissure f. **2** mus liaison f. vt **1** bredouiller. **2** lier.
slush (slʌʃ) n neige à demi fondue f.
sly (slai) adj matois, rusé.
smack[1] (smæk) n léger goût m. saveur f.
smack[2] (smæk) n claquement m. claque f. vt donner une gifle à.
small (smɔ:l) adj **1** petit, menu. **2** mesquin. **3** peu de. **smallholding** n petite ferme f. **smallpox** n petite vérole f.
smart (sma:t) vi cuire, brûler. adj **1** vif, vive. **2** fin, malin. **3** élégant, chic. n cinglant m. **smarten** vt animer. **smarten up** dégourdir.
smash (smæʃ) n **1** accident m. **2** coup écrasant m. vt briser en morceaux.
smear (smiə) n tache, souillure f. vt souiller, barbouiller.
smell* (smel) n **1** odorat, flair m. **2** odeur f. parfum m. vt, vi sentir. vt flairer.
smile (smail) n sourire m. vi sourire.
smirk (smə:k) vi minauder. n sourire affecté m.
smock (smɔk) n chemise, blouse f.
smog (smɔg) n purée de pois f. brouillard épais m.
smoke (smouk) n fumée f. vi, vt fumer.
smooth (smu:ð) adj lisse, aplani, uni. vt lisser, aplanir. **smoothen** vt lisser.
smother ('smʌðə) vt étouffer, suffoquer.
smoulder ('smouldə) vi couver, brûler lentement.
smudge (smʌdʒ) vt barbouiller, maculer. n tache f.
smug (smʌg) adj suffisant, béat.
smuggle ('smʌgəl) vt passer en contrebande.
snack (snæk) n casse-croûte m invar. **snack-bar** n snack-bar m.
snag (snæg) n **1** écueil, obstacle m. **2** accroc m. vt accrocher.
snail (sneil) n escargot m.
snake (sneik) n serpent m.
snap (snæp) n **1** claquement m. **2** coup de dents m. adj immédiat, instantané. vt **1** faire claquer. **2** casser net. **3** happer. **snapshot** n instantané m.
snarl (sna:l) vi gronder, grogner. n grondement, grognement m.

snatch (snætʃ) *vt* saisir brusquement, arracher. *n* mouvement brusque pour saisir *m*.

sneak (sni:k) *n inf* cafard *m*. *v* **sneak in** se faufiler dans. **sneak off** partir furtivement.

sneer (sniə) *n* sourire de mépris *m*. *vi* ricaner.

sneeze (sni:z) *n* éternuement *m*. *vi* éternuer.

sniff (snif) *n* reniflement *m*. *vi,vt* renifler.

snipe (snaip) *n* bécassine *f*.

snivel ('snivəl) *vi* pleurnicher.

snob (snɔb) *n* snob, prétentieux *m*.

snooker ('snu:kə) *n* jeu de billard *m*.

snoop (snu:p) *vi* fureter, fouiner.

snooty ('snu:ti) *adj* prétentieux, -euse.

snooze (snu:z) *n* somme, roupillon *m*. *vi* sommeiller.

snore (snɔ:) *vi* ronfler. *n* ronflement *m*.

snort (snɔ:t) *n* renâclement, ébrouement *m*. *vi* renâcler, s'ébrouer.

snout (snaut) *n* museau, -aux, mufle *m*.

snow (snou) *n* neige *f*. *v imp* neiger. **snowball** *n* boule de neige *f*. **snowdrift** *n* congère *f*. **snowdrop** *n* perce-neige *m or f invar*. **snowflake** *n* flocon de neige *m*. **snowman** *n* bonhomme de neige *m*. **snowplough** *n* chasse-neige *m invar*. **snowstorm** *n* tempête de neige *f*.

snub (snʌb) *n* mortification, rebuffade *f*. *vt* rabrouer, faire affront à.

snuff (snʌf) *n* tabac à priser *m*.

snug (snʌg) *adj* confortable, douillet, -ette.

snuggle ('snʌgəl) *vt* serrer. *vi* se blottir.

so (sou) *adv* 1 si, tellement. 2 ainsi. 3 le. **so much** *or* **many** autant de. ~*conj* donc. **so as to** afin de. **so that** pour que. **so-and-so** *n* 1 *inf* individu *m*. 2 ceci et cela. 3 *inf* machin *m*. **Mr So-and-so** Monsieur un tel. **so-called** *adj* soi-disant. **so-so** *adj,adv* comme ci comme ça.

soak (souk) *vt,vi* tremper.

soap (soup) *n* savon *m*. **soap-powder** *n* savon en poudre *m*.

soar (sɔ:) *vi* s'élever, monter.

sob (sɔb) *n* sanglot *m*. *vi* sangloter.

sober ('soubə) *adj* 1 sobre, modéré. 2 pas ivre.

social ('souʃəl) *adj* social, -aux. **sociable** *adj* sociable. **socialism** *n* socialisme *m*. **socialist** *adj,n* socialiste.

society (sə'saiəti) *n* société *f*.

sociology (sousi'ɔlədʒi) *n* sociologie *f*. **sociological** *adj* sociologique. **sociologist** *n* sociologue *m,f*.

sock[1] (sɔk) *n* chaussette *f*.

sock[2] (sɔk) *vt inf* donner une beigne à.

socket ('sɔkit) *n* 1 emboîture *f*. 2 *anat* alvéole, jointure *f*.

soda ('soudə) *n* soude *f*. **soda-water** *n* eau de Seltz *f*. soda *m*.

sofa ('soufə) *n* canapé *m*.

soft (sɔft) *adj* 1 mou, molle. 2 doux, douce. **soften** *vt* 1 amollir. 2 assouplir. 3 adoucir. *vi* 1 s'amollir. 2 s'attendrir.

soggy ('sɔgi) *adj* détrempé, saturé.

soil[1] (sɔil) *n* sol, terrain *m*.

soil[2] (sɔil) *vt* salir, souiller.

solar ('soulə) *adj* solaire.

sold (sould) *v see* **sell**.

solder ('sɔldə) *vt* souder. *n* soudure *f*.

soldier ('souldʒə) *n* soldat *m*.

sole[1] (soul) *adj* 1 seul, unique. 2 exclusif, -ive.

sole[2] (soul) *n* 1 *anat* plante *f*. 2 semelle *f*.

sole[3] (soul) *n zool* sole *f*.

solemn ('sɔləm) *adj* solennel, -elle.

solicitor (sə'lisitə) *n* avoué *m*.

solid ('sɔlid) *adj* solide. **solidify** *vt* solidifier. *vi* se solidifier, se figer.

solitary ('sɔlitri) *adj* solitaire.

solitude ('sɔlitju:d) *n* solitude *f*.

solo ('soulou) *n* solo *m*. **soloist** *n* soliste *m,f*.

solstice ('sɔlstis) *n* solstice *m*.

soluble ('sɔljubəl) *adj* soluble.

solution (sə'lu:ʃən) *n* solution *f*.

solve (sɔlv) *vt* résoudre. **solvent** *adj* 1 solvable. 2 dissolvant. *n* dissolvant *m*.

sombre ('sɔmbə) *adj* sombre, morne.

some (sʌm) *adj* 1 quelque, quelconque. 2 de. 3 environ. *pron* 1 certains. 2 en. **somebody** *pron* quelqu'un. **somehow** *adv* d'une façon ou d'une autre. **someone** *pron* quelqu'un. **something** *pron* quelquechose. **sometime** *adv* tôt ou tard. **sometimes** *adv* quelquefois, parfois. **somewhat** *adv* quelque peu, un peu. **somewhere** *adv* quelque part. **somewhere else** ailleurs.

somersault ('sʌməsɔ:lt) *n* saut périlleux *m*. culbute *f*. *vi* faire la culbute.

son (sʌn) *n* fils *m*. **son-in-law** *n* beau-fils, gendre *m*.

sonata (sə'nɑ:tə) *n* sonate *f*.

song (sɔŋ) *n* chant *m*. chanson *f*.

sonic ('sɔnik) *adj* sonique.

sonnet ('sɔnit) *n* sonnet *m*.

soon (su:n) *adv* bientôt, tôt. **as soon as** aussitôt que, dès que.

soot (sut) *n* suie *f*.

soothe (su:ð) *vt* calmer, apaiser.

sophisticated (sə'fistikeɪtɪd) *adj* blasé, sophistiqué.

soprano (sə'prɑːnou) *n* soprano *m*.

sordid ('sɔːdid) *adj* sordide.

sore (sɔː) *adj* 1 douloureux, -euse, irrité. 2 sensible. *n* 1 plaie *f*. 2 mal *m*.

sorrow ('sɔrou) *n* peine *f*. chagrin *m*. *vi* s'affliger.

sorry ('sɔri) *adj* 1 désolé. 2 fâché, peiné. *interj* pardon!

sort (sɔːt) *n* sorte, espèce *f*. genre *m*. *vt* assortir, trier, classifier.

sou (suː) *n* sou *m*.

souffle ('suːfleɪ) *n* soufflé *m*.

sought (sɔːt) *v* see **seek.**

soul (soul) *n* âme *f*.

sound[1] (saund) *n* son, bruit *m*. *vi* 1 sonner, retentir. 2 paraître. **soundproof** *adj* isolé, insonore.

sound[2] (saund) *adj* 1 sain, robuste. 2 solide. 3 profond.

sound[3] (saund) *vt* sonder.

soup (suːp) *n* soupe *f*. potage *m*.

sour (sauə) *adj* 1 aigre, acide. 2 revêche. *vt* aigrir. *vi* s'aigrir.

source (sɔːs) *n* source, origine *f*.

south (sauθ) *n* sud *m*. **south of France** midi *m*. ~*adj* méridional, -aux, sud *invar*. *adv* au or vers le sud. **south-east** *n* sud-est *m*. *adv* vers le sud-est. *adj* du sud-est. **southerly** *adj* du sud. **southern** *adj* du sud, méridional, -aux. **southward** *adj* du côté du sud. **southwards** *adv* vers le sud. **south-west** *n* sud-ouest *m*. *adv* vers le sud-ouest. *adj* du sud-ouest.

South Africa *n* Afrique du Sud *f*. **South African** *adj,n* sud-africain.

South America *n* Amérique du Sud *f*. **South American** *adj,n* sud-américain.

South Pole *n* pôle sud *m*.

souvenir (suːvə'nɪə) *n* souvenir *m*.

sovereign ('sɔvrɪn) *n* souverain *m*. *adj* souverain, suprême.

Soviet Union ('souvɪət) *n* Union soviétique *f*.

sow'[1] (sou) *vt* semer, ensemencer.

sow[2] (sau) *n* truie *f*.

soya bean ('sɔɪə) *n* soja *m*.

spa (spɑː) *n* station thermale *f*.

space (speis) *n* espace *m*. *vt* espacer.

spade[1] (speid) *n* bêche *f*.

spade[2] (speid) *n game* pique *m*.

Spain (spein) *n* Espagne *f*. **Spaniard** *n* espagnol *m*. **Spanish** *adj* espagnol. **Spanish** (language) *n* espagnol *m*.

span (spæn) *n* 1 empan *m*. envergure *f*. 2 portée *f*. écartement *m*. 3 durée *f*. *vt* 1 enjamber. 2 embrasser.

spaniel ('spænɪəl) *n* épagneul *m*.

spank (spæŋk) *vt* fesser. *n* fessée, claque *f*.

spanner ('spænə) *n* clef (à écrous) *f*.

spare (spɛə) *adj* 1 disponible. 2 de rechange. *vt* 1 épargner, ménager. 2 se passer de. **sparing** *adj* 1 économe, chiche. 2 modéré.

spark (spɑːk) *n* étincelle *f*. trait *m*. *vi* émettre des étincelles. **spark plug** *n* bougie d'allumage *f*.

sparkle ('spɑːkəl) *vi* étinceler, scintiller, pétiller. *n* étincellement, pétillement *m*.

sparrow ('spærou) *n* moineau, -aux *m*.

sparse (spɑːs) *adj* clairsemé, épars.

spasm ('spæzəm) *n* spasme *m*. **spasmodic** *adj* 1 spasmodique. 2 fait par à-coups. **spastic** *adj* spasmodique. *n* malade de paralysie spasmodique *m,f*.

spat (spæt) *v* see **spit.**

spatial ('speiʃəl) *adj* spatial, -aux.

spatula ('spætjulə) *n* spatule *f*.

spawn (spɔːn) *n* frai *m*. œufs (de poisson) *m pl*. *vi* frayer.

speak' (spiːk) *vi,vt* parler, dire. **speaker** *n* orateur *m*.

spear (spiə) *n* lance *f*. javelot *m*.

special ('speʃəl) *adj* spécial, -aux, particulier, -ière. **specialist** *n* spécialiste *m,f*. **speciality** *n* spécialité *f*. **specialize** *vt* particulariser. *vi* se spécialiser.

species ('spiːʃiːz) *n* espèce *f*.

specify ('spesifai) *vt* spécifier, préciser. **specific** *adj* spécifique.

specimen ('spesimən) *n* spécimen, échantillon *m*.

speck (spek) *n* 1 petite tache *f*. 2 grain *m*.

spectacle ('spektəkəl) *n* 1 spectacle *m*. 2 *pl* lunettes *f pl*. **spectacular** *adj* spectaculaire.

spectator (spek'teitə) *n* spectateur, -trice.

spectrum ('spektrəm) *n pl* **-tra** *or* **-trums** spectre *m*.

speculate ('spekjuleit) *vi* 1 spéculer. 2 méditer.

speech (spiːtʃ) *n* 1 parole *f*. 2 discours *m*. **speechless** *adj* interdit, muet, -ette.

speed (spiːd) *n* vitesse *f*. *vi* se hâter. **speedboat** *n* canot automobile *m*.

spell[1] (spel) *vt* épeler, s'écrire. **spelling** *n* orthographe *f*.

spell[2] (spel) *n* charme *m*. formule magique *f*. **spellbound** *adj* ensorcelé, charmé.

spell[3] (spel) *n* 1 période *f*. 2 tour *m*.

spend* (spend) *vt* **1** dépenser. **2** passer. **3** consacrer. **spendthrift** *adj,n* dépensier, -ière.

sperm (spə:m) *n* sperme *m*.

sphere (sfiə) *n* sphère *f*. **spherical** *adj* sphérique.

spice (spais) *n* épice *f*.

spider ('spaidə) *n* araignée *f*.

spike (spaik) *n* pointe *f*. piquant *m*. *vt* clouer.

spill* (spil) *vt* répandre, verser. *vi* se répandre.

spin* (spin) *n* rotation *f*. *vt* **1** filer. **2** faire tourner. *vi* tourner. **spin-dry** *vt* essorer.

spinach ('spinidʒ) *n* épinards *m pl*.

spine (spain) *n* colonne vertébrale *f*.

spinster ('spinstə) *n* femme non mariée *f*.

spiral ('spairəl) *n* spirale, hélice *f*. *adj* spiral, -aux.

spire (spaiə) *n* flèche *f*.

spirit ('spirit) *n* **1** esprit *m*. **2** alcool *m*. **spiritual** *adj* spirituel, -elle.

spit*[1] (spit) *vi* **1** cracher. **2** (with rain) bruiner. *n* crachat *m*. salive *f*.

spit[2] (spit) *n* broche *f*.

spite (spait) *n* rancune *f*. dépit *m*. **in spite of** malgré. **spiteful** *adj* rancunier, -ière, méchant.

splash (splæʃ) *n* éclaboussure, tache *f*. *vt* éclabousser.

splendid ('splendid) *adj* splendide. **splendour** *n* splendeur *f*.

splint (splint) *n* éclisse, attelle *f*. **splinter** *n* éclat *m*. écharde *f*. *vi* voler en éclats.

split* (split) *vt* **1** fendre. **2** diviser. *vi* se fendre. *n* **1** fente *f*. **2** division *f*.

splutter ('splʌtə) *n* bredouillement, crachement *m*. *vi* bredouiller, crachoter.

spoil* (spoil) *vt* gâter, abîmer, endommager. *vi* s'abîmer. **spoil-sport** *n* rabat-joie *m,f invar*.

spoke[1] (spouk) *n* rayon *m*.

spoke[2] (spouk) *v see* **speak.**

spoken ('spoukən) *v see* **speak.**

spokesman ('spouksmən) *n* porte-parole *m invar*.

sponge (spʌndʒ) *n* éponge *f*. *vt* éponger. **sponge on** vivre aux crochets de.

sponsor ('sponsə) *n* garant *m*. *vt* subventionner. **sponsorship** *n* parrainage *m*.

spontaneous (spon'teiniəs) *adj* spontané, automatique. **spontaneously** *adv* spontanément.

spool (spu:l) *n* bobine *f*.

spoon (spu:n) *n* cuiller, cuillère *f*. **spoonful** *n* cuillerée *f*.

sport (spo:t) *n* sport *m*. **sportive** *adj* badin. **sportsman** *n* sportif *m*.

spot (spot) *n* **1** endroit *m*. **2** tache *f*. **3** pois *m*. **4** goutte *f*. **on the spot** sur-le-champ. ~*vt* **1** tacher. **2** apercevoir. **spotless** *adj* immaculé. **spotlight** *n* projecteur *m*.

spouse (spaus) *n* époux, -ouse.

spout (spaut) *n* **1** bec *m*. **2** gouttière *f*. *vi* **1** jaillir. **2** pérorer. *vt* déclamer.

sprain (sprein) *n* entorse, foulure *f*. *vt* se fouler.

sprang (spræŋ) *v see* **spring.**

sprawl (spro:l) *vi* s'étaler, se vautrer.

spray[1] (sprei) *vt* **1** pulvériser. **2** asperger. *n* **1** atomiseur *m*. **2** jet *m*. **3** embrun *m*.

spray[2] (sprei) *n* (of flowers, etc.) brin *m*.

spread* (spred) *vt* **1** étendre. **2** répandre. **3** déployer. *vi* **1** s'étendre. **2** se répandre. *n* **1** étendue *f*. **2** diffusion *f*. **3** *inf* festin *m*.

spree (spri:) *n* fête, rigolade *f*.

sprig (sprig) *n* brindille *f*.

sprightly ('spraitli) *adj* éveillé, sémillant.

spring* (spriŋ) *n* **1** printemps *m*. **2** source *f*. **3** saut *m*. **4** ressort *m*. *vi* **1** bondir, sauter. **2** jaillir. **springboard** *n* tremplin *m*. **spring-clean** *vt* nettoyer à fond. **springtime** *n* printemps *m*.

sprinkle ('spriŋkəl) *vt* saupoudrer, arroser. *n* pincée *f*.

sprint (sprint) *n* course de vitesse *f*. sprint *m*. *vi* faire une course de vitesse.

sprout (spraut) *n* pousse *f*. germe *m*. *vi* pousser, germer, bourgeonner.

sprung (sprʌŋ) *v see* **spring.**

spun (spʌn) *v see* **spin.**

spur (spə:) *n* **1** éperon *m*. **2** stimulant *m*. **3** éperon *m*. ~*vt* éperonner. **spur on** stimuler.

spurt (spə:t) *n* **1** giclée *f*. **2** coup de collier, sursaut *m*. *vi* jaillir.

spy (spai) *n* espion, -onne. *vi* espionner. *vt* épier.

squabble ('skwobəl) *vi* se chamailler. *n* prise de bec *f*.

squad (skwod) *n* **1** *mil* peloton *m*. **2** brigade *f*.

squadron ('skwodrən) *n* **1** *mil* escadron *m*. **2** *naut* escadre *f*.

squalid ('skwolid) *adj* sale, crasseux, -euse.

squander ('skwondə) *vt* gaspiller.

square (skwɛə) *n* **1** carré *m*. **2** carreau, -aux *m*. **3** place *f*. *adj* **1** carré. **2** en ordre. **3** quitte. *vt* **1** carrer. **2** régler. **3** accorder.

squash (skwoʃ) *n* **1** écrasement *m*. cohue *f*. **2** *sport* squash *m*. *vt* écraser. *vi* s'écraser.

squat (skwot) *vi* **1** s'accroupir. **2** occuper sans titre de possession. *adj* trapu, accroupi.

squawk (skwɔːk) *vi* pousser des cris rauques. *n* cri rauque *m.*

squeak (skwiːk) *vi* **1** pousser des cris aigus, crier. **2** grincer, crisser. *n* **1** petit cri aigu *m.* **2** crissement *m.*

squeal (skwiːl) *vi* pousser des cris aigus. *n* cri aigu *m.*

squeamish ('skwiːmiʃ) *adj* **1** délicat, difficile. **2** nauséeux, -euse.

squeeze (skwiːz) *vt* **1** presser, serrer. **2** extorquer.

squid (skwid) *n* calmar *m.*

squiggle ('skwigəl) *n* tortillement *m.* fioriture *f.*

squint (skwint) *n* strabisme *m.* *vi* loucher.

squirm (skwəːm) *vi* **1** se tordre. **2** être au supplice.

squirrel ('skwɪrl) *n* écureuil *m.*

squirt (skwəːt) *vt* faire jaillir. *vi* gicler. *n* jet *m.* giclée *f.*

stab (stæb) *n* coup de couteau *m.* *vt* poignarder.

stabilize ('steibəlaiz) *vt* stabiliser.

stable[1] ('steibəl) *n* écurie *f.*

stable[2] ('steibəl) *adj* **1** stable, solide. **2** permanent. **3** constant.

stack (stæk) *n* **1** meule *f.* **2** tas *m.* **3** cheminée *f.* *vt* **1** empiler. **2** entasser.

stadium ('steidiəm) *n, pl* **-ia** *or* **-iums** stade *m.*

staff (stɑːf) *n* **1** personnel *m.* **2** bâton *m.*

stag (stæg) *n* cerf *m.*

stage (steidʒ) *n* **1** *Th* scène *f.* **2** estrade *f.* **3** phase *f.* **4** étape *f.* *vt* monter. **stage manager** *n* régisseur *m.*

stagger ('stægə) *vi* chanceler. *vt* **1** échelonner, étaler. **2** *inf* renverser, étonner. **3** faire chanceler.

stagnant ('stægnənt) *adj* **1** stagnant. **2** inactif, -ive. **stagnate** *vi* croupir.

stain (stein) *n* **1** tache *f.* **2** couleur *f.* colorant *m.* *vt* **1** souiller. **2** teindre, teinter. **stained-glass window** *n* vitrail, -aux *m.* **stainless** *adj* inoxydable.

stair (stɛə) *n* **1** marche *f.* **2** *pl* escalier *m.* **staircase** *n* escalier *m.*

stake[1] (steik) *n* **1** pieu, -eux, jalon *m.* **2** bûcher *m.* *vt* jalonner.

stake[2] (steik) *n* game enjeu, -eux *m.* mise *f.* **at stake** en jeu. ~*vt* jouer, risquer.

stale (steil) *adj* **1** rassis, vicié. **2** passé, rebattu. **3** défraîchi.

stalemate ('steilmeit) *n* **1** game pat *m.* **2** impasse *m.*

stalk[1] (stɔːk) *n* tige *f.* trognon *m.*

stalk[2] (stɔːk) *vt* traquer. *vi* marcher à grands pas.

stall[1] (stɔːl) *n* **1** stalle *f.* **2** étalage *m.* **3** *pl Th* fauteuils d'orchestre *m pl.* *vt, vi* caler.

stall[2] (stɔːl) *vt* (evade) repoussér, berner.

stallion ('stæliən) *n* étalon *m.*

stamina ('stæminə) *n* vigueur, énergie *f.*

stammer ('stæmə) *vi, vt* bégayer, balbutier. *n* bégaiement *m.*

stamp (stæmp) *n* **1** timbre *m.* **2** poinçon *m.* **3** trépignement *m.* *vt* **1** timbrer. **2** poinçonner. **3** frapper. **4** trépigner.

stampede (stæm'piːd) *n* débandade *f.* *vi* fuir en désordre.

stand* (stænd) *vi* **1** être *or* se tenir debout. **2** se trouver. **3** se maintenir. **4** représenter, signifier. **5** durer. *vt* **1** mettre. **2** supporter. *n* **1** situation *f.* **2** support *m.* **3** étalage *m.* **4** stand *m.* **stand-by** *n* **1** appui *m.* **2** ressource *f.* **standing** *n* **1** situation *f.* **2** rang *m.* **3** durée *f.* *adj* **1** debout. **2** stagnant. **3** sur pied. **4** fixe. **standstill** *n* arrêt *m.*

standard ('stændəd) *n* **1** norme *f.* **2** bannière *f.* **3** degré *m.* étalon *m.* *adj* **1** type. **2** classique. **3** courant.

stank (stæŋk) *v see* **stink.**

stanza ('stænzə) *n* stance, strophe *f.*

staple[1] ('steipəl) *n* **1** crampon *m.* **2** agrafe *f.* *vt* **1** cramponner. **2** agrafer.

staple[2] ('steipəl) *adj* principal, -aux.

star (stɑː) *n* **1** étoile *f.* astre *m.* **2** (films, etc.) star, vedette *f.* *vi* être en vedette. **starfish** *n* étoile de mer *f.*

starboard ('stɑːbəd) *n* tribord *m.*

starch (stɑːtʃ) *n* amidon *m.* *vt* empeser.

stare (stɛə) *vi* regarder fixement. *n* regard fixe *m.*

stark (stɑːk) *adj* **1** raide. **2** absolu. *adv* entièrement, tout.

starling ('stɑːliŋ) *n* étourneau, -aux, sansonnet *m.*

start (stɑːt) *n* **1** commencement *m.* **2** départ *m.* **3** sursaut *m.* *vi* **1** commencer. **2** sursauter. *vt* **1** entamer, se mettre à. **2** mettre en marche. **3** lancer. **starter** *n* mot démarreur *m.*

startle ('stɑːtl) *vt* faire sursauter, effrayer.

starve (stɑːv) *vi* mourir de faim. *vt* **1** faire mourir de faim, affamer. **2** priver.

state (steit) *n* **1** état *m.* **2** position *f.* **3** pompe *f.* *adj* **1** d'état. **2** d'apparat. *vt* **1** déclarer. **2** fixer. **stately** *adj* majestueux, -euse. **statement** *n* **1** déclaration *f.* compte rendu *m.* **2**

law déposition *f.* **3** *comm* relevé *m.* **states-man** *n* homme d'Etat *m.*

static ('stætik) *adj,n* statique *f.*

station ('steiʃən) **1** (railway) gare *f.* **2** poste *m.* **3** position *f.* rang *m.* **station-master** *n* chef de gare *m.*

stationary ('steiʃənri) *adj* stationnaire.

stationer ('steiʃənə) *n* libraire *m.* **stationer's shop** *n* papeterie *f.* **stationery** *n* papeterie *f.*

statistics (stə'tistiks) *n* statistique *f.*

statue ('stætju:) *n* statue *f.*

stature ('stætʃə) *n* stature, taille *f.*

status ('steitəs) *n* position *f.* rang *m.*

statute ('stætju:t) *n* loi *f.* statut *m.* **statutory** *adj* réglementaire.

stay[1] (stei) *n* séjour *m.* *vi* **1** rester, se tenir. **2** séjourner. **3** attendre.

stay[2] (stei) *n* support *m.* *vt* étayer.

steadfast ('stedfɑ:st) *adj* **1** constant. **2** stable, ferme.

steady ('stedi) *adj* **1** ferme. **2** soutenu, régulier, -ière. **3** rangé. *vt* raffermir. *vi* reprendre son aplomb.

steak (steik) *n* bifteck *m.* entrecôte *f.*

steal* (sti:l) *vt* **1** voler. **2** dérober. **stealing** *n* vol *m.*

steam (sti:m) *n* vapeur *f.* *vt* cuire à la vapeur. *vi* fumer. **steam-roller** *n* rouleau compresseur *m.*

steel (sti:l) *n* acier *m.* *adj* d'acier.

steep[1] (sti:p) *adj* escarpé, raide.

steep[2] (sti:p) *vt,vi* tremper.

steeple ('sti:pəl) *n* clocher *m.* **steeplechase** *n* steeple-chase *m.*

steer (stiə) *vt* diriger, conduire. **steering-wheel** *n* volant *m.*

stem[1] (stem) *n* tige *f.* *v* **stem from** provenir de.

stem[2] (stem) *vt* **1** arrêter, endiguer. **2** refouler.

stencil ('stensəl) *n* **1** pochoir *m.* **2** stencil *m.*

step (step) *n* **1** pas *m.* **2** démarche *f.* **3** marche *f.* échelon *m.* *vi* faire un pas, aller. **step-ladder** *n* marchepied *m.*

stepbrother ('stepbrʌðə) *n* demi-frère *m.*

stepdaughter ('stepdɔ:tə) *n* belle-fille *f.*

stepfather ('stepfɑ:ðə) *n* beau-père *m.*

stepmother ('stepmʌðə) *n* belle-mère *f.*

stepsister ('stepsistə) *n* demi-soeur *f.*

stepson ('stepsʌn) *n* beau-fils *m.*

stereo ('steriou) *adj,n* stéréo *m.*

stereophonic (steriə'fɔnik) *adj* stéréophonique.

stereotype ('steriətaip) *n* cliché *m.* *vt* stéréotyper.

sterile ('sterail) *adj* stérile. **sterilize** *vt* stériliser.

sterling ('stə:liŋ) *n* sterling *m.* *adj* **1** de bon aloi. **2** sterling.

stern[1] (stə:n) *adj* sévère, rigide, austère.

stern[2] (stə:n) *n* *naut* arrière *m.* poupe *f.*

stethoscope ('steθəskoup) *n* stéthoscope *m.*

stew (stju:) *n* ragoût *m.* *vt* faire cuire à la casserole. *vi* mijoter.

steward ('stju:əd) *n* **1** intendant *m.* **2** économe *m.* **3** commissaire *m.* **stewardess** *n* femme de chambre, stewardess *f.*

stick[1] (stik) *n* **1** bâton *m.* **2** canne *f.* **3** morceau de bois *m.*

stick*[2] (stik) *vt* **1** coller. **2** enfoncer. **3** *inf* mettre. **4** *sl* supporter. *vi* **1** adhérer. **2** s'embourber. **3** se coincer. **stick at** s'arrêter devant. **stick out** saillir. **stick to 1** s'en tenir à. **2** rester fidèle à.

sticky ('stiki) *adj* **1** collant. **2** *inf* difficile.

stiff (stif) *adj* **1** raide, dur. **2** pénible, difficile. **stiffen** *vt* raidir. *vi* se saidir, se guinder. **stiffly** *adv* avec raideur.

stifle ('staifəl) *vt* **1** étouffer. **2** réprimer. *vi* suffoquer.

stigma ('stigmə) *n, pl* **-mata** *or* **-as** stigmate *m.*

stile (stail) *n* échalier *m.*

still[1] (stil) *adj* **1** tranquille, calme. **2** immobile. *adv* toujours, encore. *conj* cependant, pourtant. **stillborn** *adj* mort-né. **still life** *n* nature morte *f.*

still[2] (stil) *n* alambic *m.*

stilt (stilt) *n* échasse *f.* **stilted** *adj* guindé, tendu.

stimulate ('stimjuleit) *vt* stimuler, activer.

stimulus ('stimjuləs) *n, pl* **-li** stimulant *m.* impulsion *f.*

sting* (stiŋ) *vt* piquer. *vi* cuire. *n* **1** piqûre *f.* dard *m.* **2** pointe *f.*

stink* (stiŋk) *vi* puer. *n* puanteur *f.*

stipulate ('stipjuleit) *vt,vi* stipuler.

stir (stə:) *n* **1** remuement *m.* **2** mouvement *m.* **3** *inf* remue-ménage *m* *invar.* *vt* **1** remuer. **2** agiter, susciter. *vi* remuer, bouger.

stirrup ('stirəp) *n* étrier *m.*

stitch (stitʃ) *n* **1** point *m.* maille *f.* **2** *med* suture *f.* *vt* **1** coudre. **2** *med* suturer.

stoat (stout) *n* hermine d'été *f.*

stock (stɔk) *n* **1** provision *f.* **2** stock *m.* **3** souche *f.* **4** *pl comm* titres *m pl.* actions *f pl.* **5** *cul* bouillon *m.* *adj* courant. *vt* **1** approvisionner. **2** stocker. **stockbreeding** *n* élevage *m.* **stockbroker** *n* agent de change *m.* **stock exchange** *n* bourse *f.* **stockpile** *n* stocks de réserve *m pl. vt,vi* stocker. **stocktaking** *n* inventaire *m.*

stocking (ˈstɔkiŋ) *n* bas *m.*

stocky (ˈstɔki) *adj* trapu.

stodge (stɔdʒ) *n inf* aliment bourratif *m.*

stoical (ˈstouik|) *adj* stoïque.

stoke (stouk) *vt* chauffer, entretenir.

stole¹ (stoul) *v see* **steal.**

stole² (stoul) *n* étole *f.*

stolen (ˈstoulən) *v see* **steal.**

stomach (ˈstʌmək) *n* 1 estomac *m.* 2 ventre *m. vt inf* supporter. **stomach-ache** *n* mal de ventre *m.*

stone (stoun) *n* 1 pierre *f.* 2 (of a fruit) noyau, -aux *m.* 3 (weight) stone *m. adj* de pierre. *vt* 1 lapider. 2 dénoyauter.

stood (stud) *v see* **stand.**

stool (stuːl) *n* tabouret *m.*

stoop (stuːp) *vi* 1 se pencher. 2 s'abaisser. 3 être voûté.

stop (stɔp) *vt* 1 arrêter. 2 boucher. 3 cesser. 4 retenir. *vi* s'arrêter. *n* arrêt *m.* **stoppage** *n* 1 suspension *f.* 2 obstruction *f.* **stopper** *n* bouchon *m.* **stopwatch** *n* chronomètre *m.*

store (stɔː) *n* 1 provision, réserve *f.* 2 magasin *m. vt* 1 approvisionner. 2 amasser. 3 emmagasiner. **storage** *n* emmagasinage *m.*

storey (ˈstɔːri) *n* étage *m.*

stork (stɔːk) *n* cigogne *f.*

storm (stɔːm) *n* orage *m.* tempête *f. vi* faire rage. *vt* donner l'assaut à. **stormy** *adj* orageux, -euse.

story (ˈstɔːri) *n* histoire *f.* conte, récit *m.*

stout (staut) *adj* 1 fort. 2 costaud, vaillant. 3 corpulent. *n* stout *m.* bière brune forte *f.*

stove (stouv) *n* poêle, fourneau, -aux *m.*

stow (stou) *vt* arrimer. **stowaway** *n* passager clandestin *m.*

straddle (ˈstræd|) *vi* se tenir *or* marcher les jambes écartées. *vt* chevaucher, s'affourcher sur, enfourcher.

straggle (ˈstrægəl) *vi* 1 s'éparpiller. 2 traîner. **straggler** *n* traînard *m.*

straight (streit) *adj* 1 droit, raide. 2 franc, -che. 3 en ordre. *adv* 1 droit. 2 juste. 3 directement. 4 tout droit. **straighten** *vt* 1 redresser. 2 mettre en ordre. *vi* se redresser. **straightforward** *adj* loyal, -aux, franc, -che.

strain¹ (strein) *vt* 1 tendre. 2 *med* se fouler. 3 filtrer. *vi* peiner, fatiguer. *n* 1 tension *f.* 2 *med* entorse *f.*

strain² (strein) *n* lignée, race *f.*

strand¹ (strænd) *vt,vi* échouer.

strand² (strænd) *n* brin *m.* fibre *f.*

strange (streindʒ) *adj* étrange, bizarre, singulier, -ière. **strangeness** *n* étrangeté *f.* **stranger** *n* inconnu *m.*

strangle (ˈstræŋgəl) *vt* étrangler.

strap (stræp) *n* 1 courroie *f.* 2 bande *f. vt* lier avec une courroie.

strategy (ˈstrætidʒi) *n* stratégie *f.* **strategic** *adj* stratégique.

straw (strɔː) *n* paille *f.* **that's the last straw!** ça, c'est le comble! ~*adj* de paille. **strawberry** *n* fraise *f.* **strawberry plant** fraisier *m.*

stray (strei) *vi* 1 s'égarer. 2 s'éloigner, errer.

streak (striːk) *n* 1 rayure *f.* 2 trait *m. vt* rayer, strier.

stream (striːm) *n* 1 ruisseau, -aux *m.* 2 flux *m.* 3 courant *m. vi* couler. **streamline** *vt* 1 profiler. 2 moderniser.

street (striːt) *n* rue *f.*

strength (streŋθ) *n* 1 force *f.* 2 nombre *m.* **strengthen** *vt* consolider, renforcer.

strenuous (ˈstrenjuəs) *adj* 1 énergique. 2 acharné. 3 fatiguant.

stress (stres) *n* 1 tension *f.* 2 force *f.* 3 accent *m. vt* insister sur, souligner.

stretch (stretʃ) *n* 1 étendue *f.* 2 section *f.* 3 extension *f. vt* tendre. *vi* 1 s'élargir. 2 s'étendre. **stretcher** *n* brancard *m.*

strict (strikt) *adj* 1 strict. 2 rigide. 3 sévère.

stride (straid) *vi* marcher à grandes enjambées. *n* enjambée *f.*

strike (straik) *n* 1 grève *f.* 2 coup *m. vt* 1 frapper. 2 frotter. 3 heurter. *vi* 1 sonner. 2 se mettre en grève. **striking** *adj* remarquable.

string (striŋ) *n* 1 corde *f.* 2 ficelle *f.* 3 cordon *m.* 4 chapelet *m.* 5 train *m. vt* enfiler.

stringent (ˈstrindʒənt) *adj* rigoureux, -euse.

strip¹ (strip) *vt* 1 mettre à nu, dépouiller. 2 dégarnir. *vi* se dévêtir. **striptease** *n* striptease *m.*

strip² (strip) *n* 1 bande *f.* 2 lambeau, -aux *m.*

stripe (straip) *n* 1 raie *f.* 2 bande *f. vt* rayer, barrer.

strive (straiv) *vi* 1 s'efforcer. 2 se débattre.

strode (stroud) *v see* **stride.**

stroke¹ (strouk) *n* 1 coup *m.* 2 trait *m.* 3 brassée *f.* 4 *med* apoplexie *f.*

stroke² (strouk) *vt* caresser. *n* caresse *f.*

stroll (stroul) *n* promenade *f.* tour *m. vi* flâner.

strong (strɔŋ) *adj* 1 fort. 2 solide. 3 prononcé. *adv* fort. **stronghold** *n* forteresse *f.* **strongminded** *adj* résolu, décidé.

strove (strouv) *v see* **strive.**

struck (strʌk) v see **strike.**

structure (ˈstrʌktʃə) n **1** structure f. **2** édifice m.

struggle (ˈstrʌgəl) n lutte f. vi lutter, se débattre.

strum (strʌm) vi pianoter, tapoter.

strung (strʌŋ) v see **string.**

strut[1] (strʌt) vi se pavaner.

strut[2] (strʌt) n entretoise f.

stub (stʌb) n **1** souche f. **2** bout, mégot m. vt cogner, heurter. **stub out** éteindre.

stubborn (ˈstʌbən) adj obstiné, têtu, opiniâtre. **stubborness** n entêtement m.

stud[1] (stʌd) n **1** clou à grosse tête m. **2** bouton m. **3** poteau, -aux m. vt **1** clouter. **2** parsemer.

stud[2] (stʌd) n écurie f. haras m.

student (ˈstjuːdṇt) n étudiant m.

studio (ˈstjuːdiou) n **1** Art atelier m. **2** studio m.

study (ˈstʌdi) n **1** étude f. **2** cabinet de travail m. vt étudier. **studious** adj studieux, -euse.

stuff (stʌf) n matière f. vt **1** rembourrer. **2** cul farcir. **3** empailler. **stuffing** n **1** cul farce f. **2** bourre f. **stuffy** adj **1** renfermé, mal aéré. **2** inf collet monté.

stumble (ˈstʌmbəl) vi trébucher.

stump (stʌmp) n **1** tronçon m. souche f. **2** bout m. **3** moignon m. vt inf coller.

stun (stʌn) vt **1** étourdir. **2** abasourdir. **stunning** adj **1** inf épatant. **2** étourdissant.

stung (stʌŋ) v see **sting.**

stunk (stʌŋk) v see **stink.**

stunt[1] (stʌnt) vt empêcher de croître, rabougrir.

stunt[2] (stʌnt) n **1** tour de force m. acrobatie f. **2** affaire publicitaire f.

stupid (ˈstjuːpid) adj stupide, bête.

sturdy (ˈstəːdi) adj **1** robuste. **2** hardi.

sturgeon (ˈstəːdʒən) n esturgeon m.

stutter (ˈstʌtə) vt,vi bégayer. n bégaiement m.

sty (stai) n étable f.

style (stail) n **1** style m. **2** manière f. **3** chic m. vt dénommer. **stylish** adj élégant, chic.

stylus (ˈstailəs) n stylet m.

subconscious (sʌbˈkɔnʃəs) adj,n subconscient m. **subconsciously** adv inconsciemment.

subcontract (sʌbkənˈtrækt) vt sous-traiter. **subcontractor** n sous-entrepreneur, sous-traitant m.

subdue (səbˈdjuː) vt **1** subjuguer, soumettre. **2** atténuer.

subject (n,adj ˈsʌbdʒikt; v səbˈdʒekt) n **1** sujet m. **2** matière f. adj **1** assujetti. **2** sujet, -ette. vt assujettir. **subjective** adj subjectif, -ive.

subjunctive (səbˈdʒʌŋktiv) adj,n subjonctif, -ive m.

sublime (səˈblaim) adj sublime, suprême.

submachine-gun (sʌbməˈʃiːngʌn) n mitraillette f.

submarine (sʌbməˈriːn) n sous-marin m.

submerge (səbˈməːdʒ) vt submerger. vi plonger.

submit (səbˈmit) vi se soumettre. vt soumettre, présenter. **submission** n soumission m. **submissive** adj soumis, docile.

subnormal (sʌbˈnɔːməl) adj au-dessous de la normale.

subordinate (səˈbɔːdinət) adj inférieur, accessoire. n subordonné m. vt subordonner.

subscribe (səbˈskraib) vt souscrire. vi s'abonner à. **subscription** n **1** souscription f. **2** adhésion f. **3** abonnement m.

subsequent (ˈsʌbsikwint) adj subséquent. **subsequently** adv plus tard.

subservient (səbˈsəːviənt) adj **1** obséquieux, -euse. **2** subordonné. **3** utile.

subside (səbˈsaid) vi **1** s'affaisser. **2** baisser. **3** s'apaiser.

subsidiary (səbˈsidiəri) n filiale f. adj auxiliaire, subsidiaire.

subsidize (ˈsʌbsidaiz) vt subventionner. **subsidy** n subvention f.

subsist (səbˈsist) vi subsister.

substance (ˈsʌbstəns) n **1** substance f. **2** solidité f. **substantial** adj **1** substantiel, -elle. **2** important. **substantive** n substantif m.

substitute (ˈsʌbstitjuːt) n **1** remplaçant m. **2** succédané m. vt substituer. vi remplacer. **substitution** n substitution f. remplacement m.

subtitle (ˈsʌbtaitḷ) n sous-titre m. vt sous-titrer.

subtle (ˈsʌtḷ) adj **1** subtil. **2** fin.

subtract (səbˈtrækt) vt soustraire. **subtraction** n soustraction f.

suburb (ˈsʌbəːb) n **1** faubourg m. **2** pl banlieue f. **suburban** adj suburbain.

subvert (sʌbˈvəːt) vt subvertir. **subversion** n subversion f. **subversive** adj subversif, -ive.

subway (ˈsʌbwei) n passage souterrain m.

succeed (səkˈsiːd) vt succéder. vi réussir. **success** n succès m. réussite f. **successful** adj heureux, -euse, réussi. **succession** n **1** succession f. **2** suite, série f. **successive** adj successif, -ive.

succulent (ˈsʌkjulənt) adj succulent.

succumb (səˈkʌm) vi succomber, céder.

such (sʌtʃ) adj **1** tel, telle, semblable. **2** si. **such as** tel que, comme. ~pron tel, telle.

suck (sʌk) vt,vi sucer. vt téter.

sucker ('sʌkə) n **1** inf gobeur, niais m. **2** bot rejeton m.

suction ('sʌkʃən) n succion, aspiration f.

sudden ('sʌdn) adj soudain, subit. **all of a sudden** tout à coup.

suds (sʌdz) n pl **1** mousse de savon f. **2** lessive f.

sue (suː) vt poursuivre en justice.

suede (sweid) n daim m.

suet ('suːit) n graisse de rognon f.

suffer ('sʌfə) vt **1** souffrir, éprouver. **2** supporter. vi souffrir. **suffering** n souffrance f.

sufficient (sə'fiʃənt) adj suffisant, assez de. **sufficiently** adv suffisamment, assez.

suffix ('sʌfiks) n suffixe m.

suffocate ('sʌfəkeit) vt,vi suffoquer, étouffer. **suffocation** n asphyxie f.

sugar ('ʃugə) n sucre. vt sucrer. **sugarbeet** n betterave à sucre f. **sugar cane** n canne à sucre f.

suggest (sə'dʒest) vt **1** suggérer. **2** inspirer. **suggestion** n **1** suggestion f. **2** trace f. **suggestive** adj suggestif, -ive, évocateur, -trice.

suicide ('suːisaid) n **1** suicide m. **2** (person) suicidé m. **commit suicide** se suicider.

suit (suːt) n **1** costume m. **2** poursuites f pl. **3** game couleur f. **4** requête f. vt **1** convenir à, aller bien. **2** accommoder. **suitable** adj **1** convenable. **2** approprié. **suitcase** n valise f.

suite (swiːt) n **1** suite f. **2** appartement m. **3** mobilier m.

sulk (sʌlk) vi bouder. n bouderie f. **sulky** adj maussade, boudeur, -euse.

sullen ('sʌlən) adj morose, morne.

sulphur ('sʌlfə) n soufre m.

sultan ('sʌltən) n sultan m.

sultana (sʌl'taːnə) n raisin sec (de Smyrne) m.

sultry ('sʌltri) adj étouffant.

sum (sʌm) n **1** somme f. total, -aux m. **2** calcul m. v **sum up 1** résumer. **2** classer.

summarize ('sʌməraiz) vt résumer. **summary** n sommaire, résumé m. adj sommaire.

summer ('sʌmə) n été m. **summerhouse** n pavillon m. **summertime** n été m.

summit ('sʌmit) n sommet, faîte m.

summon ('sʌmən) vt **1** convoquer. **2** sommer. **3** faire appel à. **summons** n **1** law citation f. **2** appel m. vt citer en justice.

sun (sʌn) n soleil m. vt exposer au soleil.

sunbathe ('sʌnbeið) vi prendre un bain de soleil.

sunburn ('sʌnbɔːn) n hâle m.

Sunday ('sʌndi) n dimanche m.

sundial ('sʌndaiəl) n cadran solaire m.

sundry ('sʌndri) adj divers. **all and sundry** tout le monde. **sundries** n pl frais divers m pl.

sunflower ('sʌnflauə) n tournesol m.

sung (sʌŋ) v see **sing.**

sunglasses ('sʌnglaːsiz) n pl lunettes de soleil f pl.

sunk (sʌŋk) v see **sink.**

sunlight ('sʌnlait) n lumière solaire f. soleil m.

sunny ('sʌni) adj ensoleillé.

sunrise ('sʌnraiz) n lever du soleil m.

sunset ('sʌnset) n coucher du soleil m.

sunshine ('sʌnʃain) n soleil m.

sunstroke ('sʌnstrouk) n insolation f. coup de soleil m.

suntan ('sʌntæn) n hâle m.

super ('suːpə) adj inf superbe, magnifique.

superannuation (suːpərænjuˈeiʃən) n retraite par limite d'âge f.

superb (suːˈpəːb) adj superbe, magnifique.

superficial (suːpəˈfiʃəl) adj superficiel, -elle.

superfluous (suːˈpəːfluəs) adj superflu, de trop.

superhuman (suːpəˈhjuːmən) adj surhumain.

superimpose (suːpərimˈpouz) vt superposer, surimposer.

superintendent (suːpərinˈtendənt) n directeur, surveillant m.

superior (suˈpiəriə) adj,n supérieur m.

superlative (suˈpəːlativ) n superlatif m. adj **1** suprême. **2** superlatif, -ive.

supermarket ('suːpəmaːkit) n supermarché m.

supernatural (suːpəˈnætʃrəl) adj,n surnaturel, -elle m.

supersede (suːpəˈsiːd) vt remplacer, supplanter.

supersonic (suːpəˈsɔnik) adj supersonique.

superstition (suːpəˈstiʃən) n superstition f. **superstitious** adj superstitieux, -euse.

supervise ('suːpəvaiz) vt **1** surveiller. **2** diriger. **supervision** n **1** surveillance f. **2** direction f.

supper ('sʌpə) n souper m.

supple ('sʌpəl) adj souple, pliant, maniable.

supplement (n 'sʌplimənt; v sʌpli'ment) n supplément m. vt compléter, ajouter à. **supplementary** adj supplémentaire.

supply (sə'plai) vt fournir, munir. n **1** fourniture, offre f. **2** pl vivres f pl. approvisionnements m pl.

support (sə'pɔːt) n appui, soutien m. vt **1** soutenir, appuyer, entretenir. **supporter** n **1** partisan, adhérent m. **2** sport supporter m.

suppose (sə'pouz) vt supposer. **supposed** adj prétendu. **supposedly** adv soi-disant, censément.

suppress (səˈpres) vt **1** réprimer, refouler. **2** dissimuler. **suppression** n **1** répression f. **2** étouffement m.

supreme (səˈpriːm) adj suprême. **supremacy** n suprématie f.

surcharge (ˈsəːtʃɑːdʒ) n surcharge, surtaxe f.

sure (ʃuə) adj sûr, certain. adv certainement. **surely** adv assurément, bien sûr. **surety** n **1** garant m. caution f. **2** certitude f.

surf (səːf) n ressac m.

surface (ˈsəːfis) n **1** surface f. **2** apparence f. vi remonter à la surface.

surfeit (ˈsəːfit) n surabondance f.

surge (səːdʒ) n **1** vague, lame f. **2** naut houle f. vi se soulever.

surgeon (ˈsəːdʒən) n chirurgien m. **surgery** n **1** chirurgie f. **2** cabinet de consultation, dispensaire m. **surgical** adj chirurgical, -aux.

surly (ˈsəːli) adj bourru, revêche, hargneux, -euse.

surmount (səˈmaunt) vt surmonter, maîtriser.

surname (ˈsəːneim) n nom de famille m.

surpass (səˈpɑːs) vt **1** surpasser. **2** l'emporter sur.

surplus (ˈsəːplis) n surplus, excédent m. adj excédentaire.

surprise (səˈpraiz) n surprise f. vt surprendre, étonner.

surrealism (səˈriəlizəm) n surréalisme m. **surrealist** adj,n surréaliste m.

surrender (səˈrendə) vi se rendre. vt rendre, céder. n reddition f.

surreptitious (sʌrəpˈtiʃəs) adj subreptice, clandestin.

surround (səˈraund) vt entourer, cerner. n bordure f. **surroundings** n pl milieu m.

survey (n ˈsəːvei; v səːˈvei) n **1** étude **2** levé m. **3** enquête f. vt **1** examiner. **2** arpenter.

surveyor (səˈveiə) n **1** arpenteur m. **2** surveillant m.

survive (səˈvaiv) vi survivre. vt survivre à. **survival** n survivance f. **survivor** n survivant m.

susceptible (səˈseptəbəl) adj **1** susceptible. **2** sensible.

suspect (v səˈspekt; n,adj ˈsʌspekt) vt **1** soupçonner. **2** se douter de. adj,n suspect.

suspend (səˈspend) vt suspendre. **suspense** n suspens m. **suspension** n suspension f.

suspicion (səˈspiʃən) n soupçon m. **suspicious** adj **1** méfiant, soupçonneux, -euse. **2** suspect, louche.

sustain (səˈstein) vt **1** soutenir. **2** éprouver.

swab (swɔb) n tampon, torchon m. vt nettoyer, essuyer.

swagger (ˈswægə) n **1** air important m. **2** crânerie f. vi crâner.

swallow[1] (ˈswɔlou) vt avaler, gober. n **1** gosier m. **2** gorgée f.

swallow[2] (ˈswɔlou) n zool hirondelle f.

swam (swæm) v see **swim.**

swamp (swɔmp) n marais m. vt inonder, submerger.

swan (swɔn) n cygne m.

swank (swæŋk) vi crâner. n inf prétention f.

swap (swɔp) vt troquer, échanger. n troc, échange m.

swarm (swɔːm) n essaim m. nuée f. vi **1** essaimer. **2** fourmiller.

swastika (ˈswɔstikə) n croix gammée f.

swat (swɔt) vt inf écraser.

sway (swei) vi osciller, se balancer. vt **1** agiter. **2** influencer.

swear* (swɛə) vt,vi jurer. **swearword** n juron m.

sweat (swet) n sueur, transpiration f. vi,vt suer. **sweater** n chandail m.

swede (swiːd) n rutabaga m.

Sweden (ˈswiːdn) n Suède f. **Swede** n suédois m. **Swedish** adj suédois. **Swedish (language)** n suédois m.

sweep* (swiːp) vt **1** balayer, ramoner. **2** enlever. vi **1** passer rapidement. **2** s'étendre. n **1** coup de balai m. **2** ramoneur m. **3** mouvement circulaire m. **sweeping** adj **1** large. **2** rapide. **3** radical, -aux. **4** complet, -ète.

sweet (swiːt) adj **1** doux, douce. **2** sucré. **3** charmant. n **1** bonbon m. **2** dessert m. **sweetbread** n ris de veau or d'agneau m. **sweet corn** n maïs m. **sweetheart** n amoureux, -euse. **sweet pea** n pois de senteur m. **sweeten** vt sucrer.

swell* (swel) vi s'enfler, se gonfler. vt gonfler. n naut houle f. **swelling** n enflure f.

swept (swept) v see **sweep.**

swerve (swəːv) n écart m. embardée f. vi faire un écart or une embardée.

swift (swift) adj rapide. n martinet m.

swig (swig) n inf lampée f. vt boire à grands traits.

swill (swil) vt laver à grande eau. **swill out** rincer. ~n **1** pâtée pour les porcs f. **2** lavage m. **3** lampée f.

swim* (swim) vi **1** nager. **2** tourner. **3** être inondé. vt traverser à la nage. n nage f. **swimming** n natation f. **swimming cos-**

tume *n* maillot de bain *m*. **swimming pool** *n* piscine *f*.

swindle (ˈswɪndļ) *vt* escroquer. *n* escroquerie *f*. **swindler** *n* escroc *m*.

swine (swain) *n invar* cochon *m*.

swing* (swɪŋ) *vi* **1** se balancer. **2** changer de direction. *vt* **1** balancer. **2** tourner. *n* **1** balançoire *f*. **2** oscillation *f*. **3** revirement *m*.

swipe (swaip) *inf vt* **1** cogner. **2** chiper. *n* coup *m*.

swirl (swəːl) *vi* tourbillonner. *vt* faire tournoyer. *n* remous *m*.

swish (swɪʃ) *vi* siffler, bruire. *vt* fouetter, battre, faire siffler. *n* sifflement, bruissement *m*.

switch (swɪtʃ) *n* **1** interrupteur, commutateur *m*. **2** cravache *f*. *vt* **1** aiguiller. **2** battre. **switch off/on** éteindre/allumer. **switchboard** *n* standard téléphonique *m*.

Switzerland (ˈswɪtsələnd) *n* Suisse *f*. **Swiss** *adj,n* suisse.

swivel (ˈswɪvəl) *vi* pivoter. *n* pivot *m*.

swollen (ˈswoulən) *v* see **swell**. *adj* enflé, gonflé.

swoop (swuːp) *vi* fondre, foncer. *n* descente *f*.

swop (swɔp) *n* troc *m*. *vt* échanger.

sword (sɔːd) *n* épée *f*. **swordfish** *n* espadon *m*.

swore (swɔː) *v* see **swear**.

sworn (swɔːn) *v* see **swear**.

swot (swɔt) *vi inf* bûcher.

swum (swʌm) *v* see **swim**.

swung (swʌŋ) *v* see **swing**.

sycamore (ˈsikəmɔː) *n* sycomore *m*.

syllable (ˈsiləbəl) *n* syllabe *f*.

syllabus (ˈsiləbəs) *n, pl* **-buses** *or* **-bi** programme *m*.

symbol (ˈsimbəl) *n* symbole *m*. **symbolic** *adj* symbolique. **symbolism** *n* symbolisme *m*. **symbolize** *vt* symboliser.

symmetry (ˈsimitri) *n* symétrie *f*. **symmetrical** *adj* symétrique.

sympathy (ˈsimpəθi) *n* **1** sympathie *f*. **2** condoléances *f pl*. **sympathetic** *adj* sympathique, compatissant. **sympathize** *vi* sympathiser, avoir de la compassion.

symphony (ˈsimfəni) *n* symphonie *f*.

symposium (simˈpouziəm) *n, pl* **-iums** *or* **-ia** conférence *f*. recueil *m*.

symptom (ˈsimptəm) *n* symptôme *m*.

synagogue (ˈsinəgɔg) *n* synagogue *f*.

synchronize (ˈsiŋkrənaiz) *vt* synchroniser.

syndicate (ˈsindikət) *n* syndicat *m*.

syndrome (ˈsindroum) *n* syndrome *m*.

synonym (ˈsinənim) *n* synonyme *m*. **synonymous** *adj* synonyme.

synopsis (siˈnɔpsis) *n, pl* **-ses** sommaire, résumé *m*.

syntax (ˈsintæks) *n* syntaxe *f*.

synthesis (ˈsinθəsis) *n, pl* **-ses** synthèse *f*.

synthetic (sinˈθetik) *adj* synthétique.

syphilis (ˈsifəlis) *n* syphilis *f*.

Syria (ˈsiriə) *n* Syrie *f*. **Syrian** *adj,n* syrien, -ienne.

syringe (siˈrindʒ) *n* seringue *f*. *vt* seringuer.

syrup (ˈsirəp) *n* sirop *m*.

system (ˈsistəm) *n* **1** système, réseau, -aux *m*. **2** méthode *f*. **systematic** *adj* systématique, méthodique.

T

tab (tæb) *n* **1** étiquette *f*. **2** patte *f*.

tabby (ˈtæbi) *adj* tacheté, moucheté. *n* chat tigré *m*.

table (ˈteibəl) *n* **1** table *f*. **2** plaque *f*. **3** tableau, -aux *m*. *vt* déposer. **tablecloth** *n* nappe *f*. **tablemat** *n* rond de table *m*. **tablespoon** *n* cuiller à dessert *f*. **table tennis** *n* tennis de table *m*.

tablet (ˈtæblət) *n* **1** tablette *f*. **2** comprimé *m*.

taboo (təˈbuː) *n* tabou *m*. *adj* interdit, proscrit. *vt* proscrire.

tack (tæk) *n* **1** petit clou *m*. pointe *f*. **2** *dom* point de bâti *m*. **3** *naut* bordée *f*. *vt* **1** clouer. **2** *dom* faufiler. *vi* virer.

tackle (ˈtækəl) *n* attirail, appareil *m*. *vt* s'attaquer à, aborder.

tact (tækt) *n* tact *m*. **tactful** *adj* délicat, de tact.

tactic (ˈtæktik) *n* tactique *f*.

tadpole (ˈtædpoul) *n* têtard *m*.

taffeta (ˈtæfitə) *n* taffetas *m*.

tag (tæg) *n* fiche *f*. ferret *m*.

Tahiti (təˈhiːti) *n* Tahiti *m*.

tail (teil) *n* **1** queue *f*. **2** arrière *m*. **3** pile *f*. **4** pan *m*. *vt* pister.

tailor (ˈteilə) *n* tailleur *m*. *vt* façonner.

taint (teint) *n* **1** corruption, souillure *f*. **2** trace *f*. *vt* vicier, corrompre, gâter.

take* (teik) *vt,vi* prendre. *vt* **1** conduire. **2** emporter. **3** saisir. **4** falloir. **take away** emmener. **take off 1** enlever. **2** décoller. **take-off** *n* **1** envol *m*. **2** *inf* caricature *f*. **take on** entreprendre. **take place** se passer. **take up** relever. **take-over** *n* reprise *f*. *adj* de rachat.

talcum powder (ˈtælkəm) n talc m.
tale (teil) n conte, récit m.
talent (ˈtælənt) n talent m.
talk (tɔːk) vt,vi parler. vi jaser, causer. n paroles f pl. bavardage m. conversation f. **talkative** adj bavard.
tall (tɔːl) adj 1 grand. 2 haut. 3 inf incroyable.
tally (ˈtæli) vt pointer, contrôler. vi correspondre. n pointage m.
talon (ˈtælən) n serre, griffe f.
tambourine (tæmbəˈriːn) n tambourin m.
tame (teim) adj 1 domestique, apprivoisé. 2 soumis. vt apprivoiser.
tamper (ˈtæmpə) vi **tamper with** tripoter.
tampon (ˈtæmpɔn) n tampon m.
tan (tæn) vt tanner. vi se bronzer. n hâle m.
tangent (ˈtændʒənt) n tangente f.
tangerine (tændʒəˈriːn) n mandarine f.
tangible (ˈtændʒəbəl) adj 1 tangible. 2 sensible.
Tangier (tænˈdʒiə) n Tanger m.
tangle (ˈtæŋgəl) n enchevêtrement, emmêlement m. vt embrouiller. vi s'embrouiller.
tango (ˈtæŋgou) n tango m.
tank (tæŋk) n 1 réservoir m. 2 mil char de combat m. **tanker** n 1 naut pétrolier m. 2 mot camion-citerne m.
tankard (ˈtæŋkəd) n pot m. chope f.
tantalize (ˈtæntəlaiz) vt tourmenter, taquiner.
tantrum (ˈtæntrəm) n accès de colère m.
tap[1] (tæp) vt taper. n tape f. petit coup m.
tap[2] (tæp) n robinet m. vt 1 percer. 2 vider. 3 capter.
tape (teip) n 1 ruban m. 2 tech bande magnétique f. vt 1 attacher. 2 enregistrer. **tape-measure** n mètre à ruban m. **tape-recorder** n magnétophone m.
taper (ˈteipə) n cierge m. vi s'effiler. vt effiler.
tapestry (ˈtæpistri) n tapisserie f.
tapioca (tæpiˈoukə) n tapioca m.
tar (tɑː) n goudron m. vt goudronner.
Tarmac (ˈtɑːmæk) n Tdmk bitume m.
tarantula (təˈræntjulə) n tarentule f.
target (ˈtɑːgit) n but m. cible f.
tariff (ˈtærif) n tarif m.
tarnish (ˈtɑːniʃ) vt ternir. vi se ternir. n ternissure f.
tarragon (ˈtærəgən) n estragon m.
tart[1] (tɑːt) adj 1 âpre, acerbe. 2 mordant, caustique.
tart[2] (tɑːt) n 1 tarte f. 2 sl poule f.
tartan (ˈtɑːtn) n tartan m.
task (tɑːsk) n tâche, besogne f.
tassel (ˈtæsəl) n gland m.

taste (teist) n 1 goût m. saveur f. 2 prédilection f. penchant m. ~vt goûter, déguster. **taste of** avoir un goût de. **tasteless** adj insipide, fade. **tasty** adj savoureux, -euse.
tattoo[1] (təˈtuː) n mil retraite du soir f.
tattoo[2] (təˈtuː) n tatouage m. vt tatouer.
taught (tɔːt) v see **teach.**
taunt (tɔːnt) vt se gausser de, accabler de sarcasmes. n reproche m.
Taurus (ˈtɔːrəs) n Taureau m.
taut (tɔːt) adj raide, tendu.
tautology (tɔːˈtɔlədʒi) n tautologie f.
tavern (ˈtævən) n taverne f.
tax (tæks) n 1 impôt m. contribution f. 2 charge f. vt 1 taxer. 2 imposer. 3 mettre à l'épreuve. **taxation** n impôts m. **taxpayer** n contribuable m.
taxi (ˈtæksi) n taxi m.
tea (tiː) n 1 thé m. 2 goûter m. **tea-bag** n sachet de thé m. **tea-break** n pause café f. **tea-cloth** n torchon m. **teacup** n tasse à thé f. **tealeaf** n feuille de thé f. **teapot** n théière f. **teaspoon** n cuiller à thé f.
teach* (tiːtʃ) vt enseigner, instruire, apprendre. **teacher** n 1 professeur m,f. 2 instituteur, -trice. **teacher training college** école normale.
teak (tiːk) n teck m.
team (tiːm) n 1 équipe f. 2 (of horses, etc.) attelage m.
tear[1] (tiə) n larme f. pleur m. **teardrop** n larme f. **tearful** adj en pleurs, larmoyant. **tear-gas** n gaz lacrymogène m.
tear* [2] (tɛə) vt 1 déchirer. 2 arracher. vi 1 se déchirer. 2 inf aller très rapidement. n déchirure f.
tease (tiːz) vt taquiner.
teat (tiːt) n 1 mamelon m. 2 (of a bottle) tétine f.
technical (ˈteknikəl) adj technique. **technician** n technicien m. **technique** n technique f. **technology** n technologie f. **technological** adj technologique.
teddy bear (ˈtedi) n ours en peluche, nounours m.
tedious (ˈtiːdiəs) adj fastidieux, -euse, pénible.
tee (tiː) n but m. vt surélever.
teenage (ˈtiːneidʒ) adj adolescent. **teenager** n adolescent m.
teetotal (tiːˈtoutl) adj antialcoolique. **teetotaller** n abstinent m.
telegram (ˈteligræm) n télégramme m.
telegraph (ˈteligrɑːf) n télégraphe m. vt télé-

graphıer. **telegraph pole** n poteau télégraphıque m.

telepathy (tɪ'lepəθi) n télépathıe f.

telephone ('telifoun) n téléphone m. vt,vɪ téléphoner.

telescope ('teliskoup) n télescope m. longue-vue f.

television ('teləvɪʒən) n télévɪsɪon f. **televise** vt téléviser.

telex ('teleks) n télex m.

tell* (tel) vt 1 dire, raconter. 2 discerner. vɪ porter. **tell off** réprimander.

temper ('tempə) n 1 tempérament m. humeur f. 2 sang-froɪd m. 3 colère f. 4 tech trempe f. vt 1 modérer. 2 délayer. 3 tech tremper. **temperament** n tempérament m. **temperamental** adj capricieux, -euse. **temperate** adj 1 modéré, sobre. 2 tempéré. **temperature** n température f.

tempestuous (tem'pestjuəs) adj tempétueux, -euse.

temple[1] ('tempəl) n rel temple m.

temple[2] ('tempəl) n anat tempe f.

tempo ('tempou) n tempo m.

temporal ('tempərəl) adj temporel, -elle. **temporary** adj temporaire, provɪsoɪre.

tempt (tempt) vt tenter. **temptation** n tentatɪon f.

ten (ten) adj,n dix m. **tenth** adj dixième.

tenacious (tə'neɪʃəs) adj tenace.

tenant ('tenənt) n locataɪre m,f. **tenancy** n location f.

tend[1] (tend) vɪ 1 tendre. 2 être sujet.

tend[2] (tend) vt surveiller, garder, soɪgner.

tendency ('tendənsi) n tendance f.

tender[1] ('tendə) adj 1 tendre. 2 sensible.

tender[2] ('tendə) vt offrir. **tender for** soumɪssionner pour. ~n offre, soumission f.

tendon ('tendən) n tendon m.

tendril ('tendril) n vrille f.

tenement ('tenəmənt) n appartement, logement m.

tennis ('tenis) n tennis m. **tennis court** n court de tennis m.

tenor ('tenə) n 1 mus ténor m. 2 teneur, marche f.

tense[1] (tens) adj 1 tendu. 2 raɪde. **tension** n tension f.

tense[2] (tens) n temps m.

tent (tent) n tente f.

tentacle ('tentəkəl) n tentacule f.

tentative ('tentətiv) adj 1 expérimental, -aux. 2 hésitant.

tenuous ('tenjuəs) adj ténu, mɪnce.

tepid ('tepid) adj tiède.

term (tə:m) n 1 terme m. 2 pérɪode f. 3 educ trimestre m. 4 pl conditions f pl. 5 pl rapports m pl. 6 pl facilités de paɪement f pl. vt désɪgner, nommer.

terminal ('tə:mɪnl) n 1 termɪnus m. 2 tech borne f.

terminate ('tə:mineit) vt achever. vɪ se termɪner.

terminology (tə:mi'nɔlədʒi) n termɪnologie f.

terminus ('tə:mɪnəs) n termɪnus m.

terrace ('terəs) n terrasse f.

terrestrial (tə'restrɪəl) adj terrestre.

terrible ('teribəl) adj terrible, épouvantable.

terrier ('teriə) n terrɪer m.

terrify ('terifai) vt épouvanter, effrayer. **terrific** adj formɪdable.

territory ('terɪtri) n terrɪtoire m.

terror ('terə) n terreur, épouvante f. **terrorism** n terrorɪsme m. **terrorist** n terrorɪste m,f. **terrorize** vt terrorɪser.

Terylene ('terili:n) n Tdmk Térylène m.

test (test) n 1 essaɪ m. épreuve f. 2 examen m. vt essayer, mettre à l'épreuve. **test-tube** n éprouvette f.

testament ('testəmənt) n testament m.

testicle ('testikəl) n testɪcule f.

testify ('testifai) vt témoɪgner, déclarer. vɪ déposer.

testimony ('testɪməni) n témoɪgnage m. déposɪtion f. **testimonial** n attestatɪon f.

tether ('teθə) vt mettre à l'attache. n longe f.

text (tekst) n texte m. **textbook** n manuel m.

textile ('tekstail) n 1 tɪssu m. étoffe f. 2 textile m. adj textile.

texture ('tekstʃə) n texture f. graɪn m.

Thames (temz) n Tamise f.

than (ðən; stressed ðæn) conj que, de.

thank (θæŋk) vt remercɪer. **thanks!** ɪnterj merci! **thanks to** grâce à. **thank you!** merci! **thankful** adj reconnaissant.

that (ðæt) adj 1 ce, cet, cette. 2 ce...là. conj que, afin que. pron 1 cela, ɪnf ça, ce. 2 celui-là, celle-là. 3 qui, que. 4 lequel, laquelle. 5 où. 6 dont. **that's all** voɪlà tout.

thatch (θætʃ) n chaume m. vt couvrɪr de chaume.

thaw (θɔ:) vt dégeler, décongeler, faire fondre. vɪ fondre, se décongeler. v ɪmp dégeler. n dégel m.

the (ðə; stressed ði:) def art 1 le, l' ms. la, l' fs. 2 pl les m,f pl. adv d'autant.

theatre ('θiətə) *n* 1 théâtre *m*. 2 *med* salle d'opération *f*. **theatrical** *adj* théâtrical, -aux.

theft (θeft) *n* 1 vol *m*. 2 larcin *m*.

their (ðɛə) *poss adj 3rd pers pl* leur *m,f s.* leurs *m,f pl.* **theirs** *poss pron 3rd pers pl* le *or* la leur.

them (ðəm; *stressed* ðem) *pron 3rd pers pl* 1 les. 2 eux *m.* elles *f.* 3 leur. **themselves** *pron 3rd pers pl* 1 eux-mêmes *m.* elles-mêmes *f.* 2 se.

theme (θiːm) *n* thème, sujet, motif *m*.

then (ðən; *stressed* ðen) *adv* 1 alors, en ce temps-là, à cette époque. 2 puis, ensuite. *conj* en ce cas, donc, alors.

theology (θi'ɔlədʒi) *n* théologie *f*. **theologian** *n* théologien *m*. **theological** *adj* théologique.

theorem ('θiərəm) *n* théorème *m*.

theory ('θiəri) *n* théorie *f*. **theoretical** *adj* théorique. **theorize** *vi* théoriser.

therapy ('θerəpi) *n* thérapie *f*. **therapeutic** *adj* thérapeutique.

there (ðɛə) *adv* là, y. **thereabouts** *adv* 1 par là, dans les environs. 2 à peu près, environ. **thereafter** *adv* après, ensuite, par la suite. **thereby** *adv* par ce moyen, de cette façon. **therefore** *adv* donc, par conséquent. **thereupon** *adv* là dessus, sur ce. **therewith** *adv* 1 avec cela. 2 en outre.

thermal ('θəːməl) *adj* thermal, -aux, thermique.

thermodynamics (θəːmoudai'næmiks) *n* thermodynamique *f*.

thermometer (θə'mɔmitə) *n* thermomètre *m*.

thermonuclear (θəːmou'njuːkliə) *adj* thermonucléaire.

Thermos ('θəːmɔs) *n Tdmk* bouteille Thermos, bouteille isolante *f*.

thermostat ('θəːmɔstæt) *n* thermostat *m*.

these (ðiːz) *adj pl* 1 ces. 2 ces...ci. *pron pl* ceux-ci *m pl.* celles-ci *f pl.*

thesis ('θiːsis) *n, pl* -**ses** thèse *f*.

they (ðei) *pron 3rd pers pl* 1 ils *m pl.* elles *f pl.* 2 eux *m pl.* elles *f pl.* **they say** on dit.

thick (θik) *adj* 1 épais, épaisse, gros, grosse. 2 touffu, dru. 3 *inf* stupide, bête. **thicken** *vt* épaissir, lier. *vi* 1 s'épaissir, se lier. 2 se compliquer. **thickness** *n* épaisseur *f*. **thickskinned** *adj* peu susceptible.

thief (θiːf) *n, pl* **thieves** voleur *m*.

thigh (θai) *n* cuisse *f*. **thigh-bone** *n* fémur *m*.

thimble ('θimbəl) *n* dé (à coudre) *m*.

thin (θin) *adj* 1 mince, maigre, léger, -ère. 2 rare, clairsemé. *vt* 1 amincir. 2 éclaircir. *vi* 1 s'amincir. 2 s'éclaircir. 3 amincir. **thinness** *n*

maigreur, minceur *f*. **thin-skinned** *adj* susceptible, sensible.

thing (θiŋ) *n* 1 chose *f.* objet *m.* 2 *pl* affaires *f pl.* effets *m pl.* 3 *inf* machin, truc *m.* **for one thing...for another** en premier lieu...d'autre part.

think (θiŋk) *vi* penser, réfléchir. *vt* croire, songer. **think about/of** penser à/de. **think over** réfléchir.

third (θəːd) *adj* troisième. **third party** *n* tiers *m.* **third-party** *adj* au tiers. **third person** *n* tiers *m.* troisième personne *f.* **third-rate** *adj* de qualité inférieure.

thirst (θəːst) *n* soif *f.* **thirsty** *adj* assoiffé. **be thirsty** avoir soif.

thirteen (θəː'tiːn) *adj,n* treize *m.* **thirteenth** *adj* treizième.

thirty ('θəːti) *adj,n* trente *m.* **thirtieth** *adj* trentième.

this (ðis) ce, cet, cette. *pron* 1 ceci, ce. 2 celui-ci *m.* celle-ci *f.* **this way and that** de-ci, de-là.

thistle ('θisəl) *n* chardon *m*.

thorn (θɔːn) *n* épine *f*.

thorough ('θʌrə) *adj* 1 complet, -ète, parfait. 2 profond, minutieux, -euse. **thoroughbred** *adj* pur sang *invar,* de race. *n* cheval pur sang *m.* **thoroughfare** *n* voie *f*.

those (ðouz) *adj pl* 1 ces *m,f pl.* 2 ces...là *m,f pl. pron* 1 ceux-là *m pl.* celles-là *f pl.* 2 ceux *m pl.* celles *f pl.*

though (ðou) *conj* quoique, bien que. **as though** comme si. ~*adv* cependant, pourtant.

thought[1] (θɔːt) *n* 1 pensée, idée *f.* 2 réflexion *f.* **thoughtful** *adj* 1 pensif, -ive. 2 prévenant. **thoughtless** *adj* 1 irréfléchi. 2 sans égards.

thought[2] (θɔːt) *v see* **think.**

thousand ('θauzənd) *adj,n* mille *m invar.* **a thousand** millier *m.* **thousandth** *adj* millième.

thrash (θræʃ) *vt* battre, rosser.

thread (θred) *n* 1 fil *m.* trame *f.* 2 *tech* filet, pas *m. vt* enfiler. **threadbare** *adj* usé, râpé.

threat (θret) *n* menace *f.* **threaten** *vt* menacer.

three (θriː) *adj,n* trois *m.* **three-dimensional** *adj* tridimensionnel, -elle, à trois dimensions. **three-quarters** *n* trois-quarts *invar.* **threesome** *n* ménage à trois *m*.

thresh (θreʃ) *vt* battre.

threshold ('θreʃhould) *n* seuil, pas de porte *m*.

threw (θruː) *v see* **throw.**

thrift (θrift) *n* économie, épargne *f.* **thrifty** *adj* économe, ménager, -ère.

thrill (θril) *n* frisson *m.* sensation *f. vt* faire

frissonner, émouvoir. *vi* frissonner. **thriller** *n* roman *or* film à sensation *m*.

thrive (θraɪv) *vi* 1 pousser, se développer. 2 prospérer.

throat (θrout) *n* gorge *f*. **clear one's throat** s'éclaircir la voix.

throb (θrɔb) *vi* palpiter, battre. *n* palpitation *f*. battement *m*.

throne (θroun) *n* trône *m*.

throng (θrɔŋ) *n* 1 foule, populace *f*. 2 cohue *f*. *vi* faire foule, affluer. *vt* encombrer.

throttle ('θrɔtl̩) *vt* étrangler. *n tech* papillon *m*.

through (θru:) *prep* 1 à travers. 2 pendant. 3 par. 4 à cause de. *adj* direct. *adv* 1 à travers. 2 d'un bout à autre. **throughout** *prep* 1 d'un bout à l'autre. 2 partout. *adv* de fond en comble.

throw* (θrou) *vt* jeter, lancer. **throw away** 1 rejeter. 2 gaspiller. ~*n* jet, lancement *m*.

thrush (θrʌʃ) *n* grive *f*.

thrust* (θrʌst) *vt* pousser violemment, enfoncer. *n* 1 poussée *f*. 2 coup de pointe *m*.

thud (θʌd) *n* bruit sourd *m*.

thumb (θʌm) *n* pouce *m*. *vt* feuilleter.

thump (θʌmp) *n* 1 coup sourd *m*. 2 bourrade *f*. *vt* frapper du poing.

thunder ('θʌndə) *n* tonnerre *m*. *vi* tonner. **thunderstorm** *n* orage *m*.

Thursday ('θəːzdi) *n* jeudi *m*.

thus (ðʌs) *adv* 1 ainsi, de cette manière. 2 donc, par conséquent.

thwart (θwɔːt) *vt* contrecarrer, déjouer.

thyme (taɪm) *n* thym *m*.

thyroid ('θaɪrɔid) *adj* thyroïde.

tiara (ti'ɑːrə) *n* tiare *f*.

tick[1] (tik) *n* 1 tic-tac *m*. 2 *inf* instant *m*. 3 marque *f*. trait *m*. *vi* faire tic-tac. *vt* pointer, marquer.

tick[2] (tik) *n zool* tique *f*.

ticket ('tikit) *n* 1 billet *m*. 2 étiquette *f*. **ticket collector** *n* contrôleur *m*. **ticket office** *n* guichet *m*.

tickle ('tikəl) *vt* chatouiller. *vi* démanger. *n* chatouillement *m*. **ticklish** *adj* 1 chatouilleux, -euse. 2 susceptible, délicat.

tide (taid) *n* marée *f*. courant *m*. **high/low tide** marée haute/basse. **tidemark** *n* ligne de marée haute *f*.

tidy ('taidi) *adj* bien rangé, en ordre, ordonné. *vt* ranger, mettre en ordre.

tie (tai) *vt* lier, nouer, attacher. *vi* faire match nul. *n* 1 lien *m*. attache *f*. 2 cravate *f*. 3 match nul *m*.

tier (tiə) *n* rangée *f*. étage, gradin *m*.

tiger ('taigə) *n* tigre *m*.

tight (tait) *adj* 1 tendu, raide. 2 imperméable, étanche, hermétique. 3 *inf* serré, radin. 4 *inf* ivre. *adv* 1 fermement. 2 serré. 3 hermétiquement. **tighten** *vt* serrer, reserrer, tendre. *vi* se reserrer, se tendre. **tight-fisted** *adj inf* radin, près de ses sous. **tightrope** *n* corde raide *f*. **tightrope walker** funambule *m,f*. **tights** *n pl* collant *m*.

tile (tail) *n* 1 tuile *f*. 2 carreau, -aux *m*. *vt* 1 couvrir de tuiles. 2 carreler.

till[1] (til) *prep* 1 jusqu'à. 2 que. **till now** jusqu'à présent. **till then** jusque-là. ~*conj* jusqu'à ce que.

till[2] (til) *n* caisse *f*. guichet *m*.

till[3] (til) *vt* labourer, cultiver.

tiller ('tilə) *n* barre du gouvernail *f*.

tilt (tilt) *vt* faire pencher. *vi* pencher, s'incliner. *n* pente, inclinaison *f*.

timber ('timbə) *n* bois de charpente *m*.

time (taim) *n* 1 temps *m*. 2 fois *f*. 3 heure *f*. 4 époque *f*. âge *m*. 5 mesure *f*. **in time** à temps. **on time** à l'heure. ~*vt* 1 fixer l'heure de. 2 chronométrer. 3 régler. **time bomb** *n* bombe à retardement *f*. **timekeeper** *n* chronométreur *m*. **timetable** *n* emploi du temps, horaire *m*.

timid ('timid) *adj* timide, craintif, -ive.

timpani ('timpəni) *n pl* timbales *f pl*.

tin (tin) *n* 1 étain, fer blanc *m*. 2 boîte *f*. *vt* 1 étamer. 2 mettre en boîtes. **tin-opener** *n* ouvre-boîtes *m invar*.

tinge (tindʒ) *n* teinte, nuance *f*. *vt* teinter, nuancer.

tingle ('tiŋgəl) *vi* picoter, tinter. *n* tintement, picotement *m*.

tinker ('tiŋkə) *n* chaudronnier ambulant *m*. *vi* bricoler.

tinkle ('tiŋkəl) *vi* tinter. *vt* faire tinter. *n* tintement, drelin *m*.

tinsel ('tinsəl) *n* clinquant *m*.

tint (tint) *n* teinte, nuance *f*. *vt* teinter, nuancer.

tiny ('taini) *adj* minuscule, tout petit.

tip[1] (tip) *n* extrémité *f*. bout *m*. **tiptoe** *n* pointe des pieds *f*. *vi* marcher sur la pointe des pieds.

tip[2] (tip) *vt* renverser, faire basculer. *vi* se renverser, basculer, chavirer. *n* pente, inclinaison *f*.

tip[3] (tip) *n* 1 pourboire *m*. 2 tuyau, -aux *m*. *vt* donner un pourboire. **tip-off** *n* tuyau, -aux, indice *m*.

tipsy ('tipsi) *adj inf* gris, éméché.

tire

tire ('taiǝ) vt fatiguer, lasser. vi se fatiguer. **tired** adj fatigué. **tired out** épuisé.

tissue ('tiʃuː) n 1 tissu m. étoffe f. 2 mouchoir en papier m.

title ('taitl) n 1 titre m. 2 droit m. vt intituler.

to (tǝ; stressed tuː) prep 1 à, en, vers. 2 chez. 3 pour, envers. 4 sur. 5 contre. conj pour, afin de. **to-do** n remue-ménage m.

toad (toud) n crapaud m. **toadstool** n champignon vénéneux m.

toast[1] (toust) n pain grillé m. vt,vi griller.

toast[2] (toust) n toast m. vt boire à la santé de.

tobacco (tǝ'bækou) n tabac m. **tobacconist** n marchand de tabac m.

toboggan (tǝ'bɔgǝn) n toboggan m. luge f.

today (tǝ'dei) adv,n aujourd'hui m. **a week today** aujourd'hui en huit.

toddler ('tɔdlǝ) n tout petit enfant m.

toe (tou) n orteil, doigt de pied m. **toenail** n ongle de pied m.

toffee ('tɔfi) n caramel m.

toga ('tougǝ) n toge f.

together (tǝ'geðǝ) adv ensemble.

toil (tɔil) n travail dur, labeur m. vi travailler durement.

toilet ('tɔilǝt) n 1 toilette f. 2 pl toilettes f pl. cabinets m pl. **toilet paper** n papier hygiénique m. **toilet roll** n rouleau de papier hygiénique m. **toilet water** n eau de toilette f.

token ('toukǝn) n 1 signe m. marque f. 2 jeton, bon m.

told (tould) v see **tell.**

tolerate ('tɔlǝreit) vt tolérer, supporter. **tolerance** n tolérance f. **tolerant** adj tolérant.

toll[1] (toul) n péage, droit de passage m. **tollgate** n barrière de péage f.

toll[2] (toul) n glas m. vt sonner, tinter. vi sonner le glas.

tomato (tǝ'mɑːtou) n, pl **-oes** tomate f.

tomb (tuːm) n tombe f. tombeau, -aux m.

tomorrow (tǝ'mɔrou) adv,n demain m. **day after tomorrow** après-demain m.

ton (tʌn) n tonne f.

tone (toun) n 1 ton m. 2 voix f. timbre m. 3 nuance f. vt tonifier. **tone down** adoucir.

tongs (tɔŋz) n pincettes, pinces f pl.

tongue (tʌŋ) n langue f. **tongue-tied** adj muet, muette.

tonic ('tɔnik) n fortifiant m. adj tonique. **tonic water** n eau minérale f.

tonight (tǝ'nait) adv,n ce soir m. cette nuit f.

tonsil ('tɔnsǝl) n amygdale f. **tonsillitis** n amygdalite f.

292

too (tuː) adv 1 trop. 2 aussi. 3 d'ailleurs, de plus.

took (tuk) v see **take.**

tool (tuːl) n outil, ustensile m.

tooth (tuːθ) n, pl **teeth** dent f. **toothache** n mal de dents m. **have toothache** avoir mal aux dents. **toothbrush** n brosse à dents f. **toothpaste** n dentifrice m. **toothpick** n cure-dents m invar.

top[1] (tɔp) n 1 haut, sommet m. cime f. 2 surface f. 3 dessus m. adj 1 supérieur, d'en haut. 2 principal, -aux. vt 1 coiffer. 2 dépasser. **top up** remplir. **top hat** n chapeau de forme m. **top-heavy** adj trop lourd du haut.

top[2] (tɔp) n (toy) toupie f.

topaz ('toupæz) n topaze f.

topic ('tɔpik) n sujet, thème m. matière f. **topical** adj topique, d'actualité.

topography (tǝ'pɔgrǝfi) n topographie f.

topple ('tɔpǝl) vi tomber, s'écrouler. vt faire tomber, culbuter.

topsoil ('tɔpsɔil) n terre du dessus f.

topsy-turvy (tɔpsi'tǝːvi) adv,adj sens dessus dessous.

torch (tɔːtʃ) n 1 torche f. 2 lampe électrique f.

tore (tɔː) v see **tear.**

torment (v tɔː'ment; n 'tɔːment) vt tourmenter. n tourment, supplice m.

torn (tɔːn) v see **tear.**

tornado (tɔː'neidou) n, pl **-oes** or **-os** tornade f. ouragan m.

torpedo (tɔː'piːdou) n, pl **-oes** torpille f. vt torpiller.

torrent ('tɔrǝnt) n torrent m.

torso ('tɔːsou) n torse m.

tortoise ('tɔːtǝs) n tortue f.

tortuous ('tɔːtʃuǝs) adj tortueux, -euse, sinueux, -euse.

torture ('tɔːtʃǝ) n torture f. supplice m. vt torturer, mettre au supplice.

Tory ('tɔːri) adj,n Tory m.

toss (tɔs) vt 1 lancer en l'air. 2 tirer à pile ou face. 3 hocher, agiter. vi s'agiter. n lancement, jet m.

tot[1] (tɔt) n 1 petit enfant, bambin m. 2 goutte f.

tot[2] (tɔt) vt **tot up** additionner.

total ('toutl) adj total, -aux, complet, -ète. n montant, total, tout m. **totalitarian** adj totalitaire.

totter ('tɔtǝ) vi chanceler, tituber.

touch (tʌtʃ) vt 1 toucher. 2 émouvoir. vi se toucher. n 1 toucher, tact m. 2 attouchement m. 3 touche f. **touchy** adj susceptible.

tough (tʌf) *adj* **1** dur, coriace. **2** fort. **3** raide. **toughen** *vt* durcir. *vi* s'endurcir.

toupee (ˈtuːpei) *n* toupet *m.* perruque *f.*

tour (tuə) *n* **1** voyage, tour *m.* **2** tournée *f. vt,vi* voyager. **tourism** *n* tourisme *m.* **tourist** *n* touriste *m,f.*

tournament (ˈtuənəmənt) *n* tournoi, concours *m.*

tow (tou) *vt* remorquer. *n.* remorque *f.* **towrope** *n* corde de remorque *f.*

towards (təwɔːdz) *prep also* **toward** **1** vers. **2** envers, à l'égard de. **3** pour.

towel (ˈtauəl) *n* serviette *f.* essuie-mains *m invar.*

tower (ˈtauə) *n* tour *f. vi* dominer, planer. **tower-block** *n* tour d'habitation *f.*

town (taun) *n* ville *f.* **town hall** *n* hôtel de ville *m.* **town-planning** *n* urbanisme *m.*

toxic (ˈtɔksik) *adj* toxique.

toy (tɔi) *n* jouet *m. adj* de jouet. *vi* jouer, s'amuser.

trace (treis) *n* trace *f. vt* **1** tracer. **2** suivre. **3** calquer.

track (træk) *n* **1** trace *f.* **2** piste *f.* **3** chemin, sentier *m. vt* traquer. **tracksuit** *n* survêtement *m.*

tract (trækt) *n* étendue *f.*

tractor (ˈtræktə) *n* tracteur *m.*

trade (treid) *n* **1** commerce *m.* affaires *f pl.* **2** métier *m. vt* échanger, troquer. *vi* faire le commerce. **trademark** *n* marque de fabrique *f.* **tradesman** *n* fournisseur *m.* **trade union** *n* syndicat *m.* **trade unionist** *n* syndiqué *m.*

tradition (trəˈdiʃən) *n* tradition *f.* **traditional** *adj* traditionnel, -elle.

traffic (ˈtræfik) *n* **1** circulation *f.* **2** trafic, commerce *m.* **traffic jam** *n* embouteillage *m.* **traffic lights** *n pl* feu de circulation *m pl.* **traffic warden** *n* contractuel, -elle.

tragedy (ˈtrædʒədi) *n* **1** tragédie *f.* **2** drame *m.* **tragic** *adj* tragique.

trail (treil) *n* **1** traînée *f.* **2** piste, trace *f.* **3** route *f. vt* **1** suivre à la piste. **2** traîner. *vi* traîner. **trailer** *n* **1** remorque *f.* **2** (for a film) bande publicitaire *f.*

train (trein) *n* **1** train *m.* **2** suite *f.* **3** convoi *m.* **4** traîne *f.* **5** série *f. vt* entraîner, dresser, former. *vi* s'entraîner, s'exercer. **trainee** *n* stagiaire *m,f.* **training** *n* **1** formation *f.* **2** *sport* entraînement *m.*

traitor (ˈtreitə) *n* traître, perfide *m.*

tram (træm) *n* tramway *m.*

tramp (træmp) *n* **1** vagabond, clochard *m.* **2** bruit de piétinement *m. vi* vagabonder. *vt* faire à pied.

trample (ˈtræmpəl) *vi,vt* piétiner, fouler.

trampoline (ˈtræmpəliːn) *n* trampolino *m.*

trance (trɑːns) *n* trance, extase *f.*

tranquil (ˈtræŋkwil) *adj* tranquille, serein, calme. **tranquillity** *n* tranquillité *f.* calme *m.* **tranquillizer** *n* tranquillisant, calmant *m.*

transact (trænˈzækt) *vt* traiter, faire, passer. **transaction** *n* **1** conduite *f.* **2** opération *f.*

transatlantic (trænzətˈlæntik) *adj* transatlantique.

transcend (trænˈsend) *vt* dépasser, surpasser.

transcribe (trænˈskraib) *vt* transcrire.

transfer (*v* trænsˈfəː; *n* ˈtrænsfə:) *vt* transférer, déplacer, virer. *n* transfert, déplacement *m.*

transform (trænsˈfɔːm) *vt* transformer, métamorphoser. **transformation** *n* métamorphose *f.*

transfuse (trænsˈfjuːz) *vt* transfuser. **transfusion** *n* transfusion *f.*

transistor (trænˈzistə) *n* transistor *m.*

transit (ˈtrænsit) *n* **1** passage *m.* **2** transport, transit *m.*

transition (trænˈziʃən) *n* transition *f.* passage *m.*

transitive (ˈtrænsitiv) *adj* transitif, -ive.

translate (trænzˈleit) *vt* traduire. **translation** *n* traduction *f.*

translucent (trænzˈluːsənt) *adj* translucide.

transmit (trænzˈmit) *vt* transmettre. **transmitter** *n* transmetteur, émetteur *m.*

transparent (trænsˈpærənt) *adj* **1** transparent, limpide. **2** clair.

transplant (*v* trænsˈplɑːnt; *n* ˈtrænsplɑːnt) *vt* transplanter, greffer. *n* greffe *f.*

transport (*v* trænsˈpɔːt; *n* ˈtrænspɔːt) *vt* transporter. *n* transport *m.*

transpose (trænsˈpouz) *vt* transposer.

trap (træp) *n* **1** trappe *f.* piège *m. vt* attraper, prendre au piège. *vi* trapper. **trapdoor** *n* trappe *f.*

trapeze (trəˈpiːz) *n* trapèze *m.*

trash (træʃ) *n* camelote *f.*

trauma (ˈtrɔːmə) *n* traumatisme *m.* **traumatic** *adj* traumatique.

travel (ˈtrævəl) *vi* **1** voyager. **2** aller. *vt* parcourir. *n* voyage *m.* **travel agency** *n* agence de voyages *f.* bureau de tourisme *m.* **traveller's cheque** *n* chèque de voyage *m.*

trawl (trɔːl) *vi* chaluter. **trawler** *n* chalutier *m.*

tray (trei) *n* plateau, -aux *m.*

treachery (ˈtretʃəri) *n* trahison, perfidie *f.* **treacherous** *adj* perfide, déloyal.

treacle ('tri:kəl) *n* mélasse *f*

tread° (tred) *vi* marcher. *vt* écraser, fouler. *n* 1 pas *m*. 2 *mot* chape *f*.

treason ('tri:zən) *n* trahison *f*

treasure ('treʒə) *n* trésor *m*. *vt* tenir beaucoup à. **treasurer** *n* trésorier *m* **treasury** *n* trésorerie *f*.

treat (tri:t) *vt,vi* traiter *vt* régaler *n* plaisir, régal *m*. **treatment** *n* traitement *m*

treatise ('tri:tiz) *n* traité *m*.

treaty ('tri:ti) *n* traité, accord *m*.

treble ('trebəl) *adj* 1 triple. 2 *mus* aigu -uë, de soprano. *adv* trois fois plus *vt* tripler *vi* se tripler.

tree (tri:) *n* arbre *m*.

trek (trek) *vi* 1 faire route. 2 changer de pays. *n* étape *f*.

trellis ('trelis) *n* treillis, treillage *m*. *vt* treillisser

tremble ('trembəl) *vi* trembler, frissonner *n* frisson *m*

tremendous (tri'mendəs) *adj* 1 terrible 2 *inf* énorme, immense.

tremor ('tremə) *n* tremblement *m* secousse *f*.

trench (trentʃ) *n* tranchée *f*. fossé *m*

trend (trend) *n* tendance *f*. **trendy** *adj* à la mode, dans le vent.

trespass ('trespəs) *n* infraction, violation *f*. *vi* enfreindre, violer.

trestle ('tresəl) *n* tréteau, -aux *m*. chevalet *m*.

trial ('traiəl) *n* 1 *law* jugement, procès *m*. 2 essai *m*. épreuve *f*. *adj* d'essai.

triangle ('traiæŋgəl) *n* triangle *m*. **triangular** *adj* triangulaire.

tribe (traib) *n* tribu *f*. **tribal** *adj* de tribu, tribal, -aux. **tribesman** *n* membre de la tribu *m*.

tribunal (trai'bju:nl) *n* tribunal, -aux *m*.

tributary ('tribjutəri) *adj* tributaire. *n* tributaire, affluent *m*.

tribute ('tribju:t) *n* tribut *m*.

trick (trik) *n* 1 tour *m*. 2 ruse *f*. 3 *game* levée *f*. *vt* attraper, duper. **tricky** *adj* compliqué, délicat.

trickle ('trikəl) *vi* couler, suinter. *n* filet *m*.

tricycle ('traisikəl) *n* tricycle *m*.

trifle ('traifəl) *n* 1 bagatelle *f*. 2 *cul* diplomate *m*. *vi* jouer, badiner.

trigger ('trigə) *n* détente, gâchette *f*.

trill (tril) *n* trille *m*. *vt* triller, rouler. *vi* faire des trilles.

trim (trim) *vt* 1 parer, tailler. 2 orner. *n* 1 bon ordre *m*. 2 coupe *f*. *adj* soigné, ordonné.

trio ('triou) *n* trio *m*.

trip (trip) *n* 1 excursion *f*. 2 faux-pas, croc-en-jambe *m*. *vi* faire un faux-pas, trébucher. **trip up** donner un croc-en-jambe à.

tripe (traip) *n* 1 tripe *f*. 2 *inf* camelote *f*.

triple ('tripəl) *adj* triple. *vt* tripler. *vi* se tripler. **triplet** *n* 1 trio *m*. 2 *pl* triplés *m pl*.

tripod ('traipɔd) *n* trépied *m*.

trite (trait) *adj* banal, trivial.

triumph ('traiʌmf) *n* triomphe *m*. victoire *f*. *vi* triompher, remporter un succès **triumphant** *adj* triomphant.

trivial ('triviəl) *adj* 1 insignifiant, superficiel, -elle 2 banal.

trod (trɔd) *v* see **tread.**

trodden ('trɔdn) *v* see **tread.**

trolley ('trɔli) *n* 1 chariot *m*. 2 table roulante *f*.

trombone (trɔm'boun) *n* trombone *m*.

troop (tru:p) *n* troupe *f*.

trophy ('troufi) *n* trophée *m*.

tropic ('trɔpik) *n* tropique *m*. **tropical** *adj* tropical, -aux.

trot (trɔt) *n* trot *m*. *vi* aller au trot, trottiner. **trotter** *n* pied de cochon *m*.

trouble ('trʌbəl) *n* 1 ennui *m*. difficulté *f*. 2 peine *f*. malheur *m*. 3 dérangement *m*. *vt* 1 affliger, inquiéter. 2 déranger *vi* 1 s'inquiéter. 2 se donner de la peine **troublemaker** *n* trublion *m*.

trough (trɔf) *n* auge *f*

troupe (tru:p) *n* troupe *f*

trousers ('trauzəz) *n pl* pantalon *m*.

trout (traut) *n* truite *f*.

trowel ('trauəl) *n* truelle *f*.

truant ('truənt) *n* **play truant** faire l'école buissonnière *f*

truce (tru:s) *n* trêve *f*.

truck (trʌk) *n* wagon, camion *m*.

trudge (trʌdʒ) *vi* marcher péniblement.

true (tru:) *adj* 1 vrai, exact. 2 authentique. 3 fidèle, loyal, -aux. **truly** *adv* sincèrement, vraiment.

truffle ('trʌfəl) *n* truffe *f*.

trump (trʌmp) *n* atout *m*. *vt* couper. *vi* jouer atout.

trumpet ('trʌmpit) *n* trompette *f*.

truncheon ('trʌntʃən) *n* bâton *m*. matraque *f*.

trunk (trʌŋk) *n* 1 tronc *m*. 2 (luggage) malle *f*. 3 *zool* trompe *f*. **trunk call** *n* appel interurbain *m*.

trust (trʌst) *n* 1 confiance *f*. 2 espoir *m*. 3 *comm* trust *m*. *vt* 1 se fier à, faire confiance à. *vi* 1 se confier. 2 espérer. **trustee** *n* fidéicommissaire *m*. **trustworthy** *adj* digne de confiance, honnête.

truth (tru:θ) n vérité f. **truthful** adj 1 véridique 2 vrai, fidèle

try (trai) vt 1 essayer, tenter. 2 law juger 3 éprouver **try on** essayer. **try out** essayer à fond. ~n essai m. **trying** adj vexant, contrariant.

tsar (tsɑː) n tsar m.

T-shirt n maillot à manches courtes m

tub (tʌb) n bac, baquet m.

tuba ('tjuːbə) n tuba m.

tube (tjuːb) n 1 tube, tuyau, -aux m. 2 métro m.

tuber ('tjuːbə) n tubercule f.

tuberculosis (tjuːbəːkjuˈlousis) n tuberculose f.

tuck (tʌk) vt 1 remplir. 2 relever, retrousser **tuck in** vt border vi manger à belles dents. ~n pli, rempli m

Tuesday ('tjuːzdi) n mardi m.

tuft (tʌft) n touffe, houppe, huppe f

tug (tʌg) vt,vi tirer avec effort. vt 1 tirer, traîner 2 remorquer n 1 traction, saccade f 2 naut remorqueur m

tuition (tjuːˈiʃən) n instruction f

tulip ('tuːlip) n tulipe f.

tumble ('tʌmbəl) n chute, culbute, dégringolade f. vi chuter, culbuter, dégringoler vt culbuter, faire tomber, renverser **tumbler** n grand verre m

tummy ('tʌmi) n inf ventre m

tumour ('tjuːmə) n tumeur f

tumult ('tumʌlt) n tumulte m

tuna ('tjuːnə) n thon m.

tune (tjuːn) n 1 air m. 2 mélodie, harmonie f. 3 accord m. vt accorder **tuneful** adj mélodieux, -euse, harmonieux, -euse.

tunic ('tjuːnik) n tunique f

Tunisia (tjuːˈniziə) n Tunisie f **Tunisian** adj,n tunisien, -ienne.

tunnel ('tʌnl̩) n tunnel m. galerie f.

tunny ('tʌni) n thon m

turban ('təːbən) n turban m.

turbine ('təːbain) n turbine f

turbot ('təːbət) n turbot m.

turbulent ('təːbjulənt) adj turbulent, tumultueux, -euse

turf (təːf) n 1 gazon m. 2 sport turf m **turf accountant** n bookmaker m

turkey ('təːki) n 1 dindon m 2 cul dinde f

Turkey ('təːki) n Turquie f **Turk** n turc, turque. **Turkish** adj turc, turque, de Turquie **Turkish (language)** n turc m

turmeric ('təːmərik) n curcuma m.

turmoil ('təːmɔil) n trouble, tumulte m agitation f.

turn (təːn) vt 1 tourner 2 retourner. 3 changer. 4 diriger vi 1 tourner. 2 se retourner 3 se changer **turn down** refuser. **turn off** éteindre, couper. **turn on** allumer, ouvrir. **turn out** 1 mettre à la porte. 2 éteindre. 3 s'arranger. **turn up** 1 se relever. 2 arriver ~n 1 tour m 2 virage, tournant m 3 service m. **to a turn** à point. **turning** n tournant, virage m adj tournant **turning point** n point décisif m. **turntable** n 1 plaque tournante f. 2 platine f.

turnip ('təːnip) n navet m.

turnover ('təːnouvə) n 1 chiffre d'affaires m. 2 cul chausson m

turpentine ('təːpəntain) n térébenthine f

turquoise ('təːkwɔiz) n 1 turquoise f 2 (colour) turquoise m invar. adj turquoise invar

turret ('tʌrət) n tourelle f.

turtle ('təːtl̩) n tortue de mer f.

tusk (tʌsk) n défense f croc m

tussle ('tʌsəl) n lutte, bagarre f vi lutter, se bagarrer.

tutor ('tjuːtə) n précepteur m vt instruire, donner des leçons particulières

tweed (twiːd) n tweed m

tweezers ('twiːzəz) n pince à épiler f.

twelve (twelv) adj,n douze m. **twelfth** adj douzième.

twenty ('twenti) adj,n vingt m **twentieth** adj vingtième.

twice (twais) adv deux fois

twiddle ('twidl̩) vt,vi tourner, tortiller

twig (twig) n brindille, ramille f.

twilight ('twailait) n crépuscule m

twin (twin) n jumeau, -elle adj jumelé, jumeau, -aux

twine (twain) vt tordre, enrouler vi 1 se tordre, s'enrouler 2 serpenter n ficelle f.

twinge (twindʒ) n élancement m vt,vi torturer, élancer

twinkle ('twiŋkəl) vi scintiller. n scintillement m

twirl (twəːl) vt faire tournoyer, tortiller vi tournoyer, pirouetter n 1 tournoiement m 2 pirouette f

twist (twist) vt 1 tordre, tortiller 2 se tordre. 3 déformer vi 1 se tordre, se tortiller. 2 tourner n 1 fil retors, cordon m. 2 torsion f.

twitch (twitʃ) vt donner une saccade, tirer vi se contracter, se crisper n 1 saccade f 2 convulsion f

twitter ('twitə) vi gazouiller n gazouillement m

two (tuː) adj,n deux m **two-faced** adj 1 à deux visages, hypocrite 2 sans envers **twosome** n

partie à deux f. couple m. **two-way** adj à
deux sens.
tycoon (tai'ku:n) n magnat m.
type (taip) n **1** type, genre m. **2** caractère m. vt
taper à la machine. **typewriter** n machine à
écrire f. **typical** adj typique. **typist** n dactylographe m,f.
typhoid ('taifɔid) n typhoïde f.
typhoon (tai'fu:n) n typhon m.
tyrant ('tairənt) n tyran m. **tyranny** n tyrannie
f.
tyre ('taiə) n pneu m.

U

ubiquitous (ju:'bikwitəs) adj présent partout.
udder ('ʌdə) n mamelle f. pis m.
ugly ('ʌgli) adj laid, moche. **ugliness** n laideur
f.
ukulele (ju:kə'le:li) n ukulele m.
ulcer ('ʌlsə) n ulcère m.
ulterior (ʌl'tiəriə) adj **1** ultérieur. **2** caché.
ulterior motive n motif caché m.
ultimate ('ʌltimət) adj **1** final. **2** définitif, -ive,
dernier, -ère. **3** ultime. **ultimately** adv en fin
de compte. **ultimatum** n, pl **-tums** or **-ta**
ultimatum m.
ultraviolet (ʌltrə'vaiələt) adj ultraviolet, -ette.
umbrella (ʌm'brelə) n parapluie m.
umpire ('ʌmpaiə) n arbitre m.
umpteen (ʌmp'ti:n) adj je ne sais combien.
unable (ʌn'eibəl) adj incapable.
unacceptable (ʌnək'septəbəl) adj inacceptable.
unaccompanied (ʌnə'kʌmpnid) adj seul, non
accompagné.
unanimous (ju:'nanimɔs) adj unanime.
unarmed (ʌn'ɑ:md) adj sans arme.
unattractive (ʌnə'træktiv) adj peu attrayant.
unaware (ʌnə'wɛə) adj pas au courant,
ignorant. **unawares** adv inconsciemment, au
dépourvu.
unbalanced (ʌn'bælənst) adj **1** mal équilibré. **2**
déséquilibré.
unbearable (ʌn'bɛərəbəl) adj insupportable.
unbelievable (ʌnbi'li:vəbəl) adj incroyable.
unbend* (ʌn'bend) vt **1** détendre. **2** redresser. vi
se détendre. **unbending** adj inflexible.
unbreakable (ʌn'breikəbəl) adj incassable.
unbutton (ʌn'bʌtn) vt déboutonner.
uncalled-for adj déplacé, injustifié.
uncanny (ʌn'kæni) adj mystérieux, -euse,
inquiétant.

uncertain (ʌn'sə:tn) adj incertain.
uncle ('ʌŋkəl) n oncle m.
unclear (ʌn'kliə) adj peu clair, obscur.
uncomfortable (ʌn'kʌmftəbəl) adj **1** inconfor-
table, incommode. **2** mal à l'aise.
unconscious (ʌn'kɔnʃəs) adj inconscient.
unconventional (ʌnkən'venʃnəl) adj non-con-
formiste.
uncooked (ʌn'kukt) adj cru.
uncouth (ʌn'ku:θ) adj grossier, -ière, rude.
uncover (ʌn'kʌvə) vt découvrir.
uncut (ʌn'kʌt) adj **1** non-coupé. **2** sur pied, non
taillé. **3** brut.
undecided (ʌndi'saidid) adj indécis.
undeniable (ʌndi'naiəbəl) adj indéniable,
incontestable.
under ('ʌndə) prep sous, au dessous de. adv
(au) dessous. adj de dessous, subalterne.
undercharge (ʌndə'tʃɑ:dʒ) vt faire payer un
prix trop bas.
undercoat ('ʌndəkout) n première couche f.
undercover ('ʌndəkʌvə) adj secret, -ète.
undercut (ʌndə'kʌt) vt vendre à meilleur marché que.
underdeveloped (ʌndədi'vèləpd) adj sous-
développé.
underdone (ʌndə'dʌn) adj **1** pas assez cuit. **2**
(of meat) saignant.
underestimate (ʌndər'estimeit) vt sous-estimer.
underfoot (ʌndə'fut) adv sous les pieds.
undergo* (ʌndə'gou) vt subir, éprouver.
undergraduate (ʌndə'grædjuət) n étudiant m.
underground (adv ʌndə'graund; adj,n 'ʌndə-
graund) adv **1** sous terre. **2** secrètement. adj **1**
souterrain. **2** secret, -ète. n métro m.
undergrowth ('ʌndəgrouθ) n sous-bois m.
broussailles f pl.
underhand (ʌndə'hænd) adj sournois, clandestin. adv **1** sous main, sournoisement. **2** sport
par en dessous.
underline (ʌndə'lain) vt souligner.
undermine (ʌndə'main) vt miner, saper.
underneath (ʌndə'ni:θ) prep au dessous de,
sous. adv au-dessous, par-dessous, dessous.
adj inférieur, de dessous.
underpants ('ʌndəpænts) n pl caleçon, slip m.
underpass ('ʌndəpɑ:s) n passage inférieur m.
underrate (ʌndə'reit) vt mésestimer, sous-estimer.
understand* (ʌndə'stænd) vt **1** comprendre. **2**
s'entendre à. **3** sous-entendre. **understanding** n entendement m. compréhension f.
understate (ʌndə'steit) vt minimiser. **under-**

statement n **1** amoindrissement m. **2** euphémisme m.

understudy (ˈʌndəstʌdi) n doublure f. vt doubler.

undertake* (ʌndəˈteik) vt entreprendre, assumer. **undertaker** n entrepreneur de pompes funèbres m.

undertone (ˈʌndətoun) n demi-ton m. deɪɪ..-voix f.

underwater (ʌndəˈwɔːtə) adj sous-marin.

underwear (ˈʌndəwɛə) n sous-vêtements m pl.

underworld (ˈʌndəwəːld) n **1** bas-fonds m pl.milieu m. pègre f. **2** enfers m pl.

underwrite* (ˈʌndərait) vt garantir, souscrire.

undesirable (ʌndiˈzaɪərəbəl) adj indésirable, importun.

undo* (ʌnˈduː) vt **1** détruire, réparer. **2** défaire.

undoubted (ʌnˈdautid) adj indubitable, incontestable.

undress (ʌnˈdres) vt déshabiller, dévêtir. vi déshabiller, se dévêtir.

undue (ˈʌndjuː) adj injuste, illégitime.

undulate (ˈʌndʒəleit) vi,vt onduler.

unearth (ʌnˈəːθ) vt déterrer, exhumer. **unearthly** adj surnaturel, -elle, sinistre.

uneasy (ʌnˈiːzi) adj mal à l'aise, gêné.

unemployed (ʌnimˈplɔid) adj désœuvré, en chômage. n chômeurs m pl. **unemployment** n chômage m.

unequal (ʌnˈiːkwəl) adj inégal, -aux.

uneven (ʌnˈiːvən) adj inégal, -aux, accidenté.

unfair (ʌnˈfɛə) adj injuste.

unfaithful (ʌnˈfeiθfəl) adj infidèle, déloyal, -aux.

unfamiliar (ʌnfəˈmiliə) adj peu familier, -ière, inconnu.

unfit (ʌnˈfit) adj impropre, inapte.

unfold (ʌnˈfould) vt déplier, déployer. vi se dérouler.

unfortunate (ʌnˈfɔːtʃunət) adj infortuné, malheureux,-euse.

unfurnished (ʌnˈfəːniʃt) adj non meublé.

ungrateful (ʌnˈgreitfəl) adj ingrat.

unhappy (ʌnˈhæpi) adj malheureux, -euse.

unhealthy (ʌnˈhelθi) adj malsain, insalubre.

unicorn (ˈjuːnikɔːn) n licorne f.

uniform (ˈjuːnifɔːm) adj uniforme, constant. n uniforme m.

unify (ˈjuːnifai) vt unifier.

uninterested (ʌnˈintrəstid) adj non intéressé, indifférent.

union (ˈjuːniən) n union f.

Union Jack n pavillon britannique m.

unique (juːˈniːk) adj unique.

unison (ˈjuːnizən) n unisson m.

unit (ˈjuːnit) n unité f.

unite (juːˈnait) vt unir. vi s'unir, se joindre. **unity** n unité f.

United Kingdom n Royaume-Uni m.

United States of America n Etats-Unis d'Amérique m pl.

universe (ˈjuːnivəːs) n univers m. **universal** adj universel, -elle.

university (juːniˈvəːsiti) n université f. adj universitaire.

unkempt (ʌnˈkempt) adj dépeigné, mal soigné.

unkind (ʌnˈkaind) adj dur, cruel, -elle.

unknown (ʌnˈnoun) adj inconnu, étranger.

unlawful (ʌnˈlɔːfəl) adj illégal, -aux.

unless (ənˈles) conj à moins que.

unlike (ʌnˈlaik) adj différent, peu ressemblant. **unlikely** adj invraisemblable, peu probable.

unload (ʌnˈloud) vt décharger.

unlucky (ʌnˈlʌki) adj **1** malheureux, -euse, infortuné. **2** maléfique.

unnatural (ʌnˈnætʃərəl) adj **1** anormal, -aux, monstrueux, -euse. **2** contre nature.

unnecessary (ʌnˈnesəsri) adj inutile, superflu.

unofficial (ʌnəˈfiʃəl) adj non officiel, -elle, officieux, -euse.

unorthodox (ʌnˈɔːθədɔks) adj peu orthodoxe.

unpack (ʌnˈpæk) vt **1** déballer, dépaqueter. **2** défaire. vi défaire.

unpleasant (ʌnˈplezənt) adj désagréable, déplaisant.

unpopular (ʌnˈpɔpjulə) adj impopulaire.

unravel (ʌnˈrævəl) vt effiler, effilocher. vi s'effiler, se démêler.

unreasonable (ʌnˈriːzənəbəl) adj déraisonnable.

unreliable (ʌnriˈlaiəbəl) adj sur lequel on ne peut pas compter, sujet à caution.

unrest (ʌnˈrest) n **1** inquiétude f. **2** agitation f. malaise m.

unruly (ʌnˈruːli) adj indiscipliné, insoumis.

unscrew (ʌnˈskruː) vt dévisser.

unsettle (ʌnˈsetl) vt ébranler, troubler.

unsightly (ʌnˈsaitli) adj laid.

unsound (ʌnˈsaund) adj défectueux, -euse.

unsteady (ʌnˈstedi) adj peu stable, inconstant.

unsuccessful (ʌnsəkˈsesfəl) adj infructueux, -euse, sans succès.

untangle (ʌnˈtæŋgəl) vt démêler, dépêtrer.

untidy (ʌnˈtaidi) adj mal tenu, en désordre.

untie (ʌnˈtai) vt dénouer, déficeler.

until (ʌnˈtil) conj jusqu'à ce que. prep jusqu'à. **not until** pas avant.

untrue

untrue (ʌnˈtruː) *adj* faux, fausse.
unusual (ʌnˈjuːʒuəl) *adj* inhabituel, -elle, insolite.
unwanted (ʌnˈwɔntid) *adj* indésirable.
unwell (ʌnˈwel) *adj* indisposé.
unwind° (ʌnˈwaind) *vt* dérouler.
unwrap (ʌnˈræp) *vt* désenvelopper.
up (ʌp) *adj* 1 debout, levé. 2 fini, expiré. 3 droit. *adv* 1 en haut, au haut. 2 en l'air. 3 en avance. 4 droit, debout. **up there** là-haut. **up to** jusqu'à, jusque. ~*prep* en haut de, en montant. **up and down** de haut en bas.
upbringing (ˈʌpbriŋiŋ) *n* éducation f.
upheaval (ʌpˈhiːvəl) *n* bouleversement *m*. agitation f.
uphill (ʌpˈhil) *adv* en montant. *adj* 1 en rampe. 2 ardu.
uphold° (ʌpˈhould) *vt* supporter, soutenir.
upholstery (ʌpˈhoulstəri) *n* capitonnage *m*. tapisserie f.
upkeep (ˈʌpkiːp) *n* entretien *m*.
uplift (ʌpˈlift) *vt* soulever, élever. *n* élévation f.
upon (əˈpɔn) *prep* sur.
upper (ˈʌpə) *adj* 1 plus haut, d'au-dessus, de dessus. 2 supérieur. **upper-class** *adj* de la classe supérieure. **uppermost** *adj* le plus haut, premier, -ière.
upright (ˈʌprait) *adj* 1 vertical, -aux, perpendiculaire. 2 droit.
uprising (ˈʌpraiziŋ) *n* insurrection f. soulèvement *m*.
uproar (ˈʌprɔː) *n* vacarme, tapage *m*.
uproot (ʌpˈruːt) *vt* déraciner, arracher.
upset° (*v,adj* ʌpˈset; *n* ˈʌpset) *vt* 1 renverser, culbuter. 2 déranger. 3 bouleverser. *vi* se renverser. *adj* bouleversé, ému. *n* 1 renversement *m*. 2 désordre *m*.
upshot (ˈʌpʃɔt) *n* résultat *m*. conséquence f.
upside down (ʌpsaid ˈdaun) *adv* sens dessus dessous, la tête en bas.
upstairs (ʌpˈstɛəz) *adv* en haut.
upstream (ʌpˈstriːm) *adv* en amont. *adj* d'amont.
upward (ˈʌpwəd) *adj* ascendant, montant. **upwards** *adv* vers le haut, en montant.
uranium (juˈreiniəm) *n* uranium *m*.
Uranus (juˈreinəs) *n* Uranus f.
urban (ˈəːbən) *adj* urbain.
urge (əːdʒ) *vt* 1 encourager, exciter. 2 conseiller. *n* incitation, impulsion f.
urgent (ˈəːdʒənt) *adj* urgent, pressant.
urine (ˈjuərin) *n* urine f. **urinate** *vi* uriner.
urn (əːn) *n* urne f.

298

us (ʌs) *pron* lst pers pl nous.
use (*v* juːz; *n* juːs) *vt* utiliser, employer, se servir de. **use up** épuiser, consommer. ~*n* 1 emploi, usage *m*. 2 jouissance f. **usage** *n* usage *m*. **used** *adj* 1 usagé. 2 d'occasion. **useful** *adj* utile, pratique. **useless** *adj* inutile, bon à rien.
usher (ˈʌʃə) *n* 1 (at a wedding) garçon d'honneur *m*. 2 introducteur *m*. *v* **usher in** inaugurer, introduire. **usherette** *n* ouvreuse f.
usual (ˈjuːʒuəl) *adj* usuel, -elle, habituel, -elle. **usually** *adv* d'habitude.
usurp (juˈzəːp) *vt* usurper.
utensil (juːˈtensəl) *n* ustensile, outil *m*.
uterus (ˈjuːtərəs) *n, pl* **uteri** utérus *m*.
utility (juːˈtiliti) *n* utilité f.
utmost (ˈʌtmoust) *adj also* **uttermost** extrême, dernier, -ière. *n* dernière limite f. **do one's utmost** faire tout son possible.
utter[1] (ˈʌtə) *vt* dire, pousser, proférer.
utter[2] (ˈʌtə) *adj* complet, -ète, absolu.

V

vacant (ˈveikənt) *adj* 1 vacant, libre, vide. 2 vague, distant. **vacancy** *n* 1 vacance f. 2 vide *m*.
vacate (vəˈkeit) *vt* quitter, évacuer.
vacation (vəˈkeiʃən) *n* vacances f pl.
vaccine (ˈvæksiːn) *n* vaccin *m*. **vaccinate** *vt* vacciner. **vaccination** *n* vaccination f.
vacillate (ˈvæsəleit) *vi* vaciller, chanceler.
vacuum (ˈvækjuəm) *n* vide *m*. **vacuum cleaner** *n* aspirateur *m*. **vacuum flask** *n* bouteille Thermos f.
vagina (vəˈdʒainə) *n* vagin *m*.
vagrant (ˈveigrənt) *n* vagabond *m*. *adj* vagabond, errant.
vague (veig) *adj* vague, imprécis, flou.
vain (vein) *adj* 1 vain, creux, creuse. 2 inutile. 3 vaniteux, -euse.
valiant (ˈvæliənt) *adj* vaillant, brave.
valid (ˈvælid) *adj* valide, valable. **validity** *n* validité, justesse f.
valley (ˈvæli) *n* vallée f.
value (ˈvæljuː) *n* valeur f. *vt* 1 estimer, priser. 2 tenir à, faire grand cas de. **valuable** *adj* précieux, -euse, de valeur.
valve (vælv) *n* soupape, valve f.
vampire (ˈvæmpaiə) *n* vampire *m*.
van (væn) *n* fourgon *m*. camionnette f.

vandal ('vændl) n vandale m. **vandalism** n vandalisme m.

vanilla (vəˈnilə) n vanille f.

vanish ('vænif) vi disparaître, s'évanouir.

vanity ('væniti) n vanité f.

vapour ('veipə) n vapeur, buée f.

variety (vəˈraiəti) n variété, diversité f.

various ('veəriəs) adj varié, divers.

varnish ('va:nif) n vernis m. vt vernir.

vary ('veəri) vt varier, diversifier. vi varier, différer. **variant** n variante f. **variation** n variation, différence f.

vase (va:z) n vase m.

vasectomy (væˈsektəmi) n vasectomie f.

vast (va:st) adj vaste, immense.

vat (væt) n cuve f.

Vatican ('vætikən) n Vatican m.

vault[1] (vɔ:lt) n arch 1 voûte f. 2 caveau, -aux m.

vault[2] (vɔ:lt) vt,vi sauter. n saut m.

veal (vi:l) n veau m.

veer (viə) vi tourner, changer de direction.

vegetable ('vedʒtəbəl) n légume m. adj végétal, -aux. **vegetarian** adj,n végétarien, -ienne. **vegetation** n végétation f.

vehement ('viəmənt) adj 1 véhément. 2 passionné.

vehicle ('vi:ikəl) n véhicule m.

veil (veil) n voile m. vt voiler, cacher.

vein (vein) n veine f.

velocity (vəˈlɔsiti) n vitesse f.

velvet ('velvit) n velours m.

veneer (viˈniə) n 1 placage m. 2 vernis m. vt plaquer.

venerate ('venəreit) vt vénérer.

venereal disease (viˈniəriəl) n maladie vénérienne f.

Venetian (viˈni:ʃən) adj,n vénitien, -ienne. **Venetian blind** n jalousie f.

vengeance ('vendʒəns) n vengeance f.

Venice ('venis) n Venise f.

venison ('venisən) n venaison f.

venom ('venəm) n venin m.

vent[1] (vent) n trou, orifice m. ouverture f.

vent[2] (vent) vt donner libre cours à.

ventilate ('ventileit) vt aérer, ventiler. **ventilation** n aération, ventilation f.

venture ('ventʃə) n entreprise risquée f. vt oser, se risquer à. vi risquer de.

Venus ('vi:nəs) n Vénus f.

veranda (vəˈrændə) n véranda f.

verb (və:b) n verbe m. **verbal** adj verbal, -aux.

verdict ('və:dikt) n verdict m.

verge (və:dʒ) n bord m. bordure f. v **verge on** toucher à, friser.

verify ('verifai) vt vérifier, confirmer.

vermin ('və:min) n vermine f.

vermouth ('və:məθ) n vermout m.

vernacular (vəˈnækjulə) adj vernaculaire, indigène. n 1 langue du pays f. 2 langage m.

versatile ('və:sətail) adj souple, apte à tout.

verse (və:s) n 1 vers m. 2 strophe f.

version ('və:ʃən) n version, interprétation f.

vertebrate ('və:tibreit) adj,n vertébré m.

vertical ('və:tikəl) adj vertical, -aux.

verve (və:v) n verve f.

very ('veri) adv 1 très. 2 fort, bien. 3 tout. adj 1 vrai, véritable. 2 même.

vessel ('vesəl) n 1 naut navire m. 2 récipient m.

vest (vest) n gilet, maillot (de corps) m. vt revêtir, confier. **vested** adj acquis.

vestment ('vestmənt) n vêtement m.

vestry ('vestri) n sacristie f.

vet (vet) n inf vétérinaire m. vt inf examiner.

veteran ('vetərən) n vétéran m. adj aguerri, expérimenté.

veterinary surgeon ('vetrinəri) n vétérinaire m.

veto ('vi:tou) n, pl **-oes** veto m. vt mettre son veto à, interdire.

vex (veks) vt vexer, fâcher.

via ('vaiə) prep via, par.

viable ('vaiəbəl) adj viable.

viaduct ('vaiədʌkt) n viaduc m.

vibrate (vaiˈbreit) vi vibrer. vt faire vibrer. **vibration** n vibration f.

vicar ('vikə) n curé m.

vicarious (viˈkeəriəs) adj 1 pour or par un autre. 2 délégué, par substitution.

vice[1] (vais) n vice, défaut m.

vice[2] (vais) n tech étau, -aux m.

vice-chancellor n 1 vice-chancelier m. 2 educ recteur m.

vice-president n vice-président m.

vice-versa ('və:sə) adv vice versa.

vicinity (viˈsinəti) n voisinage m. alentours m pl.

vicious ('viʃəs) adj vicieux, -euse, méchant.

victim ('viktim) n victime f. **victimize** vt prendre comme victime.

victory ('viktri) n victoire f. **victorious** adj victorieux, -euse.

video-tape ('vidiouteip) n bande magnétique vidéo f.

Vietnam (vietˈnæm) n Viet-nam m. **Vietnamese** adj,n vietnamien, -ienne.

view (vju:) n 1 vue, perspective f. 2 opinion f. vt,vi regarder. **view-finder** n viseur m.

vigil ('vidʒil) *n* veille *f*. **vigilant** *adj* vigilant, éveillé.
vigour ('vigə) *n* vigueur *f*.
vile (vail) *adj* **1** vil, infâme. **2** *inf* exécrable.
villa ('vilə) *n* villa *f*.
village ('vilidʒ) *n* village *m*.
villain ('vilən) *n* scélérat, gredin *m*.
vindictive (vin'diktiv) *adj* vindicatif, -ive.
vine (vain) *n* vigne *f*. **vineyard** *n* vignoble *m*.
vinegar ('vinigə) *n* vinaigre *m*.
vintage ('vintidʒ) *n* **1** vendanges *f pl*. **2** année *f*.
vinyl ('vainil) *n* vinyl *m*.
viola (vi'oulə) *n* alto *m*.
violate ('vaiəleit) *vt* violer, profaner. **violation** *n* violation, infraction *f*.
violence ('vaiələns) *n* violence *f*. **violent** *adj* violent.
violet ('vaiələt) *n* **1** *bot* violette *f*. **2** (colour) violet *m*. *adj* violet, -ette.
violin (vaiə'lin) *n* violon *m*.
viper ('vaipə) *n* vipère *f*.
virgin ('və:dʒin) *n* vierge *f*. *adj* de vierge, virginal, -aux.
Virgo ('və:gou) *n* Vierge *f*.
virile ('virail) *adj* viril, mâle.
virtue ('və:tju:) *n* **1** vertu *f*. **2** qualité *f*. **virtual** *adj* **1** de *or* en fait. **2** virtuel, -elle. **virtuous** *adj* vertueux, -euse.
virus ('vairəs) *n* virus *m*.
visa ('vi:zə) *n* visa *m*.
viscount ('vaikaunt) *n* vicomte *m*. **viscountess** *n* vicomtesse *f*.
vision ('viʒən) *n* **1** vision, vue *f*. **2** apparition *f*. **visible** *adj* visible. **visibility** *n* visibilité *f*. **visionary** *adj,n* visionnaire.
visit ('vizit) *n* visite *f*. *vt* visiter, rendre visite à. **visitor** *n* visiteur, -euse.
visual ('vizjuəl) *adj* visuel, -elle. **visualize** *vi* se représenter. *vt* envisager.
vital ('vaitl) *adj* vital, -aux. **vitality** *n* vitalité *f*.
vitamin ('vitəmin) *n* vitamine *f*.
vivacious (vi'veiʃəs) *adj* vif, vive, enjoué.
vivid ('vivid) *adj* vif, vive, éclatant.
vixen ('viksən) *n* renarde *f*.
vocabulary (və'kæbjuləri) *n* vocabulaire *m*.
vocal ('voukəl) *adj* vocal, -aux.
vocation (vou'keiʃən) *n* vocation *f*. **vocational** *adj* professionnel, -elle.
vodka ('vodkə) *n* vodka *f*.
voice (vois) *n* voix *f*. *vt* exprimer.
void (void) *adj* **1** vide. **2** *law* nul, nulle. **3** dépourvu. *n* vide *m*.
volatile ('volətail) *adj* volatile.

volcano (vol'keinou) *n*, *pl* **-oes** *or* **-os** volcan *m*.
vole (voul) *n* compagnol *m*.
volley ('voli) *n* volée, salve *f*. *vi* reprendre la balle de volée.
volt (voult) *n* volt *m*.
volume ('volju:m) *n* **1** volume *m*. **2** *lit* tôme *m*.
volunteer (volən'tiə) *n* volontaire *m*. *vt* offrir volontairement. *vi* s'offrir. **voluntary** *adj* volontaire, spontané.
voluptuous (və'lʌptʃuəs) *adj* voluptueux, -euse.
vomit ('vomit) *vt,vi* vomir. *n* vomissement *m*.
voodoo ('vu:du:) *n* vaudou *m*.
vote (vout) *n* vote, scrutin *m*. *vt,vi* voter.
vouch (vautʃ) *vt* affirmer, garantir. **vouch for** répondre de.
voucher ('vautʃə) *n* bon, reçu *m*.
vow (vau) *n* vœu, vœux, serment *m*. *vt* vouer, jurer.
vowel ('vauəl) *n* voyelle *f*.
voyage ('voiidʒ) *n* voyage sur mer *m*.
vulgar ('vʌlgə) *adj* vulgaire, commun. **vulgarity** *n* vulgarité *f*.
vulnerable ('vʌlnərəbəl) *adj* vulnérable.
vulture ('vʌltʃə) *n* vautour *m*.

W

wad (wod) *n* tampon, bouchon *m*. bourre *f*. *vt* capitonner, ouater. **wadding** *n* ouatage, rembourrage *m*.
waddle ('wodl) *vi* se dandiner. *n* dandinement *m*.
wade (weid) *vi* marcher dans l'eau. *vt* passer à gué. **wade through** venir péniblement à bout de.
wafer ('weifə) *n* gaufrette *f*.
waft (woft) *n* bouffée *f*. souffle *m*. *vt* porter. *vi* flotter.
wag (wæg) *n* agitation *f*. frétillement *m*. *vt* agiter, remuer. *vi* s'agiter, se remuer.
wage (weidʒ) *n* gages *m pl*. salaire *m*. *v* **wage war** faire la guerre.
waggle ('wægəl) *vt* frétiller.
wagon ('wægən) *n* chariot, wagon *m*.
waif (weif) *n* épave *f*. enfant abandonné *m*.
wail (weil) *vi* gémir, vagir. *n* cri plaintif *m*. plainte *f*.
waist (weist) *n* taille, ceinture *f*. **waistband** *n* ceinture *f*. **waistcoat** *n* gilet *m*. **waistline** *n* taille *f*.
wait (weit) *vi,vt* attendre. *n* attente *f*. **waiter** *n* garçon *m*. **waiting list** *n* liste d'attente

f. **waiting room** n salle d'attente f. **waitress**
n serveuse f.
waive (weɪv) vt renoncer à, abandonner, écarter.
wake* (weik) vi se réveiller. vt réveiller. **waken**
vt 1 réveiller. 2 éveiller. vi se réveiller.
Wales (weilz) n pays de Galles m.
walk (wɔːk) vi 1 marcher. 2 se promener. 3 aller
à pied. vt faire marcher, promener. n 1
promenade f. 2 marche f. **walking stick** n
canne f. **walkout** n grève spontanée f.
walkover n victoire facile f.
wall (wɔːl) n 1 mur m. 2 muraille f. **wallflower**
n giroflée des murailles f. **be a wallflower**
faire tapisserie. **wallpaper** n papier peint m.
wallet ('wɔlit) n portefeuille m.
wallop ('wɔləp) vt inf rosser, flanquer une volée
à. n coup vigoureux m.
wallow ('wɔlou) vi se vautrer, croupir.
walnut ('wɔːlnʌt) n noix f. **walnut tree** n noyer
m.
walrus ('wɔːlrəs) n morse m.
waltz (wɔːls) n valse f. vi valser.
wand (wɔnd) n baguette f.
wander ('wɔndə) vi errer, vaguer.
wane (wein) n déclin m. vi décliner, décroître.
wangle ('wæŋgəl) vt inf obtenir par subterfuge,
resquiller. n intrigue f.
want (wɔnt) vt 1 vouloir. 2 manquer de, avoir
besoin de. vi manquer. n 1 manque, défaut m.
2 besoin m. **for want of** faute de. **wanted**
adj 1 on demande. 2 recherché (par la police).
war (wɔː) n guerre f. vi lutter, faire la guerre.
warfare n guerre f.
warble ('wɔːbəl) n gazouillement m. vi gazouiller.
ward (wɔːd) n 1 salle f. 2 cellule f. 3 pupille
m,f. v **ward off** parer. **warden** n directeur,
gardien, conservateur m. **warder** n gardien
de prison m. **wardrobe** n garde-robe f.
warehouse ('wɔəhaus) n entrepôt m. vt emmagasiner.
warm (wɔːm) adj 1 chaud. 2 chaleureux, -euse.
vt chauffer. vi se chauffer. **warmth** n chaleur
f.
warn (wɔːn) vt avertir, prévenir. **warning** n
avertissement, préavis m.
warp (wɔːp) vt fausser, pervertir. vi gauchir, se
déformer, jouer. n 1 chaîne f. 2 voilure f.
warrant ('wɔrənt) n 1 garantie f. 2 autorisation
f. 3 mandat m. vt 1 garantir, certifier. 2
justifier.
warren ('wɔrən) n garenne f.

warrior ('wɔriə) n guerrier m.
wart (wɔːt) n verrue f.
wary ('wɛəri) adj avisé, prudent.
was (wəz; stressed wɔz) v see **be.**
wash (wɔʃ) vt laver. vi se laver. **wash down**
arroser. **wash out** 1 enlever. 2 rincer. **wash-
out** n sl fiasco, four m. **wash up** faire la
vaisselle. ~n 1 lavage m. 2 lessive f. **washbasin** n lavabo m. **washer** n rondelle
f. **washing** n 1 lavage m. 2 linge m. **washing
machine** n machine à laver f. **washing
powder** n lessive f. **washroom** n cabinet de
toilette m.
wasp (wɔsp) n guêpe f.
waste (weist) adj 1 de rebut. 2 inculte. n 1
gaspillage m. perte f. 2 rebut m. déchets m pl.
vt 1 gaspiller. 2 épuiser. vi s'user. **wasteful**
adj prodigue, gaspilleur, -euse. **wastepaper
basket** n corbeille à papier f.
watch (wɔtʃ) vt 1 observer, regarder. 2 surveiller. vi veiller. n 1 garde f. 2 montre f. 3
naut quart m. **watchdog** n chien de garde
m. **watchful** adj vigilant, attentif, -ive.
water ('wɔːtə) n eau, eaux f. vt 1 arroser. 2
abreuver. vi se mouiller. **water down** diluer.
water-closet n cabinet m.
watercolour ('wɔːtəkʌlə) n aquarelle f.
watercress ('wɔːtəkres) n cresson m.
waterfall ('wɔːtəfɔːl) n chute d'eau, cascade f.
watering-can n arrosoir f.
waterlily ('wɔːtəlili) n nénuphar m.
waterlogged ('wɔːtəlɔgd) adj imbibé d'eau.
watermark ('wɔːtəmɑːk) n filigrane m.
watermelon ('wɔːtəmelən) n pastèque f.
waterproof ('wɔːtəpruːf) adj imperméable. vt
caoutchouter.
water-ski vi faire du ski nautique.
watertight ('wɔːtətait) adj étanche.
waterway ('wɔːtəwei) n voie navigable f.
watery ('wɔːtəri) adj aqueux, -euse.
watt (wɔt) n watt m.
wave (weiv) n 1 vague f. 2 geste m. 3 ondulation f. vi 1 s'agiter. 2 onduler. 3 faire signe à.
vt 1 agiter. 2 faire signe de. **waveband** n
longueur d'onde f. **wavelength** n longueur
d'onde f. **wavy** adj onduleux, -euse.
waver ('weivə) vi 1 vaciller. 2 hésiter, fléchir.
wax[1] (wæks) n cire f. vt cirer, encaustiquer.
wax[2] (wæks) vi croître.
way (wei) n 1 voie, route f. chemin m. 2 moyen
m. façon, manière f. 3 direction f. 4 sens m. 5
point de vue f. **by the way** à propos. **this
way** par ici. **under way** en train. **wayside** n

bas-côté, bord de la route m. adj du bord de la route.
waylay* (wei'lei) vt arrêter au passage.
wayward ('weiwəd) adj entêté, fantasque.
we (wi:) pron 1st pers pl nous.
weak (wi:k) adj 1 faible. 2 infirme. **weaken** vt affaiblir. vi s'affaiblir. **weak-minded** adj faible d'esprit. **weakness** n 1 faiblesse f. 2 faible m. **weak-willed** adj sans volonté.
wealth (welθ) n 1 richesse f. 2 abondance f. **wealthy** adj riche.
weapon ('wepən) n arme f.
wear* (wɛə) vt 1 porter, mettre. 2 user. vi s'user. **wear out** 1 user. 2 épuiser. ~n 1 usage m. 2 usure f. **wear and tear** usage m.
weary ('wiəri) adj las, lasse. vt lasser, fatiguer. vi se lasser.
weasel ('wi:zəl) n belette f.
weather ('weðə) n temps m. vt survivre. **weather-beaten** adj basané. **weather forecast** n bulletin météorologique m.
weave* (wi:v) vt tisser. n tissage m.
web (web) n 1 toile f. 2 tissu m.
wedding ('wediŋ) n mariage m. noces f pl. **wedding ring** n alliance f.
wedge (wedʒ) n coin m. cale f. vt 1 coincer, assujettir. 2 serrer.
Wednesday ('wenzdi) n mercredi m.
wee (wi:) adj inf tout petit.
weed (wi:d) n mauvaise herbe f. vt désherber.
week (wi:k) n semaine f. **weekday** n jour de semaine m. **weekend** n fin de semaine f. week-end m. **weekly** adj,n hebdomadaire. adv tous les huit jours.
weep* (wi:p) vi pleurer.
weigh (wei) vt,vi peser. **weighbridge** n bascule f. **weight** n poids m. pesanteur f. **weight-lifting** n haltérophilie f.
weird ('wiəd) adj étrange, mystérieux, -euse.
welcome ('welkəm) adj bienvenu. n bienvenue f. vt souhaiter la bienvenue à.
weld (weld) n soudure f. vt souder.
welfare ('welfɛə) n bien-être m. prospérité f.
well[1] (wel) n puits m.
well[2] (wel) adv bien. **as well** aussi. ~adj bien, bon, bonne. **well-behaved** adj sage, bien élevé.
well-bred adj 1 bien élevé. 2 de race.
well-built adj costaud.
well-known adj bien connu, célèbre.
well-off adj à l'aise, riche.
well-paid adj bien payé.
well-spoken adj au langage cultivé.

302

well-worn adj usagé.
Welsh (welʃ) adj gallois. n (language) gallois m. **Welshman** n gallois m.
went (went) v see **go**.
wept (wept) v see **weep**.
were (wə:) v see **be**.
west (west) n 1 ouest m. 2 cap Occident m. adj occidental, -aux, ouest invar. adv à or vers l'ouest. **westerly** adj d'ouest. **western** adj de l'ouest, occidental, -aux. n western m. **westward** adj à l'ouest, de l'ouest. **westwards** adv vers l'ouest.
West Indies ('indiz) n Antilles f pl. **West Indian** adj,n antillais.
wet (wet) adj 1 mouillé, humide. 2 pluvieux, -euse. n pluie f. vt mouiller.
whack (wæk) n coup violent m. vt donner des coups à, rosser.
whale (weil) n baleine f.
wharf (wɔ:f) n débarcadère m.
what (wɔt) pron 1 qu'est-ce qui? qu'est-ce que? que? quoi? 2 ce qui, ce que, ce dont. adj 1 quel? quelle? 2 que, qui. interj quoi! comment! **whatever** pron tout ce qui, tout ce que, quoi, qui, quoi que. adj 1 quelque... qui, quelque... que. 2 aucun, quelconque.
wheat (wi:t) n blé m.
wheedle ('wi:dl) vt cajoler, câliner.
wheel (wi:l) n roue f. **wheelbarrow** n brouette f. **wheelchair** n fauteuil roulant m.
wheeze (wi:z) vi respirer péniblement.
whelk (welk) n buccin m.
when (wen) adv quand? conj 1 quand, lorsque. 2 où, que. **whenever** adv toutes les fois que, chaque fois que.
where (wɛə) adv 1 où? 2 où. conj,pron où. **whereabouts** adv où? n situation f. **whereas** conj 1 attendu que. 2 tandis que. **whereby** adv par lequel. **whereupon** adv sur quoi, sur ce. **wherever** adv 1 partout où, n'importe où. 2 où que.
whether ('weðə) conj si.
which (witʃ) adj 1 quel? quelle? 2 lequel, laquelle. pron 1 lequel? laquelle? 2 qui, que, dont, lequel, laquelle. 3 ce qui, ce que. **whichever** pron celui qui, celui que, n'importe lequel. adj n'importe quel, quelque...que.
whiff (wif) n bouffée f.
while (wail) conj pendant que, tandis que. n temps m. **be worth one's while** valoir la peine.
whim (wim) n caprice m.

whimper ('wɪmpə) *vi* pleurnicher, geindre. *n* pleurnichement, geignement *m*.

whimsical ('wɪmzɪkəl) *adj* capricieux, -euse.

whine (waɪn) *vi* se plaindre, pleurnicher, geindre. *n* geignement *m*.

whip (wɪp) *n* fouet *m*. *vt* fouetter.

whippet ('wɪpɪt) *n* whippet, lévrier *m*.

whir (wə:) *vi* vrombir, siffler, ronronner. *n* bruissement, ronronnement *m*.

whirl (wə:l) *n* tourbillon, tournoiement *m*. *vi* tourbillonner, tournoyer. **whirlwind** *n* trombe *f*.

whisk[1] (wɪsk) *vt* 1 agiter. 2 enlever, escamoter. *vi* s'élancer.

whisk[2] (wɪsk) *vt* fouetter, battre. *n* fouet *m*.

whisker ('wɪskə) *n* 1 (of a cat, etc.) moustache *f*. 2 *pl* favoris *m pl*.

whisky ('wɪski) *n* whisky *m*.

whisper ('wɪspə) *n* chuchotement *m*. *vi, vt* chuchoter.

whist (wɪst) *n* whist *m*.

whistle ('wɪsəl) *n* sifflement *m*. *vi, vt* siffler.

white (waɪt) *adj* blanc, -che. *n* 1 blanc *m*. 2 *cap* Blanc, -che. **whiten** *vt* blanchir. *vi* pâlir. **whitewash** *vt* badigeonner à la chaux, blanchir. *n* blanc de chaux *m*. **whiting** *n* merlan *m*.

Whitsun ('wɪtsən) *n* Pentecôte *f*.

whiz (wɪz) *vi* siffler.

who (hu:) *pron* 1 qui? qui est-ce qui? 2 qui, lequel, laquelle, celui qui. **whoever** *pron* 1 celui qui, quiconque. 2 qui, que.

whole (houl) *adj* 1 sain, intact. 2 entier, -ière. *n* tout *m*. totalité *f*. **on the whole** en somme. **wholehearted** *adj* de tout cœur, sincère. **wholemeal** *adj* complet, -ète. **wholesale** *n* vente en gros *f*. *adj* 1 de *or* en gros. 2 général, -aux. *adv* en gros. **wholesome** *adj* sain, salubre. **wholly** *adv* 1 tout à fait. 2 intégralement.

whom (hu:m) *pron* 1 qui? qui est-ce que? 2 que, lequel, laquelle, qui.

whooping cough ('hu:pɪŋ) *n* coqueluche *f*.

whore (hɔ:) *n* prostituée, putain *f*.

whose (hu:z) *pron* 1 de qui? à qui? 2 dont, de qui.

why (waɪ) *adv* pourquoi? *conj, n* pourquoi *m*. *interj* tiens!

wick (wɪk) *n* mèche *f*.

wicked ('wɪkɪd) *adj* mauvais, méchant.

wide (waɪd) *adj* 1 large. 2 vaste. 3 loin. *adv* 1 loin. 2 (tout) grand. **widely** *adv* largement, très. **widen** *vt* élargir, étendre. *vi* s'élargir. **widespread** *adj* étendu, répandu.

widow ('wɪdou) *n* veuve *f*. **widower** *n* veuf *m*.

width (wɪdθ) *n* largeur *f*.

wield (wi:ld) *vt* manier.

wife (waɪf) *n*, *pl* **wives** femme, épouse *f*.

wig (wɪg) *n* perruque *f*.

wiggle ('wɪgəl) *vt* tortiller, remuer. *vi* se tortiller.

wigwam ('wɪgwæm) *n* wigwam *m*.

wild (waɪld) *adj* 1 sauvage, farouche. 2 affolé. 3 furieux, -euse. **wildlife** *n* faune *f*.

wilderness ('wɪldənəs) *n* lieu sauvage, inculte *m*.

wilful ('wɪlfəl) *adj* entêté, volontaire.

will[1] (wɪl) *v mod aux* 1 translated by the future tense. 2 aller.

will[2] (wɪl) *n* 1 volonté *f*. vouloir *m*. 2 testament *m*. *vt* 1 vouloir, désirer. 2 léguer. **willpower** *n* volonté *f*.

willing ('wɪlɪŋ) *adj* de bonne volonté, consentant.

willow ('wɪlou) *n* saule *m*.

wilt (wɪlt) *vi* se flétrir, dépérir.

win (wɪn) *vi, vt* gagner, remporter.

wince (wɪns) *n* crispation *f*. tressaillement *m*. *vi* grimacer, tressaillir de douleur.

winch (wɪntʃ) *n* manivelle *f*. treuil *m*.

wind[1] (wɪnd) *n* vent *m*. **windfall** *n* 1 fruit tombé *m*. 2 aubaine *f*. **windmill** *n* moulin à vent *m*. **windpipe** *n* gosier *m*. **windscreen** *n* pare-brise *m* invar. **windscreen wipers** *n pl* essuie-glace *m*. **windswept** *adj* venteux, -euse, balayé par le vent. **windy** *adj* venteux, -euse.

wind[2] (waɪnd) *vt* tourner, enrouler. **wind up** remonter.

windlass ('wɪndləs) *n* treuil *m*.

window ('wɪndou) *n* fenêtre *f*. **window box** *n* caisse à fleurs, jardinière *f*. **window-dressing** *n* art de l'étalage *m*. **window-shop** *vi* faire du lèche-vitrines.

wine (waɪn) *n* vin *m*. **wineglass** *n* verre à vin *m*.

wing (wɪŋ) *n* 1 aile *f*. 2 *pl Th* coulisses *f pl*. **wing commander** *n* lieutenant-colonel d'aviation *m*. **wingspan** *n* envergure *f*.

wink (wɪŋk) *vi* cligner les yeux, faire de l'œil. *vt* cligner. *n* clignement, clin d'œil *m*.

winkle ('wɪŋkəl) *n* bigorneau, -aux *m*.

winter ('wɪntə) *n* hiver *m*.

wipe (waɪp) *vt* essuyer. *n* coup de torchon *or* d'éponge *m*.

wire ('waiə) n **1** fil de fer m. **2** dépêche f. vt **1** clôturer. **2** télégraphier. vi télégraphier.

wise (waiz) adj sage, prudent. **wisdom** n sagesse f.

wish (wiʃ) vt **1** désirer. **2** souhaiter. **3** vouloir. n désir, souhait m.

wisp (wisp) n bouchon m. poignée, mèche f.

wisteria (wis'tiəriə) n glycine f.

wit (wit) n **1** esprit m. **2** intelligence f.

witch (witʃ) n sorcière f. **witchcraft** n sorcellerie f.

with (wið) prep **1** avec. **2** de, à. **3** chez. **4** malgré.

withdraw* (wið'drɔ:) vt retirer, enlever. vi se retirer. **withdrawal** n **1** retrait m. **2** retraite f.

wither ('wiðə) vt **1** dessécher, faner. **2** foudroyer. vi se dessécher, se faner.

withhold* (wið'hould) vt **1** refuser. **2** dissimuler.

within (wið'in) adv à l'intérieur. prep **1** à l'intérieur de. **2** dans. **3** en. **4** en moins de.

without (wið'aut) prep **1** sans. **2** en dehors de. adv à l'extérieur.

withstand* (wið'stænd) vt résister, supporter.

witness ('witnəs) vt être témoin de, assister à. vi témoigner. n **1** témoin m. **2** témoignage m.

witty ('witi) adj spirituel, -elle, piquant.

wizard ('wizəd) n sorcier, magicien m.

wobble ('wɔbəl) vi ballotter, branler. n oscillation f. branlement m.

woke (wouk) v see **wake.**

woken ('woukən) v see **wake.**

wolf (wulf) n, pl **wolves** loup m.

woman ('wumən) n, pl **women** femme f. **womanhood** n état de femme m. féminité f.

womb (wu:m) n matrice f. sein m.

won (wʌn) v see **win.**

wonder ('wʌndə) vi s'étonner, s'émerveiller. vt **1** se demander. **2** s'étonner. n **1** merveille f. prodige m. **2** étonnement m. **wonderful** adj merveilleux, -euse, épatant.

wonky ('wɔŋki) adj inf branlant, patraque.

wood (wud) n bois m. **woodcock** n bécasse f. **wooden** adj **1** de or en bois. **2** raide. **woodland** n pays boisé, bois m. adj des bois, sylvestre. **woodpecker** n pic m. **woodpigeon** n ramier m. palombe f. **woodwind** n bois m pl. **woodwork** n **1** menuiserie f. ébénisterie f. **2** bois travaillé m. **woodworm** n ver du bois m.

wool (wul) n laine f. **woollen** adj de laine. **woolly** adj **1** laineux, -euse. **2** flou.

word (wə:d) n **1** mot m. **2** parole f. vt formuler, énoncer. **word-perfect** adj qui connaît parfaitement son rôle.

wore (wɔ:) v see **wear.**

work (wə:k) n **1** travail, -aux, ouvrage m. **2** œuvre f. vi **1** travailler. **2** exploiter. **3** fonctionner, marcher. **working class** n classe ouvrière f. **workman** n ouvrier m. **workmanship** n façon f. fini de l'exécution m. **workshop** n atelier m.

world (wə:ld) n monde m. **worldly** adj **1** du monde. **2** mondain. **worldwide** adj universel, -elle, répandu partout.

worm (wə:m) n ver m.

wormwood ('wə:mwud) n absinthe f.

worn (wɔ:n) v see **wear.** adj usagé. **worn out** adj **1** épuisé. **2** usé.

worry ('wʌri) vi se tracasser, s'inquiéter. vt **1** tourmenter, tracasser. **2** harceler. **don't worry!** ne vous en faites pas! ~n ennui, souci, tracas m.

worse ('wə:s) adj pire, plus mauvais. n pire m. adv pis, plus mal. **worsen** vt empirer, aggraver. vi s'empirer, s'aggraver.

worship ('wə:ʃip) vt adorer. n **1** culte m. adoration f. **2** cap Honneur m.

worst (wə:st) adj le or la pire. n pire m. **at the worst** au pis aller. ~adv le pis, le plus mal.

worth (wə:θ) adj valant, digne de. **be worth** valoir. ~n valeur f. **worthwhile** adj qui en vaut la peine. **worthy** adj digne f.

would (wəd; stressed wud) v see **will** [1].

wound [1] (wu:nd) n blessure f. vt blesser, froisser.

wound [2] (waund) v see **wind** [2].

wove (wouv) v see **weave.**

woven ('wouvn̩) v see **weave.**

wrangle ('ræŋgəl) vi se disputer, se quereller. n dispute f.

wrap (ræp) vt envelopper. **wrap oneself up** s'emmitoufler. **wrapping** n emballage m.

wreath (ri:θ) n couronne mortuaire f.

wreathe (ri:ð) vt enguirlander. vi tourbillonner.

wreck (rek) n épave, ruine f. vt faire naufrage, faire ruiner. **wreckage** n débris m. épave f.

wren (ren) n roitelet m.

wrench (rentʃ) n mouvement de torsion m. vt tordre, forcer, arracher.

wrestle ('resəl) vi,vt lutter. n lutte f.

wretch (retʃ) n **1** malheureux m. **2** scélérat m. **wretched** adj **1** misérable. **2** pitoyable.

wriggle ('rigəl) vi se tortiller, se remuer. vt tortiller. n tortillement m.

wring' (riŋ) vt tordre. n torsion f.
wrinkle ('riŋkəl) n ride f. vt rider, froncer. vi se rider.
wrist (rist) n poignet m. **wristwatch** n montre-bracelet f.
writ (rit) n acte judiciaire m.
write' (rait) vt,vi écrire. **writer** n auteur, écrivain m. **writing paper** n papier à lettres m.
writhe (raið) vi se tordre.
wrong (rɔŋ) adj 1 mauvais, mal invar. 2 incorrect, faux, fausse. **be wrong** 1 avoir tort. 2 se tromper. ~n mal, tort m. adv mal, de travers, à tort. vt faire tort à.
wrote (rout) v see **write**.
wrought iron (rɔ:t) n fer forgé m.
wrung (rʌŋ) v see **wring**.
wry (rai) adj tordu, de travers.

X

xenophobia (zenə'foubiə) n xénophobie f.
Xerox ('ziərɔks) n Tdmk machine à photocopier f. vt photocopier.
X-ray n rayon X m. vt radiographier.
xylophone ('zailəfoun) n xylophone m.

Y

yacht (jɔt) n yacht m. **yachtsman** n plaisancier m.
yank (jæŋk) vt tirer brusquement. n secousse, saccade f.
yap (jæp) vi japper. n jappement m.
yard¹ (jɑ:d) n (measurement) yard m. **yardstick** n 1 yard m. 2 mesure f. aune m.
yard² (jɑ:d) n 1 cour f. 2 chantier m.
yarn (jɑ:n) n 1 fil m. 2 histoire f.
yawn (jɔ:n) vi bâiller. n bâillement m.
year (jiə) n an m. année f.
yearn (jə:n) vi languir, soupirer. **yearning** n désir m. envie f.
yeast (ji:st) n levure f.
yell (jel) n hurlement m. vi,vt hurler.
yellow ('jelou) adj,n jaune m.
yelp (jelp) vi glapir, japper. n glapissement m.
yes (jes) adv,n oui m.
yesterday ('jestədi) adv,n hier m. **the day before yesterday** avant-hier m.
yet (jet) adv 1 encore. 2 déjà, jusqu'ici. conj cependant, malgré tout.

yew (ju:) n if m.
Yiddish ('jidiʃ) adj,n yiddish m.
yield (ji:ld) vt 1 donner, rapporter. 2 céder. vi céder, fléchir. n production f. rendement m.
yodel ('joudl) vi iouler.
yoga ('jougə) n yoga m.
yoghurt ('jɔgət) n yaourt m.
yoke (jouk) n joug m. vt accoupler.
yolk (jouk) n jaune d'œuf m.
yonder ('jɔndə) adv là-bas.
you (ju:) pron 2nd pers s 1 fam tu. 2 fam te. 3 fam toi. 4 fml vous. 5 pl vous.
young (jʌŋ) adj 1 jeune. 2 (of an animal) petit. **youngster** n jeune personne f. gosse m,f.
your (jɔ:; juə) poss adj 2nd pers s 1 fam ton, ta, tes. 2 fml votre, vos. 3 pl votre, vos. **yours** poss pron 2nd pers s 1 fam le tien, la tienne, à toi. 2 fml le or la vôtre, à vous. 3 pl le or la vôtre, à vous. **yourself** pron 2nd pers s 1 fam toi-même. 2 fam te. 3 fml vous-même. 4 fml vous. 5 pl vous-mêmes. 6 pl vous.
youth (ju:θ) n jeunesse f. **youth hostel** n auberge de la jeunesse f.
Yugoslavia (ju:gou'slɑ:viə) n Yougoslavie f. **Yugoslav** adj,n yougoslave.

Z

zeal (zi:l) n zèle m. **zealous** adj zélé, empressé.
zebra ('zebrə) n zèbre m. **zebra crossing** n passage clouté m.
zero ('ziərou) n zéro m.
zest (zest) n 1 enthousiasme, entrain m. 2 saveur f. piquant m.
zigzag ('zigzæg) n zigzag m. vi zigzaguer.
zinc (ziŋk) n zinc m.
Zionism ('zaiənizəm) n sionisme m.
zip (zip) n 1 Fermeture Éclair Tdmk f invar. 2 inf énergie f.
zither ('ziðə) n cithare f.
zodiac ('zoudiæk) n zodiaque m.
zone (zoun) n zone f.
zoo (zu:) n zoo m.
zoology (zou'ɔlədʒi) n zoologie f. **zoological** adj zoologique. **zoologist** n zoologiste m,f.
zoom (zu:m) vi vrombir. n bourdonnement m.